THE LAW OF
INSURANCE
CONTRACTS

LLOYD'S COMMERCIAL LAW LIBRARY

Interests in Goods
by Norman Palmer and
Ewan McKendrick
(1993)

The Law of Insurance Contracts
second edition
by Malcolm A. Clarke
(1994)

EC Banking Law
second edition
by Marc Dassesse, Stuart Isaacs
and Graham Penn
(1994)

THE LAW OF
INSURANCE
CONTRACTS

BY

MALCOLM A. CLARKE
M.A., LL.B., Ph.D.

Fellow of St. John's College, Cambridge
Reader in Commercial Contract Law in the University of Cambridge

SECOND EDITION

LONDON   NEW YORK   HAMBURG   HONG KONG
LLOYD'S OF LONDON PRESS LTD
1994

Lloyd's of London Press Ltd.
Legal Publishing Division
27 Swinton Street
London WC1X 9NW

USA AND CANADA
Lloyd's of London Press Inc.
Suite 308, 611 Broadway
New York, NY 10012 USA

GERMANY
Lloyd's of London Press GmbH
59 Ehrenbergstrasse
2000 Hamburg 50, Germany

SOUTH EAST ASIA
Lloyd's of London Press (Far East) Ltd.
Room 1101, Hollywood Centre
233 Hollywood Road
Hong Kong

©

Malcolm A. Clarke
1989, 1994

First published in Great Britain, 1989
Second edition 1994

British Library Cataloguing in Publication Data
A catalogue record for this book is
available from the British Library

ISBN 1–85044–551–6

Text set in 10/12pt Linotron 202 Times by
Interactive Sciences, Gloucester
Printed in Great Britain by
Hartnolls Ltd., Bodmin, Cornwall

PREFACE TO THE SECOND EDITION

I am most grateful to those who bought the first edition of this book and thus encouraged the publishers to commission a second. They will find the general plan of the book as before. The main changes are these. Chapter 2 (The Conflict of Laws) has been substantially revised to take greater account of the Rome Convention and the Directives of the (former) EC. Chapter 5 (Third Party Rights) draws the changes in the expanding boundary of the "commercial trust". Chapter 9 (The Insured and his Agent) follows *Caparo* v *Dickman* and the associated developments on the liability of the agent in tort for negligent misstatements. Chapter 15 (Construction of the Contract) records developments in the so-called doctrine of reasonable expectations. In Chapter 19 (Exceptions), discussion of the contract requirement of reasonable precautions has been extended in the light of *Sofi* v *Prudential*, *Devco* v *General* and the Ombudsman's response. Moreover, a section has been added on the impact on insurance terms of the Unfair Contract Terms Act and of the EC Directive on unfair terms in consumer contracts. Chapter 26 (Claims Procedure) has been extended to cover time limitation. Chapter 28 (Indemnity) has been extended by discussion of residual value insurance and of indemnity for the cost of preventing or mitigating loss. Chapter 30 (Payment and Non-Payment) has been revised in the light of developments in the law relating to payment by mistake and to economic duress, as regards settlements or compromises of claim, and examines recent cases on the nature of insurance payments as damages. At various points in the book, attention has been given to developments on liability policies in the United States, concerning environmental damage. Lastly, the reader will find that the Index has been refashioned and greatly expanded.

Of the many decisions of the English courts in the last five years, notable instances are *The Fanti* on section 1(3) of the Third Parties (Rights Against Insurers) Act, 1930, and "pay first" clauses; *Bradley* v *Eagle Star* and *Smit Tak* v *Youell* on liability cover; *De Souza* v *Home* on personal accident cover; *Morley* v *United Friendly* on the exception of wilful exposure to unnecessary danger; *The Good Luck* on breach of warranty; *Banque Financière* v *Westgate* on non-disclosure; *Napier* v *Ettrick* on subrogation; *Scher* v *PPB* on the application of the Policyholders Protection Act; *Punjab* v *De Boinville* on inconsistent drafting; *The Kanchenjunga* on the distinction between waiver and estoppel; and *Hiscox* v *Outhwaite* on arbitration. We follow *Pan Atlantic* v *Pine Top* as far as the Court of Appeal, however, many readers will be aware that its course has not been run.

"The overloading of judgments with massive quotations is the bane of modern jurisprudence" (*First Energy (UK) Ltd* v *Hungarian International Bank Ltd* [1993] 2 Lloyd's Rep 194, 202 *per* Steyn LJ). Something similar might be said of law books and case citation, however, readers have mostly welcomed the reference made in the first

v

edition to decisions in other jurisdictions. Although some of the older references have been deleted, they have been replaced by reference to recent decisions, drawn mostly from Australia, Canada, New Zealand and the United States. The "common law is the system of law which governs between a quarter and a third of the population of the world", said Lord Goff in 1991 ((1992) 5 JCL 1–2), and he went on to state his belief that we should "recognise that some of the more unusual features of our own law might well benefit from a decent dose of the comparative method". It is that same belief that is behind this book.

My thanks to various colleagues in Cambridge for helping me to follow the runes from Brussels and to Julian Burling for help with those from Lloyd's. I am also grateful to the publishers for their help and encouragement. The law is stated, as I believe it to be, at 1 January 1994.

Cambridge, January 1994   MALCOLM CLARKE

PREFACE TO THE FIRST EDITION

When planning this book, I was advised by the late Wilfred Getz, Q.C., to "look west", to look, as Lord Esher once put it,[1] to "America, to which we naturally look for assistance, though not for authority—on any important mercantile question which has not yet been decided in England"; and, we may add, to anticipate trends that may come to England. Once set in that direction, I went further in two respects. First, there was a natural extension to other countries of common law, notably Canada and Australia. Second, why just fill the gaps? If the unity of the common law tradition, which we have been encouraged to preserve and promote,[2] is to be maintained at all, we must take stock of what there is to preserve and promote. Eventually even established rules come under attack and may need fraternal support from allied jurisdictions. Even when a decision offers nothing new, the discussion may be illuminating. So, this book offers a selection of references to those with the time and the interest to pursue them, not only where the decisions are different but also where they are the same. It is not a book of American law[3]; it remains chiefly a book of English law.[4] If the selection can be improved, suggestions will be received gratefully. It also remains chiefly a book of general insurance law; although on the authority of Lord Blackburn[5] the general principles of insurance law apply to all insurances, marine insurance has special rules of its own, which are not discussed here.

I acknowledge with gratitude the help, much of it in the form of comments on drafts of parts of this book, of Julian Burling of the Corporation of Lloyd's, Brian Warburton of C E Heath & Co, Dr John Carter of the University of Sydney, Professor John Fleming and Professor Kevin Tierney of the University of California, and from the University of Cambridge, John Collier, Professor Gareth Jones, and John Thornely,

---

1. *Stewart* v *Merchants Marine Ins Co* (1885) 16 QBD 619, 622 (CA).

2. For example, *Hart* v *O'Connor* [1985] 2 All ER 880, 894 *per* Lord Brightman (PC); especially as regards marine insurance: *Queens Ins Co* v *Globe & Rutgers Fire Ins Co*, 263 U.S. 487, 493 *per* Holmes J (1923). "English courts always aim as far as possible at securing uniformity in regard to the law of contract between the two countries"—Lord Wright speaking of the United States of America in *Legal Essays & Addresses*, p 88.

3. In any event, for our purpose there is no such thing. Insurance law is state law. When a federal court finds a gap in the state law to be applied, it applies a synthesis of law in other state jurisdictions; for example, *Bryant* v *Standard Life & Accident Ins Co*, 348 F 2d 649 (5 Cir, 1965—life). There is occasional reference to English law, especially in cases of marine insurance.

In Canada, law is provincial law, notably legislation, with a substratum of common law based on English law. Similar legislation is found in all states except Quebec, not only to regulate the industry but also to govern contract terms. See Brown & Menezes, No 2:1:1.

4. As the writer was born in Wales, it is hoped that he may be forgiven for referring compendiously to the law or the courts of England, Wales, and, unless otherwise indicated, Scotland, as English.

5. *Thomson* v *Weems* (1884) 9 App Cas 671 (life).

as well as the Librarian and staff of the Squire Law Library. I am also in debt to my family for their patience and support.

The law is stated, as I believe it to be, at 1 June 1989.

Cambridge, September 1989   MALCOLM CLARKE

CONTENTS

3 INSURABLE INTEREST IN LIFE

4 INSURABLE INTEREST IN PROPERTY

5 THIRD PARTY RIGHTS

6 ASSIGNMENT

7 AGENTS: AUTHORITY TO BIND THE INSURED

8 AGENTS: AUTHORITY TO BIND THE INSURER

9 THE INSURED AND HIS AGENT: RIGHTS AND DUTIES INTER SE

10 THE PROPOSAL OF INSURANCE

11 CONTRACT FORMATION

12 INTERIM INSURANCE: COVER NOTES AND BINDERS

13 PREMIUM

14 THE INSURANCE CONTRACT: CONTENTS

15 THE INSURANCE CONTRACT: CONSTRUCTION

16 COVER: LOSS AND PROOF OF LOSS

17 COVER: CAUSES OF LOSS

18 THE PERIOD OF COVER

19 EXCEPTIONS

20 WARRANTIES

21 MISTAKE

22 MISREPRESENTATION

23 PART I: NON-DISCLOSURE

23 PART II: THE EFFECT OF MISREPRESENTATION AND NON-DISCLOSURE

24 ILLEGAL INSURANCE

25 CAUSATION

26 CLAIMS PROCEDURE

27 CLAIMS CO-OPERATION AND GOOD FAITH

30 PAYMENT AND NON-PAYMENT

31 SUBROGATION

CONTENTS

BIBLIOGRAPHICAL ABBREVIATIONS

Abraham—K S Abraham, *Distributing Risk*, New Haven, 1986.

Anson—Anson, *Law of Contract* (26th ed by A G Guest), Oxford, 1984.

Appleman—J A and J Appleman, *Insurance Law and Practice with Forms*, St Paul, Minnesota.

Arnould—*Arnould's Law of Marine Insurance and Average* (16th ed by Sir Michael Mustill and J C B Gilman) London, 1981.

Benjamin—Benjamin, *Sale of Goods* (4th ed by A G Guest and others), London, 1992.

Birds—J Birds, *Modern Insurance Law* (3rd ed), London, 1993.

Bower Estoppel—Bower and Turner, *The Law Relating to Estoppel by Representation* (3rd ed), London, 1977.

Bower Representation—Bower and Turner, *The Law Relating to Actionable Misrepresentation* (3rd ed) London, 1974.

Bowstead—*Bowstead on Agency* (15th ed by F M B Reynolds), London, 1985.

Brown and Menezes—C. Brown and J. Menezes, *Insurance Law in Canada* (2nd ed), Scarborough, Ontario 1991.

Butler and Merkin—J S Butler and R M Merkin, *Reinsurance Law*, London, 1988.

Cheshire & Fifoot—Cheshire, Fifoot and Furmston's *Law of Contract* (12th ed by M P Furmston), London, 1991.

Chitty—*Chitty on Contracts*, Vol 1 (26th ed by A G Guest and others), London, 1989.

Clerk & Lindsell—*Clerk & Lindsell on Tort* (16th ed by R W M Dias and others), London, 1989.

Corbin—*Corbin on Contracts*, St Paul, Minnesota, 1963.

Derrington—D Derrington and R S Ashton *The Law of Liability Insurance*, Sydney, 1990.

Dicey—*Dicey and Morris on the Conflict of Laws* (12th ed by L. Collins and others) London, 1993.

Foundations—*New Foundations for Insurance Law* (ed F D Rose), London, 1987.

Goff & Jones—Lord Goff of Chieveley and Professor G H Jones, *The Law of Restitution* (3rd ed), London, 1986.

Halsbury—*Halsbury's Laws of England* (4th ed).

Hodgin—R W Hodgin, *Insurance Intermediaries and the Law*, London, 1987.

Houseman—Houseman and Davies, *Law of Life Assurance* (10th ed), London, 1984.

Ivamy—E R Hardy Ivamy, *General Principles of Insurance Law* (6th ed), London, 1993

Ivamy Fire—E R Hardy Ivamy, *Fire and Motor Insurance* (4th ed), London, 1984.

Keeton—R E Keeton, *Insurance Law—Basic Test*, St Paul, Minnesota, 1971.

Lewison—K Lewison, *The Interpretation of Contracts*, London, 1989.

MacGillivray—MacGillivray & Parkington, *Insurance Law* (8th ed by M Parkington and others), London, 1988.

McGregor—*McGregor on Damages* (15th ed by H McGregor), London, 1988.

Mann—F A Mann, *The Legal Aspect of Money* (4th ed), Oxford, 1982.

Merkin and McGhee—R M Merkin and A McGhee, *Insurance Contract Law*, London, 1988.

PM—*The Post Magazine*, London, weekly.

Sutton—K C T Sutton, *Insuance Law in Australia and New Zealand* (2nd ed), Sydney, 1991.

Tarr—A A Tarr K-L Liew and W Holligan, *Australian Insurance Law* (2nd ed), Sydney, 1991.

Treitel—G H Treitel, *The Law of Contract* (8th ed), London, 1991.

Welford—A W B Welford, *The Law Relating to Accident Insurance* (2nd ed), London, 1932.

Williston—S Williston, *Treatise on the Law of Contracts* (3rd ed), New York, 1957.

Winfield—*Winfield & Jolowicz on Tort* (13th ed by W V H Rogers), London, 1989.

Vance—W A Vance, *Handbook on the Law of Insurance* (3rd ed), St Paul, Minnesota, 1963.

TABLE OF CASES

xlix

liii

TABLE OF LEGISLATION, DIRECTIVES AND CONVENTIONS

CHAPTER 1

INSURANCE CONTRACTS

1-1 DEFINITION OR DESCRIPTION

The English courts know an elephant when they see one, so too a contract of insurance, and talk for example, of "those who are generally accepted as being insurers".[1] What counts is not what the contract is called but its nature and content.[1a] Although insurance companies are regulated by the Insurance Companies Act 1982, the legislature has not defined insurance, for "no difficulty has arisen in practice, and therefore there has been no all-embracing definition, and the probability is that it is undesirable that there should be, because definitions tend sometimes to obscure and occasionally to exclude that which ought to be included".[2] The latter, of course, is also true of the train door and the aircraft cabin, which some people evidently find useful, perhaps because they like to know where they stand (or sit). Indeed, "where intuition alone has not been enough the English courts have resorted to remarkable agility in characterizing the facts in dispute".[3] For the writer, it is said, the task of attempting a definition is "inescapable".[4] But if the attempt on insurance is inescapable, as with early attempts to climb Mont Blanc, so too is failure. The shape, the appearance of mountains depends on the line of approach. Similarly, the appearance of insurance depends on the issue in question.

While English courts are shy of definitions, courts in the United States are less reticent, offering at least "broad" definitions. For example, insurance is, it is said, "a contract whereby, for an agreed premium, one party undertakes to compensate the other for loss on a specified subject by specified perils".[5] Canadian uniform legislation,[6] defines insurance as "the undertaking by one person to indemnify another person against loss or liability for loss in respect of a certain risk or peril to which the object of insurance may be exposed, or to pay a sum of money or other thing of value upon the

---

1. *Medical Defence Union Ltd v Dept of Trade* [1980] Ch 82, 97 *per* Megarry V-C. A similar approach can be found in *First National Bank of Eastern Arkansas v Taylor*, 907 F 2d 775, 779 (8 Cir, 1990). The case concerned banks and debt cancellation contracts.

1a. *Re Barrett* (1992) 106 ALR 549, 563 (FCA—life).

2. *Department of Trade & Industry v St Christopher Motorists' Assn* [1974] 1 Lloyd's Rep 17, 18 *per* Templeman J (mobility). Hodgin [1980] LMCLQ 14, 20. Templeman J, nonetheless relied on the "essential requirements" of insurance set out in *Prudential Ins Co v IRC* [1904] 2 KB 658, 663 *per* Channell J (life), while stressing (p 21) that this was not an exhaustive definition.

3. Brown & Menezes, No 1:2:6.

4. MacGillivray, No 1. In the same sense Birds, pp 10–11; Merkin & McGee, p A.1.1–01. *Cf* Hellner, 12 Am J Comp L 494, 495 (1963): "the approach through a formal definition leads to innumerable difficulties and, if taken seriously, unfortunate results."

5. *Newark Fire Ins. Co. v. Turk*, 6 F 2d 533, 534 (3 Cir, 1925—fire), quoting Bouvier's Law Dictionary, 1613. For other such definitions see 44 CJS p 471.

6. For example RSO Ont. 1980, c. 218, section 1, para. 30.

happening of a certain event". The California Insurance Code, section 22, defines insurance as a "contract whereby one undertakes to indemnify another against loss, damage or liability arising from a contingent or unknown event". Such definitions, mainly with indemnity rather than contingency insurance in mind,[7] require "loss" to be defined broadly and some common lawyers may find them too bland to be useful.

Insurance contracts are best seen and, if at all, defined according to the angle or line of approach, that is, the context or issue before the court. With regulatory statutes, courts are concerned with the purpose of the statute, whether, for example, this is the kind of thing that Parliament intended to regulate,[8] or to encourage (Income Tax Acts), and they examine the terms of the contract in that light. If the issue is insurable interest, courts are mainly asking whether this is the kind of thing that public policy and Parliament wish to discourage (wagering). Courts tend to look at the objective[9] of the rule of law in point and identify the agreement as insurance, or not, in the light of the objective,[10] and Keeton suggests[11] that definitions should be classified according to the purpose of the rules in issue. In England, while unwilling to define the insurance contract, the courts are willing to describe it,[12] and the rule in issue and the purpose of that rule have affected the description.

An insurance contract has been described as a contract whereby a person (insurer), usually but not always in business as such, agrees to pay money (or provide a corresponding benefit) on the occurrence of an uncertain and adverse event, in return for a money consideration, usually called a premium.

1–1A Contract

An insurance agreement must have contractual force: it must bind the insurer to pay insurance money in certain circumstances.[13] If payment is left to the discretion of the

---

7. Yet it is clear from sections 100 and 101 of the Cal Ins Code that section 22 is intended to embrace non-indemnity contingency insurance.

8. *Medical Defence Union Ltd* v *Dept of Trade* [1980] Ch 82, 96–97 *per* Megarry V-C, concerning the Insurance Companies Act 1974. The same approach, by reference to the purpose of the legislation, can be discerned in some decisions in the USA: for example, *First National Bank of Eastern Arkansas* v *Taylor*, 907 F 2d 775, 778 ff. (8 Cir, 1990); *Mutual Re* v *Great Plains Mutual Ins Co*, 750 F Supp 455 (D Kan, 1990—re).

9. For example thrift through insurance: *Gould* v *Curtis* [1913] 3 KB 84, 96 *per* Kennedy LJ (CA—life).

10. Also in this sense: Brown & Menezes No 1:2:7. For example, *Lipof* v *Florida Power & Light Co*, 596 So. 2d 1004 (Fla, 1992—liability).

11. p 545. See also pp 2 ff. For example, *Feinstein* v *A-G*, 366 NYS 2d 613, 616 (1975); *Twentieth Century Ins Co* v *Liberty Mutual Ins Co*, 965 F 2d 747, 752 (9 Cir, 1992—motor).

12. *Medical Defence Union Ltd* v *Dept of Trade* [1979] 1 Lloyd's Rep 499, 505 *per* Megarry V-C.

13. *Hampton* v *Toxteth Co-operative Provident Sy Ltd* [1915] 1 Ch 721 (CA—life).

"Its terms must bind the parties to that contract"—*New York Central Employees* v *Commercial Credit Co*, 178 NYS 2d 977, 980 (1958—motor). Any doubt about whether mutual insurance created a contract of insurance between P & I Club and member has now been dispelled; see Hazelwood, *P & I Clubs, Law and Practice* (1989), p 235. If in all other respects discussed below an agreement looks like insurance, the courts will be reluctant to find that it is not. For example in *Home Ins Co* v *Admin Asigurarilor de Stat* [1983] 2 Lloyd's Rep 674 (re) Parker J found a binding contract, notwithstanding the inclusion of an "honourable engagement" clause. *Cf* also *R* v *Cohen* (1979) 27 ALR 263, 270–271 (HCA) that the Tasmanian Motor Accidents Insurance Board with a statutory (and not contractual) duty to indemnify for certain third party liabilities was an insurer, and hence that its employees were "employed in the business of insurance" within the meaning of the eligibility clause of the relevant industrial organisation. The purpose of the inquiry may explain the statement of Mason J (pp 270–271), with whom other judges agreed, that "I very much doubt whether the existence of a contract is of itself essential to the legal concept of 'insurance'. There is much to be said for the view that it is the relationship of indemnity that exists between insurer and insured, rather than the source of that relationship, that is the essence of the concept of insurance."

debtor, it is not insurance.[14] "When a person insures, I think that he is contracting for the certainty of payment in specified events, and not merely for the certainty of proper consideration being given to his claim that a discretion to make a payment in those events should be exercised in his favour."[15]

The contract may take any form. Although a document that is generally recognised as a policy is often issued, there is no agreement on the definition of a policy, but general agreement that, unless required for the purposes of a statutory rule,[16] an insurance contract may exist without a policy.[17] Although courts often speak of policies and insurance contracts as synonymous,[17a] an insurance contract, which must therefore be distinguished from a guarantee (below, 1–2), may exist without writing of any kind. For that reason, unless the context otherwise requires, this book speaks less of insurance policies than of insurance contracts.

1–1B An Insurer in Business

It has been held[18] that the insurer must be in business as such, and that therefore an indemnity agreement with a charity is not an insurance contract. However, this decision was based on the interpretation of a statute regulating the industry, and it does not follow that for other purposes the contracts of a charitable[19] or statutory[20] body would not be regarded as insurance. In any event, an organisation is nonetheless an insurer, if insurance is a minor part of its activity,[21] or insurance is just one part of its contractual undertaking to the person insured.[22]

1–1C Money or Corresponding Benefit

In most cases, when the insured event occurs, the insurer will simply pay money to the insured. In some cases, however, the insurer (or the insured) will have a choice whether the insurer pays money or pays for benefits in kind, such as the reinstatement

14. *Department of Trade & Industry* v *St Christophers Motorists' Assn* [1974] 1 Lloyd's Rep 17, 19 *per* Templeman J (mobility); *The Vainqueur Jose* [1979] 1 Lloyd's Rep 557, 580 *per* Mocatta J (P & I). A contract is nonetheless an insurance contract if, as may be the case of mutual insurance, some benefits are available as of right and some as a matter of discretion: Tilley 17 JMLC 427, 442 (1986).

15. *Medical Defence Union Ltd* v *Dept of Trade* [1979] 1 Lloyd's Rep 499, 506 *per* Megarry V-C.

16. For example, *Hampton* v *Toxteth Co-operative Provident Sy Ltd* [1915] 1 Ch 721 (CA—life); *Hall d'Ath* v *British Provident Assn* (1932) 48 TLR 240 (PA); *cf Nelson & Co.* v *Board of Trade* (1901) 17 TLR 456.

17. For example, a Lloyd's slip, or a certificate issued under a cargo policy or a group health or life policy. The Stamp Act 1891 requires a stamp, if a policy is issued. It defines a policy in terms too broad to be helpful as an indicator of insurance: "every writing whereby any contract of insurance is made or agreed to be made."

17a. In Canada, for example, most lawyers and judges still use the terms "policy" and "contract" interchangeably, even though they are distinguished in insurance legislation: Baer, 22 Ottawa L Rev 389, 409 (1990).

18. *Hall d'Ath* v *British Provident Assn* (1932) 48 TLR 240 (PA).

19. *Re Bendix Automotive of Canada Ltd and UAW Local 195* (1971) 20 DLR (3d) 151, 159 (Ont—PHA). *Commissioner of Internal Revenue* v *Treganowan*, 183 F 2d 288 (2 Cir, 1950—life).

20. *R* v *Cohen* (1979) 27 ALR 263, 271 *per* Mason J (HCA—motor).

21. *Nelson & Co* v *Board of Trade* (1901) 17 TLR 456: a retailer promised pensions to promote the sale of tea. See also *Hampton* v *Toxteth Co-operative Provident Sy Ltd* [1915] 1 Ch 721 (CA—life). *R* v *Cohen* (1979) 27 ALR 263, 272 *per* Mason J (HCA—motor). *Cf Lipof* v *Florida Power & Light Co*, 596 So. 2d 1004 (Fla, 1992—liability), in which it was held that an employer who provided his employees with liability insurance was not an insurer.

22. *Re Bendix Automotive of Canada Ltd and UAW Local 195* (1971) 20 DLR (3d) 151, 160 (Ont—PHA).

of property damaged[23] or, in the case of mobility insurance, the services of a chauffeur for the insured who is unable to drive his motor vehicle.[24]

In *Medical Defence Union Ltd* v *Dept of Trade*[25] a member of the Union had no right to indemnity or to legal defence, but a right to ask the Union for these things, a request that had rarely been refused in the past. It was accepted by counsel that, although a benefit, this right was not a right to money or money's worth.[26] The court held that the arrangement was not insurance. Insurance is a contract "for the payment of money, or for some *corresponding* benefit".[27]

In the same case the judge, Sir Robert Megarry V–C, observed[28] that, even if the member had the right to "advice or assistance", that would not fall within the definition of insurance. It was not "money's worth . . . in the sense of being the equivalent of money".[29] It was, however, a "benefit". He continued: "If 'benefit' is the right expression, it is difficult to see why a contract to provide such advice and assistance should not be a contract of insurance." Indeed, if those who pay for the reinstatement of the fire damage or the services of a driver can be classified as insurers, why not also those who pay for advice ? The consequence, however, would be that many professional and other bodies which give their members the right to advice and assistance might thus be brought within the Insurance Companies Act. "Like Monsieur Jourdain, who was astonished to find that for 40 years he had been speaking prose without knowing it, such bodies might equally be astonished to discover that for many years they have been insurance companies carrying on insurance business without knowing it".[30] To avoid this result, the judge was compelled to the somewhat strained conclusion,[31] that one who paid for the services of a third party (such as a repairer or a driver) could be an insurer,[32] but one who provided the same services as part of his own operation (and thus paid the persons employed by him to provide that service) could not.

A problem of the same kind has confronted courts in the USA. Some courts have held that the grant of a "negative" benefit, such as the release of a debt owed to the grantor, amounted to insurance. More recent opinion, however, is against that conclusion, less because there was no benefit to the debtor than because debt cancellation contracts differ from "traditional insurance contracts" and because banks, the creditors in question, are not commonly regarded as insurers.[32a]

23. *Prudential Ins Co* v *IRC* [1904] 2 KB 658, 664 *per* Channell J (life).
24. *Department of Trade & Industry* v *St Christophers Motorists' Assn* [1974] 1 Lloyd's Rep 17 (mobility). Templeman J (pp 20–21) distinguished statements requiring the payment of money as statements to be confined to the context in which they were made, fire damage: *Rayner* v *Preston* (1881) 18 Ch D 1, 9 *per* Brett LJ (CA—fire).
25. [1980] Ch 82.
26. At the same time it was "not contended that the right was valueless" (p 92). *Cf Chaplin* v *Hicks* [1911] 2 KB 786 (CA) that the right to compete in a beauty contest, with prize money for the winner, was a valuable right, in respect of which damages could be awarded.
27. p 93, quoting *Prudential Ins Co* v *IRC* [1904] 2 KB 658, 663 *per* Channell J (life) (emphasis added). See also *Cook* v *Field*, discussed below 3–6B2.
California Physicians' Service v *Garrison*, 172 P 2d 4, 12 (Cal, 1946—PHA): "money, or its equivalent"; *idem Candell* v *US*, 189 F 2d 442, 444 (10 Cir, 1951—life). A "benefit of pecuniary value"—NY Insurance Law, section 41.
28. p 94.
29. p 96.
30. pp 96–97.
31. p 97.
32. *Department of Trade & Industry* v *St Christophers Motorists' Assn* [1974] 1 Lloyd's Rep 17 (mobility).
32a. *First National Bank of Eastern Arkansas* v *Taylor* 907 F 2d 775 (8 Cir, 1990).

The decision in *Medical Union* is best seen in the context of the question before the court, whether the services were insurance in the sense of an activity to be regulated under the Act. In a different context the provision of services might still be classified as insurance.[33]

1–1D An Uncertain Event

"The true test is not the character of the consideration agreed to be furnished, but whether or not the contract is aleatory in nature. A contract still partakes of the nature of insurance, whether the consideration agreed to be furnished is money, property or services, if the agreement is aleatory and the duty to furnish such consideration is dependent upon chance or the happening of some fortuitous event."[35]

Insurance money must be payable on an event, the occurrence of which is uncertain.[36] The uncertainty may lie not only in whether the event, such as theft, will occur but also how often and to what extent the event, for example damage to taxis,[37] will occur or when the event, for example death, will occur.[38] In the case of life insurance, "a whole life policy is an insurance against dying too soon, an endowment policy an insurance against living too long".[38a] Uncertainty is tested at the time that the contract is concluded.[39]

In England, uncertainty is tested with the benefit of omniscience, whereas in certain other countries it is tested on the basis of the knowledge of the parties to the contract.[39a] There is agreement in most countries, however, that the very nature of insurance, if not also public policy, "forbids one from obtaining insurance for a loss the insured knows is already present".[39b]

Further, in order to distinguish an ordinary obligation to pay damages for breach of contract, the occurrence of which is also uncertain at the time of contracting, it is

---

33. An inference to the contrary comes from 1981 SI No 1564, reg 23, made under the Insurance Companies Act 1982, section 2(5), whereby such activities are excluded from regulation under the Act. Further, loss prevention, with advice to that end, is widely seen as part of the role of the insurer. And in *R. v Anderson & Teskey* [1941] 1 DLR 346 (Alta) an organisation providing legal services for motorists charged with manslaughter was convicted of the offence of providing a "benefit . . . payable by an insurer" without a licence. This decision brings automobile clubs within the scope of the definition: Brown & Menezes, No 1:2:5.

35. *California Physicians' Service v Garrison*, 172 P 2d 4, 17–18 (Cal, 1946—PHA), applied in Canada in *Re Bendix Automotive of Canada Ltd and UAW Local 195* (1971) 20 DLR (3d) 151, 158 (Ont—PHA).

36. *Scottish Amicable Heritable Securities Assn Ltd v Northern Assurance Co* (1883) 11 R (Ct Sess) 287, 303 *per* Lord Moncrieff (fire); *Prudential Ins Co v IRC* [1904] 2 KB 658, 663 *per* Channell J (life); *Department of Trade & Industry v St Christophers Motorists' Assn* [1974] 1 Lloyd's Rep 17, 19 *per* Templeman J (mobility); *Medical Defence Union Ltd v Dept of Trade* [1980] Ch 82, 89 *per* Megarry V-C. *Re Barrett* (1992) 106 ALR 549, 563 (FCA—life). *Re Bendix Automotive of Canada Ltd and UAW Local 195* (1971) 20 DLR (3d) 151, 157 (Ont—PHA); *Burt v Union Central Life Ins Co*, 187 US 362, 366 *per* Brewer J (1902—life); *Commissioner of Internal Revenue v Treganowan*, 183 F 2d 288, 290 (2 Cir, 1950—life).

37. Most taxis sustain insured damage in the course of annual insurance cover: PM 23 June 1988, p 32.

38. *Prudential Ins Co v IRC* [1904] 2 KB 658, 663 *per* Channell J (life). *Idem* as regards property damage caused by subsidence: *Prudential–LMI Commercial Insurance v Superior Court*, 274 Cal Rptr 387, 401 (1990—fire); Towner, 27 Tort & Ins L J 638 (1992).

38a. *National Mutual Life Assn v FCT* (1959) 102 CLR 29, 45 *per* Windeyer J (HCA—life). Allsop, (1992) 5 Ins L J 123.

39. *Department of Trade & Industry v St Christophers Motorists' Assn* [1974] 1 Lloyd's Rep 17, 19–20 *per* Templeman J (mobility).

39a. Below 17–3A.

39b. *International Ins Co v Peabody Int. Corp*, 747 F Supp 477, 484 (ND Ill, 1990—liability). This rule is sometimes called the "known loss" doctrine.

said[40] that the insurance event must be outside the control of the insurer, or that the event giving rise to the obligation to pay is not one for which the insurer is responsible.[41]

1–1E An Adverse Event

The insurance "must be against something . . . an event which is *prima facie* adverse to the interest of the assured".[42] If the insured has an insurable interest in the subject-matter of the insurance,[43] the event will be adverse to him; but the reverse is not true. Whether or not insurable interest is an essential feature of insurance,[44] it is an essential feature of **valid** insurance in England. It is said that, whereas a wager, from which insurance must be distinguished, creates a risk, insurance distributes an existing risk. Nonetheless, one is not allowed to insure against the loss of an existing wager. These difficulties are considered in chapter 4.

The possibility that the adverse event will occur creates a risk for the insured, which the contract of insurance transfers to the insurer so that, from the insurer's side, there is also now a risk—he may gain or he may lose and it can be said that the contract is one that can be described as a "contract upon speculation".[45] Whether the insurance is indemnity insurance or contingency insurance, there must be a risk of loss[46] for the insured "and an assumption of it by another . . . Hazard is essential and equally so the shifting of its incidence. If there is no risk, or there being one it is not shifted to another or others, there can be neither insurance nor indemnity".[46a] In a case of life insurance, risk "shifting emphasizes the individual aspect of insurance: the effecting of a contract between the insurer and the insured each of whom gamble on the time the latter will die. Risk distribution, on the other hand, emphasizes the broader, social aspect of insurance as a method of dispelling the danger of a potential loss by spreading its cost throughout a group. By diffusing the risks through a mass of separate risk

---

40. MacGillivray No 6; Tarr, p 11.

41. Birds, p 12. In *Mein v US Car Testing Co,* 184 NE 2d 489, 493 (Ohio, 1961) a motor maintenance contract was held to be insurance, as it promised indemnity for loss caused by events for which the promisor was not responsible. *Idem: Gerenstein v Weiner* 164 NYS 2d 122 (1957).

42. *Lucena v Craufurd* (1806) 2 Bos & Pul 269, 301 *per* Lawrence J (hull); *Prudential Ins Co v IRC* [1904] 2 KB 658, 663, *per* Channell J (life); *Department of Trade & Industry v St Christophers Motorists' Assn* [1974] 1 Lloyd's Rep 17, 21 *per* Templeman J (mobility).

43. The subject-matter of the insurance—house, bicycle, life—has been distinguished from the subject-matter of the insurance contract, which is money: *Rayner v Preston* (1881) 18 Ch D 1, 9 *per* Brett LJ (CA—fire).

44. *Cf Medical Defence Union Ltd v Dept of Trade* [1980] Ch 82, 89–90 *per* Megarry V-C, who called it one of the "three elements in a contract of insurance". In this sense: *Home Ins Co v Bernstein*, 16 NYS 2d 45, 47 (1939—motor); *Congdon v Oneida County Grange Co-operative Fire Ins Co*, 114 NYS 2d 167 (1952—fire). However, doubt is cast on this *inter alia* by recent Australian legislation, allowing insurance without interest: see Tarr, pp 10–11.

45. *Carter v Boehm* (1766) 3 Burr 1905, 1909 *per* Lord Mansfield.

46. *Re Commonwealth Homes & Investment Co Ltd* [1943] SASR 211, 231.

46a. *California Physicians' Service v Garrison*, 172 P 2d 4, 12 (Cal, 1946—PHA), and cases cited, holding that a mere agent or distributor of funds was not an insurer. See also *Securities & Exchange Commission v Variable Annuity Life Ins Co*, 359 US 65, 71 (1958—annuity). And in Australia: *Re Barrett* (1992) 106 ALR 549, 564 (FCA—life), in which the amount to be (re)paid by the "insurer" was little more than the amount paid by the "insured" plus interest: this was not insurance but an investment service.

It is irrelevant that the insurer, for example the insurer whose premiums and investment income is high, trades without financial risk: *Flood v Irish Provident Assurance Co Ltd* [1912] 2 Ch 597 (CA Ir—life); *Commissioner of Internal Revenue v Treganowan*, 183 F 2d 288 (2 Cir, 1950—life).

shifting contracts, the insurer casts his lot with the law of averages".[47] The "elements of risk-shifting and risk-distributing are essential to a life insurance contract".[48] Although Keeton[49] saw risk shifting and distribution as the principal characteristics of insurance, he also saw that they are not peculiar to insurance. Nearly every business venture entails some allocation of risk,[50] and some of those risks may be outside the control of the parties. Something more is required to distinguish insurance from, for example, an export sale subject to licence, a merchandise warranty, a repair contract for a price fixed in advance,[51] or a contract of guarantee.[52]

While adversity is an essential of indemnity insurance,[53] it is not, it is said,[54] an essential of all insurance, notably contingency insurance[55] such as an annuity, sometimes described as the obverse of life insurance, whereby money becomes payable if the insured survives to a stated age. Some judges, such as Megarry V-C,[56] have regarded maturity as a blessing rather than a curse: a "feat of survival can hardly be called an event that is adverse to his interests". For others[57] maturity is less blessed. Adversity may lie in the precarious state of income and of health, with associated demands on savings, which old age can bring. It is not stretching words, and there is judicial support,[58] to suggest that the insurance is a provision against the "pecuniary disadvantage"[59] often associated with retirement and old age, and survival to the stated age is a simple and arbitrary contingency which determines whether the pro-

---

47. *Commissioner of Internal Revenue* v *Treganowan*, 183 F 2d 288, 291 (2 Cir, 1950—life), quoting 59 Yale LJ 780, 784.

48. *Helvering* v *Le Gierse*, 312 US 531, 539 (1940—life). The case concerned a life "insurance policy" and an annuity issued to the "insured" shortly before her death aged 80. The Supreme Court viewed them together and observed (p 542): "Here the total consideration was prepaid and exceeded the face value of the 'insurance' policy. The excess financed loading and other incidental charges. Any risk that the prepayment would earn less than the amount paid to the ['insured'] as an annuity was an investment risk similar to the risk assumed by a bank; it was not an insurance risk." See also *Ballou* v *Fisher*, 61 P 2d 423, 425 (Or, 1936); *Group Life & Health Ins Co* v *Royal Drug Co*, 440 US 205, 211 (1979); *Pilot Life Ins Co* v *Dedeau*, 481 US 41, 48 (1987—disability). Pierce, 19 Western Univ L R 165, 168 (1992) and references cited. But *cf* *Cook* v *Field*, discussed below 3–6B2.

49. p 9.

50. *Transportation Guarantee Co* v *Jellins*, 174 P 2d 625, 629 (Cal, 1946).

51. *Jellins* (above) held that a motor vehicle maintenance contract was not insurance. Generally in this sense: *Re Barrett* (1992) 106 ALR 549, 563 (FCA—life); *Vesta Ins Co* v *Amoco Production Co*, 986 F 2d 981 (5 Cir, 1993). This was the decision in *Griffin Systems Inc* v *Ohio Dept of Ins*, 575 NE 2d 803, 807 (Ohio, 1991), however, the court indicated that if the warranty had concerned defects in products provided not by the alleged insurer but by a third party the decision might have been different. *Cf* also *Mein* v *US Car Testing Co*, 184 NE 2d 489, 493 (Ohio, 1961). Moreover, an arrangement or contract whereby a party retains an insurance risk does not make that party an insurer: *Jellins*, p 632. In *Brown* v *University Nursing Home Inc*, 496 SW 2d 503 (Tenn, 1973) it was held that a contract with a nursing home to provide for an elderly patient such care "as may be required" was not an insurance contract. In *Feinstein* v *ATG*, 366 NYS 2d 613, 616 (1975) it was held that a contract for prepaid legal services was not insurance.

52. Below 1–2.

53. *Gould* v *Curtis* [1913] 3 KB 84, 95 *per* Buckley LJ (CA—life).

54. *Medical Defence Union Ltd* v *Dept of Trade* [1980] Ch 82, 93 *per* Megarry V-C.

55. *Gould* v *Curtis* [1913] 3 KB 84, 92 *per* Cozens-Hardy MR, 95 *per* Buckley LJ (CA—life). The decision that endowment insurance was insurance in the sense of statute was also reached in *Flood* v *Irish Provident Assurance Co Ltd* [1912] 2 Ch 597 (CA Ir—life). See further *Joseph* v *Law Integrity Ins Co Ltd* [1912] 2 Ch 581 (CA—life).

Cf Gray v *Kerslake* [1958] SCR 3 that an annuity contract, although contingent on the duration of life, should be seen not as insurance but as a pension arrangement.

56. *Medical Defence Union Ltd* v *Dept of Trade* [1980] Ch 82, 93.

57. Including T S Eliot: "Do not let me hear of the wisdom of old men, but rather of their folly."

58. *Gould* v *Curtis* [1913] 3 KB 84, 98–99 *per* Kennedy LJ (CA—life). See also *Prudential Ins* Co v *IRC* [1904] 2 KB 658 (life).

59. *Ibid*.

vision should be paid. A similar concern lies behind insurance against the blessing of children.[60] In any case, the Insurance Companies Act 1982 expressly applies to annuities[61] and this kind of arrangement is generally regarded as insurance.[61a]

1–1F Premium

"It must be a contract . . . for some consideration, usually but not necessarily for periodical payments called premiums."[62] It may be a fixed payment in advance of cover or, in the case of mutual insurance, a subsequent call in the light of claims experience.[63] It may be a component part of a larger payment.[64]

The calculation of the amount of premium on the basis of the chance that the contingency will occur, rather than the actual cost of the contingency after the event, is said[65] to distinguish insurance contracts from repair contracts, but does not distinguish the latter from mutual insurance. Further, the calculation of premium according to the particular risk has been denied as an essential element of insurance.[66]

1–2 GUARANTEE INSURANCE

Insurance contracts must be distinguished from performance bonds[66a] and, in particular, guarantee contracts, which may be contracts of indemnity but are not insurance contracts. In particular, a guarantee contract, whereby A guarantees that B will repay B's debt to C, must be distinguished from an insurance contract, especially credit or guarantee insurance, whereby A promises to indemnify C, if B fails to pay or repay a debt.[66b] By the Statute of Frauds, 1677, section 4, guarantees are required to be evidenced in writing and signed, if they are to be enforced; insurance contracts are often in writing but may be oral. Insurance contracts are construed strictly in favour of

---

60. Bunyon, *Life Assurance* (4th ed 1904), ch 6.

61. Schedule 1. Likewise the Cal Ins Code provides (section 100) that insurance includes life insurance, and (section 101) that life insurance includes "the granting, purchasing, or disposing of annuities".

61a. On the question when arrangements contracted with a view to investment and return can be regarded as life insurance, see Allsop, (1992) 5 Ins L J 123.

62. *Lucena* v *Craufurd* (1806) 2 Bos & Pul 269, 301 *per* Lawrence J (hull); *Prudential Ins Co* v *IRC* [1904] 2 KB 658, 663 *per* Channell J (life). *Ollendorf Watch Co* v *Pink*, 17 NE 2d 676, 677 (NY); *Re Commonwealth Homes & Investment Co Ltd* [1943] SASR 211, 231: some element of premium may be required to distinguish life insurance from a loan, the repayment of which is accelerated by the death of the lender. *Cf R* v *Cohen* (1979) 27 ALR 263, 270 *per* Mason J (HCA—motor) that a premium was not essential; but this must be seen in the context of the issue: see 1–1A above.

63. On the distinction see *Standard Steamship Owners' P & I Assn (Bermuda) Ltd.* v *Gann* [1992] 2 Lloyd's Rep 528, 531 ff per Hirst J (P & I). On mutual insurance, see Hazelwood, *P & I Clubs, Law and Practice* (London 1989).

Cf Hampton v *Toxteth Co-operative Provident Sy Ltd* [1915] 1 Ch 721 (CA—life) in which business profits were used *inter alia* to pay pensions to members whose spouses had died. The majority view was expressed by Lord Cozens-Hardy MR (pp 732–733; see also p 732 *per* Joyce J): "The arrangement . . . is nothing more than an appropriation of income." However, Phillimore LJ (dissenting p 738) replied that "this is the case with all mutual insurance societies. The profits first go in paying . . . claims".

64. *Ollendorf Watch Co* v *Pink*, 17 NE 2d 676 (NY) in which the price of a watch included a promise by the seller to replace the watch if it were stolen within 12 months.

65. MacGillivray No 2.

66. *Commissioner of Internal Revenue* v *Treganowan*, 183 F 2d 288, 291 (2 Cir, 1950—life).

66a. *Cf* also surety bonds: Goode [1988] JBL 88.

66b. Guarantee insurance also includes fidelity insurance: Kantor, (1993) 3 Ins L & P (no 2) 49; and thus bankers' blanket bond insurance: Rose, (1993) 82 BILA Journal 15.

cover,[67] but guarantees are construed strictly against the creditor.[68] Moreover, guarantees may be discharged by any compromise between creditor and debtor[69] and, it has been maintained,[70] are not subject to the doctrine of good faith.

"Contracts of guarantee are between persons who are in the positions of creditor, debtor and surety. The surety assumes the obligation to make good the default of the principal debtor either for a fee or even without a fee from motives of friendship towards the debtor. There is not usually any bargaining between the guarantor and the creditor; nor is there a payment made by the creditor. On the other hand an insurer engages to pay a loss incurred by the insured in the event of a certain contingency occurring."[71] The obligation of the insurer is said[72] to be direct, that of a guarantor is accessory. They are distinguished less by the parties' intention or their objective, for in each case the purpose is the financial security of the creditor C, but by the method employed to achieve it.[73] The contract is characterised "not upon a scrutiny of the terms used but upon an examination of its effect".[74]

Among the elements that distinguish insurance from a guarantee are whether (a) there is payment (premium) from C to A[75]; (b) if the contingency occurs, the loss ultimately falls on A[76]; (c) the risk of default is a risk with which A is or should be familiar, so that he cannot complain of non-disclosure[77]; (d) the arrangement was instigated by C, which suggests insurance, or by B, which suggests a guarantee[78]; and (e) the agreement includes or excludes a characteristic consequence.[79]

67. See below 15–5C.

68. *Blest* v *Brown* (1862) 4 De G F & J 367, 376 *per* Lord Westbury; applied in *Doe* v *Canadian Surety Co* [1937] SCR 1, 19.

69. *Dane* v *Mortgage Ins Corp Ltd* [1894] 1 QB 54 (CA—solvency). *Doe* v *Canadian Surety Co* [1937] SCR 1.

70. *North British Ins Co* v *Lloyd* (1854) 10 Ex 523, 534–535 *per* Pollock CB; *Seaton* v *Heath* [1899] 1 QB 782, 793 *per* Romer LJ (CA—solvency). MacGillivray No 714. But *cf Railton* v *Mathews* (1844) 10 Cl & Fin 934 (HL—fidelity bond); *London General Omnibus Co Ltd* v *Holloway* [1912] 2 KB 72 (CA—fidelity bond); *Trade Indemnity Co Ltd* v *Workington Harbour & Dock Board* [1937] AC 1, 17 *per* Lord Atkin.

North British (above) was applied in *Niagara District Fruit Growers Stock Co* v *Walker* (1896) 26 SCR 629, 634–635. However, in the case of guarantees there may be a limited duty of disclosure: *Churchbridge* v *London Guarantee & Accident Ins Co* [1925] 3 DLR 341 (Sask—guarantee bond). Brown & Menezes, No 1:2:9 suggest that it is limited to a duty to disclose improbable facts.

71. *The Zuhal K* [1987] 1 Lloyd's Rep 151, 155 *per* Sheen J. See also Blair 29 MLR 522 (1966). For the view that the law should draw a distinction between sureties who act for personal reasons and those that act for reward, "compensated sureties", see [1992] LMCLQ 177.

72. *Scottish Amicable Heritable Securities Assn Ltd* v *Northern Assurance Co* (1883) 11 R (Ct Sess) 287, 303 *per* Lord Moncrieff (fire); *Dane* v *Mortgage Ins Corp Ltd* [1894] 1 QB 54, 61 *per* Lord Esher MR (CA—solvency).

73. *Seaton* v *Heath* [1899] 1 QB 782, 792 per Romer LJ (CA—solvency), applied in *International Commercial Bank* v *Ins Corp of Ireland* [1991] ILRM 726 (High Ct of Ireland). See also *Yeoman Credit Ltd* v *Latter* [1961] 2 All ER 294, 296 *per* Holroyd Pearce LJ (CA).

74. *Re Law Guarantee Trust & Accident Sy Ltd* [1914] 2 Ch 617, 631 *per* Buckley LJ (CA—mortgage ins). *Cf International Commercial Bank* (above) pp 736 ff, in which the court did examine the terms to assess whether they were characteristic of insurance or of guarantee.

75. Payment from B to A is not indicative. *Cf* Blair, 29 MLR 522, 527 (1966).

76. A factor fatal to the insurance argument in *The Zuhal K* [1987] 1 Lloyd's Rep 151 was that the arrangement provided for a counter-indemnity from principal debtor to guarantor.

77. *Seaton* v *Heath* [1899] 1 QB 782, 793 *per* Romer LJ (CA—solvency), applied in *International Commercial Bank* (above) p 738. *Cf Trade Indemnity Co Ltd* v *Workington Harbour & Dock Board* [1937] AC 1.

78. International Commercial Bank (above) p 736. See also Blair, 29 MLR 522, 527 (1966), citing *Seaton* (above). In the case of guarantee C may require B to instigate the arrangement.

79. Thus a clause forbidding release of B suggests a guarantee: *Trade Indemnity Co Ltd* v *Workington Harbour & Dock Board* [1937] AC 1, 17 *per* Lord Atkin.

1–3 INSURANCE CONTRACTS

"What do they know of the law of insurance, who only the law of contract know ?" "A contract of insurance is no different from any other contract." These conflicting views come from judges in the United States 70 years ago.[80] Not surprisingly, the truth probably lies somewhere between these two statements.[80a] The insurance contract has been affected by legislation and judicial activity much more in the United States than in England.[81] In the United States, the insurers started the century under the cloud of scandal, which invited hostility and intervention.[81a] Then, at a time when in England the state was assuming some responsibility in matters of health and social welfare, in the United States the welfare programme had not begun and people depended on private insurance.[82] The expectations of the people were supported by judges, some of whom were elected by those people, and who saw themselves in varying degrees as the representatives of the people against the corporations, including the insurance companies. At the same time there were developments in the law of tort which assumed that insurers would pay the bill. Professor Fleming James[83] had instructed a generation of lawyers that the purpose of the law of torts was to distribute risks through insurance, social insurance of a kind based on private contract. The expansion of liability in tort by judges required a matched expansion of insurance cover, which if resisted by insurers, came to the same judges for decision. Still, it could be said,[84] for many purposes an insurance contract "is a contract and stands on no different basis than any other contract".

Nonetheless, Professor Kessler argued[85] that "the courts pay merely lip service to the dogma that the common law of contracts governs insurance contracts. With the help of the law of torts they nullify those parts of the law of contracts which in the public interest are regarded as inapplicable." The impact of tort, coupled with intervention by state authorities, affected insurance contracts in the United States in a number of ways, which are not found in England. (a) The court in the United States is more likely to find a contract to be an insurance contract in cases of doubt. (b) Contracts are interpreted to fulfil the reasonable expectations of the insured (below, 15–5A). (c) As the doctrine of proximate cause was stretched in tort, so the doctrine of the same name was stretched to match it (below, 25–3). (d) If the insurer was slow to pay he became liable for consequential loss under the tort of bad faith (below, 30–10). (e) In many states, including notably New York, certain classes of insurance must be contracted on a standard form approved by a regulatory body.

---

80. Quoted by Holmes, 39 U Pitt L Rev 381, 393 (1978). Even today, for example, in Ohio, "an insurance policy is a contract, and the parties' rights under the contract are purely contractual in nature": *Park—Ohio Industries Inc* v *Home Indemnity Co*, 975 F 2d 1215, 1218 (6 Cir, 1992—liability).

80a. Holmes (above).

81. Hasson, (1984) 47 MLR 505.

81a. Roe, 93 Colum. L. Rev. 639 (1993).

82. Hasson, p 521.

83. Harper & James, *The Law of Torts* (1956). See an illuminating discussion of the second edition of the book in (1987) 7 OJLS 279.

84. *Blair* v *Berkshire Life Ins Co*, 429 F 2d 996, 1000 (3 Cir, 1970—life). Also in this sense: Keeton p 2. *Aetna Ins Co* v *Eisenberg,* 185 F Supp 415, 418–419 (ED Ark, 1960), affirmed 294 F 2d 301 (8 Cir, 1961); *Moss* v *National Life & Accident Ins Co*, 385 F Supp 1291, 1295 (WD Mo, 1974—life); *Wood* v *Allstate Ins Co*, 815 F Supp 1185, 1193 (ND Ind, 1993—fire; although the contract may receive special treatment as a contract of adhesion: *Young* v *Metropolitan Life Ins Co,* 77 Cal Rptr 568 (1969—life).

85. 43 Col L Rev 629, 635 (1943). Indeed, there is a history of judicial hostility to insurance companies in the USA that is not found in England; see, for example, Works, 70 Neb L Rev 229, 244 (1991).

In England, however, it is, said Roskill LJ, "desirable that the same legal principles should apply to the law of contract as a whole and that different legal principles should not apply to different branches of that law".[86] In England,[87] as well as Australia[88] and New Zealand,[89] insurance contracts are subject to the general law of contract, albeit with some special rules, such as the duty of good faith. However, again and again courts faced with particular issues have recognised a familiar issue of contract and asserted that the rule of general contract law applies. The general law of contract provides a frame of reference, from which by education, inclination and tradition the English judge proceeds. The general law of contract provides a substratum to which the judge can resort, if a rule of "insurance law" is not apparent. It is from the perspective of general contract law that most English lawyers come to problems of insurance and it is from this perspective that this book has been written.

86. *The Hansa Nord* [1976] 1 QB 44, 71 *per* Roskill LJ (CA).
87. Beale, Bishop & Furmston, *Contract Cases and Materials* (1985) ch 1(a). *Cf* Atiyah, *Essays on Contract* (1986), ch 1; Swan, U Toronto LJ 217, 220 (1988). Moreover, insurance contracts are still seen mainly as commercial contracts. In commercial contracts classical contract theory survives. Priestley, 1 *Journal of Contract Law* 15, 17 (1988).
88. Sutton No 1.6.
89. Timmins, 7 VUWL Rev 217 (1974).

CHAPTER 2

THE CONFLICT OF LAWS[1]

2–1 THE PROPER LAW OF THE INSURANCE CONTRACT

2–1A Introduction

"Contracts are incapable of existing in a legal vacuum. They are mere pieces of paper devoid of all legal effect unless they were made by reference to some system of private law which defines obligations assumed by the parties to the contract."[2] This book is about English law, which is relevant chiefly when English law governs the contract. This chapter is concerned with identifying the law that governs the contract of insurance. The subject may arise at two stages of proceedings. First, the English court may have to ask whether it has jurisdiction in the matter: one ground of jurisdiction is that English law applies.[3] Second, if the English courts have jurisdiction on other grounds, the court, faced with a conflict of laws, will have to consider whether English law (or some other law) governs the contract.

If an insurance contract is connected with more than one system of law, there is a potential conflict between the laws concerned. In the absence of evidence that relevant foreign law is different from that of the court, the court will apply its own law,[4] the *lex fori*. If different, the court turns to the conflicts' rules of the *lex fori*, to which the insurance contract like any other contract is subject. Under the conflicts' rules of the English court, an insurance contract may be governed by any one of three different regimes.

---

1. Appleman, sections 7041 ff; Carnaham, *Conflict of Laws and Life Insurance Contracts* (2nd ed, 1958); Castel, *Canadian Conflict of Laws* (2nd ed, 1986), Nos 437–438; Collier, *Conflict of Laws* (1987), pp 143 ff; Dicey & Morris, *Conflict of Laws* (12th ed, 1993) pp 1338 ff; Ehrenzweig, *Treatise on the Conflict of Laws* (1962), pp 511 ff; Hancock, *Studies in Modern Choice-of-Law: Torts, Insurance, Land Titles* (Buffalo, 1984); Maitland-Walker, "EC Insurance Directives" (London); Merkin, "The Proper Law of Insurance and Reinsurance Contracts", *New Foundations*, p 61; Restatement (2d), Conflict of Laws, sections 192, 193; Roth, *Internationales Versicherungsvertragsrecht* (Tübingen 1985); Unger, "Life Insurance and the Conflict of Laws", 13 Int & Comp LQ 482 (1964), Wani, "Choice of Law Theory in the Courts: a Missouri Case Study", 32 St Louis Univ L J 355 (1987), Williston, section 1292A. For further references see Roth, pp 763 ff.
2. *Amin Rasheed Shipping Corp v Kuwait Ins Co* [1984] AC 50, 65 *per* Lord Diplock (hull).
3. As to jurisdiction, see below 2–9 and 2–10.
4. *Gold v Life Assurance Co of Pennsylvania* [1971] 2 Lloyd's Rep 164, 167 *per* Donaldson J (life). *Canadian Fire Ins Co v Robinson* (1901) 31 SCR 488 (fire); *Continental Casualty Co v Thompson*, 369 F 2d 157 (9 Cir, 1966—PA). For a more sophisticated view of the problem, see Schlesinger, 59 Cornell L Rev 1 (1973).

First, reinsurance contracts and contracts on risks situated outside the European Community (EC) are governed by the Rome Convention, which was enacted in England by the Contracts (Applicable Law) Act 1990[5]: below, 2–7.

Second, "general business", i.e. non-life insurance contracts, on risks situated in the EC is governed by legislation derived from an EC Directive.[6] This was enacted by the Insurance Companies (Amendment) Regulations 1990[7] and came into force on 1 July 1990 as a new section, section 92A, of the Insurance Companies Act 1982.[8] See below, 2–8.

Third, life insurance contracts on risks situated in the EC are governed by legislation derived from the Second Life Insurance Directive.[9] This was enacted by the Insurance Companies (Amendment) Regulations 1993 and came into force on 20 May 1993.

The common law rules have been largely replaced as regards contracts concluded after these regimes come into force. Even so, it is likely that English courts will fall back on common law ideas to answer various questions unsettled by the new regimes. For example, whereas the Rome Convention regulates the material validity of a contract, the EC regime for general business is silent on such matters. Further, paragraph 5(1) of Schedule 3A to the Insurance Companies Act 1982 directs the court to "apply the general rules of private international law . . . concerning contractual obligations". An English court might see this as an invitation to fall back on familiar rules of common law. Finally, it should be stressed that the new rules do not have retrospective effect and that common law still governs contracts within the scope of the Rome Convention,[10] if concluded before 1 July 1991, and to other insurance contracts on risks in the EC before the EC Directives had effect: a point of importance for life contracts. For these reasons, the first part of this chapter is devoted to the rules of common law.

2–1B The Scope of the Proper Law

In English common law, the "proper law" of the contract is "the law which governs the contract and the parties' obligations under it; it is the law which determines (normally) its validity and legality, its construction and effect, and the conditions of its discharge".[11]

5. For a useful introduction to the position for insurance contracts, see O'Dowd, *BILA Journal*, No 76, May 1991, p 13.

6. A complementary provision of the Rome Convention, art. 1.3, excludes from that Convention "contracts of insurance which cover risks situated in the territories of the Member States of the European Economic Community. In order to determine whether a risk is situated in these territories the court shall apply its internal law". The internal law of England for this purpose is found in section 96A(3) of the Insurance Companies Act 1982. Art 1.4 of the Rome Convention saves reinsurance contracts which, therefore, remain subject to the Rome Convention. Maitland-Walker, chapter 3.

7. SI 1990 No 1333.

8. See below.

9. Maitland-Walker, chapter 4.

10. Art 29.

11. *Amin* (above note 2) p 69 *per* Lord Wilberforce (hull); see also p 60 *per* Lord Diplock. As to discharge, see also *Perry* v *Equitable Life Assurance Sy* (1929) 45 TLR 468 (life). Discharge includes the determination of the place where policy monies are to be paid: *Pick* v *Manufacturers Life Ins Co* [1958] 2 Lloyd's Rep 93, 97 *per* Diplock J (life).

For certainty, though not necessarily confidence, all aspects of the contract should be governed by one system of law. In 1933, on the question of the currency for payment of dividends to shareholders, Lord Wright said this[12]: "It is established that *prima facie*, whatever is the proper law of a contract regarded as a whole, the law of the place of performance should be applied in respect of any particular obligation which is performable in a particular country other than the country of the proper law of the contract." Today, the established rule is different. Although parties are free to choose that different parts of the contract shall be governed by different systems of law, it is usually inferred or imputed that most aspects of the contract are governed by one system of law.[13] "In general, it has always been held that an insurance relationship cannot be fragmented, as the scission of a unitary contract, it has been felt, would produce great inconvenience, confusion, and difficulties."[14]

Consequently, (a) the validity of a contract is judged by its proper law.[15] This includes whether the contract can be avoided for economic duress,[16] misrepresentation or non-disclosure.[17] (b) All questions of interpretation of the insurance contract are governed by the proper law, except as regards a term of currency foreign to the proper law: all questions about the "currency in any particular country must be ascertained in accordance with the law of that country".[18] (c) Whereas the amount of money to be paid under an insurance contract is a question of substance and governed by the proper law, the mode of payment is determined by the law of the place of payment.[20] Moreover, it is inherent in the application of the proper law by the English courts that "nobody will be held liable to perform a contract, at any rate an English contract, in so far as the performance would be illegal by the law of the country in which it is to take place".[21] (d) As regards rights of suit and, in particular, the right of third parties to bring action against the insurer, the balance of opinion[22] is that this is not a matter for the *lex fori* but a matter for the proper law of the contract. Certain questions of damages,[23] and the validity of an arbitration clause[24] are also governed

12. *Adelaide Electric Supply Co Ltd* v *Prudential Assurance Co Ltd* [1934] AC 122, 151, citing *Ralli Bros.* v *CN Sota y Aznar* [1920] 2 KB 287 (CA—charterparty freight).

13. *Royal Exchange Assurance Corp* v *Sjorforsakrings AB Vega* [1901] 2 KB 567, 574 *per* Bigham J (re); *Forsik. Vesta* v *Butcher* [1986] 2 Lloyd's Rep 179, 193 *per* Hobhouse J (re).

Cf Restatement, Conflict of Laws (2d) section 188. Many states favour *dépeçage*, that is, issue-by-issue analysis. However, outside the USA the notion has found little favour: Lando, International Encyclopedia of Comparative Law, vol III, chapter 24 nos 14 ff.

14. Lenhof, *op cit*, p 553, citing *Aetna Life Ins Co* v *Dunken*, 266 US 389 (1924—life).

15. Dicey, p 1253.

16. *The Evia Luck* [1992] 1 Lloyd's Rep 115 (HL).

17. *Mackender* v *Feldia AG* [1967] 2 QB 590, 603 *per* Diplock LJ (CA— jewellers' block).

18. *Ottoman Bk of Nicosia* v *Chakarian* [1938] AC 260, 278 *per* Lord Wright (PC). *Cf Weiss* v *State Life Ins Co* [1935] SCR 461 in which the *prima facie* rule, that dollars payable in Indiana meant American dollars, was overridden by a mandatory statute of the proper law, which was also the *lex fori*.

20. *Mount Albert BC* v *Australasian Temperance & General Mutual Life Assurance Sy Ltd* [1938] AC 224 (PC).

21. *Ralli Bros* v *CN Sota y Aznar* [1920] 2 KB 287 (CA).

22. See Kaye p 809. *Cf* the insurer's rights in subrogation: in *Javed* v *British Airways plc*, 980 F 2d 1407 (11 Cir, 1993), these rights were governed by the (English) law which the parties had expressly chosen for matters of subrogation.

23. Such as remoteness: *D'Almeida Araujo Lda* v *Sir Frederick Becker & Co Ltd* [1953] 2 QB 329, relying on *Livesley* v *Horst Co* [1924] SCR 605, 610 *per* Duff J. But quantification of damages is a matter for the *lex fori: D'Almeida*, p 338 *per* Pilcher J.

24. *Hamlyn* v *Talisker Distillery* [1894] AC 202; *Spurrier* v *La Cloche* [1902] AC 446 (PC—fire).

by the proper law. Questions of procedure, however, such as pre-trial discovery of documents and estoppel, are matters for the procedural *lex fori*.[25]

2–1C Related Contracts

Contracts that are closely related contracts are presumptively governed by the same law[26]; thus "there must be a *prima facie* inference that a following policy is governed by the same law as the policy it follows".[27]

A less simple picture is found in the case of a reinsurance contract. On one view, it can be interpreted in accordance with law A, the law of the closely related primary insurance contract, but governed by a different law, law B. This was the view of Hobhouse J in *Forsik. Vesta* v *Butcher*[28]:

"Where a contract such as the present provides that its terms and conditions are to be the same as those of another contract and where its clear commercial purpose is to provide a corresponding cover to that provided by the other contract, then, unless some other powerful consideration is to intervene, the conclusion must be that there is an intention that both contracts are to be governed by the same law."

Recalling that the primary contract was governed by Norwegian law, he continued[29]:

"However, there remains something surprising and improbable about the conclusion that the Lloyd's slip and the Lloyd's policy are governed by anything other than English law . . . In the present case there is an express provision for the terms and conditions of the reinsurance contract and those of the original insurance to be the same and the reinsurance is manifestly back-to-back with the original insurance. From this one should infer a contractual intent that the legal effect of the clauses which define and limit the scope of the cover should be the same in the reinsurance and in the original insurance. When one takes into account that the parties clearly must contemplate that the original insurance is governed by Norwegian law I infer as a matter of English law that the parties intended the construction and effect of the clauses . . . shall be governed by Norwegian law. . . . The reinsurance contract itself is and remains an English law contract but it is one which is made with reference to, and on the terms of, the Norwegian law contract of original insurance."

---

25. *South Carolina Ins Co* v *Assurantie Maatschappij "De Zeven Provincien" NV* [1987] AC 24. Estoppel: *Janred Properties Ltd* v *Enit* [1989] 2 All ER 444 (CA). At one time, time limitation was seen as procedural, however, the Foreign Limitation Periods Act 1984 provides that it is a matter of substance and hence governed by the proper law. Further there is authority (*Leroux* v *Brown* (1852) 12 CB 801) that the requirement that a contract be evidenced in writing is a question of procedure; for criticism see Dicey, pp 176 ff.
Restatement (2d), section 142 (1988 revision) provides that in general:
  "(1) The forum will apply its own statute of limitations barring the claim unless the exceptional circumstances of the case make such a result unreasonable.
  (2) The forum will apply its own statute of limitations permitting the claim unless:
        (a) maintenance of the claim would serve no significant interest of the forum; and
        (b) the claim would be barred under the statute of limitations of a state having a more significant relationship to the parties and the occurrence."
26. *Armadora Occidental SA* v *Mann* [1977] 1 All ER 347, 351 *per* Kerr J (hull); *Forsik. Vesta* v *Butcher* [1988] 1 Lloyd's Rep. 19, 34 *per* Sir Roger Ormrod (CA—re); *Islamic Arab Ins Co* v *Saudi Egyptian American Reinsurance Co* [1987] 1 Lloyd's Rep 315, 320 *per* Bingham LJ (re).
27. *Du Pont de Nemours & Co* v *Agnew* [1987] 2 Lloyd's Rep 585, 591 *per* Bingham LJ (CA—liability).
28. [1986] 2 All ER 488, 504; the direct insurance was governed by Norwegian law. According to English law but not Norwegian law, breach of a warranty (24 hour watch on the fish farm insured), which caused no loss, discharged the insurer from liability.
29. pp 504–505.

This hybrid solution to the dilemma was as ingenious as it will, perhaps, be isolated.[30] The judge continued[31]:

"this conclusion is fully in accordance with the business nature of the transaction. London underwriters and brokers are seeking to market insurance contracts in foreign countries. As a matter of business they do not do this directly but make use of a local insurance company to obtain the business. The business reality is that the contract that is marketed is a local contract fronted by the local insurance company. The 90% reinsurance framework, like the profit commission and 25% brokerage payable to the brokers, is in reality only a mechanism to achieve this end. It is commercially unrealistic for reinsurers to rely on an English law consequence which forms no part of the scheme of the insurance which is being provided."

On appeal, the courts agreed with this view of the parties' intention and of the business nature of the transaction. At least one member of the Court of Appeal[32] had sympathy with the hybrid solution of the conflicts question. But most appeal judges, while not rejecting that solution outright,[33] preferred to see the issue as one of the construction of a (reinsurance) contract, entirely governed by English law. In the words of Lord Lowry[34] in the House of Lords, the question concerned the construction of a contract governed by English law, a contract in which the parties "are deemed to have used the same dictionary, in this case a Norwegian legal dictionary, to ascertain the meaning of the terms and conditions".

2–1D The Search for the Proper Law at Common Law

The doctrine of *renvoi* does not apply to contracts.[35] With insurance contracts, as with other contracts, paramount importance is given to psychological and subjective factors in the determination of the proper law[36]; in particular, the court seeks the law that gives the parties certainty and confidence.

The search for the proper law of the contract has three stages. If the court finds an answer in one stage, it does not proceed to the next.[37] The first stage is to seek an express choice of law (below, 2–2). If the court finds no express choice of law, the

30. Merkin, *op cit*, p 76 comments that the judge's problems "were of his own making. Had he taken the view that the full reinsurance clause did not permit the incorporation of anything (such as the watch clause) in the original insurance inconsistent with, or inappropriate to, the express provisions of the reinsurance contract, the reinsurers' obligation would, as a matter of English law, have remained merely to indemnify the reinsured for its liabilities under Norwegian law".

The decision was affirmed [1988] 1 Lloyd's Rep 19 (CA—re), but for a variety of reasons; for example, Sir Roger Ormrod (p 35) found an implied term in the reinsurance contract "that breach of warranty will only avoid, or permit underwriters to repudiate, the policy if breach of the same warranty will permit the reinsured to avoid the original policy". Some support, however, for the approach taken by Hobhouse J can be found (pp 32–33) in the judgment of Neill LJ (with whom O'Connor LJ agreed).

In some cases this kind of problem can be solved by incorporation of the foreign rules of law as terms of the contract: *Ex p Dever* (1887) 18 QBD 660, 668 *per* Fry LJ (CA—life), applied in *Travelers Canada* v *MacDonald* (1984) 14 DLR (4th) 88 (Ont—motor).

31. pp 503–504.

32. [1988] 1 Lloyd's Rep 19, 34 *per* Sir Roger Ormrod.

33. For example, Lord Lowry thought the hybrid view unnecessary: [1989] 1 AC 852, 911.

34. Ibid. Lords Bridge, Ackner and Griffiths agreed with Lord Lowry. See also p 891 *per* Lord Templeman.

35. *Amin Rasheed Shipping Corp* v *Kuwait Ins Co* [1984] AC 50, 62 *per* Lord Diplock (hull). Dicey, p 1204. *Reger* v *National Assn of Bedding Manufacturers Ins Trust Fund*, 372 NYS 2d 97, 118 (1975—group life).

36. Unger, p 488.

37. *Amin* (above) p 61 *per* Lord Diplock. On this case, see Stone [1984] LMCLQ 438. The three stage approach has been adopted in Australia: *John Kaldor Fabricmaker Pty Ltd* v *Mitchell Cotts Freight (Australia) Pty Ltd* (1989) 18 NSWLR 172 (mutual).

second stage is to seek an inferred choice of law (2–3). If the court finds no inferred choice of law,[38] the third stage is to seek the imputed proper law by localising the contract (2–4). Although the conceptual distinction between law inferred and law imputed is clear, its application to cases is not and particular decisions may be seen as illustrating one rule, the other or both[39]; and the same factors may be seen by one court as implicit of choice under stage two but by another court as localising the contract under stage three.[40]

2–2 COMMON LAW: EXPRESS CHOICE

If there is an express choice of law in the contract of insurance, that choice will be respected by the court.[41] So also, if the parties choose law A and state also that, if all or part (such as an arbitration clause) of the contract is unenforceable by law A, the contract shall be governed by law B.[42] In *Amin*,[43] an insurance case which has become a leading case for all kinds of contract, Lord Diplock said this:

"English conflict rules accord to the parties to a contract a wide liberty to choose the law by which their contract is to be governed. So the first step is to examine the policy in order to see whether the parties have, by its express terms, or by necessary implication from the language used, evinced a common intention as to the system of law by reference to which their mutual rights and obligations under it are to be ascertained."

2–2A Public Policy of the Forum

The effectiveness of an express choice of law has rarely been challenged in England by the judges—or by the parties to the contract, who may well be content with the commercial certainty that express choice usually provides. The exception is Lord Wright, who stated[44] that effect would be given to the parties' choice of law only if their choice was (a) *bona fide*, (b) legal and (c) a choice, which there was no reason for avoiding on grounds of public policy.[45] It is implicit in this statement, that the validity of an express choice of law is subject to the *lex fori*.[46]

This statement has generated many comments but few cases. Certainly, a choice of law clause will be disregarded by the English court, if its application would oust com-

---

38. *Bonython* v *Commonwealth of Australia* [1951] AC 201, 219 *per* Lord Simonds (PC), as interpreted by Lord Diplock in *Amin* (above), p 61.

39. Collier, p 152 pointing, for example, to *Amin* (above), in which Lord Diplock applied English law as the inferred choice of the parties, whereas Lord Wilberforce (p 69) applied English law as the imputed law, while observing that the two stages "merge into each other".

40. Collier [1983] CLJ 214.

41. *R* v *International Trustee* [1937] AC 500, 529 *per* Lord Atkin, approved in *Amin* (above) p 61 *per* Lord Diplock. For example, a choice of Russian law disadvantageous to the insured: *Perry* v *Equitable Life Assurance Sy* (1929) 45 TLR 468 (life); *Mutual Life Ins Co of New York* v *Cohen*, 179 US 262, 267 *per* Brewer J (1900—life). Restatement (2d), Conflict of Laws, section 186.

42. *The Mariannina* [1983] 1 Lloyd's Rep 12, 15 *per* Ackner LJ (CA).

43. *Amin* p 61.

44. *Vita Food Products Inc* v *Unus Shipping Co* [1939] AC 277, 290 (PC). For the view that Lord Wright's remark was intended to mean very little and that conditions (a) to (c) can be accommodated by other rules of law without negating the chosen law as the proper law, see Collier, pp 147–148.

45. The court may refuse to apply the chosen law, if that law validates a contract which, by the *lex fori*, would not be enforced because the insured lacked capacity to contract: Collier, p 164.

46. Cf *dicta* of Lord Diplock in *The Hollandia* [1983] 1 AC 565, 576. As regards the existence of a choice of law, i.e., consent, it seems that that is governed by the *lex fori*: *Mackender* v *Feldia AG* [1967] 2 QB 590 (CA).

pulsory rules of the *lex fori*.[47] In the United States, by way of comparison, the Restatement (2d), Conflict of Laws, section 187 states that the chosen law applies "unless . . . application of the law of the chosen state would be contrary to a fundamental policy of a state which has a materially greater interest than the chosen state in the determination of the particular issue" and which is the one with the most "significant relationship to the transaction and the parties" under section 188.[48] Moreover, in the case of life insurance, a choice of law will be disregarded there, if the law chosen gives the insured less protection than he would receive under the law otherwise applicable,[49] usually the law of domicile when the policy was applied for.

2–2B Connection with the Law Chosen

In England, a choice of a law, although designed to avoid a foreign system of law otherwise applicable as the imputed law, will be respected.[50] The courts will also respect a choice of a system of law having no factual connection with the contract.[51] For example, the English insured and the French insurer, who wish to escape the English rules of law concerning disclosure, may choose the law of California or New South Wales.[52] There appears to be no reported case, however, in which the chosen foreign law has been applied to a contract entirely English. Such a choice would be ignored, for example, in the United States,[53] or in France, where it would infringe the require-

---

47. The usual instance is a choice of law which, if respected, avoids a statute of the forum, such as the Carriage of Goods by Sea Act 1971: by virtue of a unilateral conflict rule in the state, when an English court is seized of a case within the scope of the Act, it must apply the Act: *The Hollandia* [1983] AC 565. *Re Mellon Estate* (1920) 53 DLR 664, 666 (Alta—life); *Reger v National Assn of Bedding Manufacturers Ins Trust Fund*, 372 NYS 2d 97, 116 (1975—group life) holding that the law of New York requiring notification to the insured of conversion rights was not mandatory public policy. See also *Foreman v Foreman Associates Ltd*, 517 F 2d 354 (9 Cir, 1975). The US Constitution "does not require a State to apply another State's law in violation of its own legitimate public policy"—*Nevada v Hall*, 440 US 410, 422 *per* Stevens J (1979). Lenhoff, pp 555 ff.

48. See below, 2–4. An example (Restatement (2d), Conflict of Laws, section 187, Comment (g)) is that of a statute designed to protect against the oppressive use of superior bargaining power.

49. Restatement (2d), Conflict of Laws, section 192 Comment (e). Courts have disregarded an express choice of the law of the insurer's place of incorporation, if its application would lead to forfeiture which would not have been permitted by a regulatory statute of the insured's place of residence: *New York Life Ins Co v Cravens*, 178 US 389, 398 *per* McKenna J (1900—life); *New England Life Ins Co v Olin*, 114 F 2d 131, 137 (7 Cir, 1940—life). Similarly, in *Oakley v National Western Life Ins Co*, 294 F Supp 504 (SD NY, 1968) the court applied the law of residence (New York) to a group life contract under a master policy governed by another law in respect of the right of the insured to notification of conversion: "New York clearly has an interest in assuring its domiciliaries are notified of the right to convert group insurance policies" (p 508). See further Ehrenzweig, op cit (note 1) p 514 and cases cited. *Cf* fraternal benefit associations: Restatement (2d), Conflict of Laws, section 192 Comment (k).

50. Dicey, p 1213.

51. *Vita Food Products Inc v Unus Shipping Co* [1939] AC 277, 290 *per* Lord Wright (PC). For example, *Anderson v Equitable Assurance Sy* (1926) 134 LT 557 (CA—life).

English courts have enforced contracts governed by foreign law, although those contracts would not have been enforceable by English law for want of consideration (*Re Bonacina* [1912] 2 Ch 394 (CA)) or as containing a contractual penalty (*Godard v Gray* (1870) LR 6 QB 139). In these cases, however, there were objective contacts with the foreign system of law.

52. It is unlikely, however, that the parties could escape the English rule of insurable interest (below, chapters 3 and 4), as this is a matter of public policy: above 2–2A.

53. In New York, for example, an express choice of law will be applied only "where the law chosen bears a reasonable relationship to the transaction"—*Reger v National Assn of Bedding Manufacturers Ins Trust Fund*, 372 NYS 2d 97, 114 (1975—group life). Under the Restatement (2d), Conflict of Laws, section 187 the chosen law applies "unless . . . the chosen state has no substantial relationship to the parties or the transaction and there is no other reasonable basis for the parties' choice . . . ".

ment that the choice be *bona fide*. Morever, the normal justification of choice of law, flexibility in the face of international competition, cannot be made in cases lacking any foreign element.[54]

In the United States, in *Boseman*,[55] group life insurance was arranged by a parent company in state A for the benefit of the employees of its subsidiary company in state B; the express choice of the law of state A was challenged in the Supreme Court— unsuccessfully. The Court considered that the employer acted as agent for the employee in all dealings with the insurer, including the procuring of the master policy, and, when the employee joined the scheme, he accepted the provisions of that policy, including the choice of law.

2–2C Floating Choice Clauses

The English courts will not apply a "floating choice of law clause", that is to say, a clause which permits one or other party to choose the proper law at a time later than the commencement of the contract. This is because the duties under a contract, indeed, the very existence of the contract cannot be determined without reference to its proper law: "contracts are incapable of existing in a legal vacuum".[56]

A similar objection is made to the "service of suit clause" whereby, in the event of a dispute, the insured may choose the competent jurisdiction[57] and submit to the law there. These clauses are enforced in the United States, as regards jurisdiction, but their effect, as choice of law clauses, is disputed.[58] The same kind of difficulty arises with the "New York suable clause" whereby, at the option of the insured, the place of issue and delivery of the policy is considered to be New York and matters arising determined in accordance with "American law". As it is clear that the option is exercisable after cover has commenced, this clause may be seen as a limited version of a floating choice clause,[59] and thus unacceptable to the English courts.

54. Batiffol & Lagarde, *Droit International Privé* (7th ed, 1983), Nos 574–575.

55. *Boseman* v *Connecticut General Life Ins Co*, 301 US 196 (1937); see also *Pound* v *INA*, 439 F 2d 1059 (10 Cir, 1971—group accident); *Reger* v *National Assn of Bedding Manufacturers Ins Trust Fund*, 372 NYS 2d 97, 115 (1975—group life).

However, more recently, using the "grouping of contacts" approach (below 2–4), and noting that this is a "take-it-or-leave-it" situation for the insured, some courts have applied the law of the insured's place of residence: *Nelson* v *Aetna Life Ins Co*, 359 F Supp 271 (WD Mo, 1973—group accident); the same result was reached by the "governmental interest" approach (below 2–4) in *Krauss* v *Manhattan Life Ins Co*, 643 F 2d 98 (2 Cir, 1981—group life).

56. *Amin Rasheed Shipping Corp* v *Kuwait Ins Co* [1984] AC 50, 65 *per* Lord Diplock (hull). See also *The Armar* [1980] 2 Lloyd's Rep 450, 455 *per* Megaw LJ (CA); *The Iran Vojdan* [1984] 2 Lloyd's Rep 380, 385 *per* Bingham J. The idea was also condemned by Kerr LJ in *Bank Mellat* v *Helleniki Techniki SA* [1984] QB 291, 301 (CA), *Nav Amazonica Peruana SA* v *Via. Int de Seguros del Peru* [1988] 1 Lloyd's Rep 116, 119 (CA), and in *The Star Texas* [1993] 2 Lloyd's Rep. 445 (CA).

The idea of detaching the substance of a dispute from a particular domestic system of law is more attractive to jurists in certain other European jurisdictions which may explain, for example, *Texaco Overseas Petroleum Co* v *Govt. of the Libyan Arab Republic* (1979) 53 Int LR 389. But *cf* in France: Batiffol & Lagarde, *Droit International Privé* (7th ed, 1983), No 571.

57. Usually within the United States of America.

58. *Capital Bank & Trust* v *Associated International Ins*, 576 F Supp 1522 (1984); *cf Edinburgh Assurance* v *Burns Corp*, 479 F Supp 138 (CD Cal, 1979), affirmed 669 F 2d 1259 (9 Cir, 1982). Objections to the clause rest chiefly on the evils of forum shopping.

59. *The Stolt Marmaro* [1985] 2 Lloyd's Rep 428, 435 *per* Goff LJ (CA—re); *cf Armadora Occidental SA* v *Horace Mann Ins Co* [1977] 2 Lloyd's Rep 406, 411 *per* Lord Denning MR (CA—hull).

2–2D Equity Clauses[60]

Arbitration clauses, notably in reinsurance contracts, may contain an "honourable engagement" or "equity" clause whereby, for example, "the arbitrators shall not be bound by the strict rule of law but should settle any differences referred to them according to an equitable rather than a strictly legal interpretation of the provisions of this agreement". In the past, courts have asked whether such clauses are contrary to public policy, as ousting the jurisdiction of the court. The answer depends on whether there is a binding contract. If the effect of the clause is that the contract is not a binding contract but a "gentleman's agreement", there is no jurisdiction to oust.[61] If there is a binding contract and a clause requires arbitration before resort to the courts, the clause is not invalid: the jurisdiction of the court is not ousted but merely postponed.[62] If the clause makes the arbitrators the final adjudicators of fact, again, public policy is not offended. If, however, it makes them final judges on questions of law, that is an attempt to oust the jurisdiction of the courts and the clause is invalid.[63]

The purpose of the rule against ouster is to retain public control over commercial arbitrations, lest the arbitrator be a law unto himself or, as Bankes LJ put it,[64] lest the arbitrator have "a free hand to decide according to law or not according to law as he . . . think fit, in other words to be outside the law". There must be a uniform standard of justice and one uniform system of law.[65] On this basis, there are two assumptions behind the rule, which affect its scope.

The first assumption is that the issue taken from the courts is a question of law. This is itself a question of law for the courts: a question of law "cannot be turned into something other than a question of law by an agreement of the parties in their agreement to arbitrate".[66] Even so, in *Eagle Star Ins Co Ltd* v *Yuval Ins Co Ltd*,[67] Lord Denning, MR, said that the equity clause there was valid, as it "only ousts technicalities and strict constructions".[68] These are not questions of law but how is a line to be drawn ? Perhaps by separating fact, which can be exclusively dealt with by the arbi-

---

60. Generally, see Mustill & Boyd, *Commercial Arbitration* (1982), pp 605 ff and references cited. The authors describe these clauses as "best reserved for transactions where the parties are contracting for a long relationship, in which the maintenance of commercial trust between the parties is reasonably assured. Equity clauses are a recipe for trouble in cases where the contract establishes sharply defined mutual obligations between parties who are briefly drawn together by a single transaction".

61. *Rose & Frank Co* v *Compton & Bros Ltd* [1925] AC. However, as Megaw J observed in *Orion Cia. Espanola d Seguros* v *Belfort Maats. voor Algemene Verzekgringeen* [1962] 2 Lloyd's Rep 257, 264 (re), if there were no contract "there would be no legally binding arbitration clause, and an 'award' would not be an award which the law would recognize". It is unlikely that this is the intention of parties to a reinsurance contract: *Home Ins Co* v *Admin Asigurarilor de Stat* [1983] 2 Lloyd's Rep 674, 676–677 *per* Parker J (re). "What they want is a contract which is rather blurred at the edges"—Mustill & Boyd, *Commercial Arbitration* (1982), p 615. *Contra* the Megaw view: *Paulsson* (1981) 30 ICLQ 358.

62. *Scott* v *Avery* (1856) 5 HLC 811.

63. *Czarnikow* v *Roth, Schmidt & Co* [1922] 2 KB 478 (CA). Mustill & Boyd, *op cit*, pp 696 ff.

64. p 484 *per* Bankes LJ.

65. p 491 *per* Atkin LJ. Also in this sense: Pearson LJ in *Tersons Ltd* v *Stevenage Development Corp* [1965] 1 QB 37, 55 (CA).

66. *Orion* (above), p 264 *per* Megaw J.

67. [1978] 1 Lloyd's Rep 357 (CA—re): a decision accepted as correct in *Home & Overseas Ins Co Ltd* v *Mentor Ins Co Ltd* [1989] 1 Lloyd's Rep 473 (CA—re).

68. *Yuval* (above) p 362; he also said that this would lessen (but not eliminate) the points on which parties could ask for a case stated. Other members of the court were silent on the question.

trators, from law (or non-technical law),[69] which cannot. Perhaps, therefore, the equity clause reflects an old distinction[70] between interpretation (fact) and construction (law), in which interpretation concerns the meaning of words[71] and construction means their legal effect, once they have been interpreted. On this basis, the arbitrators can ignore court decisions on the meaning of words but not their (legal) effect on the rights and duties of the parties; and they can ignore the ordinary and literal meaning of words, if that better accords with commercial good sense.[72]

The second assumption is that English law applies to the contract and its interpretation.[73] Even if the parties choose foreign law,[74] the Bankes view is still relevant because, in applying foreign law, the English court is not only observing the comity of nations but also observing its own public policy interest in the effective resolution of disputes. For that, the contract must from the start be subject to one system of law or another: it cannot exist in a vacuum.[75] If there is no "effective" choice, the forum decides what (recognised) system of law should be applied. Hence it seems doubtful whether, by using the equity clause, the contracting parties can choose a vacuum and ask the arbitrator to fill it, without infringing the Bankes *dictum* that, in the interests of uniformity and certainty, the arbitrator should not be a law unto himself.

In *DST* v *Raknoc*,[76] however, although the Bankes view was referred to,[77] it was not answered in detail. In *Raknoc*, the Master of the Rolls concluded[78] that an agreement of this kind would be enforced if (a) it was intended to create legally enforceable rights and duties, (b) it was certain, and (c) it was not contrary to public policy to enforce the resulting award. As to certainty, he said[79] that "the parties have left the proper law to be decided by the arbitrators and have not in terms confined the choice to national systems of law". It was enough that the arbitrators had chosen, not a recognised system of law, but "a common denominator of principles underlying the laws of various nations governing contractual relations". In the result, the parties are served with a mystery cocktail, which will not be shaken still less stirred and tested, until well after performance of the contract has commenced, performance according to duties that have yet to be determined.[80]

2–2E Incorporation

Clauses choosing law, using phrases such as "shall be governed by", "shall be con-

---

69. Generally on the difference between fact and law in arbitration, see Mustill & Boyd, *Commercial Arbitration* (1982), pp 532 ff. In Lord Denning's statement it is unclear what law is "technical". Mustill & Boyd (p 612) suggest that it might include a right to terminate the contract for a minor breach of condition, to avoid a contract for minor misrepresentation or non-disclosure, or, we may add, for immaterial breach of warranty.

70. See below, 15–1.

71. Apparently in this sense: *Overseas Union Inc* v *AA Mutual International* [1988] 2 Lloyd's Rep 63, 72 *per* Evans J (re).

72. *Home & Overseas Ins Co Ltd* v *Mentor Ins Co Ltd* [1989] 1 Lloyd's Rep 473 (CA—re).

73. Mustill & Boyd, *Commercial Arbitration* (1982), p 59.

74. *Orion* v *Belfort* [1962] 2 Lloyd's Rep 257, p 264 *per* Megaw J.

75. *Amin Rasheed Shipping Corp* v *Kuwait Ins Co* [1984] AC 50, 65 *per* Lord Diplock (hull).

76. *Deutsche Schachtbau- und Tiefbohrgesellschaft mbH* v *Ras Al Khaimah National Oil Co* [1987] 2 All ER 769 (CA); another part of the decision in this case was reversed *sub nom Deutsche Schachtbau- und Tiefbohrgesellschaft mbH* v *Shell International Petroleum Co Ltd* [1990] 1 AC 295.

77. As expressed by Megaw J in *Orion* (above).

78. p 779.

79. *Ibid*.

80. Objections to this kind of result are discussed above, 2–2C.

strued in accordance with", must be distinguished from incorporation clauses.[81] A contract governed by law A may, nonetheless, contain an incorporation clause, which brings in certain provisions of law B to regulate a specific aspect of the contract, which remains governed in general by law A.[82] Thus, cargo insurance governed by French law may use an English form and provide that certain terms shall be construed in accordance with the MIA 1906. This contract differs vitally from one governed by law B because, in the case of incorporation, if law B is changed, the contract remains one to be construed in accordance with law B as it stood at the time that it was incorporated into the contract of insurance.

2–2F The Putative Proper Law

Doubt has arisen whether the law chosen can be the putative proper law. The putative proper law is that to which reference is made to resolve whether the contract has been concluded at all or has been rendered void *ab initio*. If an express choice is operative only by virtue of the force of the contract but the choice is respected to determine whether the contract exists at all, the cart of choice is evidently before the contractual horse. Nonetheless, the putative proper law must sometimes be found and it is the law which would govern, if the contract were valid.[83] In seeking the law which would govern, i.e. the proper law, there seems no good reason why reference should not be made to the usual indicators, including the choice of the parties.[84]

A similar attitude is behind the assumption that a contract to settle a dispute arising under a contract of insurance is governed by the law that governs the contract of insurance or, if the contract is governed by more than one law (unlikely in England), the law that governs the matter in dispute.[85]

2–3 IMPLIED CHOICE

In the absence of an express choice of law, the courts seek the choice of law implicit in the contract.[86] A number of elements have been considered to imply choice, however, the importance of any one kind of element depends on the facts of the case, notably, on the impact of other elements present.

2–3A Jurisdiction or Arbitration Clauses

If a state is chosen by the parties, as the state where their disputes shall go to court or to arbitration, there is a strong inference that the law of that state is intended to apply.

---

81. Dicey, pp 1222 ff.

82. *Ex p Dever* (1887) 18 QBD 660, 668 *per* Fry LJ (CA—life); *Amin Rasheed Shipping Corp v Kuwait Ins Co* [1984] AC 50, 69 *per* Lord Wilberforce (hull); *Travelers Canada v MacDonald* [1984] 14 DLR (4th) 88 (Ont—motor).

83. *Britannia SS. Ins Assn Ltd v Ausoni Assicurazioni SpA* [1984] 2 Lloyd's Rep 98 (CA—re); *Cf Mackender v Feldia AG* [1967] 2 QB 590, 603 *per* Diplock LJ (CA—jewellers' block) that the *lex fori* should apply; this "difficult" case has been criticised on this point by Collier (pp 163–164).

84. Collier, pp 163–164; Dicey, pp 1249–1250.

85. See Fischer, 27 Tort & Ins L J 82, 83 (1991).

86. *Spurrier v La Cloche* [1902] AC 446, 450 *per* Lord Lindley (PC—fire); *Amin* (above) p 61 per Lord Diplock.

So strong was this inference once, that it could be defeated only by express choice of the law of a different state,[87] Then it was held that, even in the absence of express choice, other elements may combine to outweigh the inference of an arbitration clause.[88] Today, however, the inference remains very strong,[89]; especially in reported insurance cases,[90] *Quis elegit iudicem elegit ius*: a London judge or London arbitrator is likely to work better, if English law, with which he is most familiar, is applied.

Distinguish "mandatory" jurisdiction clauses and "permissive" jurisdiction clauses; if the latter and the option is not exercised, the clause has little effect on the implication of the proper law. In *The Stolt Marmaro*,[91] a ship owned by a Liberian company was insured via English brokers with a number of underwriters, of whom the first four were English (covering 14.5% of the risk) and the rest were from other countries, including Italy. Although the policy was issued in and delivered in London,[92] the contract provided[93] that "at the option of the assured . . . the place of issue and delivery shall be considered the City of New York and all matters arising hereunder shall be determined in accordance with American Law". Goff LJ observed[94] that this clause, known as the New York suable clause, was "the nearest thing to a choice of law clause in the policy". If the option were exercised, its terms would be applied; if not, however, the clause appeared to contemplate that, the policy having been issued in London, it would be governed by English law.[95]

For similar reasons, similar importance is attached to a "follow London" clause, whereby any negotiation with regard to claims and their settlement is undertaken, in the first instance, by the London underwriters on risk and whereby other underwriters are to follow their lead.[96] In *Armadora*,[97] the defendant was among a number of American underwriters insuring a fleet of 29 ships under policies, which were nego-

---

87. *Spurrier* (above) p 450 *per* Lord Lindley (PC—fire); *Maritime Ins Co Ltd* v *Assecuranz-Union von 1865* (1935) 52 Ll L Rep 16, 19 *per* Goddard J (re); *Tzortzis* v *Monark Line A/B* [1968] 1 Lloyd's Rep 337 (CA).

88. *Cie Tunisienne de Navigation SA* v *Cie d'Armement Maritime SA* [1971] AC 572, concerning a charterparty.

89. For example *The Mariannina* [1983] 1 Lloyd's Rep 12 (CA). *Cf* Paulsson (1981) 30 ICLQ 358.

90. Apart from *Spurrier* (above) and other cases cited in that note, see *Royal Exchange Assurance Corp* v *Sjoforsakrings A/B Vega* [1902] 2 KB 384, 394 *per* Collins MR (CA—hull); *Bankers & Shippers' Ins Co* v *Liverpool Marine & General Ins Co Ltd* (1926) 24 Ll L Rep 85 (re), in which it was not disputed that the House of Lords should apply the law of New York; *Norske Atlas Ins Co Ltd* v *London General Ins Co Ltd* (1927) 28 Ll L Rep 104 (re); *Afia Worldwide Ins Co* v *Deutsche Ruck Versicherungs AG* (1983) 133 NLJ 621 (re). *John Kaldor Fabricmaker Pty Ltd* v *Mitchell Cotts Freight (Australia) Pty Ltd* (1989) 18 NSWLR 172, 190 (mutual). *Idem* in a case of carriage of goods by sea: *The Komninos S* [1991] 1 Lloyd's Rep 371, 375 (CA), in which Bingham LJ quoted Lord Reid in *Cie Tunisienne* (above) as saying that the choice of an English arbitral forum is "an important factor and in many cases it may be the decisive factor".
Cf Sent. Anvers 16.6.1983 [1987] ETL 752 (jewellery) in which Belgian arbitrators applied Swiss law in spite of (other) contacts with Belgium.

91. [1985] 2 Lloyd's Rep 428 (CA—hull); see also *Spurrier* v *La Cloche* [1902] AC 446 (PC—fire); *Norske Atlas Ins Co* v *London General* (1927) 43 TLR 541 (re); *Maritime Ins Co Ltd* v *Assecuranz-Union von 1865* (1935) 52 Ll L Rep 16, 19 *per* Goddard J (re). For a different reading of *Spurrier* see Unger, p 486.

92. However, the court held that the contract was concluded in Italy.

93. Required if English insurers were to write American risks.

94. [1985] 2 Lloyd's Rep 428, 434.

95. *per* Goff LJ, p 434. See also *Armadora* (below), p 410 *per* Lord Denning MR.

96. An example taken from *Armadora* (below)is this: "Assurers herein shall follow Lloyd's Underwriters and/or British insurance companies in regard to amounts, terms, conditions, alterations, additions, extensions, endorsements, cancellations, surveys and settlement of claims hereunder and all matters pertaining to this insurance with or without prior notice."

97. *Armadora Occidental SA* v *Horace Mann Ins Co* [1978] 1 All ER 407.

tiated and issued in the United States and which made all premiums and claims payable there, where 39% of the entire risk was placed. 30% of the risk, however, was placed in London and all the policies contained a "follow London" clause. Although the policy before the court had its closest connection with the United States, the "follow London" clause was "a countervailing point of much importance".[98] As the policies with the London insurers were governed by English law and claims under those policies would be settled under English law, the Court of Appeal inferred that the American policies were also intended to be governed by English law.

2–3B Form and Language of the Policy

In the past, courts were ready to infer that the use of a standard form of contract in English implied a choice of English law.[99] The form of contract, although still one element to be considered,[100] is of less importance today. English forms are still widely used throughout the world but, often, in countries with sophisticated laws and experienced courts of their own. Although the English language has been described with Irish irony as the "*lingua franca* of commerce",[101] it "is a strong thing to say that, in the absence of an express choice of law clause, the proper law of all such policies is to be regarded as English".[102] Even so, if the form, such as the Lloyd's marine form, is not only in English but has clearly been drafted with reference to English law, English law is likely to be applied.[103]

In *Amin* v *Kuwait*,[104] a Liberian company resident in Dubai insured a ship with an insurer in Kuwait on the standard Lloyd's policy form,[105] which in this instance was issued in Kuwait. The contract provided for claims to be paid in Kuwait but the currency of the contract was sterling. The ship was seized in Saudi Arabia but the owner's claim for constructive total loss of the vessel was rejected by the insurer. The owner sued in England and sought leave to serve the insurer in Kuwait. Service could be allowed, if the contract was governed by English law.[106] The House of Lords held that it was governed by English law.[107] One reason was that, at the time of the contract, there was no law in force in Kuwait governing marine insurance. The parties must have intended some legal system to govern the contract and, by implication,[108] it was

98. p 409 *per* Lord Denning MR.
99. *The Adriatic* [1931] P 241 (CA).
100. *Amin Rasheed Shipping Corp* v *Kuwait Ins Co* [1984] AC 50, 70 *per* Lord Wilberforce (hull); *The Stolt Marmaro* [1985] 2 Lloyd's Rep 428, 434 *per* Goff LJ (CA—re). Generally see *Whitworth Street Estates (Manchester) Ltd* v *Miller & Partners Ltd* [1970] AC 583; *Cie Tunisienne de Navigation SA* v *Cie d'Armement Maritime SA* [1971] AC 572.
101. *The Armar* [1980] 2 Lloyd's Rep 450, 453 *per* Megaw LJ (CA).
102. *Amin* (above) p 71 *per* Lord Wilberforce.
103. In *Rossano* v *Manufacturers Life Ins Co* [1963] 2 QB 352 McNair J, finding that the proper law of a life policy was that of Ontario, was influenced in part by the fact that the policy form in English was clearly based on the law of Ontario. See also *Royal Exchange Assurance Corp* v *Sjoforsakrings A/B Vega* [1902] 2 KB 384 (CA—hull).
104. [1984] AC 50; [1983] CLJ 215.
105. Set out in Schedule 1 to the MIA.
106. RSC Ord 11 r (1)(i)(f)(iii).
107. But the House refused leave to serve; see below 2–9.
108. p 63 *per* Lord Diplock.

not that of Kuwait. The only serious alternative in this case was English law. Lord Diplock concluded[109]: "Except by reference to the English statute and to the judicial exegesis of the code that it enacts it is not possible to interpret the policy or to determine what those mutual legal rights and obligations are. So . . . the proper law of the contract embodied in the policy is English law."

2–3C Currency and Place of Payment

These contacts are of small importance, especially if the currency is widely used in international trade and thus with little implication that the law of any one state should apply.[110] As regards the place of payment, this may have some significance, unless there is more than one place of payment[111] or the place stipulated in the contract has not been used.[112]

2–3D Inference in Favorem Negotii[113]

It may be inferred that the parties intended the application of the system of law, under which all or part of the contract is valid and enforceable rather than that under which it is not[114]: *ut res magis valeat quam pereat*. In the case of contracts of insurance connected with states in which such contracts might be invalid by Muslim law, for example, courts have been ready to infer that that system of law was not the one intended by the parties.[115]

2–4 IMPUTED CHOICE: LOCALISATION

In the absence of an express or an implied choice of law,[116] the contract is localised in a system of law by the court. The quest is not for the state but for the system of law,[117] with which the contract has the closest connection. It is the duty of the court to determine for the parties what is the proper law which, as just and reasonable persons, they ought to have intended, if they had thought about the question when they made the

---

109. p 64, with whom Lords Roskill, Brandon and Brightman concurred.
110. For example *Armadora*, above, 2–3A, in which all premiums and claims were to be paid in the United States, but a "follow London" clause implied a choice of English law.
111. Dicey (11th ed.), p 1291.
112. As in *Amin*, above, 2–3B.
113. Sometimes called the principle of validation.
114. *P & O SN Co Ltd* v *Shand* (1865) 3 Moore PC (NS) 272; *Maritime Ins Co Ltd* v *Assecuranz-Union von 1865* (1935) 52 Ll L Rep 16, 19–20 per Goddard J (re).
115. *Islamic Arab Ins Co* v *Saudi Egyptian American Reinsurance Co* [1987] 1 Lloyd's Rep 315, 320 per Bingham LJ (re).
116. *Bonython* v *Commonwealth of Australia* [1951] AC 201, 209 per Lord Simonds.
117. *Rossano* v *Manufacturers Life Ins Co* [1963] 2 QB 352 (life); *Amin Rasheed Shipping Corp* v *Kuwait Ins Co* [1984] AC 50, 69 per Lord Wilberforce (hull); *Islamic Arab Ins Co* v *Saudi Egyptian American Reinsurance Co* [1987] 1 Lloyd's Rep 315, 320 per Bingham LJ (re).

contract.[118] Dicey suggested[119] that, if the contacts do not point to another system of law, the contract of insurance is governed by the law of the state in which the insurer carries on business and, if in more than one state, the law of the state where its head office is situated. However, that suggestion is aimed mainly at life insurance and derived from certain decisions on life insurance. It is argued below[120] that that is not

118. *Mount Albert Borough Council* v *Australasian Temperance & General Mutual Life Assurance Sy Ltd* [1938] AC 224, 240 *per* Lord Wright (PC).

The English rule was applied in *Imperial Life Assurance Co* v *Colmenares* (1967) 62 DLR (2d) 138, 142–143 *per* Ritchie J (Sup Ct, Canada—life).

Cf USA: It is unconstitutional for a state to impose its own law when the contact with that state is insignificant: *Home Ins Co* v *Dick*, 281 US 397 (1930—hull); *John Hancock Mutual Life Ins Co* v *Yates*, 299 US 178 (1936—life); *Allstate Ins Co* v *Hague*, 449 US 302, 313 *per* Brennan J (1981—motor); *Phillips Petroleum Co* v *Shutts*, 472 US 797 (1985). *Kogan*, 62 NYU L Rev 651, (1987). Subject to this, three different approaches are found solving a conflict of laws in the absence of express choice of law:

(i) The vested rights approach of the Restatement, Conflict of Laws (1934), which generally favours the *lex loci contractus*, found in a large but diminishing number of states.

(ii) The Restatement (2d), Conflict of Laws, section 188 provides:

"(1) The rights and duties of the parties with respect to an issue in contract are determined by the local law of the state which, with respect to that issue, has the most significant relationship to the transaction under the principles stated in section 6.

(2) In the absence of an effective choice of law by the parties (see section 187), the contacts to be taken into account in applying the principles of section 6 to determine the law applicable to an issue include:

(a) the place of contracting,

(b) the place of negotiation of the contract,

(c) the place of performance,

(d) the location of the subject matter of the contract, and

(e) the domicil, residence, nationality, place of incorporation and place of business of the parties . . .

(3) If the place of negotiating the contract and the place of performance are in the same state, the local law of this state will usually be applied . . . "

This approach, referred to as the "centre of gravity", "grouping of contacts" or "significant relationship" approach has gradually replaced the "vested rights" approach; see for example *Auten* v *Auten*, 124 NE 2d 99 (NY, 1954); *Nelson* v *Aetna Life Ins Co*, 350 F Supp 271 (WD Mo, 1973—PA). Although the Restatement talks of the "most significant relationship to the transaction" (above) "the modern trend in this area [is that] of isolating the *particular issue* and then applying the law of the state having the most significant contacts with that *particular issue*"—*Calvert Fire Ins Co* v *Unigard Mutual Ins Co*, 526 F Supp 623, 632 (D Neb, 1980—re) (emphasis added); also *American Home Assurance Co* v *American Employers Ins Co*, 384 F Supp 3, 6 (ED Pa, 1974—liability).

(iii) Under "the governmental interest analysis approach, the forum in a conflicts situation 'must search to find the proper law to apply based upon the interests of the litigants and the involved states . . . Only if each of the states involved has a 'legitimate but conflicting interest in applying its own law' will we be confronted with a 'true' conflicts case"—*Offshore Rental Co Inc* v *Continental Oil Co*, 583 P 2d 721, 723, 725 (Cal, 1978). The contacts stressed in the Restatement (2d) (above) "are not disregarded, but are examined in connection with the analysis of the interest of the involved state in the issues"—*McMullan & Son Inc* v *US Fidelity & Guarantee Co*, 162 Cal Rptr 720, 723 (Cal, 1980—liability). This approach is also found in New York and the District of Columbia: the "'inquiry focusses on the relationship of the . . . jurisdictions to the controversy, the interests involved, and whether application of foreign law would offend a strong and clearly defined local policy' . . . the Court must decide, from those found to have a conflicting interest, which State's policy would be advanced by application of its law"—*Keene Corp* v *INA*, 595 F Supp 934, 938 (D Col, 1984—liability), holding that when "the primary purpose of a rule of law [punitive damages] is to deter or punish conduct, the states with the most significant contacts are those in which the conduct occurred . . . and the defendant . . . located" (*ibid*). "Therefore, if application of a foreign decisional rule will not significantly advance the interests of the foreign state, a California court will conclude that the conflict is 'false' and apply its own law"—*Strassberg* v *New England Mutual Life Ins Co*, 575 F 2d 1262 (9 Cir, 1978—life); also *National Semiconductor Corp* v *Allendale Mutual Ins Co*, 549 F Supp 1195, 1198 (D Conn, 1982—business interruption). Horowitz, 21 UCLA 719 (1974); Posnak, 36 Am J Comp L 681 (1988). *cf* Ehrenzweig, op cit (note 1), p 781.

119. (11th ed.) pp 1289–1290.

120. No 2–4B2.

even the best rule for all cases of life insurance and that, anyway, other kinds of insurance should be treated differently.

Although the choice is imputed rather than real, the contract is localised on the basis of facts and apparent intent at the time of the contract,[121] without regard to what occurs later and might suggest closer connection with another system of law. In particular, English courts avoid an imputed proper law which "floats" until a later time when, for example, a place is chosen for the settlement of claims and the proper law crystallises as the law of that place.

"As a matter of legal logic, I find insuperable difficulty in seeing by what system of law you are to decide what, if any, is the legal effect of an event which occurs when a contract is already in existence with no proper law: but, instead with a 'floating' non-law . . . The governing law cannot fall to be decided, retrospectively, by reference to an event which was an uncertain event in the future at the time when obligations under the contract had already been undertaken, had fallen to be performed, and had been performed."[122]

2–4A Contacts

In practice, the court weighs the contacts in the case before it and chooses the law, with which the contract has the closest connection, or, in other words perhaps, seeks the contract's "centre of gravity". What is scarcely articulated in England is why one contact is more important than another; there is no guiding standard to measure the importance of a particular contact.

Reference is sometimes made to "what an ordinary, reasonable and sensible businessman would be likely to intend", i.e., "that which is 'convenient,' or, equally, that which will give 'business efficacy' to the contract".[123] These factors support, for example, the localisation of reinsurance contracts in the reinsurance market (below, 2–4B1). The convenience of the insurer, it has been decided in some cases, locates life insurance at his head office, although (see below, 2–4B2) a different factor now affects life insurance, which is such a part of the fabric of society that the state of the insured's residence has a vested interest in regulating the contract. Similarly, the cost to society of motor accidents is such that the state has an interest in the regulation of motor insurance on risks primarily located within its borders (below, 2–4B3). Again, it can be argued that in the case of consumer or personal insurance business, convenience gives way to social considerations. For example, "each nation has a legitimate interest that its nationals and permanent inhabitants be not maimed or disabled from self-support".[124]

---

121. *The Armar* [1980] 2 Lloyd's Rep 450 (CA); *The Iran Vojdan* [1984] 2 Lloyd's Rep 380, 385 *per* Bingham J. *Imperial Life Assurance Co* v *Colmenares* [1967] SCR 443 (life).

122. *The Armar* (above) p 455 *per* Megaw LJ (CA). See also *Amin Rasheed Shipping Corp* v *Kuwait Ins Co* [1984] AC 50, 65 *per* Lord Diplock (hull); *Forsik. Vesta* v *Butcher* [1986] 2 All ER 488, 504 *per* Hobhouse J (*re*); *Du Pont de Nemours & Co* v *Agnew* [1987] 2 Lloyd's Rep 585, 592 *per* Bingham LJ (CA—liability). See also above, 2–2C and 2–2D.

123. *The Assunzione* [1953] 2 Lloyd's Rep 91, 101 *per* Willmer J. When holding that the charterparty was governed by Italian law, the judge was influenced (p 102) *inter alia* by the fact that the shipowner was Italian and that it was in Italy that he could most conveniently be sued. The reference to convenience and business efficacy was approved when the decision was affirmed: [1954] P 150, 193 *per* Hodson LJ (CA).

124. *Lauritzen* v *Larsen*, 345 US 571, 586 *per* Jackson J (1952).

2–4A1 The Place of Contracting

In the past, weight has been given to the law of the place of contracting, the *lex loci contractus*,[125] often the place where the policy was signed and posted[126] in response to a proposal from the insured. This is still true of some parts of the United States; contracting is seen as a key event, whereby the parties' rights "vest" in the jurisdiction concerned.[127] In England, the *lex loci contractus* has lost its importance:

"in these days of modern methods of communication where international contracts are so frequently negotiated by telex, whether what turns out to be the final offer is accepted in the country where one telex is situated or in the country where the other telex is installed is often a mere matter of chance. In the result the *lex loci contractus* has lost much of the significance in determining the proper law of contract that it had close on 50 years ago."[128]

A related but distinct point of contact is the contract's "centre of gravity",[129] i.e., the place where the machinery, notably the broking, of the contract is to be found. This contact, which is commonly influential in connection with reinsurance contracts (below, 2–4B1), should, it has been suggested,[130] be given the same importance in connection with other insurance contracts, but case support for this suggestion is not apparent.

2–4A2 The Place of Performance

In the past, weight has also been given to the law of the place of performance, *lex loci solutionis*, the place for payment.[131] It has never been a decisive contact[132] and has little impact on insurance contracts in England today. Lord Diplock[133]:

"As respects *lex loci solutionis* the closeness of the connection of the contract with this varies with the nature of the contract. A contract of insurance is performed by the payment of money, the premiums by the assured, claims by the insurers, and, in the case of marine insurance, very often in what is used as an international rather than a national currency. In the instant case, the course of business between the insurers and the assured established before the policy now

---

125. For example *Pattison* v *Mills* (1828) 1 Dow & Cl 342, 363 *per* Lord Lyndhurst (HL—marine fire); *Maritime Ins Co Ltd* v *Assecuranz-Union von 1865* (1935) 52 Ll L Rep 16, 19 *per* Goddard J (re); *Mutual Life Ins Co of New York* v *Cohen*, 179 US 262, 265 *per* Brewer J (1900—life).
   In Canada this contact remains important, as many provinces have legislation with mandatory application to insurance contracts (usually excepting PA, sickness, life and marine insurance) deemed to be made in the province. For example, RSO 1980, c 218, sections 99–100. See further, Castel, p 565.
126. *Sanderson* v *Cunningham* [1919] 2 IR 234 [motor "Dreadnought" policy posted in England].
127. Restatement of Conflict of Laws (1934) sections 311 ff. *Cf* Restatement (2d), section 188.
128. *Amin Rasheed Shipping Corp* v *Kuwait Ins Co* [1984] AC 50, 62 *per* Lord Diplock (hull), reiterating a view he had expressed years previously: *Pick* v *Manufacturers Life Ins Co* [1958] 2 Lloyd's Rep 93, 98 *per* Diplock J (life). See also *Moss* v *National Life & Accident Ins Co*, 385 F Supp 1291, 1296–1297 (WD Mo, 1974—life). Courts in the United States have tended to apply to life insurance contracts the law of the insured's domicile rather than the *lex loci contractus*: *Zogg* v *Penn Mutual Life Ins Co*, 276 F 2d 861, 865 (2 Cir, 1960); *Fleet Messenger Service Inc* v *Life Ins Co of N America*, 315 F 2d 593, 596–597 (2 Cir, 1963).
129. See Kerr LJ in *Citadel Ins Co* v *Atlantic Union Ins Co SA* [1982] 2 Lloyd's Rep 543, 548 (re); the phrase was also used by Mustill J in *Afia Worldwide Ins Co* v *Deutsche Ruck Versicherungs AG* [1983] 133 NLJ 621 (re); and by Goff LJ in *The Stolt Marmaro* [1985] 2 Lloyd's Rep 428, 435 (re). However, its origin is probably in the United States; see above 2–4.
130. Merkin, *loc cit. Contra*: *Amin* (above), p 71 *per* Lord Wilberforce.
131. For example, Restatement of Conflict of Laws (1934).
132. For example *Jacobs & Co* v *Crédit Lyonnais* (1884) 12 QBD 589, 601 *per* Bowen LJ (CA).
133. *Amin Rasheed Shipping Corp* v *Kuwait Ins Co* [1984] AC 50, 62–63 (hull). However, a "contract made and to be performed wholly within the territory of a foreign state will normally be subject to the laws of that state and to no other", even though one party is British: *Holmes* v *Bangladesh Biman Corp* [1989] 1 Lloyd's Rep 444, 451 *per* Lord Bridge (HL).

sought to be sued upon was entered into, ignoring, as it did, the provisions in the previous policies that claims were payable in Kuwait, shows how little weight the parties themselves attached to the *lex loci solutionis*."

2–4A3 The Form of the Policy

See above, 2–3B.

2–4A4 Validity

English courts which, when seeking the implied choice of the parties, favour the system of law whereby the contract is valid rather than invalid,[134] are likely to impute choice in the same spirit. In the United States, courts may go further[135]: "the Court will protect insureds from the greater power of insurers by means of its choice of law rules . . . the reason underlying the choice of law rule is to allow the maximum protection of the insured."

2–4B Contracts

2–4B1 Reinsurance

In spite of what has been said (above, 2–3) about the search *first* for party intention, courts often start with a presumption about the localisation of a contract. An example is the tendency, in the case of international sales of commodities, to turn to the law of the state in which the market is found.[136] Similarly, in the case of reinsurance, there is a tendency to localise such contracts in the relevant market, such as London,[137] which is usually also the place of contracting,[138] or the place where the machinery,[139] notably the broking,[140] leading to the contract is located. In *Citadel*,[141] Kerr LJ stressed that

134. *Maritime Ins Co Ltd* v *Assecuranz-Union von 1865* (1935) 52 Ll L Rep 16, 20 *per* Goddard J (re). *Cf Royal Exchange Assurance Corp* v *Sjoforsakrings A/B Vega* [1902] 2 KB 348 (re), in which a jurisdiction clause pointing to England led the court to the law of invalidity.

135. *Blanco* v *Pan-American Life Ins Co*, 221 F Supp 219, 228 (SD Fla, 1963—life), affirmed 362 F 2d 167 (5 Cir, 1966). But *cf Present* v *US Life Ins Co*, 232 A 2d 863 (NJ, 1967—life).

136. *Tamari & Sons Co* v *Rothfos Beteiligungsgesellschaft mbH* [1980] 2 Lloyd's Rep 553 (CA); this factor is often reinforced, as in that case, if disputes are to be resolved by the procedures of the relevant commodity exchange.

137. *Citadel Ins Co* v *Atlantic Union Ins Co* [1982] 2 Lloyd's Rep 543 (CA); see also *Du Pont de Nemours & Co* v *Agnew* [1987] 2 Lloyd's Rep 585, 592 *per* Bingham LJ (CA—liability). Monachos [1972] JBL 206, 215, 219: such a rule has the merit that the entire risk is more likely to be reinsured under the same legal system.

The contention of Monachos (above), that reinsurance contracts are generally governed by the law of the place of the reinsured's head office, is effectively answered by Butler & Merkin, D.4.2–24 ff.

Cf USA: in *Calvert Fire Ins Co* v *Unigard Mutual Ins Co*, 526 F Supp 623, 632 (D Neb, 1980—re), the court isolated the issue (misrepresentation) and applied the law with the most significant relationship to the issue, which was the law of the place where the contract was made and the alleged misrepresentations occurred. In a case of claims against a reinsurer in liquidation, the government interest approach led to the law of the state in which the liquidation occurred (also the *lex fori*)—*American Reinsurance Co* v *Ins Commission*, 527 F Supp 444 (CD Cal, 1981).

138. This influenced Goddard J in *Maritime Ins Co Ltd* v *Assecuranz-Union von 1865* (1935) 52 Ll L Rep 16, 19 (re); Lord Denning MR in *Citadel Ins Co* v *Atlantic Union Ins Co* [1982] 2 Lloyd's Rep 543, 545 (CA); and Mustill J in *Afia Worldwide Ins Co* v *Deutsche Ruck Versicherungs AG* [1983] 133 NLJ 621 (re). Also in this sense: *Stephens* v *American Home Insurance Co*, 811 F Supp 937, 946 (SDNY, 1993—re). Place of signature and of payment: *Progressive Casualty Ins Co* v *CA Reaseguradoro Nacional de Venezuela*, 991 F 2d 42 (2 Cir, 1993—re).

139. Merkin, *loc cit*.

140. Butler & Merkin, D.4.2–27.

141. In *Citadel Ins Co* v *Atlantic Union Ins Co* [1982] 2 Lloyd's Rep 543, 548–549 (CA), Canadian insurers via brokers in New York and in London placed hull risks on the London market with Greek reinsurers; English law applied. See also in this sense *Forsik. Vesta* v *Butcher* [1988] 1 Lloyd's Rep 19, 32 *per* Neill LJ (CA—re), affirmed [1989] 1 AC 852.

the "whole of the business, both from the point of view of the defendants as reinsurers and of the reinsured plaintiffs, was run [by the broker] in London. All the documents are here, and it is only by an examination of these documents that it is possible to determine the rights and wrongs of the disputes". This is a strong factor for reinsurance contracts, in spite of another presumption that linked contracts, such as primary contracts, should be governed by the same law.[142] When there is no relevant reinsurance market, courts may resort to more general contacts, such as the place where the reinsurance certificate was issued and where claims would be paid.[143]

2–4B2 Life Insurance

In *Rossano*,[144] life insurance had been contracted by an Egyptian in Egypt. Although at first sight the contract was most closely connected with Egypt, McNair J held[145] that the contract was governed by the law of Ontario, where the head office of the insurer was situated. He said[146]: "where a resident in a territory seeks life assurance from a foreign insurance company through its local agent in that territory, it is manifest that normally he chooses the foreign company because he has faith not only in that company, but in the system of law under which it operates." However, the contract in question was made in time of war and insecurity in the Middle East by a proposer who contemplated flight. In this, as in other cases in which the law of the place of head office has been applied, that was in the interest of the insured as much (if not more) than in that of the insurer. Dicey's suggestion,[147] that *ceteris paribus* the same rule should apply as a presumption in not only all life contracts[148] but also other insurance contracts, is hard to support.

Dicey's view[149] may well be the wish of the insurer but, surely, not necessarily that of the insured. For the insurer the "'analysis of risks on the basis of the premiums is

---

142. *The Njegos* [1936] P 90. See *Vesta v Butcher* (above, 2–1C).

143. *Arkwright–Boston Manufacturers Mutual Ins Assn v Calvert Fire Ins Co*, 887 F 2d 437 (2 Cir, 1989—re)

144. *Rossano v Manufacturers Life Ins Co* [1963] 2 QB 352; [1962] 1 Lloyd's Rep 187 (life): the decision to contract was made by head office in Ontario; some premiums were paid in advance in Ontario, others in Egypt; policy money was payable in London and New York; notice of assignment had to be given to head office. A similar decision is that of Diplock J in *Pick v Manufacturers Life Ins Co* [1958] 2 Lloyd's Rep 93 (life); here too there were other contacts with the law of the insurer's head office.

A Canadian decision in this sense is *National Trust Co v Sterling Accident & Guarantee Co* (1916) QR 51 SC 481 (PA).

145. p 204.

146. p 204.

147. p 1341. The seventh edition of Dicey (1957) suggested (p 837) a "preference for the *lex loci contractus*, i.e., usually the assured's place of residence or business rather than for the law of the insurer's place of business".

148. Referred to by Unger, *loc cit* as the Continental view, but *semble* coming from Germany rather than from France: Batiffol & Lagarde, *Droit International Privé* (7th ed, 1983), p 302. The view was probably introduced to Dicey (8th ed) by Kahn-Freund. It was doubted in *Imperial Life Assurance Co v Colmenares* (1967) 62 DLR (2d) 138, 143 *per* Ritchie J (Sup Ct, Canada—life). The "Dicey view", however, was taken by McLeod, The Conflict of Laws (Calgary, 1983), p 510.

In *Rowett Leakey & Co v Scottish Provident Institution* [1927] 1 Ch 55, 69 (CA—life), Warrington LJ regarded the insurer's head office in Scotland as immaterial, as all other contacts were with England. A similar preference for the *lex loci contractus* over the law of the insurer was expressed *obiter* by Bowen LJ in *Ex p Dever* (1887) 18 QBD 660, 666 (CA). Although the *loci contractus* is not currently given much importance, these cases show that, when they were decided, the same was true of the law of the place of head office.

149. Unger, *loc cit*, p 483, citing Lando in 6 Am J Comp Law 16 (1957). Also in this sense Ehrenzweig, *op cit* (note 1) p 513.

calculated as safe only when all policies in force in one group are governed by the same rules of law.' Recognition of the fact that contracts of life insurance are standardised must therefore be of decisive importance when determining the law by which they are to be governed." Today, however, that may not even be the wish of the insurer. Many products are marketed world wide but tailored for particular markets; what is true of the motor car is in this regard true of life insurance. If the underwriter can allow for differences, for example, in the incidence of AIDS or malaria, then why not differences in law?[150] If not, it is a simple matter for the insurer to include an express choice of his own law.

Professor Unger[151] was concerned for insurers "exposed to litigation concerning contracts concluded elsewhere and having possibly no genuine links with the country where such litigation is conducted. Insurance companies are entitled to expect protection against this abuse". However, is not the insured entitled to ask why his life contract should be subject to a legal system located far away in a system of law, to which he has no links and to which he may be compelled to go to enforce his contract? If, as Dicey concedes,[152] banking contracts are generally governed by local law, why, in an age of easy communication and *bancassurance*, should there be a different rule for insurance?[153]

Accordingly, it is submitted, cases like *Rossano* are the exception rather than the rule; in stable social conditions, the location of the insured carries more weight than that of the insurer's head office. Thus, in *Buerger* v *New York Life Ins Co*,[154] life contracts made and performed in pre-revolutionary Russia with an American insurer were governed by Russian law. This is also the current trend in the United States where courts,[155] more concerned to protect the insured from the insurer than vice versa,[156] have ignored the law of the insurer and applied the law of the state of the insured in which the contract is often made and performed. Courts in more and more states have applied section 192 of the Restatement (2d), Conflict of Laws:

"The validity of a life insurance contract issued to the insured upon his application and the rights created thereby are determined in the absence of an effective choice of law by the insured in his application, by the local law of the state where the insured was domiciled at the time the policy was applied for, unless, with respect to the particular issue, some other state has a more significant relationship under the principles stated in section 6 to the transaction and the parties, in which event the local law of the other state will be applied."[157]

---

150. *Lee* v *Abdy* (1886) 17 QBD 309, 315 *per* Willes J (life).
151. Unger, p 483.
152. p 1341.
153. *Contra* Kahn-Freund, (1959) 22 MLR 195, 198.
154. (1927) 43 TLR 601 (CA). *Contra* the *situs* of the risk: MacGillivray (7th ed), No 1111. It is, however, a rule basic to the EC Convention on Contracts, below, 2–8.
155. *Northwestern Mutual Life Ins Co* v *McCue*, 223 US 234 (1912—life) and cases cited.
156. *Cf* Unger (p 488): "It is not the assured who seeks the protection of the law of the country of residence but the insurer who pleads for the application of this law since he is anxious to avoid friction with the authorities of the country in which his branch office is operating."
157. Restatement (2d), section 6 provides:
   "(1) A court, subject to constitutional restrictions, will follow a statutory directive of its own state on choice of law.
   (2) When there is no such directive, the factors relevant to the choice of the applicable rule of law include
   (a) the needs of the interstate and international systems,
   (b) the relevant policies of the forum,
   (c) the relevant policies of other interested states and the relative interests of those states in the determination of the particular issue,

This rule is thought to take account of the disparity in bargaining power between an insurance company and those whose lives it insures, and serves the purpose of any local legislation designed to protect the insured. Further, it weighs the fact that life insurance is usually solicited by local agents of insurers who, by employing these agents and by sometimes maintaining a branch office in the state of the insured's residence, might be said to submit to local law.[158]

Section 192 is subject to qualifications,[159] notably the case of group life insurance: the rights of members of the group are governed by the law of the master policy, which may not be that of their residence or domicile.[160] Generally, however, reference to the latter is justified by state interest in life insurance for family provision, investment, and security by its citizens.[161]

The relevant residence or domicile is that of the insured at the time of contracting.[162] In the case of reinstatement, it is the law of the original contract,[163] unless the policy is reinstated on different terms: in that case, the courts are likely to apply the law of domicile at the time of reinstatement.[164] Similarly, faced with a choice between the State in which the insured resided when he contracted the insurance and that in which he resided when he executed a form to change the beneficiary of the policy, the United States Federal Court has held that the validity of the form was governed by the law of the latter.[165]

2–4B3 Vehicle Insurance

As regards insurance contracts other than reinsurance, life and marine, there are few reported cases in England. In the United States, the "grouping of contacts" theory leads to the law of the state, which the parties understood would be the principal location of the insured risk and which is most intimately concerned with the outcome of the litigation.[166] If the risk is located, motor insurance is usually governed by the

---

(d) the protection of justified expectations,
(e) the basic policies underlying the particular field of law,
(f) certainty, predictability and uniformity of result, and
(g) ease in the determination and application of the law to be applied."As to constitutional restrictions referred to in section 6(1), see above, note 108.

158. Ehrenzweig, op cit (note 1) p 516. But cf the law of Michigan: *New York Life Ins Co v Agee*, 807 F Supp 53, 56 (ED Mich, 1992—life).

159. Section 192 does not apply (a) to insurance on a life other than that of the proposer: see Restatement (2d), Conflict of Laws, section 188, above, 2–4; (b) to transient residents such as military personnel; and (c) to certain aspects of the contract on any life, for example, details of performance, such as payment of premium, which may be governed by the law of the place of performance: Restatement (2d), Conflict of Laws, section 206.

160. *Boseman v Connecticut General Life Ins Co*, 301 US 196 (1937); Restatement (2d), Conflict of Laws, section 192, Comment (h).

161. Restatement (2d), Conflict of Laws, section 192, Comment (c).

162. *New England Mutual Life Ins Co v Lauffer*, 215 F Supp 91 (SD Cal, 1963); *Bernstein v Fidelity Life Ins Co*, 449 F Supp 327 (ED Mo, 1978—life); except that on the "governmental interest" approach (above, 2–4) to the conflict of laws the law of the later domicile will usually be applied in all cases: *Strassberg v New England Mutual Life Ins Co*, 575 F 2d 1262 (9 Cir, 1978—life).

163. *John Hancock Mutual Life Ins Co v Munn*, 188 F 2d 1, 3 (8 Cir, 1951—life); *Bowie v Bankers Life Co*, 105 F 2d 806, 808 (10 Cir, 1939—life).

164. Restatement (2d), Conflict of Laws, section 192, Comment (g).

165. *Blount v Bartholomew*, 714 F Supp 252 (ED Ky, 1988—life), affirmed 869 F 2d 1488 (6 Cir, 1989).

166. Restatement (2d), Conflict of Laws, section 193. It does not apply to details of performance (such as mode of payment of premium), which are governed by the law of the place where performance has taken or is to take place: *ibid*, Comment (a).

law of the place where the vehicle is mainly used, garaged, and licensed.[167] The mere possibility of interstate travel by the insured is irrelevant[168]; "The contacts with the state where the accident occurred", including the residence of the victim, "are fortuitous."[169]

For example, in *Minkoff*,[170] a motor policy sent from Pennsylvania by an insurer, incorporated in Massachusetts, for delivery to an insured resident in New York, who had responded to an advertisement by the insurer in a New York newspaper, was governed by the law of New York and covered a vehicle registered in New York, when it was in an accident in New Jersey.

If there is a change in the location of the risk during the currency of a policy, there is no change in the governing law, unless the change of location is such a change of risk that there is a change in the terms of the contract (notably premium).[171]

In the case of machines, which frequently cross state boundaries, not only motor vehicles but also aircraft and railway rolling stock, courts consider the relative importance of other contacts[172] such as the place of contracting,[173] place of performance, nationality and residence of parties.[174]

2–4B4 Fire Insurance

Fire insurance is likely to be governed by the law of the place where the property is situated.[175] However, an early case[176] suggests that if parties resident in state A there

167. *Seguros Tepeyec SA* v *Bostrom*, 347 F 2d 168, 172 (5 Cir, 1965); *American Service Mutual Ins Co* v *Bottum*, 371 F 2d 6, 12 (8 Cir, 1967); *Young* v *U.S. Fidelity & Guarantee Ins Co*, 786 F Supp 600 (SD Miss, 1991—motor). Ehrenzweig, op cit (note 1) p 518.

Cf Allstate Ins Co v *Hague*, 449 US 302 (1981—motor), in which the insured was resident in state A and commuted to work in state B; the court held that it was not unconstitutional for the courts of state B to apply their own law to the case, even though the accident did not occur in state B: "While employment status may implicate a state interest less substantial than does resident status, that interest is nevertheless important" (p 314).

168. *Peterson* v *Warren*, 143 NW 2d 560, 563 (Wis, 1966).

169. *Sotirakis* v *United Service Automobile Assn*, 787 P 2d 788, 791 (Nev, 1990—motor). See also *State Automobile Mutual Ins Co* v *Spray*, 547 F 2d 397 (7 Cir, 1977—motor); *Johnson* v *Occidental Fire & Casualty Co*, 954 F 2d 1581 (11 Cir, 1992—motor).

170. *Colonial Penn Ins Co* v *Minkoff*, 338 NYS 2d 444, 445 (1972). There was the same result in *Allstate Ins Co* v *Sullam*, 349 NYS 2d 550 (1973—motor) but by means of the "governmental interest" approach (above, 2–4). The contract could be rescinded for misrepresentation in Massachusetts but not in New York. "New York has a substantial interest in the compensation of its own citizens and more precisely in protecting them from unwarranted withdrawal of liability insurance after the damage is done . . . The prevention of unjust denial of compensation for injuries is a natural interest for New York which must look after the victims of accidents here, likely, as they are here, to be local residents, to insure payment of local hospitals and doctors, . . . to protect automobile accident victims from financially crippling medical expenses" (p 562).

171. *American Service Mutual Ins Co* v *Bottum*, 371 F 2d 6, 10 (8 Cir, 1967).

172. Restatement (2d), Conflict of Laws, section 193, Comment (a).

173. In *Roberts* v *Underwriters at Lloyd's London*, 195 F Supp 168 (D Idaho, 1961), the court applied the *lex loci contractus* (California) to a helicopter based in Idaho. See *Greer* v *Poole* (below).

174. *Cf Edinburgh Assurance Co* v *Burns Corp*, 479 F Supp 138 (CD Cal, 1979) on risks associated with salvage: it was agreed that location was inconclusive, as the tow would pass though various seas and waters. Applying the governmental interest approach, the court looked *inter alia* at the residence of the parties.

175. Both on the Restatement (2d) test of significant contact: *Keating* v *Westchester Fire Ins Co*, 290 F Supp 141 (D Wis, 1968); *Mitchell* v *State Farm Fire & Casualty Co*. 902 F 2d 790 (10 Cir, 1990—fire); and on the "governmental interest" approach: *Abels* v *State Farm Fire & Casualty Co*, 596 F Supp 1461 (WD Pa, 1984—fire). *Idem*: McLeod, The Conflict of Laws (Calgary 1983), p 511.

176. *Coffin* v *London & Edinburgh Ins Co*, 27 F 2d 616, 617 (ND Ga, 1928); the exceptional character of *Coffin* was pointed out in *Mitchell* (above) p 794. In *Greer* v *Poole* (1880) 5 QBD 272, Lush J applied English law to cargo insurance contracted by an English owner with an English insurer, although the cargo was on a French ship from Lagos to Marseille; no reasons were offered.

contract insurance on property in state B, property rarely if ever visited by the insured, the contract will be governed by the law of state A.

2–4B5 Liability Insurance

In general, liability insurance contracts will be located in the state, in which the relevant (business) operations take place.[177] Similarly, group accident insurance organised by an employer has been located at the place of employment.[178] An indemnity bond has been held subject to the law of the place where most transactions that might give rise to liability under the bond would occur.[179] Fidelity insurance has been held subject to the law of the place where the relevant employee works.[180]

The place of (business) operations, evidently relevant to professional liability, is less decisive when the insured's liability arises out of something he produces, whether it is for the use of others or it is a waste product that damages the environment. In each case, the relevant injury or damage may occur far from the place of production. Difficulties also arise if, although the liability arises at the insured's place of operations, it is just one of many places at which he operates. The paradigm problem, however, is that of an insured with a base of some kind in state A but whose liabilty arises in another state, state B. Past decisions, mostly in the USA, suggest the following pattern.

(a) *Reference to Base.* In favour of the law of state A is predictability: a single legal system for a single insurance contract, the relevant law of which is known to or asertainable by those concerned. The claim of state A is strongest when that of the other state is weakest, for example, motor (liability) insurance or cargo insurance, in which the place of the accident is fortuitous: it is just one of a number of states (B–Z) in which the liability might have arisen, and the locus has no special interest in the case, perhaps because the victim is from a third state or because the locus might be the high seas, where there is no state and the chance of injury to people is slight. Further, reference to state A has sometimes been reinforced by the consideration that the insured was resident there, as it had "an interest in seeing that [the insured's liability] coverage is protected".[181]

---

177. *Brookville Electric Co* v *Utilities Ins Co*, 142 SW 2d 803, 810 (Mo, 1940); *Raymond* v *Monsanto Co*, 329 F Supp 247 (D NH, 1971); *American Home Assurance Co* v *American Employers Ins Co*, 384 F Supp 3 (ED Pa, 1974); *Steinbach* v *Aetna Casualty & Surety Co*, 440 NYS 2d 637 (1981—aviation liability).

Cf Keene Corp v *INA*, 597 F Supp 934 (D Col, 1984—liability) in which it was held on a punitive damages claim against the insurer, taking the "governmental interest" approach (above, n 2–4), that when (p 938) "the primary purpose of a rule of law is to deter or punish conduct, the States with the most significant interests are those in which the conduct occurred and in which the principal place of business and place of incorporation of defendant are located". The *Keene* approach also means that business interruption is located where the effects are felt rather than where the interruption occurs: *National Semiconductor Corp* v *Allendale Mutual Ins Co*, 549 F Supp 1195, 1200 (D Conn, 1982—business interruption).

178. *Cunninghame* v *Equitable Life Assurance Sy*, 652 F 2d 306 (2 Cir, 1981). *Aliter* if the employees are employed in a variety of states: *Smith & Chambers Salvage* v *Insurance Management Corp*, 808 F Supp 1492, 1497 (ED Wash, 1992—workers' compensation).

179. *Exchange National Bank* v *INA*, 341 F 2d 673, 675 (2 Cir, 1965); see also *Conesco Industries Ltd* v *Conforti & Eisele Inc*, 627 F 2d 312 (D Col, 1980—surety).

180. *Baldwin Motors Inc* v *Aetna Casualty & Surety Co*, 194 A 2d 709, 712 (Conn, 1962); *Essex County State Bk* v *Fireman's Fund Ins Co*, 331 F Supp 931 (D NJ, 1971).

181. *Peavey Co* v *Zurich Ins Co* , 971 F 2d 1168, 1172 (5 Cir, 1992—liability); this was an action by the insurer against the insured to recover defence costs. Above 2–4B3

A different kind of case, in which the operational base was decisive, is *Kaldor*,[182] however, it was the base not of the insured but of the insurer. Suit was brought in New South Wales against a mutual insurer incorporated in Bermuda but operating out of London, in respect of liability cover for a customs agent. The court observed:

"For the Association emphasis was laid upon . . . the fact that the insurance was on the mutual principle, so that a large number of other persons, also insured with the Association, and located in many other countries were interested in the defendant's insurance, and the defendant was interested in their insurance. It was therefore argued that there was a real, soundly based, practical point to the rules [of the Association] being construed consistently, that is, according to the rules of one system of law. I am inclined to think that the last-mentioned factor is of some consequence in a case such as the present one; in an abstract way, it seems unlikely that a Bermuda insurer would wish to insure a Sydney company, and to wish to arrange affairs so that the proper law of the contract was the law of New South Wales, a proposition which is reinforced by a consideration of the circumstance that the defendant was one of some 700 members located in seventy countries. But similarly, it seems unlikely that a Sydney company would be likely to know much about the legal system of Bermuda, or to wish to enter into a contract, the proper law of which was Bermuda. On the other hand, both parties might have thought it fair and reasonable to make English law the proper law of the contract, particularly as it was a contract of insurance".[183]

(b) The Location. The claim of state B is strongest, when the interest of state B and the content of its law is predictable, notably when state B is the place planned for the deposit of waste, and when state B has a particular interest because of the potential damage to its people. The strongest case is that of pollution with both cause and effect in state B but, for example, the place of contracting or the head office of the insured in state A: the law of B is likely to be applied.[184] In *Leksi*,[185] a case of waste moved from A for deposit in B, the court observed:

"Common sense indicates that a state will be less willing to allow toxic wastes to be placed on its land unless it can be assured that its law will be applied in determining the respective parties for cleanup costs . . . . A corollary to New Jersey's compelling interest in the remediation of hazardous waste sites [there] is its interest in the availability of insurance coverage for the costs associated with the cleanup of those sites".

In *Leksi*, state B stood alone against state A, however, even if B is but one of states B–Z, there may be sufficient predictability to take in the interest of B–Z in local damage and danger. In *Shapiro*,[186] the insured owned clubs in various states and con-

---

182. *John Kaldor Fabricmaker Pty Ltd* v *Mitchell Cotts Freight (Australia) Pty Ltd* (1989) 18 NSWLR 172 (mutual).

183. p 190 *per* Brownie J. In view of this factor and, particularly, of a London arbitration clause, the court held that the contract was governed by English law.

184. *Chesapeake Utilities Corp* v *American Home Assurance Co*, 704 F Supp 551 (D Del, 1989—liability); *Travelers Indemnity Co* v *Allied–Signal Inc*, 718 F Supp 1252 (D My, 1989—liability). *Idem* concerning liability to employees in respect of unsafe plant in state B: *Mountain Fuel Supply* v *Reliance Ins Co*, 933 F 2d 882, 888 (10 Cir, 1991—liability).

185. *Leksi Inc* v *Federal Ins Co*, 736 F Supp 1331, 1334–1335 (D NJ, 1990—liability). See also in this sense *Johnson & Co* v *Aetna Casualty & Surety Co*, 741 F Supp 298, 301 (D Mass, 1990—liability); Pittston Co v Allianz Ins Co, 795 F Supp 678, 684 ff. (D NJ, 1992—liability); *General Metalcraft Inc* v *Liberty Mutual Ins Co* , 796 F Supp 794, 798 ff (D NJ, 1992—liability).

186. *Shapiro* v *Associated International Ins Co*, 899 F 2d 1116, 1119 ff (11 Cir, 1990—liability).

tracted umbrella insurance in respect of its liability for the premises. The court rejected "the archaic *lex loci contractus* rule" and applied the law of the place of the particular risk.

"Unlike a contract for automobile insurance where the location of the insured risk can vary as readily and as quickly as an automobile can move, the Associated policy insured against occurrences at [the particular] Club, a risk whose location was unchanging . . . . [Although] the risks covered under the Associated umbrella policy were spread out over several states the Restatement [2d Conflict of Laws, section 193, comment f] advises application of the substantive law of the state in which each individual risk is located when adjudicating issues concerning that risk, treating the comprehensive policy effectively as several different policies."

In *Shapiro*, both the risk and the claim were centred and contained within state B. A very different case is *National Starch*,[187] in which the court stated: "This case involves 21 different waste sites located in 12 different states . . . it would be unreasonable . . . to apply 12 different bodies of law to the contracts of insurance." Indeed, neither party argued for the law of the different states, perhaps because the case involved the simultaneous pursuit of action concerning all 21 sites, and, not surprisingly, "considerations of judicial economy, uniformity and certainty" led the court to apply the law of one state.[188]

Compare *Shapiro* also with *Vigen*.[189] The insured was a builder and, at the time he took insurance, it was clear that his work would be in a number of different states but not so clear which states they would be. In the circumstances, the court, which, it should be said, had a tradition of applying the *lex loci contractus*, concluded that the location of work was not the most significant contact and gave way to the contacts "bearing upon the contractual relationship between the insured and the insurer": that the "insured and insurer were Minnesota corporations; the policy was negotiated and issued in Minnesota; and the insurance premiums were paid in Minnesota".

(c) The Borderline. Although the Restatement (2d) Conflict of Laws (1971) does state that the "location of the insured risk will be given greater weight than any other single contact in determining the state of the applicable law", a significant proviso is added: "that the risk can be located, at least principally, in a single state".[190] But what is the location of a risk? In *Shapiro* (above), as regards any one incident of loss, the risk was entirely at one club in one state. The loss, however, may have its cause in one state but its effects in another. The borderline cases mostly concern defects in manu-

---

187. *National Starch & Chemical Corp v Great American Insurance Cos*, 743 F Supp 318, 322 (D NJ, 1990—liability).

188. p 323. The contest was between the law of New York, where the insurance had been broked and was managed, for example, as to payment of premiums, and the law of New Jersey, where the insured had its principal place of business. The New Jersey court applied the law of New Jersey.

189. *Vigen Construction Co v Millers National Ins Co*, 436 NW 2d 254, 257 (N D, 1989—liability).

190. This statement in relation to fire and casualty insurance has been applied to liability insurance, especially as regards the proviso.

A further qualification, however, arises out of *dépeçage*: localisation according to the issue. Distinguish, therefore, American cases such as *Cie des Bauxites de Guinée v Argonaut–Midwest Ins Co*, 880 F 2d 685 (3 Cir, 1989—liability), in which the issue was notice of claim. "As to that issue, location of the insured risk is further diminished in importance while factors like the location of the injury, the domicile of the parties, and the location of contracting and negotiation become relatively more important" (p 690). The court opted for the last of these, which was also that of the state with an interest in seeing that the insurance policies which it regulated were adhered to by the parties. See also, for example, *Broadhead v Hartford Casualty Ins Co*, 773 F Supp 882 (SD Miss, 1991—liability), in which the court isolated the issue (coverage) and did not apply the law of the location.

facture in state A, manufacture of a product which is sent out to do its damage in states B–Z.

On one side of the line is *Pepco*,[191] in which the insured was liable for damage caused by polluted equipment, which it had sold to other users in nine different states. The court rejected the law of the place of pollution because this "could result in a single insurance contract being interpreted in a multitude of different ways, depending on the law of the jurisdiction where environmental damage occurred".[192] In these circumstances, the court chose "the headquarters of the insured as the location with the most substantial interest in the controversy", especially as it was also "the center of the insured's operations" and "the location which appears to be most likely contemplated by the parties . . . as the one jurisdiction which ties all potential parties together".[193]

On the other side of the line is *Goodyear*,[194] in which the arguments successful in *Pepco*, predictability and thus cost, failed. The insured

"argues that this suit is a contract dispute and that in contract cases predictability is of paramount importance, especially for a corporation which transacts business in all fifty states. It further argues that the question of whether a policy negotiated and entered into in Georgia covers certain damages should not be determined by the chance of where an accident occurred. Goodyear claims this holds particularly true for a corporation which has paid millions of dollars in premiums for protection from [awards of punitive damages, insurable in Georgia but not in Minnesota]. If a court were to allow [Minnesota] law to void that contract, the predictability which is critical to the financial stability of a company would be frustrated".

Nonetheless, in *Goodyear Tire*, the court rejected these arguments observing[195] (a) that it was "foreseeable that an accident involving one of these products could arise in any state"; (b) that, whereas there was no doubt that Goodyear desired predictability in its insurance cover, it has omitted to obtain this certainty through a choice of law clause in the contract of insurance. Finally, the decisive factor was the governmental interest of Minnesota, where the accident occurred, "in deterring conduct which would lead to the injury of its citizens".[196]

Finally, in some cases, the balance is tipped in one direction or another by the tendency of courts to find reasons for applying its own law.[197]

2–5 ASSIGNMENT

As insurance is property, there is a contact in the *situs* of the property.[198] In the case of life insurance, this points to the insured's domicile, an important contact for the proper law governing the contract of insurance itself: above 2–4B2. The *situs* of a *debt*, however, including the debt represented by a life policy, is the place where the debt

191. *Potomac Electric Power* v *California Union Ins Co* 777 F Supp 968 (DDC 1991—liability).
192. p 972.
193. p 673.
194. *United States Fire Ins Co* v *Goodyear Tire & Rubber Co*, 726 F Supp 740, 743 (D Minn, 1989—liability).
195. p 744
196. p 745.
197. For example, *Triangle Publications Inc* v *Liberty Mutual Ins Co*, 703 F Supp 367 (ED Pa, 1989—liability).
198. This is one possible explanation of *Crosland* v *Wrigley* (1895) 73 LT 60 (life); affirmed 73 LT 327 (CA); *cf* Unger, p 486.

"is properly recoverable and can be enforced",[199] i.e., where the debtor (insurer) resides[200] or where the contract provides that the insurance money shall be payable.[201] The result is that the validity of a policy assignment is governed by the proper law of the contract (of assignment).[202] If, however, although valid by the *lex loci actus*, the assignment is not valid by the proper law, the *lex loci actus* applies.[203] Priority, in the case of successive assignments of a policy, assignments the validity of which may be governed by different systems of law, is determined not by the proper law of (any one) assignment but by the proper law of the policy.[204]

2–6 AGENCY

2–6A The Contract of Agency

The existence and scope of the agent's actual authority is a matter for the contract of agency which, like any other contract, has its proper law. In the absence of express choice, it is inferred or imputed that the agency contract is governed by the law of the place where the relationship of principal and agent is created or, in the event of alteration of an existing relationship, where it is altered.[205] If, however, the contract is concluded between principal and agent in different states and there is no one place of creation (or alteration), the court must seek the centre of gravity of the contract[206] and that is likely to be the place, in which the agent is to carry out his mandate[207]; or, if that is in more than one state, the principal's place of residence.[208]

199. *New York Life Ins Co* v *Public Trustee* [1924] 2 Ch 101, 109 *per* Pollock MR (CA—life). Dicey, pp 924 ff.; Moshinsky (1992) 109 LQR 591.
200. Unger, p 493.
201. *New York Life Ins Co* v *Public Trustee* [1924] 2 Ch 101 (CA—life); *contra* Unger, p 497. See also *Jabbour* v *State of Israel* [1954] 1 All ER 145 (fire).
202. *Pender* v *Commercial Bank of Scotland*, 1940 SLT 306 (Ct Sess—life). *Cf Lee* v *Abdy* (1886) 17 QBD 309 (life).
203. *Scottish Provident Institution* v *Cohen & Co* (1888) 16 R 112 (life), in which the Court of Session gave effect to an assignment valid in England, where it was effected, although the policy was a Scots policy and under Scots law such an assignment would have been invalid.
204. *Le Feuvre* v *Sullivan* (1855) 10 Moore 1 (PC—life); although commonly cited for this proposition, the force of the case is not great, as the issues raised by the modern law did not have to be faced.
205. *Maspons y Hermano* v *Mildred Goyeneche & Co* (1882) 9 QBD 530, 539 *per* Lindley LJ (CA), affirmed (1883) 8 App Cas 874; applied in *Ruby SS Corp Ltd* v *Commercial Union Assurance Co* (1934) 150 LT 38, 39 by Scrutton LJ (CA—marine). See also *Atlantic Underwriting Agencies Ltd* v *Cia di Assicurazione di Milano SpA* [1979] 2 Lloyd's Rep 240, in which Italian law was applied as that of the place of residence of the principal and of the place where the contract was negotiated. In this sense in the USA: *Smith & Chambers Salvage* v *Insurance Management Corp*, 808 F Supp 1492, 1497 (ED Wash, 1992—workers' compensation).
206. *Atlantic* (above). *Cf* Restatement (2d), Conflict of Laws, section 291: "the local law of the state which, with respect to the particular issue, has the most significant relationship to the parties and the transaction" under the principles in section 6 (above, note 147); a similar rule in section 293 governs ratification: *Re Petition of Ins Co*, 22 F 109 (ND NY, 1884—hull), affirmed 24 F 559 (1885).
207. *Chatenay* v *Brazilian Submarine Telegraph Co Ltd* [1891] 1 QB 79, 83–84 *per* Lord Esher MR (CA); *Employers' Liability Assurance Corp Ltd* v *Sedgwick, Collins & Co Ltd* [1927] AC 95, 109 *per* Lord Sumner; *First Russian Ins Co* v *London & Lancashire Ins Co Ltd* [1928] Ch 922, 940 *per* Romer J (re).
In *Edinburgh Assurance Co* v *Burns Corp*, 479 F Supp 150 (CD Cal, 1979—salvage risks), part reversed on other grounds 669 F 2d 1259 (9 Cir, 1982), the court applied English law to the relationship between a London broker and Californian client, in respect of the placement of risks at Lloyd's. See also Restatement (2d), Conflict of Laws, section 291, Comment (f).
In *Arab Monetary Fund* v *Hashim* [1993] 1 Lloyd's Rep 543, Evans J applied the law governing the contract of agency (Abu Dhabi) to a restitutionary claim by the principal to recover from the agent the amount of a bribe paid to the agent from London to Switzerland in US dollars.
208. Butler & Merkin, D4.3–09 by reference to *Atlantic* (above, note 205).

2–6B The Contract Mandated

Rights and duties between principal and third party (insured and insurer) are governed by the proper law of the contract concluded by the agent and with the third party[209]; for the purpose of finding the proper law, the *loci contractus* is identified on the basis that the contract was concluded by the agent.[210] The apparent authority of the agent is also governed by the proper law of that contract.[211]

2–7 THE APPLICABLE LAW OF THE CONTRACT UNDER THE ROME CONVENTION

The EC Convention on the Law Applicable to Contractual Obligations,[212] commonly referred to as the Rome Convention, was given force of law in England as the First Schedule to the Contracts (Applicable Law) Act 1990, with effect from 1 April 1991.[213] It applies to all contracts concluded after 1 July 1991.[214] The Brussels Protocol, the Third Schedule to the Act, concedes jurisdiction to the European Court of Justice on questions of interpretation of the Convention. The Rome Convention, together with the Brussels Convention of 1968,[215] is designed to eliminate forum shopping and to promote uniformity of law within the EC.[216] The Rome Convention provides a uniform regime for determining the "applicable law", that is, what common law knows as the proper law of the contract.

Subject to certain important exclusions, the rules of this Convention shall apply (Art 1.1) to all "contractual obligations in any situation involving a choice between the laws of different countries",[217] including contracts of agency, whether or not the countries concerned are members of the EC or the case has any connection with the EC, except, of course, that the case has come before a court for which the Convention is the relevant *lex fori*. The Convention also applies "in the case of conflicts between the laws of different parts of the United Kingdom".[218]

The exclusions from the Convention include arbitration agreements and choice of

---

209. Dicey, p 1458. Restatement (2d), Conflict of Laws, section 292: this is usually but not necessarily the place where the agent is authorised to act and does act in making the contract concerned: *New York Life Ins Co* v *Chapman*, 132 F 2d 688 (8 Cir, 1943—life), *cert den* 319 US 749 (1943); *Mercier* v *John Hancock Life Ins Co*, 44 A 2d 372 (Maine, 1945—life).

210. *Pattison* v *Mills* (1828) 1 Dow & Cl 342, 363 *per* Lord Lyndhurst LC (HL—hull).

211. Dicey, p 1460; even though apparent authority might be characterised as estoppel and a question of evidence for the *lex fori*.

212. Signed and ratified by Belgium, Denmark, France, Germany, Ireland, Italy, Luxembourg, Netherlands and the United Kingdom.

213. With the exception of s 2(1) insofar as it relates to the Brussels Protocol, and s 3(1), (2) and (3)(b). For an introduction to the Act, see Merkin [1991] JBL 205; Rogerson (1991) 141 NLJ 281 and 359. For a commentary on the Act, see Giuliano and Lagarde, "Report on the Convention on the Law Applicable to Contractual Obligations", O.J. 1980, No C282/1; Morse, *Current Law Statutes 1990*, c 36; Plender, *The European Contracts Convention* (London, 1991). For a German view, see Basedow and Drasch NJW 1991.785.

214. Art. 29.

215. Below 2–10.

216. The Rome Convention (Art 20) gives way to *lex specialis* concerning particular kinds of contract, such as the unilateral conflicts rules determining the scope of uniform law on particular contracts, for example, Art 1 of the Convention on the Contract for the International Carriage of Goods by Road 1956, known as the CMR.

217. It has been suggested that this includes a case, in which the only foreign element is the parties' choice of a law, with which the contract has no (other) connection: Morse, *op cit*, note to Art 1.1.

218. Contracts (Applicable Law) Act 1990, s 2(3).

court agreements,[219] and "contracts of insurance which cover risks situated in the territories" of the EC[220]: the latter are not governed by the Rome Convention but are the subject of EC Directives (below 2–8).

The applicable law is, first and foremost, the law expressly chosen by the parties. That law is not required to be the law of a Contracting State (Art 2) or one with which the parties or their contract have any (other) connection.[221] Second, in the absence of an express choice, the law is that implicitly chosen by the parties. This rule appears to be the same[222] as that at common law.[223] Thus, an arbitration clause retains its traditional importance in insurance contracts.[224] Third, in the absence of any choice, express or implied, the law is that with which the contract has its closest connection. In all cases, as is true also of English common law, the possibility of *renvoi* is excluded.[225] Although superficially similar to the common law rule, the third rule looks to a connection found in Swiss law[226] that is apparently quite different from that preferred by English common law. It is presumed (Art 4.2):

"that the contract is most closely connected with the country where the party who is to effect the performance which is characteristic of the contract has, at the time of the conclusion of the contract, his habitual residence, or, in the case of a body corporate or unincorporate, its central administration. However, if the contract is entered into in the course of that party's trade or profession, that country shall be the country in which the principal place of business is situated or, where under the terms of the contract the performance is to be effected through a place of business other than the principal place of business, the country in which that other place of business is situated."

It has been suggested that the payment of money will not normally be characteristic: "It is the performance for which the payment is due, i.e. . . . . the provision of a service, transport, insurance, . . . which usually constitutes the centre of gravity and the socio–economic function of the contractual transaction".[227] However, whereas the force of this observation is clear with regard to a contract to sell goods, it is less clear in the case, such as that of insurance, in which both parties pay or promise to pay money. In the case of indemnity insurance, the promise or payment of indemnity looms large in the minds of the parties. Alternatively, the mind of the lawyer might see good faith as most characteristic of insurance,[228] but this betrays an instinctive desire to find the conceptual identity of a legal institution with which to distinguish it from other legal institutions, and it is doubtful that this was the prime intention of the Convention. Moreover, the reciprocal and continuing duty of good faith[229] may be hard to tie down to any particular place.

Faced with this dilemma, there must be some temptation to avoid it altogether. As Article 4.2 contains no more than a presumption, an English court might be tempted to fall back on Article 4.5, whereby the presumptions are rebutted when "it appears

219. Art 1.2(d). It was not possible to reach agreement on the rules to govern arbitration agreements. Agreements on forum are regulated by Art 17 of the Brussels Convention 1968: below 2–10G.
220. Art 1.3. Other matters relating to contracts are excluded and are listed in Art 1.2.
221. This is the implication of Art 3.3.
222. Rogerson, p 359.
223. Above, 2–3.
224. Merkin [1991] JBL 205, 215. Below, 2–3A.
225. Art 15.
226. Guiliano and Lagarde, p 20, n 38. "The concept of characteristic performance essentially links the contract to the social and economic environment of which it will form part."(*Ibid.*)
227. *Ibid.*
228. Merkin & McGhee *Ibid*. D.4.2–48.
229. See below, 27–1.

from the circumstances as a whole that the contract is more closely connected with another country", and to apply common law rules of localisation.[230]

Moreover, in certain cases, the court may disregard the applicable law,[231] and

    (a) apply the mandatory rules of the law of the state with which, apart from the parties express choice, the contract is most connected[232]; or

    (b) apply the mandatory rules of the forum[233]; or

    (c) decline to apply any rules of the applicable law which conflict with the public policy of the forum.[234]

Further, in the absence of an express choice, a contract to supply services to consumers is governed by the law of the country in which the consumer has his habitual residence, if certain conditions are satisfied: Article 5. This applies to many private lines.[234a]

The Convention governs most matters concerning the interpretation of contracts, their performance and their discharge; these are specified. It governs the material validity of a contract, for example the reality of consent (Art 8), the formal validity of a contract (Art 9),[235] the mode of performance (Art 10), the consequences of breach (Art 10), limitation of actions (Art 10), capacity to contract (Art 11), assignment (Art 12), subrogation (Art 13). In particular, Art 10.1(c) provides that the applicable law governs "the assessment of damages in so far as it is governed by rules of law". Thus it appears that the applicable law governs issues of remoteness and mitigation whereas the arithmetical quantification of damages is regulated by the *lex fori*, except in so far as it can be said to fall within Art 10.1(c).[236] However, if the law of the contract turns out to be that of certain states in the USA, this provision might be thought to require an award of punitive damages or of damages for bad faith, unless the English court is excused on the basis that such an award offends public policy.[237]

The Convention does not govern the capacity of the parties to the contract,[238] or the effect of illegality on the contract.[239] If the existence of the contract is in dispute, the Convention (Art 8), like common law,[240] refers to the putative proper law. Matters procedural according to the *lex fori* are governed by that law.

Particular mention must be made of Article 12 concerning rules for voluntary

---

230. Above, 2–4.

231. Merkin [1991] JBL 205, 214.

232. Art 3.3.

233. Art 7.2.

234. Art 16, headed "Ordre public" and thus appears to envisage respect for the public policy of the forum in distinction with ordre public international, a more limited public policy common to relevant States.

234a. See discussion of Art 5 by Morse, *op cit*; and in F Reichert-Facilides and HUJ d'Oliveira (ed), *International Insurance Contract Law in the EC* (Deventer, 1993), pp 33 ff.

235. This provision looks not to the law of the forum, but classifies the issue as substantive and provides four rules, the main one being a reference to the applicable law or to the law of the place of conclusion, if the contract is concluded between parties in the same state: Art 9.1. Formal validity includes "every external manifestation required on the part of a person expressing the will to be legally bound, and in the absence of such expression of will would not be regarded as fully effective": Tizzano Report (OJ 1990 C219/1), p 28.

236. Morse *loc cit*.

237. Art 3.3 (above). As regards English public policy against punitive damage, see the Protection of Trading Interests Act 1981. Also see *Rookes* v *Barnard* [1964] AC 1129; and *Cassell & Co Ltd* v *Broome* [1972] AC 1027.

238. Art 1.2(a), but apart from partial regulation in Art 11.

239. Except to caution that only public policy that is "manifestly incompatible" with the application of a rule of law specified by the Convention may justify a court in refusing to apply that rule: Art 16.

240. Above, 2–2F.

assignment, an area of obscurity at common law. Article 12.1, which deals with the relationship between assignor and assignee, provides that the mutual obligations of assignor and assignee against the insurer shall be governed by the law which under this Convention applies to the contract between the assignor and assignee. This includes the material and formal validity of the assignment. This is similar to what is believed to be the common law rule.[241]

Article 12.2, which is concerned with the position of the debtor, i.e. the insurer, provides that the law governing the right to which the assignment relates, i.e. the law applicable to the insurance contract itself, shall determine its assignability, the relationship between the assignee and the insurer, including priority between assignees, the conditions under which the assignment can be invoked against the insurer and any question whether the insurer's obligations have been discharged.

2–8 RISKS SITUATED IN THE EC

The Convention on the Law Applicable to Contractual Obligations, known as the Rome Convention,[242] does not apply to contracts of insurance covering risks situated in member states: article 1(3). If a risk is situated in a Member State, it is governed by a different conflicts' regime emanating from the EC Council.

The object of the two directives is the free movement of services and establishment within the EC so that an insurer in one state is allowed to offer insurance in any Member State on the basis of standardised home state supervision. Further, if an insured within the EC chooses an insurer established outside the EC, in respect of a risk situated within the EC, the conflicts' rules are such as to promote the application of the substantive rules of law in his state of domicile or, in the case of a company, of its place of business.

Attempts to harmonise insurance contract law have stalled. A proposal put by the EC Commission to the EC Council in 1979[243] did not attract sufficient agreement among Member States. For this reason, the Commission turned its attention to harmonisation of the rules of private international law and sought, in particular, to limit the operation of mandatory rules of the *lex fori*.[244]

2–8A General Business

The first of two such regimes is found in the Council Directive 88/357/EEC of 22 June 1988.[245] It was given effect in England by the Insurance Companies (Amendment) Regulations 1990,[246] by means of adding certain provisions to the Insurance Companies Act 1980. These establish a new set of rules for insurance contracts, specifically, those which constitute general business, and which cover risks situated in the

---

241. Above, 2–5.
242. Above 2–7.
243. OJ 1979, C 190/2, as amended: OJ 1980, C 355/30. Smulders and Glazener CML Rev 1992.775, 777.
244. Smulders p 779. In the "insurance cases" (for example *Commission v FRG* [1986] ECR 3755) the Court of Justice held that, in the absence of harmonization of insurance contract law, states could apply domestic mandatory *lex fori* concerning insurance contracts, although the effect was a restriction on the free movement of services.
245. OJ No L172, 4.7.88, p 1. Generally, see F Reichert-Facilides and HUJ d'Oliveira (ed), *International Insurance Contract Law in the EC* (Deventer, 1993).
246. SI 1990 No 1333.

United Kingdom or another Member State of the EC.[247] Excluded are reinsurance contracts and contracts on risks situated outside the EC: these are governed by the Rome Convention.[248] Also excluded are life insurance contracts on risks situated in the United Kingdom or another Member State of the EC; these are the subject of a parallel directive[249]: below, 2–8B.

2–8A1 The Situation of Risks

Section 96A(3)(a) of the 1982 Act provides that where the insurance "relates to buildings or to buildings and their contents (in so far as the contents are covered by the same policy)," the risk is situated in the "Member State in which the property is situated".[249a]

Section 96A(3)(b) provides that "where the insurance relates to vehicles of any type", the risk is situated in the "Member State of registration".

Section 96A(3)(c) provides that "in the case of policies of a duration of four months or less covering travel or holiday risks (whatever the class concerned)", the risk is situated in the "member State where the policy holder took out the policy".

Section 96A(3)(d) provides that as regards insurance policies governed by the Act but not covered by paragraphs (a) to (c), when the policy holder is an individual, the risk is situated where he has his habitual residence and, when he is not an individual "where the establishment of the policy holder to which the policy relates is situated".

As regards establishment, section 96A(2) provides that establishment means "the head office or a branch or agency of the company"; and that any "permanent presence of such a company in a Member State shall be regarded as a branch or agency, even if that presence consists merely of an office managed by the company's own staff or by a person who is independent but has permanent authority to act for the company in the same way as an agency".

2–8A2 Applicable Law

The law applicable to contracts within the scope of the Act is set out in Schedule 3A to the Act. In contrast with the common law and with the regime of the Rome Convention,[250] the primacy of party choice is less marked, with more importance to objective factors; and among these, emphasis is placed on the residence of the insured rather than that of the insurer.

Note that under the proposed EC Third Directive on Non Life Insurance,[251] the Non Life Framework Directive, the rules in Schedule 3A would be replaced by new rules designed to simplify the current rules and, in particular, extending freedom of choice to all large risks.[252] Schedule 3A is headed "Law Applicable to Certain Con-

---

247. Section 94A(1).

248. Above, 2–1A. Reinsurance contracts are excluded from the 1982 Act by section 94A(2).

249. The Second Life Directive, 90/619. This locates the risk in the policy holder's place of habitual residence or relevant place of business. The applicable law is that of the Member State of the commitment: see below, 2–8B.

249a. For the reasons said to support this rule, see Lando in F Reichert-Facilides and HUJ d'Oliveira (ed), *International Insurance Contract Law in the EC* (Deventer, 1993), pp 102 ff.

250. Above, 2–1A.

251. 92/49/EEC: OJ L 228, 11.8.92; Bull EC 6–1992, point 1.313.

252. OJ No C 244/28, 28.9.90, Art 24.

tracts of Insurance" and is sub-headed "General Rules as to Applicable Law". Part 1[253] of Schedule 3A reads:

"General Business

1.—(1) Where the policy holder has his habitual residence or central administration within the territory of the member State where the risk is situated, the law applicable to the contract is the law of that member State. However, where the law of that member State so allows, the parties may choose the law of another country.[254]

(2) Where the policy holder does not have his habitual residence or central administration within the territory of the Member State where the risk is situated, the parties to the contract may choose to apply either—

(a) the law of the Member State[254a] where the risk is situated, or

(b) the law of the country in which the policy holder has his habitual residence or central administration.

(3) Where the policy holder carries on a business and the contract covers two or more risks relating to his business which are situated in different Member States, the freedom of choice of the law applicable to the contract extends to the laws of those Member States and of the country in which he has his habitual residence or central administration. In this sub-paragraph 'business' includes a trade or profession.

(4) Where the member States referred to in sub-paragraph (2) or (3) grant greater freedom of choice of the law applicable to the contract, the parties may take advantage of that freedom.[255]

(5) Notwithstanding sub-paragraphs (1) to (3), when the risks covered by the contract are limited to events occurring in a Member State other than the Member State where the risk is situated, the parties may always choose the law of the former State.

(6) For risks classified under classes 4, 5. 6, 7, 11 and 12 of Part I of Schedule 2, the parties to the contract may choose any law."

The risks referred to in sub-paragraph (6) are respectively indemnity cover in respect of railway rolling stock,[256] aircraft,[257] ships,[258] goods in transit,[259] and liability cover in respect of aircraft,[260] and ships.[261]

"Applicable Law in the Absence of Choice

2.—(1) The choice referred to in paragraph 1 must be expressed or demonstrated with reasonable certainty by the terms of the contract or the circumstances of the case.[262]

(2) If that is not so, or if no choice has been made, the contract shall be governed by the law

253. Schedule 3A is set out here, as amended by para. 5 of the Insurance Companies (Amendment) Regulations 1993. Since that amendment, the Schedule has been divided into 2 Parts; Part 1 concerns general business and Part II (below, 2–8B) concerns long term business.

254. The law of England (see below paragraph 5(2)(a)) does so allow, so if the policy holder has his habitual residence or central administration in England and the risk is situated in England, the parties may choose another law. The underlying thought is that, if choice is allowed, there is no need to protect the insured against a choice which deprives him of the protection of his own law: Smulders p 782. See the following note.

254a. The law of that Member is the conflicts law—but is that common law or is it the Rome Convention? See Morse in *International Insurance Contract Law in the EC* (above), p 39.

255. English law grants such freedom. See below, paragraph 5(2)(a).

256. Insurance against loss of or damage to railway rolling stock.

257. Insurance upon aircraft or upon the machinery, tackle, furniture or equipment of aircraft.

258. Insurance upon vessels used on the sea or on inland water, or upon the machinery, tackle, furniture or equipment of such vessels.

259. Insurance against loss of or damage to merchandise, baggage and all other goods in transit, irrespective of the form of transport.

260. Insurance against damage arising out of or in connection with the use of aircraft, including third-party risks and carrier's liability.

261. Insurance against damage arising out of or in connection with the use of vessels on the sea or on inland water, including third-party risks and carrier's liability.

262. That choice may be demonstrated by the circumstances of the case, appears to allow a court to refer by way of analogy to common law rules relating to implied choice.

of the country (from amongst those considered in the relevant sub-paragraphs) with which it is most closely connected.[263]

(3) Nevertheless, a severable part of the contract which has a closer connection with another country (from amongst those considered in the relevant sub-paragraphs) may by way of exception be governed by the law of that other country.

(4) A contract is rebuttably presumed to be most closely connected with the Member State where the risk is situated.[264]

Mandatory Rules

3.—(1) The fact that in the cases referred to in paragraph 1 the parties have chosen a law does not, where all the other elements relevant to the situation at the time of the choice are connected with one Member State only, prejudice the application of the mandatory rules of that member State, which means the rules from which the law of that Member State allows no derogation by means of a contract.[265]

(2) Nothing in this Part of this Schedule restricts the application of the rules of a part of the United Kingdom in a situation where they are mandatory, irrespective of the law otherwise applicable to the contract.[266]

Supplementary Provisions

4.—(1) Where a member State includes several territorial units, each of which has its own rules of law concerning contractual obligations, each unit shall be considered as a country for the purposes of identifying the applicable law.

(2) The provisions of this Part of this Schedule apply to conflicts between the laws of the different parts of the United Kingdom.

5.—(1) Subject to the preceding provisions of this Part of this Schedule, a court in a part of the United Kingdom shall act in accordance with the provisions of the Contracts (Applicable Law) Act 1990.

(2) In particular, reference shall be made to those provisions—

   (a) to ascertain for the purposes of paragraph 1(1) and (4) what freedom of choice the parties have under the law of a part of the United Kingdom; and

   (b) to determine whether the mandatory rules of another member State should be applied in accordance with paragraph 3(1) where the law otherwise applicable is the law of a part of the United Kingdom."

2–8B Life Insurance

The Second Life Insurance Directive[267] was implemented by the Insurance Companies (Amendment) Regulations 1993,[268] which came into force on 20 May 1993. It applies to contracts of insurance to which Article 1 of the First Long Term Insurance Directive applies. The regime is an interim regime pending the operation of the Third Life Insurance Directive,[269] which is expected to come into effect in 1994.

Regulation 5 amends section 94B and Schedule 3A of the Insurance Companies Act 1982. Section 94B now reads:

"(1A) The Law applicable . . . shall be determined in accordance with the provisions of part II of Schedule 3A to this Act if—(a) where the policy holder is an individual, he is habitually

---

263. Subject to the words in brackets, this appears to allow a court to refer by way of analogy to common law, however, *cf* sub-paragraph (4).

264. As regards the situation of risk, see above 2–8A1.

265. The essence of this sub-paragraph appears to be that, as at common law (above 2–2A), a choice of law will be disregarded, if its application would oust compulsory rules of the state to which all other elements in the case point, as the state with which the contract is connected.

266. What is envisaged here is overriding public policy (*règles d'application immédiates*) of the kind seen in *Regazzoni* v *Sethia (K.C.) (1944) Ltd* [1958] AC 301: Smulders p 784.

267. 79/267/EEC, OJ 1990, L 330/50.

268. SI 1993 No. 174.

269. 90/619/EEC, as amended by Directive 92/96/EEC.

resident in a Member State; or (b) where the policy holder is not an individual, the establishment of the policy holder to which the contract relates is situated in a Member State—".

(2) Subsections (1) and (1A) above do not apply in relation to a contract of reinsurance."

Part II of Schedule 3A is headed "LONG TERM BUSINESS" and reads:

"General rules as to applicable law
6. The law applicable to the contract is the law of the Member State of the commitment.[270] However, where the law of that Member State[270a] so allows, the parties may choose the law of another country.
7. Where the policy holder is an individual and has his habitual residence in a Member State other than that of which he is a national, the parties may choose the law of the Member State of which he is a national.[270b]

Mandatory Rules
8. Nothing in this part of this Schedule restricts the application of the rules of a part of the United Kingdom in a situation where they are mandatory, irrespective of the law otherwise applicable to the contract.

Supplementary Provisions
9.–(1) Where a Member State includes several territorial units, each of which has its own rules of law concerning contractual obligations, each unit shall be considered as a country for the purposes of identifying the applicable law.
(2) The provisions of this Part of this Schedule apply to conflicts between the laws of the different parts of the United Kingdom.
10.–(1) Subject to the preceding provisions of this Part of this Schedule, a court in a part of the United Kingdom shall act in accordance with the provisions of the Contracts (Appicable) Law Act 1990.[271]
(2) In particular, reference shall be made to those provisions to ascertain for the purposes of paragraph 6 what freedom of choice the parties have under the law of a part of the United Kingdom."

2–9 JURISDICTION: COMMON LAW

Before 1982, the English court had jurisdiction to hear an action *in personam*, if the defendant could be served with a writ in England or with notice of proceedings abroad.[272] If the defendant was abroad, it was possible to serve notice of proceedings on that defendant *inter alia* if the proper law of the contract were English law.[273] This is still the law for some cases but the position was modified by the Brussels Convention on Jurisdiction and the Enforcement of Judgments in Civil and Commercial Matters 1968, which was enacted in England in 1982[273a] and is considered below: 2–10. Cases within the scope of the Convention include insurance contracts (other than reinsur-

---

270. That is to say, the Member State where the insured has his habitual residence or, if he is a legal person, the Member State where is situated its establishment, to which the contract relates: Insurance Companies (Amendment) Regulations 1993, Reg. 6(2)(b); see Smulders p 786.
270a. See above, note 254a.
270b. As regards the relevant law within the United Kingdom, see Reg 9; and Morse in *International Insurance Contract Law in the EC* (above), p 48.
271. p 270. For the jurisdiction of courts in the USA over non-resident insurers, see Soiret, 28 Tort & Ins LJ 533 (1993). See above, 2–7.
272. Dicey, p 270. For the jurisdiction of courts in the USA over non-resident insurers, see Soiret, 28 Tort & Ins LJ 533 (1993).
273. RSC Ord. 11, r 1(1)(f). *Overseas Union Ins Co Ltd* v *Incorporated General Ins Ltd* [1992] 1 Lloyd's Rep 439 (CA—re). Butler & Merkin, D.4.1–01.
273a. Below, 2–10.

ance contracts). Cases outside the scope of the Convention are governed by the common law.

2–9A Forum Conveniens

The common law rules of jurisdiction are found in RSC Ord 11, r 1(1) and are outside the scope of this chapter, except to recall that, even if the proper law is English law, the English court has a discretion to decline jurisdiction,[274] if it is not the *forum conveniens*. In exercising its discretion, the court will consider various factors and, if these considerations point to a foreign court as the more appropriate forum, the general rule is that leave to serve will be refused.

A sense of the way in which the court will exercise its discretion can be gained from *Du Pont de Nemours & Co* v *Agnew*.[275] The plaintiff, whose liability for punitive damages had been established in Illinois where, however, the law did not permit insurance of such liability, sought a declaratory judgment in England against English insurers in respect of that liability. The first court considered that a stay of the proceedings in England would deprive the plaintiff of a substantial and legitimate juridical advantage, the opportunity to claim in a forum where the insurers' defence based on public policy might not succeed.[276] On appeal, Bingham LJ agreed with the result but said[277] that the correct approach

"is to compare the relative appropriateness of the English with the competing foreign forum for a just trial of the action in question. It is less important [since *Spiliada*[278]] whether a stay will deprive the plaintiff of a legitimate personal or juridical advantage . . . This aspect is to be considered as part of a more general judgment on which is the appropriate forum in the interests of all the parties and in the interests of justice."

Having considered "the general undesirability of concurrent proceedings between the same parties on the same issues in different jurisdictions",[279] "a recipe for confusion and injustice",[280] Bingham LJ considered[281] the factors connecting the case with Illinois. (a) The plaintiff's tort liability arose there; but that was chance, it might well have arisen in a different state. (b) The liability of the plaintiff had been decided by courts in Illinois, but the present matter would not be decided by the same courts, so that any court in Illinois or England would come to the present issue afresh. (c) The courts of Illinois were seized of the present dispute; this was relevant, but did not give Illinois any "*a priori* claim to the right of way". (d) Illinois was a state in which the plaintiffs carried on a substantial business; however, Du Pont is a Delaware corporation and none of the insurers were incorporated there. (e) Witnesses and evidence

---

274. For the doctrine in the USA, see *Gulf Oil Corp* v *Gilbert* 330 US 501 (1947); *Koster* v *Lumbermens Mutual Casualty Co* 330 US 518 (1947); *Piper Aircraft Co* v *Reyno* 454 US 235 (1981).
275. [1987] 2 Lloyd's Rep 585 (CA).
276. See also Bingham LJ (p 587).
277. p 588, after considering the speech of Lord Goff in *Spiliada Maritime* v *Corp Cansulex Ltd* [1987] AC 460.
278. Above.
279. p 589, namely the possibility of conflicting judgments, or an "ugly rush to get one action decided ahead of the other, in order to create a situation of *res judicata*, or issue estoppel in the latter"—*The Abidin Daver* [1984] AC 398, 423 *per* Lord Brandon.
280. *The Abidin Daver* (above) p 412 *per* Lord Diplock.
281. pp 593–594.

were more readily available and compellable in Illinois; but the issues of fact in the present case would require very little oral evidence. (f) None of the policies were broked there. Having found this review of competing factors inconclusive, Bingham LJ continued[282]:

"There is, however, one factor . . . which is in my judgment heavily in favour of the English forum. Du Pont and Endo's policies were, as I have held, governed by English law. They are accordingly entitled to such indemnity as on a proper construction of the policies English law affords them; no more, of course, but certainly no less. This court is necessarily better placed than any other to rule on that question."

From this and other cases, it appears that the court will consider some or all of the following (non–exhaustive) list of factors:

(a) When English law is the proper law of the contract, that has importance for the jurisdiction of the English courts.[283] When the main issue in a case is the construction of a policy, for example as to the scope of the cover afforded, *ceteris paribus* the appropriate forum is that of the proper law which governs such issues.

(b) The fact "that the parties have agreed in their contract that the English Courts shall have jurisdiction (albeit a non–exclusive jurisdiction) creates a strong *prima facie* case that that jurisdiction is an appropriate one; it should in principle be a jurisdiction to which neither party to the contract can object as inappropriate; they have both agreed that it is appropriate".[284]

(c) If the dispute turns on issues of fact, the location of the evidence and of the witnesses that might be called is clearly important.[285] A related factor is whether the claimant has brought the action in a forum that would unfairly inconvenience the defendant.[286]

(d) If another court is already seized of the dispute, that is relevant, although this factor does not give that court any *a priori* claim to precedence.[287] In particular, the court will consider "for how long and up to what stage of the action the foreign Court has been seised of the case".[288]

(e) "In any case in which the costs are going to involve very substantial sums of money, . . . the question of the recoverability of such costs is not an irrelevant factor. . . . The Courts of New York do not provide [the parties] with any remedy by which they can recover the costs of enforcing what they say

---

282. p 594. Subsequently, an application for an injunction against the insurers to restrain them from continuing with the proceedings in Illinois was refused: [1988] 2 Lloyd's Rep 240 (CA).

283. *Du Pont* v *Agnew* [1987] 2 Lloyd's Rep 585 (CA); *Britannia SS Assn Ltd* v *Ausonia Assicurazioni SpA* [1985] 2 Lloyd's Rep 98 (CA—re); *cf Insurance Corp of Ireland* v *Strombus International Ins Co* [1985] 2 Lloyd's Rep 138 (CA—re); *New Hampshire Ins Co* v *Strabag Bau AG* [1992] 1 Lloyd's Rep. 361, 370 per Lloyd LJ (CA); *Overseas Union Ins Co Ltd* v *Incorporated General Ins Ltd* [1992] 1 Lloyd's Rep 439 (CA –re). English law as proper law was also an important factor in *S & W Berisford plc* v *New Hampshire Ins Co* [1990] 1 Lloyd's Rep 454, 464 per Hobhouse J; *The Irish Rowan* [1989] 2 Lloyd's Rep 144, 167, *per* Purchas LJ (CA—liability); and *Arkwright Mutual Ins Co* v *Bryanston Ins Co Ltd* [1990] 2 Lloyd's Rep 70, 81, Potter J (re)

284. *Berisford* (above) p 463. *Gulf Oil Corp* v *Gilbert* 330 US 501, 508 (1947): a choice of forum should be given great weight. Also in this sense: *Piper Aircraft Co* v *Reyno* 454 US 235, 255 (1981).

285. *Du Pont* v *Agnew* (above); *Berisford* (above) p 463. *Gulf Oil* (above) pp 509–509.

286. *Piper Aircraft Co* (above).

287. *Du Pont* v *Agnew* (above); *Arkwright Mutual Ins Co* v *Bryanston Ins Co Ltd* [1990] 2 Lloyd's Rep 70 (re). *Monsanto Co* v *Aetna Casualty Co* 559 A 2d 1301, 1308 (Del, 1988—liability).

288. *Arkwright* (above) p 80, per Potter J, citing *de Dampierre* v *de Dampierre* [1988] AC 92, 108.

are their rights under these policies. It is not for the defendants to deprive the plaintiffs of the right to recover costs."[289]

(f) Special considerations arise in the case of multiple parties to the same claim. In *The Irish Rowan*,[290] a risk was insured by 77 insurers from around the world, led by a leading underwriter who was subject to the jurisdiction of the English court. The Court of Appeal held that that jurisdiction enabled the insured to bring a representative action in England, thus conferring on the English court jurisdiction over underwriters not otherwise subject to that jurisdiction. In *The Goldean Mariner*,[291] proceedings were instituted to enforce a reinsurance contract concluded in England between 46 reinsurers, of whom 44 "were insurance companies scattered around the globe"[292] and who were led by Lloyd's underwriters. The vital issue was the cause of a casualty on the high seas. Phillips J rejected an application to stay the proceedings, stating[293] that, whereas there was "no obviously appropriate forum", "one consideration outweighed all others in making London the obvious forum":

"where 'a vessel is insured on the world market with individual insurers around the globe each covering a comparatively small proportion of the risk it is vital in the interests of all concerned that if the validity of a claim has to be determined by litigation, this should occur in a single hearing binding on all concerned. This is because the costs of a contested marine insurance action can be enormous . . . . The English forum, by reason of the exorbitant provisions of O.11, r. 1(1)(j), was the only jurisdiction in which it was open to the plaintiffs to sue all the defendants'."

(g) Special considerations also arise in the case of multiple claims involving the same parties, for example, the case of a manufacturer in the USA, who is liable for clean up costs and seeks a single comprehensive declaratory judgment for all its sites against all its liability insurers on risk.[294] If the cover relates to sites in several different states, the doctrine of *forum non conveniens* may be pleaded by one or more of the insurers to argue that the consolidated suit should be dismissed and brought again as several smaller suits in the states concerned.

Against consolidation, it might be said that one of the objects of the doctrine of *forum non conveniens* is to prevent forum shopping,[295] and there is no doubt that the manufacturer will seek a declaratory judgment from a court chosen as one favourable to such claims[296] rather than one, as in the

289. *S & W Berisford plc* v *New Hampshire Ins Co* [1990] 1 Lloyd's Rep 454, 464. By contrast, it is also "a substantial advantage in a case . . . , where the sums involved are relatively small and the incidence of costs, and in particular the power of the Court to award costs against the unsuccessful party, can be a decisive factor in the parties' decision whether or not to proceed to trial": *Arkwright* (above) p 83 *per* Potter J, citing *Roneleigh Ltd* v *M II Exports Ltd* [1989] 1 WLR 619, 623 *per* Nourse LJ, 624 *per* Butler–Sloss LJ (CA).
290. *Irish Shipping Ltd* v *Commercial Union Assurance Co plc* [1989] 2 Lloyd's Rep 144 (CA—liability). Merkin [1989] LMCLQ 389.
291. [1989] 2 Lloyd's Rep 390.
292. p 392 *per* Phillips J.
293. p 400.
294. On this question, see Eilender, 90 Colum L Rev 1066 (1990).
295. *Piper Aircraft Co* v *Reyno* 454 US 235, 249 (1981).
296. Notably, a court that recognises the triple trigger basis of liability: below 17–4C2. The court is typically a state court, in which the insurer has the burden of proving that the insurance does not cover the case (usually that the pollution is not "sudden and accidental"); the sheer factual complexity of the consolidated claims, in respect of which the insurer must establish a defence, favours the claimant: Eilander p 1074.

English reinsurance cases (above), with which the affair has a strong objective connection. A second argument is that, in the absence of a clear objective connection with the chosen court, that court should not have the burden of having dumped at its door the weight of toxic litigation that belongs elsewhere.[297] A third argument is that insurance cover is "site-specific and that, therefore a review of an individual site and the examination, collection and identification of volumes of documents and witnesses that must be imported to the forum court" pose "too great of an administrative burden on both the defendants and the court".[298] The somewhat cynical suggestion has been made that this last point has been exaggerated for, if the court rules that the relevant terms of the contract, notably "sudden and accidental", are ambiguous, it can construe the contract against the insurer in the comfort of the courthouse without the inconvenience of a close look at the facts on the site.[299]

In favour of consolidation, it is argued that it avoids the cost and inconvenience of piecemeal litigation,[300] both to the litigants and to the courts of the community of states concerned, not least because the parties are more likely to reach a settlement if the issues between them are consolidated; and that the uncertainty of protracted litigation in different courts leading to inconsistent decisons is bad for the predictability commercially desirable for both manufacturers and insurers alike.[301]

(h) There is an exception to the jurisdiction of the court indicated by the balance of other factors, if the plaintiff can establish that, in the foreign court, justice could not be obtained or could be obtained only at excessive cost, delay or inconvenience.[302] The exception will be hard to prove,[303] but not impossible. In *Islamic Arab Ins Co v Saudi Egyptian American Reinsurance Co*,[304] the Court of Appeal considered that, as between a forum in England and in Saudia Arabia where insurance (except mutual insurance) is invalid by Islamic law, it was in the interests of the parties that the case be tried in England, which "has a specialist Court and specialist lawyers, which it is common ground Saudi Arabia has not".[305]

The same kind of argument may be found in a more discrete form in *Du Pont v Agnew*[306] and, perhaps, in any case, in which the issue is seen as one

---

297. Eilander p 1092.

298. Eilander pp 1074 and 1075.

299. This is the inference of Eilander p 1089. Even if the court must scrutinise the evidence, the author cited the court in *Montsanto Co v Aetna Casualty Co* 559 A 2d 1301 (Del, 1988—liability) as saying (p 1308): "A waste site can only offer a view of a 'hole or a pile'. The waste site does not offer documents or witnesses."

300. *Lumbermens Mutual Casualty Co v Connecticut Bank & Trust* 806 F 2d 411 (2 Cir, 1986—liability); *General Reinsurance Corp v Ciba–Geigy Corp* 853 F 2d 78 (2 Cir, 1988—liability).

301. Eilander pp 1079 ff.

302. *Amin Rasheed Shipping Corp v Kuwait Ins Co* [1984] AC 50, 66–68 *per* Lord Diplock, 72 *per* Lord Wilberforce (hull). See also *The Abidin Daver* [1984] AC 398, 411–412 *per* Lord Diplock; and, especially, the speech of Lord Goff in *Spiliada Maritime Corp v Cansulex Ltd* [1987] AC 460, 478 ff.

303. For example, *Insurance Corp of Ireland v Strombus International Ins Co* [1985] 2 Lloyd's Rep 138 (CA—re); and *New Hampshire Ins Co v Strabag Bau AG* [1992] 1 Lloyd's Rep 361, 370–371 per Lloyd LJ (CA), noting that there is authority "which deplores any discussion or entertainment" of the argument that the plaintiff could not get justice in the foreign court, *in casu*, Germany.

304. [1987] 1 Lloyd's Rep 315 (CA—re).

305. p 319 *per* Parker LJ.

306. [1987] 2 Lloyd's Rep 585.

of public policy. Behind that case was the possibility of an award of indemnity for punitive damages. While acknowledging that the standing and integrity of the Illinois court was beyond reproach, Bingham LJ considered[307] that, in the Illinois action attention might be diverted from policy cover under the proper (English) law to policy of another kind in Illinois, where indemnity for punitive damages cannot be enforced, and concluded that England was the more appropriate forum.

In any event, these are no more than factors: general conclusions cannot be drawn with confidence. If the balance of factors points to a foreign jurisdiction, the English court will decline to proceed. The matter is one for the discretion of the judge. An appeal can succeed only if the judge is shown to have been wrong. In *Spiliada*,[308] Lord Templeman said this:

"it seems to me that the solution of disputes about the relative merits of trial in England and trial abroad is pre-eminently a matter for the trial judge. Commercial court judges are very experienced in these matters. In nearly every case evidence is on affidavit by witnesses of acknowledged probity. I hope that in future the judge will be allowed to study the evidence and refresh his memory of the speech of . . . Lord Goff in this case in the quiet of his room without expense to the parties; that he will not be referred to other decisions on other facts; and that submissions will be measured in hours and not days. An appeal should be rare and the appellate court should be slow to interfere."

If, as in *DuPont* v *Agnew* (above), the decision of the court is that the English court is a *forum conveniens*, it does not follow from that alone that the English court is the only appropriate forum or that one of the parties to that decision will be restrained from continuing proceedings over the same dispute in a foreign court by an injunction of the English court.[309] An injunction will be granted only if "the ends of justice so require",[310] and an application for such an injunction against the insurers in that case was refused.[311]

2–10 JURISDICTION: THE BRUSSELS CONVENTION

For most purposes, jurisdiction is now governed by the Convention on Jurisdiction and the Enforcement of Judgments in Civil and Commercial Matters 1968, as supplemented by a Protocol of 1971 on interpretation, and amended by the Convention on Accession 1978. As to the latter, the original provisions for insurance "were ill-suited to the particular nature and international importance of much of the non-domestic British insurance market and they were therefore amended by the accession Conven-

---

307. p 595. While not ruling out the relevance of the public policy of Illinois, the judge observed (p 594) that "the conclusion that an insured's right to indemnity depended on the chance where the claim against him happened to be brought might well be thought to introduce an unacceptably random element into a very important contractual undertaking".

308. *Spiliada Maritime Corp* v *Cansulex Ltd* [1987] AC 460, 465. This advice was taken by the Court of Appeal and, it seems, by the editors of the law reports in *McMillan* v *New South Wales Medical Union Ltd* (18 May 1987) which was not reported. The advice was also heeded in *Irish Shipping Ltd* v *Commercial Union Assurance Co plc* [1989] 2 Lloyd's Rep 144 (CA—liability).

309. *Société Nationale Industrielle Aérospatiale* v *Lee Kui Jak* [1987] AC 871, 895 per Lord Goff.

310. *Ibid*.

311. *Du Pont de Nemours* v *Agnew* (No. 2) [1988] 2 Lloyd's Rep 240 (CA).

tion".[312] The 1968 Convention, as amended, was then enacted in England by the Civil Jurisdiction and Judgments Act 1982.[313] The Act came into effect on 1 January 1987. The matter of jurisdiction is evidently one of importance. Even within the EC, the perception is that member courts vary widely in terms of cost, the speed at which they work, and the nature and amount of awards courts might make.[314]

2–10A Interpretation

As the Convention is one designed to unify law and its meaning may be the subject of reference to the European Court of Justice, the English court must apply broad rules of interpretation, including the teleological method of interpretation which, in the view of Lord Diplock,[315] may require the court to give effect to the spirit rather than the strict letter of the text; and which, in the view of one commentator,[316] is the technical term for not taking the text of a document seriously. Lord Denning, however, took this method of interpretation very seriously:

"We must . . . put on one side our traditional rules of interpretation. . . . We ought, in interpreting this convention, to adopt the European method. . . . They adopt a method which they call . . . the 'schematic and teleological' method of interpretation. It is not really so alarming as it sounds. All it means is that the judges do not go by the literal meaning of the words or by the grammatical structure of the sentence. They go by the design and purpose which lies behind it. When they come across a situation which is to their minds within the spirit—but not the letter—of the legislation, they solve the problem by looking at the design and purpose of the legislature—at the effect which it was sought to achieve. They then interpret the legislation so as to produce the desired effect."[317]

Initially, other judges were less enthusiastic[318] but, the United Kingdom having ratified the Vienna Convention on the Law of Treaties 1969,[319] the courts are now obliged to interpret later treaties as indicated by Articles 31–33 of that Convention and thus in the light of the "object and purpose" of the text and, indeed, are doing

---

312. O'Malley and Layton, *European Civil Practice* (London, 1989), 18.02, with reference to the Schlosser Report, paras 136 ff., i.e., "Report of Professor Peter Schlosser on the Convention of October 9, 1978 on the Accession of the Kingdom of Denmark, Ireland and the United Kingdom of Great Britain and Northern Ireland to the Convention on Jurisdiction and the Enforcement of Judgments in Civil and Commercial Matters and to the Protocol on its Interpretation by the Court of Justice", OJ 1979, C.59/71 (hereafter referred to as the Schlosser Report). Note also the Jenard Report: the "Report on the Convention on Jurisdiction and the Enforcement of Judgments in Civil and Commercial Matters", by P Jenard; it is reproduced in O'Malley, Appendix 1.

Note further, by the Lugano Convention and Protocols of 16 September 1988, a Convention similar to the Brussels Convention was concluded between the 12 EC States and the six States of EFTA. To implement this Convention, the United Kingdom Parliament has passed the Civil Jurisdiction and Judgments Act 1991, however, this Act is not in force. Further, by the San Sebastian Convention of 26 May 1989, which came into force on 1 December 1991, Spain and Portugal acceded to the Brussels Convention and the Luxemburg Protocol, as amended. Between these versions of the Convention there are some differences, however, these do not appear to have a significant impact on contracts of insurance.

313. Generally, see Butler & Merkin, D.4.1–26 ff.; Collins, *The Civil Jurisdiction and Judgments Act 1982*, pp 68 ff.; Dicey, pp 349 ff.

314. *Insurance International*, February 1992 p 7.

315. *Henn & Darby* v *DPP* [1981] AC 850, 905 *per* Lord Diplock.

316. Briggs [1991] LMCLQ 10, 12.

317. *James Buchanan & Co* v *Babco Forwarding & Shipping (U.K.)* [1977] QB 208, 213 (CA).

318. *Ibid* on appeal: [1978] AC 141, 152–153 per Lord Wilberforce. Later, he took a more sympathetic view of the method: *Fothergill* v *Monarch Airlines* [1981] AC 251, 276.

319. Cmnd 4140. Generally, see Mann (1983) 99LQR 376, 377 ff; Sinclair, "The Vienna Convention on the Law of Treaties" (2nd ed, Manchester 1984).

so.[320] In the light of such statements, however, and quite apart from the volume of litigation to which the Brussels Convention has given rise, the draftsman should need little encouragement to settle questions of jurisdiction as explicitly as possible in the contract itself.

The impact of the Vienna Convention on the interpretation of the Brussels Convention, as enacted in the 1982 Act (as amended), is as follows:

(a) The courts must seek in good faith[321] the natural and ordinary meaning of the words[322] in issue in the context of the 1982 Act, including their purpose, as it appears from the Act itself.

(b) Especially but not only if the court finds ambiguity or the application of (a) leads to a result which is manifestly absurd or unreasonable, the court may resort to supplementary aids to interpretation, including the purpose of the Convention as it appears from extrinsic evidence, the legislative history,[323] learned commentaries[324] and the decisions of courts—not only of the ECJ but of courts in other jurisdictions.

2–10B The Scope of the Brussels Convention

By Article 1, the Brussels Convention applies "in civil and commercial matters". It does not apply *inter alia* to (a) "rights in property arising out of a matrimonial relationship", (b) "wills and succession", (c) "bankruptcy, proceedings relating to the winding-up of insolvent companies or other legal persons, judicial arrangements, composition and analogous proceedings" or (d) "arbitration".[325] As regards insurance contracts, Section 3 (Articles 7 ff), applies what is called a special jurisdiction.[326] However, Section 3 is not autonomous or self-contained[327] and must be read with

320. *Fothergill* (above) p 294 per Lord Scarman; *The Hollandia* [1983] 1 AC 565, 574 per Lord Diplock; *New Hampshire Ins Co v Strabag Bau AG* [1992] 1 Lloyd's Rep 361, 365 per Lloyd LJ (CA).

321. Clarke [1993] HKLJ—and references cited.

322. This is called the golden rule of construction, however, it is applies less rigidly to conventions, as they tend to be worded more loosely; *Buchanan* (above) p 160 per Lord Salmon; *Silber v Islander Trucking* [1985] 2 Lloyd's Rep 243, 245 per Mustill J.

323. *Cf Pepper (Inspector of Taxes) v Hart* [1993] A.C. 593.

324. Notably but not only the Schlosser Report and the Jenard Report (above, 2–10).

325. In *The Atlantic Emperor, Marc Rich & Co AG v Soc Italiana Impianti PA* [1989] 1 Lloyd's Rep 549, plaintiffs issued an originating summons, asking the English court to appoint an arbitrator on the behalf of the defendants, and obtained leave to serve the summons out of the jurisdiction on the defendants in Italy. The defendants applied to set aside the order giving leave on the ground *inter alia* that the dispute fell within the Convention and should therefore be resolved in Italy. The decision of Hirst J, that the Convention did not apply, was referred to the ECJ by the CA (*ibid*). The ECJ ([1992] 1 Lloyd's Rep 342) decided that, by excluding arbitration from the scope of the Convention on the ground that it was already covered by other conventions, the intention was to exclude arbitration in its entirety; hence, it excluded not only proceedings before arbitrators but also related proceedings brought before national courts, even a dispute over the existence or validity of an arbitration agreement.

In casu, the appointment of an arbitrator by a national court was a measure adopted as part of the process of setting arbitration in motion and came, therefore, within the sphere of arbitration, which was excluded from the Convention, and was within the jurisdiction of the English court. Pending the ruling of the ECJ, however, the English buyers entered an appearance in the Italian courts (other than merely to contest jurisdiction), with the result that the English court was obliged to recognise the judgment of the Italian court that there was no valid arbitration agreement: *The Atlantic Emperor (No 2)* [1992] 1 Lloyd's Rep. 624.

326. This reflects the fact that certain national laws had special rules designed to protect weaker parties against abuse of the economic power of insurance companies: Kaye, *Civil Jurisdiction and Enforcement of Foreign Judgments* (Abingdon, 1987), p 806.

327. Kaye p 805.

other provisions, which provide a path to and context for Section 3. The scope of the Convention is to be determined solely by reference to the subject-matter of the dispute.[328]

2–10B1 Forum Non Conveniens

When the Convention applies, "the Court cannot stay or strike out or dismiss proceedings on the ground of *forum non conveniens* where to do so would be inconsistent with the Convention, and that covers all cases where the defendant in proceedings in England is domiciled in England and the conflict of jurisdiction is between the jurisdiction of the English court and the jurisdiction of the courts of some other Contracting State". These are the words of Dillon LJ in *Re Harrods (Buenos Aires) Ltd*,[329] in which that question arose, except that the conflict was not with the court of a Contracting State but with that of a non-Contracting State, Argentina. The "novelty"[330] of two earlier decisions[331] was that such a rule applied not only when the natural forum was in a Contracting State but also when it was in a non-Contracting State, and even when proceedings between the same parties had already been commenced in the non-Contracting State. The earlier decisions on these points were rejected by the Court of Appeal in *Re Harrods*.

In the earlier decisions, although section 49 of the 1982 Act preserves the discretion "where to do so is not inconsistent with the 1968 Convention", the exercise of the discretion was considered to be inconsistent[332] both with the language of the Convention[333] and with the "principle and the overall intention of the Convention".[334] Although, in relation to intended defendants who are not domiciled in a Contracting State, Article 4 allows the court to apply its own rules, the Convention is designed "to achieve uniformity and to 'harmonise' the relevant procedural and jurisdiction rules of the Courts of the Contracting States". So, said the courts, the "Convention leaves no room for the application of any discretionary jurisdiction by the Courts of [England]: the availability of such a discretion would destroy the framework of the Convention

---

328. *The Atlantic Emperor* (above) p 351.
329. [1991] 3 WLR 397.
330. Briggs [1991] LMCLQ 10, 11.
331. In *Arkwright Mutual Ins Co v Bryanston Ins Co Ltd* [1990] 2 Lloyd's Rep 70 (re), which concerned action by a United States insurer against a reinsurer domiciled in England, Potter J refused to stay proceedings on account of a *lis alibi pendens* instituted by the reinsurer in New York. In *S & W Berisford plc v New Hampshire Ins Co* [1990] 1 Lloyd's Rep 454 (AR) a plaintiff incorporated in New York claimed in relation to stolen gold and gems under insurance (taken for it by another plaintiff incorporated in the United Kingdom) with the London branch of an insurer incorporated in New Hampshire. The submission, that the court in London had no jurisdiction under the Convention, because neither the plaintiff in question nor the insurer was domiciled in a Contracting State, was rejected by Hobhouse J.
332. *Berisford* (above) p 462 *per* Hobhouse J.
333. *Arkwright* (above) p 73 *per* Potter J: referred to Art 2, that "Subject to the provisions of the Convention, persons domiciled in a Contracting State *shall* . . . be sued in the Courts of that State" (emphasis added by the judge) and concluded that "it is *only* within the Convention that its limitations are to be found".
334. *Berisford* (above) p 462 *per* Hobhouse J. But *cf* Collins (1990) 106 LQR 537, who points out that in *Banco Atlantico SA v British Bank of the Middle East*, ([1990] 2 Lloyd's Rep 504 (CA)), although the point was not argued, the court proceeded on the basis that an application would be entertained to have proceedings stayed in favour of the courts of a non-Contracting State. He also points out (p 539) that, as a matter of public international law, the "Contracting States were not regulating relations with non-Contracting States".

and create lack of uniformity in the interpretation and implementation of the Convention".[335]

The effect of these decisions was that, when a case fell within the scope of the Convention and the English court had jurisdiction under the Convention, the English court might decline jurisdiction only if the Convention expressly allowed it.[336] Indeed, the inference was that, even if foreign proceedings had been commenced years before, the English court had no discretion to stay later proceedings in England. This caused consternation. "So profoundly impractical a result cannot rationally have been intended."[337] By the same reasoning, the same inference might have been drawn when the parties had a contractual agreement to bring proceedings in a non-Contracting State, as the Convention does not allow for such agreements.[338] "No rational person", it was said,[339] "can defend such a result".

To sidestep these decisions, the discretion of the English courts might have been characterised as procedural and, as such, put outside the scope of the Convention, which is concerned with jurisdiction and not with procedure: procedure remains a matter for the *lex fori*.[340] This manoeuvre may now be unnecessary. In *Re Harrods (Buenos Aires) Ltd*, the Court of Appeal took a narrower view of the purpose and construction of the Convention and upheld the English court's discretion—as regards the courts of non-Contracting States.[341] The decision, however, is the subject of an appeal to the House of Lords, which has adjourned its proceedings and referred the matter to the ECJ.[342]

2–10C The Purposes of the Convention

In *Berisford*,[343] Hobhouse J stated the primary purpose of the Convention, as stated in the preamble, to be to:

---

335. pp 462–463, with reference to paras. 76 ff of the Schlosser Report, including (para 78): "Where the Courts of several States have jurisdiction, the plaintiff has deliberately been given a right of choice, which should not be weakened by application of the doctrine of *forum non conveniens*. The plaintiff may have chosen another apparently 'inappropriate' court from among the competent courts in order to obtain a judgment in the State in which he also wishes to enforce it." Moreover, the effect of the Convention is that, in cases to which it applies, the courts of England will lose jurisdiction "based merely on service of a writ within the area of the court. To correct rules of a jurisdiction in a particular case by means of the concept of *forum non conveniens* will then be largely unnecessary".

336. Collins (1990) 106 LQR 535, 537.

337. Briggs, [1991] LMCLQ 10, 12. See also Fentiman, 26 Cornell Int L J 59 (1993).

338. Briggs (above). *Cf* the view of Collins (above) that such agreements are valid under the Convention, as Art 17, which sanctions such agreements, does not limit its approval to agreements in favour of the courts of Contracting States.

339. Briggs (above).

340. This argument is advanced by Briggs (above), with reference to the decision of the ECJ in *Hagen* v *Zeehaghe* [1990] ECR 1845, that the criteria for joinder of a third party are procedural and that, as such, they are a matter for the forum, unless the application of the *lex fori* prejudices the practical effect of the Convention. The application of English rules to stay proceedings would not, it is argued, prejudice the practical effect of the Convention. *Quaere* whether the argument has the same force as regards an application to stay proceedings in a contracting State.

341. In *Re Harrods (Buenos Aires) Ltd (No 2)* [1991] 4 All ER 348 (CA), an appeal was allowed against the decision of Harman J that the English court and not the Argentinian court was the *forum conveniens*.

342. See Fentiman, 26 Cornell Int L J 59, 61 (1993).

343. *S & W Berisford plc* v *New Hampshire Ins Co* [1990] 1 Lloyd's Rep 454, 460 (with corrections). See also *Overseas Union Ins Ltd* v *New Hampshire Ins Ltd* [1988] 2 Lloyd's Rep 63, a decision of Hirst J, which has been referred to the ECJ.

" 'implement the provisions of Article 220 of [the EEC] Treaty by virtue of which [the parties] undertook to procure the simplification of formalities governing the reciprocal recognition and enforcement of judgments of courts or tribunals;'. It is also: 'To determine the international jurisdiction of their courts, to facilitate recognition and to introduce an expeditious procedure for securing the enforcement of judgments, authentic instruments and court settlements;'.

It is part of this objective and scheme that there should be an agreement between the Contracting States as to jurisdiction which their respective courts shall exercise. If the judgments of those Courts are to be recognised and enforceable in any Convention country it is necessary to know by what criteria the validity of the exercise of jurisdiction by the Court giving the judgment or making the order is to be tested. The Convention harmonises those criteria . . . .

A further purpose of the Convention has been recognized. It is to avoid conflicts of jurisdiction[344] and inconsistent decisions between different Courts in different Contracting States. This objective is an aspect of the primary objective but it also has a validity of its own as a matter of regulating and co-ordinating the jurisdictions of the Courts of the Contracting States *inter se*."

This statement of the purposes of the Convention by Hobhouse J was considered and not contradicted by the Court of Appeal in *Re Harrods (Buenos Aires) Ltd*[345] but the court took a more limited view of how far the Convention actually went in pursuit of these purposes. In view of Article 4, which allows courts to apply their own rules to defendants not domiciled in a Contracting State, Bingham LJ[346] thought that, although the Convention was intended to reduce the number of cases, in which Contracting State A will have to recognise and enforce the judgments given in Contracting State B but in circumstances where State A would not itself have accepted jurisdiction, the Convention does not eliminate such cases altogether. Dillon LJ,[347] too, thought that, in view of Article 4, "the common basis of jurisdiction envisaged does not apply world-wide . . . . The desideratum expressed in paragraph 78 of Professor Schlosser's report that 'A plaintiff must be sure which court had jurisdiction [and that he] should not have to waste his time and money risking that the court concerned may consider itself less competent than another' is thus very obviously not met where the defendant is not domiciled in a Contracting State". Indeed, he thought, the terms of both the Schlosser Report and the Jenard Report suggested that the object was limited to uniformity for those domiciled in Contracting States. As Bingham LJ put it, if "member states were to recognise and enforce each others' judgments virtually on the nod, it was plainly desirable, so far as possible, to agree a common basis for accepting jurisdiction".[348] Dillon LJ:

"For the English court to refuse jurisdiction, in a case against a person domiciled in England, on the ground that the court of some non-Contracting State is the more appropriate Court to decide the matters in issue does not in any way impair the object of the Convention of establishing an expeditious, harmonious, and, I would add, certain procedure for securing the enforcement of judgments, since *ex hypothesi* if the English court refuses jurisdiction there will be no judgment of the English court to be enforced in the other Contracting States. Equally and for the same reason such a refusal of jurisdiction would not impair the object of the Convention

---

344. Also in this sense: *Minster Investments Ltd* v *Hyundai Precision Industry Co Ltd* [1988] 2 Lloyd's Rep 621, 623 *per* Steyn J, who also observed that the Act was intended to be "a self-contained code".
345. [1991] 3 WLR 397.
346. [1991] 3 WLR 397, 420, with whom Stocker LJ agreed (p 417).
347. p 416.
348. p 419.

that there should, subject to the very large exception of Article 4, be a uniform international jurisdiction for obtaining the judgments which are to be enforced."[349]

If Article 2 were given wide effect, the English court would be compelled to hear and decide cases, in which there was a *lis* pending in a non-Contracting State or in which the parties had agreed on exclusive jurisdiction in a non-Contracting State, although these were situations on which the relevant provisions of the Convention (Articles 17, 21 and 22) were silent. Like the commentators, Dillon LJ concluded that this "would be contrary to the intentions of the Convention. Since the Convention is merely an agreement between the Contracting States among themselves, I do not agree with Hobhouse J that the framework of the Convention would be destroyed if there were available to the English court a discretion to refuse jurisdiction, on the grounds that the courts of a non-Contracting State are the more appropriate forum, in a case in which no other Contracting State is in any way concerned".[350] In conclusion, Bingham LJ concurred with the view of commentator Collins,[351] that "the States which were parties to the Convention had no interest in requiring a Contracting State to exercise a jurisdiction where the competing jurisdiction was in a non-Contracting State". Subsequently, the Court of Appeal concluded that the appropriate forum for the particular dispute was not in England but in Argentina. The decision of the Court of Appeal, however, is now the subject of an appeal to the House of Lords, which has adjourned its proceedings and referred the matter to the ECJ.[352]

2–10D Jurisdiction: the Basis on Domicile

Article 2 of the Convention provides the basic general rule, that "persons domiciled in a Contracting State shall, whatever their nationality, be sued in the courts of that State". If, however, the defendant is not domiciled in a Contracting State, according to Article 4, "the jurisdiction of the courts of each Contracting State shall, subject to the provisions of Article 16,[353] be determined by the law of that State", which may have a different general rule.

According to Article 52, the meaning of domicile is determined by the "internal law" of the forum, with two qualifications. First, Article 52(2) provides that, if "a party is not domiciled in the Contracting State whose courts are seized of the matter, then, in order to determine whether the party is domiciled in another Contracting State, the court shall apply the law of that State". Second, Article 53 provides that for the purposes of the Convention, "the seat of a company or other legal person or association of natural or legal persons shall be treated as its domicile. However, in order to determine that seat, the court shall apply its rules of private international law".

As regards the "internal law" of England, sections 41 and 42 of the 1982 Act pro-

---

349. p 416. As the Jenard Report states (p 13): "the territory of the Contracting States may be regarded as forming a single entity: it follows, for the purpose of laying down rules on jurisdiction, that a very clear distinction can be drawn between litigants who are domiciled in the Community and those who are not."

350. p 417.

351. (1990) 106 LQR 535.

352. See Fentiman, 26 Cornell Int L J 59 (1993).

353. Article 16 gives certain courts exclusive jurisdiction regardless of domicile in certain matters, matters of no particular relevance to insurance contracts.

vide a definition of domicile,[354] a definition which is believed to be wider than that of the common law and in line with that of other Contracting States. The principal provisions are these:

"41 . . . (2) An individual is domiciled in the United Kingdom if and only if—
    (a) he is resident in the United Kingdom; and
    (b) the nature and circumstances of his residence indicate that he has a substantial connection with the United Kingdom.
42 . . . (3) A corporation or association has its seat in the United Kingdom if and only if—
    (a) it was incorporated or formed under the law of part of the United Kingdom and has its registered office or some other official address in the United Kingdom; or
    (b) its central management and control[355] is exercised in the United Kingdom."

2–10E Exceptional Cases: Special Jurisdiction

The general rule of jurisdiction with reference to domicile[356] is supplemented in a number of exceptional cases, in which there is "special jurisdiction", as set out in Articles 5, 6 and 6A. These cases of special jurisdiction, which authorise jurisdiction in addition to that of Article 2 based on the domicile of the defendant, include the following:

    (a) A person domiciled in a Contracting State may be sued in another Contracting State in respect of matters relating to a contract, in the courts for the place of performance of the obligation in question.[357] The obligations in question are "the obligations which correspond to the rights upon which the plaintiffs' action is based".[358] The matters include the question whether the alleged contract was concluded at all.[359]

    (b) A person domiciled in a Contracting State may be sued in another Contracting State, "in matters relating to tort", in the courts for the place where the harmful event occurred: Article 5(3). This place is either "the place where the damage occurred" or the "place of the event giving rise to it", at the plaintiff's option.[360] The latter is not necessarily the first event in time: the

354. On questions of domicile internal to the United Kingdom, for example, between England and Scotland, see Schedule 4 to the 1982 Act.

355. *The Rewia* [1991] 2 Lloyd's Rep 325, 328 per Leggatt J (CA).

356. Art 2, above, 2–10D

357. Art 5(1). For example, *Rank Film Distributors Ltd v Lanterna Editrice SRL*, FTLR, 14 June 1991, as regards a contract of guarantee. In that case, an argument, that the place of domicile (Art 2) should prevail over the place of performance (Art 5) as being the pre-eminent jurisdiction, was rejected by Saville J: Art 2 was expressly made subject to the provisions of the Convention , which included Art 5. Further, as regards the place of performance of a contract of employment, see *Mercury Publicity Ltd v Wolfgang Loerke GmbH*, *The Times*, 21 October 1991 (CA).

358. *Medway Packaging Ltd v Meurer Maschinen GmbH* [1990] 1 Lloyd's Rep 383, 389 *per* Hobhouse J, with reference to *De Bloos Sprl Etablissment v Bouyer SCA* [1976] ECR 1497. An appeal against the *Medway* decision was dismissed: [1990] 2 Lloyd's Rep 112 (CA).

359. *Kloeckner & Co v Gatoil Overseas Inc* [1990] 1 Lloyd's Rep 176, 195 *per* Hirst J, citing *Effer SpA v Kantner* [1982] ECR 825, 834.

360. *Handelswekerij G J Bier BV v Mines de Potasse d'Alsace SA* [1978] QB 708. In this case, it was alleged that salt deposited by the defendants in the Rhine in France had damaged the plaintiff's seedbeds in Holland. The ECJ held that the harmful event had occurred in both France and Holland and that the plaintiff could sue in the appropriate courts of either country. This decision was based on the interpretation of the Convention and, further, because that interpretation "has the advantage of avoiding any upheaval in the solutions worked out in the various national systems of law, since it looks to unification, in conformity with article 5(3) of the Convention, by way of systematisation of solutions which, as to their principle, have already been established in most of the states concerned"(p 731).

English court will ask "where in substance the cause of action in tort arises, or what the place the tort is most closely connected with".[361]

In *Minster* v *Hyundai*[362] Steyn J concluded that the essence of the cause of action, in the case before him, was "a negligent mis-statement, or negligent advice, and reliance on it, and not the historical advice which led to the mis-statement or the wrong advice". In this case, he held, the harmful event was the receipt of the negligently produced certificates of the second defendants, which the plaintiffs were intended to rely on and did rely on—in England.

In *Davenport*[363] in connection with an action based on section 151 of the Road Traffic Act 1988,[364] the argument, that jurisdiction was in Scotland where the tort of negligence occurred, was rejected by the Court of Session. The words of Article 5(3), "in matters relating to tort", had become[365] virtually synonymous with "in proceedings based on" tort. The intention behind the Convention was to confer jurisdiction, by way of exception to that based on domicile, only when the obvious convenience of the case required it. In tort, it made good sense to confer exceptional jurisdiction upon courts which had the closest connection with the place out of which the facts of the case arose. However, the dispute in *Davenport* was less about the actual tort than about the requirements of the statute. Accordingly, the only applicable ground of jurisdiction was the domicile of the defendant insurers, which was England.

(c) A person domiciled in a Contracting State may be sued in another Contracting State, as regards a dispute arising out of the operations of a branch, agency or other establishment, in the courts for the place in which the branch, agency or other establishment is situated.[366] These words are to be interpreted *eiusdem generis*.[367] To be a branch, agency or other establishment, the entity must be under some degree of control by the company over which jurisdiction is sought.[368] That degree of control is lacking, when the entity is free to organise its work without instructions from the alleged principal and to represent rival firms, and does not participate in the completion or execution of transactions but only negotiates or transmits orders to the principal.[369] Hence, if a foreign insurer contracts insurance in London through a London broker, the broker is not an agency in the sense of the Conven-

---

361. *Minster Investments Ltd* v *Hyundai Precision Industry Co Ltd* [1988] 2 Lloyd's Rep 621, 624, *per* Steyn J.
362. Above, *loc cit.*
363. *Davenport* v *Corinthian Motor Policies at Lloyd's*, 1991 SLT 774.
364. Below, 5–9.
365. As a result of the decision in Case 189/87, *Kalfelis* v *Schroeder* [1988] ECR 5565.
366. Art 5(5). Plainly, the branch etc must be the branch of the defendant: *New Hampshire Ins Co* v *Strabag Bau AG* [1990] 2 Lloyd's Rep 61, 68 *per* Potter J; affirmed: [1992] 1 Lloyd's Rep 361 (CA).
367. *De Bloos Sprl Etablissment* v *Bouyer SCA* [1976] ECR 1497.
368. *De Bloos* (above).
369. *Ets Somafer SA* v *Saar–Ferngas AG* [1978] ECR 2183; *Blanckaert* v *Trost* [1981] ECR 819. In *Somafer*, it was held that the concept implies a place of business which has the appearance of permanency, has a management and is materially equipped to negotiate business with third parties so that the latter, although knowing that there will if necessary be a legal link with the parent body, the head office of which is abroad, do not have to deal directly with such parent body but may transact business with the local entity. The relevant operations of the entity include undertakings entered into there in the name of the parent body and which must be performed in the Contracting State where the place of business is established.

tion,[370] as he obeys the instructions of the insurer only as regards the particular transaction. In *New Hampshire*,[371] Potter J concluded that, whereas the brokers may have acted as agents of the defendants:

> "for the purposes of the ordinary law of contract and/or agency, that alone is not enough to satisfy the wording of art. 5(5). In that article the word 'agency' has been interpreted and/ or defined by the European Court *eiusdem generis* with the words 'branch' or 'establishment' which appear on either side of it, so as to connote an organ or business presence which is in itself an extension or emanation of the defendant's own business and subject to its general control, rather than an independent entity whose business it is to act as agent or broker for others in relation to a particular transaction or transactions."

(d) A person domiciled in a Contracting State may be sued in another Contracting State in his capacity as settlor, trustee or beneficiary of a trust created by the operation of a statute, or by a written instrument, or created orally and evidenced in writing, in the courts of the Contracting State in which the trust is domiciled.[372]

(e) A person domiciled in a Contracting State may also be sued, when he is one of a number of defendants, in the courts for the place where any one of them is domiciled.[373]

(f) A person domiciled in a Contracting State may also be sued as a third party in any third party proceedings, in the court seised of the original proceedings.[374]

(g) A person domiciled in a Contracting State may also be sued, on a counterclaim arising from the same contract or facts on which the original claim was based, in the court in which the original claim is pending.[375]

(h) There are special rules for insurance, as follows.

2–10F Insurance

Article 2, which established the general rule of jurisdiction based on domicile, is subject *inter alia* to Article 7. Article 7 provides that in "matters relating to insurance, jurisdiction shall be determined by this Section", i.e., Section 3, Articles 7 to 12A, "without prejudice to the provisions of Article 4 and 5.5".[376] As Section 3 is an exception to the general rule in Article 2, it is for the party alleging that Section 3 applies to

---

370. *New Hampshire Ins Co v Strabag Bau AG* [1990] 2 Lloyd's Rep 61; affirmed: [1992] 1 Lloyd's Rep. 361 (CA).

371. (above) pp. 68–69, referring *inter alia* to the Schlosser Report para 150. *Cf* the Jenard Report (Art 7), which refers to a situation in which "the foreign company is represented by a person *able to conclude contracts* with third parties on behalf of the company" (emphasis added), which might include a broker. However, Jenard (*ibid*) also says that the rule "was adopted because foreign insurance companies can establish branches or agencies in other States only by putting up guarantees which in practice place them in the same position as national companies". The decision of Potter J has been affirmed: [1992] 1 Lloyd's Rep 361 (CA).

372. Art 5(6).

373. Art 6(1).

374. Art 6(2).

375. Art 6(3).

376. The effect of the reference to Art 4 is that Section 3 is limited to cases in which the defendant, whether the insurer, policy-holder or beneficiary, is domiciled in a Contracting State. Article 5 provides: "A person domiciled in a Contracting State may, in another Contracting State, be sued . . . (5) as regards a dispute arising out of the operations of a branch, agency or other establishment, in the courts for the place in which the branch, agency or other establishment is situated". On this, see O'Malley, 18.05.

prove it.[377] The questions, whether a contract is a contract of insurance or whether an issue is a matter "relating to insurance", are questions to be resolved not by national law but by interpretation of the Convention.[378]

For example, although compulsory private insurance and the liability of the MIB are said[379] to be within Section 3, insurance by the State is not, insofar as "social security" is excluded from the Convention by Article 1(3). Again, Section 3 does not apply to reinsurance,[380] which is governed by the general provisions of the Convention.[381] This is "based on the proposition that the protective aims and spirit [of Section 3] are unnecessary in relation to reinsurance contracts where such inequality of bargaining power as might on occasion exist between negotiating insurers is not to be regarded as a significant feature, or one which the Convention is concerned to obviate".[382] However, although Section 3 is intended to protect the small policy holder against a more powerful insurer,[383] the corollary, that Section 3 applies only to insurance between parties of unequal bargaining power and where the insured "contracts with an insurer on the basis of a standard term policy, and/or a situation where, typically, terms are offered by the insurers on a 'take it or leave it' basis to a person of unequal bargaining power", has been rejected.[384] Hence, apart from reinsurance, commercial insurance between parties of equal bargaining power is governed by Section 3.[385]

2–10F1 Actions Against the Insurer

An insurer domiciled in a Contracting State may be sued
- (a) in the courts of the State where he is domiciled; or
- (b) in another Contracting State, in the courts for the place[386] where the policy-holder[387] is domiciled; or
- (c) if he is a co-insurer,[388] in the courts[389] of a Contracting State in which pro-

377. *New Hampshire Ins Co* v *Strabag Bau AG* [1990] 2 Lloyd's Rep 61, 65, *per* Potter J.
378. O'Malley para 18.06. *Cf*, however, the approach taken by the ECJ in *Handelswekerij G J Bier BV* v *Mines de Potasse d'Alsace SA* [1978] QB 708.
379. Kaye, *Civil Jurisdiction and Enforcement of Foreign Judgments* (Abingdon, 1987), p 808.
380. *Citadel Ins Co* v *Atlantic Union Ins Co* [1982] 2 Lloyd's Rep 543, 549, per Kerr LJ (CA—re); *Arkwright Mutual Ins Co* v *Bryanston Ins Co Ltd* [1990] 2 Lloyd's Rep 70, 73, *per* Potter J (re), referring to para 150 of the Schlosser Report. Kaye [1990] JBL 517, 518. *Cf*, however, Collins, (1990) 106 LQR 535, 537.
381. See Butler & Merkin, p D.4.1–38.
382. *New Hampshire Ins Co* v *Strabag Bau AG* [1990] 2 Lloyd's Rep 61, 67, *per* Potter J.
383. *New Hampshire Ins Co* v *Strabag Bau AG* [1992] 1 Lloyd's Rep 361, 367 per Lloyd LJ (CA).
384. *New Hampshire* p 67 *per* Potter J, as a matter of interpretation of the Convention. He added (p 68) that "I do not regard it as axiomatic that a corporate insured, or a 'commercially strong' insured, is necessarily to be regarded as of equal bargaining power to underwriters in matters of insurance. I have in mind cases where the market may be restricted and where insurers may well be in a position to adopt a 'take or leave it' approach to applications for cover." *Idem* on appeal: p 369 per Lloyd LJ.
385. In support of this view: Kaye [1990] JBL 517, 521 ff.
386. In the case of the United Kingdom, the contracting State is the United Kingdom, and internal jurisdiction, for example, as between England and Scotland is the subject of Schedule 4 to the 1982 Act.
387. *Cf* the insured and the beneficiary: below 2–10F2 (ii). However, any claimant, whether policy-holder or not, may sue the insurer in these courts: O'Malley, para 18.14
388. *Prima facie* this could refer to any double insurance, in respect of which there might eventually be contribution between insurers; see Nicholson (below). However, the reference to a leading insurer suggests a case of a series of subscriptions to a single risk solicited by a broker, such as occurs at Lloyd's. This is partly confirmed by the Schlosser Report (para 149), which indicates that the object of this provision is to concentrate actions arising out of an insured event.
389. To facilitate concentration of related actions, this should be interpreted as meaning the particular court in which proceedings are brought against the leading insurer: Schlosser Report, para 149.

ceedings are brought against the leading insurer for the same risk[390]; or

(d) in respect of insurance of immovable property,[391] in the courts for the place where the harmful event[392] occurred; or

(e) in respect of liability insurance,[393] in the courts for the place where the harmful event[394] occurred or, if the law of the court permits it,[395] by being joined in proceedings[396] which the injured party has brought against the insured.[397]

Ground (d) under Article 9 and ground (e) under Articles 9 and 10 are expressed to be in addition to grounds (a), (b) and (c) under Article 8.[398] Moreover,

(f) any defendant, who is not domiciled in a Contracting State, is subject to jurisdiction in the court of any Contracting State in accordance with the national rules[399] of that court, apart from the Convention. However, a defendant may submit to Convention jurisdiction under Article 18 by entering an appearance, except when the appearance was entered solely to contest the jurisdiction or when another court has exclusive jurisdiction under Article 16.[400]

---

390. The reference to the same risk was added by Hobhouse J in *S & W Berisford plc v New Hampshire Ins Co* [1990] 1 Lloyd's Rep 454, 461. Generally, co-insurance refers to a single insurance contract, whereby two or more persons insure their interests, however, in the context of contribution it refers to double insurance, i.e. two or more insurance contracts on the same risk: Nicholson (1990) 3 Ins L J 218. It is in the latter sense that the term is used in the Convention: Kaye, p 812. However, *cf* O'Malley, para 18.16: here, these are not terms of art and co-insurance should be understood in both senses.

391. O'Malley (para 18.25) argues that this refers to insurance against physical damage to the property and not, for example, title insurance. In any case, as is indicated by the second sentence of Art 9, this jurisdiction "extends to movable property in cases where the building and the movable property it contains are covered by the same insurance policy. This also applies if the movables are covered by an endorsement to the policy covering the immovable property" (Jenard Report, Art 9). *Quaere* whether movable property such as bicycles, the subject of an AR extension, are "contained" in the building. However, both movable and immovable property must have been "affected by the same contingency" (Art 9), so it seems that theft of movables achieved without any damage to the building is not within Art 9.

392. *Handelswekerij G J Bier v Mines de Potasse d'Alsace* [1978] QB 708 (ECJ), discussed above 2–10E(6).

393. O'Malley (para 18.25) argues that this includes cover with a liability component, such as legal expenses insurance.

394. *Bier* (above). Although that case concerned tort, and Art 5(3), in which the words "harmful event" also occur, refers to tort, in the context of "liability" insurance, the words also refer to product liability, whether it is characterised as tortious or not.

395. This is reference via the conflict rules of the forum: Jenard Report (Art 10). The issue is likely to be determined by reference to the proper law of the contract of insurance. Such an action is permitted in Germany and Holland in some cases only: O'Malley para 18.39. Moreover, it seems that it will not generally be permitted, if the particular forum has been excluded by a term of the insurance contract: Kaye, p 861, with reference to the Schlosser Report, para 148.

396. The leading instance is thought to be that of claims arising out of road accidents.

397. Note that the Convention distinguishes the insured from the policy-holder (and the beneficiary); see below 2–10F2. The reference here to the insured would thus include a person (the policy-holder) who did not contract motor insurance but was a named person covered by the contract (O'Malley, para 18.37).

398. The precise effect of the words "in addition" (Art 9) and "also" (Art 10) is unclear: see O'Malley, paras 18.26 ff.

399. As Section 3 is subject to Art 4: Kaye, p 809.

400. Such cases include: "(1) . . . proceedings which have as their object rights *in rem* in, or tenancies of, immovable property, the courts of the Contracting State in which the property is situated; (2) . . . proceedings which have as their object the validity of . . . the decisions of their organs, the courts of the Contracting

Note that the Convention may apply, even though neither party is actually domiciled in the State, the jurisdiction of which is invoked. In *S & W Berisford plc v New Hampshire Ins Co*,[401] a plaintiff incorporated in New York claimed in relation to stolen gold and gems under insurance (taken for it by another plaintiff incorporated in the United Kingdom) with the London branch of the defendant insurer, which was incorporated in New Hampshire. The submission, that the English court had no jurisdiction under the Convention because neither the particular plaintiff nor the insurer were domiciled in a Contracting State, was rejected.[402]

2–10F2 Actions Against the Policy Holder, the Insured or Beneficiary[403]

The policy-holder,[404] the insured or a beneficiary, if domiciled in a Contracting State, may be sued

(a) in the courts of his domicile[405]; or

(b) on a counterclaim,[406] in the court in which the action brought by the insured is pending; or

(c) in the courts in which he has a branch, agency or other establishment in respect of a dispute arising out of the operations of that branch, agency or establishment.[407] Moreover,

(d) in the case of a direct action by an injured third party against the insurer, the policy–holder or the insured may be sued in the court with jurisdiction in that action, if the law[408] governing that action permits them to be joined in the proceedings: Article 10.

State in which the company, legal person or association has its seat; . . . (5) . . . proceedings concerned with the enforcement of judgments, the courts of the Contracting State in which the judgment has been or is to be enforced."

401. [1990] 1 Lloyd's Rep 454 (AR). In this case, the plaintiff, incorporated in the United Kingdom, was the parent company of the second and "real" plaintiff, incorporated in New York.

402. In view of the purposes of the Convention, on which see above, 2–10C. The judge also pointed (pp 460–461) to other indications in the Convention that it was to apply, when one or both parties were not domiciled in Contracting States.

403. Generally, see Collins, *Civil Jurisdiction and Judgments Act 1982* (London, 1983), p 70.

404. The policy-holder is not defined by the Convention, but O'Malley (para 18.08) suggests that he is the person who originally contracted the insurance. However, "policy–holder" is a translation of "preneur d'assurance". The Schlosser Report (para 152) distinguishes the latter from the assignee of rights under the insurance who is a beneficiary. Perhaps the insured differs from the others, in that he may be an assignee not just of rights but of the contract itself, however, the Schlosser Report (*ibid*) refers to this person as a "preneur d'assurance". The essential feature of the latter, according to the Jenard Report (Art 8), is that he is the other party to the contract, with whom the insurer deals and whose domicile he knows. The terms employed are not clear.

405. Art 11. This rule corresponds to the general rule under Art 2. Hence, the domicile in question is that of the insured at the time at which the proceedings are commenced: Jenard Report (Art 11). As regards this rule, O'Malley (para 18.45) argues that "defendant" in Art 11 should include not only the policy-holder, insured or beneficiary, to whom Art 11 refers, but also any other defendant sued by the insurer in matters relating to insurance, hence including an assignee of rights under the insurance contract, a loss payee and a person whose life is insured (by somebody else).

406. Art 11. In all respects which are not explicit in Art 11, the ground should be interpreted in accordance with that provided for actions not relating to insurance matters under Art 6(3), and the counterclaim should thus be a "counterclaim arising from the same contract or facts on which the original claim was based": O'Malley, para 18.47. The French text refers to *une demande reconventionelle* which, under French law, does not have to be made in the same proceedings as the original claim.

407. This appears to follow from Art 5(5), the application of which in insurance matters governed by Section 3 is preserved by Art 7.

408. The balance of opinion is that this is not the *lex fori* but the proper law of the contract of insurance: Kaye, p 809.

(e) Any defendant, who is not domiciled in a Contracting State, is subject to jurisdiction in the court of any Contracting State in accordance with the national rules[409] of that court, apart from the Convention. However, a defendant may submit to Convention jurisdiction under Article 18 by entering an appearance, except when the appearance was entered solely to contest the jurisdiction or when another court has exclusive jurisdiction under Article 16.[410]

2–10F3 Jurisdiction Agreements

Insurer and insured may agree a jurisdiction which "departs from" the provisions of Section 3, if their agreement[411] satisfies (any) one of the five conditions stated by Article 12:

(1) Under paragraph (1), the agreement is "entered into after the dispute has arisen". A dispute has arisen "as soon as the parties disagree on a specific point and legal proceedings are imminent or contemplated".[412] The assumption behind the condition is that the agreement is reached at a time when the insured can be expected to have taken independent legal advice.

(2) Under paragraph (2), the agreement "allows the policy-holder, the insured or a beneficiary to bring proceedings in courts other than those indicated" in Section 3. As the general drift of Section 3 is to protect the weak against the strong, any agreement in favour of the former is acceptable in principle.

(3) Under paragraph (3), the agreement is "concluded between a policy-holder and an insurer, both of whom are at the time of the conclusion of the contract domiciled or habitually resident in the same Contracting State, and which has the effect of conferring jurisdiction on the courts of that State even if the harmful event were to occur abroad, provided that such an agreement is not contrary to the law of that State".[413]

(4) Under paragraph (4), the agreement is "concluded with a policy-holder[414] who is not domiciled in a Contracting State,[415] except in so far as the insur-

---

409. As Section 3 is subject to Art 4: Kaye, p 809.

410. Such cases include: "(1) . . . proceedings which have as their object rights *in rem* in, or tenancies of, immovable property, the courts of the Contracting State in which the property is situated; (2) . . . proceedings which have as their object the validity of . . . the decisions of their organs, the courts of the Contracting State in which the company, legal person or association has its seat; . . . (5) . . . proceedings concerned with the enforcement of judgments, the courts of the Contracting State in which the judgment has been or is to be enforced."

411. O'Malley (para 18.51) argues that, although Art 12 is silent on the question, the agreement must satisfy the same requirements of form as prorogation of jurisdiction under Art 17: below, 2–10G.

412. Jenard report, Art 12. However, there is little agreement on the precise point at which it can be said that a dispute has arisen: see references cited by O'Malley, para 18.55.

413. This possibility was created to solve a problem raised by the procedural law of Germany: Kaye, pp 813–814.

414. It is contended that, although in other provisions of the Convention the policy-holder, the insured and the beneficiary are distinguished, this reference to the policy-holder includes a reference to the insured and the beneficiary: O'Malley, para 16.60.

415. This possibility was included at the request of the United Kingdom, in view of the importance to the United Kingdom of insurance contracts with insureds in non-Contracting States, contracts which would otherwise be subject to Section 3 of the Convention: Schlosser Report, para 137.

ance is compulsory[416] or relates to immovable property[417] in a Contracting State".

(5) Under paragraph (5), the agreement "relates to a contract of insurance in so far as it covers one or more of the risks set out in Article 12A". Being an exception to the general scheme based on domicile, Article 12A is to be construed narrowly: *Charman*.[418] Thus, in that case, the court concluded that "a jurisdiction agreement under art. 12(5) must be limited to marine risks of the type described in art. 12A, and that any agreement, such as the present, which embraced both marine and non-marine risks was impermissible and contrary to art. 12(5)", even though, as the court recognised, "this construction has drawbacks, and may, in a policy covering both marine and non–marine risks, result in duplication of litigation, in the event that the parties should agree to a specific jurisdiction for the marine risks, with the result that, contrary to the purpose expressed by Mr Jenard, the litigation will not be concentrated in one forum".[419]

As the Preamble to the Convention indicates that the purpose of the Convention is "to determine the international jurisdiction of their courts", it has been argued[420] that that and the spirit of the Convention indicate that the courts chosen under Article 12 must be courts of Contracting States.

The risks set out in Article 12A are singled out as acceptable for jurisdiction agreements between the parties, as these risks are generally insured by persons who do not need "social and economic protection".[421] Further, "the risks insured are highly mobile and insurance policies tend to change hands several times in quick succession. This leads to uncertainty as to which courts will have jurisdiction and the difficulties in calculating risks are thereby greatly increased".[422] In these circumstances, it is evidently sensible to allow the parties to settle the otherwise uncertain question of jurisdiction. The risks concern marine and aviation insurance[423] and are these:

"(1) Any loss of or damage to
    (a) sea-going ships,[424] installations situated offshore or on the high seas, or aircraft, arising from perils which relate to their use for commercial purposes,

---

416. The exception refers to insurance compulsory by the proper law, the obvious example being motor insurance. The Schlosser Report (paras 138 ff) sets out instances of insurance compulsory in the Contracting States. The Report (*ibid*) also indicates that the insurance is insurance compulsory by statute rather than, for example, under professional rules or other constraints.

417. Even if the *lex loci* permits jurisdiction agreements in such a case: Schlosser Report, para 139.

418. *Charman* v *WOC Offshore BV*, [1993] 1 Lloyd's Rep 378; *Semble* this point was not disturbed on appeal: [1993] 2 Lloyd's Rep 551 (CA).

419. p 384 per Hirst J, who pointed out (ibid) that "it is open to the parties to remedy any such disadvantage by entering into an agreement after the dispute has arisen under art. 12(1), where there is no limitation as to the subject-matter of the risks".

420. O'Malley, para 18.52.

421. Kaye, p 820.

422. Schlosser Report, para 140.

423. *Cf* insurance of risks associated with carriage by land: "no exceptional rules of any kind appeared justified" (*ibid*).

424. Ships include "hovercraft, hydrofoils, barges and lighters used at sea"; also "floating apparatus which cannot move under its own power, e.g. oil exploration and extraction installations which are moved about on water . . . . The provision also covers ships in the course of construction, but only so far as the damage is the result of a maritime risk" (Schlosser Report para 141).

    (b) goods in transit other than passengers' baggage where the transit consists of or includes[425] carriage by such ships or aircraft;

(2) Any liability, other than for bodily injury to passengers or loss of or damage to their baggage,

    (a) arising out of the use or operation of ships,[426] installations or aircraft referred to in (1)(a) above in so far as the law of the Contracting State in which such aircraft are registered does not prohibit agreements on jurisdiction regarding insurance of such risks,

    (b) for loss or damage caused by goods in transit as described in (1)(b) above;

(3) Any financial loss connected with the use or operation of ships, installations or aircraft as referred to in (1)(a) above, in particular loss of freight or charter-hire;

(4) Any risk or interest connected with any of those referred to in (1) to (3) above."[427]

2–10G. Prorogation of Jurisdiction

As regards prorogation of jurisdiction, Article 17 provides that, if "the parties, *one or more of whom is domiciled* in a Contracting State, have agreed that a court or the courts of a Contracting State are to have jurisdiction to settle any disputes which have arisen or which may arise in connection with a particular legal relationship, that court or those courts shall have exclusive jurisdiction",[428] even though the jurisdiction clause is not expressed in exclusive terms.[429] In *Berisford*,[430] Hobhouse J held that the simple clause in that case, "This insurance is subject to English jurisdiction", was not apt to oblige the parties to submit to the exclusive jurisdiction of the English court. However, there is attraction in the comment that, when parties trouble to select a particular jurisdiction, albeit without expressly qualifying their choice by reference to degrees of exclusivity, the natural inference is that the single jurisdiction selected is intended to be exclusive.[431] In any case, it is clear that there must have been a choice of jurisdiction and this has been held to mean an express, rather than implied, choice of jurisdiction.[432]

Article 17 further provides that where "such an agreement is concluded by parties, *none of whom is domiciled* in a Contracting State, the courts of other Contracting States shall have no jurisdiction over their disputes unless the court or courts chosen have declined jurisdiction".[433]

---

425. This phrase is designed to include multimodal transport. Were it otherwise, there would be "unwarranted complications for the insurance industry in drafting policies and settling claims, if a fine distinction had always to be drawn as to the section of transit in which loss or damage had occurred. Moreover it is often impossible to ascertain this" (Schlosser Report, para 142). So, even if it is clear that the loss or damage was sustained during a land phase, Art 12A applies (*ibid*).

426. It is unclear to what extent this includes the liability of shipbuilders or repairers: Schlosser Report, para 144.

427. The Schlosser Report (para 147) suggests that these include shipowner's disbursements, such as port charges. In *Charman* v *WOC Offshore BV*, [1993] 2 Lloyd's Rep 551 (CA), it was held that "interest" was not the narrow insurable interest understood by English law (see below 4–3B) but indicated any property in connection with which a risk could give rise to loss and thus property (and risks) other than those mentioned in (1) to (3). Moreover, the court rejected the argument, which had been successful in the court below ([1993] 1 Lloyd's Rep 378) that the risk or interest had to be close (accessory or ancillary) to a risk or interest mentioned in (1) to (3).

428. Emphasis added.

429. *S & W Berisford plc* v *New Hampshire Ins Co* [1990] 1 Lloyd's Rep 454, 461 *per* Hobhouse J.

430. Above.

431. Kaye [1992] JBL 47, 61.

432. *New Hampshire Ins Co* v *Strabag Bau AG* [1992] 1 Lloyd's Rep 361, 371 *per* Lloyd LJ (CA).

433. Emphasis added.

In each case, the "agreement conferring jurisdiction shall be either in writing or evidenced in writing or, in international trade or commerce, in a form which accords with the practices in that trade or commerce of which the parties are or ought to have been aware". Standard clauses inserted in a standard form document relating to the contract do not, without more, evidence the agreement of the proferee.[434]

An agreement under Article 17 has no legal force, if it is contrary to the provisions of Article 12.[435] Hence, in the case of insurance, Article 17 does not authorise jurisdiction agreements other than those listed in Article 12 (above, 2–10F3)[436] but reinforces their effect, as regards exclusivity, and limits them, as regards form. An agreement under Article 7 is immune, however, from any exercise of discretion under Articles 21 and 22.[436a]

2–10H Entering an Appearance

In addition to jurisdiction based on other provisions of the Convention, Article 18 gives jurisdiction to the court of any Contracting State "before whom a defendant enters an appearance", unless "appearance was entered solely to contest jurisdiction".[437] As the result may be that more than one court has jurisdiction, Articles 21 ff, relating to *lis pendens*,[438] apply.

2–10I Interim Relief

The Convention "requires each contracting state to make available, in aid of the courts of another contracting state, such provisional and protective measures as its own domestic law would afford if its courts were trying the substantive action. That would be harmonisation of jurisdiction, although not of remedies".[439] Under section 25(1) of the 1982 Act, the English court has a discretion[440] to grant interim relief, notably a *Mareva* injunction, where "(a) proceedings have been or are to be commenced in a Contracting State other than the United Kingdom . . . ; and (b) they are or will be proceedings whose subject-matter is within the scope of the 1968 Convention . . . ". If the defendant is domiciled in a Contracting State, interim relief may be obtained without leave for service of the writ outside the jurisdiction under RSC, Ord 11,[441] provided that the English proceedings do not concern the same cause of action as the proceedings in the other Contracting State.[442] If the defendant is not domiciled in a Contracting State, service is possible, but leave must be obtained.[443]

---

434. As regards bills of lading, see *Partenreederei m/s "Tilly Russ"* v *Haven & Vervoerbedrijf Nova NV* [1984] ECR 2417; and *The Duke of Yare, Dresser UK Ltd* v *Falcongate Freight Management Ltd* [1991] 2 Lloyd's Rep 557 (CA); Briggs [1992] LMCLQ 150, 154.
435. Art 17, paragraph 3.
436. Butler & Merkin, p D.4.1–34.
436a. *Continental Bank NA* v *Akakos Cia Nav SA*, *The Times*, 26 November 1993 (CA).
437. Or unless "another court has exclusive jurisdiction by virtue of Article 16".
438. Below, 2–10J.
439. *Republic of Haiti* v *Duvalier* [1989] 1 All ER 456, 463, *per* Staughton LJ (CA), with whom the other members of the court concurred.
440. Section 25(2): if "it is expedient for the court to grant it".
441. *Duvalier* (above).
442. RSC, Ord 11, r 1(2)(a)(i), which (*Duvalier*, above, p 463, *per* Staughton LJ) is intended to reflect Art 21 of the Convention (below 2–10J).
443. *X* v *Y* [1989] 3 All ER 689. This decision was based in part on the conclusion that the meaning of RSC, Ord 11, r 1(1)(b) had been changed from that put upon it in *The Siskina* [1977] 3 All ER 803 (HL); *sed quaere*.

2–10J Lis Pendens

Not only if the defendant enters an appearance (above, 2–10H), but also, notably, in cases of special jurisdiction (above 2–10E), the courts of more than one Contracting State may have jurisdiction under the Convention and more than one action may be brought on the same dispute. The issue of *lis pendens*, whether one court should give way to another court, is dealt with by Article 21.

As to the scope of Article 21, although domicile (see above, 2–10D) is the central platform for jurisdiction under the Convention, Article 21 makes no mention of domicile. For this reason, in *Overseas Union Ins Ltd* v *New Hampshire Ins Co*,[444] the ECJ was free to decide, as it did, that Article 21 applies not only when parties are domiciled in Contracting States (and jurisdiction is governed by the Convention) but also when a court exercises jurisdiction (under its ówn law) over a defendant, who is not domiciled in a Contracting State. The Court considered that its decision was borne out by the aim of the Convention, to promote the recognition and enforcement of judgments in Contracting States other than those in which the judgments were delivered, the protection of persons domiciled in Contracting States from exorbitant jurisdiction;[445] and that therefore it was indispensable to limit the risk of irreconcilable judgments. For these reasons, the Court concluded that Article 21 must be interpreted broadly to cover, in principle, all situations of *lis pendens* before the courts of Contracting States, irrespective of the domicile of the parties to the litigation.[446]

Compare the approach taken by the ECJ in *Overseas Union* with that of the Court of Appeal in *Owens Bank Ltd v Bracco*.[447] In a judgment given by Parker LJ, the court did not lift its collegiate head from the immediate text of the Convention. In proceedings commenced in Italy to enforce a judgment against him in St Vincent, B alleged that the judgment there had been obtained against him by fraud. In proceedings commenced in England to enforce the judgment obtained in St Vincent, B sought to have the English proceedings set aside *inter alia* on the ground of *lis pendens* in Italy. The court held that Articles 21 and 22 did not apply to proceedings for the recognition and enforcement of judgments from non-Contracting States.

This decision was reached, first, by reference to the Preamble of the Convention, which indicates, in the words not of the Preamble but of the court,[448] that it is concerned with the "reciprocal recognition and enforcement of the judgments of contracting states *inter se* . . . because it would be surprising if contracting states were seeking to affect the position of persons over whom their courts had no jurisdiction or to concern themselves with the recognition or enforcement of judgments of the courts of non-contracting states". Second, the court inferred from Article 27 that "as between a non-contracting state and a contracting state the recognition of the judgment of the non-contracting state is a matter wholly dependant upon the arrangements [outside the Convention] between the non-contracting state and the contracting state".[449] Further, even if the Convention did apply, Articles 21 and 22 did not apply, because they are "clearly directed to proceedings which may lead to a judgment, i.e.

444. Case C–351/89, 27 June 1991; [1992] 2 All ER 138; [1992] 1 Lloyd's Rep 204. On this case, see Kaye [1992] JBL 47, 51 ff.
445. See Hartley (1992) 17 Euro L Rev 75; and Kaye (above) pp 55 ff.
446. p 160; p 216.
447. [1991] 4 All ER 833.
448. p 840.
449. p 841.

original proceedings, and not to proceedings to enforce a judgment which has been obtained in original proceedings, such enforcement proceedings being expressly dealt with under Title III".[450] The decision of the Court of Appeal on this point "sits awkwardly"[451] with the court's later decision in the same case, that a decision of the Italian court (that there had been fraud) could estop the bank from enforcing its judgment in England—as a matter of common law. Moreover, this decision is scarcely in the spirit of the ECJ in *Overseas Union* (above), which underlined that the risk of incompatible judgments and the concomitant waste of effort and expense was something which the Convention was intended to prevent. It was "deceptively easy to say that the question was one concerned only with the recognition of a St Vincent judgment"[452] and thus ignore the fact that the Italian court was seised of the same issue (fraud), an issue which would require the retrial of the merits of the original case and thus squarely raised the problem of *lis pendens*.

2–10J1 The Same Cause of Action.

As enacted under the 1982 Act, Article 21 provided:

"Where proceedings involving the same cause of action and between the same parties are brought in the courts of different Contracting States, any court other than the court first seised shall of its own motion [decline jurisdiction in favour of that court.

A court which would be required to decline jurisdiction may stay its proceedings if the jurisdiction of the other court is contested."]

In the current version of Article 21, as substituted by Article 8 of the San Sebastian Convention, the words in brackets have been replaced by these:

"stay its proceedings until such time as the jurisdiction of the court first seised is established.

Where the jurisdiction of the court first seised is established, any court other than the court first seised shall decline jurisdiction in favour of that court."

In the case of contract, the ECJ has said of Article 21 that the "same cause of action means the same contract."[453]   In *Gubisch Maschinenfabrik* v *Palumbo*[454] the ECJ was concerned with an international sale of goods, a planing machine, and one action to enforce the contract in Germany and a subsequent action for annulment in Italy. The Court stated:

"Where, as in the present case, the case concerned the international sale of movable property it was apparent that the purpose of an action for the enforcement of the contract was to give effect to that contract, and that the purpose of an action for annulment and dissolution was to deprive the contract of effect. The enforceability of the contract was therefore at the centre of both proceedings. If the action for annulment or dissolution was the second action, it might even be regarded as constituting simply an argument in the defence against the first action which had been presented in the form of independent proceedings before a court in another Contracting State."

---

450. p 842.
451. Briggs, (1991) 107 LQR 531, 533.
452. Briggs, p 534.
453. *Gubisch* (below). For example, a claim for both total loss of and physical damage to cargo arising out of the same insured event and claimed under the same cause of action is likely to be subject to Art 21, even though they may be based on breach of different terms of the contract of carriage: *The Indian Grace, Republic of India* v *India Steamship Co* [1993] AC 410 (HL).
454. [1988] ECR 4861.

The Court held that Article 21 applied. *Gubisch* was applied to insurance contracts in *AGF* v *Chiyoda*,[455] on the basis that *Gubisch* had decided three things:

"First art. 21 is to be construed in the light of its purpose which is to prevent a situation where a judgment given by a Court in one Contracting State is not recognized in another Contracting State on the ground referred to in art. 27(3) namely that—'. . . it is irreconcilable with a judgment given in a dispute between the same parties in the State in which recognition is sought'.

Second, there are three conditions for the application of art. 21 and no more; the actions must be between the same parties and involve the same cause of action and the same subject-matter.

Third it is permissible to look for this purpose at the question which 'lies at the heart of the two actions' to see whether they concern the same subject-matter. The 'concept cannot be restricted so as to mean two claims which are entirely identical'."[456]

2–10J2 The Response of the Court Seized Second

Article 21 requires "any court other than the court first seized" to decline jurisdiction, unless the jurisdiction of the latter is contested, in which case the former court may merely stay its proceedings until the contest over the latter's jurisdiction has been resolved. This "rule was introduced so that the parties would not have to institute new proceedings if, for example, the court first seised of the matter were to decline jurisdiction."[457]

If the court seised second does not decline jurisdiction, is it allowed only to stay its proceedings or is it permitted or even required under Article 21 to examine whether the court first seized has jurisdiction and, if so, to what extent? In *Overseas Union Ins Ltd* v *New Hampshire Ins Co*,[458] the ECJ concluded that when, as in that case, the court seized second was not claimed to have *exclusive* jurisdiction,[459] notably exclusive jurisdiction under Article 16, the only obligation imposed by Article 21 on that court to decline jurisdiction is when it stays proceedings, an option which it may exercise only if the jurisdiction of the court first seized is contested. The objective of the stay was to avoid negative conflicts of jurisdiction, a situation in which neither court exercised jurisdiction, and it could be achieved without the second court examining the jurisdiction of the first. Moreover, as the jurisdiction of the first court might be based not only on the Convention but also on the *lex fori*, it was a matter best left to that court. Hence, the Convention neither permitted nor required the second court to examine whether the court first seized had jurisdiction.[460]

The ECJ did not have to consider the situation of a second court claiming to have jurisdiction that was exclusive under Article 17, however, that situation arose in *Kloeckner* v *Gatoil*.[461] The second (English) court was given exclusive jurisdiction by

455. *Assurances Générales de France* v *The Chiyoda Fire & Marine Co (UK) Ltd* [1992] 1 Lloyd's Rep 325 (re).

456. p 340 *per* Judge Diamond QC. He also pointed out that in *Overseas Union* (below) the ECJ had said (p 160; 216) that Article 21 "must be interpreted broadly so as to cover, in principle, all situations of *lis pendens* before courts in Contracting States irrespective of the parties' domicile". If Article 21 were limited to entirely identical claims, it "would enable parties to frustrate the purpose of art. 21 by introducing an additional party in the proceedings of the Court which is 'second seised' to enable that Court to retain jurisdiction" (p 341).

457. *Overseas Union Ins. Ltd* v *New Hampshire Ins Co.*, Case C–351/89, 27 June 1991; [1992] 2 All ER 138, 161–162; [1992] 1 Lloyd's Rep 204, 217.

458. Above.

459. The case of a second court claiming exclusive jurisdiction was the one *Kloeckner & Co* v *Gatoil Overseas Inc* [1990] 1 Lloyd's Rep. 176.

460. [1992] 2 All ER 138, 161–162; [1992] 1 Lloyd's Rep 204, 217.

461. Above.

private contract and the English court decided that it was not obliged to cede jurisdiction to the German court first seised. A conflict appears[462] between the purpose of Article 21, notably the avoidance of conflicting judgments, and the purpose of Article 17, which is to allow businessmen to avoid jurisdictional disputes and to ensure that proceedings are brought in courts of their choice.

2–10J3 Related Actions.

If the actions are not "the same" (above 2–10J1) but are "related", Article 22 requires that "any court other than the court first seized *may*, while the actions are pending at first instance, stay its proceedings"(emphasis added). The court has a discretion.

Actions, in the words of paragraph 3 of Article 22, are "related where they are so closely connected that it is expedient to hear and determine them together to avoid the risk of irreconcilable judgments arising from separate proceedings".[463] In *AGF* v *Chiyoda*,[464] however, Judge Diamond QC considered that the effect of *Overseas Union* (above, 2–10J2) is that, subject to limited exceptions, a court in one Contracting State is not permitted to review the assumption of jurisdiction by a court in another Contracting State and that, if the English court were to decide whether the action (in Italy) was a related action, that is what, indirectly, it would be doing.

As to the discretion, in *The Maciej Rataj*[465] Sheen J observed that the "circumstances to be taken into account when considering how to exercise the Court's discretion in cases of *forum non conveniens*[466] are different from the factors to be taken into account under Article 22, but the weight to be given to other proceedings must depend on the character of those proceedings and not the date of their institution". So, noting that the earlier proceedings commenced in Rotterdam by Polish carriers were a pre-emptive strike by way of forum shopping and that the resolution of those proceedings would lead to considerable delay, the judge declined to stay the proceedings in England. On appeal,[467] however, the Court of Appeal stayed the proceedings pending the answer to questions to be addressed to the ECJ.

2–10J4 The Court First Seized

The ECJ has pronounced in general terms, that "the court 'first seized' is the one before which the requirements for proceedings to become definitively pending are first fulfilled, such requirements to be determined in accordance with the national law of each of the courts concerned".[468] The Convention is not concerned with the harmonization of procedural law.[469] In England, a court cannot be seized of proceedings before it has jurisdiction over the person of the defendant or over his property.

---

462. Hartley (1992) 17 Euro L Rev 75.
463. For example, *Virgin Aviation Services Ltd* v *CAD Aviation Service*, *The Times*, 2 February 1990. Also, *The Maciej Rataj* [1992] 2 Lloyd's Rep 552 (CA).
464. *Assurances Générales de France* v *The Chiyoda Fire & Marine Co (UK) Ltd* [1992] 1 Lloyd's Rep. 325, 338–339 (re).
465. [1991] 2 Lloyd's Rep 458, 466.
466. Above 2–9A.
467. [1992] 2 Lloyd's Rep 552 (CA).
468. *Zelger* v *Salinitri* (*No 2*) [1984] ECR 2397, 2408: it was not the object of the Convention to unify such formalities, as they are closely related to the organisation of judicial procedure in each Contracting State. For a comparative survey, see *Zelger* (above).
469. *Hagen* v *Zeehaghe* [1990] ECR 1845.

As regards actions *in personam*, it was understood that the English court has "jurisdiction over all persons and companies who or which can be served with a writ which is simply a writ for service within the jurisdiction. Because such persons and companies can be served with the Queen's writ, they can be compelled to submit to orders of the court. This may be the reason why (if it be correct) a court is seized of jurisdiction from the moment when a writ is issued".[470]

However, in *The Duke of Yare*,[471] the Court of Appeal held that, in an ordinary and straightforward case, the English court is "seized of an action for the purpose of jurisdiction under Article 22 of the 1968 Convention not when the writ is issued but when it is served. This is because it is then that the proceedings become "definitively pending",[472] in that the court acquires jurisdiction and the parties become bound to perform procedural duties and suffer the prescribed consequences of default.[473] It would be:

"artificial, far-fetched and wrong to hold that the English Court is seised of proceedings, or that proceedings are decisively, conclusively, finally or definitively pending before it, upon mere issue of proceedings, when at that stage (1) the Court's involvement has been confined to a ministerial act by a relatively junior officer; (2) the plaintiff has an unfettered choice whether to pursue the action and serve the proceedings or not . . . ; (3) the plaintiff's claim may be framed in terms of the utmost generality; (4) the defendant is usually unaware of the issue of proceedings and, if unaware, is unable to call on the plaintiff to serve the writ or discontinue the action and unable to rely on the commencement of the action as a *lis alibi pendens* if proceedings are begun elsewhere; (5) the defendant is not obliged to respond to the plaintiff's claim in any way, and not entitled to do so save by calling on the plaintiff to serve or discontinue; (6) the Court cannot exercise any powers which, on appropriate facts, it could not have exercised before issue; (7) the defendant has not become subject to the jurisdiction of the Court".[474]

So, an unserved writ "is a thing writ in water".[475] It is not definitive until served, except in the case of interlocutory proceedings, notably *Mareva* injunctions.[476] A rule by reference to service has the advantage of being more consistent with the procedural laws of other EC countries, but harmonization of such laws was not an objective of the Convention[477] and this rule has disadvantages, not least the creation of uncertainty.[478]

As regards an action *in rem*, the date is either the date of the service of the writ or, in the case of a ship, the date of the arrest of the ship, whichever is the earlier.[479] In the case of a ship, the date on which the writ is issued is inappropriate, as the writ may name more than one ship, although an action may be brought against only one: the court cannot be seized of an action *in rem* until the plaintiff has decided which ship to arrest.[480]

---

470. *The Freccia del Nord* [1989] 1 Lloyd's Rep 388, 391, *per* Sheen J, citing *Russell & Co v Cayzer Irvine & Co Ltd* [1916] 2 AC 298, 302, *per* Viscount Haldane. Also in this sense: *Kloeckner & Co v Gatoil Overseas Inc* [1990] 1 Lloyd's Rep 176, 204 *per* Hirst J.

471. *Dresser UK Ltd v Falcongate Freight Management Ltd* [1991] 2 Lloyd's Rep 557 (CA); applied in *Assurances Générales de France v The Chiyoda Fire & Marine Co (UK) Ltd* [1992] 1 Lloyd's Rep. 325 (re).

472. p 567, with reference to *Zelger* (above).

473. p 566 per Bingham LJ, with whom the other members of the court agreed.

474. p 569 per Bingham LJ.

475. Briggs [1992] LMCLQ 150, 152.

476. p 569 *per* Bingham LJ.

477. *Hagen v Zeehaghe* [1990] ECR 1845.

478. Briggs (above).

479. *The Freccia del Nord* [1989] 1 Lloyd's Rep 388, 391, *per* Sheen J. In most cases, the ship is arrested before the writ is served.

480. pp 391–392, citing *The Banco* [1971] P 137, 158, *per* Megaw LJ (CA).

CHAPTER 3

INSURABLE INTEREST IN LIFE[1]

3-1 INTRODUCTION

The law requires an insurable interest in the person who contracts insurance. On this topic, life and personal accident insurance,[1a] sometimes called contingency insurance, are considered separately from indemnity insurance. Yet, in each case the reasons for having a requirement of insurable interest at all are said to be the same, the avoidance of wagers,[2] and to a lesser extent the removal of temptation to bring about the loss insured against.[3]

Indeed, in France life insurance was forbidden by the *Ordonnance de la Marine* of 1681 and was not mentioned in the civil code at all. It was "fit only, said Portalis with a sneer at the English, for a morality that is overgrown by the vile spirit of commerce".[3a] Even in England, however, life insurance was the subject of early and rare intervention by the legislature (below 3–2), as the possibility of abuse was a matter of concern.

In the United States the same reasons for the requirement of interest have been given in the past.[4] As regards life insurance, however,

1. Generally see Appleman, sections 761 ff; Houseman, p 16 ff; Keeton, section 3.5(c)T(f).
1a. Life insurance is sometimes referred to as life assurance, however, the expressions usually bear the same meaning: *Re Barrett* (1992) 106 ALR 549, 561 (FCA—life).
2. For example, Houseman, pp 24–25. *Hopkins* v *Hopkins*, 614 A 2d 96, 98 (Md, 1992—life); Vukowich, 7 Willamette LJ 1, 6 (1971).
3. For example, *Hopkins* (above); see also *Commonwealth Life Ins Co* v *George*, 28 So 2d 910, 912 (Ala, 1947—life). Appleman, sections 764 and 766; Keeton, section 3.5(e); Vukowich, 7 Willamette LJ 1, 8 (1971).
The relevance of temptation to kill has provoked some scepticism in England: "A man does not gamble on his own life to gain a Pyrrhic victory by his own death"—*Griffiths* v *Fleming* [1909] 1 KB 805, 821 *per* Farwell LJ (CA—life). The insured may of course be tempted to commit suicide to benefit those dear to him. This possibility was met by policy clauses excepting such loss, failing which the contract was declared unenforceable as contrary to public policy: *Beresford* v *Royal Ins Co Ltd* [1938] AC 586. "It cannot indeed be considered that any person, by means of an interest created in the duration of another's life, would be impelled to commit murder in this country, from fear of the law if from no other fear; but against the murder of a person in a foreign country, there might not be the same salutary check"—*per* Lord Ellenborough CJ in *Gilbert* v *Sykes* (1812) 16 East 149 (life). The reader will no doubt judge for himself whether a modern court would be so sanguine.
In *Evans* v *Jones* (1839) 5 M & W 77, a wager on the outcome of a trial was held void because (p 82 *per* Lord Abinger CB, with whom the other barons agreed) it tended to encourage the parties to pervert the course of justice.
3a. Rudden, *Disclosure in Insurance: the Changing Scene* in Lectures on the Common Law, vol. 3 (Deventer 1991), p 1.
4. *Watson* v *Massachusetts Mutual Life Ins Co,* 140 F 2d 673, 675–676 (D Colum, 1943—life), cert den 322 US 746.

"its purpose is intended not to take the gambling features out of each particular contract but to limit public opportunity to engage in a speculative business of buying and selling insurance policies on the lives of others. Such a purpose can be accomplished by imposing two safeguards which limit the class of persons who can enforce such policies—(1) They must stand in a close family or financial relationship with the person whose life is the subject of the policy. (2) They must acquire the insurance with the consent of such subject."[5]

In England, however, the main reason for requiring an interest is said to be to avoid wagering. A wager is commonly described as a contract in which neither party has an interest apart from the contract itself.[6] As wagering is defined negatively by reference to interest, we know that they are mutually exclusive; but not where the line is to be drawn between them. In truth, the requirement of interest is the language of insurance law for the more general proposition of contract law that the contract must be lawful, not only as regards questions of formality but also as regards the purposes that the parties seek to promote.[7] "A wagering contract . . . is an aleatory contract which has a harmful tendency".[8]

There is a presumption of lawfulness, i.e., of insurable interest, unless the contrary is shown. The insured is not generally required to state or specify his interest at the time of the contract. The rule "is that you must specify the subject-matter of the insurance, not your interest in it",[9] and it is reflected in the MIA, section 26(2), which provides that "The nature and extent of the interest of the insured in the subject-matter of the insured need not be specified in the policy".

The law stated in this chapter concerning insurable interest in lives applies also to personal accident (PA) insurance.[10] "Accident insurance is generally recognized to be that form of insurance which insures against an accident, with death or disability being some of the liability creating events. Life insurance is insurance against death with accidental death as one of the contingencies by which benefits accrue and incidental to the main objective."[11] However, when it comes to insurable interest, the public policy and the consequent law are the same, with the following reservation. PA insurance may cover medical expenses or loss of wages. This kind of cover is indemnity insurance and hence what is said (below 3-6D) about the extent of the interest insurable does not apply. On indemnity principles the cover is limited to the amount of the actual loss incurred.[12]

5. p 676. Thus, for example, in New York such insurance is valid only with the consent of the insured: NY Ins Law, section 146(3).
6. For example *Carlill* v *Carbolic Smoke Ball Co Ltd* [1892] 2 QB 484, 490 *per* Hawkins J, applied in *The Moonacre* [1992] 2 Lloyd's Rep 501, 510 *per* Deputy Judge Colman, QC, (yacht). Anson, p 297.
7. For example, see below, 3-3(f).
8. Patterson, 18 Colum L Rev 381, 386 (1918).
9. *Mackenzie* v *Whitworth* (1875) 10 Exch 142, 148 *per* Bramwell B (re), holding that it was unnecessary to state that the insured was reinsuring his liability on cargo. See also *Crowley* v *Cohen* (1832) 3 B & Ad 478, that the carrier could insure goods or cargo without specifying that his interest was that of a bailee; in the same sense *Palmer* v *Pratt* (1824) 2 Bing 185, 192 *per* Park J; *London & North Western Ry Co* v *Glyn* (1859) 1 El & El 652, 664 *per* Crompton J. See also *Inglis* v *Stock* (1885) 10 App Cas 263, 274 *per* Lord Blackburn.
10. *Shilling* v *Accidental Death Ins Co* (1858) 1 F & F 116.
11. *Simmons* v *Continental Casualty Co,* 285 F Supp 997, 1002 (D Neb 1968—group disability), affirmed 410 F 2d 881 (8 Cir, 1969).
Life insurance "is not a fixed obligation to pay at some future date which is undetermined. It is a series of contingent obligations to pay if death occurs during the year covered by each successive premium"—*Watson* v *Massachusetts Mutual Life Ins Co,* 140 F 2d 673, 676 (D Colum, 1943—life).
12. See below ch 28. This is true also of permanent health insurance (PHI), also found under various other names such as continuous disability, permanent sickness, income protection. Sickness benefits under accident policies are usually limited to a certain number of weeks. Moreover accident policies are normally

3–2 THE LIFE ASSURANCE ACT 1774

It "is the duty of the Court always to lean in favour of an insurable interest, if possible".[13] Nonetheless, English law, like that of the United States,[14] invalidates life insurance taken without interest. In England the legal requirement derives from the Life Assurance Act 1774. This Act does not, of course, apply in the United States,[15] but has been applied in Canada.[16] The Act prohibits insurance without interest, not only on lives but also "on any other event or events whatsoever".[17] In England the Act probably applies to any kind of insurance,[18] except marine insurance[19] and the insurance of "goods and merchandise".[20] However, the Act, it seems, does not apply to insurance of any kind at all unless the contract is recorded in a policy.[21]

Section 1 of the Act requires the insured to have an insurable interest in the life insured. Section 2 requires that the names of persons interested in the policy be stated in the policy.[22] Section 3 provides that the insured who has an interest shall recover no

annual and hence the insurer may refuse to renew or do so only at a much increased premium in the case of an accident with continuing effects. PHI deals with this situation by providing a longer term of cover both for the contract cover itself and the length of the effects.

13. *Re London County Commercial Reinsurance Office Ltd* [1922] 2 Ch 67, 79 (re) *per* Lawrence J, citing *Stock* v *Inglis* (1884) 12 QBD 564, 571 *per* Lord Brett MR (CA—cargo).

14. *Cammack* v *Lewis,* 15 Wall 643 (SC, 1873—life); *Crotty* v *Mutual Life Ins Co,* 144 US 621 (1892—life); *Grigsby* v *Russell,* 222 US 149 (1911—life). As a matter of public policy "the defense of a want of insurable interest and the consequent illegality of the insurance contract, is one that may be raised by the court though not properly pleaded"—*Midland National Bank* v *Dakota Life Ins Co,* 277 US 346, 349 *per* Justice Brandeis (1928—life). The issue cannot be excluded by an incontestable clause in the policy: *Commonwealth Life Ins Co* v *George,* 28 So 2d 910 (Ala, 1947—life), citing *Hall* v *Coppell,* 7 Wall 542, 549 *per* Justice Swayne (1869); the effect of the plea is that the contract is void and that the clause falls with the rest of the contract. See also *Aetna Life Ins Co* v *Hooker,* 62 F 2d 805 (6 Cir, 1933—life), cert den 289 US 748.

Courts in certain states have also held that the lack of interest may be pleaded by the insurer but not, for example, by contesting beneficiaries under the policy: *Feely* v *Lacey,* 322 P 2d 1104 (Mont, 1959—life); *Moran* v *Moran,* 346 NYS 2d 424 (1973—motor). In New York, however, the insurer has been estopped from pleading lack of interest: *Holmes* v *Nationwide Mutual Ins Co,* 244 NYS 2d 148 (1963—life), affirmed 245 NYS 2d 330.

15. However, in the nineteenth century courts in the United States regarded the Act as common law, which they sought to observe as common law.

16. For example, *North American Life Assurance Co* v *Craigen* (1886) 13 SCR 278 (life).

17. The Act has been invoked to outlaw a wager on share prices: *Paterson* v *Powell* (1832) 9 Bing 320; on trade relations between Great Britain and Maryland: *Mollison* v *Staples* (1778) Park 909; on so-called peace policies on the ending of the First World War: *Re London County Commercial Reinsurance Office Ltd* [1922] 2 Ch 67; on the sex of the Chevalier d'Eon: *Roebuck* v *Hamerton* (1778) 2 Cowp 737.

18. The Act applies whenever there "is a premium paid, in consideration of the insurers incurring the risk of paying a larger sum upon a given contingency"—*Paterson* v *Powell* (1832) 9 Bing 320, 329 *per* Lord Tindal CJ. *Cf* insurance of buildings: below, 4–4A.

19. Marine insurance is regulated by the MIA, section 4.

20. These are exempted by section 4 of the Life Assurance Act 1774. It seems that an insurable interest in marine cases is required by the MIA, and in other cases by the Gaming Act 1845 and the Marine Insurance Act 1788 (in so far as it applies also to goods on land).

21. *Roebuck* v *Hamerton* (1778) 2 Cowp 737. In *Good* v *Elliott* (1790) 3 TR 693, 706 Lord Kenyon CJ said that the Act was confined to wagers recorded in "written instruments". In *Morgan* v *Pebrer* (1837) 3 Bing NC 457, 466 Lord Tindal CJ said that a wager was not caught by the Act unless it assumed "the form of a policy of insurance". In *Carlill* v *Carbolic Smoke Ball Co* [1892] 2 QB 484, 493 Hawkins J said that section 2 of the 1774 Act applied "only to a policy which is a written document, and cannot apply to a contract like the present, which is created by a written proposal or offer accepted by the fulfilment by the plaintiff [by conduct] of the conditions attached to the offer". The Court of Appeal agreed that the contract in that case was not a wager, Lindley LJ dismissing the contrary contention "as not worth serious attention": [1893] 1 QB 256, 261.

22. Modified in respect of group policies by section 50 of the Insurance Companies Amendment Act 1973, whereby section 2 of the 1774 Act does not "invalidate a policy for the benefit of unnamed persons from time to time falling within a specified class or description if the class or description is stated in the

more than the value of his interest. The effect of section 3 is to bring an element of indemnity into life insurance, which is not in essence a contract of indemnity, in appropriate cases such as insurance by a creditor on the life of his debtor (below 3–7D). Moreover, if the insured has covered the full amount of his interest under one policy, he cannot recover a further amount under another policy, even though the latter amount alone is no greater than the amount of his interest. In *Hebdon* v *West*[23] the court accepted the argument of counsel that "if this were otherwise, the object of the statute would be defeated, as a small amount of insurable interest might be made the foundation for a great number of insurances, each to the amount of the whole of the interest of the insured; and, if he could recover upon each of these, it would be against the words of" section 3.

3–3 THE TRUE INSURED: LIFE INSURANCE FOR THE BENEFIT OF OTHERS

Section 2 of the Life Assurance Act 1774 requires the insertion in the policy of the name or names of the person or persons interested in the policy for whose use, or benefit or on whose account the insurance is made. This refers not only to the insured, who contracted the insurance (sometimes called the grantee), but also to third parties, who did not apparently contract the insurance, but are intended to be beneficiaries of the insurance. The purpose of the section is to defeat insurance contracted by A, who has an insurable interest, but really contracted by A for B who has none. The scheme of the Act is that the prime beneficiary of the insurance must have an interest (section 1) and, to avoid deception, be brought into the open by being named in the policy (section 2).[24] The effect of the Act is that, if A takes genuine insurance on his life, he may do so and may subsequently apply the insurance for the benefit of B, whether B has an insurable interest in the life or not. If, however, the prime intention at the time of contract is the immediate benefit not of A but of B, B must not only be named in the policy but also have an insurable interest in the life. The difficulty is to draw a line between these two situations.

In *Wainwright* v *Bland*[25] Lord Abinger CB said to the jury,

"the question in this case is, who was the party really and truly effecting the insurance. Was it the policy of Miss A ? or was it substantially the policy of W the plaintiff, he using her name for purposes of his own ? If you think it was the policy of Miss A, effected by her for own benefit, her representative is entitled to put it in force; and it would be no answer to say that she had no

policy with sufficient particularity to make it possible to establish the identity of all persons who at any given time are entitled to benefit under the policy".

23. (1863) 3 B & S 579, 590 *per* Wightman J.

24. Birds (p 43) points out that for this purpose it is enough that the immediate beneficiary should have an insurable interest, as required by section 1, without the further requirement of section 2 that the beneficiary be named in the policy: "If A insures his own life for the benefit of B, but B has an insurable interest, whether or not B is named in the policy should not affect its validity, as there is no element of gaming or wagering. If B has no interest in A's life, the policy is illegal under section 1, even if B is expressly named in the policy." However, it seems clear that both requirements of the statute must be satisfied: *Hodson* v *Observer Life Assurance Sy* (1857) 8 El & Bl 40 (life).

25. (1835) 1 M & Rob 481, 486–487; life insurance had been taken by A on her own life at the suggestion of a near relative, W, with whom she lived, and with the assistance of W's wife. A, who was impecunious, paid the premiums with money provided by W. A had also taken other life policies, two of which had been assigned shortly before her death to W. Subsequently, according to Pollock B in *M'Farlane* v *Royal London Friendly Sy* (1886) 2 TLR 755, 756, W was deported for fraud on an insurance company, it being believed that he had poisoned more than one person whose life he had insured in this way.

funds to pay the premiums; W might lend her the money for that purpose, and the policy still continue her own. But, on the other hand, if . . . you come to the conclusion that the policy was in reality effected by W; that he merely used her name, himself finding the money, and meaning (by way of assignment, or by bequest, or in some other way), to have the benefit of it himself; then I am of the opinion such a transaction would be a fraudulent evasion of the [1774 Act], and that your verdict should be for the defendants."[26]

So, the court asks whether it is A, who contracted the insurance, or B, the beneficiary, who is the "party really and truly effecting the insurance", the true beneficiary. On this kind of question, the court may be influenced by the following factors.

(a) If B has an insurable interest anyway, the question posed is largely academic,[27] although still necessary in England to satisfy the requirement of naming in section 2. The court will be slow to defeat the insurance.

(b) The payment of premiums by A establishes a *prima facie* case that A is the true beneficiary of the policy,[28] but this factor is not conclusive, especially in England.[29]

(c) In the United States courts inquire whether it was A or B who initiated the arrangement of the insurance.[30] For Professor Patterson[31] initiative was the decisive factor: having identified the evil of wagering as the pursuit of unearned gain, he continued "If, then, the initiative in procuring life insurance contracts is taken away from the persons who may gain by them, the making of such contracts cannot become a vocation and their harmful tendencies will disappear entirely or will, at the very least, be reduced to an extent as inconsiderable as the case of gifts."

(d) If B contracts insurance on the life of A, in the United States the consent of A is seen as some kind of safeguard against the abuse which the law seeks to prevent. Thus in New York the Insurance Law[32] requires the consent of the person insured except in the case of group life, accident or health insurance, the insurance of a wife by her husband and *vice versa,* and the insurance of a child under 15 by one on whom the child is dependent for support and main-

---

26. The jury decided for the defendants on this issue. A similar decision was reached by the court in *Shilling* v *Accidental Death Ins Co* (1857) 2 H & N 42 (PA) in which a son paid the premiums for a policy ostensibly for his father.
   Cf *M'Farlane* v *Royal London Friendly Sy* (1886) 2 TLR 755: a proposal on the life of M was signed by R, with whom M lived, as agent for M. M paid the first premium, R paid the rest. The plea that this was really insurance for the benefit of R, in breach of section 2, was rejected by the Divisional Court.

27. *Aetna Life Ins Co* v *France,* 94 US 561 (1877—life).

28. *North American Life Assurance Co* v *Craigen* (1886) 13 SCR 278, 283 *per* Ritchie CJ, 291 *per* Strong J (life); *Brophy* v *North American Life Assurance Co* (1902) 32 SCR 261, 266 *per* Taschereau J (life); "well established is the rule that one may not insure his own life for the benefit of another who has no insurable interest therein if the beneficiary assumes payment of the premiums or otherwise participates in or induces the transaction"—*Penn Mutual Life Ins Co* v *Slade,* 47 F Supp 219, 221 (ED Ky, 1942—life). Generally see Appleman, section 765.

29. *Wainwright* v *Bland* (above); *Brewster* v *National Life Ins Sy* (1892) 8 TLR 648 (CA—life): father's life cover paid for by daughters A and B for ultimate benefit of children of daughter C: valid insurance.
   USA in this sense: *Aetna Life Ins Co* v *France,* 94 US 561 (1877—life); *Fidelity Mutual Life Assn* v *Jeffords,* 107 F 402, 410–411 (5 Cir, 1901—life); *Feely* v *Lacey,* 322 P 2d 1104, 1107 (Mont, 1959—life). Patterson, 18 Colum L Rev 381, 401 (1918).

30. *Equitable Life Ins Co of Iowa* v *Cummings,* 4 F 2d 794, 796 (3 Cir, 1925—life); *Aetna Life Ins Co* v *Messier,* 173 F Supp 90, 95 (MD Pa, 1959—life). Canada *idem: North American Life Assurance Co* v *Craigen* (1886) 13 SCR 278, 284–285 *per* Ritchie CJ (life).

31. 18 Colum L Rev 381, 388–389, 396–397 (1918).

32. Section 146(3). If the required consent is not obtained the insurance may nonetheless be enforced: *Holmes* v *Nationwide Mutual Ins Co,* 244 NYS 2d 148 (1963—life).

tenance. However, a "statutory consent requirement is a very slight deterent [*sic*]. Consent of the insured can easily be obtained as a favor or for a slight consideration."[33] Consent as such has not influenced the courts in England, but is considered as an aspect of *bona fides* (below, (f)).

(e) If A insures his own life and immediately assigns the policy to B, it might be thought that B is the true beneficiary of the insurance and B, therefore, who should have the insurable interest required by section 1 of the Act and be named in the policy as required by section 2. The United States Supreme Court[34] once said that "The assignment of a policy to a party not having an insurable interest is as objectionable as the taking out of a policy in his name . . . The law might be readily evaded, if the policy or an interest in it could, in consideration of paying the premiums . . . be transferred so as to entitle the assignee to retain the whole of the insurance money." Yet, public policy in favour of "freedom of alienation" encourages the court to validate an assignment by an insured who wishes to dispose of his property in this way. Life insurance is one of the recognised forms of investment and self-compelled saving.[35] So far as reasonable safety permits, it is desirable to give to life policies the ordinary characteristics of property; to deny the right to sell a policy except to persons having an insurable interest in the life is to diminish the value of the policy to the insured.[36] An assignment of a policy to the highest bidder has been held valid.[37] Although not the best way of raising money, it is accepted in English practice that a person who has taken an endowment policy on his own life and who later needs to raise money may auction that policy on the secondary market in order to realise an amount higher than the surrender value.

In the United States, assignment to B soon after the insurance is contracted is generally not decisive that B is the true beneficiary.[38] Moreover, in England, assignment of the policy to B not named in the policy, even though intended when the policy was taken and carried out immediately afterwards, does not necessarily make B the true beneficiary (who must therefore satisfy the requirements of sections 1 and 2) provided that the insurance is *bona fide* (below, (f)); there may be a good motive for immediate assignment, which does not offend the purpose of the Act. Baron Pollock said[39] that

---

33. *Holmes* v *Nationwide Mutual Ins Co,* 244 NYS 2d 148, 152 (1963—life).

34. *Warnock* v *Davies,* 104 US 775, 779–780 *per* Field J (1881—life). In certain states assignment to one without an interest is always invalid: Appleman, section 856 ff. There have also been decisions that, if at the time of contract assignment to one without an insurable interest was contemplated, the contract is invalid as a wagering contract: for example *Bankers' Reserve Life Co* v *Matthews,* 38 F 2d 528, 529 (8 Cir, 1930—life). This is the view expressed by Appleman, section 857.

35. *Grigsby* v *Russell,* 222 US 149 *per* Holmes J (1911—life).

36. *Ibid.* See also Patterson, 18 Colum L Rev 381, 391 (1918).

37. *Gordon* v *Ware National Bank,* 132 F 444, 450 (8 Cir, 1904—life).

38. *Grigsby* v *Russell,* 222 US 149 (1911—life) in which the insured paid two premiums but then needed money for surgery and assigned the policy to raise money; the policy was held valid: the evils which the law sought to avoid were not incurred in such a case. See also *Midland National Bank* v *Dakota Life Ins Co,* 277 US 346 (1928—life).

39. *M'Farlane* v *Royal London Friendly Sy* (1886) 2 TLR 755, 756 (life) (emphasis added). He based this view on his reading of the law as laid down in *Wainwright* v *Bland* and *Shilling* v *Accidental Death Ins Co* (above).

Also in this sense: *North American Life Assurance Co* v *Craigen* (1886) 13 SCR 278, 284–285 *per* Ritchie CJ (life); *Brophy* v *North American Life Assurance Co* (1902) 32 SCR 261, 266 *per* Taschereau J (life). *Cf* Birds, p 44, who agrees that the line is fine but suggests (on the basis of *M'Farlane*) that it is drawn

"there is nothing to prevent any person from insuring his own life a hundred times, paying in each instance only one premium, provided it is *bona fide an insurance on his life, and, at the time, for his benefit,* and that there is nothing to prevent this being done, even though at the time when he effected the policies he had the intention of dealing with them. There is no law against this, and it is not within the evil or mischief of the statute. But if *ab initio* the policy effected in the name of A is *really and substantially intended* for the benefit of B and B only . . . [t]hat is within the evil and mischief intended to be met by the statute."

(f) Life insurance is valid if it is *bona fide*.[40] The line that separates *bona fide* insurance, as envisaged by Baron Pollock (above, (e)), from the fraud envisaged by Lord Abinger in *Wainwright v Bland* is sometimes fine.[41] In England, where this factor is more influential than any other, the position depends on the main purpose of the transaction and on whether that purpose is associated with the mischief that the statute seeks to prevent. It seems that, if the purpose is acceptable, the policy will be enforced, even though the main purpose is not life insurance but some other purpose, to which the life insurance is a means. Similarly, courts in the United States may look at the "motivating cause for taking out and assigning" the policy[42]; it is this that determines *bona fides*.[43]

In *Wainright v Bland* (above), although allegations that the beneficiary had murdered the life insured were not proven, the court had grave doubts and the jury found the policy invalid. In *M'Farlane v Royal London Friendly Sy*[44] a later court took the view that a person who insured his own life to provide security for a creditor was effecting *bona fide* insurance, and did not require the creditor to be named in compliance with section 2.

The policy is also valid when taken by the insured to provide for persons, such as relatives, after his own death and section 11 of the Married Women's Property Act 1882 authorises and facilitates the transaction of life policies by a spouse for the bene-

"between A taking out a policy in order to benefit B, and A *bona fide* effecting a policy with an intention of assigning the benefit but with no particular assignee in mind. The first case would fall foul of section 2 if B's name were not inserted and of section 1 if it was really a case of B insuring A's life in which he had no interest. The second is perfectly valid". A similar statement is made by MacGillivray No 113, but it is difficult to reconcile with some of the decisions there cited, for example, *North American Life Assurance Co v Craigen* (1886) 13 SCR 278 (life).

40. *M'Farlane v Royal London Friendly Sy* (1886) 2 TLR 755, 756 *per* Pollock B (life); *North American Life Assurance Co v Craigen* (1886) 13 SCR 278, 291 *per* Strong J (life).

41. *M'Farlane* (above) *loc cit.*

42. *Lawrence v Travelers' Ins Co*, 6 F Supp 428, 429–430 (ED Pa, 1934—life). But it seems that a distinction may be drawn between the (objective) purpose of the transaction, which governs its validity, and the "motive and intention of the parties"—*Aetna Life Ins Co v Messier*, 173 F Supp 90, 95 (Pa, 1959—life).

43. *Crotty v Mutual Life Ins Co*, 144 US 621 (1892—life); *Grigsby v Russell*, 222 US 149 (1911—life); *Aetna Life Ins Co v Hooker*, 62 F 2d 805 (6 Cir, 1933—life), *cert den* 289 US 748; *Carnes v Franklin Life Ins Co*, 81 F 2d 800 (5 Cir, 1936—life); *American Casualty Co v Rose*, 340 F 2d 469 (10 Cir, 1964—PA); *Corder v Prudential Ins Co*, 248 NYS 2d 265 (1964—life).

44. (1886) 2 TLR 755 (Div Ct—life). See also *Downes v Green* (1844) 12 M & W 481 (life). *Cf MacDonald v National Mutual Life Assn of Australasia Ltd* (1906) 14 SLT 173 (life): when F insured his own life with the sole object of raising money on the policy, by seeking a lender to buy the policy and pay the premium, the Court of Session held that the transaction was invalid under the Act. This case is distinguishable from *M'Farlane v Royal London Friendly Sy* (1886) 2 TLR 755 (life), which was not mentioned to or by the Court of Session; (a) The Court was influenced by the fact that the assignment to the lender had been agreed even before the policy had been issued (see p 174). This is unlikely to influence a court today. (b) As a loan transaction it was bogus or at least very one-sided. In return for the assignment of the policy, the life got very little: "the paltry sum of £5, which he practically received for lending his name to the transaction"—p 174 *per* Lord Ardwall.

fit of the other spouse and/or their children.[45] Thus, consistently with the purpose of the Life Assurance Act, a personal representative of the insured may enforce the policy for the estate, even though the representative[46] and the beneficiaries of the estate[47] are not named in the policy. In *Brewster* v *National Life Ins Sy*[48] Lord Esher MR said that "The father really insured his life for his own benefit, to enable him to leave money for the benefit of the children". It has also been said[49] that a policy may be effected by trustees without naming the beneficiaries under the trust, but this is doubtful.[50] Doubt about group policies, however, was resolved by section 50 of the Insurance Companies Amendment Act 1973, which provides that the beneficiaries of a group policy do not have to be named in the policy.

3–4 PERSONS WITH AN INSURABLE INTEREST IN LIFE

Insurable interest is not defined in the Act. The cases suggest that insurable interest may be of two kinds. There may be a non-pecuniary interest based in natural affection (below, 3–5) and a pecuniary interest (below, 3–6), each of which is served by the long life of the life insured.

3–5 INTEREST PRESUMED: NATURAL AFFECTION

A person's affection for himself is presumed to be such as to give him a sufficient interest to insure his own life.[51] There is, said Pollock B,

"nothing to prevent any person insuring his own life a hundred times . . . provided it is *bona fide* insurance on his life".[52] "But this", said Farwell LJ, "must be on the ground that an insurance by a man on his own life is not within the mischief of the Act. A man does not gamble on his own life to gain a Pyrrhic victory by his own death. I cannot persuade myself that such an insurance is of a pecuniary interest or . . . that if the man dies he will gain an advantage, if he lives he will suffer a loss. The loss is in both cases his own, being either of his own life or of his premiums; the pecuniary gain is his executor's . . . It is not a question of property at all."[53]

For similar reasons a person is allowed to insure those closest to him, but in England the range is limited. A husband may insure the life of his wife[54] and a wife may

---

45. See Houseman, ch 9.
46. *Wainwright* v *Bland* (1835) 1 M & Rob 478, 487 *per* Lord Abinger CB (life).
47. Houseman, p 18.
48. (1892) 8 TLR 648, 649 (CA—life). *Idem*: *North American Life Assurance Co* v *Craigen* (1886) 13 SCR 278, 284 ff *per* Ritchie CJ (life), discussing a number of early decisions in the United States to the same effect. See also *Ingersoll* v *Knights of Golden Rule,* 47 F 272 (SD Ga, 1891—life).
49. Houseman, p 18.
50. *Collett* v *Morrison* (1851) 9 Hare 162, 176 *per* Sir G J Turner (life), who thought that the name of the beneficiaries should appear on the face of the policy.
51. *Wainwright* v *Bland* (1835) 1 M & Rob 481, approved in *Griffiths* v *Fleming* [1909] 1 KB 805, 814 *per* Vaughan Williams LJ (CA—life).
USA: a person has "an unlimited insurable interest in his own life"—*Equitable Life Ins Co of Iowa* v *Cummings,* 4 F 2d 794, 796 (3 Cir, 1925—life). See also *Bankers' Reserve Life Co* v *Matthews,* 39 F 2d 528 (8 Cir, 1930—life); *Aetna Life Ins Co* v *Messier,* 173 F Supp 90 (MD Pa, 1959—life); *Aetna Life Ins Co* v *Patton,* 176 F Supp 368 (SD Ill, 1959—life).
52. *M'Farlane* v *Royal London Friendly Sy* (1886) 2 TLR 755, 756.
53. *Griffiths* v *Fleming* [1909] 1 KB 805, 821 (CA—life).
USA: there is a similar assumption in the case of own life insurance or the insurance of close relatives that natural affection is sufficient to protect the life of the insured: *Warnock* v *Davis,* 104 US 775 (1881).
54. *Griffiths* v *Fleming* [1909] 1 KB 805 (CA—life).

insure that of her husband,[55] without having to prove the reality or extent of any pecuniary interest in the life insured. This rule does not extend to the insurance of their children.[56] The only other interest of this kind recognised in England is a very limited case created by statute[57] for industrial life insurance, sometimes more accurately described as home service insurance, whereby a person may insure a parent or grandparent.

In the United States, in contrast with England, an insurable interest is recognised in all persons having a close relationship or affinity with the life, if they have a non-pecuniary interest in the continuance of the life grounded in natural affection.[58] So, a husband has an interest in the life of his wife[59] and a wife in the life of her husband [60] and this is valid in spite of subsequent divorce.[61] In some states this rule has been applied to a fiancé.[62] Controversially, it has also been applied to persons living together for a number of years as husband and wife.[63] But in a later case[64] the same court concluded that the designated beneficiary of the policy was not "so closely related at any time to [the deceased] either as fiance [sic], common law wife, putative wife, or otherwise, that she wanted him to continue to live, irrespective of monetary considerations"[65] and hence did not have an insurable interest on the ground of natural affection. On the contrary, the court considered that "her relations with the insured were meretricious and illicit . . . It is a matter of common knowledge that the practice of such relations often results in a fertile field for the breeding of violence which too frequently ends in the wanton destruction of human life."[66] Currently, in a climate of conservatism, the later case is likely to find favour.

In England, strict theory says that there is no insurable interest in the life of a coha-

---

55. *Reed* v *Royal Exchange Assurance Co* (1795) Peake Add Cas 70 (life), approved in *Griffiths* (above).
56. See below, 3–7B.
57. The Industrial Assurance and Friendly Societies Act 1948, section 2. The amount payable on death is very limited. Industrial insurance is defined in the Industrial Assurance Act 1923, section 1(2). See further Halsbury, Vol 24, Nos 201 ff. The essential requirements of this kind of insurance are (a) that premiums are payable at intervals not exceeding two months, and (b) they are paid to collectors, who call for them.
58. *Volunteer State Life Ins Co* v *Pioneer Bank,* 327 SW 2d 59, 64 (Tenn, 1959—life).
59. *Simmons* v *Continental Casualty Co,* 410 F 2d 881 (8 Cir, 1969—PA).
60. *Metropolitan Life Ins Co* v *Skov,* 51 F Supp 470 (D Or, 1943—life); *Shaw* v *Board of Administration,* 241 P 2d 635 (Cal, 1952—life); *Aetna Life Ins Co* v *Messier,* 173 F Supp 90 (MD Pa, 1959—group life).
61. The interest is tested at the time the insurance is contracted; *Metropolitan Life Ins Co* v *Skov,* 51 F Supp 470 (D Or, 1943—life); *Shaw* v *Board of Administration,* 241 P 2d 635 (Cal, 1952—life). Although earlier common law was different, the rule is now the same in Texas: *Dreesen* v *Coleman,* 531 SW 2d 201 (Tex, 1975—life). The interest is reinforced, if by the divorce settlement the party insured is required to pay maintenance to the other: *Meerwirth* v *Meerwirth,* 319 A 2d 779 (NJ, 1974—life). See also Wilmit, 73 Cornell L Rev 653 (1988).
62. *Green* v *Southwestern Voluntary Assn Inc,* 20 SE 2d 694 (Va, 1942—life); even though the engagement was later broken off: *Scherer* v *Wahlstrom,* 318 SW 2d 456 (Tex, 1958—life).
63. *Renchie* v *John Hancock Mutual Life Ins Co,* 174 SW 2d 87 (Tex, 1943—life): the "wife" had lived with the deceased for 11 years in the belief that they were legally married and the court rejected a claim by an earlier lawful wife to recover money paid under a policy benefiting his "wife".
64. *Biggs* v *Washington National Life Ins Co,* 275 SW 2d 566 (Tex, 1955—PA): the named beneficiary had lived with the deceased for five years prior to his death and was aware that the deceased had a living lawful wife. See also *Electrical Workers Benefit Assn* v *Brown,* 26 F 2d 981 (D Colum, 1928—life).
65. p 569. The court, after "hearing all the sordid evidence in this case", also rejected the alternative ground of insurable interest, that the beneficiary had reasonable expectation of pecuniary benefit from the relationship.
66. *Ibid.* The insured died as a result of gunshot wounds; however, it does not appear from the report that his death was connected with his relations with the beneficiary. But in other states evidence that the relationship was meretricious has been declined as irrelevant to the question of insurable interest: *Equitable Life Ins Co of Iowa* v *Cummings,* 4 F 2d 794 (3 Cir, 1925—life); *Northeastern Life Ins Co* v *Leach,* 213 NYS 2d 357 (1961—life).

biting "partner", although some insurers are in the practice of issuing cover in this situation. "For the avoidance of doubt", the Scottish Law Commission has recommended that "(a) . . . it should be made clear by statute that a cohabitant has an insurable interest in the life of his or her partner of the same type as he or she has in his or her own life. (b) No qualifying period of cohabitation should be required for this purpose".[66a] In the view of the Commission, a cohabitant would be likely to think of effecting an insurance policy on the life of his or her partner only if the relationship was one of some permanence.

As regards parent and child see below, 3–7. In the United States but not in England there is an insurable interest between siblings.[67] But in the absence of financial dependency there is no insurable interest between persons (except husband and wife) related by marriage[68]; or between nephew or niece and uncle or aunt[69]; or between cousins.[70]

Returning for a moment to spouses, an attempt was made to justify interest between them not only on grounds of natural affection but also on pecuniary lines. Having referred to academic opinion on the Married Women's Property Act 1882, Vaughan Williams LJ in 1907 in *Griffiths* v *Fleming* inferred[71] that

"now that a husband may reasonably look for pecuniary aid from his wife, just as formerly she looked for pecuniary aid from him, the husband plainly has a reasonable expectation, in case of need, of assistance from his wife in case she acquires and holds property, and that in such a case the same reason for not requiring affirmative proof of the existence and extent of the pecuniary interest arises where the husband is the insurer of his wife's life as arises in the case where the wife insures the husband's life."

But in the same case Farwell LJ,[72] with whom Kennedy LJ agreed, held that it was not a question of property or pecuniary interest at all, but like that on own life insurance (above): the case of spouses was not within the mischief to be defeated by the Act. He concluded[73] that the "interest appears to me to be the personal interest founded on affection and mutual assistance, and not a pecuniary interest". For the same reason the Insurance Ombudsman, writing in 1990,[73a] stated his intention to allow life insurance on a fiancé. However it seems that the mutual assistance may be partly pecuniary, for Farwell LJ cited with approval this statement by Lord Moncrief[74]:

"There is no fraud nor unfairness in such investment by insurance. But the intention plainly is that, when his wife shall die, a sum of money shall become payable to himself . . . He invests a portion of his funds or gains, upon a contingent contract, that, if he shall have the misfortune to

66a. Scottish Law Commission (No 135), *Report on Family Law*, para 16.41.
67. *Aetna Life Ins Co* v *France*, 94 US 460 (1877—life); *Supreme Assembly, Royal Sy of Good Fellows* v *Adams*, 107 F 335 (D RI, 1901—life); *Mutual Savings Life Ins Co* v *Noah*, 282 So 2d 271 (Ala, 1973—life).
68. *Carter* v *Continental Life Ins Co*, 115 F 2d 947 (D Colum, 1940—life); *Mutual Savings Life Ins Co* v *Noah*, 282 So 2d 271 (Ala, 1973—life).
69. *Commonwealth Life Ins Co* v *George*, 28 So 2d 910, 912 (Ala, 1947—life); *Peoples First National Bank & Trust Co* v *Christ*, 65 A 2d 393 (Pa, 1949—life); *Mutual Savings Life Ins Co* v *Noah*, 282 So 2d 271 (Ala, 1973—life).
70. *Bankers Reserve Life Co* v *Matthews*, 39 F 2d 528 (8 Cir, 1930—life); *Mutual Savings Life Ins Co* v *Noah*, 282 So 2d 271 (Ala, 1973—life).
71. [1909] 1 KB 805 (CA—life).
72. p 821.
73. p 823.
73a. Annual Report 1989 nos 2.31 ff.
74. *Wight* v *Brown* (1849) 11 D 459, 470. *Quaere* whether the pecuniary interest recognised by Lord Moncrief is a legal interest: below, 3–6B.

lose his wife and be then less able for labour than he was before, he may then have a fund to be paid to him for his support."

On separation or divorce, an interest based on affection is hard to sustain, however, in that situation, one may well be obliged to make maintenance payments to the other and the latter will have an interest in the life of the former, not as spouse but as debtor.[74a]

3–6 PECUNIARY INTEREST IN LENGTH OF LIFE

In cases in which there is no interest based on natural affection (above, 3–5), the insured must have an interest in the duration of the life insured, which is pecuniary (below, 3–6A) and legal (below, 3–6B) at the time of the contract (below, 3–6C).[75] If so, there is an insurable interest, but one limited in extent to the degree of pecuniary involvement (below, 3–6D).

3–6A Pecuniary Interest

The interest must be pecuniary in a reasonable sense capable of valuation in money.[76]

3–6B Legal Interest

The interest "must be a legal interest, not a mere chance or expectation",[77] so that, if the life drops, there is an effect on some right enjoyed by the insured (below 3–6B1) or he incurs a legal liability (below 3–6B2). For example, a binding promise not to enforce a debt during the life of the creditor gives the debtor a legal interest in the life of the creditor, but a gratuitous promise does not.[78]

In the United States, by contrast, it is enough that the insured has a reasonable expectation of benefit or loss dependent on the duration of human life[79]: there is an interest if

"he would in reasonable probability suffer a pecuniary loss, or fail to make a pecuniary gain, by the other's death; or (in some jurisdictions) . . . , in the discharge of some undertaking, he has spent money, or is about to spend money, for the other's support or advantage . . . Sentiment or affection is not sufficient of itself, although it may often be influential in persuading a court or jury to reach the conclusion that a beneficiary had a reasonable expectation of pecuniary advantage from the continued life of the insured."[80]

74a. Below, 3–7D. For example, *Hopkins* v *Hopkins*, 614 A 2d 96, 99 (Md, 1992—life).

75. This can be inferred from the language of section 3 of the Life Assurance Act 1771: *Halford* v *Kymer* (1830) 10 B & C 724, 728 *per* Lord Tenterden CJ; *Barnes* v *London, Edinburgh & Glasgow Ins Co* [1891] 1 QB 864, 865 *per* Lord Coleridge CJ; *Griffiths* v *Fleming* [1909] 1 KB 805, 814 *per* Vaughan Williams LJ (CA).

76. *Simcock* v *Scottish Imperial Ins Co* (1902) 10 SLT 286, 287 *per* Lord Pearson (Ct Sess—life). It "need not be capable of exact estimation in dollars and cents"—*Life Ins Clearing Co* v *O'Neill*, 106 F 800, 802 (3 Cir, 1901—life).

77. *Griffiths* v *Fleming* [1909] 1 KB 805, 820 *per* Farwell LJ (CA—life).

78. *Hebdon* v *West* (1863) 3 B & S 579, 589 *per* Wightman J (life).

79. *Warnock* v *Davis*, 104 US 775 (1881—life).

80. *Life Ins Clearing Co* v *O'Neill*, 106 F 800, 801–802 (3 Cir, 1901—life).

Thus between members of a family, who may not have an insurable interest in each other's lives based on affinity (above, 3–5), it is enough that there is a *de facto* dependence on financial support by Y on Z to give Y an insurable interest in the life of Z. So, a godchild has an insurable interest in the life of a godparent who, although not legally obliged to, looks after him.[81] A divorced woman has an insurable interest in the life of her former husband because of the continuing duty of the latter to support the child of the marriage, who is living with her.[82] However, in general, old friends do not have an insurable interest in each other's lives.[83]

3–6B1 Contingent Rights

A person with a right, the enjoyment of which is dependent on the duration of a human life, has an insurable interest in that life. In *Law* v *Indisputable Life Policy Co*,[84] for example, a father purchased from his son a legacy from a testator who had died, but which was contingent on the son's reaching the age of 30. The court was in no doubt that the father had an insurable interest in the life of his son: the benefit only began when the life attained 30. In *Parsons* v *Bignold*,[85] a father was to have the enjoyment of property for the duration of his child's life: the benefit had begun but would end when the life ended; here too the father had an insurable interest in his son's life.

3–6B2 Contingent Liability

If the incidence of a legal duty is dependent on the duration of human life, there is an insurable interest in that life. Thus a life insurer has an insurable interest in the life insured which justifies reinsurance.[86] But compare a contract of loan under which the sum is to be repaid, not on a fixed date but on a contingency, the occurrence of which is uncertain, when the agreement is made, such as repayment "when you can", or "when you get paid what you are owed by C". This is a valid agreement. Is it otherwise, if the contingency is the death of a third party? In that case is there a loan, a contract of insurance or a wager?

In *Cook* v *Field*[87] A expected to inherit property under the will of C. A contracted with B that, for an immediate payment of £2,000 by B to A, A would transfer to B the property, if and when received upon the death of C; and that if A did not inherit it or was unable to make a good title to it, A would repay the sum of £2,000 to B.[88] The agreement was impugned *inter alia* as a wager on the date of C's death, under which B

---

81. *Drane* v *Jefferson Standard Life Ins Co*, 161 SW 2d 1057, 1060 (Tex, 1942—life). See also *Commonwealth Life Ins Co* v *George*, 28 So 2d 910, 913 (Ala, 1947—life).

82. *Rio Grande Life Ins Co* v *Tichenor*, 69 F Supp 709 (ND Tex, 1947—life). Such insurance contracted prior to divorce remains valid by virtue of the interest based on affinity at the time of the contract (above, 3–5).

83. *Finn* v *Metropolitan Life Ins Co*, 16 SW 2d 922 (Tex, 1929—life).

84. (1855) 1 K & J 223, 230–231 *per* Sir W Page Wood V-C (life).

85. (1843) 13 Sim 518. See also *Swete* v *Fairlie* (1833) 6 Car & P 1. In these cases the lawful nature of the insurable interest was not challenged.

86. *Dalby* v *Indian & London Life Assurance Co* (1854) 15 CB 365, 388 *per* Parke B.

87. (1850) 15 QB 460.

88. A also agreed to assign to B as security an insurance policy on his own life.

would win if death occurred soon but lose if it occurred late.[89] The transaction was upheld.

The decision is less easy to accept in principle than in common sense. Payment of money or the equivalent on a contingency of uncertain occurrence is a feature of insurance (above, 1–1D), but it is also a feature of other transactions. Nor is it decisive that there was an element of risk: there is usually an element of risk and hence, it might be said, of wagering in every extension of credit, and indeed in every executory contract, particularly if the amount or quality of promised performance is uncertain or variable. A prominent feature of insurance is the transfer of a risk from insured to insurer, and its distribution in the wider community (above, 1–1E), and this feature was lacking in *Cook* v *Field*. Typically, the courts in that case were less concerned with whether it was insurance than with whether it was a wager, and found that it was not. The courts instinctively recognised a perfectly acceptable business arrangement. It was enough in *Cook* v *Field* that the court recognised a *bona fide* arrangement which did not therefore offend public policy.[90]

3–6C The Time of Interest

The insurable interest must exist at the time of the making of the contract of insurance.[91] Interest does not have to exist when the life drops; the following reasons have been given for this rule.

(a) The rule is sufficient to achieve the purpose of the Act, to prevent wagering policies:

> "But supposing a fair and proper insurable interest . . . to exist at the time of taking out the policy, and that it be taken out in good faith, the object and purpose of the rule which condemns wager policies is sufficiently attained; and there is then no good reason why the contract should not be carried out according to its terms. This is more manifest where the consideration is liquidated by a single premium paid in advance than where it is distributed in annual payments during the insured life."[92]

(b) Such a rule is in the nature of the life insurance contract: it is not a contract for indemnity at the time of the event (death or survival), but a contract that, in consideration of a certain annual payment, the company will pay at a

---

89. Citations included *Gilbert* v *Sykes* (1812) 13 East 150 in which the plaintiff paid the defendant 100 guineas, in return for the latter's promise to pay the plaintiff 1 guinea a day for as long as Napoleon Bonaparte should live—a dinner table wager on whether Napoleon would be assassinated. It was held void, partly because it was a wager and (*per* Bayley J at p 162) "this case has strongly illustrated the inconvenience of countenancing wagers in Courts of Justice; it occupies the time of the Court, and diverts their attention from causes of real interest and concern".

Note that in *Cook* v *Field* (above) Lord Campbell CJ objected (p 467) that the ordinary notion of life insurance was that, on the death, money was to be paid absolutely to the insured. But in the modern law it would make no difference that A's duty was to pay, not a sum of money, but to transfer a legacy: it is enough that the insurer A must pay money or money's worth: see above, 1–1C.

90. A similar difficulty arises when courts must decide whether a contract to sell futures, to sell goods at a future market price is a genuine sale or a wager on the market price: Benjamin, No 1–103.

91. *Barnes* v *London, Edinburgh & Glasgow Life Ins Co* [1891] 1 QB 864, 865 *per* Lord Coleridge CJ (life); *Simcock* v *Scottish Imperial Ins Co* (1902) 10 SLT 286, 288 *per* Lord Pearson (Ct Sess—life). *Connecticut Mutual Life Ins Co* v *Schaefer*, 94 US 457 (1877—life); *Shaw* v *Board of Administration*, 241 P 2d 635 (Cal, 1952—life); *Ducros* v *CIR*, 272 F 2d 49 (6 Cir, 1959—life). This rule was confirmed as regards the law of New York in *Herman* v *Provident Mutual Life Ins Co* 886 F 2d 529 (2 Cir, 1989—life), in which the former partners of a law firm, after the partnership had been dissolved, were held to have an interest and entitled to enforce keyman life insurance on the (former) senior partner.

92. *Connecticut Mutual Life Ins Co* v *Schaefer*, 94 US 457 (1877—life) *per* Bradley J. See also *Dalby* v *India & London Life Assurance Co* (1854) 15 CB 365, 389–390 *per* Parke B (Exch Ch—life).

future time a fixed sum calculated by them with reference to the value of the premiums which are to be paid, in order to purchase the postponed payment.[93] Hence it is enough that the insured had an insurable interest at the time that the contract was made, and it is not necessary that he have an interest when the event occurs.[94] If the latter were also required the contract of insurance would be

"completely altered in its terms and effect. It is no longer a contract to pay a certain sum as the value of a then-existing interest, in the event of death, in consideration of a fixed annuity calculated with reference to that sum; but a contract to pay—contrary to its express words—a varying sum, according to the alteration in the value of that interest at the time of the death . . . and yet the price, or the premium to be paid, is fixed, calculated on the original fixed value, and is unvarying; so that the insured is obliged to pay a certain premium every year, calculated on the value of his interest at the time of the policy, in order to have the right to recover an uncertain sum, *viz.* that which happens to be the value of the interest at the time of the death . . . He has not therefore a sum certain, which he stipulated for and bought with a certain annuity; but it may be a much less sum, or even none at all. This seems to us so contrary to justice and fair dealing and common honesty, that this construction cannot, we think, be put upon this section."[95]

As life insurance is a form of financial provision, its value should be as contracted, not reduced by reference to supposed damnification at the time of the event; were it otherwise "the meat which a man buys for his dinner should be returnable to the butcher under cost, if a friend should invite him in the meantime".[96]

(c) The rule is said[97] to follow as a matter of construction of section 3 of the Life Assurance Act 1774.

3–6D The Extent of Interest

Apart from the special cases of own life and insurance of the life of a spouse (above, 3–5), in which the full extent of the interest insured is presumed, the interest insurable is, it has been said, limited to the pecuniary value of the actual impact of the event (death or survival) on the insured, estimated at the time of the contract.[98] However, if this is the rule, it seems honoured more in breach than observance. More realistic is the view in the United States[99] that, if such an interest exists, the amount of the policy may exceed the actual value of the interest, unless so grossly disproportionate as to change the predominant character of the transaction from insurance to wager. Further, even in the case of a contingency befalling the insured himself, whose interest

---

93. *Law* v *London Indisputable Life Policy Co* (1855) 1 K & J 223, 228–229 *per* Sir W Page Wood V-C (life).
94. *Dalby* v *India & London Life Assurance Co* (1854) 15 CB 365 (re).
95. Parke B *ibid* pp 390–391, speaking of section 3 of the Life Assurance Act 1771.
96. De Morgan cited by Parke B at p 397.
97. *Dalby* v *India & London Life Assurance Co* (1854) 15 CB 365, 389 *per* Parke B (Exch Ch—re).
98. *Barnes* v *London, Edinburgh & Glasgow Life Assurance Co* [1891] 1 QB 864, 866 *per* Lord Coleridge CJ (CA—life).
99. *Watson* v *Massachusetts Mutual Life Ins Co,* 140 F 2d 673, 676 (D Colum, 1943—life); *National Life Ins Co* v *Tower,* 251 F Supp 215, 221 (D Md, 1966—life); *Bowman* v *Zenith Life Ins Co,* 384 NE 2d 949, 950 (Ill, 1978—life).

is presumed, he should not be allowed, it is said,[100] to "turn his plight into a bonanza".

3–6E The Effect of No Interest

If a contract of life insurance is made by a person without insurable interest, section 1 of the Life Assurance Act 1774 provides that the contract is "null and void to all Intents and Purposes whatsoever". In practice insurers pay rather than take the point. As the contract is void, however, a court must take notice of its nullity,[101] whether the parties plead its nullity or not. Moreover, if the insurer does plead lack of interest as a defence to an action, the availability of the defence is not conditional on the insurer's willingness to return the premiums paid.[102]

As the contract is void, the insurer is not bound to perform the contract by payment of the sum insured. If, nonetheless, the insurer pays, the right of the recipient to retain the money is controlled not by the invalidity of the contract of insurance, but by the legal effect of payment. If payment is made, ownership of the insurance money passes to the recipient.[103] In *Worthington* v *Curtis*[104] the insurer paid with full knowledge of the facts and of the insured's lack of interest in the life insured; the parties were *in pari delicto*. Mellis LJ said that "if the effect of the statute is that the Court will give no relief to any party because of the illegality of the transaction, in that case the maxim *melior est conditio possidentis* must prevail, and the party who has the money must keep it".[104a] By the same token, if the insured has paid premiums, he is unable to recover them from the insurer under a contract void for want of insurable interest.[105] Further, the policy is still an item of property, which may be disposed of by the insured or by the person in possession.[106]

3–7 LEADING CASES

3–7A Child–Parent

In general, a child has no legal rights against its parent and hence in England no insurable interest in the parent's life. In particular, a parent has no duty enforceable in the

---

100. Vukowich, 7 Willamette LJ 1, 7 (1971), citing *Batchelor* v *American Health Ins Co,* 107 SE 2d 36 (SC, 1958—PHI) in which the insured used multiple insurance to recover a weekly sum more than 10 times the wages actually lost while he was in hospital.

101. *Gedge* v *Royal Exchange Assurance Corp* [1900] 2 QB 214 (hull): the case concerned a policy with a PPI clause, void under the Marine Insurance Act 1745. See also *Royal Exchange Assurance Corp* v *Sjofor-sakrings A/B Vega* [1902] 2 KB 384, 394 *per* Lord Collins MR (CA—hull).

102. *Brophy* v *North American Life Assurance Co* (1902) 32 SCR 261, 270 *per* Taschereau J (life), distinguishing the case of illegality from that of rescission for misrepresentation or non-disclosure; see also pp 275–276 *per* Sedgewick J.

103. *A-G* v *Murray* [1904] 1 KB 165, 171 *per* Cozens-Hardy LJ (CA).

104. (1875) 1 Ch D 419 (CA—life): the insurer paid a father who had (illegally) insured the life of his son. An action by the son's creditors to recover the insurance money failed.

104a. p 425. Mellish LJ also said (p 424) that "the question who is entitled to the money must be determined as if the statute did not exist". The decision was followed on this point in *A-G* v *Murray* [1904] 1 KB 164 (CA), and applied in *Carter Bros* v *Renouf* (1962) 36 AJLR 67 (HCA). *Cf*, below, 30–5.

105. *Brophy* v *North American Life Assurance Co* (1902) 32 SCR 261, 268 *per* Taschereau J (life).

106. *Hadden* v *Bryden* (1899) 1 F (Ct of Sess) 710.

civil courts to support his or her child,[107] unless the child is the subject of a mainten-ance order by the court, in which case the child may insure the life of the parent con-cerned. It might be argued that the power of the court to order maintenance is so extensive that the very existence of the power, whether or not exercised in the particu-lar case, gives the child an insurable interest[108]; however, even if this argument were accepted, there remains the difficulty of assessing the extent of a right which has yet to be given pecuniary expression by the court.

In *Harse* v *Pearl Life Assurance Co*[109] it was argued that it was sufficient to give the child an insurable interest in the life of its parent that there was a reasonable prob-ability that the child would have to pay for its parent's funeral. The argument was rejected.[110]

In general,[111] therefore, in England a child has no insurable interest in the life of its parent. This rule, largely unchallenged in the courts, has been criticised[112] and is not found in kindred jurisdictions.[113] In practice, provision can be made for a child by the parent taking insurance on his own life and ensuring that the benefit of the policy is enjoyed by the child.[113a]

3–7B Parent–Child

It was argued in 1830 that a father had an interest in the life of his son because, if the son died, the chance of the father being maintained in old age was diminished. Reject-ing this argument, Bayley J said that, as the parish was bound to maintain him, it was a matter of indifference to the father, whether he were maintained by the parish or by the son.[114] Whether or not today's parent would agree, in England the son has no legal duty to maintain a parent,[115] and the parent has no insurable interest in the life of the son on this kind of ground.

107. *Bazeley* v *Forder* (1868) LR 3 QB 559, 565 *per* Lord Cockburn CJ; *Stopher* v *NAB* [1955] 1 QB 486, 495 *per* Lord Goddard CJ. *Cf Barnes* v *London, Edinburgh & Glasgow Life Ins Co* [1891] 1 QB 864, 866 *per* Lord Coleridge CJ (CA—life); *Northrop* v *Northrop* [1967] 2 All ER 961, 978 *per* Diplock LJ (CA).
   Cf Scotland: the parent has a duty to support the child and this is thought to give the child an insurable interest in the life of the parent. However, a step-child does not have an insurable interest in his step-parent: *Came* v *City of Glasgow Friendly Sy*, 1933 SC (Ct of Sess) 69 (industrial life).
108. In *Downing* v *Downing* [1976] Fam 288 a direct application by the child against the father was allowed.
109. [1904] 1 KB 558 (CA—life).
110. [1903] 2 KB 92; the correctness of this part of the decision was assumed in the Court of Appeal: p 562 (Lord Collins MR), p 564 (Romer LJ and Mathew LJ). A similar assumption was made by Erle J in *Shilling* v *Accidental Death Ins Co* (1858) 1 F & F 116, 121 (PA) and by Mathew LJ in *Howard* v *Refuge Friendly Sy* (1886) 54 LT 644, 646.
111. A minor exception is found in the Industrial Assurance and Friendly Societies Act 1948; see above, 3–5.
112. As "repugnant to common sense."—MacGillivray No 98.
113. USA: "The wife and the children have an insurable interest in the life of the husband and father"—*Central National Bank of Washington City* v *Hume,* 128 US 195, 205 *per* Justice Fuller (1888—life). This extends to an illegitimate child: *Hernandez* v *Supreme Forest Woodmen Circle,* 80 SW 2d 346 (Tex, 1935—life).
113a. See above 3–3 and below 5–4.
114. *Halford* v *Kymer* (1830) 10 B & C 724, 728.
115. *Barnes* v *London, Edinburgh & Glasgow Life Ins Co* [1891] 1 QB 864, 866 *per* A L Smith LJ (CA—life); *Hadden* v *Bryden* (1899) 1 F (Ct of Sess) 710.
   Cf Scotland: "By our law a parent has a right to claim aliment from his children, and this seems to me sufficient to give the parent an insurable interest in the child's life"—*Carmichael* v *Carmichael's Executrix,* 1919 SC (Ct of Sess) 636, 647 *per* Lord Dundas (life), reversed on another ground 1920 SC (HL) 195. The

The investment of the parent in the maintenance and education of the child gives the parent no insurable interest in the life of the child,[116] unless maintenance and education are made the subject of a contract between them; in that case the parent has an insurable interest in the life of the child, not because he is child, but because he is debtor.[117] A foster parent, even one who fosters a child for reward, has no such interest. Likewise in the United States, in the absence of financial dependency, affinity does not give a step-child or foster-child an interest in the life of the step-parent or foster-parent or *vice versa*.[118]

In England, there is doubt about the legality of school fees insurance (taken by a parent on the life of the child) or of travel insurance taken by a parent in respect of the child: the payment of school fees and of medical expenses may be matters of overwhelming moral obligation, but they are not in performance of obligations at law to the child. Fees are best provided for by endowment or decreasing term life insurance on the life of the parent. Travel insurance may be contracted by the parent as agent for the child.[119]

3–7C Guardian–Ward

In *Barnes*[120] it was held that the person taking care of a young relative had an insurable interest in the latter. There was an "interest in the child's life so far as to secure the repayment of the expenses incurred".[121] The decision has been doubted[122] and, indeed, it is difficult to reconcile with the decisions on parents and children (above, 3–7B).

scope of the duty determines the range of persons with an insurable interest; see MacGillivray (7th ed) Nos 100–104.

Cf USA: *Connecticut Mutual Life Ins Co* v *Schaefer*, 94 US 457 (1877—life) *per* Bradley J: "We cannot doubt that a parent has an interest in the life of a child, and vice versa . . . not merely on the ground of provision of law that parents and grandparents are bound to support their lineal kindred when they may stand in need of relief, but upon considerations of strong morals, and the force of natural affection between near kindred." *Idem: Bowman* v *Zenith Life Ins Co*, 384 NE 2d 949, 950 (Ill, 1978—life) if in good faith: "We believe the face amount of the policy is not grossly disproportionate to the extent of the plaintiff's interest. This factor is an indication that plaintiff acted in good faith in obtaining the policy." A contrary view is found in some early decisions, for example, *Life Ins Clearing Co* v *O'Neill,* 106 F 800 (3 Cir, 1901—life).

116. *Worthington* v *Curtis* (1875) 1 Ch D 419, 423 *per* Mellish LJ (CA—life).

117. Below, 3–7D.

118. *National Life & Accident Ins Co* v *Parker*, 19 SE 2d 409, 422 (Ga, 1942—life).

But there have also been decisions that a person who, although without legal obligation, stands *in loco parentis* to a child has an insurable interest in the life of the child: *Peoples First National Bank & Trust Co* v *Christ*, 65 A 2d 393 (Pa, 1949—life). This has been extended to a prospective adoptive parent, but on the basis of an interest grounded in natural affection: *Volunteer State Life Ins Co* v *Pioneer Bank*, 327 SW 2d 59, 64 (Tenn, 1959—life).

119. *Woodar Investment Development Ltd* v *Wimpey Construction UK Ltd* [1980] 1 All ER 571, 576 *per* Lord Wilberforce (HL). The contract is binding on the child as a contract for necessaries: Halsbury, Vol 24, Nos 416–417; Treitel, pp 481 ff.

120. *Barnes* v *London, Edinburgh & Glasgow Life Ins Co* [1891] 1 QB 864 (CA—life).

121. p 866 *per* Lord Coleridge CJ. This view finds some support in the USA: *Peoples First National Bank & Trust Co* v *Christ*, 65 A 2d 393 (Pa, 1949—life) in which a person standing *in loco parentis* to a child had an insurable interest in the life of the child. *Cf Anctil* v *Manufacturers' Life Ins Co* [1899] AC 604 (PC): that a "protector" did not have an insurable interest in the person under his protection.

122. For example Birds, p 40. Houseman, p 20, relegates the case to a footnote, observing that the decision was doubted by two members of the Court of Appeal in *Griffiths* v *Fleming* [1909] 1 KB 805, 819 (CA—life).

3–7D Creditor–Debtor

A creditor, including a mortgagee[123] or surety,[124] has an insurable interest in the life of his debtor and of any other person who is bound to discharge the debt.[125] The creditor insures against the debtor's death at any moment, that is, not only against the possibility of death before payment,[126] but also of death after payment.[127] In some parts of the United States the rule has been extended to give joint and several obligors an insurable interest in the lives of each other,[128] and to allow insurance on the life of a person who was expected to be a regular debtor of the creditor insured, even though there was no debt outstanding at the time of the contract.[129]

When the debtor dies, the insurance money is payable to the creditor even though the debt has already been repaid[130] or discharged, for example by bankruptcy,[131] or has been time barred.[132] For valid insurance, it is enough that the creditor has an interest at the time that the contract of insurance was concluded; what happens after that does not affect its validity: see above, 3–6C.

The extent of the creditor's interest is the subject of doubt. It is clear that the creditor can recover no more than the amount insured. It is clear that he can insure the amount of the debt (plus interest then due) when the insurance is contracted. Is it allowed to include in the amount insured a *bona fide* estimate of the cost of servicing the debt in future, including insurance premiums and future interest on the debt? In principle not: these are not sums to which the insured creditor is entitled, when he makes the contract of insurance, but expectancies, not themselves sufficient to support an insurable interest in English law (above, 3–6B). In the United States, however, expectancies can be insured; so a creditor has "an insurable interest in the life of his debtor to the extent of his debt plus the amount of the insurance premium advanced by the creditor, and if an amount in excess of the debt is received by the creditor he holds such excess in trust for the debtor or debtor's estate".[133] Only if the sum insured is extravagant by comparison with the creditor's estimated financial inter-

---

123. *Kincaid* v *Alderson*, 354 SW 2d 775 (Tenn, 1962—life).

124. *Lea* v *Hinton* (1854) 5 De G M & G 823 (life).

125. *Godsall* v *Boldero* (1807) 9 East 72; *Von Lindenau* v *Desborough* (1828) 3 Car & P 353; *Downes* v *Green* (1844) 12 M & W 481 (life); *Connecticut Mutual Life Ins Co* v *Schaefer*, 94 US 457 (1877); *Mutual Life Ins Co of New York* v *Armstrong*, 117 US 591, 598 *per* Field J (1886—life); *Grigsby* v *Russell*, 222 US 149 (1911—life); *Sachs* v *United States*, 412 F 2d 357 (8 Cir, 1969—life). Even when the debtor has not consented to the insurance on his life—*Livesay* v *First National Bank of Lockney*, 57 SW 2d 86 (Tex, 1933—life); on the significance of consent, see above, 3–3(d).

126. Even though the debtor's estate is liable for the debt, "his chance of payment depends upon the debtor remaining alive"—*Simcock* v *Scottish Imperial Ins Co* (1902) 10 SLT 286, 288 *per* Lord Pearson (Ct Sess—life). In the same sense *Godsall* v *Boldero* (1807) 9 East 72, 81 *per* Lord Ellenborough CJ.

127. *Simcock* (above)

128. *International Life Ins Co* v *Carroll*, 17 F 2d 42 (6 Cir, 1927—life).

129. *Baker* v *Keet-Rountree Dry Goods Co*, 2 SW 2d 733 (Mo, 1928—life). *Quaere* whether this would be the decision in other states.

130. *Dalby* v *Indian & London Life Assurance Co* (1854) 15 CB 365 (Exch Ch) overruling *Godsall* v *Boldero* (1807) 9 East 72; *Central National Bk* v *Hume*, 128 US 195, 205 *per* Justice Fuller (1888—life).

131. This appears consistent with the principle that discharge of a debt by bankruptcy does not render the debt void *ab initio*: *Heather & Son* v *Webb* (1876) 2 CPD 1, 8 *per* Lindley J.

Also in this sense: *Manhattan Life Ins Co* v *Hennessy*, 99 F 64 (5 Cir, 1900—life). But it has also been held that the creditor has an insurable interest to take out insurance after the discharge, for although the legal obligation may have been extinguished the moral obligation has not: *Livesay* v *First National Bank of Lockney*, 57 SW 2d 86 (Tex, 1933—life).

132. *Rawls* v *American Mutual Life Ins Co*, 27 NY App 282 (1863—life).

133. *Sachs* v *United States*, 412 F 2d 357, 364 (8 Cir, 1969—life), *cert* den 396 US 906; *Alperstein* v *National City Bank*, 103 NYS 2d 930 (1951—life).

est, immediate and future, will the insurance be void. Insurance for $3000 in respect of a $70 debt will not be enforced[134]; the amount insured must be reasonably proportionate to the amount of the debt.[135]

3–7E Debtor–Creditor

A debtor has no insurable interest in the life of his creditor. If the creditor makes a gratuitous promise not to enforce the debt during his own life, there is no interest because, although the debtor may have a reasonable expectation that the promise will be kept, he has no legal right to enforce it.[136] If, however, the creditor's promise is binding, the debtor has an insurable interest in the creditor's life.

3–7F Employer–Employee

In one way or another an employer is concerned with the life and death of his employee. First, he may be liable to and for his employee, and there is no doubt that he may insure against this liability. Second, he may be liable to the employee under a pension scheme linked to the life of the employee; that too is a liability which may be the subject of insurance by the employer. Third, group life or PA insurance arranged by an employer can be seen as insurance taken by the employee on his own life through the agency of the employer, or as insurance taken by the employer with the employee as third party beneficiary.[137] Fourth, the employer may also lose the employee's skill and labour and thus an employer has an insurable interest in the life and health of his employee to the extent of the work, to which the employer is entitled by law. Evidently, some employees are more indispensable than others,[137a] so this interest is limited to senior business executives,[138] key technicians,[139] and star performers.[140] A principal has a similar interest in the life of his agent.[141] In the United States, shareholders have an insurable interest in the life and health of senior employees of the company.[142] Conversely, there is some suggestion there that a com-

---

134. *Cammack* v *Lewis*, 82 US 643 (1873).

135. *Watson* v *Massachusetts Mutual Life Ins Co*, 140 F 2d 673, 676 (D Colum, 1943—life), *cert den* 322 US 746.

136. *Hebdon* v *West* (1863) 3 B & S 579, 584 *per* Wightman J. The court seems to have been chiefly concerned about the difficulty in estimating the value of the interest: p 585. Generally, see above 3–6B. *Cf Re Hygrade Envelope Corp*, 272 F Supp 451 (ED NY, 1967—life).

137. See the discussion in *Aetna Life Ins Co* v *Messier*, 173 F Supp 90 (MD Pa, 1959—life).

137a. *Cf Durr Drug Co* v *United States*, 22 F Supp 788 (MD Ala, 1938—life): no insurable interest in a minor shareholder who also worked for the company as a travelling salesman. The employer must have a "substantial economic interest" in the life and health of the employee.

138. *United States* v *Supplee-Biddle Hardware Co*, 265 US 189, 195 *per* Chief Justice Taft (1924—life): "Life insurance in such a case is . . . a contract of indemnity"; followed in *Wellhouse* v *United Paper Co*, 29 F 2d 886 (5 Cir, 1929—life); and *Ducros* v *Commissioner of Internal Revenue*, 272 F 2d 49 (6 Cir, 1959—life); see also *American Casualty Co* v *MSL Industries Inc*, 406 F 2d 1219 (7 Cir, 1969—life); *Empire Life Ins Co* v *Moody*, 584 SW 2d 855 (Tex, 1979—life).

139. *Simcock* v *Scottish Imperial Ins Co* (1902) 10 SLT 286 (life).

140. *Theatre Guild Productions Inc* v *Ins Corp of Ireland*, 267 NYS 2d 297 (1966—disability insurance on the actress Gertrude Berg for the play "Dear Me, the Sky is Falling").

141. *Turner & Co* v *Scottish Provident Institution* (1896) 34 SLT 146, 147 (Ct Sess): the insured "carried on a very lucrative business by means of their connection with [their selling agent] in Iceland, and . . . their profits would be greatly affected by [his] death".

142. *Mickelberry's Food Products Co* v *Haeussermann*, 247 SW 2d 731 (Mo, 1952—life). Further, in a close corporation members, by analogy with partnership, have an insurable interest in the life of each other: *Sandlin's Administratrix* v *Allen*, 90 SW 2d 350 (Ky, 1936—life).

pany may have an insurable interest in the life of a principal shareholder,[143] or creditor.[144]

In England the extent of the employer's interest is limited. In *Simcock v Scottish Imperial Ins Co*[145] Lord Pearson said that

"the value of the interest as at the date of the policy must be calculated with some reference to the legal relation subsisting between the parties. A contract of services affords a fairly sure basis of valuation. If there is no contract, the whole matter is thrown loose. It is impossible to appreciate in money the 'amount or value' of an interest whose endurance rests on sentiment or good feeling or mutual advantage."

In that case the employee had been the employer's right hand man in his business of pork butcher for many years, but his contract was a weekly contract. The court held (p 288) that the "utmost limit of the insurable interest" was the value of one week's employment. This implicitly excludes insurance against consequential loss of trading profit.[145a] However, employers in the world of entertainment may have legal rights which reflect the long term value of a star employee. For example, when footballer Ian Rush played football for Wales in 1986, his employer, Liverpool FC, demanded PA insurance cover of £3 million,[146] for that was the sale price of the footballer agreed by his employer with a football club in Italy. It might even be argued that a key player is an asset for the balance sheet:

"The argument runs that players' contracts have a definable life and an up-front value—the transfer fee—which can be amortised. Players will have a residual value at the end of their contracts: effectively the price at which they can be transferred to another club. The prospect that 5 per cent. of the club's net worth could be eliminated by an indiscreet tackle can be solved by insuring the players . . . The idea that [P], Spurs' redoubtable left back, is an intangible asset may be news to some opposing forwards; but one wonders whether the principle of capitalising key employees could be extended to other industries. What about all those equity traders, hired for expensive golden hellos on fixed term contracts? Adopting the policy would do no harm to some ailing bank balance sheets: although the residual value of a trader after a few years in these dismal markets cannot amount to much."[146a]

As regards more mundane spheres of activity, it has been suggested[147] that the value of the employer's interest in a key employee is not just the salary which the employee was entitled to earn, but the estimated loss of profit to the firm, if the employee dies. A realistic assessment of consequential loss and thus of desirable "keyman" insurance covers not only the value of the work on which the employee is engaged, but also in an appropriate case, the clientele and goodwill that he generates, and his effect on the credit rating of the business, or on stability in labour relations; but this appears to be contrary to both the letter and the spirit of the 1774 Act.

143. *Sinclair Refining Co v Long,* 32 P 2d 464, 473 (Kan, 1934—life).
144. *Re Hygrade Envelope Corp,* 272 F Supp 451 (ED NY, 1967—life): held that the company had an insurable interest in a factor who provided the company with finance.
145. (1902) 10 SLT 286, 288 (Ct Sess).
145a. p 288. The argument that the interest was limited (as it is in England) to the extent of the employer's contractual rights to the employee's services was rejected by the Supreme Court in *US v Supplee-Biddle Hardware Co,* 265 US 189 (1924). The scope of the insurable interest is limited to the extent that the employee concerned can be easily replaced. However, if there is an interest at the time of contracting the insurance, the employer may recover the sum insured, even though the employee has left his employment some time before death: *Secor v Pioneer Foundry Co,* 173 NW 2d 780 (Mich, 1970—life).
146. PM 28 August 1986, p 5; 19 February 1987, p 7.
146a. *Financial Times,* Lex column, 4 November 1989.
147. Houseman, p 22. In the USA such cover is lawful, as, regardless of legal rights, the employer may protect "a reasonable expectation of advantage or benefit from the continuance of his life"—*Warnock v Davies,* 104 US 775, 779 (1881) *per* Field J.

3–7G Employee–Employer

An employee has an insurable interest in the life of his employer to the extent of the pecuniary value of the unexpired period of his contract of employment.[148] This does not apply, of course, to a corporate employer which "has neither body to be killed nor soul to be damned", however, there seems to be no reason in principle to prohibit insurance against corporate disaster or death in the form of insolvency and liquidation.

3–7H Partners[149]

A partnership may wish a business continuation plan with an element of insurance. If partners are obliged to buy each other out, for example, on the death of one of them, they have an insurable interest in each other.[150] Ultimately the purchase may benefit the buyer, but in the short term it is a liability and it may be onerous; hence life insurance on the departing partner is allowed. If, however, surviving partners have, not an obligation, but an option to buy the deceased partner's share, there is strictly speaking no insurable interest. In such a case an alternative plan is for the partners collectively to take keyman insurance, but that too has its limits in English law (above, 3–7F).

3–7I Royalty

Wagers on the fortunes of public figures, including royalty, were among the abuses that the Life Assurance Act 1774 was to avoid. Nonetheless, this century has seen policies on the lives of royalty, for example, by theatrical producers, lest their production be cancelled as part of national mourning on the death of a monarch. It is difficult to see what legal interest the producer has to satisfy the Act, but it is equally difficult to object to such insurance on grounds of public policy. When, as in the Duchy of Cornwall, a leasehold interest terminates on the death of the royal landlord, the insurable interest is apparent.[151]

---

148. *Hebdon* v *West* (1863) 3 B & S 579 (life).

149. Similar rules apply to co-directors in companies, usually small companies. Also joint and several obligors (for example under a joint property venture) have an insurable interest in the lives of each other: *International Life Ins Co* v *Carroll*, 17 F 2d 42 (6 Cir, 1927—life). Similarly, in a close corporation or incorporated partnership, the members have an insurable interest in each other: *Sandlin's Administratrix* v *Allen*, 90 SW 2d 350 (Ky, 1936—life).

150. *Connecticut Mutual Life Ins Co* v *Luchs*, 108 US 498, 505–506 *per* Field J (1883—life); *Mutual Life Ins Co of New York* v *Armstrong*, 117 US 591, 598, *per* Field J (1886—life). Appleman, section 871.

151. George C Evans, *Insurances of the Person*, No 1A6G.

CHAPTER 4

INSURABLE INTEREST IN PROPERTY

4-1 INTRODUCTION

The insured must have an interest in the subject-matter of the insurance; he is not, however, required to state his interest at the time of making the insurance contract: above, 3–1. If he has no interest, the insurance cannot be enforced. Preliminary questions are these: (a) Who must have the interest? (b) To answer that question, we must answer another: what is the subject-matter of the insurance? (c) If a person has an interest, there is also the question of its extent.

4-1A Who is Required to have the Interest?

Clearly, the person who makes the contract of insurance with the insurer must have an interest. Further, an assignee of an insurance contract on property must also have an interest.[1] However, some doubt persists over what is required of the person who, although he cannot enforce the insurance contract, is likely to benefit indirectly from its performance.

In *Rowlands (Mark) Ltd* v *Berni Inns Ltd*[2] Kerr LJ considered the position of tenants who were likely to benefit from insurance taken by their landlords. He concluded[3] that

"Provided that a person with a limited interest has an insurable interest in the subject-matter of the insurance . . . there is no principle of law which precludes him from asserting that an insurance effected by another person was intended to enure for his benefit to the extent of his interest in the subject-matter. . . . Illustrations of relationships that may give rise to this consequence are those of bailee and bailor and mortgagee and mortgagor."

If the tenants could enforce the insurance directly, or indirectly by compelling the landlords to enforce it, their position would be like that of an insured who must have an insurable interest. Where, however, they have a contractual right to have the landlords insure the property (and to damages if they do not), and a contractual right to have insurance money used to reinstate the property (and to damages if it is not), they are at one step removed from the position of an insured; nonetheless, it appears from the proviso in this statement in the Court of Appeal that they must satisfy the requirement of interest.

---

1. *Lloyd* v *Fleming* (1872) LR 7 QB 299, 302 *per* Blackburn J (cargo). See further below, 6–3E.
2. [1985] 2 Lloyd's Rep 437 (fire); [1986] CLJ 22.
3. p 442. This aspect of the case was not challenged by counsel; no precedent was cited.

4–1B The Subject-Matter of the Insurance

To determine the existence of an insurable interest in the subject-matter of the insurance the subject-matter must be precisely defined. It has been suggested that, although insurance contracts are referred to as as though they insure something, no contract of insurance insures anything; that what is insured is the person owning or responsible for such thing against the loss which may be occasioned to him from the damage to or destruction of the thing, or from damages resulting from the use or abuse of the thing. Nonetheless, insurance is still commonly said to be "on" property, and the property perceived as the subject-matter of the insurance.[4] In most cases there is little difficulty, but there is some ambiguity in two cases, insurance of profits[5] and liability insurance.

Liability insurance is sometimes treated as something different from other kinds of insurance, but as regards insurable interest it is an insurance like any other; interest there must be. The subject-matter of liability insurance is the patrimony from time to time of the insured,[6] the patrimony which is vulnerable to the effect of his liability, *viz*, awards of damages. In short, the subject-matter is his "pocket".

To say[7] that "an individual has an unlimited interest in his own personal liability" is not correct. Liability is not the subject of the insurance; liability is the event against which cover is taken to protect the insured's pocket. It was argued before the Supreme Court of New Hampshire that the insured under a motor policy had no interest because he did not own the car. Rejecting this argument the court said,[8] correctly, that the insured "although without any title to the car, stood to suffer loss by the occurrence of the event insured against, that is, injuries to others due to his negligent operation thereof. This is enough to give him an insurable interest under a liability policy". As the court did not plan to cut off his arm to keep him off the road, the only suffering in prospect for the insured, apart perhaps from remorse, was financial; the reference to the insured was a reference to his assets. Apart perhaps from monks under vows of poverty, everyone has something, albeit just the shirt on his back, which can be taken from him. It is that which is the subject-matter of liability insurance; it is in that that an interest must and inevitably does exist.

4–1C The Extent of the Interest

A person may have an insurable interest, even though its extent is hard to quantify.[9] If the insured has an interest, the extent of his interest, the amount he may recover from the insurer and that part of the sum which he may retain are related but sometimes different amounts. However, it should be underlined from the start that he may insure the property for an amount that exceeds the value of his interest and recover that amount; but, if he does, the excess he must hold on trust for third parties whose loss it

---

4. See also below 16–1.
5. See below, 4–5N.
6. This is recognised more clearly by certain continental writers, for example, Brehm, *Le Contrat d'Assurance RC* (1983), No 3.
7. Harnett & Thornton, 48 Col LR 1162, 1171 (1948).
8. *Howe* v *Howe*, 179 A. 362, 364 (1935).
9. *Eyre* v *Glover* (1812) 16 East 218, 220 *per* Lord Ellenborough. Generally see *Chaplin* v *Hicks* [1911] 2 KB 786 (CA). Tabachnik, [1972] CLP 149, 151.

represents. He must do this because his property insurance is a contract of indemnity—he must not recover and keep for himself more than he has lost. Further, it should be underlined that more than one person may have an insurable interest in the same subject-matter[10]; indeed, the aggregate value of their interests may exceed the value of the subject-matter itself.[11]

4–1D Onus of Proof

To claim under his insurance the insured does not have to prove his interest. Lack of interest may be raised as a defence by the insurer, but that is a defence that he is slow to raise, because it is bad for the image of the industry[12] to take what is widely perceived as a technical defence, and courts are ill disposed to companies that take premium and then cry "no contract".[13] "Time was", said Buller J in 1798,[14] "when no underwriter would have dreamed of making such an objection: if his solicitor suggested a loop-hole by which he might escape he would have spurned the idea." Whether or not that is still true, it is not now entirely a matter for the insurer to decide. If he chooses to pay a claim to a man with no interest, the courts do not know and do not intervene.[14a] If, however, a claim comes before a court, whatever the issue, and it appears to the court[15] that the claimant lacks insurable interest, the court must take notice of it,[15a] for it affects public policy. Two decisions of lower courts over the last 50 years can be cited to the contrary,[16] but although these are contrary to the letter of the rule they are not contrary to its spirit; they do not violate the public policy behind the rule. Earlier decisions,[16a] one of the Privy Council, hold that the parties to

10. *Inglis* v *Stock* (1885) 10 App Cas 263, 274 *per* Lord Blackburn (cargo). The MIA, section 8 provides that "A partial interest of any nature is insurable". This includes the interests of joint tenants and common owners; *Grand Forks Seed Co* v *Northland Greyhound Lines,* 168 F Supp 882 (D ND, 1959—fire).

11. *Westminster Fire Office* v *Glasgow Provident Investment Sy* (1888) 13 App Cas 699 (fire).

12. Brown & Menezes, 4:1:7. It has been suggested by Keeton (section 3.3(a)) that it is when he suspects but cannot prove fraud that the insurer will go to court on the issue of insurable interest.

13. *Stock* v *Inglis* (1884) 12 QBD 564, 571 *per* Lord Brett MR (CA—cargo). *MacDonald* v *Canadian Accident & Fire Assurance Co* (1978) 77 DLR (3d) 746, 754 (Nova Scotia—fire).

14. *Wolff* v *Horncastle* (1798) 1 Bos & Pul 316, 320–321 (cargo).

14a. In any event, if payment has been made it may be effective in law; see above 3–6E and below, 30–5.

15. In New York a person bringing suit on an insurance policy must plead his interest: *Friscia* v *Safeguard Ins Co*, 293 NYS 2d 695 (1968—motor).

15a. See above 3–6E.

16. In *Prudential Staff Union* v *Hall* [1947] KB 685, while holding that the union had no insurable interest in the lives of its members, Morris J allowed an action against the insurer by the union on the understanding the moneys recovered would be held "on trust" for the lives. Public policy was respected. The same can be said of the decison of Diplock J in *Thomas* v *National Farmers' Union Mutual Ins Sy Ltd* [1961] 1 WLR 386 (fire).

16a. In *Anctil* v *Manufacturers' Life Ins Co* [1899] AC 604, 609 (life) the Privy Council affirmed the decision and adopted the reasoning of the Supreme Court of Canada that a clause whereby the insurance was incontestable after one year was contrary to public policy in so far as it concerned lack of insurable interest; see also *Gedge* v *Royal Exchange Assurance Corp* [1900] 2 QB 214 (hull), in which the court declined to enforce a ppi policy. Cf Canada: *Constitution Ins Co* v *Kosmopoulos* [1987] 1 SCR 2, 23 *per* Wilson J (fire) that only the insurer can raise the issue.

In the USA the force of public policy behind the requirement of insurable interest varies from state to state. For example in Louisiana, as in England, the insurer can never be estopped from raising the insured's lack of interest: *Rube* v *Pacific Ins Co of New York,* 131 So 2d 240 (La, 1961—motor). Section 287 of the Cal Ins Code provides that a waiver of interest is void.

In New York, however, a ppi policy, which would not be enforced in England, is enforceable: *F B Hall & Co Inc* v *Jefferson Ins Co*, 279 F 892 (SD NY, 1921—hull). See also *Lenfest* v *Cornwell,* 525 F 2d 717 (2 Cir, 1975—policy on anticipated profits).

the contract of insurance cannot waive interest and ask the court to respect their agreement. The doctrine of insurable interest as it is understood in England has been under attack (below 4–3B) but nobody has suggested in England that it should be abolished altogether. If, indeed, the doctrine survives and there is any sense in the reasons given for its continued existence (below 4–2), it is apparent that these are matters of public interest and it seems right that insurable interest cannot be waived by the parties.[16b]

4–2 THE REASONS FOR INSURABLE INTEREST[17]

The scope of the rule requiring an insurable interest in property can be tested against the reasons for the rule[18]; more than one reason has been suggested.

4–2A Moral Hazard

If the insured has an insurable interest, it is said, he will be less tempted to destroy the property insured.[19] This factor is sometimes called the moral hazard.[20] But it is doubtful whether the presence of an insurable interest has the effect claimed. A person who has an interest may also have a reason to destroy the property, for example, to convert an asset, which is difficult to sell on a depressed market, into cash. A person who has no interest might find it difficult to obtain cover. If he obtained cover but concealed his lack of interest, he would risk vitiation of the cover on the ground of non-disclosure. Moreover, he would face a difficult criminal task. If a person without apparent interest seeks to collect under a fire policy, this is bound to raise questions in the mind of the insurer and, if notified, of the police. Hence it is doubtful whether the moral hazard, in this sense primarily a matter for the criminal law,[21] provides a sufficient justification for the rule requiring an interest.

A less dramatic and more plausible view of moral hazard is a tendency in the insured "to underallocate to loss prevention after purchasing insurance".[22] If he does have an interest, but not otherwise, he may seek to avoid the inconvenience of loss or be induced by force of sentiment to safeguard the subject-matter of insurance.[23]

16b. In the same sense in the USA: *Froiland* v *Tritle* 484 NW 2d 310 (SD, 1992—life); see also notes to 3–2 (above). *Cf* Birds p 55.

17. Generally see Harnett and Thornton, "Insurable Interest in Property: A Socio-Economic Reevaluation of a Legal Concept", 48 Col L Rev 1162 (1948); Vukowich, "Insurable Interest", 7 Willamette LJ 1, 6 ff (1971).

18. This exercise was undertaken by the Supreme Court of Canada in *Constitution Ins Co* v *Kosmopoulos* [1987] 1 SCR 2 (fire).

19. *Howard Fire Ins Co* v *Chase,* 72 US 509 (1867—fire); *Castle Cars Inc* v *US Fire Ins Co*, 273 SE 2d 793, 794 (Va, 1981—motor).

20. "The moral hazard involves five basic objectionable elements. It is wrongful to commit destructive and evil acts. Innocent persons may be harmed and the destruction of useful property is economically wasteful. Also, the principle covering only fortuitous losses is violated. Finally, the unnatural loss skews the premium rates."—Pinzur, 1979 Insurance Counsel Journal 109, 111.

21. *Constitution Ins Co* v *Kosmopoulos* [1987] 1 SCR 2, 26 *per* Wilson J (fire).

22. Abraham, p 14.

23. Abraham, p 15. *Brown* v *Equitable Life Assurance Sy*, 766 F Supp 928, 933 (D Kan, 1991—disability).

4–2B Indemnity

A second reason given is that property insurance is indemnity insurance.[24] However, the one does not follow from the other, but rather they are both consequences of the same public policy against wagering. The requirement of indemnity, it has been said,[25] is

"not in any sense an independent policy, but merely another head of the hydra that is the policy against wagering. To the extent that a possible recovery is in excess of the insured's interest, it is a wager, and limiting indemnity to the extent of the interest is simply the way in which an insurance contract is removed from the wager category."

4–2C Wagering

The third and most prevalent reason given for the rule of insurable interest is social policy against wagering.[26] For Lord Ellenborough[27] the scope of the evil of wagering determined the scope of the insurable interest: light begins where darkness stops. Valid insurance is thus defined as any insurance that does not promote the evil of wagering, and attention rests on the meaning of wagering.

Unfortunately, conventional definitions of wagering are too wide for this purpose. For example, "to stake something of value on the issue of an uncertain event"[28] includes arrangements which are considered valid insurance contracts. Again, a wager, it has been said,[29] creates a risk for the parties, an insurance contract takes the risk already existing for one party (the insured) and, through the other party (the insurer), disperses that risk. But, as stated, this test is too wide; for example, it validates a wager (dressed as insurance) against losing another previous wager (an existing risk).

If a definition of wagering is not easily agreed, perhaps insurance should be defined by reference to the evils which the requirement of insurable interest seeks to avoid, the evils of wagering. Here too, however, no clear conception is apparent.

(a) The first statute in 1542 against gambling and other popular activities was to halt the decline in archery, hence a military purpose, as well as the avoidance of impoverishment, crime and neglect of Divine service.

(b) Among the economic objections are that gambling adds nothing to the wealth of the community. On the contrary, it diverts resources, according to a theory of diminishing marginal utility:

"Assume X, possessing a capital of £5,000, wagers £1,000 against £1,000 of Y's capital. Further assume ideally fair conditions so that X has a legitimate one to one chance of winning the wager. If X loses, his capital will be reduced to £4,000, and if he wins it will be increased to £6,000. However, in reality he will lose more if his capital is

24. For example *Foley* v *Manufacturers' & Builders' Fire Ins Co*, 46 NE 318, 319 (NY, 1897—fire).
25. Harnett & Thornton, *loc cit*, p 1183.
26. "[I]t hath been found by experience, that the making of insurances on lives, or other events, wherein the insured shall have no interest, hath introduced a mischievous kind of gaming"—preamble to the Life Assurance Act 1774. *Routh* v *Thompson* (1809) 11 East 428; and somewhat more recently: *Lonsdale & Thompson Ltd* v *Black Arrow Group plc* [1993] 2 Lloyd's Rep 428, 432 *per* J Sumption QC.
27. *Robertson* v *Hamilton* (1811) 14 East 522, 533 (hull); *The Moonacre* [1992] 2 Lloyd's Rep. 501, 510 *per* Deputy Judge Colman, QC, (yacht). *Rube* v *Pacific Ins Co of New York*, 131 So 2d 240 (La, 1961—motor). Appleman, section 2123.
28. *Shorter OED*; *Webster* has a similar definition.
29. *Cousins* v *Nantes* (1811) 3 Taunt 513, 524 *per* Lord Mansfield CJ (hull). Pinzur, Insurance Counsel Journal 109, 110 (1979).

reduced to £4,000 than he will gain if his capital is increased to £6,000. This is so because the fifth thousand of his capital provides for more urgent needs that the sixth thousand—that is, the more capital a man possesses, the less relatively important the addition of further capital becomes."[30]

There is also an element of waste, it is said, for a significant part of the insurer's costs are made up of administration which, in the case of a wager, serves no useful social purpose.[31] The reply, that man should play as well as work and that gambling is a legitimate recreation, is countered by social and ethical objections.

(c) Social objections turn on evidence that gambling generates in some people an excitement that defies moderation. In such cases the damage to relationships, particularly to family and responsibilities to the family, often become a matter of concern and burden to the rest of society.

(d) Ethical objections are many.[32] As a recreation, it is said, it is more available to the rich, who can afford it, than the poor. It encourages pleasure at the cost of pain to others. In the individual it is said to encourage egoism, covetousness and the desire to get something for nothing. It concentrates attention upon lucre and withdraws attention from worthier objects of life.[33] It makes chance the arbiter of conduct and, it is said, subverts the moral order of life.

To determine the validity of insurance by reference to the current perception of the evils of wagering involves a difficult value judgment which few English courts have undertaken.[33a] Indeed, there "seem to be many more convenient devices available to the serious wagerer".[34] Does this or any of the other alleged reasons for the rule of insurable interest provide sufficient justification for the rule? As things are, courts have lowered their sights to step carefully around precedent and have consequently lost a general sense of direction. English law requires its courts to play on firm ground; it recognises an insurable interest only when there is a legal relation to the subject-matter. In the margin between the safe ground and the sea of social evil, contracts about which the courts might have doubts are left in limbo.

4–3 THE MEANING OF INSURABLE INTEREST

For an insurable interest, English law[35] requires the insured to have, first, a relation in fact to the subject-matter of the insurance giving rise to an economic interest (below, 4–3A) and, second, a "legal or equitable relation" to the subject-matter insured

30. Harnett & Thornton, 48 Col L R 1162, 1179 and references cited.
31. Reference to social purpose is necessary to distinguish the beneficiary of inheritance, which is seen as socially desirable, as an encouragement to industry and a means of preserving the family: Patterson, *op cit*, p 387.
32. See for example the *Encyclopedia of Religion and Ethics* (ed Hastings), Vol 6, p 166. Patterson, 18 Col L R 381, 386 (1918).
33. *Amory v Gilman*, 2 Mass 1, 10 (1806). Patterson, *loc cit*.
33a. *Cf* note 27, above.
34. *Constitution Ins Co v Kosmopoulos* [1987] 1 SCR 2, 22 *per* Wilson J (fire).
35. MIA, section 5, which states the general position for both marine and non-marine insurance. In negative terms the rule is reinforced by the Gaming Act 1845, section 18: "all contracts or agreements, whether by parole or in writing, by way of gaming or wagering, shall be null and void". In the USA there are similar provisions in state legislation, for example, Cal Ins Code, section 280. As regards non-marine insurance in England , see for example *Macaura v Northern Assurance Co* [1925] AC 619, 632 *per* Lord Sumner (fire);

(4–3B). In Australia, Canada, and the USA[36] the law requires the first but not the second.

4–3A Economic Interest[37]

The property must be such that the insured may reasonably expect to benefit by the safety or due arrival of the property or to be prejudiced by its loss, damage or detention. The obvious example is that of property owned by the insured. If, however, the subject-matter is not in fact at risk in this sense,[38] or will not be when the cover purports to commence,[39] there is no economic interest and thus no insurable interest.

The requirement of economic interest is also found in the USA where in general

"a person has an insurable interest in the subject matter insured where he has such a relation or connection with or concern in, such subject matter that he will derive pecuniary benefit or advantage from its preservation, or will suffer pecuniary loss or damage from its destruction, termination, or injury by the happening of the event insured against."[40]

An interest in property is nonetheless an insurable interest because the insured is already covered against loss or damage to the property: the second insurance may be taken in case the earlier promise of indemnity prove unreliable.[41]

4–3A1 Measurable in Money

The expectation of benefit or loss must be one on which a pecuniary value can be set.[42] A benevolent interest does not suffice. Thus a trade union has no insurable interest in the property of its members.[43] Also, but less obviously, a father has no insurable interest in the tortious liability of his child.[44] The issue has also arisen when there was an interest when the insurance contract was made but, when the loss occurred (the time

36. For the position in these countries see below, 4–3B.

37. This expression comes from the United States; see, for example, the NY Ins Law, section 158, and is used by the Australian Law Reform Commission, Report No 20, Insurance Contracts, para 120. Harnett & Thornton, 48 Col L Rev 1162, 1171 (1948) talk instead of "factual expectation".

38. For example, *New Orleans & S American SS Co* v *W R Grace & Co*, 26 F 2d 967 (2 Cir, 1928— freight) *cert* den 278 US 636.

39. *Anderson* v *Morice*: below, 4–5J.

40. *Vetter Co* v *Aetna Casualty & Surety Co*, 612 F 2d 1076, 1078 (8 Cir, 1980—fire), quoting 44 CJS para 175. See also *Harrison* v *Fortlage*, 161 US 57 (1896—cargo); *Lumbermen's Mutual Ins Co* v *Edmister*, 412 F 2d 351 (8 Cir, 1969—fire); *Constantine* v *Home Ins Co*, 427 F 2d 1338 (6 Cir, 1970—breakdown insurance); *Scarola* v *INA*, 340 NYS 2d 630 (1972—motor); *Atlas Assurance Co Ltd* v *Harper, Robinson Shipping Co*, 508 F 2d 1381 (9 Cir, 1975—cargo).

The New York Ins Law, section 148, requires an insurable interest in property insured and continues that such interest "shall be deemed to include any lawful and substantial economic interest in the safety or preservation of property from loss, destruction or pecuniary damage".

41. *Hobbs* v *Hanham* (1811) 3 Camp 93, 94 *per* Lord Ellenborough (hull); *China Union Lines Ltd* v *American Marine Underwriters Inc*, 1985 AMC 1643 (2 Cir, 1985—re). If the insured has double insurance, his recovery will be limited to actual loss. See below 28–9.

42. *Halford* v *Kymer* (1830) 10 B & C 724, 728 *per* Lord Tenterden CJ (life).

43. *Prudential Staff Union* v *Hall* [1947] KB 685.

44. *Vandepitte* v *Preferred Accident Ins Corp* [1933] AC 70. At first sight it seems unrealistic to premise that a large damages claim, if pursued against the child, will have no financial impact on the parent. However, some claims are not pursued; some parents disown their children. As regards other cases, English law (below, 4–3B) asserts the additional need for a legal relation (between parent and liability) which is lacking and, in any event, there may be some doubt whether, in the event of the child's liability, the financial consequences are sufficiently probable: below, 4–3A2.

that matters), the value of the subject-matter to the insured had shrunk or was under threat.

In *Paterson-Leitch Co* v *INA*[45] the owner of some buildings claimed under a fire policy. The insurer resisted the claim because at the time of the fire the insured had contracted to have the buildings demolished, had vacated the buildings and allowed the utilities to be disconnected, thereby, contended the insurer, divesting himself of any economic interest. The insured replied that the buildings were standing at the time of the fire[46] and that no date had been set for demolition to begin. The insurer countered that, when demolition is a certainty, it is not necessary to wait until the ball hits the building to find that an insurable interest in it has been extinguished. The United States District Court held that the owner had an insurable interest at the time of the fire, observing that the demolition contract was not capable of specific enforcement[47] and that the insured could have backed out of the contract before demolition commenced.

4–3A2 Expectation: Probability

For an economic interest, at least in the United States,[48] "it is not necessary, to constitute an insurable interest, that the interest is such that the event insured against would necessarily subject the insured to loss". It is enough at the time of the contract that the peril insured against might happen and might affect the insured, unless that possibility is so remote as to be fanciful. However, if England had adopted economic interest as the sole test of insurable interest, it appears that the test would have required a "moral certainty" of loss.[49] In any case there are two contingencies here, the chance of the event and the chance that, if the event occurs, it will create loss.

As regards the chance of the event, the insured who buys cover is buying not only a contingent indemnity but also peace of mind; so, the expectation of loss must be reasonable, not in the sense that there is an objectively reasonable chance that the event will happen and affect the insured, but in the sense that it is not unreasonable to insure against it. Some chance must exist if the interest is not to be a fiction and perhaps a fiction that flaunts the rule of insurable interest.

As regards the chance that, if the event occurs, the event will affect or afflict the insured, the degree of probability required appears to be greater. Some doubt is

---

45. 366 F Supp 749 (ND Ohio, 1973). See also *Federowicz* v *Potomac Ins Co,* 183 NYS 2d 115 (1959—fire).

46. Thus distinguishing *Aetna State Bank* v *Maryland Casualty Co*, 345 F Supp 903 (ND Ill, 1972—fire). See also *Chicago Title & Trust Co* v *United States Fidelity & Guarantee Co*, 376 F Supp 767 (ND Ill, 1973—fire): the owner had no insurable interest in a building that was economically useless, having been gutted by a previous fire. *Cf American Ins Co* v *Treasurer, School District No 37, McCurtain, Oklahoma*, 273 F 2d 757 (10 Cir, 1959—windstorm).

47. Thus distinguishing *Royal Ins Co Ltd* v *Sisters of Presentation*, 430 F 2d 759 (9 Cir, 1970—fire). This was a case in which the insured (Sisters) had a legal relation to the property, but no economic interest. "Even the Sisters might have been induced to set fire to the old convent (or at least to pray for a fire) if legally enforceable rights were the sole test for insurable interest"—Pinzur, Insurance Counsel Journal 109, 117 (1979).

48. *Riggs* v *Commercial Mutual Ins Co*, 25 NE 1058, 1060 (NY, 1890—hull). In England see *Wilson* v *Jones* (1867) LR 2 Ex 139.

Distinguish the rule of proximate cause (below, ch 25), whereby in general the insured can only recover loss some of which was the inevitable result of the event insured against. Nonetheless, interest and causation may come close; see *Nieschlag & Co Inc* v *Atlantic Mutual Ins Co*, 43 F Supp 797 (SD NY, 1941); affirmed 126 F 2d 834 (2 Cir, 1942).

49. *Lucena* v *Craufurd* (1806) 2 Bos & Pul (NR) 269 (HL—marine).

raised by early English cases[50] on the insurance of profit from maritime adventures, cases which required the insured to prove that, but for the event, he would certainly have made the profit. This requirement has been rejected by the Supreme Court of the United States[51] in view of "the utter impracticality of making it, without the spirit of prophecy to determine the precise time when the vessel would arrive at her destined port". Today, a claim under liability insurance may be established by proving, not that liability was a certainty, but that the settlement of the liability suit was a *bona fide* compromise.[52] The law takes a similar view of fire claims that include the cost of measures taken to prevent the spread of fire.[52a] When it comes to a claim, the insured must prove that he actually did suffer loss,[53] but when contract of insurance is concluded, the insured has insurable interest and hence a valid contract if, should the event occur, it is probable that he will suffer loss.

4–3B Legal or Equitable Relation

If an economic interest exists, this might be thought enough. However, English law makes a further requirement, that of a legal or equitable relation to the subject-matter of the insurance, because the outer reaches of a rule based solely on economic interest were thought to be hard to define.[54] Lord Eldon said[55] that he had endeavoured in vain to find a fit definition of that which is between a certainty of benefit or loss, which is insurable, and a mere expectation, which is not, and went on to say that he could not "point out what is an interest unless it be a right in the property, or a right derivable out of some contract about the property, which in either case may be lost upon some contingency affecting the possession or enjoyment of the party". The economic interest had to be underpinned by something else which made loss (or benefit) sufficiently certain.[56] The law, however, has become uncertain and has been described as a trap for the unwary.[57]

The leading decision in England is *Macaura* v *Northern Assurance*.[58] The claimant sold the timber on his estate to a company, in which all shares were held by him or his nominees. Most of the timber was destroyed by fire; it was insured, not by the company which owned it, but by the claimant. The timber was the only substantial asset of the company. Lord Buckmaster said[59]: "at first sight . . . there really was no person

---

50. *Hodgson* v *Glover* (1805) 6 East 316; *Eyre* v *Glover* (1812) 16 East 218. *Cf Barclay* v *Cousins* (1802) 2 East 544. This confusion is found in the judgment of Lord Buckmaster in the leading case *Macaura* v *Northern Assurance Co* [1925] AC 619, 627 (fire).

51. *Patapsco Ins Co* v *Coulter*, 3 Pet 222, 239 (1830) *per* Mr Justice Johnson, who continued: "it seems difficult to perceive why, if profit be a mere excrescence [on the goods] . . . why the loss of the cargo should not carry with it the loss of the profits."

52. *Prince* v *Royal Indemnity Co*, 541 F 2d 646 (7 Cir, 1976—fire) *cert* den 429 US 1094 (1977). This can be supported on the basis that the purchaser of liability insurance is not only protecting his patrimony but also buying freedom from litigation.

52a See below, 17–2C2 and 17–2F.

53. See below, ch 28.

54. For example *Macaura* v *Northern Assurance Co* [1925] AC 619, 627 *per* Lord Buckmaster (fire).

55. *Lucena* v *Craufurd* (1806) 127 ER 630, 651–652.

56. Described as an "illusion" in view of the technical nature of property law: Brown & Menezes, 4:3:16, quoted with approval in *Kosmopoulos* v *Constitution Ins Co* [1987] 1 SCR 2, 16 *per* Wilson J (fire).

57. Keeton, p 115.

58. [1925] AC 619. Keeton (p 117) has suggested that the House was influenced by unproved allegations of fraud. The principle was applied to a partnership in *Arif* v *Excess Ins Group Ltd*, 1987 SLT 473 (fire).

59. p 625. There may be confusion in Lord Buckmaster's judgment on this aspect; see p 627 and above, 4–3A2.

other than the plaintiff who was interested in the preservation of the timber . . . He would receive the benefit of any profit and on him would fall the burden of any loss." Yet the House of Lords held that the plaintiff did not have an insurable interest in the timber. Lord Sumner said[60] that "the fact that he was virtually the company's only creditor, while the timber is its only asset, seems to me to make no difference . . . he was directly prejudiced by the paucity of the company's assets, not by the fire". He could insure the profits of the company but not the timber, the means by which any profit would be made.[61] The decision is based[62] on the premise that a creditor does not have an insurable interest in the property of his debtor,[63] and that a shareholder does not have an insurable interest in the property of the company,[64] rules based in their turn on lack of legal or equitable interest in the property.[65]

In Australia, the *Macaura* rule was rejected[66] as a technical rule "which prevented the insured from recovering the loss actually suffered by him". In particular, it was considered socially undesirable as it prevented insurance by the beneficiary under a will of property devised to him by a testator still living; and it was considered commercially undesirable as it invalidated insurance by a creditor of the profit-earning thing bought with the money lent. Advancing money for the development of a new product is not wagering but a highly regarded activity. It is not obvious why the developer can insure the prototype product but his lender cannot; nor why the owner can insure his factory against fire but his employee cannot insure the factory against consequent closure.

In Canada, the courts[67] followed *Macaura* until 1987, but the writing was on the Canadian wall: "As with any body of mature doctrine, there is a tendency for many insurance rules and principles to become separated from their functional underpinning. Concepts take on a life of their own, in which internal consistency, historical fidelity, linguistic purity, and circular or tautological explanations are more important than is any analysis of the underlying social problem."[67a] In 1987, in *Constitution Ins Co* v *Kosmopoulos*[68], in which the facts were similar to those in *Macaura*,[68a] the Supreme Court took another look at the social problem. The court considered that the twin purposes of an insurable interest were to reduce the temptation to destroy property insured and to discourage wagering; that these purposes could be sufficiently promoted by a rule based on economic interest alone, in combination with the rule

60. p 630.
61. p 628 *per* Lord Buckmaster, pp 630–631 *per* Lord Sumner by reference to *Wilson* v *Jones* (1867) LR 2 Exch 139.
62. pp 626–627 *per* Lord Buckmaster.
63. See below, 4–5M.
64. See below, 4–5L.
65. Moreover, the House considered that as a gratuitous bailee he was not liable for the timber and so an interest could not be based on bailment; *cf* below, 4–5I. In *Constitution Ins Co* v *Kosmopoulos* [1987] 1 SCR 2, 12 (fire) the court took the view that in the case of a one man company an employee could not be a bailee of his employer's property, at least while it was still in the possession and control of the employer, albeit through the instrumentality of the employee.
66. Law Reform Commission, Report No 20, Insurance Contracts, para 118 ff. Subsequently the law was changed by the Insurance Contracts Act 1984, section 17. For an account of the movement away from the *Macaura* rule in both Australia and New Zealand, see Long (1992) 7 Auckland Univ L Rev 80.
67. For example *Guarantee Co of N America* v *Aqua-Land Exploration Ltd*, 54 DLR (2d) 229 (SC—industrial AR).
67a. Baer, 22 Ottawa L Rev 389 (1990).
68. [1987] 1 SCR 2; Stuesser, 13 Can Bus LJ 227 (1987–8); Wolffe, 1989 SLT 103.
68a. The insured turned his business into a company, of which he was the sole shareholder and director, but retained insurance in his own name rather than that of the company.

requiring disclosure[69]; that the rule of indemnity was better served[70] by a notion of interest wider than the rule in *Macaura*. Further, the court thought[71] that the *Macaura* rule was too restrictive of legitimate insurance; that, for example, it was hard to justify a distinction between insurance against loss of income caused by illness, which is allowed, and loss of income caused by destruction of the employer's workplace, which is not. In conclusion, the court rejected the requirement of legal or equitable relation made by *Macaura*.

In the United States the early law[72] was like that in England. But in 1898 the Supreme Court of Massachusetts took a different position in *Hayes v Milford Mutual Fire Ins Co*.[73] The claimant obtained an exclusive agency for a small insurance company, the Atlas, to be remunerated by an agreed percentage of its premiums and profits. He took out insurance in respect of his profits under the contract of agency, the insured event being a specified level of fire losses for which the Atlas should be liable. The court held that the claimant had an insurable interest in the property insured with the Atlas. "As, in estimating the net profits [of the Atlas] losses were to be deducted, the plaintiff would have benefited by the continued existence of the property insured by the Atlas Insurance Co, and would have been injured by its destruction."[74] Since then most states have based their rule on economic interest alone.[75] Legal or equitable relation to subject-matter is relevant only to the extent that it reveals the insured's economic interest in subject-matter.[76] In California, for example, "Every interest in property, or any interest in relation thereto, or liability in respect thereof, of such a nature that a contemplated peril might directly damnify the insured, is an insurable interest."[77] From the language of the cases,[78] as well as prominent textbooks,[79] it is clear that, while a legal or equitable relation is commonly found in practice, in law it is not required.

4-4 THE TIME OF INTEREST

In marine insurance the insured must have an insurable interest at the time of the loss.[80] If so, it matters not that he had no interest at the time of contract or that since

69. pp 16, 24. Indeed the opportunity and hence temptation to destroy property may be greater in one who does have a legal or equitable relation to the property: p 25.

70. p 24.

71. p 17.

72. In *Farmers' Mutual Ins Co v New Holland Turnpike Rd Co*, 15 Atl 563 (1888) the claimant owned the road on each side of a bridge owned by the county. The claimant insured the bridge against fire. When fire occurred it claimed loss of revenue from the roads. The claim failed on the basis that the claimant had no insurable interest in the bridge.

73. 49 NE 754 (1898).

74. pp 755–756.

75. 68 Va L Rev 640 (1982).

76. *Ibid* p 659.

77. Cal Ins Code, section 281.

78. For example *Royal Ins Co v Sisters of the Presentation*, 430 F 2d 759 (9 Cir, 1970—fire); note 1971 Duke L J 479. In *American Indemnity Co v Southern Missionary College*, 260 SW 2d 269 (Tenn, 1953—burglary) a parent company was held to have an insurable interest in the property of its subsidiary.

79. For example, 44 CJS No 180. See also Hollman, "The Doctrine of Insurable Interest" [1978] Ins L J 160, 162.

80. MIA, section 6(1); the sub-section continues: "Provided that where the subject-matter is insured, 'lost or not lost,' the insured may recover although he may not have acquired his interest until after the loss unless at the time of effecting the contract of insurance the insured was aware of the loss, and the insurer was not."

the time of the loss his interest has ceased.[81] This rule probably applies to other kinds of indemnity insurance,[82] with two qualifications. First, in all other kinds of insurance, at the time of making the contract of insurance the person making it must have had a reasonable expectation of acquiring an interest. Second, in the case of insurance of real property, it is argued that statute requires that an interest also exist at the date of the policy.[83]

The general rule is said[84] to be because, first, businessmen need to arrange cover before their interest has matured. Second, by comparison with the (time of contract) rule for life insurance, property insurance being a contract of indemnity, it is right to focus on the moment of loss; but there is an element of circularity in this, for the contract is one of indemnity partly because of the requirement of interest. More important is whether requiring interest at the moment of loss best serves the public policy behind the interest rule, while minimising the consequent restriction on freedom of contract.

4-4A Land and Buildings

Most of the rules about interest in property apply not only to personal property but also to real property. However, the view is held that, in the case of real property, there are certain differences because, it is argued, real property is affected by the Life Assurance Act 1774.

Section 1 of the Act outlaws life insurance by persons lacking insurable interest or by way of gaming or wagering. Section 2 outlaws "policies on the life or lives of any person or persons, *or other event or events*,"[85] unless the policy mentions "the person or persons or names interested therein, or for whose use, benefit, or on whose account such policy is made or underwrote". Hence interest must appear at the time of the policy. Section 3 provides that the insured can recover from the insurer only the value of his own interest; he cannot recover the full value of the loss and hold any excess on trust for others. Section 4 excludes from the operation of the Act insurance on "ships, goods or merchandise".

The Act was passed at a time that knew not only life and marine insurance but also fire insurance. Hence, it is argued,[86] as section 4 does not exclude (fire) insurance on buildings, it must be affected by section 2 and section 3. In particular, if by reason of

The same rule is found in the USA: *Hooper* v *Robinson*, 98 US 528 (1879—cargo); *Ruby SS Corp* v *American Merchant Marine Ins Co*, 231 NYS 503, 509 (1928—hull), affirmed 166 NE 329 (1929); *The John Russell*, 68 F 2d 901 (2 Cir, 1934—cargo). Generally see Vukowich, "Insurable Interest: When it must Exist in Property and Life Ins", 7 Willamette LJ 1 (1971).

81. *Sparkes* v *Marshall* (1836) 2 Bing NC 761, 776 *per* Tindal CJ (cargo).

Cf Cal Ins Code, section 286; "An interest in property insured must exist when the insurance takes effect, and when the loss occurs, but need not exist in the meantime."

82. *Howard* v *Lancashire Ins Co* (1885) 11 SCR 92 (goods).

83. See below, 4-4A.

84. Keeton, section 3.3(c).

85. Emphasis added.

86. MacGillivray (7th ed), No 151; Birds, pp 46 ff. *Cf* Ivamy, *Fire*, p 180 who considers the question undecided but argues (pp 183 ff) strongly against that view. Also in the latter sense Halsbury, *Statutes*, 3rd ed, Vol 17, p 827; and Evans, 14 Melbourne U L Rev 265 (1983).

section 2 the parties must be mentioned in the policy as having an interest, i.e., an interest at the time of the contract, this requires an interest then, in lieu[87] or as well[88] as an interest at the time of loss.

Against the application of the Act to fire insurance it may be said, first, that the purposes of the interest rule are achieved by requiring an interest at the time of the loss, without regard to the time of the contract. Second, the title and short title[89] of the Act refer only to life insurance. Third, the Act is unworkable in the case of fire insurance on buildings and it is believed to be widely ignored in that context.[90] Moreover, the application of the Act to fire insurance on buildings was rejected by the Court of Appeal in *Rowlands (Mark) Ltd* v *Berni Inns Ltd* in which Kerr LJ said[91] that

"A literal application of the language of section 2 would create havoc in much of our insurance law, . . . [T]his ancient statute was not intended to apply, and does not apply, to indemnity insurance, but only to insurances which provide for the payment of a specified sum upon the happening of an insured event."

For the application of the Act it has been said[92] that primacy must be given to the clear words of the statute; it is difficult to explain the reference to "other event or events" without including fire insurance on buildings. Indeed, Kerr LJ (above) noted that although "obviously directed primarily to life insurance, the words 'or other event or events' admittedly widen its scope". However, it remains curious that such an important question has not been raised in the courts sufficiently clearly or often for the matter to be put beyond doubt and this lends force to the view of Ivamy[93] that, whatever the literal meaning of the Act, the practice of underwriters has passed it silently by with the tacit accord of the courts.[94] The danger of requiring interest at the time of the contract is that the prudent house buyer may contract insurance too soon and 20 days or 20 years later, when the house is burned down, find that he is not covered.[95]

4–4B Contingent Interests

It is said that a contingent interest can be insured, while a mere expectation of benefit cannot.[96] An estate, interest, right, liability or obligation is said to be contingent when

---

87. MacGillivray, No 24.

88. In this sense *Bank of New South Wales* v *North British & Mercantile Ins Co* (1881) 2 NSWLR 239, 244 (fire, buildings); *Caldwell* v *Stadacona Fire & Life Ins Co* (1883) 11 SCR 212 (fire). Also, *Keefer* v *Phoenix Ins Co* (1901) 31 SCR 144 (fire); *Caledonian Ins Co* v *Montreal Trust Co* [1932] SCR 581, 588 *per* Lamont J (fire).

In the USA the rule for insurance on buildings varies from state to state. The English rule is found in the law of Missouri: *Dupeck* v *Union Ins Co of America*, 216 F Supp 487 (D Mo, 1962—fire); and Alabama: *Providence Washington Ins Co* v *Stanley*, 403 F 2d 844 (5 Cir, 1968—fire). However in New York, for example, it is enough that the insured had an interest at the time of loss: *Ins Co of North America* v *Seaboard Homes Inc*, 273 NYS 2d 470 (1965—fire).

89. "An Act for regulating Insurances upon Lives and for prohibiting all such insurances except in cases where the Persons insuring shall have an interest in the Life or Death of the Persons insured."

90. Ivamy, *Fire*, p 183.

91. [1985] 3 WLR 964, 974. *Cf Re King* [1963] Ch 459 (CA—fire). The *Rowlands* view was preferred in *Siu* v *Eastern Ins Co Ltd*, *The Times*, 16 December 1993 (PC—liability).

92. MacGillivray (7th ed), No 151. See also *Re King* 485 *per* Lord Denning MR; *Sadlers' Co* v *Badcock* (1743) 26 ER 733, 756 *per* Lord Hardwicke LC. USA: see Vukowich, 7 Willamette LJ 1, 12 ff.

93. *Loc cit.*

94. See, as a possible example, *Mumford Hotels Ltd* v *Wheeler* [1964] Ch 117.

95. *Gentry* v *Hanover Ins Co*, 284 F Supp 626 (WD Ark 1966—fire); see also *Lititz Mutual Co* v *Lengacher*, 248 F 2d 850 (7 Cir, 1957—fire).

96. *Knox* v *Wood* (1808) 1 Camp 543, 545 *per* Lord Ellenborough CJ; *Stirling* v *Vaughan* (1809) 11 East 619, 628 *per* Lord Ellenborough CJ (hull); MacGillivray, No 49.

its existence depends on an uncertain event. If a contingent interest is an insurable interest which becomes actual, when the contingency occurs, can it be anything of consequence in law before that? Baron Bramwell observed that a contingent interest is no interest at all.[97] It is hard[98] to make sense of the cases. It may be that contingent interest has become shorthand for an insurable interest based on an immediate legal right the enjoyment of which was contingent on something else, often the performance of reciprocal duties by the insured.[99] The leading situations in which the cases find a contingent interest that is insurable are the right to profit and the right to freight; in each case there is an immediate right, albeit one which may not be enforced until the insured has performed his own duties. These common situations are discussed in greater detail below. As for a mere expectancy, the leading case is *Lucena* v *Craufurd*.

In *Lucena* v *Craufurd*[100] Dutch ships and cargo which had been seized and sent back to England were partly or wholly lost on the way. Commissioners, who had insured the ships, had power to deal with the ships on their arrival, dependent, however, on a triple contingency: that the ships came "into port, and his majesty's orders did not intervene to prevent their being brought in, or hostilities did not intervene to prevent their being brought in, or to change the character of the owners."[101] The House of Lords held that the Commissioners did not have an insurable interest. Lord Eldon said[102] that their expectation, "though founded upon the highest probability, was not interest . . . That which was wholly in the crown, and which it was in the power of his majesty to give or withhold, could not belong to the captors, so as to create *any right in* them."

4–5 INSURABLE INTEREST: CASES

The rule of English law, that the insured must stand in a legal or equitable relation to the subject-matter of his insurance (above 4–3B), is a rule with neither firm roots nor clear aspirations. But rule it is and to consider its impact one can but collect the cases which have satisfied the courts.

97. *Anderson* v *Morice* (1875) LR 10 CP 609, 623. In this sense Megarry & Wade, *Real Property* (5th ed), p 231.

98. I am consoled to find that Arnould, No 334, agrees.

99. Arnould, No 334, suggests that a person who has sold and parted with goods has an insurable interest in the goods contingent on rejection of the goods (or documents relating to them) by the buyer. It seems, however, that he has no insurable interest prior to rejection or stoppage in transit (see below, 4–5G5).

100. (1806) 2 Bos & Pul (NR) 269. See also *Routh* v *Thompson* (1809) 11 East 428: a policy was taken on a captured ship being sent back to England but lost *en route*. As regards interest it was contended that the captors who had insured her "had a well-grounded expectation, warranted by the practice of the Crown in similar cases, that the ship and freight, had there been no loss, would have been granted to them." Lord Ellenborough CJ stressed (p 432) that it was clear that "they had no vested right; they could demand nothing of the Crown". The court held that they had no interest.

101. p 319 *per* Lord Eldon.

102. p 323 (italics supplied). They had no legal or equitable right or duty in respect of the property prior to arrival. *Cf* the insurance of profit: below, 4–5N.

4–5A Ownership

The person who has the legal ownership of property has an insurable interest in that property,[103] even if the insured's title is defeasible.[103a] Such persons include a co-owner[104]; and a tenant for life,[105] even though the value of his interest is less than the value of the property.[106] The purchaser of stolen property, is a special case.[107]

4–5B Trust

"A trustee has a legal interest in the thing, and may therefore insure"[108] all the trust property,[109] without declaring to the insurer the nature of his interest as trustee.[110] This includes the executor of an estate; moreover, although probate "is necessary to complete his title; yet before probate he has title sufficient to enable him to insure."[111] The economic interest of the trustee lies in his desire to avoid liability for breach of trust. The beneficiary under a trust has an equitable interest in the trust property and thus he too has an insurable interest in it.[112]

4–5C Receivership

A legal interest sufficient for an insurable interest is found in the receiver in bankruptcy.[113] His duty is "to take care that the property is preserved so far as it reasonably may be for the benefit of all whom it may concern",[114] and thus to use funds in his hands to protect property for which he is responsible against normal risks, such as fire. The bankrupt retains an insurable interest in property still in his possession[115] by virtue of his possession: below, 4–5H.

---

103. *Joyce* v *Swann* (1864) 17 CB (NS) 84 (cargo). *Howard Fire Ins Co* v *Chase*, 72 US 509 (1867—fire); *Germania Fire Ins Co* v *Thompson*, 95 US 547 (1877—fire); *The Sidney*, 23 F 88 (SD NY, 1885—cargo); *Liss* v *US Fidelity & Guarantee Co*, 169 NYS 1027 (1918—theft). Cf *Simon* v *Travelers Ins Co*, 378 NYS 2d 870 (1975—motor).

103a. For example, the transferee under a transfer to defraud transferor's creditors has an insurable interest: *Canadian Credit Men's Assn* v *Stuyvesant Ins Co* (1916) 26 DLR 314 (Man—fire). See also *Re Waters*, 93 F 2d 196 (5 Cir, 1937—fire).

104. *Providence Washington Ins Co* v *Stanley*, 403 F 2d 844 (5 Cir, 1968—fire).

105. *Caldwell* v *Stadacona Fire & Life Ins Co* (1883) 11 SCR 212, 227–229 per Ritchie CJ.

106. *Castellain* v *Preston* (1883) 11 QBD 380, 400 per Bowen LJ (CA—fire); cf *Re Bladon* [1911] 2 Ch 350, 354, *per* Neville J. The extent to which the tenant for life insures is a question of construction; there is a presumption that the tenant for life, who is not obliged to insure the property but nonetheless does so, insures only for his own benefit and to the extent of his own interest: *Gaussen* v *Whatman* (1905) 93 LT 101 (fire).

107. See below, 4–5H.

108. *Lucena* v *Craufurd* (1806) 2 B & PNR 269, 324 per Lord Eldon. See also *Rhind* v *Wilkinson* (1810) 2 Taunt 237 (hull). *Babson* v *Thomaston Mutual Fire Ins Co*, 2 F Cas No 704 (Me 1874—fire); *Young* v *Union Ins Co*, 24 F 279 (D Ill, 1885—hull).

109. *Parry* v *Ashley* (1829) 3 Sim 99; *Re Betty* [1899] 1 Ch 821.

110. *Howard Fire Ins Co* v *Chase*, 72 US 509 (1867—fire), unless, of course, the nature of his interest is material to the risk and must therefore be disclosed.

111. *Stirling* v *Vaughan* (1809) 11 East 619, 629 per Lord Ellenborough CJ (hull). *Baird* v *Fidelity–Phenix Fire Ins Co*, 162 SW 2d 384 (Tenn, 1942—fire).

112. *Universal Ins Co* v *Steinbach*, 170 F 2d 303 (9 Cir, 1948—hull).

113. *Caledonian Ins Co* v *Montreal Trust Co* [1932] SCR 581, 588 per Lamont J (fire). *Thompson* v *Phenix Ins Co*, 136 US 287 (1890—fire); *Imperial Assurance Co* v *Livingston*, 49 F 2d 745 (8 Cir, 1931—fire). Cf *Cabaud* v *Federal Ins Co*, 37 F 2d 23 (2 Cir, 1930—hull).

114. *In re Newdigate Colliery Ltd* [1912] 1 Ch 468, 473 per Lord Cozens-Hardy MR (CA).

115. *Marks* v *Hamilton* (1852) 7 Ex 323, 324 per Pollock CB (fire).

4–5D Sale of Land

The seller of land, if he has conveyed it and been paid, has no further insurable interest in the land sold.[116] The owner of land, however, who has contracted to sell it but has yet to convey it, retains a legal interest sufficient to permit him to insure it[117]; the same is true of the owner prior to the conveyance of land subject to a compulsory purchase order[118] and of property while he is still responsible for it or may be entitled to retain it as a security for payment. The economic interest lies in his liability or in the utility of the property as a security for the price and as a possible source of interim revenue.

A bare legal title provides the legal relation required but there must still be an economic interest.[119] What can it be? In *Bank of New South Wales* v *North British & Mercantile Ins Co*[120] the majority of the Supreme Court of New South Wales held that, although the insured vendor retained a legal relation, on the premise that he had no duty with regard to the property, he had no economic interest[121] and so no insurable interest at the time of the fire. The minority, however, thought that an interest remained with the insured because "until the conveyance is executed the vendor is the only one who can bring ejectment; for the property is in him."[122]

Persons who have contracted to buy land have an equitable interest in the land prior to conveyance; they have therefore an insurable interest in the land.[123] The same holds for a buyer who has contracted to buy subject to a contingency or to the performance of a condition.[124]

4–5E Sale of Goods

4–5E1 Sellers of Goods

Sellers of goods have an insurable interest in goods, not only as owners [125] but also, in

---

116. *Ecclesiastical Commissioners* v *Royal Exchange Assurance Co* (1895) 11 TLR 476 (fire). *Vogel* v *Northern Assurance Co*, 219 F 2d 409 (3 Cir, 1955—fire); if the seller has been paid by the buyer, the seller holds the insurance money on trust for the buyer.

117. *Rayner* v *Preston* (1881) 18 Ch D 1 (CA—fire); *Castellain* v *Preston* (1883) 11 QBD 380, 385 *per* Brett LJ (CA—fire). *Vogel* (above); *Musselman* v *Mountain West Farm Bureau Mutual Ins Co*, 824 P 2d 271 (Mont, 1992—fire).

118. *Collingridge* v *Royal Exchange Assurance Corp* (1877) 3 QBD 173. *Chicago Title & Trust Co* v *United States Fidelity & Guarantee Co*, 376 F Supp 767 (DC Ill, 1973—fire).

119. *Commercial Union Assurance Group* v *Watson*, 91 DLR (3d) 434 (1979, SC Nova Scotia—fire); *cf* the contrary inference in *Castellain* v *Preston* (1883) 11 QBD 380, 385 *per* Brett LJ (CA—fire).

120. (1881) 2 NSWLR 239; the fire occurred between the time of contract and of conveyance.

121. p 245 and p 250.

122. p 248.

123. *Milan* v *Providence Washington Ins Co*, 227 F Supp 251 (DC La, 1964—windstorm); *Deck* v *Chautauqua County Patrons' Fire Relief Assn*, 343 NYS 2d 855 (1973—fire); *a fortiori* if the buyer is in possession of the property: *Smith* v *Jim Dandy Markets*, 172 F 2d 616 (9 Cir, 1949—fire); *Hartford Fire Ins Co* v *Cagle*, 249 F 2d 241 (10 Cir, 1957—fire).

124. *Norwich Union Fire Ins Cy. Ltd.* v *Traynor* [1972] NZLR 504 (CA—fire).

125. For example *Marks* v *Fireman's Fund Ins Co*, 175 F 222 (SD NY, 1910—cargo) affirmed 179 F 1020 (2 Cir, 1910).

some cases, as risk bearers[126] or as unpaid sellers having security rights,[127] until they have divested themselves of all rights and duties relating to the goods.[128] The unpaid seller who has parted with possession of the goods, although having a right to stop the goods in transit if the buyer is insolvent,[129] has no insurable interest in the goods, unless and until the right of stoppage is exercised.[130]

4–5E2 Buyers of Goods

He who has contracted to buy goods does not have an insurable interest in the goods,[131] unless he has them in his possession (below, 4–5H), or they are at his risk (below, 4–5J), or he has made an advance in respect of the purchase.

In *Clark* v *Scottish Imperial Ins Co*[132] a shipbuilding contract provided that the buyer would make advances in respect of the work and that he would be able to look to the ship, when completed, as security for these advances; until then, he would have neither property in nor lien on the shipbuilding. The buyer took fire insurance on the shipbuilding; prior to delivery the work was destroyed by fire. The insurer resisted his claim on the ground that he had no insurable interest in the work. The Supreme Court of Canada held that he had an insurable interest and was entitled to recover. Ritchie CJ[133] said that the contract

"was a specific appropriation of the specific property to the discharge of these particular advances . . . sufficient to bind the property in equity and clothe it with an equity in favor of the

126. *Reed* v *Cole* (1764) 3 Burr 1512 (mutual insurance on hull). See also below, 4–5J. *US* v *Lutz*, 295 F 2d 736 (5 Cir, 1961—fire). *Cf* UCC 2–501(2) whereby the seller of goods has an insurable interest "so long as title to or any security interest in the goods remains in him". Such a security interest includes reservation of title by means of conditional sale, controlling the bill of lading relating to the goods, as well as exercising a possessory lien. Note that, unlike in England, it is not enough to create insurable interest that the risk remains with the seller; on this, critically, see Stockton, 17 Vand L Rev 815, 819 (1964); also Condon [1986] LMCLQ 484, 493–494.

127. *Industrial Waxes* v *Brown*, 160 F Supp 230 (SD NY, 1957—cargo); *The Catts Co* v *Gulf Ins Co*, 723 F 2d 1494 (10 Cir, 1983—installation floater).

128. *Gillespie* v *Miller, Son & Co*, 1874 1 R (Ct Sess) 423. *Perryman Burns Coal Co Inc* v *Northwestern Fire & Marine Ins Co*, 223 NYS 559 (1927—cargo); *Dairyland Ins Co* v *Hawkins*, 292 F Supp 947 (D Iowa, 1968—motor); *York-Shipley Inc* v *Atlantic Mutual Ins Co*, 1973 AMC 584 (5 Cir, 1973—cargo).

129. Sale of Goods Act 1979, sections 44–46.

130. Arnould, No 369. *Contra* in the United States, Stockton, *loc cit*, p 824.

131. *Anderson* v *Morice* (1876) 1 App Cas 713 (cargo); the buyer had made no advance of price. *Idem* as regards an FOB buyer: *New South Wales Leather Co Pty Ltd* v *Vanguard Ins Co Ltd* (1991) 25 NSWLR 699 (cargo), criticised by Galbraith, (1993) 5 Ins LJ 177. Contrary dicta or inference have probably not survived this decision, for example, *Ebsworth* (below, note 134), p 637 *per* Brett J; *Stockdale* v *Dunlop* (1840) 6 M & W 224, 232 *per* Lord Abinger CB (cargo). In the United States the position is different. Under the UCC, section 2–501(1), the buyer of goods gets an insurable interest in those goods "by identification of existing goods to which the contract refers". Identification occurs, in the case of goods identified *in specie* at the time of contract, and in the case of unascertained goods, when the goods are shipped or otherwise designated as the goods to which the contract refers. See *Groban* v *S S Pegu*, 331 F Supp 883 (SD NY 1971), affirmed 456 F 2d 685 (2 Cir, 1972), following *Harrison* v *Fortlage*, 161 US 57 (1896), in which a buyer FOB had an insurable interest in identified tractor parts, *Cf Plata American Trading Inc* v *Lancashire*, 214 NYS 43 (1957—cargo).

132. (1879) 4 SCR 192.

133. p 205; *McQueen* v *Phoenix Mutual Fire Ins Co* (1880) 4 SCR 660, 689 *per* Henry J (fire). *Dunne* v *Phoenix Ins Co of Hartford*, 298 P 49, 51 (Cal, 1931—fire): "A purchaser of personal property has an insurable interest therein, although he has not *fully* paid the purchase price nor acquired title." (Italics supplied). See also *Ruby SS Corp* v *American Merchant Marine Ins Co*, 231 NYS 503, 509 (1928—hull) affirmed 166 NE 329 (1929).

plaintiff, and which gave [him] a privilege or claim on such property, an equitable lien in the nature of an equitable assignment for the advances made."

From *Ebsworth* v *Alliance Marine Ins Co*[134] it appears that the law in England is the same. The plaintiffs were agents who acted as consignees of cotton for resale in England from a seller in India. On one consignment the plaintiffs accepted a bill of exchange drawn on them by the seller who negotiated it with the Bank of India. Brett J observed[135] that

"This contract and position of affairs did not pass the legal property in the cotton to the plaintiffs, for that was still in the Bank of India. It did not give a present right of possession of the bill of lading, or even a right of possession of the cotton on arrival . . . the plaintiffs could not be held to be either the legal or equitable owners of the cotton."

Nonetheless he agreed that they had an insurable interest in the cotton. The Court of Common Pleas held that the plaintiffs could enforce a floating policy on the cotton. Bovill CJ said[136] that the "consignment immediately became an equitable security to the plaintiffs for the amount of their acceptance" and that they were entitled to insure in their own names the whole of the cotton.

Apart from such cases there are no decisions that the "mere" buyer has an insurable interest. It has, however, been suggested that a person with the right to possess goods has a right to sue the person in actual possession for negligence[137]; if so, it is not obvious why he should not also have a right to insure. Further, it has been stated that, although the "mere" buyer cannot insure the goods, he can insure the profit he hopes to make on the goods (below, 4–5N), even though the traditional view of that profit is the added value of the goods.[137a]

4–5F Leases

Lessor[138] and lessee[139] have an insurable interest in the property subject of the lease. This has rarely been disputed in England. Quite apart from any legal estate created by the lease or retained by the lessor, an interest may arise by virtue of possession of the property (below, 4–5H) or liability (below, 4–5K) for its fate. The lessee's interest has been held to extend to improvements made by the lessee to the property,[140] and, in the case of the lessee of one floor of a building, his liability insurance has been held to extend to parts of the building not demised to him under the lease.[140a].

---

134. (1873) LR 8 CP 596. See further, Arnould, No 378.
135. p 635.
136. pp 607–608.
137. *Transcontainer Express Ltd* v *Custodian Security Ltd* [1988] 1 Lloyd's Rep 128, 134–135 *per* Slade LJ (CA). Cf *The Aliakmon* [1986] AC 785; Clarke [1986] CLJ 382.
137a. *Ebsworth* (above) p 637 per Brett J. The view has been reiterated more recently by the Court of Appeal of New South Wales: *New South Wales Leather Co Pty Ltd* v *Vanguard Ins Co Ltd* (1991) 25 NSWLR 699 (cargo), discussed critically by Davies (1992) 5 Ins L J 159 and by Galbraith, (1993) 5 Ins L J 177, in which the basic rule against an insurable interest for the mere buyer was reaffirmed.
138. *Darrell* v *Tibbitts* (1880) 5 QBD 560 (CA—fire). *Southwestern Graphite Co* v *Fidelity & Guarantee Ins Corp*, 201 F 2d 553 (5 Cir, 1953—fire).
139. *Smith* v *Royal Ins Co Ltd*, 111 F 2d 667 (9 Cir, 1940—fire), *cert den* 311 US 676 (1940): a month to month tenancy constituting an interest in the property; *Seaboard Machinery Corp* v *Hanover Fire Ins Co*, 149 F Supp 362 (D Fla, 1957—fire), reversed on other grounds 256 F 2d 166 (1958).
140. *Modern Music Shop Inc* v *Concordia Fire Ins Co*, 226 NYS 630 (1927—fire); *Lumbermens Mutual Ins Co* v *Edminster*, 412 F 2d 351 (8 Cir, 1969—fire).
140a. In *Scottsdale Ins Co* v *Glick*, 397 SE 2d 105 (Va, 1990—liability) the insured tenant was held to have an insurable interest in other parts of the building, including a defective external staircase which collapsed with consequent injury to a fireman.

4–5G Security Interests

Persons interested in property as security may insure it; the security must be a valid security.[141]

4–5G1 Mortgage

The mortgagor of goods retains an insurable interest in the goods,[142] even if his debt is greater than the value of the goods insured.[143] The mortgagor of land retains an insurable interest in the property subject of the mortgage.[144] Even if he has sold the equity of redemption, the property right which most clearly justifies his insurable interest, the mortgagor will retain an insurable interest, if he also retains potential liability under the mortgage.[145]

As for the mortgagee, it is

"clear that a mortgagee of goods by assignment would be entitled to insure the whole of the goods in his own name, and to their full value, and, in case of loss, would be entitled to recover in his own name the full amount of the insurance, and would be a trustee for the mortgagor as to any surplus beyond the amount of his own debt."[146]

The same is true of the mortagee of land[147]; but his interest does not extend to revenue from the use or renting of the land, unless he is entitled to such revenue.[148] *Prima facie* the mortgagee insures to the extent of his debt,[149] but if allowed by the policy, he may insure the full value of the property.

If the property is damaged, the mortgagee may enforce his insurance, even though the mortgagor remains his debtor and is solvent,[150] and even though the property insured (or any other security he has)[151] remains sufficiently valuable to secure his debt: the damage has made it less a property and thus less a security: a person insuring as mortgagee insures not his debt but his security.[152] "The undertaking is that the property shall not suffer loss . . . ; that is, in effect, that its capacity to pay the mort-

---

141. For example, invalid hypothecation of a ship does not create an insurable interest in the ship for the grantee: *Stainbank* v *Fenning* (1851) 11 CB 51; *Stainbank* v *Shepard* (1853) 13 CB 418.

142. *Irving* v *Richardson* (1831) 2 B & Ad 193. MIA, section 14(1).

143. *Southwestern Graphite Co* v *Fidelity & Guarantee Ins Corp*, 201 F 2d 553 (5 Cir, 1953—fire); *Meyers* v *Norwich Union Fire Ins Sy Ltd*, 262 NYS 2d 579 (1965—fire); *White* v *Empire Mutual Ins Co*, 299 NYS 2d 998 (1969—motor).

144. *Alston* v *Campbell* (1779) 4 Bro PC 476 (HL); *Smith* v *Lascelles* (1788) 2 TR 187; *Hutchinson* v *Wright* (1858) 25 Beav 444; *Provincial Ins Co of Canada* v *Leduc* (1874) LR 6 PC 224, 244 *per* Sir Barnes Peacock. *Ottawa Agricultural Ins Co* v *Sheridan* (1880) 5 SCR 157. *Carpenter* v *Providence Washington Insurance Co*, 16 Pet 495 (SC, USA, 1842); *Royal Ins Co of Liverpool* v *Stinson*, 103 US 25 (1881—fire).

145. See below, 4–5K.

146. *Ebsworth* v *Alliance Marine Ins Co* (1873) LR 8 CP 596, 608 *per* Bovill CJ (cargo); *Samuel & Co* v *Dumas* [1924] AC 431, 444 *per* Viscount Cave (hull). MIA, section 14(1). *Cassa Maritima* v *Phoenix Ins Co*, 29 NE 962 (NY 1892—hull); *Factoring & Discount Inc* v *Central Mutual Ins Co*, 125 F Supp 627 (SD NY, 1954—motor), affirmed 216 F 2d 751 (2 Cir, 1954).

147. *Idem* concerning an heritable security on land under the law of Scotland: *Westminster Fire Office* v *Glasgow Provident Investment Sy* (1888) 13 App Cas 699.

Carpenter v *Providence Washington Ins Co*, 16 Pet. 495 (USA, 1842). The same is true of an assignee from the mortgagee: *International Trust Co* v *Norwich Union Fire Ins Sy*, 71 F 81 (8 Cir, 1895—fire); *Kelly* v *Commercial Union Ins Co*, 709 F 2d 973 (5 Cir, 1983—fire).

148. *Westminster Fire Office* v *Glasgow Provident Investment Sy* (1888) 13 App Cas 699.

149. *Royal Ins Co Ltd* v *Mylius* (1926) 38 CLR 477, 490 *per* Isaacs J (HCA—fire).

150. *Ibid*, 489 *per* Isaacs J (HCA—fire).

151. *Kent* v *Aetna Ins Co*, 82 NYS 817 (1903—fire).

152. *Mylius* (above), *loc cit*.

gage debt shall not be diminished."[153] The result is that, if there are several mort-gagees who have each insured their respective interest in a single property, which is later destroyed, the aggregate amount payable by the insurers may be greater than the value of the property, unless the insurers can and do elect to reinstate.[154] The mort-gagee's interest as mortgagee usually terminates on foreclosure and sale of the prop-erty mortgaged.[155]

Mortgagees commonly seek to secure themselves by requiring the assignment of the mortgagor's insurance. As assignees they lose protection, if for example the insurance was obtained by misrepresentation by the insured. Against this kind of threat a mort-gagee may take another policy[156] to cover the mortgagee interest, that is, loss that cannot be recovered under the policy assigned.

4–5G2 Liens and Rights of Arrest

It is generally agreed that a person with a lien on property has an insurable interest in that property.[157] More controversial is the decision in *Moran* v *Uzielli*[158] that the plaintiff, who insured a ship which was the only substantial asset of his debtor, had an insurable interest in the ship, not as creditor, but as one having a statutory right to arrest the ship in respect of his debt.

The decision has been criticised by Arnould,[159] first, because "it can hardly be maintained that a person who, if he begins an action *in rem*, will have a right to arrest, stands thereby in any 'legal or equitable relation' to the property." Secondly, it is objected that "the result would seem to be that every judgment creditor would have an insurable interest in all the property of his debtor which was capable of being taken in execution." A short response might be, why not? The answer to this question turns on the position of the creditor (below, 4–5M).

4–5G3 Pledge

In the case of a pledge of goods, the pledgor has an insurable interest [160] in view of his general property in the goods. The pledgee has an interest not only because of his pos-session (below, 4–5H) but also because he is liable for the safety of the property pledged (4–5K).

---

153. *Excelsior Fire Ins Co* v *Royal Ins Co of Liverpool* (1873) 55 NY 343, 359, cited with approval in *Mylius* (above), *loc cit*.
154. *Westminster Fire Office* v *Glasgow Provident Investment Sy* (1888) 13 App Cas 699 (fire).
155. *Westchester Fire Ins Co* v *Norfolk Building & Loan Association*, 14 F 2d 524 (8 Cir, 1926—fire); *Whitestone Savings & Loan Assn* v *Allstate Ins Co*, 321 NYS 2d 862 (1971—fire). *Cf Equitable Life Assur-ance Sy of the United States* v *Great Atlantic Ins Co*, 330 NYS 2d 840 (1972).
156. For example the Institute Mortgagees Interest Clauses Hulls for use with the Marine Policy form. Such policies were considered in *The Captain Panagos DP* [1985] 1 Lloyd's Rep 625; *The Alexion Hope* [1987] 1 Lloyd's Rep 60.
157. USA: (a) Possessory lien: *Russel* v *Union Ins Co*, 21 F Cas No 12, 146 (D Pa, 1806—cargo); *Great Lakes Transit Corp* v *Interstate SS Co*, 301 US 646 (1937). (b) Maritime lien: *Hooper* v *Robinson*, 98 US 528 (1879—hull); *F B Hall & Co Inc* v *Jefferson Ins Co*, 279 F 892 (SD NY, 1921—hull); *Eagle Star & British Dominions* v *Tadlock*, 22 F Supp 545 (D Cal, 1938—hull). (c) Builders' and contractors' lien in respect of their work: *In re San Joaquim Packing Co*, 295 F 311 (9 Cir, 1924—fire) cert den 265 US 583; *Cardinal* v *Mercury Ins Co*, 273 NYS 487 (1934—fire); *Atlantic Ins Co* v *Massey*, 381 F 2d 520 (10 Cir, 1967—builders' risks); the existence of the lien is subject to the terms of the building contract: *Ins Co of North America* v *Seaboard Homes Inc*, 273 NYS 470 (1965—fire).
158. [1905] 2 KB 555.
159. No 337.
160. *Hibbert* v *Carter* (1787) 1 TR 745.

4–5G4 Equitable Assignment

In *Wilson* v *Martin* Pollock CB said[161] that "a bill is drawn which distinctly pledges the freight. That operated as an equitable assignment of the freight and consequently the plaintiffs [acceptors] had an interest in it to the extent of their disbursements."

4–5G5 Stoppage in Transit

The seller, who has parted with ownership and possession of goods, has a right to stop the goods in transit, if the buyer has not paid him and becomes insolvent.[162] When the right is exercised, the seller resumes possession and has an insurable interest (below, 4–5H); however, until then his rights are contingent and he has no insurable interest in the goods.[163]

4–5H Possession

Possession of property,[164] including constructive possession,[165] gives an insurable interest in that property, even though someone else has a better right to the property[166] and even though the possession is wrongful.[167] The pattern was set by Lord Kenyon CJ in a case about ships captured as prize[168]:

"they had the possession of the property insured, and from that possession, certain rights and duties resulted. If it were a legal capture, the captors were entitled; if the capture were improperly made, they were liable to be called to account in the Court of Admiralty, and where they might be amerced in damages and costs. They had therefore a right to insure themselves, against the decision that might have loaded them with damages and costs."

161. (1856) 11 Ex 684, 695.
162. Sale of Goods Act 1979, sections 44 ff.
163. See above, 5E. *York-Shipley Inc* v *Atlantic Mutual Ins Co*, 474 F 2d 8 (5 Cir, 1973—cargo). *Cf Kalemian* v *Liberty Mutual Fire Ins Co*, 1963 AMC 1730.
164. *The Moonacre* [1992] 2 Lloyd's Rep 501, 512 per Deputy Judge Colman, QC, (yacht). However, in so far as this passage suggests that the use and enjoyment of the yacht was essential to a legal interest, this is to confuse the requirement of legal relation with that of economic interest. For legal relation, possession alone is enough. See also *MacDonald* v *Canadian Accident & Fire Assurance Co* (1978) 77 DLR (3d) 746 (NS—fire)—occupation of premises held in the name of the insured's wife.
165. *The Colonial Ins Co of New Zealand* v *Adelaide Marine Ins Co* (1886) 12 App Cas 128 (cargo).
Cf Curacao Trading Co Inc v *Federal Ins Co*, 50 F Supp 441 (SD NY, 1942—cargo), affirmed 137 F 2d 911 (2 Cir, 1943), *cert den* 321 US 765 (1944).
166. *Marks* v *Hamilton* (1852) 7 Ex 323 (fire). *Hudson* v *Glen Falls Ins Co*, 112 NE 728 (NY, 1916—fire); *Scarola* v *INA*, 340 NYS 2d 630 (1972—motor). Tenants in possession: *Modern Music Shop Inc* v *Concordia Fire Ins Co*, 226 NYS 630 (1927—fire); *Lumbermen's Mutual Ins Co* v *Edminster*, 412 F 2d 351 (8 Cir, 1969—fire); even though the tenancy is terminable by notice: *Commercial Union Assurance Co* v *Jass*, 36 F 2d 9 (5 Cir, 1929—fire). Finders: *Reif* v *INA*, 223 NYS 2d 101 (1961). Not trespassers and squatters: *Fidelity Phenix Fire Ins Co* v *Raper*, 6 So 2d 513 (Ala, 1941—fire), but the court said (p 515) that, if the trespasser made improvements, this might give rise to an insurable interest to the extent of any consequent lien.
167. *Lucena* v *Craufurd* (1806) 2 B & P (NR) 269, 323 *per* Lord Eldon; *Stirling* v *Vaughan* (1809) 11 East 619, 628 *per* Lord Ellenborough CJ; *Goulstone* v *The Royal Ins Co* (1858) 1 F & F 276 (fire).
USA *contra*: *Fidelity* v *Raper*, 6 So 2d 513 (Ala, 1941—fire); *Hartford Fire Ins Co* v *Carter*, 196 F 2d 992 (10 Cir, 1952—fire); *Friscia* v *Safeguard Ins Co*, 293 NYS 2d 695 (1968—motor). *Cf* also Brown & Menezes, 4:2:7. Jurisdictions that do not require a legal relation enforce the insurance of stolen property by a *bona fide* purchaser: *Castle Cars Inc* v *US Fire Ins Co*, 273 SE (2d) 793 (Va, 1981—motor); there was an economic interest measured by the purchase price; see further 68 Va L Rev 651 (1982).
168. *Boehm* v *Bell* (1799) 8 TR 154, 161 (hull). *Cf Routh* v *Thompson* (1809) 11 East 428.

It has been said that, if the possession is wrongful, there is an insurable interest only if the possession is innocent. If a villain kidnaps a champion horse and demands a ransom, courts may be understandably reluctant to enforce the villain's insurance on the horse. But one persons's possession may be more wrongful than another's, and it is better to explain the court's reaction by reference to general rules of public policy about illegal contracts,[169] than by the more shadowy public policy behind the rule of insurable interest: above, 4–2. In the case of the *bona fide* purchaser of stolen property non-enforcement of insurance has no deterrent value, as *ex hypothesi* he does not know that the property is stolen; moreover, there is little evidence that the possibility of non-enforcement will make him more careful about what he buys.[170]

4–5H1 The Right to Possess

Usually the right to possess goods is found with other rights, such as ownership. A bare right to possess is unusual, but may be found in agents. Agents in possession lack an insurable interest, not because the right to possess does not provide the legal relation required by English law, but because they lack the economic interest also required by law. Thus in *Seagrave* v *Union Marine Ins Co*[171] it was held that the nominal consignee of goods and agent of the seller lacked insurable interest in the goods, because[172] "it must be an interest such that the peril would by its proximate effect cause damage to the insured". If the person with a right to possess does have an economic interest, it has been suggested that he also has a right to sue the person in actual possession for negligence[173]; if so, in principle he would appear also to have a right to insure.

4–5I Bailment

Many non-owners such as carriers or warehousemen have possession of property as bailees; there is no doubt that bailees have an insurable interest in the property. They have rights and duties in respect of the property, in particular, they may be liable if the property is lost or destroyed.

4–5I1 Carriage and Warehousing

Commonly there is insurance of "stock in trade the property of the Insured or held by him in trust or on commission for which he is responsible". If this were always and only liability insurance, he could recover only in the event of his liability, but the courts have seen it differently.

---

169. *Cf Zinati* v *Canadian Universal Ins Co Ltd* (1984) 5 DLR (4th) 110; (1984) 12 DLR (4th) 766 (Ont—property); *Ardekany* v *Dominion of Canada General Ins Co* (1986) 32 DLR (4th) 23 (BC—theft).
170. 68 Va L Rev 640, 667 (1982).
171. (1866) LR 1 CP 305 (cargo).
172. p 320 *per* Willes J. See also *Ebsworth* v *Alliance Marine Ins Co* (1873) LR 8 CP 596, 622 *per* Bovill CJ (cargo).
173. *Transcontainer Express Ltd* v *Custodian Security Ltd* [1988] 1 Lloyd's Rep 128, 134–135 *per* Slade LJ (CA). *Cf The Aliakmon* [1986] AC 785; Clarke [1986] CLJ 382.

In *Tomlinson* v *Hepburn*[174] the insured carried cigarettes for the maker and also insured them. Without fault or liability on the part of the insured a consignment was stolen. The insurer resisted the claim on the ground that such insurance was a contract of indemnity and that the insured, having incurred no liability, had therefore suffered no loss. The House of Lords decided for the carrier: as a matter of construction the insurance was not of liability but of goods; the carrier had an interest insuring the goods and could recover the full value, provided that the insurance monies over and above the amount of his own loss (in this case none) were held on trust for the maker.[175]

The carrier has an economic interest in the goods as a means of profit or as a means of loss. Generally, one cannot insure the means of one's profit (such as a supplier's factory) unless there is a legal relation, but that relation is found here in the bailment. It is commercially convenient,[176] although theoretically unorthodox,[177] to permit bailees to insure goods in their charge; such insurance is more easily and cheaply arranged by the bailee than by the goods' owner. Some of the convenience would be lost if enforcement required not only potential loss at the time of contract but actual personal loss at the time of the event insured against. What is convenient to some, however, may be surprising to others.

4–5I2 Construction Sites

In *Petrofina (UK) Ltd* v *Magnaload Ltd*[178] the insurers of damage to construction work on an oil refinery claimed to exercise rights in subrogation against sub-contractors on the site, allegedly responsible for the damage. However, the policy identified the insured as the "contractors and/or sub-contractors". If that included the defendants, they could not be sued by the insurer (below, 31–5D). That turned on whether the defendants had a sufficient insurable interest to contract the insurance for the whole site, even though as regards much of the property, including what was damaged, they were neither owners nor bailees.

174. [1966] AC 451. See also *Crowley* v *Cohen* (1832) 3 B & Ad 478; *Waters* v *Monarch Life Assurance* (1856) 5 El & Bl 870; *Stephens* v *Australasian Ins Co* (1872) LR 8 CP 18; *Hill* v *Scott* [1895] 2 QB 713 (CA); *Maurice* v *Goldsbrough Mort & Co* [1939] AC 452 (PC—cargo); *Transcontinental Underwriting Agency SRL* v *Grand Union Ins Co Ltd* [1987] 2 Lloyd's Rep 409 (re). *Cf North British & Mercantile Ins* v *Moffatt* (1871) LR 7 CP 25 where the wording of the policy precluded cover of goods owned by persons other than the insured.
  Phoenix Ins Co of Brooklyn v *Hamilton*, 14 Wall 504 (1872—fire); *Home Ins Co of New York* v *Baltimore Warehouse Co*, 93 US 527 (1876—fire); *The Sidney*, 23 F 88 (SD NY 1885—cargo); *California Ins Co* v *Union Compress Co*, 133 US 387 (1890—fire); *US* v *Lutz*, 295 F 2d 736 (5 Cir, 1961—fire); *Keystone Fabric Laminates Inc* v *Federal Ins Co*, 407 F 2d 1353 (3 Cir, 1969—fire); *Aetna Casualty & Surety Co* v *Brunswick Corp*, 437 F 2d 838 (10 Cir, 1971—fire); *Mechaber* v *Omaha Indemnity Co*, 341 NYS 2d 58 (1973—baggage insurance); *Omaha Property Co* v *Crosby*, 756 F Supp 1380, 1384 (D Mont, 1990—motor).
175. The policy would be illegal for gaming if the insured could retain the full amount of the claim above his own loss: [1966] AC 451, 472 *per* Lord Hodson. Also in this sense *Home Ins Co* v *Baltimore Warehouse Co*, 93 US 527 (1876).
176. *Waters* v *Monarch* (1856) 5 El & Bl 870; *Tomlinson* v *Hepburn* [1966] AC 451, 477 *per* Lord Pearce.
177. See below, 5–6.
178. [1983] 2 Lloyd's Rep 91. See the critical note by Birds: [1983] JBL 497: the policy defined the insured property as that for which the insured were responsible; thus, it is argued, the interest of any insured in property not in his possession or ownership was limited to that of potential liability. *Cf Commonwealth Construction Co Ltd* v *Imperial Oil Ltd* (1977) 69 DLR (3d) 558, 562–563 *per* De Grandpre J (Sup. Ct., Canada—contractors AR). *British Traders' Ins Co Ltd* v *Monson* (1964) 111 CLR 86, 93 (HCA—fire).

As a matter of construction, the judge found that the policy covered not only liability but also the whole of the property involved; that each insured was insured not only in respect of his own property but also that of the others on site.[179]

"In the case of a building or engineering contract, where numerous different sub-contractors may be engaged, there can be no doubt about the convenience from everybody's point of view, including . . . the insurers, of allowing the head contractor to take out a single policy covering the whole of the risk . . . Otherwise each sub-contractor would be compelled to take out his own separate policy. This would mean, at the very least, extra paperwork; at worst it could lead to overlapping claims and cross claims in the event of an accident. Furthermore . . . the cost of insuring his liability might in the case of a small sub-contractor, be uneconomic . . . I would hold that the position of a sub-contractor in relation to contract works is sufficiently similar to that of a bailee in relation to goods bailed to enable me to hold, by analogy, that he is entitled to insure the entire contract works, and in the event of a loss to recover the full value of those works in his own name."[180]

Accordingly the action by the insurer against the sub-contractors failed. Lest convenience be promoted at the expense of the public policy basis for the rule of insurable interest, the insured is required to hand over insurance money for loss that is not his loss. Decisions like this have considerable implications for any kind of collaborative activity, however, in more recent decisions, the *Petrofina* principle has not been applied.

In *Stone Vickers Ltd* v *Appledore Ferguson Shipbuilders Ltd*[180a] the principle in *Petrofina (UK) Ltd* v *Magnaload Ltd* was applied to a sub-contractor supplying parts to a shipbuilding yard, even though the sub-contractor was not employed to work[180b] in the shipyard but to fabricate parts (the propellor and ancillary equipment) on its own premises. The approach, said the judge,[180c] suggested by the reasoning in earlier decisions was to "ask whether the supplier of a part to be installed into the vessel or contract works under construction might be materially adversely affected by loss of or damage to the vessel or other works". As a supplier, notably a supplier who provided boilers, "might be liable for the resultant damage by fire or explosion not only to the boilers supplied but to other parts of the vessel before the delivery of the vessel", and as delivery did not normally occur until after successful trials at sea, the answer was affirmative. The exception would be the supplier of "some relatively trivial fittings which by no stretch of the imagination could endanger the whole vessel". The judge concluded that when it comes to "the supplier under a sub-contract of a major part of the vessel the failure of which may render that supplier liable for damage to the vessel beyond the mere replacement of the defective part I can see no material difference between the position of such supplier and that of the sub-contractor who is actively engaged in construction of the vessel. Both have a pervasive interest in the entire works". Perhaps this is true in some cases, however, in the particular case, there was

179. [1983] 2 Lloyd's Rep 91, 95.

180. pp 96–97 *per* Lloyd J by reference to the *Commonwealth Construction* case (above), where the court (De Grandpre J, p 563) said: "Thus all the parties whose joint efforts have one common goal, e.g., the completion of the construction, would be spared the necessity of fighting between themselves should an accident occur involving the possible responsibility of one of them." Does the same apply to a college, a hospital, a fairground, a harbour, a factory?

180a. [1991] 2 Lloyd's Rep. 288.

180b. Except as regards a service engineer employed by the sub-contractor to supervise installation of the propellor; this was not, the judge pointed out, essential to this decision, but it provided an additional ground.

180c. p 301 *per* Anthony Colman, QC.

insufficient evidence that the sub-contractor was intended to be insured under the particular policy and an appeal from the judge's decision was allowed.[180d]

Again, in *Canadian Pacific Ltd v Base–Security Services BC Ltd*,[180e] the *Petrofina* principle was not extended to a firm responsible for security on a construction site. The reason was that, under the insurance contract, "the 'insureds' are those persons without whose contribution to the project in its entirely the project itself could not be completed. That will for the most part be trades . . . [Only] those persons whose contributions are an integral and necessary part of the construction process itself are within the definition of 'Insured' in the policy and not those whose contributions are collateral to that process".[180f] However, Colman J rallied to the defence of principle in *NOW v Dol*,[180g] in which he rejected "the suggestion that there cannot as a matter of law be an insurable interest based merely on potential liability arising from the existence of a contract between the assured and the owner of property or from the assured's proximate physical relationship", such as that involved in work on the same site, to the property of others. This property can be the subject-matter not only of liability insurance but also of property insurance.

4–513 Gratuitous Bailment

Among gratuitous bailees, especially the householder, it has been suggested that he has no insurable interest in the goods bailed in the house.[181] But the correctness of this depends on the case. If the bailee acquires no direct benefit from the bailment and is under no legal liability in respect of the property bailed, he has no insurable interest.[182] But the modern law sees in bailment a legal relation coupled with economic interest either in the benefit of use or in liability for the property bailed.

In *Horsch*[183] the insured shared a house and barn owned by his wife, and the court said[184]:

"The possession and use of the house and barns was of the utmost importance to him in providing a support for himself and his family, and their destruction was substantially as disastrous to him in his endeavors (*sic*) to support himself and his family as though he had actual title . . . The actual possession and use of property is a valuable right."

In *Goulstone*[185] the husband had an insurable interest in furniture belonging to his wife and placed in the matrimonial home; his role as occupier of the premises gave rise

---

180d. [1992] 2 Lloyd's Rep. 578 (CA).

180e. (1991) 77 DLR (4th) 178 (CA BC—AR).

180f. p 185, by reference to the *Commonwealth Construction case* (above) and to *Consolidated–Bathurst Export Ltd v Mutual Boiler & Machinery Ins Co* (1981) 112 DLR (3d) 49.

180g. *National Oilwell (UK) Ltd v Davy Offshore Ltd* [1993] 2 Lloyd's Rep 582, 611 (builders' AR).

181. *Macaura v Northern Assurance Co* [1925] AC 619, 628 *per* Lord Buckmaster (fire).

182. *Tomlinson v Hepburn* [1966] AC 451, 480.

183. *Horsch v Dwelling House Ins Co*, 45 NW 945 (Wis, 1890—fire).

184. p 946; the decision was followed in *Kludt v German Mutual Fire Ins Co*, 140 NW 321 (Wisc, 1913—fire). See also *Dubuque Fire & Marine Ins Co v Union Compress & Warehouse Co*, 146 F Supp 482 (DC La, 1956—fire) and *National Security Fire & Casualty Co v Minchew*, 372 So 2d 327 (Ala, 1979—fire) in which a man, who was living with his ex-wife in a house owned by her, was held to have an insurable interest in the house.

Cf Mercantile Ins Co v The Orphan Boy, 17 F Cas No 9, 431 (D Ohio, 1878—hull) in which it was held that a man in control of a ship belonging to his wife had no insurable interest in the ship either as master (*cf* possession above, 4–5H) or as husband; no reasons were given.

185. *Goulstone v The Royal Ins Co* (1858) 1 F & F 276.

to both potential liability and legal relation. It says much about English law that a father's household insurance may extend to the bicycle of his student son, provided that the bicycle spends one or two days a year in the father's house. That is convenient for father and son but not for any accurate assessment of risk.

Cover of this kind extends to the gold bracelet that the insured's wife keeps in her jewellery case. If the insured does not possess the bracelet or share its use with his wife, insurable interest on his part cannot be based on possession or bailment, but on, for example, theoretical liability to his wife in case of fire damage. As to economic interest, it is not obvious that he suffers direct loss, if the bracelet is lost or stolen. It has been argued that, in so far as a spouse has a "right" to money from the other's estate under legislation ensuring a minimum family provision on death, that is a right in the other's property which is insurable in the other's lifetime. But it would be curious if I could insure my wife's jewellery against the contingency of non-provision next year, but not the jewellery of my debtor against non-payment of the debt next week (below, 4–5M). It is still more curious if the insurance extends not only to her jewellery but also to the clothing in her cupboard which may have gone to dust many years before their wearer. It is surely less contrived, although less convenient, to say that the householder has no insurable interest in the private posessions of other members of the house, but nonetheless may insure them, not in his own capacity but as agent.[186]

4–5J Risk

The person at whose risk goods are dealt with has an insurable interest in those goods.[187] Usually risk follows ownership, so that there is an insurable interest as owner. However, goods may be at the risk of the buyer before he owns them and he can insure them. The economic interest is obvious, that he will suffer loss if the property is damaged or destroyed.[188] The legal relation is found in the contract to buy, in particular, his promise to pay notwithstanding the loss or damage; this provides the element of certainty of loss apparently desired by the judges, and distinguishes the case from that of the "mere" buyer (above, 4–5E2).

The leading decisions are *Stock* v *Inglis* [189] and *Anderson* v *Morice*.[190] In the latter it was agreed, in the words of Lord Selborne,[191] that "if the rice was to be at the risk of the buyer during the time of its shipment at Rangoon, the plaintiff was entitled to recover" against the insurer. In cases like this it is usually the person who has the duty under the contract of sale to insure the goods who bears the risk; the duty to insure gives rise to the insurable interest.

---

186. In this sense *Price* v *United Pacific Casualty Ins Co*, 56 P 2d 116 (Or, 1936—burglary); *Commonwealth Ins Co of New York* v *Lacey*, 214 SW 2d 899 (Tex, 1948—jewellery floater).
187. *Reed* v *Cole* (1764) 3 Burr 1512 (hull); *Inglis* v *Stock* (1885) 10 App Cas 263 (cargo).
188. See e.g., Blackburn J in *Anderson* v *Morice* (1875) 10 CP 609, 615–616 (cargo).
189. *Inglis* v *Stock* (1885) 10 App Cas 263. In such cases risk usually passes on shipment, whereas ownership may pass then or later. See also *Grain Processing Corp* v *Continental Ins Co*, 726 F 2d 403 (8 Cir, 1984—cargo).
190. (1876) 1 App Cas 713: rice was put on board a ship in Rangoon for London. Before leaving port the ship and rice sank. The buyers' action against the insurer of the goods failed. The Court of Exchequer Chamber decided against the buyers because they had neither ownership nor risk. The House of Lords was evenly divided on whether ownership or risk had passed so the decision of the court below remained. The principle of law stated in the text was accepted.
191. p 746.

4–5K Liability

He who is liable mediately or immediately at law, *inter alia,* for loss or damage to property has an insurable interest in the property concerned. Hence the insurer, who is liable to the insured in the event of loss or damage to the property which is the subject-matter of the prime insurance,[192] and can reinsure. Apparently, any promise, the effect of which is the assumption of responsibility for property, creates an insurable interest in that property.

4–5K1 The Promise to Insure

In *Heckman* v *Isaac*[193] a single lease let property A for 16 years and property B for 5 years. A global rent was set at £120 for 5 years and £100 thereafter. The lessee promised to "keep the said premises insured from loss or damage by fire . . . in the sum of 2000 pounds". There was no provision to vary this duty after 5 years. The lessor brought an action for ejectment *inter alia* for breach of the covenant to insure and a strong Court of Queen's Bench held that the covenant to insure remained in full effect throughout the 16 year term of the lease. To the defendant lessee's argument that he had no insurable interest in the property B after 5 years, Crompton J replied[194] that "the covenant to insure would give him an interest".

This dictum might suggest that, if A makes a binding promise to B to insure property in which A had thitherto had no interest of any kind, his potential liability to B gives A an insurable interest in the property. But, if so, any line between insurance and wagers would be lost. A benevolent interest in property is not enough for an insurable interest in that property.[195] In *Heckman* the two properties were taken together: Blackburn J asked, "What is the impossibility of covenanting to keep up an insurance on two sets of premises during the time that the covenantor's interest in either set continues?" It was probably essential to the decision that the lessee had and continued to have an indisputable interest in one of them. If so, the case is best seen as a precursor of the collective insurance justified by convenience and upheld in *Petrofina* (above, 4–5I).

4–5K2 The Supplier's Warranty

If A were a shipbuilder and, as part of the sale of a vessel to B, he promised free repair of latent defects discovered within one year (a common term in shipbuilding contracts), that promise is part of the contract of sale. A can insure his liability to B, and,

---

192. *Mackenzie* v *Whitworth* (1875) 1 Ex D 36 (CA). A parent has no insurable interest in respect of the liability of children, unless the parent is liable for their acts or omissions: *Vandepitte* v *Preferred Accident Ins Corp of New York* [1933] AC 70, 80–81 *per* Lord Wright (motor). But *cf Petrofina* (above, 4–5I) and *Williams* v *Baltic Ins Assn of London Ltd* [1924] 2 KB 282, 290 *per* Roche J (motor).

USA: for example, a tugowner's liability in tort: *New York* v *United States*, 1976 AMC 2253 (SD NY, 1976); liability of a forwarding agent: *The Sidney*, 23 F 88 (SD NY, 1885—cargo), appeal dismissed 139 US 331 (1891); the liability of a carrier for cargo: *Great Lakes Transit Corp* v *Interstate SS Co*, 301 US 646 (1937).

193. (1862) 6 LT 383.

194. p 385. See also in this sense *Joyce* v *Swann* (1864) 17 CBNS 84, 104 *per* Willes J (cargo); *Castellain* v *Preston* (1883) 11 QBD 380, 400 *per* Bowen LJ (CA—fire). *Cf Petrofina* above, 4–5I.

195. *Prudential Staff Union* v *Hall* [1947] KB 685 (burglary): trade union had no insurable interest in its members' property.

as we have seen,[196] in some cases at least that same liability provides the insurable interest for insurance of the property itself. The same may be true of any supplier, who has ceased to own or possess the property supplied, if he remains liable for its condition.

In *Village of Constantine* v *Home Ins Co*[197] there was a conditional sale of generators to the Village under a contract whereby the seller was obliged to insure the goods against breakdown, which he did, and against damage, which he did not. After the sale contract was sold to a bank, but the breakdown insurance was not assigned, the generators broke down. The insurer pleaded that the insured had ceased to have an insurable interest in the generators. Although the insured had not warranted the condition of the generators, the court said[198] that patently the insured

"had a real interest in the continued existence and operation of the instant machinery. As of the time of the breakdown . . . he was still liable on his undertaking to procure damage insurance. In the event he had failed to do so . . . he will become liable to the Village of Constantine for the damage. While [the insured] had neither ownership interest in the property insured nor anything to gain from it, he clearly did have something to lose. Under Michigan law we believe this was sufficient to take this insurance out of the 'wagering contract' class."

4–5L Company Shareholders

In *Macaura* v *Northern Assurance Co*[199] the House of Lords held that a shareholder, lacking any legal or equitable interest in the company's property, had no insurable interest in that property. The reason given was that it would be hard to calculate the indemnity: "the extent of his insurable interest could only be measured by determining the extent to which his share in the ultimate distribution [of assets on a winding-up] would be diminished by the loss of the asset—a calculation almost impossible to make."[200]

This difficulty could be overcome by taking a valued policy.[201] In other cases it could be overcome by a little determination. In the case of a quoted company, reference could be made to the market price; if an unquoted company, the requirements of the Companies Acts, if observed, should ensure enough information to enable calculation by a determined court. This is the position in New York.[202] It is now also the position in Canada.[203]

---

196. Above, 4–5K.

197. 427 F 2d 1338 (6 Cir, 1970). See also *Prince* v *Royal Indemnity Co*, 541 F 2d 646 (7 Cir, 1976—fire) *cert* den 429 US 1094 (1977).

198. p 1340.

199. [1925] AC 619. It has been suggested in Canada that if a company becomes dormant by being removed from the register, the assets revert to the shareholders as creditors, who then have an insurable interest in the assets: *Zimmerman* v *St Paul Fire & Marine Insurance Co* (1967) 63 DLR (2d) 282, 285 (Sask—fire).

200. p 627 *per* Lord Buckmaster.

201. See *Wilson* v *Jones* (1867) LR 2 Ex 139.

202. *Riggs* v *Commercial Mutual Insurance Co*, 25 NE 1058, 1060 (NY, 1890—hull). Followed in *Feinman* v *Consolidated Mutual Insurance Co*, 155 NYS 2d 326 (1956—liability). Similar decisions in other States include *Providence Washington Insurance Co* v *Stanley*, 403 F 2d 844 (5 Cir, 1968—fire); *Oklahoma Morris Plan Co* v *Security Mutual Casualty Co*, 323 F Supp 1057 (D Mo, 1970—fidelity) affirmed 455 F 2d 1209 (8 Cir, 1972).

Cf Heindl-Evans Inc v *Reliance Insurance Co*, 1980 AMC 2823 holding that, in Virginia, a company has an insurable interest in a yacht owned and operated by principal shareholders, when the main purpose of the yacht was to entertain in relation to company business.

203. *Kosmopoulos* v *Constitution Ins Co* [1987] 1 SCR 2 (fire).

4–5M Debt[204]

Early statements suggested that a creditor had an insurable interest in any item of his debtor's property. In *Lucena* v *Craufurd*,[205] for example, Lawrence J said:

"Interest does not necessarily imply a right to the whole or the part of a thing, nor necessarily and exclusively that which may be the subject of privation, but the having some relation to, or concern in, the subject of the insurance; which relation or concern, by the happening of the perils insured against may be so affected as to produce a damage, detriment or prejudice to the person insuring. And where a man is so circumstanced with respect to matters exposed to certain risks or dangers as to have a moral certainty of advantage or benefit but for those risks or dangers, he may be interested in the safety of the thing. To be interested in the preservation of a thing is to be so circumstanced with respect to it as to have benefit from its existence, prejudice from its destruction."

This statement, though often quoted, has not been literally applied in England. In England the creditor does not have an insurable interest in his debtor's property[206] as such,[207] even if its loss would lead to the debtor's bankruptcy. Faced with the paradigmatic problem of the Merchant of Venice, the English creditor can neither have his debtor's flesh nor insure his property (though, curiously, he can insure his flesh). His only legal right is to the debt; the ship may sink, but the right survives.[208] In England the leading case is *Macaura* v *Northern Assurance Co Ltd*[209] and the reasons given are as follows.

First, Lord Buckmaster argued that, if the creditor had an insurable interest, "it would follow that any person would be at liberty to insure the furniture of his debtor".[210] And, one might ask, why not ? The perils of this liberty are less obvious today. An "effective curb on excessive insurance is the general ability of insurance carriers to decline risks, or insert protective clauses".[211] Moreover, the range of successful claims would be limited by the rule of proximate cause.[212]

Second, "the debt was not exposed to fire nor were the shares."[213] The "probability

---

204. Patterson & McIntyre, "Unsecured Creditor's Insurance", 31 Col L R 212 (1931).

205. (1806) 2 B & PNR 269, 302.

206. *Moran* v *Uzielli* [1905] 2 KB 555; the decision was approved in *Macaura* v *Northern Assurance* [1925] AC 619, 626 (above). See also *Lowry* v *Bourdieu* (1780) 2 Dougl 468; *Stainbank* v *Fenning* (1851) 11 CB 51 (hull); *Stainbank* v *Shephard* (1853) 13 CB 418 (hull).

Similar decisions in the USA: *China Mutual Insurance Co* v *Ward*, 59 F 712 (2 Cir, 1894—hull); *Vancouver National Bank* v *Law Union & Crown Insurance Co*, 153 F 440 (D Or, 1907—fire); *Miller* v *Stuyvesant Insurance Co*, 227 NYS 326 (NY, 1928—fire); *Banco Commercial de Puerto Rico* v *Royal Exchange Assurance Corp*, 71 F 2d 933 (1 Cir, 1934—fire); *Re P B McChesney & Son*, 31 F Supp 202 (D Ky, 1940—fire); *Rube* v *Pacific Insurance Co of New York*, 131 So 2d 240 (La, 1961—motor). *Contra*, *Tischendorf* v *Lynn Mutual Fire Insurance Co*, 208 NW 917 (Wis, 1926—fire): landlord held to have an interest in his tenant's crops, by means of which the tenant would be able to pay the rent.

207. The rule is different if he has a security interest in the property: above, 4–5G.

208. *Moran* v *Uzielli* [1905] 2 KB 555, 559 *per* Walton J. This argument is weak: see below (4–5M) as regards what a creditor can do.

209. [1925] AC 619 (fire); above, 4–3B.

210. [1925] AC 619, 626. The same concern was expressed by Lord Eldon in *Lucena* v *Craufurd* (1806) 127 ER 630, 651–652.

211. Harnett & Thornton, 48 Col L Rev 1162, 1175 (1948) cited in *Kosmopoulos* v *Constitution Ins Co* [1987] 1 SCR 2, 17 *per* Wilson J (fire).

212. This is illustrated in the same case (p 630) by Lord Sumner's view that "after the fire" the plaintiff "was directly prejudiced by the paucity of the company's assets, not by the fire." However, in that situation a modern court would find that the paucity was a direct result of the fire and that therefore the prejudice was proximately caused by the fire. For a discussion of this kind of causation problem, see Pinzur, 1979 *Insurance Counsel Journal* 109, 123.

213. p 630 *per* Lord Sumner.

that if the debtor's ship should be lost he would be less able to pay his debts does not, in my judgment, give to the creditor any interest, legal or equitable, which is dependent upon the safe arrival of the ship."[214] It was conceded that a creditor could insure the life of his debtor [215] but, said Lord Buckmaster,[216] "this depends . . . upon the means and probability of payment which the continuance of a debtor's life affords to his creditors and the probability of loss which would result from his death." But most debts are a burden on the estate and it is far from clear that death of the debtor will more probably defeat the creditor than the destruction of the debtor's principal assets; the opposite may be true. The man who has just one life often keeps most of his eggs in just one basket. In any event, probability of loss is the key to the decision: without a legal or equitable relation to the ship, the probability of loss was not high enough for the House.[217] In requiring a legal or equitable relation, it was concerned to give the economic interest (in this case loss) a strict definition. The wisdom of the decision depends on whether the modern law needs to define insurable interest and thus the probability of loss in this way.

In this state of English law what can the unsecured creditor do? First, he can insure the debt itself,[218] as the debt is property the value of which is affected by what happens to assets of the debtor.

Second, the creditor can take credit insurance,[219] defined by Schedule 2 of the Insurance Companies Act 1982 as "Effecting and carrying out contracts of insurance against risks of loss to the persons insured arising from the insolvency of debtors of theirs or from the failure (otherwise than through insolvency) of debtors of theirs to pay their debts when due." But credit insurers may require the insured to take some of the risk himself.

Third, the creditor might require, as a condition of credit, that the debtor insure his property, with a clause binding the insurer that loss should be payable to the creditor (below, 5–1A). The snags with this course are that the debtor may let the cover lapse or break its warranties; and that, if the insurer pays the debtor, the debtor may dispose of the money before the creditor can get it. If the creditor requires assignment of the policy, his claim can still be defeated by misrepresentation, non-disclosure or wilful misconduct on the part of the debtor-insured. Against this possibility he can take out a separate policy on his "mortgagee interest",[220] whereby he will recover if and to the extent he is unable to recover on the property policy assigned by the debtor.

214. *Moran, Galloway & Co* v *Uzielli* [1905] 2 KB 555, 562 *per* Walton J, cited with approval by Lord Buckmaster in *Macaura* (p 626).

215. *Godsall* v *Boldero* (1807) 9 East 72. See also *Blascheck* v *Bussell* (1916) 33 TLR 74 which upheld insurance on the health of an actor engaged for a performance.

216. p 626.

217. The House did not consider the point that the value of the debt as a saleable chose in action was adversely affected by the impoverishment of the debtor.

218. In *National Filtering Oil Co* v *Citizens Insurance Co*, 13 NE 337 (NY, 1887—fire) the insured had a right to royalties on an invention, which the debtor was to exploit in the debtor's factory. It was held that the insured could insure the royalties against fire at the factory. In *Franois* v *Automobile Insurance Co of Hartford*, 37 A 2d 525 (Pa, 1944—motor) the sole beneficiary under a will had an insurable interest in the estate property between the time of the testator's death and the settlement of the estate.

219. See *Anglo-Californian Bank* v *London & Provincial Marine & General Ins Co* (1904) 10 Com Cas 1.

220. Such a policy came before Mustill J in *The Captain Panagos DP* [1985] 1 Lloyd's Rep 625, where he said (p 630) that the "general tenor and shape" of the policy "speak more of an insurance against physical damage to (and liability of) the ship, than against financial damage to the mortgagee's interests". In this case the creditor had a mortgage of the debtor's ship, so it was undisputed that, whatever the nature of the policy, he had an insurable interest in the ship.

4–5N Profit

Insurable interest in profit was an issue in international trade in the late eighteenth and early nineteenth centuries. English courts sought to prevent wagering by limiting recovery on the principle of indemnity. However, while foreign courts were ready to base indemnity on the value of goods in the market at destination, English law took[221] the prime cost of the property insured, plus the expenses of and incidental to shipping, and the charges of insurance upon the whole; as this excluded profit, merchants sought to insure profit as such.[222]

In *Lucena* v *Craufurd* Lord Eldon said:[223] "I send my ship to India; I expect profit from the voyage; if the ship is lost my expectation is defeated; but of those expected profits the law can have no consideration." This remark must be kept in the context of of the case—an uncertain profit on ships captured but not yet brought back across the Atlantic Ocean to England. Compare *Barclay* v *Cousins* in which Lawrence J said this[224]:

"Where capital is employed subject to . . . risks, in case of loss the party is a sufferor by not having used his money in a way, which might with moral certainty have made a return not only of his principal but of profit: it is but playing with words to say that there is no loss because there is no possession, and that it is but a disappointment."

So profit can be insured, but what is "moral certainty"? Whatever the answer, as a sole test of insurable interest moral certainty[225] was rejected by the majority in *Lucena*; and merchants continued to insure profit on trade without censure from the courts.[225a] Insurable profit was not confined to the resale profit on international sales, or the value of company shares. It included commission,[226] freight or ship hire charges,[227] and profits from the retail trade.[228]

4–5N1 Subject-Matter

To find the limits of profit insurance and to distinguish *Macaura* (above, 4–3B) it is necessary to be clear about the subject-matter of the insurance. At the time of contracting the insurance, the profit itself cannot be touched or identified, it is inchoate. Hence the subject-matter of insurance is not the profit but, perhaps, the right to profit, which would be lost, if, for example, the ship and cargo failed to arrive safely.

---

221. *Usher* v *Noble* (1810) 12 East 639. Lord Ellenborough indicated that, if the insured wished to cover prospective profit, he should take a valued policy.

222. *Cf* the Contract Price Clause found in fire policies today, whereby "in respect only of goods sold but not delivered for which the insured is responsible and with regard to which under the conditions of the sale the sale contract is cancelled by reason of the fire or other peril insured against . . . the liability of the Company shall be based on the *contract* price." (Emphasis added).

223. (1806) 2 Bos & Pul (NR) 269, 325.

224. (1802) 2 East 544, 547–548. It appears that, if some loss of profit is sufficiently certain at the time of contract, the amount need not be certain: *Grant* v *Parkinson* (1781) 3 Dougl 16 (cargo and hull)—*id certum est quod certum reddit potest*. Also in this sense *Eyre* v *Glover* (1812) 16 East 218.

225. On the probability of loss or gain, see below, 4–5N2.

225a. *Wilson* v *Jones* (1867) LR 2 Ex 139, 147 per Willes J.

226. *Buchanan & Co* v *Faber* (1899) 4 Com Cas 223, 226 *per* Bigham J (fees paid to ship managers).

227. MIA, section 3. *Rankin* v *Potter* (1873) LR 6 HL 83; *Robertson* v *Petros M Nomikos Ltd* [1939] AC 371; *Continental Grain Co Inc* v *Twitchell* (1945) 78 LLR 251 (CA).

228. *Re Sun Fire Assurance Co* (1834) 3 N & M 819, 820 *per* Taunton J; *City Tailors Ltd* v *Evans* (1922) 91 LJKB 379 (CA).

Lord Eldon said that he was unable to "point out what is an interest unless it be a right in the property, or *a right derivable out of some contract about the property, which in either case may be lost upon some contingency affecting the possession or enjoyment of the party.*"[229] Considerable objections can be raised to this view. (a) In some of the cases[230] there is nothing that can be called a right to profit. (b) The view does not square with the cases measuring loss by reference to actual profit lost, rather than the right to earn it, which, excepting cases when profit was certain, should be less valuable. (c) In no other instance is the requirement of legal or equitable relation satisfied by a naked contractual right.[231]

A better view is that the subject-matter of the insurance is found in the means of profit, the things which are expected to generate the profit.[232] This view reflects the historical development of profits insurance as an exercise in topping up the insurable value of goods, depressed by section 16 of the MIA, which insists that the insurable value of goods be the value at shipment: "profits may be insured, but this is on the ground that they form an additional part of the value of the goods, in which the party already has an interest."[233] Moreover, this is consistent with the judges' view of *Wilson* v *Jones*[234] as insurance on "the value of the plaintiff's shares".

In *Wilson* v *Jones*[235] the company project was to lay a cable across the Atlantic, the events insured against were adverse to the success (and profitability) of the project. The subject-matter was the claimant's shares in the company. It was thus all but certain that the occurrence of one of the events would cause loss, damage the shares. Profit or loss in the adventure would be directly reflected in the value of the shares. The insurance was enforced.

---

229. *Lucena* v *Craufurd* (1806) 2 Bos & Pul (NR) 269, 321 (italics supplied). See also *Thompson* v *Taylor* (1795) 6 TR 478 where the court held insurable a profit which, in the words of Lord Kenyon CJ (p 481), "he [the insured] had a right to receive". A similar approach can be traced in *M'Swiney* v *Royal Exchange Assurance* (1849) 14 QB 634.

230. *Grant* v *Parkinson* (1781) 3 Dougl 16; *Barclay* v *Cousins* (1802) 2 East 544; *Stockdale* v *Dunlop* (1840) 6 M & W 224; *Wilson* v *Jones* (1867) LR 2 Ex 139.

231. See above, 4–5E.

232. USA: early cases can be viewed like this; in *National Filtering Oil Co* v *Citizens' Ins Co*, 13 NE 337 (NY, 1887—fire): the insured, who had contracted for royalties from the production of a particular plant using his patent, was held to have an insurable interest in the plant. See also *Hayes* v *Milford Mutual Fire Ins Co*, 49 NE 754 (Mass, 1898—fire), which is discussed above, 4–3B.

233. *Stockdale* v *Dunlop* (1840) 6 M & W 224, 232 *per* Parke B. See also *M'Swiney* v *Royal Exchange Assurance* (1849) 14 QB 634, 661 *per* Parke B; *Smith* v *Reynolds* (1856) 1 H & N 221 approved by the CA in *Berridge* v *The Man On Insurance Co Ltd* (1887) 18 QBD 346; in *Eyre* v *Glover* (1812) 16 East 218, 220 Lord Ellenborough asked rhetorically: "Are profits any thing (*sic*) more than an excrescence upon the value of the goods beyond the prime cost?"
Note: profit must be named as the subject-matter of insurance, if it is to be covered: *Mackenzie* v *Whitworth* (1875) 1 Ex D 36, 43 *per* Blackburn J (cargo) and cases cited. See also *Re Wright & Pole* (1834) 1 Ad 7 E 621 (fire) and, arising out of the same facts *Re Sun Fire Assurance Co* v *Wright* (1834) 3 N & M 819 (fire); *Anderson* v *Morice* (1875) LR 10 CP 607, 621 *per* Blackburn J, 624 *per* Bramwell B (cargo); *Maurice* v *Goldsbrough Mort & Co* [1939] AC 452 (PC—cargo). Cf *Devaux* v *J'Anson* (1839) 5 Bing NC 519 that insurance of freight included insurance of profits on goods carried.

234. (1867) LR 2 Ex 139, 146 *per* Willes J.

235. *Ibid* pp 145–146 *per* Willes J. Cf Arnould, No 328 that the authority of this case is doubtful since the decision in *Macaura* v *Northern Assurance Co* [1925] AC 619; *idem* Hasson, 8 Can Bus LJ 114, 116 (1983). In *Macaura* the House distinguished (but did not overrule) *Wilson* v *Jones* as a case of insurance, not on company property, but on shares: pp 627–628 *per* Lord Buckmaster.

As regards the case of insurance of freight, which has been allowed[236] for many years, Ashurst J affirmed in 1794 that "if the insured have no title to the ship they have no interest in the freight."[237] Over a century later, insurance of freight was justified as "an interest in the goods akin to an insurance on profits."[238] More recently, Lord Wright said[239] that he could see "no legal obstacle" to a clause, the intention of which was "to provide that the owner's interest in the profit-earning capacity of his ship, which is certainly a good interest in a business sense, should be deemed a sufficient insurable interest for the purposes of the policy." The legal relation is provided by a property interest in the ship, the means of earning profit. Commercial interest is provided by the probability of loss, if the ship is damaged or lost. Freight can now be insured under the MIA, section 3, without reference to the property that earns it. Outside the field of the MIA, the corollary is that in principle, when there is no property interest in the means of profit, the profit is "naked" profit and cannot be insured in England.

On this basis the dairy must insure its profits as the increased value of its cows, the writer his royalties by means of his word processor, the concert pianist his fees by means of his piano.[240] When one comes to the painter and his brushes, the strain of the exercise is overwhelming and the resultant mirth fractures the argument. However, the argument is the product of the need to meet commercial need without offending the rule in *Macaura* (above, 4–3B).

4–5N2 Commercial Interest: Future Profit

Future profit means profit to be made, perhaps by means of things in which the insured already has a proprietary right, but via contracts yet to be concluded. Although Ivamy calls insurance on future profits anomalous but well recognised,[241]

---

236. *Simmes v Marine Insurance Co*, 22 F Cas No 12,862 (D Columbia, 1825); *Hart v Delaware Insurance Co*, 11 F Cas No 6,150.

237. *Camden v Anderson* (1794) 5 TR 709, 711. Although strictly speaking only a shipowner has an insurable interest in freight (Arnould, No 344), charterers also insure the profit they hope to make by subfreight: Arnould, No 320.

USA: absent any requirement of property interest in the ship, there is no such difficulty about insurance of freight: *Tweedie Trading Co v Western Assurance Co*, 179 F 103 (2 Cir, 1910); *Booth-American Shipping Co v Importers & Exporters Insurance Co*, 9 F 2d 304, 305 (2 Cir, 1925).

238. *New Orleans & South American SS Co v W R Grace & Co*, 26 F 2d 967, 969 (2 Cir, 1928) adopting Arnould (11th ed), No 232.

239. *Robertson v Petros M Nomikos Ltd* [1939] AC 371, 384. This opinion was adopted by Goddard LJ, sitting as an additional judge, in *Papadimitriou v Henderson* (1939) 55 TLR 1035, while observing warily that "as a rule cases which deal with freight insurance raise questions of difficulty".

240. Of course, just as comedians, actors and football stars insure various parts of their anatomy, the pianist may insure his hands; this is non-indemnity insurance and does not give rise to the same theoretical difficulties.

241. p 26. See also Hickmott, *Interruption Insurance* (1982), p 4; Riley, *Consequential Loss & Business Interruption Insurance* (5th ed 1981) No 19. In New York, for example, the managing owner of a ship may insure future profit: *The Regent*, 57 F Supp 242 (D NY, 1944—insurance of profits). Moreover, in England, the Insurance Companies Act 1982, Schedule 2, recognises the business of Miscellaneous Financial Loss insurance as including "Effecting and carrying out contracts of insurance against . . . (a) risks of loss to the persons insured attributable to interruptions of the carrying on of business carried on by them or to reduction of the scope of business so carried on."

there must be some doubt about profits on deals that have yet to be concluded,[242] as the loss, if the insured event occurs, is insufficiently certain. In practice cover is offered in PPI (Policy Proof of Interest) policies,[243] although in the cold legal light of day the policy proves nothing, and the courts consider each case on its merits.[244]

---

242. It has been said that freight can be insured only if it has been contracted for: *Continental Grain Co Inc* v *Twitchell* (1945) 78 LL L Rep 251 (CA). Arnould, Nos 320, 336, 351 ff. Some cases to this effect cited by Arnould may be explained by the terms of the policy. In *Buchanan & Co* v *Faber* (1899) 4 Com Cas 223 (insurance on "disbursements") brokers could not insure profit hoped for as the hope was slight. In *Cheshire & Co* v *Vaughan Bros & Co* (1920) 123 LT 487 (CA) warehousemen could not insure profit they hoped to make on expected goods; see also *Flint* v *Flemyng* (1830) 1 B & Ad 45, 48 *per* Lord Tenterden CJ. *Brown* v *Jerome*, 298 F 1 (9 Cir, 1924). The mere expectancy of an option to purchase cannot be insured by a tenant at will: *Van Cure* v *Hartford Fire Ins Co*, 253 A 2d 663 (Pa, 1969—fire).

243. See, for example, Hardacre PM, 12 June 1986, p 50.

244. Compare, for example, *Buchanan & Co* v *Faber* (1889) 4 Com Cas 223 and *Gedge* v *Royal Exchange Assurance Corp* [1900] 2 QB 214. MIA, section 4(2)(*b*).

CHAPTER 5

THIRD PARTY RIGHTS

5-1 INTRODUCTION

This chapter is concerned with the right, if any, of a third party, i.e. a person who is not a party to the contract between insurer and insured, to benefit from the contract. In England the position of the third party at common law is poor, being caught by the rule of privity of contract[1]: no one may enforce all or part of a contract, to which he is not a party.

In particular, in England, as in Canada,[2] if the insurer is insolvent, the insured has no right of action against a solvent parent company of the insurer[2a] or against a reinsurer with whom the insurer has placed all or part of the risk. In the United States many jurisdictions permit a third party to enforce a contract, including an insurance contract, made for his benefit.[3] Even in the USA, however, the primary insured has no right of action on his insurer's contract with a reinsurer: "The general rule is that the contract of insurance and that of reinsurance remain totally distinct and unconnected".[4] Moreover, the reinsurance contract is a contract of indemnity; that being so, if the primary insurer, being insolvent, has not paid its insured, that insurer has not suffered the loss that triggers the liability of the reinsurer.[5] It is otherwise if (a) the reinsurance contract purports to benefit the primary insured[6] or (b) the primary insurance contract assigns to the insured a right to claim against the reinsurer.[7] It has been held in New York,[8] however, that any such benefit cannot be implied but that the "cut-through" clause to this effect must be an express term of the reinsurance con-

---

1. *Dunlop Pneumatic Tyre Co Ltd* v *Selfridge & Co Ltd* [1915] AC 847.
2. *Re Treverton* (1987) 45 DLR (4th) 712 (Ont—re). Equally, but for different reasons, a reinsurer is not entitled to a declaration that the primary insurance contract is invalid: *Meadows Indemnity Co* v *Ins Corp of Ireland plc* [1989] 2 Lloyd's Rep 298 (CA—re).
2a. *Cf* USA: the court may pierce the corporate veil of the insurer, if it is but a dummy under the domination and control of the parent: *Stephens* v *American Home Assurance Co*, 811 F Supp 937, 955–956 (SD NY, 1993—re).
3. Williston, Nos 356 ff. Rest Contracts 2d sections 304 and 311c. In states that did not have this rule at common law, statutes have provided for enforcement in specific areas of law.
4. *Consumer Benefit Assn* v *Lexington Ins Co*, 731 F Supp 1510, 1513 (MD Ala, 1990—re). In the same sense: *Allendale Mutual Ins Co* v *Crist*, 731 F Supp 928 (WD Mo, 1989—re); *Klockner Stadler Hurter Ltd* v *Ins Co of the State of Pennsylvania*, 785 F Supp 1130 (SD NY, 1990—AR); *Travelers Indemnity Co* v *Household Int Inc*, 775 F Supp 518 (D Conn, 1991—liability).
5. *Turner & Boisseau* v *Marshall Adjusting Corp*, 775 F Supp 372, 380 (D Kan, 1991).
6. *Crist* (above).
7. *Klockner* (above).
8. *Unigard Sec. Ins Co* v *North River Ins Co*, 949 F 2d 630 (2 Cir, 1991—re), to be brought before the New York Court of Appeals: 580 N.Y.S. 2d 193 (1992).

tract. Moreover, the insured has no right of discovery of documents containing reinsurance arrangements.[9]

Exceptions to the privity rule in the insurance context are considered below (5–1B). Apart from the exceptions, if the insured wishes to extend the benefit of the insurance to a third party, he must contract not only on his own behalf but as agent for that party, in which case the latter is a third party no longer but a party to the contract. If that cannot be done because the identity of the third party is not yet known, the solution may be to contract a composite contract[10] for the benefit of all persons of a certain kind, interested and to become interested.

If the insurer does pay insurance money to which the third party payee, although the latter could not have sued for it, he may keep it, unless it is shown that (a) this was not the true intention of the parties to the contract of insurance, or (b) the third party took the benefit solely as a nominee or agent for the insured.[11] Unless one of these two exceptions applies, the third party is permitted to keep the benefit because it is a gift, which has been perfected and which, once properly executed, cannot be revoked.[12]

In England, as in most other countries of common law, the limits on the enforcement of the insurance contract by third parties are set largely by that part of the traditional rule of privity of contract, which says that no person may enforce a contract to which he is not a party.[13] The traditional rule was re-examined by the High Court of Australia in *Trident General Ins Co Ltd* v *McNiece Bros Pty Ltd*.[14] Liability insurance taken for a limestone crushing plant was, it was held, intended to extend to the plant, and to all contractors and sub-contractors engaged on construction work at the plant. The main contractor sought to enforce the insurance[15] although not a party to it.[16] The Court of Appeal[17] held that the action succeeded on the basis that at common law the beneficiary of an insurance contract can sue on the contract, even though not a party to the contract and providing no consideration. The appeal to the High Court of Australia was unanimously dismissed, but reasons differed.

Four judges in the High Court found a trust (below 5–2). Three judges,[18] however,

---

9. *Rhône-Poulenc Rorer, Inc* v *Home Indemnity Co*, LEXIS 14111 (ED Pa, 1 October 1991). For subsequent stages in this litigation, see the decision of the same court dated 6 August 1993: LEXIS 10852.

10. As regards composite policies, see below 27–2D and 30–4.

11. See the discussion of this possibility by Du Parcq LJ in *Re Schebsmann* [1944] Ch 83, 105–106 (CA).

12. *Beswick* v *Beswick* [1968] AC 58, 96 *per* Lord Upjohn, approving *Re Schebsmann* [1944] Ch 83 (CA); in the latter case see, for example, pp 92–93 *per* Lord Greene MR. Generally on this point see Halsbury Vol 20, para 55.

13. *Dunlop Pneumatic Tyre Co Ltd* v *Selfridge & Co Ltd* [1915] AC 847.

14. (1988) 62 ALJ 508. For the implications of this decision, see Kincaid [1989] CLJ 243. *Trident* was applied in *Nitschke* v *Rossair Pty Ltd* (1989) 97 FLR 54, 67 (SA 1989—liability) to cover a pilot under an airline's policy "as a person for whose benefit the policy enures, and a person whose legal liability is covered by the policy, has the right to enforce it"; and in *Barroora Pty Ltd* v *Provincial Ins Ltd* (1992) 26 NSWLR 170, to fire insurance at the suit of one with a charge on the insured property.

15. The contractor had been held liable to an injured workman.

16. The facts were in 1979, and hence before the operation of the Insurance Contract Act 1984 (Cth): section 48 enables a third party to enforce any contract of insurance, if he is specified as a person to whom insurance cover is provided.

17. (1987) 8 NSWLR 270: McHugh JA, with whom the other two judges agreed.

18. Mason CJ, Wilson and Toohey JJ. Gaudron J also dismissed the appeal, on the view (p 537) that "a promisor who has accepted an agreed consideration for a promise to benefit a third party comes under an obligation to the third party to fulfil that promise and the third party acquires a right to bring an action to secure the benefit of that promise. The right of the third party is not a right to sue on the contract: rather, it is a right independent of, but ordinarily corresponding in content and duration with, the obligation owed

grasped and throttled the traditional nettle by allowing a direct action by the third party against the insurer. They noted general dissatisfaction with the privity rule, and that partial solutions did not work well enough (trust), or did not cover all situations of need (specific performance and estoppel). They thought it unjust that the third party should not be able to sue, especially as in many cases, including the present, the party would have relied on that possibility by refraining from taking his own insurance cover. Of the three judges,[19] two stated obiter that the right of action should extend to *any* kind of contract, and be subject to any defences available against the promisee. The third judge, for reasons similar but tempered by more respect for precedent, gave a narrower judgment in favour of a direct action on a liability insurance contract by an identified third party.[20]

Traditional objections to direct enforcement by a third party were raised and dismissed. (i) As regards the risk of double recovery, this was thought slight, as joinder of all parties to the first action would make the decision binding on all concerned. (ii) As regards the argument that the promisee should be free to agree with the promisor a discharge or modification of the contract, it was thought that the right of a third party to sue could be subordinated to the right of the contracting parties to rescind or modify the contract, which would be lost only if he had relied on the promise to his detriment.[21] An English court is unlikely to follow this lead. Courts there are bound by decisions of the House of Lords, which has had the opportunity to overthrow the rule but has declined to do so, leaving it the more entrenched.[22]

5–1A Loss Payable Clauses

Some policies direct that the insurance money shall be paid to a named third party, such as a creditor of the insured. Such a clause, known as a loss payable clause, "gives no rights to the loss payee unless it also constitutes or evidences an assignment of the assured's rights under the policy or evidences the fact that the designated person is an

---

under the contract by the promisor to the promisee". The source of the obligation, he said, was in restitution. He concluded (p 538) that "Where the consideration is wholly executed in favour of a promisor under a contract made for the benefit of a third party a rule that the third party may not bring action to secure the benefit of the contract permits of the possibility that the promisor may be unjustly enriched to the extent that the promise is not fulfilled". He relied on general statements in *Pavey & Mathews Pty Ltd v Paul* (1987) 162 CLR 221; and *Brook's Wharf & Bull Wharf Ltd v Goodman Bros* [1937] 1 KB 534, 545 *per* Lord Wright MR (CA).

19. Mason CJ and Wilson J.

20. If identified "in terms that evidence an intention on the part of insurer and assured that the policy will indemnify" the third party contractor "and it is reasonable to expect that such a contractor may order its affairs by reference to the existence of the policy . . . " : Toohey J, p 536.

21. *Cf* Rest 2d Contracts, section 311(3).

22. *Dunlop Pneumatic Tyre Co Ltd v Selfridge & Co Ltd* [1915] AC 847, 853 *per* Lord Haldane; *Midland Silicones Ltd v Scruttons Ltd* [1962] AC 446; *Beswick v Beswick* [1968] AC 58; *Woodar Investment Development Ltd v Wimpey Construction UK Ltd* [1980] 1 All ER 571 (HL). See also *Vandepitte v Preferred Accident Ins Corp* [1933] AC 70 on appeal from Canada. In Australia see *Wilson v Darling Stevedoring & Lighterage Co Ltd* (1956) 96 CLR 43. In *Trident* Brennan J and Deane J thought the rule too well established to be thrown out. In Canada see *Greenwood Shopping Plaza Ltd v Beattie* (1980) 111 DLR (3d) 257 (Sup Ct.). As regards English law, see also the Law Commission Consultation Paper No 121, *Privity of Contract: Contracts for the Benefit of Third Parties* (HMSO, London 1991); and discussion of that Paper: Degeling (1993) 6 JCL 177.

Cf USA: third parties can sue in their own name on contracts made for their benefit—Rest 2d Contracts (1979) ch 14. Also in Scotland: *Carmichael v Carmichael's Executrix* [1920] SC (HL) 195; *Allan's Trustees v Lord Advocate* [1971] SC (HL) 45. McBryde, *The Law of Contract in Scotland* (1987), ch 18. Also in Australia: *Barroora Pty Ltd v Provincial Ins Ltd* (1992) 26 NSWLR 170 (fire).

original assured".[22a] A simple form of loss payee clause, however, is not as an assignment of the policy proceeds.[22b] Such a clause purports to benefit a third party, the loss payee, and is subject to the rule of privity against enforcement by the third party, and subject to the exceptions to or evasions of that rule in the law of insurance discussed in the pages that follow. Moreover, the loss payee can be in no better position than the insured through whom he is, if at all, entitled to the insurance money.[22c]

5–1B Exceptions to the Privity Rule

In certain situations Parliament has intervened and given the third party a statutory right of action on the policy: below, 5–4, 5–8, and 5–9. Apart from these statutes, the usual device employed is the trust. In principle the trust may be found with respect to any kind of insurance; in practice, it occurs mostly with regard to life insurance, apart from the "commercial trust" of goods, which is probably not a trust at all: below, 5–6. As regards life insurance, there may be

(a) An express trust declared in the policy of insurance: below, 5–2.
(b) An assignment of a policy to trustees to hold on trusts declared by the insured who arranged the policy. As to assignment see chapter 6. In other respects the effectiveness of this device depends on the general law of trusts.
(c) The purchase of the policy from the insured, who first contracted it, by the third party, who pays the premiums and thus benefits from a resulting trust: below, 5–3.
(d) A statutory trust under the Married Women's Property Act 1882, section 11: below, 5–4.

5–2 EXPRESS TRUST

An express trust may be found in the policy, usually a life policy.[23] For an express trust there must be (a) trust property, the benefit of the policy, (b) persons identified

---

22a. *The Angel Bell, Iraqi Ministry of Defence* v *Arcepey Shipping Co SA* [1979] 2 Lloyd's Rep 491, 497 *per* Donaldson J (hull). Arnould, No 259. *Guerin* v *Manchester Fire Assurance* (1898) 29 SCR 139, 149 *per* Sir Henry Strong CJ (fire).

In the United States certain of these clauses are enforceable by the payee, for example, *Fruehauf Trailer Co* v *Stuyvesant Ins Co*, 141 F Supp 65 (D Minn, 1956—motor). That was a case of a mortgage clause and a distinction has been drawn between a mortgage clause, which creates a separate contract between mortgagee and insurer, and a "mere" loss payee clause, which does not create a contract between payee and insurer and which, as in England, is not enforceable by the payee: *Vargas* v *Nautilus Ins Co*, 811 P 2d 868 (Kan, 1991—fire).

22b. *Canadian Imperial Bank of Commerce* v *Ins Corp of Ireland* (1991) 75 DLR (4th) 482 (BC, 1990—business interruption).

22c. In *Ressler* v *White*, 968 F 2d 1478 (2 Cir, 1992), for example, as the insured's claim in respect of a gold robbery was fraudulent, the loss payee could not recover either. *Cf Foremost Ins Co* v *Allstate Ins Co*, 486 NW 2d 600 (Mich 1992—motor), in which deliberate destruction of a motor home by the insured did not affect the rights of the line holder who, by implication, had a separate contract with the insurer; see *Fruehauf* (above).

23. *Re Harrington Motor Co* [1928] 1 Ch 105 (CA—motor). Generally, see Houseman ch 9. In Scotland, however, a clear statement in a policy that it is for the benefit of a third party is sufficient to make the policy enforceable by that third party: *Carmichael* v *Carmichael's Executrix*, 1920 SC (HL) 195.

In the United States the rule permitting third parties to enforce contracts made for their benefit obviates in most jurisdictions any need for the device of express trust; it is enough that a life policy is expressed to be for the benefit of a third party, for the latter to have a vested interest which he can enforce: *Nance* v *Hilliard*, 101 F 2d 957 (8 Cir, 1939—life); *American Casualty Co* v *Rose*, 340 F 2d 469 (10 Cir, 1964—life); *Wargo* v *Wargo*, 265 NYS 2d 37 (1965—life). See further, Appleman, section 7717.

as beneficiaries of the trust, (c) a clear purpose for the trust, and (d) a clear intention to create a trust.

A trust may be created in favour of the third party. Indeed, in the past, the Court of Appeal has suggested the use of this device as a means of creating third party rights under an insurance contract. It is essential, however, that the words to this effect are clear and unambiguous.[24] In The High Court of Australia in *Trident*,[24a] four judges[24b] based their judgment on implied trust. In England, courts have been slow to imply a trust of a promise.[24c]

"It is true, that by the use of possibly unguarded language, a person may create a trust, as Monsieur Jourdain talked prose, without knowing it, but unless an intention to create a trust is clearly to be collected from the language used and the circumstances of the case, I think that the court ought not to be astute to discover indications of such an intention."[25]

Reasons for their reluctance are, first, a trust once created is not revocable by the promisee/trustee.[25a] Second, there is the difficulty of ascertaining intention to create a trust.[25b] Third, "serious duties and obligations rest on any person claiming to be insured, which necessarily involve consent and privity of contract".[25c]

Technical language is not necessary to create a trust, for it is axiomatic that "Equity regards the intention rather than the form". Little doubt arises, if the benefit of the policy is expressed to be held "in trust for" or "upon trust to pay" the third party. By contrast, it is not enough that the policy is expressed to be "for the benefit of" the third party[26]; or "for or on behalf of" the third party[27]; or that the policy states that the insurance money should be paid to the third party[28]; or that the policy is expressed to take effect, as if subject to section 11 of the Married Women's Property Act 1882, in circumstances to which that section does not in terms apply.[29]

24. Halsbury, Vol 48, Nos 542 ff.

24a. *Trident General Ins Co Ltd* v *McNiece Bros Pty Ltd* (1988) 62 ALJ 508, above, 5–1.

24b. *Ibid* Brennan J, Deane J, Dawson J and, as an alternative basis, Toohey J.

24c. A trust of a promise was found in *Williams* v *Baltic Ins Assn Ltd* [1924] 2 KB 282 (motor); and *Harmer* v *Armstrong* [1934] 1 Ch 65 (CA); but reluctance to infer a trust is clear from *Re Schebsmann* [1944] Ch 83 (CA) and *Beswick* v *Beswick* [1968] AC 58, as well as cases cited below. There is a limited exception for the enforcement of shipbrokers' commission: *Les Affréteurs Réunis SA* v *Walford (London) Ltd* [1919] AC 801; *The Helvetia-S* [1960] 1 Lloyd's Rep 540.

25. *Re Schebsmann* [1944] Ch 83, 104 *per* Du Parcq LJ (CA).

25a. See especially *Green* v *Russell* [1959] 2 QB 226 (CA—PA), also Law Revision Committee (6th Interim Report) 1937, Cmd 5449. para 47. *Cf Wilson* v *Darling Island Stevedoring & Lighterage Co Ltd* (1956) 95 CLR 43, 67 *per* Fullagar J: "a revocable trust can be enforceable in equity while it subsists."

25b. Cmd 5449 para 44. Corbin 46 LQR 12, 17 (1930); Stoljar, 13 NZUL Rev 68, 83 (1988). The trust solution was rejected by the Australian Law Reform Commission Report No 20.

25c. *Vandepitte* v *Preferred Accident Ins Corp* [1933] AC 70, 81 (PC—motor).

26. *Re Burgess's Policy* (1915) 113 LT 443 (life); *Re Sinclair's Life Policy* [1938] Ch 799; *Re Foster* (1938) 54 TLR 993 (life—"child deferred policy"); *Green* v *Russell* [1959] 2 QB 226, 241 *per* Romer LJ (CA—group accident); *Re Foster's Policy* [1966] 1 WLR 222, 227 *per* Plowman J (life). Such wording is, however, effective to create a statutory trust: below, 5–4.

Cf Scotland, where such wording is effective to create a right enforceable by the third party: *Carmichael* v *Carmichael's Executrix*, 1920 SC (HL) 195.

27. *Re Webb* [1941] Ch 225, 234 *per* Farwell J (life).

28. *Cleaver* v *Mutual Reserve Fund Life Assn* [1892] 1 QB 147, 152 *per* Lord Esher MR (CA—life), followed on this point in *Re Engelbach's Estate* [1924] 2 Ch 348 (life). See also *Re Foster's Policy* [1966] 1 WLR 222, 227 *per* Plowman J (life). *Cf Re A Policy No 6402 of the Scottish Equitable Life Assurance Sy* [1902] 1 Ch 282, criticised by Eve J in *Re Engelbach's Estate* [1924] 2 Ch 348, 354.

29. *Re Clay's Policy* [1937] 2 All ER 548, 550 *per* Farwell J. In this case the policy was expressed to be for the benefit of a wife, to whom section 11 applied, and also of an adoptive child, to whom the section did not apply. The reference in the policy to section 11 could be explained by the intention to benefit the wife. However, it is submitted that, if the policy had been expressed only to benefit the adoptive child, to whom the

If an express trust of the policy or of monies payable under the policy has been created, the third party beneficiary should invite the trustee, who contracted the policy, to carry out the trust in his favour. If the trustee refuses to hand over insurance money to the third party, he may sue the trustee for the money. If the trustee refuses to sue the insurer to recover money due under the policy, the third party beneficiary is "entitled to sue in his own name in presence of the trustee, whom he may make a defendant".[30]

5–2A Group Insurance

In *Bowskill* v *Dawson*[31] a company set up a scheme under which trustees took out a group life policy on behalf of the company's employees. Romer LJ looked at the terms of the scheme and said[32] that the employees

"may be regarded as beneficiaries under a voluntary trust (albeit a conditionally revocable one), established by [the company] for their benefit. The frequent references in the clauses which I have cited to the 'claims' and 'rights' and entitlement of the members or their legal representatives permit, I think, of no other conclusion."

In particular, he concluded[33] that the representatives

"had more than mere expectancies, . . . they had rights which the courts would recognize and enforce; and although those rights were conferred upon them by the scheme itself they were such as to entitle them as *cestuis que trust* to call upon the trustees to perform the trusts of the deed under which they benefited and to seek the intervention of the court if need arose. . . . Indeed, it may well be that, had the insurance company refused to pay and the trustees declined to sue, the defendants themselves could have sued the [insurance] company adding the trustees as defendants."

In the case of a scheme such as that in *Bowskill*, the intention to create a trust must be clear enough to overcome the scepticism of the court on two points. The courts ask, first, why should a donor (such as the employer) have bound himself irrevocably to make a gift (of insurance money) at some uncertain date in the future? Second, why should a donor bind himself (to the third party donee) to pay premiums to the insurer for an indefinite period?[34] Whereas in *Bowskill* v *Dawson* (above) alteration of the scheme was carefully controlled and, by clear implication, in other circumstances excluded, the position in another case, *Green* v *Russell*,[35] was quite different: in that case Romer LJ pointed out that[36] "There was nothing to prevent [the employer] at any time, had he chosen to do so, from surrendering the policy and receiving back a

section did not apply, it would have been more difficult to conclude that the insured did not wish to create a trust in favour of the child. See also *Re Burgess's Policy* (1915) 113 LT 443 (life).

30. *Royal Exchange Assurance* v *Hope* [1928] 1 Ch 179, 185 *per* Tomlin J. In the USA the beneficiary under a life policy has a vested interest from the time that the contract of insurance takes effect: *Central Bank of Washington City* v *Hume*, 128 US 195 (1888); *New York Life Ins Co* v *Halpern*, 47 F 2d 935 (WD Pa, 1931—life); *Morton* v *United States*, 457 F 2d 750 (4 Cir, 1972—life).

31. [1955] 1 QB 13 (CA).

32. pp 26–27.

33. p 28.

34. *Re Webb* [1941] Ch 225, 238 *per* Farwell J (life); *Re Schebsmann* [1944] Ch 83, 104 *per* Du Parcq LJ (CA).

35. [1959] 2 QB 226 (CA): a similar question arose in respect of group accident insurance. In this case the policy stated that the insured employer was "the absolute owner of the policy and shall not be bound to recognize any equitable or other claim to or interest in the policy". The Court of Appeal held *inter alia* that an employee, covered by the policy, had no right to the insurance money.

36. p 241; see also p 236.

proportionate part of the premium which he had paid". It was more plausible that he should intend to be completely free to change his mind than to be completely bound to keep up the insurance. Nonetheless, "if, according to the terms of the policy, a time does come when the grantee ceases to have any beneficial interest in it, then . . . it is not very difficult to imply a trust for the person for whose benefit the policy is expressed to have been taken out".[37]

5-3 RESULTING TRUST

If a policy taken out by A is purchased by B, who then pays the premiums to continue the policy, there is a rebuttable presumption that B has a beneficial interest in the policy, enforceable by B as a resulting trust.[38]

5-4 THE MARRIED WOMEN'S PROPERTY ACT 1882[39]

In 1860, it was possible to create a trust of the benefit of an insurance policy in favour of one's family, but difficult to do.[40] After the death of the bread-winner there was a need for family provision, which would not be entirely swallowed by his debts. This need was greatest among the less rich, who were also less likely to have the desire or the means to get the legal advice necessary to draft a trust.[41] Parliament tried to meet the need in section 10 of the Married Women's Property Act 1870: a provision "to enable a trust to be created appropriating policy moneys for the spouse or children of the insured without his going to the trouble of executing a trust deed."[42] Section 10 was replaced by section 11 of the Married Women's Property Act 1882,[43] to the same end, but extending the provision to insurance by a wife in favour of her husband: even if the bread-winner survived, it was recognised that the loss of the spouse, who had looked after the home, could result in expense to the survivor.

5-4A The Scope of Section 11

Section 11 provides:

"A married woman may effect a policy upon her own life or the life of her husband for her own benefit; and the same and all benefit thereof shall enure accordingly.

---

37. *Re Foster's Policy* [1966] 1 WLR 222, 229 *per* Plowman J (life): the insured took a life policy, described as Early Provident Insurance, "on the life of and for the benefit of" his daughter, then aged two. When the daughter reached the age of 25, the beneficial interest would lie solely with the daughter. The court held that the policy gave rise to a trust in favour of the daughter on the money payable after she had reached 25. See also *Re Webb* [1941] Ch 225, 239 *per* Farwell J (life).
38. See discussion in *Re Schebsmann* [1944] Ch 83, 104-105. See further MacGillivray, No 1270 (p 603).
39. Generally see Houseman, ch 9.
40. See above, 5-2.
41. Finlay, *Contracts for the Benefit of Third Persons* (1939), pp 81–82.
42. *Cousins* v *Sun Life Assurance Sy* [1933] 1 Ch 126, 133 *per* Lord Hanworth MR (CA).
43. The Act does not apply in Scotland or Northern Ireland. In Scotland similar provisions are found in the Married Women's Policies of Assurance (Scotland) Act 1880, as amended by the Married Women's Policies of Assurance (Scotland) (Amendment) Act 1980. Under Scots law no valid trust can be created without delivery of the policy: *Jarvie's Trustee* v *Jarvie's Trustees* (1887) 14 R 411; however intimation to the beneficiary that the policy is in his favour constitutes a notional delivery that satisfies this requirement: *Allan's Trustees* v *Lord Advocate*, 1971 SC (HL) 45. In Northern Ireland section 11 was replaced by provisions of the Law Reform (Husband and Wife) Act (Northern Ireland) 1964.

A policy of assurance effected by any man on his own life, and expressed to be for the benefit of his wife, or of his children, or of his wife and children, any of them, or by any woman on her own life, and expressed to be for the benefit of her husband, or of her children, or of her husband and children, or any of them, shall create a trust in favour of the objects therein named, and the moneys payable under any such policy shall not, so long as any object of the trust remains unperformed, form part of the estate of the insured, or be subject to his or her debts:

Provided, that if it shall be proved that the policy was effected and the premiums paid with intent to defraud the creditors of the insured, they shall be entitled to receive, out of the moneys payable under the policy, a sum equal to the premiums so paid. . . ."[44]

5–4A1 The Life of the Insured

The purpose of section 11 might have been furthered by extending the section to any life, the ending of which would give rise to a need for family provision. As a means of provision for others, section 11 is limited to a policy on the life of the insured, so, a person cannot use section 11 in respect of the life of a rich aunt on whom that person or his children depend.[45] Usually the policy is a life policy; however, a policy may be within the scope of section 11, even though it covers events other than death,[46] such as accidental injury, and even though it excludes death by certain causes. It is uncertain whether it is possible for spouses to make a joint policy effective under section 11.[47]

5–4A2 The Range of Beneficiaries

The purpose of section 11 suggests that the beneficiaries should be the insured's dependants, those whose need the Act was intended to meet in the event of his death. However, the scope of section 11 is both broader and narrower than this. First, it is not necessary to show actual need on the part of the beneficiary, either actual need at the time of death[48] or potential need perceived at the time the policy is taken. What is essential is simply a relationship, that of "spouse" or of "child". This relationship need not exist either at the time of the policy (the section may benefit a future child or wife) or at the time of death (the beneficiary may have died before the insured) for in the latter case it cannot be said that the purpose of the trust has come to an end.[49] Second, the section does not help all those in need, only spouses and children. It does not extend to "partners" or cohabitants, although the Scottish Law Commission has recommended a change in the law on this point.[49a]

It has been suggested[50] that, if a policy purports to benefit both persons who are within the scope of section 11 and persons who are not, the section will not assist any of them. However, it is submitted that the better view[51] is that *ceteris paribus* the trust for the former will be effective under the Act; and even as regards the latter the words used may be sufficient to create an express trust without resort to the Act.

44. The rest of the section is set out below, 5–4B.
45. In any event he may lack insurable interest: see above, 3–5B.
46. *Re Gladitz* [1937] Ch 588 (PA).
47. See further, Houseman, pp 191–192.
48. Such a requirement was dismissed as unreasonable by Kekewich J in *Re Browne's Policy* [1903] 1 Ch 188, 190.
49. *Cousins v Sun Life Assurance Sy* [1933] 1 Ch 126, 138 *per* Lawrence LJ (CA).
49a. As regards the Married Women's Policies of Assurance (Scotland) Act 1880: Scottish Law Commission (No 135), *Report on Family Law*, para 16.45
50. MacGillivray, No 1398 (p 651) with reference to *Re Parker's Policies* [1906] 1 Ch 526 which, it is submitted, does not clearly support the suggestion.
51. Houseman, p 192. In this sense *Re Clay's Policy* [1937] 2 All ER 548, 550 *per* Farwell J, to whom *Re Parker's Policies* (above) was not cited.

5–4A3 The Proviso: Intent to Defraud Creditors

Although section 11 refers to fraud, it is doubtful whether this alludes to fraud in the strict common law sense. Given the context, it is more likely that it refers to fraud as it is understood in the law of bankruptcy.[52] If so, the proviso operates when the policy is effected with the intent that the beneficiary will get money which would (not might) otherwise go to creditors. Whereas it is one of the purposes of the section that there should be some money for the family, in spite of creditors, it seems that, when the insured effects the policy, he must be able to pay not only the premium but also his debts as they fall due. Nonetheless, it appears that a trust effective under section 11 cannot be set aside as fraudulent under sections 340 and 423 of the Insolvency Act 1986.

5–4A4 Benefit Expressed

One purpose of section 11 was to facilitate a family trust. So, "for the benefit of" my wife, words that are inadequate to create an express trust,[53] give rise to a trust under the section; so does a term that the sum insured or "all claims" shall be payable to the appropriate beneficiary.[54] Moreover, "it may be that if a policy expressed to be under the Act is capable of two constructions, one within and the other not within the powers of the Act, the former might be considered by the light of the Act to be the true construction."[55] Still, in times of social mobility such as the present people are advised to anticipate a conflict of laws by making an express reference to section 11.[56]

5–4A5 The Identity of the Beneficiaries

Section 11 refers to the "objects therein named", that is to the persons designated in the policy, a question of construction in each case.[57] In other contexts a reference to "my wife" would suggest a reference to the person who was lawful wife[58] at the time of the reference.[59] However, in the light of the purpose of the Act and of the policy, it is here taken to mean the person who is wife when the insured dies.[60] Still, a reference to "my wife Lilian" must, of course, mean that wife and no other. In such a case the

---

52. Generally, see *Re Kushler Ltd* [1948] Ch 248 (CA). Halsbury, Vol 3, Nos 231 ff and 908 ff.
53. Above, 5–2A.
54. *Re Gladitz* [1937] Ch 588: Bennett J (*dubitante*) following *Re Fleetwood* [1926] Ch 48 and *Griffiths* v *Fleming* [1909] 1 KB 805 (CA).
55. *Re Seyton* (1887) 34 Ch D 511, 514 *per* North J, speaking of the Act of 1870, which that of 1882 replaced.
56. Houseman, p 171.
57. *Re Browne's Policy* [1903] 1 Ch 188, 190 *per* Kekewich J; *Cousins* v *Sun Life Assurance Sy* [1933] 1 Ch 126, 139 *per* Romer LJ (CA)
58. This question is governed by the usual rules of the conflict of laws: *Metropolitan Life Ins Co* v *Chase*, 189 F Supp 326 (NJ, 1960—life), affirmed 294 F 2d 500 (3 Cir, 1961).
59. This is the rule in the USA: *Federal Life Ins Co* v *Tietsort*, 131 F 2d 448 (7 Cir, 1942—life).
60. *Re Browne's Policy* [1903] 1 Ch 188; *idem* in respect of the 1870 Act: *Re Collier* [1930] 2 Ch 37. See also *Re Parker's Policies* [1906] 1 Ch 526.
USA: the courts will give effect to a separation agreement, whereby one party is to retain the benefit of insurance on the life of the other, such agreement overriding a subsequent change in the nomination of beneficiary: *Life Assurance Sy of the United States* v *Jones*, 679 F 2d 356 (4 Cir, 1982—life). There may be a rule of law to similar effect, for example, in Missouri: *Glover* v *Metropolitan Life Ins Co*, 664 F 2d 1101 (8 Cir, 1981—life).

policy creates a vested interest in Lilian at the time of the policy, not an interest contingent on her surviving the insured.[61]

A reference to "my children" is a reference to children of the insured of whichever marriage alive at the time of death.[62] Children include illegitimate children[63] and also children adopted by the insured under an adoption order.[64] It does not extend to other dependents, such as children of the home who have been informally adopted[65] or "grandchildren or other remote descendants".[66]

5–4B The Effect of Section 11

Although the operation and effect of a trust under section 11 is much like that of an express trust, it does have some distinguishing features. If there is more than one beneficiary, they take in accordance with any effective appointment or apportionment in the policy,[67] by will or by deed. If there is none, they benefit in equal shares as joint tenants[68]: the argument that, in the case of a policy for the benefit of spouse and children, the spouse should benefit for life with remainder to the children, has been rejected.[69] The joint tenants are those beneficiaries alive on the death of the insured: any benefit which might have gone to a beneficiary, who predeceased the insured, is shared among the survivors.[70]

The interest of the beneficiary may be made contingent, for example, contingent on the beneficiary surviving the insured.[71] If the contingency does not occur, the benefit reverts to the insured or his estate.[72]

If the benefit under the policy is not exhausted by the trust, there is a resulting trust of the balance in favour of the insured and his estate.[73] If the purposes of the trust fail, there is a resulting trust in favour of the insured and his estate. In the event of divorce between the insured and a beneficiary of a statutory trust, the court granting the

61. *Cousins v Sun Life Assurance Sy* [1933] 1 Ch 126 (CA); the court refused the declaration sought by the insured that, wife Lilian having died, he had the sole beneficial interest in the policy and could surrender it. *A fortiori* if there is a reference in the policy to the beneficiary's personal representatives: *Prescott v Prescott* [1906] 1 IR 155. *Aliter* if the policy refers to a beneficiary "if then living": *Cleaver v Mutual Reserve Fund Life Assurance* [1892] 1 QB 147 (CA).
USA: if "my wife Lilian" can be identified, she benefits under the policy, even though she is not in law the wife of the insured: *Prudential Ins Co v Taylor*, 46 F Supp 115 (WD La, 1942—life); *Nicholson v Hartford Life Ins Co*, 233 NYS 2d 64 (1962—life).
62. *Re Browne's Policy* [1903] 1 Ch 188.
USA: the same rule is found with regard to not only the child by a former wife but to the stepchild of a former wife—*Mutual of Omaha Ins Co v Walsh*, 395 F Supp 1219 (Mo, 1975—life). *Cf New York Life Ins Co v Beebe*, 57 F Supp 754 (My, 1944—life).
63. Family Law Reform Act 1969, section 19(1).
USA: *idem* as a matter of the ordinary use of language: *Metropolitan Life Ins Co v Thompson*, 368 F 2d 791 (3 Cir, 1966—life), *cert den* 388 US 914 (1967).
64. Adoption Act 1958, section 14(3); this has been replaced by section 39 of the Adoption Act 1976.
65. *Re Clay's Policy* [1937] 2 AER 548; Farwell J took a literal interpretation of the section.
66. *Bowen v Lewis* (1884) 9 App Cas 890, 915 *per* Lord Blackburn, when construing "child" in a will; *semble* the construction is the same under section 11. See Anderson, (1993) 22 Anglo-Am L Rev 221.
67. For example, *Re Parker's Policies* [1906] 1 Ch 526.
68. Cases to this effect under the 1870 Act: *Re Seyton* (1887) 34 Ch D 511, followed in *Re Davies' Policy Trusts* [1892] 1 Ch 90 and *Re Griffiths' Policy* [1903] 1 Ch 739. For the same decision under the 1882 Act see *Re Browne's Policy* [1903] 1 Ch 188.
69. Accepted in *Re Adam's Policy Trust* (1883) 23 Ch D 525.
70. *Re Seyton* (above).
71. *Re Takimidis' Policy Trusts* [1925] 1 Ch 403; *Re Fleetwood* [1926] Ch 48.
72. *Re Collier* [1930] 2 Ch 37 (applying the Act of 1870).
73. *Cleaver v Mutual Reserve Fund Life Assn* [1892] 1 QB 147 (CA).

decree has power, as in the case of express trust, to make an order varying or discharging any settlement, including life insurance, made on the parties to the marriage.[74]

Section 11 of the Married Women's Property Act 1882 further provides[75]:

" . . . The insured may by the policy, or by any memorandum under his or her hand, appoint a trustee or trustees of the moneys payable under the policy, and from time to time appoint a new trustee or new trustees thereof, and may make provision for the appointment of a new trustee or new trustees thereof, and for the investment of the moneys payable under any such policy. In default of any such appointment of a trustee, such policy, immediately on its being effected, shall vest in the insured and or his legal representatives, in trust for the purposes aforesaid. The receipt of a trustee or trustees duly appointed, or, in default of any such appointment, or in default of notice to the insurance office, the receipt of the legal personal representatives of the insured shall be a discharge to the office for the sums secured by the policy, or for the value thereof, in whole or in part."

5–5 THE BROKER'S UNNAMED PRINCIPAL

In *Provincial Ins Co of Canada* v *Leduc*[76] it was held to be "clear that an agent who insures for another with his authority may sue in his own name" for the benefit of others interested.[77] The contention that that rule is confined to marine insurance has been rejected.[78] The basis of the rule may lie in the fiduciary nature of the relation between agent and principal.[79] If so, this is also the basis of the right of an ordinary trustee to enforce an insurance contract concluded on behalf of a beneficiary of the trust.[80] Alternatively, the agent's right of action may be seen as an instance of commercial specialty: below, 5–6C5.

5–6 THE COMMERCIAL TRUST

A person with an insurable but limited interest in goods may insure those goods and, in the event of loss, recover the full amount of the loss or damage; then, having deducted the amount of his own loss, he holds the balance for others with an interest in the goods. He has been called a commercial trustee.[81]

74. Matrimonial Proceedings and Property Act 1970, section 27.
75. For detail the reader is referred to Houseman, pp 200 ff; MacGillivray, Nos 1422 (p 661) ff.
76. (1874) LR 6 PC 224, 244 *per* Sir Barnes Peacock (hull). Bowstead, p 433.
77. *Lloyd's* v *Harper* (1880) 16 Ch D 290, 315 *per* James LJ, 321 *per* Lush LJ (CA). Lush LJ (*ibid*) considered that, unlike *Hepburn* (below 5–6), the third party principal "has a right, if he pleases, to take action himself and sue upon the contract made by the broker for him, for he is a principal party to the contract". The rule as stated by Lush LJ finds modern support *en passant* in *Woodar Investment Development Ltd* v *Wimpey Construction UK Ltd* [1980] 1 All ER 571, 576–577 *per* Lord Wilberforce, 585 *per* Lord Russell (HL); and *Siu* v *Eastern Ins Co Ltd, The Times*, 16 December 1993 (PC—liability).
78. *Transcontinental Underwriting Agency SRL* v *Grand Union Ins Co Ltd* [1987] 2 Lloyd's Rep 409 (re).
79. *Woodar* (above) p 585 *per* Lord Russell (HL). Alternatively the basis may be that of commercial specialty (below, 5–6C5).
80. *Woodar* (above) p 585.
81. MacGillivray, No 172. *Cf General Accident* v *Midland Bank* [1940] 2 KB 388, 405 *per* Lord Greene MR (CA—fire), applied in *Woolcott* v *Sun Alliance & London Ins Co Ltd* [1978] 1 Lloyd's Rep 629 (fire): When more than one person is interested in property, these persons may insure under a single policy; both their interests and their potential loss differ, so theirs is not a joint interest or a joint policy: it is an insurance by two or more persons for their respective interests; see below 30–4. In this situation, unlike that now under consideration, these persons are parties to the contract of insurance.
Concerning, joint or composite insurance, see below, 30–4

In *Waters* v *Monarch Life Assurance Co*[82] the plaintiff insured property, his own and that of third parties, in his warehouse. The insurers were held liable to the plaintiff not only for the value of the plaintiff's own property and of his lien on the property of the third parties, but to the full value of the latter. A century later, *Waters* was applied in *Tomlinson (Hauliers) Ltd* v *Hepburn*[83]: cigarettes, insured by carriers, were stolen from the carriers' vehicle without liability on the part of the carriers. Although the carriers had insured at the insistence of the owners of the cigarettes, it was accepted that they did so not as agents of the owners but in their own name. Although they had suffered no loss, the House of Lords held that they could recover from the insurer the full amount of the loss, holding the money for the owners. The owners could not compel the insured carriers to recover the full value, but once the carriers had done so they were accountable to the owners for the insurance money. In such cases the courts have been influenced by the following factors.

First, the solution is commercially convenient:

"The practice of the mercantile community as well as of underwriters has also, we believe, been entirely in accordance with this view of the law; and there is manifest convenience in it, that it saves a multiplicity of insurances upon the same subject-matter, and avoids the necessity for any nice distinctions as to the precise interest of the several parties."[84]

Second, the premium paid to the insurer by the insured was calculated on the basis of potential liability for the full value of the goods.[85]

Third, as a bailee was permitted to recover the full value of the goods from a tortfeasor in an action for negligence[86] or conversion, it "would seem irrational, therefore, if he could not also insure for their full value".[87]

---

82. (1856) 5 El & Bl 870 (fire). Similar decisions in the USA include *Re Podolsky*, 115 F 2d 965 (3 Cir, 1940—fire); *Sutton Carpet Cleaners Inc* v *Firemen's Ins Co of Newark*, 68 NYS 2d 218 (1947—fire); *Dawson* v *United States*, 203 F 2d 201 (5 Cir, 1953—fire); *Old Colony Ins Co* v *Lampert*, 129 F Supp 545 (NJ, 1955—fire), affirmed 227 F 2d 520 (3 Cir, 1955); *Keystone Fabric Laminates Inc* v *Federal Ins Co*, 407 F 2d 1353 (3 Cir, 1969—fire).

As in England, the *rationale* varies. One basis that is not found in England is that a third party is entitled to sue on a contract for his benefit and may therefore have better rights against the insurer than the insured. *Aetna Ins Co* v *Eisenberg*, 188 F Supp 415 (ED Ark, 1960—fire), affirmed 294 F 2d 301 (8 Cir, 1961): the third party bailor had a direct action against the insurer of goods held by a furrier and was unaffected by false declarations of value made to the insurer by the furrier, because the insurer, having failed to check the declarations carefully, was estopped from raising this defence to an action by the third party.

83. [1966] AC 451 (goods in transit). See also *Maurice* v *Goldsborough, Mort & Co Ltd* [1939] AC 452 (PC—fire). In *Framar Money Management Pty Ltd* v *Territory Ins Office* (1986) 87 FLR 251 (NT—fire) *Hepburn* was applied to insurance by a company of the property of other companies in the same group of companies. It was applied in New Zealand in *Entec Service Ltd* v *Neuchâtel Swiss Gen Ins Co Ltd* (1990) ANZ Ins Cases, no 60–969 (cargo); and *Guardian Royal Exchange* v *Roberts* (1991) 6 ANZ Ins Cases, no 61–031 (motor).

84. *Ebsworth* v *Alliance Marine Ins Co* (1873) LR 8 CP 596, 612 *per* Bovill CJ (cargo). See also *Waters* v *Monarch* (1856) 5 El & Bl 870, 881 *per* Lord Campbell CJ: "It would be most inconvenient in business if a wharfinger could not, at his own cost, keep up a floating policy for the benefit of his customers." This statement was approved in *Hepburn* p 467 *per* Lord Reid, with whom Lord Guest and Lord Wilberforce concurred. See also Lord Pearce *ibid* (p 477 and p 481); *LNWR* v *Glyn* (1859) 1 El & El 652, 661 *per* Wightman J (fire).

85. *LNWR* v *Glyn* (1859) 1 El & El 652, 661 *per* Wightman J (fire).

86. *The Winkfield* [1902] P 42 (CA), a case of maritime collision, in which the bailee was not liable for the collision to the bailor. It has been suggested that this decision has been restricted by the Torts (Wrongful Interference) Act 1977, section 8, to cases in which the third party (bailor) cannot be identified: Halsbury, Vol 45, No 1477.

87. *Tomlinson (Hauliers) Ltd* v *Hepburn* [1966] AC 451, 480 *per* Lord Pearce; see also p 468 *per* Lord Reid (goods in transit).

These decisions appear to conflict with well established rules of law. First, although the bailee has an insurable interest in the goods by virtue of his potential liability to the bailor,[88] it might be said that the underlying policy against wagering is offended, when he is allowed to recover an amount in excess of his actual loss. The answer[89] is that there can be no objection if, as *Hepburn* decided, the insured is required to hold the surplus money over and above his own loss for third party interests. Second, in the case of damages the principle of indemnity means that no plaintiff may recover loss that he himself has not suffered: *The Albazero*,[90] in which Lord Diplock acknowledged[91] the rule in *Hepburn* as a mercantile exception.

5–6A The Trustee Insured

For the application of *Hepburn* the insured must be a bailee[92] or mortgagee[93] or person in analogous position,[94] that is, a person,

    (a) who has an insurable interest of his own in the property subject-matter of the insurance; and

    (b) who is in such relation to the subject-matter that it is sensible and convenient that he should be able to insure and recover for others who have suffered loss from the insured event but who are not parties to the contract of insurance.

5–6B Insurance Terms

The contract of insurance must purport to cover property in which the third party has

---

88. See above, 4–5I.
89. *Robertson* v *Hamilton* (1811) 14 East 522, 532–533 *per* Lord Ellenborough CJ (marine); approved in *Hepburn* by Lord Pearce (p 478). In the same sense in *Hepburn* p 468 (Lord Reid) and p 477 (Lord Pearce).
90. [1977] AC 774.
91. p 846. See also *Hepburn*, pp 470–471 *per* Lord Reid.
92. *Tomlinson (Hauliers) Ltd* v *Hepburn* [1966] AC 451.
93. *Garden* v *Ingram* (1852) 23 LJ Ch 478 (fire); *Nichols & Co* v *Scottish Union & National Ins Co*, 885 14 R (Ct Sess) 1094 (fire). The issue has arisen relatively infrequently as regards mortgagees of land, in view of the practice of reinstatement encouraged by the Fires Prevention (Metropolis) Act 1774, section 83: below, 5–7 and 29–3. For discussion of other instances, see *Lonsdale & Thompson Ltd* v *Black Arrow Group plc* [1993] 3 All ER 648, 655 *per* J Sumption QC (fire), in which the rule was applied to lessor and lessee.
USA: insurance by the mortgagor or mortgagee in part for the benefit of the other is more common than in England. See for example *Westchester Fire Ins Co of New York* v *Norfolk Building & Loan Assn*, 14 F 2d 524 (8 Cir, 1926—fire). The third party may have better rights than the insured: *City-Wide Knitwear Processing Co Inc* v *Safeco Ins Co of America*, 366 NYS 2d 81 (1973—fire).
94. *Hepburn*, p 481 *per* Lord Pearce. The category of persons includes a joint owner—*Page* v *Fry* (1800) 2 Bos & Pul 240 (cargo). MIA, section 14(2) provides: "A mortgagee, consignee, or other person having an interest in the subject-matter insured may insure on behalf and for the benefit of other persons interested as well as for his own benefit." This is intended as an enactment of the common law rule in *Ebsworth* v *Alliance Marine Ins Co* (1873) LR 8 CP 596 (marine). Arnould, No 380, suggests that the effect is a trust of the insurance money in the hands of the insured in favour of the third party. The rule was extended to a lessor in *Lonsdale & Thompson Ltd* v *Black Arrow Group plc* [1993] 2 Lloyd's Rep. 428 (fire).

an interest.[95] If so, it is unnecessary to seek further the intention of the insured.[96] However, if it is proved that the insured did not in fact intend to insure for the third party, the insured cannot recover in respect of it.[97] Moreover, if a term of the contract of insurance requires goods held by the insured as bailee to be specifically insured as such, this must be done.[98]

Words which indicate an intent to benefit a third party include "goods his own in trust or on commission",[99] "merchandise the insureds' own property or held by them in trust or on commission for which they may be liable".[100] However, the same intention may be deduced from other terms of the policy, such as premium,[101] or from the trade context.[102]

5–6C The Basis of Enforcement by the Third Party

The rights of third parties in respect of the insurance or the insurance money in cases of commercial trust depend on the legal basis of those rights; in England this is far from clear. There is a number of possibilities.

5–6C1 Liability Cover

In many cases the insured was under a duty to the third party to insure the property to its full value.[103] Hence it might have been said that the subject-matter of insurance

---

95. *Armitage* v *Winterbottom & Hextall* (1840) 1 Man & G 130 (fire); *Martineau* v *King* (1872) LR 7 QB 436 (fire); *Ebsworth* v *Alliance Marine Ins Co* (1873) LR 8 CP 596, 609 *per* Bovill CJ (cargo); *Boston Fruit Co* v *British & Foreign Marine Ins Co* [1906] AC 336 (hull); *Samuel & Co Ltd* v *Dumas* [1923] 1 KB 592, 614 *per* Bankes LJ, 625 *per* Scrutton LJ; affirmed [1924] AC 431 (hull). *Cf Re Harrington Motor Co* [1928] Ch 105 (CA—liability).

Cf Scotland: it has been held that, when bailees, without instructions from or the knowledge of the bailor, insured goods in their possession "their own, in trust or on commission", this created no enforceable rights in the bailor to the insurance money paid to the bailee in respect of damage to the goods: *Dalgleish* v *Buchanan & Co* (1854) 16 D 332, 336–338 *per* Lord Ivory, whose opinion was approved in *Ferguson* v *The Parish Council of the City Parish of Aberdeen*, 1916 SC 715. In these cases the courts appeared to require a duty in the bailee towards the bailor to insure the goods. *Cf Gillespie* v *Miller, Son & Co*, 1874 1 R (Ct Sess) 433 (fire) in which the court was divided over whether a duty was necessary. In the USA a duty to insure is unnecessary: *United States* v *INA*, 65 F Supp 401 (WD SC, 1946—fire), affirmed 159 F 2d 699 (4 Cir, 1947).

96. *Tomlinson (Hauliers) Ltd* v *Hepburn* [1966] AC 451, 482 *per* Lord Pearce. As regards marine insurance *cf* Arnould, Nos 249 and 250. Generally, *cf Vandepitte* v *Preferred Accident Ins Corp of New York* [1933] AC 70 in which the Privy Council required on the part of the insured intention to benefit the third party; the decision has been criticised on this and other points: 33 Colum L Rev 749 (1933); Finlay, *Contracts for the Benefit of Third Persons*, pp 40 ff.

97. *Hepburn* (above), p 482 *per* Lord Pearce. *British Traders' Ins Co Ltd* v *Monson* (1964) 111 CLR 86, 96 (HCA—fire). *Board of Education of Raleigh County* v *Winding Gulf Collieries*, 152 F 2d 382 (4 Cir, 1945—fire), *cert* den 328 US 844 (1946).

98. *London & North Western Railway* v *Glyn* (1859) 1 El & El 652; *South Australian Ins Co* v *Randall* (1869) LR 3 PC 101 (fire).

99. "Goods in trust" means, not goods held upon trust in equity, but simply goods with which the insured has been entrusted: *Waters* v *Monarch Fire & Life Assurance Co* (1856) 5 E & B 870, 880 *per* Lord Campbell CJ. *Re Podolsky*, 115 F 2d 965 (3 Cir, 1940—fire).

100. *Maurice* v *Goldsborough, Mort & Co Ltd* [1939] AC 452 (PC). *Cf North British & Mercantile Ins Co* v *Moffatt* (1871) LR 7 CP 25: goods belonging to the insured or "for which they are responsible". The goods in question were outside the policy.

101. *Maurice* (above).

102. *Yangtsze Ins Assn Ltd* v *Lukmanjee* [1918] AC 585.

103. For example *Ebsworth* v *Alliance Marine Ins Co* (1873) LR 8 CP 596; reversed (1874) 43 LJCP 394n. *Maurice* v *Goldsborough, Mort & Co Ltd* [1939] AC 452 (PC); *Tomlinson (Hauliers) Ltd* v *Hepburn* [1966] AC 451. *Cf* in Scotland: *Dalgleish* v *Buchanan & Co* (1854) 16 D 332; *Ferguson* v *The Parish Council of the City Parish of Aberdeen*, 1916 SC 715.

was the insured's liability arising out of that duty. On this basis there are no difficulties with general rules of contract law, such as privity.[104] The third party enforces the duty of the insured, which exists *ex hypothesi*. However, this explanation does not hold for the cases[105] in which the subject-matter of the insurance was not liability, but property. Moreover, in other cases the present rule was applied, even though there was no duty to the third party to insure the property.[106]

5–6C2 Agency

Before *Hepburn*,[107] the insured bailee would probably have been seen[108] as making the contract of insurance not only for himself but also as agent for the third party.[109] The courts have generally been ready to imply an agency, if there are good commercial reasons for it.[110] As for the present rule, sometimes courts have discussed it in terms of agency[111] and there is no doubt that the third party as principal can enforce the contract made for him by the insured.[112] But this was not the basis of the decision in *Hepburn*,[113] in which agency was explicitly ruled out. Further, analysis as agency falters on the general rule that there can be ratification of agency, only if the principal could have made the very same contract at the time of ratification: this is said to preclude ratification of insurance in respect of loss that has already occurred. If that is right, a *Hepburn* decision can be based on agency, only if the exception to the general rule against ratification after loss, which is found in marine insurance,[114] were extended to non-marine insurance; but the marine exception is thought to be anomalous,[115] and its extension a matter of doubt.[116]

5–6C3 Trust of the Insurer's Promise to Pay

This explanation sees the insured as trustee of the insurer's promise to pay; the beneficiary is the third party who, as such, can enforce the trust, i.e., can compel the trustee insured to enforce the contract of insurance on his behalf.[117] If there is a trust of an agreement, "the trustee then can take steps to enforce performance to the beneficiary by the other contracting party as in the case of other equitable rights. The

---

104. For example, *Woodar Investment Development Ltd* v *Wimpey Construction UK Ltd* [1980] 1 All ER 571, 591 *per* Lord Scarman (HL).
105. Notably *Hepburn* (above).
106. For example, *Waters* v *Monarch* (1856) 5 El & Bl 870, 881 *per* Campbell LCJ.
107. Above, 5–5.
108. There is a hint from the House of Lords that this is the usual way of solving this kind of problem: *Woodar Investment Development Ltd* v *Wimpey Construction UK Ltd* [1980] 1 All ER 571, 576 *per* Lord Wilberforce (HL). See further Finlay, *Contracts for the Benefit of Third Persons* (1939), pp 96 ff.
109. Unless the principal was unascertained at the time that the contract was made: Finlay, *loc cit.*
110. *The Eurymedon, Satterthwaite & Co Ltd* v *New Zealand Shipping Co Ltd* [1975] AC 154; *Godina* v *Patrick* [1984] 1 Lloyd's Rep 333, 336 *per* Hutley J (HCA)
111. For example *Waters* v *Monarch* (1856) 5 El & Bl 870, 881 *per* Lord Campbell CJ. See also *Robertson* v *Hamilton* (1811) 14 East 522, 533–534 *per* Lord Ellenborough CJ; *Cochran & Son* v *Leckie's Trustee* (1906) 8 F (Ct Sess) 975; *Williams* v *Baltic Ins Assn of London Ltd* [1924] 2 KB 282, 289 *per* Roche J (motor).
112. For example, *Cochran* (above).
113. *Tomlinson (Hauliers) Ltd* v *Hepburn* [1966] AC 451, 479 *per* Lord Pearce.
114. *Williams* v *North China Ins Co* (1876) 1 CPD 757 (CA—freight).
115. *Ibid* p 766 *per* Lord James MR.
116. See further below, 7–4D1.
117. *Robertson* v *Hamilton* (1811) 14 East 522, 532 *per* Lord Ellenborough CJ: the insured "may recover upon this policy as trustees for those who are interested with themselves."

action should be in the name of the trustee; if, however, he refuses to sue, the bene-ficiary can sue, joining the trustee as a defendant".[118] In the absence, however, of an express trust, a trust must be implied. In the general law in recent times the courts have rarely implied a trust of a promise,[119] notably because, in the absence of an express trust, it is not easy to convince a court that the trustee (insured) intended to tie his hands in this way.[120] This reason is not entirely persuasive in the present situation, so the implication of such a trust cannot be totally ruled out.

5–6C4   Trust of the Insurance Money

If the insured recovers the full amount of the loss from the insurer, a trust may be imposed on the money to the extent that it exceeds the amount of the insured's own loss, a trust in favour of third parties who have suffered loss from the insured event. In other words "the effect of the plaintiffs' insuring and recovering in their own names would be to place them in the position of trustees for the other parties interested, as to any surplus beyond the amount of their own claim".[121]

Early insurance cases allowed a restitutionary action by the third party against the insured for money had and received to the third party's use.[122] Were it otherwise, the insured would be unjustly enriched to the extent that the insurance money in his hand exceeded the amount of his own loss. Significantly, perhaps, this seems to have been in the mind of Lord Pearce in *Hepburn*[123] when he said that the insured "were intended to be trustees of the benefit of that policy and of any recovery effected under it" for the third party.

In *Re E Dibbens & Sons*,[124] Harman J explained the meaning of the "trust". He noted that a "fiduciary" obligation "can run from the full rigour of trusteeship", which the present case is not, "down to a much lower duty, merely a duty to account for moneys actually come into your hands". In the present case, "one does not have here a true trust relationship at all: one has a relationship of fiduciary obligation which can be satisfied out of the insurance fund available to pay those persons who contracted to have their goods insured *to the amount which they required to be insured* if the fund will go so far",[124a] but not to the full value of the goods if that were a higher amount. In that case, the insured warehousing firm was in creditors' voluntary liquidation after a large fire had destroyed the firm's warehouse. Those customers who had paid for insurance had a prior right to be paid from the insurance moneys held by the liquida-

118. *Vandepitte* v *Preferred Accident Ins Co of New York* [1933] AC 70, 79 *per* Lord Wright (PC—motor); the Board did not find that a trust had been intended in the particular case.
119. See above, 5–2.
120. Treitel, pp 564–565.
121. *Ebsworth* v *Alliance Marine Ins Co* (1873) LR 8 CP 596, 629 *per* Bovill CJ concerning a consignee of goods.
122. *Gillett* v *Mawman* (1808) 1 Taunt 137, 140 *per* Lord Mansfield CJ (fire); *Sidaways* v *Todd* (1818) 2 Stark 400 (fire); accepted but not applied in view of the facts in *Armitage* v *Winterbottom & Hextall* (1840) 1 Man & G 130 (fire).
123. *Tomlinson (Hauliers) Ltd* v *Hepburn* [1966] AC 451, 476; *idem* p 480. See also *LNWR* v *Glyn* (1859) 1 El & Bl 652, 660–661 *per* Wightman J; *Ebsworth* v *Alliance Marine Ins Co* (1873) LR 8 CP 596, 629 *per* Bovill CJ (cargo); *Gillespie* v *Miller, Son & Co*, 1874 1 R (Ct Sess) 423, 433 *per* the Lord Justice-Clerk (fire); *The Albazero* [1977] AC 774, 845–846 *per* Lord Diplock. *British Traders' Ins Co Ltd* v *Monson* (1964) 111 CLR 86, 102–103 (HCA—fire). *Sutton Carpet Cleaners Inc* v *Firemen's Ins Co of Newark*, 68 NYS 2d 218, 225 (1947—fire), affirmed 78 NYS 2d 565 (1948). Generally in English law, see *Saunders* v *Vautier* (1841) Cr & Ph 240.
124. [1990] BCLC 577; Adams [1992] JBL 291.
124a. pp 582–583.

tor. As regards those customers who had not paid for insurance, the duty of the firm to store and redeliver goods was covered entirely by contract: their rights required no fiduciary obligation, they were owed none and were no more than general creditors of the firm.

5–6C5 Commercial Specialty

The emphasis on commercial convenience, together with a reluctance by the courts in some cases to explain the "commercial trust" in terms of established concepts, gives some colour to another explanation. In the general law of contract, if it is clear that a commercial practice exists in favour of third party rights, the defeat of which would cause widespread inconvenience, and that the parties to a case have based their dealing on it, the courts will do what they can to sanction the practice.[125] The rule applied in *Hepburn* has been described as "appropriated from the law merchant",[126] and the action by the insurance agent for his principal (above, 5–5) has also been mentioned[127] as a matter of "trade usage".

5–7 THE FIRES PREVENTION (METROPOLIS) ACT 1774

Section 83 of this Act provides that "in order to deter and hinder ill-minded persons from wilfully setting their house or houses or other buildings on fire with a view of gaining to themselves the insurance money, whereby the lives and fortunes of many families may be lost or endangered," fire insurers are "authorised and required" to expend the insurance money, as far as it will go, on the reinstatement of the house or building. This provision applies,

   (a) if the insurer has "grounds of suspicion" that the owner, occupier or other person who has insured the building has been guilty of fraud, or of wilfully setting the building on fire, or

   (b) if the insurer is requested to do so by a "person interested in or intitled unto" the building.

     In each case there is an exception, if

    (i) within 60 days after the adjustment of his claim, the insured gives "sufficient security" to the insurer that the insurance money will be spent on reinstatement; or

    (ii) within the same period of time the insurance money is "settled and disposed of to and amongst all the contending parties, to the satisfaction and approbation" of the insurer.

  As regards (a), "grounds of suspicion" that the insured has been guilty of "fraud" or arson, this situation has not arisen in the courts. The insurer is likely to stipulate in

---

125. Concerning bankers' commercial credits: *Malas v British Imex Industries Ltd* [1958] 2 QB 127, 129 *per* Jenkins LJ (CA); *Alan (WJ) & Co Ltd v El Nasr Export & Import Co* [1972] 2 QB 189, 208 *per* Lord Denning MR (CA). See also *United Dominions Trust Ltd v Kirkwood* [1966] 2 QB 431 (CA). Generally see Anson, p 432. But now see *The Aramis* [1989] 1 Lloyd's Rep 213, 219 *per* Stuart-Smith LJ (CA).

126. *The Albazero* [1977] AC 774, 846 *per* Lord Diplock, who also said that the doctrine of subrogation was such an exception based on the law merchant.

127. Bowstead, p 433.

the contract and, if sufficiently suspicious, exercise an option of reinstatement or, absent such a stipulation, to refuse to pay.[128] As regards (b) see below, 29–3A.

5–7A The Scope of Section 83

(a) Section 83 applies only to fire insurance, and to a fire insurer who is liable to pay insurance money to the insured in respect of fire loss to the building concerned.[129] If the insurer is requested to reinstate after he has settled the claim, the insurer is liable no longer and the request is too late.[130]

(b) Section 83 applies to "offices for insuring houses or other buildings". Although the purposes of the section may be relevant to other kinds of property, section 83 does not apply to other property, such as furniture,[131] contents of buildings,[132] or tenant's fixtures, to which the landlord has no immediate right.[133]

(c) Section 83 applies to the "governors or directors of the several [fire] insurance offices". From this it has been deduced[134] that the duty does not apply to members of Lloyd's, who until recently were in no legal sense a company. However, the concept of a company as a legal body distinct from its human members was not clear in 1774.[135] Moreover, the duty in section 83 is imposed not on the company as such but on the leading human agents of the company. Further, in 1774 fire business was not transacted at Lloyd's.[136] A purposive construction of section 83, which has been applied on the geographical scope of the section (below, 5–7B), suggests that the section should apply to Lloyd's.

5–7B Geographical Scope

Originally, as the short title of the Act suggests, section 83 applied only to certain parts of London. A purposive construction by the courts extended it to all parts of the United Kingdom; the evil giving rise to the Act, said Lord Cranworth LC,[137] was not confined to London. Lord Watson, however, thought[138] that it did not extend to Scotland, because the Act was brought in to amend previous legislation which did not apply to Scotland. But, if Lord Cranworth was right to extend the Act from London to

128. *Cf Simpson* v *Scottish Union Ins Co* (1863) 1 H & M 618 in which the insurer was suspicious but nonetheless reached a settlement with the insured lessee, against the wishes of the third "person interested", the lessor.

129. *Matthey* v *Curling* [1922] 2 AC 180, 198 *per* Atkin LJ.

130. *Simpson* v *Scottish Union Ins Co* (1863) 1 H & M 618, 628 *per* Sir W Page Wood, V-C; *Rayner* v *Preston* (1881) 18 Ch D 1, 7 *per* Cotton LJ (CA).

131. *In re Quicke's Trusts* [1908] 1 Ch 887.

132. *Sinnot* v *Bowden* [1912] 2 Ch 414.

133. *Ex p Gorely* (1864) 4 De G J & S 477.

134. *Portavon Cinema Co Ltd* v *Price & Century Ins Co Ltd* [1939] 4 All ER 601, 608 *per* Branson J.

135. See for example, Gower, *Principles of Modern Company Law* (5th ed, 1992), ch 2 ff.

136. Around the end of the eighteenth century a few underwriters at Lloyd's wrote fire insurance until for taxation reasons, the business ceased to be profitable. By and large fire risks were written by the companies until 1870 when a small fire market at Lloyd's had been revived: A. Brown, *Cuthbert Heath* (London, 1980), p 63.

137. *Ex p Gorely* (1864) 4 De G J & S 477, 480; applied in *Re Quicke's Trusts* [1908] 1 Ch 887; *Sinnott* v *Bowden* [1912] 2 Ch 414.

138. *Westminster Fire Office* v *Glasgow Provident Investment Sy* (1888) 13 App Cas 699, 716.

Watford, the same logic suggests that the Act should apply to Scotland. It has been applied in certain Commonwealth jurisdictions.[139]

5–7C Persons Interested

The right to initiate reinstatement on the part of the insurer is given to "persons interested or intitled unto" the building concerned. This has three possible meanings: (a) If the sole purpose of the Act were to deter the ill-minded insured, tempted to fire the property, this suggests that a person interested is anyone who might have a public interest in deterrence. (b) The purpose of the section, being not only to inhibit arson but also to protect persons interested, suggests all persons who might be damnified, if the insured fires the building and pockets the insurance money; this points not only to those with an insurable interest in law but also persons affected consequentially, such as the assembler who depends on components manufactured in the building insured. (c) An insurance view is that a person interested is any person with an insurable interest in law in the property.[140] For the caselaw, see below, 29–3A.

5–7D Procedure

The insurer has no duty to reinstate until he has "grounds for suspicion" or he has received a request from a "person interested or intitled". Enforcement of the duty has not come before the courts on the first ground and only rarely on the second.

   In the case of a request, the request must be clear. In *Simpson* v *Scottish Union Ins Co*[141] the plaintiff let two houses to tenants who, in accordance with the agreement, insured the houses, which were later burned down. The plaintiff, in the words of Sir W Page Wood, V-C,[142]

"went to see the secretary of the insurance offices, and claimed to be entitled to the benefit of the policy, and to have the amount applied towards the rebuilding the houses, and said that he relied on the office paying nothing to the tenants; to which the secretary agreed. There was no reference, on this occasion, to the statute . . . Throughout, the plaintiff is not requesting the company to lay out the money in the manner prescribed by the Act of Parliament, but claiming to be the person really interested under the policy."

The court held that there had been no "distinct request", as required by the Act. Nor could such a request be made later for "if the owner does not make this request before a settlement with the tenant, he cannot insist upon it afterwards."[143]

5–7E The Effect of Section 83

The effect intended for section 83 is the reinstatement of the building, as far as the insurance money will go, in the form it enjoyed before the fire (below, 29–2D). If it is done at the request of a "person interested", that person is not regarded as a person

---

139. Australia: *Royal Ins Co* v *Mylius* (1926) 38 CLR 477 (the HCA applied a provision based on section 83); *Goldman* v *Hargrave* [1967] 1 AC 645 (PC applied section 86 of the 1774 Act).
   Section 86 of the 1774 Act was applied in Canada in *Southern Ry. Co* v *Phelps* (1884) 14 SCR 132; and section 83 in *Re Alliance Assurance Co Ltd* (1960) 25 DLR (2d) 316 (BC).
140. See above, 4–5D.
141. (1863) 1 H & M 618.
142. p 627.
143. p 628.

insured under the policy for the purposes of double insurance.[144] If the insurer declines to accede to the request for reinstatement, it is not clear whether there is an effective remedy against him.[145]

5–8 THE THIRD PARTIES (RIGHTS AGAINST INSURERS) ACT 1930[146]

If a person who had liability insurance became bankrupt (or, in the case of a company, went into liquidation) the person to whom he was liable (the third party) was compelled to prove in the bankruptcy with the other creditors, unless, of course, he had previously managed to obtain judgment and levy execution against the bankrupt insured.[147] The feeling that this was unjust was intensified by the advent of motor vehicles and the injuries in which they were instrumental, and led[148] to the Third Parties (Rights Against Insurers) Act 1930, under which the claimant has a direct right of action against the insurer: the insured's claim is abstracted from the bankruptcy and transferred to the third party.[149]

In states that do not insist on privity of contract, it may be enough for the contract of insurance to purport to benefit a third party for that third party to have a right of action against the insurer.[150] In other states, such as England, a similar result has been achieved in specific situations by statute,[151] in particular, the Act of 1930 (above) and the Road Traffic Act of 1988.[152] Otherwise the third party, notably the victim, has no right of action against the liability insurer.[153]

Section 1 of the 1930 Act provides that, if (a) a person is insured under a contract of insurance against liability to third parties and (b) he becomes bankrupt or makes a composition or arrangement with his creditors, his rights against the insurer in respect of liability that he has incurred to a third party are "transferred and vested in the third party to whom the liability was incurred". The section is expressed to apply also to companies; for the purposes of this chapter henceforth any reference, apart from that

144. *Portavon Cinema Co Ltd* v *Price & Century Ins Co Ltd* [1939] 4 All ER 601.
145. See below, 29–3A.
146. Calabresi, "Economic Analysis of Law", 69 Iowa L Rev 832 (1984).
147. For example, *Re Harrington Motor Co Ltd* [1928] Ch 105 (CA).
148. *Jones* v *Birch Bros Ltd.* [1933] 2 KB 597, 612 *per* Greer LJ (CA—motor); *McCormick* v *National Motor & Accident Ins Union Ltd* (1934) 49 Ll L Rep 361, 363 *per* Scrutton LJ (CA—motor).
149. *Re Compania Merabello San Nicholas SA* [1973] Ch 75, 90–91 *per* Megarry J; see also *Re Allobrogia SS Corp* [1978] 3 All ER 423.
150. *Central Mutual Ins Co* v *Tartar*, 92 F 2d 839 (6 Cir, 1937—motor); *New Amsterdam Casualty Co* v *Jones*, 135 F 2d 191 (6 Cir, 1943—liability); *Chapin Owen Co Inc* v *Newman*, 107 NYS 2d 941 (1951—cargo); *Rappaport* v *Phil Gottlieb-Sattler*, 114 NYS 2d 221 (1952), affirmed 111 NE 2d 647 (1953); *Babcock & Wilcox Co* v *Parsons Corp*, 298 F Supp 898 (D Neb—machinery floater). However, there is no right of action by the original insured against the insurer's reinsurer: *A/S Ivarans Rederei* v *Puerto Rico Ports Authority*, 617 F 2d 903 (1 Cir, 1980); on this, see above, 5–1.
151. For example the NY Ins Law, art 167(b) gives a right of action to the third party if "judgment against the insured . . . in an action brought to recover damages for injury sustained or loss or damage occasioned during the life of the policy or contract, shall remain unsatisfied at the expiration of thirty days from the serving of notice of entry of judgment upon the . . . insured, and upon the insurer . . . " As the precondition is less dramatic than the insolvency required by the English Act of 1930, the statute has been applied in a wider range of situations; for example, it has allowed a direct action by the consignee of goods against the carrier's liability insurer: *Cicero Construction Corp* v *United States Fire Ins Co*, 41 NYS 2d 719 (1943—cargo).
152. Below, 5–9. Section 151 of this Act applies to the case of motor insurance, whether the insured is bankrupt or not. It does not take away any rights that the third party may have under the Act of 1930.
153. *Re National Motorship Corp*, 96 F 2d 88 (2 Cir, 1938—hull); *Gutride* v *General Reinsurance Corp*, 4 NYS 2d 387 (1938—re).

in a particular decision of the courts, to bankruptcy should be taken to include *mutatis mutandis* a reference to the liquidation or receivership of companies.

5–8A A Contract of Insurance

The Act applies when there is a contract of insurance,[154] which includes mutual insurance.[155]

5–8B Insolvency

The Act applies (i) in the case of a person, in the event of his "becoming bankrupt or making a composition or arrangement with his creditors", or (ii) in the case of a company, "in the event of a winding-up order being made, or a resolution for a voluntary winding up being passed . . . or of a receiver or manager of the company's business or undertaking being duly appointed, or of possession being taken by or on behalf of the holders of any debentures secured by a floating charge, of any property comprised in or subject to the charge".

The Act does not apply in the case of a company which is "wound up voluntarily merely for the purposes of reconstruction or of amalgamation with another company".[156] Nor does the Act apply in any case to a company which has been completely wound up, if in that case there is no longer any means by which the existence and amount of liability can be established.[157] Moreover, the third party has no right to prevent a settlement between the insured and the insurer for an amount that is inadequate to cover the likely liability of the insured to the third party, even though the practical effect of the settlement is that the insured is insolvent.[158]

The Act applies to foreign corporations, if they can be wound up in England under sections 221 ff of the Insolvency Act 1986. For this there must be a sufficient connection with the jurisdiction, that is, not whether the corporation has a place of business here, but *inter alia* whether it has "assets here to administer and persons subject or at least submitting to the jurisdiction who are concerned or interested in the proper administration of the assets"[159] over whom jurisdiction is exercisable.[160] If the claim in question against the insurer is the only such asset, it must be shown that the claim has a reasonable possibility of success.[161]

5–8C Liability of the Insured

There must be liability, which is covered by the terms of a policy (below, 17–4). It is not enough to have a claim against the insured; the third party must have established

---

154. See above, 1–1.
155. *Re Allobrogia SS Corp* [1978] 3 All ER 423 (P & I).
156. Section 1(6).
157. *Bradley* v *Eagle Star Ins Co* [1989] 1 All ER 961 (HL—liability).
158. *Normid Housing Assn Ltd* v *Ralphs* [1989] 1 Lloyd's Rep 265 (CA—liability). The position in that case might have been different, if the insured had owed a duty to the claimant to insure the liability. *Quaere* the position if the settlement were in bad faith.
159. *Banque des Marchands de Moscou (Koupetschesky)* v *Kindersley* [1951] Ch 112, 126 *per* Lord Evershed MR (CA). The common law position has been changed by decisions under the Brussels Convention 1968 (above 2–70); see Dicey, Rule 157.
160. For example *Re Compania Merabello San Nicholas SA* [1973] Ch 75.
161. *Re Allobrogia* (above).

his claim in proceedings against the insured.[162] If the liability of the insured has not been established, the third party should proceed as follows:

"If there is an unascertained claim for damages in tort, it cannot be proved in the bankruptcy; nor in the liquidation of the company. But nevertheless the injured person can bring an action against the wrongdoer. In the case of a company, he must get the leave of the court. No doubt leave would automatically be given. The insurance company can fight an action in the name of the wrongdoer. In that way liability can be established and the loss ascertained. Then the insured person can go against the insurance company."[163]

If the insured had been wound up, until recently, suit could not be brought against the insured, and the third party lost his right against the insurer.[164] This position was changed by section 141 of the Companies Act 1989, amending section 651 of the Companies Act 1985, so that a dissolved company can be restored to the register within 20 years of the commencement of the section (16 November 1989) in order that it may be sued. By section 651, in its original form, petitions for restoration to the register had to be brought within two years. This was too short in cases of long tail insurance, such as cases of asbestosis, cancer and pollution. The effect of section 141 is that, in cases of actions for damages for personal injury (including any disease and any impairment of a person's physical condition) or of actions under the Fatal Accidents Acts, the period during which petitions for restoration may be brought is extended to 20 years. Restoration by the court in response to a petition is discretionary.[165]

5–8D Rights against the Insurer

There must, of course, be liability cover. The Act does not apply, if the liability falls within a policy exception,[166] or cover is available only at the discretion of the insurer.[167]

---

162. *Bradley* v *Eagle Star Ins Co Ltd* [1989] AC 957, 960 *per* Lord Brandon (liability); *Post Office* v *Norwich Union Fire Ins Sy Ltd* [1967] 2 QB 363 (CA—liability). As to the meaning of liability cover see 17–4A.
    USA: the contract often requires that judgment be obtained against the insured as a condition precedent to the liability of the insurer: such conditions have been enforced, for example, *Ayers* v *Hartford Accident & Indemnity Co*, 106 F 2d 958 (5 Cir, 1939—liability); *Arsht* v *Hatton*, 80 F Supp 149 (ED Pa, 1948—motor); *Sumait* v *Capital Fire & Casualty Co*, 296 F 2d 108 (9 Cir, 1961—motor). The meaning of "judgment" is a matter for state law. In Pennsylvania, for example, judgment has not been finally obtained until any pending appeal has been decided: *Arsht* (above). In Ohio "final judgment" means "a judgment which brings a suit to a conclusion . . . which bars recovery in any other litigation between the parties on the same claim."—*Ranallo* v *Hinman Bros. Construction Co*, 49 F Supp 920, 924 (ND Ohio, 1942—motor), affirmed 135 F 2d 921 (6 Cir, 1943), *cert den* 320 US 745 (1943); this includes a judgment by default or a judgment entered by the agreement of the parties (*ibid*).
    163. *Post Office* v *Norwich Union Fire Ins Sy Ltd* [1967] 2 QB 363, 375 *per* Lord Denning MR (CA—liability). Salmon LJ (p 378): "from a broad commercial point of view I can well understand why the insurers do not want their name to appear on the record as defendants . . . it would mean that the cause lists would contain the names of many defendant insurance companies; and this could not be good for their business."
    Cf "The law maintains the fiction that the insured is the real party in interest at the trial of the underlying . . . action in order to protect the insurance company against overly sympathetic juries."—*Thrasher* v *United States Liability Ins Co*, 278 NYS 2d 793, 799 (1967—motor). See further Kalven, 19 Ohio State LJ 158 on the behaviour of juries. In England juries are rarely found in such cases and the judges deny that the shadow of the insurer affects the liability of the insured: *Davie* v *New Merton Board Mills Ltd* [1959] AC 604, 627 *per* Viscount Simonds. *Cf* Atiyah, *Accidents, Compensation and the Law* (4th ed), pp 232 ff.
    164. *Bradley* v *Eagle Star Ins Co Ltd* [1989] AC 957 (HL—liability).
    165. See McGee (1991) 1 Ins Law & Practice 26.
    166. For example, injury intentionally inflicted.
    167. *The Vainqueur José* [1979] 1 Lloyd's Rep 557, 580 *per* Mocatta J (P & I). Discretionary benefits are still found in P & I Rules, for example, liability incurred under a towage contract.

It is said that the third party can have no better right than the insured against the insurer. The effect of section 1 has been described as a statutory assignment,[168] which implies, as courts have said,[169] that the third party steps into the shoes of the insured. However, in England "it is not all the rights and liabilities of the insured under the contract of insurance which are transferred to the third party, only the particular rights in respect of the liability incurred by the insured to the third party".[170] From this two limits appear. First, it is not the entire cover under the contract of insurance that is assigned; the insured may need cover against liability to other third parties. Second, there is no assignment of rights in respect of matters not closely connected with the insured's liability to the third party concerned, hence for example no reorientation of the insurer's rights of set-off for non-payment of premiums.[171]

5–8E Defences to Claims

Rights transferred to the third party are subject to all defences available to the insurer on the question of the insurer's liability to pay. The third party takes his wrongdoer and his wrongdoer's insurance as he finds them. That the insurer should have any fewer rights or any greater liability with respect to the third party than contracted for with the insured wrongdoer, was not acceptable either to the legislator or to the judge in England: the third party cannot "have the plums without the duff".[172] Although the statutory right of action bypasses the insured and the other creditors and is his own, the claimant's rights against the insurer are those originally enjoyed by the insured. Hence, it is clear that, if the insurance was vitiated by the misrepresentation,[173] non-disclosure[174] or breach of warranty by the insured, cover can be rescinded in the face of the third party.[175] The rights transferred are transferred subject to any conditions or qualifications affecting those rights.[176] To take a further example, the limitation period begins to run not when the insured was declared bankrupt but (at the earlier date) when the insured's cause of action against the insurer arose.[177]

"Courts of law, unless constrained by the most unambiguous legislation, would . . . be slow to fix upon the insurers an obligation, even of limited indemnity, in cases in which the insurers should establish that they had entered into no indemnity."[178] This statement assumes, first, that the important sides of the triangle are the relationships

---

168. For example *Greenlees* v *Port of Manchester Ins Co Ltd*, 1933 SC 383, 400 *per* Lord Alness, 411 *per* Lord Murray (motor).

169. *The Padre Island* [1984] 2 Lloyd's Rep 408, 414 *per* Leggatt J (P & I).

170. *Murray* v *Legal & General Assurance Sy Ltd* [1970] 2 QB 495, 503 *per* Cumming-Bruce J (employers' liability).

171. *Murray* (above).

172. *The Padre Island* [1984] 2 Lloyd's Rep 408, 414 *per* Leggatt J (P & I); see also *Farrell* v *Federated Employers' Ins Assn Ltd* [1970] 2 Lloyd's Rep 170, 173 *per* Lord Denning MR (CA—liability).

173. *Greenlees* v *Port of Manchester*, 1933 SC 383 (motor); *McCormick* v *National Motor & Accident Ins Union Ltd* (1934) 40 Com Cas 76 (CA—motor).

174. *Cleland* v *London General Ins Co Ltd* (1935) 51 Ll L Rep 156 (CA—motor).

175. However, these defences are not available to the insurer in the case of (compulsory) motor insurance: Road Traffic Act 1988, section 151(1): below, 5–9.

176. *Post Office* v *Norwich Union Fire Ins Sy Ltd* [1967] 2 QB 363, 374 *per* Lord Denning MR, 376 *per* Harman LJ (CA—liability); *Murray* v *Legal & General Assurance Sy Ltd* [1970] 2 QB 495, 503 *per* Cumming-Bruce J (employers' liability).

177. *Lefevre* v *White* [1990] 1 Lloyd's Rep 569 (motor).

178. *Greenlees* v *Port of Manchester Ins Co Ltd*, 1933 SC 383, 389 *per* Lord Moncrieff (motor); see also *McCormick* v *National Motor & Accident Ins Union Ltd* (1934) 40 Com Cas 76, 84 *per* Scrutton LJ (CA—motor).

between third party and insured, and between insurer and insured; second, that liability insurance is chiefly something for the protection of the insured. However, if the emphasis is put on the public purpose to compensate the third party, such as the road victim, the third side of the triangle becomes more important. "Instead of tort law being the primary vehicle for ensuring payment of compensation to accident victims, with liability insurance as an ancillary device to protect the insured, insurance becomes the primary medium for the payment of compensation . . . "[179] Over time, courts have become less willing to allow the third side of the triangle to be constrained by the other two. In England this is true of compulsory insurance; for example, under the Road Traffic Act 1988[180] defences of misrepresentation and non-disclosure available to the insurer against the insured are not available against the third party. In the United States a similar attitude surfaces in the courts,[181] when the policy is consciously interpreted in favour of the third party[182]; liability insurance being "permeated with a public interest"[183] the third party may have better rights against the insurer than the insured.

A distinction might have been made between the scope of cover, the insurer's promise to pay, and the procedural conditions for invoking that promise, such as notice of loss. But the English courts have considered that a duty shorn of its procedural safeguards would be a different duty, so the third party, like the insured, has to observe the claim conditions. Moreover, Parliament does not appear to have been concerned whether the third party is reasonably placed to observe those conditions and thus benefit from the insurance. The defences that have most troubled third parties have been those concerning arbitration (below, 5-8E1), notice (5–8E2), "pay first"clauses (5–8E3), and lack of co-operation (5–8E4).

5–8E1 Arbitration

The policy may provide that it shall be a condition precedent to the liability of the insurer that the insured's claim shall have been submitted to arbitration to determine, for example, the amount of liability. This provision is binding on the third party.[184] It has been seen as an essential mode of measuring the extent of cover under the particular contract of insurance.[185]

If the third party is too poor to go to arbitration, that is unfortunate. Faced with a third party who was thus "gravely hampered in establishing his case", Clauson LJ

---

179. Atiyah, *Accidents, Compensation and the Law* (4th ed, 1987), p 226.
180. Section 151(1). See below, 5–9.
181. For example, *Roland* v *Allstate Ins Co*, 370 F 2d 289, 292 (5 Cir, 1966—motor)
182. *Lewis* v *Manufacturers' Casualty Ins Co*, 107 F Supp 465, 476 (WD La, 1952—motor); *Southeastern Fire Ins Co* v *Helton*, 192 F Supp 441, 445 (SD Ala, 1961—motor).
183. *New Amsterdam Casualty Co* v *Jones*, 135 F 2d 191, 196 (6 Cir, 1943). See also *Barrera* v *State Farm Mutual Automobile Ins Co*, 456 P 2d 674 (Cal, 1969—motor); *Bourget* v *Government Employees' Ins Co*, 13 F Supp 367, 370 (Conn, 1970). This attitude is usually found in relation to compulsory insurance.
184. *Freshwater* v *Western Australia Assurance Co Ltd* [1933] 1 KB 515 (CA—motor); *Greenlees* v *Port of Manchester Ins Co Ltd*, 1933 SC 383 (motor); *Cunningham* v *Anglian Ins Co Ltd*, 1934 SLT 273 (motor); *Dennehy* v *Bellamy* [1938] 2 All ER 262 (CA—motor); *Smith* v *Pearl Assurance Co Ltd* [1939] 1 All ER 95 (CA—motor); *The Padre Island* [1984] 2 Lloyd's Rep 408 (P & I). *Chernick* v *Hartford Accident & Indemnity Co*, 87 NYS 2d 534 (1959—motor).
185. The insurer's "promise to indemnify was not a mere promise to indemnify, but a promise to indemnify to this extent—by paying the sum which shall be found by the arbitrator to be due."—*Dennehy* v *Bellamy* [1938] 2 All ER 262, 264 *per* Greer LJ (CA—motor).

observed[186] that poverty is "a personal disability in no way connected with the contractual rights or obligations". While seeking to protect the third party from the poverty of the insured wrongdoer, Parliament showed no intention to protect him from his own.

5–8E2 Notice Clauses

The policy may provide that any communication received by the insured, such as a writ, affecting the liability insured must be communicated to the insurer "immediately on receipt thereof". It is not unlikely that an insured who is bankrupt or in liquidation will be less than diligent in observing the fine print of the policy,[187] and that persons formerly authorised to give or receive notices on behalf of the insured are no longer willing or competent to do so.[188] Moreover, notice of events, such as an accident that *may* give rise to a claim, notice which the insurer may have received prior to the bankruptcy, does not constitute notice that it *will* be followed by a claim.[189] Nonetheless, failure by the insured to observe a notice clause is a defence available to the insurer against the insured and, it has been held, against the third party claiming under the Act. Thus, in *Hassett*[190] a letter with the third party's writ remained unopened at the registered office of the insured company, the office of an accountant who no longer worked for the company. The third party's action against the insurer failed for want of notice to the insurer. Moreover, later decisions[191] have confirmed this position, whether or not the insurer has been prejudiced by lack of notice. Allowance for the difficulties faced by an insolvent insured in giving the notice required can be made only when the policy requires *reasonable* notice, as the court will then consider those difficulties in assessing whether notice has been given in time.[192]

If the third party can identify the insurer, the obvious step is to notify him directly of the claim: complete information from an alternative and reliable source is sufficient.[193] But this may not be permitted on a proper construction of the contract of insurance.[194]

186. *Smith* v *Pearl Assurance Co* [1939] 1 All ER 95, 98 (CA—motor); he went on to suggest that consideration be given to amending the Act.
187. In spite of the duty imposed on the insured by section 2 of the 1930 Act to give information.
188. For example, *The Vainqueur José* [1979] 1 Lloyd's Rep 557 (P & I).
189. *Ibid* p 566 *per* Mocatta J. In *Pioneer Concrete (UK) Ltd* v *National Employers Mutual General Ins Assn Ltd* [1985] 1 Lloyd's Rep 274 the third party gave the insurer formal notice of his claim but not of his subsequent service of writ on the insured. Bingham J held that the purpose of notice predicated that the insurers must receive notice, not only, as stated in the policy, of an "accident" and a "claim" but also of any subsequent "proceedings".
190. *Hassett* v *Legal & General Assurance Sy Ltd* (1939) 63 Ll L Rep 278 (liability). *Idem*: *Clements* v *Preferred Accident Ins Co*, 41 F 2d 470 (8 Cir, 1930—accident); *Royal Indemnity Co* v *Watson*, 61 F 2d 614 (5 Cir, 1932—motor); *Fireman's Fund Indemnity Co* v *Kennedy*, 97 F 2d 882 (9 Cir, 1938—motor). More recently some hostility to such clauses is found; for example, if an insurer has unequivocally refused to defend the action against the insured, the insurer can no longer insist on notice: *Capitol Indemnity Corp* v *St Paul Fire & Marine Ins Co*, 357 F Supp 399 (WD Wis, 1972—professional indemnity).
191. *Farrell* v *Federated Employers' Ins Assn Ltd* [1970] 1 Lloyd's Rep 129, 136 *per* Mackenna J; [1970] 2 Lloyd's Rep 170, 175 *per* Megaw LJ (CA); *The Vainqueur José* [1979] 1 Lloyd's Rep 577, 566 *per* Mocatta J (P & I); *Pioneer Concrete (UK) Ltd* v *National Employers' Mutual General Ins Assn Ltd* [1985] 1 Lloyd's Rep 274. See further below, 26–2E.
192. See below, 26–2E3.
193. *Barrett Bros (Taxis) Ltd* v *Davies* [1966] 2 Lloyd's Rep 1 (CA—motor).
194. For example, *The Vainqueur José* [1979] 1 Lloyd's Rep. 557, 565 *per* Mocatta J (P & I).
In the United States, if the insurer has notice, it has been held irrelevant that notice was not received or given in strict accordance with the policy: *Babcock & Wilcox Co* v *Parsons Corp*, 298 F Supp 898 (D Neb, 1969—machinery floater).

5–8E3 Pay First Clauses

Section 1(3) of the 1930 Act, which is designed to prevent the parties to the contract of insurance from contracting out of the Act, provides that, in so far as any contract of liability insurance "purports, directly or indirectly, to avoid the contract or to alter the rights of the parties thereunder upon the happening of" events mentioned in section 1(1), notably the insolvency of the insured, the "contract shall be of no effect". Contracts of mutual insurance commonly contain a "pay first" (or "pay to be paid") clause, that before the insurer is to be liable under the insurance the insured shall discharge his liability to the third parties. English courts were once divided on whether the clause is contrary to section 1(3),[195] but the House of Lords in *The Fanti*[196] has decided that the clause is not. In that case, the Court of Appeal held that, although indeed the clause did not offend section 1(3), it should be struck down because its performance had become impossible. The House of Lords agreed on the first point but not on the second. The condition had to be fulfilled.[197] The result is that, when the insured has not discharged a liability to the third party claimant, and his liability insurance contains a clause of this kind, payment to the third party is a condition of his rights against the insurer, and if the insured is wound up before payment, no cause of action against the insurer has accrued to the insured and no right of indemnity against the insurer can be transferred to the third party claimant. The main bones of contention in *The Fanti* were as follows.

First, as regards the contention, that the clause has the effect, directly or indirectly, of avoiding the contract of insurance or of altering the rights of the parties under the contract, on the insured being wound up, Lord Brandon noted that both Saville J and the Court of Appeal had rejected this contention, and stated that they were right to do so.[198] In particular, he shared the view of Saville J,[199] that whereas an insolvent insured would be unlikely to pay the third party, that "does not result, directly or indirectly, from any alteration of the [insured's] rights under his contract of insurance, it results rather from the [insured's] inability, by reason of insolvency, to exercise those rights".[200] What is affected by the situation is not the insured's rights but the ability of the insured in practice to enforce them and then only in certain cases.

Second, the contrary view[201] proceeded from the premise that there was a liability

---

195. Such clauses are rendered nugatory in New York by NY Ins Law, section 167.1(b). In most parts of the USA such conditions, known as "no-action" clauses, have been outlawed by legislation: Hazelwood, *P & I Clubs, Law and Practice* (Lloyd's of London Press Ltd, 1989), p 241.

196. *Firma C–Trade SA* v *Newcastle Protection & Indemnity Assn* [1991] 2 AC 1. Appeals from the decision of Staughton J in *The Fanti* [1987] 2 Lloyd's Rep 299, that the clause was contrary to section 1(3) and from the decision of Saville J in *The Padre Island* [1987] 2 Lloyd's Rep 529, that it was not, were taken together by the Court of Appeal: [1989] 1 Lloyd's Rep 239; the first was dismissed and the second allowed. From each of these decisions appeals were allowed by the House of Lords and are hereafter referred to together as *The Fanti*. In the House, judgments were delivered by Lord Brandon, with whom Lord Keith, Lord Ackner, Lord Goff and Lord Jauncey agreed; by Lord Goff, with whom Lord Ackner also agreed; and by Lord Jauncey.

197. On measures that might be taken to "outflank" the decision of the House of Lords, see Smallwood, P & I International, October 1991 p 17.

198. p 29. The House thus rejected the view of Slade J in *Re Allobrogia SS Corp* [1978] 3 All ER 423, 433 that the clause offended the spirit of the Act and that the clause "would have the substantial effect of avoiding the contract or of altering the rights of the parties *on the insolvency of the company*".

199. [1987] 2 Lloyd's Rep 529, 535.

200. pp 28–29. *Idem* p 37 *per* Lord Goff.

201. *Re Allobrogia SS Corp* [1978] 3 All ER 423.

covered by the insurance but, thought Lord Brandon,[202] "on the ordinary and natural construction" of the contract terms, the insured was not entitled to be indemnified until the liability had been discharged. A further premise was that the clause is a procedural condition of the insurance, and not a term delimiting the scope or existence of cover.[203] The line between terms delimiting scope and procedural and other conditions of the contract of insurance is not always clear. In the case of liability insurance, it can be argued, subject of course to the terms of the particular contract of insurance, that the insured event has not occurred until the insured's patrimony has been diminished by payment[204] of the liability to the third party; that therefore there was no pre-existent cover to be "avoided" or right to be "altered" by the pay first clause.

Third, as regards the effect of the Act when insurance contained the clause, the view of Staughton J and of the Court of Appeal, that what was transferred to the third party was a right to indemnity contingent on payment *by the third party*, was rejected by Lord Brandon.[205] The legislature did not intend to put the third party in any better position as against the insurer than the insured, and the insured had no right to indemnity at all, until he, the insured, had performed the condition of payment. Moreover, Lord Goff rejected the argument, that performance of the condition of payment had become futile and hence could be brushed aside: "I know of no general rule that the mere fact that a condition becomes impossible of performance renders the condition of no effect. Whether it does so must depend on the construction of the contract; and it may well be that, as here, the fact that it cannot be performed will simply mean that it is never fulfilled".[206]

A fourth point surfaced for the first time in the Court of Appeal and was refined and elaborated before the House, an impressive argument, said Lord Goff, which he called the "equity point". He summarised the argument thus:[207]

"(1) The purpose of the condition of prior payment was to prevent a member from making a profit from his insurance cover by receiving payment from the [insurer] but failing to pay the third party. This problem does not arise if [an insured] is being wound up, because on winding up the assets are held for creditors; nor does it arise if the [insurer] makes payment direct to the third party.
(2) If [an insurer] (as it may do) makes payment direct to the third party, it thereby discharges the [insured's] liability to the third party and so fulfils the condition that the [insured] (on whose behalf the [insurer] has paid) must have paid the third party's claim. In such a case, the [insurer] cannot rely on the circular argument that payment had not already been made. If payment direct to the third party will satisfy the condition of prior payment, it follows that the [insurer] is contractually bound either to pay the [insured] who has in fact paid the claim or simply to pay the claim direct to the third party.[208]

202. p 27.
203. Thus, for example, a duty to go to arbitration to settle such questions as the amount of loss has been seen as an inherent part of the cover promised: *Elliott v Royal Exchange Assurance Co* (1867) LR 2 Exch 237 (fire); *Caledonian Ins Co v Gilmour* [1893] AC 85. 95 *per* Lord Watson (fire).
204. In this sense *Seguros Tepeyec SA v Bostrom*, 347 F 2d 168, 173 (5 Cir, 1965—motor); *Smith v Transit Casualty Co*, 81 F Supp 661, 667 (ED Tex, 1968—motor), affirmed 410 F 2d 210 (5 Cir, 1969). Brehm, *Le Contrat d'Assurance RC* (1983). But this is not the prevalent view in English law: below, 17–4A.
205. p 29; see also p 32 per Lord Goff.
206. pp 32–33. This objection was also raised in the first edition of this book, 5–8E3, text at note 220.
207. pp 33–34.
208. At this point, however, the argument appears to assume what it seeks to prove, that the insurer is bound to pay, whereas the insurer is bound to pay only when the third party has been paid. The argument does not correspond with the contractual reality. In practice the insurer may pay the third party, thus waiving the condition of payment by the insured, but is not obliged to do so: p 35 *per* Lord Goff.

(3) If however the [insurer] is not so bound, and the condition of prior payment operates at law to exclude the [insurer's] obligation to pay [the insured] who has not in fact paid the third party's claim, equity will resolve the deadlock by requiring the [insurer] either to pay the third party direct or to pay the [insured] for the purpose of his paying the third party, and thereby ensuring that both the condition precedent and the [insurer's] obligation are satisfied. The basis on which equity intervenes is as follows.

(a) At common law, a contract of indemnity gave rise to an action of assumpsit for unliquidated damages for failing to prevent the indemnified person from suffering damnum by paying the third party. A condition of prior payment was implicit in the contract.

(b) Equity, though recognising the existence of the condition, would not allow reliance on it when the effect would be to defeat the indemnity altogether rather than to achieve the object of the condition, i.e. to ensure that the liability in respect of which the indemnity existed was indeed discharged. This is because equity looks to the substance rather than to the form of a transaction.

(c) The mere fact that the contract contained a condition of prior payment cannot displace the equity. On the contrary, the condition is a prerequisite of the operation of the equitable doctrine.

(d) Although the equity may be displaced by language which reveals the parties to have intended the result which applying the condition will have, it will not be excluded by words directed to another problem, e.g. preventing the [insured] from making a profit from the [insurer's] payment by receiving it and yet not paying the third party's claim.

(e) Procedurally, it was never necessary to invoke the equity by applying for specific equitable relief. It originally operated by a decree of specific performance of the contract of indemnity. Nowadays, following the Chancery Amendment Act 1858 (Lord Cairns's Act) and the Supreme Court of Judicature Act 1873, relief can take the form of a judgment for the relevant money sum."

The argument rested on the foundation, that an implied condition existed at common law and had been overriden in the past by equity, and failed when that foundation was denied by Lord Goff.[209] Whereas he accepted that equity had intervened to ensure that a contract of indemnity was performed, "by means of what is effectively a decree of specific performance of the contract of indemnity",[210] if such a condition had existed, such intervention by equity would not have occurred. When, as in the case before the court, a condition of payment existed, the condition was effective to displace the equity: it would be "contrary to principle that equity should grant specific performance of the contract inconsistently with the terms of the contract".[211] Accordingly, there was no precedent for equitable intervention of the kind contended for by counsel.

Finally, with reference to the view of Stuart-Smith LJ,[212] that the condition enabled any liability insurer to drive a coach and horses through the Act, Lord Goff considered that "this statement both exaggerates the danger and ignores the policy underlying the 1930 Act".[213] The Act did not purport to give third parties any greater rights than those enjoyed by the insured under the contract of insurance. Whereas in the case of motorists and employers, insurance was compulsory and Parliament had provided that clauses in the contract of insurance which defeat the purpose of the insurance will be ineffective,[214] this is not the case of the shipowner and his liability to third

209. p 35; see also p 41 *per* Lord Jauncey.
210. p 36.
211. *Ibid.* Also in this sense, Michel and Congdon [1989] LMCLQ 495, 496.
212. *The Fanti* [1989] 1 Lloyd's Rep 239, 259 (CA). In the same sense: *Re Allobrogia SS Corp* [1978] 3 All ER 423, 433 *per* Slade J.
213. p 38.
214. For example, the Road Traffic Act 1988, ss 148–150, below, 5–9B.

parties.[215] The condition antedates the 1930 Act and was not included in the contract of insurance to evade the Act.[216]

5–8E4 Lack of Co-operation with the Insurer

In the United States the insurance contract commonly obliges the insured to co-operate with the insurer in respect of claims.[217] The courts have been reluctant to allow the insurer to plead lack of co-operation by the insured as a defence to a direct action against the insurer by a third party. In particular, the courts have insisted that, to be a defence, the lack of co-operation must be "substantial".[218] In 1966 the Court of Appeals of New York said[219]:

"The burden of proving lack of co-operation of the insured is placed upon the insurer (Ins Law, art. 167, subd. 5). Since the defense of lack of co-operation penalizes the plaintiff for the action of the insured over whom he has no control, and since the defense frustrates the policy of this State that innocent victims of motor vehicle accidents be recompensed for the injuries inflicted upon them,[220] the courts have consistently held that the burden of proving the lack of co-operation is a heavy one indeed. Thus, the insurer must demonstrate that it acted diligently in seeking to bring about the insured's co-operation[221]; that the efforts employed by the insurer were reasonably calculated to obtain the [insured's] co-operation[222]; and the attitude of the insured, after his co-operation was sought, was one of 'willful and avowed obstruction'[223]."

5–8F The Effect of Section 1

5–8F1 The Transfer of Rights

If section 1 applies, the effect, it is said,[224] is a statutory assignment of the insured's rights in respect of the particular claim[225] to the extent necessary to achieve the object

---

215. p 39.

216. Lord Goff (p 36) was attracted by the explanation that "in a mutual insurance association such as a P & I club, it is essential that members should be able to assume the financial probity of other members, because all of them are insurers as well as insured. To that end it is customary to require each member to discharge his own liability before he can be indemnified against it by the club. Each member is, after all, running his own business; it is up to him to make sure that a claim against him is well founded, and the best way of ensuring that is to require him first to pay the claim before seeking indemnity from the club".

217. Concerning this duty, see below, 29–2E.

218. *Home Indemnity Co* v *Finley*, 261 F Supp 318, 321 (ED Ark, 1966—motor). See also *Weiby* v *Marfell*, 172 F Supp 397 (D Minn, 1958—motor), affirmed 273 F 2d 327 (8 Cir, 1960); *Gutnick* v *Long Island Ins Co*, 283 NYS 2d 947 (1967—accident), affirmed 293 NYS 2d 701 (1968).

219. *Thrasher* v *United States Liability Ins Co*, 278 NYS 2d 793, 800 (1967—motor). *Cf* earlier cases allowing the insurer to plead lack of co-operation, even if the insurer had not been prejudiced thereby: *National Grange Mutual Liability Co* v *Fino*, 212 NYS 2d 684 (1961).

220. The court cited *Wallace* v *Universal Ins Co*, 238 NYS 2d 379 (1963—motor), affirmed 244 NYS 2d 779 (1963); *Kehoe* v *Motorists Mutual Ins Co*, 246 NYS 2d 827, 828 (1964—motor).

221. The court cited *Amatucci* v *Maryland Casualty Co*, 267 NYS 2d 41 (1966—motor); *Rosen* v *United States Fidelity & Guarantee Co*, 260 NYS 2d 677 (1965—motor); *National Grange Mutual Ins Co* v *Lococo*, 248 NYS 2d 150 (1964—motor), affirmed 261 NYS 2d 50 (1965).

222. The court cited *National Grange* v *Lococo* (above); *Wallace* v *Universal* (above).

223. The court cited *American Surety Co* v *Diamond*, 154 NYS 2d 918 (1956—motor).

In the USA insurers have also pleaded lack of co-operation by the third party: *US Fidelity & Guarantee Co* v *Wyer*, 60 F 2d 856 (10 Cir, 1932—motor); *Wright* v *Farmers Automobile Inter-Ins Union*, 102 P 2d 353 (Cal, 1940—motor); *Nationwide Mutual Ins Co* v *Tillman*, 161 So 2d 604 (Miss, 1964); *Kirk* v *Home Indemnity Co*, 431 F 2d 554 (7 Cir, 1970—motor); *Olenick* v *Govt Employees Ins Co*, 328 NYS 2d 50 (1971—motor). The cases divide on whether the insurer must prove that he was prejudiced by the lack of co-operation.

224. *Post Office* v *Norwich Union Fire Ins Sy Ltd* [1967] 2 QB 363, 376 *per* Harman LJ, 377 *per* Salmon LJ (CA—liability).

225. *Murray* v *Legal & General Assurance Sy Ltd* [1970] 2 QB 495, 503 *per* Cumming-Bruce J (employers' liability).

of the Act, to safeguard the interests of the third party. The third party has a direct action[226] against the insurer. More particularly:

(a) The insured is still able to claim under the policy in respect of insured loss apart from the liability to the third party in question.[227]

(b) The third party is not affected by a right of set-off, for example in respect of arrears of premiums, available to the insurer against the insured.[228] In the United States, in contrast, it has been held that the third party may plead an estoppel against the insurer, an estoppel arising out the insurer's dealings with the insured.[229]

(c) It has been suggested[230] that, to the extent that the third party gets rights against the insurer, the third party loses his rights, let us say in tort, against the insured wrongdoer. This is the inference of section 1(4) of the Act. Behind the suggestion is concern that, having recovered from the insurer, the third party should not be able to recover again in respect of the same loss.

This concern appears unjustified in the case of a third party who has recovered in full from the insurer: he is unlikely to trouble to prove in the bankruptcy or liquidation of the insured, who, in most cases, would lack the funds to pay. There remains, however, the case of the solvent company mentioned in section 1(1)(b), whose insurer is insolvent. While it is clear that generally an action may be brought in tort to recover damages, irrespective of any insurance cover enjoyed by the plaintiff in respect of the loss or damage for which he brings the action, the premise is that the plaintiff has paid for this cover by his premiums and should not be deprived of the full benefit of his prudence.[231] This premise does not apply in the present situation, in which the premiums have been paid not by the third party but by the wrongdoing insured. The purpose of the Act suggests that the transfer of rights from insured to third party should not defeat the rights of the third party against the insured, unless the rights transferred have been effective to compensate the third party. If the third party retains rights against the insured, when his compensation is limited by the terms of the policy (section 1(4)(b)), why not also when his compensation is limited or illusory by the insolvency of the insurer?

5–8F2 Co-operation with the Third Party

By section 2 of the 1930 Act the insured or his representative is obliged, at the request of the third party, to give "such information as may reasonably be required by him for

---

226. *Greenlees* v *Port of Manchester*, 1933 SC 383 (motor). *Cf* Michel [1987] LMCLQ 228, 230.
227. Section 1(4).
228. *Murray* (above).
229. In *Jones* v *Zurich General Accident & Liability Ins Co*, 121 F 2d 761 (2 Cir, 1941—employers' liability) it was held that, by defending the action against the insured, the insurer was estopped from a subsequent plea that the liability was not covered by the policy. See also *Wheeler* v *Lumbermen's Mutual Casualty Co*, F Supp 193 (Me, 1933—motor); *Hoosier Casualty Co* v *Fox*, 102 F Supp 214 (ND Iowa, 1952—motor).
230. MacGillivray, No 1994, citing cases under section 5 of the Workmen's Compensation Act 1906, such as *Re Pethwick Dix & Co* [1915] 1 Ch 26. In the same sense Finlay, *op cit*, p 109.
231. See for example *Bradburn* v *GWR* (1874) LR 10 Exch 1, 3 *per* Piggott B. For a similar rule as regards an occupational pension see *Parry* v *Cleaver* [1970] AC 1.

the purpose of ascertaining whether any rights have been transferred" to him, for example, whether there was liability insurance at all and, if so, its terms. He must also give any such information relevant to the enforcement of such rights, for example, the address of the insurer or his agent. In each case this includes a duty to allow the third party to inspect documents.[231a] Further, if there is "reasonable ground for supposing" that the third party does get rights under the Act, he is owed a similar duty of information by the insurer.[231b] However, these duties arise only if there is a liability of the kind mentioned in section 1. The third party who, before commencing proceedings wishes to know whether the defendant has liability cover has no right under section 2 to that information.[231c]

5–8F3 Waiver

By section 3 of the Act, if a case falls within section 1, no agreement, waiver, assignment, payment or other disposition made or agreed between the insured and the insurer shall be effective to defeat or affect rights transferred to the third party under section 1.

5–9 THE ROAD TRAFFIC ACT 1988, SECTION 151

With the Third Parties (Rights Against Insurers) Act 1930 came the belief, that persons injured or killed in road accidents through the fault of another would be compensated, whether the wrongdoer was impecunious or not, by direct action against the wrongdoer's insurer.[232] But this belief was soon dispelled by insurers, whose exceptions and warranties, binding on insured and third party[233] alike, not only limited the liability of the insurer but did so in a way which sowed the seeds of uncertainty. As regards motor insurance, the rights of the third party against the insurer were to be increased by section 10 of the Road Traffic Act 1934. This was replaced by sections 148 and 149 of the Road Traffic Act 1972.[234] The Road Traffic Act 1972 was replaced by the Road Traffic Act 1988 and, as regards action against the insurer by a third party, substantially similar provisions are found in sections 143 ff of the Act of 1988.

5–9A The Scope of Section 151

    (a) Judgment must have been given against the insured. Judgment is not complete so long as execution has been stayed pending an appeal[235] or as long as it may be set aside.[236]

231a. Section 2(3).
231b. Section 2(2).
231c. *Nigel Upchurch Associates* v *The Aldridge Estates Investment Co Ltd* [1993] 1 Lloyd's Rep 535.
232. *Adams* v *London General Ins Co* (1932) 42 Ll L Rep 56, 58 *per* Swift J (motor); *Zurich General Accident & Liabilty Ins Co Ltd* v *Morrison* [1942] 2 KB 53, 61 *per* Goddard LJ (CA). Finlay, p 102
233. Above, 5–8E
234. As amended by the Motor Vehicles (Compulsory Insurance) Regulations 1987, SI No 2171, designed to implement part of the Second EC Directive on Motor Insurance. The regulations came into force on 31 December 1988.
235. Section 152(1)(*b*).
236. *Windsor* v *Chalcraft* [1939] 1 KB 279, 289, *per* Slesser LJ (CA) in a dissenting judgment: *semble* the majority did not differ with him on this point. The decision of the majority was that under a general rule of procedure—*Jacques* v *Harrison* (1884) 12 QBD 165 (CA), the insurer could have a judgment in default against the insured set aside and obtain permission to defend.

(b) Notice of "bringing of the proceedings" must have been had by the insurer "before or within seven days after the commencement of the proceedings in which judgment is given".[237] Lawton J explained[238] the reasons for requiring notice:

> "Insurers may have repudiated liability as against their assured but they may have their own reasons for taking over control of any litigation there may be. It may well be that if the facts are gone into, for example, a plaintiff may have no grounds of claim at all and unless the insurers have notice of the commencement of proceedings, they are not in a position to intervene. It is important from the insurers' point of view, too, that they should have notice not later than seven days after the commencement of proceedings because of the danger of judgment in default of appearance being given against a defendant assured."

As to the source of notice, in practice, the insurer will have "had notice" from the third party, but the Act is so worded that notice may come from any source,[239] including therefore the court itself, if the insurer decided to seek that kind of information from the court.

As to the content of the notice, the wording of section 151(1)(b), which contemplates that such notice may be given before proceedings have been commenced, suggests that it is unnecessary (for it may be impossible) to give details of the proceedings themselves.[240] A firm expression of intention to commence proceedings in respect of a specified accident would suffice[241] but notification "that a claim may be made is not notification of the commencement of proceedings".[242] Nor is a letter from the third party's solicitors that, unless the insurer "will be dealing with the matter on a full liability basis, we will advise our client to institute proceedings" against the insured.[243] Neither communication is a clear notice "of proceedings": that proceedings have been commenced or definitely will be. Only that will suffice in view of the purpose of notice,[244] to enable the insurer to avoid liability by bringing an action for a declaration[245] and, if so entitled,[246] to take over the defence of the proceedings against their insured. So, in contrast, a letter that unless the insurer agrees to deal "with the matter on a full liability basis, we have been instructed by our clients to commence proceedings" would be notice enough.[247]

The proceedings of which notice must be given are legal proceedings.[248] Where litigation involves more than one claim, the proceedings in question are those which

---

237. Section 152(1)(a).
238. *McGoona v MIB* [1969] 2 Lloyd's Rep 34, 47 (motor).
239. *Harrington v Pinkey* [1989] 2 Lloyd's Rep 310, 316, *per* Sir Denis Buckley (CA—motor).
240. *Ceylon Motor Ins Assn Ltd v Thambugala* [1953] AC 584, 593: this decision of the Privy Council concerned similar provisions in force in Ceylon. *Idem*: *Harrington v Pinkey* [1989] 2 Lloyd's Rep 310, 315, *per* Woolf LJ (CA—motor).
241. *Thambugala* (above) *loc cit*.
242. *McGoona* (above) *loc cit* (emphasis added). *Idem*: *Weldrick v Essex & Suffolk Equitable Ins Sy Ltd* (1949) 83 Ll L Rep 91, 102 *per* Birkett J (motor).
243. *Harrington v Pinkey* [1989] 2 Lloyd's Rep 310 (CA—motor) as regards the corresponding provision, section 149(2)(a), of the 1972 Act. The victory of the Lloyd's underwriters was a technical victory and Woolf LJ expressed the hope that they would nonetheless pay the (relatively small) claim. Subsequently, they did pay the claim, but also required payment of their costs.
244. pp 312–313 *per* Woolf LJ. The second of the purposes was also acknowledged by Lawton J in *McGoona v MIB* [1969] 2 Lloyd's Rep 34, 47 (motor).
245. Below, 5–9C
246. Below, 17–4E.
247. *Ceylon Motor Ins Assn Ltd v Thambugala* [1953] AC 584.
248. *Herbert v Railway Passengers Assurance Co* (1938) 60 Ll L Rep 143, 146 *per* Porter J (motor).

institute the claim which, if successful, will give rise to liability covered by the policy: in the event of claims and counter-claims, the moment is the commencement of the proceedings in which the judgment (above (a)), referred to in section 151(1), was given.[249]

  (c) The liability, in respect of which judgment has been sought, must be liability which is covered by the policy in question and liability required to be covered by section 145(3)(*a*): liability "in respect of the death or bodily injury to, any person or damage to property caused by, or arising out of, the use of the vehicle on a road" in Great Britain.[250]

  (d) The policy, under which indemnity is sought from the insurer, must have been issued by an authorised insurer.[251] It must also be in force as between insurer and insured.[252]

5–9B Restrictions on Cover

One of the points, on which the legislator of 1932 wanted to remedy the defects perceived in the Third Parties (Rights Against Insurers) Act 1930, was the right of the insurer to plead contract exclusions against the third party.[253] So, section 148(1) declares to "be of no effect" so much of the contract "as purports to restrict" the insurance by reference to any of the following matters listed in section 148(2):

  (a) The age or physical or mental condition of persons driving the vehicle. It has been held that a term, that the insured should use all care and diligence to avoid accidents, did not fall within (a), even when the insured impaired his physical and mental condition by getting drunk.[254]

  (b) The condition of the vehicle.[255]

  (c) The number of persons that the vehicle carries.

  (d) The weight or physical characteristics of the goods that the vehicle carries. A term that the vehicle may be used for business X but not for business Y does not fall within (d).[256]

  (e) The times at which or the areas in which the vehicle is used.

  (f) The horsepower or cylinder capacity or value of the vehicle.

  (g) The carrying on the vehicle of any particular apparatus.

  (h) The carrying on the vehicle of any particular means of identification.[257]

  Further, the third party is not affected by any term of the policy whereby liability shall cease "in the event of some specified thing being done or omitted to be done

---

249. *Cross v British Oak Ins Co Ltd* (1938) 60 Ll L Rep 46, 48, 49 *per* Du Parcq J (motor).
250. By section 145(4) the policy is not required to cover certain kinds of loss, in an attempt to co-ordinate cover with other contracts of insurance, but including (f) "any contractual liability", and (b) "insurance for more than £250,000 in respect of all such liabilities as may be incurred in respect of damage to property caused by, or arising out of, any one accident involving the vehicle".
251. Section 145(2).
252. Section 152(2)(*c*).
253. Above, 5–8E.
254. *National Farmers' Union Mutual Ins Sy Ltd v Dawson* (1941) 70 Ll L Rep 167 (motor).
255. For example *Liverpool Corp v Roberts* [1964] 2 Lloyd's Rep 219 (motor).
256. *Jones v Welsh Ins Corp Ltd* (1937) 59 Ll L Rep 13 (motor).
257. Other than any means of identification required by or under the Vehicles (Excise) Act 1971.

after the happening of the event giving rise to a claim under the policy".[258] This provision is intended to avoid the difficulty created for the third party by, for example, notice clauses in respect of the 1930 Act.[259] It also outlaws terms, whereby the insurance cover is ineffective, if the insured admits liability to the third party.

Again, the insurer is not allowed to plead a contract requirement that the driver have a driving licence,[260] or that the "vehicle had been stolen or unlawfully taken"[261] unless, in the latter case, the third party was "allowing himself to be carried in or upon the vehicle" and knew when the journey commenced that the vehicle was stolen or unlawfully taken.

Finally, as regards a policy designed to limit the use of a vehicle to non-commercial use, section 150[262] contains criteria of non-commercial operation. The criteria are such that lift sharing arrangements in private cars are not treated as commercial use.

All other terms, which do not fall within the prohibited categories (above), are valid against the third party, such as a term that the vehicle shall not be used for purposes connected with the motor trade.[263]

It is a feature of section 148(1) that the restrictions are of no effect, whether framed as exceptions or as warranties. They must, however, be restrictions—which may be an accident of policy drafting. To take the example of a term about area of use, if there is cover in the United Kingdom (i.e., the United Kingdom of Great Britain and Northern Ireland), except for Northern Ireland, the latter is framed as a restriction and thus appears to be of no effect.[264] If, however, cover is defined in purely positive terms to be for Great Britain (thus incidentally not extending to the province of Northern Ireland), there is a valid "restriction" or delimitation of cover to Great Britain.[265]

5–9C Avoidance

The insurer must pay, even though as regards the insured the insurer is entitled to "avoid or cancel"[266] the policy, notably on grounds of misrepresentation or non-disclosure, unless in such cases the insurer obtains a court declaration that he is entitled to avoid the policy "on the ground that it was obtained (i) by the non-disclosure of a material fact, or (ii) by a representation of fact which was false in some material par-

---

258. Section 148(5). An arbitration clause may be enforced against the third party, because it does not cause liability to cease or prevent liability arising, but merely defers any judgment that might establish liability: *Freshwater* v *Western Australian Ins Co* [1933] 1 KB 515 (CA—motor).

259. Above, 5–8E2.

260. Section 151(3).

261. Section 151(4).

262. These provisions were added by the Transport Act 1980, section 61. *Cf Wyatt* v *Guildhall Ins Co Ltd* [1937] 1 KB 653 (motor).

263. *Gray* v *Blackmore* (1933) 47 Ll L Rep 69 (motor).

264. Section 148(1)(*e*).

265. See the situation in *Provincial Ins Co Ltd* v *Morgan* [1933] AC 240. *Cf Bright* v *Ashfold* [1932] 2 KB 153: the Divisional Court held that a "restriction" on cover for motor bikes carrying a passenger, unless a side-car was attached (to the motor bike), was not an exception within section 38 of the Road Traffic Act 1930, which corresponds to section 148 of the 1988 Act. This seems correct, in view of the wording of the subsection; however, the reasoning of Lord Hewart CJ (p 158) is a threat to the operation of section 148: "This was a condition which circumscribed the operation of the policy from the beginning. There was, therefore, no policy of insurance against third party risks at all in force."

266. Section 151(5). For examples concerning non-disclosure by the insured of convictions for dangerous driving or drunken driving, see *Merchants' & Manufacturers' Ins Co Ltd* v *Davies* [1938] 1 KB 196 (CA—motor); *Guardian Assurance Co Ltd* v *Sutherland* [1939] 2 All ER 246 (motor); *Zurich General Accident & Liability Ins Co* v *Leven* 1940 SC 406 (motor).

ticular".[267] Thus, what is taken from the insurer by one hand of Parliament appears to have been given back by another; however, the rebate is conditional (below, 5–9C2) and the insurer may prefer not to be seen to be taking it back.

Parliament was reluctant to enforce insurance obtained by misrepresentation or non-disclosure.[268] But Parliament was also concerned that a third party might find himself without compensation as a result of the conduct of the insured, when contracting the insurance, conduct over which the third party had no control. A compromise emerged: insurers may raise the misrepresentation or non-disclosure of the insured, but only if (a) there were extra-contractual grounds for avoidance, and (b) the insurer takes, and is seen to take, the initiative of obtaining a court declaration.

5–9C1　Grounds of Avoidance

The insurer may avoid the contract only if "he was induced to make the contract of insurance by some material non-disclosure or misrepresentation which, by ordinary insurance law, and not merely by reason of some special stipulation which he has put in his form of policy, entitles him to avoid the contract".[269] The effect appears to be to negative the operation of basis clauses[270] and confine the insurer to misrepresentation[271] or non-disclosure[272] of facts that are material.

The assumption appears to have been that the grounds of avoidance in law are more serious or more stringent than those under the terms of the contract; however, this is not necessarily true.[273] It was also assumed that non-disclosure, for example, is essentially different from a breach of condition. Of course, conceptually this is true, but practically, especially from the standpoint of the third party, the distinction is less clear. A condition that my car is not covered for use in Northern Ireland might be caught by section 148(2)(e), so that the cyclist injured there by my negligence at the wheel has an action against my insurer; but, it appears, if I renew my cover and fail to disclose my intention of going to reside in the province and the same accident occurs, my insurer can plead section 152(2) and refuse payment to the cyclist, however injured, outraged and mystified the cyclist might be.

5–9C2　Court Declaration

To avoid the insurance the insurer must obtain a court declaration under section 152(2). To obtain a declaration he must (a) commence the proceedings leading to this declaration within three months of the commencement of proceedings against the insured[274]; and (b) give notice of his commencing proceedings for a declaration to the

---

267. Section 152(2). This is also the rule, when the insured is unable to recover under the policy, because the loss or damage is the result of his own wilful act: *Hardy* v *MIB* [1964] 2 QB 745 (CA—motor).
268. *Guardian Assurance Co Ltd* v *Sutherland* [1939] 2 All ER 246 (motor).
269. *Merchants' & Manufacturers' Ins Co Ltd* v *Hunt* (1941) 68 Ll L Rep 117, 120 *per* Scott LJ (CA—motor).
270. *Zurich General Accident & Liability Ins Co* v *Leven*, 1940 SC 406, 414 *per* Lord Normand (motor). See below, 20–2B2.
271. See below, 22–3A.
272. See below, 23–5.
273. See notes 271 and 272.
274. Section 152(2). For example, *Durrant* v *Maclaren* [1956] 2 Lloyd's Rep 70 (motor).

third party within seven days of commencing them.[275] As to the purpose of notice, Scott LJ referred[276] to the

"danger of the injured party being deprived of the pecuniary safeguard . . . without his knowledge, and even by collusion between the insurer and the insured. It was essential that he should have notice of any such action by the insurer, and also to be given the right to appear in it and there defend his rights".

Further, in the view of Goddard LJ,[277]

"if an insurer was intending to repudiate a policy, it was only fair that the injured third party should know the grounds on which repudiation was sought before he went to the expense of endeavouring to establish his claim against the insured, who, if not entitled to indemnity, might be unable to satisfy a judgment. It was to prevent an injured party incurring further useless expense."

5–9D The Effect of Section 151

The insurer must pay the judgment, plus costs and any sum payable in respect of interest on the amount of the judgment.[278] To the extent that the sum includes an amount, for which the insurer was not liable under the terms of the policy, because of restrictions of the kind described above (5–9B), the insurer may recover that amount from the insured.[279]

If in spite of the 1988 Act the third party is not compensated, he may recover under the current agreement between the Secretary of State for the Environment and the Motor Insurers Bureau (MIB). The current agreement is that of 21 December 1988.[280] It applies to compulsory motor insurance cover,[281] if judgment has been obtained by the third party victim[282] against those responsible for the loss.[283] The third party recovers the amount of the judgment plus costs up to a ceiling, as regards property damage, of £250,000. The MIB is not liable to a victim who knew or should have known that the person responsible was uninsured.

---

275. Section 152(3). The recipient of notice may become a party to the proceedings whereby the insurer seeks a declaration: see further *Merchants' & Manufacturers' Ins Co Ltd* v *Hunt* (1941) 68 Ll L Rep 117 (CA—motor). As regards the contents of notice see *Zurich General Accident & Liability Ins Co* v *Morrison* [1942] 2 QB 53 (CA—motor).

276. *Merchants' & Manufacturers' Ins Co Ltd* v *Hunt* (1941) 68 Ll L Rep 117, 120 (CA—motor).

277. *Zurich* v *Morrison* (above), p 62.

278. Section 151(5).

279. Section 148(4).

280. See Bragg (1991) 1 Ins L & P 42.

281. It does not cover liability arising out of the use of vehicles on areas not falling within the definition of road under the current Road Traffic Act. Hence it does not apply to a lorry in the London Dock Area: *Buchanan* v *MIB* [1955] 1 WLR 488.

282. Hence, to the extent that the victim chooses to seek compensation under his own first party insurance, the liability of the MIB is reduced and there are no rights in subrogation against the latter.

283. It does not apply to the driver who is the victim of the negligence of the owner of the vehicle that the victim is driving, as the user of the vehicle is excluded from the risks compulsorily insured: *Cooper* v *MIB* [1985] 1 All ER 449 (CA).

CHAPTER 6

ASSIGNMENT

6-1 INTRODUCTION

Rights under a contract of insurance are choses in action.[1] Common law did not permit the assignment of choses in action, but eventually assignment was permitted by statute (below, 6–2 and 6–3). Meanwhile, an informal assignment was enforced by equity (below, 6–4) and equitable assignment has survived the introduction of the statutory modes of assignment.[2]

Life policies were made assignable under the Policies of Assurance Act 1867, and marine policies under the Marine Insurance Act 1868. The assignment of marine policies is now governed by the Marine Insurance Act 1906 (MIA) section 50.[3] The assignment of life policies can still be effected under the Act of 1867; however, life policies together with other choses in action are also assignable under section 136 of the Law of Property Act 1925 (LPA),[4] as well as in equity.[5] It is a poor comment on this montage that Houseman[6] advises the insurer that, even if the assignee appears to have made out title under section 136, the safest course is not to pay, unless he can also establish title under the Act of 1867.

The mode of assignment must be that of equity or of the appropriate statute. Assignment of the subject-matter of the insurance, such as a house[7] or a motor vehicle,[8] does not carry with it an insurance contract on that property, unless there is express or implied agreement to assign the insurance contract,[9] implemented in the appropriate mode. Quite apart from a defect in the mode of assignment, assignment

---

1. *Re Moore* (1878) 8 Ch D 519 (CA—life).
2. *Brandt's Sons & Co* v *Dunlop Rubber Co Ltd* [1905] AC 454, 461 *per* Lord Macnaghten.
3. On the rules particular to the assignment of marine contracts see Arnould, Nos 253 ff.
4. Slight doubt is raised by MacGillivray, No 1293 (p 613).
5. Policies issued under the Friendly Societies Acts are assignable in equity, notwithstanding legislative provisions for nomination of a person to take the benefit of the policy: *Re Griffin* [1902] 1 Ch 135 (CA—life).
6. p 116.
7. *Mildmay* v *Folgham* (1799) 3 Ves Jun 471, 474 *per* Loughborough LC (fire); *Rayner* v *Preston* (1881) 18 Ch D 1 (CA—fire). *Royal Ins Co Ltd* v *Mylius* (1926) 38 CLR 477, 490 *per* Isaacs J (HCA—fire). *Caledonian Ins Co* v *Montreal Trust Co* [1932] SCR 581, 585 *per* Lamont J (fire). *Newark Fire Ins Co* v *Turk*, 6 F 2d 533 (3 Cir, 1925—fire); *Milchem Inc* v *Smith Well Service Inc*, 351 F Supp 1307 (ED La, 1972—dual interest floater).
An attempt to deal with the problems raised by *Rayner* (above) for the buyer and seller of land is found in section 47 of the LPA, which, it is said, assigns not the contract of insurance but the benefit of the contract in cases of land transfer: Birds, pp 157 ff. *Cf* MacGillivray, No 1629.
8. *Peters* v *General Accident Fire & Life Assurance Corp Ltd* [1938] 2 All ER 267 (CA—motor); *Semple* v *State Farm Mutual Automobile Ins Co*, 215 F Supp 645 (ED Pa, 1963—motor).
9. MIA, section 15.

may be in performance of a contract to assign, which like any other contract may be vitiated by flaws in contracting; these are beyond the scope of this chapter.

A distinction is made[10] between (a) assignment of the (entire) contract of insurance, and (b) assignment of the right to recover insurance money under the contract.[11] (a) must also be distinguished from (c), the conclusion of a new contract between insurer and "assignee".[12] It may be difficult to distinguish (a) from (c), but it can be said that the consent of the insurer to the assignment is not of itself enough to indicate a new contract.[13] In (a) and (c) the assignee becomes the insured under the contract, whether it be the old contract or a new contract, and the assignor drops out, a change described as a novation,[14] while in (b) the assignor remains the insured. This difference produces differences in the consequences of assignment (below, 6–6). In any case, any contract which is normally assignable may be made expressly non-assignable.[15]

For (a) and (b), the cases of assignment, there are differences in the rules that govern the mode of assignment. First, as regards some kinds of insurance (a) may not be possible at all[16] or not possible without the consent of the insurer (see below, 6–3D); in (b) the insurance contract as such is unchanged[17] and, while notice must be given to the insurer, his consent is not normally required.[18] Second, in most cases of property insurance, (a) must occur at the same time as assignment of the property insured (see below, 6–3E). Third, in (a) but not (b)[19] the assignee must have an insurable interest in the subject-matter of the insurance. Case (b) in most if not all respects and case (a), except as detailed in this paragraph, are subject to the ordinary rules of assignment of choses in action.[20]

6–2 THE POLICIES OF ASSURANCE ACT 1867

By section 5 of the Act, the mode of assignment is endorsement on the policy or a separate instrument in or to the effect of words set out in the Schedule to the Act. By section 3 "written notice of the date and purport" of the assignment must be given to the insurer at a place of business specified in section 3 and to be specified (section 4) on the policy, such notice being effective in questions of priority only when received

10. Brown & Menezes No 17:3:1; Halsbury, Vol 25, No 650; MacGillivray, No 1615; Sutton, No 2.114. *Cf* Merkin & McGee, p D.1.1–04.

11. Whether or not loss recoverable under the insurance has occurred at the time of assignment: Ivamy, pp 476–477.

12. For example, *Springfield Fire & Marine Ins Co* v *Maxim* [1946] SCR 604 (fire). *Ellis* v *INA*, 32 F 646, 650 (SD Iowa, 1887—fire), approved in *Virginia-Carolina Chemical Co* v *Sundry Ins Cos*, 108 F 451, 456 (D SC, 1901—fire).

13. *Mercantile Finance Corp Ltd* v *New Zealand Ins Co Ltd* [1932] NZLR 1107, 1112 *per* Reed J (Sup Ct—motor).

14. For example *Gill* v *Yorkshire Ins Co* (1913) 24 WLR 389, 399 (Man—livestock).

15. See below, 6–3D.

16. Thus in *Peters* v *General Accident Fire & Life Assurance Corp Ltd* [1937] 4 All ER 628, 633 (motor), affirmed [1938] 2 All ER 267 (CA), Goddard J said that while it was impossible for an insured to assign a motor policy, he could assign his "right to receive money under it". The same is true of life insurance.

17. *Springfield Fire & Marine Ins Co* v *Maxim* [1946] SCR 604, 618 *per* Rand J (fire).

18. *Springfield* (above) *loc cit.* Schneideman v *Barnett* [1951] NZLR 301, 306 *per* Adams J (Sup Ct—fire).

19. For example a contingent right to insurance money under a liability policy (in respect of liability already incurred) may be assigned to creditors: *North America Accident Ins Co* v *Newton* (1918) 57 SCR 577. Ivamy, p 476.

20. *Lloyd* v *Fleming* (1872) LR 7 QB 299, 302–303 *per* Blackburn J (cargo).

by the insurer. By section 6, the person who gave notice may require the insurer to deliver a written acknowledgement of receipt of notice.

In 1867 the only kind of assignment known to the law was equitable assignment, so section 1 identifies the assignee, who by that section is empowered to sue, as a person now or later becoming entitled, by assignment or other derivative title, to a life policy and having the right in equity to receive policy monies and give effective discharge for such. The right to receive in equity

"does not mean a right depending on the validity of the policy; it means that, supposing the contract of assurance to be free from fraud, and otherwise valid, the derivative title of the assignee to this chose in action is such as would in Equity have entitled him to sue on it if the Act had not been passed. The qualification was introduced to guard against the assignee obtaining a better title than he would have had if he was suing in the name of the party who made the policy".[21]

Hence, as with other kinds of assignment (below, 6–6), assignment under this Act is subject to equities. However, unlike assignment under section 136 of the LPA (below, 6–3), assignment under the Act of 1867 may be part of the insured's interest in the policy.

6–3 THE LAW OF PROPERTY ACT 1925

Section 136 of the LPA, re-enacting section 25(6) of the Judicature Act 1873, provides:

"(1) Any absolute assignment by writing under the hand of the assignor (not purporting to be by way of charge only) of any debt or other legal thing in action, of which express notice in writing has been given to the debtor, trustee or other person from whom the assignor would have been entitled to claim such debt or thing in action, is effectual in law (subject to equities having priority over the right of the assignee) to pass and transfer from the date of such notice—
    (a) the legal right to such debt or thing in action;
    (b) all legal and other remedies for the same;
    (c) the power to give a good discharge for the same without the concurrence of the assignor:
Provided that, if the debtor, trustee or other person liable in respect of such debt or thing in action has notice—
    (a) that the assignment is disputed by the assignor or any person claiming under him; or
    (b) of any other opposing or conflicting claims to such debt or thing in action;
he may, if he thinks fit, either call upon the persons making the claim thereto to interplead concerning the same, or pay the debt or other thing in action into court under the provisions of the Trustee Act, 1925.
(2) This section does not affect the provisions of the Policies of Assurance Act, 1867."

Section 136 applies to any debt or other chose in action[23] including, therefore, rights under a contract of insurance, unless the chose can be transferred only by compliance with another statute. It applies only to an existing chose in action.[24] The purported assignment of a future debt can operate only as an assignment in equity.[25] There can

---

21. *Scottish Amicable Life Assurance Sy* v *Fuller* (1867) IR 2 Eq 53, 56 (life). See further on this Act Houseman, pp 114 ff.
23. This term includes all rights the assignment of which a Court of Law or Equity would before the Judicature Act 1873, have considered lawful: *King* v *Victoria Ins Co Ltd* [1896] AC 250, 254 *per* Lord Hobhouse (PC—cargo).
24. It is, however, possible to assign rights that mature in the future, if those rights are based on a presently existing contract: *Earle Ltd* v *Hemsworth RDC* (1929) 140 LT 69 (CA).
25. *Holt* v *Heatherfield Trust Ltd* [1942] 2 KB 1, 5 *per* Atkinson J.

be no assignment of rights which do not yet exist or belong to the assignor. Under a contract of insurance the insured has present rights which are assignable, whether or not an insured loss has occurred. Conversely, there can be no assignment of a right that has ceased so that, if the insured sells goods insured, the goods insurance lapses and cannot later be assigned to the buyer[26]: if there is to be assignment under section 136, it must be at the time of sale.

6–3A Form and Intention

Assignment must have been intended. Intention is ascertained by the substance rather than the form of what is said or done. A mere instruction to the insurer to pay a third party is ambiguous, and does not without more indicate intention to assign: it may be no more than a mandate which can be summarily revoked by the insured.[27]

Assignment must be absolute. Assignment of a chose to a lender until reassigned is absolute; assignment until the debt is repaid or assignment subject to any condition is not.[28] Assignment to an assignee on trust for a third person is absolute.[29] In general assignment is absolute, if it leaves the insurer in no doubt thereafter to whom the legal right assigned has been transferred.[30] Subject to this, assignment by way of mortgage is possible under section 136.[31]

Assignment must be in writing and that writing must be signed by the assignor.

6–3B Communication to the Assignee

Communication to the assignee is not specified by section 136, however, it is generally required, although the reason is hard to pin down. Perhaps it is necessary to complete a gift,[32] or to perfect the transaction in a way analogous to the delivery of a chattel,[33] or it may be just convenient as evidence of intention to assign.[34]

6–3C Notice to the Insurer

Notice must be given to the insurer in writing. It must contain material information: enough to make it plain who is entitled to be paid,[35] if the insured event occurs. Notice may be given at any time prior to suit to enforce the rights assigned,[36] and it may be

---

26. *North of England Pure Oil-Cake Co v Archangel Maritime Ins Co* (1875) LR 10 QB 249 (cargo); applied in *Caledonian Ins Co v Montreal Trust Co* [1932] SCR 581 (fire).
27. *Timpson's Exors v Yerbury* [1936] 1 KB 645, 658 *per* Lord Wright MR (CA).
28. *Re Williams* [1916] Ch 1 (CA—life). Treitel, p 579 ff.
29. *Comfort v Betts* [1891] 1 QB 737 (CA).
30. *Durham Bros v Robertson* [1898] 1 QB 765, 773 *per* Chitty LJ (CA).
   In Alberta similar legislation has been applied to assignment by way of mortgage: *Wilton v Rochester German Underwriters Agency* [1917] 2 WWR 782 (Alta—fire); *Taylor v Equitable Fire & Marine Ins Co* [1918] 1 WWR 676 (Alta—fire). But the prevailing view in Canada is said to be that any assignment to secure a debt, though absolute in form, is not to be treated in substance as absolute: Brown & Menezes, No 17:2:4, citing *Dominion Creosoting Co v Nickson Co* (1916) 55 SCR 303.
31. *Tancred v Delagoa Bay* (1889) 23 QBD 329.
32. *Timpson's Exors v Yerbury* [1936] 1 KB 645, 657–658 *per* Lord Wright MR (CA), who also suggested that communication by post was not achieved until receipt.
33. Treitel, p 583.
34. *Curran v Newpark Cinemas Ltd* [1951] 1 All ER 295 (CA).
35. *Van Lynn Developments Ltd v Pelias Construction Co Ltd* [1969] 1 QB 607, 613 *per* Lord Denning MR (CA).
36. *Bateman v Hunt* [1904] 2 KB 530 (CA).

given by the assignee.[37] Notice is not effective until received by the insurer.[38] Without notice there can be no assignment under section 136, although it may be effective in equity (below, 6–4). If the other requirements of section 136 have been met, the effect of notice is to complete assignment under section 136.

6–3D The Consent of the Insurer

In general, the law does not require the consent of the debtor to an assignment of the debt, but with the reservations, that a contract may effectively prohibit assignment without the consent of the debtor[39] and personal contracts by their very nature cannot be assigned without consent.[40] A contract is personal if the debtor is willing to perform the contract only in favour of one particular creditor. The insurer's concern with his insured lies in the risk and so an insurance contract is personal in this sense, if the assignment and change of creditor involve a significant change of risk. In practice this means that cargo insurance contracts[41] can be assigned without consent; that motor contracts,[42] perhaps livestock contracts,[43] and certainly fire contracts cannot.[44] A fire contract is

"a personal contract of indemnity . . . It is insurance against certain risks, and among them, what is called the moral risk of the insured. It is limited also to the interest of the insured in the subject matter. To say of a reciprocal relationship, that the insured could by his own act substi-

37. *Bateman* (above); *Holt* v *Heatherfield Trust Ltd* [1942] 2 KB 1, 4 *per* Atkinson J. *Cf Williams* v *Atlantic Assurance Co* [1933] 1 KB 81, 106 *per* Slesser LJ (CA—cargo) who accepted that there might be express notice *pendente lite* but also said that "a tender of notice of the assignee as a party and an amended pleading is not in itself an express notice within the meaning of s.136; it is at most an indirect and adjectival notice".

38. *Holt* (above). It is enough to give notice to the local agent as the channel of communication, but *quaere* whether it is effective then or within a reasonable time thereafter, i.e., time for transmission to head office: *Re Hennessy* (1842) IR 5 Eq 259 (life). The later time is suggested by analogy with the LPA, section 196. *Cf Laidlaw* v *Hartford Fire Ins Co* (1916) 10 WWR 1063, 1067 (Alta—fire) that it is enough to give notice to a local agent.

39. *Brice* v *Bannister* (1878) 3 QBD 569, 581 *per* Bramwell LJ (CA); *Re Birkbeck Permanent Benefit Building Sy* [1913] 2 Ch 34, 37 *per* Neville J (guarantee). *Prima facie* a contractual restriction does not apply to assignment by a person on whom property has devolved by operation of law and who is under an obligation to assign: *ibid* p 38.

40. *Peters* v *General Accident Fire & Life Assurance Corp Ltd* [1938] 2 All ER 267, 270 *per* Sir Wilfred Greene MR (CA—motor). *Central Union Bk* v *New York Underwriters' Ins Co*, 52 F 2d 823, 824 (4 Cir, 1931—fire).

41. In the case of cargo insurers "it is immaterial to them in whom the interest vests at the time of loss"— *North of England Pure Oil-Cake Co* v *Archangel Maritime Ins Co* (1875) LR 10 QB 249, 254 *per* Cockburn CJ (cargo). Also, it has been said, an employer's liability contract: *Siu* v *Eastern Ins Co Ltd*, *The Times*, 16 December 1993 (PC—liability); *sed quaere*.
Moreover, a windstorm contract is not a personal contract, the risk being beyond the control of the insured, and can be assigned without the consent of the insurer: *Swihart* v *Missouri Farmers Mutual Tornado Cyclone & Windstorm Ins Co*, 138 SW 2d 9, 15 (Mo, 1940).

42. A "contract of that kind is in its very nature not assignable . . . That appears to me to be altering *in toto* the character of the risk"—*Peters* v *General Accident Fire & Life Assurance Corp Ltd* [1938] 2 All ER 267, 269 *per* Sir Wilfred Greene MR (CA—motor), even though it may extend liability cover to persons driving with the consent of the insured . . . *Idem* an employers' liability contract: *Rendelman* v *Levitt*, 24 SW 2d 211, 213 (Mo, 1930).

43. *Gill* v *Yorkshire Ins Co* (1913) 24 WLR 389, 399 (Man—livestock).

44. *Carpenter* v *Providence Washington Ins Co*, 16 Pet 495, 503–504 *per* Story J (SC, 1842—fire); *Central Union Bk* v *New York Underwriters' Ins Co*, 52 F 2d 823, 824 (4 Cir, 1931—fire).
If the insurer consents in the case of fire insurance, the court may well infer that a new contract altogether (but on the terms of the old contract) has been concluded with the "assignee", so that the latter takes free of equities: *Springfield Fire & Marine Ins Co* v *Maxim* [1946] SCR 604 (fire). See below, 6–6(d).

tute a new party to the contract, and thereby change the moral risk and the interest in the subject matter is to misconceive the nature of the contract."[45]

Less obviously, perhaps, the same is probably true of assignment by the insurer. Certainly in the case of long term business, the insurer is chosen carefully on the basis of his record and apparent solvency. A claimant should not have to find that the insurer had transferred it to an unknown and insolvent company, as once happened to annuitants in Florida.[45a] Although it is common to talk of the assignment of life insurance, or transfer of the ownership of the policy,[46] for the same reasons the contract (and risk) cannot be assigned: the assignment that commonly occurs is an assignment of the right to the insurance money,[47] an assignment that involves no change of risk. Nor is there a change in the contract of insurance itself, so the consent of the insurer is not required.[48] In principle the same is true of other insurance contracts, such as fire contracts.[49]

In practice the matter is often regulated by terms of the contract. A term requiring notice of assignment to the insurer clearly envisages the possibility of assignment, and by inference, it has been held,[50] does not require consent. Moreover, a term prohibiting assignment does not prevent the insured creating a trust of the benefit of insurance money in favour of third parties[51] and, in view of the reasons for it, a term requiring the consent of the insurer has been construed to apply to assignment of the insurance but not to assignment of the right of action after loss has occurred.[51a] If consent is required but not obtained, the effect, if any, of a purported assignment is a question of construction of the contract.[51b]

Subject to the terms of the contract, when consent is required, it may take any form. An insurer who accepts renewal premium from an assignee will be estopped from denying consent.[52]

6–3E The Assignee

In the case of assignment of the contract, for example property insurance, the assignee

---

45. *Springfield* (above) p 618 *per* Rand J (fire). The restriction concerns voluntary assignment. A fire contract may, of course, be assigned by operation of law (below, 6–5), for example, to a trustee in bankruptcy: *Re Carr and Sun Fire Ins Co* (1897) 13 TLR 186 (CA—fire).

45a. (1992) Vol 6 Insurance International No 7 p 7 concerning "assumption reinsurance".

46. *Central Union Bk v New York Underwriters' Ins Co*, 52 F 2d 823, 824 (4 Cir, 1931—fire); *Webster v State Mutual Life Assurance Co*, 50 F Supp 11, 17–18 (SD Cal, 1943—life). A standard clause, which forbids assignment except with the written consent of the insurer, is not infringed by assignment of the insurance money: *Travelers Indemnity Co v Israel*, 354 F 2d 488 (2 Cir, 1965—fire). *Cf Senese v Senese*, 121 NYS 2d 498, 503 (1953—life): "An assignment of life insurance policies . . . vests in the assignee *all* the rights and liabilities set forth in the policy" (emphasis added). This does not appear to be the general view.

47. Ivamy, p 477. Together with any bonuses or other accretions to the policy: *Gilly v Burley* (1856) 22 Beav 619; money payable under an extension of the insurance: *Royal Exchange Assurance v Hope* [1928] Ch 179 (CA—life); or substituted insurance: *Nesbitt v Berridge* (1863) 4 De G J & Sm 45 (life).

48. *McPhillips v London Mutual Fire Ins Co* (1896) 23 OAR 524 (fire).

49. *Canadian Bk of Commerce v Wawanesa Mutual Ins Co* [1924] 3 WWR 822 (Sask—fire). *Carpenter v Providence Washington Ins Co*, 16 Pet 495, 502 *per* Story J (SC, 1842—fire).

50. *Re Birkbeck Permanent Benefit Building Sy* [1913] 2 Ch 34 (guarantee).

51. *Re Turcan* (1888) 40 Ch D 5, 10 *per* Cotton LJ (CA—life).

51a. *In re San Juan Dupont Plaza Hotel Fire Litigation*, 789 F Supp 1212, 1216 (D Puerto Rico, 1992—liability).

51b. *Linden Gardens Trust Ltd v Lenesta Sludge Disposals Ltd* [1993] 3 All ER 417, 428 *per* Lord Browne-Wilkinson (HL), with reference to Goode (1979) 42 MLR 553.

52. *Murchie v Victoria Ins Co* (1885) 4 NZLR SC 114, 123–124 *per* Prendergast CJ (fire).

must have an insurable interest in the property at the time of the assignment.[53] If he buys the property before the assignment of the insurance, the assignment is ineffective because, if the seller lost all interest of his own by the sale, it will have lapsed[54] Yet, if the assignee acquires the property after the assignment of the insurance, the insurance is invalid if, having still to acquire the property, the assignee lacked insurable interest in the property at the time of the assignment. The result is that for an effective assignment in the case of the sale of property the insurance must be assigned at the time of sale.[55] There seems no reason why the property transfer should be absolute, such as sale, or that the insurance should be limited to the property transferred, but transfer and assignment must be at the same time. In any event, it is not necessary that the assignee should have given consideration for the assignment.[56]

6–4 EQUITABLE ASSIGNMENT

Choses in action, including rights under an insurance contract, are assignable in equity, unless the chose can be transferred only by compliance with a statute. Equity distinguished equitable choses, such as the interest in a trust fund, and legal choses,[57] such as the right under an insurance contract: requirements for the latter are less stringent (below, 6–4A).

The assignment of a future debt, impossible under section 136 (above, 6–3), is possible as an assignment in equity[58]; at common law there can be no assignment of rights which do not yet exist or belong to the assignor. Moreover, the assignment of less than an absolute interest or of part of a debt, impossible under section 136, is possible in equity.[59] Under a contract of insurance the insured has present rights which are assignable, although their full value may not yet have matured. There can be no assignment, however, of a right that has ceased: if the insured sells goods insured and thereby loses any insurable interest in them, the insurance lapses[60] and cannot later be assigned to the buyer.[61] Assignment must be at the time of sale: on this point equity does not differ from section 136 (above, 6–3E).

---

53. *Lloyd* v *Fleming* (1872) LR 7 QB 299, 302 *per* Blackburn J (cargo). In principle, however, it should be sufficient that at the time of assignment he had a reasonable prospect of acquiring an insurable interest.

In the case of the assignment of insurance money, the insured remaining a party to the contract, it is not required that the assignee should have an insurable interest in the property insured: *McPhillips* v *London Mutual Fire Ins Co* (1896) 23 OAR 524 (fire).

54. *North of England Pure Oil-Cake Co* v *Archangel Maritime Ins Co* (1875) LR 10 QB 249 (cargo). The rule is now found (MIA, section 51) for marine contracts, if before or at the time of transfer, the insured transferor has not "expressly or impliedly agreed to assign the policy". *Mobilia* v *Security Taxpayers Mutual Ins Co*, 90 NYS 2d 895 (1949—liability), affirmed 99 NYS 2d 856.

55. *North of England* (above) p 254 *per* Cockburn CJ, and p 255 *per* Quain J (cargo).

56. *Re Westerton* [1919] 2 Ch 104.

57. This term includes all rights the assignment of which a court of law or equity would before the Judicature Act 1873 have considered lawful: *King* v *Victoria Ins Co Ltd* [1896] AC 250, 254 *per* Lord Hobhouse (PC—cargo).

58. *Tailby* v *Official Receiver* (1888) 13 App Cas 523, 533 *per* Lord Watson; *Holt* v *Heatherfield Trust Ltd* [1942] 2 KB 1, 5 *per* Atkinson J.

59. *Williams* v *Atlantic Assurance Co* [1933] 1 KB 81, 100 *per* Greer LJ (CA—cargo). The same is true of assignments which in this respect do not satisfy MIA, section 50: *The Evelpidis Era* [1981] 1 Lloyd's Rep 54, 64 *per* Mocatta J (P & I). *Continental Assurance Co* v *Conroy*, 111 F Supp 370, 378 (D NJ, 1953—life) and cases cited.

60. *Rogerson* v *Scottish Automobile & General Ins Co Ltd* (1931) 41 Ll L Rep 1 (HL—motor): the insurance was tied to a particular vehicle.

61. *North of England Pure Oil-Cake Co* v *Archangel Maritime Ins Co* (1875) LR 10 QB 249 (cargo).

6-4A Form and Intention

Whereas any disposition of an equitable interest must be in writing, a contractual right is not an equitable interest, and its assignment in equity does not require writing or any particular form.[62] Delivery of the policy to the assignee will suffice[63] as a matter of form, if intention to assign is clear. Even in the absence of delivery, an agreement to assign may have effect in equity.[64] In practice, assignment of insurance is often indorsed on the policy.

When an assignment is in writing, it need not contain words of assignment. "It may be couched in the language of command. It may be a courteous request. It may assume the form of mere permission. The language is immaterial if the meaning is plain. All that is necessary is that the debtor should be given to understand that the debt has been made over by the creditor to some third person".[65] There must be clear evidence of intention to assign.[66] This will be inferred, if the insured indicates that his dealings with the assignee have been such that the assignee now has a *right* to the benefit of the contract.[67] Intention has also been inferred from the term of a contract to sell the subject-matter of insurance, whereby the purchaser was obliged to pay the unearned premium.[68]

6-4B Communication to the Assignee

It is generally assumed that an assignment is ineffective unless communicated to the assignee. In England the reason for the rule is not clear (see above, 6-3B). In the United States it has been suggested that communication and failure to dissent to a voluntary assignment amount to acceptance of the gift.[69]

6-4C Notice to the Insurer

To assign the contract, notice of the assignment must be given to the insurer. It must be clear in substance and when seen in its context.[70] "The language is immaterial if the meaning is plain. All that is necessary is that the debtor should be given to understand that the debt has been made over by the creditor to some third person,"[71] "that the debt and *the right to receive it* have been transferred to the third party".[72] As regards the detail and accuracy of the notice, it must contain all material information, enough

---

62. *Cook v Black* (1842) 1 Hare 390 (life). *Contra*: *Howes v Prudential Assurance Co* (1883) 49 LT 133 (life). *Wollpert v O'Brien,* 85 NYS 2d 660 (1948—life); *Franklin Life Ins Co v Falkingham*, 229 F 2d 300 (7 Cir, 1956—life).

63. *Cook v Black* (1842) 1 Hare 390 (life); *Le Feuvre v Sullivan* (1855) 10 Moore 1, 13 *per* Knight-Bruce LJ (PC—life); *Shaw v Foster* (1872) LR 5, HL 321, 340 *per* Lord Cairns; *Thomas v Harris* [1947] 1 All ER 444 (CA—life). *Cf* Scotland: *Scottish Provident Institution v Cohen & Co* (1886) 16 R 117 (Ct Sess—life). *Re Crothers* [1930] VLR 49 (SC—life). *Canadian Bk of Commerce v Wawanesa Mutual Ins Co* [1924] 3 WWR 822 (Sask—fire). *Wollpert v O'Brien*, 85 NYS 2d 660 (1948—life).

64. *Wilder v Watts* 138 F 426, 432 (D SC, 1905—fire); *Phoenix Mutual Life Ins Co v Birkelund*, 195 P 2d 5, 10 (Cal, 1946—life).

65. *Brandt's Sons & Co v Dunlop Rubber Co Ltd* [1905] AC 454, 462 *per* Lord Macnaghten.

66. *Andrews v Andrews* 97 F 2d 485, 487 (8 Cir, 1938—life).

67. For example *Talcott Ltd v Lewis & Co Ltd* [1940] 3 All ER 592, 595 *per* MacKinnon LJ (CA).

68. *Caledonian Ins Co v Montreal Trust Co* [1932] SCR 581 (fire).

69. *Woodward v United States*, 106 F Supp 14, 28 (ND Iowa, 1952—life).

70. *Smith v SS "Zigurds" Owners* [1934] AC 209, 213–214 *per* Lord Atkin.

71. *Brandt's Sons & Co v Dunlop Rubber Co Ltd* [1905] AC 454, 462 *per* Lord Macnaghten.

72. *Talcott Ltd v Lewis & Co Ltd* [1940] 3 All ER 592, 595 *per* MacKinnon LJ (CA) (emphasis added).

to make it plain to the insurer to whom he should pay[73] insurance money that might fall due under the contract in question. It is generally enough to give notice to the local agent of the insurer as the appropriate channel of communication.[74]

As regards the assignment of the right to insurance money the position is similar. "Absence of notice does not affect the efficacy of the transaction as between the assignor and the assignee. Until notice be given the assignment is an equitable assignment."[75] However, notice is required to "perfect" or "complete"[76] the rights of the equitable assignee against the insurer,[77] for, until he has received notice of the assignment, the insurer is entitled to assume that payment to the insured will discharge his duty under the contract.

6-4D The Consent of the Insurer

Equity follows the law, as stated (above, 6-3D) in respect of assignment under section 136 of the LPA, with one exception: whereas at law a contractual prohibition on assignment is effective, in equity it is not.[78]

6-4E The Assignee

The assignee is not required to have an insurable interest.[79] However, for assignment in equity, unlike assignment under section 136 (above, 6-3E), consideration must have moved from assignee to assignor.[80] A voluntary assignment is ineffective in equity, unless it is complete, i.e., the assignor has done all that he alone can do to perfect the assignee's title, although something remains to be done which can be done by someone else,[81] or, perhaps, it can be said that the assignor has constituted himself a trustee for the assignee.[82]

6-5 ASSIGNMENT BY OPERATION OF LAW

If the insured dies, his rights pass to his personal representatives.[83] If the insured is declared bankrupt, his things, including things in action, "are deemed to have been assigned to the trustee" in bankruptcy.[84] Insurance contracts, including contracts

---

73. *Whittingstall v King* (1882) 46 LT 520. The rule is probably the same as that at common law: Megarry, 72 LQR 321 (1956).

74. *Re Hennessy* (1842) IR 5 Eq 259 (life). See below, 26-2D.

75. *Holt v Heatherfield Trust Ltd* [1942] 2 KB 1, 4 *per* Atkinson J; see also *Cook v Black* (1842) 1 Hare 390, 394 *per* Wigram V-C (life); *Dufaur v Professional Life Assurance Co* (1858) 25 Beav 599 (life); *Warner Bros Records Inc v Rollgreen Ltd* [1976] QB 430, 441 *per* Lord Denning MR (CA). *Laidlaw v Hartford Fire Ins Co* (1916) 10 WWR 1063 (Alta—fire).

76. *Re Hennessy* (1842) IR 5 Eq 259 (life).

77. *Warner Bros Records Inc v Rollgreen Ltd* [1976] QB 430 (CA).

78. *Re Turcan* (1888) Ch D 5 (CA—life). *Cf Linden Gardens Trust Ltd v Lenesta Sludge Disposals Ltd* [1993] 3 All ER 417, 428 per Lord Browne-Wilkinson (HL).

79. *Ashley v Ashley* (1829) 3 Sim 149 (life). *Robinson v Exchange National Bk*, 28 F Supp 244, 248 (ND Okl, 1939—life).

80. *Chowne v Baylis* (1862) 31 Beav 351 (life); *Re Westerton* [1919] 2 Ch 104, 111 *per* Sargant J.

81. *Re Rose* [1952] Ch 499 (CA).

82. In this sense Houseman, pp 108 ff; MacGillivray, No 1299 (p 616), No 1329 (p 624), citing *inter alia* *Thomas v Harris* [1947] 1 All ER 444 (CA—life).

83. *Doe d, Pitt v Laming* (1814) 4 Camp 73 (fire).

84. Insolvency Act 1986, section 311(4). *Idem* if a company is liquidated: the chose is assigned to the liquidator: *Re Harrington Motor Co Ltd* [1928] Ch 105 (CA—motor). The freedom of the trustee or liquidator to deal with the insurance is limited by the Third Parties (Rights against Insurers) Act 1930, section 1(1).

which are incapable of voluntary assignment, may be assigned by operation of law.[85] Further, if a contractual restriction on assignment is by its own terms inapplicable in the case of assignment by operation of law, that is construed to permit assignment by the assignee, such as a personal representative, if he was under an obligation to assign.[86]

Unless provided for in the contract, the benefit of property insurance does not pass directly to legatees of the property. If, after the death of the insured but before distribution of the estate, the property is damaged, a legatee of property is not able to enforce the insurance[87]; but the personal representatives, it has been said,[88] are trustees of the insurance for the legatees. If, however, the property is lost before the death of the insured, the loss falls on the legatees in that the insurance money is part of the insured's general estate.[89] So too, if the insured and his property perish at the same time: the insurance money is part of the general estate.[90]

6–6 THE EFFECT OF ASSIGNMENT

(a) *Suit.* If the assignment is under section 136 of the LPA, the effect is to transfer the legal right to the subject-matter of the assignment, all legal and other remedies for the same, and the power to give a good discharge to the insurer without the concurrence of the assignor. The assignee may sue in his own name.[91]

If the assignment is equitable, the assignee acquires the so-called "beneficial" interest in the insurance but not the right to sue; he must sue with the assignor as co-plaintiff with his consent or, if he does not consent, join the assignor as co-defendant with the insurer; in any event, the insurer may insist that in any action by the assignee the assignor is joined.

(b) *Liability to Pay.* In the case of assignment of the contract, whether the assignment is under section 136 or in equity,[92] the insurer becomes liable to the assignee and ceases to be liable to the assignor.[93] The interest in the contract passes "wholly"[94] to the assignee. The amount recoverable from the insurer is measured by the loss suffered by the assignee; if he recovers in excess of his actual loss, he does not hold the surplus for the assignor.[95]

In the case of assignment of the right to insurance money, the assignor remains a party to the contract and (when relevant) it is his loss that is the measure of indemnity; yet, only the assignee can give the insurer a good discharge for payment.[96] Further, in

---

85. *Hood's Trustees* v *Southern Union General Ins Co Ltd* [1928] Ch 793 (CA—motor). In the same general sense: *Imperial Enterprises Inc* v *Fireman's Fund Ins Co*, 35 F 2d 287 (5 Cir, 1976—fire).
86. *Re Birkbeck Permanent Benefit Building Sy* [1913] 2 Ch 34, 38–39 *per* Neville J (guarantee).
87. *Mildmay* v *Folgham* (1797) 3 Ves Jun 471 (fire).
88. *Durrant* v *Friend* (1851) 5 De G & Sm 343, 346 *per* Parker V-C. Ivamy, p 352, n 15.
89. *Durrant, loc cit.*
90. *Ibid.*
91. *Cf* Assignment under the Policies of Assurance Act 1867: under section 1 the assignee is "at liberty to sue in the name of" the person entitled to the policy of life insurance.
92. Treitel, p 585 and cases cited.
93. *Cottage Club Estates Ltd* v *Woodside Estates Co (Amersham) Ltd* [1928] 2 KB 463, 467 *per* Wright J.
94. *Landauer* v *Asser* [1905] 2 KB 184, 189 *per* Lord Alverstone CJ (cargo).
95. *Landauer* (above). *Cf Williams* v *Atlantic Assurance Co* [1933] 1 KB 81, 97 *per* Scrutton LJ (CA—cargo).
96. MacGillivray, No 1619.

principle it is the assignor who is liable to pay premiums.[97] Whether the assignee may or must perform any procedural conditions or other conditions precedent to payment is a matter of construction of the contract.[98] If the insurer mistakenly pays insurance money to the assignor or to a fourth party, the assignee may claim the amount from the insurer, or from the person (assignor or fourth party) to whom the money has been paid.[99]

(c) *Good faith*. The insurer owes a duty of good faith to the insured, and hence to the original insured and to an assignee of the contract; however, in the case of assignment of insurance money, the duty is owed to the original insured, who remains a party to the insurance contract, and not to the assignee.[100] Thus, in one case,[101] although the hull insurer owed no duty to the assignee mortgagee to advise him that the insured owner was trading outside the limits of the insurance contract as a matter of good faith, he did owe such a duty as a matter of contract.

(d) *Equities*. Whether the assignment is of the insurance contract or of the insurance money, the assignee takes rights subject to any equities,[102] claims or defences which the insurer has against the insured. These include a right to terminate the contract in case of a fraudulent claim by the insured,[103] to refuse a claim if notice is given too late[104] or because at the time of assignment the assignor had become an enemy alien,[105] or to avoid the contract for misrepresentation or non-disclosure,[106] or to terminate the contract for breach of warranty,[107] or to defend a claim on the basis of illegal conduct by the assignor.[108] Such a claim or defence is good against the assignee, even though he took the insurance *bona fide* for value and without knowledge of the facts giving rise to the claim or defence.[109] The assignee's rights being derivative, he can be in no better position than his assignor.[110]

When the assignment is of insurance money, the assignor remains a party to the contract of insurance, and the assignee takes subject not only to defences arising

---

97. *Robinson* v *Exchange National Bk*, 28 F Supp 244, 250 (ND Okl, 1939—life).

98. *North America Accident Ins Co* v *Newton* (1918) 57 SCR 577, 580 *per* Angin J concerning whether the assignee could or should pay the third party claimant before recovery of money contingently due under a liability contract.

99. *McEntire* v *Potter* (1889) 22 QBD 438 (marine).

100. *The Good Luck* [1988] 1 Lloyd's Rep 514, 546 *per* Hobhouse J (P & I), affirmed [1989] 2 Lloyd's Rep 238 (CA—hull). Birds [1989] JBL 348. This point did not arise for decision in the House of Lords: [1992] 1 AC 233 (HL).

101. *The Good Luck* (above): the ship of that name was insured with the defendant club and mortgaged to the plaintiff bank. As required by the mortgage, the benefit of the insurance was assigned to the bank, and the club gave a Letter of Undertaking to the bank, whereby the club promised to advise the bank promptly if the club "cease to insure" the ship. The House of Lords held that this promise was part of a contract enforceable against the club. *Cf Scottish Equitable Life Assurance Sy* v *Buist* (1877) 4 R (Ct Sess) 1076, 1081–1082 *per* Lord President Inglis.

102. *Mangles* v *Dixon* (1852) 3 HLC 702.

103. *Re Carr and Sun Fire Ins Co* (1897) 13 TLR 186 (CA—fire). *North British & Mercantile Ins Co* v *Tourville* (1895) 25 SCR 177 (fire).

104. *Re Carr* (above).

105. *Bank of New South Wales* v *South British Ins Co Ltd* (1920) 4 Ll L Rep 266, 384 (CA—cargo).

106. *Pickersgill & Sons Ltd* v *London & Provincial Marine & General Ins Co Ltd* [1912] 3 KB 614 (hull). *Venner* v *Sun Life Ins Co* (1889) 17 SCR 394 (life); *Springfield Fire & Marine Ins Co* v *Maxim* [1946] SCR 604 (fire).

107. *Boyce* v *Phoenix Mutual Life Ins Co* (1887) 14 SCR 723 (life). *Otsego Aviation Service* v *Glen Falls Ins Co*, 3 NYS 2d 454 (1948—aviation), affirmed 102 NYS 2d 344 (1951).

108. See below, 24–5 ff.

109. *Pickersgill* (above).

110. *Bank of New South Wales* (above) pp 384 and 385 *per* Bankes LJ (CA—cargo). *Carpenter* v *Providence Washington Ins Co*, 16 Pet 495, 503 *per* Story J (SC, 1842—fire).

before assignment but also defences arising after assignment.[111] In this situation the assignee is so vulnerable that it has been suggested that the insurer may owe a duty to the assignee to advise him that the insurance is voidable. In one case[111a] the judge observed *obiter* that if it was clear that the contract was voidable, there might "then be a duty of communication to those whom the company know to be interested in the policy. It would not be consistent with good faith that they should, in the circumstances, go on receiving the premiums on a policy that they intended to challenge in the end".

When the insurance contract has been assigned, however, the assignor insured drops out and the assignee is unaffected by defences conceded later by the assignor.[112] In Canada and the United States, assignment of the contract may be seen as the conclusion of a new contract with the "assignee", with the important difference that the "assignee" is unaffected by the conduct, whether past or present, of the "assignor".[113]

In any case, the assignee may acquire a better position than the assignor, taking free of equities, by consent of the insurer. This may arise, first, if the insurer's consent to "assignment" has been obtained, as in the case of fire insurance, and the court infers that a new contract altogether (but on the terms of the old contract) has been concluded with the "assignee", so that the latter takes free of equities arising from the old contract.[114] Second, to make the insurance contract more attractive as a security, the contract itself may provide for assignment free of some or all equities. Thus a life contract, unenforceable by the representative of an insured who committed suicide, may be enforceable by a *bona fide* assignee.[115]

6–7 PRIORITY BETWEEN ASSIGNEES

Whether the assignment in issue is legal or equitable,[116] priority is determined by rules of equity developed for equitable assignees. Assignees rank in the order in which notice of their assignment is given to the insurer.[117]

An assignee gains priority over an earlier assignee under the following cumulative conditions:

111. *Amicable Sy* v *Bolland* (1831) 2 Dow & Cl 1 (HL—life); *The Litsion Pride* [1985] 1 Lloyd's Rep 437 (hull). *Cf* mortgage clauses in fire contracts, designed to overcome this problem.
111a. *Scottish Equitable Life Assurance Sy* v *Buist* (1877) 4 R (Ct Sess) 1076, in which the life contract was induced by fraudulent misrepresentation, per Lord President (1081–1082). *Cf The Good Luck* [1988] 1 Lloyd's Rep 514 (P & I): the insurer owes no such duty to a mortgagee—affirmed: [1989] 2 Lloyd's Rep 238 (CA).
112. Such as an agreement compromising an insurance claim: *Hood's Trustees* v *Southern Union General Ins Co Ltd* [1928] Ch 793 (CA—motor). *Cf* loss by an excepted cause brought about by the assignor: a claim by the assignee fails, not under the present rule, but because the loss is uninsured: for example, *Jackson* v *Forster* (1860) 1 El & El 463 (Exch Ch—life).
113. *Springfield Fire & Marine Ins Co* v *Maxim* [1946] SCR 604 (fire); *London & Midland General Ins Co* v *Bonser* [1973] SCR 10 (fire); *Re National Bank of Canada* (1988) 53 DLR (4th) 519 (Alta—fire). Brown & Menezes, No 17:3:5. Ocean *Accident & Guarantee Corp Ltd* v *Southwestern Bell Telephone Co*, 100 F 2d 441 (8 Cir, 1939—liability), *cert den* 306 US 658.
114. See previous note.
115. *Cook* v *Black* (1842) 1 Hare 390, 394 *per* Wigram V-C (life); *Dufaur* v *Professional Life Assurance Co* (1858) 25 Beav 599 (life); *Rowett, Leakey & Co* v *Scottish Provident Institution* [1927] 1 Ch 55 (CA—life).
116. In *Newman* v *Newman* (1885) 28 Ch D 674, 680–681 (life), North J rejected the argument that an assignment and notice under the Policies of Assurance Act had priority over an earlier equitable assignment.
117. *Dearle* v *Hall* (1828) 3 Russ 1.

(a) His assignment is for value.[118] Although in consequence a voluntary assignee, including a trustee in bankruptcy,[119] cannot gain priority over an earlier assignee, he cannot be overtaken by a later assignee, if he has given notice (formal or informal) to the insurer.[120]

(b) He has had no notice,[121] actual or constructive,[122] of the earlier assignment at the time of his own assignment.[123]

(c) He has been misled by and induced to take the assignment by the conduct of the earlier assignee in leaving the policy with the assignor[124] *or* he has given formal notice of his assignment to the insurer, before the insurer has knowledge of the earlier assignment.[125] Formal notice[126] of the assignment must be in writing, specifying the policy concerned. If insurance money has been paid into court, the effect of formal notice is achieved by obtaining a "stop order".[127]

118. *McPhail* v *John Hancock Mutual Life Ins Co*, 108 F Supp 902 (WD Ky, 1952—life).

119. *Re Anderson* [1911] 1 KB 896.

120. *Re Russell's Policy Trusts* (1872) LR 15 Eq 26 (life).

121. *Re Holmes* (1885) 29 Ch D 786 (CA); *Newman* v *Newman* (1885) 28 Ch D 674 (life); *Re Weniger's Policy* [1910] 2 Ch 291 (life). See also *McPhail* (above).

122. The assignee has constructive knowledge of an earlier equity, if he is put on inquiry, notably, if the assignor is unable to produce the policy or give a good explanation for his inability to do so: *Spencer* v *Clarke* (1878) 9 Ch D 137 (life); *Re Weniger's Policy* [1910] 2 Ch 291 (life).

123. *Mutual Life Assurance Sy* v *Langley* (1886) 32 Ch D 460 (CA).

124. *Shropshire Union Ry & Canal Co* v *The Queen* (1875) LR 7 HL 496, 509 *per* Lord Cairns. *Contra*, MacGillivray, No 1313 (p 620), unless he also fails to give notice to the insurer. In this sense *Fidelity Mutual Life Ins Co* v *City National Bk*, 95 F Supp 276, 283 (ND W Va, 1950—life): no "equitable estoppel" against the earlier assignee in these circumstances.

125. *Dearle* v. *Hall* (1828) 3 Russ 1, applied in *Wood* v *Duncombe* [1893] AC 369.

126. Although informal notice does not give priority over an earlier assignee, it may provide the insurer with knowledge of the assignment, so that it cannot be overtaken by later assignments: *Lloyd* v *Banks* (1868) LR 3 Ch App 488.

127. *Stephens* v *Green* 2 Ch 148 (CA).

CHAPTER 7

AGENTS: AUTHORITY TO BIND THE INSURED

7–1 THE AGENTS

7–1A Introduction

Brokers and other insurance intermediaries independent of any one insurer are generally agents of the insured.[1] The role of the Lloyd's broker as agent of the insured rather than of the insurer, although criticised, has been confirmed.[1a] The agent of the insured may be remunerated by commission deducted from premium before it is sent on to the insurer, but this is done as a matter of convenience and does not make the agent the agent of the insurer.[2] Recent changes in the practice and the law relating to insurance intermediaries have polarised the profession, and the picture now is one of fewer independents and more agents more or less overtly representing insurers.

7–1B Polarisation[3]

Persons arranging insurance for others, apart from employees of an insurer, are called insurance intermediaries. There are two types of intermediary for both life and other business, tied agents and independent intermediaries. Independents who wish to be called insurance brokers must register under the Insurance Brokers (Registration) Act of 1977. A tied agent, also called a company representative in the case of life insurance, may offer life insurance with only one insurance group, or non-life insurance with up to six insurers. An independent is free to deal with any number of insurers. All intermediaries, including part-time intermediaries such as estate agents, must opt for one of these two categories. The independent is seen as primarily the agent of the insured, while a tied agent is essentially the agent of the insurer.

As regards regulation of intermediaries:

(a) independents who register as brokers are regulated by the Insurance Brokers

---

1. *Bancroft* v *Heath* (1900) 5 Com Cas 110, 115 *per* Mathew J (fire); affirmed (1901) 6 Com Cas 137 (CA).

USA *idem*: *Eagle Star* v *Tadlock*, 22 F Supp 545 (SD Cal, 1938—hull); *Edinburgh Assurance Co* v *Burns Corp,* 479 F Supp 138 (CD Cal, 1979—marine), in part reversed on other grounds, 669 F 2d 1259. See also *Hesselberg* v *Aetna Life Ins Co*, 75 F 2d 490 (8 Cir, 1935—life), *cert* den 296 US 625. Sometimes the broker acts for both insured and insurer: see below, 7–1D. See also Appleman, section 8722.

1a. *Roberts* v *Plaisted* [1989] 2 Lloyd's Rep. 341 (CA—fire); *Pryke* v *Gibbs Hartley Cooper Ltd* [1991] 1 Lloyd's Rep 602 (financial guarantee).

2. *Rozanes* v *Bowen* (1928) 32 Ll L Rep 98, 101 *per* Scrutton LJ (CA—jewellery). This view of English law was also taken in *Edinburgh Assurance Co* v *Burns Corp,* 479 F Supp 138 (CD Cal, 1979—marine).

3. My thanks to Jenny Frost of the Association of British Insurers for guiding me through the polar mist.

Registration Council, set up under the 1977 Act, which has published rules including a Code of Conduct.

(b) Under the Financial Services Act 1986, there are special rules governing the selling of investment business.[4] A tied agent, who must arrange business with only one "marketing group", is controlled by the insurance company to which he is tied, and the company is controlled by the Securities and Investments Board (SIB) or the appropriate Self-Regulating Organisation (SRO). Independent intermediaries must be authorised and hence controlled by the SIB or an appropriate SRO (usually the Financial Intermediaries, Managers and Brokers Regulatory Association—FIMBRA). They can also be authorised by a Recognised Professional Body (RPB) if their investment business does not exceed a certain percentage of their total business (percentages currently adopted are 20 per cent or 25 per cent). In the case of insurance brokers, the appropriate RPB is the Insurance Brokers Registration Council.

(c) As regards general insurance, independent intermediaries (other than brokers), tied agents and employees of insurance companies involved in selling insurance are all governed by the Code of Practice for the selling of General Insurance, prepared and published by the Association of British Insurers (ABI).[5]

(d) As regards both life insurance and non-life insurance, insurance intermediaries currently face further regulation of their activity upon the implementation of the EC Recommendation of 18 December 1991.[5a]

7–1C Incidental Agents

Persons such as solicitors, accountants,[6] estate agents, building societies and motor dealers, who retail insurance as part of a package in which insurance is not the main element, have tended to have links with particular insurers, but have been in principle independent. Since the Financial Services Act 1986 (FSA) these incidental agents must be independent intermediaries or be linked only to one insurer or marketing group in respect of investment insurance, which includes most types of life insurance. The professional bodies for solicitors and for accountants have decided that, if any of their members wish to be intermediaries, they must be independent intermediaries, both for life and for non-life business. If these persons do not wish to be intermediaries, their role may be reduced to that of introducers who pass clients to independent intermediaries without themselves giving investment advice. If, however, a person introduces investment customers to an insurer regularly and for remuneration, he would be regarded as himself carrying on investment business and would need to be a company representative.

---

4. Under the Financial Services Act 1986, investment insurance is defined as all life insurance and pension products (other than purely protection policies such as creditor insurance, short-term temporary insurance or non-profit PHI), personal pensions (except deposit-based schemes) and unit trusts. However, if a life insurance company is a member of the Life Assurance and Unit Trust Regulatory Organisation (LAUTRO), its company representatives must comply with LAUTRO rules as regards term assurance and non-profit PHI, even though these are not investment business as defined in the Act.

5. The Code applied to both new and existing intermediaries from 1 July 1989.

5a. 92/48/EEC, OJ No L 19/32, 28 January 1992.

6. Gaselee, PM 3 April 1986, p 19.

7-1D Dual Agency

Classification of agents is not exclusive. A person may act for both insurer and insured. For example, if a broker, *prima facie* the agent of the insured, tells the insured that he is covered, that may be just a matter of report by an agent to his principal. However, brokers may also have an (implied actual) agency to contract interim insurance for the insurer. Lord Diplock said in *Stockton* v *Mason*[7]:

"There must be every day thousands of cases, not only in motor insurance but in other forms of non-marine insurance, where persons wishing to become insured or wishing to transfer an insurance ring up their brokers and ask for cover or ask for fresh cover or ask to transfer the cover from an existing vehicle to another. In every case they rely upon the broker's statement that they are covered as constituting a contract binding upon the insurance company. In that sort of conversation they are speaking, in the absence of special circumstances, to the broker as agent for the insurance company, and the broker, in dealing with the matter, is acting as agent for the insurance company."

A similar willingness to interpret the situation in a way that protects the insured and, more particularly, third parties with claims against the insured is found in the United States,[8] where dual agencies are also found and are generally allowed, if there is no conflict of interest or inconsistency of duty.[9] To decide whether an agent is acting for insurer or insured at any given time, courts in Illinois, for example, look at "(1) who set him in motion first, (2) who could control his actions, (3) who paid him, and (4) whose interest he was to protect".[9a]

7-1E Sub-Agents

If the insured's agent has authority to appoint another agent to carry out part of the mandate and does so, the appointment may create a contract of agency between the appointee and the insured. Alternatively, the appointee may be a sub-agent contracting only with the agent and undertaking to execute part of the agent's mandate with the insured. In general, an agent is not allowed to appoint another to carry out his

7. [1978] 2 Lloyd's Rep 430, 432 (CA—motor): the insured exchanged his car and instructed his broker to transfer existing insurance from the old to the new; the broker said "Yes, that will be alright". The insured assumed that the terms would be the same, but unknown to him the new cover did not extend to authorised drivers, such as the insured's son, who drove the car negligently and injured the plaintiff. The judge's decision that the insurer was not liable was reversed by the Court of Appeal because a "broker in non-marine insurance has implied authority to issue . . . to enter into as agent for the insurer contracts of interim insurance" (p 431 *per* Lord Diplock). See also below, 12–2. As regards duties under dual agencies see below, 9–4B.

8. For example *GAFLAC* v *Browne*, 217 F 2d 418 (7 Cir, 1954—motor); *Western Casualty & Surety Co* v *Lund*, 234 F 2d 916 (10 Cir, 1956—motor); *US Fire Ins Co* v *Cannon*, 349 F 2d 941 (8 Cir, 1965—motor); *Martinex* v *Great American Ins Co*, 286 F Supp 141 (WD Tex, 1968—motor); *Travelers Indemnity Co* v *US*, 393 F Supp 79 (Or, 1974). Appleman, sections 8721, 8735.

9. *Conlon Coal Co* v *Westchester Fire Ins Co* 16 F Supp 93 (MD Pa, 1936—fire), affirmed 92 F 2d 162 (3 Cir, 1937); cert den 302 US 751; *Passarello* v *Lexington Ins Co*, 740 F Supp 933 (D Conn, 1990—fire).

Cf the more relaxed view in Oklahoma, where dual agencies are permitted unless the agent received an improper profit, or the agent had an improper motive, or the insured knew or should have known that the insurer was being deceived: *Bailey* v *Gulf Ins Co*, 389 F 2d 889 (10 Cir, 1968—fire). See also *Owens* v *Aetna Life & Casualty Co*, 654 F 2d 218 (3 Cir, 1981—professional liability), cert den 454 US 1092: the agent was held to be agent of the insured even though he also solicited insurance for a company.

9a. *Hardin, Rodriquez & Boivin Anesthesiologists, Ltd* v *Paradigm Ins Co*, 962 F 2d 628, 635 (7 Cir, 1992—liability). In that case the factors were evenly balanced, as the insured sought cover through the agent and relied on the agent to protect its interest, but the insurer paid the agent and instructed the agent to prepare binders for the insured.

mandate,[10] unless the appointment is limited to ministerial acts not involving discretion, or the principal knows that delegation is intended, or the nature of the mandate (for example insurance in a foreign market) necessitates delegation, or delegation is customary in the context. For one or more of these reasons the insured's agent usually has authority to delegate. Whether he has actually done so is a question of fact in the light of general principles of agency.[11]

7–2 ACTUAL AUTHORITY

The agent may have actual authority to contract for the insured: this depends on evidence of the relationship between insured and agent,[11a] of which the insurer may be unaware. If there is no actual authority, there may yet be apparent authority (below, 7–3), with the result that the insured is bound. In the case of apparent authority, the appearance is decisive.

Actual authority may be express or implied. If the insured instructs his agent to make a particular proposal, the agent has express authority to make that contract. Actual authority is implied if, for example, the insured instructs the agent to make a certain kind of contract and it can be implied from that instruction, which does not mention it expressly, that the agent is authorised to contract a particular contract. Alternatively, one can say that the express instruction "extends to all subordinate acts which are necessarily or ordinarily incidental to the exercise of his express authority".[12] Actual authority is implied too, when the agent is given a general role: the agent has implied actual authority to do all things normally done by a person with that role.

In particular, an agent instructed to arrange cover is implicitly authorised to agree the precise form and content of the policy to be issued.[13] He is also authorised to disclose or describe matters material to the risk,[14] and to give all information necessary for effecting the cover.[15] If the instructions require the agent to contract in a particular market, the agent is implicitly authorised to act in accordance with the customs of that market.[16] If "an agent is employed to effect a policy of insurance, and he does effect it, and there is a loss, and the insured sends him the policy, then the agent is the agent of the insured to collect the amount of the loss".[17] An agent instructed to cancel a policy has authority to fix the date of cancellation.[18] If any instructions from his princi-

---

10. See Bowstead, ch 4. Rest 2d Agency section 5.

11. For example *The Okeanis* [1986] 1 Lloyd's Rep 195 (hull).

11a. *The Choko Star* [1990] 1 Lloyd's Rep 516 (CA).

12. Halsbury, Vol 1, No 736; Bowstead, pp 108 ff. *Spann* v *Commercial Standard Ins Co*, 82 F 2d 593 (8 Cir, 1936—motor); Rest Agency 2d, section 35.

13. So, for example, an agent instructed to arrange travel cover to France is implicitly authorised to specify a particular route or journey in or to France: *Zurich General Accident & Liability Ins Co Ltd* v *Rowberry* [1954] 2 Lloyd's Rep 55 (CA).

14. *Bancroft* v *Heath* (1901) 6 Com Cas 137 (CA—fire). *Hayat Carpet Cleaning Co* v *Northern Assurance Co Ltd*, 69 F 2d 805 (2 Cir, 1934—burglary); *Amalgamated Mutual Casualty Co* v *Schultz*, 207 NYS 2d 890 (1960—motor).

15. *Allen* v *Universal Automobile Ins Co Ltd* (1933) 45 Ll L R 55, 58 *per* Lord Wright sitting as an additional High Court judge (motor).

16. *Graves* v *Legg* (1857) 2 H & N 210. *Aliter* of course if the instruction is clearly inconsistent with the market custom.

17. *Legge* v *Byas* (1901) 7 Com Cas 16, 19 *per* Walton J (livestock).

18. *Nobile* v *Travelers Indemnity Co*, 176 NYS 2d 585 (1958—motor).

pal are ambiguous and the agent interprets them in good faith, albeit in a sense not intended by his principal, the latter is bound.[19]

In the United States, when a broker is engaged to obtain insurance and he does so, he exhausts his authority and his mandate does not give him authority, for example, to alter or cancel the insurance, unless the insured entrusts his insurance affairs to the broker in a general way: if the mandate is to maintain certain cover as seems best, the authority extends to alteration and cancellation.[20] In particular, it has been held that, if the agent is allowed to keep possession of the policy, that implies authority to cancel it.[21]

7–2A Knowledge and Notice

The knowledge of the agent is the knowledge of his principal, the insured, as regards matters within the scope of the mandate.[22] So, notice to the agent is notice to the insured as regards all matters in respect of which the agent is acting for the insured at the time of notice.[23]

7-3 APPARENT AUTHORITY

If an agent, who lacks actual authority to contract, is held out as having that authority, and it is reasonable for the insurer to rely on that representation and he does rely on it, the insured is bound by the act of the agent. Apparent authority of this kind, sometimes called ostensible authority, can be distinguished from implied actual authority (above 7–2): in a particular case they may be coextensive, but this is not necessarily so.[24] If the agent is given a particular role, he has both apparent and implied actual authority to do all things normally associated with that role, unless the authority bestowed departs from the norm: in that case his apparent authority is the same as before but his actual authority differs. The basis of apparent authority is said to be estoppel.[25]

---

19. *Weigall* v *Runciman* (1916) 85 LJKB 1187. *Quaere* whether the agent should seek clarification from his principal. See below, 9–5A.

20. *Smith* v *Firemen's Ins Co*, 104 F 2d 546 (7 Cir, 1939—fire); *Holbrook Institutional Ins Co*, 369 F 2d 236 (7 Cir, 1966—motor). It may include authority to receive a notice of cancellation from the insurer: *Schwabach & Co* v *Gulf Shipside Storage Corp*, 173 F Supp 105 (ED La, 1959—goods), but only if this is a necessary step in obtaining further insurance: *Tarleton* v *De Veuve*, 113 F 2d 290, 299 (9 Cir, 1940—fire), cert den 312 US 691; *Bituminous Casualty Corp* v *Aetna Ins Co*, 414 F 2d 730 (8 Cir, 1972—fire). *Cf. Wisconsin Barge Line Inc* v *Coastal Marine Transport Co*, 285 F Supp 264 (ED La, 1968—hull), affirmed 414 F 2d 872 (5 Cir, 1969).

21. The court in *Holbrook* (above) was prepared to assume this, noting, however, the contrary view in *Spann* v *Commercial Standard Ins Co*, 82 F 2d 593 (8 Cir, 1936—motor).

22. *Blackburn* v *Haslam* (1888) 21 QBD 144 (marine); *Blackburn, Low* v *Vigors* (1887) 12 App Cas 531 (marine). *Gelb* v *Automobile*, 168 F 2d 774 (2 Cir, 1948—hull); *Merchants Fire* v *Lattimore*, 263 F 2d 232 (9 Cir, 1959—personal property floater); *Jet Setting* v *Toomey*, 459 NYS 2d 751 (1983—jewellers AR). As regards the duty of disclosure see below, 23–8B.

23. *All States Trailer Co* v *American Ins Co*, 234 F 2d 783 (7 Cir, 1956—fire).

24. *The Choko Star* [1990] 1 Lloyd's Rep 516, 524 per Parker LJ, 525 per Slade LJ (CA). Generally see the references given below, 8–3.

25. *Cf* USA, where estoppel and apparent authority are distinguished: Rest Agency 2d, section 8c.

7–3A Representation

It must be held out as a fact that the agent has authority, and it must be done by a person having actual authority in the matter,[26] i.e., by the insured or his authorised representative. Holding out may be by words or by conduct: "If you find conduct—standing by—of the principal, even though it is not communicated to the other party—and this conduct leads the other party to believe that the agent has authority, that is enough to bind the principal."[27]

7–3B Reliance

The representation that the agent has authority must be relied upon by the insurer. There can be no reliance by one who has notice that the agent lacks authority; notice may be actual[28] or constructive. Constructive notice may arise in the following alternative ways:

(a) If from previous dealings the insurer has had notice (actual or constructive) of a limit on the authority of the insured's agent, that may be enough to affect him with constructive notice in current dealings.[29] The insurer is affected, if the previous dealings should have suggested to him that the limit was usual and if the current dealing is sufficiently similar to those previous dealings to suggest that the same limit operates.

(b) The insurer may have enough notice from the circumstances of the case to be put on inquiry so that, if he does not make that inquiry, he is not permitted to assert his own reliance.

(c) If the insured is a company, the insurer may be deemed to have notice from the public documents of the company of limits on the authority of the agent. This kind of notice has been largely abolished by statute and will not occur often.[30]

7–3C Misfeasance

These rules on apparent authority apply even though the agent or employee is acting in breach of instructions[31] or is fraudulent.[32]

7–4 RATIFICATION

A contract not within the actual or apparent authority of the agent may nonetheless bind the principal, the insured, if later ratified by him.[33]

---

26. *A-G for Ceylon* v *Silva* [1953] AC 461 (PC); *British Bank* v *Sun Life* [1983] 2 Lloyd's Rep 9 (HL); *Armagas Ltd* v *Mundogas SA* [1986] AC 717, 778 *per* Lord Keith.

27. *Eagle Star* v *Spratt* [1971] 2 Lloyd's Rep 116, 128 *per* Lord Denning MR (CA—re). As to whether a company officer may be held out, not to make decisions (e.g., to insure,) but to communicate the fact that others have made the decision, see below, 8–3A1.

28. Thus the insurer who has received a request from the insured to continue cover cannot rely on apparent authority of the agent to cancel it: *Holbrook* v *Institutional*, 369 F 2d 236, 240 (7 Cir, 1966—motor). See also *Smith* v *Firemen's*, 104 F 2d 546 (7 Cir, 1939—fire).

29. By analogy with cases concerning notice of contractual terms: *Kendall & Sons* v *Lillico & Sons Ltd* [1969] 2 AC 31. Clarke [1976] CLJ 51, 59 ff.

30. The possibility is discussed in relation to insurance companies: below, 8–3B3.

31. *Re Economic Fire* (1896) 12 TLR 142 (fidelity).

32. See below, 8–3D.

33. Halsbury, Vol 1, Nos 756 ff; Bowstead, pp 51 ff; Appleman, sections 8761 ff.

7–4A The Appearance

In his dealings with the insurer the agent must have purported[34] to act on behalf of the insured,[35] although it is not essential that the particular insured be identified at the time.[36] When the agent is acting for an unnamed principal, it is controversial whether it must be possible to discover the identity of the principal. As regards marine insurance Arnould[37] contends that

"it is sufficient to show that the person effecting the policy was intending to insure on behalf of persons having an insurable interest of the same nature as that of the person who later seeks to ratify, or acquiring such an interest at some time during the risk. Any other view would give rise to considerable practical difficulties."

It should be enough that the principal falls within a clearly defined class, for which the agent purported to act, and that the agent is able to disclose to the insurer any facts material to the risk. It is enough that the principal can be identified generically though not individually. Whether such a rule extends to non-marine insurance is not entirely clear. Perhaps it does, with the qualification that the insured must have had an insurable interest in the subject-matter of the insurance at the time of the agent's concluding the contract.[38]

7–4B The Capacity of the Insured

The insured must have had the capacity to make the contract at the time of the contract.[39] In particular a corporate insured must have had legal existence at the time.[40] The Companies Act 1985, as amended by section 130 of the Companies Act 1989, provides in section 36C:

"(1) A contract which purports to be made by or on behalf of a company at a time when the company has not been formed has effect, subject to any agreement to the contrary, as one made with the person purporting to act for the company or as agent for it, and he is personally liable on the contract accordingly."[41]

---

34. The purport is the agent's intent, as it appeared to the insurer; a principal may ratify a contract, although the agent secretly and fraudulently intended to take the benefit of the contract himself: *Re Tiedemann and Ledermann Frères* [1899] 2 QB 66.

35. *Keighley, Maxsted & Co* v *Durant* [1901] AC 240; *The Moonacre* [1992] 2 Lloyd's Rep. 501, 515 per Deputy Judge Colman, QC, (yacht): while it is possible for the act to be ratified by an unnamed principal, it cannot be ratified by an undisclosed principal. Further, any attempted contract of insurance providing cover for an undisclosed principal would be vitiated by non-disclosure of a material fact, the identity of the principal.

36. *Routh* v *Thompson* (1811) 13 East 274, 285 per Lord Ellenborough CJ (hull).

37. No 243. See for example *Boston Fruit Co* v *British & Foreign Marine Ins Co* [1906] AC 336 (hull); and *National Oilwell (UK) Ltd* v *Davy Offshore Ltd* [1993] 2 Lloyd's Rep 582, 596–597 per Colman J (builders' AR). Rest Agency 2d, section 87.

38. Bowstead, pp 61–63. *Lyell* v *Kennedy* (1889) 14 App Cas 437. Contrary *dicta* are said to include words of Willes J in *Watson* v *Swann* (1862) 11 CB (NS) 756, 771 (cargo), but his words were general and seen in the context of the case, notably that the "agent" did not purport to contract for anyone else, it is not clear that the judge had the present problem in mind.

39. Acts *ultra vires* a company cannot be ratified: *Ashbury Railway Carriage & Iron Co* v *Riche* (1875) LR 7 HL 653. Halsbury, Vol 7, No 706. Nor acts which are illegal: *La Banque Jacques-Cartier* v *La Banque d'Epargne Montréal* (1887) 13 App Cas 111 (PC).

40. *Kelner* v *Baxter* (1866) LR 2 CP 174.

41. *See Phonogram Ltd* v *Lane* [1982] QB 938 (CA). Halsbury, Vol 7, No 724; and Palmer's Company Law (London, 1993) no 3.003.

7–4C Form and Intent

Ratification by the insured may be express or implied, which includes acquiescence.[42] Ratification "must be either with full knowledge of the act to be adopted, or with intention to adopt it at all events and under whatever circumstances."[43]

If the insured is a company, ratification must be by the appropriate organ of the company. If the contract has been made in excess of authority by the board, ratification must be by the shareholders.[44] If by an executive director, ratification must be by the board; if by an agent, who is not a director, ratification must be by the board or by an executive director with actual authority in the matter.

7–4D The Time of Ratification

The insured must ratify the act before the time due for the performance of the duty to which the contract commits him, notably, the payment of premium, unless of course the agent has paid on his behalf. In any event he must ratify within a reasonable time.[45] The insured must also ratify while there is an act to ratify, i.e., before the agreement has been rescinded by the agent and the insurer.[46] Once the insured has indicated to the insurer that he will not ratify the act, he cannot change his mind.[47]

7–4D1 Ratification After Loss

Ratification must occur before it has become unlawful. In particular, it is said to be impossible in law to ratify after loss, except in marine insurance,[48] if the insured at the time of ratification has knowledge of the loss: *Grover* v *Mathews*.[49] In that case Hamilton J acknowledged that ratification was possible in marine insurance but this, he said

---

42. It is enough that (a) the insured was "told of the insurance, and expressed no objection to it" *per* Lord Mansfield in *French* v *Backhouse* (1771) 5 Burr 2727, 2729 (hull); *Hoover* v *Millers National Ins Co*, 135 P 2d 846 (Wa, 1943); or (b) the insured raised no objection to his being debited with premium: *Robinson* v *Gleadow* (1835) 2 Bing (NC) 156 (hull); Arnould, No 243; *Hatfield* v *Minden Bank & Trust Co*, 361 So 2d 901 (La, 1978—fire); or (c) the insured accepted or enforced benefits under the policy: *Yeargin* v *Farmers Mutual Ins Assn*, 234 SE 2d 856 (Ga, 1977—fire).

43. *Phosphate of Lime Co* v *Green* (1871) LR 7 CP 43, 57 *per* Willes J. See also *Fitzmaurice* v *Bayley* (1856) 6 El & Bl 868.

44. For ratification by shareholders it is necessary that "distinct, plain and clear notice" of the contract in excess of authority "in the shape of a report or the like, was brought home to them"—*Re Athenaeum Life Assurance Co* (1858) 27 LJ Ch 829, 834 *per* Page-Wood VC (life). See also *Phosphate of Lime Co Ltd* v *Green* (1871) LR 7 CP 43, 63 *per* Brett J.

45. *Re Portuguese Consolidated Copper Mines Ltd* (1890) 45 Ch D 16 (CA).

46. *Walter* v *James* (1871) LR 6 Ex 124. However, unilateral repudiation by the insurer, which is not accepted, does not prevent ratification by the insured, for ratification is said to be retroactive and an unaccepted repudiation is ineffective: *Bolton Partners* v *Lambert* (1888) 41 Ch D 295 (CA), criticised in *Fleming* v *Bank of New Zealand* [1900] AC 577, 587 *per* Lord Lindley (PC). See discussion of this principle in Bowstead, pp 74–75.

47. *McEvoy* v *Belfast Banking Co Ltd* [1935] AC 24.

48. MIA, s 86 enacting the effect of earlier cases: *Routh* v *Thompson* (1811) 13 East 274 (hull); *Hagedorn* v *Oliverson* (1814) 2 M &S 485; there was no objection in these cases that the principal knew of loss at the time of ratification. The objection was raised, however, in *Williams* v *North China Ins Co* (1876) 1 CPD 757 (CA—freight), in which it was said by Cockburn CJ (p 764) that the earlier cases were "much too strong and of too long standing to be got over". *Idem* Lord Jessell MR (p 766). Arnould, No 244.

49. [1910] 2 KB 401 (fire): the claimants' piano factory was insured at Lloyd's and shortly before expiry their agent arranged a renewal with the same insurer. Two days after expiry the factory was destroyed by fire. The claimants ratified the renewal, but this was held ineffective.

in a short judgment,[50] "was an anomalous rule which it was not, for business reasons, desirable to extend". The arguments on the issue include these:

(a) Cases in England,[51] it is argued, are against extension. It has been said[52] that a *dictum* of Lord Campbell[53] favours extension, but it is submitted that it is not clear.[54] It has been suggested[55] that in *Mackie v European Assurance Co*[56] "an insured ratified a policy, after loss, with a different insurer from the insurer with whom it was apparently originally concluded". However, the issue was not clearly put to the court. In a key passage[57], there is a suggestion that the insured instructed the agent to obtain fire insurance, regardless of the insurer: if so, the agent fulfilled his original mandate and there was no question of ratification of something different. If, on the contrary, the agent had exceeded his mandate by dealing with insurer B rather than insurer A, then it is possible to support the decision, but either as a case of apparent authority[58] or as a case of ratification of the interim insurance before loss. In Canada[59] and the United States,[60] however, it is clear that ratification of non-marine insurance after loss has been allowed.

(b) It has been argued that it is in the nature of insurance that the loss should be a possibility but not a certainty: "a person could not insure with knowledge of the loss; consequently he cannot ratify."[61] The contrary argument is that, if the effect of ratification is retroactive[62] to the time of the agent's act concluding the contract, it is at that time that the elements of disclosure and certainty are to be tested; and it is at that time that public policy is to be satisfied: subsequent knowledge of the insured is irrelevant.

(c) The marine rule, it is said, unduly favours the insured: if the risk has been run without loss, he may decline to ratify and to pay premium; if loss occurs

---

50. [1910] 2 KB 401, 404; the "business reasons" were not specified. See also Pollock B in *Williams v North China Ins Co* (1876) 1 CPD 757 (CA—freight), the leading case for the marine rule, which he referred to (p 770) as "an exception to the general rule founded on principle".Support, however, for the extension of the marine rule to non-marine insurance is found in Bowstead, Nos 78–79.

51. *Grover & Grover Ltd v Mathews* [1910] 2 KB 401 (fire): by Branson J in *Portavon Cinema Co v Price & Century Ins Co* [1939] 4 All ER 601, 607 (fire). *Grover* was "accepted" *obiter* by Roche J in *Graham v Western Australian Ins Co Ltd* (1931) 40 Ll L Rep 64, 67 (re).

52. MacGillivray, No 370; and see *Goulding* (below).

53. *Waters v Monarch Fire & Life Ins Co* (1856) 5 El & Bl 871, 878 (fire).

54. The *dictum* was unnecessary to the decision. It has been plausibly argued that Lord Campbell's reference to ratification refers not to a contract of insurance but to a trust: see *Goulding v Norwich Union Fire Ins Sy* [1948] 1 DLR 526, 533 *per* Gordon JA (fire); but *cf* Anderson JA (*ibid*, pp 535–536).

55. MacGillivray (7th ed), No 360, n 41.

56. (1869) 21 LT 102.

57. p 105, col 2; see also p 104, col 1: the agent having "effected for them no less than 160 policies; being a man with whom they were perfectly satisfied and as to whose discretion they had no reason to complain—they leave it to him to accept or reject what he thinks fit".

58. By clothing the agent with detailed information about, for example, the layout of the subject-matter insured.

59. *Goulding v Norwich Union Fire Ins Sy* [1948] 1 DLR 526 (Sask—fire); *Spencer v Continental Ins Co* [1945] 4 DLR 593 (BC—fire).

60. *Marqusee v Hartford Fire Ins Co*, 198 F 475 (2 Cir, 1912—fire); applied in *Automobile Ins Co v Barnes-Manley Wet Wash Laundry*, 168 F 2d 381 (10 Cir, 1948). Appleman, section 8764. This view was preferred by Colman J, although unnecessary to his decision, in *National Oilwell (UK) Ltd v Davy Offshore Ltd* [1993] 2 Lloyd's Rep 582, 608 (builders' AR).

61. Unsuccessful argument of counsel in *Williams v North China Ins Co* (1876) 1 CPD 757, 762–763 (CA—freight).

62. There is some doubt about this premise; see below, 7–4E.

he may ratify and recover.[63] In reply, it is said[64] that the insurer is aware of the position when dealing with the agent and therefore cannot complain.

(d) The *Grover* rule, unlike the marine rule, accords with "the general principle that one who ratifies a contract must have power to make such a contract himself at the time of ratification".[65]

7–4E The Effect of Ratification

The effect of ratification is to put the insured in the position he would have been in, if the agent's acts had been authorised from the beginning. Ratification is said to be retroactive,[66] unless the agent contracted "subject to ratification". In the latter case, but not the former, intervening repudiation by the insurer is effective to forestall ratification and prevent the formation of a binding contract of insurance.[67]

7–5 AGENCY OF NECESSITY[68]

7–5A The Agency

Without any authority, actual or apparent, the agent may contract insurance for the insured, because the agent believes insurance to be necessary in the interests of the insured. This might arise in the case of a bailee of goods who, being unable to contact the owner, insures the goods against fire. If, however, the bailee is a voluntary bailee, his role may carry with it an implied mandate to insure the goods; in that case, he does so not as an agent of necessity but as one with implied actual or apparent authority. For a true agency of necessity there are three requirements:

(a) It must have been impossible or impracticable to communicate with the insured.[69]

(b) Insurance must have been necessary for the insured, that is, a commercial necessity,[70] "a reasonable business course to take".[71]

(c) The agent must have acted *bona fide*[72] in the interests of the insured.

---

63. Lord Ellenbrough CJ was conscious of this possibility when affirming the marine rule in *Hagedorn* v *Oliverson* (1814) 2 M & S 485, 490 (hull); so too was Le Blanc J (p 491).

64. *Marqusee* v *Hartford Fire Ins Co*, 198 F 475, 477 (2 Cir, 1912—fire); however, the court was influenced by the possibility, not found in England (above, 7–4D), that the insurer could withdraw prior to ratification by the insured.

65. *Williams* v *North China Ins Co* (1876) 1 CPD 757, 766 *per* Lord Jessell MR (CA—freight). Without further citation, the principle is accepted in Bowstead, pp 73 and 78. However, the alleged principle stands or falls with the *Grover* rule, to which it is closely linked.

66. *Bolton Partners* v *Lambert* (1888) 41 Ch D 295 (CA), criticised in *Fleming* v *Bank of New Zealand* [1900] AC 577, 587 *per* Lord Lindley (PC). See discussion of this principle in Bowstead, pp 74–75.
   In the USA *Bolton* was not followed in *Marqusee* v *Hartford Fire Ins Co*, 198 F 475 (2 Cir, 1912—fire).

67. *Warehousing & Forwarding Co Ltd* v *Jafferali & Sons Ltd* [1964] AC 1 (PC).

68. Generally see Bowstead pp 84 ff; Halsbury, Vol 1, No 724.

69. *Springer* v *GWR Co* [1921] 1 KB 257 (CA); *The Choko Star* [1990] 1 Lloyd's Rep 516 (CA).

70. *Prager* v *Blatspiel Stamp & Heacock Ltd* [1924] 1 KB 566, 572 *per* McCardie J.

71. *Springer* v *GWR Ry* [1921] 1 KB 257, 267 *per* Scrutton LJ (CA). *Cf* Cotton LJ in *Atlantic Mutual Ins Co* v *Huth* (1880) 16 Ch D 474, 481: "it is not sufficient that the [agent] thought he was doing the best for all concerned."

72. *Tronson* v *Dent* (1853) 8 Moore 419, 452 *per* Sir John Patteson (PC). The duty to act *bona fide* is applied to all agents: below, 9–4.

7–5B The Commercial Trustee

Distinguish from the agent of necessity the "agent", often a bailee for reward with an insurable interest in property, who contracts insurance on that property in his own name for the benefit of a third party (the insured).[73] He contracts the insurance personally and to the extent that loss payable under the policy exceeds his own loss he holds the balance on trust for those whose loss it is.

When a person takes a policy, and is named in that policy, it is a matter of intention, notably but not exclusively[74] by reference to the terms of the policy, whether he is insured, perhaps co-insured, or whether he is acting as agent for another person, the true insured under the policy.[75]

---

73. See above, 5–6.
74. *Boston Fruit Co* v *British Foreign & Marine Ins Co* [1906] AC 336, 338 *per* Lord Loreburn; *Samuel & Co Ltd* v *Dumas* [1924] AC 294 (hull); *Graham Joint Stock Shipping Co* v *Merchants Marine Ins Co* [1924] AC 294 (hull).
75. *Tomlinson (Hauliers)* v *Hepburn* [1966] AC 451 (cargo); *The Yasin* [1979] 2 Lloyd's Rep 45, 53–54 *per* Lloyd J (cargo).

CHAPTER 8

AGENTS: AUTHORITY TO BIND THE INSURER[1]

8-1 INTRODUCTION

The general law of agency applies to the agents of insurers.[2] The onus of proving that a person acted as agent of an insurer is on the person alleging it.[3] In the world of insurance, where there may be many links in a chain between the one who suffers loss and the one who is asked to pay, this may be a matter of complexity. The insurer is bound by the acts of an agent, if the act is within the actual authority (below, 8–2) or apparent authority (below, 8–3) of the agent, or if the act is subsequently ratified by the insurer (below, 8–4).

8-2 ACTUAL AUTHORITY

The insurer is bound by the acts of his agent within the scope of his actual authority as agent. Actual authority may be express or implied. If the insurer appoints an agent to negotiate and contract with a particular person on particular terms, the agent has express authority to that effect.[4] If the insurer appoints an agent to a particular position in the insurance company, the appointee has implied actual authority to make such contracts as are usually made by a person in that position.[5] Alternatively, one can say that an appointment to that position amounts to express authority to do "all subordinate acts which are necessarily or ordinarily incidental to the exercise of his express authority".[6]

Whether express or implied, if the mandate requires the agent to act in a particular market, the agent is implicitly authorised to act in accordance with the customs of the market.[7] Whether express or implied, the agent's authority depends on evidence of the relationship between the insurer and the agent[8] and, in the case of an appointment reference to the terms of appointment or to evidence of what is usual in an appoint-

---

1. R. Hodgin, *Insurance Intermediaries: Law & Regulation* (London, 1993).
2. *Globe Mutual Life Ins Co v Wolff*, 95 US 326 (1877—life); *Jones v Bankers Life Co*, 31 F 2d 989 (4 Cir, 1942—life). Appleman, No 8672. Hodgin, p 3. But *cf* Hasson (1991) 18 Can Bus LJ 473, 475.
3. *Globe & Rutgers Fire Ins Co v McGinnis*, 29 F 2d 357 (9 Cir, 1928—fire).
4. If the instructions are ambiguous and the agent acts on them in good faith in a sense not intended by the insurer, the insurer is bound by the agent's acts: *Weigall v Runciman* (1916) 85 LJKB 1187.
5. *Hely-Hutchinson v Brayhead Ltd* [1968] 1 QB 549, 583 *per* Lord Denning MR (CA).
6. Halsbury, Vol 1, No 736. Bowstead, pp 108 ff. Appleman, Nos 8671 ff, 8861 ff.
7. *Graves v Legg* (1857) 2 H & N 210.
8. *The Choko Star* [1990] 1 Lloyd's Rep. 516 (CA).

ment of that kind.[9] Evidence of what is usual will now be found in the codes of practice affecting intermediaries.[10]

8–2A Usual Authority

The usual authority of agents appointed to a position turns on current practice,[11] some of which has been considered by the courts. What follows must be read with appropriate caution,[12] as reported decisions are never entirely abreast of practice. In the past, the authority of the agent has increased with his distance from the head office of the insurer and with the need for speed in the business concerned.[13] Modern methods of communication make these factors less significant. Regulation of those offering insurance has resulted in a polarisation of agents between those who represent insurers and those who do not.[14]

8–2A1 Local Agents of the Insurer

(a) *Proposals.* A local agent, it has been said,[15] has authority to "negotiate the terms of a proposal for an insurance and to induce the person who wished to insure to make the proposal. He was the agent of the company to obtain a proposal which the company would accept." That means "to receive the proposal and put it into shape"[16]: to settle the terms of the proposal, but not to settle or conclude (with the proposer on behalf of the insurer) the terms of the contract of insurance itself.[17] He does, however, have authority to *explain* the terms of the insurer's policy: below, 8–3C. Disclosure of information by the proposer to the agent should, one might think, amount to disclosure to the insurer, but this is a difficult issue and it is discussed separately (below, chapter 10). Local agency carries with it authority to receive notice of loss.[18]

(b) *Contracting.* The local agent does not usually have authority to make the full

9. *Hambro* v *Burnand* [1904] 2 KB 10, 19 *per* Sir Richard Henn Collins MR (CA—guarantee policy at Lloyd's). *Bigalke* v *Mutual Life Ins Co of New York*, 34 SW 2d 1019 (Mo, 1931—life); *Downs* v *Del Regno*, 325 NYS 2d 320 (1971—employers' liability). Appleman, No 8673.
10. See, for example, Hodgin, ch 2. The codes lack the force of law and their enforcement with respect to company representatives, for example, is left to the insurance company concerned.
11. *Cf* the suggestion of King J in Canada in *Manufacturers Accident Ins Co* v *Pudsey* (1897) 27 SCR 374, 379 (PA) that it depends on what "a prudent and ordinarily sagacious and experienced person (with no reason to think otherwise) might expect [the agent] to do or to be authorized to make in respect of the particular business." For practice in the United States see 44 CJS ss 150 ff. For an English view of the position of agents in New York see *Excess Life Assurance Co Ltd* v *Firemen's Ins Co of Newark* [1982] 2 Lloyd's Rep 599, 612 ff *per* Webster J (fidelity).
12. *Brook* v *Trafalgar Ins Co Ltd* (1946) 79 Ll L Rep 365, 368 *per* Tucker LJ (CA—motor).
13. For example *Rossiter* v *Trafalgar Life Assurance Assn* (1859) 27 Beav 377 (interim life assurance contracted in Australia for an English insurer). Arnould, Nos 232 ff. *O'Brien* v *Union Ins Co*, 2 F 586, 588 (D Minn, 1884—life): general agent of foreign insurer held to have authority to waive term as to premium. Appleman, No 8672.
14. Gray, *New Foundations*, pp 19 ff. Hodgin, ch 2 and ch 3. See further above 7–1B.
15. *Bawden* v *London, Edinburgh & Glasgow Assurance Co* [1892] 2 QB 534, 539 *per* Lord Esher MR (CA—PA).
16. *Bawden* (above), p 540 *per* Lindley LJ.
17. *Levy* v *Scottish Employers' Ins Co* (1901) 17 TLR 229.
18. *Marsden* v *City & County Assurance Co* (1866) LR 1 CP 232 (plate-glass).

contract of insurance.[19] However, in modern practice he may well have authority to issue interim insurance[20]; so does the independent intermediary[21] who is normally agent for the insured. The employee of an agent has no authority to make interim insurance,[22] except of course in a purely ministerial capacity[23] under the authority of his employer, or as a sub-agent, if such an appointment is permitted.

If an agent has authority to contract interim insurance, that does not imply authority to alter the terms of interim insurance, whether as to the scope of cover,[24] the payment of premium,[25] or notice of claims.[26] However, courts have sometimes held the insurer to, for example, an alteration of terms on the basis that he is estopped from setting up the agent's lack of authority.[27] If the agent has authority to make a contract, he has also authority to receive notice from the insured terminating the contract.[28]

(c) *Waiver* . . . A branch office, being an agency more important than an individual, has been held[29] authorised to waive breaches of duty by the insured. But the more

19. *Linford* v *The Provincial Horse & Cattle Ins Co* (1864) 34 Beav 291 (cattle); *Zurich General Accident & Liability Ins Co Ltd* v *Buck* (1939) 64 Ll L Rep 115 (motor); *Stockton* v *Mason* [1978] 2 Lloyd's Rep 430, 431 *per* Lord Diplock (CA—motor).
In Canada in *World Marine & General Ins Co Ltd* v *Leger* [1952] 1 DLR 755 (fire) the Supreme Court held that the canvassing agent who collects premiums has no authority to contract. *Cf Manufacturers Accident Ins Co* v *Pudsey* (1897) 27 SCR 374, 379 *per* King J (PA) concerning renewal by an agent on unauthorised terms: "The possession of blank policies and renewal receipts signed by the president and other principal officers [of the insurance company] is some evidence of a general agency to complete the contract." See also *Kline* v *Dominion Ins Co* (1912) 9 DLR 231 (Sup. Ct.—fire) that "general" agents may contract insurance, but that their authority to make contracts is greater than their authority to alter the terms of the contract.
In the United States an agent with power to contract is described as a "general" agent: see Appleman, Nos 8691 ff; 44 CJS, ss 150 ff.
20. *Stockton* v *Mason* (above). See also below, ch 12
21. *Stockton* v *Mason* (above). The broker does not, any more than the tied agent, have authority to make the full contract: *Zurich General & Liability Ins Co Ltd* v *Buck* (1939) 64 Ll L Rep 115 (motor).
22. *Summers* v *Commercial Union Ins Co* (1881) 6 SCR 19 (fire); *Canadian Fire Ins Co* v *Robinson* (1901) 31 SCR 488 (fire).
23. *Rossiter* v *Trafalgar Life Assurance Assn* (1859) 27 Beav 377, 381 *per* Sir John Romilly MR (life).
24. *Wilkinson* v *GAFLAC* [1967] 2 Lloyd's Rep 182 (motor). *Cf Rocklebank* v *Sugrue* (1831) 5 Car & P 21 (hull) the agent was permitted to alter the voyage mentioned in policies; the insurer was bound.
In *Globe Mutual Life Ins Co* v *Wolff*, 95 US 326 (1877) a life insurance policy provided that it could be forfeited for late payment of premium, and that agents could not waive forfeiture. "The Company, by its course of dealing, had, notwithstanding the provision of the policy, left the matter to be determined by its local agent, to whom the renewal receipts were intrusted." The agent habitually gave renewal receipts whenever premiums were paid after time. The Supreme Court held that "the Company ought not, in common justice, to be permitted to allege such forfeiture against one who has acted upon the belief, and subsequently made the payment." The insurer was liable under the policy. See also *Automobile Underwriters Corp* v *Graves*, 489 F 2d 625 (8 Cir, 1973—motor).
25. *Acey* v *Fernie* (1840) 7 M & W 151, 155 *per* Parke B (life).
26. *Brook* v *Trafalgar Ins Co Ltd* (1946) 79 Ll L Rep 365 (CA—motor): the agent was not authorised to waive a term that notice of loss had to be given to head office. Such waiver was also excluded by the terms of the policy.
27. In *Holdsworth* v *Lancashire & Yorkshire Ins Co* (1907) 23 TLR 521 (employers' liability): the policy was altered at the behest of the insured and with the consent of the canvassing agent and the branch office, but not the head office. Applying *Wing* (below) Bray J held the insurance company bound by the alteration, however, on the basis that the company was estopped from denying the authority of the canvassing agent (not the local office), because they had received premiums with constructive knowledge via the agent that the policy had been changed.
28. *Re Solvency Mutual Guarantee Co* (1862) 6 LT 574, 575 *per* Wood V-C.
29. *Wing* v *Harvey* (1854) 5 De G M & G 265 (life). See also *Splents* v *Lefevre* (1864) 11 LT 114 (life).
In *Ayrey* v *British Legal & United Provident Assurance Co Ltd* [1918] 1 KB 136 (life) the court allowed waiver of non-disclosure by the insurer's superintendent, who was also district manager, but he did not have authority to vary the terms of the contract, *per* Lawrence J (p 140) and Atkin J (p 141). *Cf Comerford* v

195

important the policy term in question, the slower the courts to find that the agent has authority to waive it, especially if it amounts to waiver of forfeiture: the result of waiver is the revival of the insurance cover, something too close to the making of new contracts of insurance,[30] something which agents are not generally authorised to do.[31]

(d) *Premium*. The insurer's agent has authority, it is said,[32] to receive premium for the insurer and in practice the intermediary, agent of the insured, may also have authority to receive it for the insurer.

8–2A2 Head Office

Non-executive directors of companies, including insurance companies, acting alone have no usual authority as directors to contract for the company[33]: they can only act collectively as a board.[34] Executive directors acting individually have the authority usually associated with their post. However, the position of the chief executive or managing director gives its holder usual authority to make any contract within the powers of the company.[35]

8–2A3 Lloyd's

At Lloyd's, the active underwriter of a syndicate, like the managing agent from whom he derives his authority, has authority to contract all the ordinary business of an underwriter at Lloyd's,[36] subject to the terms of his appointment by the syndicate. If the appointment limits his authority, he still has apparent authority to contract all ordinary business: below, 8–3. In the case of "lineslips", which are arranged by a Lloyd's broker, and "consortia", a leading (active) underwriter has authority to contract for other (active) underwriters in respect of certain kinds of business, such as professional indemnity business. In addition, persons, such as coverholders under binding authorities, outside Lloyd's may have been given delegated authority to make contracts on behalf of Lloyd's underwriters; this has been increasingly practised in recent years.

According to Lloyd's byelaw No. 5 of 1989, a consortium means "a group of underwriters and, as the case may be, insurance companies who have agreed that in respect

---

Britannic Assurance Co Ltd (1908) 24 LT 593 (life) in which Bray J held that a branch superintendent did have authority to vary the amount of the insurance.

30. *Acey v Fernie* (1840) 7 M & W 151 (life). *Atlas Assurance Co v Brownell* (1899) 29 SCR 537 (fire).

31. *Linford v The Provincial Horse & Cattle Ins Co* (1864) 34 Beav 291 (cattle).

32. Cockerell & Shaw, pp 57–58. However, in the general law of agency an agent to sell goods does not usually have authority to receive the price: *Linck, Moeller & Co v Jameson & Co* (1885) 2 TLR 206 (CA); *Butwick v Grant* [1924] 2 KB 483.

33. *Rama Corp Ltd v Proved Tin & General Investments Ltd* [1952] 2 QB 147.

34. It is in this sense that Scrutton LJ observed that "the directors . . . were the only persons who could 'settle' the contracts" of insurance: *Newsholme Bros v Road Transport & General Ins Co* [1929] 2 KB 356, 370 (CA—motor).

35. *Re County Life Assurance Co* (1870) 5 Ch App 288 (life). In *Montreal Assurance Co v M'Gillivray* (1859) 13 Moore 87, the respondent sought to enforce a contract of fire insurance, in respect of which, the insurer's manager, who lacked authority to do so, had given the insured extra time in which to pay premium. The Privy Council decided against the respondent's claim, because she had constructive notice of limits on the power of the manager. However, such notice has now been abolished as regards registered companies (below, 8–3B3), and given the observation of Sir John Coleridge (p 123) that such a manager had "very large powers and a wide discretion", it seems that today his contract would have bound the insurer. See also *ibid*, p 124.

36. *Hambro v Burnand* [1904] 2 KB 10 (CA—guarantee). See the Lloyd's Binding Authorities Byelaw (No 9 of 1990); and *Arbuthnott v Fagan* (Commercial Court, 12 October 1993).

of a specific class of insurance business certain named or otherwise designated under-writers or insurance companies within that group may accept risks on behalf of all members of the group in accordance with the terms of the agreement between them". According to byelaw No. 7 of 1993, an active underwriter means, "in relation to a syndicate, the person at or deemed by the Council or Committee [of Lloyd's] to be at, the underwriting box with principal authority to accept risks on behalf of the members of the syndicate".

8–3 APPARENT AUTHORITY[37]

If an agent is held out as having authority to act for the insurer, and the insured places reasonable reliance on that holding out, the insurer is bound by the agent's act. Apparent authority of this kind, sometimes called ostensible authority, can be distinguished from implied actual authority (above 8–2): in a particular case they may be coextensive, but this is not necessarily so.[37] If the agent is given a particular role, he has both apparent and implied actual authority to do all things normally associated with that role, unless the authority bestowed departs from the norm: in that case his apparent authority is the same as before but his actual authority differs. The basis of apparent authority is said to be estoppel.[38]

8–3A Representation

It must be held out as a fact[39] that the agent has authority, and the holding out must be done by a person having actual authority in the matter,[40] i.e., by the insurer or his authorised representative. It cannot be done by the agent whose authority is in question.[41] Holding out may be by words or by conduct, even "passive" conduct: "If you find conduct—standing by—of the principal, even though it is not communicated to

---

37. *The Choko Star* [1990] 1 Lloyd's Rep 516, 524 per Parker LJ, 525 per Slade LJ (CA). Generally see *Mahony* v *East Holyford Mining Co Ltd* (1875) LR 7 HL 869; *Freeman & Lockyer* v *Buckhurst Park Properties Ltd* [1964] 2 QB 480 (CA); *Hely-Hutchinson* v *Brayhead Ltd* [1968] 1 QB 549 (CA); *The Ocean Frost, Armagas Ltd* v *Mundogas SA* [1986] AC 717, 777 per Lord Keith. Halsbury, Vol 1, No 819; Bowstead, pp 92 ff, 284 ff.

Early insurance cases include *Haughton* v *Ewbank* (1814) 4 Camp 88 (marine); *Mackie* v *European Assurance Sy* (1869) 21 LT 102, 105 per Malins V-C (fire), applying *Wing* v *Harvey* (1854) 5 De G M & G 265 (life).

In the United States see for example *Pacific Mutual Life Ins Co* v *Barton*, 50 F 2d 362 (5 Cir, 1931—life), cert den 284 US 647. Rest Agency 2d, sections 8 ff. Appleman, No 8674.

38. *Willis, Faber & Co Ltd* v *Joyce* (1911) 27 TLR 388 (marine) per Scrutton J; *Freeman & Lockyer* v *Buckhurst Park Properties Ltd* [1964] 2 QB 480, 503 per Diplock LJ (CA). The basis of apparent authority in estoppel is disputed, but this is the prevailing view in England: Bowstead, p 290.

In the United States apparent authority is partly based on estoppel: Rest Agency 2d, section 8, but estoppel is distinguished from the present rule.

39. If the representation involves the interpretation of a document, that may be a representation not of a fact but of law. See further below, 8–3C.

40. *A-G for Ceylon* v *Silva* [1953] AC 461 (PC); *British Bank of the Middle East* v *Sun Life Assurance Co of Canada (UK) Ltd* [1983] 2 Lloyd's Rep 9 (HL); *The Ocean Frost, Armagas Ltd* v *Mundogas SA* [1985] 1 Lloyd's Rep 1, 66–67 per Robert Goff LJ: [1986] AC 717, 778 per Lord Keith.

41. *The Ocean Frost* (above) p 390 per Lord Keith. *Annapolis Fire & Marine Ins Co* v *Rich*, 212 A 2d 249 (My, 1965); *National Surety Corp* v *Inland Properties Inc*, 286 F Supp 173, 180 (ED Ark, 1968—guarantee), affirmed 416 F 2d 457 (8 Cir, 1969).

the other party—and this conduct leads the other party to believe that the agent has authority, that is enough to bind the principal."[42]

If the agent is appointed to a defined role, say managing director, he has the usual authority associated with that role[43]: authority to do all things *intra vires* the company. This is actual authority, express or implied.[44] However, to the extent that the company (usually through the board) makes his authority more limited than usual, the agent nonetheless has apparent authority[45] to do what is usually associated with the role of managing director, unless and to the extent that the limit is known to the insured.[46]

So, if the Lloyd's Policy Signing Office issues a policy in the name of an underwriter, the latter may be bound even on matters reserved by that underwriter, for the issue of a commitment on those matters is within the apparent authority of the LPSO.[47] Again, if an agent is appointed by the insurer to renegotiate an insurance contract, the agent's renegotiation binds the insurer, in spite of any reservations about the terms communicated privately to the agent but not to the insured.[48] There is, how-

42. *Eagle Star Ins Co Ltd* v *Spratt* [1971] 2 Lloyd's Rep 116, 128 *per* Lord Denning MR (CA—re). *Employers Liability Assurance Corp Ltd* v *Glen Falls Ins Co*, 70 P 2d 682, 684 (Ariz, 1970—liability). For example the issue to an agent of (a) blank policies: *Pacific Mutual Life Ins Co* v *Barton*, 50 F 2d 362 (5 Cir, 1931—life), cert den 284 US 647; *First Trust & Deposit Co* v *Middlesex Mutual Fire Ins Co*, 8 NYS 2d 936 (1940—fire), affirmed 31 NE 2d 510 (1940); or (b) other documents bearing the name of the insurer: *Meyers* v *Lawyers Title Ins Co*, 33 NYS 2d 33 (1972—title insurance), affirmed 304 NE 2d 371 (1973). However, simply leaving an employee alone in a branch office does not hold out that employee as having authority to make a contract of insurance: *Globe & Rutgers Fire Ins Co* v *McGinnis*, 29 F 2d 357 (9 Cir, 1928—fire): the employee was a young lady typist, and the court seemed to infer that it should have been obvious that she was not the kind of person who would be authorised to contract.

43. *Manufacturers Accident Ins Co* v *Pudsey* (1897) 27 SCR 374, 380 *per* King J (PA). *Globe & Rutgers Fire Ins Co* v *McGinnis*, 29 F 2d 357 (9 Cir, 1928—fire).

44. Concerning implied actual authority, see above, 8–2.

45. *Wilkinson* v *GAFLAC* [1967] 2 Lloyd's Rep 182, 191 *per* Commissioner Heilbron (motor). The same principle governs the case in which the agent's authority ended altogether: *Willis, Faber & Co Ltd* v *Joyce* (1911) 27 TLR 388 (marine): the termination of authority of Lloyd's underwriting agent unknown to plaintiff: insurer bound, *per* Scrutton J applying *Scarf* v *Jardine* (1882) 7 App Cas 345.

In *Manufacturers Accident Ins Co* v *Pudsey* (1897) 27 SCR 374 the insurer issued an instruction rescinding the previous practice of its agents to give credit for premiums, but this change was not communicated to the insured. Four years after the change the agent gave credit for renewal of an accident policy and the company was held bound by the Supreme Court of Canada.

See also *Massachusetts Bonding & Ins Co* v *Parsons Electric Co*, 1 F 2d 264 (8 Cir, 1932—motor); *Brady* v *Metropolitan Life Ins Co*, 4 NYS 2d 581 (1939—industrial life), affirmed 20 NYS 2d (1940); *Warren* v *New York Life Ins Co*, 37 F Supp 358 (WD La, 1941—life), affirmed 128 F 2d 671 (5 Cir, 1942); *Seventi* v *New York Fire Ins Co*, 253 F Supp 670 (WD Pa, 1966—fire); *Downs* v *Del Regno*, 325 NYS 2d 320 (1971—employer's liability).

46. *Wilkinson* (above). *New York Life Ins Co* v *Rutherford*, 284 F 707 (9 Cir, 1922—life), cert den 262 US 744. An example of holding out is to place blank proposal forms with the agent: *First Trust* v *Middlesex Mutual Fire Ins Co*, 18 NYS 2d 936 (1940—fire). See further Appleman, No 8678.

47. *Eagle Star Ins Co Ltd* v *Spratt* [1971] 2 Lloyd's Rep 116, 128–129 *per* Phillimore LJ (CA—re). *Thomas* v *Prudential Ins Co of America*, 104 F 2d 480, 482 (4 Cir, 1939—life): "The authority of agents of life insurance companies, so far as the public with whom they deal is concerned, is controlled not so much by the terms of their employment or by the terms of the policies, which they procure, as by the things which the principal permits them to do by the nature and extent of the business for which they are employed and permitted to carry on." See also Rest Agency 2d, section 32, applied in *McGowan* v *Prudential Insurance Co of America*, 253 F Supp 415 (WD Pa, 1966—PA).

48. In *Re County Life Assn* (1870) LR 5 Ch App 288 (life) the managing director, P, and directors were appointed by the articles of the insurance company. The directors resolved that the company should not carry on business, thus revoking the actual authority of P to make contracts. Yet P issued 350 policies over two years and it was argued for the insured that the directors (who alone had actual authority to conduct business) must be taken to have acquiesced. The company was held bound. See also *Eagle Star Ins Co Ltd* v *Spratt* [1971] 2 Lloyd's Rep 116 (CA—re).

ever, a kind of communication by insurer to insured: the actual appointment of the agent to the negotiation, together with the silence on any reservations of terms or authority, is a representation to the insured that this agent has full powers to negotiate the matter.

8–3A1 Authority to Communicate

If an agent lacks actual authority, with two exceptions the insurance company is not bound simply because somebody says that it is i.e. that he or the agent who purported to act for the company does have authority.[49] The first clear exception is when this is said by one with actual authority to do the act in question for the company (above, 8–3A). The second but doubtful exception is when it is said by one with actual authority to say it, i.e., to communicate to the outside world the decisions of those in (high) authority in the company.

This role of high priest or communicator might be performed by a person such as the company secretary. If what the secretary tells the world is not true, can the company be nonetheless bound by what he says? Is it a sufficient holding out by the board that the communicator is actually (or apparently) authorised to communicate such matters? An affirmative answer might be based on modern recognition of the role of the secretary,[50] the recognition that life moves too quickly to require every corporate decision to be formally authenticated by seals or by the full array of directors' signatures. The same can be said of the insurer's local office.[51] However, contrary arguments are compelling: first, there is a *via media* between a collection of signatures and total trust by the outsider (insured) in what the agent or secretary says.[52] Second, to allow the secretary to bind the company as communicator would undermine the basic idea of agency that the principal should be liable only for what he has authorised or allowed to appear authorised. "It would indeed be strange if a servant who had no [apparent] authority to conclude a transaction were to be held to have [apparent] authority to communicate that that very transaction had been approved by his master."[53]

Even if a particular agent has been used as the medium of communication in the past, thus having had actual authority in the past to communicate the company's decision, it does not follow from this "that the principal has thereby represented that the agent has authority to communicate such approval in relation to future transactions, with the effect that the principal will be bound to such communication".[54] So, the same rules apply to authority to communicate decisions as to other acts performed

---

49. *British Bank of the Middle East* v *Sun Life Assurance Co of Canada (UK) Ltd* [1983] 2 Lloyd's Rep 9 (HL).
50. The contrary decision of *Houghton & Co* v *Nothard Lowe & Wills Ltd* [1927] 1 KB 246 (CA), in which the secretary's communication was ineffective, must now been seen in the light of *Panorama Developments (Guildford) Ltd* v *Fidelis Furnishing Fabrics Ltd* [1971] 2 QB 711 (CA), in which the enhanced role of the modern secretary was recognised.
51. *Berryere* v *Firemen's Fund Ins Co* (1965) 52 DLR (2d) 603 (Man—motor).
52. *British Bank of the Middle East* (above).
53. *The Ocean Frost, Armagas Ltd* v *Mundogas SA* [1985] 1 Lloyd's Rep. 1, 37 *per* Dunn LJ (CA).
54. *Ibid*, p 67 *per* Robert Goff LJ.

on behalf of the insurer.[55] For example, a branch manager may have authority to communicate the decision of head office.[55a]

8–3B Reliance

The representation that the agent has authority must be relied upon by the insured.[56] There can be no reliance by one who has notice that the agent lacks authority; notice may be actual[57] or constructive. Constructive notice may arise as follows: (a) The insurer has given sufficient notice, notice of which the insured should have been aware but was not (below, 8–3B1); or (b) the insured has enough notice from the circumstances of the case to be put on inquiry so that, if he does not make that inquiry, he is not permitted to assert his own reliance (8–3B2); or (c) the insured is deemed to have notice from the public documents of the insurance company (8–3B3).

8–3B1 Sufficient Notice

(a) *Documents*. (i) Receipts: Early cases suggest that the insured should have notice of any limit on the agent's authority which is stated on the premium receipt.[58] However, the general law now suggests that this is correct only if the insured should realise that the receipt is more than a mere receipt for money paid,[59] i.e., that he can be expected to look and see what it says. (ii) Policy: No such doubt arises about the terms of a policy already in the possession of or available to the insured: any limit therein on the authority of an agent, for example, authority to alter its terms, is thereby notified to the insured,[60] and is effective subsequently. It does not affect what might have happened before the insured had access to the policy terms.[61] (iii) Proposal Form: The proposer is taken to have sufficient notice of what is stated on the proposal form, which he signs.[62] However, the more the limit on the agent's authority

55. *The Ocean Frost, Armagas Ltd* v *Mundogas SA* [1986] AC 717, 778 *per* Lord Keith.
Cf USA: the presence of the company seal on a document apparently that of the company may be conclusive that the document was indeed authorised by the company: *American Employers Assurance Co* v *Christman Bros Co*, 78 NW 750.
55a. *First Energy (UK) Ltd* v *Hungarian International Bank Ltd* [1993] 2 Lloyd's Rep 194 (CA), concerning a bank.
56. *The Ocean Frost* (above) p 390 *per* Lord Keith. *World Marine & General Ins Co Ltd* [1952] 1 DLR 755, 761 *per* Kerwin J (SC—fire).
57. *Towle* v *National Guardian Assurance Sy* (1861) 30 LJ Ch 900, 916 *per* Turner LJ (CA) : notice that the agent lacked authority to issue a premium receipt in the form in question because of the notice on the receipt itself, of which it seemed the insured was aware. See also *Wilkinson* v *GAFLAC* [1967] 2 Lloyd's Rep 182 (motor).
58. *Acey* v *Fernie* (1840) 7 M & W 151, 155 *per* Parke B (life); *Towle* v *National Guardian Assurance Sy* (1861) 30 LJ Ch 900, 916 *per* Turner LJ (guarantee).
59. *Richardson, Spence & Co Ltd* v *Rowntree* [1894] AC 217. Clarke [1976] CLJ 51, 56.
60. *Horncastle* v *Equitable Life Assurance Sy of USA* (1906) 22 TLR 735 (CA—life); followed in *Comerford* v *Britannic Assurance Co Ltd* (1908) 24 TLR 593 (life). *Commercial Union Assurance Co* v *Margeson* (1899) 29 SCR 601 (fire); *Hyde* v *Lefaivre* (1902) 32 SCR 474 (fire). *Knickerbocker Life Ins Co* v *Norton*, 96 US 234 (1878—life); *Mutual Benefit Health & Accident Assn* v *Lyon*, 95 F 2d 528, 533 (8 Cir, 1938—PA); *Richardson* v *Prudential Ins Co of America*, 217 NYS 2d 300 (1961—life). For decisions hostile to such clauses see Appleman, No 8673. However, the insured has a "duty" to read his policy and to know what it says: below, 11–2A2
61. *Olley* v *Marlborough Court Ltd* [1949] 1 KB 532 (CA). *Abbott* v *Prudential Ins Co of America* 24 NE 2d 87, 89 (NY, 1939—industrial life).
62. *Levy* v *Scottish Employers Ins Assn* (1901) 17 TLR 229 (PA). *New York Life Ins Co* v *McCreary*, 60 F 2d 355 (8 Cir, 1932—life); *Braman* v *Mutual Life Ins Co*, 3 F 2d 391 (8 Cir, 1934—life). In England, this is reinforced by the rule of general law that the signatory is bound by terms in the document signed: *L'Estrange* v *Graucob Ltd* [1934] 2 KB 394. See further below, 10–3.

departs from the authority such a person usually has, the greater the degree of notice that must be given by the insurer.[63] Moreover, the proposer's signature to the form does not prevent his denying notice of its contents, if the insurer (or his agent) knew or should have known that the proposer was blind or otherwise unable to read the form.[64]

(b) *Previous Dealings*. If from previous dealings the insured has had notice (actual or constructive) of the limit on the authority of the insurer's agent, that may be enough to affect him with similar notice in current dealings.[65] The insured is thus affected, if the previous dealings should have suggested to him that the limit was usual and if the current transaction is sufficiently similar to those previous dealings to suggest that the same limit operates.

(c) *Custom*. If there is a general custom that a certain kind of agent has a certain kind of authority, the custom supports the normal rule about the usual authority of agents: above, 8–2A. However, there may be a local custom that deviates from usual practice, and a person may be affected with knowledge of the local custom and hence knowledge of a deviant limit on the agent's usual authority.[66] The consumer is unlikely to be affected with such knowledge, except perhaps through the knowledge of his own agent.

8–3B2 Inquiry

The insured cannot say that he relied on the apparent authority of the agent, if the circumstances were such as to put a reasonable man in his position on inquiry,[67] for example, if the terms of the cover offered were patently unusual,[68] or if the proposal was one which, to the knowledge of the proposer, was one which might give the insurer pause for thought, and it was not clear from circumstances the agent's representation that the insurer had had the opportunity to give due consideration to the proposal.[69]

---

63. By analogy with notice of contractual terms: *Crooks* v *Allen* (1879) QBD 38, 40 *per* Lush J; *Thornton* v *Shoe Lane Parking Ltd* [1971] 2 QB 163 (CA); *Interfoto Picture Library Ltd* v *Stiletto Visual Programmes Ltd* [1989] QB 433 (CA).

64. *Thompson* v *LMS Ry* [1930] 1 KB 41, 46–47 *per* Sankey LJ (CA). *Cf Budd* v *P & O SN* [1969] 2 Lloyd's Rep 262, 274–275 *per* Paull J. As regards the proposal of insurance see 10–3A.

65. By analogy with cases concerning notice of contractual terms: *Kendall & Sons* v *Lillico & Sons Ltd* [1969] 2 AC 31. Clarke [1976] CLJ 51, 59 ff.

66. *Baines* v *Ewing* (1866) LR 1 Ex 320 (hull): Liverpool shipowners were taken to know the Liverpool custom that insurance agents had limits on the sum they could insure. Bramwell B (p 323): the shipowners "have to rely on . . . the defendant having . . . held out the broker as his agent generally to sign policies. But in fact he only held him out as having the ordinary authority of a Liverpool broker." This *dictum* indicates another way of seeing the case: the contract made was not within the scope of the holding out.

67. *Howard* v *Patent Ivory Manufacturing Co* (1888) 38 Ch D 156; *The Ocean Frost, Armagas Ltd* v *Mundogas SA* [1986] AC 717.

In the USA the question is whether a reasonably prudent person would have been misled: *Dyer* v *Labedzki*, 179 NYS 2d 984, 986 (1958—workmen's compensation). See also *First Trust & Deposit Co* v *Middlesex Mutual Fire Ins Co*, 8 NYS 2d 936 (1940—fire), affirmed 31 NE 2d 510 (NY, 1940). *Cf Western Millers Mutual Ins Co* v *Williams*, 231 F 2d 425 (5 Cir, 1956—fire).

In *Jones* v *Bankers Life Co*, 31 F 2d 989, 994 (4 Cir, 1942—life), it was said that the claimant failed for he "closed his eyes to the circumstances which were known to him, or observable by ordinary attention, thereby attempting to gain for himself an advantageous position as a result of his ignorance". Applying the law of North Carolina, the court applied the principle that "the means of knowledge is equivalent to actual knowledge and that a party who has the opportunity for ascertaining facts cannot remain supine or inactive and thereby assert a want of knowledge".

68. *The Ocean Frost* (above).

69. For example, *Attleboro Mutual Ins Co* v *Grange Mutual Ins Co*, 611 A 2d 76 (Me, 1992—fire).

8–3B3 Constructive Notice of Public Documents

(a) *Common Law*. At common law all persons, including the insured, are taken to know the contents of the public documents of the insurance company, which include a statement of the objects of the company. If an act is *ultra vires* the company, it is not binding on the company.[70] Such acts should be distinguished from acts *intra vires* the company but *ultra vires* the agent, such as the executive director.[71] The latter acts could be binding on the company under the doctrine of apparent authority, unless the limit on the director's powers appeared from the public documents of which the insured was deemed to have notice, with the result that the company was not bound.[72]

As regards the public documents of large companies, it is unlikely that a limit on the authority of directors will be stated with such specificity that the reader of the document would know, without further information, that authority has been exceeded in a particular case. The articles might require, for example, that notice of a director's appointment should be given to certain people, but the outsider, such as the insured, would have no means of knowing whether this article had been observed; nor is he obliged to investigate. In most situations, a

"distinction is to be drawn between that which is apparent on the face of the [public document] which every contracting party must know, as here, that the policy is to be under seal, and what is only the result of . . . certain internal arrangements of the company, the compliance with which the contracting party has a right to assume".[73]

However, this assumption cannot be made, if the breach of article is (or should be) apparent to the insured. If there is a provision in the articles of the insurance company that all policies must be under seal, an insured, who knew this and saw that his policy was without seal, would also know that authority had been exceeded. He is deemed to have knowledge of this kind.

(b) *Statute*. Sections 35, 35A and 35B of the Companies Act 1985 contain new provisions[74] to implement Article 9 of the First EC Directive on Company Law. Section 35(1) provides: "The validity of an act done by a company shall not be called into question on the ground of lack of capacity by reason of anything in the company's memorandum."   Instead of an outright abolition of the doctrine of *ultra vires*, this provision seeks the same effect in what has been described as "an oddly oblique manner".[75] The common law rule restriction on the legal capacity of companies survives, but neither the company nor an insured contracting can question the validity of the company's acts on that ground.

Section 35A deals with the power of a director to bind the company: "(1) In favour

---

70. *Ashbury Railway Carriage Co v Riche* (1875) LR 7 HL 653; *Small v Small* (1884) 10 App Cas 119.

71. *Rolled Steel Products (Holdings) Ltd v British Steel Corp* [1985] 2 WLR 908 (CA).

72. *Ernest v Nichols* (1857) 6 HL Cas 401, 419 *per* Lord Wensleydale. Limits that have been imposed include the requirement of a policy: *Montreal Assurance Co v M'Gillivray* (1859) 13 Moore 87 (PC—fire); a particular form of insurance policy: *Hambro v Hull & London Fire Ins Co* (1858) 3 H & N 789 (cargo, freight): *Re Athenaeum Life Assurance Sy* (1858) 27 LJ Ch 829 (life); *cf Prince of Wales Assurance Co v Harding* (1858) El Bl & El 183, 214 *per* Lord Campbell CJ (life); limits on who might be insured: *Re Arthur Average Assn for British, Foreign & Colonial Ships* (1875) LR 10 Ch App 542 (hull mutual). See further Halsbury, Vol 7, No 737.

73. *Re Athenaeum Life Assurance Co* (1858) 27 LJ Ch 829, 833 *per* Page-Wood V-C (life). See also *Prince of Wales Assurance Co v Harding* (1858) El Bl & El 183 (life). This is the internal management rule of Company Law: *Royal British Bank v Turquand* (1856) 6 E & B 327; Halsbury, Vol 7, No 713.

74. The Companies Act 1989 s 108 (1) amending the original and much criticised section 35 of the Companies Act 1985.

75. R R Pennington, *Company Law* (6th ed, London 1990), p 97.

of a person dealing with a company in good faith, the power of the board of directors to bind the company, or authorise others to do so, shall be deemed to be free of any limitation under the company's constitution.''

8–3C Misinterpretation of Policy Terms

If the insured has notice of the existence of a term or a clause limiting the authority of the agent, a further question may arise: is the insurer bound by what the agent says about the meaning of the term? In particular, how is the insured affected by a false representation by the agent that the term allows him to bind the company? The answer is bound up with the more general question, whether the insurer is bound by what his agent says about any of the terms of the contract and their meaning.

Early cases decide that the insurer is not bound by what the agent says, on the basis that the agent has no authority to alter the terms of the contract.[76] These early cases can be explained in that it should have been obvious to the insured that the agent was changing the terms. The present issue premises that the insured and, usually, also the agent believe otherwise. Further, recent cases (above, 8–3A1) confirm that an agent cannot increase his own authority by simply asserting that authority. These can be distinguished in that they concern assertions of fact on matters outside the scope of the agent's authority rather than the meaning of documents, the explanation of which may well be within the agent's authority.

Recent cases in the general law[77] suggest that, if the term in question is one which the insured found difficult to understand,[78] he acts reasonably in relying on the interpretation of the agent. Indeed, the ABI Code of Practice requires intermediaries to "explain all the essential provisions of the cover afforded by the policy, or policies which he is recommending", and to "draw attention to any restrictions and or exclusions applying to the policy". Moreover, although there are thousands of policies and, it is said by the Institute of Insurance Brokers, that it is easy to make mistakes, the Institute has recognised the responsibility of the profession by launching a policy wording analysis service to help its members perform this role.[79] Against this background, it is submitted, the law is that the term is deemed to say what it is represented as saying by the agent.[80] If the buyer of goods may rely on the salesman's statements about the goods, why not also the buyer of insurance? In the USA the answer is clear:

"It strains credulity to believe that the managers of any insurance company would *actually* (not merely on paper) so limit the authority of the company's soliciting agents as to, in effect,

---

76. *Comerford* v *Brittanic Assurance Co Ltd* (1908) 24 TLR 593 (life); see further, above, 8–2A1.

77. *Curtis* v *Chemical Cleaning & Dyeing Co* [1951] 1 KB 805, 809 *per* Denning LJ (CA); *Mendelssohn* v *Normand Ltd* [1970] 1 QB 177 (CA): Denning LJ clearly regarded the agent as acting within the scope of his apparent authority. Edmund Davies LJ agreed with Denning LJ. Phillimore LJ took the line found in *Curtis*, one based on a *dictum* of Scrutton J in *L'Estrange* v *Graucob Ltd* [1934] 2 KB 394, that a person was bound by what he signed, unless there was fraud or misrepresentation, so that the effect of misrepresentation is to eliminate the whole clause, not to bind the principal to a new or different clause. In *Mendelssohn* v *Normand* (above), it is possible to say, as Denning LJ appeared to say, that the effect of the misrepresentation was to create a new duty on the employer to look after the car and contents; however, the decision could also have been reached (as *per* Phillimore LJ), by saying that the misrepresentation eliminated the exemption clause, leaving the bailment duty to revive of its own motion as a basis for the liability of the principal.

78. If the term is clear, the insured is bound by it as it stands: *Collins* v *Howell-Jones* [1981] EGD 207 (CA). Bowstead, p 308.

79. PM 13 May 1993, p 3.

80. This view of *Curtis* is also that taken by J Carter, *Unequal Bargaining* (Oxford, 1991), p 44.

instruct each to say to his prospects, 'Let me take your application for a . . . policy, but I cannot tell you what it covers".[81]

'Given the realities of the insurance business in which applications and certificates describe complex rights and obligations, it is to be expected that the average person will depend on the agent to explain everything. This is the way people buy insurance in the real world. We point out that an insurance company may protect itself in large part . . . through the improved training and supervision of its agents'.[82]

Nonetheless, any statement of the law on this question, whether law in England or the USA, must start from the two propositions that the insured's agent is not obliged to explain the terms of a policy[82a] and that the insured is deemed to read relevant documents, notably the policy, and, up to a point at least, to understand them.[82b] These two propositions are subject, however, to the following cases, which tend to show, as suggested above, that, if the agent does say what the term means and if the insured acts reasonably in relying on the agent's interpretation, the relevant term is then deemed to say what it is represented as saying.

From *Joel*[83] it is clear that a medical examiner has authority to explain the questions in the proposal form, questions which, with the answers given, become terms of the contract. The explanation colours the answers and thus the terms. In *Kaufmann*[84] a claim was defended on the ground that it concerned loss while the car was in private use, a use not covered by the policy. Deciding for the claimant, Roche J held that private use was covered by the policy, but that, anyway, the insurer was estopped by its agent's representation that such use was covered. In *Graves*[85] the defendant's motor policy limited cover to an area within a 75-mile radius of his address. At the time of his

81. *Vernon Fire & Casualty Ins Co* v *Thatcher*, 285 NE 2d 660, 670 (Ind, 1972—fire).

82. *Ellingwood* v *NN Investors Life Ins Co*, 805 P 2d 70, 76 (NM, 1991—life). The responsibility of insurers has been recognised in England, for example, in the heavy fines which have been imposed on insurers by LAUTRO in respect of misstatements by agents selling policies: PM, 11 November 1993, p 2.

82a. Below, 9–5C; but *cf* the ABI Code of Practice quoted above and discussed below, 8–3C(d).

82b. See below, 11–2A2.

83. *Joel* v *Law Union & Crown Ins Co* [1908] 2 KB 863 (CA—life).

84. *Kaufmann* v *British Surety Ins Co Ltd* (1929) 33 Ll L Rep 315 (motor). Also in this sense: *London Life Assurance Co* v *Baker* (1987) 34 DLR (4th) 340 (NB—disability). *Cf*, however, *Gates* v *City Mutual Life Assurance Sy Ltd* (1986) 160 CLR 1 (HCA—life).

85. *Automobile Underwriters Corp* v *Graves* 489 F 2d 625 (8 Cir, 1973—motor). See also *Fidelity & Casualty Co* v *Phoenix Manufacturing Co*, 100 F 604 (7 Cir, 1900—liability); *White* v *Liberty Mutual Ins Co*, 309 NYS 2d 819 (1970—aviation); *Cornell, Howland, Hayes & Merryfield Inc* v *Continental Casualty Co*, 65 F 2d 22 (9 Cir, 1972—liability); *Iowa National Mutual Ins Co* v *City of Osawatomie*, 458 F 2d 1124 (10 Cir, 1972—fire); *Heinson* v *Porter*, 772 P 2d 778 (Kan, 1989—homeowner's); *Ellingwood* v *N.N. Investors Life Ins Co*, 805 P 2d 70, (NM, 1991—life); *Nichols* v *Shelter Life Ins Co*, 923 F 2d 1158, 1161 and cases cited (5 Cir, 1991—medical); *Bill Brown Construction Co* v *Glen Falls Ins Co*, 818 SW 2d 1 (Tenn, 1991—cargo). Pierce 19 Western Univ L R 507 (1992). For the same decision against the insurer on the basis of a brochure: *Weinberg* v *INA*, 388 NYS 2d 69 (1976—liability).

Alternatively, the claim may be against the insurer for damages: *Smith* v *New York Life Ins Co*, 208 F Supp 240 (SD Iowa, 1962—life), where the court said (p 242) that the insurer "is bound by the statement of [the agent] that the plaintiff could get the commuted value [of the annuity] in an emergency", and awarded the insured damages for deceit to the amount of the commuted value. In *Thomas* v *American Workmen*, 14 SE 2d 886, 887 (1941) the Supreme Court of South Carolina said; "In the case before us, we have an ignorant negro woman, with an equally ignorant husband and with no circumstances to incite suspicion, dealing with a representative of the defendant [insurer] who was well informed, and who . . . fraudulently misrepresented the provisions of the policy in material particulars . . . The policy of the courts is, on the one hand, to suppress fraud, and on the other, not to encourage negligence and inattention to one's own interest. Either course has obvious dangers. But the unmistakable drift is toward the just doctrine that a wrongdoer cannot shield himself from liability by asking the law to condemn the credulity of the ignorant and unwary." The court affirmed the lower judgment that the defendant was liable for damages for the conduct of the agent. See also *Equitable Life & Casualty Co* v *Lee* 310 F 2d 262 (9 Cir, 1942—life); *Rempel* v *Nationwide Life Ins Co*, 323 A 2d 193 (Pa, 1974—life).

proposal he asked the insurer's agent about this policy restriction and was told, that, if he went outside it "once in a while" he would still be covered. Following an accident outside the 75-mile radius the insurer sought a declaration of no coverage. The United States' Court of Appeals held[86] that "such a statement to an applicant for insurance by an agent who is shown to be generally authorized to represent an insurer serves to create an oral contract of insurance which binds the agent's principal to provide insurance coverage consistent with the agent's representation". In that case the agent had authority to issue interim cover beyond the 75-mile limit.

The nature of the rule in issue here is estoppel. In England in *Hiscox* v *Outhwaite* (No 3),[87] although in the end the point did not arise for decision, Evans J stated his conclusion that "Given a right to claim under the reinsurance contract, that is to say, an independent and pre-existing cause of action, an estoppel may prevent the reinsurers from denying that particular facts lie within the scope of the contract, notwithstanding that a claim may succeed which otherwise would fail for being outside it". In the USA in *Hully* v *Aluminum Co of America*[88], the court held[89] that (i) waiver was "inapplicable since there was no unilateral intent imputable to the insurance company to relinquish a known right under the policy"; (ii) "[r]eformation of the contractor's policy is not a proper remedy since there was no mutual intent or actual agreement of the parties"; and (iii) "the insurance company is precluded by estoppel from taking advantage of such exclusion in the contractor's policy". A more extended discussion of estoppel in insurance cases is to be found below (26–4), but certain points require mention here.

(a) *The Authority of the Agent.* In *Kaufmann* and in *Graves* (above) the agent had actual authority to make contracts but, as the decisions were based on estoppel, actual authority was not essential. If the insured does not or cannot be expected to realise that the contract terms are being modified, what counts is not actual or apparent authority to contract but actual or apparent authority to explain the meaning of (apparently unmodified) terms. In England, the issue has been obscured by the emphasis put upon signature by the proposer of a proposal form which was other than that represented by the agent. However, in some of the cases, at least, it was held that, if the proposer would not have understood the form, he was entitled to trust what was said about the form by the agent, whether the proposer had read it or not.[90] It is more or less explicit in these decisions that the agent had authority to explain the form and, in so far as the answers were warranties, to explain the terms of the contract.

(b) *Reasonable Reliance.* In general, the person seeking insurance is taken to know the contents of the policy[91] and to understand the ordinary language of the policy. He "has no right to rely upon an agent's patently absurd interpretation of a policy. He

---

86. 489 F 2d 625, 629 (8 Cir, 1973—motor).
87. [1991] 2 Lloyd's Rep 524, 535 (re).
88. 143 F Supp 508 (SD Iowa, 1956).
89. pp 512–513. Reliance by the insured is essential: *St Joseph Bank & Trust Co* v *Sun Ins Co*, 80 F Supp 890 (D Ind, 1974).
90. See below, 10–3A. In the United States a general agent or a policy-writing agent has actual authority to interpret policies: *Cadez* v *General Casualty Co*, 98 F 2d 535 (10 Cir, 1961—employer's liability), *cert* den 369 US 861, but (*ibid*) a soliciting agent does not have authority to interpret contracts of insurance. See also *Union Life Ins Co* v *Burk*, 169 F 2d 235 (10 Cir, 1948—employer's liability); and *Cavallo* v *Metropolitan Life Ins Co*, 62 NYS 2d 618 (1965—life) in which the New York court reached the same result on the ground that the scope of cover was a question of law, and therefore a matter which the agent was not authorised to explain.
91. See below, 11–2A2.

ordinarily may rightfully rely, however, upon an agent's interpretation that is plausible and not in patent conflict with the printed policy although legally untenable".[92] Reliance must be reasonable and in good faith.[93]

(c) *Representations of Law.* Any prediction that the insurer will be estopped by what his agent says about the terms of the insurance cannot be made with total confidence in England, as the interpretation of a document has been regarded as a question of law,[94] and there can be no estoppel on the basis of (mis)statements of law.[95] However, estoppel is possible if the question is one of private rights, as this is generally regarded not as law but fact.[96] Further, a distinction has been drawn between the contents of a document (fact) and the interpretation of a document (law). Obviously this is a difficult line to draw, for a statement of a document's contents is based on conclusions about its meaning. There is some evidence that, provoked by the unreality[97] of the rule against allowing legal action based on misstatements of law, the courts are moving that line to confine the rule.[98] If this trend is confirmed, an insurer may be estopped under English law by his agent's interpretation of the policy. A trend of this kind is found in the United States[99]:

"Statements of an agent rarely are given as opinions but rather as statements of fact. It scarcely seems reasonable that a layman should be expected to know enough law to appreciate that a flat statement such as 'your policy is now in effect' or 'this policy covers both cars' is one of law and not one of fact. It seems more reasonable for insurers to be responsible for the utterances of their representatives, and thus to have an incentive to regulate them more closely than for the courts to rescue them from an agent's overzealous misstatements, whether they be of fact or law."

(d) *Silence: Failure to Explain.* Any doctrine based on estoppel assumes a positive representation by the party estopped, and so it is with the decided cases discussed above. In practice, however, good insurance practice, as expressed in the Association of British Insurers' Code of Practice for intermediaries, goes further: it requires the intermediary to explain the terms of the contract and, in particular, to draw attention to any restrictions and any exclusions applying to the policy. The Code does not have the force of law, however, in at least one case it offered sufficient footing for the Ombudsman to decline to allow an insurer to rely on an exclusion, to which the atten-

---

92. *Flamme* v *Wolf Ins. Agency*, 476 NW 2d 802, 807 (Neb, 1991—motor); see also *Barhonovich* v *American National Ins Co*, 947 F 2d 775 (5 Cir, 1991—life). There will, of course, be no estoppel, if the claimant is unable to show that he relied on the representation because, for example, the error in it was obvious: *Colvin* v *Metropolitan Life Ins Co* [1936] 2 DLR (Ont—life).
93. *Hully* (above).
94. *Harse* v *Pearl Life Assurance Co* [1904] 1 KB 558, 563 *per* Lord Collins MR (CA—life policy). See further references in Bower, *Estoppel*, No 43, n 4.
95. *Kai Nam* v *Ma Kam Chan* [1956] AC 358 (PC) with reference to *Territorial & Auxiliary Forces Assn* v *Nichols* [1949] 1 KB 35: a statement by a landlord's agent to the tenant about the effect of a tenancy was held by the Court of Appeal to be law. Scott LJ (p 50): the statement was "that they were controlled premises. That is not a representation of fact; it is a statement of the result obtained by applying the provisions of the Acts to the circumstances of the case."
96. *Cooper* v *Phibbs* (1867) LR 2 HL 149, 170 *per* Lord Westbury.
97. The rule rests on public policy that no person should be allowed to rely on his own mistake about the law of the land. While this serves the purpose of the criminal law, it is less obvious why each citizen should be expected to know the mass of complex civil law. The rule was criticised *obiter* by Lord Denning MR in *André et Cie SA* v *Ets Michel Blanc & Fils* [1979] 2 Lloyd's Rep 427, 431–432.
98. As regards relief for misrepresentation of law see below, 22–2B3. See also a representation concerning the meaning of a settlement offered by an insurer to a claim: *Horry* v *Tate & Lyle Refineries Ltd* [1982] 2 Lloyd's Rep 416. Clarke [1989] JBL.
99. Appleman, section 8874.35.

tion of the claimant had not been drawn by the insurer's agent.[100] In effect, the contract was treated as if the exclusion had not been written.

8–3D Misfeasance

The same rules apply if the agent is acting in breach of instructions[101] or is fraudulent.[102] Neither disobedience nor fraud *per se* takes his act outside the scope of his apparent authority. If the act is, however, outside the scope of the (actual or) apparent authority of the agent, the insurer is not liable, even if the opportunity to commit the act arose out of the agency.[103]

8–4 RATIFICATION

A contract, which is not within the actual or apparent authority of the agent, may nonetheless bind the insurer, if the insurer later ratifies it.[104]

8–4A The Appearance

In his dealings with the insured the agent must have purported[105] to act on behalf of the insurer,[106] although it is not essential that the particular insurer be identified at the time.

8–4B The Capacity of the Insurer

The principal (the insurer) must have had the capacity to do the act at the time of the act.[107] Thus a corporate insurer must have had legal existence at that time.[108] These rules have little practical impact on insurance companies. However, it may follow that a new member at Lloyd's, who joins a syndicate with effect from a certain date, can-

---

100. The Insurance Ombudsman, Annual Report 1991, para 2.18. Concerning the possibility of a legal "duty to speak", see *The Stolt Loyalty* [1993] 2 Lloyd's Rep 281.

101. *Re Economic Fire Office Ltd* (1896) 12 TLR 142 (fidelity): when an agent gave a receipt for a premium, which had not been paid, the insurer was estopped from resisting an action by the insured; the insured (employer) was unaware of the non-payment by the (employee) whose fidelity was insured and whose duty it was to pay the premium.

102. Below, 10–5.

103. *Ruben v Great Fingall Consolidated* [1906] AC 439. A *dictum* of Lord Loreburn in this case (p 443) is the basis for the proposition that a company can never be bound by a forged document. However, this is probably incorrect, if the agent who forges the document is acting within his apparent authority.

104. Bowstead pp 15 ff; Halsbury, Vol 1, Nos 756 ff. Rest Agency 2d, sections 82 ff; Appleman, section 8766.

105. The purport is the agent's intent, as it appears to the insured; a principal may ratify a contract, although the agent secretly and fraudulently intended to take the benefit of the contract himself: *Re Tiedemann and Ledermann Frères* [1899] 2 QB 66. *Watson v US Fidelity & Guarantee Co*, 27 F 2d 1355 (9 Cir, 1970—motor).

106. *Keighley, Maxsted & Co v Durant* [1901] AC 240: while it is possible for the act to be ratified by an unnamed principal, it cannot be ratified by an undisclosed principal, i.e., one of whose existence the insured is unaware because the agent himself appears to be contracting as sole principal.

107. Acts *ultra vires* a company cannot be ratified: *Ashbury Railway Carriage & Iron Co v Riche* (1875) LR 7 HL 653. Halsbury, Vol 7, No 706. But a company may ratify an act *intra vires* the company performed by a person at a time when the company lacked the proper organ or officer to perform the act: *Ward & Co Ltd v Samyang Navigation Ltd* [1975] 2 All ER 424 (HL).

108. *Kelner v Baxter* (1866) LR 2 CP 174. Companies Act 1985, s 36C: see above, 7–4B.

not lawfully ratify business contracted before that date, if such acts by an unlicensed person, being then illegal,[109] would not have been enforced by the courts.[110]

8–4C Form and Intent

Ratification may be express or implied. It must occur "either with full knowledge of the act to be adopted, or with intention to adopt it at all events and under whatever circumstances".[111] For example, the insurer who receives and retains premium obtained by an agent acting in excess of his authority, with knowledge of that excess, ratifies the agent's acts.[112]

Ratification must, however, be by the appropriate organ of the insurer. If the insurer is a company and the directors exceed their powers, usually ratification must be by the shareholders by an ordinary resolution in general meeting. For ratification by the acquiescence of shareholders there must be[113] "distinct, plain and clear notice" that the contract in excess of authority "in the shape of a report or the like, was brought home to them". However, it is neither necessary nor possible

"to prove that every shareholder had notice or such a knowledge of the facts as amounts to notice. It is sufficient to shew that facts were made known to the shareholders, into the effect of which they might and ought to have inquired, and to which they ought to have objected at the time, unless they intended to adopt the transaction."[114]

8–4D The Time of Ratification

The insurer must ratify the act of the agent within a reasonable time.[115] If the contract of insurance stipulates a time for the commencement of contractual performance, it has been said that in the interests of certainty ratification must occur prior to that time[116]; in the case of insurance that means before cover is due to begin. This view is controversial.[117]

"There can be no ratification until the purported principal is aware of the transaction concerned . . . The matter was complex and, in view of this and of the fact that ratification, if operative at all, could not prejudice but merely benefit the insured, it was not, in my judgment, too late."[118]

In any event the insurer must ratify the act before the act has become one which he cannot lawfully perform,[119] and before the act has been undone.[120]

---

109. *La Banque Jacques-Cartier* v *La Banque d'Epargne Montréal* (1887) 13 App Cas 111 (PC).

110. See below, 24–3A.

111. *Phosphate of Lime Co* v *Green* (1871) LR 7 CP 43, 57 *per* Willes J. See also *Reuter* v *Electric Telegraph Co* (1856) 6 El & Bl 341; *Fitzmaurice* v *Bayley* (1856) 6 El & Bl 868. *US Fidelity & Guarantee Co* v *Anerson Construction Co*, 60 F 2d 172 (9 Cir, 1958—surety bonds).

112. *Globe Mutual Life Ins Co* v *Wolff*, 95 US 326 (1877—life); *Weaver* v *Metropolitan Life Ins Co*, 545 F Supp 74 (ED Mo, 1982—life).

113. *Re Athenaeum Life Assurance Co* (1858) 27 LJ Ch 829, 834 *per* Page-Wood V-C (life).

114. *Phosphate of Lime Co Ltd* v *Green* (1871) LR 7 CP 43, 63 *per* Brett J.

115. *Re Portuguese Consolidated Copper Mines Ltd* (1890) 45 Ch D 16 (CA).

116. *Metropolitan Asylums Board* v *Kingham & Sons* (1890) 6 TLR 217, 218 *per* Fry LJ (CA). See also *Dibbins* v *Dibbins* [1896] 2 Ch 348.

117. See discussion in Bowstead, pp 77–79.

118. *Bedford Ins Co Ltd* v *Instituto de Resseguros do Brasil* [1985] QB 966, 987 *per* Parker J (re).

119. *Grover* v *Mathews* [1910] 2 KB 401: for the question whether there can be ratification (by the insured) after loss, see above, 7–4D1.

120. As where, for example, agent and insured rescind their agreement: *Walter* v *James* (1871) LR 6 Ex 124; however, unilateral repudiation by one of them, say the insured, does not prevent ratification, for ratification is said to be retroactive: below, 8–4E.

If the insurer intimates to the insured that he does not intend to ratify the act of the agent, he is bound by his election and cannot ratify later.[121]

8-4E The Effect of Ratification

The effect of ratification is to put the insurer in the position he would have been, if the agent's act had been authorised when it was performed. Ratification is said to be retroactive,[122] unless the agent contracted "subject to ratification". In the latter case alone intervening repudiation by the insured is effective to forestall ratification and prevent the formation of a binding contract with the insurer.[123]

8-5 WARRANTY OF AUTHORITY

If the insurer's agent indicates that he has authority to bind the insurer, but he does not have that authority, and the insured relies on that indication and consequently suffers loss, the agent may be liable to the insured: (a) if the agent is fraudulent he may be liable in the tort of deceit[124]; (b) if the agent is negligent he may be liable in tort for negligent misstatement[125]; (c) if the agent is fraudulent, negligent or entirely innocent, he may be liable for breach of warranty of authority.[126]

For liability for breach of warranty of authority there are these requirements: first, the agent must represent by words or by conduct that he[127] has authority to act in the way in question on behalf of the insurer. If he purports to act as agent he is taken to have represented that he has authority to act.

Second, the insured must have been induced by the agent's representation to act in a way in which he would not otherwise have acted if this representation had not been made. There will be no liability for breach of the warranty, if the insured knows all the material facts from which the agent's authority or its extent may be inferred, or if the agent expressly disclaims present authority.[128]

If there is breach of the warranty, the insured may recover consequent loss as damages. If, however, the insured was also in breach of a condition of the insurance

---

121. *McEvoy* v *Belfast Banking Co Ltd* [1935] AC 24.

122. *Bolton Partners* v *Lambert* (1888) 41 Ch D 295 (CA), criticised in *Fleming* v *Bank of New Zealand* [1900] AC 577, 587 *per* Lord Lindley (PC). See discussion of this principle in Bowstead, pp 74–75. *Bolton* was not followed in *Marqusee* v *Hartford Fire Ins Co*, 98 F 475 (2 Cir, 1912—fire).

123. *Warehousing & Forwarding Co of E Africa Ltd* v *Jafferali & Sons Ltd* [1964] AC 1 (PC).

124. If fraud can be proved, the insured might prefer an action based in deceit, rather than negligent misstatement or warranty of authority, as the damages recoverable may be greater: *Doyle* v *Olby (Ironmongers) Ltd* [1969] 2 QB 158 (CA). Concerning deceit, see also below, 11–3C1.

In the USA there may also be a breach of fiduciary duty owed by the insurer's agent to the insured, where there is a confidential relationship giving rise to a duty of disclosure. See *Edwards* v *Travelers Ins Co*, 563 F 2d 105 (6 Cir, 1977—motor). Cf *Moses* v *Manufacturers' Life Ins Co*, 298 F Supp 321 (D SC, 1968—life), affirmed 407 F 2d 1142 (4 Cir, 1969), *cert den* 396 US 827, in which it was held that no fiduciary duty was owed to the insured by the insurer.

125. *Rust* v *Abbey Life Assurance Co Ltd* [1978] 2 Lloyd's Rep 386 (life). As regards negligent misstatement, see also below, 9–2A.

126. *Yonge* v *Toynbee* [1910] 1 KB 215 (CA). Generally see Bowstead, pp 457 ff. The warranty of authority was applied to the case of an insurer's agent by the House of Lords in *Harris* v *McRobert* (1924) 19 Ll L Rep 135, 136 *per* Viscount Cave (fire).

127. Action will also lie when the defendant has represented that, not he, but a third person has authority; *M'Dougall* v *Colonial Bank of Australasia* (1869) 38 LJPC 49.

128. *Halbot* v *Lens* [1901] 1 Ch 344.

policy, his loss would have occurred whether the agent's representation of authority were true or not; the insured's loss is not consequent upon the agent's breach and the agent is not liable.[129] For historical reasons the action based on a warranty of authority is regarded as contractual rather than tortious, and the amount of damages is measured accordingly.

---

129. *Harris* v *McRobert* (1924) 19 Ll L Rep 135 (HL—fire). See also below, 9–6A.

CHAPTER 9

THE INSURED AND HIS AGENT: RIGHTS AND DUTIES INTER SE[1]

9-1 INTRODUCTION

The conduct of agents is regulated both by statute and by codes of conduct.[2] Codes provide little consolation for the proposer or the insured (referred to in this chapter as the client) if they are not observed; it is with the civil liability of the one to the other— chiefly the liability of the agent to the client, that this chapter is concerned. In particular, if the client does not get the contract of insurance, which the agent agreed to procure, and if the client then suffers loss which he would not have suffered if the mandate had been performed, he may seek compensation from the agent. Although beyond the title of this book, the picture is incomplete without discussion of (a) the rights of the client against the agent of the insurer for breach of warranty of authority[3]; and (b) the rights of the client against his own agent, usually a broker, for breach of duty as agent.

The nature of the agent's duties depends on their basis, which may be in contract, in tort or in equity fiduciary duty. It is generally assumed that the agent may be liable concurrently in contract and tort[4]: in most cases the extent of the liability will be the same.[5] However, one point of practical difference should be signalled at the start. The effect of the Latent Damage Act 1986 (section 14A of the Limitation Act 1980) is that the limitation period for an action in tort is extended: whereas the general rule is six years from accrual of the causes of action, these provisions allow suit in tort within three years from the time that the claimant acquired knowledge of the relevant facts.

---

1. Generally see Bowstead, ch 5; Hanley, *The Law of Insurance Broking* (1990); Harnett, *Responsibilities of Insurance Agents and Brokers* (1986); Hodgin, ch 3; Jackson & Powell, *Professional Negligence* (1987), ch 7; Mance, (1993) 82 BILA Journal 32.

2. Notably conduct of business rules made under the Financial Services Act 1986; and the General Insurance Business—Code of Practice, drawn up by the Association of British Insurers. See also the Insurance Brokers Registration Council (Code of Conduct) Approval Order 1978, SI 1978, No 1394. On such matters generally see Birds, pp 178 ff; Hodgin, ch 5.

3. See above, 8-5.

4. For example *Strong and Pearl* v *Allison & Co Ltd* (1926) 25 Ll L Rep 504, 507 *per* Greer J (yacht); *Osman* v *Moss Ltd* [1970] 1 Lloyd's Rep 313 (CA—motor); *Cherry* v *Allied Ins Brokers Ltd* [1978] 1 Lloyd's Rep 274, 280 *per* Cantley J (consequential loss). Jackson & Powell, *op cit*, No 7.07. More recently, in the *Superhulls Cover* case, *Youell* v *Bland Welch & Co Ltd* [1990] 2 Lloyd's Rep 431, 439 (re), Phillips J confirmed the assumption that the agent may be liable concurrently in contract and in tort, pointing out that the same point had been made earlier by O'Connor LJ in *Forsik. Vesta* v *Butcher* [1988] 1 Lloyd's Rep 19, 23 (CA—re). Also in this sense: *Macmillan* v *Knott Becker Scott* [1990] 1 Lloyd's Rep 98, 101 *per* Evans J (liability); *Punjab National Bank* v *De Boinville* [1992] 3 All ER 104 (CA).
Idem in Canada: *Wilcox* v *Norberg & Wiggins Ins Agencies Ltd* [1979] 1 WWR 414, 433 (BC—fire); *cf Nunes Diamond* v *Dominion Electric Protection Co* [1972] SCR 769; *Brown & Menezes*, 3:4:10. Le Bouthillier, (1992) 24 Ottawa L Rev 649.

5. *Brown & Menezes*, 3:4:3.

Further, another difference may be that the contract of agency has a limiting effect not only on the agent's duty of care,[6] actionable in tort, but also on the scope of his duties as a fiduciary.[7]

9–1A Sub-agents

For simplicity this chapter refers only to agents. In general, what is said here about agents applies also to sub-agents, but with one important exception: when the agent employs a sub-agent to carry out an appropriate part of the mandate, there is no contract between client and sub-agent,[8] and any liability of the sub-agent to the client must be in tort (below, 9–2) or for breach of fiduciary duty (below, 9–4). The agent remains liable for the failure of the sub-agent to perform the contractual duties of the mandate.[9]

9–2 LIABILITY OF THE AGENT IN TORT

For an action in tort the claimant, let us say the client, must establish either deceit or negligence. For deceit, the claimant must establish that the agent made a fraudulent statement which caused him loss. A statement is fraudulent[10] if made with knowledge that it is untrue, made without belief in its truth, or made recklessly, not caring whether it is true or not.

For negligence, the claimant must establish that the agent owed him a duty of care, broke that duty and that as a result the proposer suffered loss of a reasonably foreseeable type.[11] In general, no duty is owed to a person whose loss is purely economic, except when the loss is caused by negligent misstatement.[12] Nor is there a duty or, at least, liability for breach of the duty, if the agent has made an effective disclaimer: below, 9–2E.

For such a duty to arise there must be a negligent misstatement by an informed person to or for an identifiable claimant, which is reasonably relied on by the claimant. In other words currently in vogue,[13] first, the agent and the claimant must have "a relationship characterised by the law as one of proximity". This relationship will generally exist between the agent and an identifiable claimant, particularly, if the purpose of the advice is known to the agent, the advice is communicated directly to the claimant and if the claimant is likely to act on it.[14] Second, the situation must be "one in which the court considers it fair, just and reasonable that the law should impose a duty".[15] If

6. *Norwich City Council* v *Harvey (Paul Clarke)* [1989] 1 All ER 1180 (CA).
7. *Kelly* v *Cooper* [1992] 3 WLR 936 (PC).
8. Bowstead, p 131; except when it is part of the agent's mandate to appoint a person (i.e., another agent rather than a sub-agent) to act directly for the principal: *ibid*.
9. For example *The Okeanis* [1986] 1 Lloyd's Rep 195, 201 *per* Bingham J (hull). For umbrella arrangements at Lloyd's, known as piggybacks or flags of convenience, see *Johns* v *Kelly* [1986] 1 Lloyd's Rep 468.
10. *Derry* v *Peek* (1889) 14 App Cas 337. On the damages recoverable for deceit see *Doyle* v *Olby (Iron-mongers) Ltd* [1969] 2 QB 158 (CA); *Smith Kline* v *Long* [1988] 3 All ER 887 (CA).
11. If there is a duty and a breach of that duty, the type of loss suffered in consequence will usually have been reasonably foreseeable. For foreseeability, sometimes referred to as causation in law, the reader is referred to general works.
12. *Hedley Byrne & Co Ltd* v *Heller & Partners Ltd* [1964] AC 465, 502–503 *per* Lord Morris, 514 *per* Lord Hodson. For the position in New York, see Bass and Maccarrone, 28 Tort & Ins LJ 646 (1993).
13. *Caparo Industries plc* v *Dickman* [1990] 2 AC 605, 618 per Lord Bridge.
14. *Ibid* p 638 per Lord Oliver.
15. *Ibid* p 618 per Lord Bridge. See *Macmillan* v *Knott Becker Scott* (below, 9–2C2).

reliance is reasonable, these two requirements are usually satisfied,[16] unless there is some strong countervailing consideration of public policy against liability.[17]

Although what is fair and reasonable in a particular case is a question of law,[18] this requirement enables a court to take account of the particularity of a context or of a relationship, and to preserve judicial discretion in the face of new developments. In the general law of negligence, the courts have retreated from general principles and announced their intention to develop the law incrementally[19] and by reference to traditional categories of case.[20] Likewise, within the broad band of special relationships giving rise to a duty of care with respect to advice, "in the recent cases on negligent misstatement in the House of Lords, there is a strong current of emphasis upon the specific situation in which the statement is made".[21] What is expected of an auditor may be more or less than what is expected of an insurance agent or an investment adviser. One important factor is that the courts are unlikely to use tort to break an established mould or pattern of liability created by contract.[22]

9–2A Negligent Misstatement

A misstatement is an untrue statement. A statement connotes words rather than conduct.[23] Hence while a duty may arise if the agent tells the claimant proposer what to write or that what he, the agent, has written, is what is required, it is less clear that a duty will arise if the agent fills the form and hands it to the proposer to sign without comment on the contents.[24] Usually the statement is one made by the agent to the client, but it may also be one made for the client to a third party, such as the insurer.[25]

There is negligence, if the conduct of the agent falls below the level of care and skill to be expected of an agent of that kind, having regard in particular to the current practices of the profession, including codes of conduct: below, 9–3A.

16. See below 9–2D.
17. In other situations public policy may intervene to negate a duty, for example the case of the cartographer or the author of a legal textbook! Examples from decisions of the courts include: (a) The purpose of a statement, so that even if reliance is foreseeable and reasonable, that alone is insufficient, if reliance by person such as the claimant is outside the purpose: *Caparo* (above); *The Morning Watch* [1990] 1 Lloyd's Rep 547. (b) The insurability of the defendant's liability: *Caparo* (above) p 643 *per* Lord Oliver. (c) It is not fair and reasonable for the plaintiff to rely on a statement, if it is clear that the opinion it contains is provisional: *McNaughton (James) Paper Group Ltd* v *Hicks Anderson & Co* [1991] 1 All ER 134, 146 *per* Neill LJ (CA), concerning "draft accounts".
18. *Macmillan* v *Knott Becker Scott* [1990] 1 Lloyd's Rep 98, 109 per Evans J (liability).
19. *Murphy* v *Brentwood DC* [1991] 1 AC 398, 461 (HL) *per* Lord Keith (HL).
20. *Caparo* v *Dickman plc* [1990] 2 AC 605, 635 *per* Lord Oliver.
21. *Morgan Crucible Co plc* v *Hill Samuel Bank Ltd* [1990] 3 All ER 330, 334 per Hoffmann J, citing *Caparo* (above) pp 617–618 *per* Lord Bridge.
22. See *Macmillan* v *Knott Becker Scott*, below, 9–2C2. This point reflects a significant development in the law of negligence, whereby the scope or existence of a duty of care is influenced by the contractual setting in which it arises. See *Tai Hing Cotton Mill* v *Liu Chong Bank* [1986] AC 80, 107 *per* Lord Scarman (PC); *Norwich CC* v *Harvey* [1989] 1 All ER 1180 (CA); *Pacific Associates Inc* v *Baxter* [1989] 2 All ER 159 (CA). Adams and Brownsword (1990) 10 LS 12.
23. *Argy Trading Development Co Ltd* v *Lapid Developments Ltd* [1977] 3 All ER 785, 800 *per* Croom-Johnson J (fire).
24. It is doubtful whether the law would distinguish in this regard between the doctor who tells his patient what drug he will prescribe for him and the doctor who simply writes (perhaps illegibly) on a prescription form and hands it to the patient.
25. *Ministry of Housing & Local Govt.* v *Sharp* [1970] 2 QB 223 (CA); *Lawton* v *BOC Transhield Ltd* [1987] 2 All ER 608.

9–2B An Informed Person

The essence of the client's case against the agent's case is that the client's reliance on the agent's advice was reasonable (below 9–2D) or, in other words, that the advice was likely to be acted on. For this, it has been said, the agent must be or appear to be an informed person. An informed person is a person

"in a sphere in which a person is so placed, that others could reasonably rely upon his judgment or his skill or upon his ability to make careful inquiry, a person who takes it upon himself to give information or advice to, or allows his information or advice to be passed on to, another person who, as he knows or should know, will place reliance upon it".[26]

Such persons may include persons negotiating contracts,[27] financial advisers,[28] and insurance brokers.[29]

9–2C An Identifiable Claimant

An identifiable claimant is one with whom the informed person (above, 9–2B) has a special relationship or, in other words used by Lord Oliver in *Caparo*,[30] a relationship of proximity. He is one who, as the informed person knows or should know, will place reliance upon his statements.[31] In other words, again those of Lord Oliver in *Caparo*, there will be a relationship of proximity, if:

"(1) the advice is required for a purpose, whether particularly specified or generally des-
        cribed, which is made known, either actually or inferentially, to the adviser at the
        time when the advice is given,
  (2) the adviser knows, either actually or inferentially that his advice will be communi-
        cated to the advisee, either specifically or as a member of an ascertainable class, in
        order that it should be used by the advisee for that purpose,
  (3) it is known, either actually or inferentially, that the advice so communicated is likely
        to be acted on by the advisee for that purpose without independent inquiry".

Although it may difficult to establish such a relationship between auditors and investors (*Caparo*), there is little difficulty between agent and insured when in direct contact with each other, and not least when the agent helps a proposer to complete the proposal.[32]

The agent for the insured may also owe a duty to "third parties",[33] i.e., to persons other than his client, i.e., to the insurer (9–2C1), to a person intended by his client to

---

26. *Hedley Byrne & Co Ltd* v *Heller & Partners Ltd* [1964] AC 465, 503 *per* Lord Morris; see also p 514 *per* Lord Hodson. The rule was limited (by a majority of 3–2) in *Mutual Life & Citizens Assurance Co Ltd* v *Evatt* [1971] AC 793 (PC) to cases in which the defendant was in the "business" of providing such advice. The case of the insurance agent is, arguably, within this limit. In any event the limit was rejected: *Esso Petroleum Co Ltd* v *Mardon* [1976] QB 801 (CA); *Chaudry* v *Prabhakar* [1988] 3 All ER 718 (CA).

27. *Esso Petroleum Co Ltd* v *Mardon* [1976] QB 801 (CA); *Howard Marine & Dredging Co Ltd* v *Ogden (Excavations) Ltd* [1978] QB 574 (CA).

28. *Hedley Byrne* (above).

29. *Cherry* v *Allied Insurance Brokers* [1978] 1 Lloyd's Rep 274. *Fine's Flowers* v *General Accident* (1974) 49 DLR (3d) 641 (Ont).

   A similar duty was imposed on insurers in *Banque Keyser Ullmann SA* v *Skandia (UK) Ins Co Ltd* [1987] 1 Lloyd's Rep. 69; but rejected on appeal: [1988] 2 Lloyd's Rep 513 (CA); [1991] 2 AC 249.

30. *Caparo Industries plc* v *Dickman* [1990] 2 AC 605, 638 *per* Lord Oliver.

31. *Hedley Byrne & Co Ltd* v *Heller & Partners Ltd* [1964] AC 465, 503 *per* Lord Morris. Direct contact between claimant and defendant is not necessary: *Smith* v *Bush* [1990] 1 AC 831.

32. *Reid* v *Traders General Insurance Co* (1963) 41 DLR (2d) 148 (NS—motor). As to when an agent has this role, see below, 10–2.

33. Generally, see *Ministry of Housing & Local Govt.* v *Sharp* [1970] 2 QB 223 (CA); *Lawton* v *BOC Transhield Ltd* [1987] 2 All ER 608.

benefit from the insurance (9–2C2), and to the recipient of a document put into circulation, such as the subscriber to a slip at Lloyd's (9–2C3).

9–2C1 Insurers

Early statements[34] indicate that the agent of the insured owes no duty of care to the insurer. Today, however, when an agent makes a negligent misstatement while acting in the course of his authority to make a contract, the principal is liable under the Misrepresentation Act 1967, section 2(1), while the agent may be liable in tort for the negligent misstatement.[35] When the agent is acting within the scope of his authority, the insurer can avoid the insurance contract (or reject the claim) and is unlikely to suffer loss. An action in tort remains a possibility, when the agent has not acted within the scope of his authority or, to take a different and particular instance, perhaps also when a Lloyd's broker gives a signing indication to one writing a line on the slip proffered by the broker.[36]

9–2C2 Intended Beneficiaries

In the United States, agents, who have wrongfully failed to obtain insurance cover, have been held liable to third parties intended to benefit from the insurance.[37] In England, the rule of privity of contract blocks liability in contract to the third party; however, the agent may be liable to the third party in tort. In *Ross* v *Caunters*[38] Megarry V-C decided that when a person undertakes to a client to carry through a transaction which is to benefit a third party, the duty of care which binds the agent to his client is one which may be extended to the third party. For such a duty there are the following requirements.[39] First, there must be a close degree of proximity; the agent's contemplation of the third party must be actual, nominate and direct: see above, 9–2C. Second, this proximity must be a product of the duty of care owed to the insured, with no conflict between the interests of the insured and of the third party as regards the performance of the mandate. Third, there must be no spectre of imposing on the agent an uncertain and unlimited liability: the third party must be the whole or part of a determinate and very limited class, although it is not necessary that the agent should know the precise identity of the third party.[40] Fourth, an action by the third party is

---

34. *Empress Assurance Corp Ltd* v *CT Bowring & Co Ltd* (1905) 11 Com Cas 107, *per* Kennedy J (re); *Glasgow Assurance Corp Ltd* v *Symondsen & Co* (1911) 16 Com Cas 109, 110 *per* Scrutton J (re).
35. *The Skopas, Resolute Maritime Inc* v *Nippon Kaiji Kyokai* [1983] 2 All ER 1, 4 *per* Mustill J; Owen [1984] CLJ 27.
36. *The Zephyr* [1984] 1 Lloyd's Rep 58 (re). On appeal this question did not fall to be decided, but the doubt expressed by Mustill LJ ([1985] 2 Lloyd's Rep 529, 537–538), i.e., that the undertaking was essentially contractual rather than tortious, is persuasive.
  Cf also *Pryke* v *Gibbs Hartley Cooper Ltd* [1991] 1 Lloyd's Rep 602 (re), in which *Empress Assurance* (above) was applied, however, it was held that a Lloyd's broker owed a duty of care to Lloyd's underwriters.
37. *Gothberg* v *Nemerovski*, 208 NE 2d 12 (Ill, 1965); *Hamer* v *Kahn*, 404 So 2d 847 (Fla, 1981).
38. [1980] Ch 297; followed in *Gartside* v *Sheffield, Young & Ellis* [1983] NZLR 37 (CA), but not in *Seale* v *Perry* [1982] VR 193. USA: the agent may be liable in these circumstances in tort: *Duggan* v *Rooney*, 749 F Supp 234 (D Kan, 1990—life).
39. *Ross* v *Caunters* [1980] Ch 297, as distinguished in *Clarke* v *Bruce Lance & Co* [1988] 1 All ER 364 (CA). *Ross* v *Caunters* was upheld by the Court of Appeal in *White* v *Jones* ([1993] 3 All ER 481). In each case the defendant was a solicitor.
40. See Baughen (1992) 8 PN 99 discussing *Smith* v *Claremont Haynes & Co, The Times* 3 September 1991.

unlikely to succeed, if the agent is also liable to the insured for the same loss and there is a risk that the agent might have to pay damages twice over.

Failure of the fourth requirement was just one of the reasons why the claims by third parties were struck out in *Verderame*.[41] The claims were based in tort against not only the insurer but also the broker and by not only the company, which had sought cover, but also the two sole directors and shareholders of the company. The Court of Appeal granted the application of the broker to have the claims of the latter against them struck out because, whereas the broker owed a duty to the company, the broker did not owe a duty to the company's shareholder or directors.

In *Macmillan* v *Knott Becker Scott*[42] Evans J held that a Lloyd's broker, whose negligence in the arrangement of liability insurance was assumed, was not liable to a third party (underwriting syndicate), to whom the insured (another Lloyd's broker now in liquidation) was liable, in circumstances in which the insurance, if it had been properly arranged, would have covered that liability. Although there was no question of double jeopardy,[43] and although the third party's loss was foreseeable and there was the necessary degree of proximity between broker and third party,[44] it was not just and reasonable that the broker should owe a duty to the third party: the attendant liability "would disturb the balance of legal relationships established by the different contracts, in this quintessentially commercial context".[45] To disturb the contractual structure would not matter, however, "if the requirements of justice or even commercial convenience so required. Such were the circumstances in *Ross* v *Caunters*, in which the Vice-Chancellor was clearly influenced by the fact that the intended beneficiary under the will, who alone suffered any loss, would have no way of securing the lost benefit unless the negligent solicitor was liable to him".[46] In the instant case the claimant could sue the liquidator of the insured and the liquidator could claim to recover that loss from the defendant broker. The decision thus falls in with earlier cases which, in the view of the judge, showed that "where there is a contractual chain or structure of an established kind the Courts are unlikely, to put it no higher, to hold that duties of care arise in favour of other parties, absent any direct contractual link, in respect of pure economic loss".[47]

By contrast, in *Punjab National Bank* v *De Boinville*[48] a broker was held liable to the assignee of insurance, where the broker knew that the insurance had been contracted on the instructions and for the benefit of the assignee. The claimant bank confirmed a letter of credit and in that connection agreed to negotiate bills of exchange drawn on Sudanese buyers *inter alia* on the security, first, of a promise by the Bank of Sudan that the bills would be honoured at maturity and, second, of insurance against non-fulfilment of that promise. The insurance was taken out by the buyers and, as anticipated by all relevant parties including the brokers, assigned to the claimant bank. Staughton LJ observed that, in terms of the law after *Caparo*[49] and *Murphy*,[50]

41. *Verderame* v *Commercial Union Assurance Co plc* [1992] BCLC 793 (CA—theft).
42. [1990] 1 Lloyd's Rep 98.
43. p 101.
44. p 108.
45. p 110.
46. *Ibid*.
47. p 105. See also *Pryke* v *Gibbs Hartley Cooper Ltd* [1991] 1 Lloyd's Rep 602 (re).
48. [1992] 3 All ER 104.
49. *Caparo Industries plc* v *Dickman* [1990] 2 AC 605, 618 *per* Lord Bridge.
50. *Murphy* v *Brentwood DC* [1991] 1 AC 398 (HL).

"to hold that a substantial creditor of an insurance broker's client is necessarily owed a duty of care in tort might well be more than a justifiable increment" extending the established category of duty owed by a broker.[51] However, an extension would be justified as regards a "specific person who [the broker] knows is to become an assignee of the policy, at all events if (as in this case) that person actively participates in giving instructions for the insurance to the broker's knowledge".[52] In this case it was against the very possibility that a remedy against the client/buyers would be worthless that the claimant bank required insurance and assignment.

9–2C3 Documents in Circulation

In *The Zephyr*[53] it was argued that, if a broker owed a duty of care with regard to a signing indication made to the leading underwriter, the duty was also owed to other subscribers to the slip. Mustill LJ observed[54] that

"a representation contained in a document which the marker [sic] knows is intended to be put in circulation may found a liability if the document comes into the hands of a third party who relies upon it, if the circumstances are such as to show that the possibility of such reliance was within the contemplation of the maker."

9–2D Reliance

The claimant must have placed reasonable reliance on the statement, and his reliance must have been a real and substantial though not necessarily decisive cause[55] of the claimant's loss; an exception is found in *Ross v Caunters*[56] in which the breach of duty must have caused loss, but actual reliance is not required. Reliance is not reasonable nor caused by the misstatement, if the untruth should have been discovered by the claimant or his agents.[57]

9–2E Disclaimer by the Agent

If the informed person disclaims liability in clear terms, that disclaimer is effective,[58] either as a defence to suit or to negate the existence of any duty of care at all. If the disclaimer operates as a defence, it is seen as an exclusion of liability subject[59] to the Unfair Contract Terms Act 1977, whereby the exclusion is ineffective in so far as it is

---

51. Emphasis added. Mann LJ and Dillon LJ agreed with the judgment given by Staughton L J.

52. *Idem per* Dillon LJ. Staughton LJ added: "In such a case there is a rather greater degree of proximity than that which existed between the solicitor and the beneficiary under the will in *Ross v Caunters* [1980] Ch 297, for the beneficiary may have known nothing of the will or the solicitor and would not have derived any benefit from it if it had later been revoked." *Macmillan v Knott Becker Scott* (above) was not mentioned.

53. [1985] 2 Lloyd's Rep 529 (CA—re); the argument was rejected on the facts. *Cf* also *Pryke v Gibbs Hartley Cooper Ltd* [1991] 1 Lloyd's Rep 602 (re).

54. p 539. He continued: "A statement in a bill of lading as to the order and condition of the goods shipped might fall into this category".

55. *J E B Fasteners Ltd v Marks Bloom & Co* [1983] 1 All ER 583 (CA); *The Arta* [1983] 2 Lloyd's Rep 405. *Sulzinger v Alexander Ltd* (1971) 24 DLR (3d) 137 (Ont).

56. Above, 9–2C. This difference stems from the basis of *Ross v Caunters*, not in the tort of negligent misstatement but in broader principles derived from the duty of care and the tort of negligence.

57. *The Arta* [1983] 2 Lloyd's Rep 405.

58. *Hedley Byrne & Co Ltd v Heller & Partners Ltd* [1964] AC 465.

59. A disclaimer was subject to the Act in *Smith v Bush* [1990] 1 AC 831.

unreasonable.[60] If, however, it negates the very existence of the duty, there being no duty to exclude, it is not subject to the Act at all.[61]

9–2F Limitation of Actions

If the cause of action brought against an agent is breach of contract, whether or not that breach is said to amount to negligence,[62] the limitation period is that stated by section 5 of the Limitation Act 1980: six years from the date on which the cause of action accrued.

If the cause of action brought against the agent is the tort of negligence, including negligent misstatement, the limitation period is stated by section 14A of the Limitation Act 1980: not more than "six years from the date on which the cause of action accrued"[63] or "three years from the starting date", whichever period expires later. The cause of action accrues when the claimant suffers loss as a result of the agent's breach of duty. The starting date is the earliest date on which the claimant "had both the knowledge required for bringing an action for damages in respect of the relevant damage and a right to bring such an action".[64]

As regards the starting date and the requisite knowledge,[65] the material facts are "such facts about the damage as would lead a reasonable person who had suffered such damage to consider it sufficiently serious to justify his instituting proceedings for damages against a defendant who did not dispute liability and was able to satisfy a judgment".[66] In *Iron Trade Mutual Ins Co Ltd* v *J K Buckenham Ltd* the "damage" was the fact that the reinsurance contracts were voidable, so the question for the court became "when did the plaintiffs have sufficient knowledge of the facts concerning the voidability of the contract as would lead a reasonable person to consider it sufficiently serious to justify the taking of proceedings?"[67]

As regards the time when the cause of action accrued, this is an issue that arose in both *Iron Trades Mutual* (above) and *Islander Trucking Ltd* v *Hogg, Robinson & Gardner Mountain (Marine) Ltd*.[68] Action was brought both for breach of contract and in tort against brokers in respect of insurance that did not pay because of misrepresentation and non-disclosure by the brokers who placed it. The brokers sought to

---

60. On factors affecting reasonableness see Yates & Hawkins, *Standard Business Contracts* (London, 1986).

61. In terms of section 2(2) there is no "liability for negligence" to exclude. This view, which is not new, was applied in *Harris* v *Wyre Forest DC* [1988] QB 835 (CA), but was rejected in *Smith* v *Bush* [1990] 1 AC 831.

62. Not being an action in respect of personal injuries to which section 11 applies. And not being an action framed in contract, where the alleged breach of contract was founded on negligent conduct: *Iron Trade Mutual Ins Co Ltd* v *J K Buckenham Ltd* (below). For criticism of this decision, see O'Dair (1992) 55 MLR 405, 409 ff.

63. This is also the general period for actions in tort: under the Limitation Act 1980 section 2, an action founded on tort shall not be brought after the expiration of six years from the date on which the cause of action accrued.

64. Section 14A(5). By section 14A(10), "a person's knowledge includes knowledge which he might reasonably have been expected to acquire (a) from facts observable or ascertainable by him; or (b) from facts ascertainable by him with the help of appropriate expert advice which it is reasonable for him to seek; but a person shall not be taken by virtue of this subsection to have knowledge of a fact ascertainable only with the help of expert advice so long as he shall have taken all reasonable steps to obtain (and, where appropriate, to act on) that advice".

65. Section 14A(5).

66. Section 14A(6).

67. [1990] 1 All ER 808, 824 per Kenneth Rokison QC, sitting as a Deputy Judge of the High Court.

68. [1990] 1 All ER 826. The claim concerned carriers' liability insurance.

have the action in tort struck out, as being time barred, on the basis that the cause of action accrued when the voidable insurance had been contracted. The claimants argued that their action was in time, as the cause of action did not accrue until the insurance had been actually avoided. It was held in each case that the cause of action accrued when the broker procured a contract of insurance that was voidable rather than valid: this was when the claimants suffered financial loss,[69] as the contract of insurance afforded them lesser contractual rights and was less valuable than that which the brokers were required to procure,[70] even though the extent of the loss would not become apparent until later, if and when the insurers elected to avoid the contract.

These decisions followed earlier decisions concerned with the negligence of solicitors,[71] which may "be put on one or both of two bases. The first is because the chose in action which the client acquires . . . is regarded as a form of property . . . and which is found to be devalued, that is to say worth either nothing or less than it would be worth if free from the defect which has resulted from the solicitor's negligence. The second possible basis is perhaps this: in the case of a claim against a solicitor . . . the plaintiff is entitled to recover for economic loss, as distinct from any injury to person or property cases".[72] The analogy with the negligence of solicitors was close for, if, having unwittingly contracted a voidable insurance contract, the insured "was then negligently advised by the solicitor that the policy was effective and not voidable it would be unsatisfactory if, for the purposes of a claim against the solicitor, he was held to have suffered damage but for the purposes of a claim against the broker he was held not to have done so sufficiently to support a negligence claim".[73]

9–3 LIABILITY OF THE AGENT IN CONTRACT

Agency arises by agreement, which may or may not be embodied in a binding contract between principal (the client) and agent. In the case of insurance agency, a contract is commonly assumed to exist and to which the ordinary principles of the law of contract apply.[74] If so, it is obvious that there is a contractual obligation to carry out the mandate, for example, to arrange insurance cover.[75] The scope of the mandate is a question of fact, but certain instructions imply duties that are not necessarily articulated.[76] It is a matter of interpretation of the promise in each case whether the agent has

69. *Forster* v *Outred & Co* [1982] 2 All ER 753 (CA).
70. The claimants did not receive that which the brokers ought to have obtained for them, but something different, something less valuable: see in this sense *Baker* v *Ollard & Bentley* (1982) 126 SJ 593 (CA); *Moore & Co Ltd* v *Ferrier* [1988] 1 All ER 400, 410 *per* Dunn LJ, 411 *per* Bingham LJ (CA).
71. Respectively *Forster* and *Baker* (above).
72. *Islander Trucking* (above) p 831 *per* Evans J.
73. p 834 *per* Evans J.
74. *Marker* v *Preferred Fire Ins Co*, 506 P 2d 1163 (Kan, 1973—tornado).
75. As regards the general law of agency, this proposition is developed in Bowstead, pp 138 ff. USA *idem: Flournoy* v *Hewgley*, 234 F 2d 213 (10 Cir, 1956—life).
76. See above, 7–2 and 7–3. In New York an agent instructed to procure is not obliged to volunteer advice outside the immediate scope of the mandate: *Callahan* v *American Motorists Ins Co*, 89 NYS 2d 1005 (1968); the court rejected the argument that the agent, who procured a homeowner's policy, and who knew that the insured also conducted business from the premises, should have ensured that the client was covered against risks incidental to business use: the client had not requested business cover and the agent had no reason to believe that he was the client's only agent.

undertaken to achieve the task in question, or to use best endeavours, reasonable care and skill, to that end.[77]

Although it is generally assumed that there is a contract between client and agent, this assumption is not without technical difficulty: what is the consideration moving from client to agent? We may distinguish four situations.

(a) In the first situation the mandate is, for example, to arrange insurance, to handle a claim, or to make a report on the client's existing insurance arrangements and the agent receives remuneration from the proposer himself.[78] There is clearly a contract between client and agent.

(b) The second situation is a less simple version of the first: the agent does various things for the client, including arranging insurance, receiving payment for the entire service.[79] There is clearly a contract between client and agent.

(c) In the third, common and simple situation the agent agrees to seek insurance for the client, and the agent is paid commission, if and when a contract of insurance is concluded. This might be seen as a contract, whereby, if the agent finds acceptable insurance, either the client promises to pay a sum which will be shared by insurer and agent, or a sum to the insurer, from whom the agent will eventually receive commission. The agent receives no money consideration directly from the client, for it is generally assumed[80] that the agent is paid commission by the insurer. Indeed, the client is not generally bound to take[81] one or other of the policies of insurance suggested by the agent, so that the agent earns commission. *Prima facie* the client is not bound to do anything that will produce the benefit (commission), which the agent wants. Before the insurance has been concluded, the most that can be said is that the client provides the agent with an opportunity to earn commission.[82] The value of that opportunity depends on the seriousness of the client. Is he therefore obliged to be serious, and not capricious?

There is no general duty in English law to perform contracts in good faith.[83] An

---

77. *Eagle Star Ins Co Ltd* v *National Westminster Finance Australia Ltd* (1985) 58 ALR 165, 174 *per* Lord Roskill (PC). Compare *Transport & Trading Co Ltd* v *Olivier Co Ltd* (1925) 21 Ll L Rep 379 and *Avondale Blouse Co Ltd* v *Williamson & Town* (1948) 81 Ll L Rep 492.

78. *Turpin* v *Bilton* (1843) 5 Man & G 455: broker, remunerated by client (p 466), to effect marine insurance; action clearly based in contract (p 470). Similar cases are *Hurrell* v *Bullard* (1863) 3 F & F 445 (hull); *Transport & Trading Co Ltd* v *Olivier & Co Ltd* (1925) 21 Ll L Rep 379 (hull).

79. For example to repair and insure a vehicle: *McNeil* v *Millen & Co* [1907] 2 IR 328 (CA); to insure and sell goods: *Callander* v *Oelrichs* (1838) 5 Bing (NC) 58 (cargo); also *Great Western Ins Co* v *Cunliffe* (1874) LR 9 Ch App 525 (re); *Hood* v *West End Motor Car Packing Co* [1917] 2 KB 38 (CA—cargo).

80. For example *Cunliffe* (above) p 539 *per* Mellish LJ.

81. *Friedman* v *Markman*, 201 NYS 2d 743 (1960—life); *Arden* v *Freydberg*, 214 NYS 2d 400 (1961—life). The same is true of renewal: *Beidler & Bookmyer Inc* v *Universal Ins Co*, 134 F 2d 828 (2 Cir, 1943—cargo).

82. The opportunity to earn a reward is itself of economic value and can constitute consideration: *Chaplin* v *Hicks* [1911] 2 KB 786 (CA).
"The consideration which flows to the broker in return for his promise to procure insurance is said to be the expectation of the broker of receiving a commission or profit when the insurance policy is obtained"—*Marker* v *Preferred Fire Ins Co*, 506 P 2d 1163, 1168 (Kan, 1973—tornado). But the court continued (*ibid*): "The agreement by the proposed insured to pay the premium and accept a delivered policy is a real and not just a technical consideration." A similar statement is found in *Lawrence* v *Francis*, 267 SW 2d 306, 309 (Ark, 1954—fire).
Consideration might also be found in a promise by the client not to employ another agent to carry out the mandate, at least for a reasonable time, or a promise to release the agent from his obligation (below, 9–4B) not to make a profit from the performance of his fiduciary duty as agent.

83. *Interfoto Picture Library* v *Stiletto Visual Programmes Ltd* [1989] QB 433, 439 (CA). Clarke [1993] HKLJ 318.

alleged contract to negotiate a contract in good faith has been held void for uncertainty.[84] One view is that the principal will only be liable for preventing the agent from earning his remuneration when the implication of a promise that he will not do so is necessary to give business efficacy to the contract, or otherwise to effect the intention of the parties.[85] In general, the courts are unlikely to imply a duty as a matter of business efficacy which requires a proposer to justify his decision not to go ahead with an insurance proposal.[86] The exception is when the mandate is relatively specific about the act to be done or the cover to be obtained and the agent carries out that mandate: then it has been held that the client is liable to the agent, if he refuses to go ahead and enable the agent to earn commission, and the damages were the amount of commission lost.[87]

The awkwardness of this analysis suggests that contract is not the best legal basis for the duties of the agent. Still, it is commonly assumed both by writers[88] and by courts[89] that the agent is liable to the client in contract. Moreover, the current trend is to reaffirm the proposition that, if the claimant has suffered economic loss, his claim should be in contract rather than in tort.[90] Accordingly this chapter proceeds on the basis that this assumption is correct; that the agent has a contractual duty to carry out his mandate.

(d) A fourth situation arises, when there is a contract between agent and client, for example, to procure insurance. The agent does so and later promises to do something else, but does not do it. An action for breach of the later promise may be met with the defence, lack of consideration. Decisions in the United States suggest that this defence will succeed, unless the later act was contemplated as something the agent might be expected to do as part of the earlier contract[91]; or the later act was part of a

84. See references below, 11–3C1.
85. Bowstead, pp 210 ff.
86. "The mere fact that a prospective customer requests proposals from a broker places the customer under no obligation to accept the proposal when made . . . Any and all proposals may be rejected for any reason and without reason."—*Hanley* v *Marsh & McLennan*, 117 P 2d 69, 73 (Cal, 1941—fire). See also *inter alia Arden* v *Freydberg*, 214 NYS 2d 400 (1961—life).
87. *Smyth, Sandford & Gerard Inc* v *Missouri-Kansas-Texas Ry Co*, 72 F 2d 216 (2 Cir, 1934)
88. For example, Hodgin, p 50.
89. For example, *O'Connor* v *Kirby & Co* [1971] 1 Lloyd's Rep 454, 460 *per* Megaw LJ (CA—motor); *Wilson* v *Avec Audio-Visual Equipment Ltd* [1974] 1 Lloyd's Rep 81, 82 *per* Edmund Davies LJ (CA—burglary); *Ackbar* v *Green & Co Ltd* [1975] QB 582 (motor). *Ogden & Co Pty Ltd* v *Reliance Fire Sprinkler Co Pty Ltd* [1975] 1 Lloyd's Rep 52, 67 (NSW—liability), holding that the broker was under an implied contractual term to exercise reasonable care and skill; it left open (pp 73–74) whether in these circumstances there could also be an action in tort. *Cf Norwest Refrigeration Services Pty Ltd* v *Bain Dawes Pty Ltd* (1984) 157 CLR 149 (HCA—hull).
In some cases a broker has been found guilty of both a breach of contract and of negligence: *Strong and Pearl* v *Allison & Co Ltd* (1926) 25 Ll L Rep 504, 507 *per* Greer J (yacht). See also *Osman* v *Moss Ltd* [1970] 1 Lloyd's Rep 313 (CA—motor); *Cherry* v *Allied Ins Brokers Ltd* [1978] 1 Lloyd's Rep 274, 280 *per* Cantley J (consequential loss).
USA: the agent is potentially liable in contract and in negligence: *MacDonald* v *Carpenter & Pelton Inc*, 298 NYS 2d 780 (1969—fire); *Fli-Back Co* v *Philadelphia Manufacturers Mutual Ins Co*, 12 F 2d 214, 217 (4 Cir, 1974—business interruption); or negligent misstatement: *Fiorentino* v *Travelers Ins Co*, 548 F Supp 1364 (ED Pa, 1978—liability)
90. See, for example, *The Zephyr* [1985] 2 Lloyd's Rep 529, 538 *per* Mustill LJ (CA—re).
91. *Marker* v *Preferred Fire Ins Co*, 506 P 2d 1163 (Kan, 1973—tornado): a subsequent promise, to notify the client when the insurance expired so that the client (not the agent) could arrange renewal, was not binding; it would have been different, if the agent could have expected to handle the renewal and earn commission. See also *Williams Fruit Co* v *Hanover Ins Co*, 74 P 2d 577 (Wash, 1970—fire).
An English court is likely to take the same view on the ground that, unless the later act could be implied as part of the earlier contract, there was no consideration, the earlier consideration provided by the client being past consideration and hence no consideration: *Re Casey's Patents* [1892] 1 Ch 104 (CA).

continuing relationship, such that the agent could expect to be remunerated at a date later than the act in question, for example, by commission on renewal of insurance.[92]

9–3A Care and Skill

Whether his duty is based in contract or in tort, the agent does not usually promise absolutely to carry out his mandate but to exercise reasonable care, skill[93] and speed[94] to that end. Reasonable speed is assessed with reference to the difficulty of performing the mandate, the day and the time.[95] The standard of care and skill traditionally required of a contractual agent was greater than that required of a gratuitous agent. At a general level, it is now clear[96] that the level of care and skill expected is the same, whether the agency is based on a contract or not and whether the agent is an insurance agent or any other kind of agent.[97] Still, a court may derive assistance from the ABI Code of Practice for All Intermediaries: because it is part of the context in which an insurance agent operates, and because, in deciding whether a professional man has been negligent, a court should be careful not to adopt too high or too perfectionist a standard, reference to the Code helps the court to adopt a realistic standard.[98]

The kind of care and skill is that which can reasonably be expected of a person having the skill (and knowledge) that can reasonably be expected of an insurance agent at that time.[99] However, if agents step outside the borders of insurance agency and, for example, advise on matters of law affecting insurance, it has been held[100] that they "are responsible for seeing that they are equipped with a reasonable degree of skill and a reasonable stock of information so as to render it reasonably safe for them to give that particular piece of advice". Within the field of insurance agency, conduct will be assessed *inter alia* by reference to the normal practice of agents in a given situation.[101] If the profession is divided, but as many skilful and experienced agents would

---

92. *Marker* (above).

93. *Smith* v *Cologan* (1788) 2 TR 188n (cargo) in which Buller J said that the foundation of the action against the agent was negligence. See also *Holland* v *Russell* (1863) 4 B & S 14, 16 *per* Erle CJ (hull). *Baxter & Co* v *Jones* (1903) 6 OLR 360 (Ont—fire). *Consolidated Sun Ray Inc* v *Lea*, 276 Supp 132 (ED Pa, 1967—fire), affirmed 401 F 2d 650 (3 Cir, 1968), *cert* den 393 US 1050.

94. *London Borough of Bromley* v *Ellis* [1971] 1 Lloyd's Rep 97 (CA—motor). *Cf United Mills Agencies Ltd* v *Harvey, Bray & Co* [1951] 2 Lloyd's Rep 631, 638 *per* McNair J (fire) in which the non-performance of an instruction by the proposer was viewed as a question of negligent failure to appreciate the nature of the instruction.

95. *Cock, Russell & Co* v *Bray, Gibb & Co Ltd* (1920) 3 Ll L Rep 71, 72 *per* Bailhache J.

96. *Forsik Vesta* v *Butcher* [1988] 1 Lloyd's Rep 19 (CA—re), affirmed [1989] AC 582. See also *Smith* v *Cologan* (1788) 2 TR 188n (cargo) *per* Buller J, with whom Lord Kenyon agreed in *Wilkinson* v *Coverdale* (1793) 1 Esp 75, 76 (fire). *Cf Chaudry* v *Prabhakar* [1988] 3 All ER 718 (CA).

97. *Harvester Trucking Co Ltd* v *Davis*, [1991] 2 Lloyd's Rep 638, 643 per Judge Diamond (goods in transit).

98. *Ibid.*

99. *Connecticut Fire Ins Co* v *Kavanagh* [1892] AC 473, 480 *per* Lord Watson (PC—fire). *Butler* v *Scott* 417 F 2d 471, 473 (10 Cir, 1969—fire).

100. *Sarginson Bros* v *Keith Moulton & Co Ltd* (1942) 73 Ll L Rep 104, 107 *per* Hallett J, who went on to point out that brokers could always place a caveat on their advice or consult a solicitor. *Idem: Fanhaven Pty Ltd* v *Bain Dawes Northern Pty Ltd* [1982] 2 NSWLR 57, 65.

101. For example, (a) to insert a particular clause: *Mallough* v *Barber* (1815) 4 Camp 150 (hull); (b) if cover of an established type is sought, the agent must get the usual terms for that kind of cover: *Vale & Co* v *Van Oppen & Co Ltd* (1921) 37 TLR 367 (cargo); unless, of course, the parties agree that the agent shall seek different terms: *Yuill* v *Scott Robson* [1907] 1 KB 685 (cargo). See also *Harvester Trucking* (above).

have agreed with the judgement of the agent impugned as would not, that judgement does not fall below the standard required.[102]

The care to be exercised by an agent with the requisite skill and knowledge depends on negligence factors, such as (a) the probability of loss if care is not taken; (b) the amount of loss if care is not taken; (c) the susceptibility of the proposer; and (d) the general practice followed by a responsible section of the profession. On this point the codes of practice[103] adopted by the profession will be of special importance. If, for example, the agent knows that the proposer's understanding of affairs or of the English language is poor, he must take special steps to ensure that the client's needs are covered and that the client has understood the agent's advice.[104]

9-4 THE FIDUCIARY DUTIES OF THE AGENT

Agents generally owe the duties of a fiduciary. As a person owing fiduciary duties, the insurance agent owes a duty of care and skill (above, 9-3A), as well as a duty to act *bona fide* (below, 9-4A), while not placing himself in a position in which his fiduciary duty to the client may conflict with his own interests, in particular, his duties (in which he has the interest of remuneration) to other clients (below, 9-4B).

9-4A Bona Fides

The agent must act *bona fide* in what he believes to be the interests of his client.[105] The greater the reliance placed by the client on the agent's advice and judgement, the greater the scope for his discretion, and it is then that the duty to act *bona fide* is important.

9-4B No Conflict of Duty and Interest

"It is an inflexible rule of a Court of Equity that a person in a fiduciary position, . . . is not, unless otherwise expressly provided, entitled to make a profit; he is not allowed to put himself in a position where his interest and duty conflict."[106] But there is controversy over when this conflict occurs. On the stricter view, it is enough that there is a

---

102. *Chapman* v *Walton* (1833) 10 Bing NC 57, 63–64 *per* Tindal CJ (cargo); *Robinson* v *Post Office* [1974] 2 All ER 737, 745 *per* Orr LJ (CA); *Luxmoore-May* v *Messenger May Baverstock* [1990] 1 All ER 1067 (CA).

103. *Harvester Trucking Co Ltd* v *Davis*, [1991] 2 Lloyd's Rep 638, 643 per Judge Diamond (goods in transit).

104. *Osman* v *Moss Ltd* [1970] 1 Lloyd's Rep 313, 315 *per* Sachs LJ (CA—motor); *cf* p 318 *per* Phillimore LJ. See also *O'Connor Kirby & Co* [1971] 1 Lloyd's Rep 454, 459 *per* Karminski LJ (CA—motor). Generally see *Geier* v *Kujawa* [1970] 1 Lloyd's Rep 364. However, the circumstances may permit the agent to assume that a proposer will take steps to have, for example, letters explained to him by a third party.

105. This follows from his designation as a fiduciary: *Cook* v *Deeks* [1916] 1 AC 554 (PC). "The relationship between a competent insurance broker and his client is a relationship of personal trust and confidence"—*Lynd* v *Heffernan*, 146 NYS 2d 113, 115 (1955—liability). See also *Fli-Back Co Inc* v *Philadelphia Manufacturers Mutual Ins Co*, 502 F 2d 214, 217 (4 Cir, 1974—business interruption).

106 *Bray* v *Ford* [1896] AC 44, 51 *per* Lord Herschell.

mere possibility of conflict.[107] The other view is that there can be no breach of duty unless there is a "real sensible possibility" of conflict of duty and interest.[108]

On the stricter view, but not the other, certain collateral transactions are barred to the agent. For example, an assessor, having persuaded the client to adopt his *bona fide* advice not to accept reinstatement of damaged property, cannot then buy the salvaged property himself—the mere possibility of acquisition himself might be thought to have affected the nature and force of his advice. Again, an agent may not be allowed to use information received in the course of his agency to speculate in the shares of his client.

An agent in actual or potential breach of this duty may safeguard his position by disclosing it to his principal and obtaining his consent,[109] unless the agent has also broken his duty of *bona fides*.[110]

9–4B1 Competing Employment

Agents rarely act solely for one client. If the agent may serve two masters, there remains the question whether he can do so at the same time or in quick succession without conflict leading to breach of duty to one or both. In *Anglo-African Merchants Ltd* v *Bayley*,[111] counsel conceded that in all matters relating to the placing of the insurance the broker is the agent of the proposer, but argued that, when a claim arose, the same broker may become the agent of both insured and insurer. Megaw J applied a statement by Scrutton LJ[112] and concluded[113] that if

"an insurance broker discloses to his client that he wishes to be free to act in the way suggested, and if the would-be insured, fully informed as to the broker's intention to accept such instructions from the insurers and as to the possible implications of such collaboration between his agent and the opposite party, is prepared to agree that the broker may so act, good and well. In the absence of such express and fully informed consent, in my opinion it would be a breach of duty on the part of the insurance broker so to act."

107. *Keech* v *Sandford* (1726) Cas Temp King 61; *Parker* v *McKenna* (1874) LR 10 Ch 96, 124–125 *per* James LJ; *Boardman* v *Phipps* [1967] 2 AC 46, 123 *per* Lord Hodson, p 103 *per* Lord Cohen; *Industrial Development Consultants Ltd* v *Cooley* [1972] 2 All ER 162. Generally see Jones (1968) 84 LQR 472, 473–474 and cases cited. The force of this view depends significantly on whether and to what extent fiduciaries, including agents, are subject to the same strict rules as trustees; see Sealy [1962] CLJ 69.
   USA: similar statements can be found in cases concerning company directors, for example, *Irving Trust* v *Deutsch*, 73 F 2d 121 (2 Cir, 1934); *Guth* v *Loft Inc*, 5 A 2d 503 (Del, 1939).
108. Jones (1968) 84 LQR 472, 478, citing *Boardman* v *Phipps* [1967] 2 AC 46, 124 *per* Lord Upjohn (dissenting). It is possible to find support for this view in *Queensland Mines Ltd* v *Hudson* (1978) 52 AJLR 399 (PC), also reported by Sullivan, 42 MLR 711 (1979); however, the decision might also be seen as breach under the strict view, but breach cured by disclosure to the party to whom the duty was owed i.e., the company represented by its shareholders acting informally.
109. *Regal Hastings Ltd* v *Gulliver* [1967] 2 AC 134n.
110. *Cook* v *Deeks* [1916] 1 AC 554 (PC); *Parke* v *Daily News Ltd* [1962] Ch 927. Above, 9–4A.
111. [1970] 1 QB 311, 322–323: When a Lloyd's underwriter (unsuccessfully) pleaded non-disclosure by the plaintiff insured, the (general) brokers and the Lloyd's brokers, both brokers being held (p 318) agents of the insured, made their files available to the underwriter. Further, the Lloyd's broker commissioned an assessor's report on the plaintiff's claim and refused to show it to the plaintiff insured, conduct which was condemned by the judge. See also *North & South Trust Co* v *Berkeley* [1971] 1 WLR 470 (goods in transit); *Eagle Star Ins Co Ltd* v *Spratt* [1971] 2 Lloyd's Rep 116, 133 *per* Megaw LJ (CA—re); *Forsik Vesta* v *Butcher* [1986] 2 Lloyd's Rep 179, 195 *per* Hobhouse J (re). Generally see Bowstead, pp 34 ff, 188 ff.
112. *Fullwood* v *Hurley* [1928] 1 KB 498, 502. See also *North & South Trust* v *Berkeley* [1971] 1 WLR 470, 482–484 *per* Donaldson J. Generally see Halsbury, Vol 1, No 787.
   USA: The agent must avoid conflict of duty and interest: *American Eagle Fire Ins Co* v *Burdine*, 200 F 2d 26 (10 Cir, 1952—fire). If there is a possibility of conflict, consent is required: *Westchester Fire Ins Co* v *Conlon*, 92 F 2d 160 (3 Cir, 1937—fire), *cert den* 302 US 751: acquiescence may be enough.
113. [1970] 1 QB 311, 322–323

As to the implications of such collaboration, Lord Jauncey has warned that, as the consent of the principal must be given in the knowledge of the conflict, that implies knowledge that as a result the agent "may be disabled from disclosing to each party the full knowledge which [the agent] possesses as to the transaction or may be disabled from giving advice to one party which conflicts with the interest of the other".[113a]

If the agent acts in breach of this duty, his action is not a nullity.[114] The position[115] is that (a) the agent is liable to the client (the true principal) for loss resulting from the agent's inability, due to the conflict of duties, fully to perform his duty to the client: below, 9–6A. (b) The client may have an action to compel the agent to account and hand over any benefit received in the course of the unlawful agency: below, 9–6B. (c) If the agent has been mandated to make a contract between the client and the person for whom he has been acting unlawfully as agent, the client may rescind the contract: below, 9–6D. However, (d) the principal cannot obtain disclosure of documents obtained by the agent in the course of the unlawful agency, although the documents concern the client.[116]

9–4B2 No Secret Profits

Fiduciaries are treated like trustees.[117] A "person in a fiduciary position . . . is not, unless otherwise expressly provided, entitled to make a profit".[118] Clearly, an agent may be paid for his services,[119] often by the person to whom he owes the fiduciary duty, and this is consistent with his fiduciary role in so far as the payment is received with the knowledge and consent of the client.

In the absence of such consent fiduciaries have been required to surrender secret payments by way of commission,[120] which the law sees as bribes.[121] There is a bribe whenever a gift is made to an agent in order to induce the agent to act in favour of the donor in relation to transactions between the donor and the agent's principal, the client, without the knowledge and consent of the latter.[122] It will be observed that "gift" includes not only commission but also benefits in kind and any other material

113a. *Clark Boyce* v *Mouat* [1993] 4 All ER 268, 273 (PC), concerning a solicitor who acts for both sides in a property transaction.
114. *North & South Co* v *Berkeley* [1971] 1 WLR 470, 485 *per* Donaldson J.
115. *Ibid* with reference to *In re a Debtor* (No 229 of 1927) [1927] 2 Ch 367; *Taylor* v *Walker* [1958] 1 Lloyd's Rep 490 and the cases there cited.
116. This was the decision in *North & South* (above); Donaldson J rejected (a) the assumption that the information must be disclosed to the client even though the agent would not have been able to obtain the information, if such disclosure were likely or even possible; (b) the argument that information was property and for that reason a benefit for which the agent could be required to account; (c) the premise of that argument that the information was acquired as agent for the client. However, the premise was, it is submitted, correct. The scope of an agent's fiduciary duty is determined, not by the agent's intention (to act for A rather than B) at the time of the act, but by the scope of the duty he has undertaken to the client, the true principal. See further Kay and Yates, 35 MLR 78 (1972).
117. Hanbury & Maudsley, *Modern Equity* (12th ed, 1985), p 577.
118. *Bray* v *Ford* [1896] AC 44, 51 *per* Lord Herschell.
119. *Phipps* v *Boardman* [1967] 2 AC 46.
120. *Brown* v *IRC* [1965] AC 244 (solicitor not allowed to retain interest on clients' account); *Mahesan* v *Malaysia Govt Officers Cooperative Housing Sy* [1979] AC 374 (PC: agent bribed to make purchase). Generally see Bowstead, pp 185 ff; Goff & Jones, pp 632 ff.; and in Canada: Shepherd, *The Law of Fiduciaries*, ch 19.
USA *idem*: *Re Browning's Estate*, 22 NYS 2d 652 (1940—fire), affirmed 24 NYS 2d 1001, 25 NYS 2d 797: agent cancelled fire cover and procured new cover which carried higher commission.
121. *Industries & General Mortgage Co Ltd* v *Lewis* [1949] 2 All ER 573, 575 *per* Slade J.
122. *Hovendon & Sons* v *Millhof* (1900) 83 LT 41, 43 *per* Romer LJ; see also *Industries & General Mortgage Co Ltd* v *Lewis* [1949] 2 All ER 573, 575 *per* Slade J.

incentive.[123] It is irrelevant that nobody concerned had a corrupt or improper motive.[124] As regards the insurance industry, it has been claimed that the obligation has neither been understood nor applied in 200 years[125]; it is nonetheless part of English law.

As regards commission, a distinction has been made in the past between brokers and other agents acting for the insured[126]:

"if one instructed an agent to effect an insurance for him and that agent received a commission, without any agreement, express or implied, that the commission should be for his own benefit, the commission belonged to the person whose property was being insured, and not to the agent. Of course, if one employed an insurance broker it might fairly be inferred that he was to have the commission. On the other hand, if one employed a solicitor it was not his business, and the solicitor was accountable to his client."

Each kind of agent is required to act *bona fide* in the interests of his principal (above, 9–4A).

(a) Brokers' commission is said to be lawful by usage,[127] or by implied agreement.[128]

If brokers' commission is lawful by usage, the proposer is bound by the usage because he chooses to deal in the context in which the usage prevails. Actual knowledge of the usage is unnecessary: if the practice is generally known and acquiesced in by those in the particular market, a newcomer who enters the market must take its practices as he finds them.[129]

If, however, the lawfulness of commission rests on implied agreement, it can be argued that the proposer must have actual knowledge of the commission. If so, how much knowledge? It seems enough that he knows or should know that commission is paid by insurers; he need not know the amount.

"If a person employs another, who he knows carries on a large business, to do certain work for him as his agent with other persons, and does not choose to ask him what his charge will be, and in fact knows that he will be remunerated not by him but by the other persons—which is very common in mercantile business—and does not choose to take the trouble of inquiring what the amount is, he must allow the ordinary amount which agents are in the habit of charging."[130]

If, however, the rule is based on genuine, though implied, agreement, it is difficult to see why brokers should be in a better position than other agents of the insured, whose commission is lawful only if the insured has full knowledge of the material facts which must, surely, include the amount of the commission (see below, (b)).

In the code drawn up by the Insurance Brokers Registration Council[131] example (6) provides that brokers shall, on request, disclose to any client who is an individual and

---

123. Hence this includes, for example, incentives such as hospitality, telephone facilities paid for the insurer, and discounts.

124. *Taylor* v *Walker* [1958] 1 Lloyd's Rep 490, 512 *per* Havers J (motor).

125. Dinmore, *PM Special Report on Incentives*, 24 April 1986, p 32.

126. *Workman & Army & Navy Cooperative Supply Ltd* v *London & Lancashire Fire Ins Co* (1903) 19 TLR 360, 362 *per* Kekewich J (fire).

127. *Green & Son Ltd* v *Tughan & Co* (1913) 30 TLR 64 (cargo).

128. *Workman* (above).

129. *Baring* v *Stanton* (1876) 3 Ch D 502, 506 *per* Mellish LJ (CA—hull). Law Commission, CP No. 124, 3 April 1992, para 3.4.19.

130. *Great Western Ins Co* v *Cunliffe* (1874) LR 9 Ch App 525, 539 *per* Mellish LJ (re); see also p 537 *per* James LJ; *Baring* v *Stanton* (1876) 3 Ch D 502 (CA—hull). See also *Swale* v *Ipswich Tannery Ltd* (1906) 11 Com Cas 88, 896–897. In this sense Bowstead, p 186.

131. Insurance Brokers Registration Council (Code of Conduct) Approval Order 1978, SI 1978, No 1394. On the merits of disclosure see Gray, *New Foundations*, pp 19 ff.

who is, or is contemplating becoming, the holder of a United Kingdom policy of insurance, the amount of commission paid by the insurer under any relevant policy of insurance. In the same code, example (11) provides that brokers shall disclose to the client any payment received as a result of securing on behalf of the client any service additional to the arrangement of a contract of insurance. Now, it seems likely that disclosure will be required by law.

(b) Other Agents' Commission. At common law agents other than brokers are in breach of duty to the client, if they receive commission, unless they disclose the commission to the principal and he acquiesces in its payment.[132] Acquiescence by the client can occur only if he has full knowledge of the material facts.[133] This suggests not only knowledge that commission is paid to the agent but also knowledge of the amount, however, in a recent case in which the decision did not turn on the point, Leggatt J stated his view that knowledge of the amount was not necessary.[134]

(c) Information. Whether broker or other agent, there remains the question whether information obtained while acting for one client can be used to act on behalf of another client. Once again, the answer depends on whether the use of the information raises a conflict of duty and interest in respect of the two clients.[135] Further, and regardless of such a conflict, an agent is not allowed to disclose information acquired as agent, if it is confidential.[136] It is confidential if (a) it is imparted in confidence, and (b) it is not common knowledge.[137] If the use in question is publication, there is a defence that publication was in the public interest, usually because the information concerned fraud, crime or breach of a code of conduct.[138]

9–5 SPECIFIC ASPECTS OF THE AGENT'S DUTY

9–5A Instructions: Discretion

The agent must carry out what he knew or should have known were the wishes of the client[139] to the letter.[140] If the agent is unable to carry out the instructions in full, for example, to obtain cover on the terms desired by the client, it may be no breach of

---

132. *Swale* v *Ipswich Tannery Ltd* (1906) 11 Com Cas 88: Kennedy J held that X, employed *inter alia* to arrange his employer's insurance, could be dismissed for taking a secret commission from the insurers. The judge referred (p 96) to the "obvious impropriety of the double position and the conflict of duties".

133. *Re Haslam & Hier-Evans* [1902] 1 Ch 765, 772 *per* Stirling LJ (CA); *Jacobus Marler Estates* v *Marler* (1916) 85 LJPC 167. The rule derives from the law of trusts: *Randall* v *Errington* (1805) 10 Ves Jun 423 in which Sir William Grant MR required (p 427) disclosure of the price at which a trustee bought trust property. See also *Life Assn of Scotland* v *Siddall* (1861) 3 De GF & J 58, 74 *per* Turner LJ, whose view was approved by Lord Campbell LC (p 77). See further Goff & Jones, pp 637 ff.

134. *Anangel Atlas C.N. S.A.* v *Ishikawajima–Harima Heavy Industries Co Ltd* [1990] 1 Lloyd's Rep 167, 170.

135. Hanbury & Maudsley, *op cit*, pp 588–589. See above, 9–4B.

136. *Harris Trustees Ltd* v *Power Packing Services (Hermit Road) Ltd* [1970] 2 Lloyd's Rep 65: the claimant was appointed to assess fire damage at a warehouse. The client (warehouseman) allowed the claimant to approach persons whose goods were damaged in the fire, provided that he did not disclose that the warehouseman was underinsured as regards goods in his warehouse. Paull J held that the client was entitled to terminate the agency for breach of a duty not to disclose confidential information.

137. *Seager* v *Copydex Ltd* [1967] 1 WLR 923 (CA). Generally see Goff & Jones, pp 659 ff.

138. *Initial Services Ltd* v *Putterill* [1968] 1 QB 396 (CA); *Dunford & Elliott Ltd* v *Johnson & Firth Brown Ltd* [1977] 1 Lloyd's Rep 505 (CA); *A-G* v *Guardian Newspapers (No 2)* [1990] AC 109. Generally see Cripps, *The Legal Implications of Disclosure in the Public Interest* (1987).

139. *GAFLAC* v *Minet & Co Ltd* (1943) 74 Ll L Rep 1 (CA—re).

140. *Ireland* v *Livingston* (1872) LR 5 HL 395, 414 *per* Martin B (cargo). See also *Fomin* v *Oswell* (1813) 3 Camp 357 (marine).

duty by the agent to obtain cover on the best terms possible[141]; the extent of the agent's discretion depends on the instructions and on the circumstances of the case. If the agent does have discretion it is enough[142] that he exercises it *bona fide* (above, 9–4A) and without negligence (above, 9–3A), and that he obtains terms that a reasonable and prudent professional insurance agent would have obtained in the circumstances.[143]

In any event, the agent must put a reasonable interpretation on the instructions received from the client.[144] Lord Chelmsford said[145] that

"if a principal gives an order to an agent in such uncertain terms as to be susceptible of two different meanings, and the agent *bona fide* adopts one of them and acts upon it, it is not competent to the principal to repudiate the act as unauthorized because he meant the order to be read in other than the sense of which it is equally capable."

However, if the ambiguity is apparent and time permits, it appears that the agent should seek clarification before acting.

9–5B Choice of Insurer

The agent is under a duty to select an insurer who offers favourable rates.[146] This does not necessarily mean the insurer who offers the cheapest rate,[147] however, if the rate were among the most expensive, the agent would be open to the charge of breach of fiduciary duty.[148] Further, the insurer must be one who is reasonably believed to be solvent[149] and to warn the insured client, if the insurer chosen has become unlikely to be able to pay,[150] although even courts in the USA do not expect an insurance agent to detect financial flaws that have escaped the rating agencies.[151] It has also been suggested[152] that agents

"ought to be under a duty at all times to all classes of insured to advise and warn about particular insurers, not just as to their financial stability but also as to the suitability of particular poli-

---

141. *Waterkeyn* v *Eagle Star & British Dominions Ins Co Ltd* (1920) 5 Ll L Rep 42 (insolvency); *King* v *Chambers & Newman (Ins Brokers) Ltd* [1963] 2 Lloyd's Rep 130 (jewellery).
142. *Moore* v *Mourgue* (1776) 2 Cowp 480 (cargo); *Comber* v *Anderson* (1808) 1 Camp 523 (cargo).
143. *Fiorentino* v *Travelers Ins Co*, 548 F Supp 1364, 1370 (ED Pa, 1978—liability).
144. *Ireland* v *Livingston* (1872) LR 5 HL 395, 414 *per* Martin B (cargo): "the question is, what is the natural, grammatical, fair, and reasonable meaning". See also *Vale* v *Van Oppen* (1921) 37 TLR 367 (cargo); *United Mills Agencies Ltd* v *Harvey, Bray & Co* [1951] 2 Lloyd's Rep 631 (fire).
145. *Ireland* (above) p 416 (cargo). *Madsen* v *All State Ins Co*, 760 F Supp 1389 (D Or, 1991—liability).
146. *Smyth, Sanford & Gerard Inc* v *Missouri-Kansas-Texas Ry Co*, 72 F 2d 216 (2 Cir, 1934).
147. *Ibid*: the court held that premium was not the only factor, and the fact that the client had found a cheaper policy than that procured by the broker did not establish negligence by the broker.
148. See above, 9–4B2.
149. *Dixon* v *Hovill* (1828) 4 Bing 665, 668 *per* Park J (cargo). There must be "no reason for supposing" that the insurer was not a responsible and solvent person: *Hurrell* v *Bullard* (1863) 3 F & F 445, 453 *per* Cockburn CJ (hull). *National Boat Corp* v *John Doe Ins Co*, 1979 AMC 2274 (MD Fla, 1979); *Sternoff Metals Corp* v *Vertecs Corp*, 693 P 2d 175 (Wash, 1984). Montgomery, 18 JMLC 395 (1987).
150. *Osman* v *Moss Ltd* [1970] 1 Lloyd's Rep 313 (CA—motor). *Beck Helicopters Ltd* v *Edward Lumley & Sons* (1990) 6 ANZ Ins Cases, no 60–995 (High Ct, NZ—aviation). The agent must "acquire the requested coverage with a reliable company who can and will properly and promptly pay claims when due"—*Butler* v *Scott*, 417 F 2d 471 (10 Cir, 1969—fire); *Brown* v *Poritzky*, 283 NE 2d 751 (NY 1972—fire); *First Alabama Bk* v *First State Ins Co* 899 F 2d 1045, 1068 (11 Cir, 1990—liability). Rest 2d, Agency, para 3(2).
151. *May* v *United Services Assn*, 884 SW 2d 666 (Tex, 1992—PHI).
152. Birds, p 174. *Cf First Alabama Bk* v *First State Ins Co* 899 F 2d 1045, 1069 (11 Cir, 1990—liability), which appears to go further in requiring the agent to inform the client about the options available to him, although those other than the cover selected by the agent were not, in the opinion of the agent, appropriate for the client.

cies and their general record in treating their insured, for example, as to their generosity in paying claims."

However, it has been held[153] that the agent does not guarantee that the insurer will not make unfounded resistance to a claim, and is thus not liable to his client for the legal costs incurred in suit against the insurer.

9–5C Policy Interpretation

If the agent is to advise on the suitability of a policy, he must understand its terms.[154] However, it has been held that the broker has no duty to give advice about the contents or meaning of policies, perhaps because these may be questions of law,[155] unless he chooses to offer advice, for example, in response to a question from the client.[156] Moreover, there is the further qualification that, if the agent agrees to find cover for a particular risk or meet a particular need, there is the clear implication that, unless expressly indicated by the agent, the policy procured does cover the risk or meet the need;[157] this also carries the implication that the terms of the policy have the meaning desired. Thus, it was held in a hull case[158] that the agent had a duty to warn the client that, unless he had the vessel surveyed, a clause in the proposed insurance would exclude cover. It is the duty of the agent, when the policy is issued, to read it and check that it is the cover required.[159] Although the insured is required to read his policy and be familiar with its terms,[160] he is not required to check that it complies with the instructions that he gave his agent:

"when a broker is employed to effect an insurance, especially when the broker is employed as a person of repute and experience, the client is entitled to rely upon the broker carrying out his instructions, and is not bound to examine the documents drawn up in performance of those instructions and see whether his instructions have, in fact, been carried out by the broker. In many cases the principal would not understand the matter, and would not know whether the document did in fact carry out his instructions. Business could not be carried on if, when a person has been employed to use care and skill with regard to a matter, the employer is bound to use his own care and skill to see whether the person employed has done what he was employed to do."

153. *Ciaramitaro* v *Gough & King Inc*, 250 F 2d 943 (1 Cir, 1958—hull).
154. *Offshore Production Inc* v *Republic Underwriters Ins Co* 910 F 2d 224, 231 (5 Cir, 1990—builders' risks).
155. See 22–2B3.
156. *Sarginson Bros* v *Moulton & Co Ltd* (1942) 73 Ll L Rep 104; *Harvester Trucking Co Ltd* v *Davis* [1991] 2 Lloyd's Rep 638, 643 per Judge Diamond (goods in transit). *Fries-Breslin Co* v *Bergen*, 176 F 76, 79 (3 Cir, 1909—fire): the *dictum* suggests that the agent must offer the advice, if requested, *sed quaere*. See also *Farber* v *Great American Ins Co*, 406 F 2d 1228 (7 Cir, 1969—motor).
Cf the ABI Code of Practice which requires intermediaries to explain the terms of the contract: above 8–3C(d).
157. *Offshore Production Inc* v *Republic Underwriters Ins Co* 910 F 2d 224, 230 (5 Cir, 1990—builders' risks).
158. *Norwest Refrigeration Services Pty Ltd* v *Bain Dawes Pty Ltd* (1984) 157 CLR 149 (HCA—hull).
159. *Dickson & Co* v *Devitt* (1916) 86 LJKB 315 (hull). Also *Norwest Refrigeration* (above); *Rudd Paper Box Co* v *Rice* (1912) 3 DLR 253, 254 (Ont—fire); see also *Peter Unruh Construction Co Ltd* v *Kelly-Lucy Cameron Adjusters Ltd* [1976] 4 WWR 419, 423 (Alta—liability), relying on *Wilkinson* v *Coverdale* (1793) 1 Esp 76; *Landry* v *Anderson* (1977) 16 NBR (2d) 700 (NB—motor); *Elliott* v *Ron Dawson & Associates (1972) Ltd* (1982) 139 DLR (3d) 323, 327 (BC—property), rejecting the argument that the insured was contributorily negligent in failing to read the policy; *cf Hudson Turner Furs Ltd* v *American Ins Co* (1964) 43 DLR (2d) 322, 333 (Ont—furrier's block).
USA: "a claim based upon the negligence of the agency to properly provide coverage is . . . not affected by the insured's failure to read and understand the policy": *Grigsby* v *Mountain Valley Ins Agency*, 795 SW 2d 372, 374 (Ky, 1990—fire).
160. See below, 11–2A2.

This was said in *Dickson v Devitt*,[161] which was concerned with causation. The question in issue was whether, in failing to check the documents, the plaintiff "was negligent in the conduct of his business in a respect which broke the chain of causation".[162] Generally, the client's assumption that the documents carry out his instructions will not have that effect, unless perhaps "the defect is so obvious that it springs to the eye",[163] or the point is one on which the insured is better placed to check the contents than the agent, such as a schedule of items insured.[164]

In all this, it appears that some degree of legal knowledge can be expected of the agent.[165] As to the skill to be expected, see above, 9–3A. Given the high standards now expected of the profession, the acceptance of concurrent liability in contract and in tort and the centrality in tort of the idea of reasonable reliance, the consumer of insurance, like the consumer of widgets, if he finds that the product does not work (the insurer does not pay) is likely to turn not against the maker (the insurer) but against the retailer (the agent). Retailers of insurance in England might note what has been recently said[166] of their colleagues in Canada: "In describing the broker's duty there has been some reference to the standards in the industry. However, most authorities describe the broker's duty in language which closely mimics the American doctrine of giving effect to the insured's reasonable expectations."[167]. Nonetheless, in England some regard has been shown to the standards of the industry as set by the ABI.[168]

9–5D Disclosure to the Insurer

When arranging insurance the agent must disclose material facts to the insurer.[169] In *Dunbar*[170] the clients' loss was not covered as a result of non-disclosure by their brokers; in their claim against the brokers they were entitled to be put in the position they would have occupied, if the insurance had been obtainable and valid. The agent's duty of disclosure to the insurer is limited to facts about the risk that the agent knew or should have known[171]; but what he knows depends on what he must find out and, on this the law draws a difficult line between statements and omissions.

As regards statements, in *O'Connor v Kirby*[172] the client signed a proposal of motor

161. Above, p 317 per Atkin J, applied by Phillips J in *Youell v Bland Welch & Co Ltd* [1990] 2 Lloyd's Rep 431, 453 (re).
162. *Youell* (above) p 454. In the general law, clearly a failure to check may break the chain of causation: *McInerny v Lloyd's Bank* [1974] 1 Lloyd's Rep 246 (CA). It will be otherwise—and this, it seems, is the understanding between client and broker—only when the defendant "has warranted that he need not—there is no necessity to—take the very precautions for the failure to take which he has" suffered the loss claimed: *Hadley v Droitwich Construction Co* [1968] 1 WLR 37, 43 per Winn LJ, a view approved by Lord Diplock in *Lambert v Lewis* [1982] AC 225, 276.
163. *General Accident v Minet* (1942) 72 Ll. L Rep 48, 62 per Atkinson J (re); affirmed (1942) 74 Ll.L.Rep 1 (CA).
164. *Motors Ins Co v Bud's Boat Rental* 917 F 2d 199, 205 (5 Cir, 1990—liability).
165. In this general sense: *Park v Hammond* (1816) 6 Taunt 495. Jackson & Powell, *op cit* No 7.13.
166. Baer, 22 Ottawa L Rev 389, 413 (1990).
167. The doctrine of reasonable expectations is discussed below, 15–5B.
168. *Harvester Trucking Co Ltd v Davis*, [1991] 2 Lloyd's Rep 638, 643 per Judge Diamond (goods in transit).
169. *British Citizens Assurance Co v Wooland & Co* (1921) 8 Ll L Rep 89 (re); *Coolee Ltd v Wing, Heath & Co* (1930) 47 TLR 78 (liability).
170. *Dunbar v A & B Painters Ltd* [1985] 2 Lloyd's Rep 616 (liability).
171. *Lyons v Bentley Ltd* (1944) 77 L Ll Rep 335 (burglary: insurance history—there is no suggestion that the agent should have asked the proposer about it). As regards disclosure see further below, 23–8B.
172. [1971] 1 Lloyd's Rep 454 (CA—motor).

insurance, prepared by the agent, stating untruly that the vehicle was normally kept in a garage. The responsibility was that of the client rather than that of the agent[173]; it was for the client rather than the agent to check that the statement was true. In general terms this is asserted by the brokers' code of conduct.[174] The agent is entitled to assume that, before the client signs the form, the client reads and approves what has been written,[175] however, the same assumption cannot be made about what has not been written.

As regards omissions, in the later case of *Warren* v *Sutton & Co*[176] the plaintiff asked his agent to arrange motor cover for a trip to France with a friend as co-driver. The agent did not ask about and the plaintiff did not disclose the driving record of the friend, which was bad; the insurer rescinded the contract. The agent, however, was held liable to the plaintiff: he, "was under a duty to obtain cover for [the friend], if possible, to make such enquiries as were necessary to that end and to make a suitable statement" to the insurer.[177] In another case, the Supreme Court of Victoria stated that if "his client may be at risk of having his insurance cover avoided for non-disclosure, the broker must have a duty to inform himself of sufficient of the business activities of his client to carry out his duties adequately and in particular to prevent the avoidance of liability under any policy written".[178] As regards significant or novel commercial risks at least, English law may well be the same.

9–5E Notifying the Client

The agent is obliged to notify his client that the insurance cannot be obtained, or that there is some hitch in the arrangements,[179] which takes the situation outside the scope of the agent's discretion to act without consultation (above, 9–5A). The purpose of notification is to afford the client an opportunity to make alternative plans, perhaps to find insurance elsewhere,[180] if he can. However, notification is not required until the agent has had a reasonable time to ascertain by the exercise of reasonable diligence

173. The same is true, if the client confirms the contents of the document by a separate communication: *Commonwealth Ins Co* v *Groupe Sprinks SA* [1983] 1 Lloyd's Rep 67, 82 *per* Lloyd J.

174. Found in the Insurance Brokers Registration Council (Code of Conduct) Approval Order 1978, SI 1978, No 1394.

175. *O' Connor* (above, note 116), p 461 *per* Megaw LJ. See below, 10–3.

176. [1976] 2 Lloyd's Rep 276 (CA—motor).

177. p 284 *per* Sir John Pennycuick; Browne LJ (p 281) distinguished misrepresentation and non-disclosure, *sed quaere*. In *McNealy* v *Pennine Ins Co Ltd* [1978] 2 Lloyd's Rep 18 (CA) low premium motor insurance was only available to certain professions. The broker failed to ensure that the proposer qualified and was held liable to the latter. Waller LJ (p 21) said that it was the duty of the agent "to make as certain as he reasonably could that the [proposer] came within the categories acceptable to the" company. See also *Ogden & Co Pty Ltd* v *Reliance Fire Sprinkler Co Pty Ltd* [1975] 1 Lloyd's Rep 52, 69 (NSW—liability).

178. *Helicopter Resources Pty Ltd* v *Sun Alliance Australia Ltd*, unreported but discussed by Hetherington (1992) 5 Ins L J 86, 89.

179. *Smith* v *Lascelles* (1788) 2 TR 187 (cargo). See also *Callander* v *Oelrichs* (1838) 5 Bing NC 58 (cargo); *Avondale Blouse Co Ltd* v *Williamson & Town* (1948) 81 Ll L Rep 492; *Cherry* v *Allied Ins Brokers Ltd* [1978] 1 Lloyd's Rep 274 (consequential loss). *Eagle Star Ins Co Ltd* v *Nat Westminster Finance Australia Ltd* (1985) 58 ALR 165, 174 *per* Lord Roskill (PC). *Fine Flowers Ltd* v *General Accident Assurance Co* (1977) 81 DLR (3d) 139 (Ont); *Reardon* v *Kings Mutual Ins Co* (1981) 120 DLR (3d) 196 (NS—fire). *Gulf-Tex Brokerage Inc* v *McDade*, 433 F Supp 1015 (SD Tex, 1977—hull); *Haeuber* v *Can-do*, 666 F 2d 275 (5 Cir, 1982—P & I). The same decision has been reached when the insurer refused unexpectedly to renew a policy: *Unger* v *Twin City Fire Ins Co*, 10 NYS 2d 853 (1960—fire), affirmed 216 NYS 2d 663; *Prince* v *Royal Indemnity Co*, 41 F 2d 646 (7 Cir, 1976—fire), *cert* den 429 US 1094; *Honeycutt* v *Kendall*, 549 F Supp 802 (D Del, 1982—motor); or to provide additional cover: *MacDonald* v *Carpenter & Pelton Inc*, 298 NYS 2d 780 (1969—fire).

180. *Smith* v *Lascelles* (1788) 2 TR 187 (cargo).

whether he can carry out the original mandate according to instructions.[181] If the agent is able to carry out the mandate in general but with significant differences of detail, for example by obtaining cover but not on the terms that the client might have expected[182] or "if the only insurance which the agent is able to obtain contains unusual, limiting or exempting provisions",[183] it seems that the agent must draw the client's attention to the terms available: the agent must "discuss the nature of the problem with him and take reasonable steps either to obtain alternative insurance, if any is available, or alternatively to advise the client as to the best way of acting so that his business procedures conform to any requirements laid down by the policy".[184] If not, the agent will be liable for consequent loss.[185] The same is true of renewal on terms different from the terms which the client expected.[186]

By contrast, if the mandate is taking its expected although perhaps difficult course, there is no duty to keep the client informed of the problems that arise, for example, the insurer's insistence on a survey of the property.[187] Nor is the agent obliged to notify the client when the instructions have been carried out, although in practice he may do so.

"That seems to me to be good business and prudent office management, but on the evidence I am completely unable to hold that it is part of the duty owed by the broker to the client so to notify him, in the sense that a failure to notify him would involve him in legal liability . . . It seems to me to put quite an intolerable and unreasonable burden on a broker to say that as a matter of law, apart from prudent practice, he is bound to forward the cover note as soon as possible. It is no doubt prudent to do so, both to allay the client's anxiety and possibly to enable the client to check the terms of the insurance. That is a very different thing from saying it is part of his duty."[188]

By the same token, the client, who has paid a year's premium for motor insurance and received a temporary cover note but hears nothing more from his agent, is entitled to assume that the policy has been obtained.[189]

9–5F Renewal

An agent mandated to contract insurance is not authorised to renew it, unless the mandate is of a broader kind, for example, to keep certain property covered.[190] This is

181. *MacDonald* (above) p 783.
182. For example, the duration of cover: *Youell* v *Bland Welch & Co Ltd* [1990] 2 Lloyd's Rep 431 (re); and cancelling cover as instructed but sooner than expected, so that the client was uninsured: *Cherry* v *Allied Ins Brokers Ltd* [1978] 1 Lloyd's Rep 274 (consequential loss); see also *King* v *Chambers & Newman Ltd* [1963] 2 Lloyd's Rep 130 (jewellery). *Haeuber* v *Can-do*, 666 F 2d 275 (5 Cir, 1982—P & I).
183. *Harvester Trucking Co Ltd* v *Davis*, [1991] 2 Lloyd's Rep 638, 643 per Judge Diamond (goods in transit);
184. *Ibid*.
185. *Cherry* (above). *Sea Fever Corp* v *Hartford Fire Ins Co*, 1983 AMC 1276 (D Mass, 1982—hull).
186. *Mint Security Ltd* v *Blair* [1982] 1 Lloyd's Rep 188, 199–200 *per* Staughton J. *Cf Michaels* v *Valentine* (1923) 16 Ll L Rep 244.
187. *Avonale Blouse Co Ltd* v *Williamson & Geo Town* (1948) 81 Ll L Rep 492 (burglary); see also *King* v *Chambers & Newman (Ins Brokers) Ltd* [1963] 2 Lloyd's Rep 130 (jewellery).
188. *United Mills Agencies Ltd* v *Harvey, Bray & Co* [1951] 2 Lloyd's Rep 631, 643 *per* McNair J (fire).
189. *Osman* v *Moss Ltd* [1970] 1 Lloyd's Rep 313, 316 *per* Sachs LJ (CA—motor).
190. See above, 7–2. In *Mathew* v *Maughold Life Assurance Co Ltd* (1987) 3 Prof Neg 98 (CA) a solicitor who had arranged term life insurance for a client as part of a tax avoidance scheme was held liable to the client for failing to remind him to exercise an option to renew the insurance.

said[191] to be because "a reasonable man checks his insurance annually". There is also force in the view found in Minnesota that, in the absence of special circumstances, the agent has no duty at the time of renewal to update the cover or to enquire whether changes have occurred in the position of the insured or his property which would affect cover.[192] An "agent has no duty beyond what he or she has specifically undertaken to perform for his client". In particular, the "agent has no 'ongoing duty of surveillance' ", because the insured is in a position to ask about changes that might affect cover whereas the agent is not well placed to discover such changes on his own initiative.[193] An exception might be made for an unsophisticated insured who habitually relied upon the agent for advice.[194]

The insurer is not obliged to send a renewal notice, nor perhaps the agent to send a reminder. However, the position probably depends on the particular relationship between client and agent. There is force in the Canadian view[195] that, if an agent has renewed a policy or sent reminders in the past, he undertakes a duty in law to renew the policy or at least to advise the client that it is about to expire.

9–5G Accounts

The agent must account for all monies, such as money payable under the policy, received for the client insured.[196] Lord Ellenborough[197]:

"If an insurance broker keeps the policy in his hands, he shall be presumed to promise, that he will collect the sums due from the underwriters upon a loss happening . . . [and] to bring the underwriters to a settlement of the loss, according to the usage of trade in this respect."

Once the insurance money has been (actually or notionally)[198] received by the agent, an action for money had and received will be available to the client against the agent.[199]

9–6 REMEDIES

9–6A Damages

If the agent breaks one of his contractual or tortious duties to the client, the client may recover damages from the agent in respect of loss caused by the agent's breach.[200] If

---

191. *Argy Trading Development Co Ltd* v *Lapid Developments Ltd* [1977] 3 All ER 785, 800 *per* Croom-Johnson J, holding that a landlord who had maintained a block fire policy for the benefit of the tenant was not obliged to notify the tenant when his cover had ceased. This decision can be explained: the landlord was not a professional broker: Hodgin, p 66. However, see also *Hudson Turner Furs Ltd* v *American Ins Co* (1964) 43 DLR (2d) 322, 333 (Ont—furrier's block).
192. *Gabrielson* v *Warnemunde*, 443 NW 2d 540 (Minn, 1989—homeowner's): the existing insurance did not cover watercraft of the kind later acquired by the insured.
193. pp 543–544.
194. pp 544–545.
195. *Morash* v *Lockart & Ritchie Ltd* (1978) 95 DLR (3d) 647, 655 (NB—fire).
196. *Dixon* v *Hammond* (1819) 2 B & Ald 310 (hull). Generally Bowstead, pp 197 ff.
197. (1810) 2 Camp 545.
198. As where it is an account entry between insurer and agent.
199. *Andrew* v *Robinson* (1812) 3 Camp 199 (hull); *Wilkinson* v *Clay* (1815) 6 Taunt 110 (hull); *Roberts* v *Ogilvy* (1821) 9 Price 269 (hull); *McEntire* v *Potter* (1889) 22 QBD 438 (hull).
200. *Cahill* v *Dawson* (1857) 3 CB NS 106 (cargo). *Ogden & Co Pty Ltd* v *Reliance Fire Sprinkler Co Pty Ltd* [1975] 1 Lloyd's Rep 52, 76 (NSW—liability).

the loss stems from the agent's failure to conclude a contract of the kind sought by the client, it is enough that in consequence the insurer has declined to pay the loss; the client does not have to sue the insurer as a precondition of a claim against the agent.[201]

If the agent would have failed to procure the insurance sought, because such insurance was not available, *prima facie* the agent is not liable, as his failure did not cause the insured loss.[202] Even so, it is still "necessary to assess what course the client could have followed and would have followed".[203] If the evidence is that the insured would not have pursued the activity that led to loss in the absence of cover, the agent's failure regains a causal role.

Again, if the agent fails to conclude a contract which, if "concluded", would have been void, the agent is not liable to the client,[204] if the loss would not have been covered anyway.[205] If, however, in such a case the contract would have been not void but voidable, the "Court must next consider . . . what were the chances that an insurance company of the highest repute and reputation . . . , notwithstanding their strict legal rights, would, as a matter of business, have paid up under the policy".[206] *Prima facie* the client has suffered loss and it is for the agent to prove otherwise.[207]

The duty of the agent is not only to procure cover but also to advise about cover and it is in this context that questions may arise of contributory negligence on the part of the insured. In the *Superhulls Cover* case[208] Phillips J held that, by failing to inform the plaintiff insurers about a clause in a reinsurance contract, the defendant brokers were in breach of duty to the plaintiffs, and "that the insurers owed no duty to the brokers to read the insurance wording with skill and care and to draw attention to any inadequacies in the cover".[209] However, he continued: "It does not follow from this that the insurers were not guilty of 'neglect of what would be prudent in respect of their own interests' ".[210] In this case the plaintiff insurers had been negligent and, although their negligence did not break the chain of causation between the brokers breach and the loss,[211] it contributed to that loss and liability was apportioned under the Law Reform (Contributory Negligence) Act 1945.[212]

The judge stressed[213] that the personnel involved on behalf of the plaintiff insurers were marine underwriters of great experience, and it does not follow that a layman

---

201. *Curaçao Trading Co Inc* v *William Stake & Co*, 1 F Supp 181 (SD NY, 1945—cargo).
202. *Rayden Engineering Corp* v *Church*, 151 NE 2d 57 (Mass, 1958—PA); *MacDonald* v *Carpenter & Pelton Inc*, 298 NYS 2d 780 (1969—fire): a claimant whose broker had failed to obtain additional cover had to show that such cover was obtainable.
203. *Cee Bee Marine Ltd* v *Lombard Ins Co Ltd* [1990] 2 NZLR 1, 6 (CA—fire).
204. *Cheshire & Co* v *Vaughan Bros & Co* [1920] 3 KB 240, 258 *per* Atkin LJ (CA), in spite of evidence that the insurer would not have taken the point.
205. *Graham* v *Milky Way Barge Co*, 923 F 2d 1100 (5 Cir, 1991 – liability), in which the insured was in breach of warranty, fulfilment of which is in English law a condition precedent to cover.
206. *Fraser* v *Furman Productions Ltd* [1967] 2 Lloyd's Rep 1, 11 *per* Diplock LJ (CA—liability), applied in *Dunbar* v *A & B Painters Ltd* [1986] 2 Lloyd's Rep 38 (CA—liability).
207. *Everett* v *Hogg, Robinson & Gardner Mountain (Ins) Ltd* [1973] 2 Lloyd's Rep 217, 223 *per* Kerr J (re). See also *Fraser* (above). The different treatment of void and voidable contracts is cogently criticised by MacGillivray, No 392.
208. *Youell* v *Bland Welch & Co Ltd* [1990] 2 Lloyd's Rep 431, 446 (re), affirmed [1992] 2 Lloyd's Rep. 127 (CA);
209. p 460. On this point, see also above, 9–5C.
210. *Ibid*, citing *Swan* v *North British Australasian Co* (1863) 2 H & C 175, 182 *per* Blackburn J
211. As, for example, in *McInerny* v *Lloyds Bank Ltd* [1974] 1 Lloyd's Rep 246 (CA).
212. *Forsik Vesta* v *Butcher* [1988] 1 Lloyd's Rep 19 (CA—re).
213. p 462.

will be found contributorily negligent, if he fails to appreciate the policy obtained by his agent does not meet his needs or fulfil his instructions: above, 9–5C.[214]

As regards the measure of damages, if the action is based on breach of contract, the plaintiff client is to be put in the position he would have enjoyed, if the agent had performed his mandate. If the action is based in tort, the plaintiff client is to be put in the position he would have enjoyed, if the tort, usually negligence, had not occurred.[215] In most cases, the normal rules of remoteness of loss apply and, for most purposes, the types of loss recoverable by the client and the measure of damages are the same, whether the basis of the action is contract or tort. However, if the tort in question is not negligence but deceit, it is established that the claimant may recover all consequential loss, whether that kind of loss was reasonably foreseeable and hence not too remote or not, unless the chain of causation between the tort and the loss was broken by a *novus actus interveniens*.[216] To the surprise of commentators, it has now been held[217] that the same rule applies in an action based on section 2(1) of the Misrepresentation Act 1967. Subject to this, recoverable loss includes:

(a) premium paid[218];
(b) the amount of insurance money, which would have been recovered from the insurer, if the breach of duty by the agent had not occurred[219];
(c) consequential loss.

In *Osman* v *Moss Ltd*[220] an agent, who failed to warn his client to obtain motor cover, was held liable for the amount of a fine imposed on the client for driving uninsured. In *Ramwade Ltd* v *Emson & Co Ltd*,[221] however, an agent who had failed to cover a lorry, was not liable for the client's expense in hiring a substitute lorry while the client was out of pocket.

In *Ramwade*[222] the expense was refused as having been caused (a) by the impecuniosity of the client on the principles of *Liesbosch*[223] and (b) the failure of the agent to

---

214. Still, the general rule appears to be that it "is the duty of a policyholder to educate himself concerning matters of insurance coverage": *Howell* v *Bullock* 764 SW 2d 422, 424 (Ark, 1989—motor). This is accepted in England by the Ombudsman as regards private lines: The Insurance Ombudsman, Annual Report 1990, para 2.1. Generally, see below, 11–2A2. An exception arises, if the insured is not able to appreciate the significance of the wording of the policy or he has been led by the agent to believe that the terms of the policy are different: *Elliott* v *Ron Dawson & Associates (1972) Ltd* (1982) 139 DLR (3d) 323, 327 (BC—property).

215. This will also be the measure in the case of misuse of confidential information: *Dowson & Mason Ltd* v *Potter* [1986] 2 All ER 418 (CA).

216. *Doyle* v *Olby (Ironmongers) Ltd* [1969] 2 QB 158 (CA).

217. *Royscott Trust Ltd* v *Rogerson* [1991] 3 All ER 294 (CA). For arguments against this decision, see Brown and Chandler [1992] LMCLQ 40.

218. *Osman* v *Moss Ltd* [1970] 1 Lloyd's Rep 313 (CA—motor).

219. *Cahill* v *Dawson* (1857) 3 CB NS 106 (cargo); *Smith* v *Price* (1862) 2 F & F 748, 752 *per* Erle CJ (cargo); *Strong and Pearl* v *Allison & Co* (1926) 25 Ll L Rep 504, 508 *per* Greer J (yacht); *Osman* (above); *Ackbar* v *Green & Co Ltd* [1975] QB 582 (motor); *Cherry Ltd* v *Allied Ins Brokers Ltd* [1978] 1 Lloyd's Rep 274 (consequential loss); *McNealy* v *Pennine Ins Co Ltd* [1978] 2 Lloyd's Rep 18 (CA—motor); *Dunbar* v *A & B Painters Ltd* [1986] 2 Lloyd's Rep 38 (CA—liability); *Ramwade Ltd* v *Emson & Co Ltd* (1987) 2 Prof Neg 197, 199 *per* Parker LJ (CA—motor). *Butler* v *Scott*, 417 F 2d 471 (10 Cir, 1969—fire); *Manning* v *Tiffany Brokers Inc*, 454 NYS 2d 498 (1982—fire) *Hancock Bank* v *Travis*, 580 So 2d 727 (Miss, 1991—credit disability); *Flamme* v *Wolf Ins Agency*, 476 NW 2d 802 (Neb, 1991—motor).
Cf Charles v *Altin* (1854) 15 CB 46, 63 *per* Jervis CJ (freight). *Cf* also *Webster* v *De Tastet* (1797) 7 TR 157 (insurance of wages illegally earned); *Cohen* v *Kittell* (1889) 22 QBD 680.

220. [1970] 1 Lloyd's Rep 313 (CA—motor); the client also recovered the amount of premium paid and the amount of his civil liability to another motorist, together with costs.

221. (1986) 3 Prof Neg 197 (CA).

222. p 199, *per* Parker LJ.

223. *Liesbosch Dredger* v *Edison SS* [1933] AC 448.

pay promptly what the insurer would have paid. As to (a), it is not obvious why the tortfeasor should take the risk of a weak skull but not of a weak wallet. The rule has been criticised as illogical[224] and modern courts[225] tend to distinguish it: *Ramwade* is an exception. As to (b), we have been told[226] that the duty to pay damages is a secondary obligation created by the contract, breach of which may not itself be a cause of action,[227] but is still a cause of loss. As to both (a) and (b), it being accepted (above) that, if the agent breaches his contract to procure cover, the amount of a loss which should have been covered is not too remote, surely it is not stretching the contemplation of the parties at the time of the contract to include that the client would be out of pocket for longer than if the loss had been insured.[228]

9–6B Account for Profit

The agent in breach of fiduciary duty must account for his profit and surrender secret profit, such as secret commission, to the proposer.[229] He must do this, even though the latter has not suffered as a result of the breach of duty: it is enough that the fiduciary agent has been unjustly enriched.[230]

9–6C Restitution

If secret commission is reflected in the price of the insurance, the proposer may recover the amount of the commission from the insurer as money had and received. In *Hovendon & Sons* v *Millhoff* [231] the agent was mandated to purchase goods, and the Court of Appeal assumed as against the defendant that "the true price of the goods as against him and the purchaser . . . be less than the price paid".[232] It is that extra element in the price that the defendant is ordered to pay back. If this rule applies to secret insurance commission, it will have to be shown that the insurance in question could have been bought at a premium lower by the amount of commission reclaimed.[233] In any event, the proposer cannot recover the amount both from the insurer and the agent: he must choose.[234]

---

224. Winfield & Jolowicz *Tort* (13th ed, London 1989), p 149.

225. For example *Dodds Properties (Kent) Ltd* v *Canterbury CC* [1980] 1 All ER 928, 940–941 *per* Donaldson LJ (CA), followed in *Archer* v *Brown* [1984] 2 All ER 267.

226. *Photo Production Ltd* v *Securicor Transport Ltd* [1980] AC 827.

227. *The Lips* [1988] AC 395, 424 *per* Lord Brandon: "There is no such thing as a cause of action in damages for late payment of damages." He cited no precedent. See a critical note by Mann, 104 LQR 3 (1988); and Clarke, [1992] LMCLQ 287.

228. Mann, *loc cit*, p 5.

229. *Morison* v *Thompson* (1874) LR 9 QB 480; *Mahesan* v *Malaysia Government Officers' Cooperative Housing Sy Ltd* [1979] AC 374 (PC). Bowstead, pp 186–187; Sealy [1963] CLJ 119, 128 ff.

230. *Reading* v *A-G* [1951] AC 507; *Boardman* v *Phipps* [1967] 2 AC 46. As to whether there is a constructive trust of the profit in favour of the principal, thus giving him advantage in the event of the agent's bankruptcy, see *A-G for Hong Kong* v *Reid* (1993) 143 NLJ 1569 (PC); Millett [1993] RLR 7.

231. (1900) 83 LT 41 (CA).

232. p 43, *per* Romer LJ.

233. See in particular Smith LJ (pp 42–43) and Williams LJ (p 43). It is not necessary to show this, if the action is brought against the agent, for it is not necessary between agent and principal that the latter should have suffered loss as a result of the breach of duty: *Boardman* v *Phipps* [1967] 2 AC 46.

234. *Mahesan* v *Malaysia Government Officers' Cooperative Housing Sy* [1979] AC 374 (PC).

9–6D Rescission

The client may terminate his contract with the agent on the ground of breach of contract.[235] The client is released from all outstanding duties to the agent.[236]

If the agent has received a secret commission in connection with concluding a contract with a third party, such as the insurer, the client may rescind the contract of insurance on the ground of non-disclosure.[237]

9–6E Injunction

Where appropriate the client may obtain an injunction to restrain the breach or further breach of duty, for example, the misuse of confidential information obtained from the client.[238]

9–7 THE RIGHTS OF THE AGENT AGAINST THE CLIENT

9–7A Remuneration

The agent is entitled to the remuneration agreed with his client. If none has been agreed, the agent is entitled to a reasonable sum.[239] In many cases, however, it is implied in the relationship that he shall receive no remuneration from the client, but shall be free to earn commission from the insurer on any contract of insurance (or renewal) made.[240]

If the client breaks his contract with the agent, with the result that the agent loses commission or the opportunity to earn it, the agent may claim damages from the client: he is entitled to be placed in the position in which he would have been, if the contract had been performed.[241] *Ceteris paribus* he will be able to recover the lost commission from the client.[242]

When remuneration comes not from the insurer but from the proposer, common law requires that the activity of the agent shall have been the effective cause of the achievement of the mandate.[243] When the agent is contractually obliged not to achieve the object of the mandate, for example effect insurance, but to exercise

---

235. *Swale* v *Ipswich Tannery Ltd* (1906) 11 Com Cas 88; *Harris Trustees Ltd* v *Power Packing Services (Hermit Road) Ltd* [1970] 2 Lloyd's Rep 65 (fire assessor).

236. *Andrews* v *Ramsay & Co* [1903] 2 KB 635. Nor will the principal be obliged to reimburse the agent's expenses: *Barron* v *Fitzgerald* (1840) 6 Bing NC 201 (life)—in this case the agent was in breach not of his fiduciary duty but of his duty of care and skill; however, the decision that he could not recover the amount of premiums paid for the principal would apply equally to breach of fiduciary duty.

237. *Taylor* v *Walker* [1958] 1 Lloyd's Rep 490: The insured appointed X, an assessor, to negotiate a claim against an insurer in respect of personal injuries received in a motor accident. He settled the claim for the figure negotiated by the assessor unaware that the assessor had received a commission from the insurer. See also *Panama & South Pacific Telegraph Co* v *India Rubber, Gutta Percha, & Telegraph Co* (1875) 10 Ch App 515; *Rowland* v *Chapman* (1901) 17 TLR 669.

238. *Cranleigh Precision Engineering Ltd* v *Bryant* [1965] 1 WLR 1293; *Speed Seal Products Ltd* v *Paddington* [1986] 1 All ER 91 (CA). Generally Goff & Jones, pp 659 ff.

239. *Allen & Co Ltd* v *Holmes Ltd* [1969] 1 Lloyd's Rep 348 (CA). Bowstead, pp 210 ff. Halsbury, Vol 1, Nos 799 ff. *Smyth, Sanford & Gerard Inc* v *Missouri-Kansas-Texas Ry Co*, 72 F 2d 216 (2 Cir, 1934); *Tanenbaum Co* v *Sixth Av*, 48 NYS 2d 415 (1944—fire), affirmed 62 NE 2d 390 (1945).

240. See above, 9–3.

241. *Johnson & Higgins* v *Harper Transport Co*, 228 F 730 (D Mass, 1915—hull).

242. *Ibid*.

243. *Millar* v *Radford* (1903) 19 TLR 575 (CA); applied in *McNeil* v *Law Union & Rock Ins Co Ltd* (1925) 23 Ll L Rep 314 (liability). Bowstead, pp 227 ff.

reasonable diligence to that end (above, 9–3), the common law rule is modified by the express or implied terms of the mandate.

9–7B Reimbursement and Indemnity

In the general law an agent is entitled to reimbursement by his principal of all expenses incurred in carrying out his mandate.[244] He is also entitled to be indemnified against any liability reasonably incurred in carrying out his mandate. The basis of these rights is an implied term of the contract and, in the context of insurance, the practices of the industry may limit the implication of these terms, it being understood that expenses are a business cost to be covered by the commission earned. However, one expense that might be incurred by the agent is the premium: if he has paid premium to the insurer on behalf of the client, he is entitled to recover that from the client.[245]

9–7C Lien

The agent has a possessory lien on the property of his principal in respect of any lawful claims that he has against the latter arising out of the agency.[246] In particular, the insurance agent will have on a policy in his possession a lien which, it has been held,[247] entitles him to decline to deliver it to the insured until paid the amount of premium owed.

---

244. Bowstead, pp 246 ff. Halsbury, Vol 1, No 807.

245. *Dixon* v *Hovill* (1828) 4 Bing 665 (cargo); *Power* v *Butcher* (1829) 10 B & C 329 (hull). The agent does not usually incur personal liability for the premium: *Wilson* v *Avec Audio-Visual Equipment Ltd* [1974] 1 Lloyd's Rep 81, 82–83 *per* Edmund Davies LJ (CA—burglary). *Bleicher* v *Heeter*, 4 NW 2d 897 (Neb, 1942—fire). But *cf Ruby SS Co* v *Johnson & Higgins*, 18 F 2d 948 (2 Cir, 1927—hull), *cert* den 275 US 544, in which the courts declined to follow English practice. *Cf* also *Alliance Ins Co* v *City Realty Co*, 52 F 2d 271 (MD Ga, 1932—fire).Cf also Lloyd's practice: *Universo Ins Co of Milan* v *Merchants' Marine Ins Co Ltd* [1897] 2 QB 93 (CA—re).

246. Bowstead, pp 256 ff.; Halsbury, Vol 1, Nos 810 ff.

247. *Levy* v *Barnard* (1818) 8 Taunt 149 (cargo); *Fisher* v *Smith* (1878) 4 App Cas 1 (cargo). In marine insurance the lien extends to the general balance of the account between agent and insured: MIA s 53(2); Arnould, No 195. *Semble* it has not been settled whether this rule extends to non-marine insurance. As to whether the agent has a particular lien on premium money already paid by the proposer, see Bowstead, p 258.

CHAPTER 10

THE PROPOSAL OF INSURANCE[1]

10-1 INTRODUCTION

The proposal, sometimes called the application, is completed by the proposer who seeks insurance on a form usually drafted by the insurer. It functions as an offer to contract made by the proposer,[2] as well as a statement of matters affecting the risk, which may induce the insurer to contract[3]; and, if a contract is concluded, a basis clause[4] in the proposal makes it a source of terms in the contract of insurance. Although apparently the instrument of the proposer, the form is frequently completed by the proposer with the assistance of the insurer's agent, who may even fill it in for him.[5] This chapter considers the following questions: Who should bear the consequences of an error in the form? What is the effect of statements entered by the agent in the form, which conflict with statements by the proposer to the agent, or of material facts which are disclosed to the agent but not recorded in the form?

The answers depend on how the court identifies the legal issues involved. On the surface the issues are (1) whether the agent was acting as agent of the insurer or of the insured, when helping the proposer to complete the form or when receiving information about the risk; or, if the insured has signed the form, (2) whether he should be bound by the consequences of his signature. Further, if the proposal is duly completed but corrupted en route (by the agent), this has been seen[6] as raising a question of whether there is sufficient correspondence between offer and acceptance to form a

---

1. Hodgin, pp 34 ff; Merkin, "Transferred Agency in the Law of Insurance", 13 Anglo-American Law Rev 33 (1984); Tan Lee Meng, "Insurance Agents and the Proposal Form," 17 Mal L R 104 (1975), with reference to the law of England, Malaysia and Singapore; Tedeschi, "Assured's Misrepresentation and the Insurance Agent's Knowledge of the Truth", 7 Is LR 475 (1972), with reference to the law of England, Israel, France, Italy and West Germany; Timmins, "Misrepresentation in Insurance Proposal Forms Completed by Agents", 7 VUW Law Rev 217 (1974), with reference to the law of England, Australia, New Zealand and the United States.
2. See below, 11–1.
3. See below, 22–2.
4. See below, 20–2B2.
5. For example the Insurance Ombudsman's Report, 1985, p 6. Cf the General Insurance Business—Code of Practice for all Intermediaries, prepared by the Association of British Insurers, which came into effect on 1 January 1989: Part 1, C provides that "The intermediary shall, in obtaining the completion of the proposal form or any other material: (1) avoid influencing the prospective policyholder and make it clear that all the answers or statements are the latter's own responsibility; and (ii) ensure that the consequences of non-disclosure and inaccuracies are pointed out to the prospective policyholder by drawing his attention to the relevant statement in the proposal form and by explaining them himself to the prospective policyholder".
6. For example, *Phoenix* v *Berechree* (1906) 3 CLR 946, 957–958 *per* Griffiths CJ (HCA—life).

contract. But usually the dominant issue is the force of signature and the allocation of risk.[7]

10–2 TRANSFERRED AGENCY

When the issue is seen as one of agency, some courts find "transferred agency": that, when helping the proposer to fill the form, the agent is then acting not as agent for the insurer but as agent for the proposer.[8] Hence, the statements in the form are the responsibility of the proposer alone and any information that comes to the agent's attention at that time cannot be attributed via the agent to the insurer, unless it is actually put in the form.

The leading case of this kind is *Newsholme*.[9] The agent's mandate from the insurer was "to procure persons to take out insurance policies with the insurance company and to obtain from them duly filled in and signed proposal forms."[10] He was not authorised to complete forms and there was no evidence that the insurer knew that he did so. A proposal form for the insurance of a bus was signed by the proposer, having been completed incorrectly by the agent; although told the truth by the proposer, for reasons that were unclear the agent wrote untrue answers. The Court of Appeal held that, when completing the form, he was not the agent of the insurer but merely the amanuensis of the proposer; that the agent's knowledge of the truth was not attributable to the insurer; and that therefore the insurer could avoid liability on the policy in view of the untrue statements in the proposal.

One objection to the decision is that agency for the proposer rather than the insurer is an uncomfortable inference from the facts. The agent is not a solicitor, to whom the proposer has brought the form for explanation and advice. It is often the agent who approaches the proposer with the encouragement or acquiescence of the insurer, and it is the agent who is best placed to explain what is in the insurer's form. In almost any

---

7. In the general law of contract see Treitel, pp 22 ff.

8. *Biggar* v *Rock Life Assurance Co* [1902] 1 KB 516, 524 *per* Wright J (accident); *McMillan* v *Accident Ins Co Ltd*, 1907 SC 484; *Newsholme Bros* v *Road Transport & General Ins Co Ltd* [1929] 2 KB 356, 369 *per* Scrutton LJ (CA—motor). See also *Dunn* v *Ocean Accident & Guarantee Corp Ltd* (1933) 50 TLR 32 (CA—motor): although Lord Hanworth MR agreed with Avory J that the agent was the agent of the proposer (to whom he was married), the decision rests more easily on the basis of fraud (below, 10–5B).

Cf Maye v *Colonial Mutual Life Assurance Sy Ltd* (1924) 35 CLR 14 (life) in which the HCA treated the question as one of agency but found that the agent filled the form as agent of the insurer.

Moreover, in Ireland s 51(1) of the Insurance Act 1989 provides that, when he helps the proposer to complete the proposal, an insurance agent shall be deemed to be acting as the agent of the insurer.

9. *Newsholme Bros* v *Road Transport & General Ins Co Ltd* [1929] 2 KB 356. The decision has been applied in a number of cases, all of which, however, have distinguishing features:

For example in *Dunn* v *Ocean Accident & Guarantee Corp Ltd* (1933) 50 TLR 32 (CA—motor) the agent was secretly married to the plaintiff proposer and there was a clear suggestion of collusion. In *Facer* v *Vehicle & General Ins Co Ltd* [1965] 1 Lloyd's Rep 113 (motor) an additional ground was a special clause. In *Newsholme* itself the proposer was aware that some of the statements in the form were untrue: [1929] 2 KB 356, 365 *per* Scrutton LJ. There was a hint of fraud; see *per* Scrutton LJ (pp 375–376) reflecting a view of fraud by an agent that is probably not the law today: see above, 8–3C.

However, transferred agency was accepted by the Supreme Court of Canada in *Billington* v *Provincial Ins Co* (1879) 3 SCR 182 (fire), discussed below, 10–3; see also in this sense *Reid* v *Traders General Ins Co* (1963) 41 DLR (2d) 148 (NS—motor).

10. This finding of the arbitrator was criticised by the court (for example by Scrutton LJ at pp 365–366) as unclear.

other context, the agent would be seen as the agent of the person who proffers the form for signature.[11] Indeed, there is the anomaly that, if he misrepresents the terms of a proposed settlement of claim, the agent acts for the insurer,[12] but that, if he misrepresents the terms of the proposed insurance itself, he acts for the proposer. Worse, even while procuring the insurance, the agent may switch roles from Jekyll to Hyde and back again, perhaps several times.[13]

In *Wilkinson*[14], the Supreme Court of the United States rightly observed that the proposer

"looks to and relies upon the agent who has persuaded him to effect insurance as the full and complete representative of the company, in all that is said or done in making the contract. Has he not a right so to regard him?"

The court noted the argument that the agent filled the form as the agent of the insured and continued:

"But to apply such a doctrine, in its full force, to the system of selling policies through agents, which we have described, would be a snare and a delusion, leading, as it has done in numerous instances, to the grossest frauds, of which the insurance corporations receive the benefits, and the parties supposing themselves insured are the victims . . . The powers of the agent are, *prima facie*, co-extensive with the business intrusted (*sic*) to his care, and will not be narrowed by limitations not communicated to the person with whom he deals."

Yet another objection to *Newsholme* is that the Court of Appeal asked if the agent had actual authority in that case to act for the insurer when filling the form and, finding none, concluded without more that the agent must be acting for the proposer. This did not follow. The Court appeared[15] to jump the question whether the agent had *apparent* authority[16] to act for the insurer in this respect and, if so, whether the insurer was thus bound by the actions or knowledge of the agent. The reason for the jump is not hard to find. The apparent authority of an agent cannot affect the insurer unless the proposer relies on it.[17] In *Newsholme* reliance on the agent was negated because

---

11. *Curtis* v *Chemical Cleaning & Dyeing Co Ltd* [1951] 1 KB 805 (CA). Treitel, p 223. Law reform committees in England, Australia, Canada and New Zealand have recommended legislation that the agent be regarded as representing the insurer in this context: Hodgin pp 38–39. See also decisions in the United States in which it was held that insurance cover took effect in the terms represented to the proposer by the insurer's agent: above, 8–3C.

Cf Joel v *Law Union & Crown Ins Co* [1908] 2 KB 863 (CA—life): it was not disputed that the doctor, appointed by the insurer to submit a medical report on the basis of questions answered and signed by the proposer, was acting as the agent of the insurer: the doctor had written instructions to put the questions, and fill in the answers "with any necessary explanations" (*per* Vaughan Williams LJ p 874).

12. The *Newsholme* view appears to overlook the possibility that the agent may act concurrently for both insurer and proposer: *Horry* v *Tate & Lyle Refineries Ltd* [1982] 2 Lloyd's Rep 416 (employers' liability).

13. Tedeschi, pp 477 ff.

14. *Union Mutual Life Ins Co* v *Wilkinson*, 13 Wall 222 (1872—life). For a case in which a limitation on the authority of the agent to act for the insurer in connection with the proposal was nonetheless effective see *Aetna Life Ins Co* v *Moore*, 231 US 356 (1913). Generally see 45 CJS, sections 728 ff.

15. In *Newsholme Bros* v *Road Transport & General Ins Co Ltd* [1929] 2 KB 356 the leading judgment of Scrutton LJ stressed that the particular agent lacked actual authority (p 365; see also Greer LJ, p 377). There was but passing reference to general practice, evidence of apparent authority, although the evidence suggested (p 362) that the agent might have had apparent authority to fill the form: "It is inevitable in such a course of business that the agent employed to get proposals will sometimes fill in or assist in filling in answers on the form."

16. Generally see above, 8–3. On this ground, *Newsholme*, described (p 632) as the "high point of the insurer being shielded from knowledge gained by a canvasser", was readily distinguished in *Farrell* v *National Mutual Life Assn of Australasia Ltd* [1991] 2 Qd R 624 (disability).

17. Bowstead, p 414.

the proposer was treated as if he knew that the agent had put false information in the form[18]—because the proposer had signed it. It is submitted that the true foundation of the decision is less the role of the agent than the impact of signature (below, 10–3).

A third objection to *Newsholme* is that, even if the agent does act for the proposer when filling the form, it does not necessarily follow that information (for example about risk) acquired, when acting for the proposer, cannot be attributed via the agent to the insurer[19]; or that, when acting once again for the insurer in transmitting the completed form to the insurer, that information does not then become that of the insurer.[20] It would be odd, if information acquired before transmission of the form could never be attributed to the insurer but a different rule applied to similar information acquired later.[21]

The "transferred agency" approach to the proposal form has produced curious results out of line with the general law of agency. This, it is submitted, may be because the real issue is not agency but the attribution of fault and the allocation of risk in respect of a signed document.[22]

10–3 THE IMPORTANCE OF SIGNATURE

In *Newsholme*[23] Scrutton LJ spoke of

"a conflict, which is visible in the authorities cited to us, between the desire to hold the insurer, who employs an agent to bring him business, liable for anything that agent does in procuring business, and, on the other hand, the contention that a man who signs a promise that certain written statements are true and the basis of his contract, which statements, if he read them before signing, he would know to be untrue, cannot claim to vary his contract by omitting that promise and misstatement."

18. Because he could not deny his signature; see [1929] 2 KB 356, 364–365 *per* Scrutton LJ; 378 *per* Greer LJ.

19. In *Newsholme* (above) p 370 Scrutton LJ appears to have proceeded on the basis that the knowledge of an agent authorised to procure contracts but not to conclude them could not be attributed to his principals. *Contra* Tedeschi, *op cit*, pp 482 ff.

"While the agent may have lacked authority from the CML to fill up the proposal on behalf of Deaves, he nevertheless received, as part of his function as a representative of CML information . . . relevant to the risk. Having received such information, *and the signed proposal not being contradictory of it*, the CML is to be treated as itself possessing that knowledge "—*Deaves* v *CML Fire & General Ins Co Ltd* (1979) 53 ALJR 382, 392 *per* Stephen J (HCA—fire) (italics supplied). The judge went on to adopt a similar statement in Ivamy (3rd ed, p 523), now found (in the 6th ed) at p 579. *Contra* Merkin, 13 Anglo-American L Rev 33 (1984), 42.

20. *Cf Blackburn, Low & Co* v *Vigors* (1887) 12 App Cas 531. 537 *per* Lord Halsbury (re); *Taylor* v *Yorkshire Ins Co* [1913] 2 IR 1, 21 *per* Pallas CB (stallion); *Banque Keyser Ullmann DSA* v *Skandia (UK) Ins Co Ltd* [1987] 1 Lloyd's Rep 69. 95 *per* Steyn J. In the view of Bowstead (p 415), the position of an agent who switches on and off is unclear. See further below, 23–9A2.

21. As it does: *Wing* v *Harvey* (1854) 5 De GM & G 265 (life). *Cf* also *Ayrey* v *British Legal & United Provident Assurance Co* [1918] 1 KB 136 (life). *Blackley* v *National Mutual Life* [1972] NZLR 1038 (CA—life). See also *Golding* discussed below, 10–3B. It should make no difference whether knowledge acquired by an agent in the course of his agency is acquired before the contract or not: *Holdsworth* v *Lancashire & Yorkshire Ins Co* (1907) 23 TLR 521, 523 *per* Bray J.

22. In this sense *Deaves* v *CML Fire & General Ins Co Ltd* (1979) 53 ALJR 382, 392 *per* Stephen J (HCA—fire). Hodgin, p 35.

23. *Newsholme Bros* v *Road Transport & General Ins Co Ltd* [1929] 2 KB 356 (CA—motor). The same idea is sometimes expressed in terms of the parol evidence rule, for example, *Newsholme* (above), pp 379–380 *per* Greer LJ.

In the same sense as the text: *Merchants' Mutual Ins Co* v *Lyman*, 15 Wall 664 (SC, 1873—hull).

A person is generally bound by the contents of a document that he has signed.[24]

"Every presumption in law is in favour of holding that a man knows what he is putting his subscription to, and if he did not read what he was signing *sibi imputet*. Any other rule would be most dangerous to the certainty of transactions based on signed documents. If a man signing a document chooses to take the risk of trusting that another person has drawn up the document according to his instructions, he must take the consequences if there are statements above his signature which are false."[25]

This is a general rule of law, which has the merit of being clear and which applies to insurance contracts. If the proposer signs a proposal form without reading it, in general, he is bound by what he has signed whatever he might have said to the agent. In English insurance law the leading case of this kind is *Newsholme*,[26] in which the Court of Appeal was influenced by a leading case in the United States, *New York Life Ins Co v Fletcher*.[27]

In *Fletcher*, the proposer of life insurance answered questions put by the agent and told him *inter alia* that he suffered from diabetes; this was not inserted in the form by the agent, who was fraudulent. The proposer signed but did not read or check what had been inserted. After his death a claim on the policy failed. One reason, commonly mentioned in later cases, was that the form contained an effective limit on the authority of the agent to receive information. However, if that limit was effective, it was as a result of the signature:

"It was his duty to read the application he signed. He knew that upon it the policy would be issued, if issued at all. It would introduce great uncertainty in all business transactions, if a party making written proposals for a contract, with representations to induce its execution, should be allowed to show, after it had been obtained, that he did not know the contents of his proposals, and to enforce it, notwithstanding their falsity as to matters essential to its obligation and validity. Contracts could not be made or business fairly conducted, if such a rule should prevail."[28]

24. In respect of formal documents: *Saunders v Anglia Building Society* [1971] AC 1004; *Norwich & Peterborough Building Society v Steed (No 2)* [1993] 1 All ER 330 (CA); and in respect of less formal documents: *L'Estrange v Graucob Ltd* [1934] 2 KB 394; see also *United Dominions Trust Ltd v Western* [1976] QB 513 (CA).

25. *McMillan v Accident Ins Co*, 1907 SC 484, 491 *per* the Lord Justice-Clerk; see also p 493 *per* Lord Stormont-Darling. In England: *Biggar v Rock Life Assurance Co* [1901] 2 KB 516, 524 *per* Wright J (life). USA: *New York Life Ins Co v Fletcher*, 117 US 519, 529 (1886) *per* Field J (life); *Jakobson Shipyard Inc v Aetna*, 775 F Supp 606 (SD NY, 1991—liability); and *Jones v New York Life & Annuity Corp*, 985 F 2d 503, 508 (10 Cir, 1993—life). See further *Vance*, pp 261-262.

26. Above, 10–2. The document, having been authenticated by signature, is decisive; thus Greer LJ (*ibid* pp 379–380), having stressed the importance of signed writing, continued: "it does not seem to matter whether the verbal statements which are relied upon are made to [the agent] or are made to the directors of the company". *Semble* it does not matter, in his view, whether the agent is acting for the proposer or the insurer, for the document is decisive. See also *Life & Health Assurance Assn Ltd v Yule* (1904) 6 F 437 (Ct Sess—liability).

In Canada see *Blanchette v CIS* (1973) 36 DLR (3d) 561 (Sup Ct.—fire and liability).

27. 117 US 519 (1886). See also *Billington v Prudential Ins Co of America*, 254 F 2d 428 (7 Cir, 1958—life).

28. 117 US 519, 529 *per* Field J (1886). See also *Maier v Fidelity Mutual Life Assn*, 78 F 566 (6 Cir, 1897—life); *Aetna Life Ins Co v Moore*, 231 US 543 (1913—life); *Maryland Casualty Co v Eddy*, 239 F 477 (6 Cir, 1917—PA); *Bankers' Reserve Life Co v Yelland*, 41 F 2d 684 (9 Cir, 1930—life); *Telford v New York Life Ins Co*, 69 P 2d 835 (Cal, 1937—life). Although not followed in all the state courts, *Fletcher* has been followed in recent times at federal level: for example, *Commercial Ins Co of Newark v Smith*, 417 F 2d 1330 (10 Cir, 1969—disability); and *Barciak v United of Omaha Life Ins Co*, 777 F Supp 839 (D Colo, 1991—life).

In some later cases, however, *Fletcher* has been limited to cases of fraud, so that even when the proposer tells the agent the truth but signs without checking a form fraudulently and falsely completed by the agent, the insurer is estopped from setting up the false statement: for example, *Bank Sav. Life Ins Co v Butler*, 38 F 2d 972 (8 Cir, 1930—life); *Velez Gomez v SMA Life Assurance Co*, 793 F Supp 378, 384 (D Puerto Rico,

A similar result for similar reasons was reached in Canada in *Billington* v *Provincial Ins Co*,[29] in spite of the fact that the agent had greater authority than most agents, *viz*, authority to grant temporary insurance cover himself. *Billington* concerned insurance against fire on machinery in store. The proposer told the agent that there was another policy which might extend to the goods. The agent agreed to check this possibility and complete the form, which he received from the proposer signed in blank. The other policy did cover the goods, but the agent did not make the promised check or mention the earlier policy in the proposal. Eventually the insurer met a claim with a plea of non-disclosure of the other policy. The Supreme Court of Canada decided against the claim:

"Instead of getting himself the precise information required to enable him to make a proper application, as was his interest and duty to the Company, [the proposer] trusts to [the agent] to get it for him. Surely he must take the consequences of any neglect on [the agent's] part."[30]

These cases premise an assumption of risk by the signatory and, by implication, the consent of an independent will. Yet it is not immediately obvious why the proposer, who does not know the agent, assumes the risk of the agent's fraud, forgetfulness or incompetence, while the insurer, who appointed or commissioned the agent, does not; on the contrary, "it is more reason that he that employs and puts a trust and confidence in the deceiver should be loser than a stranger."[31] The more so when, for reasons of poor education, intelligence or health, the proposer is no match for the agent. This may be why today many jurisdictions in the United States have rejected a strict rule based on signature, holding that the proposer who signed without reading what he had signed was not necessarily negligent[32]; and that, unless he was fraudulent, he would not be estopped by his signature of a proposal from pleading what he had told the agent.[33] In England, the position of the proposer is less favourable. Yet even in England developments in the law at large suggest that in three situations (below, 10–3A to 10–3C) the binding effect of signature has been loosened by considerations of fault and the re-allocation of risk.

10–3A The Vulnerable Proposer

If the person signing was illiterate, blind, senile or incapacitated, the early law did not allow the profferor to set up his signature against him.[34] More recently, this rule has been applied only to "those who are permanently or temporarily unable through no fault of their own to have without explanation any real understanding of the purport of a particular document, whether that be from defective education, illness or innate incapacity".[35] This extends to anyone whose lack of education or capacity makes him

1992—disability). In such cases, the emphasis is not on the force of signature but on the role of the agent as agent of the insurer.
   29. (1879) 3 SCR 182. See also *Jumna Khan* v *Bankers & Traders Ins Co Ltd* (1925) 37 CLR 451 (HCA—fire). Cf *Moxness* v *Cooperative Fire & Casualty Co* (1979) 95 DLR (3d) 365 (Alta—motor).
   30. pp 199–200.
   31. *Western Australian Ins Co Ltd* v *Dayton* (1924) 35 CLR 355, 377 *per* Isaacs ACJ (HCA—motor).
   32. *New Jersey Mutual Life Ins Co* v *Baker*, 94 US 610 (1876—life); *Weiss* v *Mutual Indemnity Co*, 145 NW 2d 171, 173 (Wis, 1966—hospital); *Schneider* v *Washington National Ins Co*, 437 P 2d 798, 810–811 (Kan, 1968—PHI).
   33. *Rapides Club* v *American Union Ins Co*, 35 F 2d 253 (WD La, 1929—fire); *Fruge* v *Woodmen of World Life Ins Co*, 70 So 2d 539 (La, 1965—life); *Rea* v *Hardware Mutual Casualty Co*, 190 SE 2d 708 (NC, 1972—motor).
   34. *Thoroughgood's case* (1548) 2 Co Rep 9a.
   35. *Saunders* v *Anglia Building Society* [1971] AC 1004, 1016 *per* Lord Reid.

unable to understand the technical language or jargon of the form. "There are degrees of understanding and a person who is a great expert in some subjects may be like a child in relation to other subjects."[36] On this basis, some courts have held that in appropriate circumstances a signatory acts reasonably in relying on the advice or assurances of the agent, and is not at fault if, thus reassured, he takes no further steps to check what he has been told.[37]

From this it appears that he who signs a proposal of insurance is bound only by what, if he had read it or, perhaps, taken reasonable steps to have it explained to him,[38] he would have understood.[39] In Newsholme[40] Scrutton LJ observed that he could "understand a contention that Newsholme was induced to sign by the representation of [the agent], that these answers were what the insurance company required", but on the particular facts of the case "such a contention would be difficult to sustain in view of Newsholme's knowledge that the answers were untrue".[41] This, it is submitted, is the line that marks a path between the cases following Newsholme (above, 10–2) and the cases following Bawden[42] (below). The feature of the latter is that, even if the proposer had read what was written in the form, he would not have realised that anything was wrong, either because he was led to think that the form gave the information required[43] or because he lacked the capacity to know better.[44]

In Bawden[45] the proposer could sign his name, but was illiterate. Patently he had only one eye. He took accident insurance through an agent, who had no authority to conclude contracts of insurance but did have authority to negotiate such contracts and to settle the form of proposals.[46] The details filled by the agent were accurate but the form, which the proposer signed, contained a printed declaration that "I . . . have no physical infirmity, nor are there any circumstances that render me peculiarly liable to

---

36. *Saunders, loc cit.*
37. *Curtis v Chemical Cleaning & Dyeing Co Ltd* [1951] 1 KB 805 (CA). *Western Australian Ins Co Ltd v Dayton* (1924) 35 CLR 355, 374 ff *per* Isaacs ACJ (HCA—motor).
38. *Adamos v New York Life Ins Co*, 5 F Supp 278 (WD Pa, 1933—life).
39. Also in this sense Ivamy, p 579.
40. *Newsholme Bros v Road Transport & General Ins Co Ltd* [1929] 2 KB 356, 364–365 *per* Scrutton LJ (CA—motor).
41. The knowledge in that case appears to be knowledge presumed from signature.
42. *Bawden v London, Edinburgh & Glasgow Assurance Co* [1892] 2 QB 534, as viewed in *Taylor v Yorkshire* [1913] 2 IR 1, 16 *per* Palles CB. See also *New York Life v Fletcher*, 117 US 519, 532–533 (1886) *per* Field J. *Life & Health Assurance Assn Ltd v Yule* (1904) 6 SCR 437, 441; *Blanchette v CIS* (1973) 36 DLR (3d) 561, 577 (Sup. Ct., —fire and liability).
43. See cases cited at the end of this section under (c)
44. See cases cited at the end of this section under (a) and (b).
45. [1892] 2 QB 534. See also *O'Connor v Kirby & Co* [1971] 1 Lloyd's Rep 454, 458 *per* Davies LJ (CA—motor). *Cf Telford v New York Life Ins Co*, 69 P 2d 835 (Cal, 1937—life) in which the court declined to attribute knowledge to the insurer via a doctor, who had been appointed to examine the proposer, that the proposer had had a breast removed. *Cf* also *Johnson v Mutual Benefit Health & Accident Assurance Assn*, 168 NYS 2d 879 (1958—PA).
Bawden was distinguished on its facts in *Newsholme Bros v Road Transport & General Ins Co Ltd* [1929] 2 KB 356, 375 and 380 and, it was thought, shunted into a siding of legal history. So Bowstead (p 417) suggests that *Newsholme* represents the prevailing view. However, *Bawden* was approved by the Court of Appeal in *Brewster v National Life Sy* (1892) 8 TLR 648 (life) and in *Stone v Reliance Mutual* [1972] 1 Lloyd's Rep 469, 475 *per* Lord Denning MR. *Bawden* was applied in *Hough v Guardian Fire & Life Assurance Co Ltd* (1902) 18 TLR 273 (fire); *Holdsworth v Lancashire & Yorkshire Ins Co* (1907) 23 TLR 521 (accident); *Thornton-Smith v Motor Union Ins Co Ltd* (1913) 30 TLR 139 (motor); *Keeling v Pearl Assurance Co Ltd* (1923) 129 LT 573 (life); *Paxman v Union Assurance Sy Ltd* (1923) 39 TLR 424 (motor); *Kaufmann v British Surety Ins Co Ltd* (1929) 33 Ll L Rep 315 (motor); and *Mahomed v Anchor Fire & Marine Ins Co* (1913) 48 SCR 547, 554 by Duff J (fire). See also *Cruikshank v Northern Accident*, discussed below, 23–9A2.
46. For example [1892] 2 QB 534, 539 *per* Lord Esher MR; later cases have doubted this conclusion.

accidents". His claim in respect of loss of the remaining eye was resisted by the insurer.

The Court of Appeal decided for the insured. It took a general, rather than segmentary, view of the negotiations: it saw the agent as the agent of the insurer throughout. The main problem was signature of the document which, read literally, was untrue. The court's solution lay in construction. Lord Esher MR[47]:

"The proposal must be construed as having been negotiated and settled by the agent with a one-eyed man. In that sense the knowledge of the agent was the knowledge of the company. The policy was upon a printed form which contained general words applicable to more than one state of circumstances, and we have to apply those words to the particular circumstances of this case."

So, viewed as a proposal from a patently one-eyed man, who in effect was saying that he had no other infirmity, it was not inaccurate.[48]

Bawden was approved in *Stone* v *Reliance Mutual Ins Sy Ltd*,[49] where there was clear evidence of company policy that the agent should put the questions and write the answers[50] and the insurer was held liable. The insurer was unable to plead non-disclosure (of a previous fire claim) because "It was their own agent who made the mistake. It was he who ought to have known better."[51] Having noted that the insurer could have discovered the mistake from records, Lord Denning MR said[52]:

"No doubt it was Mrs Stone's mistake too. She ought to have read through the questions and answers before she signed the form: but she did not do so. Her mistake, however, was excusable, because she was of little education, and assumed that the agent would know all about the previous policies and that there had been claims under them."

Likewise in the USA, if the proposer discloses information to the agent, for example treatment for high blood pressure, but is assured by the agent that it does not matter, for example because it had occurred too far in the past, a plea of non–disclosure will fail.[53]

In Canada, a similar concern about the vulnerability of the proposer can be seen in *Mahomed* v *Anchor Fire & Marine Ins Co*.[54] The proposer signed in blank a proposal of fire insurance on merchandise, furniture and fixtures, leaving it to Mr Freeze, the

---

47. pp 539–540. See also Lindley LJ p 541. *Cf* Kay LJ (p 542): "the condition that the statements in the proposal are to form the basis of the contract do not apply at all, because knowledge is to be imputed to the company of the fact that Bawden only had one eye."

48. This view of the case was taken in *Newsholme* v *Road Traffic & General* [1929] 2 KB 356, 381–382 by Greer LJ, with implicit reference to *Smith* v *Wilson* (1832) 3 B & D 728 (seen in context, "1,000 rabbits" really meant 1,200 rabbits!).

49. [1972] 1 Lloyd's Rep 469 (CA—fire & theft). See also *Raymond* v *Zeringue*, 422 So 2d 534 (La, 1982—motor).

50. So, in *Vrbancic* v *London Life Ins Co* (1991) 76 DLR (4th) 68 (Ont, 1990—life), *Stone* was followed and *Bawden* distinguished on the ground that the agent was acting for the insurer. *Stone* was also applied in *Bell* v *Australian Eagle Ins Co Ltd* (1990) 6 ANZ Ins Cases, no 60–983 (FCA—life).

51. p 475 *per* Lord Denning MR; see also p 476 *per* Megaw LJ.

52. [1972] 1 Lloyd's Rep 469, 474; see also p 476 *per* Megaw LJ. And *Lloyds Bank plc* v *Waterhouse* [1991] Fam Law 23 in which a person was not bound by his signature of a guarantee because the bank, to which it was given, had given a misleading reply to his questions about its scope.

53. *Ward* v *Durham Life Ins Co*, 381 SE 2d 698 (NC, 1989—life). Also in this sense: *American Life Ins Co* v *Mahone* (below, 10–3C); *Hawaian Life Ins Co Ltd* v *Laygo*, 884 F 2d 1300 (9 Cir, 1989—life); *Guy* v *Commonwealth Life Ins Co*, 894 F 2d 1407 (5 Cir, 1990—medical expenses).

54. (1913) 48 SCR 547. See also *Great Northern Ins Co* v *Whitney* (1918) 44 DLR 433 (Sup Ct—livestock): the proposer's sight was "not good and he did not check the statement" in his proposal, so the erroneous statement of value inserted by the agent was not the proposer's "fault" (p 436). The decision in favour of the proposer could not be supported in England today, but for the fact that there was ambiguity in the question to which the erroneous reply was made.

defendant's manager, to complete the form by apportioning the sum insured between the three kinds of property. This he did incorrectly and this led to his company pleading overvaluation to resist a claim. The Supreme Court decided for the claimant. This decision is difficult to reconcile with those in which the proposer, who left a blank form with the agent to be completed by the agent, was bound by the contents.[55] The difference in *Mahomed* may lie in the technical nature of the information to be inserted: it appears that, even if the proposer had checked the apportionment, she would not have understood whether it was correct or not,[56] not least because her English was poor.[57] In any event, it seems to have been a matter that was reasonably left to the insurer.

We can conclude that, in the cases in which the proposer has been allowed to deny his signature, the proposer was vulnerable on one or more of these points:

    (a) inability to read, or to read English[58];

    (b) inability to understand the meaning of questions or statements in the form[59];

    (c) induced belief that he had disclosed all that he needed to disclose.[60]

In England, however, the force of signature remains strong.[61] Point (a) is unlikely to excuse. While the instances may be expanded in future, points (b) and (c) have excused the signatory mainly as regards,

    (i) the scope of the cover proposed[62]; and

    (ii) the meaning of questions forming the basis of a medical report[63]: the signatory is bound by the answers he makes in the form, but in the sense in which the questions were explained to him by the doctor acting for the insurer, and

---

55. *Billington* v *Provincial Ins Co* (1879) 3 SCR 182 (fire) discussed above 10–3.

56. Unlike many agents, Mr Freeze had authority to conclude contracts, but it does not appear that the decision turned on this. *Cf Jumna Khan* v *Bankers & Traders* (1925) 37 CLR 451 (below, 10–4) in which the contentious part of the form was such that, if the proposer had asked for it to be read out, he would have understood that it was wrong. *Semble* this was not the case in *Mahomed*.

57. Stressed at p 549.

58. *Bawden* v *London, Edinburgh & Glasgow Assurance Co* [1892] 2 QB 534 (CA); *Stone* v *Reliance Mutual Ins Sy Ltd* [1972] 1 Lloyd's Rep 469 (CA—fire and theft). *Reserve Life Ins Co* v *Meeks*, 174 SE 2d 585 (Ga, 1970— hospital).

59. *Joel* v *Law Union & Crown Ins Co* [1908] 2 KB 863 (CA—life); *Keeling* v *Pearl Assurance Co Ltd* (1923) 129 LT 573, 575 per Bailhache J (life). *Mahomed* v *Anchor Fire & Marine Ins Co* (1913) 48 SCR 547 (fire). *Sias* v *Roger Williams Ins Co*, 8 F 183 (D NH, 1881—fire); *Pacific Mutual Life Ins Co* v *Snowden*, 58 F 342 (8 Cir, 1893—PA); *Carrollton Furniture Mfg Co* v *American Credit Indemnity Co*, 115 F 77 (2 Cir, 1902—credit).

60. *Bawden* (above); *Hough* v *Guardian Fire & Life Assurance Co Ltd* (1902) 18 TLR 273 (fire); *Stone* (above). Insurance Ombudsman's Annual Report for 1985, pp 6–7.

Western Australian Ins Co Ltd v *Dayton* (1924) 35 CLR 355 (HCA—motor); *Deaves* v *CML Fire & General Ins Co Ltd* (1979) 53 ALJR 382, 396 per Mason J (HCA—fire). *Lewis* v *Northern Assurance Co Ltd* (1956) 4 DLR (2d) 496 (Ont—motor). *Eames* v *Home Ins Co*, 94 US 621 (1877—fire); *Continental Life Ins Co* v *Chamberlain* 132 US 305 (1889—life); *Standard Life & Accident Ins Co* v *Fraser*, 76 F 705 (9 Cir, 1896—PA); *Bass* v *Farmers Mutual Protective Fire Ins Co*, 68 P 2d 302, 304 (Cal, 1937—fire); *Green* v *South Western Voluntary Assn Inc*, 20 SE 2d 694, 697 (Va, 1942—life); *Pitcher* v *World Ins Co*, 42 NW 2d 735 (Mich, 1950—disability); *Boggio* v *Californian-Western States Life Ins Co*, 239 P 2d 144 (Cal, 1952—life); *Lipsky* v *Washington National Ins Co*, 152 NW 2d 702 (Mich, 1967—hospital).

61. *Saunders* v *Anglia Building Society* [1971] AC 1004.

62. *Kaufmann* v *British Surety Ins Co Ltd* (1929) 33 Ll L Rep 315, 319 per Roche J (motor). Generally see *Curtis* v *Chemical Cleaning & Dyeing Co Ltd* [1951] 1 KB 805 (CA). Treitel, p 223. See further above, 8–3C.

63. *Joel* v *Law Union & Crown Ins Co* [1908] 2 KB 863 (CA—life). *Mutual Benefit Life Ins Co* v *Robison*, 58 F 723 (8 Cir, 1893—life); *New York Life Ins Co* v *Russell*, 77 F 94 (8 Cir, 1896—life).

the insurer cannot plead a misstatement, the inaccuracy of which was caused by the doctor making the report.[64]

In these situations it seems reasonable for the proposer to ask the profferor what his document means. The allocation of risk to the insurer is reinforced by the rule of construction *contra proferentem*.

The counsel of perfection may yet argue that the reasonable proposer should not trust the devil to explain his own pact, that nothing should be signed without independent advice. If so, a distinction may be necessary between, first, the illiterate or blind and, second, the unaware. It may be said that the first, being aware of the risk of signature, should seek independent advice or explanation and, if they do not, should be responsible for any error which this precaution would have revealed. A handicap which makes it more difficult to fulfil a duty does not excuse the duty[65]: it has been held[66] in the United States that a proposer, whose English was such that he did not understand the questions put, should have asked for explanation,[67] and the contention that he could not be held to the statements in the form failed. In contrast, the second group will not be held to signature in such cases, if "reasonably" unaware of the risk.

10–3A1 The Industrial Assurance Act 1923

The Act applies to industrial assurance, that is, life insurance at premiums received through collectors at intervals of less than two months. By section 20(4),[68] if the proposal is completed partly or wholly by the collector, the insurer is not entitled to question the validity of the contract on the ground of any misstatement contained in the proposal, except as regards a statement about the health of the assured.

10–3B Transmission of the Proposal

The proposer is normally expected to read through the proposal at the time of signature, and is committed to what he should have read and understood at that time (above, 10–3). But misstatements or omissions in the proposal may be the result of what occurs after the proposal has left the proposer for transmission to the insurer. In cases like this, courts are influenced by whether the proposer had a reasonable opportunity to check the contents of the proposal after it had left him.

The proposer's position is weak when the form is signed by the proposer wholly or partly in blank for completion by the agent. The risk of error or fraud by the agent is assumed by the proposer; he is estopped by his signature of the form, as completed by

---

64. USA in this sense: *Variety Homes Inc v Postal Life Ins Co*, 287 F 2d 320 (2 Cir, 1961—life). *Cf Phillips-Morefield v Southerm States Life Ins Co*, 66 F 2d 29 (5 Cir, 1933—life).

65. *Mills v Reserve Life Ins Co*, 335 SW 2d 955, 957 (Ky, 1960—PHI).

66. *Adamos v New York Life Ins Co*, 5 F Supp 278 (WD Pa, 1933—life); the court underlined that the questions were intelligible to a person with a normal command of English, and that it considered the application fraudulent.

If the proposer does not understand the questions he should seek clarification from the agent and, if he does not, cannot later deny his signature on the ground that he was confused: *Nationwide Mutual Fire Ins Co v Dungan*, 634 F Supp 674 (SD Mo, 1986—homeowners').

67. There are signs that the court would have been content with an explanation from the agent, but *quaere*.

68. Section 20(4), as amended by the Industrial Assurance and Friendly Societies Act 1948, section 9(2) and the Financial Services Act 1986, section 139 (2).

the agent.[69] His position is stronger when he signs a completed form, which unexpectedly requires alteration, or which is altered without his knowledge after it has been delivered to the agent for transmission to the insurer.

In *Golding* v *Royal London Auxiliary*[70] the claimant signed a proposal of fire insurance, without reading it. However, he did read a duplicate left behind by the agent and noticed an omission to disclose a previous fire. A few days later he informed the agent of the omission to mention the previous fire, but the agent forgot to pass the information to the appropriate officer of the company, which issued a policy. The insurer's defence to a claim, a defence based on the omission, failed.

If the agent in *Golding* had been told of the fire prior to completion and signature of the form, but the form had not mentioned the fire, it is clear that the proposer's signature would have overridden the oral statement to the agent and he would have been held to the omission.[71] The essential point about *Golding* is that the mention post-dated signature and, perhaps, that the proposer was no longer well placed to check that the agent had done what was required. In *Golding* the agent had a duty to transmit the information, the breach of which estopped the insurer from relying on the omission. Distinguish *Billington*[72] in which the agent was provided not with the relevant information but with the means of acquiring it. It appears that in *Billington* it was the duty of the proposer to acquire the information[73] and in leaving it to the agent he assumed the risk that it might not be acquired and passed on to the insurer. In *Golding* it was the duty of the proposer to give the information, which he did although late, and the duty of the agent as agent of the insurer to transmit it.

At the very least *Golding* supports the proposition that if, as is usual, the agent has authority to procure and transmit proposals, the proposer is entitled to trust the agent to transmit the proposal properly and, in particular, without fraud.[74] He is entitled to assume that a properly completed form will not be altered by the agent during transmission without his consent.[75] Further, *Golding* and *Stipcich* (below, 10–4B) decide that the proposer is entitled to trust the agent to record and transmit information aris-

---

69. *Newsholme Bros* v *Road Transport & General Ins Co Ltd* [1929] 2 KB 356 (CA—motor); *United Dominions Trust Ltd* v *Western* [1976] QB 513 (CA). *Billington* v *Provincial Ins Co* (1879) 3 SCR 182 (fire); *Blanchette* v *CIS* (1973) 36 DLR (3d) 561 (Sup. Ct.—fire and liability). *Golden Rule Ins Co* v *Lease*, 755 F Supp 948 (D Colo, 1991—PHI).
  On this point some earlier decisions to the contrary must be regarded as doubtful: *Holdsworth* v *Lancashire & Yorkshire Ins Co* (1907) 23 TLR 521 (liability); *Thornton-Smith* v *Motor Union Ins Co Ltd* (1913) 30 TLR 139 (motor).
70. (1914) 30 TLR 350. Also *Blanchette* v *CIS Ltd* (1973) 36 DLR (3d) 561 (Sup Ct—fire and liability).
  Cf cases that information given to a soliciting agent after the contract in question has been concluded is not knowledge which is attributable to his principal, the insurer; for example *Hare & Chase* v *National Surety*, 49 F 2d 447 (SDNY, 1931—guarantee).
71. See above, 10–3.
72. *Billington* (above); see also above, 10–3. *Cf Moxness* v *Cooperative Fire & Casualty Co*, 95 DLR (3d) 365 (Alta—motor).
73. But the agent's duty to transmit it.
74. As to the special problems raised by fraud, see below, 10–5.
75. *Mutual Reserve Fund Life* v *Farmer*, 47 SW 850 (Ark, 1898—life).
  Cf Phoenix Assurance Co Ltd v *Berechree* (1906) 3 CLR 947: the plaintiff signed a completed proposal of fire insurance. It was taken away by the insurer's agent who deleted a word inserted at the time of signature and interlined a substitute answer which overstated the plaintiff's interest in the property insured. The High Court of Australia held that the defendant insurer was not bound by the agent's conduct and that the claim on the policy failed. However, it is submitted that to the extent that the decision turns on estoppel (for example p 959) or on the liability of companies for fraudulent agents (pp 961–962), the law has now changed to a degree that would give a different decision in such a case; see above, 8–3D.

ing after the form has passed from proposer to agent, even though the (late) arrival of the information is in some degree the fault of the proposer.

10–3C Non-Reliance on the Proposal

The binding effect of deeds is commonly justified by reference to the need for certainty and to the operation of estoppel. With less conviction and with less consistency the same is said of documents signed[76]: the signatory is said to represent that he adopts the contents,[77] or that he has assented to the contents,[78] which, in the context of a proposal form, means that he has assented to the statement inserted by or on the advice of the agent as his own statement and representation which, if untrue, will justify rescission by the insurer. When, in reality, there is no such representation or assent on the part of the proposer as regards (all or) part of the proposal, there is an opening which the courts have taken to soften the effects of signature. A person should not generally be bound by his apparent assent when the other party knows that that person did not really assent at all.[79] Thus, there is no reliance by the insurer on a statement in the proposal which is obviously erroneous and which the proposer evidently did not intend to make.[80]

This can explain cases like *Bawden*[81] in which the agent sees a one-eyed man sign a form stating that he has no physical infirmity. It was also the explanation accepted by the Louisiana court, when an applicant on crutches signed a statement that he was in sound health: the agent's acceptance of the form as it stood (and failure to enquire about the reason for the crutches) was regarded as a waiver of the matter.[82]

A more difficult case of this kind is that of the proposal statement based on information supplied by third parties. Generally, if a third party provides information which is adopted by the proposer and entered in the form, the insurer relies on adoption by the proposer, who is estopped in that regard by his signature.[83] However, in some cases it cannot be said that the the insurer relies on the proposer. In *Union Mutual Life Ins Co of Maine* v *Wilkinson*[84] the proposer of life insurance was asked about the death of his mother. The proposer professed ignorance, but the agent questioned an old woman present who gave him false information which the agent entered in the proposal, which the proposer signed. The insurer pleaded the false statement,

---

76. Above, 10–3. As regards the influence of estoppel *cf McCutcheon* v *MacBrayne Ltd* [1964] 1 WLR 125, 134 *per* Lord Devlin (HL).

77. *Harris* v *GW Ry* (1876) 1 QBD 515, 530 *per* Blackburn J.

78. *Roe* v *Naylor (No 1)* [1917] 1 KB 712, 716 *per* Atkin J; *L'Estrange* v *Graucob Ltd* [1934] 2 KB 394, 403 *per* Scrutton LJ (CA).

79. *Hitchman* v *Avery* (1892) 8 TLR 698. *Cf Blay* v *Pollard & Morris* [1930] 1 KB 628 (CA). Spencer [1973] CLJ 104, 114–116; Vorster, 103 LQR 274, 275 (1987). *Colonial Investment Co* v *Borland* (1911) 1 WWR 171, 189 (Alta), affirmed (1912) 2 WWR 960 (SC); *Tilden Rent-a-Car Co* v *Clendenning* (1978) 83 DLR (3d) 400 (Ont); *Gallant* v *Sun Alliance Ins Co* (1984) 4 DLR (4th) 180 (NB—motor). Waddams, 49 Can Bar Rev 578, 590 (1971), and *Law of Contracts* (2nd ed, 1984), p 233; Holahan, 31 U Pittsburgh L Rev 547 (1970).

80. *Keeling* v *Pearl Assurance Co Ltd* (1933) 129 LT 573 (life).

81. Above 10–3A.

82. *Swain* v *Life Ins Co of Louisiana*, 537 So 2d 1297 (La, 1989—life). See also *Ross* v *Western Fidelity Ins Co* 872 F 2d 665 (5 Cir, 1989—health); *Ellingwood* v *N.N. Investors Life Ins Co*, 805 P 2d 70, 76–77 (NM, 1991—life). *Aliter*, if there is evidence of bad faith: *Monarch Life Ins Co Ltd* v *Pierce, Fenner & Smith Inc*, 708 F Supp 674 (ED Pa, 1989—life).

83. *Keeling* (above) p 574 *per* Bailhache J (life). See also below, 22-2C2.

84. 13 Wall 222 (1872). In this sense generally Williston, section 1518.

but the Supreme Court of the United States rejected the defence. Mr Justice Miller said:

"the parol testimony makes it clear beyond a question, that this party did not intend to make that representation when he signed the paper, and did not know he was doing so . . . If . . . we suppose the [insurer] to have been an individual, and to have been present when the application was signed, and soliciting the insured to make the contract of insurance, and that the insurer himself wrote out all these representations, and was told by the plaintiff and his wife that they knew nothing at all of this particular subject of inquiry, and that they refused to make any statement about it, and yet knowing all this, wrote the representation to suit himself, it is . . . clear that for the insurer to insist that the policy is void because it contains this statement, would be an act of bad faith and of the grossest injustice and dishonesty."

Wilkinson was applied in *American Life Ins Co* v *Mahone*[85]: a form proposing life insurance asked whether the proposer was "temperate". In the words of the Supreme Court, the "answer was not 'Yes' but 'I never refuse a drink' or 'I always take my drinks' and that the answer 'Yes' was improperly written down [by the agent] without the knowledge or consent" of the proposer. The court rejected a defence based on false representation, adding

"Nor do we think it makes any difference that the answers as written were subsequently read to [the proposer] and signed by him. [He] had a right to assume that the answers he did make were accepted as meaning, for the purpose of obtaining the policy, what [the agent] stated them in writing to be."

10–4 CLAUSES

The rule whereby the knowledge acquired by the agent of the insurer is the knowledge of the insurer can, it has been said,[86] be changed by the terms of the contract. These terms usually say that the knowledge of the agent shall not be imputed to the insurer or that, if the form is filled in any part by any person other than the proposer, that person shall be deemed to be the agent of the proposer. These terms are exemption clauses,[87] if they relieve the profferor (insurer) of a liability which would otherwise fall upon him. As exemption clauses they are potential prey of rules evolved by the courts to curb exemptions prior to the Unfair Contract Terms Act 1977 (the relevant parts of which do not apply to contracts of insurance), rules which remain as a substratum of common law.

10–4A Notice

The general law requires that contract terms, including attempts to limit the authority of agents, be sufficiently brought to the attention of the other party,[88] especially if the

---

85. 88 US 593 (1875)

86. *McMillan* v *Accident Ins Co*, 1907 SC 484, 492. Such a clause was decisive in *Levy* v *Scottish Employers'* (1901) 17 TLR 227 (PA). The operation of a clause was an additional ground in *Facer* v *Vehicle & General* [1965] 1 Lloyd's Rep 113 (motor) where the clause read: "if any particular is filled in by an other person, such person shall be deemed to be [the proposer's] agent and not the agent of the Company."

New York Life Ins Co v *Fletcher*, 117 US 519, 530 *per* Field J (1886); *Aetna Life Ins Co* v *Moore*, 231 US 356 (1913—life); *Maryland Casualty Co* v *Eddy*, 239 F 477 (6 Cir, 1917—PA). The rule may be displaced by state legislation: *Union Indemnity Co* v *Dodd*, 21 F 2d 709 (4 Cir, 1927—life).

87. Cf *Overbrooke Estates Ltd* v *Glencombe Properties Ltd* [1974] 3 All ER 511 and criticisms of that decision: Coote [1975] CLJ 17; Treitel, p 346.

88. *Mendelssohn* v *Normand Ltd* [1970] 1 QB 177 (CA); Coote [1975] CLJ 17. *Whitney* v *Great Northern Ins Co* (1917) 32 DLR 756, 759 (Alta—livestock), affirmed [1918] SCR 543. *Union Mutual Life Ins Co* v *Wilkinson*, 13 Wall 222 (1871—life), discussed above, 10–3C.

term is unusual or unexpected.[89] However, if the proposer has signed a form containing the clause, *prima facie* he is bound by the clause, whether he has actual notice of it or not.[90]

The rule of binding signature is subject to an exception, in part the work of Lord Denning, if the nature of the term or document signed is misrepresented by the profferor and the signatory reasonably relies on that representation.[91] It was probably this exception that Lord Denning had in mind in *Stone* v *Reliance Mutual Ins Sy Ltd*.[92] He brushed an exemption clause aside saying[93] that an innocent misrepresentation by the agent that the form was correctly filled in "may debar a person from relying on an exception". While it is true in general that a person may plead misrepresentation, even though he was negligent in relying upon it,[94] it is submitted that when it concerns a proposal of insurance, Lord Denning's rule will only operate if the proposer was acting reasonably in relying on what the agent said. Thus the effect of the exemption turns on the broad question of the assessment of fault and allocation of risk which runs through this chapter. It is an instance of the broader proposition that, if the proposer relies reasonably on what the agent says about the terms of an insurance document (notably the policy), the document is taken to say what it is represented to say.[95]

10–4B Strict Construction

Such clauses will be construed strictly against the insurer.[96] A striking example of strict construction is found in a leading decision of the United States Supreme Court: *Stipcich* v *Metropolitan Life Ins Co*.[97] The insured applied for life insurance but, before his application had been accepted, discovered that he had a duodenal ulcer; he informed the appropriate agent of the insurer and the policy was issued. To a claim on the policy the insurer pleaded a clause that the authority of the agent procuring the application did not extend to varying any term or waiving any condition or to receiving information sought by questions in the application other than embodied in the proposal. The court rejected this plea, stating[98] that the agent

"when the insured communicated the information to him, did not purport to vary any term or waive any condition of the proposed insurance contract; he did not acquiesce in a variation of the application; *nor in connection with the preparation* of the written application did he receive any information not written into it. The insured merely communicated information *supplementing* the application, to the designated agent of the company . . . "

89. *Thornton* v *Shoe Lane Parking Ltd* [1971] 2 QB 163 (CA); *Interfoto Picture Library Ltd* v *Stiletto Visual Programmes Ltd* [1989] QB 433 (CA). *Tilden Rent-a-Car Co* v *Clendenning* (1978) 83 DLR (3d) 400 (Ont) and cases cited.
90. *L'Estrange* v *Graucob Ltd* [1934] 2 KB 394. *New York Life Ins Co* v *Fletcher*, 117 US 519 (1886—life), discussed above, 10–3.
91. *Curtis* v *Chemical Cleaning & Dyeing Co Ltd* [1951] 1 KB 805 (CA). *Ellingwood* v *NN Investors Life Ins Co*, 805 P 2d 70, (NM, 1991—life).
 Cf Canadian Indemnity Co v *Okanagan Mainline Real Estate Board* [1971] SCR 493, 500: "A party who misrepresents, albeit innocently, the contents or effect of a clause inserted by him into a contract cannot rely on the clause in the face of his misrepresentation."
92. [1972] 1 Lloyd's Rep 469 (CA—fire).
93. p 475. See Merkin, *op cit* 49
94. *Redgrave* v *Hurd* (1881) 20 Ch D 1 (CA).
95. See above, 8–3C.
96. Generally, see below, 15–5C.
97. 277 US 311 (1928).
98. p 319 *per* Justice Stone (emphasis added).

10–5 FRAUD BY THE AGENT

Fraud and the opportunity to commit fraud are no more than factors among others in the assessment of fault and the allocation of risk. On the one hand the law

"requires that the insured shall not only, in good faith answer all the interrogatories correctly, but shall use reasonable diligence to see that the answers are correctly written. It is for his interest to do so, and the insurer has the right to presume that he will do it. He has it in his power to prevent this species of fraud and the insurer has not."[99]

On the other hand, it is by the insurer that the agent is appointed and sent to procure proposals. Nonetheless, it has been suggested that the normal rules (above, 10–3 to 10–4) do not apply, if the agent has been fraudulent. This suggestion finds little modern support, unless the proposer is aware of the agent's fraud; cases in which he was aware should be separated from cases in which he was not.

10–5A Proposer Unaware of the Agent's Fraud

In *Newsholme*[100] Scrutton LJ said: "If the answers are untrue and [the agent] knows it, he is committing a fraud which prevents his knowledge being the knowledge of the insurance company." Unqualified statements like that, made without reference to the knowledge of the proposer, are difficult to reconcile not only with a later decision of the House of Lords[101] but also with an earlier decision of the Court of Appeal.

In *Hambro* v *Burnand*[102] a leading underwriter at Lloyd's had actual authority to contract on behalf of other underwriters. It was argued[103] by the latter that

"if it appears, on inquiry into the motives which existed in the agent's mind, that he intended, in making the contract, to misuse for his own ends the opportunity given to him by this authority, and apply it to a purpose, which, if the principal had known of it, he would not have sanctioned, then, because the agent was so influenced by improper motive, the principal is not liable upon the contract made by him."

The Court of Appeal rejected this argument and held the principals bound because[104] "it would be impossible . . . for the business of a mercantile community to be carried on, if a person dealing with an agent was bound to go behind the authority of the agent in each case, and inquire [into] his motives."

Today too, an agent does not cease to bind his principal simply because he is fraudulent.[105] On the contrary, if the agent is acting within his apparent authority, the principal is bound by his act, even if fraudulent.[106] The question is simply whether the proposer should reasonably have regarded the agent as having authority to do what-

---

99. *New York Life Ins Co* v *Fletcher*, 117 US 519, 533 *per* Field J (1886—life).

100. *Newsholme Bros* v *Road Transport & General Ins Co Ltd* [1929] 2 KB 356, 375–376 (CA—motor). See also *Biggar* v *Rock Life Assurance Co* [1901] 2 KB 516 (life).

101. *The Ocean Frost* [1986] AC 717.

102. [1904] 2 KB 10 (solvency insurance).

103. See pp 19–20.

104. p 20 *per* Lord Collins MR; *idem* pp 25–26 *per* Mathew LJ. The court relied on *Bank of Bengal* v *Fagan* (1849) 7 Moo PC 61, 74 *per* Lord Brougham; *Bryant* v *Quebec Bank* [1893] AC 170, 180 *per* Lord Macnaghten.

105. Generally see Bowstead, art 77.

106. *Lloyd* v *Grace, Smith & Co* [1912] AC 716, 725 *per* Lord Loreburn (solicitor liable for documentary fraud by his clerk), applied to a case of life insurance by Isaacs ACJ in *Maye* v *Colonial Mutual Life Assurance Sy Ltd* (1924) 35 CLR 14, 34 (HCA). See also *Slingsby* v *District Bank Ltd* [1932] 1 KB 544 (CA); *Uxbridge Permanent Building Sy* v *Pickard* [1939] 2 KB 248 (CA); *Briess* v *Woolley* [1954] AC 333; *The Ocean Frost* [1986] AC 717; *United Bk of Kuwait* v *Hammond* [1988] 3 All ER 418 (CA). Bowstead, p 230.

ever he was doing, notably helping him to complete the proposal in the way he did.[107] If the proposer realises that the agent is defrauding his principal, the proposer should also realise that the agent is acting outside his authority.

10–5B Proposer Party to the Agent's Fraud

If the proposer is aware or should have been aware of the agent's fraud, he is not in a position to argue that the insurer is bound by the fraudulent act or advice of the agent, for clearly the agent has neither actual nor apparent authority to act in this way. Consequently the proposer cannot set up the act or advice of the agent as a ground for denying the normal consequences of his signature to the proposal form.

In particular, "notice to an agent is not notice to the principal where it be quite certain that the agent would not disclose the matter."[108] It is like posting a letter in a hollow tree. The rule is obvious, the justifications various. The proposer is not acting *uberrima fidei*. He cannot be said to rely on the apparent authority of the agent. Moreover, it would be contrary to public policy for the courts to enforce a contract obtained by the proposer by fraud.[109]

---

107. Winfield & Jolowicz, *op cit*, p 589
108. *Re Fitzroy Bessemer Steel* (1884) 50 LT 144, 147 *per* Kay LJ (CA). See also *Hambro* v *Burnand* [1904] 2 KB 10, 25 *per* Romer LJ (solvency insurance). Bowstead, p. 335.
109. *Begbie* v *Phosphate Sewage* (1875) LR 10 QB 491; *Brown Jenkinson & Co* v *Percy Dalton (London)* [1957] 2 QB 621 (CA). *Southern Farm Bureau Casualty Ins Co* v *Allen* 388 F 2d 126 (5 Cir, 1967—motor).

CHAPTER 11

CONTRACT FORMATION

11–1 OFFER

The rules of law governing the formation of contracts of insurance are those which govern the formation of most other contracts.[1] Their application to contracts at Lloyd's gives special difficulties, which are discussed separately (below, 11–3).

Most contracts of insurance are bilateral contracts between insurer and insured. In law their contract is made when the offer of one party, most often the insured, is accepted by the other party, the insurer. If the insurer is not willing to accept the offer, he may respond with a counter-offer, which may then be accepted by the insured. However, the insured may meet the counter-offer with a further offer of his own, for acceptance by the insurer. This process continues until the counter-offer of the one or other is finally accepted or rejected.[2]

Simple cases might run like this. A person interested in taking insurance responds to advertising or to a quotation from an insurer (invitations to treat), by making a proposal of insurance (offer) to the insurer, who accepts it (Case A). If, however, the insurer responds with policy terms which are not part of the offer, that response is a counter-offer, which the proposer may accept (Case B); this might arise if the premium cannot finally be calculated until the insurer has considered the proposal. If the proposer rejects the insurer's counter-offer and comes back with a further proposition, he makes a further counter-offer, which the insurer may accept (Case C) or reject, and so on. However,

"When the negotiations extend over a period, the principle is that the whole course of the negotiations must be considered in order to see whether or not full agreement on all the material terms was reached at any stage, and if it is contended that this happened at a particular point, then the Court must also have regard to the subsequent events in order to determine whether or not this contention has been established."[3]

---

1. See Anson, chapter 2; Treitel, chapters 2 and 4. In the USA also, general rules of the law of contract apply: e.g. *Shattuck* v *Mutual Life Ins Co*, F Cas No 12,715 (D Mass, 1878—life); *Mofrad* v *New York Life Ins Co*, 206 F 2d 491 (10 Cir, 1953—life); *Lynn* v *Farm Bureau Mutual Auto Ins Co*, 264 F 2d 921, 925 (4 Cir, 1959—motor).

2. The template of offer and acceptance is no more than a guide: *Rust* v *Abbey Life Assurance Co Ltd* [1978] 2 Lloyd's Rep 386, 392 *per* C M Clothier QC (property bonds). The analysis of a transaction in such terms "may be relevant for the purpose of ascertaining whether there is a consensus between the relevant parties upon a mutual bargain and for answering other consequential questions, but once the consensus upon a mutual bargain has been demonstrated that [i.e. the demonstration] suffices."—*The Zephyr* [1984] 1 Lloyd's Rep 58, 72 *per* Hobhouse J (re). Stoljar [1988] CLJ 193.

3. *CTI Inc* v *Oceanus Mutual Underwriting Assn (Bermuda) Ltd* [1984] 1 Lloyd's Rep 476 505, *per* Kerr LJ (CA—containers).

Returning to the simple scenario of contract formation, there is an offer when the offeror indicates by words or conduct that, if the offeree assents, he, the offeror, is ready to be legally bound[4] by a certain arrangement stated, expressly or implicitly, in the offer. The offer, therefore, implies two features: a certain arrangement (below, 11–1A) and a definite expression of intention (11–1B). It must also be open for acceptance (11–1C).

11–1A A Certain Arrangement

Unless the parties know what they are committing themselves to, the courts are slow to infer intention to contract and hence slow to infer that an alleged offer is indeed an offer in law, unless the offer (and hence the contract) is certain in content. Uncertainty arises in two ways: in what the parties have said—ambiguity (below, 11–1A1), and in what the parties have not said—incompleteness (below, 11–1A2). Courts approach uncertainty in a positive spirit, expressed in the maxim *ut res magis valeat quam pereat*: this is the abbreviated form of a maxim that a liberal construction should be put upon documents, so as to uphold them, if possible, and carry into effect the intention of the parties.

11–1A1 Ambiguity

Ambiguity in the terms of the agreement, unless in terms of very minor significance, is generally fatal to enforcement of the contract. Although the ambiguity may be the product of carelessness and does not suggest a lack of intention to contract, the courts cannot give effect to intention which is unclear and, as they will not guess what the parties might (or should) have intended, the "agreement" will not be enforced.[5]

11–1A2 Incompleteness

As it makes no sense that parties should intend to be bound by an arrangement that is incomplete, a proposal that is incomplete is not an offer in law. This follows. however, only if the missing term is an essential term. Terms essential to insurance contracts are as follows:

    (a) Terms, without which it is presumed that there was no intention to contract, terms which indicate the parties to the contract,[6] the kind of risk,[7] the sub-

---

4. Intention to be legally bound may be rebutted by the words used; so, when a newspaper offered "free insurance" but stated that "this free insurance scheme does not involve any contractual liability" the newspaper was not liable to the reader who claimed cover: *Woods* v *Cooperative Ins Sy*, 1924 SC 692.

5. *Colonial Ins Co* v *Adelaide Marine Ins Co* (1886) 12 App Cas 128 (PC—cargo); *Scammell & Nephew Ltd* v *Ouston* [1941] AC 251. *Liverpool & London & Globe Ins Co* v *Wyld* (1877) 1 SCR 604, 629–630 *per* Richards CJ (fire).

6. *Davidson* v *Global General Ins Co* (1965) 48 DLR (2d) 503, 507 (Ont—fire), quoting MacGillivray (4th ed) para 673. *Zannini* v *Reliance Ins Co* 590 NE 2d 457 (Ill, 1992 – property). Appleman, section 7122.

    When an agent represents more than one insurer, the law of California requires that he designate the insurer for whom he contracts, if a binder is to have legal effect: *Granco Steel Inc* v *Workmen's Compensation Appeals Board*, 436 P 2d 287, 291 (Cal, 1968—workmen's compensation).

    Cf the practice of reinsurance at Lloyd's whereby reinsurance may be agreed as a package, to be offered to an insured, whose identity is not yet known: below, 11–3E.

7. *Murfitt* v *Royal Ins Co Ltd* (1922) 10 Ll L Rep 191, 194 *per* McCardie J (fire).

ject-matter at risk, and the amount of insurance.[8] These are terms particular
to the contract in question, which cannot without more be implied by the
court and must therefore be expressed by the parties.

(b) Terms, essential to the business efficacy of that kind of contract of insurance,
such as the duration of cover, which, if not expressed, will be readily
implied.[9] For example, it is commonly inferred that for fire, accident and
burglary insurance the period of cover will be a year.

(c) Other terms fall between (a) and (b): they can be implied in some contracts
but not in others. Thus the geographical limits of cover are implicit in some
contracts but not, for example, in the case of war risks.[10] The same is true of
premium, which depends on whether the particular risk is a standard risk for
which there is an ascertainable market rate.[11]

Subject to this, the gaps in the arrangement may be filled by resort to implied terms
(below, 11-1A3) or terms settled indirectly (11–1A4).

11–1A3 Implied Terms

Implied terms are categorised according to their source.

(a) Terms are said to be implied by law, when they are implied by statute[12] or by
the courts. Terms will be implied by the courts only if they are necessary to
give business efficacy to the contract.[13]

(b) Terms may be implied from previous dealings between the particular parties.[14]

(c) Terms may be implied by the operation of trade custom, i.e., the custom of
the insurance industry. Generally such terms must be certain, reasonable,[15]
universal in the trade context, and contrary neither to law nor to the express
terms of the contract. It is a custom of the insurance market, of which even
the consumer is assumed to have notice,[16] that insurers have standard terms.
This is also true of the rules of a mutual insurance association and, in this
connection, the insured is considered to have the knowledge and thus the
notice of his agent.[17]

Allied to this, is the important proposition that the proposal of the intending
insured is presumed to be on the basis of the insurer's standard terms (if any) for the
kind of risk proposed.

---

8. *Phoenix Ins Co v Schulz*, 80 F 337 (4 Cir, 1897—fire); *Ellingwood v NN Investors Life Ins Co*, 805 P 2d
70 (NM, 1991 – life); *Zannini* (above).
9. *Eames v Home Ins Co*, 94 US 621 (1877—fire).
10. *American Airlines Inc v Hope* [1973] 1 Lloyd's Rep 233 (CA—aviation), affirmed on other points
[1974] 2 Lloyd's Rep 301 (HL).
11. *Allis-Chalmers Co v Maryland Fidelity & Deposit Co* (1916) 114 LT 433 (HL—fidelity). *Res–Care
Development v Oakes Agency Inc*, 758 F Supp 1191 (WD Ky, 1989). See below, 11-1A4.
12. For example, MIA, sections 36 ff.
13. *Liverpool CC v Irwin* [1977] AC 239. Phang [1993] JBL 242.
14. *Hillas & Co Ltd v Arcos Ltd* (1932) 147 LT 503 (HL); *American Airlines Inc v Hope* [1972] 1 Lloyd's
Rep 253, 261 *per* Mocatta J (aviation). *Eames v Home Ins Co*, 94 US 621 (1877—fire); *Hartford Fire Ins Co
v Tatum*, 5 F 2d 169 (5 Cir, 1925—fire).
15. Unreasonable terms may be implied, if it can be shown that, in addition to meeting the other requirements of trade terms, they were actually known to both parties.
16. *Parker v SE Ry* (1877) 2 CPD 416, 422 *per* Mellish LJ. Clarke [1976] CLJ 51, 55 ff.
17. *Organ v Conner*, 792 F Supp 693 (D Alaska, 1992—hull): Alaskan fisherman bound by London arbitration clause.

In *General Accident Ins Corp* v *Cronk*[18] the defendant submitted a proposal of accident insurance to the insurer who purported to accept the proposal by sending a policy, which contained terms not mentioned in the proposal. The defendant later argued that, as the terms of the policy did not correspond with those of the proposal, the insurer had rejected the proposal and made a counter-offer, to which the proposer had not consented, so that no contract had been formed. Rejecting this argument and finding for the plaintiff insurer, the Divisional Court held that the proposal must be taken to have been on the basis of the ordinary form of policy issued by the insurer. Hence the proposal did correspond with the terms of the policy sent and by sending it the insurer had accepted the offer contained in the proposal.

The presumption, that a proposal is on the standard terms of the insurer concerned, may be confirmed by a clause in the proposal form. The presumption does not apply, however, in each of the following circumstances:

(a) The insurer has no standard terms for the risk proposed.

(b) The proposal refers to terms other than insurers' standard terms for that kind of business.[19]

(c) The insurer indicates before any contract is concluded that the usual terms will not apply.[20] Evidently, if the insurer sends a policy on terms different from his own standard terms,[21] that cannot be acceptance of a proposal based on his standard terms, so the insurer's response in that case is a counter-offer.

(d) The proposer has been misled by the insurer or his agent about the contents of the standard terms. If this occurs, in principle the terms apply as they have been represented to be.[22]

(e) The standard terms of the cover are not available for examination by the proposer. He need not have actual knowledge of those terms but, for knowledge to be presumed, he must have the means of knowledge.[23] His means of knowledge include the knowledge and facilities of his agent or broker.[24]

Further, it should be noted that a limited degree of control over insurers' standard terms may be exercised by the EC Commission under article 85 of the EC Treaty.

---

18. (1901) 17 TLR 233. See also *Star Fire & Burglary Ins Co Ltd* v *Davidson & Sons Ltd* (1902) 5 F (Ct of Sess) 83, 86 *per* Lord Young (fire); *Sanderson* v *Cunningham* [1919] 2 Ir R 234 (motor); *Rust* v *Abbey Life Assurance Co Ltd* [1978] 2 Lloyd's Rep 386; [1979] 2 Lloyd's Rep 334, 339 *per* Brandon LJ (CA—property bonds). *Action Scaffolding Ltd* v *AMP Fire Ins & Gen Ins Co* (1990) 6 ANZ Ins Cases, no 60–970 (motor). *Cf Canning* v *Farquhar* (1886) 16 QBD 727, 733 *per* Lindley LJ (CA—life).
USA: the proposal is presumed to "contemplate such form of policy, containing such conditions and limitations as are usual in such cases, or have been used before between the parties"—*Eames* v *Homes Ins Co*, 94 US 621 (1877—fire); see also *Zannini* (above 11–1A2); and *Progressive Casualty Ins Co* v *CA Reaseguradora Nacional de Venezuela*, 802 F Supp 1069, 1076 (SD NY, 1992—re). Appleman, section 7125.
19. *Adie & Sons* v *The Insurance Corp Ltd* (1898) 14 TLR 544 (fire).
20. *McCutcheon* v *David MacBrayne Ltd* [1964] 1 Lloyd's Rep 16 (HL).
21. *Sanderson* v *Cunningham* [1919] 2 Ir R 234, 239 *per* Sir James Campbell (motor); *S E Lancashire Ins Co Ltd* v *Croisdale* (1931) 40 Ll L Rep 22: the defendant proposer applied for insurance on his buses on the basis of a premium rebate term in the standard form; in the policy sent, however, that term had been deleted. Macnaghten J held that the defendant was not bound (to accept the policy sent or to pay premiums).
22. See above, 8–3C.
23. The Statement of Insurance Practice, 1977 (HC Deb, Vol 931, No 98, Cols 217–220): "unless the prospectus or the proposal form contains full details of the standard cover offered . . . the proposal form shall include a statement that a copy of the policy form is available on request."
The insured must have "a reasonable opportunity to ascertain the contents of the policy"—*Dickens* v *St Paul Fire & Marine Ins Co*, 95 SW 2d 910, 913 (Tenn, 1936—fire).
24. *Sanderson* v *Cunningham* [1919] 2 Ir R 234, 242 *per* O'Connor LJ (motor).

Article 85 contains a broad prohibition on anti-competitive agreements and practices. A block exemption proposed by the Commission in 1993 concerns standard forms of policy and standard wording.[24a] These must be available to the public and must state that their use is not compulsory.

11–1A4 Terms Settled Indirectly: Terms TBA

Under the maxim *certum est quod certum reddi potest*[25] courts give effect[26] to terms, which have not been settled by the parties themselves and stated in the contract but incorporated in the contract by reference. The reference may be to the market or to a nominated person. A notable example of this device is the practice at Lloyd's of stating a term, such as premium,[27] TBA (to be arranged).

Generally, the law does not enforce an agreement a term of which remains to be settled by the future agreement of the parties: it is in the nature of people that future agreement may not be reached, so it is not sufficiently certain that the matter can be made certain.[28] *Prima facie*, therefore, a term that premium shall be agreed in future by the insurer and insured is uncertain and no contract of insurance at such a premium can be enforced.[29] Nonetheless, it is generally believed that insurance for a premium TBA is enforceable.

In *Greenock SS Co v Maritime Ins Co Ltd*.[30] Bigham J concluded[31] that, in the case of a premium TBA, the parties "must ascertain what premium it would have been reasonable to charge. If they cannot do it by agreement, they must have recourse to a Court of law". As regards marine insurance, the matter was subsequently settled by section 31(1) of the MIA: "Where an insurance is effected at a premium to be arranged, and no arrangement is made, a reasonable premium is payable." As regards non-marine insurance, a similar result has been achieved by analogy and by liberal construction.[32] The corollary is, however, that a clause for premium TBA is ineffective, if there is evidence of contrary intention by the parties,[33] or if no reasonable com-

---

24a. Commission Regulation (EEC) No 3932/92, OJ No L398/7, entered into force on 1 April 1993. See Green, (1993) 3 Ins L & P 62.

25. That is certain which can be made certain.

26. *Aetna Ins Co v Licking Valley Milling Co*, 19 F 2d 177, 180 (6 Cir, 1927—fire); *New England Ins Co v Cummings*, 164 F Supp 553 (SD Miss, 1958—fire).

27. Other examples are commencement date and geographical limits.

28. *Loftus v Roberts* (1902) 18 TLR 532; *Mallozzi v Carapelli Spa* [1976] 1 Lloyd's Rep 407 (CA). *Quaere* the effect on this rule of *Sudbrook Trading Estate Ltd v Eggleton* [1982] 3 All ER 1 (HL).

29. In this sense *Christie v North British Ins Co* (1825) 3 Sh & D (Ct of Sess) 519 (fire); doubted in *American Airlines Inc v Hope* [1972] 1 Lloyd's Rep 253, 260–261 by Mocatta J (aviation).

30. [1903] 1 KB 367 (hull).

31. p 375. He cited no precedent, however, thought it like the well established case of the sale of goods at a reasonable but unnamed price.

32. *Liberian Ins Agency Inc v Mosse* [1977] 2 Lloyd's Rep 560, 568 *per* Donaldson J (cargo). This construction is consistent with that in *Sudbrook Trading Estate Ltd v Eggleton* [1982] 3 All ER 1 (HL). USA: a striking example is an unambiguous clause in medical insurance whereby the insurer determines "acceptable medical practice" and hence the scope of cover afforded: *Kekis v Blue Cross and Blue Shield of Utica*, 815 F Supp 571 (ND NY, 1993).

33. *American Airlines Inc v Hope* [1973] 1 Lloyd's Rep 233 (CA—aviation). In this case, a war risk extension, at an additional premium and geographical limits TBA, was held by Mocatta J to be enforceable in principle. On the facts, however, he held that it was not intended to be applied in default of agreement, *inter alia* because there was no reasonable commercial rate for the area in question. The decision was affirmed: [1973] 1 Lloyd's Rep 233 (CA); and on other points [1974] 2 Lloyd's Rep 301 (HL).

mercial rate can be ascertained, i.e. there is no market price, for the kind of risk in question.[34]

A further dimension is added, if the term is TBA (to be agreed) L/U (leading underwriter). The effect of this is that Lloyd's underwriters, who have followed the leading underwriter, agree to be bound by any future arrangement he makes as to the terms in question. This provision is effective[35] and exemplifies the same general rule. It is enough between the following underwriters and the insured that a term can be made certain by reference to the decision of a third party (the leading underwriter).[36] Hence, in a case like this, the clause would be effective, even if there was no general market rate for the kind of risk in question: reference to the market is unnecessary.

11–1B Definiteness

To be a legal offer, the proposal and any other relevant document must indicate a definite willingness to be bound on the part of the offeror. This is a matter of construction of the document. Also, there must be no reason to infer from the surrounding circumstances, in which the document is generated, that it is contrary to commercial sense that the profferor should intend to be bound without more. For example, literature issued by insurers inviting proposals will not normally be construed as an offer, which can be converted into a contract of insurance by anyone who responds with acceptance, as it makes little sense that an insurer would be willing to be bound without first assessing the particular risk. A similar inference may be drawn from the past practice of the particular parties.[37]

11–1B1 Coupon Insurance

An exception is found in the case of coupon insurance: the coupon issued by the insurer is an offer, accepted by the act of the insured[38] in sending the coupon to the insurer or by the performance of any other act required by the offer contained in the coupon.

In the United States, a similar rule has been applied to insurance dispensed by machine and to insurance transacted by post. In *Fritz* v *Old American Ins Co*[39] H received by post a brochure from the defendant insurer, which solicited accident insurance, described the proposed policy in detail, and was accompanied by an application form. No medical examination was required. H completed the form and sent it to the insurer, with the required premium. After receipt of the form by the insurer and

---

34. *Liberian* (above); *Hope* (above); also *Kirby* v *Cosindit SpA* [1969] 1 Lloyd's Rep 75, 79 *per* Megaw J (builders' risks). This conclusion is consistent with *May & Butcher* v *R* [1934] 2 KB 17n (HL).

35. *Hope* (above).

36. *Arcos Ltd* v *Aronsen* (1930) 36 Ll L Rep 108; *Sudbrook Trading Estate Ltd* v *Eggleton* [1982] 3 All ER 1 (HL). USA: a striking example is an unambiguous clause in medical insurance whereby the insurer determines "acceptable medical practice" and hence the scope of cover afforded: *Kekis* v *Blue Cross and Blue Shield of Utica*, 815 F Supp 571 (ND NY, 1993).

37. *Hope* (above): the question was whether aircraft destroyed at Beirut were covered by a war risks extension TBA L/U. Absent express agreement, it was argued for the insured that premium could be implied at a reasonable commercial rate to be fixed by arbitration or by the court. This argument was rejected *inter alia* because the implication was inconsistent with evidence of party intention drawn from their past contracting practice (p 241; also [1972] 1 Lloyd's Rep 253, 261 *per* Mocatta J).

38. *Shanks* v *Sun Life Assurance Co of India* (1896) 4 SLT 65 (accident); *General Accident, Fire & Life Assurance Corp* v *Robertson* [1909] AC 404, 411 *per* Lord Loreburn LC (life).

39. 354 F Supp 514 (SD Tex, 1973).

before a policy was sent to him, H was killed, at which time, argued the insurer, the contract had not been completed. While accepting that in general a proposal had to be accepted by the insurer to form a contract, the Federal Court held that contracting by post required a different rule. "Because defendant operated by mail, no human agent was available to refute or confirm the reasonable expectations engendered by the brochure in the mind of the applicant." In spite of conflicting statements in the brochure[40] the court held that the insured was entitled to assume cover when he sent the form. "Thus, to maintain the concept of two informed contracting parties, it is logical to impose a greater duty on the insurance company to explain clearly and completely its policy in the advertising brochure."[41] Applying the law of Texas, the Federal Court held[42] that "the brochure and application constitute an offer by the insurance company. Deposit of a completed application into the mails is acceptance by the individual. And coverage under the policy begins immediately upon acceptance."[43]

In that case it was significant that the brochure was detailed, leaving nothing for negotiation, that would normally be negotiated, that the insurer required no information other than that on the application, and that to market the insurance the insurer had dispensed with a human agent.

11–1C The Offer must be Open

The offer must be open for acceptance at the time of acceptance. An offer once made is presumed to be open for acceptance, subject to the following:

- (a) Rejection of offer terminates the offer from the time that the rejection is received by the offeror. A counter-offer is regarded as a rejection.[44] The insurer may reject an offer, including an offer of renewal, at will and without giving reasons for rejection.[45]
- (b) Revocation of the offer by the offeror terminates the offer.[46] If the offeror follows a proposal with a different proposal for the same risk, a revocation of the first will usually be inferred.[47] Revocation may be effected at any time before the offer has been accepted, by actual communication to the offeree.[48]
- (c) An offer comes to an end, if unaccepted within any period of time for acceptance stipulated in the offer. If the stipulated period ends on a Sunday, it has

---

40. p 516.

41. The brochure stated that the policy would not be effective until issued. This provision was not, in the view of the court, prominent or clear enough to defeat the reasonable expectations of the insured.

42. p 518.

43. The court relied on cases to similar effect concerning (a) insurance solicited by post: *Klos* v *Mobil Oil Co*, 259 A 2d 889 (NJ, 1969—PA); (b) the terms of machine-dispensed flight insurance: *Lachs* v *Fidelity & Casualty Co*, 118 NE 2d 555 (NY, 1954—PA); *Steven* v *Fidelity & Casualty Co*, 377 P 2d 284 (Cal, 1962—life). *Cf Merrill* v *Fidelity & Casualty Co*, 304 F 2d 27 (6 Cir, 1962—life); *First National Bk of Chicago* v *Fidelity & Casualty Co*, 428 F 2d 499 (7 Cir, 1970—PA).

44. *Jones* v *Daniel* [1894] 2 Ch 332; *Honeyman* v *Marryatt* (1857) 6 HLC 112. *First National Bk of Quincy* v *Hall*, 101 US 43 (1880); *Equitable Life Assurance Sy* v *McElroy*, 83 F 631 (8 Cir, 1897—life); *McNicol* v *New York Life Ins Co*, 149 F 141 (8 Cir, 1906—life).

45. *Harding* v *Ohio Casualty Ins Co*, 41 NW 2d 818 (Minn, 1950—surety); *Madden* v *Indiana Lumbermen's Mutual Ins Co*, 451 SW 2d 764 (Tex, 1970—motor).

46. *Canning* v *Farquhar* (1886) 16 QBD 727, 731 *per* Lord Esher MR (CA—life).

47. *Travers* v *Nederland Life Ins Co*, 104 F 486 (8 Cir, 1900).

48. *Byrne* v *Van Tienhoven* (1880) 5 CPD 344. *Goldberg* v *Colonial Life Ins Co*, 134 NYS 2d 865 (1954, life).

been held[49] that the offer may be accepted the following day. In the absence of a stipulation, it may be inferred simply from the passage of time that the offer has lapsed.[50] The length of time depends on the kind of insurance.

(d) An offer may be conditional. Failure of a condition express or implied, subject to which the offer was made, terminates the offer.[51] Thus an offer by the insurer is generally conditional on there being no material change in the risk between the time of offer and the time of acceptance; if there were a change, it "could not fairly be regarded as a continuing offer which [the proposer] was entitled to accept".[52] For example, an offer of life or health insurance is made on the assumption that there has been no material change in health between offer and acceptance,[53] and an offer of fire insurance is made on the assumption that there the property has not been damaged by fire in the same period.[54]

11–2 ACCEPTANCE

To complete a contract the offer must be accepted. The acceptance must be unequivocal (below, 11–2A), correspond with the offer (11–2C), it must be genuine (11–2D), unconditional (11–2E), and be communicated to the offeror (11–2F).

11–2A Unequivocal Acceptance

Acceptance must be unequivocal. No particular form is required. Acceptance may be expressed in words, in speech[55] or in writing,[56] or it may be implied from conduct,[57]

---

49. *Tiller* v *McCarthy* (1982) 131 DLR (3d) 734 (Nfld—motor).
50. *Ramsgate Victoria Hotel Co Ltd* v *Montefiore* (1866) LR 1 Ex 109.
51. *Financings Ltd* v *Stimson* [1962] 1 WLR 1184 (CA); *The Elbe Ore* [1986] 1 Lloyd's Rep 176.
52. *Canning* v *Farquhar* (1886) 16 QBD 727, 733 *per* Lindley LJ (CA—life). USA: there too it has been held that a proposal of life insurance is "revoked" by the death of proposer prior to acceptance: *Paine* v *Pacific Mutual Life Ins Co*, 51 F 689, 692 (8 Cir, 1892—life).
53. This was the case of the insurer's counter-offer in *Canning* (above). A more difficult example is *Looker* v *Law Union & Rock Ins Co Ltd* [1928] 1 KB 554: "acceptance" of a life proposal contained the clause: "The risk of the company will not commence until receipt of the first premium; and the directors meanwhile reserve the power to alter or withdraw the acceptance." The proposer fell ill and sent the premium. An action against the insurer failed. (1) Acton J accepted the argument (p 559) "that the acceptance is made in reliance upon the continued truth of the representations" about the risk, notably the proposer's health; and (2) that there had been non-disclosure of the change in health. The premise is that there was no contract until payment of premium, an inference from the term of the "acceptance" reserving a *locus poenitentiae* to the directors. Their acceptance was best seen as an offer subject to a condition (no change in risk), a condition which had failed; the offer therefore lapsed and was no longer extant to be accepted. This is the view of the situation taken by Lindley LJ in *Canning* (above), p 733.
54. *Independent Fire Ins Co* v *Lea*, 782 F Supp 1144, 1155 (ED La, 1992—fire).
55. *Bhugwandass* v *Netherlands India Sea & Fire Ins Co* (1888) 14 App Cas 83 (PC—cargo). *British Traders Ins Co Ltd* v *Queens Ins Co* [1928] SCR 9 (fire). *Commercial Mutual Marine Ins Co* v *Union Mutual Ins Co*, 60 US 318 (1857—re).
56. *Mackie* v *European Assurance Sy* (1869) 21 LT 102 (fire); *Adie & Sons* v *Ins Corp Ltd* (1898) 14 TLR 544.
57. *Rust* v *Abbey Life Assurance Co Ltd* [1978] 2 Lloyd's Rep 386; [1979] 2 Lloyd's Rep 334 (CA—property bonds). *Constitution Life Ins Co* v *Thompson & Son Inc*, 475 SW 2d 165 (Ark, 1972—life): payment of premium accepts counter-offer.

such as the execution of a policy[58] or a demand for premium[59] or an acceptance of premium[60] by the insurer. Neither payment of premium[61] nor delivery of policy,[62] however, are essential to contract formation, unless required by the terms of the offer, although acceptance of premium is strong evidence of contract and that some kind of cover has begun for, otherwise, the proposer is getting little or nothing for his money.[63]

Indeed, in the USA "the 'doctrine of interim insurance' is based upon the reasonable expectations of the insured, the rationale being that the insured reasonably expects that he is getting something when he pays his initial premium to the insurance company"[64] even though the cover may be terminated later, if the risk is found unacceptable: below 11–2E(e). Until then, in the knowledge that he has paid premium and with the belief that he is immediately covered, the proposer is less likely to withdraw the application during the period of investigation, and the insurer has the use of the money. These advantages to the insurer are such that the Supreme Court of California has ruled that cover continues until the premium has been returned, and even covers the event (such as death) if it occurs before return of premium but after the insured has been notified of the insurer's decision against cover.[65]

11–2A1 Formality and Cancellation

If the contract has been formed, specific performance of a promise to deliver a policy

---

58. Execution is sufficient to render the policy "signed, sealed and delivered", even though the policy was not sent to the insured: *Xenos* v *Wickham* (1866) LR 2 HL 296 (hull). See also *Roberts* v *Security Co Ltd* [1897] 1 QB 111, 115 *per* Lopes LJ (CA—burglary); *Pearl Life Assurance Co* v *Johnson* [1909] 2 KB 288 (life); *cf McElroy* v *London Assurance Corp* (1897) 24 R (Ct of Sess) 288 (fire).

Aliter, if the terms require "issue", i.e. "it is ready for delivery to the opposite party, and actual notice of that readiness has been given to them" *per* Lord Sumner in *Allis-Chalmers Co* v *Fidelity & Deposit Co* (1914) 111 LT 327, 329 (HL—fidelity).

USA: for the meaning of policy delivery, see Appleman, section 7157.

59. *Xenos* (above), p 308 *per* Piggott B (hull); *Lishman* v *Northern Maritime Ins Co* (1875) LR 10 CP 179, 182 *per* Piggott B.

60. *Solvency Mutual Guarantee Co* v *Froane* (1861) 7 H & N 5, 15 *per* Bramwell B (guarantee); *Canning* v *Farquhar* (1886) 16 QBD 727, 731 *per* Lord Esher MR (CA—life); *Re Norwich Equitable Fire Assurance Sy* (1887) 57 LT 241, 243 *per* Kay J (re).

Aliter, if the acceptance of the premium is conditional: *Gladney* v *Paul Revere Life Ins Co*, 895 F 2d 238 (5 Cir, 1990—disability); or if, although premium has been paid, it appears that significant terms have not been settled: *Souter* v *State Mutual Life Assurance Co*, 273 F 2d 921 (4 Cir, 1960—life).

61. *Wooding* v *Monmouthshire & S. Wales Mutual Indemnity Sy Ltd* [1939] 4 All ER 570 (HL—employers' liability). *Eames* v *Home Ins Co*, 94 US 298 (1877—fire); *Cummings* v *New England Ins Co*, 266 F 2d 888 (5 Cir, 1959—fire). In practice, this is more likely to be true of fire than life insurance: *Equitable Life Assurance Sy* v *McElroy*, 83 F 631, 638 (8 Cir, 1897—life).

62. *Bhugwandass* v *Netherlands India Sea & Fire Ins Co* (1888) 14 App Cas 83 (PC—cargo). *El Dia Ins Co* v *Sinclair*, 228 F 833 (2 Cir, 1915—fire); *Cummins* v *New England Ins Co*, 266 F 2d 888 (5 Cir, 1959—fire); *Bituminous Casualty Corp* v *Aetna Ins Co*, 332 F Supp 860 (ED Mo, 1971—fire), affirmed 461 F 2d 730 (8 Cir, 1972).

Aliter, if required by the terms of the offer: *Prudential Ins Co of America* v *Rickley*, 245 F 2d 881 (10 Cir, 1957—life). Delivery to the insured's agent is constructive delivery to the insured: *Jackson National Life Ins Co* v *Receconi*, 827 P 2d 118 (NM, 1992 –life).

63. *Zurich Life Ins Co* v *Davies* (1981) 130 DLR (3d) 748, 751 (Sup Ct, Canada—life). *Idem Smith* v *Westland Life Ins Co*, 539 P 2d 433 (Cal, 1975—life).

64. *Duggan* v *Massachusetts Mutual Life Ins Co*, 736 F Supp 1072, 1075–1076 (D Kan, 1990—life), citing Appleman, section 7237. See also *Smith* (above) p 441.

65. *Smith* (above) p 443. This will be so, unless very clear language is used to the contrary; *Gonzalez* v *John Hancock Mut Life Ins Co*, 927 F 2d 659 (1 Cir, 1991—life).

will be ordered, if necessary.[66] However, unless a particular form of contract is clearly required by the contract itself or by a constitutional rule of the insurance company, of which the insured has notice, no particular form of contract is required for validity between insurer and insured. Even when the charter of an insurance company required its agreements, policies and other instruments to be in writing, the Supreme Court of the United States construed this requirement as applying "only to executed contracts or policies of insurance, by which the Company is legally bound to indemnity against loss, and not to those initial or preliminary arrangements which necessarily precede the execution of the formal instrument."[67] The reason is practicality, the need to offer speedy cover.[68]

In England, one clear exception concerns the contract of marine insurance, which is inadmissible in evidence unless embodied in a policy in accordance with the MIA.[69] Freedom of form is qualified in two other ways. First, no action can be brought on a guarantee, unless it is in writing "and signed by the party to be charged therewith".[70] Second, in the case of life or equivalent insurance, the insurer may be required to send a statutory notice advising the insured of his right to cancel the contract within a "cooling-off" period.[71]

11–2A2 The Silent Proposer

To be acceptance of an offer conduct must be positive: silence, generally ambivalent conduct, is not normally sufficient,[72] unless there is previous agreement[73] that silence shall be regarded as consent. It is then a small step from agreement (that silence is consent) to an inference of a "duty" in the proposer to respond. In the United States but not in England, the insurer who fails to respond to a proposal within a reasonable time may find that he is bound by cover on the terms proposed (below, 11–2A3). In England the courts have had to consider the significance of silence, when a proposer "accepts" and retains a policy without demur. There is more than one possibility in law.

    (a) The policy may be a counter-offer, rejecting the proposal as well as any terms inconsistent with the policy, which may have been discussed by the parties.[74] If the period of retention is short, there is no acceptance and no

---

66. *Bhugwandass* (above). *Commercial Mutual Marine Ins Co* v *Union Mutual Ins Co*, 60 US 318 (1857—re); *Franklin Fire Ins Co* v *Colt* 87 US 560 (1875—fire); *Union Central Life Ins Co* v *Phillips*, 102 F 19 (8 Cir, 1900—life).

67. *Franklin Fire Ins Co* v *Colt*, 87 US 560 (1875—fire); applied in *Eames* v *Home Ins Co*, 94 US 621 (1877—fire). See also *Moore* v *Palmetto State Life Ins Co*, 73 SE 2d 688 (SC, 1952—life). Appleman, sections 7123, 7126.

68. *Franklin Fire* (above).

69. See section 22, which also provides that the policy may be executed and issued at the time when the contract is concluded or later.

70. Statute of Frauds 1677, section 4.

71. There are two distinct regimes requiring notice. One is that of the Insurance Companies Act 1982, sections 75 ff and regulations made thereunder. The other is that of the Financial Services (Cancellation) Rules 1977, which are now made by the Securities and Investment Board under the Financial Services Act 1986, section 51. Where relevant the latter regime, which offers more protection to the insured, supersedes the former.

72. *Felthouse* v *Bindley* (1862) 11 CB (NS) 869. See further Treitel, pp 30 ff, *Equitable Life Assurance Sy* v *McElroy*, 83 F 631 (8 Cir, 1897—life).

73. "if you do not hear from me by 1 June, you may assume . . . "

74. See below, 11–2C.

contract. If the period of retention is long, the court may infer assent by the insured.[75]

(b) There may have been prior informal agreement on the terms of insurance, with which the policy terms are inconsistent. If the insured retains the policy without demur for long enough, a court might say that he has lost or waived his "right" to object to the terms of the policy[76] and to seek rectification.[77] Until then, the insured has "every reason" to think that the policy will correspond with the proposal and any interim insurance, and these prevail,[78] especially if the insured cannot read [79] or the insurer has failed to contact the insured, when requested, to discuss a supposed discrepancy in the policy,[80] or the insured was misled by the insurer about the terms of the policy.[81] Nonetheless, in most cases, there will come a time when it can be said that the insured is bound by the terms of the policy sent.

Both (a) and (b) suggest that the insured has a duty to read his policy[82] and this is true,[83] even of the insured consumer,[84] however, not immediately on receipt: he will

75. See *Rust* v *Abbey Life Assurance Co Ltd* [1978] 2 Lloyd's Rep 386, 393 *per* C M Clothier QC; [1979] 2 Lloyd's Rep 334, 340 *per* Brandon LJ (CA—property bonds); in this case the recipient held the policy for five months before objecting to its terms. *Green* v *Beneficial Life Ins Co*, 383 P 2d 770 (Or, 1963—life); *Parks* v *American Casualty Co*, 572 P 2d 801 (Ariz, 1977—disability).

76. For example, *National Benefit Trust Ltd* v *Coulter*, 1911 1 SLT 190, 193 *per* Lord Ardwall. This suggests that a person may become contractually bound by reason of estoppel and reliance by the other party. See *Metropolitan Life Ins Co* v *Whitler*, 172 F 2d 631 (7 Cir, 1949—life); *McDaniel* v *California-Western States Life Ins Co*, 181 F 2d 606 (5 Cir, 1950—life), *cert den* 340 US 822.

In England this is not yet the law: *Centrovincial Estates plc* v *Merchant Investors Assurance Co Ltd [1983] Com LR 158 (CA)*. But compare *The Henrik Syf* [1982] Lloyd's Rep 456; *The Uhenbels* [1986] 2 Lloyd's Rep 294; *A-G of Hong Kong* v *Humphreys Estate Ltd* [1987] 2 All ER 387 (PC). In Australia see *Waltons Stores Ltd* v *Maher* (1988) 62 ALJR. 110 (HCA).

77. Below, 14–3D.

78. *Liverpool & London & Globe Ins Co* v *Wyld* (1877) 1 SCR 604, 628–629 *per* Richards CJ, 639 *per* Ritchie J.

79. MacGillivray, No 243. In *Dickens* v *St Paul Fire & Marine Ins Co*, 95 SW 2d 910, 913 (Tenn, 1936) the claimant had insured his house against fire, having received a policy which misstated the ownership of the house, the mistake of an agent of the insurer who had not troubled to investigate the matter by speaking to the insured and, presumably, did not have actual knowedge (although he might have guessed) that the claimant was illiterate. The claimant did not discover the mistake in the policy. The court stressed (p 913) that the agent "elected to proceed independently and on his own responsibility" and the court allowed the bill to reform the policy in accordance with the true title to the house. It may be that there was no person to whom the insured could reasonably have gone for advice on the contents of the policy.

Cf Slater v *Fidelity & Casualty Co*, 98 NYS 2d 28 (1950—life): a person took machine vended trip policies at the airport and was held bound by their terms, whether he understood them or not. This echoes an idea found in earlier English cases, that the court should take into consideration any diminution of the means of information which is tolerated by the claimant for his own convenience: *Marriott* v *Yeoward Bros* [1909] 2 KB 987, 993.

80. *Dickens* (above), *loc cit*.

81. *Curtis* v *Chemical Cleaning & Dyeing Co Ltd* [1951] 1 KB 805 (CA). See further above, 8–3C. *McMaster* v *New York Life Ins Co*, 183 US 25 (1901): on receipt of a life policy the insured was told by the agent that its terms were the same as those of the application; in fact they differed as to commencement date. The Supreme Court held that the terms of the application prevailed: the insured was under no duty to read the policy (p 39).

82. This is accepted by the Ombudsman as regards private lines: The Insurance Ombudsman, Annual Report 1990, para 2.1. In this sense in the USA: *Reeves* v *State Farm Fire & Casualty Co*, 539 So 2d 252 (Ala, 1989—liability); *Shindler* v *Mid-Continent Life Ins Co*, 768 SW 2d 331, 334 (Tex, 1989—life); *Greene* v *Lilburn Agency Inc*, 383 SE 2d 194 (Ga, 1989—theft); *Shepard* v *Keystone Ins Co* 743 F Supp 429 (D Md, 1990—homeowner's); *Sutherland* v *NN Investors Life Ins Co*, 897 F 2d 593 (1 Cir, 1990—group health): even on renewal, at least, when the insured is told there are changes. Cf *McMaster* (above).

83. See also above 8–3B1, 8–3C and 9–6A, and below 14–3D(a), 26–2E4 and 30–6A.

84. The Insurance Ombudsman, Annual Report 1992, para 7.4.

not be affected by terms purporting to operately adversely to him immediately, especially if they are unexpected or unusual.[85] Further, when the discrepancy reflects an error which the insured subsequently seeks to have rectified, it appears that the law is more indulgent of the insured and that only gross negligence by the insured, in failing to find or correct the error, will bar rectification.[86]

11–2A3 The Silent Insurer

In the United States it has been held[87] that, if an insurer fails to accept or reject a proposal with reasonable promptness and thus induces the proposer to believe that he is covered and not to seek cover elsewhere, the insurer is considered to have impliedly accepted the proposal. However, these decisions must be seen in the context of the general rule found in the United States but not in England, whereby an obligation may be incurred by estoppel, if there is reasonable reliance on the undertaking of the obligor by the obligee.[88]

Further, in many parts of the United States, the insurer has an extra-contractual duty to respond to a proposal within a reasonable time; breach is the tort of negligence.[89] The insurer is "bound to furnish the indemnity which the state has authorized it to issue, or to decline to do so within such a reasonable time as will enable the applicant to act intelligently upon rejection".[90] A reasonable time is question of fact in each case. An application for travel insurance requires the insurer to be particularly prompt, as the period of risk is likely to be short[91] and imminent. If it appears that delay has occurred, the onus is on the insurer to prove that it was a reasonable delay.[92]

---

85. *State Farm Mutual Automobile Ins Co* v *Khoe*, 884 F 2d 401 (9 Cir, 1989—health): a term that. although the premium had been paid, there was no cover until a full policy had been issued. In English law see *Thornton* v *Shoe Lane Parking* [1971] 2 QB 163 (CA); *Interfoto Picture Library Ltd* v *Stiletto Visual Programmes Ltd* [1988] 1 All ER 348 (CA)

86. See below, 14–3D(a).

87. *National Bk of Commerce* v *Royal Exchange Assurance*, 455 F 2d 892 (6 Cir, 1972—hull). See also *American Life Ins Co* v *Hutcheson*, 109 F 2d 424 (6 Cir, 1940—life), cert den 310 US 625, in which, however, the insurer had also received a premium; *cf Schultz & Co* v *Camden Fire Ins Assn*, 106 NE 2d 272, 275 (NY, 1952—goods in transit): "Silence operates as an assent, and creates an estoppel, only when it has the effect to mislead. There must be such conduct on the part of the insurer as would, if it were not estopped, operate as a fraud on the party who has taken, or neglected to take, some action to his own prejudice in reliance upon it."

Prima facie no such estoppel is likely to arise, if the insurer has made it clear that there can be no insurance until a proposal has been approved: *Braman* v *Mutual Life Ins Co*, 73 F 2d 391 (8 Cir, 1934—life); *Martin* v *Equitable Life Assurance Sy*, 58 NYS 2d 848 (1945—life); *Reese* v *American National Ins Co*, 175 F 2d 793 (5 Cir, 1949—life); but *cf Bellak* v *United Home Life Ins Co*, 211 F 2d 280 (6 Cir, 1954—life).

88. Williston, section 91, section 98.

89. More recently, in respect of life insurance at least, the duty has been relocated in the law of contract because, if action is brought in contract, the insurance money goes directly to the beneficiary, whereas, if action is brought in tort, the money goes to the estate and the beneficiary may have to compete with creditors: Hasson, 18 Can Bus L J 473, 476 (1991).

90. Appleman, section 7226, cited with approval in *Travelers Ins Co* v *Anderson*, 210 F Supp 735 (WD SC,1962—trip insurance). See also *American Life Ins Co* v *Hutcheson*, 109 F 2d 424 (6 Cir, 1940—life), cert den 310 US 625. *Semble* for the tort to be committed it is usually necessary that the insurer have received the premium: *Salter* v *Security & Benefit Life Ins Co*, 235 F Supp 901 (ED Mich, 1964—life).

The duty of prompt decision is not found in some states, including New York: *Mietus* v *Prudential Ins Co*, 169 NYS 2d 386 (1957—life); *Cavallo* v *Metropolitan Life Ins Co*, 262 NYS 2d 618 (1965—life); Arkansas: *Killpack* v *National Old Line Ins Co*, 229 F 2d 851 (10 Cir, 1956—life); and Virginia: *Burgess* v *Charlottesville Savings & Loan Assn*, 349 F Supp 133 (WD Va, 1972—life).

91. *Travelers* v *Anderson* (above) p 738. In some states statute may stipulate a period of time after which a proposal becomes the basis of a contract.

92. *Bellak* v *United Home Life Ins Co*, 211 F 2d 280, 283 (6 Cir, 1954—life).

11–2B Mode of Acceptance

When the offeror stipulates a particular mode of acceptance, the offeree may accept by that mode or by any other mode which is apparently as good, i.e., which satisfies the apparent concerns of the offeror, for example, as to speed, proof or confidentiality, in stipulating that mode.[93] If, however, the offeror stipulates a mode of acceptance as exclusive, that mode must be followed in any event. Further, if the insurer as offeror requires the signature of a form by the proposer, the latter must observe that requirement, if the insurer is to be bound.[94]

11–2C Correspondence between Offer and Acceptance

If the terms of "acceptance" differ from the terms of the offer, the first question is whether there is any real inconsistency: sometimes insurers respond to a proposal offer with a policy in general terms that are not tailored to the proposal but which can be reconciled with it.[95] For example, in *Conheeney* v *Westgate Ins Co Ltd*,[96] an insurer responded to a proposal of liability insurance for a sole trader with a standard policy which was wide enough to cover persons in his employment. Here was no real inconsistency; the wider cover was "surplus to requirements", was clearly in excess of the cover that the proposer had paid for, and was ignored. Distinguish real inconsistency, which is most likely to arise when the non-correspondence is between proposal and response as regards terms in the latter, to which the responding insurer has given actual attention, such as conditions or premium.

If there is real inconsistency, the response is not an acceptance in law but may be one of two other things. First, it may be no more than a tentative move to see if the offeror will contract on some or all the new terms introduced by the offeree. A move of this kind does not reject the original offer and, if the move is unacceptable to the offeror, the offeree may withdraw it and, if so inclined, accept the original offer. Second, if the offeree's move is not tentative but firm, it is a counter-offer which rejects and extinguishes the original offer.

In *Allis-Chalmers Co* v *Fidelity & Deposit Co*[97] the plaintiff's request for fidelity insurance on their Paris manager was an offer. The defendant insurer "accepted" by sending a policy. The manager absconded with money belonging to the plaintiff, who then paid the premium required by the policy. If the policy sent was an acceptance completing a contract, the loss might have been covered. However, the policy contained terms not found in the plaintiff's original offer, so the House of Lords held that sending the policy was not acceptance but counter-offer, accepted only when the plaintiff paid the premium—too late to cover the loss. The question in each case is "whether or not a reasonable person in the position of the recipient would regard the

---

93. *Manchester Diocesan Council for Education* v *Commercial & General Investments Ltd* [1970] 1 WLR 241.
94. *McDonald* v *Mutual Life Ins Co*, 108 F 2d 32 (6 Cir, 1939—life), cert den 309 US 679.
95. *Izzard* v *Universal Ins Co* [1937] AC 773, 780 per Lord Wright (motor).
96. High Court 1989, unreported.
97. (1916) 114 LT 433. *Cf Cronk* (above, 11–1A3) in which the proposer's offer was deemed to be on the standard terms in the offeree insurer's policy, thus avoiding non-correspondence of offer and acceptance. In *Allis-Chalmers* it could not be inferred that the insurer's standard terms were to be read in to the offer (p 434).
USA: On this point, see *Mutual Life Ins Co* v *Young's Administrator*, 90 US 85 (1874—life); *Aetna Indemnity Co* v *Crowe Coal & Mining Co*, 154 F 545 (8 Cir, 1907—fidelity), *cert* den 207 US 589; *McDonald* v *Metropolitan Life Ins Co*, 108 F 2d 32 (6 Cir, 1939—life), cert den 309 US 679.

response as introducing a new term into the bargain, and not as a clean acceptance of the offer".[98]

11–2D Genuine Acceptance

The consent of each party and, in particular, the acceptance of the offeree must be genuine. If one or both are sufficiently mistaken about the terms of the contract or the nature of the subject-matter, a contract of insurance apparently formed may be vitiated by mistake. See chapter 21 on Mistake.

11–2E Unconditional Acceptance

Acceptance, notably acceptance by an insurer, may be conditional—in more than one sense, according to the intention. Distinguish, first, cases in which there is no agreement: if the "condition" of acceptance was not expected by the offeror, and it could not in any sense be found, express or implied, in his own offer, the "acceptance" is a counter-offer (below, case (a)) and there is no contract at that point. Distinguish, second, where the condition was expected (because it had been negotiated) or should have been expected (because it was part of standard terms) and that condition qualifies the acceptance of the insurer. In such cases there is agreement, but either there is no immediate contract (below, case (b)) or there is a contract but it does not have full effect (below, cases (c) and (d)) until the condition is met. Common examples are acceptance subject to payment of premium, subject to delivery of the policy, or subject to favourable medical report. Such conditions are most common and most likely to delay the formation of the contract in life insurance. In fire, motor and burglary insurance, the common practice is to grant temporary cover until matters of this kind have been settled. Even so, the insurance may sometimes be conditional, for example, burglary cover subject to the installation of a burglar alarm.[99]

(a) If "acceptance" is conditional in the sense that it contains terms not found in the offer, with which there is real inconsistency (above, 11–2C), the "acceptance" does not correspond with the offer and is itself a counter-offer. In *Canning* v *Farquhar*[100] Canning's proposal was "accepted" by the insurer but with a clause not found in the offer, that "No assurance can take place until the first premium is paid". Canning died and his agent tendered the premium to the insurer. The Court of Appeal held that there was no contract. Lindley LJ said[101]: "It is true that there has been an acceptance of Canning's offer, but he had not at this time assented to the company's terms; and until he had assented there was no contract binding the company. The company's acceptance of Canning's offer was not a contract but a counter offer."

(b) If there is agreement on the terms proposed but there is also agreement that no contract shall come into existence until a condition is satisfied, that is

---

98. *Lark* v *Outhwaite* [1991] 2 Lloyd's Rep 132, 139 per Hirst J (re).
99. For example *Irma Hosiery Co* v *Home Indemnity Co*, 276 F 2d 212 (3 Cir, 1960—burglary).
100. (1886) 16 QBD 727. On counter-offers see further above, 11–2A2 and 11–2C.
101. p 733. A different analysis of the situation was made by Lord Esher MR (p 731). The company's counter-offer would be revoked, before it could be accepted by the agent, by the operation of an implicit condition subject to which it was made, that the risk had not changed.

called a condition precedent.[102] This kind of condition is most common in life insurance,[103] and is illustrated by the term "no cover until premium has been paid", as in *Canning* (above). Case (b) differs from (a) in that there is agreement, and from (c), (d) and (e) in that there is no contract.

(c) If there is a contract of insurance from the time of agreement but no cover until a condition is satisfied, that is a a contract subject to a suspensive condition. Case (c) differs from (a) and (b) in that there is a contract, so neither party can unilaterally withdraw without liability for breach of contract. Moreover, as the duty of disclosure impinges when the contract is made, the contract cannot be avoided for undisclosed facts arising between the conclusion of the contract and the commencement of cover, unless the contract warrants no change in the risk in that period.[104] Case (c) differs from (d) and (e) in that there is no cover, until the condition is satisfied.

Case (c) is illustrated by *Sickness & Accident Assurance Assn* v *General Accident Assurance Corp*,[105] in which one insurer sought from another contribution to payment made under a liability policy. This raised the question whether the defending insurer was liable at all to the insured on the date of insured loss. The insured had made an offer (proposal) to the defender, who had accepted on terms that there would be no insurance until premium was paid; premium was paid after the date of loss. The Lord Ordinary said[106] that

"the contract was concluded for an insurance to cover the [date of loss], subject, however, to the suspensive condition that no insurance shall be held to be effected until the premium was paid . . . but the fact that [a loss] occurred on the first day would not . . . have entitled the defender to refuse to accept the premium."

Thus he held that defender had contracted insurance, however, the insurance did not cover the loss. His decision was affirmed by the Court of Session but the analysis is less clear.[107]

---

102. *Canning* (above), p 731 *per* Lord Esher MR, 734 *per* Lopes LJ. See also *Equitable Fire & Accident Office Ltd* v *The Ching Wo Hong* [1907] AC 96 (PC—fire). *Burks* v *Colonial Life & Accident Ins Co*, 98 F Supp 149 (MD Ga, 1951—life); *Irma Hosiery Co* v *Home Indemnity Co*, 276 F 2d 212 (3 Cir, 1960—burglary).

103. "Where no policy of life insurance has been issued, and no premium has been paid, there is a strong presumption that there was no contract, and no intention to contract"—*Equitable Life Assurance Sy* v *McElroy*, 83 F 631, 638 (8 Cir, 1897—life). See also *Paine* v *Pacific Mutual Life Ins Co*, 51 F 689 (8 Cir, 1892—life). Today, however, it has been said that courts are reluctant to find against cover, and seize ambiguity or equitable principles to aid a finding of interim insurance: see Brenner, 22 Tort & Ins L J 388 (1987) Thus in *State Farm Mutual Automobile Ins Co* v *Khoe*, 884 F 2d 401 (9 Cir, 1989—health): a term that, although the premium had been paid, there was no cover until a full policy had been issued was ignored as this did not meet the reasonable expectations of the insured. However, it is a general rule in the USA that conditions precedent must be strictly met and that the doctrine of substantial performance, which applies to the fulfilment of ordinary terms of a contract, does not apply to conditions precedent: *Hardin, Rodriquez & Boivin Anesthesiologists Ltd* v *Paradigm Ins Co*, 962 F 2d 628, 636 (7 Cir, 1992—liability).

104. This possibility is illustrated by *Harrington* v *Pearl Life Assurance Co Ltd* (1914) 30 TLR 613, 614 *per* Buckley LJ (CA—life). As to the time of the duty of disclosure, see below, 23–4.

105. (1892) 19 R 977. See also *Canning* (above, note p 731 *per* Lord Esher MR (CA—life)). USA: see *Kohen* v *Mutual Reserve Fund Life Assurance Co*, 28 F 705 (ED Miss, 1886—life); and *Rigdon* v *Marquette Casualty Co*, 163 So 2d 442 (La, 1964—fire), in which the operation of a new policy was subject to the suspensive condition of the cancellation of previous policies.

106. (1892) 19 R 977, 981–982.

107. While two judges thought there was a "preliminary" contract, but no cover, there is some uncertainty about the view of Lord Adam (p 986).

(d) A further possibility, which finds some support in *Sickness & Accident* (above) is that of a preliminary contract[108] at the time of agreement, under which the insurer promises to issue a policy, i.e., to make the main contract later, if the condition, such as a favourable medical report, is satisfied, and also to grant immediate but temporary cover pending the outcome of the condition. The grant of immediate cover separates case (d) from (c), while (d) differs from (e) in that (d) contemplates two distinct contracts, the preliminary or temporary contract and later the main contract. One consequence of (d) is that the insured has a duty of disclosure in respect of the main contract, notably as to interim changes in the risk, up to the time the main contract is concluded. "An agreement to undertake to relieve against risks necessarily assumes that when it comes to be fulfilled by issuing the policy the events are still risks,"[109] and, if they are still risks that they are the same risks. Temporary contracts of insurance like this are well known in relation to non-life insurance in both England and the United States, where they are often called binders.[110]

(e) In contrast with case (d), a preliminary contract which is superseded by the main contract, case (e) is that of a "main" contract from the beginning subject, however, to a condition—the possibility of termination by the insurer under specified circumstances: that condition is a condition subsequent. For example, life cover might be given from the time of agreement but with the possibility of subsequent rejection by the insurer, when he has had time fully to assess the risk. The effect of rejection, in particular, whether and when it operates retrospectively, is a matter of construction.

Case (e) was in issue in *Rivota*,[111] in which the plaintiff applied for insurance on his own life, paid a premium for interim cover and received a "conditional receipt". Before his proposal was approved or rejected he was killed. The United States' District Court held that the proposal was an unaccepted offer: no cover. This decision was reversed by the Court of Appeals, saying[112] that there were

"three potential solutions to the problem created by a rejection subsequent to death or serious change in insurability. These were: (1) to give retroactive effect to the rejection regardless of the reason therefor (i.e., to treat the binder as evidencing nothing more than a mere offer); (2) to treat the binder as a binding policy of temporary insurance during the interim, regardless of the applicant's insurability; and (3) to give effect to the rejection 'only where, on as objective a basis as possible, it is reasonable to say that the rejection is based on the circumstances which existed at the time of the application'."[113]

---

108. Although the same effect can be achieved by a continuing warranty; see *Harrington* v *Pearl Life Assurance Co Ltd* (1914) 30 TLR 613 (CA—life).

109. *Sickness* case (above, 11–2E(c)), p 985.

110. These are discussed below in chapter 12.

111. *Rivota* v *Fidelity & Guarantee Life Ins Co*, 497 F 2d 1225 (7 Cir, 1974). See also *Miller* v *Republic National Life Ins Co*, 714 F 2d 958 (9 Cir, 1983—life). Appleman, section 7237. *Zurich Life Ins Co* v *Davies* (1981) 130 DLR (3d) 748, 751 (Sup. Ct., Canada – life).

112. p 1228.

113. *American National Bk & Trust Co* v *Certain Underwriters at Lloyd's London*, 444 F 2d 640, 643 (7 Cir, 1971—PA). Widiss, 75 Iowa L Rev 1096, 1100 ff (1990).

11–2F Communication of Acceptance

Generally, acceptance is not effective to complete a contract until the fact of acceptance is communicated to the offeror.[114] Communication connotes receipt. However, the requirement of communication, being one made for the benefit of the offeror, may be waived by the offeror.[115]

There are degrees of waiver. First, an offeror who communicates his offer by post (or other non-instantaneous mode of communication) impliedly authorises the offeree to use the same medium,[116] and takes upon himself the risks of that mode of transmission. The consequence is that in this case the acceptance is effective not on receipt but on sending[117] and, if the acceptance is lost or delayed in transmission, there is nonetheless a valid contract of insurance from the time of sending.[118] The offeror has not waived acceptance but has waived the benefit of the general rule, whereby acceptance is ineffective until actually received.

Second, the offeror may waive the requirement of communication altogether: once there is evidence that the offeree intends to accept, there is a contract, whether the offeror knows about it or not. Waiver may be inferred from market practice. Thus, a proposal of hull insurance may be accepted by the insurer's issue of the policy.[119] Waiver will be inferred in the particular case, if it is manifestly in the interest of the insured waivor not to wait on the sending or communication of acceptance of his offer. Thus, an insurer's offer to renew motor insurance was accepted by the insured's driving a car within the scope of the cover offered, for otherwise he would have been driving without the insurance required by law.[120] Again, in *Shanks* v *Sun Life Assurance Co*[121] a man contracted accident insurance by sending a completed coupon cut from a newspaper. Two days after that insurance expired, the insured was accidentally killed. In his possession was a similar coupon issued by the same insurer for the next period of cover. This was enough for the court to hold that he had accepted the offer in the coupon for the next period.

11–2G Retraction of Acceptance

In England it is unsettled whether an acceptance may be withdrawn. The possibility of withdrawal is taken seriously by English writers only when the acceptance is sent by a

---

114. *Brinkibon Ltd* v *Stahag Stahl und Stahl Warenhandelsgesellschaft mbH* [1982] 1 Lloyd's Rep 217 (HL). On communication, see below 23–3C. *Paine* v *Pacific Mutual Life Ins Co*, 51 F 689 (8 Cir, 1892—life); *Goldberg* v *Colonial Life Ins Co*, 134 NYS 2d 865 (1954—life).

115. *Carlill* v *Carbolic Smoke Ball Co* [1893] 1 QB 256 (CA).

116. See above, 11–2B.

117. It is submitted that the common law rule is accurately expressed by the Malaysian Contract Ordinance 1950: put in the course of transmission, so as to be out of the power of the sender.

118. *Adams* v *Lindsell* (1818) 1 B & Ad 681; *Henthorn* v *Fraser* [1892] 2 Ch 27 (CA); *Sanderson* v *Cunningham* [1919] 2 Ir R 234 (motor). USA: *Tayloe* v *Merchants' Fire Ins Co*, 9 How 390 (Sup. Ct., 1850—fire); *National Quicksilver Corp* v *World Ins Co*, 139 F 2d 1 (8 Cir, 1943—workmen's compensation).

Acceptance is not effective on sending, if the acceptance is lost or delayed by the fault of the offeree, something of which the offeror is not taken to have assumed the risk; see Treitel, pp 26–27.

119. *Xenos* v *Wickham* (1860) LR 2 HL 296. See also *Roberts* v *Security Co Ltd* [1897] 1 QB 111 (CA—burglary).

120. *Taylor* v *Allon* [1966] 1 QB 304. See also *Rust* v *Abbey Life Assurance Co Ltd* [1978] 2 Lloyd's Rep 386: there was acceptance of an offer to buy a property bond by the prompt allocation of units to the offeror, such allocation being more advantageous if done that day, rather than the next.

121. (1896) 4 SLT 65. See also *Law* v *George Newnes Ltd* (1894) 21 R 1027 where mere possession of or subscription to the newspaper was held sufficient for accident insurance (Lord Young *dubitante*, p 1027, perhaps because it was unclear whether the "insured" was aware of the offer of insurance).

non-instantaneous mode of communication and is overtaken by the withdrawal, so that the offeror has not acted on the acceptance.[122] This has been the decision of courts in the United States.[123] One established case affecting insurance in England is the limited statutory right of the proposer to change his mind: above, 11–2A1.

11–3 THE FORMATION OF CONTRACTS AT LLOYD'S

11–3A The Traditional Course of Business[124]

He who proposes insurance at Lloyd's must act through a Lloyd's broker.[125] The broker prepares a slip, that is, a sheet of paper recording the essentials of the risk proposed. The broker, as the agent of the proposer,[126] takes the slip around the market at Lloyd's seeking subscriptions to the risk offered by the slip. Any subscribing underwriter[127] signifies acceptance of (usually a small part of) the risk offered, by placing his syndicate stamp on the slip and initialling it. The broker continues until the amount of the risk has been fully subscribed.[128] Usually, a policy on the terms of the slip is issued later by the Lloyd's Policy Signing Office. The issue of a policy is not a condition of the formation[129] or validity of the insurance and, in some cases, no policy is issued at all.[130] The policy, once issued, is evidence of a series of separate contracts between the insured and each member of each syndicate, whose underwriter has initialled the slip.[131] The position is the same, whether the contracts are of insurance or of reinsur-

---

122. Treitel, pp 27–28. Hudson, 82 LQR 169 (1966).

123. *Calhoun*, 391 F 2d 535 (4 Cir, 1968—life): a person applied to take life insurance as part of an investment plan. The insurer replied that he qualified for the scheme, a mistake, which the insurer corrected and notified the proposer before the latter had relied on the initial response. It was held that there was no contract.

    Cf Centrovincial Estates plc v *Merchants Investors Assurance Co Ltd* [1983] Com. L.R. 158 (CA), in which this view was rejected—but, see note 76 above.

124. This description is general and does not apply to every kind of business at Lloyd's. See further Arnould, Nos 163 ff; Horton Rogers, 14 Anglo-American L Rev 33.

125. Lloyd's Act 1982, section 8(3). Business may be shown to syndicates by non-Lloyd's brokers under the aegis of Lloyd's brokers, in accordance with umbrella arrangements: the slip is prepared by the former in accordance with the arrangement; for example, see *Johns* v *Kelly* [1986] 1 Lloyd's Rep 468 (liability). Lloyd's Byelaw (No 6 of 1988)—Umbrella Arrangements.

    At the time of writing, the course of business at Lloyd's is changing rapidly. For example, personal lines, motor and life business may be placed at Lloyd's directly by an outside agent, who has been guaranteed by a Lloyd's broker. See the Insurance Intermediaries Byelaw (No 8 of 1990) and the Binding Authorities Byelaw (No 9 of 1990). I am most grateful to Julian Burling of the Solicitors Department at Lloyd's for helping me to keep abreast of developments.

126. *American Airlines Inc* v *Hope* [1974] 2 Lloyd's Rep 301, 304 *per* Lord Diplock (HL—aviation); *Roberts* v *Plaistend* [1989] 2 Lloyd's Rep 341 (CA—fire); *Pryke* v *Gibbs Hartley Cooper Ltd* [1991] 1 Lloyd's Rep 602 (financial guarantee). For criticism of this analysis of the role of the broker, see below 23–3C. However, his role is qualified (a) as regards payment of premium: the underwriter looks to the broker rather than the insured; and (b) in some aspects of reinsurance: Reynolds [1984] LMCLQ 376, discussing *The Zephyr, General Accident Fire & Life Assurance Corp* v *Tanter* [1984] 1 Lloyd's Rep 58 (re).

127. The underwriter is an employee of an underwriting agent, who acts on behalf of a syndicate of individual underwriters, called "names", whether a natural person or, from 1994, a corporate body.

128. . . . or, more usually, oversubscribed, the amount of each subscription being later written down. Oversubscription is discussed below, 11–3C

129. *Thompson* v *Adams* (1889) 23 QBD 361 (cargo).

130. In the case of reinsurance the only record may be the slip. As to formality and when the law requires a policy, see above, 11–2A1.

131. *Fennia* [1983] 1 QB 856, 864 *per* Kerr LJ (CA). *Fennia* concerned a partially subscribed amendment slip for cover on goods in transit, which the insured sought to cancel. The result of cancellation would have been that the underwriter's liability on a loss which had just occurred would have been much greater under the original insurance than under the amended insurance. It was held by the Court of Appeal that the

ance, whether the slip is an original slip or a slip to amend existing cover, or whether the risk is marine or non-marine.[132]

In March 1992, the Joint Market Initiative (JMI) was launched by the Institute of London Underwriters (ILU), members of the London Insurance and Reinsurance Market Association (LIRMA), certain Lloyd's syndicates, and brokers in the Lloyd's Insurance Brokers Committee (LIBC). Paper slips will continue to be used, however, the JMI provides a placing support system that allows the preparation of a risk package or proposal on screen, and thus an electronic version of the traditional slip, which can be taken around the market on screen. Evidently, this is an innovation of considerable commercial significance, however, its institution does not appear to change the basic legal analysis of business at Lloyd's.

11–3B The Moment of Contract

In *Jaglom* v *Excess Insurance Co Ltd*[133] the court said that each subscription was an offer to insure, which the proposer accepted, however, not before the entire risk had been subscribed. This analysis was rejected by the Court of Appeal in *Fennia*[134] because that was not the intention of the Lloyd's insurance market "and the legal analysis must accord with their intention".[135] In that case, the Court of Appeal held[136] that, when the broker presents the slip on behalf of the insured, that is an offer, which the underwriter accepts *pro tanto* when he initials the slip; at that moment a contract of insurance comes into existence with that underwriter. This is the currently accepted analysis, however, it is too simple to accommodate all the difficulties arising out of business at Lloyd's.

11–3C Oversubscription: Signing Down

The first difficulty arises out of the possibility of oversubscription. To accommodate oversubscription, the formation of the contract (above, 11–3B) is subject to the contingency that the amount of cover accepted by the underwriter may be signed down, i.e., proportionately reduced if, at the end of its journey around the market, the slip has attracted similar acceptances for more than 100 per cent of the risk.[137] However, although "the broker may legitimately continue to obtain further subscriptions, and hence to increase the degree of signing down, after the risk has attached. . . . if the vessel [insured] suffers a casualty while the slip is being taken round the market, the extent of signing down is to be determined at the moment when the loss is known to the insured or the broker, since thereafter the risk can no longer properly be offered to further underwriters."[138]

insured was not entitled to cancel the amendment. See also *Touche Ross & Co* v *Baker* [1992] 2 Lloyd's Rep 207 (HL—liability).

132. *Fennia* (above), pp 865–866 *per* Kerr LJ.

133. [1972] 2 QB 250. This case concerned a slip for burglary cover, the terms of which were changed in the course of its subscription by various underwriters.

134. *General Reinsurance Corp* v *Forsak Fennia Patria* [1982] QB 1022; [1983] 1 QB 856 (CA).

135. pp 866–877 *per* Kerr LJ, who found some support in *Morrison* v *Universal Marine Ins Co* (1873) LR 8 Ex 197, 199 *per* Honyman J (hull and freight).

136. p 867 *per* Kerr LJ. See also *Grover & Grover Ltd* v *Mathews* [1910] 2 KB 401; *Eagle Star Ins Co Ltd* v *Spratt* [1971] 2 Lloyd's Rep 116, 124 *per* Lord Denning MR (re). MIA, section 21.

137. *Fennia* (above), p 865 and p 867 *per* Kerr LJ.

138. p 531 *per* Mustill LJ. Any contract of insurance obtained after a loss was known to the insured or his broker would be voidable for non-disclosure.

The difficulty in law is that, when the offer is accepted by each underwriter (except the last to subscribe), the amount of cover provided by each underwriter is subject to revision to an unknown degree and hence, it might be said, his contract lacks the certainty required by law. One answer is that the amount of cover, like, for example, price or premium, has been referred to the decision of third parties (in this situation that of subsequent underwriters).[139] This answer is open to the objection that the degree of oversubscription and thus the degree of writing down depends on the energy and will of one party, the insured through his broker. This objection is partly answered by pointing to provisions in contracts (other than insurance) that allow one party to choose between a number of performance options, so that the final terms are left to him; these are usually enforced.[140] However, the courts are slow to imply such a provision, if the option could be exercised by one party in a manner prejudicial to the other.[141] This point is partly answered by the Lloyd's practice, whereby the broker gives the underwriter a signing down indication (below, 11–3C1), i.e., an estimate of the degree to which the slip will be oversubscribed in the end and hence of the percentage of the risk that the particular underwriter will have to bear.[142]

11–3C1 The Signing Down Indication: Liability of the Broker

When giving a signing down indication, the broker is not acting on behalf of the insured.[143] Any liability resulting from a false signing indication does not affect the contract of insurance consequently concluded between the underwriter and the broker for the insured.[144] The broker's liability on the signing down indication might be based on one or more of the following grounds.

   (a) *Collateral Contract*: One possibility is a contract collateral to the contract of insurance, whereby in return for the subscription (making the contract with the insured) the broker promises to exercise best endeavours[145] to obtain sufficient subscriptions to sign the slip down to the stated percentage.[146] In principle this view of the broker's liability is open to doubt. A "contract" to negotiate[147] or *bona fide* to negotiate[148] is void for uncertainty, but chiefly on the ground that these arrangements were little different from agreements to agree, which are traditionally void.[149] These decisions concerned a promise

---

139. *Id certum est quod certum reddi potest*: see above, 11–1A4. It is also possible to agree alternative performance, for example, "1000 dollars or the market price on 1 June, whichever is the greater": *Renton & Co* v *Palmyra Trading Corp* [1957] AC 149; [1955] 2 Lloyd's Rep 722. This was accepted in *Fennia* (above, 11–3B) by Staughton J (p 1038) and not challenged on appeal.

140. For example the seller FOB may choose his port: *Boyd & Co Ltd* v *Louca* [1973] 1 Lloyd's Rep 209. Another answer may lie in (contractual) duties of good faith: Clarke, [1993] HKLJ 318.

141. *Bushwall Properties Ltd* v *Vortex Properties Ltd* [1976] 2 All ER 283 (CA).

142. See discussion in *The Zephyr* [1985] 2 Lloyd's Rep 529, 531–532 *per* Mustill LJ (CA—re).

143. *The Zephyr* [1984] 1 Lloyd's Rep 58, 82 *per* Hobhouse J, a conclusion apparently not challenged on appeal: [1985] 2 Lloyd's Rep 529 (CA).

144. *The Zephyr* (above).

145. *The Zephyr* (above), p 537 *per* Mustill LJ.

146. *Ibid*, pp 537–539 *per* Mustill LJ. The consideration received by the broker for such a contract lies in his financial interest in the brokerage: [1984] 1 Lloyd's Rep 58, 82 *per* Hobhouse J.

147. *Courtney & Fairbairn Ltd* v *Tolaini Bros (Hotels) Ltd* [1975] 1 All ER 716 (CA), approved in *Walford* v *Miles* [1992] 2 AC 128.

148. *Mallozzi* v *Carapelli SPA* [1976] 1 Lloyd's Rep 407 (CA); *idem Walford* v *Miles* (above); nor an implied term to use best endeavours to reach a mutually acceptable conclusion: *The Scaptrade* [1981] 2 Lloyd's Rep 425; affirmed [1983] 1 All ER 301 (CA).

149. *Courtney* (above), p 720 *per* Lord Denning MR, with whom Lord Diplock (p 720) agreed.

to negotiate with the other party to the alleged contract. Uncertainty is less evident when, as at Lloyd's, the negotiation is not with the party to the alleged contract, but with third parties (other underwriters).[150]

(b) *Tort: Negligence*: In *The Zephyr*[151] the Court of Appeal decided against a duty of care actionable in tort. The negligence alleged lay in failure to exercise best endeavours to achieve the signing down indication; it was assumed[152] that lack of best endeavours could be equated with lack of reasonable care.

> "The complaint is that [the broker] did not perform the acts necessary to transform expectation into reality, with the result that the [reinsurers] were held to the terms of their contracts with the reinsured as written, rather than the attenuated form which would have resulted from a signing-down . . . [The promise] bears to my mind no resemblance to the kind of obligation to avoid doing something badly, which is at present the subject-matter of the English law of negligence."[153]

In this case: the broker had begun to collect subscriptions, but had stopped, being "too busy with other matters".[154] Mustill LJ concluded[155]:

> "I grant that the demarcation between misfeasance and non-feasance appears old-fashioned, and indeed, artificial to this extent, that doing something badly may often involve a neglect to carry out an act which would turn bad performance into adequate performance. But the present is not the case."

On the assumption that there was no contract, the court was disinclined to find a duty actionable in tort: contract and tort have different domains[156] and contract should be protected from the presumptuous tort of negligence.[157] In the summer of 1985 *Junior Books Ltd v Veitchi & Co Ltd*,[158] to which Mustill LJ referred, was still being seen in some quarters as allowing actions in the tort of negligence for purely economic loss. However, a retreat from *Junior Books* had already begun[159] and has continued since.[160] The judgment of Mustill LJ in *The Zephyr* is in the same direction.

> "In reality, the fault of the brokers lay in a continuing failure to perform a positive undertaking. Once any contractual background is subtracted, I do not see how such a right of action can be sustained without holding that if the relationship between the parties is of the right kind, the law of England recognizes the enforceability of a gratuitous promise."[161]

150. The situation has some features of a common (and enforceable) commercial agency. Moreover, there would be less difficulty in defining and enforcing a duty to exercise best endeavours, if there were a duty to perform in good faith, as in Rest Contracts (2d), section 230.

151. (above), pp 537–539 *per* Mustill LJ.

152. p 534.

153. p 538. Concerning liability for non-feasance, see *Smith v Littlewoods Organisation Ltd* [1987] AC 241.

154. p 533. *Cf Mercer v SE & Chatham Ry Co* [1922] 2 KB 549. Further it appears from *Anns v London Borough of Merton* [1978] AC 728 that a duty of inspection may be broken either by negligent inspection or failure to inspect at all.

155. p 538.

156. *Groom v Crocker* [1939] 1 KB 194 (CA).

157. In recent times this tort has been more evident in cases of professional misjudgement: *Midland Bank Trust Co Ltd v Hett, Stubbs & Kemp* [1979] Ch 384; *Forster v Outred & Co* [1982] 2 All ER 753 (CA), discussed critically by Kaye, 100 LQR 680 (1984).

158. [1983] 1 AC 520.

159. *Tate & Lyle Ltd v GLC* [1983] 2 AC 509.

160. *The Aliakmon* [1986] AC 785; *Simaan General Contracting Co v Pilkington Glass Ltd* (No 2) [1988] QB 758 (CA); *Murphy v Brentwood D.C.* [1991] 1 AC 378. In Canada, however, the Supreme Court has moved the other way: *Norsk Pacific Steamship Co Ltd v Canadian National Ry* [1992] 1 SCR 1021.

161. *The Zephyr* (above, note 132), p 538.

In other words, this was a "contract situation"—broken promise causing purely economic loss, and, if there was no contract, there was no action in the tort of negligence.

  (c) *Tort: Negligent Misstatement*: Economic loss is recoverable in tort *inter alia* for negligent misstatement,[162] but can there be an actionable misstatement of one's own intentions? An action has succeeded in respect of pre-contract negotiations.[163] The Lloyd's broker is a skilled person on whose signing-down indication it is customary, reasonable, and reasonably foreseeable that an identifiable plaintiff, the reinsurer, will rely.[164] The broker might be liable therefore, if he did not have reasonable grounds for believing that he would fulfil the signing down indication; in the context of negligent misstatement many statements of present fact (e.g., credit, the risks of a surgical operation) are only solicited as signs of the future. But, if one can make a negligent misstatement about one's intentions, i.e., in effect about one's ability to perform a (contractual) promise, tort crosses into the field of contract and, although negligent misstatements were not directly in issue in *The Zephyr*,[165] this incursion into the field of contract was not welcomed (above (a)) by the Court of Appeal.

  (d) *Tort: Deceit*: In *The Zephyr*[166] the "signing indication was indeed a representation of present fact: namely that [the broker] honestly believed on reasonable grounds that he would be able to sign the slip down to the stated proportion," but a representation that was true. The inference is that, if the representation had been untrue, he would have been liable to the underwriter in the tort of deceit.[167]

11–3D Partial Subscription and Subscription on Different Terms

Further difficulties of market practice at Lloyd's are as follows: (a) The broker fails to obtain contracts of insurance for 100 per cent of the risk (partial subscription) and the insured wishes to cancel the contracts obtained and perhaps look elsewhere for insurance. (b) The broker can obtain contracts for 100 per cent of the risk only by agreeing different terms with different underwriters: but "market practice abhors a slip on different terms; it is possible but daft,"[168] being administratively unsatisfactory to the Lloyd's market.

  To meet these difficulties, it has been argued that there is a custom of the Lloyd's market that the insured has an option to rescind the contracts already agreed, before the risk offered has been fully subscribed. This argument succeeded before Staughton

---

162. *Hedley Byrne* v *Heller* [1964] AC 465. Indeed, it was from the latter case that Hobhouse J had pinned a duty of care on the broker in *The Zephyr* [1984] 1 Lloyd's Rep 58, 84–85, but a broad duty covering both negligent activity and negligent statement. On developments in this field, see above, 9–2.

163. *Esso Petroleum Co Ltd* v *Mardon* [1976] QB 801 (CA); this might be seen as a special case, which would have been decided differently on this point, if it had been governed by the Misrepresentation Act 1967.

164. *Cherry Ltd* v *Allied Ins Brokers Ltd* [1978] 1 Lloyd's Rep 274.

165. [1985] 2 Lloyd's Rep 529 (CA).

166. (above), p 538 *per* Mustill LJ.

167. *Derry* v *Peek* (1889) 14 App Cas 337; *Edgington* v *Fitzmaurice* (1885) 29 Ch D 459, 482 *per* Bowen LJ (CA).

168. *Fennia* (below), p 1039 *per* Staughton J.

J in *Fennia*[169] but was rejected on appeal. There was insufficient evidence of any such custom. The two difficulties remain.[170]

The decision in *Fennia* against a contract subject to an option of rescission turned on the evidence of custom in the market but, in any event, there is some doubt whether such an arrangement is possible in law. Whereas a custom cannot depart from mandatory rules of law,[171] it has been said that trade custom may override non-mandatory rules of law to the extent of giving binding force to an arrangement that would otherwise be unenforceable.[172] Even so, there must be doubt whether the trade custom alleged in *Fennia* could produce a binding contract. The situation might be seen and thus supported as a promise to do X if I manage to do Y[173] but it is more likely to be seen as a "contract" subject to a unilateral and uncontrolled option of rescission, a contradiction of legal terms. The law will enforce an option to rescind, if it is triggered by an event outside the control of the insured.[174] But in the alleged custom at Lloyd's the trigger is not entirely outside his control; and a promise to exercise "best endeavours" to obtain subscriptions may lack the certainty required for enforceability in law.[175]

At Lloyd's, in the absence of an established custom, the situation

"is likely in practice to be resolved by the underwriters acceding to a request by the brokers concerned to cancel the contract concluded by the signature of the slip, subject in some cases to payment of a 'time on risk' premium . . . No doubt underwriters who operate in the London insurance market will value the goodwill of brokers who operate in the same market. It is not surprising, therefore, that . . . underwriters who have subscribed a slip may not ordinarily in practice stand on their strict rights, but will, as a matter of grace, permit cancellation. There is,

169. [1982] 2 QB 1022.

170. [1983] 1 QB 856 (CA). There are other ways of dealing with these difficulties: (1) One solution might be that each underwriter made an offer which could not be accepted by the insured until the risk was fully subscribed on the same terms. This solution was adopted by Donaldson J in *Jaglom v Excess Ins Co Ltd* [1972] 2 QB 250 but not followed by the Court of Appeal in *Fennia*. The *Jaglom* solution appears to create two further difficulties: (a) The offer of each underwriter could be revoked before acceptance, when the proposal had been fully subscribed on the same terms—an obvious disadvantage to the proposer—unless it could be said that the subsequent activity of the broker in seeking full subscription was something desired by the underwriter, so that the business might proceed, and hence gave consideration for a promise by the underwriter to keep the offer open. Donaldson J (in *Jaglom*, pp 257–258) thought this difficulty a nice point founded on the ancient doctrine of consideration which the market would disdain to take.
(b) Acceptance of an offer must normally be communicated by the offeree to the offeror. In Lloyd's practice this would not occur: the broker who had obtained full subscription on the same terms and was thus in a position to accept the offers of all the underwriters subscribed, would not communicate acceptance to them. This might be validated by a custom that communication of acceptance had been implicitly waived by the offeror. (2) A second solution might be that each contract with each underwriter was formed at the time of his subscription, but was subject to a condition subsequent that the risk be fully subscribed (or that it be subscribed on the same terms): if it were not, the contract would be terminated by failure of the condition. Difficulties in the way of this solution are as follows. (a) The fulfilment of the condition is governed by the subsequent effort and activity of the insured through his broker, whereas a true condition subsequent operates independently of the will of the parties. (b) It cannot easily be said that, if there is no market practice in favour of an option of rescission, a condition subsequent of this kind can be implied as a matter of business efficacy: *Fennia* [1983] 1 QB 856, 873 *per* Kerr LJ.

171. *Cunliffe-Owen v Teather & Greenwood* [1967] 1 WLR 1421; *Anglo-African Merchants Ltd v Bayley* [1970] 1 QB 311.

172. For example, it has been contended that an established commercial custom in favour of the enforcement of third party rights will be respected, as an exception to the rule of privity of contract: Anson, p 375. See above, 5–6C5.

173. However, it has been argued that there may be a binding contract to sell subject to procuring an export licence, or a contract to buy subject to finance: Lindgren, *Time in the Performance of Contracts* (2nd ed), Nos 519, 599 ff.

174. *Cannon v Miles* [1974] 2 Lloyd's Rep 129 (CA).

175. See above, 11–3C1(a).

however, the world of difference between a course of conduct that is frequently, or even habitually followed in a particular commercial community as a matter of grace and a course which is habitually followed because it is considered that the parties concerned have a legally binding right to demand it."[176]

If the broker fails to get 100 per cent subscription on the same terms, he can persuade but cannot compel prior subscribers to accept cancellation.[177]

11–3E Reinsurance of a Risk not yet Insured

"A practice has developed whereby a broker instructed to obtain a primary cover will on his own initiative approach potential reinsurers to obtain from them in advance a binding promise to provide reinsurance for whatever person may subsequently write a line on the primary cover and desire to reinsure the whole or part of that line. The reinsurer conveys this promise by initialling a percentage line on a slip, which identifies the subject-matter, the nature of the risk and the value. The slip does not identify the reinsured and could not do so: for at the stage when the potential reinsurer is approached, it is not known whether the primary insurance will ever be written at all, and if so by whom; or whether any of the primary insurers will desire to effect reinsurance; or whether any insurer who does desire to reinsure will be willing to do so with the reinsurer whom the broker has approached, and on the terms which he has offered. With this promise 'at large' in his pocket, the broker can offer to an underwriter a package consisting of the opportunity to take a line on the primary cover, and at the same time to place an order for reinsurance."[178]

The effect is that by initialling the slip the reinsurer makes an offer of reinsurance, which the broker is authorised to transmit to an insurer (the reinsured). When an insurer orders reinsurance from that broker within the terms of the reinsurer's offer, the offer has been accepted and a contract of reinsurance concluded,[179] in spite of possible objections deriving from the general law of contract. The first objection, that no contract can be concluded until the reinsured's acceptance has been communicated to the reinsurer (offeror), has been rejected[180] by reference to party intention and implied waiver of communication. The second objection, the possibility that the offer might be revoked at any time before it has been accepted,[181] has been countered by some evidence of market practice that, once the reinsurer has made an offer of reinsurance, he cannot unilaterally resile from it.[182] Such a practice might be supported in law by a collateral contract whereby, in return for the reinsurer's promise to keep the offer open, the broker undertook to exercise best endeavours to procure acceptance of the offer.[183] On the remaining problem, that of reinsurance orders which exceed the amount of reinsurance on offer, Hobhouse J said this[184]:

"if the broker has only obtained subscriptions to the [reinsurance] slip totalling, say, 10 per cent

---

176. *Fennia* (above), p 874 *per* Slade LJ. The willingness of an underwriter to agree cancellation would depend on the effect of such agreement, notably, the effect if, as in *Fennia*, there is an intervening loss before the slip is fully subscribed: *ibid*, pp 870–871 *per* Kerr LJ.
177. The other possibility, which commonly occurs, is to test the market by circulating a "quotation slip".
178. *The Zephyr* [1985] 2 Lloyd's Rep 529, 532 *per* Mustill LJ (CA—re).
179. *The Zephyr* [1984] 1 Lloyd's Rep 58, 71 *per* Hobhouse J (re); this point was not appealed, however, this analysis was apparently accepted by Mustill LJ : [1985] 2 Lloyd's Rep 529, 533.
180. p 72.
181. *Byrne* v *Van Tienhoven* (1880) 5 CPD 344.
182. *The Zephyr* [1984] 1 Lloyd's Rep 58, 80 *per* Hobhouse J, who declined to express a concluded view on the question.
183. On the enforceability of this kind of promise, however, see above, 11–3C(a).
184. *The Zephyr* [1984] 1 Lloyd's Rep 58, 72.

of value and he then in succession takes three orders for reinsurance for lines of 5 per cent of value without meanwhile obtaining additional subscriptions, is the third order effective and to what extent? The third order can only confer rights on the person giving the order if he is allowed to displace in part the rights against the reinsurers of those who gave the earlier orders. Before the third order was made the first two persons were fully reinsured; it was submitted that no later order could alter this . . . The answer to the question, on my example, of the effect of the third order depends upon a determination of the capacity of the broker by accepting the third order to affect the rights of those who gave earlier orders. If the broker does have that capacity, then their rights are affected; if not, they are not and a purported acceptance of the third order is nugatory. It is not merely the giving of an order which completes the contractual nexus but it also requires that the broker should accept that order."

On the evidence, he concluded that the broker's agency was more than a simple agency for the reinsured.[185] However, he went on to reject the argument that the broker was agent for the reinsurer[186]:

"The contractual machinery which was throughout being used was facultative reinsurance on a slip. The actual contract of insurance was the contract (or contracts) in the slip. As I have said earlier the nature of this contract both in accordance with the practice of the market and the law is that the broker is the agent of the insured not the insurer [of the reinsured and not the reinsurer]." The judge continued[187]: "If [the broker] says he has reinsurance when he has not or if he says he will get it when he knows he cannot, he will be in breach of his obligations to his client [the insurer]. Similarly if he accepts an order for reinsurance from a subsequent [insurer] when he has accepted orders from earlier [insurers] which exhaust the reinsurance cover which he has available he is in breach of his duty to those earlier underwriters and may be liable to them."

11–4 CONTRACT RENEWAL

The renewal of existing insurance is the conclusion of a new contract of insurance for a further period of time on the same risk and on broadly the same terms as before but, perhaps, with slight changes concerning, for example, premium.

11–4A Variation of the Insurance Contract

Distinguish, as a matter of fact based on the intention of the parties, renewal and variation. In the case of renewal, but not variation, the insured is subject to a full duty of disclosure, as if he were contracting the insurance for the first time.[188]

11–4B Continuation of Insurance

Distinguish renewal of insurance, which is commonly from year to year, from the continuation of insurance for a longer period but subject to forfeiture for non-payment of periodic premiums. The common case of continuation is life insurance, which continues until the life drops or a term of years passes, but the same principles apply to any insurance which continues conditionally on the payment by the insured of instal-

---

185. p 73.
186. p 80, citing *Glasgow Assurance Co* v *Symondsen* (1911) 16 Com Cas 109 (re). This is an odd conclusion in view of the practice, described above, whereby the broker prepares a package of cover with the reinsurer, and then markets this "product" to primary insurers.
187. p 81.
188. See ch 23.

ments of premium during the period of cover; it may be a case of insurance for one year but quarterly payment of premium, or for a longer period with payments every year.[189]

Property insurance is usually for a limited period, after which the insurer may decline the risk; the same is true of personal accident insurance.[190] In the case of life insurance, a risk that increases year by year, the courts were reluctant to allow the insurer that option; for this "very special category of contract"[191] there is a presumption of continuity of contract until the life drops[192] or a stated term of years has passed, subject to forfeiture under strictly construed and controlled conditions. In what the market usually calls life assurance each periodic premium is "part consideration of the entire insurance for life . . . The value of insurance for one year of a man's life when he is young, strong and healthy, is manifestly not the same when he is old and decrepit. There is no proper relation between the annual premium and the risk of assurance for the year in which it is paid."[193] This raises a strong inference that the initial contract is to continue. The result is that there is "a contract made once for all with a condition to be performed *de anno in annum*, and if the condition is not performed in any year the contract is at an end".[194]

Ultimately, however, the line is drawn between renewal and continuation not by any *a priori* classification of the insurance contract as life or not but according to contract terms.[195] In particular, it is a case of renewal when the insurer has a clear option not to renew for a further period of cover,[196] and a case of continuation when the insured has a clear option to renew. The contract is also decisive of associated issues. In the case of health insurance, the insured may have a right to renew but the insurer may have a right to alter terms of the contract, notably, the amount of premium. It is significant, perhaps, that in a case of this kind a court in the United States declined to interfere with the contract terms even when it accepted that the term in question, which concerned premium, was considered unfair.[197]

When construing a contract of insurance, it is legitimate for a court to have regard to the purpose of the insurance.[198] This is evident in the case of life insurance. The point has also been made when insurance was intended to cover an operation of unknown length; it was argued in *Jones Construction Co v Alliance Assurance Co Ltd*[199] that the cover, although referring to an (arbitrary) period of time, was automatically self-extending until the operation had been completed. Although the argument

189. For example, three years: *Phoenix Assurance Co Ltd v Four Courts Hotel Ltd* [1935] IR 628 (Ireland—fire).
190. *Stokell v Heywood* [1897] 1 Ch 459 (PA).
191. *Law Accident Ins Sy Ltd v Boyd*, 1942 SC 384, 391 *per* Lord Cooper (motor).
192. *New York Life Ins Co v Statham*, 93 US 24 (1876), approved in *McMaster v New York Life Ins Co*, 183 US 25 (1901—life). See also *Frank v Sun Life Assurance Co* (1893) 20 Ont AR 564, 567 (life).
193. *Statham* (above) 23 L Ed 789, 791 *per* Bradley J.
194. *Re Anchor Assurance Co* (1870) 5 Ch App 632, 638 *per* Lord Hatherley LC (life); *Statham* (above), p 793 *per* Strong J: "life insurance is a peculiar contract. Its obligations are unilateral. It contains no undertaking of the insured to pay premiums; it merely gives him an option to pay or not, and thus to continue the obligation of the insurers, or terminate it at his pleasure"
195. For example, *Pritchard v Merchant's & Tradesman's Mutual Life Assurance Sy* (1858) 3 CB (NS) 622, 640 *per* Williams J, 643 *per* Willes J (life); *Stuart v Freeman* [1903] 1 KB 47 (CA—life).
196. For example, *Stokell v Heywood* [1897] 1 Ch 459, 464 *per* Kekewich J (PA); *Jones Construction Co v Alliance Assurance Co Ltd* [1961] 1 Lloyd's Rep 121, 131 *per* Danckwerts LJ (CA—contractors AR).
197. *Compton v Aetna Life Ins & Annuity Co*, 956 F 2d 256 (11 Cir, 1992—PHI): the court enforced a term which enabled the insurer to increase the premium by 500 per cent in one year.
198. See below, 15–3B.
199. [1961] 1 Lloyd's Rep 121 (CA—contractors AR).

was given serious consideration by the Court of Appeal, it failed in the face of the language of the particular contract.[200]

11–4C Reinstatement after Lapse

Distinguish renewal of insurance from reinstatement after lapse, a possibility found in life policies: if the policy has lapsed, for example it has been forfeited for non-payment of premium, the contract may allow the former insured to revive the policy without the full rigmarole of entering a totally new contract. In law this is an option which can be exercised and accepted by the former insured within a certain period of time and on certain conditions, such as satisfactory proof of good health. If the insured exercises the option in accordance with its terms, there is a (reinstated) contract[201] and it is not open to the insurer to decline cover, unless the insured demands new terms not found in the lapsed policy or declinature is authorised by the option itself.[202] Whatever the terms of the clause, as reinstatement rests on the formation of a new contract[203] of insurance, it follows from general principles[204] that there can be no reinstatement if the life has already dropped.

11–4D Renewal Notice

Although a contract of insurance may refer to the possibility of a further period of cover beyond that contracted for, renewal is the formation of a new contract of insurance[205] and is governed by the normal legal rules on formation.[206] In particular, when the insurer sends a renewal notice to the insured, this is usually regarded as an offer of cover for the further period for acceptance (or rejection) by the insured. In the case of motor insurance, however, it has been stated that the insurer who offers renewal implicitly waives the usual right to have acceptance of the offer before contract is formed, with the result that an insured who responds to the renewal notice as if he considered himself insured, by motoring as usual, may be deemed to have accepted the offer.[207]

The right of the insurer not to offer cover for a further period is often stated in the original policy.[208] Indeed, in the absence of contrary statute, the insurer has an absolute right to refuse to renew the policy, whatever his motives for refusal.[209] It follows

---

200. A clause "extensions covered at a premium to be arranged" was hardly more successful in *Kirby* v *Cosindit SpA* [1969] 1 Lloyd's Rep 75 (builders' risks), but this was in part due to the difficulty (see 11–1A4) in that situation in agreeing a premium.

201. *Kirkpatrick* v *South Australian Ins Co Ltd* (1886) 11 App Cas 177, 179 *per* Lord Hobhouse (PC—fire).

202. *Knights Templars' & Masons' Life Indemnity Co* v *Jacobus*, 80 F 202 (7 Cir, 1897—life).

203. *Handler* v *Mutual Reserve Fund Life Assn* (1904) 90 LT 192, 194 *per* Mathew LJ (CA—life). See also *Edge* v *Duke* (1849) 18 LJ Ch 183 (life).

204. See ch 21. Also it has been held that if, after the time of forfeiture the life drops, there can be no waiver of forfeiture by the insurer without full knowledge of the facts, including of course the death of the insured: *Bennecke* v *Connecticut Mutual Life Ins Co*, 105 US 355 (1881—life).

205. *Last* v *London Assurance Corp* (1884) 12 QBD 389, 400 *per* Day J (life and fire); *Stokell* v *Heywood* [1897] 1 Ch 459 (PA); *Law Accident Ins Sy Ltd* v *Boyd* 1942 SC 384 (motor). *DeMezey* v *Milwaukee Mechanics' Ins Co* [1945] 1 WWR 644 (Alta—fire); in Canada the matter is now governed by state legislation.

206. See above, 11–1 and 11–2.

207. *Taylor* v *Allon* [1966] 1 QB 304 (motor).

208. For example *Simpson* v *Accidental Death Ins Co* (1857) 2 CB (NS) 257 (PA).

209. *Harding* v *Ohio Casualty Ins Co*, 41 NW 2d 818, 822 (Minn, 1950—surety), even though the effect was to deprive the insured of his livelihood as a detective.

that the insurer is not obliged to send a renewal notice. In the words of the United States Supreme Court[210]

"The insured knew or was bound to know, when his premiums became due . . . The reason why the Insurance Company gives notice to its members of the time of payment of premiums is to aid their memory and to stimulate them to prompt payment. The Company is under no obligation to give such notice and assumes no responsibility by giving it."

Moreover, if the insurer does send a renewal notice, the insurer is not obliged to ensure that it reaches the insured who, for example, has changed his address.[211]

Exceptions may arise as follows: First, a contract term requiring notice may be implied from previous dealings.[212] In a life contract, the term is not a duty sounding in damages but a procedural term, which must be obeyed by the insurer before another duty, the insured's duty to pay premium, matures.

Second, the insured might argue that there has been waiver of punctual payment: that, especially in the face of a life policy with forfeiture for non-payment of premium, a past practice of sending notice in advance of the forfeiture date waives the insured's duty to pay until the usual notice is sent; and that the past practice has lulled him into a sense of security of which the insurer should not be allowed to take advantage.[213] In England, this kind of argument must overcome the reluctance of the courts to infer waiver from negative conduct.[214] Moreover, the argument has still less force in the case of insurance, which is annually renewable and which the insurer is not obliged to renew. An English court would have particular difficulty in seeing the inactivity of the insurer, who fails to send a notice, as agreement to a new contract of insurance.[215] Nonetheless, the Supreme Court of Nebraska has found waiver in the case of renewable insurance. The insurer waived his right to require the insured "to assume the burden of keeping track of premium-due dates".[216] Insurers have responded with clauses such as: "We are under no obligation to send you any renewal notice or other notice that your policy term is coming to an end, and the receipt of any such notice by you shall not be deemed to be a waiver of this provision on our part."

11–4D1 Renewal Terms

Being a new contract, in theory, the terms of the renewal may be entirely new. However, although in general the insured is expected to read his documents (above,

---

210. *Thompson* v *Knickerbocker Life Ins Co*, 104 US 252, 258 *per* Bradley J (life). See also *Union Mutual Life Ins* v *Mowry,* 96 US 544 (1877). In many parts of the United States notice is now a statutory requirement, especially as regards renewal of life insurance: Appleman, sections 8161 ff.

211. *Windus* v *Lord Tredegar* (1866) 15 LT 108 (HL—life).

212. Cases sometimes cited are not conclusive: *New York Life Ins Co* v *Eggleston*, 96 US 572 (1878—life); *Phoenix Mutual Life Ins Co* v *Doster*, 106 US 30, 36 *per* Harlan J (1882—life); *Minnick* v *State Farm Mutual Automobile Ins Co*, 174 A 2d 707 (Del, 1961—motor). These cases are distinguishable, for the first concerned a notice concerning the agent to whom premium should be paid, and the second and third the amount of premium. The first two cases concerned life contracts which could not function unless such notice were given.
    Courts have also been willing to imply a term regardless of past practice: *Doster, loc cit*; *Minnick* (above); *Pester* v *American Family Mutual Ins Co*, 186 NW 2d 711 (Neb, 1971—motor).

213. "It is a common practice followed by insurance companies with a view to retaining and furthering their business. It is likewise a practice with which the general public is familiar and upon which it has come to depend"—*Pester* v *American Family Mutual Ins Co*, 186 NW 2d 711, 713 (Neb, 1971— motor. See also *Palomar Ins Corp* v *Guthrie*, 583 So 2d 1304 (Ala, 1991—motor).

214. *The Scaptrade* [1983] 1 Lloyd's Rep 146 (CA), affirmed [1983] 2 AC 694.

215. See above, 11–2A3.

216. *Minnick* (above); *Pester* (above) p 713.

11–2A2), he is also entitled to presume that, apart from the level of premium and the dates, the insurance is on broadly the same terms as before. If the insurer intends otherwise, he must give clear notice of the new terms[217]: the general obligation of an insured to read through his contract does not apply to fix him with notice of new terms on renewal.[218] This duty may devolve upon the agent who handles the renewal. It seems that the practice of sending with the renewal documents a letter, which explains and thus highlights the changes in the contract, is sufficient notice of those changes.[219]

---

217. *Burnett* v *Westminster Bank Ltd* [1966] 1 QB 742 (CA). *Stowe Township* v *Standard Life Ins Co*, 507 F 2d 1332 (3 Cir, 1975—life); *Mountain Fuel Supply* v *Reliance Ins Co*, 933 F 2d 882, 890 (10 Cir, 1991—liability); *Midway National Bk* v *Bollmeier*, 474 NW 2d 335 (Minn, 1991—liability); *Federal Deposit Ins Corp* v *American Casualty Co of Reading*, 814 F Supp 1032 (D Wyo, 1991—liability).
218. *Wyckoff* v *Standard Fire Ins Co*, 936 F 2d 1474 (6 Cir, 1991—fire).
219. *St Paul Fire & Marine Ins Co* v *FDIC*, 765 F Supp 538 (D Minn, 1991—liability).

CHAPTER 12

INTERIM INSURANCE: COVER NOTES AND BINDERS

12-1 INTRODUCTION

The purpose of interim insurance, called a binder in the United States[1] and often recorded in a cover note in England, is to give the insurer time to assess the risk and to decide whether to commit himself to offer cover (here called "the policy") over a longer period, while offering interim cover to the proposer—especially when his need for cover is pressing. If, having considered the proposal fully, the insurer does not want the risk, he is not obliged to make the longer commitment required by the policy. Interim insurance is beneficial to the insured, who has immediate cover[2] in order, for example, to use the car he has just bought. It is beneficial to the insurer, for the facility of interim cover increases the chance that he will get business at minimum cost in investigating risks, without sacrificing altogether the option of refusing an undesirable policy proposal. It is most common in respect of fire and motor risks, however, it may also be found on lives, particularly in the United States.[3]

The effect of interim insurance depends on the wording of the agreement. Usually the agreement is itself a contract of insurance and is distinct from the contract of insurance on the same risk which may follow it and be recorded in the policy; the first is regulated by the cover note or binder and the second by the policy.[4] From the nature of interim insurance as a distinct contract, a number of consequences follow.

12–1A Interim Cover

The insured is covered for the duration of the interim insurance. For this cover the insured pays premium and, in addition, it has sometimes been inferred that the insured promises to refrain from applying for a policy from any other insurer on the same risk.[5]

---

1. Compare (1) the "binder" used to describe the agreement whereby an agent has authority from a Lloyd's underwriter to issue cover notes on behalf of the latter: *Julien Praet et Cie SA v H G Poland Ltd* [1960] 1 Lloyd's Rep 416, 428 *per* Pearson J (motor). (2) The Lloyd's slip which is temporary evidence of cover for the full period and is later evidenced by a binding policy: *Thompson v Adams* (1889) 23 QBD 361, 365–368 *per* Mathew J (fire).
2. *Queens Ins Co v Parsons* (1881) 7 App Cas 96, 124 *per* Sir Montague Smith (PC—fire).
3. Generally, see 44 Yale LJ 1223 (1935); 60 Harv LR 1164 (1947); Widiss 75 Iowa L Rev 1096 (1990).
4. *Neil v S E Lancashire Ins Co Ltd* 1932 SC 35, 38 *per* Lord Mackay, p 40–41 *per* Lord Alness (motor). USA: see *Pennsylvania Casualty Co v Upchurch*, 139 F 2d 892, 893 (5 Cir, 1943—motor).
5. *Western National Ins Co v Le Claire*, 163 F 2d 337 (9 Cir, 1947—fire).

12–1B Disclosure

When contracting interim insurance the insured owes a duty of disclosure to the insurer. It is essentially the same as the duty owed in respect of contracting the main policy[6]; in each case, the duty of disclosure impinges at the time at which the contract in question is made. Failure to disclose material facts arising between making the interim contract and the policy may affect the validity of the latter, but not that of the former.

12–1C Commencement

The rules governing the commencement of interim cover are similar to those governing commencement of the main policy. In particular, interim insurance may be affected by problems of conditional contract formation (above, 11–2E); this is seen mostly in cases of life insurance and hence more often in the United States than in England. In the United States there are two main kinds of interim insurance (binders) on lives.[7]

First, "insurable risk" or "satisfaction" binders provide that insurance cover begins at the time of premium payment or medical examination. This is a contract of insurance subject to a condition subsequent: it will be terminated *ab initio*, if it later appears that by objective standards of insurability the proposer was not insurable at the date at which interim cover began. Subject to this, if he dies after that date but before the commencement of the main policy, he is covered by the binder.[8]

Second, "approval" binders stipulate that there is no cover at all until the proposal is approved by the insurer. When approved, cover dates retrospectively from the time of the proposal or the medical examination, as stipulated. This is a contract of insurance subject to a condition precedent: no binding contract until approval. If the proposer dies after proposal or examination but before approval, he is not covered. This is evidently less favourable to the proposer than a satisfaction binder (above).

Which type of binder is in issue remains a question of interpretation, in which ambiguities will be construed against the insurer [9] and hence the tendency is to see a satisfaction binder rather than an approval binder. In particular, courts now infer interim cover, if there is a mere application (proposal) plus immediate payment of premium and, in some jurisdictions, if in the circumstances the applicant might reasonably expect to be covered at once.[10]

12–2 AUTHORITY TO GRANT INTERIM COVER

Interim insurance is usually made by an agent, who must have authority from his principal, the insurer, to grant such insurance. Authority[11] may be actual authority, which may be express or implied, or apparent authority.

6. *Mayne Nickless Ltd* v *Pegler* [1974] 1 NSWLR 228 (motor), rejecting the argument that, in the case of an interim insurance contract made rapidly for a short period, a lesser duty should suffice. For criticism of this aspect of the decision see Birds, 40 MLR 79 (1977). On disclosure see ch 23.
7. See 13 Williston, section 1568, p 372. 63 Yale LJ 523.
8. For example *Ransom* v *Penn Mutual Life Ins Co*, 274 P 2d 633 (Cal 1954—life); *cf Simpson* v *Prudential Ins Co of America*, 177 A 2d 417 (Md, 1962—life): cover only if the deceased was "objectively insurable" in the interim period.
9. *Ransom* v *Penn Mutual Life Ins Co*, 274 P 2d 633 (Cal, 1954—life).
10. *Gaunt* v *John Hancock Mutual Life Ins Co*, 160 F 2d 599 (2 Cir, 1947), *cert* den 331 US 849. *Idem* in Canada: *Zurich Life Ins Co* v *Davies* [1981] 2 SCR 670 (life). See Brenner, 22 Tort & Ins L J 388 (1987) and below, 12–3.
11. See chapter 8.

12–2A Implied Authority

Authority to contract interim insurance has been implied from the very position of a person as insurance broker. In a motor case, Lord Diplock said[12]: "A broker in non-marine insurance has implied authority to issue on behalf of the insurer or enter into as agent for the insurer contracts of interim insurance which are normally recorded in cover notes." In the United States, authority has been readily implied by the courts in view of "the reasonableness of power for instant action by the agent to meet the exigencies of public demand and sharp competition for immediate and effective insurance".[13]

12–2B Apparent Authority

An agent has apparent authority, when he is held out by the insurer as having authority to contract interim insurance and that is relied on by the insured.[14]

A person, to whom the insurer has supplied cover notes, is considered to have either implied or apparent authority to grant interim cover.[15] Authority will be implied, if possession of the cover notes is evidence of the insurer's actual intention that the agent should contract interim insurance. Authority will be apparent, if the insurer did not have any such intention but to allow possession of the notes holds out the agent to the world as having such authority.

Reliance by the insured on the holding out will normally be inferred from the insured's entering the contract. Reliance will be lacking, when the insured knew or should have known that the agent lacked authority to contract interim insurance because, for example, such agents did not normally have that authority[16] or the agent's lack of authority was clearly stated in the proposal or the interim receipt.[17]

12–3 FORM

Interim insurance may be in any form; it may be oral,[18] for example by telephone, but it is usual to evidence the contract with a document—a binder or cover note.[19] Even

12. *Stockton* v *Mason* [1978] 2 Lloyd's Rep 430, 431 (CA—motor). *Grant* v *Reliance Mutual Fire Insurance Co* (1879) 44 UCQB 229, 233 (fire). See further, above, 8–2.

13. *Bankers Indemnity Ins Co* v *Pinkerton*, 89 F 2d 194, 199 (9 Cir, 1937—fire), *cert den* 302 US 704. Further, when the agent has authority to charge premium from the time of the proposal, it has been inferred that cover commenced at that time and hence that the agent also had authority to contract interim insurance: *National Liberty Ins Co* v *Milligan*, 10 F 2d 483 (9 Cir, 1926—fire).

14. See above, 8–3.

15. *Mackie* v *The European Assurance Sy* (1869) 21 LT 102 (fire); *Murfitt* v *Royal Ins Co Ltd* (1922) 38 TLR 334, 336 *per* McCardie J (fire). However, it has been held that the agent does not have authority to alter the terms of the cover note: *Rossiter* v *Trafalgar Life Ins Assn* (1859) 27 Beav 377 (life). *Grimmer* v *Merchants' & Manufacturers' Fire Ins Co* [1932] 2 DLR 621 (NB—fire).

16. *Linford* v *Provincial Horse & Cattle Ins Co* (1864) 34 Beav 291 (livestock). Today, however, it seems that authority is usually presumed: see *Stockton* v *Mason*: above 12–2A.

17. *Levy* v *Scottish Employers Ins Co* (1901) 17 TLR 229 (PA). In view of *Stockton* v *Mason* (above), a modern court might require such a term to be specially drawn to the attention of the insured: *Mendelssohn* v *Normand Ltd* [1970] 1 QB 177 (CA).

18. *Murfitt* v *Royal Ins Co* (1922) 38 TLR 334, 335 *per* McCardie J (fire); *Parker & Co (Sandbank) Ltd* v *Western Assurance Co*, 1925 SLT 131 (fire); *Stockton* v *Mason* [1978] 2 Lloyd's Rep 430, 432 *per* Lord Diplock (CA—motor). *Cf Davies* v *National Fire & Marine Ins Co* [1891] AC 485 (PC—fire). *Grimmer* v *Merchants' & Manufacturers' Fire Ins Co* [1932] 2 DLR 621 (NB—fire); *Hochbaum* v *Pioneer Ins Co* [1933] 1 WWR 403 (BC—fire). *Lesavoy Industries Inc* v *Providence Washington Ins Co*, 174 NYS 2d 55 (1958—fire); *National Investors Fire & Casualty Co* v *Pacific Indemnity Co*, 359 F 2d 203 (10 Cir, 1966—fire); *Wells* v *Connecticut General Life Ins Co*, 469 F 2d 1231 (10 Cir, 1972—group life).

19. Sometimes called "interim receipt", a description that does not do justice to its importance.

when there is such a document, however, the terms of interim insurance may also be found in other related documents, for example, a notice to the insurer.[20]

Whether a document is evidence of the terms of interim insurance rather than, for example, a mere receipt for premium, is a matter of construction. This difficulty arises more frequently in the United States. A clear denial of cover in a document must be respected,[21] but any ambiguities in the document are construed strictly against the insurer.[22] Courts are reluctant to allow the insurer to take premium for no return and, in some states, it has been held that "where a premium has been paid there is insurance coverage regardless of other stipulations in the application or receipt".[23]

12–4 TERMS

Interim insurance must[24] have the terms essential to any contract of insurance (above, 11–1A): subject-matter, risk, premium, duration and amount.[25] As to premium, if necessary the figure will be implied from the market or other circumstances.[26] As to duration, it will be implied that the interim insurance is to continue for a reasonable time, i.e., until the policy proposal has been accepted or rejected[27] and, if rejected, until notice of rejection has been received by the proposer: below, 12–5B.

The terms may be set out in the cover note (or binder) but, in addition, general rules of actual or constructive notice apply, and the interim insurance may be subject to policy terms not set out in the note itself.

A clause in the note incorporating the usual terms of the relevant policy will be enforced.[28] In the United States some courts have held that, even in the absence of an express clause to that effect, the interim insurance is deemed to contain the terms found in the standard terms, if any, of the policy for which the proposer has applied.[29] In England, as regards interim motor cover to bridge a gap between cover on the old

---

20. *Liverpool & London & Globe Ins Co* v *Wyld and Darling* (1877) 1 SCR 147 (fire).
21. *Killpatrick* v *National Old Line Ins Co*, 229 F 2d 851 (10 Cir, 1956—life); *Machinery Center Inc* v *Anchor National Life Ins Co* (10 Cir, 1970—life).
22. *Liberty National Life Ins Co* v *Hamilton*, 237 F 2d 235 (6 Cir, 1956—life).
23. *Hamilton* (above), p 240. See also *Jones* v *John Hancock Mutual Life Ins Co*, 416 F 2d 829, 832 (6 Cir, 1969—life); *Smith* v *Westland Life Ins Co*, 539 P 2d 433 (Cal, 1975—life). *Contra: Recupito* v *Inter-Ocean Ins Co*, 362 F Supp 577 (ED Pa, 1973—life), affirmed 492 F 2d 1238 (3 Cir, 1974). See further, Appleman, section 7121; and above, 12–1C.
24. *Murfitt* v *Royal Ins Co* (1922) 38 TLR 334 (fire). *New England Ins Co* v *Cummings*, 164 F Supp 553 (SD Miss, 1958—fire); *State Farm Mutual Automobile Ins Co* v *Fields*, 325 F Supp 1135 (WD Mo, 1970—motor).
25. *Bankers Indemnity Ins Co* v *Pinkerton*, 89 F 2d 194, 197 (9 Cir, 1937—motor).
26. *Preferred Risk Fire Ins Co* v *Neet*, 90 SW 2d 39 (Ky, 1935—fire); *Cummings* v *New England Ins Co*, 266 F 2d 888 (5 Cir, 1959—fire).
27. *Parlier Fruit Co* v *Fireman's Fund Ins Co*, 311 P 2d 62 (Cal, 1957—fire).
28. *Citizens Ins Co* v *Parsons* (1881) 7 App Cas 96 (PC—fire); *GAFLAC Ltd* v *Shuttleworth* (1938) 60 Ll L Rep 301, 308 *per* Humphries J (motor). See also cases in which the cover note referred to the proposal form which referred to the usual terms of the policy and the latter were held to apply to the cover note: *Wyndham Rather Ltd* v *Eagle Star Ltd* (1925) 21 Ll L Rep 214 (CA—burglary); *Houghton* v *Trafalgar Ins Co Ltd* [1953] 2 Lloyd's Rep 18 (motor), affirmed on different grounds [1954] 1 QB 247 (CA). *M'Queen* v *Phoenix Mutual Ins Co* (1979) 29 UCCP 511 (fire).
29. *Pinkerton* (above); *Parlier* (above); *Carideo* v *Phoenix Assurance Co*, 317 F Supp 607 (ED Pa, 1970—yacht); *Zannini* v *Reliance Ins Co* 590 NE 2d 457 (Ill, 1992—property); *Progressive Casualty Ins Co* v *C A Reaseguradora Nacional de Venezuela*, 802 F Supp 1069, 1076 (SD NY, 1992—re)—provided that the terms are indeed usual.
    In the case of renewal, it has been presumed that any interim insurance is on the terms of the previous policy: *Massachusetts Bonding & Ins Co* v *Parsons Electric Co*, 61 F 2d 264 (8 Cir, 1932—motor).

car and cover on a new one, it is clear that interim cover on the new car is implicitly on the old terms.[30] As regards interim cover on a risk that is newly proposed, the position is less clear. It can be argued from general principle[31] that people should know that insurers grant interim insurance with the intention that the usual policy terms apply. Moreover, if a proposal form implicitly incorporates the usual terms of the policy applied for,[32] it is a small step to the same inference about a cover note on the same risk.[33]

The inference may work both for and against the insured. In one case,[33a] the interim insured applied for life cover of 500,000 dollars without having been made aware that the interim cover was only 100,000. The court held that the proposer, who had paid a month's premium for the main policy, was entitled to assume that the interim cover was for the full amount.

Whether the reference in interim insurance to the standard terms of the relevant policy is express or implied, incorporation of the terms of the policy is limited as follows.

(a) Interim insurance does not normally include a statement in a proposal form, to which the standard terms of the policy applied for refer, especially if the form is completed after the interim cover was granted[34]: this is the combined effect of the rules of constructive notice and of strict construction.

(b) Interim insurance does not normally include unusual or unexpected terms of the policy, even if usual in the policy of the particular insurer, unless specially drawn to the attention of the insured.[35]

(c) Interim insurance does not normally include any of the standard policy

---

30. *Stockton v Mason* [1978] 2 Lloyd's Rep 430 (CA—motor).
31. *Hood v Anchor Line Ltd* [1918] AC 837; *Thomson v LMS Ry Co* [1930] 1 KB 41 (CA); *Gray v LNE Ry Co*, 1930 SC 989.
32. *General Accident Ins Corp v Cronk* (1901) 17 TLR 233.
33. In this sense *Wyndham Rather Ltd v Eagle Star Ltd* (1925) 21 Ll L Rep 214, 215 *per* Sargant LJ (CA—burglary). *King v Allstate Ins Co*, 906 F 2d 1537 (11 Cir, 1990 – yacht).
Cf Re Coleman's Depositories [1907] 2 KB 798: the plaintiff submitted a proposal of employer's liability cover. On 28 December he received a cover note from an agent, which contained no conditions. On 2 January a workman was injured and the employer was liable. On 3 January his proposal was accepted by the defendant insurer and a policy sealed; on 9 January that policy was delivered, purporting to cover the plaintiff from 1 January and requiring, as a condition of cover, immediate notice of any accident. Notice of the accident on 2 January was not given until 14 March, the day before the injured workman died. The insurer repudiated liability for breach of the notice condition.
It was assumed that on 2 January the situation was governed not by the note but by the policy (Fletcher Moulton LJ, p 806). Counsel for the insurer contended (p 802) that the employer "cannot rely on the note, which was not upon the face of it subject to any conditions, for they went to arbitration under the policy". This did not appear to be disputed. Argument turned on whether the employer had sufficient notice of the notice condition as a term of the policy and, if so, whether it was a condition precedent.
The Court of Appeal held that the employer had insufficient notice. Constructive notice seems to have been ruled out. Vaughan Williams LJ (p 804), with whom Buckley LJ agreed (p 812), asked "How is the employer to know of these conditions unless they inform him?" He concluded (p 805) that "the risk undertaken . . . for the period prior to the delivery of the policy did not impose upon the employer the obligation to give immediate notice of the accident". See also *Parker & Co (Sandbank) Ltd v Western Assurance Co*, 1925 SLT 131 (fire).
33a. *Poston v National Fidelity Life Ins Co*, 399 SE 2d 770 (SC, 1990—life).
34. *Neil v S E Lancashire Ins Co* (below).
35. *Thornton v Shoe Lane Parking Ltd* [1971] 2 QB 163 (CA); *Interfoto Picture Library Ltd v Stiletto Visual Programmes Ltd* [1989] QB 433 (CA). *Inn Cor International Ltd v American Home Ins Co* (1973) 42 DLR (3d) 46 (Ont), discussed below, 12–5C.

terms, if copies are not reasonably accessible to the insured who wants to see them.[36]

(d) Interim insurance does not include policy terms which are clearly inappropriate to temporary cover, such as terms governing renewal.[37]

If loss occurs in the interim period, the loss is governed not by the terms of the policy but by the terms of the interim insurance.[38]

If the interim insurance incorporates terms of the policy in question, they apply as they would then and not as they might have applied in the light of something that occurred later. *A fortiori*, if, having considered the proposal, the insurer wishes to impose policy terms additional or different to those expressed or implied in the interim insurance, the new elements do not apply retrospectively.

In *Neil* v *SE Lancashire Ins Co*[39] the pursuer took temporary motor omnibus cover against third party risks, "subject to the usual terms and conditions of the Company's Policy". Two days after a person had been injured by the bus, the pursuer completed a proposal form for the main policy, in which, it was alleged, one of his statements was untrue. Some days after that a policy was issued, which contained a basis clause making the truth of the proposal a condition of liability. To dispute liability, the insurer argued in the alternative (1) that the policy (and terms) superseded the cover note retroactively to include the time of the accident, and (2) that, if not the policy but the cover note applied at the time of the accident, it incorporated the basis clause and thus the warranty alleged to have been broken. Rejecting these arguments, Lord Mackay said[40]: "on principle I fail to see how such an interim protection can in accordance with either equity or justice be avoided because of something which happened later."

12–5 TERMINATION OF INTERIM COVER

12–5A Stated Period

Interim insurance ends in accordance with its terms, for example, after a stated period of time such as 7, 14, 21 or 28 days.[41] But if, through the fault of the insurer or his agent, a decision on the main proposal is delayed beyond the stated period, it has been held in Canada that the interim insurance remains in force.[42]

12–5B Refusal of the Main Proposal

If the main policy proposal is rejected,[43] interim insurance ends on notice of rejection from the insurer,[44] if and when such notice is received by the proposer.[45] If, however,

---

36. This seems to be a rule of the general law: Clarke [1976] CLJ 51, 72–77.

37. See *Neil* v *S E Lancashire Ins Co* (below).

38. *Liverpool & London & Globe Ins Co* v *Wyld and Darling* (1877) 1 SCR 604 (fire).

39. 1932 SC 35.

40. p 42. See also Lord Ormidale p 42 and Lord Hunter pp 43–44; and *Wetherell* v *Sentry Reinsurance*, 743 F Supp 1157, 1170 (ED Pa, 1990—re).

41. See further, chapter 18.

42. *Patterson* v *Royal Ins Co* (1867) 14 Gr 169, 171 (fire), applied in *Niagara District Mutual Fire Ins Co* (1876) 23 Gr 139 (fire).

43. A request for further medical tests or examinations does not amount to rejection of an application for life cover: *Ransom* v *Penn Mutual Life Ins Co*, 274 P 2d 633 (Ca, 1954—life).

44. *Stockton* v *Mason* [1978] 2 Lloyd's Rep 430, 431 *per* Lord Diplock (CA—motor).

45. *Mackie* v *European Assurance Sy* (1869) 21 LT 102, 104 *per* Malins VC; *Holwell Securities Ltd* v *Hughes* [1974] 1 All ER 161 (CA). See also *Mayne Nickless* (below).

the note expresses cover to last for a number of days, *expressum facit cessare taci-tum*:[46] so it seems that termination on notice of rejection occurs within the stated period only if that too is expressly stipulated.

In New South Wales[47] it has been held that interim cover, which is expressed to be "subject to . . . a satisfactory proposal for your insurance", contains a condition subsequent with retroactive effect: if the main proposal is refused, the interim cover is avoided *ab initio*. The court inferred that, in case the proposal turned out to be one which no prudent insurer would reasonably accept, the insurer could not have intended to be unconditionally on risk in the interim. For the insured, however, this conclusion must create interim uncertainty and deprive interim insurance of many of its apparent advantages. It raises not only the possibility that an "insured" is uncompensated for an interim loss, which he believed was covered, but encourages the insurer to insist *ex post facto* that the proposal was unsatisfactory, a position that the "insured" or his representative may be poorly placed to dispute. In these circumstances, it must be questioned whether the insured has sufficient notice[48] of the term or, if he does, whether it is sufficiently unambiguous to overcome the rule of construction *contra proferentem*.

12–5C The Issue of a Policy

If the main proposal is accepted, interim insurance ends when the policy is issued.[49] If the policy terms differ from those of the main proposal, the issue of the policy does not conclude the main insurance contract: it is a counter-offer.[50] In that case the interim insurance remains in force until it ends for other reasons,[51] unless the terms of the counter-offer are patently unacceptable to the proposer: this may be seen as implicit termination of the interim cover by notice from the insurer.

12–5D Termination by the Insured

Interim insurance ends, if terminated by the insured before it would otherwise have ended.[52] Active negotiation with insurer B does not necessarily imply an intention to terminate interim insurance with insurer A on the same risk.[53]

---

46. There is a contrary suggestion from Malins V-C in *Mackie* (above), p 104.

47. *Mayne Nickless Ltd* v *Pegler* [1974] 1 NSWLR 228, 241 (motor) as an alternative ground, citing *Head* v *Tattersall* (1871) LR 7 Exch 7 (sale of horse) and *Kodak (Australia) Pty Ltd* v *Retail Traders Mutual Indemnity Ins Assn* (1942) 42 SR (NSW) 231, 235.

USA: such cover is common and known as a "satisfaction" binder; cover may be defeated *ab initio*: see above, 12–1C.

48. See above, 12–4(b).

49. *Roberts* v *Security Co Ltd* [1897] 1 QB 111, 115 *per* Lopes LJ (CA—burglary).

50. See above, 11–2A2 and 11–2E(a).

51. *Liverpool & London & Globe Ins Co* v *Wyld and Darling* (1877) 1 SCR 604, 639 *per* Ritchie J, p 648 *per* Strong J (fire). This case was applied in *Inn Cor International Ltd* v *American Home Ins Co* (1973) 42 DLR (3d) 46 (Ont): a firm proposed life insurance on four executives. The insurer issued a policy with an unexpected term which excluded cover on the executives, and which passed unnoticed by the firm and its broker. One of the executives died five months later. It was held that the insurer was liable: the restrictive term of the policy did not supersede the binder. There was "an effective commitment . . . which could not be altered by the terms of the policy subsequently issued without express notice of the variation to the policy holder." (pp 49–50). The court did not specify whether the commitment was based on the binder or on the policy construed in conformity with the binder. See also *Canadian Casualty & Boiler Ins Co* v *Hawthorne* (1907) 39 SCR 558, 565 (water leakage); *James* v *Ocean Accident & Guarantee Co* (1921) 70 DLR 576 (BC—burglary).

52. *Mackie* v *European Assurance Sy* (1869) 21 LT 102, 104 *per* Malins V-C (fire).

53. *Mackie* (above). *Cf. Taylor* v *Allon* [1966] 1 QB 304 (motor).

CHAPTER 13

PREMIUM

13–1 INTRODUCTION

In contracts of insurance the consideration provided by the insured is usually money,[1] and is usually referred to as premium.

It is not in the nature of an insurance contract that premium should be payable at any particular point of time in relation to the period of cover.[2] The time for payment is regulated by the terms of the particular contract. Premium may be paid at the beginning of the period of cover or in instalments, usually not more than four,[3] during the period of cover. An exception arises in the case of mutual insurance, when consideration lies in the promise to pay calls, sometimes described as assessments,[4] made later by the mutual insurance society; calls are paid with regard to the collective liability in a cover period past.[5] The effect of late payment is generally governed by the terms of the contract.[6]

13–2 THE AMOUNT OF PREMIUM

The amount of payment in the case of mutual insurance is unascertained until the cover period has ended. In the case of premium payable in respect of other kinds of insurance, the amount is usually set at the beginning, except in the case of premium to be arranged (TBA). In that or any other case[7] in which premium is not set at the time

---

1. *Prudential Ins Co v Inland Revenue Commissioners* [1904] 2 KB 658, 663 *per* Channell J (life). In *British Marine Mutual Ins Co v Jenkins* [1900] 1 QB 299, 302–303 (hull mutual): Bigham J accepted "as very improbable but . . . legally possible" that consideration might be finding someone else to promise to pay money. See above, 1–1F. USA: generally, see Appleman, sections 7831 ff.

2. *Holliday v Western Australian Ins Co Ltd* (1936) 54 Ll L Rep 373, 376 *per* Branson J (fire).

3. If the number of instalments of premium exceeds four the agreement may be subject to the Consumer Credit Act 1974: see section 16(5) of the Act and para 3 of the Consumer Credit (Exempt Agreements) Order 1977 (SI 1977, No 326). See further, MacGillivray, No 927.

4. The term "assessment" is more commonly employed in the United States. Everything turns on the interpretation of the rules of association. On the operation of assessments generally, see 44 CJS 367 ff.

On the distinction between an obligation to pay calls, including supplementary calls, and an obligation to pay fixed premium, see *Standard Steamship Owners' P & I Assn (Bermuda) Ltd. v Gann* [1992] 2 Lloyd's Rep 528, 531 ff per Hirst J. (P & I).

5. *British Marine Mutual Ins Co v Jenkins* [1900] 1 QB 299, 302 *per* Bigham J (hull); *Thomas v Richard Evans & Co Ltd* [1927] 1 KB 33, 52 *per* Lord Hanworth MR (CA—employers' liability).

6. As to lateness and whether time is of the essence of the contract, see below, 13–8.

7. A further illustration is found when the contract provides for a variation of the amount of premium during a period of cover, variations triggered by a specified increase or decrease in the risk insured; for example, insurance on cargo "to be valued as interest shall appear"—*Pollock v Davidson*, 19 F Cas No 11,254 (D Pa, 1799—cargo).

of contract but left to the hazard of future agreement between the parties, the contract may be void for uncertainty,[8] unless (a) the contract has an effective mechanism for deciding premium later, as in the case of mutual insurance, or (b) the contract is interpreted as meaning that the insured shall pay a reasonable sum, which the court can ascertain by reference to the market,[9] as in the case of an effective TBA clause.

13–3 THE PLACE OF PAYMENT

The insured, like any other debtor, is obliged to seek out his creditor, the insurer, and pay him at his residence or place of business.[10] In principle, therefore, payment must be made to the insurer at his head office.[11] In practice, however, the place of payment may be indicated in the policy, or past practice in respect of payment by the particular insured may authorise payment to an agent of the insurer. If in the past the insurer has accepted payment of premium via an agent, although the latter may not be expressly authorised to receive premium for the insurer, the insurer will be estopped from asserting that payment to the agent is not payment to the insurer.[12] Otherwise, the insured's broker, for example, is not an agent of the insurer to receive premium.[13] In cases of doubt, it may be the duty of the insurer to notify the insured of the agent authorised to receive payment,[14] failing which, the insured who does not pay is not in default.

The place of payment is important not only for the decision whether payment has been made but also whether the court has jurisdiction over disputes arising out of the contract of insurance.[15]

8. USA: if the parties fail to agree, the court will fix the premium, provided that that intervention is not expressly or implicitly limited by party intention as found in the terms of the agreement: *Oriental Mutual Ins Co* v *Wright*, 23 How 401; 16 L Ed 524, 528 *per* Nelson J (1860—cargo). Generally, see Rest 2d Contracts, section 33(e). The readiness to intervene is greater than in England: see above, 11–1A4. In some states premium is fixed by government regulation.

9. *National Surety Corp* v *Brunswick Corp*, 391 F 2d 26 (5 Cir, 1968—fire). See above, 11–1A4.

10. *Rein* v *Stein* [1892] 1 QB 753, 758 *per* Kay LJ (CA); see also *Robey* v *Snaefell Mining Co Ltd* (1887) 20 QBD 152; *Drexel* v *Drexel* [1916] 1 Ch 251, 260 *per* Neville J; *Bremer Oeltransport GmbH* v *Drewry* [1933] 1 KB 753, 766 *per* Slesser LJ (CA). Halsbury, Vol 9, Nos 490 ff; Mann, p 76. USA: no excuse that insured sought authorised agent but agent was not in his office: *Blumer* v *Kirkman Corp*, 241 P 2d 17 (Cal, 1952); *Fabian* v *Kennedy*, 333 F Supp 1001 (ND W Va, 1971).

11. *Krebs* v *Security Trust & Life Ins Co*, 56 F 294, 296 (D Or, 1907—life); *Deeren Milliken Research Corp* v *Textured Fibres Inc*, 310 F Supp 491 (D SC, 1970).

12. Even if the agent is a broker and thus primarily the agent of the insured: *Kelly* v *London & Staffordshire Fire Ins Co* (1883) Cab & E 47 (fire).

In the USA also, there has been a practice of receiving payment via agents in spite of a policy requirement of payment to head office: *Morey* v *New York Life Ins Co*, 17 F Cas no 9,795 (SD Miss, 1873—life); *Southern Life Ins Co* v *McCain*, 96 US 84 (1878 life); *State Life Ins Co* v *Murray*, 159 F 408 (3 Cir, 1908—life). In *McCain* it was held *inter alia* that if an (unauthorised) agent notified the insurer that he had received premium, which he was holding for the insurer, and for more than a month the insurer was silent and did not object, the insurer was estopped from denying the authority of the agent to receive the premium.

13. Insured's broker not the agent of the insurer for the purpose of payment, so that when the insured paid her broker in time but the broker did not pay the insurer within the time allowed, the insurance was forfeited: *Becker* v *Exchange Mutual Fire Ins Co*, 165 F 816 (ED Pa, 1908—fire).

14. *Tankexpress A/S* v *Cie Financière Belges des Pétroles SA* [1949] AC 76, 100 *per* Lord Uthwatt as regards payment of hire under a charterparty. *Seamans* v *Northwestern Mutual Life Ins Co*, 3 F 325 (D Minn, 1880—life).

15. *Robey* v *Snaefell Mining Co Ltd* (1887) 20 QBD 152. Goode, *Payment Obligations in Commercial and Financial Transactions* (1983), p 25

13-4 THE MODE OF PAYMENT

Payment must be in the form stated in the contract. In principle, if the contract is silent, payment must be in cash,[16] unless payment by other means, notably by cheque, is expressly or implicitly authorised in connection with the contract.[17] The larger the sum the more astute the courts in inferring that cash was not intended,[18] especially in the United States. In practice, the general rule, which appears to apply equally to insurance contracts, is that "payment or offer of payment in any manner current in the ordinary course of business satisfies the requirement unless the obligee demands payment in legal tender and gives any extension of time reasonably necessary to procure it".[19] Payment or tender of payment must be of the full amount due: part payment is without effect.[20]

If an agent has authority to receive premiums, it is within his implied actual or apparent authority to accept a note or cheque instead of cash.[21] If payment by cheque is not authorised, but a cheque is accepted and honoured, that amounts to payment.[22] Moreover, payment dates not from the time it was honoured but from the time that the cheque was received by the insurer or his agent.[23] In Canada it has been claimed that the "rise in use of cheques and negotiable instruments makes the old cases concerned with authorization to receive such payments obsolete".[24]

If payment by cheque is the authorised mode, but the cheque is not honoured, the legal position depends on whether payment by cheque was intended by the parties to be conditional payment or absolute payment.[25] The presumption made in the past, that the intention was that payment was conditional,[26] has recently been rejected as a

---

16. *Finch* v *Brook* (1834) 1 Bing (NC) 253, 257 *per* Tindal CJ: "there must be an actual production of the money, or a dispensation of such production". See further *Sweeting* v *Pearce* (1861) 9 CB (NS) 534, 540 *per* Bramwell B (hull); *Pape* v *Westacott* [1894] 1 QB 272, 279–280 *per* Lindley LJ (CA); *Pollway Ltd* v *Abdullah* [1974] 2 All ER 381, 383 *per* Roskill LJ (CA).

Cash usually means legal currency. In *Hoffman* v *John Hancock Mutual Life Ins Co*, 92 US 161 (1876—life) it was held that the agent who took a horse in lieu of cash was acting outside his apparent authority. See also *Huron College* v *Union County Trust Co*, 77 F 2d 609 (8 Cir, 1935); *Central Life Ins Co* v *Johnson*, 73 P 2d 1152 (Okl, 1937—life); *Raney* v *Piedmont Southern Life Ins Co*, 387 F 2d 75 (8 Cir, 1967—life). Generally, see Appleman, sections 8004 ff; and 8017 ff.

17. *Johnston* v *Boyes* [1899] 2 Ch 73. *Phillips* v *Lagaly*, 214 F 2d 527 (10 Cir, 1954—motor).

18. Mann, pp 71 ff, especially cases cited at note 56, in particular, *Mardorf Peach & Co Ltd* v *Attica Sea Carrier Corp* [1977] AC 850, 880 *per* Lord Salmon.

19. Rest 2d Contracts, section 249. *Simmons* v *Swan*, 275 US 113, 116 (1927) *per* Holmes J.

20. *Slocum* v *New York Life Ins Co*, 228 US 364 (1913—life); *Hilson* v *Sun Life Assurance Co*, 32 F 2d 989 (5 Cir, 1943—life).

21. *Manufacturers Accident Ins Co* v *Pudsey* (1897) 27 SCR 374 (PA), accepting *Tayloe* v *Merchants Fire Ins Co*, 50 US 390 (1850—fire). But *cf Sweeting* v *Pearce* (1861) 9 CB(NS) 534, 535 *per* Wightman J (hull): must be cash; and *Acey* v *Fernie* (1840) 7 M & W 151: an agent to receive premium has no actual or apparent authority to vary contract terms, for example as to time or mode of payment. See also *Montreal Assurance Co* v *M'Gillivray* (1859) 13 Moore 87 (PC—fire).

22. *Bridges* v *Garrett* (1870) LR 5 CP 451, 454 *per* Cockburn CJ (Exch Ch). *Indemnity Ins Co* v *Watson* 16 P 2d 760 (Cal, 1933—liability); *Raney* v *Piedmont Southern Life Ins Co*, 387 F 2d 75 (8 Cir, 1967—life).

23. *Marreco* v *Richardson* [1908] 2 KB 584 (CA). See also below, 13–7.

24. Brown & Menezes, No 7:6:8.

25. *Goldshede* v *Cottrell* (1836) 2 M & W 20. *Raney* v *Piedmont Southern Life Ins Co*, 387 F 2d 75, 78 (8 Cir, 1967—life): this is a question of fact for the jury.

26. *Marreco* v *Richardson* [1908] 2 KB 584, 589 *per* Sir Gorell Barnes, 592–593 *per* Farwell LJ (CA). It is not, however, a rule of law, and in the case of payment by credit card it has been held that payment is absolute: *Re Charge Card Services Ltd* [1989] Ch 497 (CA).

Central Life Ins Co v *Johnson*, 73 P 2d 1152 (Okl, 1937—life); *Colonial Life & Accident Co* v *Wilson*, 246 F 2d 922 (5 Cir, 1957—PA), cert den 355 US 927. See also *Raney* (above).

general rule by the Court of Appeal.[27] Each method of payment has to be considered in the light of the consequences and other circumstances attending that kind of payment.[28] It remains to be seen how this decision affects the payment of premium by cheque.

Absolute payment is intended when the delivery of the cheque is itself the payment of premium, whether the cheque is honoured by the drawee or not. If a particular mode of payment is requested by the payee for his own convenience, there is a presumption that payment by that mode is absolute.[29]

Conditional payment is intended when the delivery of the cheque as performance of the contractual duty of payment is conditional on the cheque's being honoured so that, if it is not honoured, there has been no payment of premium and the insured's duty of payment has not been discharged.

13-5 THE PERSON

Payment must be to the insurer or to an agent with actual or apparent authority to receive payment of premium for the insurer.[30] In particular, an agent issued by the insurer with official receipts,[31] or an agent with authority to contract interim cover[32] or to secure new insurance or renewal of old insurance[33] has authority (implied actual or apparent) to receive premiums for the insurer.[34] In the USA, courts are divided on whether an employer has authority to receive a premium for the insurer in respect of group insurance organised by the employer for employees.[35] As to brokers generally, in some parts of the USA, when an insurer issues a policy to a broker for transmission to the insured, the broker has authority to receive the premium for the insurer. Unless invested with authority on such a ground or, of course, holding actual authority from the insurer, the insured's agent has no authority to receive payment on behalf of the insurer, and no payment occurs until he remits the money to the insurer or to a person with authority to receive it. If, in spite of a contrary term in the insurance contract, the insurer accepts premiums paid via the insured's broker, the insurer has waived the term of the contract and may be estopped from denying that payment to the broker was contract payment.[36] As regards mode of payment, see above, 13-4.

27. *Re Charge Card Services Ltd* [1989] Ch 497 (CA). Such a rule remains the rule in many parts of the USA: for example, *Progressive Preferred Ins. Co* v *Brown*, 413 SE 2d 430, 432–433 (Ga, 1992—motor).

28. p 707 *per* Browne-Wilkinson V-C.

29. *Anderson* v *Hillies* (1852) 12 CB 499.

30. *Wing* v *Harvey* (1854) 5 De G M & G 265 (life). Generally, see above, 8–2 and 8–3.

31. *Wing* v *Harvey* (above).

32. *Rossiter* v *Trafalgar Life Assurance Assn* (1859) 27 Beav 377 (life).

33. *Marshall* v *Western Canada Fire Ins Co* (1911) 18 WLR 68 (Sask—fire).

USA: a soliciting agent (and *a fortiori* a general agent) has authority to receive premium: *American Family Mutual Ins Co* v *Bach*, 471 SW 2d 474 (Mo, 1971—motor). Generally on this see Appleman, sections 7981 ff.

As regards the role of an employer under a group policy for employees, see *Blue Cross-Blue Shield* v *Thornton*, 325 So 2d 187 (Ala, 1976—hospitalisation).

34. *Lezak* v *National Grange Mutual Ins Co*, 233 NYS 2d 607 (1962—motor); *Foundation Reserve Ins Co* v *Wesson*, 447 SW 2d 436, 438–439 (Tex, 1969—motor); *Chapman Motor-Sales Inc* v *National Savings Ins Co*, 26 SW 2d 592, 597 (Tex, 1982—motor). *Cf Constand Industries Pty Ltd* v *Norwich Winterthur Ins (Australia) Ltd* (1986) CLR 226 (HCA—cargo).

35. *Clements* v *Continental Casualty Ins Co*, 730 F Supp 1120, 1123 (ND Ga, 1989—PA).

36. *Mannheim Ins Co* v *Chipman*, 124 F 950 (SD NY 1903—cargo).

Payment must be by the insured or his agent,[37] or any third person contemplated by the contract; for example, in the case of solvency insurance, premium may be made payable by the person whose solvency is insured and, in the case of life insurance, by a beneficiary under the will of the life insured[38] and, when the policy is used as security for a loan, by the lender.[39] In the case of payment of a life premium after the life has dropped by a personal representative of the deceased,[40] that is a good payment,[41] unless contrary to the terms of the contract.[42] In the event of payment by an unauthorised person, that is not the payment required by the contract of insurance and it may be refused by the insurer.[43]

If the insurer receives payment from the wrong person, the insured may ratify the act of payment and the law considers that premium has been paid.[44] It is uncertain whether ratification must be within the contractual period for payment. The general law of agency is that ratification of an act is ineffective, if it is essential to the validity of the act that it should be done within a certain time and ratification occurs after that time.[45] Until ratification there has been no valid (contractual) payment.[46] Still, it seems that the outcome depends chiefly on the response of the insurer. If the insurer rejects the payment or, if, having initially accepted it, he returns it before ratification, there has been no payment. If he keeps the money paid, he may not be allowed to sue the insured for premium, for that would be a "fraud" on the third party.[47] It is submitted[48] that the same principle should prevent the insurer keeping the money and yet forfeiting the insurance. Alternatively, it might be said that there has been waiver[49] by the insurer of all strict contractual requirements for payment of premium.

In principle, the rules of law governing payment are the same, whether payment is made by the insured or by his agent. Modern practice centres on the intermediary. In England, it has been claimed[50] that "if the insurers accept the credit of the broker and

37. Including a bank or credit card company under a standing order to pay the premium when it falls due: *Market* v *Travelers Ins Co*, 10 F 2d 1202 (10 Cir, 1974—PA). Generally see Appleman sections 8011 ff.

38. See above, 3–3.

39. If authorised by the loan contract: *Farquharson* v *Pearl Assurance Co Ltd* [1937] 3 All ER 124 (life).

USA: a standard mortgage clause to this effect is enforced; however, it has been disputed whether the mortgagee is obliged on demand to pay premiums, if the mortgagor defaults; see *General Credit Corp* v *Imperial Casualty & Indemnity Co*, 5 NW 2d 145 (Neb, 1959—motor).

40. Although not an agent, he is the person appointed by the deceased in his will or, in the case of intestacy, by the court under statute to execute the will, which often stipulates the discharge of debts, or to administer the estate.

41. *Provident Savings Life Assurance Sy* v *Taylor*, 142 F 709 (3 Cir, 1906—life).

42. It is suggested that this is the basis of early cases in which payment by personal representatives was insufficient: *Want* v *Blunt* (1810) 12 East 183, 191 *per* Lord Ellenborough CJ (life); *Simpson* v *Accidental Death Ins Co* (1857) 2 CB (NS) 257, 295–296 *per* Cresswell J (PA). See also *Stuart* v *Freeman* [1902] 1 KB 47, 54 *per* Romer LJ (CA—life).

43. *Marsh* v *Pedder* (1815) 4 Camp 257. *Adams* v *Napa Cantina Wineries*, 94 F 2d 694 (9 Cir, 1938).

44. *Marsh* v *Pedder* (1815) 4 Camp 257. See also *Royal Exchange Assurance* v *Hope* [1928] Ch 179, 194 *per* Sargant LJ (CA—life). *Adams* v *Napa Cantina Wineries*, 94 F 2d 694 (9 Cir, 1938).

45. Bowstead, p 72. Rest 2d Agency, para 90.

46. Above, 7–4 ff.

47. *Welby* v *Drake* (1825) 1 C & P 557; *Hirachand Punamchand* v *Temple* [1911] 2 KB 330 (CA).

48. As a matter of agency, Bowstead, pp 76–77 is against this submission, but it finds support in the Comment on Rest 2d Agency, para 90.

49. If the insured relies on the insurer's acceptance of payment, for example, by cancelling his own arrangements to make payment, it could be argued that there is waiver of the contractual requirements as to who pays. But waiver must be unequivocal, and for this reason perhaps the insurer will not be precluded from returning the payment until he has had a reasonable opportunity to consider the situation: *McConnell* v *Provident Savings Life Assurance Sy*, 92 F 769 (6 Cir, 1899—life).

50. MacGillivray, No 933.

look to him alone for payment of the premium, the agreement with the broker for a monthly account must be a waiver of all conditions in the policy requiring punctual payment by the insured". The insured, however, has little idea of the relationship between insurer and broker. Caution counsels the initial assumption that payment to the insured's agent is not payment to the insurer. Moreover, unless authorised by the insurer, an agent who debits himself in his periodical account with that insurer does not thereby pay on behalf of any one (or more) insured.[51] We must look for a point in the dealings between agent and insurer at which it can be said that the premium has been paid in respect of a particular policy and a particular insured.

In contrast, in the United States, for many years past more emphasis has been placed on the impression gained by the insured:

"if the agent be authorized to receive the premium, an agreement between the applicant and the agent that the latter shall be responsible to the company for the amount, and hold the applicant as his personal debtor therefor, is a waiver of the stipulation in the policy that it shall not be binding till the premium is received by the company or its accredited agent".[52]

13–6 RIGHT TO PREMIUM

Premium paid to an agent is held for the agent's principal subject to the terms of the agency agreement. For example, when an agency agreement provided that money received as agent shall be "at all times the property of, and received for, and on account for and in trust to pay the same to" the insurer, the court applied the provision,[53] even though the agent in question was a broker and primarily the agent of the insured.

13–7 RECEIPT OF PAYMENT

Payment is not effective until the amount has been received by the insurer. In the case of payment by cash, there is payment when the cash is handed to him. In the case of a cheque as cash, there is payment when his account is credited, so as to give him the unconditional right to the immediate use of the money credited.[54] In the case of cheque in lieu of cash (above, 13–4), there is payment when the cheque is delivered to

---

51. *London & Lancashire Life Assurance Co* v *Fleming* [1897] AC 499 (PC—life). As regards the special customary role of the broker at Lloyd's, see *Universo Ins Co of Milan* v *Merchants Marine Ins Co Ltd* [1897] 2 QB 93 (CA—re). Arnould, Nos 168 ff. *Cf Stuyvesant Ins Co* v *Sussex Fire Ins Co*, 90 F 2d 281 (3 Cir, 1937—fire), cert den 302 US 742. *Cf* also *Menzies* v *Security of General Ins Co (NZ) Ltd* (1991) 6 ANZ Ins Cases, no 61–029 (NZ—yacht).

52. May, *Insurance*, p 526, as cited with approval in *Yonge* v *Equitable Life Assurance Sy*, 30 F 902, 904 (ED Tenn, 1887—life).

53. *Vehicle & General Ins Co Ltd* v *Elmbridge Insurances* [1973] 1 Lloyd's Rep 325 (motor). See also *Re A/G of Canada and Northumberland General Ins Co* (1987) 36 DLR (4th) 421 (Ont), affirmed (1988) 52 DLR (4th) 383: when the insurer became insolvent, the insured was unable to recover premium paid to and still in the hands of the broker.

54. *The Brimnes* [1975] QB 929, 948 *per* Edmund Davies LJ (CA). *Cf The Chikuma* [1981] 1 All ER 652 (HL) and critical comment by Mann, 97 LQR 379 (1981).

As regards inter-bank transfers see Goode, *Commercial Law* (London, 1982), ch IV. As regards transfers between accounts at the same bank, payment is made when the bank accepts the insured's instructions and does whatever is required to initiate the bank's transfer process: *Momm* v *Barclays Bank International Ltd* [1977] QB 790.

the insurer.[55] If the insurer has received money intended as payment, payment has been made, even though the money paid is in respect of more than one premium or is in excess of the amount due, and has not been specifically appropriated by the insurer to the policy in question.[56]

Charter hire for ships is paid, it has been held,[57] when money is sent by post or similar means to the payee in such manner and time that it would normally reach the payee by the requisite date. Does the same rule apply to the payment of insurance premiums? At the very least, the sending of premium by post must be expressly or implicitly authorised by the insurance contract.[58] However, it does not follow from authorisation of a certain mode of transmission, that payment is in any sense effective on being sent, and it is not clear at all that the charter rule should be applied to insurance payments. The charter decision, being based on an inference about the intention of the particular parties in the light of their past conduct,[59] is distinguishable. The decision may also be unsafe: as payment had always reached the payee's agents by the due date in the past,[60] it is not clear why the court inferred party intention (especially that of the payee) that posting in time would always be sufficient. The effect of the decision was to place the risk of loss or delay in transmission on the payee and, if a rule like this is to be adopted in other cases, it must be clear that a payee such as the insurer did indeed accept that risk [61] or that the risk should be on the insurer rather than the insured as a matter of implied term. Such a term is attractive in that, first, the risk to the insured (forfeiture) is greater than the risk to the insurer; and, second, the insured will have a more manageable task to prove sending by post than receipt. However, it can hardly be said that such a term is essential to give the contract business efficacy, as the law requires,[62] so it is not all clear that the charter rule applies to insurance.

55. Subject to 13–4, above: *The Brimnes* (above). See also *Charles* v *Blackwell* (1877) 2 CPD 151, 158 *per* Cockburn CJ (CA); *Pape* v *Westacott* [1894] 1 QB 272, 279–280 *per* Lindley LJ (CA); *Clay Hill Brick & Tile Co Ltd* v *Rawlings* [1938] 4 All ER 100. Mann, *loc cit*, p 79. *American Credit Indemnity Co* v *Champion Coated Paper Co*, 103 F 609 (6 Cir, 1900—credit insurance).
56. *Kirkpatrick* v *South Australasian Ins Co Ltd* (1886) 11 App Cas 177 (PC—fire). The language of the court suggests that the decision turned on the intention of the parties. A court today might prefer to give relief against forfeiture on the basis that the insurer was bound to appropriate money in its possession for the payment of premiums: below, 13–11B.
57. *Tankexpress A/S* v *Cie Financière Belge des Pétroles SA* [1949] AC 76. A similar statement of law can be found in *Mutual Reserve Fund Life Assn* v *Tuchfield*, 159 F 833, 839 (6 Cir, 1908—life). Moreover, in *Tayloe* v *Merchants' Fire Ins Co*, 50 US 390 (1850—fire) it was held that, when the insured was instructed to send a cheque for the premium, the payment was effective on being sent. The decision may have been coloured by (1) a clause that there was no insurance until premium was paid, and (2) the impression given to the insured, that if he sent his cheque "no other step would be necessary to give effect to the insurance of the property" (p 402). Generally, however, in the United States the act of sending, for example by post, does not amount to payment: see note 63 below.
58. Authorisation will be readily inferred: when a debtor was authorised to "remit" payment, it was held that this implicitly authorised payment by post: *Mitchell-Henry* v *Norwich Union Life Ins Sy* [1918] 2 KB 67 (CA).
59. [1949] AC 76, 93 *per* Lord Porter, 97 *per* Lord Wright, 101 *per* Lord Uthwatt. Moreover as regards international payment in 1939 "there was no better way of sending it than by post" (p 105 *per* Lord du Parcq).
60. See for example [1949] AC 76, 92 *per* Lord Porter. Generally, see Mann, p 74. *Tankexpress* (above) was applied in *American River Lines Inc* v *Central Soya Co Inc*, 524 F Supp 246 (ND Miss, 1981), but in the latter case, unlike *Tankexpress*, payment had reached the creditor late on several occasions in the past.
61. The practice between the parties in *Tankexpress* (above) was treated as something akin to waiver; modern law requires that any waiver be unequivocal to a degree which, it is suggested, is not found in that case as regards receipt of payment after the due date.
62. See below, 14–2E.

In the United States the general rule is that payment is ineffective until received,[63] unless a different rule can be inferred from past dealings[64] or the insurer has permitted payment by post:[65] it is effective on sending in that neither late arrival nor loss in the post justifies forfeiture, however, in the latter case the insured will have to still to pay.[66]

If premium, correct in amount[67] and in mode of payment, is tendered to but declined by the insurer, that does not amount to payment[68] but the fact of tender is a defence[69] to any move by the insurer to forfeit the insurance on the ground of non-payment of premium. If payment of the amount of premium is made into court, one consequence will be that the cost of any action by the insurer to recover that premium falls on the insurer.[70]

13–8 THE TIME OF PAYMENT

Premium must be paid at the time stipulated in the contract of insurance. If no time has been stipulated, the premium must be paid within a reasonable time.[71] In the event of waiver[72] of the insured's obligation to pay on time, the insurer may call for payment at any later time, subject to the ordinary rules about revocation of waiver,[73] or the insurer may deduct it from any payment of insurance money.[74]

In the general law of contract, time of payment is not of the essence of the contract, unless the contract clearly indicates otherwise or the creditor has given reasonable notice to the debtor. As regards life insurance contracts, however,

"in most policies there is an express condition that the policy shall be void in the event of default in the payment of any instalment,[75] but . . . such a condition is wholly unnecessary, the punc-

---

63. *Blumer* v *Kirkman Corp*, 241 P 2d 17 (Cal, 1952); *Colonial Life & Accident Co* v *Wilson*, 246 F 2d 922 (5 Cir, 1957—PA), cert den 355 US 927.

64. *Krebs* v *Security Trust & Life Ins Co*, 156 F 294 (D Or, 1907—life) and *Mutual Reserve Fund Life Assn* v *Tuchfield*, 159 F 833, 839 (6 Cir, 1908—life); in those cases, unlike *Tankexpress* (above), the past practice had been for the debtor (insured) to post the premium so that it necessarily arrived after the due date.

65. *Colonial* v *Wilson* (above); *Estate of Hauer* v *Aetna Casualty & Surety Co*, 893 F 2d 782, 786 (5 Cir, 1990—motor).

66. *Tayloe* (above), p 403 *per* Nelson J (1850—fire); *Estate of Hauer* (above).

67. *Dixon* v *Clark* (1848) 5 CB 365.

68. The insurer "himself precluded a complete performance, by refusing to receive it"—*Dixon* v *Clark* (1848) 5 CB 365, 377 *per* Wilde CJ. Generally, see Mann, pp 71–72, 326–327. *Cf* MacGillivray, No 932.

69. *Farquharson* v *Pearl Assurance Co Ltd* [1937] 3 All ER 124: the creditor, who had taken life assurance on the life of his debtor, fearing that the debtor would not pay the premium, offered it to the agent of the insurer, who declined it in preference for expected payment by the debtor. The debtor died before payment. Singleton J, rejecting the defence that the policy had lapsed by non-payment of premium, said (p 132) that "it would be inequitable . . . if the insurance company having had that offer of payment to its agent and manager, who was authorised to receive payments . . . was able to say in law that there is neither tender [of payment] nor anything equivalent to tender". See also *Williams* v *British Marine Mutual Ins Assn Ltd* (1886) 57 LT 27, 30 *per* Willes J (hull); *Honour* v *Equitable Life Assurance Sy* [1900] 1 Ch 852 (life).

70. *Dixon* v *Clark* (1848) 5 CB 365.

71. *Kirby* v *Cosindit SpA* [1969] 1 Lloyd's Rep 75 (builders' risks).

72. As to waiver of punctual payment see below, 13–11A.

73. In particular, he must give reasonable notice: *Tankexpress A/S* v *Cie Financière Belge des Pétroles SA* [1949] AC 76, 98 *per* Lord Wright, 104 *per* Lord du Parcq. Note that this is now seen as a case not of waiver but of promissory estoppel: below 26–4A1.

74. *Roberts* v *Security Co Ltd* [1897] 1 QB 111, 115 *per* Lord Esher MR (CA—burglary).

75. Such conditions are generally enforced by the courts: *Thompson* v *Knickerbocker Life Ins Co*, 104 US 252, 258 *per* Bradley J (1881—life).

tual payment of every part of the premium being a condition precedent to the liability of the company."[76]

This was decided because "promptness of payment is essential in the business of life insurance. All the calculations of the insurance company are based on the hypothesis of prompt payments. They not only calculate on the receipt of the premiums when due, but on compounding interest upon them."[77]

13–8A Days of Grace

Days of grace refer to an extra period of time to pay premium allowed to the insured by the contract. *Prima facie* the days are consecutive calendar days. This is the rule in Canada.[78] However, in some parts of the United States, if the days of grace end on a Sunday, the period continues until the next business day.[79] The premise, less sound today that in times past, is that payment on Sunday is impossible.

In a life contract, the effect is usually that the contract remains in force during the days of grace, although the premium has not been paid on time; time is not of the essence of the contract until the days of grace have expired. If the life drops during the days of grace and before the next premium has been paid, there is cover.[80]

In other classes of insurance, however, if the unpaid premium is for renewal of cover, which is not automatic, the effect of the days of grace may be one of two kinds. (a) There is no cover but an offer to renew cover, which starts if and when the offeree accepts the offer and pays premium.[81] The offer lapses after the period of days has passed. (b) There is interim cover,[82] until the offeree insured decides to contract for the full renewal period or not; this is the usual interpretation in the case of motor insurance.

---

76. *Frank* v *Sun Life Assurance Co* (1893) 20 OAR 564, 567 *per* Burton JA (Ont—life). *Sheridan* v *Phoenix Life Assurance Co* (1858) El Bl & El 156 (life), upheld *sub nom Phoenix Life Assurance Co* v *Sheridan* (1860) 8 HLC 745.
USA: time is of the essence: *Jackson* v *Mutual Life Ins Co of New York*, 186 F 447 (8 Cir, 1911—life); *Travelers Ins Co* v *Wolfe*, 78 F 2d 78 (6 Cir, 1935—life and disability), cert den 296 US 635; *Travelers Ins Co* v *Castro*, 341 F 2d 882 (1 Cir, 1965—life). Generally, see Appleman, section 7951. On anniversary dates see Appleman, section 7953.
77. *New York Life Ins Co* v *Statham*, 93 US 24; 23 L Ed. 789, 791 *per* Bradley J (1876—life); *Klein* v *New York Life Ins Co*, 104 US 88, 91 *per* Woods J (1881—life).
78. *Firth* v *Western Life Assurance Co* (1957) 8 DLR (2d) 129 (Sup Ct—life).
79. *Friedman* v *Group Hospitalisation, Inc*, 220 F 2d 827 (D Colum, 1955—PHI); *Whisman* v *American Mutual Ins Co*, 128 NW 2d 539 (Mich. 1964—motor). Appleman, section 7960.
80. *Stuart* v *Freeman* [1903] 1 KB 47 (CA—life). "The scheme of the policy is that it shall be for a year, and shall be kept alive till default" (p 53 *per* Lord Collins MR). The court disapproved *dicta* in *Pritchard* v *Merchants' Mutual Life Assurance Sy* (1858) 3 CB (NS) 622 (life) to the effect that in life contracts the term giving days of grace was no more than an offer to renew, without interim cover (for example p 643 *per* Willes J).
USA in the sense of Lord Collins: *New York Life Ins Co* v *Statham* 93 US 24 (1876—life); *Provident Savings Life Assurance Sy* v *Taylor* 142 F 709 (3 Cir, 1906—life); *Lincoln National Life Ins Co* v *Bastian*, 31 F 2d 859 (4 Cir, 1929—life); *Miller* v *Aetna Life Ins Co*, 437 A 2d 1224 (Pa, 1981—PA). Generally see Appleman, section 7959.
81. For example *Tarleton* v *Staniforth* (1794) 5 TR 695 (fire): "the allowance of the 15 days was merely given for the purpose of saving the expence (*sic*) of a new policy and a new stamp" (*per* Kenyon CJ p 700); also *Simpson* v *Accidental Death Ins Co* (1857) 2 CB (NS) 257 (PA).
82. See ch 12. An early example is *Salvin* v *James* (1805) 6 East 571.

13–9 THE EFFECT OF NON-PAYMENT

Non-payment of premium is non-performance of a basic contractual duty by the insured. Premium due but unpaid is an outstanding debt, enforceable in the usual ways except that it is not a ground for the arrest of the debtor's ship.[83]

Many insurance contracts provide that, until premium is paid, there shall be no insurance cover.[84] As a provision of this kind will not be implied,[85] in other cases of non–payment, cover commences at the time of the contract[86] and continues until lateness of payment becomes of the essence.[87] Once that time has come, however, non-payment is default, whatever the reasons for or circumstances surrounding non-payment.[88]

Thus, it is no excuse that the insured was too ill to attend to his affairs and to pay the premium and that his wife was unaware of the existence of the policy;[89] or that payment was prevented by the outbreak of war.[90] One exception to strict insistence on payment is that, if insured loss occurs under a binding insurance contract before premium is due "it appears to be an idle form that he should have to tender the premium . . . when he had a claim for so much larger an amount . . . allowing in account the amount of the premium".[91] Another exception occurs, if payment would not have been late but for the fault of the insurer[92] including, in appropriate cases, the failure of the insurer to deliver the required policy.[93] In the case of continuing insurance and non-payment of a premium the same rules apply. Moreover, if a policy lapses for non-payment of premium, subject to contrary contract terms, the insurer is not obliged to give the insured notice of forfeiture.[94]

13–10 REPUDIATION BY THE INSURER

In the event of a wrongful refusal by the insurer to accept or retain proper payment of premium, the insurer cannot repudiate liability on the basis of non-payment of premium: that would be to allow him to take advantage of his own wrong.[95] On the con-

---

83. *Bain Clarkson Ltd* v *Owners of Sea Friends* [1991] 2 Lloyd's Rep 322 (CA—hull): the Court of Appeal held that a claim for premium by Lloyd's brokers was not a claim by an "agent in respect of any disbursements made on account of a ship" within the meaning of section 20(2)(p) of the Supreme Court Act 1981.

84. See above, 11–2E and below, 18–2A4.

85. *Kelly* v *London & Staffordshire Fire Ins Co* (1883) Cab & E 47 (fire).

86. Below, 18–2.

87. Above, 13–8.

88. *Tankexpress A/S* v *Cie Financière Belge des Pétroles SA* [1949] AC 76, 91 *per* Lord Porter, and p 94 *per* Lord Wright.

89. *Klein* v *New York Life Ins Co*, 104 US 88 (1881—life).

90. *New York Life Ins Co* v *Statham* 93 US 24 (1876—life). Generally, see Appleman, section 8232.

91. *Roberts* v *Security Co Ltd* [1897] 1 QB 111, 117 *per* Rigby LJ (CA—burglary). *Provident Savings Life Assurance Sy* v *Taylor*, 142 F 709 (3 Cir, 1906—life). *Aliter* if insurance money payable under policy A but premium due under policy B: *Union Life Ins Co* v *Brewer*, 309 SW 2d 740 (Ark, 1958—PA).

92. *In re Preston's Will*, 328 NYS 2d 405 (1972—life) and cases cited.

93. However, delivery of the wrong policy by mistake does not relieve the insured from the obligation to accept the correct policy or from the obligation to pay the premium: *General Accident Ins Corp* v *Cronk* (1901) 27 TLR 233 (motor).

94. *Long* v *Monarch Accident Ins Co*, 30 F 2d 929 (4 Cir, 1929—PA); *Unigard Mutual Ins Co* v *Fox*, 236 SE 2d 851 (Ga, 1977—motor).

95. *Daff* v *Midland Colliery Owners Mutual Indemnity Co* (1913) 82 LJKB 1340, 1349 *per* Lord Moulton (HL—employers' liability).

trary, the insurer in that case is liable for breach of contract[96] and the insured is released from the obligation to pay.[97] The situation was discussed in *Honour* v *Equitable Life Assurance Sy*.[98] Buckley J refused to grant an injunction restraining the insurer from declining the premiums tendered under a life contract. He also held that there could be no declaration that the policy was valid before a claim under the policy had arisen. Further, he observed[99] that, although the insured had an immediate right to damages for breach of contract by the insurer who refused to receive premium, if there were no claim at that time, the damages would be nil.[100]

13–11 RELIEF

"Courts of equity, indeed, in appropriate cases relieve against failure to pay on a stipulated day, but, in so doing, they do not affect to modify the terms of the bargain, though they alter the result of failure to comply with them."[101] That was said in England; stronger statements are found in the United States, for example: "Forfeitures are so odious in law that they will be enforced only where there is the clearest evidence that such was the intention of the parties."[102] Such words suggest a general willingness to relieve against forfeiture on broad equitable grounds; but it is not so in England (below, 13–11C), where the courts have offered the insured only more limited assistance by means of waiver (13–11A) and a rule of appropriation (13–11B).

13–11A Waiver[103]

In this context, waiver is an unequivocal representation[104] by the insurer that he will not insist upon the requirement of payment of premium before cover; or that, although aware[105] of facts giving rise to forfeiture, he will not forfeit the insurance. In each of these cases the law may require that the representation has been relied upon by the insured. If the waiver is seen as a form of election, reliance is unnecessary, whereas, if it is seen as a kind of estoppel, reliance is essential.[106] In practice the insured will argue both waiver and estoppel. If there is reliance, it usually takes the

96. *Honour* v *Equitable Life Assurance Sy* [1900] 1 Ch 852, 855 *per* Buckley J (life). See also *Day* v *Singleton* [1899] 2 Ch 320; *Southern Foundries Ltd* v *Shirlaw* [1940] AC 701.
97. *Re Albert Life Assurance Co* (1870) LR 9 Eq 703 (life). *First Texas Prudential Ins Co* v *Ryan*, 82 SW 2d 635 (Tex, 1935—life); *Order of Railway Conductors of America* v *Quigley*, 83 SW 2d 701 (Tex, 1935—life).
98. [1900] 1 Ch 852 (life).
99. p 855.
100. *Ibid*. He also said that the damages awarded would be nil "because the policy was worth nothing". In many cases this would be untrue as, for example, the policy would have surrender value, or value as security.
101. *Tankexpress A/S* v *Cie Financière Belge des Pétroles SA* [1949] AC 76, 100 *per* Lord Uthwatt.
102. *Union Life Ins Co* v *Brewer*, 309 SW 2d 740, 744 (Ark, 1958—PA).
103. The general requirements of waiver are discussed in greater detail in relation to breach of warranty (below, 20–7), and breach of procedural condition (below, 26–4).
104. *Bremer* v *Vanden* [1978] 2 Lloyd's Rep 109 (HL).
105. "Knowledge means, that the fact was present in the mind at the time"—*Kelly* v *Solari* (1841) LJ Ex 10, 12 *per* Lord Abinger CB (life); see also *Busteed* v *West of England Fire and Life Ins Co* (1857) 5 Ir Ch Rep 553, 571 *per* Rt Hon Thomas Smith MR (life). Analogy with waiver of rescission suggests that it is enough that the insurer knows facts justifying forfeiture, whether or not he has drawn the inference that forfeiture would be justifed: below, 23–5B1.
USA: *Knights of Pythias of the World* v *Kalinski*, 163 US 289, 298 *per* Brown J (1896—life); *Beatty* v *Mutual Reserve Fund Life Assn*, 75 F 62, 71 (9 Cir, 1896—life).
106. See below, 26–4A1.

form of carrying on with the contract and failing to make alternative provision. In many cases both in England and the United States, the presence or absence of some kind of reliance has been decisive.[107]

Even so, in the United States the Supreme Court has pronounced strongly for a readiness to find waiver[108]:

"Forfeitures are not favored by the law. They are often the means of great oppression and injustice. And, where adequate compensation can be made, the law in many cases, and equity in all cases, discharged the forfeiture, upon such compensation being made. It is true, we held . . . that, in life insurance, time of payment is material, and cannot be extended by the courts against the assent of the Company. But where such assent is given the courts should be liberal in construing the transaction in favor of avoiding a forfeiture."

The representation giving rise to waiver may occur in different ways.

(a) If the insurer, entitled to payment in cash, accepts another mode of payment such as a cheque, he thereby waives his right to payment of that premium in cash.[109] It does not follow that the insured may pay the next premium in cash; that depends on a course of dealings which affects the contract term on payment.[110]

(b) There is waiver if the insurer declines an offer of (proper) payment by A in the expectation, unfulfilled in the event, of payment by B.[111]

(c) If the insurer has accepted late payment of premiums in the past, reasonable notice that prompt payment will be required in the future kills any contention that the strict premium requirement has been waived for the future.[112] In the absence of such notice, courts in the United States have held that past indulgence suffices to waive punctuality in future. The insurer

"ought not to be permitted to make an outward show of continued leniency, repeated with such uniformity, or in such manner, as to put another off his guard, and then afterwards, by a sudden change in his course of conduct, declare a forfeiture, when the other party has been misled, and is helpless to avert the consequences."[113]

107. *The Scaptrade* [1983] QB 529, 536 *per* Robert Goff LJ (CA) concerning forfeiture of a charter for non-payment of hire. *Newbon* v *City Mutual Life Assurance Sy Ltd* (1935) 52 CLR 723, 734–735 (HCA—life).
In the USA "A company may waive the payment of a premium when it is due, but the basis of waiver is estoppel; and unless the company does or omits some act whereby the assured has just ground to believe and does believe, and acts on the belief, that the corporation will make, continue, or restore a contract without the payment of premium, there is no estoppel, and there can be no waiver"—*Equitable Life Assurance Sy* v *McElroy*, 83 F 631, 638 (8 Cir, 1897—life); *Smith* v *New England Mutual Life Ins Co*, 3 F 769, 772 (3 Cir, 1894—life); *Becker* v *Exchange Mutual Fire Ins Co*, 365 F 816, 820 (ED Pa, 1908—fire). *Blanton* v *John Hancock Mutual Life Ins Co*, 345 F Supp 168 (ND Tex, 1971—life), affirmed 463 F 2d 421 (5 Cir, 1972): waiver of timeous payment and estoppel are the same.
108. *Knickerbocker Life Ins Co* v *Norton*, 96 US 234; 24 L Ed 689, 692 *per* Bradley J (1878—life). See also, for example, *In re Preston's Will*, 328 NYS 2d 405 (1972—life).
109. For example, *Bell Bros* v *Hudson Bay Ins Co Ltd* (1911) 44 SCR 419 (fire).
110. See above, 13–4 and below, 13–11A(c).
111. *Farquharson* v *Pearl Assurance Co Ltd* [1937] 3 All ER 124, 132 (life): Singleton J rejected the defence that the policy had lapsed by non-payment of premium mainly on the ground that there had been tender of payment. He also agreed (*ibid*) with the arbitrator that the manager had waived the premium.
112. *Laing* v *Commercial Union Assurance Co Ltd* (1922) 11 Ll L Rep 54 (fire). *Tankexpress A/S* v *Cie Financière Belge des Pétroles SA* [1949] AC 76, 98 *per* Lord Wright.
USA: it is submitted that this is the main explanation in *Smith* v *New England Mutual Life Ins Co*, 63 F 769, 772 (3 Cir, 1894—life); and *Schmerz* v *United States Life Ins Co*, 118 F 250, 257 (3 Cir, 1902—life).
113. *Beatty* v *Mutual Reserve Fund Life Assn* 75 F 62, 70 (9 Cir, 1896—life). See also *Hartford Life & Annuity Ins Co* v *Unsell*, 144 US 439 (1892—life); *Bergdorf* v *Allstate Ins Co*, 541 So 2d 716, 717 (Fla, 1989—PA); *Saunders* v *Lloyd's of London* 779 P 2d 249, 253–254 (Wash, 1989—property). *Idem* in Canada: *Peart* v *Prudential Ins Co* (1987) 47 DLR (4th) 728 (Sask—life).

In England today, it is doubtful whether past indulgence amounts to a representation that waives the duty of prompt payment in future. The doubt arises from decisions in the general law that past indulgence is equivocal, but these were decisions in market situations of such constant change that it could not be inferred, that because the creditor waived punctuality this month, he would do likewise next month.[114] In the case of insurance, if past acceptance of late payment, for example under a life contract, had occurred only after the insurer had required evidence of good health (in effect a case of reinstatement), it could not be inferred that the same would happen in future without at the very least similar evidence.[115] However, if past acceptance of late payment had occurred without apparent demur, hesitation or inquiry, it is possible to contend that the insurer has waived punctuality in the future.[116] The question turns on whether the circumstances of past indulgence, its frequency and the way in which it was expressed, can reasonably be relied upon by the insured as an unequivocal waiver of punctual payment in future.

A clear case is that of the insured, who was also an agent of the insurer, who took a number of policies in respect of his business, and a practice developed of periodic settlement of outstanding premiums less commission.[117] The obvious convenience of this practice suggested that it would be followed in future, as the convenience was mutual. So much so that the case for the insured was stronger than waiver and the court found a course of dealings that modified the strict terms of the individual insurance contracts.

(d) Acceptance of premiums after breach by the insured of any condition giving rise to forfeiture, including the case of late payment of premium, is a waiver of that forfeiture.[118] But there is no waiver by acceptance of late premium in respect of a period of cover prior to breach[119]; the insurer might wish to receive what he has earned and still be free of the risk thereafter, so it cannot be said that acceptance is an unequivocal waiver of the right of forfeiture.

(e) Ivamy has suggested[120] that, if the insurer hands to the insured a policy stating that premium has been paid, the company is estopped from pleading non-payment to defeat a claim on that policy. It is difficult to see how a mere recital in the policy, of which the proposer may be unaware, can found an

114. *The Scaptrade* [1983] QB 529 (CA). This case concerned payment of hire under a charterparty and must be seen in that context: see pp 535–536 *per* Robert Goff LJ. See also *Nichimen Corp* v *Gatoil Overseas Inc* [1987] 2 Lloyd's Rep 46 (CA).

115. *Thompson* v *Knickerbocker Life Ins Co*, 104 US 252, 259–260 (1881—life). *Redmond* v *Canadian Mutual Aid Assn* (1891) 18 OAR 335, 340 (life).

116. There was waiver in *Spoeri* v *Massachusetts Mutual Life Ins Co*, 39 F 752 (ED Mo, 1889—life) in which one-half of past premiums had been accepted between one and four weeks late.

117. *Holliday* v *Western Australian Ins Co Ltd* (1936) 54 Ll L Rep 373 (fire).

118. *Hemmings* v *Sceptre Life Assn Ltd* [1905] 1 Ch 365 (life); *Ayrey* v *British Legal & United Provident Assurance Co Ltd* [1918] 1 KB 137 (life). *Beasant* v *Northern Life Ins Co* [1923] 2 DLR 1086 (Man—life). *Phoenix Mutual Life* v *Raddin*, 120 US 183, 196 *per* Gray J (1886—life); *Knights of Pythias of the World* v *Kalinski*, 163 US 289 (1896—mutual life); *Duncan* v *Missouri State Life Ins Co*, 160 F 646 (8 Cir, 1908—life); see also cases cited below, 23–18, on waiver of rescission. In the case of mutual insurance it has been held that the acceptance of a call made after the right to forfeiture has arisen gives rise to waiver: *Beatty* v *Mutual Reserve Fund Life Assn*, 75 F 62, 72 (9 Cir, 1896—life). Appleman, section 9273.

119. *McGeachie* v *North American Life Ins Co* (1893) 23 SCR 148 (life). *Duncan* v *Missouri State Life Ins Co*, 60 F 646 (8 Cir, 1908—life); even if the payment of past premium is prompted by a renewal notice: *Holland* v *Federal Kemper Ins Co*, 553 A 2d 450 (Pa, 1989—motor).

120. p 206.

estoppel in the absence of an unequivocal representation by the insurer[121] and, in particular, actual and reasonable reliance by the proposer.[122] The issue of a policy, which states that there is no cover until premium has been paid but also that premium has been paid, to a proposer, who knows that he has not paid, has been described as a "contradiction",[123] and should not found an estoppel. However, if, knowing that premium has not been paid, the insurer makes a clear representation that non-forfeiture will not occur, that may be seen as waiver (in the sense of election) regardless of any reliance by the waivee.[124]

Exceptionally, the insurer may be estopped by the issue of a policy, if, first, the policy is a Lloyd's policy, where the custom is that the underwriter is paid not by the insured but by the broker and thus the contention, that the insured who received such a policy relied upon the representation that premium had been paid, carries more conviction.[125] Second, if the policy is under seal, the insurer is estopped as regards an assignee of the policy for value.[126]

(f) The issue of a renewal receipt stating (untruly) that premium has been paid may estop the insurer from forfeiting the policy for non-payment,[127] even though the policy provides that the insurance shall not be binding until premium is paid.[128] For estoppel, unlike waiver,[129] there must always be reliance on the representation and reliance must be reasonable.[130]

13–11B Appropriation

In the United States the "general rule is that an insurer is not justified in declaring a forfeiture of an insurance policy for the nonpayment of a premium when, at the time such premium accrues, the insurer is indebted to the insured, either for dividends declared or other funds which it may have in its hands belonging to the policy holder",

---

121. In *Western Assurance Co* v *Provincial Ins Co* (1880) 5 OAR 190, 193 (re) the argument, that the insurer was bound by the recital, was rejected because "it is manifest upon the face of the policy that it was not intended to be a binding instrument until payment of the premium".

122. *Cf Roberts* v *Security Co Ltd* [1897] 1 QB 111 (CA—burglary) in which it was held that the insurer was thus estopped, although the executed policy had not been handed to the insured, who was unaware of its contents. The decision was doubted in *Equitable Fire & Accident Office Ltd* v *The Ching Wo Hong* [1907] AC 96, 101 *per* Lord Davey (PC—fire). See also *Newis* v *General Accident Fire & Life Assurance Corp* (1910) 11 CLR 620 (HCA—fire). *Roberts* was cited with apparent approval in *Mutual Reserve Life Ins Co* v *Heidel*, 161 F 535, 537 (8 Cir, 1908—life), but distinguished. *Roberts* might be justified as a case not of estoppel but of waiver, for which reliance is not required: see below, 26–4A1.

123. *Western Assurance Co* v *Provincial Ins Co* (1880) 5 OAR 190, 197 (re).

124. See further on this kind of waiver, below, 26–4A1.

125. MIA, section 54, provides that "Where a marine policy effected on behalf of the insured by a broker acknowledges the receipt of the premium, such acknowledgement is, in the absence of fraud, conclusive as between the insurer and the insured, but not as between the insurer and broker".

126. LPA, section 68(1), "A receipt for consideration money, or other consideration in the body of a deed or endorsed thereon shall, in favour of a subsequent purchaser, not having notice that the money or other consideration thereby acknowledged to be received was not in fact paid or given, wholly or in part, be sufficient evidence of the payment or giving of the whole amount thereof."

127. *Howell* v *Kightley* (1856) 21 Beav 331, 335 *per* Lord Romilly MR (fire).

128. *Tennant* v *Travelers' Indemnity Ins Co*, 31 F 322 (ND Cal, 1887—life).

129. See below, 26–4A1.

130. *Handler* v *Mutual Reserve Fund Life Assn* (1904) 90 LT 192, 194 *per* Collins MR (CA—life).

because in such circumstances "it would be inequitable for an insurance company to forfeit a policy".[131] The insurer must appropriate the amount of the premium, if "the company actually has in its hands at the time funds which are absolutely due and payable"[132] to the insured. The duty of appropriation, which is also found in England, arises as follows:

(a) If the insured pays too much money as premium to the insurer, the insurer will be obliged to apply the relevant part to the payment of premium.[133] In the United States the same has been held, when the insured mistakenly paid too little,[134] but this ruling may only apply if the insured is entitled to extend cover for less than the usual (often annual) period.

(b) Accumulated dividends are available for appropriation to the payment of dividend,[135] even though they have been retained by the insurer as security for a loan to the insured.[136] However, dividends due under policy A will not be appropriated to pay premium due under policy B.[137]

(c) If the contract provides that the policy has a surrender value, that value may be applied to the payment of premiums.[138] Surrender value means the amount, which an insurer has contracted or is prepared to pay during the currency of the contract, in consideration of being thereafter relieved of the liability dependent on the continuance of premiums paid.[139] In some parts of the United States statute obliges the insurer to apply any surrender value to unpaid premiums. In England the contract of insurance may contain a similar provision.

(d) If the insured has an outstanding claim against the insurer, he may insist, subject to the contract, that the premium be set off against the claim.[140]

---

131. *American National Ins Co v Yee Lim Shee*, 104 F 2d 688, 694 (9 Cir, 1939—life), cert den 308 US 592. See also *State Life Ins Co v Mitchell*, 126 F 2d 867 (8 Cir, 1942—life). Generally see Appleman, sections 8271 ff.

132. *Long v Monarch Accident Ins Co*, 30 F 2d 929, 930 (4 Cir, 1929—PA).

133. *Kirkpatrick v South Australasian Ins Co Ltd* (1886) 11 App Cas 177 (PC—fire), with reference to the intention of the parties. A modern court might prefer to give relief against forfeiture on the basis that the insurer was bound to appropriate money in its possession for the payment of premiums.
    USA in this sense: *United States v Morrell*, 204 F 2d 490 (4 Cir, 1953—life), cert den 346 US 857.

134. *American National Ins Co v Yee Lim Shee*, 104 F 2d 688, 694 (9 Cir, 1939—life).

135. *General American Life Ins Co v Stephens*, 130 F 2d 511 (9 Cir, 1942—life), cert den 317 US 683.

136. *Baker v Northwestern Mutual Life Ins Co*, 55 P 2d 663 (Cal, 1945—life); *State Mutual Life Assurance Co v Fleischer*, 186 F 2d 358 (8 Cir, 1951—life). *Aliter* if profits were not to be apportioned between policy holders until later: *McCampbell v New York Life Ins Co*, 288 F 465 (5 Cir, 1923—life), cert den 262 US 759. *Quaere* whether dividends must have been declared: Appleman, section 8281.

137. *First National Bank of Wichita Falls v State Life Ins Co*, 80 F 2d 499 (5 Cir, 1935—life).

138. *Aliter* if the contract contains no such provision: *Equitable Life Assurance Sy v Reed* [1914] AC 587 (PC—life).

139. *Reed* (above), p 597 *per* Lord Dunedin.

140. *Williams v British Marine Mutual Ins Assn Ltd* (1886) 57 LT 27 (hull): this case concerned calls outstanding under the rules of a mutual association. But in *Simpson v Accidental Death Ins Co* (1857) 2 CB (NS) 257, the insured died during the days of grace allowed for the payment of premium in respect of an accident policy. His executors paid the premium after the days had expired, and claimed under the policy contending (p 295) that "payment of premium was not necessary to keep the policy alive; for, that the event on which the sum insured was to be paid having happened within the twenty-one days, it was in effect paid, as the [insurers] might deduct it out of the sum which was in their hands payable to the plaintiff". This contention was rejected *inter alia* because (p 296 *per* Cresswell J) the premium was unpaid after the days of grace, i.e., a rejection of the premise of the contention that a set-off and hence payment had already occurred during that period. Alternatively the court considered (*ibid*) that the insured had no right to the renewal of the policy for the period including the days of grace, without the agreement of the insurers, which had not occurred.

In any event, the insurer has no duty to appropriate funds to unpaid premium in the following circumstances.

(i) The funds are not sufficient to pay premium for at least the minimum period of time for which the insured is entitled to insure under the policy.[141]

(ii) The insurer is not free to apply the funds in this way. This is so, if the insured directs that the funds shall not be applied to premium[142] or, if the insurer is not free to appropriate the funds under the terms of the contract of insurance[143]: if the contract directs that surplus funds shall be applied in some other way, by implication that excludes appropriation to the payment of premium.[144]

13–11C Relief against Forfeiture

The insured, who loses his life policy because he has not paid premium in time, may appeal to the equitable doctrine of relief against forfeiture, however currently the appeal is unlikely to be fruitful. Although, it has been said that equity "has an unlimited and unfettered jurisdiction to relieve against contractual forfeitures and penalties",[145] "there has undoubtedly been some fluctuation of authority as to the self-limitation to be imposed or accepted on this power."[146]

These statements come from judgments in the House of Lords in *Shiloh Spinners Ltd* v *Harding*.[147] From these a leading writer[148] at the time was able to deduce a broad doctrine of relief, as follows:

(a) The court will consider the conduct of the parties.[149] In particular there will be relief against forfeiture for non-payment of premium, if the non-payment is induced by the insurer.[150] In New York, for example, negligence by the

---

141. *Dias* v *Farm Bureau Mutual Fire Ins Co*, 155 F 2d 788 (4 Cir, 1946—fire).
142. *American National Ins Co* v *Yee Lim Shee*, 104 F 2d 688, 694 (9 Cir, 1939—life).
143. *Williams* v *Union Central Life Ins Co*, 291 US 170 (1933—life). This case is restrictive, for Hughes CJ concluded (pp 179–180) that the insurer was not obliged to apply dividend to the payment of premium because he had no right to do so without the consent of the insured. See further *United States* v *Morrell*, 204 F 2d 490 (4 Cir, 1953—life).
144. *Morrell* (above).
145. *Shiloh Spinners Ltd* v *Harding* [1973] AC 691, 726 *per* Lord Simon; *contra* p 700 *per* Lord Diplock. On the general nature of the doctrine see Harpum [1984] CLJ 134. USA: Rest Contracts 2d, section 229.
146. *Shiloh* (above), p 722 *per* Lord Wilberforce. In that case the House of Lords reaffirmed "the right of courts of equity in appropriate and limited cases to relieve against forfeiture for breach of covenant or condition where the primary object of the bargain is to secure a stated result which can effectively be attained when the matter comes before the court, and where the forfeiture provision is added by way of security for the production of that result".
147. Above.
148. Snell, *Principles of Equity* (28th ed, 1982), p 530; a similar suggestion in the previous edition of Snell was approved in *Starside Properties Ltd* v *Mustapha* [1974] 2 All ER 567, 571 by Edmund Davies LJ (CA). *Semble*, this is still the view taken in Australia: Davies [1990] Australian Bus L Rev 328, by reference to *Stern* v *McArthur* (1988) 165 CLR 489.
149. Whether, for example, the non-payment was wilful. *Hill* v *Barclay* (1811) 18 Ves Jun 56, 62 *per* Lord Eldon; *Shiloh Spinners Ltd* v *Harding* [1973] AC 691, 722–723, 725 *per* Lord Wilberforce; 726 *per* Viscount Dilhorne; *BICC plc* v *Burndy Corp* [1985] 1 All ER 417 (CA).
150. In *Knight* v *Rowe* (1826) 2 Car & P 245 the landlord sought forfeiture of a lease for breach of a covenant to insure. The defendant had insured the premises, but not as required by the lease, the discrepancy having been induced by the landlord. Forfeiture was refused.

insurer has excused the insured, if it has led to non-payment of premium.[151] Evidently this situation is close to that of waiver or estoppel.[152]

(b) When the object of the right of forfeiture is "essentially to secure the payment of money, equity has been willing to relieve on terms that the payment is made with interest, if appropriate, and also costs."[153] As regards insurance, the object of forfeiture is undoubtedly to secure payment.[154]

(c) The court will take into account any disparity between the value of the property forfeited and the damage to the person seeking forfeiture caused by non-payment of the money due.[155] For example, in the case of endowment insurance, under which the main benefits to the insured are in later years, disparity may be great, unless forfeiture is accompanied by payment to the insured of the surrender value of the policy at an adequate figure.

On the basis of *Shiloh*, it appeared that the court was free to consider the justice of the particular case and to order relief, if justice required it. Since *Shiloh*, however, courts have doubted the breadth of the equitable relief, and a number of objections to relief have been raised.

13–11C1 The Importance of Certainty

One objection lies in the decision in *The Scaptrade*, that the doctrine does not apply to commercial transactions because it would undermine the certainty necessary in such transactions.[156] However, many insurance contracts cannot be described as commercial. Morever, the better view, which has recently gained some support, is that the commercial character of the transaction, although highly relevant (as an obstacle) to the grant of relief, does not automatically rule it out altogether.[157]

13–11C2 The Importance of Punctuality of Payment

An older objection to relief against forfeiture was expressed by Lord Hardwicke LC in *Rose* v *Rose*[158]

"Equity will relieve against almost all penalties whatsoever; against non-payment of money at a certain day; against forfeitures of copyholds: but they are all such cases where the Court can do

---

151. *In re Preston's Will*, 328 NYS 2d 405 (1972—life) and cases cited.
152. There is more than a suggestion of an approach in terms of waiver in some of the forfeiture cases: for example *BICC plc* v *Burndy Corp* [1985] 1 All ER 417, 428 *per* Kerr LJ (CA).
153. *Shiloh Spinners Ltd* v *Harding* [1973] AC 691, 722.
154. *Klein* v *New York Life Insurance Co*, 104 US 88, 91 *per* Woods J (1881—life) quoted below, 13–11C2.
155. *Shiloh* (above) pp 723–724 *per* Lord Wilberforce.
156. *Scandinavian Trading Tanker Co A/B* v *Flota Petrolera Equatoriana* [1983] QB 529; [1983] 2 AC 694 (time charter). Lord Diplock (p 699, p 704) approved reasons given by Robert Goff LJ in the Court of Appeal. The doctrine was held inapplicable to a commercial licence in *Sport International Bussum BV* v *Inter-Footwear Ltd* [1984] 1 All ER 376, 384 by Oliver LJ who also stressed the "importance of certainty in commercial transactions, the necessity for both parties to know where they stand without the delays involved in investigations about whether the court will grant relief". The decision was affirmed [1984] 2 All ER 321 (HL); Lord Templeman (p 325) declined to define the boundaries of the doctrine but adopted part of the judgment of Oliver LJ in which (p 384) the latter stressed the need for certainty and the avoidance of delay.
157. *BICC plc* v *Burndy Corp* [1985] 1 All ER 417, 428 *per* Dillon LJ (CA). In favour of the less rigid approach: Harpum (1984) 100 LQR 369; Goff & Jones, p 475.
158. (1756) Amb 331, 332.

it with safety to the other party; for if the Court cannot put him into as good condition as if the agreement had been performed, the Court will not relieve."

This aim is not literally achieved. Lord Eldon observed[159]:

"The Court has very long held in a great variety of classes of cases, that in the instance of a covenant to pay a sum of money the Court so clearly sees, or rather fancies, the amount of damage, arising from non-payment at the time stipulated, that it takes upon itself to act, as if it was certain, that giving the money five years afterwards with interest it gives a complete compensation."

Money today is usually better than money tomorrow, so interest is adequate compensation only on the basis that it is enough to put the party in, not exactly, but substantially as good a condition as if the agreement had been performed. In any event, relief is more difficult to justify, if time of payment of premium is of the essence of the contract, and it is in this form that the objection to relief has appeared in the United States.

Lord Hardwicke's objection was applied in the United States Supreme Court in *Klein v New York Life Insurance Co.*[160] In *Klein* the court accepted earlier authority[161] that the time of payment was of the essence of the contract. The court premised that time was of the essence because premiums were finely and competitively calculated on the assumption that they would be paid punctually; but it is a premise that rests on the effect on the insurer of lateness under all its contracts, not the effect of lateness in the particular case. Woods J said[162]:

"If the insured can neglect payment at maturity and yet suffer no loss or forfeiture, premiums will not be punctually paid. The companies must have some efficient means of enforcing punctuality. Hence their contracts usually provide for the forfeiture of the policy upon default of prompt payment of the premiums. If they are not allowed to enforce this forfeiture, they are deprived of the means which they have reserved by their contract of compelling the parties insured to meet their engagements."

However, acceptance of the premise, that the possession of a weapon is justified as a general deterrent, does not carry with it acceptance of its indiscriminate use in each and every case of default. In England, the courts asked to grant relief have focused not on the general effect of relief but on the desirability of relief in the particular case.[163]

Even if time is of the essence in respect of each and every payment of premium in each and every insurance contract, it is not sure that that is a bar to relief. The authority of the main decision against relief[164] has been described as suspect,[165] and it is a decision of the Privy Council not binding on the English courts. Other cases support the possibility of an extension of time to perform the contract, in spite of breach of an

---

159. *Hill v Barclay* (1811) 18 Ves Jun 56, 59–60.
160. 104 US 88 (1881—life). In this case the premiums were unpaid because the insured was too ill to attend to his affairs, and his wife was unaware of the existence of the policy. Nonetheless the Supreme Court held that the insurer was entitled to forfeit the policy.
161. *New York Life Insurance Co v Statham*, 93 US 24 (1876—life). On whether time of payment of premium is of the essence see above, 13–8.
162. 104 US 88, 91.
163. See for example *Shiloh Spinners Ltd v Harding* [1973] AC 691, 724 *per* Lord Wilberforce.
164. *Steedman v Drinkle* [1916] 1 AC 275; followed in *Brickles v Snell* [1916] 2 AC 599 (PC). Also in this sense *Sport International Bussum BV v Inter-Footwear Ltd* [1984] 1 All ER 376, 385 *per* Oliver LJ (CA).
165. Jones and Goodhart, *Specific Performance* (1986), p 46.

essential time stipulation.[166] As a matter of precedent, therefore, there is no absolute bar to relief solely because time of payment is of the essence.[167]

13–11C3 Proprietary and Possessory Rights

A further objection to relief against forfeiture in insurance cases is the view that relief is limited to contracts involving the transfer of property rights. Although one statement of Lord Wilberforce in *Shiloh Spinners Ltd* v *Harding*[168] appeared to discard any such limit on relief, it has since been stated by Lord Diplock that the Wilberforce statement "was never meant to apply generally to contracts not involving any transfer of proprietary or possessory rights, but providing for a right to determine the contract in default of punctual payment of a sum of money payable under it".[169] This raises two issues; first there is an issue of precedent: what did Lord Wilberforce mean? Second, on what principle should contracts be distinguished in the way suggested by Lord Diplock?

As precedent, this restatement of the thought of Lord Wilberforce is in reality the thought of Lord Diplock[170] and we are left with a conflict between the views of two distinguished judges, neither of which was absolutely necessary to the decision in question. Moreover, Lord Diplock's hostility to the doctrine of forfeiture should be seen in the context of a case of dog eating dog over a juicy but very particular commercial bone.[171] Nonetheless, since Lord Diplock's statement it has been assumed[172] in England that relief is confined to "contracts concerning the transfer of proprietary or possessor rights . . . as opposed to merely contractual rights"[173], although it is an assumption that is built on foundations which are beginning to show their age.

As a matter of principle, limiting relief to cases of proprietary or possessory rights rests on the premise that relief is linked to the remedy of specific performance,[174] and that specific performance is also limited to cases of proprietary or possessory rights.

166. *Re Dagenham (Thames) Dock Co* (1873) 8 Ch App 1022; *Stockloser* v *Johnson* [1954] 1 QB 476, 501 *per* Romer LJ (CA); *Starside Properties Ltd* v *Mustapha* [1974] 1 WLR 816 (CA). *Legione* v *Hately* (1983) 46 ALR 1 (HCA). See discussion of these cases in Jones and Goodhart, *loc cit*.

167. In this sense Corbin, section 714.

168. [1973] AC 691.

169. The *Scaptrade, Scandinavian Trading Tanker Co A/B* v *Flota Petrolera Equatoriana* [1983] 2 AC 694, 702 *per* Lord Diplock. The rights may relate to real or to personal property: *BICC plc* v *Burndy Corp* [1985] 1 All ER 417 (CA).

170. Lord Diplock's interpretation of the mind of Lord Wilberforce was based on his speech in *The Laconia* [1977] AC 850, 869–870; however, while it is clear that Lord Wilberforce did not mean forfeiture to apply to time charters, beyond this it is very difficult to deduce from that judgment what he really thought about other contracts.

171. See especially *The Scaptrade* (above) p 703 *per* Lord Diplock. He noted that one of the purposes of hire was to fund the operation of the next period of the charter. Later (p 704) he cautioned that "the reasoning in my speech has been directed exclusively to time charters that are not by demise".

172. Given the limits imposed on the power to grant relief against forfeiture since *Shiloh* (above), but that the power to strike out a clause as penal has fewer limitations, the inference is that whereas the two rules share the same origins, they have developed differently. These differences were considered by the Court of Appeal in *Jobson* v *Johnson* [1989] 1 All ER 621; Harpum [1989] CLJ 370.

173. *BICC plc* v *Burndy Corp* [1985] 1 All ER 417, 427–428 *per* Dillon LJ (CA); see also p 429 *per* Kerr LJ.

174. *The Scaptrade* (above) p 701 *per* Lord Diplock. Harpum (1984) 100 LQR 369, 371: if relief "would amount to a specific performance of the contract in question (as it almost invariably will), then relief against forfeiture should of course be refused, unless the contract is one of the category, unusual in purely commercial transactions, that is specifically enforceable".

This was true in the nineteenth century, but not in the eighteenth,[175] and then only in order to complement common law without usurping its jurisdiction; hence the maxim of the time that there would be no specific performance if damages at common law were an adequate remedy.[176] In the last decade of the twentieth century, the fusion of law and equity should mean that demarcation problems are a thing of the past, and there seems to be no good reason why specific performance or relief against forfeiture, if appropriate on the justice of the case,[177] should be limited to situations involving the transfer of proprietary or possessory rights. If relief is available to the instalment purchaser of land,[178] why not also to the instalment buyer of life insurance, who may, of course, have bought that insurance mainly as the means of buying his land? "The common feature in all these cases is that a penal provision is involved and the court grants relief against the forfeiture which would otherwise follow therefrom in such circumstances as justice requires."[179] As regards insurance contracts, the question has yet to be finally settled in England. By contrast, in Texas, for example, the position is clear: "Insurance policies are contracts governed by the same rules as other contracts [citation]. A court of equity may set aside a forfeiture and may compel specific performance of agreements with reference to such policies."[180] Even in England, however, the Insurance Ombudsman has given relief in extreme cases.[181]

13–12 NO RETURN OF PREMIUM

In principle, the insured has no right to a return of premium, unless the insurer has wrongfully repudiated the contract[182] or induced the contract by misrepresentation or non-disclosure. In the words of Lord Mansfield,[183]

"if the risk of that contract of indemnity has once commenced, there shall be no apportionment or return of premium afterwards. For though the premium is estimated, and the risk depends upon the nature and length of the voyage, yet, if it has commenced, though it be only for twenty-four hours or less, the risk is run; the contract is for the whole entire risk, and no part of the consideration shall be returned".

175. For example *Ball* v *Coggs* (1710) 1 Bro Parl Cas 140. Jones and Goodhart, *Specific Performance* (1986) p 6.
176. Jones and Goodhart, p 18.
177. Jones and Goodhart, p 21, citing *inter alia The Stena Nautica (No 2), CN Marine Inc* v *Stena Line A/B* [1982] 2 Lloyd's Rep 336, 348 *per* May LJ (CA).
178. *Starside Properties Ltd* v *Mustapha* [1974] 2 All ER 567 (CA); *cf* Harpum (1984) 100 LQR 369, 373 ff. USA in this sense, for example, *Cheney* v *Libby*, 134 US 68 (1890); *Ward* v *Union Bond & Trust Co*, 243 F 2d 476 (9 Cir, 1957).
179. *Starside* (above), p 574 *per* Edmund Davies LJ. *Cf* the doctrine of penalties, from which the doctrine of forfeiture must, in the current state of English law, be distinguished: *Jobson* v *Johnson* [1989] 1 All ER 621; Harpum [1989] CLJ 370.
180. *First Texas Prudential Insurance Co* v *Ryan*, 82 SW 2d 635, 637 (Tex, 1935—life).
Cf Canada: state legislation contains a general power of equitable relief against forfeiture, but the courts have been slow to apply this power to the forfeiture of insurance policies for breach of condition. An exception is *Bonne* v *Irvine*, 31 Man R (2d) 81 (Man, 1985—motor), discussed by Baer, 17 Ottawa L Rev 631, 661 ff (1985).
181. For example, the case of the insured, who was terminally ill and who did not receive the insurer's letter warning him that premiums were overdue: The Insurance Ombudsman, Annual Report 1992, para 7.6.
182. Appleman, sections 8352 ff.
183. *Tyrie* v *Fletcher* (1777) 2 Cowp 666, 668 *per* Lord Mansfield (hull). See also *Provident Savings Life Assurance Sy* v *Bellew* (1904) 35 SCR 35 (life). *Jones* v *St Paul Fire & Marine Ins Co*, 118 F 2d 237 (5 Cir, 1941—fire), applying *inter alia Tyrie* v *Fletcher* (above); *Rellim Construction Co* v *Automobile Ins Co*, 29 NYS 2d 313 (1941—fire). Appleman, section 8351.

This, according to Couch,[184] is because the "danger incurred may be greater in any one moment than during the entire remaining period of insurance, and it would be extremely difficult, at the least to apportion the premium".

The consequence is that, if the insurance cover ends with destruction of property insured,[185] or breach of warranty,[186] no premium is recoverable for the unexpired period of cover. The Law Reform (Frustrated Contracts) Act 1943, which contains a different rule for other contracts, does not apply to insurance contracts.[187] Further, if a single contract of insurance with a single premium covers property A and property B, and the cover on A is lawful, but the cover on B is unlawful, for example for lack of interest, there is no return of premium proportionate to the cover on B.[188]

The rule rests on the principle that consideration, although disproportionately low in relation to premium paid, has been received and has not totally failed, and therefore the insured may recover no part of the premium. The insurer provides consideration as soon as he comes on risk, even though no insurance money becomes payable to the insured.[189] Moreover, if the insurer does pay the insured but recovers the entire amount by way of subrogation from a third party, the insurer has provided consideration nonetheless by having been on risk and the insured may not recover premium.[190]

13–12A Exception: Divisible Risk

Implicit in Lord Mansfield's statement (above, 13–12) is an exception for the risk that is not entire but divisible: the case of a single contract of insurance covering separately identifiable risks. Thus, if the insurance attaches for property A but not for property item B, the insured may recover premium in respect of B but not A.[191] Most cases in the English courts have been early and have concerned marine insurance,[192] but the principle applies also on land.

Divisible risks are identified in the same way as divisible obligations under other kinds of contract.[193] If there is a single gross premium, for example, that implies an obligation that is not divisible but entire.[194] Again, an insurance for a year requiring premium at x per month is divisible into monthly parts, but an insurance for a year requiring a premium at x for the year, albeit payable in instalments during the year, is

184. *Insurance*, Vol 3, section 709 cited with approval in *Thomas v Baker & Co*, 60 F 2d 1057, 1060 (ED Pa, 1932—credit).

185. Whether by an event covered by the insurance or not: *Bermon v Woodbridge* (1781) 2 Doug 781, 789 *per* Lord Mansfield (hull). However, the loss of premium has been held to be recoverable as loss (which is not too remote) in a negligence action against the person who damaged or destroyed the property concerned: *Patel v London Transport Executive* [1981] RTR 29 (CA).

186. *Jones v St Paul Fire & Marine Ins Co*, 118 F 2d 237 (5 Cir, 1941—fire); *Foster Wheeler Corp v Home Ins Co*, 421 NYS 2d 363 (1979). *Cf* cases in which premium has been recovered in spite of breach of warranty: *Fidelity-Phenix Fire Ins Co v Queen City Bus & Transfer Co*, 3 F 2d 784 (4 Cir, 1925—motor); *Lane v Travelers Indemnity Co*, 383 SW 2d 955 (Tex, 1964—fire).

187. Section 2(5).

188. *Canadian Pacific Ry Co v Ottawa Fire Ins Co* (1907) 39 SCR 405 (liability).

189. The insurer will normally incur transaction costs but these are not part of the consideration.

190. *Darrell v Tibbitts* (1880) 5 QBD 560, 562 *per* Brett LJ (CA—fire).

191. MIA, section 84(2).

192. See Arnould, Nos 1326 ff. Although the intention of the parties is important, much turns on trade custom; see Arnould, No 1327.

193 Glanville Williams (1941) 57 LQR 373 and 490.

194. Arnould, No 1328.

an entire insurance for the year. Further, early marine cases[195] suggest that insurance obligations may be divisible by cause of loss. Thus, householder's "comprehensive" cover may be divisible in respect of fire, liability and so on; and a war risks extension may be a divisible part of a standard life contract.[196]

13–12B Exception: Contract Terms

The policy may provide for the return of a proportionate part of premium in specified circumstances; such provisions have been enforced, for example, when the insurer has elected to terminate the insurance.[197]

13–12C Exception: No Risk No Premium

The corollary of the general rule (above, 13–12) was spelled out by Lord Mansfield[198]:

"where the risk has not been run, whether its not having been run was owing to the fault, pleasure or will of the insured, or to any other cause, the premium shall be returned: because a policy of insurance is a contract of indemnity. The underwriter receives a premium for running the risk of indemnifying the insured, and whatever cause it be owing to, if he does not run the risk, the consideration, for which the premium or money was put into his hands, fails, and therefore he ought to return it."

In these circumstances, the insured may recover premiums by an action for money had and received.[199] For example, if premiums have been paid by mistake for cover that was not obtained,[200] or under protest to maintain cover while a dispute over premium is resolved in the insured's favour, the insured may recover them.[201] If the con-

---

195. In *Stevenson* v *Snow* (1761) 3 Burr 1237 (hull) the voyage fell into 2 distinct stages, first cabotage to Portsmouth, then an ocean voyage in convoy: the latter was a distinct risk. However, the decision, that premium for the second stage was recoverable, can be explained as turning on an express term that, if the ship did not reach Portsmouth in time to join the convoy, the insurance would cease.

196. In *Provident Savings Life Assurance Sy* v *Bellew* (1904) 35 SCR 35 a standard policy was issued with an extension to cover military service in South Africa in the "army of Great Britain in time of war", for an extra premium. The insured arrived in South Africa after the war there had ended and sought but failed to recover the extra premium. The majority of the Supreme Court interpreted the policy in such a way that the war risk had begun, so the insurer was on risk for the extension; see Nesbitt J (pp 44–45). However, the implication of all the judgments is that, if the war risk had not begun, premium would have been severable and returnable.

In *Occhipinti* v *Boston Ins Co*, 72 So 2d 326 (La, 1954) in respect of a policy incorporating both fire and associated premium insurance and a total loss by fire, the court held that the insured could recover a proportionate part of premium paid for premium insurance. *Cf Thomas* v *Baker & Co*, 60 F 2d 1057, 1060 (ED Pa, 1932—credit): "where the subject-matter of insurance is divided into separate risks, if the premium or consideration paid be single and entire, the contract must be held to be entire". In this case credit insurance was granted for a basic premium, with an additional premium based on sales volume, but held not apportionable.

In *Elias* v *Firemen's Ins Co*, 420 SE 2d 504 (SC, 1992—fire) a single policy, which covered both car and house for separate amounts of premium, was held divisible, so that cancellation (for non-payment of premium) of the motor part did not affect cover under the fire part.

197. *Sun Fire Office* v *Hart* (1889) 14 App Cas 98 (PC—fire). A more recent example is *The M Vatan* [1987] 2 Lloyd's Rep 416 (re).

198. *Tyrie* v *Fletcher* (1777) 2 Cowp 666, 668 (hull). See also *Thomson* v *Weems* (1884) 9 App Cas 671, 682 *per* Lord Blackburn (life). MIA, section 84(1). See also discussion of Lord Mansfield's statement in *Kansas City College of Osteopathic Medicine* v *Employers Surplus Lines Ins Co* (below, note 211).

199. *Stevenson* v *Snow* (1761) 3 Burr 1237, 1240 *per* Lord Mansfield CJ (hull).

200. *New York Life Insurance Co* v *Talley*, 72 F 2d 715 (8 Cir, 1934—life). But when the contract contains a waiver of premium clause in case of disability, and a disabled insured has paid premium by mistake, these have sometimes been treated as voluntary premiums and irrecoverable: *Columbia National Life Ins Co* v *Goldberg*, 158 F 2d 971 (6 Cir, 1947—life), cert den 331 US 820.

201. *Talley* (above); *Kentucky Home Mutual Life Ins Co* v *Duling*, 190 F 2d 797 (6 Cir, 1951—life).

tract is rescinded for misrepresentation, it is avoided *ab initio* and the insured may recover premiums paid,[202] unless the contract provides otherwise (below). Premium is also recoverable, if the contract is not concluded, because agreement is never reached[203] or apparent agreement is void *ab initio* because of mistake[204] or because the transaction was *ultra vires* the insurance company.[205] Again, if the cover has commenced but an exception operates for an entire premium period, the insurer is off risk during that period and the premium for that period may be recovered.[206]

To this exception there is an exception. Although consideration from the insurer has failed, there is no return of premium, when there has been fraud[207] or illegality[208] on the part of the insured or his agents and, also perhaps, when he who pays premium assumes the risk that cover will commence.[209] Further, if the contract provides that in the event of misrepresentation or non-disclosure by the insured, whether fraudulent or not, the contract shall be avoided and the premiums forfeited, the courts will give effect to that provision.[210]

This kind of exception to recovery has been extended in the United States. In the *Osteopathic College* case[211] it was a condition of an agreement to finance an extension to the College that the College should obtain a surety bond. After several months of negotiation, the College reached a unique bond agreement with the defendant. After contract but before cover had begun, the College found a better finance deal (on different terms) and sought to cancel the bond and recover premium paid. One reason against recovery[212] was that, while Lord Mansfield's general rule (no risk no pre-

202. *Anderson v Fitzgerald* (1853) 4 HLC 484, 508 *per* Lord St Leonards (life); *Anderson v Thornton* (1853) 8 Ex 425 (cargo). MIA, section 84(3)(a). Likewise in cases of misrepresentation by the insurer: *Mutual Reserve Life Ins Co v Foster* (1904) 20 TLR 715 (HL—life); *Refuge Assurance Co Ltd v Kettlewell* [1909] AC 243 (life).
  As to whether the insured may initiate rescission in respect of his own misrepresentation in order to recover premiums, see below.

203. *Fowler v Scottish Equitable Life Assurance Sy* (1858) 28 LJ Ch 225 (life). *Forster v INA*, 139 F 2d 875 (2 Cir, 1944—cargo).

204. See ch 21.

205. For instances of this see Ivamy, p 216, note 5. Recent developments in the law relating to the powers of companies make such cases unlikely.

206. *Koplovitz v New York Life Ins Co*, 101 NYS 2d 745, 747 (1947—life).

207. *Anderson v Thornton* (1853) 8 Ex 425 (cargo). MIA, section 84(1) and (3)(*a*). Arnould, Nos 1329 ff. *Ray v United States*, 121 F 2d 416 (7 Cir, 1941—war risks); see further *Bavisotto v United States*, 18 F Supp 355 (WD NY, 1937—war risks) and cases cited.

208. See ch 24.

209. This is one view of early authority that, if an agent contracts insurance and pays premium for his principal without authority to do so and his act is not ratified by the principal, the agent may not recover premium. *Hagedorn v Oliverson* (1814) 2 M & S 485, 492 *per* Bayley J (hull): "I think the [agent] never could have recovered back the premium from the underwriter, because of the uncertainty whether [his principal] would adopt the assurance, in respect of which the underwriter would have incurred the risk." See also p 491 *per* Le Blanc J; and *Routh v Thompson* (1811) 13 East 274, 290 *per* Bayley J (hull).

210. For example, *Thomson v Weems* (1824) 9 App Cas 671 (life); *Broad & Montague Ltd v S E Lancashire Ins Co Ltd* (1931) 40 Ll L Rep 328 (motor).

211. *Kansas City College of Osteopathic Medicine v Employers Surplus Lines Ins Co*, 581 F 2d 299 (1 Cir, 1978).

212. The other reason was that consideration had not failed: although cover had not begun, there was little doubt that the College had received valuable consideration in so far as the bond had enabled the College to perform an essential condition of the first finance agreement. However, the College argued that insurance law was distinct from general contract law and, in particular, that insurance was governed quite literally by the rule of Lord Mansfield, "no *risk* no premium", whether the risk not having been run "was owing to the fault, pleasure, or will of the insured, or to any other cause": *Tyrie v Fletcher* (1777) 2 Cowp 666, 668 (hull) (emphasis added). The argument was rejected: the rule "no risk no premium" is a slogan for a rule of general law as most commonly applied to insurance contracts, the rule that, if consideration has totally failed, money paid may be recovered in an action for money had and received.

mium) had been adopted in the United States,[213] his indulgence of "the will and pleasure of the insured" had not; and that the College should

"not be able to compel a return of its full premium because its own wilful and self-interested act prevented the risk from attaching to a carefully bargained for contract. Despite the fact that this was an insurance transaction we do not believe it should be immunized from the increasingly recognized contract law principle of an implied contractual duty to co-operate and facilitate the performance of mutual promises".[214]

A general duty of co-operation is found in England[215] and, unless Lord Mansfield's *dictum* is applied literally, could be used to reach a similar decision there; but it should be noted that the Federal Court was not suggesting that "in all or even in most traditional insurance contexts, a self-interested decision which prevents the risk from running, in and of itself, must limit the rule requiring the return of premiums".[216] The court was influenced by the nature of the agreement, the parties' equality of bargaining power, and the transaction costs to the insurer of negotiating the agreement and obtaining reinsurance.

13–12D Overpayment

If by mistake the insured pays too much premium, he may recover the excess. For example, if liability insurance premium is calculated on the basis of the amount of wages paid in a certain period of time, any over payment for that period must be returned.[217]

---

213. Cases cited, p 302.
214. p 303; citations included Williston, *Contracts* (3rd ed) section 887 at pp 427–431. If the duty of co-operation is broken an action lies for damages: *Lovell* v *St Louis Mutual Life Ins Co*, 111 US 264 (1884—life), citing *United States* v *Behan*, 110 US 338 (1884).
215. *Southern Foundries (1926) Ltd* v *Shirlaw* [1940] AC 701. See below, ch 27.
216. pp 303–304.
217. In *DeBellis Enterprises Inc* v *Lumbermen's Mutual Casualty Co*, 390 A 2d 1171 (NJ 1978—fire) when a premium was paid on the basis of an interest greater than actually enjoyed by the insured, he could recover a proportionate part.
In *Commissioners of Leonardtown* v *Fidelity & Casualty Co*, 270 A 2d 788 (Md, 1970) premiums paid under a fidelity bond after the limit of the company's liability has been reached could be recovered. See also *New York Life Insurance Co* v *Talley*, 72 F 2d 715 (8 Cir, 1934—life); *Kentucky Home Mutual Life Ins Co* v *Duling*, 190 F 2d 707 (6 Cir, 1951—life).
In the case of multiple marine insurance giving rise to over-insurance, there may be a return of premium under the MIA, section 84(3)(*f*); see Arnould, No 408.

CHAPTER 14

THE INSURANCE CONTRACT: CONTENTS

14-1 THE CONTRACT, AND THE PAROL EVIDENCE RULE

This book is about insurance contracts, for which the law does not in general require any particular form (above, 11–2A1). Nonetheless, in most cases the contract is recorded in a document, which is usually called a policy. To construe the policy, the reader must first know whether the policy stands alone. When are the terms of the contract of insurance or the meaning of the terms in the policy found by evidence of party intention emanating from outside the policy? This is a question of evidence, not a question of construction, but it is a necessary precursor of any discussion of rules of construction.[1]

The answer begins with the parol evidence rule, in which "parol evidence" means not evidence by word of mouth but any evidence extrinsic to the document in question. The rule is that, if there is a document which looks like the whole of the contract, i.e., a document that contains all the terms of the kind one would expect in that kind of contract and which has a degree of formality that suggests the document is significant to those who made it, such as a policy of insurance, there is a presumption that that is the whole of their contract and evidence will not be admitted to add to, vary or contradict that document.[2]

The rule is commonly justified, first, as promoting certainty[3]; and, second, as a common sense inference about human intention: it reflects an assumption about how people normally think and behave.[4] Although my wife keeps addresses on scattered

---

1. Further, once the contents of the contract have been ascertained, there remains the possibility that one of the terms has been included by mistake, giving rise to an action to rectify the document recording the contract: below, 14–3.

2. Generally, see *Mercantile Bank of Sydney* v *Taylor* [1893] AC 317 (surety); *Mercantile Agency Co Ltd* v *Flitwick Chalybeate Co* (1897) 14 TLR 90 (HL); *Jacobs* v *Batavia & General Plantation Trust* [1924] 1 Ch 287, affirmed [1924] 2 Ch 329. Wedderburn [1959] CLJ 58, 59–64; Treitel, pp 176 ff; Lewison, no 207.

3. In 1976 the Law Commission (WP No 70) recommended the abolition of the parol evidence rule, partly because the certainty the rule had once produced had been undermined by the uncertainty created by the exceptions to the rule. Ten years later, however, the Law Commission (Report No 154, Cmnd 9700) advised against legislative change: "it is not a rule of law which, correctly applied, could lead to evidence being unjustly excluded" (para 2.7).
The rule is applied in Canada: Waddams, 12 Can Bus L J 207 (1986). As for the USA, if the policy recites that it contains the entire contract of insurance, "nothing can be added to the contract as written, by construction or otherwise, except such terms as may be imposed upon the parties by operation of some valid and applicable law with reference to which the parties are deemed to have contracted"—*Pink* v *Georgia States Inc*, 35 F Supp 437, 444 (MD Ga, 1940—motor); for example *Port of Portland* v *Water Quality Ins Syndicate*, 549 F Supp 233 (D Or, 1982—liability). Appleman, sections 1233 ff; Rest 2d Contracts, sections 209 ff; Williston, sections 573 ff.

4. *Davies* v *National Fire & Marine Ins Co* [1891] AC 485, 496–497 *per* Lord Hobhouse (PC—cargo). Law Commission Report No 154 (Cmnd 9700), para 2.13.

scraps of paper, most people gather them in one special place; equally, most people keep any formal record of important mutual promises in one place rather than six.

An insurance policy is a paradigm of a formal document to which the parol evidence rule has been applied,[5] mainly, it has been thought, in the interests of the insured. In *Weston* v *Ames*[6] the insurer pleaded that cover was subject to a limit not recorded in the policy. The Court of Common Pleas accepted the contention of counsel that to admit such evidence would place a merchant in a dangerous situation,

"for his only knowledge of the terms of the contract of assurance is derived from the policy which is put into his hands: if that, which persuades him he is secure, because it purports to cover his risk, can be explained away by parol testimony, he lies wholly at the mercy of the broker."

The corresponding danger to the insurer is small. The policy is his and, if his agent exceeds his mandate, any allegation by the insured of terms collateral to the policy (or cover note) usually fails for want of authority on the part of the agent who might have agreed the term.[7]

Such is the significance of the policy, that the rule has been applied to exclude evidence found in cover notes[8] and in *Youell* v *Bland Welch & Co Ltd*,[9] Phillips J refused to look at a Lloyd's slip in order to resolve an ambiguity in the policy based on the slip. Although he accepted that "the Court should know the commercial purpose of the contract and this in turn presupposes knowledge of the genesis of the transaction, the background, the context",[10] and that "the writing of the slip was part of the factual matrix out of which the policy evolved", the "drafting of the slip formed no part of the relevant matrix in this case. That matrix was the background to the commercial adventure that formed the subject matter of the contract, not the mechanism by which the parties set about negotiating and reaching agreement".[11] The judge refused to consider the slip for the following reasons.

The first reason was a fear of opening floodgates. If "prior written agreements or drafts were admitted in evidence as an aid to construction the result would be that the Courts would often be called upon to consider a profusion of documents in cases where there was an issue as to the true construction of the final version of the contract".[12] Second, the slip is unlikely to assist the court. "An insurance slip customarily sets out a shorthand version of the contract of insurance, in terms which may be neither clear nor complete."[13] Third, the slip may not be definitive.

"Where, as here, the slip provides for the formal wording to be agreed by the leading under-

---

5. *Burges* v *Wickham* (1863) 3 B & S 669, 696 *per* Blackburn J (hull); *Reliance Marine Ins Co* v *Duder* [1913] 1 KB 265, 273 *per* Kennedy LJ (CA—re); *Marine Ins Co Ltd* v *Duder* (1944) 77 Ll L Rep 224, 234–235 *per* Atkinson J (re). *Carpenter* v *Providence Washington Ins Co*, 16 Pet 495, 510 *per* Story J (USA Sup Ct, 1842—fire).
6. (1808) 1 Taunt 115 (cargo). See also *Anglo-Californian Bank Ltd* v *London & Provincial Marine & General Ins Co Ltd* (1904) 10 Com Cas 1 (solvency); *Horncastle* v *Equitable Life Assurance Sy* (1906) 22 TLR 735 (CA—life); *British Equitable Assurance Co Ltd* v *Baily* [1906] AC 35 (life).
7. For example *Levy* v *Scottish Employers' Ins Co* (1901) 17 TLR 229 (PA). But see above, 8–3C.
8. *Levy* (above).
9. [1990] 2 Lloyd's Rep 423 (re), affirmed [1992] 2 Lloyd's Rep. 127 (CA); applied in *St Paul Fire & Marine Ins Co (UK) Ltd* v *McConnel Dowell Contractors Ltd* (Commercial Court, 14 May 1993).
10. p 427, citing *The Diana Prosperity* [1976] 2 Lloyd's Rep 620, 624 *per* Lord Wilberforce (HL). On this question, see also 15–3B(a).
11. p 428.
12. *Ibid*. Cf renewal: the court might consider the contract renewed: *Balfour* v *Beaumont* [1982] 2 Lloyd's Rep 493; affirmed [1984] 1 Lloyd's Rep 272 (CA—re).
13. p 429.

writer, the other subscribers to the risk anticipate and agree that the leading underwriter will, on their behalf, agree the final wording that will spell out their rights and obligations. If differences between the wording of the slip and that of the formal contract which is embodied in the policy give rise to the possibility that the natural meaning of the slip differs from that of the policy, the natural assumption is and should be that the wording of the policy has been designed the better to reflect the agreement between the parties. To refer to the slip as an aid to the construction of the policy runs counter to one of the objects of replacing the slip with the policy."[14]

Still, statements, notably statements by the insured, which are excluded by the parol evidence rule, may have legal consequences. First, if the statement was intended by the parties to be in the contract, the policy may be rectified to include it: below, 14-3. Second, if untrue, the statement may give the other party a remedy for misrepresentation: below, chapter 22.

14–2 EXCEPTIONS TO THE PAROL EVIDENCE RULE

The presumption that the policy is complete is rebuttable,[15] and hence parol evidence will be admitted in the following circumstances; these are the so-called exceptions to the parol evidence rule.

14–2A No Contract

The presumption that the document records the whole of the contract of insurance rests on the premise that there is a valid contract which the policy records; this premise can be attacked by parol evidence. So, parol evidence will be heard in support of the contention that (a) no binding contract was intended,[16] or (b) the contract is voidable,[17] or (c) the contract is void.[18]

If, for example, an agent misrepresents the cash value of a life policy in contradiction of the terms of the policy,[19] it is open to the insured to bring evidence of what was said by the agent in order to avoid the policy on the ground of misrepresentation.[20]

A small but difficult extension of this exception is to allow parol evidence of party agreement that the policy should not come into force until a condition has been satisfied. It is difficult because, if their agreement takes the form of a suspensive condition, there is a contract and the parol condition is a term of that contract inconsistent with the terms of the policy; admission of evidence of this (contradictory) term is difficult to justify. Admission is easier to justify in principle, however, if the term is not a condition suspending an existing contract but a condition precedent to (the very existence

---

14. *Ibid*. Also in this sense *Prenn* v *Simonds* [1971] 1 WLR 1381, 1384 *per* Lord Wilberforce (HL).

15. *Cf* MIA, section 22, whereby a contract of marine insurance must be embodied in a policy which complies with the Act.

16. This is unlikely if an insurance policy has been issued; see in relation to contracts of sale *Haryanto* v *Man (Sugar) Ltd* [1986] 2 Lloyd's Rep 44, 59 *per* Lloyd LJ (CA).

17. *Morris* v *Baron & Co* [1918] AC 1. *Investors Preferred Life Ins Co* v *Abraham*, 375 F 2d 291 (10 Cir, 1967); *Rempel* v *Nationwide Life Ins Co*, 323 A 2d 193 (Pa, 1974—life), affirmed 370 A 2d 366 (1977).

18. *Bank of Australia* v *Palmer* [1897] AC 540. *Carpenter* v *Providence Washington Ins Co*, 16 Pet 495, 510 *per* Story J (USA Sup Ct, 1842—fire).

19. *Horncastle* v *Equitable Life Assurance Sy* (1906) 22 TLR 735 (CA); *British Equitable Assurance Co Ltd* v *Baily* [1906] AC 34. *Aliter* if the proposer reasonably relies on the advice: see above, 8–3C.

20. *Baily* (above) p 41 *per* Lord Lindley (life). See ch 22.

of) a contract which, *ex hypothesi*, does not yet exist: the condition is "outside the contract altogether"[21] and no question of contradiction of contract terms arises.

14–2B Special Meaning

Evidence is admissible to show that policy wording is used not in its ordinary sense but in a special sense, unless the policy expressly excludes extrinsic evidence of that kind.[22]

First, a word may be used in a technical sense. Important examples in insurance policies include "all risks" (below, 17–3) and "riot" (below, 19–3E), to which the insurance industry and consequently insurance law give a meaning which is not that of ordinary usage (below, 15–2B). In a similar spirit, the court admits evidence to explain the meaning of abbreviations or acronyms.[23]

Second, words will be given their local meaning.[24] In the United States this has been taken a stage further.

"In the process of interpretation of the terms of a contract the court can frequently get great assistance from the interpreting statements made by the parties themselves or from their conduct in rendering or in receiving performance under it. Parties can, by mutual agreement, make their own contracts; they can also, by mutual agreement, remake them. The process of practical interpretation and application, however, is not regarded by the parties as a remaking of the contract; nor do the courts so regard it. Instead, it is merely a further expression by the parties of the meaning that they give and have given to the terms of their contract previously made."[25]

This approach to contracts, called the rule of practical application, has been applied in the USA to the construction of insurance contracts,[26] usually in cases of ambiguity[27]: in general, the rule has not been used to contradict the terms of the contract. In England, however, once the contract is concluded "an impenetrable curtain comes down which totally obscures all subsequent events";[28] nor is the court bound to observe the parties' subsequent agreement on the meaning of a clause.[29] As a matter

---

21. *Anglo-Californian Bank Ltd* v *London & Provincial Marine & General Ins Co Ltd* (1904) 10 Com Cas 1, 12 *per* Walton J (solvency). See also *Wallis* v *Littell* (1861) 11 CB 369, 375 *per* Erle CJ; *Xenos* v *Wickham* (1866) LR 2 HL 296, 311–312 *per* Blackburn J (hull). Generally see *Pym* v *Campbell* (1856) 6 E & B 370.

22. *De Monchy* v *Phoenix Ins* (1929) 33 Com Cas 197 (cargo). For example "This policy shall constitute the entire contract between the parties"—*Commonwealth of Puerto Rico* v *Pan American Life Ins Co*, 307 F Supp 1065 (D Puerto Rico, 1969—life).

23. *American Airlines Inc* v *Hope* [1973] 1 Lloyd's Rep 233, 245 *per* Roskill LJ (CA—aviation: "tba L/U").

24. *Woodfall* v *Pearl Assurance Co Ltd* [1919] 1 KB 593, 602 *per* Bankes LJ (CA—PA): insured's statement of occupation construed "as understood in the district". See also *Pelly* v *Royal Exchange Assurance Co* (1757) 1 Burr 341, 350 *per* Lord Mansfield (hull); *Clift* v *Schwabe* (1846) 3 CB 437, 470 *per* Parke B (life); *Gibson* v *Small* (1853) 4 HLC 353, 397 *per* Parke B (hull); and *Smith* v *Wilson* (1832) 3 B & D 728 in which evidence was admitted to show that by local custom "1,000 rabbits" meant 1,200 rabbits. Generally, see Arnould, Nos 64 ff.

25. Corbin, section 558.

26. "Assuming that there is ambiguity in this contract, then the practical construction placed upon it by the parties is of controlling importance"—*Hawkeye Casualty Co* v *Rose*, 181 F 2d 157, 159 (8 Cir, 1950—motor). See also *New York Life Ins Co* v *Tolbert*, 55 F 2d 10 (10 Cir, 1932—life), cert den 285 US 551; *Rice Oil Co* v *Atlas Assurance Co Ltd*, 102 F 2d 561 (9 Cir, 1939—fire); *Great West Casualty Co* v *Truck Ins Exchange*, 358 F 2d 883 (10 Cir, 1966—motor).

27. *Randolph* v *Fireman's Fund Ins Co*, 124 NW 2d 528 (Iowa, 1963—liability).

28. *The Good Helmsman* [1981] 1 Lloyd's Rep 377, 416 *per* Watkins LJ (CA).

29. *The Insurance Co of Africa* v *Scor (UK) Reinsurance Co Ltd* [1985] 1 Lloyd's Rep 312, 319 *per* Stevenson LJ (CA—re).

of construction of contracts in general,[30] or insurance contracts in particular,[31] English courts have refused to refer to the conduct of the parties subsequent to the making of the contract. However, the courts do consider conduct amounting to estoppel, and a result not unlike that of the American rule of practical application (or even variation of the contract) can come about through estoppel by convention[32]: if the parties act as if chalk means cheese, they may be estopped from asserting that it is not.

Third, evidence of trade or other usage will be admitted[33] to add to the contract although not to contradict it.[34] The custom must be so well known and acquiesced in that everyone making a contract in that situation can reasonably be presumed to have imported that term into the contract[35]; if so, a person may be bound by the custom, although in fact ignorant of it.[36]

An example arises when the policy covers certain kinds of activity by the insured: the normal inference is that "the words of the policy are intended to be construed so as to conform to the usual and ordinary method of pursuing the adventure"[37] and, if necessary, evidence will be heard about what that method is. But the scope of cover will not be extended to cover a customary practice which occurs only on a contingency, which the parties to the contract of insurance have not foreseen.[38] Again, when a term of the contract of insurance has been broken, a court may be called to decide whether that breach is sufficiently serious or of a nature to terminate cover. Initially, the court must seek the intention of the parties as expressed in the policy: is it a breach of warranty? If the policy is not clear, "regard must be had to the surrounding circumstances . . . [and] this means having regard to the nature of the transaction and the known course of business".[39]

14–2C Contrary Intention: Collateral Terms

As the parol evidence rule is based on a presumption about party intention, it may be rebutted by evidence of contrary intention of what have been called "collateral

---

30. *James Miller & Partners Ltd* v *Whitworth Street Estates (Manchester) Ltd* [1970] AC 583; *Wickman Ltd* v *Schuler AG* [1974] AC 235.

31. *Union Ins Sy of Canton Ltd* v *Wills & Co* [1916] 1 AC 281, 288 *per* Lord Parmoor (PC—cargo). *AIU Ins Corp* v *FMC Corp*, 274 Cal Rptr 820, 832 (Cal, 1990—liability), as regards views expressed in litigation unconnected with the instant case and subsequent to the formation of the contract.

32. *Amalgamated Investment & Property Ltd* v *Texas Commerce International Bank Ltd* [1982] QB 84 (CA); *The Vistafjord* [1988] 2 Lloyd's Rep 343 (CA). Treitel, pp 111 ff. As to the doctrine of "practical application" or "practical construction", see, for example, *Continental Casualty Co* v *Rapid-American Corp*, 609 NE 2d 506, 511 (NY, 1993—liability).

33. *Robertson* v *French* (1803) 4 East 130, 135 (marine); see also *Hart* v *Standard Marine Ins Co* (1889) 22 QBD 499, 502–503 *per* Bowen LJ (CA—hull).

34. *Blackett* v *Royal Exchange Assurance Co* (1832) 2 C & J 244, 249–250 *per* Lord Lyndhurst CB (hull): "usage may be admissible to explain what is doubtful, it is never admissible to contradict what is plain." See also *Hall* v *Janson* (1855) 4 E & B 500, 509–510 *per* Lord Campbell CJ (freight); *Beacon Life & Fire Assurance Co* v *Gibb* (1862) 1 Moore 73, 97 *per* Lord Chelmsford. *Con-Stan Industries Pty Ltd* v *Norwich Winterthur Ins (Australia) Ltd* (1986) 160 CLR 226, 236–238 (HCA—transit). *Nance* v *United States*, 430 F 2d 662 (9 Cir, 1970—life); *Eagle-Picher Industries Inc* v *Liberty Mutual Ins Co*, 682 F 2d 13, 17 (1 Cir, 1982—liability).

35. *Con-Stan* (above), *loc cit.*

36. *Ibid.*

37. *Pearson* v *Commercial Union Assurance Co* (1876) 1 App Cas 498, 508 *per* Lord Penzance (fire).

38. *Pearson* (above), pp 505–506 *per* Lord Chelmsford: The House of Lords held that a fire policy on a ship while it was lying at a named place and taken to a drydock did not extend to the time when it was lying in the river having paddles removed as customary, for that was an unexpected operation.

39. *Yorkshire Ins Co Ltd* v *Campbell* [1917] AC 218, 225 *per* Lord Sumner (PC—cargo).

terms".[40] Such evidence will not readily be admitted, lest the rule itself becomes the exception. Much depends on the force of the appearance of the document[41]: in the case of insurance policies the appearance of completeness and finality may be marked and the admission of contrary evidence correspondingly rare.

Collateral terms are added to other contracts when the formal contract is in standard form and it is impossible or inconvenient to write in the collateral term at the time the standard form of contract was used.[42] Circumstances like this are not found in normal insurance practice. However, the exception may be when the scope of a policy is extended during its currency and thus after the policy (plus schedules etc) has been agreed, and a loss occurs within the scope of the extension but not of the original cover, before an amended schedule had been drawn up and sent to the insured: evidence would be admitted of the extension agreement.[43] Another exception is when the printed terms of documents less important than the policy, such as a proposal form, are overridden by the express statements made by the agent of the insurer.[44]

14–2D Collateral Documents

The existence of a policy will not prevent reference to other documents, such as riders[45] or indorsements,[46] attached to the policy itself. One suggestion,[47] however, is that indorsements on the back of the policy are not part of the contract, unless expressly referred to in the body of the policy.

Further, the court will refer to the proposal form,[48] or any other document,[49] if

40. *Gillespie Bros & Co* v *Cheney, Eggar & Co* [1896] 2 QB 59, 62 *per* Lord Russell CJ. See Wedderburn, *loc cit* (above, note 2).

41. Treitel, p 177.

42. The *Stoomvaart* case (1920) 122 LT 295 (HL—hull). This might explain the decision in *Rozanes* v *Bowen* (1928) 32 Ll L Rep 98 (CA—jewellery) that statements in the proposal form were part of the contract, even though the policy did not expressly incorporate them. In the general law see, for example, *De Lassalle* v *Guildford* [1901] 2 KB 215 (CA); *Evans & Son (Portsmouth) Ltd* v *Merzario Ltd* [1976] 1 WLR 1078 (CA); *Brikom Investments Ltd* v *Carr* [1979] QB 467 (CA). Sometimes the courts have avoided this kind of analysis but achieved the same result by finding a collateral contract, for example, *City & Westminster Properties (1934) Ltd* v *Mudd* [1959] 1 Ch 129. *Cf Moss* v *Norwich & London Ins Assn* (1922) 10 Ll L Rep 395 (CA—employers' liability) which is sometimes seen as a case of collateral term, but which is perhaps better seen as a case of ambiguity.

43. *Smith* v *Eagle Star & British Dominions Ins Co Ltd* (1934) 47 Ll L Rep 88 (employers' liability).

44. *Ellingwood* v *NN Investors Life Ins Co*, 805 P 2d 70, (NM, 1991—life). In England, see *Mendelssohn* v *Normand Ltd* [1970] 1 QB 177 (CA). Generally, see above, 8–3C.

45. *Aetna Ins Co* v *Houston Oil & Transport Co*, 49 F 2d 121 (5 Cir, 1931—hull), cert den 284 US 628.

46. *Heath* v *Durant* (1844) 12 M & W 438 (cargo); *Stoomvaart* case (1920) 122 LT 295 (HL—hull). *Littrall* v *Indemnity Ins Co*, 300 F 2d 340 (7 Cir, 1962—liability), cert den 370 US 919; *Perth Amboy Drydock Co* v *New Jersey Manufacturers' Ins Co*, 270 NYS 2d 819 (1966—employers' liability).

47. In England case support for this is thin. It can be inferred from a statement of Best CJ in *Everett* v *Desborough* (1829) 5 Bing 503, 517 (life). It finds some support in the general law: *Ryan* v *Oceanic SN Co Ltd* [1914] 3 KB 731, 747-748 *per* Vaughan Williams LJ (CA); *Roe* v *Naylor Ltd* [1917] 1 KB 712, 714–715 *per* Bailhache J. Clarke [1976] CLJ 51, 77.

In the USA there is support in *The Majestic*, 166 US 375 (1897). Also, in *Pink* v *Georgia Stages Inc*, 35 F Supp 437 (D Ga, 1940—motor) terms on the back of the policy were held not part of the contract, in the absence of a reference to those terms in the body of the policy, or signature on the back; *idem Ehrke* v *N American Life & Casualty Co*, 24 NW 2d 640 (SD, 1946—health). In *Lewis* v *Fidelity & Casualty Co*, 24 Cal Rptr 388 (Cal, 1962—motor) the court disregarded terms adverse to the insured printed on the policy in a corner box. Appleman, section 7526; Williston, sections 90B and 900.

48. *Salvin* v *James* (1805) 6 East 571 (fire); *Re George and Goldsmiths' & General Ins Burglary Ins Assn* [1899] 1 QB 595 (CA—burglary); *Yorkshire Ins Co* v *Campbell* [1917] AC 218, 222 ff *per* Lord Sumner (cargo).

49. *Worsley* v *Wood* (1796) 6 TR 710 (fire); *Newcastle Fire Ins Co* v *Macmorran & Co* (1815) 3 Dow 255 (HL—fire). *Iowa Life Ins Co* v *Lewis*, 187 US 335 (1902—life); *LaFavor* v *American National Ins Co*, 155

expressly referred to and incorporated by the policy itself. As to the mode of reference, mere recital in the policy of the existence of other documents is insufficient to incorporate them[50]: there must be words of incorporation, such as a statement in the policy that the proposal shall be the basis of the contract.[51] Consequently, prospectuses and similar promotional literature, including summaries of cover, are not normally part of the contract of insurance,[52] although they are not without importance, as they may be used to construe the policy in accordance with the reasonable expectations of the insured[53] or be the basis of argument based on misrepresentation.

When the document in question is the articles of association of the insurance company, it has been held that the insured will be automatically bound by subsequent changes in the articles incorporated into his policy, if the policy purports to be subject to later amendments to the articles. Relevant articles have concerned the duty of a shipowner, member of a mutual insurance association, to keep part of his ship uninsured[54]; and the right of policyholders participating in the profits of the insurance company to a distribution of profits without deduction.[55] It may be doubted whether an insured will be bound by later alterations in the articles which reduce the normal benefits of the insured under a life insurance contract.[56] Further, whatever the insurance, courts today are likely to require that the insured be given good notice of any change.[57]

14–2E Implied Terms

Terms not part of the contract will be implied by law[58]; some are mandatory but those affecting insurance contracts are not. Non-mandatory terms, which might otherwise be implied, can be excluded from the contract expressly or implicity, if they are inconsistent with express terms.[59] Implied terms are usually classified according to their source. The first source is custom, notably, trade usage (above, 14–2B). The second is

NW 2d 286 (Minn, 1967—health). *Cf Bryant* v *Standard Life & Accident Ins Co*, 348 F 2d 649 (5 Cir, 1965—life).

50. *Wheelton* v *Hardisty* (1857) 8 El & Bl 232 (life). *Cf South Staffordshire Tramway Co* v *Sickness & Accident Assurance Assn* [1891] 1 QB 402 (CA—liability). *Cf* also *Salvin* v *James* (1805) 6 East 571, 580 (fire): Lord Ellenborough CJ took account of an advertisement published by the insurer to clarify the terms of the policy.

51. See below, ch 20.

52. *Grieb* v *Equitable Life Assurance Sy*, 189 F 498 (ED Pa, 1911—life); *Blos* v *Bankers Life Co*, 283 P 2d 744 (Cal, 1955—life); *Commercial Credit Equipment Corp* v *Evans*, 302 So 2d 727 (La, 1974—debt insurance).

53. For example in *Dubosz* v *State Farm Fire & Casualty Co*, 458 NE 2d 611 (Ill, 1983) a pictorial representation of water damage cover prevailed over more limited policy terms. See also *INA Life Ins Co* v *Brundin*, 533 P 2d 236 (Alaska, 1975—PA); *Weinberg* v *INA*, 388 NYS 2d 69 (1976—PA); *Sparks* v *Republic National Life Ins Co*, 647 P 2d 1127 (Ariz, 1982—health). See further below, 15–5B.

54. *Muirhead* v *Forth & North Sea SS Mutual Ins Assn* [1893] AC 72 (P & I).

55. *British Equitable Assurance Co Ltd* v *Baily* [1906] AC 35. *Lloyd* v *Supreme Lodge Knights of Pythias*, 98 F 66 (7 Cir, 1899—life).

56. *Knights Templars' & Masons' Life Indemnity Co* v *Jarman*, 104 F 638 (8 Cir, 1900—life); *Wells* v *Metropolitan Life Ins Co*, 13 NYS 2d 22 (1939—life); *Bloom* v *North Pacific Beneficial Assn*, 193 NW 2d 244 (ND, 1971—health).

57. *Burnett* v *Westminster Bank Ltd* [1966] 1 QB 742 (CA). *American Life & Accident Ins Co* v *Clarke*, 407 SW 2d 433 (Ky, 1966—life).

58. *Gibson* v *Small* (1853) 4 HLC 353.

59. *Fowkes* v *Manchester & London Life Assurance Assn* (1863) 3 B & S 917, 930 *per* Blackburn J (life); *Anglo-Californian Bank Ltd* v *London & Provincial Marine Ins Co Ltd* (1904) 10 Com Cas 1, 12 *per* Walton J (solvency guarantee).

statute, in England a source irrelevant[60] to insurance contracts other than marine insurance contracts.[61] The third source is party intention: the implication of matters too obvious to be stated in the written contract. The third source is sub-divided[62] into those which are truly based on party intention, and hence unlikely to be found in contracts of insurance, and those that are really the work of the court, applying rules of judge-made law in the guise of party intention, when such terms are necessary to give business efficacy to the contract of insurance.[63] In so far as this third source provides judge-made rules of law, they are outside the scope of the parol evidence rule[64]; in so far as they are truly based on party intention, they can be seen as exceptions to the parol evidence rule.

Examples include an implied term that the subject-matter of the insurance exists[65]; that, when the insured has a duty to the insurer to preserve any claims against a third party, to which the insurer might be subrogated, the cost of preservation should be borne by the insurer[66]; and in the case of mutual insurance, that the policy shall be subject to the rules of the mutual insurance association, in so far as they are consistent with the policy.[67]

14–2F Ambiguity

Evidence will be admitted to explain words or phrases which are ambiguous.[68] In the past a distinction was drawn between patent ambiguity and latent ambiguity. "A patent ambiguity is such as exists or appears on the face of the writing itself, while a latent ambiguity arises when the writing upon its face appears clear and explicit but there is some collateral matter which makes the meaning uncertain".[69] At one time extrinsic evidence was admitted only in the case of patent ambiguity. However, more recently Lord Simon observed[70] that "the distinctions between patent ambiguities, latent ambiguities and equivocations as regards the admissibility of extrinsic evidence are based on outmoded and highly technical and artificial rules and introduce absurd refinements". So, even if the words of the document are perfectly clear, for example the description of the subject-matter of insurance, the courts have nonetheless admitted evidence of the surrounding facts to show that words superficially clear are in fact ambiguous. For example, viewed alone the description of the subject-matter of fire insurance as No 16 Highfield Avenue, London, might seem clear, until evidence was adduced that there were two such addresses in London.[71]

---

60. *Cf* Canada and USA where terms may be implied by state statute.
61. The MIA implies certain warranties: Arnould nos 705 ff.
62. For a more subtle division see G L Williams (1945) 61 LQR 385, 401.
63. *Yorkshire Ins Co Ltd* v *Nisbet Shipping Co Ltd* [1962] 2 QB 330, 340 *per* Diplock J (hull). Generally see *The Moorcock* (1889) 14 PD 64; *Liverpool CC* v *Irwin* [1977] AC 239. Phang [1993] JBL 242.
64. For example, one view of the duty of good faith is that it rests on an implied term: see below, 23–1A.
65. The parties may contract out of this in a policy on property "lost or not lost": *Yorkshire Ins Co Ltd* v *Nisbet Shipping Co Ltd* [1962] 2 QB 330 (hull).
66. *The Mammoth Pine* [1986] 3 All ER 767 (PC—cargo).
67. For cases in the United States to this effect see 44 CJS, section 303.
68. On the meaning of ambiguity see further, below, 15–5.
69. *Western Casualty & Surety Co* v *Harris Petroleum Co*, 220 F Supp 952, 954 (SD Cal, 1963—motor).
70. *Schuler AG* v *Wickman Machine Tool Sales Ltd* [1974] AC 235, 268. Any distinction between latent and patent ambiguities was also disregarded in *Watcham* v *AG for the East Africa Protectorate* [1919] AC 533 (PC).
71. *Hordern* v *Commercial Union Ins Co* (1887) 56 LJPC 78 (fire).

14-2G Rectification

The parol evidence rule is no bar to evidence that the policy does not accurately reflect the agreement of the parties.[72] However, rectification is not a true exception to the parol evidence rule: the deed is not added to, varied or contradicted, but corrected[73]; see below, 14-3.

14-3 RECTIFICATION

If the policy (or other document) does not accurately record the terms of the contract of insurance agreed by the parties, the court may rectify it to record their true agreement; general rules of law apply.[74] When exercising this discretionary remedy, which originated in equity, it is not the contract which is rectified but the document that records the contract.[75]

14-3A Proof: Onus and Form

"The Court requires the mistake to be proved with a high degree of conviction before granting relief. There are sound policy reasons for this. The Court is reluctant to allow a party of full capacity who has signed a document with opportunity of full inspection, to say afterwards that it is not what he meant. Otherwise, certainty and ready enforceability would be hindered by constant attempts to cloud the issue by reference to precontractual negotiations."[76] "The graver the character of the conduct involved, no doubt the heavier the burden of proof may be".[77] It is not, however, necessary to establish the mistake beyond reasonable doubt.[78]

72. *Barrow* v *Barrow* (1854) 18 Beav 529.
73. *Craddock Bros* v *Hunt* [1923] 2 Ch 136, 151 *per* Lord Sterndale, MR: "After rectification the written agreement does not continue to exist with a parol variation; it is to be read as if it had been originally drawn in its rectified form." USA *idem: Rempel* v *Nationwide Life Ins Co*, 370 A 2d 366, 371 (Pa, 1977—life).
74. *Schongalla* v *Hickey* 149 F 2d 687 (2 Cir, 1945—life), cert den 326 US 736; *Continental Ins Co* v *Cotten*, 427 F 2d 48 (9 Cir, 1970—fire). In the United States rectification is usually referred to as reformation; see Appleman, sections 7607 ff; Williston, section 1568.
75. *Mackenzie* v *Coulson* (1869) LR 8 Eq 369, 375 *per* Sir William James, V-C; *Rose (London) Ltd* v *Pim, Jnr & Co Ltd* [1953] 2 QB 450 (CA); *The Olympic Pride* [1980] 2 Lloyd's Rep 67, 72 *per* Mustill J. Generally see Halsbury, Vol 16, No 1235.
76. *The Olympic Pride* [1980] 2 Lloyd's Rep 67, 73 *per* Mustill J. See also *Beaumont* v *Bramley* (1822) Turn & R 41, 51 *per* Lord Eldon; *Fowler* v *Fowler* (1859) 4 De G & J 250, 264 *per* Lord Chelmsford, LC; *Spalding* v *Crocker* (1897) 13 TLR 396 (hull); *Pasquali & Co* v *Traders & General Ins Assn* (1921) 9 Ll L Rep 514, 515 *per* Rowlatt J (cargo); *Jocelyne* v *Nissen* [1970] 2 QB 86 (CA).
"The party seeking reformation of an instrument is required to prove his case by very strong, clear, and convincing evidence"—*American Employers Ins Co* v *St Paul Fire & Marine Ins Co Ltd* [1978] 1 Lloyd's Rep 417, 421 (ND W Va, 1977—P & I). See also *Columbian National Life Ins Co* v *Black*, 35 F 2d 571 (10 Cir, 1929—life); *Mutual of Omaha Ins Co* v *Russell*, 402 F 2d 339 (10 Cir, 1968—flight insurance), cert den 394 US 973; *Excess Life Assurance Co Ltd* v *Firemen's Ins Co* [1982] 2 Lloyd's Rep 599, 607–608 *per* Webster J, applying the law of New York (fidelity).
77. *Bates (Thomas) & Son Ltd* v *Wyndham's (Lingerie) Ltd* [1981] 1 All ER 1077, 1086 *per* Buckley LJ; see also p 1090 *per* Brightman LJ (CA).
78. *Earl* v *Hector Whaling Ltd* [1961] 1 Lloyd's Rep 459, 468 *per* Holroyd Pearce LJ (CA); *cf Beaumont* v *Bramley* (1822) Turn & R 41, 51 *per* Lord Eldon; *Gagnière & Co* v *Eastern Co* (1921) 8 Ll L Rep 365, 366 *per* Bankes LJ (CA—cargo).
USA: More than a mere preponderance of evidence is required: *Hanes* v *Roosevelt National Life Ins Co*, 452 NE 2d 357 (Ill, 1983—life). However, it has also been asserted that to establish mistakes in insurance policies less proof is required than in the case of other kinds of document: *Jewell* v *United Fire & Casualty Co*, 131 NW 2d 276, 280 (Wis, 1964—liability); *Johnson* v *United Investors' Life Assurance Co*, 263 NW 2d 770, 774 (Iowa, 1978—life). This view is accepted by Williston, section 1568B, p 434 and p 450.

The proof may take any form, including oral evidence,[79] but must be convincing. What is necessary is some outward expression of agreement that can be proved to the court. If the term in that agreement, in accordance with which rectification is sought, was tacit or implied, the clarity of proof that a court of equity requires is unlikely to be found: the court, concerned about certainty in business matters, will not rectify the policy to accord with "what it might be convinced they would have agreed had they known this or that".[80] Commonly, reference is made to documents preceding the policy, such as a slip,[81] proposal form,[82] or other document.[83]

14–3B Common Agreement

For rectification to be ordered, there must have been a prior common agreement in terms different from those recorded in the policy.[84] The prior agreement does not have to be legally binding,[85] but it must have been authorised by the principals concerned. If the insurer's agent and the insured agree terms that are more generous to the insured than the standard terms of the insurer embodied in the policy that is subsequently issued to the insured, there is no question of rectification unless the agent had authority,[86] actual or apparent, to make a contract of insurance on the terms agreed.[87]

Further, the prior common agreement, in accordance with which rectification is sought, must have been unchanged[88] between the time of the agreement and the issue

79. For example *Aetna Life Ins* v *Brodie* (1880) 5 SCR 1 (life), where the insurer seeking rectification was aided by the unlikely nature of the term (premium rate) in the policy, as it was "utterly unreasonable and absurd, and such as no sane business man would, in the ordinary course of business enter into" (p 18 *per* Ritchie CJ).
80. *Pasquali & Co* v *Traders' & General Ins Assn* (1921) 9 Ll L Rep 514, 515 *per* Rowlatt J: it was agreed to cover goods in the free port of Copenhagen and this was recorded in the policy; congestion in the port led to the goods being stored in a warehouse just outside the free port area. While it was certain that, had this contingency been known to the parties, they would have extended cover or, had they thought of it after the placement of the goods, altered the policy, they did neither. Rowlatt J declined to rectify the policy to cover the goods outside the free port.
81. For example *Letts* v *Excess Ins Co* (1916) 32 TLR 361 (PA); *Gagnière & Co* v *Eastern Co* (1921) 8 Ll L Rep 365 (CA—cargo); *Wilson, Holgate & Co Ltd* v *Lancashire & Cheshire Ins Corp Ltd* (1922) 13 Ll L Rep 486 (cargo); *Eagle Star & British Dominions Ins Co Ltd* v *Reiner* (1927) 27 Ll L Rep 173 (re).
82. For example *Collett* v *Morrison* (1851) 9 Hare 162 (life); *Griffiths* v *Fleming* [1909] 1 KB 805, 817 *per* Farwell LJ (CA—life); *Sun Life Assurance Co of Canada* v *Jervis* [1943] 2 All ER 425 (CA—life).
83. Such as (a) promotional material issued to induce people to contract the insurance: *British Equitable Assurance Co Ltd* v *Baily* [1906] AC 35, 41 *per* Lord Lindley (life); *Jervis* (above); or (b) the standard terms or regulations of the insurance company: *Solvency Mutual Guarantee Co* v *Freeman* (1861) 7 H & N 17, 24 *per* Bramwell B (guarantee); *Aetna Life Ins* v *Brodie* (1880) 5 SCR 1 (life); or (c) previous policies: *Rogers* v *Whittaker* [1917] 1 KB 942 (fire).
Particular difficulties of evidence may arise on renewal, when the insured seeks rectification on the terms of a previous policy but the insurer contends that the insured was given notice of a change (intended by the insurer) in the terms of cover. See above, 11–4E.
84. *Collett* v *Morrison* (1851) 9 Hare 162 (life); *Fowler* v *Scottish Equitable Life Assurance Sy* (1859) 28 LJ Ch 225 (life); *Letts* v *Excess Ins Co Ltd* (1916) 32 TLR 361 (PA); *Commercial Union Assurance Co PLC* v *Sun Alliance Ins Group PLC* [1992] 1 Lloyd's Rep 475 (re).
Columbian National Life Ins Co v *Black*, 35 F 2d 571 (10 Cir, 1929—life); *Ensedrch Corp* v *Shand, Morhan & Co.*, 952 F 2d 1484, 1503 (5 Cir, 1992—liability).
85. *Xenos* v *Wickham* (1866) LR 2 HL 296, 324 *per* Lord Cranworth (hull); *United States* v *Motor Trucks Ltd* [1924] AC 196, 200 *per* Lord Birkenhead (PC); *Jocelyne* v *Nissen* [1970] 2 QB 86 (CA); *The Olympic Pride* [1982] 2 Lloyd's Rep 67, 72 *per* Mustill J.
86. See ch 8.
87. For example, *Kelly-Dempsey & Co* v *Century Indemnity Co*, 77 F 2d 85 (10 Cir, 1935—liability).
88. *Crane* v *Hegeman-Harris Co Inc* [1939] 1 All ER 662, 664 *per* Simonds J; *Pindos Shipping Corp* v *Raven* [1983] 2 Lloyd's Rep 449, 452 *per* Bingham J (yacht).

of the policy, so that, when the policy is issued in terms differing from the prior agreement, it can be inferred that the issue of the policy in those terms was a mistake.

14–3C Mistake

For rectification to be ordered, here must have been a mistake in the policy. Distinguish the case in which the parties have recorded the right terms in the policy but those terms, identical in both policy and in prior agreement, were adopted for the wrong reasons,[89] such as a miscalculation of premium or a mistake about whether the cover was sufficient for the needs of the insured. The mistake must lie in the belief that the policy accurately records the prior agreement. The mistake may be either unilateral or common to both parties. If common, that "does not necessarily mean that it must arise in the same way on each side. Very often the mistake of one party occurs in the writing and of the other in the signing of the document, but the mistaken belief is common to both".[90]

14–3C1 Unilateral Mistake

A unilateral mistake arises when one party alone is mistaken and, in addition, the other party is aware that the first is mistaken. In the case of common mistake, the court is mending a document so that it accurately records the subjective agreement of the parties. In the case of unilateral mistake, this is not true and the nature of the remedy has changed. The key to unilateral mistake is an element of sharp practice by the party aware of the mistake and the basis appears to be a species of equitable estoppel[91]: the conduct of the defendant has been such as to make it inequitable that he should be allowed to object to the rectification of the document. There are four requirements[92]:

    (a) One party must have made a mistake about the terms of the policy—that it did or did not contain an agreed term.

    (b) The other party must have been aware of the mistake.[93] Such awareness may

---

89. *American Airlines Inc* v *Hope* [1974] 2 Lloyds Rep 301, 307 *per* Lord Diplock (HL—aviation). See also *Barrow* v *Barrow* (1854) 18 Beav 529; *Rose (London) Ltd* v *Pim Jnr & Co Ltd* [1953] 2 QB 450 (CA). *Cf Re Butlin's Settlement Trusts* [1976] Ch 251, 260 *per* Brightman J. *Hayes* v *Travelers Ins Co*, 93 F 2d 568 (10 Cir, 1937—life); *Aetna Ins Co* v *Paddock*, 301 F 2d 807 (5 Cir, 1962—AR installation floater).

90. *The Olympic Pride* [1980] 2 Lloyd's Rep 67, 72 *per* Mustill J. *Aetna Casualty & Surety Co* v *Crawford*, 370 F 2d 917 (5 Cir, 1967—export credit insurance).

91. Snell, *Principles of Equity* (25th ed, 1960), p 569, adopted in *Roberts & Co Ltd* v *Leicestershire County Council* [1961] Ch 555, 570 *per* Pennycuick J. See also *Bates (Thomas) & Son Ltd* v *Wyndham's (Lingerie) Ltd* [1981] 1 All ER 1077, 1085–1086 *per* Buckley LJ, 1090 *per* Eveleigh LJ (CA); *The Nai Genova* [1984] 1 Lloyd's Rep 353, 364–365 *per* Slade LJ (CA). Cartwright, 103 LQR 594, 618 (1987); Megarry, 77 LQR 313, 315 (1961).

92. *Bates* (above) p 1086 *per* Buckley LJ, with whom Brightman LJ (p 1090) concurred (CA). See also *Roberts* (above); *Riverlate Properties Ltd* v *Paul* [1975] Ch 133, 140 *per* Russell LJ (CA); *The Olympic Pride* [1980] 2 Lloyd's Rep 67, 72 *per* Mustill J; *The Nai Genova* [1984] 1 Lloyd's Rep 353, 359–360 *per* Slade LJ (CA).

93. It was said in *Bates* (above), p 1086 by Buckley LJ that the document did not accurately record the agreement "by reason" of the plaintiff's mistake, as if the inaccuracy in the document must in some sense have been caused by the plaintiff's error. This element is not found in the decisions relied upon by Buckley LJ (*Roberts* and *Riverlate*) and it is difficult to see why the result should differ according to whether, for example, the typist, who made the error in the document, was employed and supervised by the plaintiff or by the defendant. Probably "by reason of" the plaintiff's mistake means no more than that the document would not have been adopted, if the plaintiff had observed the discrepancy between the document and the prior agreement.

be attributed to the insurer through the knowledge of his agent.[94] When, however, one party is mistaken and the other is not mistaken but is unaware of the first party's mistake, the parties being at cross purposes, rectification will not be ordered.[95]

    (c) The other party must have omitted to draw the mistake to the notice of the party mistaken.

    (d) The mistake must have been calculated to benefit the party who was aware of it.[96] Requirement (d) is necessary in the view of some judges to show the element of sharp practice which justifies intervention.[97]

14–3D Defences

As an equitable remedy, rectification is subject to some of the bars to equitable relief.

    (a) A person loses the right to rectification if, with knowledge of the mistake, he affirms the contract in a way inconsistent with the subsequent exercise of that right. If the insured, for example, having discovered the error in the policy, nonetheless seeks to enforce the contract of insurance, without first or concurrently[98] seeking to have the policy rectified, he loses the right to rectification.[99] The same has been said of the insurer who, in similar circumstances, issues and sends a policy to the insured.[100]

    It is not entirely clear whether there may be affirmation in ignorance of the error in the policy. For affirmation to bar an equitable remedy, notably rescission, knowledge of the facts giving rise to the remedy is usually required. As regards rectification the rule is probably the same.[101] It might be argued that, if the party should have known the truth, he may be taken to have known and to have affirmed; see also lapse of time (below, (b)). In England, constructive knowledge of the right to rescind has not been enough to bar rescission[102] and it would be odd if that were otherwise with rectification. However, the real and more specific issue is whether, on receipt of

94. *Raymond* v *Zeringue*, 422 So 2d 534 (La, 1982—motor).

95. *Stanton & Stanton Ltd* v *Starr* (1920) 3 Ll L Rep 259 (burglary); *Riverlate* (above).

"Where the minds of the parties have not met there is no contract, and hence none to be rectified"— *Hearne* v *New England Mutual Marine Ins Co*, 20 Wall 488, 490 (1874—hull); *Electro Battery Mfg Co* v *Commercial Union Ins Co*, 762 F Supp 844 (ED Mo, 1991 – motor).

96. *Cf* Eveleigh LJ in *Bates* (above), p 1090, who thought it sufficient to satisfy requirement (d) that "the inaccuracy of the instrument as drafted would be detrimental to the other party, and this may not always mean that it is beneficial to the one who knew of the mistake".

97. *Bates* (above, note 81), p 1086 *per* Buckley LJ. See also *The Nai Genova* [1984] 1 Lloyd's Rep 353, 361–362 *per* Slade LJ (CA). *Columbian National Life Ins Co* v *Black*, 35 F 2d 571 (10 Cir, 1929—life); *Preferred Accident Ins Co* v *Onali*, 43 F Supp 227, 231 (D Minn, 1942—motor), affirmed 125 F 2d 580 (8 Cir, 1942); *Rolane Sportswear Inc* v *United States Fidelity & Guarantee Co*, 407 F 2d 1091, 1096 (6 Cir, 1969— fire). A failure to explain to the proposer the legal effect of a term in the contract is not sharp practice of the kind required to justify rectification: *Harlach* v *Metro Property & Liability*, 602 A 2d 1007 (Conn, 1992— motor).

98. At one time it was thought that the plaintiff could not seek both rectification and specific performance of an agreement in the same proceedings. This view has been rejected: *Craddock Bros* v *Hunt* [1923] 2 Ch 136 (CA).

99. *Dawsons Ltd* v *Bonnin* [1922] 2 AC 413, 431–432 *per* Viscount Cave (motor); *Roberts* v *Anglo-Saxon Ins Assn Ltd* (1927) 137 LT 243, 246 *per* Scrutton LJ (CA—motor).

100. *Xenos* v *Wickham* (1866) LR 2 HL 296, 324 *per* Lord Cranworth (hull).

101. *Rider* v *State Farm Mutual Automobile Ins Co*, 513 F 2d 780 (10 Cir, 1975—motor) requiring awareness of the defect in the policy before the right to rectification could be affected.

102. See below, 23–18B1.

the policy, the insured is to be expected to read the policy and discover the mistake. If the nature of the mistake is such, that no insured who read the policy would realise that there was a mistake, clearly he lacks the requisite knowledge. In most cases, perhaps, the mistake would be apparent. Older decisions suggest that in such cases, on receipt of his policy, the insured should have read it and found the error [103]; moreover, the balance of precedent is that the insured cannot object to a policy that contains terms he did not expect, unless he does so quite soon after receipt: above, 11–2A2. However, when the point is made against an insured who seeks an equitable remedy, equity is more indulgent of the insured. Negligence does not bar rescission by a representee who, but for his negligence, would have discovered the untruth of the representation.[104] The same is probably true of a person who, but for his negligence, would have discovered the mistake in the policy. In the United States, it has been said, "negligence is not in itself a defense, else there would be no ground for reformation for mistake, as mistakes nearly always presuppose negligence".[105]

Note also that, in the United States, the plea of mistake and the demand for rectification (reformation) of the policy are not barred by an incontestable clause in the policy. An action for reformation "is not a contest of the policy, but a prayer to make a written instrument speak the real agreement of the parties".[106]

(b) Lapse of time is sometimes raised as a bar to equitable remedies but the

---

103. *Foster* v *Mentor Life Assurance Co* (1854) 3 El & Bl 48, 76 *per* Coleridge J (life); *Mackenzie* v *Coulson* (1869) LR 8 Eq 368, 375 *per* James V-C (cargo). See further above, 11–2A2; and *Provident Savings Life Assurance Sy* v *Mowatt* (1902) 32 SCR 147, 155 *per* Taschereau J (life) in which the insured sought unsuccessfully to have the policy rectified seven years after its delivery.

104. *Redgrave* v *Hurd* (1881) 20 Ch D 1 (CA). Treitel, pp 301 ff. See below, 22–3D.

105. *Columbia National Ins Co* v *Black*, 35 F 2d 571, 575 (10 Cir, 1929 – life). See also *Hearne* v *Marine Ins Co*, 20 Wall 488 (1874—hull) in which the Supreme Court took the view that, if there was prior agreement, the insured was entitled to assume that his policy recorded that agreement accurately. Also *Liverpool & London & Globe Ins Co* v *Crosby*, 83 F 2d 647 (6 Cir, 1936—fire), cert den 299 US 587; *Kansas City Life Ins Co* v *Cox*, 104 F 2d 321 (6 Cir, 1939—life); *Schweitzer* v *American Casualty Co*, 226 NYS 2d 267 (1962— burglary); *Harbor Ins Co* v *Urban Construction Co*, 990 F 2d 195 (5 Cir, 1993—liability). This is especially so on renewal or the substitution of a mortgagee: *Connecticut Fire Ins Co* v *Oakley Improved Building & Loan Co*, 80 F 2d 717 (6 Cir, 1936—fire), cert den 298 US 687.

But, on the general point, cf *Fidelity & Guarantee Fire Corp* v *Bilquist*, 108 F 2d 713 (9 Cir, 1940—fire).

Further, some courts there have held that relief will be refused to a negligent plaintiff if (i) he has been grossly or culpably negligent: *Parker* v *Title & Trust Co*, 33 F 2d 505 (9 Cir, 1956—title insurance); *Jewell* v *United Fire & Casualty Co*, 131 NW 2d 276, 289 (Wis, 1964—liability); or (ii) the other party would be unfairly prejudiced by rectification: *Black* (above); *Kansas City Life Ins Co* v *Cox*, 104 F 2d 321 (6 Cir, 1939—life); *Preferred Accident Ins Co* v *Onali*, 43 F Supp 227, 233 (D Minn, 1942—motor).

106. *Black* p 577 (above). See also *Prudential Ins Co of America* v *Strickland*, 187 F 2d 67 (6 Cir, 1951— life); *Freestone* v *Prudential Ins Co of America*, 139 F Supp 665 (ND Iowa, 1956—life); *Mutual Life Ins Co of New York* v *Simon*, 151 F Supp 408 (SDNY, 1957—life).

Cf *Richardson* v *Travelers Ins Co*, 71 F 2d 699, 701 (9 Cir, 1948—life), where the insured relied successfully on the clause, to resist rectification after 20 years of a policy which gave him double the benefit intended. The court said: "the origin of the clause may be found in the competitive idea of offering to policyholders assurance that their dependents would be the recipients of a protective fund rather than a lawsuit . . . Logically the coverage of this clause should extend to [all] those defenses of the insurer which could be conceivably raised within the contractual period of contestability . . . If this seems harsh, it must be remembered that the insurer himself agreed not to raise these defenses as an inducement to prospective policyholders." The court may also have been influenced by the fact that the clerical error was made by the insurer's employees.

better view is that it is an aspect of affirmation.[107] The court in New York has concluded[108] that "mere delay has been recognised as insufficient to bar reformation". It is submitted that this is also the law of England.

(c) Equitable relief is barred if it is impossible to return the parties to the *status quo ante*. For example, if there is loss covered by the terms of the policy, the insurer cannot seek rectification in terms that exclude that loss. In one such case the court observed[109] that

"Had this suit been brought before the loss destroyed the hangar, . . . the company would have been in a position to offer a refund for the premiums, and the [insured] would have been able to contract with some other insurer for the protection of its building. At this time it is impossible to put the parties in *status quo ante*."

14–3E Consequences

The insurance contract is enforced on the terms originally agreed.[110] The insured may demand a policy in conformity with those terms.[111] It follows that the insured may also reject a policy document that does not conform with those terms. But a mistake in the policy for which the insurer is responsible does not entitle the insured to terminate the contract of insurance altogether, to refuse to accept a correct policy[112] or to refuse to pay the premium.[113]

---

107. See above, this section and below, 23–18B. Some courts have spoken of delay as a defence, but coupled with knowledge, hence a bar akin to affirmation: *Black* (above); *Rider* v *State Farm Mutual Automobile Ins Co*, 514 F 2d 780 (10 Cir, 1975—motor).

108. *Simon* (above) p 412: after eight years or even after 20 years, citing *Black* (above) and *Metropolitan Life Ins Co* v *Oseas*, 27 NYS 2d 65 (1941—life), affirmed 46 NE 2d 348 (1942). However, the court may be less sympathetic to an insurer: *Metropolitan Life Ins Co* v *Asofsky*, 38 F Supp 464, 466 (D NJ, 1941—life).

109. *Royal Ins Co Ltd* v *City of Morgantown*, 98 F Supp 609 (ND W Va, 1951—fire); see also *Rolane Sportswear Inc* v *United States Fidelity & Guarantee Co*, 407 F 2d 1091, 1096 (6 Cir, 1969—fire).

110. *Collett* v *Morrison* (1851) 9 Hare 162, 173 *per* Turner V-C (life), cited with approval by Farwell LJ in *Griffiths* v *Fleming* [1909] 1 KB 805, 817 (CA—life). *Canada Casualty & Boiler Ins Co* v *Hawthorne* (1907) 39 SCR 558, 565 *per* Davies J. Also *Black* (above).

111. *Pallison* v *Mills* (1828) 1 Dow & Cl 342, 361 *per* Lord Lyndhurst LC (HL—hull).

112. *General Accident Corp* v *Cronk* (1901) 17 TLR 233 (liability).

113. *Solvency Mutual Guarantee Co* v. *Freeman* (1861) 7 H & N 17, 24 *per* Bramwell B (guarantee); *Cronk* (above).

CHAPTER 15

THE INSURANCE CONTRACT: CONSTRUCTION[1]

15-1 INTENTION

Lord Ellenborough CJ[2]:

"[T]he same rule of construction which applies to all other instruments applies equally to this instrument of a policy of insurance, *viz*, that it is to be construed according to its sense and meaning, as collected from the terms used in it, which terms are themselves to be understood in their plain, ordinary and popular sense, unless they have generally in respect to the subject matter, as by the known usage of trade, or the like, acquired a peculiar sense distinct from the popular sense of the same words; or unless the context evidently points out that they must . . . be understood in some other special and peculiar sense."

This was said in 1803 but it remains broadly true today. In particular, insurance contracts are subject to the same rules of construction as other commercial documents,[3] and are thus construed with less meticulous attention to the actual words used than, for example, a specially drafted conveyance, unless, by the same token, the court is concerned with a clause in the policy, which is not in standard form but has been written by the parties.[4] It is this that has led to the suggestion that reinsurance contracts should be construed differently from other insurance contracts, i.e. those on standard

---

1. In the United States some (but not all) commentators draw a distinction between interpretation of contracts and construction of contracts: Rest Contracts 2d, para 200. In a leading article, 64 Colum L Rev 833, 833–835 (1964), Patterson said that "the process of interpretation often consists merely of the direct application of the symbols [contract words etc] used to the factual situation", whereas construction "is a process by which legal consequences are made to follow from the terms of the contract and its more or less immediate context, and from a legal policy or policies that are applicable to the situation." As illustrations of construction he gave the implication of terms when the contract was vague, construction *contra proferentem* in case of ambiguity, and court refusal to give literal application to an unconscionable term. In the courts, for example: "Construction of an insurance policy—the process of determining its legal effect—is a question of law for the court. Interpretation—the process of determining the meaning of words used—is also a question of law for the court unless it depends on extrinsic evidence or a choice among reasonable inferences to be drawn"—*McDonald Industries Inc v INA*, 475 NW 2d 607, 618 (Iowa 1991—liability). The distinction is also found in *Life Ins Co of Australia Ltd v Phillips* (1925) 36 CLR 60, 78 *per* Isaac J (HCA—life). However, it is not generally found in English courts today and is not followed in this book.
2. *Robertson* v *French* (1803) 4 East 130, 135 (marine).
3. *Smith* v *Accident Ins Co* (1870) LR 5 Ex 302, 307 *per* Martin B (life); *Hart* v *Standard Marine Ins Co* (1889) 22 QBD 499. 501 *per* Bowen LJ (CA—hull); *Yorkshire Dales SS Co Ltd* v *Minister of War Transport* [1942] AC 691, 713 *per* Lord Wright (hull). *Consolidated-Bathurst* v *Mutual Boiler* [1980] 1 SCR 888, 899 *per* Estey J. Brown & Menezes, No 6:4:3. *Liverpool & London* v *Kearney*, 180 US 132 (1901—fire); *Shepherd* v *Mutual Life Ins Co*, 63 F 2d 578 (8 Cir, 1933—life); *Kaun* v *Industrial Fire & Casualty Ins Co*, 436 NW 2d 321, 324 (Wis, 1989—motor). See further Appleman, section 7381 and cases cited; Lightstone, 23 Cal W L Rev 125, 128 ff (1987).
4. Arnould, No 83.

331

terms, as "reinsurance involves two sophisticated business entities", sophisticated in the very business of insurance, "who bargain at arm's length".[5]

This chapter takes a cautious view of construction in the United States. Scrutton LJ once said[6]: "I am not impressed by the fact that a different view has been taken by American courts on American policies. Those courts frequently differ from ours on the construction of mercantile documents. English courts construe documents by the light of English decisions." That was in 1919. Today the same is true: decisions can be found applying most of the rules found in England; however, for example, the development in many States of a rule that implements the reasonable expectations of the insured (below, 15–5B) has produced some decisions that are unlikely to influence an English court.[7]

Yet, in each country of common law the primary rule of construction of the contract of insurance is that construction must give effect to the intention of the parties.[8] In *Polpen Shipping Co Ltd v Commercial Union Ins Co Ltd*[9] Atkinson J said: "I am told that I have to give the words 'ship or vessel' their natural and ordinary meaning, but probably it would be more accurate to say that I must give them the meaning intended by the parties to this policy." In apparent contrast, in an earlier case Denman J said[10]: "The question, in this and other cases of construction of written instruments, is, not what was the intention of the parties, but what is the meaning of the words they have used." This, however, was because the only evidence of intention in that case lay in the words used. If it is a proper case for the admission of evidence extrinsic to the policy of party intention (above, 14–2), perhaps contrary to the primary meaning of the words used, intention is paramount. Subject to this, the courts presume that the words are used in their ordinary sense.[11]

5. Thomas, "Utmost Good Faith in Reinsurance: A Tradition in Need of Adjustment" 41 Duke LJ 1548, 1553 (1992).
6. *Re Hooley Hill Rubber & Chemical Co Ltd and Royal Ins Co* [1920] 1 KB 257, 272 (CA—fire).
7. On the law in the United States see Appleman, sections 7381 ff; Liedermann, "Insurance Coverage Disputes in the United States" [1986] LMCLQ 79.
8. *Tarleton v Staniforth* (1794) 5 TR 695, 699 *per* Lord Kenyon CJ (fire); *Want v Blunt* (1810) 12 East 183, 187 *per* Lord Ellenborough CJ (life); *Braunstein v Accidental Death Ins Co* (1861) 1 B & S 782, 799 *per* Blackburn J (PA); *M'Cowan v Baine & Johnson* [1891] AC 401, 403 *per* Lord Selborne (hull). *Bull v Sun Life Assurance Co*, 141 F 2d 456 (7 Cir, 1944—life); *Tennessee Corp v Hartford Accident & Indemnity Co*, 463 F 2d 548 (5 Cir, 1972—liability).
9. [1943] KB 161, 164 (hull). See also *Borradaile v Hunter* (1843) 5 Man & G 639, 653 *per* Maule J (life).
10. *Rickman v Carstairs* (1833) 5 B & Ad 651, 663 (marine), cited with approval by Lord Chelmsford in *Beacon Life & Fire Assurance Co v Gibb* (1862) 1 Moore (NS) 73, 97 (fire). See also *Drinkwater v Royal Exchange Assurance Corp* (1767) Wilm 282, 286–287 *per* Lord Wilmot CJ (fire); *Re George and Goldsmiths' & General Burglary Assn* [1899] 1 QB 595, 611 *per* Collins LJ (CA—burglary). Lewison, no 1.03.
The intention of the parties is "as established by the written contract"—*Prudential Ins Co of America*, 126 F 2d 607, 610 (10 Cir, 1942—PA). See further Appleman, section 7385 and cases cited at note 74.
11. *Pearson v Commercial Union Assurance Co* (1863) 15 CB (NS) 304, 313 *per* Erle CJ (fire); *Thompson v Equity Fire Ins Co* [1910] AC 592, 597 *per* Lord Macnaghten (PC—fire); *Petrofina (UK) Ltd v Magnaload Ltd* [1983] 2 Lloyd's Rep 91, 95 *per* Lloyd J (contractors AR); *Ashville Investments Ltd v Elmer Contractors Ltd* [1988] 2 All ER 577, 581 *per* May LJ (CA); *Glasgow Training Group Ltd v Lombard Continental plc*, 1989 SLT 375 (storm). Lewison no 4.01.
Queensland Govt Rail & Electric Power Transmission Pty Ltd v Manufacturers' Mutual Ins Ltd [1969] 1 Lloyd's Rep 214, 218 *per* Windeyer J (HCA—contractors AR), who also suggested that the "ordinary meaning of words today is not to be ascertained by etymology"; he preferred a definition of "faulty" provided by Doctor Johnson.
Aschenbrenner v United States Fidelity & Guarantee Co, 292 US 80 (1934—PA); *Rouse v Greyhand Rent-A-Car Inc*, 506 F 2d 410 (5 Cir, 1975—motor); *Casey v Highlands Ins Co*, 600 P 2d 1387 (Idaho, 1979—burglary); *Lumber & Wood Products Inc v New Hampshire Ins Co*, 807 F 2d 916, 919 (11 Cir, 1987—cargo). For the extensive caselaw to this effect see Appleman, section 7384, note 56; and 44 CJS, section 294.

15–2 THE ORDINARY MEANING

"When I use a word", Humpty Dumpty said in a scornful tone, "it means just what *I* choose it to mean—neither more nor less."[12] This is not the rule of construction that governs insurance contracts. The presumption is that words are to be given their ordinary meaning, whether that is what the insurer had in mind or not,[13] especially when it is the insurer who seeks to reject the ordinary meaning and when the document is a standard form of document written by the insurer himself.[14] The presumption is expressed in various ways by the courts: words should be given their natural,[15] plain,[16] popular,[17] common sense,[18] primary[19] meaning; also the meaning that would be placed on the words by an "ordinary man of normal intelligence and average knowledge of the world",[20] a very modest description of the judiciary,[21] who must read policies in the way of the ordinary man. The view of the ordinary man sometimes enables the courts to give up the pursuit of precise definition and to construe words as a matter of impression.[22]

The ordinary meaning is presumed to be that of the dictionary,[23] and in accord with grammatical orthodoxy. However, as usual, dictionaries must be used with caution.[24] "An unabridged comprehensive dictionary definition lists every conceivable usage of words, including those that are arcane, archaic and obscure." With these words, the

12. Lewis Carroll, *Through the Looking Glass*, quoted in *McMillan v State Mutual*, 922 F2d 1073, 1077 (3 Cir, 1990—life).
13. *Ibid.*
14. *M/S Aswan Engineering Establishment Co Ltd v Iran Trades Mutual Ins Co Ltd* [1989] 1 Lloyd's Rep 289, 293 *per* Hobhouse J (liability).
15. *Stanley v Western Ins Co* (1868) LR 3 Exch 71, 75 *per* Martin B (fire); *Thomson v Weems* (1884) 9 App Cas 671, 687 *per* Lord Watson (life); *Lake v Simmons* [1927] AC 487, 508 *per* Viscount Sumner (jewellery); *Rapp Ltd v McClure* [1955] 1 Lloyd's Rep 292, 293 *per* Devlin J (burglary); *Commonwealth Smelting Ltd v Guardian Royal Exchange Assurance Ltd* [1984] 2 Lloyd's Rep 608, 611 *per* Staughton J (material damage).
16. *Robertson v French* (1803) 4 East 130, 135 *per* Lord Ellenborough CJ (marine); *Re George and Goldsmiths' & General Burglary Ins Assn* [1899] 1 QB 595, 610 *per* Collins LJ (CA—burglary); *Jason v British Traders' Ins Co Ltd* [1969] 1 Lloyd's Rep 281, 290 *per* Fisher J (motor).
17. *Robertson* (above), *loc cit*; *Stanley v Western Ins Co* (1868) LR 3 Exch 71, 73 *per* Kelly CB (fire). *Lumber & Wood Products Inc v New Hampshire Ins Co*, 807 F 2d 916, 919 (11 Cir, 1987—cargo).
18. *Re George* (above), *loc cit*; *Hales v Reliance Fire & Accident Ins Corp Ltd* [1960] 2 Lloyd's Rep 391, 396 *per* McNair J (fire).
19. *Allen & Sons Billposting Ltd v Drysdale* (1939) 65 Ll L Rep 41 (subsidence); *Princette Models Ltd v Reliance Fire & Accident Ins Corp Ltd.* [1960] 1 Lloyd's Rep 49, 56 *per* Pearson J (goods in transit).
20. *Yorke v Yorkshire Ins Co Ltd* [1918] 1 KB 662, 666 *per* McCardie J (life), holding that "sober and temperate" referred to the use or misuse of alcohol, but not of drugs. *Cf* reference to the "understanding of business people"—*Lowenstein & Co Ltd v Poplar Motor Transport (Lymm)* [1968] 2 Lloyd's Rep 233, 238 *per* Nield J (goods in transit): this might be seen as the ordinary and popular meaning tempered by the context of the business.
21. *Barnett & Block v National Parcels Ins Co Ltd* [1942] 1 All ER 221, 223 *per* Atkinson J (burglary), affirmed 73 Ll L Rep 17 (CA).
22. *Merchants Marine Ins Co Ltd v North of England P & I Assn* (1926) 26 Ll L Rep 201, 203 (CA—hull), considering whether a floating crane was a "ship or vessel", Scrutton LJ suggested that with a ship as with an elephant one knows when one sees one. See also *Emanuel & Son Ltd v Hepburn* [1960] 1 Lloyd's Rep 304, 308 *per* Pearson J (strikes contingency: "physical loss or damage or deterioration").
23. *Clift v Schwabe* (1846) 3 CB 437, 458 *per* Wightman J (life: "suicide"); *Barnett & Block v National Parcels Ins Co Ltd* [1942] 1 All ER 221, 223 *per* Atkinson J (burglary: "garage"), affirmed 73 Ll L Rep 17 (CA); *Mills v Smith* [1963] 1 Lloyd's Rep 168, 175 *per* Paull J (householders' comprehensive: "accident"); *Kumar v Life Ins Corp of India* [1974] 1 Lloyd's Rep 147, 149 *per* Kerr J (life), where on both ordinary and technical usage a Caesarean delivery was an "operation"; *Commonwealth Smelting Ltd v Guardian Royal Exchange Assurance Ltd* [1984] 2 Lloyd's Rep 608, 611 *per* Staughton J ("explosion"). Lewison no 4.03.
24. USA: dictionary definitions are not controlling, but they are persuasive: *Aschenbrenner v United States Fidelity & Guarantee Co*, 292 US 80, 85 (1934—PA).

Pennsylvania court preferred what it regarded as the common usage of the term ("smoke"), as it appeared in the context of the particular contract,[25] although the dictionary may indicate a primary meaning which, it might be said, is the ordinary meaning.

Having found the ordinary meaning, a court applies it literally, even if the effect appears unreasonable, for there is a presumption that words are intended to mean what they say.[26] Faced with an exception in a case of liability insurance Hobhouse J affirmed[27] that

"even if these policies were unbusinesslike, such a consideration does not provide an escape from the clear contractual provision. These policies represent a bargain freely entered into between insured and underwriter, and it is not for the Court to remake that bargain, even if it were to think that a different bargain would have been better".

The presumption in favour of the ordinary and literal meaning assumes that an ordinary meaning can be found—an assumption made by the movement in favour of "plain language", which has been strong in the United States and is found also in England.[28] Talk of "plain language" insurance contracts may be little more than an exercise in marketing insurance; it may be important that the consumer thinks he knows what his cover is, even if the thought is delusion—he may never discover otherwise and the insurer may prefer to leave it that way. If, however, "plain" means "intelligible", the next question is, to whom? If it be to the insured, the approach resembles that of the problematical rule in favour of the reasonable expectations of the insured: below, 15–5B. If "plain" means intelligible to the market or to the legal profession, the presumption in favour of the ordinary meaning is the first of several necessary rules of construction: below, 15–2A and 15–2B.

In any event, draftsmen are sometimes careless or incompetent, and the search must go beyond the ordinary meaning of the words used. "In construing these instruments we must always look for what was the intention of the parties without confining ourselves to a strict grammatical construction; for it is impossible in many instances so to construe them, without departing widely from the object intended."[29] So, further rules are needed, and in practice the presumption in favour of the ordinary meaning, even if unambiguous,[30] gives way in many cases, as follows.

First, some words, such as "premises"[31] have no natural or ordinary meaning when viewed in isolation, and must be understood in their wider context: below, 15–3. Second, if the effect of the ordinary meaning is unreasonable, the court will be more

---

25. *K & Lee Corp v Scottsdale Ins Co*, 769 F Supp 870, 873 (ED Pa, 1991—fire). *Emanuel & Son Ltd v Hepburn* [1960] 1 Lloyd's Rep 304, 308 *per* Pearson J (strikes contingency). *Cf Price & Co v A1 Ships' Small Damage Ins Assn Ltd* (1889) 22 QBD 580, 584 *per* Lord Esher MR (CA—hull): "to say that the language of these Lloyd's policies can be construed altogether according to strict grammar is . . . next to impossible." Justice Holmes, 12 Harv L R 417 (1899). See also Patterson, "The Interpretation and Construction of Contracts", 64 Colum L Rev 833, 838 ff (1964); Brown & Menezes, No 6:4:1.

26. *Borradaile v Hunter* (1843) 5 Man & G 639, 663 *per* Coltman J (life); *Winspear v Accident Ins Co Ltd* (1880) 6 QBD 42, 45 *per* Lord Coleridge CJ (PA); *Cassel v Lancashire & Yorkshire Accident Ins Co Ltd* (1885) 1 TLR 495, 496 *per* Pollock CB (PA).

27. *Cooke & Arkwright v Haydon* [1987] 2 Lloyd's Rep 579, 582, affirmed *ibid* (CA).

28. But see above, at note 25.

29. *Marsden v Reid* (1803) 3 East 572 *per* Lawrence J (cargo). See also *Glen's Trustees v Lancashire & Yorkshire Accident Ins Co Ltd*, 1906 8 F (Ct of Sess) 915 (PA). *Hake v Eagle Picher Co*, 406 F 2d 893 (7 Cir, 1969—liability).

30. Arnould, No 104.

31. *Mint Security Ltd v Blair* [1982] 1 Lloyd's Rep 188, 193–194 *per* Staughton J (cash in transit), citing *Maunsell v Olins* [1975] AC 373, 383–384 *per* Viscount Dilhorne.

than ready to find ambiguity, and thus feel free to avoid an unreasonable result: below, 15–4 and 15–5. Third, in an appropriate case, a purely literal interpretation, which may also be the ordinary meaning, gives way to the technical meaning of words: below, 15–2A and 15–2B.

15–2A Technical Meaning: Precedent

If the meaning of the words used has been previously settled by the courts, it can be inferred that the parties intend the words to bear that meaning. Precedent is respected,[32] not only when the policy words are exactly the same as those previously settled but also when the court regards them as substantially the same[33]; the same is true of words used in a statute.[34] It is assumed that the draftsman works with a view to certainty of sense and standardisation[35] of terms. "Courts should be chary in interfering with the interpretation given to a well-known document and acted on for any considerable period of time",[36] and courts are ready to assume that, as in the case of a statute, a phrase has been used in the same sense as it was in previous contracts of insurance on the same risk.[37] In this respect, at least, even American courts are kind to the insurance companies and the clumsiness and caution of the draftsman. Judge Posner:

"The puzzle is easily solved once the method of creating contracts is understood. Concerned to minimize uncertainty, insurance companies are very reluctant to change terminology whose meaning has been fixed in litigation or approved by the State agencies that regulate insurance [in certain States]. They prefer to create new coverage not by drafting a new contract from scratch but instead in modular fashion: standard terms whose meaning has been tested in litigation or blessed by regulators are shuffled to create the particular package of insurance protection that the customer desires .... God forbid that it should draft new language!"[38]

However, although precedent is respected, the court is not bound by the doctrine of *stare decisis* to follow it.[39]

32. *Clift* v *Schwabe* (1846) 3 CB 437, 470 *per* Parke B (life); *Glen* v *Lewis* (1853) 8 Ex 607, 619 *per* Parke B (fire); *Andersen* v *Martin* [1908] AC 334, 340 *per* Lord Halsbury (hull); *Becker, Gray & Co* v *London Assurance Corp* [1918] AC 101, 108 *per* Lord Dunedin (HL—cargo). Of course, if the decision in the later case is to be the same, not only the words but also the facts must be the same: *Re Calf and Sun Ins Office* [1920] 2 KB 366, 382 *per* Atkin LJ (CA—burglary). *Government Employees Ins Co* v *United States*, 349 F 2d 83 (10 Cir, 1965—motor), cert den 382 US 1026; *Mutual of Enumclaw* v *Wilcox*, 843 P 2d 154 (Idaho, 1992—liability). In *Roy* v *State Farm Mutual Automobile Ins Co*, 954 F 2d 392 (6 Cir, 1992—motor) this decision was reached on the basis of the doctrine of reasonable expectations (below 15–5B).
33. *Lawrence* v *Accidental Ins Co Ltd* (1881) 7 QBD 216, 220 *per* Denman J (PA).
34. For example in *Laurence* v *Davies* [1972] 2 Lloyd's Rep 231, 233 (motor) Dunn J held that in the context of motor insurance, compulsory under the Road Traffic Acts, "motor car" did not have the ordinary meaning, but the meaning in the Acts and thus included a van. See also *Polpen Shipping Co Ltd* v *Commercial Union Ins Co Ltd* [1943] KB 161, 164 *per* Atkinson J (hull); *Navigators & General Ins Co Ltd* v *Ringrose* [1962] 1 All ER 97, 98 *per* Holroyd Pearce LJ (CA—dinghy insurance), but *cf* 100 *per* Davies LJ; *Mills* v *Smith* [1963] 1 Lloyd's Rep 168, 175 *per* Paull J (householders' comprehensive).
35. *Re Etherington and Lancashire & Yorkshire Accident Ins Co* [1909] 1 KB 591, 597 *per* Williams LJ (CA—PA); *Louden* v *British Merchants' Ins Co Ltd* [1961] 1 Lloyd's Rep 154, 157–158 *per* Lawton J (motor).
36. *Re Hooley Hill Rubber and Royal Ins Co* [1920] 1 KB 257, 269 *per* Bankes LJ (CA—fire: "explosion"). In "commercial cases it is, I think, of the highest importance that authority should not be disturbed"—*Atlantic Shipping & Trading Co Ltd* v *Dreyfus & Co* [1922] 2 AC 250, 257 *per* Lord Dunedin.
37. *Vancouver General Hospital* v *Scottish & York Ins Co* (1988) 55 DLR (4th) 360 (BC—liability), with reference to statements by Lord Wilberforce in *Prenn* v *Simmonds* [1971] 3 All ER 237, 239–240 (HL).
38. *Continental Casualty Co* v *Pittsburgh Corning Corp*, 917 F 2d 297, 299 per Judge Posner (7 Cir, 1990—liability).
39. *Ashville Investments Ltd* v *Elmer Contractors Ltd* [1988] 2 All ER 577, 582 *per* May LJ (CA).

15–2B Technical Meaning: Trade, Legal or Scientific Usage

If a word has a technical meaning, there is a presumption that it was intended in its technical meaning, whether that meaning is the language of the law or of science[40] or the usage found in a trade or industry. But it is too sweeping to say that the technical meaning always prevails over the ordinary meaning. Some courts are reluctant to sanction new technical definitions at the expense of the ordinary meaning.[41] The cases, in which the technical meaning has prevailed, can be categorised (and limited) as follows:

(a) Cases concerning terminology of the criminal law[42]: the technical sense is respected; however, if the word, for example "consent", has been defined not only in the criminal law but also in other branches of the law, the former definition will not necessarily govern[43]; a similar hesitation is found when the policy covers events in more than one jurisdiction.[44]

(b) Cases in which the policy makes it very clear that a technical sense is intended.[45] But a policy term, that a "condition" of the policy to be performed by the insured is to be construed in a technical sense as a condition precedent to the liability of the insurer, may not be taken literally.[46]

(c) Cases in which both parties were familiar with the trade or context from which the technical sense of the word derived.[47] In the latter instance, the

40. *Kumar* v *Life Ins Corp of India* [1974] 1 Lloyd's Rep 147, 149 *per* Kerr J (life), where on both ordinary and technical usage a Caesarean delivery was an "operation". *Canton Ins Office Ltd* v *Independent Transport Co*, 217 F 213 (9 Cir, 1914—hull); *Reliance Ins Co* v *Orleans Parish School Board*, 322 F 2d 803 (5 Cir, 1963—fire), cert den 377 US 916. UCC, section 1-205.

41. *Starfire Diamond Rings Ltd* v *Angel* [1962] 2 Lloyd's Rep 217, 219 *per* Lord Denning MR and Upjohn LJ (CA—jeweller's block). *Minier* v *Travelers Indemnity Co*, 159 F Supp 230 (SD Ill, 1958—employers' liability); *Riefflin* v *Hartford Steam Boiler Inspection & Ins Co*, 521 P 2d 675 (Mont, 1974—boiler); *Webb* v *Allstate Life Ins Co*, 536 F 2d 336 (10 Cir, 1976—life).

42. This may reflect the assumption of public policy that ordinary people are familar with the criminal law. Examples include: *Saqui & Lawrence* v *Stearns* [1911] 1 KB 426, 436 *per* Farwell LJ (CA—burglary: "theft"); *Debenhams Ltd* v *Excess Ins Co Ltd* (1912) 28 TLR 505 (fidelity: "embezzlement"); *Re Calf and Sun Ins Office* [1920] 2 KB 366, 380–382 *per* Atkin LJ (CA—burglary: "entry"); *London & Lancashire Fire Ins Co* v *Bolands Ltd* [1924] AC 836 (burglary: "riot"), a decision that has attracted much criticism: below, 19–3D; *Grundy (Teddington) Ltd* v *Fulton* [1981] 2 Lloyd's Rep 666 (burglary: "theft"), affirmed [1983] 1 Lloyd's Rep 16 (CA); *Deutsche Genossenschaftsbank* v *Burnhope* [1993] 2 Lloyd's Rep 518 ("theft"). Generally, see Wasik [1986] JBL 45. Lewison no 4.08.

For criticism see *Algemeene Bankvereeniging* v *Langton* (1935) 40 Com Cas 247, 259 *per* Maugham LJ (CA—Lloyd's Bankers' Policy): "very few commercial men in this country are fully aware of the fact that in order entirely to apprehend the meaning of that word ["larceny"] you must go through more than 100 closely printed pages of Archbold . . . " see also *Nishina Trading Co Ltd* v *Chiyoda Fire & Marine Ins Co Ltd* [1969] 2 QB 449, 462 (CA—cargo) where Lord Denning MR doubted whether ordinary commercial men would intend to bring in "all the eccentricities of the law of larceny".

Cf Pan Am World Airways Inc v *Aetna Casualty & Surety Co*, 505 F 2d 989 (2 Cir, 1974—aviation): the court held that international law did not govern the word "war", but did provide a starting point for inquiry.

43. *Singh* v *Rathour* [1988] 2 All ER 16, 20 *per* May LJ (CA—motor). Wilkinson, 138 NLJ 519 (1988).

44. *Equitable Trust Co of New York* v *Henderson* (1930) 47 TLR 90.

45. *Sturge* v *Hackett* [1962] 1 Lloyd's Rep 626 (CA—householder's comprehensive). The insured is on notice and must, if necessary, take advice about the meaning of the words in the policy.

46. *Re Bradley and Essex & Suffolk Accident Indemnity Sy* [1912] 1 KB 415 (CA—employers' liability). In the general law, see *Wickman Machine Tool Sales Ltd* v *Schuler AG* [1974] AC 235.

47. For example in *Scragg* v *UK Temperance & General Provident Institution* [1976] 2 Lloyd's Rep 227 the amount payable under a life policy was limited, if the insured died as a result of "motor racing". Having held (p 229) that the "sprint event" as a result of which the insured died was "motor racing" in ordinary English, Mocatta J found that, in the sport, "motor racing" was used in a technical sense that did not include a "sprint event" and that the insurer was aware of this (p 233). He concluded that the limitation did not apply to the death of the insured. The judge (p 230) distinguished the case of the person who "entered a market such as the Stock Exchange through a broker and was accordingly bound by its customary usages

technical or special sense is also the ordinary sense (cf above, 15–2) in the particular (trade) context.[48]

A technical meaning will not be applied in the following circumstances:

(d) Cases in which the ordinary meaning of a word differs from the technical meaning, and one party to the contract cannot be expected to be familiar with the technical meaning.[49] It has been stressed that, "before an insurance company can avail itself of a legal technical meaning of a word or words, it must be clear that *both* parties to the contract intended that the language have a legal technical meaning".[50]

For example, it was for this reason that an American court rejected the insurer's argument that "damages" in liability insurance were limited to common law damages awarded by way of compensation, and did not extend to clean-up costs incurred in obedience to a court order. However, courts in the USA are divided on this issue, and one contrary view is that there are "many words, phrases or paragraphs in a standard insurance contract that a first time reader does not understand"[51] and that is to be expected: the insured should take advice, if he does not understand techical words, and, in general, is presumed to have intended technical terms to have their technical meaning, whether he actually understands them or not.

(e) Cases in which the policy itself states that words, which would otherwise bear a technical meaning, are not intended to have their technical meaning.[52]

(f) Cases in which the context of the policy indicates that a technical meaning was not intended: for example insurance on subject-matter abroad, where the technical sense of the words is not employed.[53] This case may be a variant of (d).

15–3 CONTEXT

The ordinary meaning of words is the meaning when read not in isolation but in con-

---

and trade meanings." See also *M'Cowan* v *Baine* [1891] AC 401, 407–408 *per* Lord Watson. *Canton Ins Office Ltd* v *Independent Transport Co*, 217 F 213 (9 Cir, 1914—hull); *New York Life Ins Co* v *Federal National Bank of Shawnee*, 143 F 2d 69 (10 Cir, 1944—life); *Reliance Ins Co* v *Orleans Parish School Board*, 322 F 2d 803 (5 Cir, 1971—fire). See further Appleman, section 7388.

48. *Robertson* v *French* (1803) 4 East 130, 135 *per* Lord Ellenborough CJ (marine); *Price & Co* v *A1 Ships' Small Damage Ins Ltd* (1889) 22 QBD 580, 584 *per* Lord Esher MR (CA—hull: "average"); *Anglo-African Merchants Ltd* v *Bayley* [1969] 1 Lloyd's Rep 268, 277–278 *per* Megaw J (AR: "new" clothes).
   Semble aliter unless it appears that both parties intended to use the words in their technical sense.

49. In *De Maurier (Jewels) Ltd* v *Bastion Ins Co Ltd* [1967] 2 Lloyd's Rep 550, 557 (jewellers' AR) Donaldson J held that, in the case of a company, a car "owned by the insured" included cars held on hire-purchase, for a "reasonable assured" would describe them as "the company's cars". See also *Scragg* (above).

50. *Boeing Co* v *Aetna Casualty & Surety Co*, 784 P 2d 507, 513 (Washington, 1990—liability) (emphasis added). See also *AIU Ins Corp* v *FMC Corp* 274 Cal Rptr 820, 832 (Cal, 1990—liability: "damages").

51. *Patrons Oxford Mutual Ins Co* v *Marois*, 573 A 2d 16, 19 (Me, 1990—liability). See also *Sturge* v *Hackett* (above).

52. *Re George and Goldsmiths' & General Burglary Ins Assn Ltd* [1899] 1 QB 595, 601 *per* Lord Russell CJ (CA—burglary: "loss or damage by burglary or housebreaking, as hereinafter defined . . . ").

53. In *Algemeene Bankvereeniging* v *Langton* (1935) 40 Com Cas 247 the Court of Appeal considered a Lloyd's Bankers' Policy covering banking in Belgium and concluded that the words "fire, burglary, theft, robbery, or hold-up" should not be construed in a technical sense according to English law (see p 259 *per* Maugham LJ).

text.[54] The context is a series of circles: the phrase, the sentence, the paragraph, the part of the policy, the whole of the policy, and then, outside the policy itself, the past dealings of the parties, the trade context, and the objects which the policy was intended to achieve. The court moves outward through the circles until it is satisfied that it has found the meaning intended by the parties.

15–3A The Context Inside the Policy

The meaning of a word or phrase may be affected by its place in the policy: the phrase,[55] the sentence,[56] the paragraph,[57] or the entire policy,[58] including the recital.[59] Sometimes, a word viewed in the context of a paragraph is seen as generically similar to other matters there enumerated, and this mode of construction is close to the *eiusdem generis* rule of construction (below, 15–3A1). Further, and especially when looking at the context of the entire policy, the court presumes that the parties intended internal consistency in the use of language.[60] The presumption of consistency

54. *Lake* v *Simmons* [1927] AC 487, 499 *per* Viscount Haldane (jewellery).

55. *Emmanuel & Son Ltd* v *Hepburn* [1960] 1 Lloyd's Rep 304, 309 *per* Pearson J (strikes contingency: "physical loss or damage or deterioration").

56. Examples include *Curtis & Sons* v *Mathews* [1919] 1 KB 425, 430 *per* Bankes LJ (CA—fire): an exception of fire caused by "destruction by the Government" "had reference to deliberate destruction, that is to say, deliberate in the same sense as confiscation, the word immediately preceding it, would be deliberate"; *Hales* v *Reliance Fire & Accident Ins Corp Ltd* [1960] 2 Lloyd's Rep 391, 396 *per* McNair J: to construe "inflammable" in a shopkeepers' fire policy the judge had regard to the context of the word in a warranty aimed at factors that might increase the risk. In *De Maurier (Jewels) Ltd* v *Bastion Ins Co Ltd* [1967] 2 Lloyd's Rep 550, 560 (jewellers' AR) Donaldson J construed car "lock" in the context of a warranty concerned with the security of jewellery left in a car, and held that it must mean a lock providing greater security than those found on ordinary production cars.

In *Hart* v *Standard Marine Ins Co* (1889) 22 QBD 499, 502 *per* Bowen LJ, 503 *per* Fry LJ (CA—hull) it was suggested that the meaning of a word such as "iron" might differ according to whether it was found in an affirmative description, such as the scope of cover, or in a warranty or exception; *sed quaere*.

Queensland Govt Rys & Electric Power Transmission Pty Ltd v *Manufacturers' Mutual Ins Ltd* [1969] 1 Lloyd's Rep 214, 218 *per* Windeyer J (HCA—contractors AR): the meaning of "fault" depends on whether it concerns a person or a thing, such as a bridge; in the former case it connotes blame, in the latter it does not.

See also *Hooper* v *Accidental Death Ins Co* (1860) 5 H & N 546, 559 *per* Wightman J (PA); *Rogers* v *Whittaker* [1917] 1 KB 942, 943 *per* Sankey J (fire: "military power"); *Shell International Petroleum Co Ltd* v *Gibbs* [1983] 1 Lloyd's Rep 342, 348 *per* Lord Roskill (HL—cargo). But some courts have been reluctant to construe in context: *Re United London & Scottish Ins Co Ltd* [1915] 2 Ch 167 (PA) in which the Court of Appeal rejected the argument that in the exception, accident caused by "medical or surgical treatment, or fighting, ballooning, racing, self-injury, or suicide, or anything swallowed, administered or inhaled", the word "inhaled" meant "voluntarily inhaled". Warrington LJ (p 172): "Directly you depart from the literal meaning of the words you embark upon a sea of difficulties and speculations which ought I think to be avoided." See also *Coles* v *Accident Ins Co Ltd* (1889) 5 TLR 736 (CA—PA).

57. For example *Kearney* v *General Accident Fire & Life Corp* [1968] 2 Lloyd's Rep 240, 244 *per* Nield J (employers' liability).

58. *Drinkwater* v *Royal Exchange Assurance Corp* (1767) Wilm 282, 286 *per* Lord Wilmot CJ (fire); *Hamlyn* v *Crown Accidental Ins Co Ltd* [1893] 1 QB 750 (CA—PA); *Equitable Fire & Accident Office Ltd* v *The Ching Ho Wong* [1906] AC 96, 100 *per* Lord Davey (PC—fire); *Hansford* v *London Express Newspaper Ltd* (1928) 44 TLR 349 (PA: "vehicle" included bicycle); *Jaglom* v *Excess Ins Co Ltd* [1971] 2 Lloyd's Rep 171, 176 *per* Donaldson J (jewellery AR).

59. *Notman* v *Anchor Assurance Co* (1858) 4 CB (NS) 466, 480 *per* Cockburn CJ (life); *Blasheck* v *Bussell* (1916) 33 TLR 74 (CA—loss).

60. For example *South Staffordshire Tramways Co Ltd* v *Sickness & Accident Assurance Assn Ltd* [1891] 1 QB 402, 408 *per* Fry LJ (CA—liability); *Hamlyn* v *Crown Accidental Ins Co Ltd* [1893] 1 QB 750 (CA—PA); *Daff* v *Midland Colliery Owners Mutual Indemnity Co* (1913) 82 LJ KB 1340, 1351 *per* Lord Moulton (HL—workmen's compensation); *Pennsylvania Co for Insurances on Lives and Granting Annuities* v *Mumford* [1920] 2 KB 537, 543 *per* Lord Sterndale MR (CA—Lloyd's "Banks" Policy); *Lake* v *Simmons* [1927] AC 487, 507 *per* Viscount Sumner (jewellery); *Gale* v *Motor Union Ins Co* [1928] 1 KB 359 (motor).

in the whole of the policy is closely linked to consideration of the purpose[61] or the subject-matter of the insurance.[62]

15–3A1 Eiusdem Generis[63]

A word may be construed by reference to the meaning of words used with it, in particular, as being generically similar to other words in the same context, whether that context be the phrase, the sentence, the paragraph or even, less commonly, the whole of the policy. Construction *eiusdem generis* the whole policy becomes in effect construction by reference to the object of the whole policy[64]: see further below, 15–3B(c).

Most commonly the *eiusdem generis* rule is applied as a rule of construction that

"where a particular enumeration is followed by such words as 'or other', the latter expression ought, if not enlarged by the context, to be limited to matters *eiusdem generis* with those specially enumerated. The canon is attended with no difficulty except its application. Whether it applies at all, and if so, what effect should be given to it, must in every case depend upon the precise terms, subject-matter, and context of the clause under construction."[65]

It is clear from these words of Lord Watson that the rule is not applied automatically whenever a series of words includes or is followed by words wider in meaning

61. *Cornish* v *Accident Ins Co Ltd* (1889) 23 QBD 452, 456 *per* Lindley LJ (CA—PA). See further below, 15–3B(c).

62. *Hales* v *Reliance Fire & Accident Ins Corp Ltd* [1960] 2 Lloyd's Rep 391, 396 *per* McNair J (fire); *Exchange Theatre Ltd* v *Iron Trades Mutual Ins Co Ltd* [1984] 1 Lloyd's Rep 149, 151 *per* Eveleigh LJ (CA—fire).

63. Sometimes referred to as *noscitur a sociis* (for example in *Broom's Legal Maxims* (10th ed), pp 396—401), but sometimes treated as a rule distinct from the latter (for example MacGillivray, Nos 1088–1089).

USA: the rule is employed less often than in England. See *Ocean Accident & Guarantee Corp Ltd* v *First National Bank*, 84 SW 2d 1111 (Tex, 1935—burglary); *Rintoul* v *Sun Life Assurance Co*, 142 F 2d 776 (7 Cir, 1944—life); *Livingston* v *Nationwide Mutual Ins Co*, 295 F Supp 1122 (D SC, 1969—motor), affirmed 419 F 2d 837.

64. In *Sangster* v *General Accident & Employers Liability Corp Ltd* (1896) 24 R (Ct of Sess) 56, 57 with reference to an exception in a PA policy of exposure to unnecessary danger, the Lord Ordinary said: "But a general clause of exclusion is not to be read in a sense inconsistent with the main purpose of the policy, which is to insure against accident. If this clause were read literally, it would exclude the great majority of accidents." His decision that an expert swimmer drowned in a Highland loch was not within the exception was affirmed by the Court of Session in these words of Lord Robertson (p 58) based on the *eiusdem generis* rule: the exception follows "an enumeration of specific cases, and the kind of case intended to be embraced by the general words must be such as the cases specifically enumerated. Now, the characteristic of the specifically enumerated cases is this, that in them the danger was obvious". See also *Chandris* v *Isbrandtsen-Moller Co Inc* [1951] 1 KB 240, 244–245 *per* Devlin J.

65. *Sun Fire Office* v *Hart* (1889) 14 App Cas 98, 103-104 *per* Lord Watson (PC—fire). Examples of policy construction *eiusdem generis* include: *Watchorn* v *Langford* (1813) 3 Camp 422, 423 *per* Lord Ellenborough (fire): "linen" in the phrase "stock in trade, household furniture, linen, wearing apparel and plate", meant household linen. *Elliot* v *Royal Exchange Assurance Co* (1867) LR 2 Exch 237, 245 *per* Martin B (fire): arbitration clause seen like other clauses as a condition precedent. *Thames & Mersey Marine Ins Co Ltd* v *Hamilton, Fraser Co* (1887) 12 App Cas 484: "perils of the seas . . . and all other perils, losses and misfortunes" did not include damage to a donkey-engine. *Curtis* v *Mathews* [1919] 1 KB 425, 430 *per* Bankes LJ (CA—fire): "destruction", like the events in the words around it, notably "confiscation", connoted deliberate loss or damage; *cf Re United London & Scottish Ins Co Ltd* [1915] 2 Ch 167 (CA—PA). *King* v *Travellers' Ins Assn Ltd* (1931) 48 TLR 53 (baggage): whether furs within "jewelry, watches, fieldglasses, cameras and other fragile or specially valuable articles". *The Lapwing* [1940] P 112 (hull): stranding in drydock was *eiusdem generis* cover against perils of the sea. *Young* v *Sun Alliance & London Ins Ltd* [1976] 2 Lloyd's Rep 189 (CA—storm): "flood" in "storm, tempest or flood" meant "something which has some element of violence, suddenness or largeness about it" (p 191 *per* Shaw LJ).

But *cf Wimpey Construction (UK) Ltd* v *Poole* [1984] 2 Lloyd's Rep 499; note Birds [1985] JBL 166: in the phrase "negligent act, error or omission", it might have been thought that "negligent" qualifies not only "act" but also "error or omission", however, in that case Webster J held otherwise.

than the rest. The rule is no more than a corrective to the tendency of the draftsman, whose mind is focused on a particular matter, to use words which, if construed literally, would have an effect wider than he intended. But that is a tendency, not an inevitable reflex, and if, for example, the other words in the collocation do not come within a genus, that is one factor to suggest that the more general words should not be limited by the *eiusdem generis* rule of construction.[66] Again, if the general words come first, and are followed by a specific enumeration within the scope of the general words, a court may construe the latter as exhaustive of the genus described in the general words.[67]

15–3A2 Expressio Unius[68]

It is an established rule of the construction of documents that the express mention of one thing may imply the exclusion of another.[69] Thus, if one policy condition is expressed to be a condition precedent of cover and another condition is not, the first is construed as a condition precedent but the second is not.[70] If, however, it appears that the contract has been patched together by incorporating terms from various sources rather than drafted as an interconnected whole, the court will be slow to draw this kind of inference.[71]

15–3A3 Deleted Clauses

Can it be argued that *expressio unius* (above, 15–3A2) has a natural complement in a rule that the court may look at clauses, which have been deleted, to discern party intention about the meaning of the clauses that have been left in the policy? Form may be given to art not only by uniting parts to form a whole but also by sculpting the shape from something else; so also the work of the draftsman, who, starting with the rough shape in standard form, outlines his intent both by what he inserts and by what he takes away. If the draftsman's tool is a word processor, the court may not have much evidence of what was taken away; the present question is most acute in the case of "blue pencil" deletion of a more traditional kind, which obscures but does not eradicate the original words.

---

66. *Sun Fire Office* v *Hart* (1889) 14 App Cas 98, 104 *per* Lord Watson (PC—fire); *Chandris* v *Isbrandtsen-Moller Co* [1951] 1 KB 240, 244 *per* Devlin J. The court declined to apply the rule in *Cole* v *Accident Ins Co Ltd*, 5 TLR 736 (CA—life); *Re United London & Scottish Ins Co Ltd* [1915] 2 Ch 167 (CA—PA); *Rogers* v *Whittaker* [1917] 1 KB 942, 944–945 *per* Sankey J (fire); *Ewing & Co* v *Sicklemore* (1918) 35 TLR 55 (CA—goods in transit).

67. *Ambatielos* v *Anton Jürgens Margarine Works* [1923] AC 175.

68. *Expressio unius est exclusio alterius*, sometimes stated as *expressum facit cessarae tacitum*.

69. Generally see *Broom's Legal Maxims* (10th ed), pp 443 ff; Lewison no 6.05. *New* v *Mutual Benefit Health & Accident Assn*, 76 P 2d 131 (Cal, 1938—health); *American Fidelity & Casualty Co* v *Indemnity Ins Co*, 195 F Supp 648 (DC Ohio, 1961—motor), affirmed 308 F 2d 697.

70. *Stoneham* v *Ocean, Ry & General Accident Ins Co* (1887) 19 QBD 237, 239–240 *per* Mathew J, 241 *per* Cave J (PA); see also *Re Coleman's Depositories Ltd and Life & Health Assurance Assn* [1907] 2 KB 798, 812–813 *per* Buckley LJ (CA—employers' liability); *Home Ins Co* v *Victoria-Montreal Fire Ins Co* [1907] AC 59, 64 *per* Lord Macnaghten (PC—re). Cf *Reid & Co Ltd* v *Employers' Accident & Livestock Ins Co Ltd*, 1899 1 F (Ct of Sess) 1031 (liability) in which the court declined to hold that a policy with a condition avoiding the policy for fraudulent misrepresentation excluded avoidance for misrepresentations that were not fraudulent.

71. *Netherlands Ins Co Ltd* v *Ljunberg & Co AB* [1986] 3 All ER 767, 771 per Lord Goff (PC—cargo).

In the general law, there are cases for such a rule[72] and cases against it,[73] however, these cases contain little discussion of the merits of the rule and little reference to other cases, in which the point has arisen, except perhaps to acknowledge that a conflict of cases exists. The balance of cases in England appears to favour reference to the deletion,[74] although a distinction may have to be made between the deletion of standard terms and the rejection of terms previously drafted.

As regards the deletion of standard terms, Diplock J said this[75]:

"Where there is a standard form of words familiar to commercial men and contained in a printed form in general use, . . . it seems unreal to suppose that when the contracting parties strike out a provision dealing with a specific matter, but retain other provisions, they intend to effect any alteration other than the exclusion of the provision struck out. I cannot, *prima facie* at any rate, ascribe to them any intention of altering the meaning of the words in the provisions which they have chosen to retain . . . but, while I think that I must look first at the clause in its actual form without the deleted words, if I find the clause ambiguous, I think that I am entitled to look at the deleted words to see if any assistance can be derived from them in solving the ambiguity . . . "

As regards the rejection of terms previously drafted, a caveat was expressed by Lord Reid[76]:

"If the words were first inserted by the draftsman of the agreement and then *deleted before signature* then I have no doubt that they must not be considered in construing the agreement. They are in the same position as any other preliminary suggestion put forward and rejected before the final agreement was made."

Compare, however, the more recent decision of the Court of Appeal *Punjab National Bank* v *De Boinville*,[77] in which the court held "that, if the parties to a concluded agreement subsequently agree in express terms that some words in it are to be replaced by others, one can have regard to all aspects of the subsequent agreement in

72. Cases concerning the construction of charterparties: *Gray* v *Carr* (1871) LR 6 QB 522, 529 *per* Cleasby J; *Stanton* v *Richardson* (1874) LR 9 CP 390, 392 *per* Cockburn CJ; *Baumvoll Manufactur von Scheibler* v *Gilchrist & Co* [1892] 1 QB 253, 256 *per* Lord Esher MR (CA); *Caffin* v *Aldridge* [1895] 2 QB 648, 650 *per* Lord Esher MR and Lopes LJ (CA); *Rowland SS Co Ltd* v *Wilson & Co Ltd* (1897) 2 Com Cas 198, 200 *per* Bruce J; *London Transport Co Ltd* v *Trechmann Bros* [1904] 1 KB 635, *per* Lord Collins MR (CA); *Taylor* v *Lewis* (1927) 28 Ll L Rep 329, 330 *per* Lord Alness (Ct Sess.); *The Anastasia* (1933) 46 Ll L Rep 1, 6 *per* Scrutton LJ (CA); *Thomasson Shipping Co Ltd* v *Peabody & Co of London Ltd* [1959] 2 Lloyd's Rep 296, 304 *per* McNair J; *London & Overseas Freighters Ltd* v *Timber Shipping Co SA* [1972] AC 1, 15–16 *per* Lord Reid. Other cases in this sense include : *Sanday & Co* v *McEwan & Co* (1922) 10 Ll L Rep 459, 460 *per* Bankes LJ (CA—sale CIF); *Mottram Consultants Ltd* v *Sunley & Sons Ltd* [1975] 2 Lloyd's Rep 197, 209 *per* Lord Cross (HL—building contract).
73. Cases concerning the construction of charterparties: *Inglis* v *Buttery* (1878) 3 App Cas 552, 569 *per* Lord Hatherley, 576 *per* Lord Blackburn; *SS "Lyderhorn" Co Ltd* v *Fox & Co* [1909] 2 KB 929, 941 *per* Farwell LJ (CA); *Cia Nav Termar SA* v *Tradax Export SA* [1965] 1 Lloyd's Rep 198, 204 *per* Mocatta J. This view is preferred by *Scrutton on Charterparties* (19th ed), p 21. Other cases in this sense include: *Manchester Ship Canal Co* v *Horlock* [1914] 1 Ch 453, 463–464 *per* Eve J (ship sale); *Sassoon & Sons Ltd* v *International Banking Corp* [1927] AC 711, 721 *per* Viscount Sumner (PC—documentary credit).
74. *Cf* Australia and Canada, where the balance of authority seems to be against reference to deletions: Young (1993) 67 ALJ 228.
75. *Dreyfus & Cie* v *Parnaso Cia Nav SA* [1959] 2 QB 498, 513 (charterparty), reversed on other grounds: [1960] 2 QB 49. The reader may wish to consider whether the meaning of Diplock J's *dictum* is changed by restoring the words omitted by the quotation.
76. *London & Overseas Freighters Ltd* v *Timber Shipping Co SA* [1972] AC 1, 15 (emphasis added). His distinction is between what have been called the communings prior to contract, which must not be considered, and the circumstances at the time of contract, which may be considered: for example, *Taylor* v *Lewis* (1927) 28 Ll L Rep 329, 330 *per* Lord Alness (Ct Sess). *Cf* Lewison no 2.04.
77. [1992] 1 Lloyd's Rep 7, 33 per Staughton LJ (CA—cargo); Hudson [1992] LMCLQ 10, 303. *Cf* 15–3B(a), below.

341

construing the contract, including the deletions even in a case which is not, or not wholly, concerned with a printed form". Currently, the trend is to look behind documents at their history.

15–3A4 Sections of the Policy

Although there is a presumption of consistency of meaning throughout the contract,[78] when a policy has different sections of cover, one might think[79] that the meaning of the exception would be tailored to the section and thus vary according to the section, for example, that a condition requiring reasonable care by the insured would be given a very narrow construction in the section of a contract covering liability,[80] but a wider meaning in other sections.[81] However, it seems that, if the exception or condition is expressed in a general part of the policy which purports to apply to all sections of the cover, it will be given the same meaning in all sections, even though the purpose of each section might suggest that a different meaning would be appropriate.[82]

15–3B The Context Outside the Policy

A natural break occurs on the outskirts of the policy, a break imposed by the parol evidence rule (above, 14–1), although some courts require little persuasion to look further. Other courts, however, will do so only if there is ambiguity in the policy. Relevant evidence outside the policy varies from case to case.

    (a) The court may look at the past trade dealings between the parties. Thus, the court looks at documents such as the proposal, whether it was expressly incorporated in the policy or not,[83] as well as, in the case of a renewal, the insurance contract which has been renewed.[84] Generally, however, the court does not look at drafts that preceded the final contract[85] or, if a Lloyd's policy has been issued, the slip on which it was based.[86] Nor, in principle, does the court consider the conduct or views of the parties subsequent to the conclusion of the contract: above, 14–2B.

    (b) The court may look at the wider trade context.[87] A notable instance is that, if the relevant words have a customary meaning, or a settled meaning by the

---

78. Above, 15–3A.
79. In this sense: Tompkinson BILA Journal No 76 (1991) p 8.
80. Below 19–2A1.
81. Below 19–2D2; but cf 19–2A2.
82. Sofi v Prudential Assurance Co Ltd [1993] 2 Lloyd's Rep 559 (CA—AR).
83. For example Samuelson v National Ins & Guarantee Corp Ltd [1984] 3 All ER 107, 108 per Esyr Lewis QC (motor).
84. Balfour v Beaumont [1982] 2 Lloyd's Rep 493, affirmed [1984] 1 Lloyd's Rep 272 (CA—re)
85. Youell v Bland Welch & Co Ltd [1990] 2 Lloyd's Rep 423, 428 per Phillips J (re), discussed above 14–1; affirmed [1992] 2 Lloyd's Rep 127 (CA). Idem: Vancouver General Hospital v Scottish & York Ins Co (1988) 55 DLR (4th) 360, 366 (BC—liability). Cf Punjab (above, 15–3A3).
86. Youell (above).
87. For example in Lowenstein & Co Ltd v Poplar Motor Transport (Lymm) Ltd [1968] 2 Lloyd's Rep 233, 238 (goods in transit) to decide whether a duty "cannot be complied with" Nield J took account of the practices of the haulage industry. Other examples include: Clift v Schwabe (1846) 3 CB 437, 469 per Parke B (life); Birrell v Dryer (1884) 9 App Cas 345, 353–354 per Lord Watson (hull: "no St Lawrence"); Yangtsze Ins Assn v Indemnity Mutual Marine Assurance Co [1908] 2 KB 504, 509 per Farwell LJ (CA—re: "contraband of war"); Yorkshire Ins Co Ltd v Campbell [1917] AC 218, 225 per Lord Sumner (PC—cargo); Wulfson v Switzerland Ins Co [1940] 3 All ER 221, 223 per Atkinson J (goods "in store"); S C A (Freight) Ltd v Gibson [1974] 2 Lloyd's Rep 533, 535 per Ackner J (goods in "transit").

universally understood usage and practice of the London insurance market, that overrides any contrary interpretation.[88] The court's willingness to look at a trade context may also explain statements that a clause must receive a business-like interpretation,[89] for this usually means an interpretation which is commercially sensible in the particular trade context. However, the same result can be achieved without apparent offence to the parol evidence rule by confining attention to the use of language within the policy and finding that it has the special sense used in the (wider) trade context (above, 15–2B).

(c) The court may construe the contract in the light of the objects which the contract was intended to achieve.[90]

For example, in *Fraser*[91] a duty in an accident policy to take "reasonable precautions to prevent accidents and disease" was construed in the light of the commercial purpose of the insurance as being limited to a duty not to be reckless. And in *Cornish*[92] Lindley LJ said "The object of the contract is to insure against accidental death and injuries, and the contract must not be construed so as to defeat this object, nor so as to render it practically illusory." This statement has been adopted in Canada[93]:

---

88. *Phillips & Stratton* v *Dorintal Ins Ltd* [1987] 1 Lloyd's Rep 482, 487 *per* Steyn J (re). See also *The Leegas* [1987] 1 Lloyd's Rep 471, 474–475 *per* Hirst J (hull).

89. *Hydarnes SS Co* v *Indemnity Mutual Marine Ins Co* [1895] 1 QB 500, 504–506 *per* Lord Esher MR (CA—freight); *Westminster Fire Office* v *Reliance Marine Ins Co* (1903) 19 TLR 668 (CA—cargo); *Martin of London Ltd* v *Russell* [1960] 1 Lloyd's Rep 554, 565 *per* Pearson J (cargo); *Home & Overseas Ins Co Ltd* v *Mentor Ins Co (UK) Ltd* [1989] 1 Lloyd's Rep 473, 486 *per* Parker LJ (CA—re); *Abrahams* v *Mediterranean Ins & Reins Co Ltd* [1991] 1 Lloyd's Rep 216, 235–236 per Parker LJ (CA—re).

90. The court must look to the "general scope and design" of the policy: *Drinkwater* v *Royal Exchange Assurance Corp* (1767) Wilm 282, 287 *per* Lord Wilmot CJ (fire). Generally, see *Prenn* v *Simmonds* [1971] 1 WLR 1381, 1384–1385 per Lord Wilberforce (HL).
In *Borradaile* v *Hunter* (1843) 5 Man & G 639, 653 (life) Maule J construed "suicide" in the light of the object of the exception in which it appeared to protect the insurer against any temptation in the insured to self-destruction. *Idem* Erskine J (p 658).
In *Rapp Ltd* v *McClure* [1955] 1 Lloyd's Rep 292, 293 (burglary), to decide the meaning of "warehouse", Devlin J said: "In each case the court is concerned to construe the word in the context in which it is to be found having regard to the purpose for which it is used." He then proceeded to take account of the object of the policy in the clause under review, which was the security of the goods.
Other examples are found in *Sangster* v *General Accident & Employers Liability Corp Ltd* (1896) 24 R (Ct of Sess) 56, 57 (PA) *per* the Lord Ordinary; *Lake* v *Simmons* [1927] AC 487, 509 *per* Viscount Sumner (jewellery); *Wulfson* v *Switzerland Ins Co* [1940] 3 All ER 221, 223, 225 *per* Atkinson J (goods "in store"); *Yorkshire Dale SS Co Ltd* v *Minister of War Transport* [1942] AC 691, 713 *per* Lord Wright (hull); *Starfire Diamond Rings Ltd* v *Angel* [1962] 2 Lloyd's Rep 217, 220 *per* Upjohn LJ (CA—jewellers' block); *Lowenstein & Co Ltd* v *Poplar Motor Transport (Lymm) Ltd* [1968] 2 Lloyd's Rep 233, 238 *per* Nield J (goods in transit); *S C A (Freight) Ltd* v *Gibson* [1974] 2 Lloyd's Rep 533, 535 *per* Ackner J (goods in transit); *The Leegas* [1987] 1 Lloyd's Rep. 471 (hull). *M W Wilson (Lace) Ltd* v *Eagle Star Ins Co Ltd*, 1993 SLT 938, 944 *per* Lord McCluskey; *National Oilwell (UK) Ltd* v *Davy Offshore Ltd* [1993] 2 Lloyd's Rep 582, 604 *per* Colman J (builders' AR).
New England Mutual Life Ins Co of Boston v *Olin*, 114 F 2d 131 (7 Cir, 1940—life); *Standard Accident Ins Co* v *Newman*, 47 NYS 2d 804 (1944—motor); *Hake* v *Eagle Picher Co*, 406 F 2d 893 (7 Cir, 1969—liability). *Golden Eagle Liberia Ltd* v *St Paul Fire & Marine Ins Co*, 685 F Supp 393, 396 (SD NY, 1988: "accident"—liability). Further, it has been held, by analogy with non-conforming goods, that if policy terms do not effect the broad purpose of the insurance, the insurer has broken an implied warranty that the policy shall be fit for its purpose: *C & J Fertilizer Inc* v *Allied Mutual Ins Co*, 227 NW 2d 169, 177–178 (Iowa, 1975—burglary).

91. *Fraser* v *Furman (Productions) Ltd* [1967] 1 WLR 898, 905 (CA—PA). Also in this sense: *Morley* v *United Friendly Ins plc* [1993] 3 All ER 47, 52 per Neill LJ (CA—PA).

92. *Cornish* v *Accident Ins Co* (1889) 23 QBD 452, 456 (CA—PA).

93. *Consolidated-Bathurst* v *Mutual Boiler* [1980] 1 SCR 888, 901 *per* Estey J; see also *Indemnity* v *Excel* [1954] SCR 169, 177–178 (liability).

"an interpretation which defeats the intentions of the parties and their objective in entering into the commercial transaction in the first place should be discarded in favour of an interpretation of the policy which produces a sensible commercial result. It is trite to observe that an interpretation of an ambiguous contractual provision which would render the endeavour on the part of the insured to obtain insurance protection nugatory, should be avoided."

A further example is the statement that reinsurance contracts will be construed in accordance with their "spirit and intention"[94] so as to be not inconsistent with the concept of reinsurance[95] and in line with the primary risks reinsured.[96] Of course, a case may cross the line between (b) and (c), when the purpose of a policy has to be discovered in the context of the trade.

15–4 ABSURDITY

If the rules of construction outlined above lead to an absurd meaning, the courts must, it has been said,[97] give effect to that meaning. The corollary is that the courts will not construe contracts of insurance in such a way as to produce a reasonable result, unless that result also happens to be justifiable on other grounds of construction—at least, as regards commercial contracts. As regards insurance contracts made by persons in their private capacity that come before the Ombudsman, he and his colleagues require the insurer to observe good insurance practice and, although insurance contracts were excluded from the Unfair Contract Terms Act 1977, "this was on the understood basis that the industry would observe the spirit of the legislation. Accordingly it must surely be recognised as one of the principles of good insurance practice that terms of the policy, being in a standard form contract with a consumer, should not be relied upon unless they satisfy the statutory test of 'reasonableness' ".[98] Moreover, even the courts consider that a "construction of the policy producing . . . a bizarre result should not be adopted in the absence of necessity".[99] Most courts are readily persuaded that that cannot have been the real intention of the parties and strive to avoid an absurd construction, in various ways.

First, the court may strive to find an ambiguity in the wording (below, 15–5), which gives it licence to construe against the absurdity.[100] Second, the court may take a more direct approach. Even in the absence of literal ambiguity, an "unreasonable result must be a relevant consideration. The more unreasonable the result the more unlikely

94. *Home Ins Co* v *Victoria & Mutual Fire Ins Co* [1907] AC 59, 65 *per* Lord Macnaghten.
95. *Forsik Vesta* v *Butcher* [1989] 1 AC 852, 897 per Lord Griffiths (re).
96. *Forsik Vesta* v *Butcher* [1989] 1 AC 852, 895 per Lord Griffiths, 909 per Lord Lowry (re); *Youell* v *Bland Welch & Co Ltd* [1992] 2 Lloyd's Rep 127, 132 per Staughton LJ, 138 per Beldam LJ (CA—re).
97. *Farr* v *Motor Traders Mutual Ins Sy* [1920] 3 KB 669, 673 *per* Bankes LJ (CA—motor).
98. Insurance Ombudsman, Annual report 1990, para 2.4.
99. *Strang Pty Ltd* v *NZI Ins Australia Ltd* [1990] VR 1016, 1021 (liability). In England a construction contended for by the insured was dismissed as "absurd", which would "make the insurance impossible to rate" by Mustill LJ in *Smidt Tak Offshore Services Ltd* v *Youell* [1992] 1 Lloyd's Rep 154, 159, (CA—liability).
100. *Barnard* v *Fisher* [1893] 1 QB 340, 342 *per* Lindley LJ (CA—fire): "When you have a clause which is consistent with the ordinary habits of men if you interpret it one way, and which is utterly inconsistent with their ordinary habits if you interpret it another, I prefer the former interpretation, that is, supposing the language admits of a double intepretation." In this case this led the court to a construction in favour of the insurer. See also *Gold Coast Bakeries (Qld) Pty Ltd* v *Heat & Control Pty Ltd* [1992] 1 Qd R 162, 170 (liability).

it is that the parties can have intended it".[101] In that situation the absurdity *per se* leads the court to look outside the words of the policy to the objects of the policy (above, 15–3B),[102] or to the dictates of "realism'[103] or of "business necessity"[104] or of "business efficacy".[105] It is sometimes said[106] that the courts will generally put a reasonable construction on the terms of the policy. But it is not the role of the court to make a reasonable contract for them,[107] and it is safer to say that the courts will seek to avoid a construction that is unreasonable (or absurd)[108] and, incidentally, that for similar reasons the court will ignore an obvious grammatical error.[109]

101. *Wickman Machine Tool Sales Ltd* v *Schuler AG* [1974] AC 235, *per* Lord Reid, cited with approval by Lord Lowry in *Forsik Vesta* v *Butcher* [1989] 1 AC 852, 910 (re). See also *Canada SS Lines Ltd* v *R* [1952] AC 192, 208 *per* Lord Moreton (PC); *Gillespie Bros Ltd* v *Bowles Transport Ltd* [1973] QB 400, 421 *per* Buckley LJ (CA); *Photo Production Ltd* v *Securicor Transport Ltd* [1980] AC 827, 851 *per* Lord Diplock. Lewison no 6.13.

102. In *Pioneer Concrete (UK) Ltd* v *National Employers' Mutual General Ins Assn Ltd* [1985] 1 Lloyd's Rep 274 (liability) the issue was whether there had been timeous notice of any "accident or claim or proceedings". The insured argued that these events should be read disjunctively, so that notice of any one alone, for example notice of proceedings, would suffice, even notice of proceedings years after the accident. Bingham J noted (p 278) that the insured "accepts the absurdity of this construction, but contends that this is, after all, the insurers' form and is to be construed against them." Rejecting this construction he said (*ibid*): "The obvious commercial purpose of this clause is to enable the insurer to perform his role as *dominus litis* and to investigate accidents and claims at the earliest possible opportunity, and that purpose would clearly be frustrated by the construction contended for."

In *Trew* v *Railway Passengers' Assurance Co* (1861) 6 H & N 839, 844 (PA) Cockburn CJ said "We ought not to give to those policies a construction which will defeat the protection of the insured in a large class of cases."

See also *Borradaile* v *Hunter* (1843) 5 Man & G 639, 657 *per* Erskine J (life); *Re Athenaeum Life Assurance Co ex p Eagle Ins Co* (1858) 4 K & J 549, 555 *per* Page V-C (life); *Lion Ins Assn* v *Tucker* (1883) 12 QBD 176, 190 *per* Lord Brett MR (CA—hull mutual); *Australian Agricultural Co* v *Saunders* (1875) LR 10 CP 668, 674 *per* Bramwell B (cargo); *Cornish* v *Accident Ins Co Ltd* (1889) 23 QBD 453, 456 *per* Lindley LJ (CA—PA); *Sangster's Trustees* v *General Accident Assurance Corp Ltd* 1896 24 R (Ct of Sess) 56, 57 *per* Lord Stormonth-Darling (PA).

103. In *Lowenstein & Co Ltd* v *Poplar Motor Transport (Lymm) Ltd* [1968] 2 Lloyd's Rep 233, 238 (goods in transit) per Nield J.

104. *Ibid*.

105. *Petrofina (UK) Ltd* v *Magnaload Ltd* [1983] 2 Lloyd's Rep 91, 95 (contractors' AR) per Lloyd J. See also *Pearson* v *Commercial Union Ins Co* (1876) 1 App Cas 498, 507 *per* Lord Penzance (hull); *Hydarnes SS Co* v *Indemnity Mutual Marine Ins Co* [1895] 1 QB 500, 505–507 *per* Lord Esher MR (CA—freight); *Westminster Fire Office* v *Reliance Marine Ins Co* (1903) 19 TLR 668 (CA—cargo).

106. *Pim* v *Reid* (1843) 6 Man & G 1, 20 *per* Tindal CJ (fire); *Borradaile* v *Hunter* (1843) 5 Man & G 639, 657 *per* Erskine J (life); *Connecticut Mutual Life Ins Co* v *Moore* (1881) 6 App Cas 644, 648 *per* Sir Robert Collier (PC—life); *Century Bank of New York* v *Mountain* (1914) 112 LT 484, 486 *per* Kennedy LJ (CA—securities).

107. *Sulphate Pulp Co Ltd* v *Faber* (1895) 11 TLR 547 (fire); *Re George and Goldsmiths' & General Burglary Ins Assn* [1899] 1 QB 595, 609–610 *per* Collins LJ (CA—burglary); *Abrahams* v *Mediterranean Ins & Reins Co Ltd* [1991] 1 Lloyd's Rep 216, 237 per Parker LJ (CA—re)..

108. *North British & Mercantile Ins Co* v *London, Liverpool, & Globe Ins Co* (1877) 5 Ch D 569, 576 *per* Lord Jessel MR (CA—goods). See also *Braunstein* v *Accidental Death Ins Co* (1861) 1 B & S 782 (PA); *London Guarantie Co* v *Fearnley* (1880) 5 App Cas 911, 916 *per* Lord Blackburn (fidelity); *Home Ins Co of New York* v *Victoria-Montreal Fire Ins Co* [1907] AC 59, 64 *per* Lord Macnaghten (PC—re); *Re Coleman's Depositories Ltd* [1907] 2 KB 798, 807 *per* Fletcher Moulton LJ (CA—liability), followed in *Farrell* v *Federated Employers Ins Co Ltd* [1970] 1 WLR 1400 (CA—liability); *Hulton & Co Ltd* v *Mountain* (1921) 37 TLR 869, 870 *per* Bankes LJ (CA—liability); *Martin of London Ltd* v *Russell* [1960] 1 Lloyd's Rep 554, 565 *per* Pearson J (cargo); *Pine Top Ins Co Ltd* v *Unione Italiana Anglo-Saxon Reinsurance Co Ltd* [1987] 1 Lloyd's Rep 476, 480 *per* Gatehouse J (re).

109. In *Glen's Trustees* v *Lancashire & Yorkshire Accident Ins Co Ltd* 1906 8 F (Ct of Sess) 915, 918 (PA) Lord Dunedin said that the clause "if taken literally . . . is meaningless, but reading it as a whole . . . it is also clear that the confusion is due to grammatical error . . . I think we should read the stipulation as if the word 'not' was omitted." Similarly, in *American Airlines Inc* v *Hope* [1974] 2 Lloyd's Rep 301, 305 *per* Lord Diplock (HL—aviation), an erroneous negative, the product of a typing error, was ignored.

15–5 AMBIGUITY

It is commonplace that ambiguity in the policy gives the court licence to decide what the words mean or should mean and thus, usually, to put on them a construction that favours the insured. But, what is ambiguity? What is clear to one man may be unclear to another. Ambiguity in an insurance contract is objectively ascertained by the particular court.[110] A document is not necessarily ambiguous because courts in past cases have taken a different view of the words,[111] still less so merely because a different view of the words is taken by the parties to the instant dispute[112] or even that the contract is almost illegible,[113] if it can be read and comprehended by the court seized of the case. A document is

"not ambiguous by reason only that it is difficult of construction. If it is finally held to bear a particular construction, that must govern its legal meaning, notwithstanding any difficulty that the courts might have felt in arriving judicially at the construction; it is only ambiguous when, after full consideration, it is determined judicially that no interpretation can be given to it."[114]

Although in principle ambiguity is determined by the court, i.e., by the objective scrutiny of persons trained to read legal documents, a court determined to find ambiguity (and hence to favour the insured) will find ambiguity through the eyes of the insured, by applying the standard of construction of the ordinary man. There is, of course, scant difference between the reasonable insured and the ordinary man. This

---

110. *Higgins* v *Dawson* [1902] AC 1. On the distinction between patent and latent ambiguity see Lewison no 7.02.

USA: Ambiguity is a question of law for the court: *Peterson* v *Lexington Ins Co*, 753 F 2d 1016 (11 Cir, 1985—hull). But "an insurance contract is ambiguous, even if a careful, expert reading of the entire document might resolve that ambiguity, so long as there exists some internal documentary support for the insured's interpretation which a reasonable person, unacquainted with the niceties of insurance, might similarly interpret"—*Marston* v *American Employers Ins Co*, 439 F 2d 1035, 1039 (1 Cir, 1971—liability). This kind of statement is associated with the doctrine of reasonable expectations (below, 15–5B) which enables the courts to disregard clauses that the insured could not understand.

111. *Graingrowers Warehouse Co* v *Central National Ins Co*, 711 F Supp 1040, 1044 (ED Wash, 1989—casualty); *Peerless Ins Co* v *Wells*, 580 A 2d 485, 488 (Vt, 1990—liability): the court seized of the question makes up its own mind; but *cf Smith* v *Hughes Aircraft Corp*, 783 F Supp 1222, 1225 (D Ariz, 1991—liability).

112. *Kane* v *Royal Ins Co of America*, 768 P 2d 678, 680 (Colo, 1989—AR). In England, see *Budd* v *P & O Steam Navigation Co Ltd* [1969] 2 Lloyd's Rep 262, 274–275 *per* Paull J. But, in the case of proposals, which may become part of the policy, the questions must be "in such terms as can be understood by the persons who are likely to be required to answer them, which includes persons of humble rank and perhaps not the highest intelligence"—*Hales* v *Reliance Fire & Accident Corp* [1960] 2 Lloyd's Rep 391, 396 *per* McNair J.

113. In *Koskas* v *Standard Marine Ins Co Ltd* (1926) 25 Ll L Rep 363 (cargo) Sankey J disregarded a clause, because it was in very small print. On appeal this view was censured, at least as regards the clause in question, the possibility being admitted that in a true case of illegibility a clause might be disregarded: (1927) 27 Ll L Rep 59, 61 *per* Bankes LJ, 62 *per* Scrutton LJ. See also *Derby Cables Ltd* v *Frederick Oldridge Ltd* [1959] 2 Lloyd's Rep 140, 149 *per* Winn J.

114. *Higgins* v *Dawson* [1902] AC 1, 10 *per* Lord Davey. This statement, made in a case about a will, has been applied to insurance: *American Airlines Inc* v *Hope* [1973] 1 Lloyd's Rep 233, 250 *per* Roskill LJ (CA—aviation).

USA: As in England, a contract is not ambiguous merely because it is complex: *State Farm Mutual Auto Ins Co* v *Fermahin*, 836 P 2d 1074, 1077 (Hawaii, 1992—motor). A policy clause is ambiguous, when it is fairly susceptible of more than one reasonable meaning: *Walker* v *Fireman's Fund Ins Co*, 268 F Supp 899 (D Mont, 1967—motor); *Farm Bureau Mutual Ins Co Inc* v *Horinck*, 660 P 2d 1374, 1378 (Kan, 1983—liability); *Michigan Chemical Corp* v *American Home Ins Co*, 728 F 2d 374, 378 (6 Cir, 1984—liability).

has been demonstrated in the United States,[115] where this approach has become part of the doctrine of reasonable expectations (below, 15–5B). It is not law in England, where complexity is not equated with ambiguity; nor is it the law in all jurisdictions of the United States.[116] However, even in England, some courts have been quick to find ambiguity in policies of insurance, in order to apply the canon of construction *contra proferentem*.[117] Indeed, there is a danger that the canon will be used to create the ambiguity[118] that then justifies the (further) use of the canon: the cart (or the canon) gets before the horse in the pursuit of the insurer. Orthodoxy, however, insists that the *contra proferentem* rule must not be allowed to defeat the clear meaning of the words used.[119]

If the courts do find ambiguity in the words of the contract, they sometimes conduct a genuine examination of extrinsic evidence to find objective party intention. More often, the courts resort at once[120] to rules of construction unfavourable to the insurer, as follows.

15–5A Liberal Construction

"If there be a doubt, we think of all instruments that come before us, none requires a more liberal construction than a life policy."[121] Liberality cannot be applied in a vacuum and the court may use other canons of construction,[122] such as reference to the objects of the policy (above, 15–3B), in order to decide the true direction in which

---

115. *Gaunt* v *John Hancock Mutual Life Ins Co*, 160 F 2d 599, 602 *per* Judge Learned Hand (2 Cir, 1947—life), cert den 331 US 849; *Biebel Bros Inc* v *United States Fidelity & Guarantee Co*, 522 F 2d 1207 (8 Cir, 1975); *Standard Venetian Blind Co* v *American Empire Ins Co*, 469 A 2d 563 (Pa, 1983—liability); *Baybutt Construction Corp* v *Commercial Union Ins Co*, 455 A 2d 914 (Me 1983—liability); *Keene Corp* v *INA*, 597 F Supp 946, 950 (D Colum, 1984—liability). Generally, see Meyer, 36 Maine L Rev 179; Appleman, section 7384, note 62 and cases cited.

116. See Meyer, *loc cit*.

117. Below 15–5C. *Cf* USA: ambiguity alone is the basis of construction against the insurer without resort to the intermediate step of construction *contra proferentem*: Miller 88 Colum L Rev 1849 (1988).

118. *Cornish* v *Accident Ins Co Ltd* (1889) 23 QBD 453, 456 *per* Lindley LJ (CA—PA); *Cole* v *Accident Assurance Co Ltd* (1888) 5 TLR 736, 737 *per* Lindley LJ (CA—PA); *Yorkshire Ins Co Ltd* v *Campbell* [1917] AC 218, 223 *per* Lord Sumner (PC—cargo); *London & Lancashire Fire Ins Co Ltd* v *Bolands Ltd* [1924] AC 836, 848 *per* Lord Sumner (burglary).

Shepherd v *Mutual Life Ins Co*, 63 F 2d 578 (8 Cir, 1933—life); *Sulzbacher* v *Travelers Ins Co*, 137 F 2d 386 (8 Cir, 1943—PA); *Otten* v *Stonewall Ins Co*, 511 F 2d 143 (8 Cir, 1975—health); *Hofing GMC Truck Inc* v *Kay Wheel Sales Co*, 543 F Supp 414 (ED Pa, 1982—liability); *Viger* v *Commercial Ins Co*, 707 F 2d 769, 773 (3 Cir, 1983—liability); *Schering Corp* v *Home Ins Co*, 712 F 2d 4, 9 (2 Cir, 1983—liability).

119. *Alder* v *Moore* [1960] 2 Lloyd's Rep 325, 329 *per* Sellers LJ (CA—health). Courts have often stressed that there must first be genuine ambiguity: *Cole* v *Accident Ins Co Ltd* (1888) 5 TLR 736 (CA—PA); *Passmore* v *Vulcan Boiler & General Ins Co Ltd* (1936) 54 Ll L Rep 92, 94 *per* Du Parcq J (motor); *Jason* v *British Traders Ins Co Ltd* [1969] 1 Lloyd's Rep 281, 290 *per* Fisher J (PA); *Marzouca* v *Atlantic & British Commercial Ins Co Ltd* [1971] 1 Lloyd's Rep 449 (PC—fire).

Stolberg v *Pearl Assurance Co Ltd* [1970] 2 Lloyd's Rep 421 (BC—liability); *Pickford & Black Ltd* v *Canadian General Ins Co* [1976] 2 Lloyd's Rep 108 (Sup. Ct. Canada—liability). *Sentinel Life Ins Co* v *Blackmer*, 77 F 2d 347 (10 Cir, 1935—PA), cert den 296 US 602; *Hill* v *Standard Mutual Casualty Co*, 110 F 2d 1001 (7 Cir, 1940—motor); *Trinity Universal Ins Co* v *Cincinnati Ins Co*, 513 F 2d 915 (6 Cir, 1975—motor); *Schenectady County* v *Travelers Ins Co*, 368 NYS 2d 894 (1975—liability).

120. In *Acands* v *Aetna Casualty & Surety Co*, 764 F 2d 968, 973 (3 Cir, 1985—liability) the court specifically rejected the argument that ambiguous provisions of an insurance contract should not be resolved against the insurer, unless extrinsic evidence fails to resolve the ambiguity.

121. *Sheridan* v *Phoenix Life Assurance Co* (1858) El, Bl & El 156, 166 *per* Pollock B (life).

USA in this sense: *Strohmann* v *Mutual Life Ins Co*, 300 US 435 (1937—life); *Lloyds America* v *Ferguson*, 116 F 2d 921 (5 Cir, 1941—motor); *Farm Bureau Mutual Ins Co* v *Waugh*, 188 A 2d 889 (Me, 1963—motor). See further, Appleman, sections 7401 ff.

122. *Ashville Investments Ltd* v *Elmer Contractors Ltd* [1988] 2 All ER 577, 581 *per* May LJ (CA).

liberality lies.[123] In practice, this approach has effects similar to construction *contra proferentem* (below, 15–5C), i.e., construction against the insurer.[124]

15–5B The Reasonable Expectations of the Insured

It has been suggested in Scotland that the policy should be construed in accordance with the reasonable expectations of the insured.[125] In England, however, the courts have been slow to take this line as a general principle of construction, as it leads to uncertainty.

"The weakness of the reasonable expectation principle is its dependence on the notion of reasonableness. Despite many judicial expeditions to find him, the reasonable man has not been reduced to captivity. In truth, as any man on the Clapham omnibus could tell us, the reasonable man does not exist at all."[126]

"The law is concerned with legal obligations only and the law of contract only with legal obligations created by mutual obligations between contractors—not with the expectations, however reasonable, of one contractor that the other will do something that he has assumed no legal obligation to do."[127]

Nonetheless, such a principle has been vigorously applied in the United States (below, 15–5B1): once it is accepted that the general law of contract "seeks primarily to protect the reasonable expectations of the parties induced by promise-making",[128] it is a natural thing to construe their promises in such a way; and even in England, where contract lawyers have begun to talk about the protection of the parties' expectations,[129] and in Ireland, where the Supreme Court has interpreted a life contract by reference to the "officious bystander" test,[130] there are some trends in this direction (below, 15–5B2).[131]

15–5B1 Decisions in the United States

In the United States the principle has produced decisions which are unlikely in England.[132] In particular, it has been used to disregard unambiguous exceptions, of which

123. For example *Pearson* v *Commercial Union Assurance Co* (1876) 1 App Cas 498, 507 *per* Lord Penzance (hull): "In construing the meaning and extent of this 'liberty' [to go into dry dock] I think great latitude should be allowed . . . In construing such terms, it is always to be borne in mind that the object of insurance is indemnity from the risks attending some commercial adventure or operation which the owner of the subject of insurance is engaged upon; and it is well understood by both parties that the desire and object of the insured is that the policy should extend to all such risks, of the character insured against, as may arise by the adventure or operation being carried out in the usual and ordinary manner."

124. *Pelly* v *Royal Exchange Assurance Co* (1757) 1 Burr 341, 349 *per* Lee CJ (marine). In parts of the USA, this appears to be a reflex response; criticised by Miller 88 Colum L Rev 1849 (1988).

125. *Sangster's Trustees* v *General Accident Assurance Corp Ltd*, 1896 24 R (Ct of Sess) 56, 57 *per* Lord Stormonth-Darling (PA),

126. Baker [1979] CLP 17, 33. *Cf*, however, *Port-Rose*: below, 19–2A2.

127. *Lavarack* v *Woods* [1967] 1 QB 278, 294 *per* Diplock LJ (CA).

128. Holmes, 39 U Pittsburgh L Rev 381, 396 (1978).

129. Mainly as regards the award of damages: for example, Treitel p 831.

130. *Keating* v *New Ireland Assurance Co plc* [1990] IR 383, 395 (life). The test is that associated with MacKinnon LJ in *Shirlaw* v *Southern Foundries* (1926) Ltd [1939] 2 KB 206, 227 (CA), affirmed [1940] AC 701.

131. Adams and Brownsword (1991) 54 MLR 281. The doctrine has been recognised in general terms in Canada: *Reid Crowther & Partners Ltd* v *Simcoe & Erie General Ins Co* (1993) 99 DLR (4th) 741, 752–753 (Sup Ct—liability).

132. The doctrine has been defined by Keeton, 83 Harv L Rev 961, 967 (1970): "The objectively reasonable expectations of applicants and intended beneficiaries regarding the terms of insurance contracts will be honoured even though painstaking study of the policy provisions would have negated those expectations." Further it is said that policy clauses, which are contrary to the expectations of the insured, should not be

the consumer was unaware,[133] because they are, in the view of the court, unconscionable.[134]

It is, however, a principle that is found in the law of some States but not others;[135] it is not a doctrine of federal common law.[136]

The principle has been supported on various grounds:

   (a) It induces the insurer to give the prospective insured better information about the kind of cover available, and the insured will then make more efficient use of his resources.

   (b) It promotes equity, if the insurer has created misleading expectations about cover.

   (c) It promotes effective risk spreading.[137]

Excessive application of the reasonable expectations approach has been criticised[138]:

   (a) It increases uncertainty, particularly by inconsistency between State jurisdictions, and so increases the cost of insurance, as well as leading to delay in settlement of claims.[139]

   (b) "The response of the insurance industry has been a shrinkage of capacity and redoubled efforts at redrafting and restricting coverages. Insureds are now confronting the dilemma of more tightly drawn and limited contracts with

---

enforced, even if the insured was aware of them: Keeton, s 6(3)(a), p 358. The chances of court intervention are in proportion to the insurer's causal responsibility for and knowledge of the expectation: Abraham, 67 Va L Rev 1151, 1197 (1981). Further, it has been suggested that the expectations are significantly influenced by the premium: the more the insured has to pay the more he may (reasonably) expect to get: Keeton, 83 Harv L Rev 961, 975 (1970).

Generally, writers see Keeton, para 6.3(a); Abraham, ch 5; also 67 Va L Rev 1151 (1981), suggesting *inter alia* that the doctrine parallels doctrines in the general law of contract; Lashner, 57 NYULR 1175 (1982). Appleman, No 7386, note 98.35. Also, Ware, 56 U of Chicago L Rev 1461 (1989), in which the author argues that the problems the doctrine purports to solve are not real problems, and that the implementation of the doctrine is damaging to both economic efficiency and freedom (and certainty) of contract; and Widiss, 75 Iowa L Rev 1096, 1110 ff (1990), in which the author is critical of the application of the doctrine to interim insurance.

133. For example, *Steven* v *Fidelity & Casualty Co*, 377 P 2d 284, 288 (Cal, 1962—life); *Gerhardt* v *Continental Ins Co*, 225 A 2d 328 (NJ, 1966—liability); *C & J Fertilizer* v *Allied Mutual Ins Co*, 227 NW 2d 169 (Iowa, 1975—burglary); *Collister* v *Nationwide Life Ins Co*, 388 A 2d 1346 (Pa, 1978—life); *Stewart* v *Bohnert's Estate*, 162 Cal Rptr 126, 129 (1980—liability).

134. *Steven* (above); *Kievet* v *Loyal Protective Life Ins Co*, 170 A 2d 22 (NJ, 1961—PA).

135. It has been suggested by Lashner (above, pp 1090 ff) that in some States of the United States the courts have retreated from this degree of intervention, and now limit it to cases of ambiguity. For example, *Casey* v *Highlands Ins Co*, 600 P 2d 1387 (Idaho, 1979—burglary); *Clark-Peterson Co* v *Independent Ins Associates Ltd*, 492 NW 2D 675, 677 (Iowa, 1992—liability). There is little enthusiasm for the doctrine in New York: *Emons Industries Inc* v *Liberty Mutual Fire Ins Co*, 567 F Supp 335, 339 and cases cited (SD NY, 1983—liability). Still less enthusiasm among insurers such as William O Bailey, president of Aetna Life & Casualty Co, quoted by Liederman [1986] LMCLQ 79, 80–81: "courts will misinterpret language wilfully as they constantly search for more and more money to deal with societal problems which a decade ago we took care of through the tax mechanism on the part of the government."

In Canada the doctrine has gained ground: Baer, 22 Ottawa L Rev 389, 410 ff (1990). An idea of that kind was previously implanted on Canadian soil by legislation on fire insurancce which allows the court to condemn any exclusion, condition or warranty as "unjust or unreasonable."

136. *Federal Deposit Ins. Corp.* v *Zaborac*, 773 F. Supp. 137, 147 (CD Ill, 1991—liability).

137. Generally see Abraham, pp 114 ff with reservations pp 127 ff; and 67 Va L Rev 1151, 1168 ff (1981), concluding that the most acceptable basis is (b).

138. Abraham, p 122ff, 128 ff.

139. See, for example, *Standard Venetian Blind Co* v *American Empire Ins Co*, 469 A 2d 563 (Pa, 1983—liability); note 89 Dick LR 549 (1985).

little room for interpretation and little more than a Pyrrhic victory gained from past judicial grants of broad coverage for obsolete wording."[140]

(c) It ignores the true intention of the parties in commercial lines insurance, where there has been genuine bargaining.[141]

In the United States the expectations cases can be divided into two groups. In the first group, an expectation was generated by the particular insurer, usually by creating a misleading impression. Generally, the impression will be created when the contract is concluded, however, it has been held that the doctrine may apply to expectations aroused later than that.[142] In the second group, the expectation was less that of the parties than that of the court, which did not expect or wish to see that kind of clause in that kind of (insurance) contract: in short judicial legislation thinly disguised.[143] As regards the first group but not the second, converging lines of cases in England may lead English law to the point reached in the United States.

In the first group of cases are decisions that, if insurance is sold under a name that suggests cover wider than that actually offered, the American court will enforce the insurance to an extent that meets the expectations of the insured. In *Kievet* v *Loyal Protective Life Ins Co*[144] "accident" insurance was sold to a man of 48, who later suffered an accidental blow on the head which triggered latent Parkinson's disease. The insurer pleaded an exception of "disability or other loss resulting from or contributed to by any disease or ailment". The court noted that people would expect this kind of accident to be covered and that, if it were not covered, the insurance would be of little value to a man of 48. The court refused to read the exception literally, for, if it did, "the policy would be of little value to him since disability or death resulting from accidental injury would in all probability be in some sense contributed to by the infirmities of old age",[145] holding that the accident was covered by the policy. Thus judicial attack has two fronts. First, literally construed the insurance does not achieve its main purpose, for example accident cover. Second, it is assumed that the ordinary man does not read the fine print (containing the exceptions), but bases his expectations on the large print, including titles such as "Products Liability", "All Risks", which are then taken to be a statement of general cover.[146] In the application of the principle the

---

140. Liederman [1986] LMCLQ 79; also in this sense: Powell 71 Neb L Rev 1194, 1222 ff (1992).

141. Liederman, p 86. Thus in *National City Bank* v *St Paul Fire & Marine Ins Co* 435 NW 2d 57, 64 (Minn, 1989—bankers' blanket bond) the court refused to apply the doctrine *inter alia* because it "cannot be said that there is unconscionability due to unequal bargaining power when the parties are a major national bank and an insurance company. Nor is lack of insurance expertise a factor".

142. *AIU Ins Co* v *FMC Corp* 274 Cal Rptr 820, 831 (1990—liability).

143. Abraham p 104, p 109; Powell 71 Neb L Rev 1194, 1223 (1992).

144. 170 A 2d 22 (1961). See also *Silverstein* v *Metropolitan Life Ins Co*, 254 NY 81, 85 (PA), in which Cardozo CJ adopted a similar construction of the policy in order to avoid "contradiction and absurdity"; and *Lacks* v *Fidelity & Casualty Co*, 118 NE 2d 555 (NY 1954—PA) in which flight insurance, excepting cover on charter flights, was offered from a vending machine placed in front of the sales counter of a charter airline. See further *Gaunt* v *John Hancock Mutual Life Ins Co*, 160 F 2d 599 (2 Cir, 1947—life), cert den 331 US 849; *C & J Fertilizer* v *Allied Mutual Ins Co*, 227 NW 2d 169 (Iowa, 1975—burglary); Milstein, 64 Geo LJ 987 (1976); *Rordan* v *Auto Club*, 422 NYS2d 811 (1979); *Baker* v *Nationwide Mutual Ins Co*, 551 NYS 2d 387, 389 (1990—travel). *Virginia Ins Reciprocal* v *Forest County General Hospital*, 814 F Supp 535, 537 (SD Miss, 1993—liability).

145. 170 A 2d 22, 30 (1961).

146. See, for example, *Wise* v *Westchester Fire Ins Co*, 463 F 2d 386 (10 Cir, 1972—motor); *Vale Chemical Co* v *Hartford Accident & Indemnity*, 490 A 2d 896 (Pa, 1985—liability), applied in *Acands Inc* v *Aetna Casualty & Surety Co*, 764 F 2d 968 (3 Cir, 1985—liability). However, this kind of contention has failed when the policy prominently instructed the insured to read its terms carefully, for example, *Employers Reins Corp* v *Sarris*, 746 F Supp 560 (ED Pa, 1990—liability).

courts will consider whether the insured was told of an important but obscure provision, and whether it was one known to the public generally.[147]

15–5B2 England: Misleading Impression

There is more than one line of cases in England that might converge on the same point to produce law similar to that in the first group of cases in the United States.

First, there are cases concerning rectification of unilateral mistake[148]: if the insurer knowingly allows the insured to contract insurance under a mistaken belief about its terms, the contract will be rectified (and enforced) in accord with the belief of the insured.[149]

Second, there are cases that a contractual document is taken to say what it is represented as saying.[150] The result is that, if an agent of the insurer leads the proposer to expect that a document contains term X, when the reality is that it contains term Y, it may be enforced as if it contained X rather than Y.

Third, the profferor of contract terms is not allowed to rely on clauses misleadingly presented by the document itself[151]; inconspicuously printed in non-contractual written material,[152] or "tucked away at the end of the policy".[153] The insured is entitled to expect a contract "that would be free of disguised or concealed limitations".[154] However, although Clauson LJ referred[155] to a "duty" of the motor insurer to make clear any term adverse to the insured, in *Smit Tak*,[156] at least as regards commercial insurance between parties or comparable bargaining power, Mustill LJ rejected a contention of this kind: "the fact that it was called an 'Umbrella' policy, and was plainly designed to scoop up liabilities not covered by the underlying . . . policies does not mean that it should be understood as giving [the insured] protection against all misfortunes not insured elsewhere. This would be absurd and would make the policy impossible to rate." A duty to highlight and explain conditions is one matter, but a duty not to conceal them is another and is well established in law.

---

147. *Atwater Creamery Co* v *Western National Mutual Ins Co*, 366 NW 2d 271 (Minn, 1985—burglary).

148. Abraham (p 119) finds a basis for the expectations cases in doctrines of equity: "First, if the insurer knew or should have known of the insured's expectations, the equities weigh heavily in favor of holding it responsible for fulfilling them. The principle underlying reformation [rectification] would then apply. The policy would be reformed to conform to the insured's expectations. Second, if the insurer also created or helped create those expectations, equity would suggest even more strongly that those expectations be fulfilled. The insurer would be estopped to deny the truth of the expectations it had induced."

149. Some judges require inequitable conduct by the insurer. See further above, 14–3C1.

150. See above, 8–3C. For development of these arguments, see Clarke [1989] JBL 389.

151. In *Ryan* v *Oceanic SN Co Ltd* [1914] 3 KB 731, 747-748 (CA), Vaughan Williams LJ thought that the defendant could not plead a term printed below the point where the contractual part of the document appeared to end. See further Clarke [1976] CLJ 51, 77.

152. In *Stephen* v *International Sleeping-Car Co Ltd* (1903) 19 TLR 621 the defendant was not allowed to plead a clause on a voucher on the same side of the paper as 22 advertisements.

153. *Woolfall & Rimmer Ltd* v *Moyle* [1942] 1 KB 66, 73 (CA—employers' liability). Also in this sense in respect of personal lines: Insurance Ombudsman, Annual Report 1990 para 2.4; see also para 2.6. For this kind of argument in another contractual context, see Macdonald, "Exclusion Clauses", 12 LS 277 (1992).

See also the rule that, if in a document an early clause is followed by a later clause which destroys altogether the earlier clause, the later clause is to be rejected as repugnant: *Forbes* v *Git* [1922] 1 AC 256, 259 *per* Lord Wrenbury (PC). *Semble* this rule does not exist as such in the United States: *Citizens Mutual* v *Liberty Mutual*, 273 F 2d 189 (6 Cir, 1959).

154. *Parsons* v *Canadian Indemnity Co* (1982) 135 DLR (3d) 359, 364 (NS)—homeowner's).

155. *English* v *Western* [1940] 2 KB 156, 165 (CA—motor).

156. *Smit Tak Offshore Services Ltd.* v *Youell* [1992] 1 Lloyd's Rep. 154, 159 (CA—liability).

Fourth, Professor Abraham has suggested[157] that expectations cases such as *Kievert*[158] resemble the English doctrine of fundamental breach, which occurs *inter alia* when a seller delivers something fundamentally different from what was contracted for. Presumably, Professor Abraham has in mind the modern exemplar of Lord Abinger's discrimination between peas and beans, that "in the true meaning of words a car that will not go is not a car at all".[159] If a man promises peas, he must deliver peas. If a man promises a car he must deliver a car. If an insurer promises accident cover, that is what he must provide. It will be recalled that the doctrine of fundamental breach was evolved primarily to limit the effect of exemption clauses and is now based on construction of the contract.[160] It is distinguishable though not distinct from construction *contra proferentem*. By the latter a narrow but literal construction is put upon the clause. By the doctrine of fundamental breach, the court starts from the premise, that literally construed the clause applies, but declines to give it literal effect because the result would be absurd.[161] Certainly, when things are sold, the courts will apply this doctrine if the thing delivered is totally unsuitable for the purpose stipulated.[162] More generally, an exemption will be construed so as not to defeat the main purpose of the transaction.[163] The present suggestion is that insurance is sold like any other product and should be subject to the same rules of law; hence, perhaps the view of the House of Lords that a reinsurance contract must be construed so as to be not inconsistent with the concept of reinsurance.[164]

It remains to be seen whether these strands will be brought together in England to form a rule of reasonable expectations applied to insurance contracts. When this kind of contention was put to the Court of Appeal in *Smit Tak*,[165] Mustill LJ observed that, if "English law is moving in this direction it plainly has a very long way to go, but if traces of such a doctrine can be discerned it is because . . . certain sorts of insurance are 'sold like any product and should be subject to the same rules of law'. . . . Anything further from the present case is hard to imagine. This policy was not a commodity sold to lay consumers by sophisticated insurers, but a one–off contract placed at arm's length."[166] Evidently, an argument based on reasonable expectations would carry more force in the case of personal lines.[167]

15–5C Construction Contra Proferentem

"There are two well established rules of construction, although one is perhaps more often relied on with success than the other. The first is that, in case of doubt, wording in a contract is to be construed against a party who seeks to rely on it in order to diminish or exclude his basic obli-

---

157. p 236, note 18.
158. Above, 15–5B1.
159. *Karsales (Harrow) Ltd* v *Wallis* [1956] 2 All ER 866, 869 *per* Birkett LJ (CA).
160. *Photo Production Ltd* v *Securicor Transport Ltd* [1980] AC 827.
161. *UGS Finance Ltd* v *National Mortgage Bank of Greece* [1964] 1 Lloyd's Rep 446, 453 *per* Pearson LJ (CA).
162. *Tor Line AB* v *Alltrans Group of Canada Ltd* [1984] 1 All ER 103 (HL); Clarke [1984] CLJ 32.
163. *Neuchatel Asphalte* v *Barnett* [1957] 1 WLR 356, 360 *per* Denning LJ (CA).
164. *Forsik Vesta* v *Butcher* [1989] 1 AC 852, 895 *per* Lord Griffiths, 909 *per* Lord Lowry (re). See also *Cornish* v *Accident Ins Co* (1889) 23 QBD 452, 456 *per* Lindley LJ (CA—PA).
165. *Smit Tak Offshore Services* v *Youell* [1992] 1 Lloyd's Rep 154 (CA—liability) .
166. p 159, with reference to this section of the first edition of this book. The insurance in the case was liability cover *inter alia* for salvage and wreck removal.
167. Insurance Ombudsman, Annual Report 1990 para 2.4; see also para 2.6.

gation, or any common law duty which arises apart from contract. The second is that, again in case of doubt, wording is to be construed against the party who proposed it for inclusion in the contract: it was up to him to make it clear."[168]

As the judge here quoted observed,[169] in "the vast majority of cases the two rules will lead to the same result", and in this section of the book the rules are considered as one.

In most insurance cases, the rule is applied in its second form and against the insurer. In principle, however, the rule may also operate against the insured, first, as regards any words of contract for which he is primarily responsible,[170] including state-

168. *Youell* v *Bland Welch & Co Ltd* [1992] 2 Lloyd's Rep 127, 134 per Staughton LJ (CA—re).
169. *Ibid*. Although the judge expressed doubt, it appears that it is to the second that the maxim *verba chartarum fortius accipiuntur contra proferentem* refers; see *Broom's Legal Maxims* (10th ed), pp 402 ff. The same effect is sometimes achieved by the so-called "fair and reasonable construction", in effect construction in favour of the insured. In *Fowkes* v *Manchester & London Life Assurance & Loan Assn* (1863) 3 B & S 917, 929-930 Blackburn J, having referred to the rule *contra proferentem*, continued: "the above rules apply, and [the words] ought to be construed in that sense in which a prudent and reasonable man on the other side would understand them." See also *Pim* v *Reid* (1843) 6 Man & G 1, 20 per Tindal CJ (fire); *Borradaile* v *Hunter* (1843) 5 Man & G 639, 657 per Erskine J (life); *Braunstein* v *Accidental Death Assurance Co* (1861) 1 B & S 782 (PA) in which Crompton J (pp 797–798) decided by reference to reasonable construction, and Blackburn J (p 799) reached the same conclusion by construction *contra proferentem*. The rule has been of less importance in marine than in other branches of insurance: Arnould, No 112. *Cf Spooner & Sons Inc* v *Connecticut Fire Ins Co*, 314 F 2d 753, 755 (2 Cir, 1963—hull), cert den 375 US 818: the rule "is particularly applicable to a time policy of marine insurance".
In Canada the rule is applied: for example, *Cansulex Ltd* v *Reed Stenhouse Ltd* (1986) 70 BCLR 273, 312 (liability). *Idem* in the USA: , *Stiptich* v *Metropolitan Life Ins Co*, 277 US 311 (1928—life); *Aschenbrenner* v *United States Fidelity & Guarantee Co*, 292 US 85 (1934—PA); *Stroehmann* v *Mutual Life Ins Co*, 300 US 435 (1937—life); *Marston* v *American Employers Ins Co*, 439 F 2d 1035 (1 Cir, 1971—liability); *Vargas* v *INA*, 651 F 2d 838 (2 Cir, 1981—aviation). Corbin, sections 559, 559A. The rule is only applied in favour of the insured, when the identity of the insured has been determined; it does not apply in favour of a person, to assist his (preliminary) contention that he is a beneficiary of the insurance contract: *McBroome-Bennett Plumbing Inc* v *Villa France Inc*, 515 SW 2d 32 (Tex, 1974—contractors' builder's risk); *Atlas Assurance Co Ltd* v *General Builders Inc*, 600 P 2d 850 (NM, 1979—property damage). Note that in the United States third parties have rights as third parties, which are not enjoyed in England: Rest 2d Contracts, ch 14.
Examples of the application of the rule *contra proferentem* include: *Fowkes* v *Manchester & London Life Assurance & Loan Assn* (1863) 3 B & S 917 (life): "untrue" statement by insured meant one that was fraudulent or designedly untrue; *Simmonds* v *Cockell* [1920] 1 KB 843, 845 per Roche J (theft): warranty that premises "always occupied" did not mean never unattended, but used for occupation; *Lake* v *Simmons* [1927] AC 487, 508–509 per Viscount Sumner: exception of jewellery "entrusted" was limited to delivery to a person with a species of fiduciary duty, and did not apply to any person to whom the goods were handed over; *English* v *Western* [1940] 2 KB 156, 163–164 per Slesser LJ (CA—motor): exception of "any member of insured's household" limited to household of which insured was head; *Houghton* v *Trafalgar Ins Co Ltd* [1953] 2 Lloyd's Rep 503 (CA—motor): exception while car is "conveying any load in excess of that for which it was constructed" limited to vehicles for which a weight load was specified; *Woolford* v *Liverpool CC* [1968] 2 Lloyd's Rep 256, 258–259 (PA) Roskill J declined to limit "cover any injury" to injury customarily covered; *Lane* v *Spratt* [1969] 2 Lloyd's Rep 229, 237 per Roskill J (goods in transit): "reasonable precautions to prevent accidents" did not extend to vetting the insured's staff; *S & M Hotels Ltd* v *Legal & General Assurance Sy Ltd* [1972] 1 Lloyd's Rep 157 (householder's comprehensive): condition of "proper state of repair" not breached by inadequate supports during reconstruction.
170. *Cf* USA: it is said that such words are not construed against either party: *US Shipping Board* v *Aetna Casualty & Surety Co*, 98 F 2d 238 (D Colum, 1938—bond); *Nieschlag* v *Atlantic Mutual Ins Co*, 43 F Supp 797 (SD NY, 1941—cargo), affirmed 126 F 2d 834 (2 Cir, 1942), cert den 317 US 640. Certainly, this will be true of standard clauses vetted and approved by State officials, however, something like the English rule is found when the clauses have been drafted by the insurer: *Standard & Poors Corp* v *Continental Casualty Co*, 718 F Supp 1219, 1221 (SD NY, 1989—liability). On one view this is construction not less strict but even stricter against the insurer: ambiguity alone is the basis of construction against the insurer without resort to the intermediate step of construction *contra proferentem*: Miller 88 Colum L Rev 1849 (1988). However, something like the English view is found in other cases: "ambiguous language is construed against the party who caused the uncertainty to exist": *AIU Ins Co* v *FMC Corp*, 274 Cal Rptr 820, 831 (1990—liability).

ments defining the scope of the risk[171] of the kind found in the Lloyd's slip[172] prepared by a Lloyd's broker. Second it applies to terms originally drafted by the underwriter but adopted by the insured through his broker for the particular contract.[173] The rule is unlikely, however, to be applied against the unskilled insured whose statements, usually in response to questions framed by the insurer, become terms of the contract.[174]

In early days, the rule was justified as extending insurance cover and thus promoting the efficiency or expansion of trade.[175] Today, the justification lies in the presumption that the party drafting the words looks to his own interests and no greater benefit to himself[176] (or burden to the other) can have been intended than he has made clear, above all, clear to the other party. In the United States, the rule has also been justified as an equitable response to the standard form contract.

"In the case of personal lines insurance, the disparate position between the parties to the contract is concededly most evident. The layman is usually untrained and unsuspecting of the nuances of insurance coverages. Equitable principles, therefore, dictate that the contract be interpreted as a layman would interpret the wording . . . "[177]

From statements like this, one might expect the speed with which the courts resort to construction *contra proferentem* to be in some proportion to the need to protect the insured. Although the vulnerability of the insured is a connected but distinct consideration from that of whether the particular contract was adopted in a standard form prepared by the insurer or actually negotiated, the vulnerability of the particular insured may drive the court to greater severity in its construction *contra proferentem*,[178] with the corollary that such construction will be softer when parties have equal bargaining power.[179] In England, certainly, this is true when a form of words is drafted by a body

171. *Birrell* v *Dryer* (1884) 9 App Cas 345, 352 *per* Lord Blackburn (hull); *Condogianis* v *Guardian Assurance Co* [1921] 2 AC 125, 130–131 *per* Lord Shaw (PC—fire).

172. *A/S Ocean* v *Black Sea & Baltic General Ins Co Ltd* (1935) 51 Ll L Rep 305, 307 *per* Greer LJ (CA—hull), applied in *Bartlett & Partners Ltd* v *Meller* [1961] 1 Lloyd's Rep 487 (goods in transit); see also *De Maurier (Jewels) Ltd* v *Bastion Ins Co Ltd* [1967] 2 Lloyd's Rep 550, 559–560 *per* Donaldson J (jeweller's AR); *American Airlines Inc* v *Hope* [1973] 1 Lloyd's Rep 233, 250 *per* Roskill LJ (aviation); *Balfour* v *Beaumont* [1982] 2 Lloyd's Rep 493, 503 *per* Webster J (aviation); *Ikerigi CN SA* v *Palmer* [1991] 1 Lloyd's Rep 400, 416 per Hobhouse J (freight). However, if the insurer amends the slip prepared by the insured, the amendment is construed against the insurer: *Dunn* v *Campbell* (1920) 4 Ll L Rep 36. 39 *per* Bankes LJ (CA); *Jaglom* v *Excess Ins Co Ltd* [1971] 2 Lloyd's Rep 171, 177 *per* Donaldson J (AR).

173. *McDermott International Inc* v *Lloyd's Underwriters of London*, 944 F.2d 1199, 1207 (5 Cir, 1991—AR installation floater).

174. For example *Condogianis* v *Guardian Assurance Co Ltd* [1921] 2 AC 125 (PC—fire).

175. *Pelly* v *Royal Exchange* (1757) 1 Burr 341, 349 *per* Lee CJ (hull); *Newbury* v *Armstrong* (1829) 6 Bing 201, 202 *per* Tindal CJ (guarantee). The rule against absurdity (above, 15–4) is still justified on grounds of business necessity.

176. *Quia stipulatori liberum fuit verba late concipere*: the person stipulating should take care fully to express that which he proposes shall be done for his own benefit—Broom, *Legal Maxims* (10th ed), pp 402 ff. See for example *Notman* v *Anchor Assurance Co* (1858) 4 CB (NS) 466, 481 *per* Cockburn CJ (life); *Simmonds* v *Cockell* [1920] 1 KB 843, 845 *per* Roche J (theft). *Wawanesa Mutual Ins Co* v *Bell* (1957) 8 DLR (2d) 577, 583–584 *per* Locke J (Sup Ct—motor); *Paddleford* v *Fidelity & Casualty Co*, 100 F 2d 606 (7 Cir, 1938—fidelity), *cert den* 306 US 664; *United National Ins Co* v *Waterfront Realty Corp*, 777 F Supp 254, 257 (SDNY, 1991—liability). See further Appleman, section 7401, note 2 and cases cited.

177. Liederman [1986] LMCLQ 79, 84.

178. In England, as regards the construction of statements made by a proposer to the insurer's medical examiner, Fletcher Moulton LJ said "It is a case in which the principle of taking such a document as this '*contra proferentes*' ought to be applied in the strongest way, in view of the confidential character of the interview and the relations created thereby"—*Joel* v *Law Union & Crown Ins Co* [1908] 2 KB 431.

179. *Eagle Leasing Corp* v *Hartford Fire Ins Co*, 540 F 2d 1257, 1261 (5 Cir, 1976—P & I); *Loblaw Inc* v *Employers' Liability Assurance Corp*, 446 NYS 2d 743 (1981—liability); *Garcia* v *Truck Ins Exchange*, 682 P 2d 1100, 1105–1106 (Cal, 1984—liability).

on which the interests of both insurer and insured were represented[180]; in that case, the courts will be slow to use rules of construction against the insurer to disturb the allocation of risk suggested by the ordinary meaning of the contract terms.[181] Similarly, in New York, the rule does not apply between insurers themselves because they "are sophisticated business entities, familiar with the market in which they deal and armed with relatively equivalent bargaining power".[182]

From this it does not follow, however, that the heart of the court will always harden to the man of affairs.[183] Parties do not always bring their bargaining power to bear on a particular contract. In Pennsylvania, for example, the "rule favoring the insured applies even if the insured is a commercial or business entity, and therefore, presumably knowledgeable about contracts and their legal implications".[184] "The critical fact remains that the policy in question is a standard form policy prepared by the company's experts, with language selected by the insurer. The specific language in question was not negotiated, therefore, it is irrelevant that some corporations have company counsel. Additionally, this standard form policy has been issued to big and small businesses throughout the State. Therefore it would be incongruous for the court to apply different rules of construction based on the policyholder."[185] Bargaining power is not a factor that provokes construction *contra proferentem* so much as one which, given the presence of a profferor and a profferee, affects the severity with which the rule of construction is applied.

In the general law of England *contra proferentem* has been a canon of construction of second resort, one employed when other aids to interpretation do not lead to the meaning of the words.[186] When confronted with insurance contracts, however, courts have been ready to use the canon as a weapon of first strike against ambiguity, it being "extremely important with reference to insurance, that there should be a tendency rather to hold for the insured than for the company, where any ambiguity arises upon the face of the policy."[187] This is important, notably, in life insurance, for otherwise it would

"lead a vast number of persons to suppose that they have made a provision for their families by an insurance on their lives, and by payment of perhaps a very considerable proportion of their

180. *Tersons Ltd* v *Stevenage Development Corp* [1963] 2 Lloyd's Rep 333, 368 *per* Pearson LJ (CA).
181. *Photo Production Ltd* v *Securicor Transport Ltd* [1980] AC 827; *Mitchell (Chesterhall) Ltd* v *Finney Lock Seeds Ltd* [1983] QB 284 (CA), affirmed [1983] 2 AC 803.
182. *United States Fire Ins Co* v *General Re Corp*, 949 F 2d 569, 574 (2 Cir, 1991—liability).
183. For example *Metal Scrap & By-products Ltd* v *Federal Conveyors Ltd* [1953] 1 Lloyd's Rep 221, 227 *per* Croom-Johnson J (goods in transit).
184. *Federal Kemper Ins Co* v *Jones*, 777 F Supp 405, 409 (MD Pa, 1991—liability).
185. *Boeing Co* v *Aetna Casualty & Surety Co*, 784 P 2d 507, 514 (Washington, 1990—liability). See also *Acands Inc* v *Aetna Casualty & Surety Co*, 764 F 2d 968, 973 (3 Cir, 1985—liability); *McNeilab Inc* v *North River Ins Co*, 645 F Supp 525 (SD NY, 1986—liability); *Keating* v *National Union Fire Ins Co*, 754 F Supp 1431, 1437 (CD Cal, 1990—liability).
186. *Lindus* v *Melrose* (1858) 3 H & N 177, 182 *per* Coleridge J (Exch Ch). Broom, *loc cit* citing 1 Duer Insurance 210.
In Canada and USA the rule is still said to be one of last resort, but usually this has been said in cases of equal bargaining power: *Stevenson* v *Reliance* [1956] SCR 936, 953 *per* Cartwright J (motor); *Consolidated-Bathurst* v *Mutual Boiler* [1980] 1 SCR 888, 901 *per* Estey J; *Schering Corp* v *Home Ins Co*, 712 F 2d 4, 10 (2 Cir, 1983—liability).
187. *Fitton* v *Accidental Death Ins Co* (1864) 17 CBNS 122, 134–135 *per* Willes J (PA). See also *Re Etherington and Lancashire & Yorkshire Accident Ins Co* [1909] 1 KB 591, 596 *per* Vaughan Williams LJ (CA—PA).

income, when in point of fact, from the very commencement, the policy was not worth the paper upon which it was written."[188]

Still, the rule *contra proferentem* does not justify an unreasonable construction in order to favour the insured. The Privy Council in *Condogianis* v *Guardian Assurance Co Ltd*[189] declined to adopt the "extreme literalism"[190] argued by the insured, because it was a view of the words that was beyond "the limits of reasonable interpretation".[191] Nor does the court adopt the *most* reasonable view: that might not be *contra proferentem* at all. English law cannot be far from the law of New York where, in a case of ambiguity, the insured prevails if he establishes *any* reasonable interpretation in support of his position; if the insurer is to prevail he must establish that his interpretation is the *only* reasonable interpretation.[192]

For example, in *Advance (NSW) Ins Agencies* v *Matthews*,[193] the claim was resisted because one of the joint insured had not disclosed a previously rejected claim in response to a question in the proposal, asking whether "you" had ever had a claim rejected. The claimants argued *contra proferentem* and persuaded the lower courts that, in the case of "a joint policy the word 'you' should be taken to mean the jointure composed of all the components [and that] on the true construction of the question it only covers the situation where [both] have had a claim rejected".[194] The High Court of Australia, however, stressed the purpose of the inquiry and came to the eminently reasonably conclusion against the claimants that "you" meant "either of you".[195]

The rule *contra proferentem*, it has been said, will not be applied, if the result is contrary to law and, more specifically, if the construction works a wrong to a third party.[196] As this rule of construction usually works against the insurer, it is likely to

---

188. *Anderson* v *Fitzgerald* (1853) 4 HLC 484, 507 *per* Lord St Leonards (life); see also *Joel* v *Law Union & Crown Ins Co* [1908] 2 KB 863, 886 *per* Fletcher Moulton LJ (CA—life); *Re Etherington and Lancashire & Yorkshire Accident Ins Co* [1909] 1 KB 591, 596 *per* Vaughan Williams LJ (CA—PA). In *Condogianis* v *Guardian Assurance Co Ltd* [1921] 2 AC 125, 130 (PC—fire) Lord Shaw said of a term derived from the proposal form: "Where an ambiguity exists, the contract must stand if an answer has been made to the question on a fair and reasonable interpretation of that question. Otherwise the ambiguity would be a trap against which the insured would be protected by courts of law."
189. [1921] 2 AC 125 (PC—fire): the insured had argued that as his statement in the proposal, that he had made a previous claim, was literally true, it should be treated as true, although materially false, because he had omitted mention of another claim. This construction was rejected. See also *National Protector Fire Ins Co Ltd* v *Nivert* [1913] AC 507, 513 *per* Lord Atkinson (PC—fire); *English* v *Western* [1940] 2 KB 156, 166 (CA—motor) *per* Goddard LJ, dissenting, in favour of the insurer.
190. [1921] 2 AC 125, 131 *per* Lord Shaw.
191. *Ibid*, p 132 *per* Lord Shaw. USA in this sense: *Eagle Leasing Corp* v *Hartford Fire Ins Co*, 540 F 2d 1257, 1263 (5 Cir, 1976—P & I). However, the onus is on the insurer to show that the insured had no reasonable basis for his belief or construction: *Collister* v *Nationwide Life Ins Co*, 388 A 2d 1346 (Pa, 1978—life).
192. *Lachs* v *Fidelity & Casualty Co*, 118 NE 2d 555 (NY, 1954—airplane trip), adopted in *Steven* v *Fidelity & Casualty Co*, 377 P 2d 284 (Cal, 1962—life); *Pan American World Airways Inc* v *Aetna Casualty & Surety Co*, 505 F 2d 989, 1021 (2 Cir, 1974—aviation); [1975] 1 Lloyd's Rep 77, 99; *Vargas* v *INA*, 651 F 2d 838 (2 Cir, 1981—aviation); *Loblaw Inc* v *Employers' Liability Assurance Corp*, 446 NYS 2d 743, 745 (1981—liability). See also *Hill* v *Standard Mutual Casualty Co*, 110 F 2d 1001 (7 Cir, 1940—motor); *Collister* v *Nationwide Life Ins Co*, 388 A 2d 1346 (Pa, 1978—life); *McCormick & Co Inc* v *Empire Ins Group*, 878 F 2d 27, 31 (2 Cir, 1989—liability); *US Fidelity & Guarantee Co* v *Fireman's Fund Ins Co*, 896 F 2d 200 (6 Cir, 1990—liability); *Chen* v *Metropolitan Ins Co*, 907 F 2d 566 (5 Cir, 1990—PA). Some of these cases were discussed by Webster J in *Excess Life Assurance Co Ltd* v *Firemen's Ins Co* [1982] 2 Lloyd's Rep 599, 610 (fidelity). See further, Appleman, section 7401, note 9 and cases cited.
193. (1989) 63 ALJR 365 (HCA—homeowner's).
194. pp 366–367.
195. p 369.
196. Broom's *Legal Maxims* (10th ed), p 407.

favour rather than wrong third parties who might have an interest in the enforcement of the insurance. It will be otherwise only when the rule is used against the insured for statements of his which become terms of the policy.

15–6 QUALIFICATION AND INCONSISTENCY

If the contract contains terms that appear to be inconsistent, contradictory or mutually repugnant, the court first attempts to reconcile the terms.[197] The position in this and other respects is the same between terms in the original contract and words in a subsequent endorsement.[198]

Inconsistency must be distinguished from multiplicity. In the United States, certain courts determined to aid the insured have been quick to find internal inconsistency between exclusions of cover, and have seized on this to reduce the scope of the exclusions.[199] Many decisions of this kind would be seen in England as contrary to the rule, a rule also recognised in the United States, that each exclusion "is meant to be read with the insuring agreement independently of every other exclusion. The exclusions should be read *seriatim*, not cumulatively. . . . There is no instance in which an exclusion can properly be regarded as inconsistent with another exclusion, since they bear no relationship with one another."[200] The meaning must be sought first within the confines of the clause in question: see above 15–3A.

Inconsistency must also be distinguished from deliberate qualification by the draftsman: a common technique of documentary drafting defines a concept, such as a duty, by stating a broad proposition and then reducing its scope by qualification.[201]

To distinguish inconsistency, which is unintentional, from qualification, which is intentional, courts consider the degree of apparent contradiction and the way it appears in the document. If, for example, the policy covers travel in Europe but then excepts travel in Europe, that is a contradiction and a nonsense—of a stark and simple kind that is unlikely to arise. If, however, the contract covers States A to F, then excepts State D, is that a contradiction or a qualification? The answer must be sought first within the confines of the clause but, as indicated (above 15–3B), in certain cases the answer may depend on the main purpose of the contract or, in the legal currency of the United States, the reasonable expectations of the insured.

In the *Century* case,[202] the Century bank had a policy with cover in several sections,

---

197. *Benignae facienda sunt interpretationes propter simplicitatem laicorum ut res magis valeat quam pereat* (Co Litt 36a), more usually known as *ut res magis valeat quam pereat*: Broom's *Legal Maxims* (10th ed), p 361. For example *Beacon Life & Fire Assurance Co v Gibb* (1862) 1 Moore (NS) 73 in which the Privy Council applied a fire policy, including the word "premises", to a ship.
  USA in this sense: *Keystone Fabric Laminates Inc v Federal Ins Co*, 407 F 2d 1353 (3 Cir, 1969—fire).
198. *New Market Investment Corp v Fireman's Fund Ins Co*, 774 F Supp 909 (Pa, 1991—cargo).
199. For example *Baybutt Construction Corp v Commercial Union Ins Co*, 455 A 2d 914 (Me, 1983—liability); Meyer, 36 Maine L Rev 179 (1984). See also *Federal Ins Co v P A T Homes Inc*, 547 P 2d 1050 (Ariz, 1976—liability).
200. *Weedo v Stone-E-Brick Inc*, 405 A 2d 788, 795 (NJ, 1979—liability). See also *Biebel Bros Inc v United States Fidelity & Guarantee Co*, 522 F 2d 1207, 1212 (8 Cir, 1975—liability).
201. Generally, Coote, *Exception Clauses*, ch 1. Keeton, section 4.1(a). This approach to a motor policy can be seen in *Davidson v Guardian Royal Exchange Assurance* [1979] 1 Lloyd's Rep 406, 409 *per* Lord Kissen (Ct Sess); and in the USA in *Hermitage Ins Co v Action Marine*, 816 F Supp 1280 (ND 1LL, 1993—liability).
202. *Federal Insurance Co v Century Federal Savings & Loan Assn*, 824 P 2d 302 (NM, 1992—financial institutions cover).

one of which was called "Mortgage Holder's Insurance" and the second of three heads of cover was against failure of a mortgagor to provide valid fire insurance on property mortgaged to the bank. This occurred but the insurer refused to pay, pointing to an (unfulfilled) "condition" of the cover, that the bank should "verify the actual existence of valid insurance" on the mortgaged property. The Supreme Court of New Mexico accepted the bank's argument that the cover was "in irreconcilable conflict with the verification condition".[203] It rejected the argument of the insurer for a mutual accommodation of the two clauses, whereby the condition qualified the cover by requiring the bank to take reasonable steps to verify. That was not what the clause said: "the policy provides on one page that it covers a loss when hazard insurance does not exist and, four pages later, requires the insured to verify that valid insurance exists".[204] This, said the court, was a case of contradiction or repugnancy and the condition should be disregarded so as to fulfil the reasonable expectations of the insured.

In England, the court is less likely to disregard a condition of this kind altogether than to find some narrow construction which leaves it in the contract but out of harm's way, even if on a literal view of the condition it denies cover altogether. In this connection as regards contracts in general, Pearson LJ once spoke of a "rule of construction . . . to give the contract that business efficacy which the parties as reasonable men must have intended it to have", to cope with "standard terms of contract containing exception clauses drawn in extravagantly wide terms, which would produce absurd results if applied literally".[205] Thus, in another case concerning towage, an exception for the consequences of "omission or default" did not excuse performance (towage) altogether—that would be a contradiction that denied the existence of a contract at all—but applied only to failure to take precautions when purporting to perform the contract.[206] In a further case, an insurance case, if the condition were to be construed in isolation, "it would follow", as Goddard LJ observed, "that the underwriters were saying: 'We will insure you against your liability for negligence on condition that you are not negligent' ".[207] To resolve this apparent contradiction, the court in that case held covered the insured employer, who had appointed competent staff and had thus performed a condition requiring "reasonable precautions to prevent accidents", notwithstanding negligence by the staff in question which led to an accident, for which the employer as employer was liable.

If, indeed, "the later clause does not destroy but only qualifies the earlier, then the two are to be read together and effect is to be given to the intention of the parties as disclosed by the deed as a whole."[208] Either, one can say, there is really no inconsistency at all or, another way of looking at the same document, there is but apparent inconsistency, which is resolved in favour of the more specific provision by limiting the

203. p 305. The same court went further along the same line of interpretation in an earlier case, in which the insuring clause was against loss caused by accidental discharge of water from a plumbing system, but there was an exclusion as regards damage due to water below ground. As "substantial *parts* of *many* plumbing systems" are below ground, the court decided for the insured: *King* v *Travelers Ins Co*, 505 P 2d 1226 (NM, 1973). See also *Western Heritage Ins Co* v *Chava Trucking*, 991 F 2d 651 (10 Cir, 1993—liability).
204. p 306
205. *UGS Finance* v *National Mortgage Bank of Greece* [1964] 1 Lloyd's Rep. 446, 453 (CA). See also above, 15–4.
206. *The Cap Palos* [1921] P 458 (CA).
207. *Woolfall & Rimmer Ltd* v *Moyle* [1942] 1 KB 66, 76. See also the restrictive construction put upon a condition that the insured shall exercise reasonable care to prevent the insured loss: below 19–2A1
208. *Forbes* v *Git* [1922] 1 AC 256, 259 *per* Lord Wrenbury (PC).

broader provision *pro tanto*.[209] For example, health cover may be world wide, except States A and B.[210] However, there is a presumption that a proviso or qualification is confined in effect to the last antecedent clause.[211]

Even in England, an inconspicuous qualification may be disregarded altogether, however, on a slightly different ground:

"It is true that the document must be read as a whole, and that wide and comprehensive words of obligation imposed on the underwriters in the body of the policy may be cut down by subsequent clauses in the document, but, . . . a policy of this kind is not to be approached with the idea that a large part of the benefit of the insurance which any employers would obviously wish to get, and which is at the outset given in wide terms, is to be eliminated by a 'condition' tucked away at the end of the policy in the context in which this condition is to be found, for, be it observed, all the other conditions relate to matters of comparatively minor importance."[212]

In case of real or substantial inconsistency or contradiction in an insurance contract, the rules of construction that may apply are as follows.

15–6A Inconsistency: First In . . .

If there is real inconsistency, there is an old rule of construction that favours the term that appears first. "If in a deed the earlier clause is followed by a later clause which destroys altogether the obligation created by the earlier clause, the later clause is to be rejected as repugnant and the earlier clause prevails."[213] This rule has been criticised as "a mere rule of thumb, totally unscientific and only to be resorted to when all else fails."[214] It is singularly inappropriate to insurance policies in which the customary style of drafting does not necessarily put the most important terms first. Indeed, there is or was another rule that pointed in the opposite direction: that, 'if two sections of the same statute are repugnant, the known rule is that the last must prevail'. What was recently said of that rule might also be said of the old rule of construction : 'If there ever was such a principle, it is long since obsolete. Such a mechanical approach to the construction of statutes is altogether out of step with the modern purposive approach to the interpretation of statutes and documents."[215] The courts are reluctant to let the policy take away with one clause what it appears to have granted with another clause.[216]

---

209. *Izzard v Universal Ins Co Ltd* [1937] AC 773, 780 *per* Lord Wright (motor); *Commercial Ins Co v Burnquist*, 105 F Supp 920, 935 (ND Iowa, 1952—health); *Consolidated Electric Coop v Employers Mutual Liability Ins Co*, 106 F Supp 322 (D Mo, 1952—liability).

210. For another example, motor cover may be subject to conditions, such as the maintenance of the vehicle in efficient condition. *New India Assurance Co Ltd v Yeo Beng Chow* [1972] 1 WLR 786 (PC—motor).

211. *Rintoul v Sun Life Assurance Co*, 142 F 2d 776 (7 Cir, 1944—life), *cert den* 323 US 776.

212. *Woolfall & Rimmer Ltd v Moyle* [1942] 1 KB 66, 73 *per* Lord Greene MR (CA—employers liability). See also above, 15–5B2. It is submitted that the last point in the quotation, that the contradictory clause kept poor company, was not essential to the decision.

213. *Forbes v Git* [1922] 1 AC 256, 259 *per* Lord Wrenbury (PC). Lewison no 8.08.

214. Odgers, p 72. *Cf* the conflicting rule of construction below, 15–6D. *Cf* the USA, where, it is said, priority depends not on chronological order but on the search for intention and the purpose of the policy: for example, *Citizens Mutual Automobile Ins Co v Liberty Mutual Ins Co*, 273 F 2d 189 (6 Cir, 1959—motor); *Government Employees Ins Co v Lally*, 327 F 2d 568 (4 Cir, 1964—motor).

215. *Re Marr* [1990] Ch 773, 784, per Nicholls LJ, with whom the other members of the Court of Appeal agreed,

216. See also the cases on misleading impression, above, 15–5B2.

15–6B Words Written and Words Printed

In case of inconsistency between printed words and words written or typed in for the particular contract, on which the parties have deliberated, the latter prevail because they have been the subject of deliberation.[217] In particular, a proper endorsement will prevail over the standard terms in the main body of the policy[218] unless, perhaps, the policy and indorsement are presented at the same time as a single package and the indorsement is not specifically negotiated or adverted to.[218a]. Further, the court will disregard the printed words of a standard form of policy which are clearly inapplicable to the particular contract of insurance.[219]

15–6C The Main Purpose of the Contract

Words have been rejected if they are inconsistent with the main purpose of the contract. For example, when the carriage of goods overland was insured on a form prepared for carriage by sea, the court ignored words appropriate only to carriage by sea.[220]

15–6D Policy and Proposal

In the case of inconsistency between the proposal, incorporated into the policy as the basis of the contract, and the terms expressed in the policy itself, the latter prevail,[221]

217. *Robertson* v *French* (1830) 4 East 130, 136 *per* Lord Ellenborough CJ (hull and cargo); *Foster* v *Mentor Life Assurance Co* (1854) 3 E & B 48, 82 *per* Lord Campbell CJ (life); *Joyce* v *Realm Marine Ins Co* (1872) LR 7 QB 580, 583 *per* Blackburn J (re); *Cunard SS Co Ltd* v *Marten* [1902] 2 KB 624, 627 *per* Walton J (liability); *St Paul Fire & Marine Ins Co* v *Morice* (1906) 22 TLR 449, 450 *per* Kennedy J (cargo); *Farmers' Co-op Ltd* v *National Benefit Assurance Co Ltd* (1922) 13 Ll L Rep 417, 530, 533 *per* Atkin LJ (CA); *Kaufmann* v *British Surety Ins Co Ltd* (1929) 33 Ll L Rep 315, 318 *per* Roche J (motor).

    Aetna Ins Co v *Houston Oil & Transport Co*, 49 F 2d 121 (5 Cir, 1931—hull), cert den 284 US 628; *Marston* v *American Employers Ins Co*, 439 F 2d 1035 (1 Cir, 1971—liability); *Argonaut Ins Co* v *National Indemnity Co*, 435 F 2d 718 (10 Cir, 1971—motor). Appleman, section 7522.

    The decision might have been reached on this basis in *Hennor Co Inc* v *Superior Fire Ins Co*, 39 F 2d 477 (D NY, 1930—fire), but the court relied on a broader rule that any contradiction or inconsistency between clauses of the policy will be resolved in favour of the insured. This rule has also been applied, for example, in *Oswega Soy Products Corp* v *Home Ins Co*, 94 NYS 2d 301 (1945—fire); *Silberg* v *California Life Ins Co*, 521 P 2d 1103 (Cal, 1974—medical expenses).

    218. For example *San-Nap-Pak Manufacturing Co* v *Firemen's Ins Co*, 47 NYS 2d 542 (1944—transportation policy), affirmed 51 NYS 2d 579; *Henderson* v *Trans-continental Mutual Ins Co Inc*, 227 F 2d 106 (5 Cir, 1955—motor); *Argonaut Ins Co* v *National Indemnity Co*, 435 F 2d 718 (10 Cir, 1971—motor); *Elston* v *Shell Oil Co*, 376 F Supp 968 (D La, 1973—motor), affirmed 495 F 2d 1371 (5 Cir, 1974); *Alaska Rural Electric Coop Assn* v *Insco Ltd*, 785 P 2d 1193 (Ala, 1990—liability).

    218a. *Simon* v *Shelter General Ins Co*, 842 P 2d 236, 241 (Colo, 1992—liability).

    219. *Hydarnes SS Co* v *Indemnity Mutual Marine Assurance Co* [1895] 1 QB 500, 506 *per* Lord Esher MR, 509 *per* Rigby LJ (CA—freight); *Western Assurance Co* v *Poole* [1903] 1 KB 376, 389 *per* Bigham J (hull); *South British Fire & Marine Ins Co* v *Da Costa* [1906] 1 KB 456, 460–461 *per* Bigham J (re); *Home Ins Co* v *Victoria-Montreal Fire Ins Co* [1907] AC 59, 64 *per* Lord Macnaghten (PC—re); *Yorkshire Ins Co Ltd* v *Campbell* [1917] AC 218, 224 *per* Lord Sumner (PC—cargo); *Mountain* v *Whittle* [1921] 1 AC 615, 630 *per* Lord Sumner (hull). *Aitken* v *Gardiner* (1956) 4 DLR (2d) 119, 142 (Ont). *Traders & General Ins Co* v *Champ*, 226 F 2d 829 (9 Cir, 1955—motor).

    220. *Baring Bros* v *Marine Ins Co* (1894) 10 TLR 276 (CA); see also *Robinson Gold Mining Co* v *Alliance Ins Co* [1902] 2 KB 488 (CA); *Home Ins Co* v *Victoria-Montreal Fire Ins Co* [1907] AC 59, 64–65 *per* Lord Macnaghten (PC—re) and above, 15–3B.

    In the general law see cases on carriage by sea, such as *Glynn* v *Margetson & Co* [1893] AC 351, 357 *per* Lord Halsbury, and *Sze Hai Tong Bank Ltd* v *Rambler Cycle Co Ltd* [1959] AC 576, 587 *per* Lord Denning (PC). *Traders & General Ins Co* v *Champ*, 226 F 2d 829 (9 Cir, 1955—motor). Lewison no 8.09.

    221. *Australian Widows' Fund Life Assurance Sy Ltd* v *National Mutual Life Assn Ltd* [1914] AC 634, 642 *per* Lord Parker (PC—re); *Kaufmann* v *British Surety Ins Co Ltd* (1929) 33 Ll L Rep 315, 318 *per* Roche J (motor); *Izzard* v *Universal Ins Co Ltd* [1937] AC 773, 779–780 *per* Lord Wright (motor).

as being later and thus "more expressive of the final minds of the parties,"[222] as well as being recorded more formally. For similar reasons, in *Punjab National Bank* v *De Boinville*[223] absent a contention that the policy should be rectified, Hobhouse J declined to look at the relevant Lloyd's slip in order to interpret the policy. Such an approach would be "wrong in law. The purpose of a policy was to state the actual and complete terms of the contract of insurance".

The application of this principle may appear to conflict with that discussed above, 15–6B. In *Conheeney* v *Westgate Ins Co Ltd*,[224] the liability policy was couched in standard terms wide enough to cover the claimant's vicarious liability for the negligence of his employee, however, reference to the proposal made it clear the claimant had sought and paid for cover on the basis that he was a self-employed one-man business, and that was the decision of the court.

15–6E Policy and Certificate

Inconsistency may be found between the terms of a master policy and certificates, which have been issued to various persons intended to benefit from the master policy. For example, an employer may arrange group life or health insurance for his employees, and issues certificates to the employees. A shipper of goods in bulk may insure the bulk, but sell parts of the bulk CIF to various buyers, giving them certificates of insurance in respect of their part.[225]

If the certificate appears to be a complete statement of the insurance contract, subject to contrary terms in the certificate, that should preclude reference to the policy at all. The first reason is the application of the parol evidence rule (above, 14–1), especially if, as often happens, the certificate contains a statement that it shall take the place of the policy.[226] The second reason, particularly if such a statement is found in the certificate, is that the buyer has not been given sufficient notice of the terms which are stated in the policy but not in the certificate.[227]

If the certificate is evidently not a complete statement of the terms of the contract of insurance, the courts have compared the contents of certificate and policy and held in case of conflict, usually in favour of the insured, that the certificate prevailed. A number of arguments support this conclusion. First, the contradictions between policy and certificate create ambiguity and any ambiguity must be resolved against the insurer by construction *contra proferentem*.[228] Second, in the case of cargo insurance the certificate is put into circulation as a document of international trade, which will be relied on by buyers of the goods; efficient business practice predicates that the

---

222. *Kaufmann* v *British Surety Ins Co Ltd* (1929) 33 Ll L Rep 315, 318 *per* Roche J (motor). *North American Accident Ins Co* v *Anderson*, 100 F 2d 452 (10 Cir, 1938—PA); *Gurley* v *Life & Casualty Co*, 132 F Supp 289 (D NC, 1955—life), affirmed 229 F 2d 326 (4 Cir, 1956).

223. [1992] 1 Lloyd's Rep 7; an appeal against his decision was dismissed: *ibid*.

224. High Court, 1992 (unreported).

225. See, for example, *Manbre Saccharine Co Ltd* v *Corn Products Co Ltd* [1919] 1 KB 198.

226. *De Monchy* v *Phoenix Ins Co* (1928) 33 Com Cas 197, 204 *per* Scrutton LJ (CA—cargo). However, he accepted (p 206) the possibility that the insured might rely on a term in the policy but not in the certificate, if it was a term adverse to the insurer; see also Sankey LJ (p 209). *Cf New York & Oriental S/S Co* v *Automobile Ins Co*, 37 F 2d 461 (2 Cir, 1930—freight).

227. *De Monchy* (above), p 205 *per* Scrutton LJ, p 210 *per* Sankey LJ, both citing with approval *Graham Bros AG* v *St Pauls Ins Co*, 204 NYS 551 (1924—cargo).

228. *Koskas* v *Standard Marine Ins Co Ltd* (1927) 32 Com Cas 160, 163 *per* Scrutton LJ (CA—cargo): the policy, unlike the certificate, made prompt notice of claim a condition precedent, and was thus more favourable to the insurer than the certificate.

buyer should not have to refer to the policy.[229] So, an insurer who puts such a certificate into circulation may be estopped from denying or qualifying the terms of the certificate by reference to terms of the policy.[230] A similar contention can be maintained in respect of other kinds of insurance.[231] Third, the certificate should prevail, as being the later of the two documents; it has been seen as a modification of the original contract contained in the master policy.[232]

One certificate, which may appear incomplete, is that issued under group health insurance. In the United States, the certificate has little apparent contractual importance, being no more than evidence[233] of the holder's right to cover provided by the master policy. Usually, the holder cannot ascertain his rights without reference to the policy. The two documents are construed together.[234] In case of conflict, however, the certificate has been held to prevail,[235] especially if the conflict arises from a change in the master policy, which has not been notified to the holder of the certificate,[236] or there are terms which the court can use to find an estoppel against the insurer.[237]

15–6F Promotional Material

There is some suggestion that a policy will be construed in the light of promotional material.[238] Evidently, a clear statement that, in the event of any discrepancy between the material and the policy, the latter prevails, will be given effect.[239]

229. *De Monchy* (above), p 204 *per* Scrutton LJ, and p 212 *per* Russell LJ (CA—cargo).
230. *St Paul Fire & Marine Ins Co* v *Balfour*, 168 F 212, 216 (9 Cir, 1909—cargo). See also cases below on group insurance.
231. *Parks* v *Prudential Ins Co of America*, 103 F Supp 493 (ED Tenn, 1951—health).
232. *St Paul Fire & Marine Ins Co* v *Pure Oil Co*, 58 F 2d 393 (SD NY, 1932—open policy on cargo).
233. *Boseman* v *Connecticut General Life Ins Co*, 301 US 196 (1937—health); *Van Ostrand* v *National Life Ins Co*, 371 NYS 2d 51 (1975—life).
234. *Fagan* v *John Hancock Mutual Life Ins Co*, 200 F Supp 142 (D Kan, 1961—life).
235. *Parks* (above). See also *Binkley* v *Manufacturers Life Ins Co*, 471 F 2d 889 (10 Cir, 1973—life), cert den 414 US 877; *Life Ins Co of N America* v *Lee*, 519 F 2d 475 (6 Cir, 1975—group disability); *Van Vactor* v *Blue Cross Assn*, 365 NE 2d 638 (Ill, 1977—group health).
236. *Parks* (above).
237. In *Parks* (above) the court underlined the policy clause, that the insurer "will issue to the employer to be delivered to the insured an individual certificate setting forth the protection to which such person is entitled" and observed (p 497): "By the terms of the group policy the defendant has said to the plaintiff 'these two certificates represent the protection and benefits to which you are entitled under the group policy'". Thus in *Humphrey* v *Equitable Life Assurance Sy*, 432 P 2d 746, 751 (Cal, 1967—life) the court accepted that the insurer "was estopped from showing that the coverage of the policy was more limited than that of the certificate . . . This result is easily justified upon the grounds that the individual certificate is the only document which the employee sees or is given at any time and that the insurer who drafts the instrument in language it selects, cannot thereafter complain that it does not express the intention of the parties." See also *Lecker* v *General American Life Ins Co*, 525 P 2d 1114, 1118 (Hawaii, 1974—group PA). Cf *Van Ostrand* v *National Life Ins Co*, 371 NYS 2d 51 (1975—life), in which a certificate expressly made subject to the master policy, was controlled by the latter in case of conflict. This did not preclude the possibility of estoppel if, for example, the insurer misrepresented the contents of the policy (p 55).
238. *Baker* v *Nationwide Mutual Ins Co*, 551 NYS 2d 387, 390 (1990—travel).
239. *Blue Cross and Blue Shield of Virginia* v *Wingfield*, 391 SE 2d 73 (Va, 1990—group health).

CHAPTER 16

COVER: LOSS AND PROOF OF LOSS

16–1 THE NATURE OF COVER AND LOSS

Cover is the insurer's promise to pay in certain circumstances. The circumstances, sometimes called the event insured, are defined by the insurance contract; there are usually at least three elements.

The first element is an event affecting the insured, usually visiting him with loss: destruction, damage, death, injury and so on; see below, 16–2. Also an insured event, which may or may not be seen as loss, is survival to age X in term life insurance. There is a trend to single composite contracts of insurance covering a wide range of events or of kinds of loss; see, for example, contractors' all risks, publicans' all risks or the widening scope of householders' insurance. Usually, however, there are two further elements which define and thus limit the scope of cover.

The second element is the subject-matter of the insurance, usually a named person or property identified specifically or generically.[1] Property insurance may be divided into two kinds by the market, insurance on tangible property, including specific items of money, and insurance on intangible wealth, known as pecuniary loss insurance. The same legal rules apply to each kind of property insurance, in particular, both kinds of insurance are classified by lawyers as indemnity insurance. Insurance of tangible property has been traditionally divided by the market according to cause of loss (for example, fire) or the kind of property (for example, livestock, plate-glass, marine, house, fidelity[1a]). Pecuniary loss insurance includes[2] cover against the insolvency of debtors, loss sustained by guarantors under their contracts of guarantee, consequential loss (sometimes described as business interruption),[3] and loss to the insured in the form of unforeseen expense.

The third element is the cause of the loss covered, sometimes called the risk in a narrow sense: for example fire, accident, death (both the cause and the effect), theft, riot, peril of the seas; see chapter 17.

Rules of law do not necessarily depend on market classification. A basic distinction is made by lawyers between insurance of the person and insurance of property, for the latter is a contract of indemnity but the former is not. Yet discussion of the law requires some regard to market classification for, if a classification mark or concept is used and litigated, its meaning or construction is a matter of contract. So, for

---

1. See also above 4–1B.

1a. Fidelity insurance, which does not fit easily into either category, is not insurance on the fidelity of employees, but insurance on certain property (for example in a shop) against the risk of infidelity of employees.

2. Hall, *Property and Pecuniary Insurances* (CII 1981), sections 1B, 10A.

3. See Riley and Cloughton, *Business Interruption and Insurance* (7th ed, 1991).

example, chapter 17 attempts to define key risks: death (17–1), fire (17–2), all risks (17–3), liability (17–4), and accident (17–5). Other concepts, for example the precise line between employers' liability and public liability, are too detailed for a book of this kind and are left to specialist works. Moreover, there is little purpose in attempting to define "person" and "property" for these concepts are too broad to be useful: the insurance contract will define the person as Mr X, the insured and the property concerned as, say, his motor vehicle, of model X and registration number A653 JEB: the work of definition is left entirely to the particular contract and the policy that records it.

To obtain cover in the sense of payment, to activate the insurer's undertaking to pay, the insured claimant must prove loss (below, 16–2) which was caused (below, chapter 25) by events covered by his insurance contract (below, chapter 17). The exact onus of proof depends on the cover and the contract terms (below, 16–3). The mode of proof is discussed as an aspect of claims procedure (below, chapter 26).

16–2 LOSS

The idea of loss arises in the familiar, general and non-technical sense of financial loss, as well as in the narrower sense of deprivation loss.

16–2A Financial Loss

The more common and wider meaning of loss is any loss, damage or deprivation suffered by the insured as a consequence of an event insured against, and which leaves him financially poorer than he was before. That is the sense in which the word is used elsewhere in this book, unless the context indicates otherwise. That is the sense, in the case of indemnity insurance,[4] in which the insured must prove loss to found a claim.

16–2A1 The Time of Loss

If loss occurs during the period of cover,[5] there is loss, although the subject-matter[6] is (unexpectedly) recovered later, or the full extent of loss is not apparent or has not developed until after the period of cover.[7] However, in the case of non-marine insurance, if there is no loss at all during the cover period, there is no right of recovery, however inevitable such loss might have seemed during that period[8]—unless the contract indicates otherwise, or unless the marine doctrine of constructive total loss, which includes loss which has yet to occur but is "appearing to be unavoidable",[9] applies to non-marine insurance.

---

4. See chapter 28. On the difference between indemnity insurance and non-indemnity insurance see below, 31–3A. On the meaning of loss in liability insurance, see below, 17–4A.
5. See chapter 18. The contract may also require the occurrence of the event causing loss to be within the period: *Kelly* v *Norwich Union Fire Ins Sy Ltd* [1989] 2 All ER 888 (CA—property).
6. For example jewellery, for which a thorough search had been made, and which was thought lost, was found; the insurer provided substitute jewellery in lieu and could not rescind this arrangement when the original jewellery was found: *Holmes* v *Payne* [1930] 2 KB 301.
7. *Knight* v *Faith* (1850) 15 QB 649 (hull); *Andersen* v *Marten* [1908] AC 334, 338 *per* Lord Loreburn, LC (hull). *Snapp* v *State Farm Fire & Casualty Co*, 24 Cal Rptr 44 (1962—fire); *Keene Corp* v *INA*, 667 F 2d 1034, 1045 (Colum, 1981—liability).
8. *Hough* v *Head* (1885) 55 LJ QB 43 (CA—freight). Still less, if loss is not inevitable but likely or seriously threatened: *Moore* v *Evans* [1918] AC 185 (jewellery AR).
9. MIA, section 60(1). For example, *Fooks* v *Smith* [1924] 2 KB 508 (cargo).

16–2A2 Constructive Total Loss (CTL)

There is no doubt that, if a policy provides that the insured shall recover in the case of CTL, effect will be given to that provision. Equally, there is no doubt that in marine insurance as a matter of law loss includes not only actual total loss[10] but also CTL. In general terms CTL means[11] (a) that the actual total loss appears to be unavoidable; or (b) that the subject-matter can only be preserved and recovered at an expenditure that would exceed the value of the subject-matter after that expenditure had been incurred. Type (a) includes deprivation loss which is accepted in the general law of insurance (below, 16–2B).[12] However, it has been stated firmly that, unless expressly provided for in the contract otherwise, CTL is a concept confined to marine insurance.

Marine insurance was distinguished by Lord Atkinson in *Moore* v *Evans*[13]:

"Marine insurance grew out of the necessities of maritime trade and commerce. It dealt with the hazardous enterprise of the navigation of the sea by ships carrying cargo for reward . . . It is founded upon the practices of merchants . . . One can readily understand that those willing to adventure, who had possessed themselves of expensive but money-making chattels like ships for the purpose of their adventures, should, if they insured, be protected as far as possible from having their capital locked up unprofitably in ships whose fate they were unable actually to ascertain and prove."

This may prove too much. It may have been obvious in 1917 why shipowners should have had their capital released more quickly than jewellers. It is not obvious today why venture capitalists in, for example, civil or aeronautical engineering should not be treated like shipowners; indeed some companies operate in both fields. It is not obvious why dates contaminated by sewage may be "lost", if it happens in port,[14] but not "lost", if it happens in a canal. The courts have been responsive to the idea of commercial loss[15] in other contexts, including frustration[16], because if "there is a reasonable probability from the nature of the interruption that it will be of indefinite duration, they ought to be free to turn their assets, their plant and equipment and their business operations into activities which are open to them, and to be free from commitments which are struck with sterility for an uncertain future period." This being so, why not show the same consideration here too?

In *Moore* v *Evans*[17] Bankes LJ said that, while concepts of marine insurance do not apply as such to other kinds of insurance, some considerations material to CTL may also arise in the other branches of insurance. There appears to be little reason in prin-

---

10. MIA, section 57.

11. MIA, section 60. In the case of a CTL the insured has the choice of treating the loss as a partial loss or of abandoning the subject-matter to the insurer (section 61). If he chooses abandonment, he must give notice to the insurer (section 62). Notice is required in most but not all cases (section 62(7)), so it is not a prerequisite or essential component of CTL: *Moore* v *Evans* [1916] 1 KB 458, 469 *per* Bankes LJ (jewellery AR); *Robertson* v *Nomikos Ltd* [1939] AC 371, 381 *per* Lord Wright (hull); *The Kyriaki* [1993] 1 Lloyd's Rep 137, 151 *per* Hirst J (hull). For extensive discussion of the meaning of CTL see Arnould, Nos 1160 ff.

12. This can be inferred from the response of Lord Atkinson in *Moore* v *Evans* [1918] AC 185, 192 (jewellery) to *Roux* v *Salvador* (1835) 3 Bing NC 266 (hull).

13. [1918] AC 185, 193 ff. Lord Atkinson regarded the decision in *Campbell & Phillips Ltd* v *Denman* (1915) 21 Com Cas 357 (goods in transit) to apply CTL to non-marine insurance as "strange" (p 197).

14. *Asfar* v *Blundell* [1896] 1 QB 123 (CA—freight).

15. Such a notion in connection with a policy on timber trapped in a warehouse in Antwerp during World War I was articulated by Bailhache J in *Mitsui* v *Mumford* [1915] 2 KB 27, 34 (goods in transit), but the correctness of his view was doubted by Lord Atkinson in *Moore* v *Evans* [1918] AC 185, 196 (jewellery AR).

16. *Denny, Mott & Dickson Ltd* v *James B Fraser & Co Ltd* [1944] AC 265, 278 *per* Lord Wright.

17. [1916] 1 KB 458, 469; this passage passed without censure in the House of Lords: [1918] AC 185.

ciple why the courts should not extend the notion of CTL to non-marine insurance, if to do so would be useful; nonetheless, the tenor of opinion in the House of Lords in that case was against it, and courts have not done so.[18]

16–2A3 The Nature of Loss

Loss does not include injury to feelings or sensibilities. Hence, while damages may be recovered for injured feelings or distress in tort and, sometimes, for breach of contract, no such sum is recoverable as "loss" under a contract of insurance. It is not possible to insure the artistic value of property as such,[19] although insurers sometimes accept the insured's own valuation of property, such as collectibles, in the knowledge that the estimate may err on the side of sentiment.[20] In general, the nature of loss in cases of indemnity insurance is firmly financial.

The contract may limit cover further to "physical" loss, in which case goods which have suffered no physical impairment but have lost value have not suffered loss.[21] However, loss includes loss of use not only when there is deprivation of the property concerned [22] but also when it is still there: it has been held in New York that there may be "loss" of a human limb without actual amputation; it is enough for "loss", that there has been loss of use.[23]

16–2A4 Consequential Loss

Unless the policy provides otherwise,[24] loss does not extend to consequential loss. In the leading case of *Theobald*,[25] the claimant bookseller was injured; consequently he was unable to pursue his business and lost profit. It was held that the amount of the profit was not loss recoverable under his accident policy. Three reasons have been offered for this well established conclusion.

First, it has been said that the definition of loss does not include consequential loss because it is difficult for the insurer of the subject-matter lost to assess his exposure. But the availability of consequential loss insurance suggests that this is no longer true.

A second reason, sometimes offered,[26] is that consequential loss is too remote: that

18. For example, in *ICI Plc* v *MAT Transport Ltd* [1987] 1 Lloyd's Rep 354, 358–359 Staughton J declined to apply CTL to land transport, stating that in England it is a concept largely peculiar to the law of marine insurance.

19. *Richard Aubrey Film Productions Ltd* v *Graham* [1960] 2 Lloyd's Rep 101, 103 *per* Winn J: no indemnity under an all risks policy in respect of sorrow at the loss of a film "the child of the artistic conception".

20. PM 11 March 1993 p 27.

21. *Glen Falls Ins Co* v *Covert*, 526 SW 2d 222 (Tex, 1975).

22. *Covert* (above) was distinguished in *Gatti* v *Hanover Ins Co*, 601 F Supp 210 (ED Pa, 1985—AR), affirmed 774 F 2d 1151 (3 Cir, 1985): physical loss included seepage of water for which the insured had been metered and had paid: "not only did the plaintiff suffer pecuniary loss, it suffered physical loss when the water leaked into the ground." (p 211).

23. *Mifsud* v *Allstate Ins Co*, 456 NYS 2d 316 (1982—PA): as a result of an injury while entering a revolving door, the bone in the insured's arm had detached from his shoulder so that it hung by the tissue. The policy defined loss as "severance", but the court said (p 317) that "severance does not mean amputation . . . to sever may limit its use, but not necessarily cause amputation". Having found ambiguity, the court construed against the insurer and found it sufficient that there was severance of the bone.

24. Cover for consequential loss, such as loss of profit or business interruption. For discussion of this kind of cover and of the standard policy forms, see Riley, *op cit* (above, note 3).

25. *Theobald* v *Railway Passengers' Assurance Co* (1854) 10 Exch 45. In *Re Wright and Pole* (1834) 1 Ad & E 621: fire insurance on an inn did not cover profit lost while the inn was being rebuilt. See also in this sense *Shelbourne & Co* v *Law Investment & Ins Corp Ltd* [1898] 2 QB 626 (river insurance on barges); *Maurice* v *Goldsborough, Mort & Co Ltd* [1939] AC 452 (PC—fire).

26. *Theobald* (above), pp 57–58 *per* Pollock CB.

it is not the direct or proximate consequence of the event covered.[27] However, while this may be true in some cases, in others it is not: it was an inevitable consequence of the accidental injury to Mr Theobald that he would lose *some* business, hence it can be said that all the loss of business was proximately caused by the injury: see below, 25–4A.

A third reason, perhaps the most convincing reason, is that the insurer has not calculated on the basis that he is exposed to loss of profit or other consequential loss. In *Theobald* Pollock CB said[28] that "what the insurance company *calculate on* indemnifying the party against is the expense, pain and loss immediately connected with the accident, and not remote consequences that may follow according to the business or profession of the passenger". By custom and practice therefore it is established that there is no cover against consequential loss, unless specifically included.

So, whether an insurance contract covers consequential loss is a matter of the terms of the contract concerned. The insurance industry's notion of consequential loss is quite different from that of the lawyer.[29] Further and for the same reason, if the contract does cover consequential loss, unless otherwise specified, that expression does not include certain items of loss, which a lawyer might think not too remote: for example, the difference in value of stock at the time of the damage and the value at the time of subsequent replacement, depreciation of undamaged stock, the cost of making the insurance claim, litigation costs arising out of the event insured, failure to recover debts as a result of the destruction of records, and loss of goodwill.[30]

16–2B Deprivation Loss

The meaning of deprivation loss depends on the context, not only the immediate context of the policy but also that of the practices and purposes of the kind of insurance.[31] For example, marine insurance on cargo is concerned with loss of an adventure, it has been said,[32] while non-marine insurance is concerned with loss of goods; the courts will be slow to apply the special rules about loss in marine insurance to non-marine insurance.[33] Subject to this, the general definition of deprivation loss is located in a band between two extreme positions.[34] On one side, temporary deprivation of the subject-matter is not loss,[35] unless the effect is that the subject-matter perishes. If there is no reason to suppose that the insured will not get the subject-matter back (in substantially the same condition), although the time is uncertain, he has failed to

27. The issue was discussed in terms of causation in, for example, *Shelbourne* (above); and *Molinos de Arroz* v *Mumford* (1900) 16 TLR 469 (war cover on goods).

28. *Theobald* (above), *loc cit* (emphasis added).

29. See "Solon", PM 22 June 1989 p 26, pointing out that there may be an exclusion of consequential loss in what used to be referred to (and still is by many in the industry) as a consequential loss policy.

30. Hall, *op cit* (above, note 2), section 10H.

31. *Moore* v *Evans* [1917] 1 KB 458, 471 *per* Bankes LJ (CA—jewellery AR)

32. *The Bamburi* [1982] 1 Lloyd's Rep 312, 318 *per* Staughton J (hull); see also *Euro-Diam Ltd* v *Bathurst* [1987] 2 All ER 113, 118 *per* Staughton J (goods in transit), affirmed [1988] 2 All ER 23 (CA).

33. *Moore* v *Evans* [1918] AC 185, 194 *per* Lord Atkinson (jewellery AR). See also above, 16–2A2.

34. Bankes LJ, *loc cit*. See also *Anderson* v *Wallis* (1813) 2 M & S 240, 247 *per* Lord Ellenborough (cargo).

35. Bankes LJ, *loc cit*.

prove loss.[36] On the other side, it is not necessary for the insured to prove a certainty that he will not get the subject-matter back.[37] Between these points defining loss is difficult, perhaps undesirable.[38]

In a particular case, it is first necessary to ask what has been lost and whether that is the property insured: this turns on careful scrutiny of the terms of the contract. Even words that seem simple, such as "loss . . . of the motor car insured" have given rise to litigation.[39] Second, it is necessary to consider whether reasonable steps have been taken to recover the subject-matter and, if so, whether recovery is still uncertain.[40] Although there must be a thorough search for things mislaid,[41] it is not always necessary to take legal action to recover subject-matter, still less to pursue the matter to the highest courts.[42]

16–2C Damage

Damage usually refers to a changed physical state. In "common parlance", it means "mischief done to property",[43] but the precise definition depends on the context in which the word is used.[44] For example, scallops, which are perfectly fit for immediate consumption but have been raised to a temperature, which has shortened their shelf life, may be damaged scallops for the insured who does not want them for immediate consumption but for sale in a foreign market.[45] The goods have become less valuable than they were before, however, for there to be damage in the sense of an insurance contract, it will also be necessary to produce the report of a food laboratory that a

---

36. *Moore* v *Evans* [1917] 1 KB 458, 473 *per* Bankes LJ (CA—jewellery AR), affirmed by the House of Lords [1918] AC 185: the insured was unable to prove that the jewellery, although in enemy territory, was not still in safe keeping, and that he would not recover it at the end of the war. *Cf Mitsui* v *Mumford* [1915] 2 KB 27 (cargo) and discussion of that case in *Moore* v *Evans* [1918] AC 185, pp 194 ff *per* Lord Atkinson.
37. *Moore* (above), p 471 *per* Bankes LJ.
38. *Webster* v *GAFLAC Ltd* [1953] 1 QB 520, 529 *per* Parker J (motor). See also *Holmes* v *Payne* [1930] 2 KB 301, 310 *per* Roche J.
39. *Eisinger* v *GAFLAC Ltd* [1955] 2 Lloyd's Rep 95. In *Webster* v *GAFLAC Ltd* [1953] 1 KB 520 the insured delivered his car to X for sale to Y. X sold it but kept the proceeds of sale. The insurer of the car argued that this was not loss of the car but loss of title or loss of the proceeds of sale; and that, in any event, loss had to be certain. These arguments were rejected by Parker J who, having heard evidence that the claimant had consulted the police and been advised that recovery of the car was hopeless, decided that the car had been lost within the meaning of the policy. See also *Richard Aubrey Film Productions Ltd* v *Graham* [1960] 2 Lloyd's Rep 101, 102 *per* Winn J (AR).
40. *Webster* (above), p 532 *per* Parker J (motor); *Holmes* v *Payne* [1930] 2 KB 301, 310 *per* Roche J.
41. *Holmes* (above).
42. *Webster* (above), *loc cit*.
43. *Smith* v *Brown* (1871) 40 LJQB 214, 218 *per* Cockburn CJ. "Damage to", "when used in relation to goods, is a physical alteration or change, not necessarily permanent or irreparable, which impairs the value or usefulness of the things said to be damaged. It follows that not every physical change to goods would amount to damage": *Ranicar* v *Frigmobile Pty Ltd* (1983) Tas R 113, 116. Derrington & Ashton, *The Law of Liability Insurance*, pp 321 ff.
Policies sometimes underline the point by reference to "property damage", which excludes, for example, actual or potential liability, i.e., damage to the insured's "pocket": *Snug Harbour Ltd* v *Zurich Ins*, 968 F 2d 538 (5 Cir, 1992—liability).
44. *Swansea Corp* v *Harpur* [1912] 3 KB 493, 505 *per* Fletcher Moulton LJ (CA). Thus "loss or damage in *connexion* with the goods", under the Hague Rules for carriage by sea, includes economic loss: *Goulandris Bros* v *Goldmann & Sons* [1958] 1 QB 74, 105 per Pearson J. A recent case under an insurance contract is *Cementation Piling & Foundations Ltd* v *Aegon Ins Co Ltd* [1993] 1 Lloyd's Rep 527 (contractors AR), concerning "physical loss or damage to the property insured".
45. *Ranicar* v *Frigmobile Pty Ltd* [1983] Tas R 113 (Tasmania—cargo).

physical change has occurred in the scallops. Moreover, as insurance does not cover ordinary wear and tear (or in some cases inherent vice),[46] the change must be one which was not inevitable in the speed of its development.

As damage refers to a change in the physical state of property, it does not generally refer to the cost of preventing such a change: for that amount to be recoverable, it must be separately insured. Moreover, damage cover does not imply any sort of duty to prevent loss; although the contract may impose a duty to minimise loss which *has* occurred,[47] courts are slow to find such a duty still less a duty to prevent loss in the first place: negligent failure to prevent it is a prime case of what insurance is for (below, 19–2A).

So, no damage, no indemnity for damage. If an insurance contract is in force while the condition of the equipment is dangerous but expires before the equipment explodes or catches fire, there can be no claim for injury or damage, as this did not occur during the period of cover.[48] Again, there is no damage in a plumbing system that is expected to leak but has yet do so[49] or in a floor which is defective when put down and which will have to be repaired or replaced.[50] In contrast, according to a court in Illinois,[51] a building that contains asbestos insulation is damaged—not because of the inevitable cost of removal but because parts of the building apart from the insulation itself have been contaminated by asbestos fibres. Similarly, in the law of negligence, English lawyers have been firmly reminded that a building with a wall,

---

46. See below, 17–3A1.

47. If there is such a duty, the law is likely to imply a duty for the insurer to indemnify the insured against the cost: below, 28–8G.

48. In this sense: *Young* v *INA*, 870 F 2d 610 (11 Cir, 1989—liability) and cases cited at p 611. The court distinguished cases involving exposure to harmful chemicals during the insurance period, as in the latter exposure was deemed to be an injury. See also *Schlosser* v *INA*, 600 A 2d 836 (Md, 1992—liability).

49. *Eljer Mfg Inc* v *Liberty Mutual Ins Co*, 773 F Supp 1102 (ND Ill, 1991—liability), unless the insurance covers physical deterioration in the pipes prior to the leak, which in this case was excluded from cover (p 1112). The cover in this case was for liability for "property damage", which was defined as "physical injury to or destruction of tangible property". The insured sought a declaratory judgment that the injury occurred not when the system began to leak or when it was recognised to have reduced the value of the property, in which it was installed, but when it was first installed in that property. Although the insured was unsuccessful in the District Court, it succeeded on appeal to the Circuit Court: 972 F 2d 805 (7 Cir, 1992). The court (p 809, *per* Judge Posner) accepted that the ordinary meaning of the words required a "harmful change in appearance, shape, composition, or some other physical dimension of [the thing] . . . But these nice, physicalistic . . . distinctions have little to do with the objectives of parties to insurance contracts. The purpose of insurance is to spread risks and by spreading cancel them". The court proceeded to interpret the contract to ensure spread, i.e. in favour of cover. In period B, risks insured in period A become uninsurable, as potential claims emerge; the purpose is to spread, so tie loss to A to ensure cover. Although the court insisted (p 812) that it "did not think that every time a component part fails, the resulting injury can be backdated to the date of installation", one result is uncertainty. Its reasoning overlooks the desire of insurers for predictable risks, so that a realistic premium can be assessed, unless, as Judge Posner suggests, it is better (law) that the risk should be transferred from the claimant, whose claim emerges in period B, to the insurer and on to other insureds. In this scenario, the insurer is less a business (with investors wanting a return) than a transfer mechanism serving a social purpose. This is the kind of thought that fuels the current hostility to claims made cover. A secondary argument was based on the history of the phrase in the standard form of liability policy. It seems highly unlikely that an English court would ignore the ordinary meaning of the words of the insurance contract in this way. Indeed, it seems unlikely that *Eljer* will be followed in other parts of the USA: *In re San Juan Dupont Plaza Litigation*, 989 F 2d 36 (1 Cir, 1993—liability).

50. *Ohio Casualty Ins Co* v *Bazzi Construction Co Inc*, 815 F 2d 1146 (7 Cir, 1987—liability); see also *In Re San Juan Dupont Plaza Hotel Fire Litigation*, 802 F Supp 624, 645 (D Puerto Rico, 1992—liability). *Cf Junior Books Ltd* v *Veitchi Co* [1983] AC 520.

51. See *Eljer* (above) p 1109, and cases cited. Towner 27 Tort & Ins L J 638, 648 (1992) suggests that this decision may be exceptional and, indeed, the decision was reversed on appeal: see above.

that will collapse unless repaired, is not a damaged building until the collapse occurs or, at least, until warning cracks appear,[52] even though the collapse is imminent.[53]

One can sympathise with the argument that it would be "an equivocal type of justice which would hold that the defendant [insurer] would be compelled to pay out, let us say, the sum of $100,000 if the plaintiff [insured] had not prevented what would have been inevitable, and yet not be called upon to pay the smaller sum which the plaintiff actually expended to avoid a foreseeable disaster". However, the law is concerned here not with distributive justice but with the interpretation of a contract. So, this argument was rejected in Maryland, shortly and simply, because justice does not "justify the construction of an insurance policy to provide coverage where none exists under the clear language of the policy".[54]

In negligence cases, the question is whether the risk should be transferred to the tortfeasor. In insurance cases, the comparable question is whether the risk has been assumed by the insurer, and this is a matter of contract: it depends on intention and on traditional ways of calculating and thus of classifying risks. Even in tort cases unaffected by contract, courts are sensitive to the argument that to impose liability for economic loss is to release a flood that could not be controlled,[55] in the classic words of Cardozo CJ, "liability in an indeterminate amount for an indeterminate time to an indeterminate class".[56] Similarly, insurers must deal with categories of loss, the incidence and cost of which can be predicted.[57] The similarity stops here, as insurers do not appear to agree with judges, that the incidence of economic loss cannot be predicted,[58] however, that is not the immediate point: what counts for the insurer is that he knows where is—that he is dealing with a category of loss which he can rate.

If then what counts above all is the contract, it must also be said that a construction

---

52. *Murphy* v *Brentwood DC* [1991] 1 AC 398. Grubb [1984] CLJ 111; Stapleton (1988) 104 LQR 213, 389. A similar view has been taken of damage to human beings caused by asbestos dust: below 17–4C1. *Cf* the law of nuisance: in the case of equipment, such as gas equipment in a dangerous condition, English law has recognised that the potential for destruction amounts to a continuous (and dangerous) state of affairs culminating but not confined to the eventual explosion: *Midwood & Co Ltd* v *Manchester Corp* [1905] 2 KB 597 (CA); *Spicer* v *Smee* [1946] 1 All ER 489.

53. *Murphy* (above). *Cf* decisions in California which regard imminent damage as damage for insurance cover: Towner 27 TILJ 638, 648 (1992).

54. *Schlosser* v *INA*, 600 A 2d 836, 839 (Md, 1992—liability). See also *DeRose* v *Albanys Ins Co*, 792 F Supp 973 (D NJ, 1992—hull) in which a claim for damage inflicted to prevent sinking, which was substantially likely, failed as it was not damage "directly caused by sinking". But *cf Intel Corp* v *Hartford Co*, 952 F2d 1551, 1566 (9 Cir, 1991—liability). On the recoverability of the cost of prevention, see below 28–8G.

55. For example, Lord Bridge in *Caparo Industries plc* v *Dickman* [1990] 2 AC 605, 621. Moreover, the "infliction of physical injury to the person or property of another universally requires to be justified. The causing of economic loss does not"—*Murphy* (above) p 487 per Lord Oliver. "The real concern of the House was . . . to preserve the distinction between tort and contract"—Cherniak & Stevens, 20 Can. Bus L J 164, 174 (1992). See also Dias & Markesinis, *Tort Law* (2nd ed., 1988) pp 62 ff. Arguably, in a market economy, the distribution of economic loss is best left to the parties (by contract), and courts should not interfere (with the tort of negligence), especially courts such as the current House which purport to sweep policy points under the carpet of "proximity" or fudge the issues with talk of foreseeability and fairness. However, it can also be said that the "essential problem in *Murphy* is that it takes an ideological stance against the possibility of recovery for pure economic loss and unduly limits the inquiry as to when judicial loss-shifting is appropriate": Cherniak & Stevens p 176.

56. *Ultramares Corp* v *Touche* 255 NY 170, 179 (1931).

57. Thus damage to aircraft, for example, is commonly insured under one contract: Margo, Aviation Insurance (2nd ed, 1989) ch 11. Diminution of the value of aircraft is the subject of a quite different contract: Below, 28–8F. So are the financial consequences of loss of use: Margo *loc cit*. However, it has been held that "property damage" includes loss of use of the property concerned: *Hofing GMC Truck Inc* v *Kay Wheel Sales Co*, 543 F Supp 414 (ED Pa, 1982—liability) concerning the theft of a motor vehicle.

58. After the decision in *Junior Books Ltd* v *Veitchi Co* [1983] AC 520 insurance was offered in the London market against liability for economic loss.

of the contract, which encourages the insured not to take steps to prevent loss but to let events take their course until loss insured occurs, is wasteful and often damaging to the insurer. That is why, in one important case at least, fire, the very meaning of fire has developed to include damage inflicted (e.g. by water) and cost incurred to prevent fire damage, provided that actual damage by fire is imminent and *inevitable*. This may well be in the interests of the insurer as the lesser evil as it results in lower indemnity and, therefore, it is what he has been taken by the courts to mean by fire. Perhaps there are more such cases, however, such special cases apart,[59] preventive cost is not the subject of indemnity unless the insurer, whether to reduce exposure or to encourage business, manifests his intention to bring it within the scope of the cover provided by the contract.

16–3 THE GENERAL ONUS OF PROOF

Onus of proof in insurance cases matters most at two stages of debate. First, it matters when a client wants to know whether to pursue a line of argument, claim or defence. Second, it matters when a claim has gone to court, and the court has heard all the evidence but is unable to decide how the loss occurred. The court must decide who had to prove what and, therefore, who has failed to meet the burden of proof and must lose the argument.

It should not be forgotten that the practical burden of proof is affected not only by the formal allocation of onus, which is sometimes called the legal burden of proof[60] and is the subject of this part of the chapter, but also by the definition and scope of the peril, whether peril covered or peril excepted,[61] and by the causal connection, which is required by the law or by the contract, between the peril and loss.[62]

16–3A The Insured Must Prove Loss Within Cover

The insured must prove that the loss claimed was caused by an event (peril) covered by the policy.[63] Loss by a peril covered by the policy must be proved on the balance of probabilities.[64] It is sometimes said that the insured must make a *prima facie* case; in so far as this implies something less than the balance of probabilities on the evidence then before the court, this is probably wrong.[65] If there is loss but the evidence is equally consistent with causation by a peril covered and by a peril excepted or not insured against, the insured fails.[66] In this connection *post hoc* is not *propter hoc*.[67]

---

59. See below 28–8G.
60. *The Torenia* [1983] 2 Lloyd's Rep 210, 215 *per* Hobhouse J.
61. Below, chapters 17 and 19.
62. See below, 25–9B.
63. *British & Foreign Marine Ins Co Ltd* v *Gaunt* [1921] 2 AC 43, 58 *per* Lord Sumner (cargo). See also *Moore* v *Evans* [1916] 1 KB 458 (CA—jewellery AR); *Regina Fur Co Ltd* v *Bossom* [1958] 2 Lloyd's Rep 425, 428 *per* Lord Evershed MR (CA—AR). *Candler* v *London & Lancashire Guarantee & Accident Co* (1963) 40 DLR (2d) 408 (Ont—PA).
64. *Richard Aubrey Film Productions Ltd* v *Graham* [1960] 2 Lloyd's Rep 101, 102 *per* Winn J (AR). See also *Whitehead* v *Mullett* (1946) 79 Ll L Rep 410 (jewellery AR) which shows the importance of reliable evidence from the insured; and *Anderson* v *Scottish Accident Ins Co*, 1889 17 R (Ct of Sess) 6 (PA).
65. *Macbeth & Co* v *R* (1916) 115 LT 221, 222 *per* Bailhache J (hull). See below, 16–3B1.
66. *Neter & Co Ltd* v *Licenses & General Ins Co Ltd* [1944] 1 All ER 341, 343 *per* Tucker J (cargo).
67. *Anderson* v *Norwich Union Fire Ins Sy* [1977] 1 Lloyd's Rep 253 (CA): evidence that a roof collapsed 13 days after exceptional rainfall did not establish rain as cause. See also *Anderson* v *Scottish Accident Ins Co*, 1889 17 R (Ct of Sess) 6 (PA). *Canadian Railway Assurance Co* v *Haines* (1911) 44 SCR 386.

16–3B The Response of the Insurer

16–3B1 Traverse

"I think that a defendant—whether he is an underwriter or any other kind of defendant—is entitled to say, by way of defence, 'I require this case to be strictly proved, and admit nothing'. Where such is the form of the pleading, it is not only obligatory upon the defendants but it is not even permissible for them to proceed to put forward some affirmative case which they have not pleaded or alleged; and it is not, therefore, right that they should, by cross-examination of the plaintiffs or otherwise, suggest such an affirmative case . . . in practice, no doubt sometimes the line is often a little narrow between evidence which is properly directed to challenging the evidence of the plaintiff upon some relevant issue, and evidence which may, upon analysis, turn out to be direct evidence of credit"[68]

and thus of an exception which has not been formally pleaded.

16–3B2 Exceptions: to be Proved by the Insurer

If the insurer defends with a contract exception, he must prove that exception.[69] For example, a contract requirement that the insured 'shall take all reasonable steps to safeguard the property insured' has been seen as an exception of (gross) negligence, so the claimant is not required to prove care as a condition precedent of cover but it is for the insurer, if he wishes and can do so, to prove (gross) negligence by the insured.[70] The onus on the insurer is to prove the exception on the balance of probabilities,[71] but that onus will be heavier when the defence alleges fraud or wilful misconduct, such as arson, by the insured.[72] If the insurer defends by reference to one exception, he does not thereby waive his right to rely later on other exceptions.[73]

16–3C The Distinction between Perils and Exceptions

It is easy to state that the claimant proves the peril that caused his loss, while the operation of an exception, like any other defence, must be proved by the insurer. The difficulty is to know when proof of the peril (by the claimant) is complete and proof of exception (by the insurer) should begin: the point at which the legal onus of proof passes from insured to insurer. This is a question of finding not a point in time (for in

---

68. *Regina Fur Co Ltd* v *Bossom* [1958] 2 Lloyd's Rep 425, 428 *per* Lord Evershed MR (CA—AR). See also *The Dias* [1972] 2 QB 625, 647 *per* Cairns LJ (CA). These lines are not always observed; the degree of latitude allowed by the court may depend on its sympathy or antipathy to the parties. See, for example, *The Popi M, Rhesa Shipping Co SA* v *Edmunds* [1985] 2 Lloyd's Rep 1 (HL—hull); Clarke [1985] CLJ 359.

69. *Munro Brice* v *War Risk Association* [1918] 2 KB 78 (hull), reversed on different grounds: [1920] 3 KB 94 (CA). See also *Stormont* v *Waterloo Life & Casualty Assurance Co* (1858) 1 F & F 20 (life); *Gorman* v *Hand In Hand Ins Co* (1877) IR 11 CL 224 (fire); *Re National Benefit Assurance Co* (1933) 45 Ll L Rep 147 (cargo AR); *Fraser* v *Furman (Productions) Ltd* [1967] 1 WLR 898, 905 *per* Diplock LJ (CA—liability); *Canadian Railway Assurance Co* v *Haines* (1911) 44 SCR 386 (PA); *Candler* v *London & Lancashire Guarantee & Accident Co* (1963) 40 DLR (2d) 408 (Ont—PA). *Home Benefit Association* v *Sargent*, 142 US 691, 700 *per* Blatchford J (1892—life); *National Union* v *Fitzpatrick*, 133 F 694, 697 (5 Cir, 1905—life); *American Indemnity Co* v *Sears, Roebuck & Co*, 195 F 2d 353, 356 (6 Cir, 1952—liability); *Lipiner & Son Inc* v *Hanover Ins Co*, 869 F 2d 685 (2 Cir, 1989—AR); *State Farm Fire & Casualty Co* v *Martin*, 872 F 2d 319 (9 Cir, 1989—homeowner's).

70. *Sofi* v *Prudential Assurance Co Ltd* (CA, 6 March 1990—AR). A similar decision was reached in *Vosten* v *The Commonwealth* [1989] 1 Qd R 693, 704 (liability).

71. See above, 16–3A.

72. *The Ny-Eeasteyr* [1988] 1 Lloyd's Rep 60, 62 (hull). See further below, 17–2H1.

73. *Schiff Associates Inc* v *Flack*, 435 NYS 2d 972, 974 (1980—liability); *Zappone* v *Home Ins Co*, 447 NYS 2d 911, 915 (1982—motor); for other cases in New York to this effect see Kroll, (1987) Insurance & Reinsurance Law International, pp 32–33. *Cf* below. 26–4D(c).

practice proof may be made intermittently and in parallel) but a question of the amount or extent of the proof provided, when viewed as a whole. If cover is X except Y, for example, fire damage not caused by riot and if the insured proves fire damage, must he also prove that it was not caused by riot? This depends in part on the wording and construction of the contract.[74] Subject to that, however, the position is as follows.

16–3C1 Specific Exceptions

If the scope of the exception is narrower than the scope of cover, it is enough that the insured has proved that his loss was caused by a peril that is covered. It is for the insurer, if he can, to show that the loss was caused by the exception.[75]

For example, it is usually enough for the insured to show that his property was damaged by fire; it is for the insurer to show that the fire damage was caused by an exception, such as riot or inherent vice in the subject-matter of the insurance.[76] The scope of the exception (fire damage caused by riot or inherent vice) is narrower than the scope of the cover (fire from whatever cause). Again, it is enough for the insured to prove that his ship was lost by perils of the sea; it is for the insurer to prove that it was sunk by enemy submarines and thus within a war risk exception.[77] The scope of the exception (sinking by war risk) is narrower than the cover (loss at sea from any cause).

16–3C2 General Exceptions

If, unlike the specific exception (above) the exception is general, that is, the exception qualifies the whole scope of the cover, the insured cannot make a case against the insurer, unless he brings himself within the promise as qualified[78]: he must prove not only the operation of the peril but also the non-operation of the exception.

An example of a general exception is an excess of £50 in a motor policy. Whenever the insured suffers loss and from whatever cause, there will always be the possibility that his loss is less than £50; so, it must always be part of any claim that the loss exceeded £50. Similarly, if the first layer of loss is placed with insurer A and the next layer with insurer B, no claim can be made against insurer B without proof that the entire loss exceeded the amount of the first layer.

16–3C3 Contract Terms

Whether an exception is specific or general is a matter of the interpretation of the contract.[79] It is possible therefore for the draftsman to change the onus of proof, both as to the degree of proof that must be brought[80] and as to the range of matters that must be put in evidence.

74. See the general discussion of this problem by Bailhache J in *Munro Brice* v *War Risk Association* [1918] 2 KB 78 (hull).
75. *Munro Brice* (above), p 81 *per* Bailhache J. *Candler* v *London & Lancashire Guarantee & Accident Co* (1963) 40 DLR (2d) 408 (Ont—PA).
76. *The Galatia* [1979] 2 All ER 726 (cargo).
77. *Munro Brice* (above). See also cases concerning all risks insurance: below 17–3B.
78. *Munro Brice* (above), pp 88–89 *per* Bailhache J.
79. *Munro Brice* (above), pp 88–89 *per* Bailhache J.
80. For example *A B* v *Northern Accident Ins Co Ltd*, 1896 24 R 258: the Court of Session held reluctantly that the claimant doctor had failed to produce the "best evidence available", as required by the contract of insurance, for he refused disclosure in breach of medical etiquette.

In the general law, if a contract contains a promise, which the law usually regards as absolute, and also an exception, for example *force majeure*, the plaintiff promisee proves breach of the promise (failure to deliver, cause unspecified), then the defendant promisor proves, if he can, the exception (earthquake, government prohibition etc). But all this may be changed by drafting. If the promise is recast so that the exception is brought into the definition of the basic promise,[81] for example, by requiring the promisor not simply (and absolutely) to deliver but (merely) to exercise due diligence to that end, the plaintiff promisee must prove not only failure to deliver but also the promisor's lack of diligence. Just as the photographer makes his negative image by eliminating with chemicals the other parts of the whole area, so also the plaintiff must make the outline of his case by eliminating matters which in a differently worded contract would be exceptions. Drafting may achieve the same effect in insurance contracts as in other contracts; but in insurance law this shift has been more or less marked according to the branch of insurance, the drafting technique employed, and the willingness of the court to interpret the policy as a whole.[82] The possibilities are endless but a number of instances follow.

First, if, for example, there is cover against fire, generally the claimant makes a case by proving fire damage; it is for the insurer, if he wishes, to prove the defence of arson by the insured. But if, for example, there is cover against "accidental fire", the insured does not make a *prima facie* case, without providing at least some evidence that the fire was an accident, and hence *inter alia* that there was no arson.[83] Again, if there is cover for "accidental bodily injury", disease excepted, and proof of injury or death, the court will not presume that it was accidental: if the cause was unknown the claimant has failed to make a case.[84] If, however, there is proof of death and of the cause of death, in the absence of grounds for suspicion, there is a presumption that the death was accidental.[85]

A second and less subtle possibility is found in *Spinney's (1948) Ltd* v *Royal Ins Co Ltd*.[86] The clause, the "reverse burden clause", read: "In any action, suit or other proceeding, where the [insurer] alleges that by reason of the [excepted causes] any loss or damage is not covered by this insurance, the burden of proving that such loss or damage is covered shall be upon the Insured." The intention of the draftsman was to require the insured to disprove relevant exceptions on demand of the insurer, thus reversing the normal onus of proof. The judge was not sympathetic[87]:

"The validity of the clause is not in doubt[88] . . . but it should not be construed in such a sense as to make the policy unworkable. In my judgment, the insurers cannot bring the clause into play simply by asserting that the loss was excluded by a particular exception, and challenging the insured to prove the contrary. They must prove evidence from which it can reasonably be argued that (a) a state of affairs existed or an event occurred falling within an exception, and (b)

---

81. This "definitional" view of exclusions has been accepted in the courts: *Kenyon Son & Craven Ltd* v *Baxter, Hoare & Co Ltd* [1971] 1 WLR 519, 522 *per* Donaldson J; *The Angelia* [1973] 1 WLR 210, 230 *per* Kerr J; *Photo Production Ltd* v *Securicor Transport Ltd* [1980] AC 827, 851 *per* Lord Diplock. See further Coote, *Exception Clauses*; Yates and Hawkins, *Standard Business Contracts* (London, 1986), Nos 6A(2) ff.
82. For example *Schiff Associates Inc* v *Flack*, 435 NYS 2d 972, 974 (1980—liability).
83. For example, in *Jefferson Terminal Corp* v *Home Ins Co*, 42 NYS 2d 392 (1942—fire) the claimant was required to prove not just fire but fire not caused by explosion.
84. For example, *Weyerhaeuser* v *Evans* (1932) 43 Ll L Rep 62 (death from blood poisoning).
85. See below, 17–1.
86. [1980] 1 Lloyd's Rep 406 (fire).
87. p 426 *per* Mustill J (emphasis added). In this case the insurers nonetheless succeeded in their defence.
88. The judge cited *Levy* v *Assicurazioni Generali* [1940] AC 791 (PC—fire), in which the Board accepted that the onus of proof might be entirely reversed by the words of the policy.

the excepted peril directly or indirectly caused the loss. It is only when an *arguable case* of this nature is made out that the insured is required to disprove it."

A third possibility is for the draftsman to tip the balance of probabilities. The contract may require, as a condition precedent to payment by the insurers, proof of loss by the claimant "satisfactory to the directors of the Company".[89] In an unusually strong reaction, courts have declined to construe phrases like this literally but have construed them as limited to such evidence as the insurer "might reasonably require",[90] thus introducing an element of good faith.[90a]

Fourth, particular difficulty arises if the draftsman stipulates "conditions" of cover: that there shall be cover, for example against theft of goods in transit, provided that the vehicle was fitted with certain anti-theft devices. It has been argued in France that the fulfilment of such matters is a precondition of cover, which must be proved by the claimant, although the highest court in France[91] has rejected this contention. An English court would probably do the same: preconditions of liability like that would be construed as warranties, the breach of which provides a defence to the insurer and must be proved by the insurer.[92]

16–3C4 Combined Perils

If the insured proves loss within the cover and the insurer proves that some but not all of the loss was caused by an excepted peril, it has been said that the onus is on the claimant to prove the extent of the loss caused by the peril covered; without this proof, the claim fails entirely.[93]

16–3C5 Exceptions to an Exception

If the insurer has proved an exception, but the contract makes this exception subject to a further exception, which is narrower in scope than the principal exception, the further exception must be proved by the insured. In other words, the rules set out above apply in a second phase. Thus, when life cover was subject to an exception of suicide except when the claimant was an assignee for valuable consideration, the

---

89. *Braunstein* v *Accidental Death Ins Co* (1861) 1 B & S 782.

90. *Ibid* p 795 *per* Wightman J. In the same sense *ibid* p 797 *per* Compton J; *Moore* v *Woolsey* (1854) 4 E & B 243, 256 *per* Lord Campbell (life); *London Guarantie* v *Fearnley* (1880) 5 App Cas 911, 916 *per* Lord Blackburn (fidelity). *Cf Doyle* v *City of Glasgow Life Assurance Co* (1884) 53 LJ Ch 527: although a court had ruled that the life should be deemed dead under statute (6 Anne c 72), the judge of the insurance action held that the insurer was acting reasonably in requiring further proof of death before paying the claim.

90a. See Clarke [1993] HKLJ 318.

91. *Cour de Cassation* 22.4.1986, *Nouveau Recueil du Havre* No 10 p 170.

92. Below, 20–6A.

93. *Stanley* v *Western Ins Co* (1868) LR 3 Ex 71, 75 *per* Martin B (fire cover, excepting loss caused by explosion).

Cf actions on contracts of carriage: if the claimant makes a case against the carrier, and the carrier is able to prove an exception which accounts for some of the loss, the carrier is liable in full unless he proves also the extent of loss caused by the exception: *Gosse Millerd Ltd* v *Canadian Government Merchant Marine Ltd* [1929] AC 223, 241 *per* Viscount Sumner; *The Torenia* [1983] 2 Lloyd's Rep 210, 218–219 *per* Hobhouse J. *Insurance Co of North America* v *SS Georgis* [1983] AMC 1916, 1923 (SD NY, 1983).

status of the claimant as such an assignee had to be proved by the claimant.[94] Again, cover for loss of rent caused by premature fading in carpets was excepted when connected to failure of products of the insured—unless that in turn was caused by a "sudden and accidental" injury to the insured's product: the latter, it was held, was an exception to an exception and its operation has to be proved by the insured.[95]

---

94. *Rowett Leckey & Co* v *Scottish Provident Institution* [1927] 1 Ch 55, 69 per Warrington LJ (CA—life). On the nature and role of exceptions to exceptions, see below 19–1A.

95. *Marglen Industries Inc* v *Aetna*, Lexis 3347 (Cal, 1992).

CHAPTER 17

COVER: CAUSES OF LOSS

17–1 DEATH

Death is normally proved by certificate issued by a responsible person who has inspected the body of the deceased. If the body cannot be found, the claim must include other evidence of death. For example, in the case[1] of a person lost at sea with the *SS Titanic*, it was sufficient to produce an affidavit that the insured had been on board at the time of sinking and had not been seen among the survivors.

It should be enough for the claimant to prove the death of the life insured, but the law of insurance requires a little more. The evidence of death must be such that there is no reason to suppose[2] that it was suicide or death by any other cause not covered by the policy. The law does not, however, require the claimant to disprove any such exception, such as suicide.[3] In the absence of evidence suggesting otherwise, there is said to be a presumption that the death was accidental,[4] for example, if a man is found drowned in a river[5] but not if his death was due to an overdose of drugs.[6] If suicide is expressly excepted, the insurer must prove suicide on the balance of probabilities.[6a]

Death must occur during the period of cover. The moment of death may be uncertain. In *Kepler* v *Georgia International Life Ins Co*[7] it was held that the insured, who suffered a massive heart attack with substantial brain damage and remained in a persistent and vegetative state with brain stem function but without heart function for 11 months until a court ordered the termination of food and hydration, died at the latter time and hence after his life insurance had expired. The court observed that the moral and emotional dimensions of this problem should not be underestimated. A "family should not be asked to balance their love for a family member against their needs in the future for life insurance proceeds. A family should not be forced by economic difficulties to file a petition for termination which conflicts with their religious or ethical beliefs simply to preserve an insurance benefit."[8] Nonetheless, "under any acceptable

---

1. *National Trust* v *Sterling* (1916) QR 51 SC 481, 488 (PA).
2. *Harvey* v *Ocean Accident & Guarantee Corp* [1905] 2 Ir R 1 (life).
3. *Boyd* v *Refuge Assurance Co Ltd*, 1890 17 R 955, 957 *per* Lord MacDonald (Ct Sess—life).
4. *Boyd* (above), *loc cit*; *London Life Ins Co* v *Trustee, Lang Shirt Co Ltd* (1929) SCR 117 (PA). *New York Life Ins Co* v *Gamer*, 303 US 161, 170 *per* Butler J (life): "the presumption is not evidence and ceases upon substantial evidence to the contrary". See also *Fidelity & Guarantee Co* v *Blum*, 270 F 946 (9 Cir, 1921—PA). *Cf* MacGillivray, No 1601; and *Clark* v *NZI Life Ltd* [1991] 2 Qd R 11, 16–17 (life).
5. *Trew* v *Railway Passengers' Assurance Co* (1861) 6 H & N 839, 845 *per* Lord Cockburn CJ (Exch Ch—PA). See also *Boyd* (above); *Ballantine* v *Employers Ins Co of Great Britain Ltd* (1893) 21 R (Ct Sess) 305 (PA).
6. *Prudential Ins Co* v *Gutowski*, 113 A 2d 579, 586 (Del, 1955—life).
6a. *Clark* v *NZI Life Ltd* [1991] 2 Qd R 11 (life). Generally, see above 16–3B2.
7. 538 So 2d 941 (Fla, 1989—life).
8. p 942.

definition of 'death,' Mr Kepler did not die before the expiration of his life insurance policy".[9]

17–2 FIRE

17–2A Ignition

Although people sometimes say that there is no smoke without fire, that is not true of insurance. In insurance contracts damage by "fire" means damage by ignition.[10]

"Fire is always caused by combustion, but combustion does not always cause fire . . . In Webster's Dictionary 'fire' is defined as 'the evolution of light and heat in the combustion of bodies.' No definition of fire can be found that does not include the idea of visible heat or light, and this is also the popular meaning of the word. The slow decomposition of animal and vegetable matter in the air is caused by combustion . . . Still we never speak of these processes as 'fire'. And why? Because the process of oxidation is so slow that it does not . . . produce a 'flame or glow'."[11]

Thus, the charring of corn by hot light bulbs is not fire.[12] Electrical arcing is not itself fire.[13] Although in practice some insurers pay, scorching alone is not covered by insurance against fire. Similar difficulties arise with regard to the warping or melting of plastic goods caused by heat. Significantly, however, fire cover includes damage incurred to prevent property insured being imminently damaged by fire, even though the damage inflicted does not involve ignition: it is in nobody's interest that there should be any encouragement to delay such measures so that the damage is insured. In *The Knight of St. Michael*[14] property was damaged by water poured on it to prevent fire. Gorell Barnes J said:

"fire did not actually break out, but it is reasonably certain that it would have broken out, and the condition of things were such that there was an actual existing state of peril of fire . . . The danger was present, and, if nothing were done, spontaneous combustion and fire would follow in natural course."

17–2B Causes of Fire

If property insured is damaged by fire, in general, the damage is covered by fire insurance whatever the cause, whether it be lightning,[15] spontaneous combustion,[16] human

---

9. *Ibid.*

10. *Everett* v *London Assurance* (1865) 19 CB (NS) 126, 133 *per* Byles J. See further Ivamy, *Fire*, p 68; Bragg (1992) 2 Ins L & P 34. *Morley* v *Employers' Liability Assurance Corp* [1939] OWN 204 (motor). *Schumacher Oil Works* v *Hartford Fire Ins Co*, 239 F 2d 836 (5 Cir, 1956—fire).

11. *Western Woollen Mill Co* v *Northern Assurance Co*, 139 F 637, 639 (8 Cir, 1905—fire), cert den 199 US 608: damage to wool by water, which caused spontaneous combustion with smoke and great heat but no visible flame or glow, held not fire. In the same sense: *Young* v *Waterloo Mutual Fire Ins Co* [1955] 5 DLR 35, 42 (Ont—fire).

12. *The Buckeye State*, 39 F Supp 344 (WD NY, 1941).

13. *Aetna Ins Co* v *Getchell Steel Treating Co*, 395 F 2d 12 (8 Cir, 1968—fire).

14. [1898] P 30, 34: freight was insured against perils of "fire . . . and of all other perils, losses and misfortunes". The insured lost freight, because part of the coal heated and had to be discharged before it caught fire. The decision, that the loss was covered by the insurance, was approved in *Symington* v *Union Ins Sy of Canton* (1928) 34 Com Cas 23 (CA—cargo). See further below 17–2C2.

15. *Gordon* v *Rimmington* (1807) 1 Camp 123 (hull).

16. *Tempus Shipping Co Ltd* v *Dreyfus & Co Ltd* [1930] 1 KB 699, 708 *per* Wright J. *Glen Falls Ins Co* v *Linwood Elevator*, 130 So 2d 262 (Miss, 1961—fire). Note, however, that in a particular case the loss may be excepted as a case of inherent vice: *Boyd* v *Dubois* (1811) 3 Camp 133 (cargo); see further, below 17–3A1.

negligence,[17] or even arson.[18] The exception is fire damage resulting from an explosion.[19] It is common for fire contracts to deal expressly with explosion, confirming the common law rule that explosion is not covered by fire insurance. The reason for special treatment of explosion and hence the special meaning given to "fire" lies in the attitude of insurers in the nineteenth century to explosion, notably from munitions factories: it is a special risk to be specially dealt with.

17–2C Consequences of Fire

If there is a fire, which is covered, the insurance also covers most immediate consequences of the fire. However, cover of the consequences is parasitic in the sense that there must first have been some ignition damage covered by the insurance.

The leading example is that of smoke damage: if there is a fire that is covered, the cover includes consequent smoke damage to the same property.[20] In Wisconsin, smoke damage has been held to include the effect of vapour from toxic chemicals,[21] but this decision was subsequently doubted in Pennsylvania. The later court pointed out that while "smoke may result from some chemical reactions, the common usage of the term refers to the products of combustion and, more importantly, to matter that is visible."[22]

Other examples include water damage from consequent melting of ice and snow,[23] or from rain which enters the damaged building,[24] physical damage inflicted by falling masonry and debris[25] and the effects of firefighting: below, 17–2F.

In contrast, theft and looting during a fire, not being proximately caused by the fire, are not normally covered.[26] However, it has been held in the United States that, if fire prevents the rescue of property from other perils, the consequent loss was caused by fire.[27]

---

17. *Harris* v *Poland* [1941] 1 KB 462 (fire). See below, 17–2G
18. See below, 17–2G.
19. *Everett* v *London Assurance* (1865) 19 CB (NS) 126; *Re Hooley Hill Rubber & Chemical Co Ltd* [1920] 1 KB 257, 274 *per* Duke LJ (CA—fire). See further below, 17–2E.
   Cf Feeny & Myers v *Empire State Ins Co*, 228 F 2d 770 (10 Cir, 1955)—the insurance covered fire caused by an oil well blowout, for, although blowouts were excepted, "there can be loss from a blowout without fire ensuing" (p 771), fire was covered and the exception could be construed *contra proferentem*.
20. *The Diamond* [1906] P 282.
21. *Henri's Food Products* v *Home Ins Co*, 474 F Supp 889 (ED Wis, 1979—fire).
22. *K & Lee Corp* v *Scottsdale Ins Co*, 769 F Supp 870, 873 (ED Pa, 1991—fire). The court held that ethyl acetate vapour was not smoke.
23. Ivamy, *Fire*, p 69.
24. *Vintix P/Y* v *Lumley Gen Ins Ltd* (1991) 24 NSWLR 627 (fire).
25. *Re Hooley Hill Rubber & Chemical Co Ltd* [1920] 1 KB 257, 271–272 *per* Scrutton LJ (CA—fire). *Pruitt* v *Hardware Dealers' Mutual Fire Ins Co*, 112 F 2d 140 (5 Cir, 1940—fire).
26. In this sense *Marsden* v *City & County Assurance Co* (1865) LR 1 CP 232 (plate glass).
   Cf USA: such loss has been held within fire cover: *Denham* v *La Salle-Madison Hotel Co*, 168 F 2d 576, 581 (7 Cir, 1948—fire).
   Cf also *Levy* v *Baillie* (1831) 7 Bing 349 (fire) in which it seems to have been assumed that such loss would be within a fire policy.
27. In *Princess Garment Co* v *Fireman's Fund Ins Co*, 115 F 2d 380 (6 Cir, 1940—fire) adjacent fire prompted police to clear the property insured, so that it was not possible to minimise flood damage to the latter.
   In *Norwich Union Fire Ins Sy Ltd* v *Bd of Commissioners of Port of New Orleans*, 141 F 2d 600 (5 Cir, 1944—fire) damage to machinery made it impossible to air undried corn, so that it deteriorated; the loss was held covered by a fire policy.
   In *Palmer & Sons* v *Lumber Mutual Fire Ins Co*, 100 NYS 2d 988 (1950) fire damage to machinery prevented working of timber before it became too damp to be used; the loss was held covered by the fire policy.

17–2C1 Friendly Fires

The court in *Austin* v *Drewe*[28] held that cover did not extend to heat damage (without ignition of the property damaged by heat), when the source of the heat was a fire (ignition) deliberately started to further an industrial process and at all times contained in the place intended.[29] Although a standard fire policy in the United States[30] covers "all direct loss by fire", courts there have been influenced[31] by *Austin* v *Drewe* to make a distinction between a "friendly" fire and a "hostile" fire: "a hostile one must extend from the place where it belongs and must pass beyond the limits assigned for it, and be an independent combustion wholly outside the original agency in which it was intended to burn."[32] Fire, said Scrutton LJ, "within the meaning of a fire policy means a fire which has broken bounds".[33]

In *Harris* v *Poland*[34] property was concealed in a cold grate, where later a fire was lit, damaging the property. Although the fire was in the right place, the property was not. The damage, it was held, was covered by fire insurance. The decision, which is likely to be the same in England if property falls on a friendly fire and is damaged, can be reconciled with statements in *Austin* v *Drewe*[35] but not with the others quoted above, as the fire was at all times in the grate and had not "broken bounds". Nor can it be reconciled with a later and wider view found in the United States that a hostile fire is one that is out of control, whether it is in its proper place or not[36]; it cannot be said that the fire in *Harris* v *Poland* was out of control. Contracts should be drafted with this in mind.

17–2C2 Adjacent Property

It has been suggested[37] that, for cover of consequences such as smoke, there must have been actual ignition of the property insured; and that, if ignition is confined to adjacent property not covered by the insurance contract, the cover will not extend to

---

28. (1816) 6 Taunt 434. *Austin* v *Drewe* was accepted in *Morley* v *Employers' Liability Assurance Corp* [1939] OWN 204, 205 (motor); *Young* v *Waterloo Mutual Fire Ins Co* [1955] 5 DLR 35 (Ont—fire).

29. p 461 per Gibbs CJ. The same is true of damage by cigarette burns.

30. The New York Standard Fire Policy, adopted in most parts of the USA.

31. Ingram [1987] Tort & Ins L J 312, 313. It was not followed in *Wasserman* v *Caledonian-American Ins Co*, 95 NE 2d 547 (Mass 1950—fire).

32. *Pacific Fire Ins Co* v *Anderson Co*, 47 F Supp 90, 92 (SD Idaho, 1942—fire). See also *Davis* v *Law Union & Rock Ins Co*, 1 NYS 2d 344 (1937—fire); *Giambalvo* v *Phoenix Ins Co of Hartford*, 36 NYS 2d 598 (1942—fire). More recently some courts have extended fire cover to fires that have not escaped: Ingram, *op cit*, p 321.

Cases that the fire must be "hostile", rather than "friendly": *Princess Garment Co* v *Fireman's Fund Ins Co*, 115 F 2d 380 (6 Cir, 1940—fire); *Reckler* v *British American Assurance Co*, 85 NYS 2d 183 (1949—fire); *Barcalo Manufacturing Co* v *Firemen's Mutual Ins Co*, 263 NYS 2d 807 (1965—fire).

33. *Upjohn* v *Hitchens* [1918] 2 KB 48, 51 (fire).

34. [1941] 1 KB 462.

35. In cases like *Harris* courts in the USA have seen a friendly fire and hence no cover: *Owens* v *Milwaukee Ins Co*, 123 NE 2d 645 (Ind, 1955—fire), citing *Austin* v *Drewe* but not *Harris* v *Poland*. Further, see Ingram [1987] Tort & Ins L J 312, 319.

36. *Barcalo* (above); see also *Fiorito* v *California Ins Co*, 114 NW 2d 661 (Minn, 1962—fire). These cases decide that damage to an oven or a furnace, when the fire within becomes too hot, is fire damage.

37. Ivamy, *Fire*, p 72. In this sense *Hobbs* v *Guardian Assurance Co* (1886) 12 SCR 631, 636–637 *per* Henry J; doubted in *Edwards* v *Wawanesa Mutual Ins Co* (1959) 17 DLR 2d 229, 231 (BC—motor).

Contra: MacGillivray, No 1868, n19. Ivamy rests his suggestion on the apparent analogy with the decision in *Everett* v *London Assurance* (1865) 19 CB (NS) 126, that a fire policy did not cover damage by concussion emanating from an explosion in a neighbouring factory. This decision was probably influenced by the view at the time that the proximate cause was usually the last cause in point of time, a view that is no longer tenable: see below, 25–3.

the consequences such as smoke damage to the property insured. But unless the risk is clearly limited in this way by the contract, this suggestion does not sit easily either with principles of causation or with cases on the point.

In *Johnston* v *West of Scotland Ins Co*[38] a fire in an adjacent property left a gable of that property, in the words of the Lord President, "tottering for a day or two" before it fell and damaged the adjacent property insured. The Lord Ordinary expressed the opinion that, if the fire were the proximate cause of loss, it did not have to be the actual instrument of loss. The Court of Session held that the loss was covered by the insurance.

Again, in *Symington* v *Union Ins Sy of Canton*[39] fire broke out on the quay at Algeciras. The insured cargo of cork was damaged by water poured on to it in a reasonable and successful attempt to prevent the fire spreading to the cork. The Court of Appeal held that the damage to the cork was covered by the insurance. Greer LJ said[40]:

"The next question is whether or not the loss was caused by fire within the policy; and, in my judgment, it is right to say that the cause of the loss was the fire. It is quite true that fire never touched the goods . . . But it has long been decided, and for a long time acted upon in relation to fire insurance on land, that damage by water done to save the consequence of fire . . . can be held to be the consequence of the fire and within a policy of fire insurance . . . There was . . . an actual peril of fire though no actual fire affected the claimant's goods."

In contrast, in *Liverpool & London & Globe Ins Ltd* v *Canadian General Electric Co Ltd*,[41] firemen directed water into a storage tank of epoxy resin in the mistaken belief that an explosion (covered by the insurance) was about to occur. In fact and with the benefit of hindsight, it was found that there was no imminent peril of explosion and no reasonable apprehension of one. With reference to English cases, to the effect that the rule "does not touch losses incurred in a mistaken attempt to avoid a peril in fact non-existent",[42] the Supreme Court of Canada held that the damage done by the water was not covered. In the language of *Symington* quoted above, there was no "actual peril of fire". Although a negligent response to an actual peril is normally covered,[43] a logical but curious line is drawn, whereby a negligent or merely erroneous assessment of the imminence or actuality of the peril is not.

Ultimately, much depends on the approach of the court, which in turn depends, first, on the wording of the contract. It may be necessary to distinguish cases approached as "damage by fire", in which the fire must be the immediate instrument of loss, from cases approached as damage "caused by fire" in which it is unnecessary for the property to have suffered ignition, if it has been damaged in some other proximate way (for example by water or smoke). The conclusion also depends, second, on the way the court defines fire as cause. One court may see fire as "ignition and/or inevitable consequences", such as smoke, while another court prefers to see ignition as an event distinct from smoke damage. If fire on property A leads to smoke damage

38. (1828) 7 Shaw 52: the fire policy was issued "against loss or damage by fire on a tenement and room". In the same sense: *Princess Garment Co* v *Fireman's Fund Ins Co*, 115 F 2d 380 (6 Cir, 1940—fire).
39. (1928) 34 Com Cas 23. The insurance was against fire and perils *eiusdem generis* with fire, so the decision might have been safely taken under the general words. The judgment of Scrutton LJ (pp 31-32) can be read on this basis.
40. pp. 35–6.
41. (1981) 123 DLR (3d) 513 (Sup Ct Canada — fire).
42. *Watson & Son Ltd* v *Fireman's Fund Ins Co* [1922] 2 KB 355, 359 *per* Rowlatt J (fire): also *The Knight of St Michael* (above 17–2).
43. Below 19–2A and 25–4B.

on property B, the first court will see a fire on property B, when the second court will not.[44]

17–2D Fire Causing Explosion

If a fire covered by the insurance leads inevitably to explosion, the damage by explosion is covered—although the policy commonly excludes this kind of loss.[45] Cases that appear to decide differently turn on the wording of the exceptions.

In *Stanley v Western Ins Co*[46] fire insurance excluded "loss or damage by explosion, except for such loss or damage as shall arise from explosion by gas". A small fire led to a big explosion and more fire, in a ratio of 1:12:6. Kelly CB took a broad view of the policy: "The company make themselves liable for any loss occasioned by fire as ordinarily understood, but not for loss caused by explosions, the mischievous and destructive results of which are so well known."[47] From this perspective, he concluded that the parties did not intend cover for any explosion unless occasioned by illuminating gas (which this was not). The claim in respect of the explosion and *subsequent* fire failed.[48]

The *Stanley* case was followed 50 years later by the Court of Appeal in *Re Hooley Hill*.[49] Buildings were insured against fire in terms similar to those in *Stanley*. A fire broke out, and after 20 minutes the heat of the fire caused an explosion that destroyed the property insured. The Court of Appeal held that the damage attributable to the explosion was not covered by the policy. It was argued for the insured, as one might expect, that the fire was the proximate cause of the whole loss for, according to the decision of the House of Lords in *Leyland Shipping*[50] handed down two years earlier, the proximate cause was the efficient cause, the one that necessarily sets the other causes in operation. For the insurers, however, it was argued that the *Leyland* rule had been excluded by unambiguous language in relation to the exception of explosion. Bankes LJ[51] thought that an "explosion without any antecedent or consequent fire does not seem to have been in the contemplation of the parties at all", so the exception of explosion was intended to include the antecedent fire. Further, the court thought the case indistinguishable from *Stanley*, a decision "unchallenged and presumably acted on for fifty years."[52] Thus, the decision rests on the construction of the contract, a construction generous to insurers in the light of the modern rule of construction *contra proferentem* (above, 15–5C).

The decision in *Re Hooley Hill* is of doubtful importance today. (a) It rests in part on *Stanley* in which the problem of causation was not discussed. (b) The reasoning

---

44. See further below, 25–9B.

45. Gamlen and Francis, *Fire Insurance*, (7th ed., 1991) ch 4.

46. (1868) LR 3 Ex 71. The sequence of events appears more clearly from the report in 37 LJ Ex 73.

47. p 75. He dismissed the argument that the insurer should be liable if a fire caused the explosion as "ingenious" and not the true construction of the particular document.

48. The insurer was held liable for the relatively small amount of damage done by the original fire (see p 76).

49. *Re Hooley Hill Rubber & Chemical Co Ltd* [1920] 1 KB 257.

50. *Leyland Shipping Co v Norwich Union Fire Ins Society* [1918] AC 350. See below, 27–4(c).

51. p 268–9. See also Scrutton LJ (p 273) who felt compelled to the decision in order to give some relevance to the exception of explosion.

52. p 270 *per* Bankes LJ.

takes little account of other cases[53] in which an excepted cause which followed inevitably from a peril insured is disregarded. (c) It can be distinguished as a decision on the construction of the particular policy.[54] (d) It was later stated in the Privy Council that, subject to any clear contract exceptions, fire insurance normally covers loss by explosion consequent on fire.[55] If an electrical fault starts a small fire in his garage which leads to a large explosion in his car, with more fire following in the adjoining lounge, the householder would be surprised to be told that he had not suffered damage by fire and the court today is likely to agree.

17–2E Explosion Causing Fire

If fire causes explosion, that is covered as fire loss: above, 17–2D. If, however, there is explosion causing fire, the fire is treated not as fire but as explosion and the loss is not within fire cover.[56] This is sometimes explained as the result of a special and narrow meaning given to "fire" in policies of insurance: above, 17–2B. An alternative explanation lies in the rules of causation: when explosion causes fire, there is fire indeed but it is proximately caused by something else, the explosion, and is consequently not itself the proximate cause of the loss.[57] In any event, explosion causing fire is commonly excluded expressly, except as regards explosion of boilers and of gas.[58]

The position is the same whether the explosion and fire began on the premises insured or on neighbouring premises. It has been suggested[59] that, if an explosion in property A led to fire in property B, there would be loss by fire, for the explosion would be too remote a cause. It is difficult, however, to see why fire, which knows few boundaries and which crosses a line in the law of property, breaks a chain of causation in law, logic or physics. If a cause is proximate in law, it matters not that a fence lies between cause and effect.

The meaning of "explosion" is to be sought in the context of the contract, in particular, in relation to other events, such as fire and lightning, which the contract appear to distinguish from explosion as a cause of loss.[60] In *Commonwealth Smelting*

53. For example *Fitton* v *Accidental Death Ins Co* (1870) LR 5 Ex 302 (accident); *Mardorf* v *Accident Ins Co* [1903] 1 KB 584 (PA); *Re Etherington and Lancashire & Yorkshire Accident Ins Co* [1909] 1 KB 591 (CA—PA). See also *Leyland Shipping Co* v *Norwich Union Fire Ins Society* [1918] AC 350, 369 *per* Lord Shaw. None of these cases concerned fire insurance, which some courts have treated as *sui generis*.

54. See in particular [1920] 1 KB 257, 271 *per* Scrutton LJ.

55. *Curtis & Harvey (Canada) Ltd* v *North British & Mercantile Ins Co* [1921] 1 AC 303, 309–310 *per* Lord Dunedin (PC—fire), approving *Hobbs* v *Guardian Assurance Co* (1886) 12 SCR 631 (fire). In the same sense *Shea and Foubert* v *Halifax Ins Co* (1958) 17 DLR 2d 667 (Ont—motor). *Waters* v *Merchants' Louisville Ins Co*, 11 Peters 213, 225 *per* Story J (Sup. Ct. USA, 1837—hull); *Texas City Terminal Ry Co* v *American Equitable Assurance Co*, 130 F Supp 843 (SD Tex, 1955—fire); *Commercial Standard Ins Co* v *Feaster*, 259 F 2d 210 (10 Cir, 1958—fire).

Cf Mitchell v *Potomac Ins Co*, 183 US 42 (1903)—the Supreme Court held that a fire policy, which excepted explosion, did not cover the case of a lighted match which caused an explosion.

56. *Boiler Inspection & Ins Co of Canada* v *Sherman-Williams Co Ltd* [1951] AC 319 (PC—PA). *Equity Oil Co* v *National Fire Ins Co*, 247 F 2d 393 (10 Cir, 1957—fire).

57. See below, 25–4. In particular, note that the operation of rules of causation can be changed by enlarging (for example explosion includes consequent fire) or restricting the definition of the event which is postulated as the cause of loss: below, 25-9.

58. Gamlen and Francis, *Fire Insurance*, (7th ed., 1991) ch 4.

59. Ivamy, *Fire*, p 72. The suggestion can be supported by interpretation of the contract, whereby "explosion" means explosion on the property insured and not, by implication, explosion elsewhere.

60. *Commonwealth Smelting Ltd* v *Guardian Royal Exchange Assurance Ltd* [1984] 2 Lloyd's Rep 608, 612 *per* Staughton J (material damage).

Ltd v *Guardian Royal Exchange Assurance Ltd*[61] Staughton J defined explosion as "an event that is violent, noisy and . . . caused by a very rapid chemical or nuclear reaction, or the bursting out of gas or vapour under pressure". This definition, which comes from Webster and the *Encyclopaedia Britannica*, was quoted by Parker LJ on appeal with apparent approval.[62] In that case an impeller in the blower house of a smelting complex failed, shattering the casing and leading to a sudden release of air which had been under pressure in the blower house. The courts looked at the policy but found no assistance. While Staughton J used the definition quoted above, Parker LJ preferred an approach of first impression[63]; the result was the same, that this was not a case of loss by explosion. Further, said Parker LJ[64]:

"one might say that some of the damage . . . was at any rate contributed to by an explosion, namely the explosion of the air from its confinement within the casing, the casing having been shattered by the entirely independent operation of the failure of the impeller. However, even so, it appears to me that the proximate and effective cause of all the damage was the failure of the impeller and not the explosion."

If this is correct, cases of explosion are restricted, for in many cases the explosion of popular imagination is proximately caused by something else which would not be described as explosion.

17–2F Associated Loss: Firefighting

Fire includes not only measures taken to prevent fire reaching the property insured (above 17–2A) but also

"any loss resulting from an apparently necessary and *bona fide* effort to put out a fire, whether it be by spoiling the goods by water, or throwing the articles of furniture out of [a] window, or even the destroying of a neighbouring house by an explosion for the purposes of checking the progress of the flames."[65]

Loss probably includes payments made for such measures.[66]

17–2G Fire Deliberately Caused

Fire cover does not include arson by the insured,[67] but fire loss caused negligently by the insured is covered by fire insurance,[68] "otherwise such policies would practically

---

61. [1984] 2 Lloyd's Rep 608, 612. An eruption without any chemical reaction is not generally an explosion: *Liverpool & London & Globe Ins Ltd* v *Canadian General Electric Co Ltd* (1981) 123 DLR (3d) 513 (Sup Ct—fire).
62. [1986] 1 Lloyd's Rep 121,124 (CA)—but without being expressly adopted.
63. p 126, giving the only reasoned judgment in the Court of Appeal.
64. *Ibid.*
65. *Stanley* v *Western Ins Co* (1868) LR 3 Ex 71, 74 *per* Kelly CB (fire), approved in *Canada Rice Mills Ltd* v *Union Marine & General Ins Co* [1940] AC 55, 71 *per* Lord Wright (PC—cargo). See also *Ahmedbhoy Habbibhoy* v *Bombay Fire & Marine Ins Co Ltd* (1912) 29 TLR 96 (PC); *Symington* v *Union Ins Sy of Canton* (1928) 139 LT 386 (CA—cargo), above 17–2C2; *The Diamond* [1906] P 282. *Commercial Union Assurance Co Ltd* v *Planters Coop Assn*, 252 P 2d 146 (Okl, 1952—fire); *McDonough* v *Hardware Dealers Mutual Fire Ins Co*, 448 F 2d 870 (1 Cir, 1971—fire).
66. MacGillivray, No 1877.
67. *The Alexion Hope* [1988] 1 Lloyd's Rep 311 (CA—mortgagee ins).
68. *Busk* v *Royal Exchange Assurance Co* (1818) 2 B & Ald 73 (hull); *Shaw* v *Robberds* (1837) 6 Ad & E 75 (fire); *Harris* v *Poland* [1941] 1 KB 462 (fire). Cf *City Tailors Ltd* v *Evans* (1921) 38 TLR 230, 233–234 *per* Scrutton LJ (CA—fire), who suggested that the insured was obliged at common law to use diligence to minimise loss, once a fire had begun.
USA: negligence is covered: *Waters* v *Merchants' Louisville Ins Co*, 11 Peters 213 (Sup Ct, USA, 1837—hull); *Rosa* v *Ins Co of the State of Pennsylvania* [1970] 2 Lloyd's Rep 386 (9 Cir, 1970—hull).

be of little importance, since, comparatively speaking, few losses of this sort would occur which could not be traced back to some carelessness, negligence, or inattention."[69] The position of the insured who fires his property while drunk is uncertain in English law, but as regards PA insurance the English courts have been slow to characterise drunken behaviour as recklessness rather than "mere" negligence.[70] Further, fire does not imply accidental fire, so it is not for the claimant to prove its accidental character,[71] but for the defendant underwriter, if so minded, to prove that the insured fired his own property.[72] The claimant benefits from a presumption of innocence of crime,[73] which also affects the onus of proof on the insurer who defends a claim with the allegation of arson: below, 17–2G4.

Fire caused by arson, the intentional act of a third party,[74] including a servant,[75] agent,[76] or relative[77] is covered, provided that it occurred without the authorisation or the connivance of the insured and that the act of the the third party in question cannot in any other way be attributed to the insured.

17–2G1 Arson by a Co-insured

In the United States, it has been held[78] that fire caused by arson on the part of one insured prevents recovery by an innocent co-insured. The reason is not that the loss is outside cover but public policy[79] against wilful misconduct. One strand of public

69. *Waters* (above) p 220 *per* Story J. See also *Federal Ins Co v Tamiami Trail Tours*, 117 F 2d 794, 796 (5 Cir, 1941—fire); *Reckler v British American Assurance Co*, 85 NYS 2d 183 (1949—fire); *General Mills v Goldman*, 184 F 2d 359 (8 Cir, 1950—fire).

70. *Marcel Beller Ltd v Hayden* [1978] 1 Lloyd's Rep 472 (motor).

71. *The Alexion Hope* (above). *Aliter*, of course, if the policy cover is expressly limited to "accidental fire", for example, *Musgrove v Pandelis* [1919] 2 KB 43 (CA—fire).

72. *Thurtell v Beaumont* (1824) 1 Bing 339 (fire); *Upjohn v Hitchens* [1918] 2 KB 48, 58 *per* Scrutton LJ (CA—fire); *City Tailors Ltd v Evans* (1921) 38 TLR 230, 233 *per* Scrutton LJ (CA—profits); *Beresford v Royal Ins Co Ltd* [1938] AC 586, 595 *per* Lord Atkin (life); *Slattery v Mance* [1962] 1 Lloyd's Rep 60, 61 *per* Salmon J (hull).

73 The presumption is referred to, for example, by Swift J in *Herbert v Poland* (1932) 44 Ll L Rep 139, 142 (fire). *London Life Ins Co v Trustee, Lang Shirt Co Ltd* [1929] SCR 117 (life). In *Gorman v Hand In Hand Ins Co* (1877) IR 11 CL 224, 231 Pallas CB said that there was reason to suggest that the fire might have been started deliberately, but nonetheless that this had to be proved on balance by the defendant insurers, who were unable to do so.

74. *Upjohn v Hitchens* [1918] 2 KB 48 (CA—fire cover against the action of enemy aircraft). *Merchants Ins Co v Lilgeomont*, 84 F 2d 685 (8 Cir, 1936—fire); *Orient Ins Co v Parkhill*, 170 F 2d 510 (5 Cir, 1948—fire); *Hanover Fire Ins Co v Argo*, 251 F 2d 80 (5 Cir, 1957—fire); *Charles Stores Inc v Aetna Ins Co*, 428 F 2d 989 (5 Cir, 1970—fire); *Richardson v Providence Washington Ins Co*, 237 NYS 2d 893 (1963—fire: vendor insured could recover, when property burned by purchaser, under policy issued to vendor and purchaser "as interest may appear").

75. *The Ikerian Reefer* [1993] 2 Lloyd's Rep 68 (hull). *Charles Stores* (above); *Owl & Turtle v Travelers Indemnity Co*, 554 F 2d 196 (5 Cir, 1977—fire).

Cf marine insurance: arson by the master or crew would be barratry and not within fire cover: *Waters v Merchants' Louisville Ins Co*, 11 Peters 213, 219–220 (Sup Ct, USA, 1837—hull).

76. *Glen Falls Ins Co v Sherritt*, 95 F 2d 823 (4 Cir, 1938—fire); however, there is a suggestion that, if the agent had had general charge of the property burned, the fire claim would have failed: *Sternberg v Merchants' Fire Assurance Corp*, 6 F Supp 541 (ED Wis, 1934—fire).

77. *Midland Ins Co v Smith* (1881) 6 QBD 561 (fire—arson by the wife of the insured). *Glen Falls Ins Co v Sherritt*, 95 F 2d 823 (4 Cir, 1938—fire: arson by the son of the insured); *Buffalo Ins Co v Amyx*, 262 F 2d 898 (10 Cir, 1958—fire: arson by the brother of the insured).

78. *Federal Ins Co v Wong*, 137 F Supp 232 (SD Cal, 1956—fire).

79. See below, 24–5B. Also *Sullivan v American Motorists Ins Co*, 605 F 2d 169 (5 Cir, 1979—fire). It is also seen as breach of the duty of good faith: *Hargove v American Century Ins Co*, 125 F 2d 225 (10 Cir, 1942—fire); or as contrary to the intention of the parties: *California Ins Co v Allen*, 235 F 2d 178 (5 Cir, 1956—fire).

policy is that the insured arsonist should not profit from his own wrong.[80] Hence, in California it has been held that an innocent wife could not recover in respect of fire damage to property held in common with her husband, who had deliberately burned it[81]; but in another case,[82] in which the arsonist husband died in the blaze and was not in a position to benefit directly from the insurance, the co-insured wife recovered under the fire insurance. However, the "no benefit" strand of public policy is weak, and it is not evident that a modern English court would reach similar decisions.

In England, Viscount Cave stated[83] that, if two persons insured under one policy had interests that were separate and distinct, the wilful misconduct of the one would not affect the rights of the other. Thus, if two partners insure partnership property, arson by one does not prevent recovery by the other.[84] *A fortiori*, arson by the mortgagor of property mortgaged does not prevent recovery by the mortgagee, if the mortgage clause gives him a separate contract.[85]

However, Viscount Cave also said: "It may well be that, when two persons are jointly insured and their interests are inseparably connected so that a loss or gain necessarily affects them both, the misconduct of one is sufficient to contaminate the whole insurance".[86] This statement and the distinction it draws have been adopted in Canada.[87] The impact of joint insurance on claims is discussed more generally below, 27–4.

17–2G2 Arson by a Corporation

An insured corporation can commit arson only through the act or connivance of the *alter ego* of the corporation. In England, the *alter ego* is the person with the power to make managerial decisions without further reference; however, there are signs that the *ego* may have a variable identity according to context and the public policy in issue. In the United States, arson by a corporation means arson by a person having control and management of the corporation[88]; when, however, a corporation is the subject of bankruptcy proceedings, the corporation has been identified with the bankruptcy trustee and arson by the former controller was covered by the corporation fire

---

80. See below, 24–5A2.
81. *Allen* (above).
82. *Safeco Ins Co* v *Kartsone*, 510 F Supp 856 (D Cal, 1981—fire). Also in this sense: *Reed* v *Federal Ins Co*, 528 NYS 2d 355 (1988—fire). In some jurisdictions the result between co-insured depends on whether the interest is joint (the innocent co-insured cannot recover) or not (the co-insured can recover). In other jurisdictions it depends simply on whether the co-insured is innocent: see *Winter* v *Aetna Casualty & Surety Co*, 409 NYS 2d 85 (1978—fire). The latter view prefers a decision based on equity rather than on the technicalities of property law.
83. *Samuel & Co Ltd* v *Dumas* [1924] AC 431, 445–446 (hull).
84. *Higgins* v *Orion Ins Co Ltd* (1985) 17 DLR (4th) 90 (Ont—fire).
85. *Caisse Populaire de Deux Rives* v *Sté d'Assurance contre l'Incendie de la Vallée du Richelieu* (1984) 19 DLR (4th) 411 (Que—fire).
86. Above.
87. *Scott* v *Wawanesa Mutual Ins Co* (1989) 59 DLR (4th) 660, 674 (Sup Ct— fire); *Peters* v *Fireman's Fund Ins Co* (1992) 93 DLR (4th) 637, 639 (NWT—fire).
88. If the insurance is taken in the name of a corporation, there is no cover, if the subject-matter is intentionally burned by the president of the corporation: *Midwest Seafood Inc* v *Truck Ins Exchange*, 431 F Supp 1197 (ED Mo, 1977—fire), affirmed 573 F 2d 1314 (8 Cir, 1978). *Idem: Kimball Ice Co* v *Hartford Ins Co*, 18 F 2d 563 (4 Cir, 1927—fire) as regards a general manager holding a quarter of the capital stock and having exclusive control and management of the property; but *cf Fidelity-Phenix Fire Ins Co* v *Queen City Bus & Transfer Co*, 3 F 2d 784 (4 Cir, 1925—fire).

insurance.[89] It appears that arson by a debtor or creditor of the corporation does not bar recovery, even though the arsonist may benefit indirectly in his capacity as debtor or creditor; compare the position of the co-insured: above 17–2G1.

17–2G3 Legitimate Fires

Public policy against arson may permit recovery in respect of the deliberate destruction of property insured in exceptional cases. First, fire may be deliberately started for a higher good. Examples include the fire break to block the march of a greater fire; and the ship that was deliberately burned by the master, so that it would not fall into enemy hands.[90] Second, in the case of a "friendly" fire which is started deliberately but which has unintended effects, those effects may be covered by fire insurance. Thus when the insured lit a fire in the grate of her home, forgetting that she had hidden some jewellery there, the loss was covered by a fire policy.[91]

17–2G4 Arson by the Insured: Onus of Proof

In *Hornal* v *Neuberger Products Ltd* Denning LJ said[92]:

"So, also in civil cases, the case may be proved by a preponderance of probability, but there may be degrees of probability within that standard; the degree depends on the subject-matter. A civil court, when considering a charge of fraud, will naturally require for itself a higher degree of probability than that which it would require when asking if negligence is established. It does not adopt so high a degree as a criminal court, even when it is considering a charge of a criminal nature; but still it does require a degree of probability which is commensurate with the occasion."

The Denning view[93] has been used in Canada to support the contention that the court must be satisfied that "the facts are such as to make it reasonably probable, having due regard to the gravity of the suggestion, that the act was in fact committed".[94] The Denning view has also been quoted with approval by the Supreme Court of South Australia.[95] However, the Court also adopted a statement in an earlier Australian case,[96] that, whereas the allegation had to be proved "merely on the balance of proba-

---

89. *In re JTR Corporation*, 958 F 2d 602 (4 Cir, 1992—fire)—even though the arson occurred between the time that the petition was filed and the trustee appointed.

90. *Gordon* v *Rimmington* (1807) 1 Camp 123. See further above, 17–2F.

91. *Harris* v *Poland* [1941] 1 KB 462 (fire). See above, 17–2C1.

92. [1957] 1 QB 247, 263 (CA). This statement was followed in *S & M Carpets (London) Ltd* v *Cornhill Ins Co Ltd* [1981] 1 Lloyd's Rep 667 (fire), affirmed [1982] 1 Lloyd's Rep 423 (CA); *Watkins & Davies Ltd* v *Legal & General Assurance Soc Ltd* [1981] 1 Lloyd's Rep 674 (fire); *The Litsion Pride* [1985] 1 Lloyd's Rep 437, 479 *per* Hirst J (hull); *McClean Enterprises Ltd* v *Ecclesiastical Ins Office Plc* [1986] 2 Lloyd's Rep 416 (fire); *Polivitte Ltd* v *Commercial Union Assurance Co Plc* [1987] 1 Lloyd's Rep 379 (material damage). See also *Herbert* v *Poland* (1932) 44 Ll L Rep 139 (fire); *CN Santi SA* v *Indemnity Marine Assurance Co Ltd* [1960] 2 Lloyd's Rep 469, 473 *per* Pearson J and cases cited (hull); *Slattery* v *Mance* [1962] 1 Lloyd's Rep 60, 63 *per* Salmon J (yacht); *Grunther Industrial Developments Ltd* v *Federated Employers Ins Assn Ltd* [1976] 2 Lloyd's Rep 259, 271 *per* Roskill LJ (CA—fire); *The Captain Panagos DP* [1986] 2 Lloyd's Rep 470, 511 *per* Evans J (hull); *The Ikerian Reefer* [1993] 2 Lloyd's Rep 68, 71 *per* Cresswell J (hull); and cases to this effect in Australia and New Zealand, cited by Tarr, 1 Ins L J 42, 59 (1988). In Canada a similar decision is *Tsalamatas* v *Wawanesa Mutual Ins Co* (1982) 141 DLR (3d) 322 (Ont—fire).

A case requiring proof beyond reasonable doubt is *Thurtell* v *Beaumont* (1823) 1 Bing 339 (fire).

93. As expressed in *Bater* v *Bater* [1952] 2 All ER 458, 459.

94. *Lewis* v *Royal Ins Co* (1990) 67 DLR (4th) 74, 76, 77 (NS—fire), concluding that "the words 'proof of a more cogent character' are by no means synonymous with 'proof beyond reasonable doubt'."

95. *Sheldon* v *Sun Alliance Australia Ltd* (1990) 53 SASR 97, 133–134 (fire).

96. *Lemmer* v *Bertram* (1971) 2 SASR 397, 400. Also in this sense: *Lewis* (above) pp 78–79.

bilities, the sufficiency of proof may well be affected by the presumption of innocence". This appears to mean that, although the total effect of the evidence, which is
often circumstantial, must indicate arson on the balance of probabilities, the pieces of
evidence that are put in the balance, such as the imminent liquidation of the insured
company and the presence of the managing director in the vicinity of the factory just
before fire broke out at 2 a.m, must be established on something more than the
balance of probability. In contrast, in the USA, although a higher degree of proof has
been demanded,[97] it has been said that such a rule is not appropriate there and that
most jurisdictions are satisfied with "a mere preponderance of the evidence".[97a] The
preponderance of legal opinion, however, is that, if the insurer alleges arson, his onus
of proof will be affected in some way and affected adversely, but in what way is hard
to predict with precision. So, it is scarcely surprising that in view of "the difficulty of
winning and the odium of losing, many insurers admit to paying out against their
better judgement".[98]

If, indeed, there is some kind of change in the burden of proof whenever an effective defence by the insurer to a fire claim may amount to a finding of crime, why not
also in any case in which the defence is that the claimant has deliberately damaged his
property or scuttled his ship, and that therefore the claim is fraudulent? Indeed, this is
so in cases of marine insurance.[99] It appears, however, that a line is drawn between a
case in which the defendant insurer proves wilful misconduct, such as arson, to which
the Denning onus applies, and cases in which the claim is equally unsuccessful but on
the more muted ground that the claimant has failed to prove the accidental character
of his loss, as required, for example, in the case of all risks insurance:[100] to conclude
that the claimant has not proved an accident may suggest that he has been guilty of
wilful misconduct, but does not establish it. Further, the courts have also been less
demanding of the insurer, requiring something less than the Denning onus, when the
allegation by the insurer is the fraud of a third party[101] or the suicide by the insured.[102]

17–3 ALL RISKS

All risks cover does not mean cover literally against all risks.[103] First, there is a practical limit to those risks to which the particular subject-matter in its particular location is

---

97. For example in *McGory* v *Allstate Ins Co*, 527 So 2d 632 (Miss, 1988—fire), the court required "clear
and convincing evidence" of the arson alleged.

97a. Ball, 59 Miss LJ 245 (1989).

98. N Michael Clarke, (1989) 29 Brit J Criminology 1, 14.

99. *CN Santi SA* v *Indemnity Marine Assurance Co Ltd* [1960] 2 Lloyd's Rep 469, 473 *per* Pearson J and
cases cited (hull); *Slattery* v *Mance* [1962] 1 Lloyd's Rep 60, 63 *per* Salmon J (yacht); *The Litsion Pride*
[1985] 1 Lloyd's Rep 437, 480 *per* Hirst J (hull); *The Ny-Eaasteyr* [1988] 1 Lloyd's Rep 60 (hull). See below,
27–2A.

However, the case of scuttling ships is controversial and possibly *sui generis*; Arnould, No 1357, con-
cludes that the onus is like that in a criminal case: *The Olympia* (1924) 19 Ll L Rep 255, 257 *per* Lord Birkenhead LC, who in *The Arnus* (1924) 19 Ll L Rep 95, 97 said of a defence of scuttling, that it must be an
"irresistible inference"; see also *The Gloria* (1936) 54 Ll L Rep 35, 50 *per* Branson J (hull); *The Zinovia*
[1984] 2 Lloyd's Rep 264, 272 *per* Bingham J (hull).

100. See below, 17–3B.

101. *Hurst* v *Evans* [1917] 1 KB 352 (jewellery AR); *Greaves* v *Drysdale* (1936) 55 Ll L Rep 95, 101 *per*
Greer LJ (burglary).

102. *Dominion Trust Co* v *New York Life Ins Co* [1919] AC 254 (PC—life).

103. Among the British public there is a widespread belief that the term "all risks" can be taken literally;
consequently there have been moves in Parliament to extend the Unfair Contract Terms Act 1977 to insurance contracts.

exposed; limits on the range of risks are usually built in to the risk situation. Second, there is usually a contractual limit: an all risks policy usually contains an express exception of particular risks.[104] Third, there is a conceptual limit: English law imposes limits as part of the definition of all risks cover. These limits, which are sometimes called implied exceptions,[105] are that loss must be fortuitous,[106] and lawful[107] to insure. Similar limits are found in the United States.[108] Subject to these limits, all risks means all risks, even though the policy may highlight certain specific risks,[109] unless, of course, the policy makes it clear that, for example, the reference is made to all risks of a certain and limited kind.[110] An obvious example is (all) perils of the sea.[111]

17–3A Fortuity

Loss is fortuitous unless (i) it was inevitable (below, 17–3A1) at the beginning—the beginning of cover or at the time that the contract is made, as appropriate to the case,[112] or (ii) it was caused by the wilful misconduct of the insured (below, 17–3A2).

17–3A1 Inevitable Loss

All risks insurance is not cover against all causes of loss but against all risks of loss: it "covers a risk not a certainty".[113] In the United States, this is because "Public policy requires that this be so . . . If it is inevitable that there will be loss, whether by the insured's own misconduct or by the inherent nature and qualities of the object of the insurance, it is against public policy to insure against that inevitable loss".[114] In Eng-

---

104. For example, Institute Cargo Clauses (A), cls 4.2 and 4.4
105. See below, 19–1A.
106. Also described as "accidental".
107. *British & Foreign Marine Ins Co Ltd* v *Gaunt* [1921] 2 AC 41, 57 *per* Lord Sumner (cargo).
108. In the United States all risks cover has been defined as embracing all risks which are fortuitous and which are not excluded by the contract: *Mellon* v *Federal Ins Co*, 14 F 2d 997 (SD NY, 1926—AR); *States SS Co* v *Aetna Ins Co*, 1985 AMC 2749, 2752 (ND Cal, 1985—marine AR); *Adams-Arapahoe* v *Continental Ins Co*, 891 F 2d 772, 774 (10 Cir, 1989—AR). The same description is found in *Gatti* v *Hanover Ins Co*, 601 F Supp 210 (ED Pa, 1985—AR), affirmed 774 F 2d 1151 (3 Cir, 1985), which adds (p 211) "except those caused by the willful (*sic*) act of the insured".
  All risks have been equated with "external causes"—*Avis* v *Hartford Fire Ins Co*, 195 SE 2d 545 (NC, 1973—homeowners' AR); *Goodman* v *Fireman's Fund*, 600 F 2d 1040, 1042 (4 Cir, 1979—hull AR). Generally see Cozens and Bennett, 20 Forum 222 (1984–5).
109. *Schloss Bros* v *Stevens* [1906] 2 KB 665, 673 *per* Walton J.
110. An example given by Walton J (p 672) is a reference "to include all risks of craft" which does no more than extend (specific) cover granted on goods while on board ship to the same goods while on lighters or landing craft.
111. A less obvious example perhaps is life insurance: all risks of death (above, 17–1). However, life insurance is subject to different rules, for example, it is not inherent in the concept of life insurance that death should not be caused by the wilful misconduct of the insured, ie, suicide. It has been argued that even suicide is accidental in the law of insurance, for it is accidental from the point of view of the third party beneficiary of the policy: Keeton, p 290.
112. This question has not been the subject of close examination in English cases.
113. *British & Foreign Marine Ins Co Ltd* v *Gaunt* [1921] 2 AC 41, 57 *per* Lord Sumner (cargo). See also a statement by Walton J, approved by the House in *Gaunt*, in *Schloss Bros* v *Stevens* [1906] 2 KB 665, 673: "all losses by any accidental cause of any kind . . . There must be a casualty." See further *Regina Fur Co Ltd* v *Bossom* [1958] 2 Lloyds Rep 425, 434 *per* Sellers LJ (CA—AR: furs). As regards marine insurance this is confirmed by MIA, section 55(2)(of2]c)
  The statement by Lord Sumner (above) was approved in *Mellon* v *Federal Ins Co*, 14 F 2d 997, 1002 (SD NY, 1926—cargo AR). See also *Avis* v *Hartford Fire Ins Co*, 195 SE 2d 545 (NC, 1973—homeowners' AR); *Goodman* v *Fireman's Fund*, 600 F 2d 1040 (4 Cir, 1979—hull AR); *States SS Co* v *Aetna Ins Co*, 1985 AMC 2749, 2752 (ND Cal, 1985—marine AR).
114. *Underwriters Subscribing to Lloyd's* v *Magi Inc*, 790 F Supp 1043, 1047 (ED Wa, 1991—AR).

land, however, express cover against, for example, inherent vice is enforceable,[115] so the rule, although similar in effect, is based not on public policy but on the definition of cover and the notion of risk.

"Fish designed for human consumption, if unfit for consumption when shipped, would inevitably be condemned. Hence there would be no insurable risk of loss but a certainty of loss. To hold otherwise would be to impose upon the insurer a guaranty of the good quality of the fish as and when packed by the shipper, which liability under the policy the insurer had not assumed."[116]

The effect is to exclude loss suffered before the date at which the element of risk is assessed. Further, an allied effect is the exclusion of loss which, although it has not occurred at that date, has become inevitable at that date. All risks "cannot, of course, be held to cover all damage however caused, for some damage as is inevitable from ordinary wear and tear and inevitable depreciation is not within the policies".[117]

Ordinary wear and tear, which is not covered, must be distinguished from damage resulting from abuse which, unless the circumstances amount to wilful misconduct (below, 17–3A3), is covered.[118] Excluded also, with ordinary wear and tear, is inherent vice, a defect in the subject-matter tending to its loss, damage or destruction[119] which was present at the time cover commenced and materialises during the period of cover. It lacks fortuity: it was always going to happen, sooner or later,[120] during the period of cover—in the particular case.

In *Noten BV* v *Harding*[121] it was argued that, as the consignment was one of a number of similar consignments, in which the damage had occurred sometimes but not other times, the damage was not inevitable and hence not a case of inherent vice. This argument was rejected by Bingham LJ,[122] saying that damage "may be caused by inherent vice without being inevitable". This statement should be seen, however, in

115. *Soya GmbH* v *White* [1983] 1 Lloyd's Rep 122, 126 *per* Lord Diplock (HL—cargo).

116. *Greene* v *Cheetham*, 293 F 2d 933 (2 Cir, 1961—cargo AR). See also *Mellon* (above), p 1002.

117. *Gaunt* (above), p 46 *per* Lord Birkenhead LC; applied in *Avis* v *Hartford Fire Ins Co*, 195 SE 2d 545, 547 (NC, 1973—homeowners' AR). For example, corrosion: *Central Louisiana Electric Co* v *Westinghouse Electric Corp*, 579 So 2d 981 (La, 1991—boiler). See also *Gatti* v *Hanover Ins Co*, 601 F Supp 210, 211 (ED Pa, 1985—AR), affirmed 774 F 2d 1151 (3 Cir, 1985): "an event which so far as the parties to the contract are aware, is dependent on chance". Towner 27 TILJ 638, 652 (1992).

118. *Johnson & Towers Baltimore Inc* v *Vessel "Hunter"*, 802 F Supp 1343, 1350 (D Md, 1992—yacht).

119. Inherent vice in English common law means some defect latent in the thing itself which "by its development tends to the injury or destruction of the thing carried": *Blower* v. *GW Ry* (1872) LR 7 C.P. 655, 662 *per* Willes J; *Kendall* v *London & South–Western Ry* (1872) LR 7 Ex 373. It concerns "ordinary processes going on in the things": *Carriage by Sea* (12th ed, London, 1971), para 15. If, however, the source of contamination was external to the chemicals common law would see a vice but not an inherent vice. In *Noten BV* v *Harding*, Phillips J ([1989] 2 Lloyd's Rep 527) held that goods (leather gloves in cardboard cartons), from which the moisture condensed to the walls of the container, and which were then wetted (and became mildewed and mouldy) by drips of condensation, did not suffer from inherent vice, for (p 531) "the sweat water has gone, as it were, into the universe on its own, even if it has come from those particular goods that are insured. It has set up a life of its own and has achieved an identity of its own; and I think it has merited the appellation of an external cause . . . ." On that premise, the decision was, no doubt, correct. However, this decision was reversed by the Court of Appeal: the real or dominant cause was not something external to the goods but the excessive moisture in the goods when shipped: [1990] 2 Lloyd's Rep 283, 288 *per* Bingham LJ. This apart, the defendant carrier does not have to prove the precise nature of the vice, it is enough that the loss or damage was caused by some propensity of the goods of the kind described: *Bradley* v *Federal S N Co* (1927) 27 Ll L Rep 395, 399 *per* Viscount Sumner (HL).

120. For example *Berk & Co Ltd* v *Style* [1955] 2 Lloyd's Rep 382 (cargo AR). The exclusion of inherent vice in principle from all marine insurance cover is confirmed by MIA, section 55(2)(of2]c).
A similar implicit exclusion of inherent vice is found in the United States: *Greene* (above).

121. [1990] 2 Lloyd's Rep 283.

122. P 289, with whom the other members of the Court of Appeal agreed. He cited Arnould para 782.

the context of his conclusion that there may be inherent vice in a particular case, although damage was not inevitable in all consignments of that kind.[123]

17–3A2 Knowledge

Neither fortuity nor certainty of loss can be established without making certain assumptions about the information available and hence about the time at which the certainty (or fortuity) is to be established.

First, all things decay or deteriorate sooner or later. What counts for the case to be outside the cover is not certainty of loss or damage but certainty of loss or damage during the insurance period. The evidence in one case was that "there is a certainty of subsidence from the moment that mining operations begin at any location". If that "precludes fortuity, there could never could be coverage for subsidence damage", a conclusion contrary to current insurance practice.[124]

Second, certainty of loss may be evident to a tester with the benefit of hindsight but not to one at the time when the venture or the cover began. In everyday language, a risk is something about to be taken and yet to be resolved, so, an insurance risk can only properly be appreciated from the perspective of a point in time before the risk has been run. At that time, it may appear that the weather will be favourable and the inherent vice will not develop while cover lasts; or that the defect would be dealt with in time to arrest its progress or to prevent loss. If loss is not certain at that time, there is not a certainty of loss but a risk of loss.[125]

Third, should the element of risk (or its absence) be assessed with the benefit of omniscience, or with the knowledge of the parties? In the case of life insurance (all risks of death) or health insurance, there is cover if, in the absence of an operative basis clause, the insured dies of a latent condition of which he was unaware at the time of the contract. In the case of PA insurance too, the accidental character of what occurs is assessed largely from the viewpoint of the insured.[126] Why not also when the insurance covers the life and health of property ? The "objective" assessment with the benefit of omniscience does not seem appropriate [127] but it does seem to reflect the current state of English law.

In a recent development, courts in the United States have preferred a "subjective" approach, whereby all risks insurance covers loss, although inevitable, if this was unknown to the insured. In the *Bauxites* case,[128] plant defectively designed and constructed collapsed. The lower court held against the insurance claim: "Such a loss can-

123. *Cf* Galbraith (1991) 4 Ins L J 143.

124. *INA* v *US Gypsum Co*, 870 F 2d 148, 152 (4 Cir, 1989—AR).

125. This kind of distinction was discussed in *Soya GmbH* v *White* [1982] 1 Lloyd's Rep 136, 150 by Donaldson LJ (CA—cargo); this point was left open on appeal: [1983] 1 Lloyd's Rep 122 (HL).

126. Cozens & Bennett, 20 Forum 222, 242 (1984–5) 136. See below, 17–5D; but *cf* 17–5F3.

127. Indeed students are taught from day one that, while risk is incapable of precise definition, it is generally subjectively assessed; see for example, Dickson, *Introduction to Insurance* (1984), No 1A1 (CII Tuition Service).

128. *Compagnie des Bauxites de Guinée* v *INA*, 724 F 2d 369 (3 Cir, 1983). A subjective approach is also found in respect of all risks cover on domestic property damaged by earth movement: *Millers Mutual Fire Ins Co* v *Murrell*, 362 SW 2d 868 (Tex, 1962); approved in *Employers Casualty Co* v *Holm*, 393 SW 2d 363, 368 (Tex, 1965—homeowners' AR); *INA* v *US Gypsum Co*, 870 F 2d 148, 151 (4 Cir, 1989—AR). "These decisions represent the clear trend of authority" *Adams-Arapahoe* v *Continental Ins Co* 891 F 2d 772, 775 (10 Cir, 1989—AR); *Underwriters Subscribing to Lloyd's* v *Magi Inc*, 790 F Supp 1043, 1048 (ED Wa, 1991—AR). By contrast but not necessarily by corollary, "public policy forbids one from obtaining insurance for a loss the insured knows is already present": *International Ins Co* v *Peabody Int Corp*, 747 F Supp 477, 484 (ND Ill, 1990—liability).

not be accidental or fortuitous, for it was predictable and certain that a defectively designed building such as the one involved here would fail and collapse, when subjected to forces in excess of those erroneously calculated."[129] The Court of Appeals started from the Restatement of Contracts[130] that "a fortuitous event . . . is an event which so far as the parties to the contract are aware, is dependent on chance". From this perspective, it found that, as the insured was ignorant of the defect, the claim should succeed.[131]

The inherent limits on the scope of all risks cover do not, therefore, follow easily from the notion of risk. In cases of inherent vice, the ruling against the insured might be justified on the basis that loss was the inevitable result of occurrences prior to the period of cover.[132] Perhaps it is safer to say that the meaning of all risks is somewhat idiosyncratic and is best explained as being what the insurance market understands and intends by all risks. Moreover, an objective approach to the scope of cover can be supported on the basis of commercial certainty. "The commercial purpose of the use of standard form policies (i.e, legal certainty as to the risk they cover) would be defeated if their construction varied from case to case according to the different circumstances",[133] including of course the actual knowledge of the particular insured.

17–3A3 Wilful Misconduct

Loss or damage caused by the wilful misconduct of the insured is not covered.[134] This rule differs from the requirement of fortuity in the sense of risk (above, 17–3A1) in that the latter is assessed at the beginning of the adventure, whereas wilful misconduct may occur at any time during the insurance period and its effect on the subject-matter may only be inevitable when the conduct occurs.

This rule can be seen as an implied exception to all risks cover, which reflects not only party intention but also the more general rule of public policy that, in general, cover should not extend to loss or damage deliberately caused by the insured.[135] It

---

129. 554 F Supp 1080, 1084 (WD Pa).

130. Section 291 (1932).

131. The summary judgment of the lower court was reversed; the case was remanded for decision whether the loss (22 million dollars) was excluded by an exception of inherent vice.

The Court of Appeals distinguished (724 F 2d 369, 373) the older marine cases as turning on the application of an express exception of inherent vice: in particular *Greene* v *Cheetham*, 293 F 2d 933, 936–937 (2d Cir, 1961—cargo AR). *Mellon* v *Federal Ins Co*, 14 F 2d 997 (SD NY, 1926—AR) was distinguished as depending on a narrow construction of the policy.

132. For example in *British & Foreign Marine Ins Co Ltd* v *Gaunt* [1921] 2 AC 41, 47 Lord Birkenhead LC cites with approval a statement by Walton J in *Schloss Bros* v *Stevens* [1906] 2 KB 665, 673, that "all risks of land and water" "were intended to cover all losses by an accidental cause of any kind occurring during the transit".

A trace of such reasoning is found in a comparable case in the United States: *Greene* v *Cheetham*, 293 F 2d 933, 936–937 (2d Cir, 1961—cargo AR).

133. *Soya GmbH* v *White* [1983] 1 Lloyd's Rep 122, 125 *per* Lord Diplock (HL—cargo). *Cf Soya GmbH* v *White* [1982] 1 Lloyd's Rep 136, 150 *per* Donaldson LJ (CA—cargo): the defence based on certainty of loss, which the judge distinguished from that of inherent vice, "is in any event subject to the qualification that it must be a certainty which is, or should be, known at least to the assured".

134. *British & Foreign Marine Ins Co Ltd* v *Gaunt* [1921] 2 AC 41, 52 *per* Viscount Finlay, and 57 *per* Lord Sumner (cargo). As regards marine insurance this is confirmed by MIA, section 55(2)(a). *Avis* v *Hartford Fire Ins Co*, 195 SE 2d 545, 549 (NC, 1973—homeowners' AR); *Gatti* v *Hanover Ins Co*, 601 F Supp 210 (ED Pa, 1985—AR), affirmed 774 F 2d 1151 (3 Cir, 1985).

Loss caused by the wilful misconduct of third parties is within all risks cover: *London & Provincial Leather Processes Ltd* v *Hudson* [1939] 2 KB 724; see also *Australia & New Zealand Bank Ltd* v *Colonial & Eagle Wharves Ltd* [1960] 2 Lloyd's Rep 241 (cargo AR).

135. Below 24–5B

stands in contrast with the general presumption that cover does extend to loss caused by the negligence of the insured.[136] Between intention and negligence, common lawyers place gross negligence and recklessness. Wilful misconduct, however, is something different again, mostly because of a concern with the actual awareness of the person concerned and because the objective probability of loss is not decisive. There is wilful misconduct at common law if a person's conduct increases the risk of loss and that person is actually aware of this.

That definition, however, has been developed largely in the context of the carriage of goods to answer the question whether and when the carrier should be deprived of contract defences to liability for loss.[137] In that context, wilful misconduct means reprobate conduct. In the context of insurance, both the question and in consequence the meaning of wilful misconduct are different. The focus shifts from the actual intention of the actor insured to the supposed intention of the insurer. The question becomes whether the insurer has assumed the risk of the insured's conduct; and the meaning of wilful misconduct takes in conduct by the insured that is usually reprobate—but not always.

In *The Wondrous*,[138] the insured shipowner could have secured the release of the ship by the payment of sums of money to the port authority, sums which in theory but not in practice would have been recoverable from the charterer as damages for breach of contract. In these circumstances, Hobhouse J held[139] that the loss of hire was not fortuitous and hence not covered by his insurance.

"where a situation comes about as a result of the voluntary conduct of the assured, it would not normally be described as fortuitous. It did not happen by chance but by the choice of the assured. Put another way, it would be in the ordinary course that, if the owners of a vessel do not pay the port dues for which they are liable to the port authority . . . the vessel will not be cleared. For the purposes of the law of insurance, in the absence of express agreement to the contrary, a policy should not be construed as covering the ordinary consequences of voluntary conduct of the assured arising out of the ordinary incidents of trading; it is not a risk."

This being so, is there a further implied exception to all risks cover when loss, although not intended by the insured, is loss that "he has brought upon himself" through gross negligence or recklessness? Could an exception be implied because, whatever the insured actually intended or expected, he is considered to have intended the natural or probable consequences of his acts or omissions?[140]

Let us take, for instance, the case of property seized. In England, burglary insurance has not been enforced in respect of uncustomed jewellery as a matter of public policy[141] and there can be little doubt that, if the jewellery had not been taken by

---

136. Below 19–2A.

137. Clarke, *International Carriage of Goods: CMR* (2nd ed London, 1991), no 107. These cases were applied to builders' AR insurance in *National Oilwell (UK) Ltd* v *Davy Offshore Ltd* [1993] 2 Lloyd's Rep 582, 621 ff by Colman J.

138. *Ikerigi CN SA* v *Palmer* [1991] 1 Lloyd's Rep 400, affirmed on other grounds: [1992] 2 Lloyd's Rep 566 (C.A.).

139. P 416. The conduct of the insured was a refusal to pay charges incurred by the insured. Such conduct would not include refusal to pay charges owed by a third party (*ibid*).

140. See below, 19–2B and 24–5B. Note also the exception found in some contracts of insurance concerning loss that is "intended or expected" by the insured.

141. Below 24–5A2. *Cf Commercial Union Ins Co* v *Sponholz*, 866 F 2d 1162 (9 Cir, 1989—AR): a claim in respect of a trawler seized by the police as stolen property failed, although there was no suggestion of any misconduct on the part of the insured. The decision turned on the construction of the contract. The court distinguished casualty insurance, such as this, from title insurance. "It is not reasonable to interpret a policy

burglars but by the customs authorities, a claim on all risks insurance would have also failed. If, however, the seizure is at the hands of public enemies, rioters and the like, the loss is commonly regarded as fortuitous and covered. But, if the seizure is a private step taken by a creditor, what then? If the seizure is by the creditor of a third party to whom the insured property has been entrusted, the loss is covered.[142] If, however, the creditor is the creditor of the insured, it has been held in the United States[143] that, whereas the seizure is "loss", it is not fortuitous: "there is nothing fortuitous about the fact that a creditor . . . would resort to the courts to obtain collateral for unpaid debts. Nor is such a business dispute outside the parties' realm of control." In England, the decision would likely be the same. Insurance is presumed to cover the negligence of the insured but not his recklessness or, it appears, his fecklessness.

17–3B Proof of All Risks

In view of the implied exceptions to all risks cover (above, 17–3A), the English courts might have held that the insurance cover extended (literally) to all risks, but was subject to exceptions for loss that was not accidental or, as is synonymous here, loss that was not fortuitous;[144] and that like any other exceptions[145] these had to be proved by the insurer. In reality, however, as long as the exception is implied, the accidental character of the event can be seen as an integral part of the cover, and some courts, to a degree at least, want it to be proved by the insured.[146]

In the leading case of *Gaunt*,[147] Lord Birkenhead, LC, said that the claimant "discharges his special onus when he has proved that the loss was caused by some event covered by the general expression, and he is not bound to go further and prove the exact nature of the accident or casualty which, in fact, occasioned his loss". It is enough that an accident might be "inferred".[148] In other words, the claimant benefits

---

so broadly that it becomes another type of policy altogether . . . [T]he contract will be given such construction as will fairly achieve its object of providing indemnity for the loss to which the insurance relates." (p 1163).

142. *London & Provincial Leather* v *Hudson* [1939] 2 KB 724 (AR).

143. *Intermetal Mexicana SA* v *INA*, 866 F 2d 71, 77 (3 Cir, 1989—AR). The court also objected that the loss was a certainty; *sed quaere*.

144. That was the decision, for example, in *Quattrociocchi* v *Albany Ins Co*, 1983 AMC 1152 (ND Cal, 1982—cargo): once the claimant had shown damage to the goods evident at destination, it was for the insurer to show inherent vice. In the same sense: *Antwerp 26.6.1986*, [1986] ETL 348.

145. Above, 16–3B2.

146. For example, in a case of cover against all risks from any external cause, the claimant had to disprove plausible internal causes, such as unseaworthiness: *Heindl-Evans* v *Reliance Ins*, 1980 AMC 2823 (ED Va, 1979—hull AR); but the District Court held that the onus of dealing with the possibility of wear and tear was on the defendant insurer.

147. *British & Foreign Marine Ins Co Ltd* v *Gaunt* [1921] 2 AC 41, 47; see also p 52 *per* Viscount Finlay and p 58 *per* Lord Sumner. *Cf*, however, *The Popi M* [1985] 1 Lloyd's Rep 1, 5, in which Lord Brandon said of an allegation of perils of the sea (marine all risks) that if the claimants were to discharge their onus of proof, they must "condescend to particularity in the matter": this statement should be kept in the context of the particular decision.

The words of Lord Birkenhead have been accepted as an accurate statement of the law in the United States: *Jewelers Mutual Ins Co* v *Balogh*, 272 F 2d 889 (5 Cir, 1959—jewellery); *Texas Eastern Transmission Corp* v *Appleton & Cox Corp*, 579 F 2d 561, 564 (10 Cir, 1978—property AR). Keeton, p 272. See also *Morrison Grain Co Inc* v *Utica Mutual Ins Co*, 632 F 2d 424, 430 (5 Cir, 1980—cargo AR).

148. Lord Birkenhead and Viscount Finlay, *loc cit*. Other judges may have had stronger proof by the claimant in mind: Lord Sumner (p 58) required that the claimant's evidence must "reasonably show" that the loss was due to a casualty. According to Atkin LJ in the same case in the Court of Appeal ([1920] 1 KB 903, 913), it was enough that the accidental character of the loss could be inferred on the balance of probabilities.

from a presumption that the loss was accidental. "Indeed, it would appear that all risk insurance arose for the very purpose of protecting the insured in those cases where difficulties of logical explanation or some mystery surrounded the disappearance of property."[149] From these statements, the onus of proof in an all risks claim differs little, if at all, from that in any other claim. If difference there is, it lies mainly with the proof of the implied exceptions.

If the normal onus of proof applied, the implied exceptions (wear and tear, inherent vice and wilful misconduct) would have to be proved on the balance of probabilities by the insurer.[150] In practice, the English court can be persuaded against the claim by something less, by an appeal to a mixture of evidence and intuition that leaves the court not in a state of conviction but of suspicion. If the claimant cannot allay that suspicion, his claim fails.

Some courts are more open to persuasion and more prone to suspicion than others[151] and decisions of this kind make poor precedent.[152] In *Hurst* v *Evans*,[153] for example, deciding against a claim on cover against jewellery all risks (except breakage and theft), Lush J said[154]:

"[I]t was for the plaintiff to prove that the loss was one against which the defendant had agreed to indemnify him. The plaintiff has not proved that. He has proved a loss, but has left, to say the least, the gravest suspicion whether his own servant was not the cause of the loss."

Again, in *Theodorou* v *Chester*,[155] deciding against a claim on cover against cargo all risks, Croom-Johnson J went further, perhaps further than the law permits,[156] saying that the defendant insurers

"have put everything in issue and have in effect said to the plaintiff 'Prove your case,' but they have done something else, which, . . . they are also fully entitled to do. They are entitled to present to the Court all sorts of theories, suggestions and all the rest of it, not with a view to accepting any onus, but simply with a view to saying: 'Now, then, here are all these possibilities. You, the plaintiff must see to it that these reasonable other explanations are negatived by your evidence, so that you do not leave anything unproved or unsustained by the case which you make to the Court."

However, the possibilities suggested by the defendant had to be plausible, not just in theory but also in relation to the particular facts, for the judge did require some evi-

---

149. *Betty* v *Liverpool & London & Globe Ins Co Ltd*, 310 F 2d 308, 311 (4 Cir, 1962—goods AR), cited in *Atlantic Lines Ltd* v *American Motorists Ins Co*, 547 F 2d 11, 13 (2 Cir, 1976—container AR).
150. Above, 16–3C2.
151. An illustration is found in the different approaches of the Court of Appeal and House of Lords to a case of marine all risks (perils of the sea) in *The Popi M, Rhesa Shipping Co SA* v *Edmunds* [1984] 2 Lloyd's Rep 555; [1985] 2 Lloyd's Rep 1 (hull); see Clarke [1985] CLJ 359.
152. *Cf The Marel* [1992] 1 Lloyd's Rep 402 (hull), in which *The Popi M* (above), a decision that turned on its particular facts, was followed.
   Cf Wenhold v *Royal Ins Co*, 197 F Supp 75 (D Mass, 1961—hull); *Heindl-Evans* v *Reliance Ins*, 1980 AMC 2823 (ED Va, 1979—hull AR); *Weber* v *New Hampshire Ins Co*, 480 So 2d 672 (Fla, 1985—hull). For cases on this kind of question in Australia and the United States see Parks, 14 JMLC 159, 186 (1983).
153. [1917] 1 KB 352. Other parts of the judgment go too far unless seen in the context of the particular claim; in this sense MacGillivray, No 1557. See also *Moore* v *Evans* [1916] 1 KB 458, 465 where, in deciding that the claimant had not met his burden of proof, Swinfen Eady LJ seems to have been influenced by the possibility that the loss was caused by an excepted peril.
   Cf Aetna Ins Co v *Hattersley*, 1984 AMC 2837 (D Or, 1983—hull).
154. [1917] 1 KB 352, 357.
155. [1951] 1 Lloyd's Rep 204, 238, purportedly in application of the principles in *Gaunt*, quoted above.
156. *Cf Regina Fur Co Ltd* v *Bossom* [1958] 2 Lloyd's Rep 425 (CA—furs AR).

dence from the defendants "to start the ball rolling".[157] The purpose of the evidence was no more than to "cast doubt"[158] on the evidence of the plaintiff.

17–4 LIABILITY

17–4A Loss

Liability insurance is "any insurance protection which indemnifies liability to third persons",[159] thus providing cover against a consequent depletion of the insured's assets. In Australia, according to section 11(7) of the Insurance Contracts Act 1984, it is a contract of general insurance that provides cover in respect of the insured's liability for loss or damage to another person.[160] The range of liability may well be limited by the contract of insurance. Cover in respect of liability for breach of contract, for example, is commonly excluded,[161] even if the circumstances also give rise to liability in tort.[162]

The contract is a contract of indemnity[163] and, in principle therefore, the insurance does not oblige the insurer to pay until the insured has suffered loss.[164] The loss to the insured which triggers the liability of the insurer is primarily a matter for the terms of the contract of insurance.[165] The contract commonly refers to the liability of the insured. When does this occur?

One view is that no loss has occurred to the insured until he is "out of pocket", i.e. until the insured has actually compensated the victim. This view has some practical advantages. The limitation period for any action against the insurer commences relatively late. Moreover, the later the liability of the insurer, the less the likelihood that the insurer will enjoy what is perceived as adverse publicity being named in litigation.

A second and quite different view is that property subject to a claim is worth less

---

157. [1951] 1 Lloyd's Rep 204, 239. *Cf* Parks, 14 JMLC 159, 188 (1983): "the underwriters' explanation must be supported by some evidence; merely arousing a suspicion will not do". Parks cites *Wenhold* v *Royal Ins Co*, 197 F Supp 75 (D Mass, 1961—hull).

158. [1951] 1 Lloyd's Rep 204, 259.

159. *Quinlan* v *Liberty Bank Co*, 575 So 2d 336, 339 (La, 1990—liability).

160. Derrington & Ashton, *The Law of Liability Insurance* (Sydney 1990) pp 47–48.

161. Even when the insurance contract does not expressly exclude cover for liability in contract, it has been held that the words of cover, "all sums which the insureds shall become legally obligated to pay", have the same effect: *Fragomeno* v *Ins Co of the West*, 255 Cal Rptr 111 (1989—liability). Further, in that case it was held (p 264) that the insureds' liability arising out of a tortious action was not covered, if it emanated from breach of a contract, such as a lease.

162. *Canadian Indemnity Co* v *Andrews & George Co Ltd* [1952] 4 DLR 690 (Sup Ct Canada—product liability); *Dominion Bridge Co Ltd* v *Toronto General Ins Co* [1963] SCR 362; [1964] 1 Lloyd's Rep 194 (Sup Ct Canada—contractors' liability).

163. *British Cash & Parcel Conveyors Ltd* v *Lamson Store Service Co Ltd* [1908] 1 KB 1006, 1014–1015 *per* Fletcher Moulton LJ (CA). Concerning contracts of indemnity, see chapter 28.

164. *West Wake Price & Co* v *Ching* [1957] 1 WLR 45, 49 *per* Devlin J (liability). *Cf Quinlan* (above) p 348, in which the majority distinguished indemnity and liability insurance: "Under a liability policy (in the narrow sense) the insurer is required to make payment although the insured has not yet suffered loss, for by definition the purpose of the liability policy is to shield the insured from being required to make any payment on the claim for which he is liable . . . Under an indemnity contract, by way of contrast, the insurer is only required to indemnify or make whole the insured after he has sustained actual loss, meaning after the insured has paid or been compelled to make payment." In this sense, many English policies are liability but not indemnity insurance; the latter would be instanced by a contract with a pay when paid clause.

165. In a case of cover for "liability imposed by law", it was held that the insurer was liable for the amount of a reasonable settlement agreed by the insured: *Shore Boat Builders Ltd* v *Canadian Indemnity Co* (1974) 51 DLR (3d) 628 (BC—liability); the court observed (p 631) that the insured was "clearly liable", but that the "absence of a formal judgment recognizing" his liability was without significance.

than property that is not[166]: the insured is "worth less" as soon as the claim is made,[167] albeit by an amount less than the amount of the claim. On this view, the insurer becomes liable to the insured when the insured becomes liable to the victim. Moreover, a practical argument for this view is that, if the insurer is not liable until later, the insurer is not obliged to take a view and, until he knows that view, the insured may find it difficult to reach a wise decision on whether to settle the claim.[168]

A third view, which takes a middle line between these two views,[169] is the one taken by English law. According to the Court of Appeal in *Post Office v Norwich Union Fire Ins Sy Ltd*,[170] "the insured only acquires a right to sue [the insurer] for the money when his liability to the injured person has been *established* so as to give rise to a right of indemnity . . . either by judgment of the court or by an award in arbitration or by agreement". Although not without critics,[171] the third view was confirmed by the House of Lords in *Bradley*:[172] the insured cannot sue for "indemnity from the insurers unless and until the existence and amount of his liability to a third party has been established by action, arbitration or agreement". No doubt the insurer will be content to await the decision or settlement before having to pay. The principle must be applied with commercial common sense and in a way that accommodates the context, including the contract, and, in this spirit, the following suggestions have been made.

First, if liability to the victim is disputed by the insured and litigated and thus, it might be said, liability has yet to be established, this does not prevent the initiation of third party proceedings against the liability insurer: "the Judge will give his decision in the main action before he decides in the third party proceedings. So, the liability of

---

166. A dramatic illustration was found in the adverse impact on the share prices of certain American tobacco companies of litigation by the representatives of smokers who had died of cancer; prices fell not only when liability was established but also when suit was brought: *The Economist*, Vol 304, No 7513 (29 August 1987) p 60. *Cf West Wake Price & Co v Ching* [1957] 1 WLR 45, 49 *per* Devlin J (liability).

167. Hence the practice, for example, of banks in making provision against bad debts. In English accounting practice, if a risk of loss is at least probable, standard practice requires accrual. This would include impending claims and, of course, legal costs which will have to be paid, whether the claim is successful or not. Practice requires that provision should be made when accounting, although the contingency has not become a certainty and although the precise amount is not yet known: Cabourn-Smith and Cohen, "Accounting for Contingencies", *Accountants Digest*, No 113.

168. This and other arguments are developed by Derrington & Ashton, *The Law of Liability Insurance*, pp 342 ff.

169. The first view was rejected in *Johnson v Salvage Assn* (1887) 19 QBD 458, 460–461 *per* Lindley LJ (CA—hull).

170. [1967] 2 QB 363, 373 *per* Lord Denning MR (CA—liability), (emphasis added). See also *West Wake Price & Co v Ching* [1957] 1 WLR 45, 49 *per* Devlin J (liability); *Brice v Wackerbarth (Australasia) Pty Ltd* [1974] 2 Lloyd's Rep 274, 277 *per* Roskill LJ (CA—liability). *Penrith City Council v GIOS* (1991) 24 NSWLR 564 (liability). A similar view has been taken in relation to the issue of time limitation in respect of contracts of indemnity: see *County & District Properties Ltd v Jenner & Son Ltd* [1976] 2 Lloyd's Rep 728 and cases cited. *Cf* Harman LJ in the *Post Office* case (p 376) who accepted the view in *Hood's Trustees v Southern Union General Ins Co Ltd* [1928] 1 Ch 793 (CA—liability) that rights against the insurer arise at the time of the wrongdoing or occurrence. USA: see above, 5–8C note 162.

171. In a critical note, MacGillivray (7th ed), No 1982, argued that the *Post Office* case should be confined to context, i.e., cases arising under the Third Parties (Rights against Insurers) Act 1930. In later editions, the editors accept the decision as correct. The view in the 7th edition appears to have been accepted in *Re St Paul Fire & Marine Ins Co and Guardian Ins Co* (1983) 1 DLR (4th) 342, 359 (Ont—liability). *Cf* the view in the context of general average: *Chandris v Argo Ins Co Ltd* [1963] 2 Lloyd's Rep 65, 73–74, 76–77 *per* Megaw J (hull). *Cf* also *Hood's Trustees v Southern General Ins Co Ltd* [1928] 1 Ch 793, 801 *per* Tomlin J (motor), approved by Harman LJ dissenting: [1967] 2 QB 363, 376. For similar difficulties in the law of tort see Stapleton, 104 LQR 213, 389 (1988).

172. *Bradley v Eagle Star Ins Co Ltd* [1989] AC 957, 966 *per* Lord Brandon, with whom the other members of the court agreed (liability). *Bradley* has been accepted on this point in Victoria: *Strang Pty Ltd v NZI Ins Australia Ltd* [1990] VR 1016, 1020 (liability).

the insured will have been ascertained".[173] Moreover, in such circumstances of disputed liability, the insurer may have nonetheless an immediate duty to aid the insured in his defence, if the contract imposes such a duty (below, 17–4E). Even a clause that "No action shall lie against the Insurer . . . until the amount of the Insured's obligation to pay shall have been finally determined" neither prevents nor postpones the operation of a contractual duty of the insurer to defend the insured in the action by the victim.[174]

Second, a flexible view may have to be taken of the establishment of liability. In *Smit Tak*,[175] Mustill LJ indicated that the insured might have incurred a "liability . . . contractual or otherwise" without the intervention of a court: "since the Ruler is the fount of laws in Dubai, if the Letter [to the insured] had begun with the words: 'I am directed by the Ruler to order . . . ', or something on the same lines, the result would have been a legal obligation to raise the wreck, and the claim under the umbrella policy would have been hard to resist". In that case, however, the insured were "over a barrel" but the barrel was commercial (and permitted by law) rather than legal (in the exercise of legal powers) and, in these circumstances, the decision was that the legal liability of the insured had not been established.

Courts in the USA have taken a different view of an insured in that position. Removal of a wreck was "compulsory by law", it was held,[176] not only when removal was directed by government order but also when it was a reasonable course "under a cost-benefit analysis taking into consideration the *probable* cost of removal and both the *likelihood* and amount of liability which *could* be imposed for failing to remove the wreck". This construction differs from that in England not only in relation to the probability of the consequences but also in that "liability" refers both to liability to the government and also liability to private persons. The reasoning is that to restrict compulsion "to the mandate of a governmental agency rather than according the usual significance of the generalized command of a statute or judicial decision narrows the meaning of the term" unjustifiably, as it made little sense that the insured and his insurer "be exposed to repeated damage claims without being able to rely on policy coverage to eliminate the hazard, unless a governmental agency ordered removal".[177] Whereas the English court appears to have looked at the words of cover in isolation, the American court took account of other parts of the policy, not only other parts of the cover but also an express duty of "salvage".[178]

Third, an agreed settlement must be one that, to a degree at least, "establishes" liability, as stated in the *Post Office* case (above). In *Corbin* v *Payne*,[179] the insured "settled legal proceedings", apparently based on nuisance, brought by the owner of

---

173. *Brice* v *Wackerbarth (Australasia) Pty Ltd* [1974] 2 Lloyd's Rep 274, 275 *per* Lord Denning MR (CA—liability).

174. *Great West Steel Industries Ltd* v *Simcoe & Erie General Ins Co* (1979) 106 DLR (3d) 347 (Ont—liability).

175. *Smit Tak Offshore Services* v *Youell* [1992] 1 Lloyd's Rep 154, 159 (CA—liability); however, the court held that the letter from the Dept of Ports and Customs (DPC), which "instructed" the insured to remove the wreck, did not have this character as the DPC had no power to order the removal. The DPC had the sanction to withdraw the insured's licence to operate in Dubai, but this would not have been a loss covered by the insurance.

176. *Cf Grupo Protexa SA* v *All American Marine Slip*, 954 F 2d 130, 138 (3 Cir, 1992—marine) with emphasis added.

177. p 137.

178. On duties of this kind, see below 28–8G.

179. *The Times*, 5 November 1991, (CA—liability).

neighbouring land, in order to carry on using a noisy machine. Although, said Mustill LJ, if the action had proceeded to judgment, the insured might have had a claim on his liability insurer, in this case, he did not. To read the cover as entitling the insured to purchase at the insurer's expense the liberty to go on using a noisy and possibly dangerous machine, which he had chosen to bring on to his land and instal near his neighbour's residence, was far removed from the tenor and intent of the contract of insurance.

In any event, it has also been held that the insurer cannot grasp the nettle himself by seeking a declaration that his insured is not liable to the third party in question: he has no *locus standi*.[180]

17–4B The Event

The incidence of loss, both as to its nature and its timing, should be distinguished from the event that brings the case within the scope of a particular period of cover: that event is specified in the contract.[180a]

The event may be the incidence of loss itself, which in English law is the establishment of the insured's legal liability (above, 17–4A), or it may be an earlier event which marks a significant stage in the process leading to the incidence of loss. In the past, that event was usually the occurrence giving rise to the insured's liability, such as an act of negligence on his part. Whereas a positive act of negligence is likely to be of short duration and thus easy to pin to a relevant period of time, negligence by omission can be regarded as continuing and attributable to any contract of insurance in force during its continuance.[181] This is one factor that has encouraged the development and use of claims-made contracts, which specify the event as the claim by a third party victim[182] arising out of the occurrence.[183]

"Occurrence policies provide coverage against liability arising out of acts of the insured occurring during the policy period, no matter when a claim is eventually lodged against the insured.

180. *Meadows Indemnity Co* v *The Insurance Corp of Ireland plc* [1989] 2 Lloyd's Rep 298 (CA—re).
180a. Derrington & Ashton, *The Law of Liability Insurance*, pp 291 ff.
181. In *Levine* v *Lumbermen's Mutual Casualty Co*, 538 NYS 2d 263 (1989—liability) it was held that delay by a law firm in taking a procedural step was covered by one of the firm's malpractice policies, although that particular policy was in force neither at the beginning of the period of delay nor at the end: "the malpractice in question consisted of a continuous error and omission of the law firm to prosecute the underlying action". (p 264). See also *Interstate Fire & Casualty Co* v *Archdiocese of Portland*, 747 F Supp 618, 625 (D Or, 1990—liability), in which the occurrence was negligent supervision over a number of years during which the supervisee committed several acts of sexual molestation.
182. *Cf* contracts under which the event is not a claim by third party against the insured but, in substance, (circumstances justifying) a claim against the insurer: Derrington & Ashton, *The Law of Liability Insurance* (1990), p 283. In essence this is an occurrence contract in which the occurrence is the incidence of loss suffered by the insured.
183. For an historical account of this shift and, in particular, judicial resistance in the United States on the basis of the doctrine of reasonable expectations, see Frame, 60 Temple LQ 165 (1987). A majority of states have adopted the commercial general liability form made available for voluntary adoption by the Insurance Service Office (ISO), which includes a claims-made policy.
A variant, which is closer to the occurrence policy than the claims-made policy, is the "discovery" policy: for example, *Brown Construction Co Inc* v *D & M Mechanical Contractors*, 222 So 2d 93 (La, 1969—professional liability).
In some states it has been held that a claims-made policy will not be a true claims-made policy and will be contrary to public policy, unless it provides unlimited retroactive cover, without a limit such as cover to the effective date of the policy or of the first such policy taken by the insured: for example *Zuckerman* v *National Union Fire Ins Co*, 495 A 2d 395 (NJ, 1985—professional liability); *cf Sparks* v *St Paul Ins Co*, 495 A 2d 406 (NJ, 1985—professional liability). Frame, 60 Temple L Q 165, 172 ff (1987). This, of course, undermines the reason for using a claims-made policy.

Pricing occurrence coverage requires prediction of claims that will be made in the future. Yet the past is not necessarily a very reliable gauge of the future, especially where demographics and claims consciousness are changing. Thus, in fields where claims may not be brought for many years—medical malpractice or toxic torts, for example—pricing occurrence policies is highly speculative because expected losses are hard to predict.

Claims-made policies, on the other hand, cover the insured against all claims that are made during the policy period, regardless of when the activity giving rise to the claim occurred. Claims-made pricing requires much less prediction of the future because only the claims that will be filed during the forthcoming policy period need be predicted."

The difference between the two kinds of policies is that the insurer bears the risk of an uncertain claims future under an occurrence policy; a claims-made approach shifts much of that risk back to the insured.[184] For instance, the discovery by a manufacturer, by reason of the claim of even a single consumer, that it has produced thousands of units of a product that is hazardous raises enormous implications for future insurability of that manufacturer. In light of the known potential for future claims of a similar nature faced by the manufacturer, the manufacturer will face either skyrocketing premiums for coverage, or a complete refusal to grant or renew coverage at all. Alternatively, insurers may agree to grant or renew a liability insurance policy but exclude coverage for liability arising out of the type of defect that has been discovered. In short, "claims-made" or "discovery" policies, by placing insurers in the position of obtaining extensive information about potential claims before commencing (or renewing) the coverage of an insured, enable insurers to avoid having to indemnify insureds for a significant proportion of the potential claims that exist as of the date of commencement (or renewal) of coverage".[185]

Consequently, there has been something of a reaction against policies of this kind. In Belgium, for example, they are illegal.[186] In the USA, the common front taken by reinsurers, when negotiating with primary insurers, which led to the change in wording from occurrence policies to claims made policies, has been condemned in the Supreme Court as unlawful collusion.[186a]

17–4C Occurrence

The occurrence that triggers liability cover varies from contract to contract, so there is an issue of interpretation in each case.[187]

17–4C1 The Nature of the Occurrence

The occurrence which triggers liability under the contract of insurance is stated in that contract of insurance, and close attention must be given to what it says.

The most common example of liability is that arising out of the insured's negligence.

---

184. Abraham 71 Va L Rev 403, 413 (1985); also Abraham, p 159; Kroll, 22 UCLA L Rev 925 (1975); Frame, 60 Temple LQ 165, 178 ff (1987); Wetterstein, 3 Ins LJ 172, 180 ff (1990). For a similar account of the background in England see for example PM 14 May 1987, pp 43 ff.

185. *Reid Crowther & Partners Ltd* v *Simcoe & Erie General Ins Co* (1993) 99 DLR (4th) 741, 749 (Sup Ct—liabililily). *Burns* v *International Ins Co*, 709 F Supp 187, 190–191 (ND Cal, 1989—liability), affirmed 929 F 2d 1422 (9 Cir, 1991) and subsequently followed: Chamberlain 28 Tort & Ins L J 90, 98 ff. (1992). Moreover, an "insurance company can establish its reserves without having to consider the possibilities of inflation beyond the policy period, upward–spiralling jury awards, or later changes in the definition and application of negligence": *Pacific Employers Ins Co* v *Superior Court* 270 Cal Rptr 779, 785 (Cal App, 1990—liability). See also in this sense Kroll, *op cit* pp 929 ff; and Pierce, 19 Western Univ L R 165, 167 (1992).

186. Law of 25 June 1992, art 78.

186a. See *Hartford Fire Ins Co* v *California*, 113 S Ct 2891 (1993).

187. For example, *British General Ins Co Ltd* v *Mountain* (1919) 1 Ll L Rep 605, 606–607 (HL—re); *The Diane, Global Tankers Inc* v *Amercoat Europa NV* [1977] 1 Lloyd's Rep 61, 65 *per* Kerr J (guarantee insurance).

Cover "in respect of any act of neglect, default or error" covers negligence[188] but not fraud or dishonesty.[189] Decisions to this effect turned, in the first place, on the construction of the terms of the contract of insurance, however, there is also the influence of public policy against cover for intentional wrongdoing.[190] Moreover, liability "arises at the time of the accident, when negligence and damage coincide".[191] The damage may be damage to property (see above, 16–2C) or damage to people, i.e., bodily injury. It has been held[192] in the United States that "bodily injury" means "any localized abnormal condition of the living body" and that, in the example of asbestosis, there was injury when the very first tissue damage occurred as a result of inhalation of asbestos fibres; see also below, 17–5H1.

Currently, controversy in the USA centres on cover in respect of liability for the cost of cleaning up pollution. Perhaps there is a lesson in the history of litigation in the USA, where the occurrence insured under the standard CGL policy is (liability for) "bodily injury" and "property damage" "caused by accident". The idea of accident persists, as does general agreement that loss is accidental if, as the policy requires, it was unexpected and unintended.[193] However, this, together with other developments in the wording of the policy, has given rise to much litigation.[194]

17–4C2 The Time of the Occurrence

Once the occurrence that triggers the liability of the insurer has been identified, the time of that occurrence decides whether it falls within the period of cover. The answer is usually simple in cases of motor accidents but less so when the occurrence concerns damage, disease or injury of a kind that may be more or less latent for many years, such as asbestosis or cancer. Unless ambiguous, the wording of the contract should be decisive, however, in the United States, it has been admitted by some courts[195] that wording will be less decisive in cases of personal injury than in cases of property damage, and that issues of public policy affect the court's decision.[196] Not surprisingly, therefore, the decisions are not consistent.

(a) *Exposure*. Certain courts have decided that loss occurs when the victim is

188. Generally, see Jess, *The Insurance of Professional Negligence Risks: Law and Practice* (2nd ed, London 1989).

189. *Davies* v *Hosken* (1937) 53 TLR 798 (liability); *West Wake Price & Co* v *Ching* [1957] 1 WLR 45, 47 *per* Devlin J (liability). The same has been held in respect of an "errors or omissions" policy: *Warrender* v *Swain* [1960] 2 Lloyd's Rep 111 (NSW—liability).

190. See above, 17–3A3, and below 24–5B. A recent instance in Florida is *Windmill Pointe Village Club Assn Inc* v *State Farm General Ins Co*, 779 F Supp 596, 598 (MD Fla, 1991—liability), in which (on both grounds) there was no cover in respect of liability for intentional acts of racial discrimination. On this, see 24–7.

191. *Post Office* v *Norwich Union Fire Ins Sy Ltd* [1967] 2 QB 363. 373 *per* Lord Denning MR (CA—liability). In the same sense: *Keating* v *National Union Fire Ins Co*, 754 F Supp 1431 (CD Cal, 1990—liability).

192. *Insurance Co of North America* v *Forty-Eight Insulations Inc*, 451 F Supp 1230 (ED Mich, 1978); 633 F 2d 1212 (6 Cir, 1980), cert den 454 US 1109, applying the law of Illinois and New Jersey. But *cf Eagle-Picher Industries Inc* v *Liberty Mutual Ins Co*, 682 F 2d 12, 19 (1 Cir, 1982—product liability); and *Keene Corp* v *INA*, 667 F 2d 1034, 1043 (Col, 1981—product liability). For the position in Australia, see Derrington & Ashton, *The Law of Liability Insurance*, pp 316 ff.

193. For example, *Hartford Co* v *US Fidelity & Guarantee Co*, 962 F 2d 1484, 1488 (10 Cir, 1992—liability).

194. See, for example, Abraham, 88 Colum L Rev 942 (1988); Marrs 26 Tort & Ins L J 662 (1991); Kolesar, 68 Notre Dame L Rev 549, 552 ff. (1993); and for an English view, Clarke [1994] JBL —.

195. *Dow Chemical Co* v *Associated Indemnity Corp*, 724 F Supp 474, 482 (ED Mich, 1989—liability).

196. p 485.

exposed to the activity or circumstance, which gives rise to the action against the insured.[197] Reasons are, first, that

"cumulative disease cases are different from the ordinary accident or disease situation. [T]he underlying theory of tort liability is that the asbestos manufacturers continually failed to warn the asbestos workers . . . The insurance policies before us are comprehensive general liability policies which are designed to insure the manufacturers against products liability suits. The contracting parties would expect coverage to parallel the theory of liability."[198]

Second, if there is any doubt about what the policy means, courts should interpret it so as to promote cover.[199]

(b) *Injury in Fact*. Close attention to the policy wording, which is the primary source of guidance on this kind of issue,[200] reveals that the time of occurrence may be at a point between exposure (above (a)) and manifestation (below (c)): the "injury in fact theory" looks to the time when injury or damage actually occurs,[201] in those cases in which there is a significant lapse of time between exposure and manifestation. An obvious argument against the injury in fact theory is the difficulty of proving the time it occurred.[202] In any event, a latent condition of injury or damage in the subject–matter of the insurance, person or property, must be distinguished from a potential for injury or damage in something else which threatens the subject-matter of the insurance but which does not constitute a state of damage in the subject-matter itself; see above 16–2C.

(c) *Manifestation*. The theory that there is no occurrence of injury until it becomes manifest was rejected by the courts opting for the exposure theory (above, (a)). One argument against the manifestation theory is that it is a "cut-and-run concept", which has the effect of reducing cover: "insurers would refuse to write new insurance for the insured when it became apparent that the period of manifestations, and hence a flood of claims, was approaching."[203] In the view of the court in the *Insulations* case,[204] the adoption of a manifestation basis would make it all but impossible for a company which

197. *Insurance Co of North America* v *Forty-Eight Insulations Inc*, 451 F Supp 1230 (ED Mich, 1978); 633 F 2d 1212 (6 Cir, 1980), *cert* den 454 US 1109: this case concerned insurance against product liability for "bodily injury", in the particular case asbestosis, under the law of Illinois and New Jersey. The court affirmed that bodily injury meant (p 1222) "any localized abnormal condition of the living body" and that injury occurred when the very first tissue damage occurred as a result of inhalation of asbestos fibres. On "bodily injury", see also, below 17–5H1.

With similar effect, some contracts cover events *originating* in the insurance period: see Derrington & Ashton, *The Law of Liability Insurance*, p 293.

198. p 1219. This decision was followed in *Porter* v *American Optical Corp*, 641 F 2d 1128 (5 Cir, 1981—product liability), rejecting the manifestation theory (below, 17–4C2(c)), the more easily because the policy defined occurrence as an accident or event or a continuous or repeated exposure to conditions which cause or result in bodily injury.

199. pp 1219–1220. The terms " 'bodily injury' and 'occurrence' are inherently ambiguous as applied to the progressive disease context before us" (p 1222), thus allowing the court to interpret the cover broadly. See further on the ambiguity of such contracts: 97 Harv L Rev 739, 740 ff. (1984).

200. *Dow Chemical Co* v *Associated Indemnity Corp*, 724 F Supp 474, 480 (ED Mich, 1989—liability). This approach is also prevalent in New York: *Maryland Casualty Co* v *Grace & Co*, 794 F Supp 1206, 1215 (SD NY, 1991—liability).

201. p 478.

202. p 485.

203. *Ibid*.

204. *Dow Chemical Co* v *Associated Indemnity Corp*, 724 F Supp 474, 480 (ED Mich, 1989—liability).

had manufactured asbestos to obtain cover for product liability, lest the effects of earlier exposure manifest themselves in the imminent insurance period. Further, analogy with the issue of time limitation, which is associated with the time of discoverability or manifestation,[205] has been suggested in Australia[206] but was rejected in the *Insulations* case: in limitation cases, the effect of choosing the (earlier) time of exposure was against liability and against compensation for the victim, whereas the effect of choosing the time of exposure for insurance was more likely to mean that the manufacturer was insured and able to pay the victim.[207] The court also rejected the manifestation theory, as a matter of construction of the particular contract, on the ground that[208] "No doctor would say that asbestosis occurred when it was discovered".

Yet, the manifestation theory was adopted in *Eagle-Picher*.[209] The case is distinguishable from *Insulations* (above) (i) on the language of the policy[210]; (ii) on the view of the medical evidence in the case, that injury in a clinical sense did not occur at the time of exposure and that such injury was not inevitable at the time of first exposure[211]; and (iii) in that Eagle-Picher was uninsured prior to 1968, the period in which most of the injury-producing exposure occurred.[212]

(d) *Triple Trigger.* The triple trigger theory, also referred to as the "multiple trigger"theory,[213] extended the collective liability of insurers in long tail situations by fixing liability on any insurer whose policy was in force (i) at the time of initial exposure, or (ii) during continued exposure, or (iii) at the time of manifestation.[214] In *Keene*,[215] the leading case, the court took the line that

---

205. See below, 26–5.
206. Derrington & Ashton, *The Law of Liability Insurance*, pp 291 ff.
207. p 1222.
208. *Ibid* p 1219.
209. *Eagle-Picher Industries Inc* v *Liberty Mutual Ins Co*, 682 F 2d 12 (1 Cir, 1982—product liability). The court was influenced (p 20) by analogy with PHI decisons, but this analogy was doubted in *Keene Corp* v *INA*, 667 F 2d 1034, 1043 (Col, 1981—product liability): "In the areas of workmen's compensation, health insurance, and statutes of limitation, the concept of 'injury' performs a function that is different from its function in the context of comprehensive general liability policies." See further the note at p 1043 and discussion at p 1045; and below 17–5F2: English courts have also drawn a distinction between statutory cover for workmen and private PA insurance. In the USA, see further *Prudential–LMI Commercial Ins* v *Superior Court*, 274 Cal Rptr 387, 403 (Cal, 1990—property), in which the manifestation theory was applied to a first party case, from which a third party liability situation was distinguished.
210. The policy in *Eagle-Picher* distinguished between the event causing injury and the resulting injury or disease, and the court found this significant (p 19); see also pp 23–24. The same is true of *American Motorists Ins Co* v *Squibb & Sons Inc*, 406 NYS 2d 658 (1978—product liability) in relation to a drug that caused cervical cancer.
211. *Eagle–Picher* (above) pp 19 and 23.
212. p 23.
213. For example, *Dow Chemical Co* v *Associated Indemnity Corp*, 724 F Supp 474, 483 (ED Mich, 1989—liability).
214. *Keene Corp* v *INA*, 667 F 2d 1034 (Col, 1981—product liability): even though the policy provided that the "injury" and not the occurrence that causes injury must fall within the policy period. For a similar approach to gradual damage by seepage and subsidence, see *California Union Ins Co* v *Landmark Ins Co*, 193 Cal Rptr 461 (Cal, 1983). See Hook, 21 Tort & Ins L J 393 (1986); and Powell 71 Neb L Rev 1194 (1992), who argues that the triple trigger approach is inappropriate in many cases of pollution. In any event, a distinction is drawn between third party liability cases such as that and first party cases, with a narrower liability rule in the latter: *Prudential–LMI Commercial Ins* v *Superior Court*, 274 Cal Rptr 387, 403 (Cal, 1990 – property).
215. Above, pp 1040–1041.

different insurers were on risk at different times during the development of the asbestos-related diseases; that the policies did not solve the difficulties of interpretation arising out of that kind of situation; and that therefore the policies should be interpreted "in a manner that is equitable and administratively feasible and that is consistent with insurance principles, insurance law, and the terms of the contracts themselves", not forgetting the reasonable expectations of the insured.[216] For the insured's "rights under the policies to be secure", not only manifestation but "both inhalation exposure and exposure in residence must also trigger coverage". The court concluded[217] that "each insurer on the risk between initial exposure and the manifestation of the disease is liable to [the insured] for indemnification and defense costs."

17–4D Claims-Made

Cover on the basis of claims made against the insured poses questions similar to those posed by cover that is occurrence based (above, 17–4C), notably whether (a) the substance or nature of the claim is within the insurance cover: below, 17–4D1; (b) whether the claim has arisen during the insurance period: below, 17–4D2; and (c) if there is such a claim, what matters are covered by the claim: 17–4D3. The meaning of claim is a matter of interpreting the contract; meaning may be affected by context.[218] Subject to this, a claim usually means a claim against the insured.

17–4D1 The Nature of the Claim

In *West Wake Price & Co* v *Ching*,[219] Devlin J, faced with the question whether the contract term "claim" referred to a single claim for money, based on three distinct grounds in law (causes of action), or whether it referred to the three claims in law, advanced as grounds for the claim for money, said this[220]:

"I think that the primary meaning of the word 'claim'—whether used in its popular sense or in a strict legal sense—is such as to attach it to the object that is claimed; and is not the same thing as the cause of action by which the claim may be supported or as the grounds on which it may be based."

Having found support for his opinion in the Oxford Dictionary, he conceded that the word is also used in the looser sense of "contention" and "it is often used by lawyers as if it meant the same thing as cause of action. It is quite natural to speak of a claim in fraud or a claim in negligence."[221] The latter sense, he thought, might be more workable, especially in the contract before him, which covered liability for negligence but not liability for fraud, to which he referred to illustrate the point:

"Thus, a claim in negligence comes into existence when an allegation of negligence is made and

---

216. p 1041 and 1046. On the doctrine of reasonable expectations see above, 15–5B.
217. p 1041.
218. *West Wake Price & Co* v *Ching* [1957] 1 WLR 45, 55 *per* Devlin J (liability).
219. [1957] 1 WLR 45 (liability).
220. p 55. Parts of the statement by Devlin J were approved by Stocker LJ in *Thorman* v *NHIC* [1988] 1 Lloyd's Rep 7, 15 (CA—professional liability); and in Australia by Derrington & Ashton, *The Law of Liability Insurance* (1990), p 282. USA in this general sense: *Evanston Ins Co* v *Security Ins Co*, 715 F Supp 1405, 1412 (ND Ill, 1989—liability).
221. Also in this sense, for example, *Gyler* v *Mission Ins Co*, 514 P 2d 1219, 1221 (Cal, 1973—liability).

continues until the allegation fails or succeeds; a claim in the sense of a cause of action must always be inside or outside the policy for the whole of its life. A claim for a sum of money, however, may start outside the policy if it is based solely on fraud; perhaps be brought within the policy if a charge of negligence is added; and then disappear from the scope of the policy if the charge of negligence is disproved at the trial."

Having considered the policy, especially the QC clause, Devlin J preferred[222] the first and ordinary meaning of claim, i.e., claim for money; and in a later case Stocker LJ[223] stated firmly that "the cause of action is not, itself, a claim but the necessary vehicle for its legal enforcement".

The meaning of "claim" is often affected by the context of the policy. *Soole* v *Royal Ins Co Ltd*[224] concerned insurance against the possibility that land for development might be subject to a restrictive covenant. It was argued that to claim meant to initiate a process of demand and included the first assertion of a right against the insured. Rejecting this argument Shaw J said[225]:

"the reason or motive for insuring is, of course, the possibility or threat of actual loss, but unless and until the possibility becomes an actuality or the threat becomes effective, the indemnity provided under a policy is inoperative. It is only the incidence of the risk insured against that gives rise to a liability of the insured. In the instant case the bare assertion of a purported claim to enforce the restrictive covenant might create a temporary concern, but nothing more."

This part of the judgment is in line with the *Post Office* case,[226] which was not cited to the court. As suggested above,[227] it is difficult to accept the premise that the assertion of a claim has no significant impact on the insured for, if the insured had tried to sell the land in question for the kind of development he himself had in mind, its price would have been affected by the incipient claim to enforce the covenant[228]; hence there was loss to the insured at that time. The judge continued in a vein which, it is submitted, distinguishes the case as one turning on the terms of the policy as to loss covered[229]: "Only if it was pursued and established and put into effect so as to give rise to loss or damage or expense to the insured of a character falling within one or other of the five categories set out in the indemnity clause would the liability of the insurer arise at all." The categories set out concerned loss or expense arising out of court proceedings, from which it followed that there was no loss within the meaning of that policy until the claim had got to court. This leads to the trite conclusion that, in general, claim means claim of a kind contemplated by the contract of insurance.[230]

17–4D2 The Time of the Claim

If there is a claim in the sense covered (above, 17–4D1), it must fall within the insurance period. In many cases, once the meaning of "claim" has been decided, the time

222. p 57.
223. *Thorman* (above), p 16.
224. [1971] 2 Lloyd's Rep 332.
225. p 337.
226. Above, 17–4A.
227. *Ibid.*
228. Assuming, of course, that the impending claim was known to potential purchasers.
229. [1971] 2 Lloyd's Rep 332, 337. In the result the judgment was for the insured—even though, when proposing the insurance, he had not mentioned to the insurer that he had taken counsel's opinion (which had been favourable to him) on the strength of the claim to enforce the covenant against him. Proceedings to enforce the covenant against the insured were instituted 18 days after the insurance period commenced.
230. This explains the decision of McNair J in *Australia & New Zealand Bank Ltd* v *Colonial & Eagle Wharves Ltd* [1960] 2 Lloyd's Rep 241, 255 (cargo AR), and distinguishes it from that of Devlin J in *West Wake* above. See also *Trollope & Colls Ltd* v *Haydon* [1977] 1 Lloyd's Rep 244 (CA—contractors liability).

of the claim will be obvious. Still, in other cases, it may be necessary to determine the point at which a contention or complaint has become a claim within cover. The possibilities include (a) the occurrence of a state of affairs which may give rise to injury and liability later[231]; (b) the occurrence of a state of affairs which may justify a claim; (c) the occurrence of a state of affairs which does justify a claim; (d) notification of (b) to the insured, in other words, mere allegation; (e) notification of (c) to the insured; and (f) the institution of proceedings against the insured. The courts may not draw all these distinctions and the cases are better approached by combining (a) to (c) into "potential claims", which differentiates the policy little from an occurrence based policy, by combining (d) and (e) as "assertion of claims", and treating (f) separately.

(a) *Potential Claims*. McNair J[232] saw only a limited choice between "the right to make a claim as in the expression 'A has a claim on B' " and the "assertion of a right as in the expression 'A has made a claim on B' ", a choice to be made by interpreting the particular contract of insurance.[233] In the case, the judge preferred the former view, which he amplified as the occurrence of a state of affairs which justifies a claim: a potential claim in the sense of (c), (above).[234]

Although it is often only a small step back in time from point (c) to point (a), the occurrence of a state of affairs which may give rise to injury and litigation,[235] point (a) can hardly have been the intention of those who drafted liability cover on the basis of claims made rather than occurrence. For one thing, it would invite overreaction on the part of the insured, the so-called "U-Haul method of notice", i.e., "reporting every potential corporate activity or incident which could engender future claims, in the hope of preserving the policy-holder's right to 'tail coverage' later on." [236]

In one such case, a trustee in bankruptcy registered claims on every matter the bankrupt company had ever handled. The court observed that, if "the trustee had reason to believe that the firm's work in a given case would lead to liability, it was entitled under the policy to inform the insurer within the period of coverage and so ensure indemnity if the potential came to pass. An effort to lodge claims on everything, to extend indefinitely the coverage of a 15-month policy, has no effect; it is merely vexatious".[237] If claim does mean potential claim, the potential must be real.

231. In *Gyler* v *Mission Ins Co*, 514 P 2d 1219 (Cal, 1973—professional liability) a policy clause in these terms was held ambiguous, so that the court could interpret the policy in favour of (the insured's reasonable expectations of) cover. See also *Katz Drug Co* v *Commercial Standard Ins Co*, 647 SW 2d 831 (Mo, 1983—professional liability); *Reid Crowther & Partners Ltd* v *Simcoe & Erie General Ins Co* (1993) 99 DLR (4th) 741, 754ff (Sup Ct—liability).

232. *Australia & New Zealand Bank Ltd* v *Colonial & Eagle Wharves Ltd* [1960] 2 Lloyd's Rep 241, 255 (cargo AR); this view was approved in *Trollope & Colls Ltd* v *Haydon* [1977] 1 Lloyd's Rep 244, 249 *per* Cairns LJ (CA—liability); *Reid Crowther & Partners Ltd* v *Simcoe & Erie General Ins Co* (1993) 99 DLR (4th) 741, 754 ff (Sup Ct—liability).

233. McNair J, *ibid*; he was concerned with an excess clause whereby the insurer was only "to pay the excess of £100 each and every claim" and held that this meant, not claim on the insured by third parties, but claim by the insured on the insurer.

234. Also in this sense: *Gyler* v *Mission Ins Co*, 514 P 2d 1219, 1221 (Cal, 1973—professional liability)— "claims maturing during the policy period whether or not the claim is actually asserted during that period".

235. PM 14 May 1987, p 45.

236. William L Mather, President of the North American Risk and Management Sy, reported in PM 10 Sept 1987, p 19.

237. *Home Ins Co* v *Cooper & Cooper Ltd*, 889 F 2d 746, 750 (1989—liability).

(b) *Assertion of Claim*. Given the deliberate drafting of claims-made cover to replace occurrence as the basis of recovery and the desire of the insurer to be in a position to control affairs, there is much to be said for the market view[238] that there is a claim, when there is notification by the third party of a potential claim.[239]

Objections to this view include (i) the practical difficulty in deciding the point at which a complaint about a product or a service becomes the assertion of a legal right[240]; and (ii) the insured, who has retired (and is less able to pay premiums), may face claims that disturb the tranquility of his retirement in respect of what he did when he was working,[241] and will need run-off insurance to cover this possibility.[242]

(c) *The Institution of Proceedings*. In *Thorman* v *NHIC*[243] a professional liability policy (in section 1) provided cover dependent "upon a claim being made against the insured during the period of the policy".[244] It was held that claim meant either the issue of a writ or its service. The decision should be seen in the context of a policy whereby the insurer was also liable (in section 8) in respect of a claim outside the period which arose out of an occurrence during the period and of which the insured had given the insurer notice. On any view there was an insured claim,[245] and the presence of section 8 enabled the court to give what might be thought a narrow view of the meaning of claim in section 1.

17–4D3 *The Scope of a Claim*

If there is an insured claim, there is the further question of what the claim includes. In *Thorman* v *NHIC*[246] Sir John Donaldson MR approached the issue through examples:

238. PM 14 May 1987, p 43. This is the position taken by decisions in California: Pierce, 19 Western Univ L R 165, 172 (1992).

239. In *Hoyt* v *St Paul Fire & Marine Ins Co*, 607 F 2d 864 (9 Cir, 1979—professional liability) the policy read: "If claim is made or suit is brought against the Insured, the Insured shall immediately forward to the Company every demand, notice summons or other process received by him or his representative." This clause was enforced as (p 867) "the 'claim' contemplated is unambiguously in the nature of a demand or notice". See also *Cornell, Howland, Hayes & Merryfield Inc* v *Continental Casualty Co*, 465 F 2d 22 (9 Cir, 1972—professional liability). *Re St Paul Fire & Marine Ins Co and Guardian Ins Co* (1983) 1 DLR (4th) 342, 359 (Ont—liability); *Reid Crowther & Partners Ltd* v *Simcoe & Erie General Ins Co* (1993) 99 CLR (4th) 741, 758 (Sup Ct—liability).
Alternatively claim might be defined to embrace a notification by the insured to the insurer, thus bringing within a given period of cover, for example, the expected claims from the public at large arising out of a defective batch of products or out of a fire caused by a product in the last few days of the cover period. Unless the insured can obtain cover under a current policy by notification, he is likely to have to bear the loss himself. However, this interpretation may be resisted by insurers as a step back to underwriting on an occurrence basis.

240. See, for example, *Link & Co* v *Continental Casualty Co*, 470 F 2d 1133 (9 Cir, 1972—professional liability), cert den 414 US 829. In *Hoyt* v *St Paul Fire & Marine Ins Co*, 607 F 2d 864 (9 Cir, 1979—professional liability) it was held that a request for an explanation was not a claim, even a request from the claimant's lawyer.

241. This objection cut no ice in *Livingston Parish School Board* v *Fireman's Fund American Ins Co*, 282 So 2d 478 (La, 1973—professional liability) in the face of an unambiguous clause.

242. Such insurance is available at a reduced premium: Frame, 60 Temple LQ 165, 182 (1987).

243. [1988] 1 Lloyd's Rep 7 (CA).

244. p 9 *per* Sir John Donaldson MR; see also p 11, col 2; but *cf* p 10, col 1.

245. p 12 *per* Sir John Donaldson MR. For the facts see below, 17–4D3. *Cf* California where "a formal lawsuit is not required before a claim is made": Pierce, 19 Western Univ L R 165, 172 (1992).

246. [1988] 1 Lloyd's Rep 7, 11–12 (CA—professional liability). See also Derrington & Ashton, *The Law of Liability Insurance* (1990), p 283.

"An architect has separate contracts with separate building owners. The architect makes the same negligent mistake in relation to each. The claims have a factor in common, namely the same negligent mistake, and to this extent are related, but clearly they are separate claims. Bringing the claims a little closer together, let us suppose that the architect has a single contract in relation to two separate houses to be built on two separate sites in different parts of the country. If one claim is in respect of a failure to specify windows of the requisite quality and the other is in respect of a failure to supervise the laying of the foundations, I think that once again the claims would be separate. But it would be otherwise if the complaint was the same in relation to both houses. Then take the present example of a single contract for professional services in relation to a number of houses in a single development. A single complaint that they suffered from a wide range of unrelated defects and a demand for compensation would, I think be regarded as single claim. But if the defects manifested themselves *seriatim* and each gave rise to a separate complaint, what then? They might be regarded as separate claims. Alternatively, later complaints could be regarded as enlargements of the original claim that the architect had been professionally negligent in his execution of his contract. It would, I think, very much depend upon the facts."

In *Thorman,* the architect and his insurer were advised within the insurance period of complaints about brickwork and, although a writ was issued by the complainant endorsed in general terms, the insured architect understood this to refer only to the brickwork. But, a subsequent statement of claim made outside the policy period specified complaints not only about brickwork but also about other defects. Steyn J held that the only claim within the insurance period concerned brickwork; and that the insurance did not therefore cover the other defects. As to the other defects, his decision was reversed by the Court of Appeal. "What matters is what claim was being made by the building owners, not what claim was perceived by the insured . . . the issuing of the [generally endorsed] writ also constitutes a claim covering all matters subsequently particularized in the statement of claim and in the Scott Schedule."[247] Otherwise, the insured would be exposed to uninsured loss, if a claimant issued a writ in general terms but declined to give details until later, when the policy in force at the time of the writ had expired.[248]

17–4D4 Notice of Claims

Liability policies commonly require the insured to give to the insurer notice of claims affecting the insured. The purpose is to enable insurers to investigate a claim early, before the trail of evidence becomes cold, to control proceedings to the mutual advantage of insurer and insured, and to take steps to obviate future liability.[249] The policy may provide, for example, that the insurer must be notified when a claim against the insured is "likely".[250] Subject to the terms of the policy, the insured will not be

---

247. p 12 *per* Sir John Donaldson MR; see also pp 16–17 *per* Stocker LJ. It did not matter that the insured's perception was reasonable; or that the claimant had not particularised the other heads of complaint (*ibid*). There was, however, a letter from the claimant to the insured within the policy period suggesting that the complaints might not be confined to brickwork.
248. pp 12–13 *per* Sir John Donaldson MR.
249. *Commercial Union Ins Co* v *International Flavors & Fragrances Inc*, 822 F 2d 267, 271 (2 Cir, 1987—product liability). Concerning the purposes of notice, see also, below 26–2E4.
250. *Moore* v *Canadian Lawyers Ins Assn* (1992) 95 DLR (4th) 365 (NS—liability).

required to give notice to the insurer, if he is unaware of the relevant information[251] or if the information received and alleged to require notice is trivial[252] or unimportant.[253] When the insured does have to give notice to the insurer, the information to be contained in the notice depends *prima facie* on the meaning of claim: above, 17–4D1. In general, the notice must be given within a reasonable time of the insured having acquired the relevant information; and, if the claim occurs within the insurance period, the insured has performed his duty although his notice is given within a reasonable time but outside the period. Attention has been drawn, however, to certain contracts which require, as a condition of cover, that not only the claim but also the notice be within the insurance period.[254] On notice generally, see further, above, 5–8E2 and below, 26–2.

17–4E The Duty to Defend

In England the insurer has no duty to defend the insured against liability claims,[255] unless the contract specifically imposes it. It is commonly provided that the insurer shall be entitled to defend the action and settle the claim against the insured; however, such clauses do not give the insured a right to be defended by the insurer nor the insurer a duty to defend.[256] Even so, it is

"everyday practice in third party proceedings for the third party [insurer] to support the defendant in his defence, to protect himself against the defendant's claim for indemnity. It is for third parties to decide the line that they will take. Usually they will do well just to watch and see how the evidence comes out, and then make up their minds as to the line they will take."[257]

Although overlapping in practice, what triggers the contractual duty to defend, usually some kind of notice to the insurer, should be distinguished from what triggers cover under the policy: above, 17–4C and 17–4D. In most parts of the United States the position is the same: no duty to defend unless required by contract.[258] If a duty exists, in California, for example, contracts are interpreted strictly against the insurer and the duty to defend arises as soon as the insurer is notified of facts which give rise

---

251. *Commercial Union Ins Co* v *Flavors & Fragrances*, 633 F Supp 646 (SD NY, 1986—product liability), reversed on other grounds 822 F 2d 267 (2 Cir, 1987).

252. *Link & Co* v *Continental Casualty Co*, 470 F 2d 1133, 1139 (9 Cir, 1972—professional liability), cert den 414 US 829.

253. Because for example the insured has a *bona fide* belief in its non-liability: *Flavors & Fragrances* (above), p 271.

254. Pierce, "Professional Liability Insurance: The Claims Made and Reported Trap", 19 Western Univ L R 165 (1992). Although attractive to the market as they cost less, these policies "provide a technical escape hatch by which the insurance company can deny coverage" and are thus contrary to social policy: *Ins Co of Pa* v *Associated International Ins Co*, 922 F 2d 516, 523 (9 Cir, 1990—re). The trap is sprung most sharply if a claim is made against the insured by the filing of suit against him of which he is unaware. Whether such a trap might exist in England depends on the time at which the claim is "made": above 17–4D2. On the position in Australia, see Hill (1993) 5 Ins LJ 218; and Mann (1993) 9 PN 15.

255. *Brice* v *Wackerbarth (Australasia) Pty Ltd* [1974] 2 Lloyd's Rep 274, 277 *per* Roskill LJ (CA—liability).

256. On the duty to defend in general see Appleman, sections 4681 ff; for Louisiana see Jensen, 47 La L Rev 85 (1986). Canada appears to follow the USA: see Brown & Menezes, ch 12:5:2.

257. *Brice* (above), p 276 *per* Lord Denning MR.

258. For example, *Brown* v *Lumbermen's Mutual Casualty Co*, 390 SE 2d 150 (NC, 1990—motor).

to potential liability under the policy.[259] One might think that the possibility of liability must be real[260]; but some courts in Canada and the United States have held that it is enough to trigger the duty to defend that a (mere) allegation of liability has been made. If there is doubt, it is the duty not of the insured but of the insurer to investigate the substance of the complaint.[261] For example, cases decide that the duty to defend and, if appropriate, to investigate "arises whenever the allegations of the underlying complaint fall within the scope of the coverage",[262] or just one of several allegations fall within the scope of the coverage.[263] It is enough that an allegation states a cause of action "that gives rise to the possibility of a recovery under the policy. There need not be a probability of recovery".[264] The reason given is that to "allow the insurer to avoid providing defense on questionable claims would frustrate one of the insured's basic purposes in procuring insurance coverage—protection from the expenses of litigation".[265] Moreover, it has been held in California that, if the insurer is obliged to defend, the insurer must defend "all of the claims involved in the action, both covered and noncovered, until the insurer produces undeniable evidence supporting the allocation of a specific portion of the defense cost to a noncovered claim."[265a]

In the case of excess insurance, the insurer is not obliged to defend until his layer has been reached.[266] It is implicit in the relatively low premium charged for excess insurance that any duty to defend is mainly the duty of the primary insurer. Moreover, any other rule would "transmogrify the policy into one guaranteeing the [performance] of whatever primary insurer the insured might choose".[267] Conversely, however, unless the contract stipulates otherwise, a duty to defend does not cease when the policy limits on the amount of liability cover have been reached.[268] With the

259. *Gray* v *Zurich Ins Co*, 419 P 2d 168, 177 (Cal, 1966—liability); the court was influenced by the doctrine of reasonable expectations, more followed in the United States than in England: see above, 15–5B. In the same sense as *Gray*: *Previews Inc* v *Californian Union Ins Co*, 640 F 2d 1026 (9 Cir, 1981—professional liability). The insurer must defend even though some heads of claim are outside the scope of the cover: *St Paul Fire & Marine Ins Co* v *Sears, Roebuck & Co*, 603 F 2d 780 (9 Cir, 1979—liability).

260. In this sense *Texaco Inc* v *Hartford Accident & Indemnity*, 453 F Supp 1109, 1112 (ED Okl, 1978—liability) and cases cited.

261. *Perkins* v *Hartford Ins Group*, 932 F 2d 1392 (11 Cir, 1991—liability).

262. *Commercial Union Ins Cos* v *Jedamich Enterprises Inc*, 536 NYS 2d 523, 525 (1989—liability). It is enough that the case comes "arguably" within the cover: *Allstate Ins Co* v *Freeman*, 443 NW 2d 734, 737 (Mich, 1989—liability).

See also *United States Fidelity & Guarantee Co* v *Roser Co Inc*, 585 F 2d 932, 936 (8 Cir, 1978—product liability); *idem: Rhodes* v *Chicago Ins Co*, 719 F 2d 116, 119 (5 Cir, 1983—professional liability); *Alert Centre* v *Alarm Protection Services*, 967 F 2d 161, 163 (5 Cir, 1992—liability). *Idem:* in Canada: *Prudential Life Ins Co Ltd* v *Public Ins Corp* (1976) 67 DLR (3d) 521, 524 (Man—liability);

263. *Golotrade Shipping & Chartering Inc* v *Travelers Indemnity Co*, 706 F Supp 214, 218 (SD NY, 1989—liability); *Titan Holdings Syndicate Inc* v *City Of Keene*, 898 F 2d 265 (1 Cir, 1990—liability); *Sauer* v *Home Indemnity Co* 841 P 2d 176, 181 (Alaska, 1992—liability). But only if the various allegations are sufficiently "intertwined": *Board of Trustees of Michigan University* v *Continental Casualty Co*, 730 F Supp 1408, 1413 (WD Mich, 1990—liability).

264. *Allstate Ins Co* v *Mugavero*, 537 NYS 2d 961, 963 (1989—liability); see also *Klaesen Bros Inc* v *Harbor Ins Co*, 410 So 2d 611, 613 (Fla, 1982—liability) and cases cited.

265. *Black* v *Fireman's Fund American Ins Co*, 767 P 2d 824, 830 (Idaho, 1989—liability).

265a. *Horace Mann Ins Co* v *Barbara B*, 846 P 2d 792, 795–796 (Cal, 1993—educator's liability).

266. *Revco DS* v *Gov Employees Ins Co*, 791 F Supp 1254, 1273–1274 (ND Ohio, 1991 — liability), affirmed 968 F 2d 1216 (6 Cir, 1992). On the division of the duty between primary and excess insurer see Bollar, 17 Pacific L J 283 (1985); Fredericks, 70 Marquette L Rev 285 (1987).

267. *Revco* p 1274.

268. *Maryland Casualty Co* v *Grace & Co*, 794 F Supp 1206, 1221 (SD NY, 1991—liability).

exception perhaps of excess insurance, the general effect of the cases in the USA is that the duty to defend has become broader than the duty to indemnify.[269]

17–4E1 Conduct of the Defence

If the insurer defends, whether by choice or by duty, he must do it properly. Just as a fire insurer who reinstates insured property may be liable for the quality of the work,[270] a liability insurer may be liable for negligent conduct of settlement negotiations and defence.[271]

Insurers can decide the tactics to be pursued, provided that "they do so in what they *bona fide* consider to be the common interest of themselves and the insured".[272] The insurer is likely to want to choose the solicitor to conduct the defence. However, the insured may insist on a solicitor of his own choice as well, at least if he faces criminal prosecution,[273] or if there is conflict of interest between insurer and insured (below, 17–4E4). A solicitor, not only one chosen by the insured but also one chosen by the insurer, owes a duty of care to the insured. However,

"The duty of the solicitor so nominated to the insured for whom he is to act cannot of course be the same as that which arises in the ordinary case of a solicitor and client, where the client is entitled to require the solicitor to act according to his own instructions. The whole object and usefulness of these provisions would be defeated if the insured were to be entitled to interfere with the conduct of the proceedings in that way. The insured in my opinion is not entitled to complain of anything done by the solicitors upon the instructions, express or implied, of the insurers, provided that it falls within the class of things which the insurers are . . . entitled to do under the terms of the policy."[274]

17–4E2 Information

The solicitor chosen by the insurer must keep the insured informed to such extent as is reasonably necessary,[275] in particular, he must inform him of any possible conflict of interest between the insurer and insured[276] and, if requested to do so, produce for the insured all documents relating to the action in his possession, custody or control, either during or after the action by the third party victim.[277]

When two parties concur in instructing a solicitor to give legal advice and for this purpose they communicate information to the solicitor in confidence, they have a joint privilege in that information, which cannot be asserted by the one against the other

269. *Prudential Life Ins Co Ltd* v *Public Ins Corp* (1976) 67 DLR (3d) 521, 524 (Man—liability). Brown & Menezes, ch 12:5:3. *Val's Painting & Drywall Inc* v *Allstate Ins Co*, 126 Cal Rptr 267, 271 (Cal, 1976—liability), citing *Gray* v *Zurich Ins Co*, 419 P 2d 168, 177 (Cal, 1966—liability). Also *Keene Corp* v *INA*, 667 F 2d 1034, 1050 (Col, 1981—product liability); *Commercial Union Ins Co* v *International Flavors & Fragrances Inc*, 822 F 2d 267, 273 (2 Cir, 1987—product liability); *Commercial Union Ins Cos* v *Jedamich Enterprises Inc*, 536 NYS 2d 523 (1989—liability).
270. Below 29–2D.
271. *Parich* v *State Farm Mutual Co*, 919 F 2d 906 (5 Cir, 1990—motor)
272. *Groom* v *Crocker* [1939] 1 KB 194, 203 *per* Sir Wilfred Greene MR (CA): the court held that the solicitor was not entitled to admit the insured's negligence, negligence denied by the insured.
273. *Barratt Bros (Taxis) Ltd* v *Davies* [1966] 2 Lloyd's Rep 1, 5 *per* Lord Denning MR (CA—motor).
274. *Groom* (above), pp 202–203; see also *per* Scott LJ, pp 222–223. The terms of the insurance contract must be regarded as incorporated into the contract between the insured and the solicitor: *Brown* v *Guardian Royal Exchange Assurance Co* (31 July 1992, unreported).
275. p 222 *per* Scott LJ.
276. p 227 *per* Mackinnon LJ.
277. *Re Crocker* [1936] Ch 696.

but which, equally, cannot be waived by one in favour of a third party without the consent of the other.[278] Although most obviously true of a joint retainer, it is not irrelevant to the instant situation between liability insurer and his insured, in which a court is likely to see the situation as one not of joint retainer but of distinct and separate contracts with the solicitor.[279] Indeed, the legal position may well be similar, a conflict of interest arises between the two parties. When a conflict emerges, the question becomes acute, whether insurer and insured have a joint privilege in the relevant information or whether it is the privilege of the insured alone. What is to be done then depends very much on the terms of the contract of insurance and, consequently, on the terms of the solicitor's retainer.[280] It is not uncommon for insurance contracts to seek to limit the circumstances in which it can be refused access to the information.

17–4E3 Costs

Liability insurance commonly covers the costs of the insured's defending the claim. The extent of this cover is a matter of interpretation [281] of the contract which, for example, may limit this cover to costs incurred with the consent of the insurer.[282] In the absence of an express clause about costs, the amount of costs (reasonably) incurred by the insured in defending the claim will be a proper matter for indemnity,[283] subject to the other terms of the policy[284] and subject to the usual rules about mitigation.[285]

It remains to be seen whether, in the case of multiple claims against the insured, the insurer can settle large claims first so to exhaust the limit of indemnity under the insurance, and thus to avoid payment of not only the rest of the claims which bring the aggregate above the limit but also of the relatively large aggregate of defence costs that might be associated with those claims.

17–4E4: Conflict of Interests: Insurer and Insured

A conflict of interests or a conflict of duty and interest arises, first, when the claim against the insured is likely to result in an award of damages in excess of the policy limit, unless the insurer settles within that limit,[286] but the insurer estimates that his interests are better served by a fight, which the insured does not want: quite apart

---

278. *Brown* (above).
279. *Ibid.*
280. *Ibid.* Generally, the court will bear in mind the insurer's interest in knowledge of the circumstances surrounding the claim and the insured's interest, underwritten by the policy, in protecting his legal position, which implies free communication with "his" solicitor. In the instant case, the judge (Judge Diamond, QC) was also influenced by the fact that the retainer was separate and not joint; that the insurer had not admitted liability to the insured; and that the insurance contract did not limit the insured's freedom to forbid the solicitor to communicate confidential information to the insurer, once a conflict of interests had arisen. Consequently, the decision was in favour of the insured.
281. For example, *British General Ins Co Ltd* v *Mountain* (1919) 1 Ll L Rep 605 (HL—re). *Losier* v *St Paul Mercury Indemnity Co* (1957) 6 DLR (2d) 686 (Ont—motor). On whether the insurer is obliged to pay costs as they arise or when the litigation ends, see Oettle & Howard, 22 Tort & Ins L J 337 (1987).
282. For example, costs (defending a libel action) incurred with the consent of the insurer, such consent not to be unreasonably withheld: *Hulton & Co Ltd* v *Mountain* (1921) 8 Ll L Rep 249 (CA—liability).
283. *Forney* v *Dominion Ins Co Ltd* [1969] 1 WLR 928, 935 *per* Donaldson J (liability).
284. For example, *Xenos* v *Fox* (1869) LR 4 CP 665 (Exch Ch—hull).
285. See below, 28–8G.
286. *Bogard* v *Employers Casualty Co*, 210 Cal Rptr 578 (1985—homeowner's liability); *St Paul Fire & Marine Ins Co* v *Roch Bros Co*, 639 F Supp 134, 139 (ED Pa, 1986—professional liability).

from the financial risk of losing at a level above the policy limits, the insured's commercial reputation may be damaged by being seen to fight.[287] Alternatively, the insured may consider that his reputation is better served by fighting a claim which the insurer considers it expedient to settle. The terms of the contract may empower the insurer to settle the claim, whether the insured agrees or not, and in England such a clause has been enforced,[288] however, it does not follow that the insurer can settle without any regard to the interests of the insured.

Courts in the United States speak of the insurer's duty to settle,[289] if that is in the interests of the insured. In general, an "insurer has a 'very great duty' to settle within the limits of the policy".[290] This duty has been based on contract,[291] although its content is one of reasonable care,[292] and sometimes it has been based less on contract than on the duty of good faith.[293] In any event, when the question comes up, the insurer's counsel has "a duty to communicate to [the insured] his evaluation of the . . . claim, the conflicting interests involved, and the right to consult with an independent counsel, or to request that [the insurer] discuss these matters with [the insured] prior to settlement".[294] Moreover, good faith requires that the insurer keep the insured informed of the progress of negotiations with the third party.[295]

Second, a conflict may arise when cover is uncertain, however, it is also uncertain when such a conflict has arisen. On one view, there is a conflict as soon as the insurer decides[296] that the case raises the question whether or not liability, if established, is within the scope of the policy. If that is right, there is conflict whenever the insurer reserves the right to dispute cover or requires the insured to concede a non-waiver

---

287. For example, his credit may be damaged as long as there is an outstanding liability against his name: *Consolidated American Ins Co v Mike Soper Marine Services*, 951 F 2d 186, 191 (9 Cir, 1991—liability).

288. *Beacon Ins Co Ltd v Langdale* [1939] 4 All ER 204 (CA—motor). The decision whether to defend or settle may be referred to the arbitration of counsel under a "QC clause": see *West Wake Price & Co v Ching* [1957] 1 WLR 45 (liability); Jess, *A Guide to the Insurance of Professional Negligence Risks*, p 207.

As regards authority between insurer (reinsured) and reinsurer to settle an insurance claim brought by the primary insured against the insurer see *Insurance Co of Africa v Scor (UK) Reinsurance Co Ltd* [1985] 1 Lloyd's Rep 312 (CA). See further, below 27–4.

289. Abraham, pp 189 ff. See further Keeton, 67 Harv L Rev 1136 (1954); Cohen, 27 U Pittsburgh L Rev 726 (1966); Papetti, 60 Geo Wash L Rev 1931 (1992); and, in particular, Syverud, 76 Va L Rev 1113 (1990) and as regards the position in Australia, see Mullins (1991) 4 Ins L J 83.

290. *Kunkel v Continental Casualty Co*, 866 F 2d 1269, 1275 (10 Cir, 1989—liability). Also in this sense: *Diblasi v Aetna Life & Casualty Co*, 542 NYS 2d 187, 191 (1989—liability); *Corrado Bros Inc v Twin City Fire Ins Co*, 562 A 2d 1188, 1191 (Delaware, 1989—workmen's compensation); and *Ranger Ins Co v Home Indemnity Co*, 741 F Supp 716, 722 (ND Ill, 1990—re), where the court also said that the rule should be applied "sparingly . . . since trial attorneys are not endowed with the gift of prophecy so as to be able to predict the precise outcome of personal injury litigation" (*ibid*). In California, the insurer who fails to accept a reasonable settlement offer within the limits of the cover, is liable for all damages resulting from that failure: *Consolidated American Ins Co v Mike Soper Marine Services*, 942 F2d 1420 (9 Cir, 1991—liability).

291. *Pacific Employers Ins Co v PB Hoidale Co*, 789 F Supp 1117, 1123 (D Kan, 1992—liability). *Cf* the current analysis of the general duty of good faith as a duty imposed by law rather than implied in contract, below, 23–1A

292. *Dumas v State Farm Mutual Automobile Ins Co*, 274 A 2d 781 783–784 (NH, 1971—motor) and cases cited.

293. *Reisen v Aetna Life & Casualty Co*, 302 SE 2d 529 (Va, 1983—motor).

294. *Corrado* (above) p 1193. However, although this duty had been broken in this case, the resulting settlement was, in the view of the court, both reasonable and in good faith.

295. *Peckham v Continental Casualty Ins Co*, 895 F 2d 830, 840 (1 Cir, 1990—motor). See also *St Paul Fire & Marine Ins Co v Edge Memorial Hospital*, 584 So 2d 1316 (Ala, 1991—liability).

296. *San Diego Navy Federal Credit Union v Cumis Ins Sy*, 208 Cal Rptr 494, 502 (1984).

agreement.[297] On a more conservative view, there is no conflict unless there is actual rather than potential conflict,[298] notably when the insurer actually disputes[299] whether the insured's liability is covered by the policy, or the interest of the insurer would be furthered by a less than vigorous defence to the action against the insured.[300] In any event, the English court is likely to imply a term, if one is not express, that if evidence emerges which may provide the insurer with a ground for refusing to pay the insured, the solicitor must immediately inform both insurer and insured.[301]

In situations of conflict, and if the insurer has a duty to defend, the position in California[302] and New York[303] is as follows. First, the insurer cannot avoid his duty to defend by pleading or creating a conflict of duty and interest.[304] Second, the insurer must pay reasonable value for an independent lawyer chosen by the insured; otherwise the insurer has not fully carried out his contractual duty to defend the insured.[305] This has been thought desirable to maintain public confidence in the judicial process.[306] In England, regulations[307] to implement EC Directive 87/344/EEC apply to legal expenses insurance, defined as being the effecting and carrying out of contracts of insurance against risks of loss to the insured attributable to their incurring legal expenses, and thus, it seems, including legal expenses ancillary to other kinds of insurance,[308] but subject to certain express exceptions.[309] Regulation 6 provides that certain "rights shall be expressly recognised in the policy". First, the insured "shall be free to choose" a lawyer to "defend, represent or serve" his interests, where "recourse is had to a lawyer". Second, the insured "shall be free to choose a lawyer . . . to serve his interests whenever a conflict of interests arises". Evidently, the insured may be unaware of a conflict, so regulation 9 requires the insurer to give the insured written notice informing him of his rights.

As to the general nature of the insurer's duty at common law in the face of a conflict

---

297. *Chi of Alaska, Inc* v *Employers Reinsurance Corp*, 844 P 2d 1113 (Alaska, 1993—liability). Abraham, pp 196 ff; Lightstone, 23 Cal W L Rev 125 (1986).

298. *St Paul Fire & Marine Ins Co* v *Roch Bros Co*, 639 F Supp 134, 139 (ED Pa, 1986—professional liability): this point is reached when the insurer "urges" that the claim is not covered.

299. *Bogard* v *Employers Casualty Co*, 210 Cal Rptr 578 (1985—homeowner's liability).

300. *Nandorf Inc* v *CNA Ins Cos*, 479 NE 2d 988, 992 (Ill, 1985—liability).

301. *Brown* v *Guardian Royal Exchange Assurance Co* (31 July 1992, unreported).

302. *Executive Aviation Inc* v *National Ins Underwriters*, 94 Cal Rptr 347 (1971—aviation liability); *Previews Inc* v *Californian Union Ins Co*, 640 F 2d 1026, 1028 (9 Cir, 1981—professional liability) and cases cited; *San Diego Navy Federal Credit Union* v *Cumis Ins Sy*, 208 Cal Rptr 494 (1984).

303. *New York State Urban Development Corp* v *VSL Corp*, 738 F 2d 61, 65 (2 Cir, 1984—liability) and cases cited.

A policy clause that the insurer shall be entitled to participate in the selection of an independent lawyer will be enforced, as long as the insurer discharges its duty of good faith and the lawyer selected is truly independent: *New York State Urban Development Corp* v *VSL Corp* 738 F 2d 61, 65 (2 Cir, 1984—liability); otherwise the right of the insured to have a free choice of lawyer is said to be absolute (*ibid*).

304. *San Diego Navy Federal Credit Union* v *Cumis Ins Sy*, 208 Cal Rptr 494, 501 (1984), following *Tomerlin* v *Canadian Indemnity Co*, 394 P 2d 571 (Cal, 1964—liability); and *Gray* v *Zurich Ins Co*, 419 P 2d 168 (Cal, 1966—liability).

305. Keeton, 67 Harv L Rev 1136, 1170 (1954).

306. Anon, 114 U Pa L Rev 734, 738 (1966).

307. SI 1990/1159. The regulations were part of the price of opening the German legal expenses insurance market to foreign competition: Fitzimmons, (1990) 1 Euro Bus L Rev 83.

308. Fitzimmons, *loc cit*.

309. For example, legal expenses insurance contracts concerning disputes or risks arising from or in connection with the use of seagoing vessels.

of interests, in *Diblasi*,[310] in which the issue was the propriety of a settlement, the New York court said that "the law imposes upon the carrier the obligation of good faith which is basically the duty to fairly consider the insured's interests as well as its own in making the decision as to settlement". Again, in *Corrado*,[311] the Delaware court required any settlement to be "both in good faith and reasonable".[312] But the court rejected the argument that the insurer was a fiduciary. That concept "is more aptly applied in legal relationships where the interests of the fiduciary and the beneficiary incline towards a common goal and in which the fiduciary is required to pursue solely the interests of the beneficiary of the property".[313] Between insurer and insured, the potential "clash of interests is clearly not compatible with the concept of a fiduciary".[314] However, some courts have gone further[315] than an ordinary duty of good faith: in every insurance contract, it is said, there is an implied duty of good faith and fair dealing whereby each refrains from preventing the other from receiving the full benefits of the contract,[316] a duty not unfamiliar to lawyers in England.[317]

17–4E5 Conflict of Interests: Insurers

The duty of good faith in relation to liability claims, it has been held, is owed only to the insured. Courts in the United States, however, are divided over whether a primary insurer owes such a duty directly to an excess insurer on the same risk,[318] although the latter may be subrogated to the rights of the insured against the primary insurer for breach of duty under the contract of insurance, including the duty owed to the insured to settle.[319]

If there are two insurers obliged to defend the insured and their interests conflict because, for example, each claims that any loss must be indemnified by the other, it

310. *Diblasi* v *Aetna Life & Casualty Co*, 542 NYS 2d 187, 191 (1989—liability). The "duty of good faith requires an insurer to give equal consideration to the protection of the insured's interests as its own interests": *Hartford Accident & Indemnity Co* v *Aetna Casualty & Surety Co*, 792 P 2d 749, 752 (Ariz, 1990—motor); *idem*: *Glenn* v *Fleming*, 799 P 2d 79, 85 (Kan, 1990—motor).

311. *Corrado Bros Inc* v *Twin City Fire Ins Co*, 562 A 2d 1188, 1191 (Delaware, 1989—workmen's compensation).

312. *Ibid*.

313. p 1192. See also in this sense: *Almon State Farm Fire & Casualty Co*, 724 F Supp 765, 766 (SD Cal, 1989—property damage); *Hassard, Bonnington, Roger & Huber* v *Home Ins Co*, 740 F Supp 789 (SD Cal, 1990—liability).

314. p 1192.

315. In this sense: Lightstone, 23 Cal W L Rev 125 (1986), who objects that the court has not interpreted the contract but extended and rewritten it; that in the case of conflict the insured is adequately protected by the duty of good faith; and that the cost of liability insurance to the insured will be much increased to provide a facility that he does not want.

316. For example *Crisci* v *Security Ins Co*, 426 P 2d 173, 176 (Cal, 1967—PA); *Guin* v *Ha*, 591 P 2d 1281 (Alaska, 1979—professional liability); *Gruenberg* v *Aetna Ins Co*, 510 P 2d 1032 (Cal, 1973—fire). See further, below, 27–1 and 30–10. The same *rationale* has been accepted in Canada: Brown & Menezes, No 12:5:16.

In South Australia the insured has obtained an injunction against the solicitors appointed by the insurer to defend him to restrain them from making use (breach of confidence) of a statement that he had made to them in connection with the defence in a subsequent recourse action by the insurers against the insured: *State Govt Ins Commission (SA)* v *Paneros* (1988) 5 ANZ Ins Cases 60–857 (SA).

317. *Day* v *Singleton* [1899] 2 Ch 320; *Southern Foundries Ltd* v *Shirlaw* [1940] AC 701.

318. Against: *Great Southwest Fire Ins Co* v *CNA Ins Cos*, 557 So 2d 966, 969 ff (La, 1989—liability). For: *Great American Ins Co* v *International Ins Co*, 753 F Supp 357, 363 (MD Ga, 1990—motor); *Ranger Ins Co* v *Home Indemnity Co*, 741 F Supp 716, 722 (ND Ill, 1990—re); *California Union Ins Co* v *Excess Ins Co*, 780 F Supp 1010 (SD NY, 1991 — liability).

319. *Ibid*.

has been held in Canada[320] that the insurers must agree a lawyer acceptable to each other and to the insured, failing which the insured may appoint a lawyer to conduct his defence and require the insurers to reimburse costs reasonably incurred. In England, to comply with the duty to implement EC Directive 87/344/EEC, regulations[321] were brought into effect on 1 July 1990 and apply to "all legal expenses insurance business".[322] A legal expenses insurance contract must be the subject of a separate policy or of a separate section of a policy. By regulation 5, an insurance company carrying on legal insurance business must adopt at least one of three specified arrangements designed to avoid conflicting interests with parts of its own business concerned with other classes of insurance. One of these arrangements is that the insurer shall, "in the policy, afford the insured the right to entrust the defence of his interests, from the moment that he has the right to claim from the insurer under the policy, to a lawyer of his choice".[323]

17–4F Waiver

If the insurer does defend the action against the insured, although the duty of indemnity is distinct from the duty to defend,[324] the insurer is advised to protect himself from the argument that, by defending, he is estopped from denying liability to indemnify. For estoppel[325] (a) there must be an unequivocal representation (that, if the insured is liable to the claimant, the insurer is liable on the policy), and (b) the insured must have acted on the representation. Generally, the representation must be positive rather than negative but the same effect may be given to inactivity in context.[326] For example, in *Reid* v *Campbell Wallis Moule & Co Pty Ltd*,[327] the judge concluded that

"there can be no question that underwriters knew of the rights which the policy gave them. They must be taken also to have known by 16 December 1988 all the facts which were capable of bearing on the question of their liability to indemnify the defendants. I am bound to find that underwriters had a reasonable time before 21 February to make a decision to decline indemnity in reliance on the exclusion clause and to communicate it to the defendants. Their failure to communicate it before 21 February, knowing that a trial had been fixed for 2 March, is powerful evidence, in the absence of an explanation for the delay, of an election inconsistent with a decision to decline liability. When that is combined with the failure in the circumstances to inform the defendants that the trial date had been fixed I am of opinion that the objective evidence of a decision not to decline liability becomes overwhelming".

In many situations, however, the defence of the insured is not an unequivocal admission that, if the defence fails, there must be liability under the policy.[328] The defence of the insured may be but an expedient first line of resistance for the insurer; it is not necessarily the last. However, the stronger the last line of defence based on

---

320. *Prudential Life Ins Co Ltd* v *Public Ins Corp* (1976) 67 DLR (3d) 5, 527 (Man—liability).
321. SI 1990/1159.
322. Subject to exceptions, including insurance contracts concerning a dispute arising out of the use of seagoing vessels.
323. The reference to a "lawyer of his choice", suggests that the "freedom to choose" mentioned in regulation 6, although it immediately follows the relevant part of regulation 5, is distinct.
324. *Great West Steel Industries Ltd* v *Simcoe & Erie General Ins Co* (1979) 106 DLR (3d) 347 (Ont—liability).
325. See discussion of waiver and estoppel below, 26–4.
326. In particular, see 26–4D.
327. [1990] VR 859, 874 (liability), with reference to the judgment of Fenton Atkinson LJ in *Allen* v *Robles* [1969] 2 Lloyd's Rep 61, 64 (CA—motor).
328. For example *Soole* v *Royal Ins Co Ltd* [1971] 2 Lloyd's Rep 332, 339–340, 342 *per* Shaw J (liability).

breach of the insurance contract, the stronger the force of any representation implicit in defending the insured against the victim for, if the insurer knows that the insured has broken a warranty which vitiates cover, it is likely to make little sense to defend an insured to whom he is no longer obliged; if he does, the insured may be entitled to assume that the insurer has waived the breach of warranty.[329]

To avoid doubt and misunderstanding, and to preserve its position the insurer may wish to follow the practice found in Canada and the United States of proceeding with the defence on the basis of a "non-waiver" agreement with the insured. A non-waiver agreement is a bilateral contract between insurer and insured, usually in writing, providing that the insurer will defend the action while reserving its right to assert later that it is not liable under the insurance contract. It is distinguished from a reservation of rights, which is similar but less formal.[330] Such agreements have been upheld; moreover, it has been held that, if an insured refused to agree a reservation of rights, the insurer was entitled to refuse to defend.[331] However, such agreements have been construed strictly against the insurer. In particular, an agreement has been interpreted as inoperative when the interests of the insured were evidently in conflict with those of the insurer.

In *Federal Ins Co* v *Matthews*[332] the insurer was defending an action in the United States by denying that the insured was drunk, while in British Columbia the same insurer was seeking a declaration that it was not liable under the same policy because the insured was drunk. The Canadian court concluded[333]:

"To give to the non-waiver agreement an interpretation which would result in the insurer being able to place its own interest at variance with that of the insured would be to lead to an injustice, and in construing the agreement it should be assumed that the parties did not intend to accomplish an unjust result if the words are equally consistent with any other conclusion".

17-5 PERSONAL ACCIDENT[334]

The meaning of "accident" depends in part on the wording of the contract concerned. Indeed, it is sometimes said that wording is conclusive, so that case cannot be compared with case, unless the wording is the same,[335] and that, if it is not, the judge can disregard an earlier decision, which might otherwise be thought to govern. This is more often convenient than convincing. However, whatever the wording, the meaning of accident is influenced by public policy factors, sometimes in the guise of refer-

---

329. *Fraser* v *Furman (Productions) Ltd* [1967] 1 WLR 898, 909 *per* Diplock LJ (CA—employers' liability). *Federal Ins Co* v *Matthews* (1956) 3 DLR (2d) 322 (BC—motor). *Schiff Associates Inc* v *Flack*, 435 NYS 2d 972, 975 (1980—professional liability); *Commercial Union Ins Co* v *International Flavors & Fragrances Inc*, 633 F Supp 646, 650–651 (SD NY, 1986—product liability).

330. Lightstone, 23 Cal W L Rev 125 (1986).

331. *Clement* v *Marathon Oil Co*, 724 F Supp 431 (ED La, 1989—liability), with reference to *Ezell* v *Hayes Oilfield Construction Co Inc*, 693 F 2d 489 (5 Cir, 1982—liability), cert den, 464 US 818 (1983).

332. (1956) 3 DLR (2d) 322 (BC—motor); see pp 340–341 and cases cited.

333. p 342.

334. Generally see Welford, *Accident Insurance* (2nd ed, 1932); MacGillivray, ch 26; Davidson "Accidents, Accidental Means and Wilful Exposure to Risk" [1984] JBL 391. Appleman, sections 352, 392, 421 ff and 531 ff.

335. For example, the ambivalent judgment of Atkinson J in *Smith* v *Cornhill Ins Co* [1938] 3 All ER 145, 150 (PA).

ence to the view of the man in the street.[336] In the result, there is some inconsistency of decision but not enough, it is submitted, to rule out the attempt in this part of the chapter to draw general guidelines.

The meaning of "accident" also depends in part on the context in which it comes, notably, the kind of insurance. We are here mainly concerned with PA insurance; the meaning of accident, for example, in marine insurance[337] and all risks cover[338] is similar but one cannot say confidently that it is exactly the same, especially when applied under pressure of public policy. A striking example is offered by the litigation in the USA to recover the cost of cleaning up pollution under the Comprehensive General Liability (CGL) Policy, especially as it stood before 1986. Although the dumping of toxic waste would appear to have been an intentional act on the part of many insured manufacturers and thus, in ordinary speech, anything but accidental, many courts have been persuaded nonetheless that the pollution was "sudden and accidental" and thus covered.[339]

17-5A Related Questions

Before attempting to define "accident" (below, 17-5C), certain related concepts need to be distinguished.[340] If in the events leading to injury there is a deliberate act of the insured, an insurer might raise the character of that act as a defence in not one but three related but different ways.

(a) *Not Accident.* The insurer may argue that, although the policy covers "accident", the insured's deliberate act was so significant in the events described as an accident, that it deprives those events (of which the deliberate act is part) of accidental character. For example, he may argue that the injury was not accidental because at the time the insured was driving his car in a reckless manner. This argument, which of course is central to the present discussion, will usually succeed, if the injury was the expected or probable result of the insured's deliberate act: below, 17-5C. The "significance of this word 'accidental' is best perceived by a consideration of the relation of causes to their effects. The word is descriptive of means which produce effects which are not their natural and probable consequences."[341]

(b) *Not Caused by Accident.* The notion of accident should be distinguished from issues of causation raised by the events leading up to the accident. As a matter of causation, probability of injury, which deprives the event itself of accidental character in (a), is evidently a looser causal link than inevitability

---

336. For example, *Fenton* v *Thorley & Co Ltd* [1903] AC 443 (workers' compensation); *Weyerhaeuser* v *Evans* (1932) 43 Ll L Rep 62 (PA); *Marcel Beller Ltd* v *Hayden* [1978] 1 Lloyds Rep 472, 477 *per* Judge Fay (PA).

In the USA similar references are found, for example, to "the average man . . . in common speech"— *Ocean Accident & Guarantee Corp Ltd* v *Penick & Ford Ltd*, 101 F 2d 493, 497 (8 Cir, 1939—machinery breakdown insurance); *Miller* v *Continental Ins Co*, 389 NYS 2d 565 (1976).

337. See, for example, *Scrutton on Charterparties* (19th ed) pp 227-228.

338. Above, 17-3A.

339. See Hawke and Nudds, 17 Anglo-American L Rev 239, 246 (1988); and Eilander, 90 Colum L Rev 1066 (1990). On "accidental damage" to property, see *Valcrane Pty Ltd* v *Mercantile Mutual Ins (Australia) Ltd* (1988) 9 Qd Lawyer 178 (motor); *Golden Eagle Liberia Ltd* v *St Paul Fire & Marine Ins Co*, 685 F Supp 393 (SD NY, 1988—liability).

340. Failure to make the distinction causes difficulty, see, for example, *Gray* v *Barr* [1971] 2 QB 554 (CA—liability). Rendall, 9 Manitoba L J 101, 104-105 (1979).

341. *Western Commercial Travelers' Assn* v *Smith*, 85 F 401, 405 (8 Cir, 1898—PA).

of injury, which is the usual external link between an insured event (such as accident) and the injury suffered by the insured. The latter is governed by the doctrine of proximate cause, which justifies an argument by the insurer that the real cause of the insured's loss was something outside the insured event (accident) and, therefore, something not covered by the insurance: see below, 25–9B1.

(c) *Not Allowed*. Yet another defence is that the claim should fail, because the insured deliberately caused or risked the injury, to allow his claim would encourage him (and others) to do it again, and this would be contrary to public policy. This is an argument, which is distinct from those in (a) and (b), and the success of which depends not on definitions or on the probability of injury in the particular case but on the impact of factors of public policy (see below, 24–5B).

17–5B Intentional Injury

(a) *The Role of Intention*

Injury is not caused by accident, if it is the intended[342] or inevitable[343] (as good as intended) result of the conduct of the insured. In *Gray* v *Barr*, the insured, holding a loaded gun, grappled with the victim. This was a deliberate act but that alone was not decisive. What counted was that, in the view of Lord Denning, it led "inexorably" to injury which was not therefore accidental.[344]

The relevant intention, however, is that of the insured. Injury is caused by accident, if it is intentionally inflicted by a third party, who attacks him.[345] Further, if there is an accidental injury, the policy covers the effects of any consequent and intentional medical treatment: below, 17-5G1.

(b) *The Nature of Intention*

Injury is caused by accident, however, if, although the inevitable result of the conduct of the insured, it was not intended by the insured because he lacked the mental capacity to form the intention. Suicide while temporarily insane is accidental,[346] provided that the insured was incapable of making a "meaningful choice", *viz.*, if he suffered delusions such that he did not understand the physical consequences of his actions or when he suffered from an "insane impulse", and was "unable to resist doing the act in issue, i.e. lacks volitional capacity".[347] Distinguish, however, the inability to

---

342. *Miss Jay Jay* [1987] 1 Lloyd's Rep 32, 36 *per* Lawton LJ (CA—hull: "external accidental means"). *Western Commercial Travelers' Assn* v *Smith*, 85 F 401 (8 Cir,1895—PA); *Radius* v *Travelers' Ins Co*, 87 F 2d 412 (9 Cir, 1937—life); *Roller* v *Stonewall Ins Co*, 801 P 2d 207 (Wash, 1990—motor).

343. *Miss Jay Jay* (above), p 38 *per* Slade LJ.

344. [1971] 2 QB 554, 566–567 (CA). *Cf* the view that if events leading to injury are initiated by an intentional act, that cannot be accidental: this view seems mistaken: below, 17–5F1.

345. Schoolmaster killed by pupils: *Trim Joint District School Board of Management* v *Kelly* [1914] AC 667 (workmen's compensation); insured torpedoed in wartime: *Letts* v *Excess Ins Co* (1916) 32 TLR 361 (PA).

Insured shot during altercation: *Robinson* v *United States' Mutual Accident Assn*, 68 F 825 (ED Mo, 1895—life); *Hensley* v *Life Ins Co of North America*, 551 F 2d 35 (3 Cir, 1977—PA). *Cf Lewis* v *INA*, 416 F 2d 1077 (5 Cir, 1969—PA) discussed below 17–5E3.

346. *Accident Ins Co* v *Crandal*, 120 US 527 (1886—PA).

347. *Erie Ins Exchange* v *Stark*, 962 F 2d 349, 356 (4 Cir, 1992—fire).

distinguish right from wrong, which does not itself rule out the ability to form the relevant intention,[348] although the inability to reach a "balanced decision" on any matter of significance might do so.[349] In *Kirkham*,[350] the suit was in tort in respect of the suicide of a person in the custody of the police. A defence of *volenti non fit injuria* failed. Lloyd LJ observed that when "a man of sound mind commits suicide, his estate would be unable to maintain an action" against the custodian, however, in the instant case, the deceased was not of sound mind because, although his suicide was "a deliberate and conscious act" and he was thus "sane in the legal sense", he was suffering from clinical depression.[351] For these reasons, it is likely that a claim under PA insurance in those circumstances would have succeeded.

The reality of intention is objectively assessed. It has sometimes been said in Canada that injury, which viewed objectively is not accidental, is nonetheless to be regarded as accidental in law, if the insured was not actually conscious or aware that he was courting danger: 17–5F2. This is not the law in England.

17–5C Accident: An Unexpected and External Fortuity

In the USA, "this word 'accidental' is best perceived by a consideration of the relation of causes to their effects".[352] In England too, the law looks at the sequence of events leading to the injury.[353] There is an accident, if injury results which, from the standpoint of the insured at the beginning of that sequence of events, is "fortuitous and unexpected".[354] Conversely, "an effect which is the natural and probable consequence of an act or a course of action is not an accident,"[355] that is, if it follows more

348. *Ibid.*
349. *Kirkham* v *Chief Constable of the Greater Manchester Police* [1990] 2 QB 283, 295 *per* Farquharson LJ (CA).
350. Above.
351. p 290. The other members of the Court agreed with him. *Cf Erie* (above): in that case, the insured suffered severe reactive depression after his son's death and attempted to destroy himself by setting fire to the family home; but these circumstances alone were not enough to take the case outside an exclusion of "intentional acts".
352. *Western Commercial Travelers' Assn* v *Smith*, 85 F 401, 405 (8 Cir, 1895—PA).
353. *Hamlyn* v *Crown Accidental Ins Co Ltd* [1893] 1 QB 750 (CA). *City of Fulton* v *Great American Indemnity Co*, 174 NYS 2d 690, 698 (1958), affirmed 181 NYS 2d 780 (1958).
354. Welford p 268, quoted with approval in *De Souza* v *Home & Overseas Ins Co Ltd, The Times*, 19 September 1990 (CA—PA). See also *Miss Jay Jay* [1987] 1 Lloyd's Rep 32, 36 *per* Lawton LJ (CA—hull: "external accidental means").
In Michigan, similarly, an "accident is an undesigned contingency, a casualty, a happening by chance, something out of the usual course of things, unusual, fortuitous, not anticipated, and not naturally to be expected": *Allstate Ins Co* v *Freeman*, 443 NW 2d 734, 740–741 (Mich, 1989—liability).
355. *Western Commercial Travelers' Assn* v *Smith*, 85 F 401, 405 (8 Cir, 1895—PA). Also in this sense, *Glenlight Shipping Co Ltd* v *Excess Ins Co Ltd*, 1983 SLT 241, 243 *per* Lord Robertson (Ct Sess—PA); *National & General Ins Co Ltd* v *Chick* [1984] 2 NSWLR 86, 99 (PA); *Mutual Life Ins Co* v *Dodge*, 11 F 2d 486, 488 (4 Cir, 1926—life); *Zurich General Accident & Liability Ins Co Ltd* v *Flickinger*, 33 F 2d 853 (4 Cir, 1929—PA); *Radius* v *Travelers' Ins Co*, 87 F 2d 412 (9 Cir, 1937—life); *Lang* v *Metropolitan Life Ins Co*, 115 F 2d 621 (7 Cir, 1940—PA); *Burr* v *Commercial Travelers Mutual Accident Assn*, 67 NE 2d 248 (NY, 1946—life); *Kuckenberg* v *Hartford Accident & Indemnity Co*, 226 F 2d 225 (9 Cir, 1955—liability); *Hathaway* v *Commercial Ins Co*, 380 NYS 2d 529 (1976—PA).
An accident is "an event that takes place without one's foresight or expectation: an undesigned, sudden, and unexpected event": *City of Fulton* v *Great American Indemnity Co*, 174 NYS 2d 690 (1958—PA); *American Casualty Co* v *Minnesota Farm Bureau Service Co*, 270 F 2d 686 (8 Cir, 1959—liability). In 1966, the National Bureau of Casualty Underwriters and The Mutual Insurance Rating Bureau revised the standard comprehensive liability policy in respect of "an accident . . . which results, during the policy period in bodily injury or property damage neither expected nor intended from the standpoint of the insured". This interpretation appears to have become the residual rule of law: *Saint Calle* v *Prudential Ins Co*, 815 F Supp 679 (SD NY, 1993—life). An alternative approach has been an express exception, for example, of loss

often than not.[356] Thus, courts have ruled out accident, if there is "a deliberate and reckless courting of the risk"[357]; or if the result was intended by the insured: above, 17–5B(a). Moreover, if some injury is intended or expected and thus not accidental, there is no accident even if the extent of the injury was unexpected or improbable[358]: if the insured on a beach holiday gets sunstroke, which is regarded as disease rather than accident, it makes no difference that it results unexpectedly in his death.[359] One important corollary of all this is that an accident is nonetheless an accident because it is caused by the negligence of the insured.[360]

More particularly, there is an accident, first, where the injury is the natural or probable result in or on the person of the insured of a fortuitous and unexpected occurrence in the life of the insured, which is external to the person of the insured: "for instance, where the assured is run over by a train, or thrown from his horse whilst hunting, or injured by a fall, whether through slipping on a step; or otherwise; or where the assured drinks poison by mistake, or is suffocated by the smoke of a house on fire; or by an escape of gas, or is drowned whilst bathing".[361] To take the first case, given the unexpected impact of the train, the crushed bones are a probable consequence. Still, in all these cases, the expected effect in or on the body was immediately triggered by an unexpected external occurrence and the injury is accidental.

There is an accident, second, where the injury is the fortuitous and unexpected result in or on the person of the insured of a cause that is a natural or probable occurrence in the life of the insured, which is external to the person of the insured: "for instance, where a person lifts a heavy burden in the ordinary course of business and injures his spine, or stoops down to pick up a marble and breaks a ligament in his knee, or scratches his leg while putting on a stocking, or ruptures himself while playing golf. In this case the element of accident manifests itself, not in the cause, but in its result".[362] To take the last case, golf may be a normal part of the insured's life but the rupture is unexpected. In all these cases, the unexpected effect in or on the body was immediately triggered by an everyday external occurrence and the injury is accidental.

The same might be said of many instances of illness and disease, however, illness and disease are excluded from the concept of accident by a line of distinction that is

---

caused "wilfully, intentionally or maliciously". On such clauses see Wilcox, 32 Wayne L Rev 1523 (1986). On attempts in New Zealand to avoid the "Serbonian Bog", see Rishworth [1990] NZ Recent Law Rev 109.

356. *Western Commercial Travelers' Assn* v *Smith*, 85 F 401, 406 (8 Cir, 1895—PA).

357. Baer, 17 Ottawa L Rev 631, 666 (1985) and cases cited. Notably *Candler*, below 17–5E1. *Idem: Gray* v *Barr* [1971] 2 QB 554, 586 *per* Phillimore LJ (CA—liability).

358. *Kuckenberg* v *Hartford Accident & Indemnity Co*, 226 F 2d 225 (9 Cir, 1955—liability), applied in *American Casualty Co* v *Minnesota Farm Bureau Service Co*, 270 F 2d 686 (8 Cir, 1959—liability). Further see Wilcox, 32 Wayne L Rev 1523, 1526 (1986) and cases cited.

359. *De Souza* v *Home & Overseas Ins Co Ltd, The Times*, 19 September 1990 (CA—PA).

360. *Cornish* v *Accident Ins Co Ltd* (1889) 23 QBD 543, 457 *per* Lindley LJ (CA—PA); *Gray* v *Barr* [1971] 2 QB 554, 579 *per* Salmon LJ (CA—liability); *Marcel Beller Ltd* v *Hayden* [1978] 3 All ER 111, 116 *per* Judge Fay (PA). *Canadian Indemnity Co* v *Walkem Machinery & Equipment Ltd* [1976] 1 SCR 309, 316 *per* Pigeon J; *Pickford & Black Ltd* v *Canadian General Ins Co* [1977] 2 SCR 261; [1976] 2 Lloyd's Rep 108, 112 and cases cited (liability). *Voisin* v *Royal Ins Co* (1988) 53 DLR (4th) 299 (Ont—PA). *Travelers' Ins Co* v *Randolph*, 78 F 754, 766 ff (6 Cir, 1897—PA): *Ocean Accident & Guarantee Corp Ltd* v *McLung*, 84 F 2d 844 (10 Cir, 1936—PA); *Cross* v *Zurich General Accident & Liability Co*, 184 F 2d 609 (7 Cir, 1950—liability); *American Family Life Co* v *Bilyeu*, 921 F 2d 87 (6 Cir, 1990—PA).

361. Welford, p 269, quoted with approval in *De Souza* v *Home & Overseas Ins Co Ltd, The Times*, 19 September 1990 (CA—PA).

362. Welford, pp 268 ff, quoted with approval in *De Souza* (above). See also *Hebert* and *Barry*, below 17–5F2.

sometimes very fine.[363] If "the deceased, without design, had slipped, and caused an abrasion of the skin, as he was walking down the street, or had punctured the skin of his foot by stepping on a nail in his room, or had pierced it with a nail in his shoe as he was drawing it upon his foot, there could have been no doubt that these injuries were produced by accidental means; and it is difficult to understand why an abrasion of the skin caused by wearing new shoes, does not fall within the same category."[364]

The distinction is hard to draw but has been justified on the ground that illness or disease is the "natural result of a natural cause". Modern man may take a less fatalistic view of his condition, but the modern insurer maintains the distinction to preserve a traditional classification of risk: illness (or disease) and accident are different risks.

17–5D The Time and Nature of Assessment

It has been suggested that injury is accidental, if it was neither intentional, probable nor expected, when considered from the standpoint of the time when the sequence of events begins: above, 17–5C. The choice of time is important and is usually the time of some act or omission on the part of the insured. Evidently, what is probable or expected depends on the information to be taken into account and, therefore, on the time at which it is assessed.

The time chosen might be one after the event, and the information might be all the information subsequently available to the court: the position of hindsight. The court might consider, for example, the insured's predisposition to illness, although unknown to the insured at the time of the accident.[365]

"[I]n the strictest sense and dealing with the region of physical nature there is no such thing as an accident. The smallest particle of dust swept by a storm is where it is by the operation of physical causes and which if you knew beforehand you would predict with absolute certainty that it would alight where it did."

Having said this,[366] Lord Halsbury LC went on to reject this approach to the definition of accident.[367] The relevant information is determined objectively by reference to the knowledge of the ordinary reasonable man at the time of the accident: "the test of what is expected is whether an ordinary reasonable man would not have expected the occurrence, it being irrelevant that a person with expert knowledge, for example of medicine, would have regarded it as inevitable."[368]

---

363. Although he thought that a rupture when the insured was playing golf was an accident, Welford (p 269) thought that a heart attack when he was running to catch a train was not an accident but a manifestation of disease. *Sed quaere*: both could be seen as an internal weakness triggered to a state of injury by an external stimulus.

364. *Western Commercial Travelers' Assn* v *Smith*, 85 F 401, 406 (8 Cir, 1895—PA) and cases cited. See also *Preferred Accident Ins Co* v *Combs*, 76 F 2d 775 (8 Cir, 1935); *Ins Co of N American* v *English*, 395 F 2d 854 (5 Cir, 1968). *Cf Kerns* v *Aetna Life Ins Co*, 291 F 289 (8 Cir, 1923); and *Sloboda* v *Continental Casualty Co* [1938] 3 DLR 166 (Alta—PA), in which an external contact (a shoe) caused a blister and that lead to infection and death, but the case was not regarded as an accident.

365. For example *Re Scarr* [1905] 1 KB 387.

366. *Brintons Ltd* v *Turvey* [1905] AC 230, 233. *Preferred Accident Ins Co* v *Clark*, 144 F 2d 165, 168 (10 Cir, 1944).

367. Some decisions can be understood only on the basis that the court has rejected the hindsight approach; for example, *Hamlyn* v *Crown Accident Ins Co Ltd* [1893] 1 QB 750 (CA—PA), below, 17–5F1.

368. Halsbury, Vol 22 (3rd ed), No 294, adopted in *Canadian Indemnity Co* v *Walkem Machinery & Equipment Ltd* [1976] 1 SCR 309 (liability); and *Cansulex Ltd* v *Reed Stenhouse Ltd* (1986) 70 BCLR 273 (BC—liability).

17–5D1 The Time of the Accident

A distinct point, which a court must sometimes pin down, is the time of the accident. An element of fortuity is essential to the sequence of events leading to injury but it does not follow that the accident occurred at the time of the fortuity. On the contrary, the courts generally find that an accident does not occur until there is some injury or other loss.

In *Pickford & Black Ltd* v *Canadian General Ins Co*,[369] a contractor's public liability insurance was limited to accidents occurring in Canada. In Halifax, Nova Scotia, the insured contractor negligently stowed cargo on a ship bound for Ghana but it was outside Canadian waters, when the cargo shifted and was damaged. The Supreme Court of Canada held that the accident occurred outside Canada and hence outside the scope of the cover. On a natural and ordinary meaning of the words used, what mattered was not where the accident was caused (Canada) but where it occurred (outside Canada).[370]

Unless the wording is clear, the answer depends in part on why the court asks the question and what the court wants to achieve. If the question before the court is whether the accident falls within the cover period and answer A gives the insured cover but answer B does not, the courts are more likely to give answer A.[371] This is seen in the decision of a Californian court,[372] for example, that the "occurrence" of an accident was the later time during cover when the complaining party was actually damaged, rather than the time of the wrongful act initiating the sequence of events, gradual seepage and subsidence; and in an English case,[373] in which a person suffered lead poisoning during the insurance period but did not die until later; death was seen as an extension of actual damage occurring during the policy period. In each case the entire injury or damage was covered.

17–5E Public Policy: Relative Recklessness

Injury resulting from reckless conduct by the insured is not accidental: above, 17–5C. As with breach of the duty of care in the law of tort, recklessness is a relative notion which is shaped in part by value judgments more or less reflecting public policy. There is much to be said for the view,[374] however, that "accident" should be defined clearly rather than flexibly and that, if courts wish to introduce public policy, they should do so more overtly.

17–5E1 The Social Utility of the Activity

The courts are more likely to find cover, if the objectives pursued by the insured at the time of the "accident" were "worthy". Action leading to injury, which is reckless if

---

369. [1977] 1 SCR 261; [1976] 2 Lloyd's Rep 108. See also *State Farm Fire Co* v *Thomas*, 756 F Supp 440, 443 (ND Cal, 1991—liability). *Cf Cansulex* (above), in which the damage (corrosion) was continuous and began inside Canada: held that the accident occurred in Canada.

370. [1976] 2 Lloyd's Rep 108, 112 *per* Ritchie J. The trial judge had construed accident as "accident due to the operations of the insured", and thus felt able to follow the chain of causation back to Halifax, finding there in the negligent stowage a sufficient connection with Canada. The Supreme Court did not agree.

371. See further, above, 17–4C.

372. *California Union Ins Co* v *Landmark Ins Co*, 193 Cal Rptr 461, 465 (Cal, 1983—liability).

373. *Mayer & Sherratt* v *Cooperative Ins Sy Ltd* [1939] 2 KB 627 (CA—employers' liability). See further, below, 18–1B.

374. Davidson [1984] JBL 391, 397.

undertaken to show off, may not be regarded as reckless if undertaken for a useful purpose[375] or if taken out of necessity.[376]

For example, in *Lester*,[377] holding that the death of a national guardsman while on duty was accidental, the US Court of Appeals observed: "In the pursuit of duty he simply exposed himself to the hazard of the service. He may have contemplated death or injury as possible, or *even probable*: but, if he did, this would not take him out of the protection of his accident insurance." Compare *Candler*[378]: to demonstrate his nerve, the insured balanced on a parapet on the thirteenth floor of a hotel and fell to his death. The High Court of Ontario held that this was not an accident, saying,[379] that the decision would have been different, however, if the parapet had crumbled or if the action had been undertaken for some "useful purpose". For similar reasons, courts in the USA have held that death playing the "precarious and ridiculous game of Russian Roulette" is not accidental, even though death was no more than foreseeable.[380]

17–5E2 General Practice

Courts are influenced by the common practices of the context or trade in which the accident occurred.[381]

17–5E3 Anti-Social Conduct

The court may decline cover to conduct of which it strongly disapproves. In such cases injury, which is no more than reasonably foreseeable and which therefore would normally be accidental, may be held non-accidental and uninsured.

---

375. Merkin & McGee, p B.8.2–04, citing *Pugh v London, Brighton & S Coast Ry* [1896] 2 QB 248 (CA—disability); *Neil v Travelers' Ins Co* (1885) 12 SCR 55, 63 *per* Strong J (PA); *Canadian Ry Accident Ins Co v McNevin* (1902) 32 SCR 194, 204 *per* Sedgewick J, 210 *per* Mills J (PA). *Travelers' Ins Co v Seaver*, 19 Wall 531 (Sup Ct USA, 1874—PA); *Baker v Life & Accident Ins Co*, 298 SW 2d 715, 717 (Tenn, 1957—PA); *Ramsden v Egan*, 458 NYS 2d 1 (1982—PA).

376. *Southard v Railway Passengers' Assurance Co*, 22 F Cas No 13,182 (D Conn, 1868—PA).

377. *Interstate Business Men's Accident Assn v Lester*, 257 F 225, 230 (8 Cir, 1919—PA), cert den 250 US 662 (1919)—emphasis added.

378. *Candler v London & Lancashire Guarantee & Accident Co* (1963) 40 DLR (2d) 408. See also *Allred v Prudential Ins Co*, 100 SE 2d 226 (NC, 1957).

See also cases concerning variations of "Russian Roulette": in *Ramsden v Regan*, 458 NYS 2d 1 (1982), the New York court held that the insured had been "wilfully negligent" and hence could not recover under an accidental death benefit statute. The court may have been influenced by the fact that the insured was a policeman (off duty) whose training should have led him to know better. Other such cases are *Baker v Life & Accident Ins Co*, 298 SW 2d 715, 717 (Tenn, 1957—PA); *Koger v Mutual of Omaha Ins Co*, 163 SE 2d 672 (W Va, 1968—PA); *Nicholas v Provident Life & Accident Ins Co*, 457 SW 2d 536 (Tenn, 1970—PA). Cf *National & General Ins Co Ltd v Chick* [1984] 2 NSWLR 86 (NSW—PA) in which a similar death was held accidental because (p 100) there was no deliberate risk that the gun would fire, the insured (negligently) believing that the chamber was empty. Also in the latter sense: *Gulf Life Ins Co v Nash*, 97 So 2d 4 (Fla, 1957—life).

379. (1963) 40 DLR (2d) 408, 422–423.

380. See *Ramsden v Regan* (above).

381. *Pacific Mutual Life Ins Co v Snowden*, 58 F 342 (8 Cir, 1893—PA); *Baker v Life & Accident Ins Co*, 298 SW 2d 715, 717 (Tenn, 1957—PA).

(a) *Provocation*. In *Lewis* v *INA*[382] the insured came home in the middle of the night and ejected the woman, with whom he had been living, striking her as he did so; she shot him dead with the pistol, which he had previously given her. The court held that his death was not an accident: "Texas law is clear to the effect that a person who should *reasonably have foreseen* that his conduct might provoke the use of deadly force against him cannot be said to have encountered accidental death."[383]

(b) *Drugs*. In *Jones* v *Prudential Ins Co*[384] the insured put a bag over his head, sniffed nail varnish remover "for kicks" and died. The Ontario court held that this was not an accident because he "knew or ought to have known that death might well ensue".[385] In the United States, there are similar decisions concerning death during autoerotic practices with drugs,[386] although a more tolerant attitude than can be expected today was found in 1976 in *Miller*[387]: the court decided that the death of the 20-year-old insured from an overdose of heroin was covered by a group policy against death from bodily injuries caused by accident; the US Court of Appeals said[388]:

> "In today's society, the knowledge has been forced upon us that heroin and other drugs are most often taken to induce a temporary aura of relaxation and well-being completely incompatible with any desire on the part of the users to depart life. When we add to that fact that the brotherly admonition that 'it is bad for you' is likely to make as small an impression on the drug users as do, for example, the regularly ignored official government warnings about the dire effects of cigarette smoking, can it be said that the trial court did not have a right to conclude that Douglas Miller, in injecting drugs into his bloodstream, did so without any thought of death in mind? We think not . . . He may have used bad judgment, he *may have been reckless* but everything points to the fact that he did not want to bring bereavement and sadness to his mother."

(c) *Alcohol*. Alcohol has been has not been viewed in the same way as other drugs. For example, in New York in *Morgan* v *Indemnity Ins Co*,[389] the court held that death by an overdose of sleeping pills was accidental but death by overindulgence with alcohol was not; but in Missouri in *Commercial Ins Co* v

---

382. 416 F 2d 1077 (5 Cir, 1969—PA). Likewise, in *Davis* v *Equitable Life Assurance Sy*, 114 NYS 2d 814 (1952—PA), the court held that the death of the insured was not an accident because he "should have foreseen" that, when he threatened his wife with a knife, "some type of force was likely to be applied in retaliation" (p 815). See also in similar vein: *Occidental Life Ins Co* v *Holcomb*, 10 F 2d 125 (5 Cir, 1925—life); *Freed* v *Protective Life Ins Co*, 405 F Supp 175 (SD Miss, 1975—life), affirmed 551 F 2d 861 (5 Cir, 1977—PA). *Cf Railway Mail Assn* v *Mosely*, 211 F 1 (6 Cir, 1914—life); *Wade's Estate* v *Continental Ins Co*, 514 F 2d 304 (8 Cir, 1975—PA); *John Hancock Mutual Life Ins Co* v *Dutton*, 585 F 2d 1289 (5 Cir, 1978—life).

383. 416 F 2d 1077, 1079 (emphasis added). See also *Aliff* v *Travelers Ins Co*, 734 F Supp 232, 235 (WD Va, 1990—PA).

384. (1971) 24 DLR (3d) 683. In England, in *Beller (Marcel) Ltd* v *Hayden* [1978] QB 694, the court declined to follow this decision in the case of driving a vehicle under the influence of alcohol; see below, 17–5E3(c).

385. p 688.

386. *Runge* v *Metroplitan Life Ins Co*, 537 F 2d 1157 (4 Cir, 1976—life); *Sigler* v *Mutual Benefit Ins Co*, 506 F Supp 542 (SD Iowa, 1981—PA); *International Underwriters Inc* v *Home Ins Co*, 662 F 2d 1084 (4 Cir, 1981—PA). In such cases, it is usually enough that death should have been (merely) "foreseen" by the insured, for a finding that death was not accidental. *Cf Connecticut General Life Ins Co* v *Tommie*, 619 SW 2d 199 (1981—PA) in which the Texas court applied a similar test but decided that death was accidental.

387. *Miller* v *Continental Ins Co*, 389 NYS 2d 565 (1976). See also *Marsh* v *Metropolitan Life Ins Co*, 388 NE 2d 1121 (Ill, 1979—PA); and *Johnson* v *Mutual of Omaha Ins Co* (1982) 139 DLR (3d) 358, 369 (Ont—PA), affirmed (1984) 8 DLR (4th) 640 (Ont).

388. pp 566–567 (emphasis added).

389. 90 NE 2d 228 (1951—PA); see also *Chen* v *Metropolitan Ins Co*, 907 F 2d 566 (5 Cir, 1990—PA).

Orr,[390] the jury decided that the insured alcoholic, who choked to death on his own vomit after drinking, had suffered an accident that was[391] "unusual, unexpected and unforeseen".

One of the few reported cases in England is *Beller (Marcel) Ltd* v *Hayden*.[392] On Christmas Eve 1975, the insured drove from pub 1 to a party, from there to pub 2, and was driving back to pub 1 when, on a bend that may have been damp but was not icy, he turned the car over and was killed. In his bloodstream was more than three times the amount of alcohol permitted (to drivers) by law.[393] Was it an accident? The court, finding little help in precedent,[394] held that the insured did not intend to kill himself and therefore the result was accidental. This is perhaps a charitable view,[395] which sits uneasily with other decisions holding that the results of recklessness are not accidental above, 17.5C. It is true but not enough to say that, as he approached the fatal bend, he did not intend to kill himself: it gives to subjective intention of the insured at the very last moment in a sequence of acts and omissions an importance that is not generally recognised in this branch of English law: below, 17–5F3. At some earlier point in the evening, the insured must have made the decision to have the drink that "took him over the limit", knowing that he would probably drive his car later on, and then another and then another, thus initiating or at least pushing forward the chain of events to the moment when he started the last journey to his death. Clearly, what is to be expected depends on the time at which the matter is assessed (above, 17–5D), and the choice of time largely determines the answer: it is not obvious that the court here chose the right time and the court did not explain its choice.

(d) *Crime.* If the insured is injured while committing a crime, it is either treated as a case of accident like any other or, if public policy influences the decision at all, the case is treated in the same way as any other involving illegality: the court balances the public policy factors in issue: below, 24–5A.

The first approach is seen in many of the cases (above (b) and (c)) con-

---

390. 379 F 2d 865 (8 Cir, 1967—PA).

391. p 874. See also *Tracy–Gould* v *Maritime Life Assurance Co* (1992) 89 DLR (4th) 726 (NS—life), affirmed (1992) 98 DLR 741.

392. [1978] QB 694; [1978] 1 Lloyd's Rep 472 (PA). A similar decision in Canada is *Mutual of Omaha Ins Co* v *Stats* (1978) 87 DLR (3d) 169, (Sup Ct, Canada), discussed below, 17–5F3, and by Rendall, (1978) 9 Manitoba LJ 101; also see *McConkey Imperial Life Ins Co* [1973] ILR 579 (Ont—motor); *Insurance Corp of British Columbia* v *Casey* (1985) 63 BCLR 387 (motor), discussed by Wexler, 20 UBCL Rev 305 (1986).

USA: see *Miller* v *American Casualty Co*, 377 F 2d 479 (6 Cir, 1967—PA). In contrast, the courts of Tennessee have held that such a case is "a foreseeable result of a voluntary and unnecessary act or course of conduct of the insured" and as such not accidental: *Hobbs* v *Provident Life & Accident Ins Co*, 535 SW 2d 864, 866 (1975—PA).

In other contexts, driving under the influence of alcohol (*Boral Resources (Queensland) Pty Ltd* v *Pyke* (1989) 5 ANZ Ins Cas 60–942) or fatigue (*Jones* v *Bencher* [1986] 1 Lloyd's Rep 54) has been condemned as "wilful misconduct".

393. In evidence, his friend said that he had had about eight rum and cokes in a period of five hours; the pathologist thought it was about 17. The legal limit was 80 mgs of blood alcohol per 100 millilitres of blood; most people are incapable of dealing with an emergency at 150 millilitres; the deceased had 261.

394. While regarding himself as bound by *Gray* v *Barr* [1971] 2 QB 554 (CA—PA), the judge (p 75) found three different views of the law on this issue on that case and, therefore, felt free to adopt a view of his own which, however, was not unlike that of Salmon LJ in *Gray* (p 580).

395. It may be significant that the ultimate decision was for the insurer under an exception of "death or disablement directly or indirectly resulting from . . . the insured person's own criminal act".

cerning alcohol and other drugs. Another case is *Harrington*,[396] in which the insured died in a road accident while seeking to evade arrest by the police for kidnap and rape. The Canadian court found that "that, although the deceased intended to escape the police by speeding away in his car, there is no evidence that he intended to kill himself as a result of his actions, and therefore his death was accidental within the meaning of the life insurance contract at issue. His death was not the rational and probable consequence of his intended act of flight".[397]

The second approach is seen in *Brown*,[398] in which the Mississippi court held that a woman, who perished painfully in the house fire that she had started, died an accidental death. The court rejected the insurer's defence based on public policy. "The primary reason to deny benefits to an insured under the public policy doctrine is to prevent that insured from reaping the rewards of his own misconduct. Obviously, such a denial would serve the public policy concerns of deterring crime. However, in this case, the beneficiary is innocent to the act. No one contends that the plaintiff", who was co-insured, "played any role in his wife's criminal scheme. Rather, he paid monthly premiums to the insurance company and reasonably expected that he would receive the proceeds of the policy. Against this backdrop, where a beneficiary is innocent of any wrongdoing, the concern of encouraging crime is outweighed by these considerations."[399]

17–5F Possible Variations

17–5F1 Accidental Means and Accidental Results

The decision sometimes turns on whether it is the chain of events (means), which is accidental, or whether it is the final result (loss, damage, death or injury), which is accidental. This distinction is drawn in Canada and some parts of the United States but it has not been influential in England. In English law (above 17–5C), if the chain is composed of probable events, the result is no less probable than the weakest link in the chain. If at the appropriate point prior to the result it can be said that the result is probable, the (chain of) events (means) leading to that result must be no less probable.[400] In England, therefore, the interpretation is the same, whether the policy talks of an accidental result, such as injury or death, or refers to a result brought about "by accidental means".

---

396. *Harrington* v *New England Mutual Life Ins Co*, 873 F 2d 166 (7 Cir, 1989—life).

397. p 169. *Cf Oakes* v *Sun Life Assurance Co* (1979) 93 DLR (3d) 80 (BC—life); and *Wawanesa Mutual Ins Co* v *Thomas* (1982) 139 DLR (3d) 56 (NS—motor). The court in *Harrington* indicated (p 168) that, if death had resulted from the victim's act of self-defence, the decision might have been different; and emphasised (p 169) that the case was about a contract dispute between an innocent beneficiary and an insurance company—an insurance company which could easily have included a (common) clause that prohibited recovery where death was caused by "participation in felony"; see *Bilyeu* (below).

398. *Brown* v *American International Life Co*, 778 F Supp 912 (SD Miss, 1991—PA).

399. p 918. In that case, the court pointed out that there was no clause against recovery. In *American Family Life Co* v *Bilyeu*, 921 F 2d 87, 89 (6 Cir, 1990—PA), the accident policy contained an exclusion of death occurring "during the commission of a crime", however, the court held the insured covered, although he was intoxicated and driving at excessive speed when his car hit a tree, because, the court considered, people would regard burglary, robbery and murder as "crime" but not drunken driving.

400. *City of Fulton* v *Great American Indemnity Co*, 174 NYS 2d 690, 697 (1958—PA). *Cf Candler* v *London & Lancs Guarantee & Accident* (1963) 40 DLR (2d) 408, 414 (PA). The distinction was doubted in *Tracy-Gould* v *Maritime Life Assurance Co* (1992) 98 DLR (4th) 741 (NS—life).

In the leading English case of *Hamlyn* v *Crown Accident Ins Co Ltd*,[401] the insurance covered "any bodily injury caused by violent, accidental, external and visible means". The insured bent forward in his shop to pick up a marble from the sloping floor and wrenched a ligament in his knee. The insurer argued that it was the means and not the result which must be unintended and thus accidental; that he intended to bend and therefore the result was not brought about by accidental means. The insured argued that it was an accident because, although he intended to bend, he did not intend to wrench his knee. The Court of Appeal held that it was an accident, Lord Esher MR saying[402]: "He did not mean to wrench his knee, and that would not be the ordinary result of such an action." Lopes LJ said[403]: "The cause of the injury was accidental in the sense that the injury was a casualty, unforeseen and unexpected." Similarly, if the insured "twisted his knee playing tennis and the injury caused blood clots that embolized to his lungs and killed him", then "the means of death—the injury to the knee—would be an accident, and the death would be covered".[404]

Support for the distinction between means and results can be found in Australia,[405] Canada[406] and, although less often than before,[407] in the United States.[408] However, in many of these cases the examination of "means" has focused on the initial conduct of the insured (or other original "cause"[409]), which was found to be intentional conduct by the insured and, as such, was a (separate) ground for a decision against accident (below, 17–5F2).[410] For example, if the insured intended to drink the bottle of whisky, got drunk and died by asphyxiation when he choked on his own food, although the result (death) was not expected, the means (intoxication) were intentio-

---

401. [1893] 1 QB 750. See also *Mills* v *Smith* [1964] 1 QB 30, 39 *per* Paull J (liability); *Glenlight Shipping Co Ltd* v *Excess Ins Co Ltd*, 1983 SLT 241, especially p 245 *per* Lord Stott (Ct Sess—PA).

402. p 753. *Cf* A L Smith LJ (p 755), who looked to the means rather than the result: it was "accidental, for getting into the particular position in which the injury could happen was not done on purpose".

403. p 754.

404. *Senkier* v *Hartford Life & Accident Ins Co*, 948 F 2d 1050, 1052 (7 Cir, 1991—PA).

405. *National & General Ins Co Ltd* v *Chick* [1984] 2 NSWLR 86 (PA). Sutton, p 132. In *Chick*, the insured obviously intended to put the gun to his head and to pull the trigger (in the belief that there was no bullet in the firing position). To find the means accidental, the court had to rely on the unexpected discharge in the fraction of a second between his pulling the trigger and death. *Cf Australian Casualty Co Ltd* v *Federico* (1986) 160 CLR 513 (HCA—disability), which appears to take the English position.

406. *Smith* v *British Pacific Life Assurance Co* (1965) 51 DLR 2d 1 (Sup Ct—PA); *Leontowicz* v *Seaboard Life Ins Co*, 58 A R 66 (Alta, 1984—PA), criticised by Baer, 17 Ottawa L Rev 631, 667 (1985) as "irresponsible pedantry masquerading as reluctant but loyal acceptance of higher authority". In *Leontowicz*, p 102, the court preferred "the robust attitude adopted by the English courts in dealing with worker's compensation", but felt bound by *Smith*. Subsequently, the distinction was maintained in *Aguilar* v *London Life Ins Co* (1990) 70 DLR (4th) 510 (Man—PA), but rejected in *Tracy–Gould* v *Maritime Life Assurance Co* (1992) 89 DLR (4th) 726 (NS—life), in which *Smith* was distinguished.

407. Ingram and Ostfeld, 12 Florida State U L Rev 1 (1984). Cases, which reject or avoid the distinction between means and result, include *United States Fidelity & Guarantee Co* v *Blum*, 270 F 946, 954 (9 Cir, 1921—PA); *Lang* v *Metropolitan Life Ins Co*, 115 F 2d 621 (7 Cir, 1940—PA); *Minton* v *Stuyvesant Life Ins Co*, 373 F Supp 33 (D Nev, 1974—life); *Florama* v *Monumental Life Ins Co*, 447 F Supp 354 (ND Ill, 1978—PA).

In particular, the distinction between means and result has not been followed in New York: *Preferred Accident Ins Co* v *Clark*, 144 F 2d 165 (10 Cir, 1944—PA); *Burr* v *Commercial Travelers Mutual Accident Assn*, 67 NE 2d 248, 252 (NY 1946—life); *Miller* v *Continental Ins Co*, 389 NYS 2d 565 (1976—PA).

408. *Landress* v *Phoenix Mutual Life Ins Co*, 291 US 491 (1934—PA); *Commercial Travelers' Ins Co* v *Walsh*, 228 F 2d 200 (9 Cir, 1955—PA); *Prudential Life Ins Co* v *Gutowski*, 113 A 2d 579 (Del, 1955—life); *American Casualty Co* v *Gerald*, 369 F 2d 829 (4 Cir, 1966—CA).

409. In this sense: 45 CJS No 753(b).

410. *Dubuque Fire & Marine Ins Co* v *Caylor*, 249 F 2d 162, 165 (10 Cir, 1957—construction equipment); *Commercial Ins Co of Newark* v *Orr*, 379 F 2d 865, 870 and cases cited (1967); Ingram and Ostfeld, 12 Florida State ULR 1, 6 (1984).

nal and the case was not one of accident.[411] English law takes a different view of intentional conduct of the insured initiating the chain of events and this, it seems, is the real point of difference. From the premise that the intentional character of the insured's initiating act is not conclusive against an accidental result (above 17–5B), English law regards the distinction between means and results as unworkable and shares the view of Cardozo J[412] that, if adopted, the distinction would "plunge this branch of the law into a Serbonian Bog".

17–5F2 Intentional Conduct

In English law, intention deprives loss (including injury) of accidental character, if the loss was the intended result of the insured's act: above, 17–5B. In Canada and some parts of the United States, some decisions go further: conduct is not accidental, if the chain of events was initiated by intentional conduct on the part of the insured, whether or not the result was either intended or probable.

In *Smith*,[413] for example, the insured rocked a motor car stuck in a snow drift, suffered a heart attack and died. The Supreme Court of Canada held that this was not an accident, because the insured intended to exert himself by rocking the car. In *Benante*,[414] the United States court held that, when the insured ran to catch an aeroplane and suffered a heart attack, that was not an accident: he intended to run.[415] One difficulty about decisions like these is that nearly every injury is preceded by an intentional act on the part of the insured which, with the benefit of hindsight, appears to be more or less related to the injury that follows and that, if these decisions are applied

411. This was the unsuccessful contention of the insurer in *Tracy–Gould* v *Maritime Life Assurance Co* (1992) 89 DLR (4th) 726 (NS—life).

412. Dissenting in *Landress* (above), p 499. In 1966, the National Bureau of Casualty Underwriters and The Mutual Insurance Rating Bureau revised the standard comprehensive liability policy in respect of "an accident . . . which results, during the policy period in bodily injury or property damage neither expected nor intended from the standpoint of the insured". One purpose of the revision was to clarify the law on the alleged distinction between accidental means and results. The effect is thought to be that loss is accidental unless the insured intended both the act and the loss: Wilcox, 32 Wayne L Rev 1523, 1525 (1986). The interpretation of this clause, which has given rise to much litigation, is affected by public policy and notions of illegality; see below, 24–5B. In any event, courts now prefer the view of Cardozo J: *Wickman* v *Northwestern National Ins Co*, 908 F 2d 1077, 1086 (1 Cir, 1990—life). *Cf Groves* v *AMP Fire & Gen Ins Co (NZ) Ltd* [1990] 1 NZLR 124 (PA).

413. *Smith* v *British Pacific Life Assurance Co* (1965) 51 DLR 2d 1 (PA) following *Columbia Cellulose Co* v *Continental Casualty Co* (1964) 42 DLR 2d 401 (Sup Ct—PA). *Cf Voisin* v *Royal Ins Co* (1988) 53 DLR (4th) 299, 304 (Ont—PA).

In England, a similar decision is *Re Scarr* [1905] 1 KB 387: the insured did not know that he had a weak heart. In the course of his job he exerted himself to remove a drunk from the premises and this resulted in his death from a heart attack. Bray J held this was not an accident, for he intended to exert himself to remove the drunk. In all the circumstances, including the heart condition, ignorance of which, the judge held, made no difference, there was no fortuity: the heart attack was the "natural and direct" consequence of his intended conduct and thus not an accident. Also in this sense: *Clidero* v *Scottish Accident Ins Co* (1892) 19 R 355 (Ct Sess—PA). *Long* v *Colonial Mutual Life Assurance Sy* [1931] NZLR 528 (PA).

414. *Benante* v *Allstate Ins Co*, 477 F 2d 553 (5 Cir, 1973—PA).

415. *McMahon* v *Mutual Benefit Health & Accident Assn*, 206 P 2d 292 (1945), which held that, when there is (1) an intentional act (the administration of anaesthetic), (2) a pre-existing bodily condition (thrombosis)) which, as a result of the act, caused (3) unexpected death, the death was not by accidental means; and that, even if the surgeon was in error, the decision would have been the same, because the act was intentional. In *Zinn Equitable Life Ins Co*, 107 P 2d 921 (1940—life), however, the same court said that it was an accidental death, if the intentional act had occurred during an operation necessitated by infection. Why, therefore, did the *McMahon* court not consider what gave rise to the operation (for herniated discs)?

A similar view of intention was taken in *Shanberg* v *Fidelity & Casualty Co*, 158 F 1 (8 Cir, 1907—PA); *Nellenback* v *Metropolitan Life Ins Co*, 3 NYS 2d 657 (1938—PA); *Johnson* v *National Life & Accident Ins Co*, 90 SE 2d 36 (Ga, 1955—PA); and *Blumenthal* v *New York Life Ins Co*, 172 NYS 2d 757 (1958—PA).

literally, few mishaps in human affairs will be accidents; the man who buys accident insurance will get very little cover for his money.[416]

Uneasy with reasoning found in cases like *Smith* (above), other courts have sought to soften its effects. In *Hebert* v *Hughes Tool Co*,[417] the insured company manager had a massive heart attack in his office at the age of 49, as the result of arteriosclerosis and job-related stress. The court held that this was a case of illness rather than accident but indicated that, if the attack had been preceded by the slightest incident, even a minor one such as tripping over a couch,[418] precipitating death, the decision might have been different. Earlier, in *Flickinger*,[419] a death during the prohibition era was held accidental because the insured "intended, it is true, to drink the cocktails which he did drink and which caused his death, but he did not intend to drink poisonous wood alcohol, and did not know that wood alcohol was contained in what he was drinking". The initiating act was seen not as drinking (intended) but as drinking wood alcohol (unintended), with accidental results.

Better, it is submitted, to disregard the intentional character of the initiating act, except in so far as that bears on probability of injury (above, 17–5B). Support is found in *Barry*[420]: a doctor aged 30 jumped four feet from a platform, injured his duodenum and died. While excluding death from disease, the insurance covered "death . . . occasioned by bodily injuries alone effected through external, violent, and accidental means". The Supreme Court of the United States held that the death was covered by the policy. Mr Justice Blatchford stressed that, although the doctor intended to jump, he might land in an unintended way and any injury sustained could still be an accident.[421] More recently, in *Romanosky*,[422] the insured, having been ejected from a discotheque by bouncers, fired buckshot at the front door of the club; he intended to damage the door and not, as occurred, to injure a person inside the club. The insurer pleaded an exclusion relating to bodily injury that was "expected or intended" by the insured. The court in New York decided for the insured on the basis that the injuries were the "accidental result of [the insured's] intentional act".[423]

The rule in *Barry* is also the rule in England. Apart from *Hamlyn* (above, 17–5F1),

---

416. The actual decisions, as well as that in *Hebert* (below), are more easily justifed as cases not of heart "attack" but of heart disease: the intentional and perfectly normal act (pushing or running) was but the final and perfectly normal straw in the life of a man suffering from disease—which is therefore not a case of accident below, 17–5G.

417. 539 So 2d 789 (La, 1989—accidental death).

418. p 791. Stress (and the events producing it) is not such an accident (p 792).

419. *Zurich General Accident & Liability Ins Co* v *Flickinger*, 33 F 2d 853, 854 (4 Cir, 1929—PA). See also *Commercial Travelers' Ins Co* v *Walsh*, 228 F 2d 200 (9 Cir, 1955—PA).

420. *Mutual Accident Assn* v *Barry*, 131 US 100 (1889) See also *Mutual Life Ins Co York* v *Dodge*, 11 F 2d 486 (4 Cir, 1926—life); *Lang* v *Metropolitan Life Ins Co*, 115 F 2d 621 (7 Cir, 1940—PA); *Cross* v *Zurich General Accident & Liability Ins Co*, 184 F 2d 609 (7 Cir, 1950—liability); *Hathaway* v *Commercial Ins Co*, 380 NYS 2d 529 (1976—PA); *Miller* v *Continental Ins Co*, 389 NYS 2d 565 (1976—PA); *Golden Eagle Liberia Ltd* v *St Paul Fire & Marine Ins Co,* 685 F Supp 393, 397 (SD NY, 1988—liability); *Brown Foundation* v *St. Paul Ins Co*, 814 SW 2d 273 (Ky, 1991—liability); *Hairston* v *Liberty National Life Ins Co*, 584 So 2d 807 (Ala, 1991—life); *Village of Morrisville* v *US Fidelity & Guaranty Co*, 775 F Supp 718 (D Vt, 1991—liability); *Vorheers* v *Preferred Mutual Ins Co*, 607 A 2d 1255, 1261 (NJ, 1992—liability).

421. p 110. He also concluded (p 121) that death would not be an accident if it were "such as follows from ordinary means, voluntarily employed, in a not unusual or unexpected way".

422. *Barry* v *Romanosky* 538 NYS 2d 14 (1989—liability). Apparently, this position has been taken consistently by the courts in Massachusetts: Boyle and O'Malley, 25 New England L Rev 827, 831 (1991). Also in this sense: *Groves* v *AMP Fire & General Ins Co (NZ) Ltd* [1990] 1 NZLR 124 (PA).

423. p 16. The possibility that enforcement of the insurance might be contrary to public policy (below 24–7B) was not discussed.

this view is found in *Fenton*[424]: a workman was ruptured while over-exerting himself to turn a wheel in the course of his employment. The House of Lords held that this was an accident under the Workmen's Compensation Act 1897. An accident, in the words of Lord Macnaghten, was a mishap "which is not expected or designed".[425] It was "any unexpected personal injury".[426] The argument that this could not be an accident, because the workman intended to exert force to turn the wheel was decisively rejected. "The fallacy of the argument" said Lord Robertson[427] "lies in leaving out of account the miscalculation of forces, or inadvertence to them, which is the element of . . . mishap." Moreover,[428] Lord Macnaghten was influenced by the purpose of the legislature in relation to the workplace: if an intentional act by a workman could never give rise to an accident and to compensation, "it would not conduce to honesty or thoroughness in work. It would lead men to shirk and hang back, and try to shift a burthen which might possibly prove too heavy for them on to the shoulders of their comrades." If this is true of the workplace, it must to a degree be true also of other situations, for which people take insurance. Indeed, it can be argued that one of the purposes of insurance is to provide a degree of security which promotes enterprise.[429]

Although their relevance to ordinary insurance cases has been doubted, cases on workmens' compensation have been relied upon in a number of cases of ordinary insurance[430] as far afield as Australia, where the High Court observed that Lord Macnaghten's definition of accident (above), "although propounded in a Workmens' Compensation Act case, has commonly been accepted as applicable to the use of the word in public liability and other insurance policies".[431] A constant refrain in both PA cases and in cases under the Acts is that there must be something "unintended and unexpected".[432]

In England, however, the doubts about the relevance of workmen's compensation cases to ordinary insurance must be taken seriously. First, it is said that the workmen's cases may be coloured by the drafting of the policy[433]—but it is true today of all kinds of insurance that the meaning of a word is subject to the colour it acquires from the context of the policy,[434] and to interpretation in favour of the insured.[435] The second doubt is more serious and turns on the purpose of the legislation, which, as inter-

---

424. *Fenton* v *Thorley & Co Ltd* [1903] AC 443. See also the discussion of intention by Lord Sumner in *Samuel & Co Ltd* v *Dumas* [1924] AC 431, 463 (hull).
425. p 448 *per* Lord Macnaghten.
426. p 451 *per* Lord Shand. Lord Robertson (p 452) stressed that the word "accident" should be given its popular and ordinary meaning.
427. p 452. See also p 446 *per* Lord Macnaghten.
428. p 447.
429. For example, Cockerell, *Insurance*, chapter 1.
430. For example, *Weyerhaeuser* v *Evans* (1932) 43 L L Rep 62 (PA); *Smith* v *Cornhill Ins Co* [1938] 3 All ER 145 (PA); *Glenlight Shipping Co Ltd* v *Excess Ins Co Ltd*, 1983 SLT 241 (Ct Sess—life). If the policy uses the words of legislation, "injury or damage caused by accident", it will be assumed that the same meaning was intended: *Mills* v *Smith* [1964] 1 QB 30, 36 *per* Paull J (liability), counsel in *Smith* v *Cornhill* (above). See also *Mutual Of Omaha Ins Co* v *Stats* (1978) 87 DLR (3d) 169, 182 (Sup. Ct. Canada).
431. *Australian Cas Co Ltd* v *Federico* (1986) 160 CLR 513, 527 (HCA—PA), cited in *Suncorp Ins* v *Ploner* (1989) 12 Qd Lawyer Reps 57, 60 (motor), affirmed [1991] 1 Qd R 69 (FC).
432. Willis's, *Workmen's Compensation Acts* (37th ed, 1945), pp 8 ff.
433. *Ibid*, p 449, *per* Lord Macnaghten and pp 454–455 *per* Lord Lindley. See also the view of Lord Sumner in *Samuel & Co Ltd* v *Dumas* [1924] AC 431, 464 (hull), that the illumination in such cases was "dim", and that it was better to proceed by the "light of reason". See further *Wicks* v *Dowell & Co Ltd* [1905] 2 KB 225, 229 *per* Lord Collins MR (workmen's compensation).
434. MacGillivray, No 1762.
435. See above, 15–5A and 15–5C.

preted by the courts, is avowedly generous to workmen particularly in cases that general insurance might see as cases not of accident but of illness.

Most recently, doubts were expressed in *DeSouza* [436] by Mustill LJ: the range of diseases covered by the Workmen's Compensation Acts had been limited, the judges were tempted to exercise ingenuity in devising an error of law when the arbitrator's decision (final) on a question of fact seemed unjust, and the courts role as instruments of a new social policy was unfamiliar, with the result that it was impossible today to reconstruct the judicial atmosphere which existed when these decisions were made. The judge discerned in the reports of those cases "a desire to see that the widows of men who had died through working hard on their employer's behalf should not be left without redress", which "led the courts on several occasions to call for the words of the statute to be given a 'popular' or 'loose' meaning". In other words, but not his words, the courts construed then, as some might now, in favour of the insured and in line with the reasonable expectations of the insured. [437] Those who took the benefit of labour also bore some of the risk. If the workman was not compensated under the Acts, he would probably not be compensated at all. These are considerations that do not apply to ordinary PA insurance, which is a cheap and useful product that will be withdrawn if it is stretched too far into the deeper waters of PHI.

17–5F3 Lack of Awareness

"A person may have been negligent or even grossly negligent but at the time that the person performed the acts in question he might never have thought himself to be negligent. If, on the other hand, the person realized the danger of his actions and deliberately assumed the risk of it . . . his actions could not be characterised as accidental." [438]

A lack of awareness of risk has been used by some courts to characterise as accidental the consequences of acts influenced by alcohol or other drugs: if the insured courts a danger deliberately [439] and is injured, there is no accident, but if he does so while drunk or drugged the result is an accident. More generally, a rule of this kind turning on awareness has been applied in Canada and has brought an element of subjectivity into the test of accident, which is not found in England. [440]

In *Stats*, [441] the insured, Mrs Brown, was "grossly intoxicated", when the car that she was driving hit a wall in central Toronto, and she and her passenger died. The trial judge held that this was not an accident, for she "had to know" that a casualty was the probable consequence of driving in the manner and circumstances that she did. On appeal, however, it was said in the Supreme Court that the

"impairment [in her faculties] which, of course, must have existed, had not been plain to either

---

436. *De Souza* v *Home & Overseas Ins Co Ltd*, *The Times*, CA, 19 September 1990.
437. See above, 15–5B.
438. *Stats* (below p 183). Cf a more objective approach in *Voisin* v *Royal Ins Co* (1988) 53 DLR (4th) 299, 303, (Ont—PA).
439. See for example *Candler* above, 17–5E1; also *Trynor Construction Ltd* v *Canadian Surety Co* (1970) 10 DLR (3d) 482 (NS—motor); *Oakes* v *Sun Life Assurance Co* (1979) 93 DLR (3d) 80 (BC—life),
440. *De Souza* v *Home & Overseas Ins Co Ltd*, *The Times*, 19 September 1990 (CA—PA). Cf *Beller Ltd* v *Hayden* [1978] QB 694 discussed above, 17–5E3(c); and *Glenlight Shipping Co Ltd* v *Excess Ins Co Ltd*, 1983 SLT 241, 245 *per* Lord Stott (life).
USA: accident "is not a subjective term. Thus, the perspective of the insured . . . is not a relevant inquiry": *Roller* v *Stonewall Ins Co*, 801 P 2d 207, 210 (Wash, 1990—motor). However, in New York in *Miller* v *Continental Ins Co*, 389 NYS 2d 564, 566 (1976) the court pointed to lack of awareness to aid its decision that the death of a 20 year old from an overdose of heroin was an accident.
441. *Mutual of Omaha Ins Co* v *Stats* (1978) 87 DLR (3d) 169 (Sup. Ct.).

other witnesses or the late Mrs Brown herself and ...[at] the time of her death all the impairment which had previously existed became active and in truth seemed to deprive the late Mrs Brown of any intelligence or judgment whatsoever."[442]

This gallant view of events allowed the court to conclude that the insured did not know what she was doing. After rejecting an argument, that the meaning of "accident" differed between accident and indemnity policies, and making a ritual reference to "the ordinary language of the people",[443] the court distinguished the case of an insured who deliberately courted danger and held that Mrs Brown had suffered an accident.

So, in Canada as in England, there is no accident if the injury is a probable or expected consequence, with the exception in Canada of the insured who did not actually appreciate the risk.[444]

The Canadian exception has been confirmed in *Yanush*.[445] Students returned to their hall of residence in the early hours of the morning and, being unable to awaken a room-mate, they piled paper on top of him and one of them set fire to it, with consequent injury to the sleeper and damage to the hall. Liability cover was limited to damage caused by accident. Having considered *Stats*, the Ontario court found that "Yanush was at best negligent and probably grossly negligent when he lit his Bic lighter. However, when he performed that act he never thought of himself as negligent, nor did he realize the danger of his actions, nor did he deliberately assume the risk of it . . . . It follows, therefore, that the occurrence was an 'accident'."[446]

17–5G Disease

The effect of disease is not covered by personal accident insurance; this follows either as an inherent feature of the meaning of accident or as the result of an express exception.

For there to be disease, the condition must have some degree of duration: thus it has been held,[447] that a fainting spell induced by lack of food was not disease but "a mere temporary disturbance or enfeeblement".

Disease is an abnormal condition of the human body. Ageing, however, is normal, as is the menopause, which is not therefore disease.[448] Whether the effects of arteriosclerosis are accidental or not may depend on the degree to which it is found in the insured and on his age.[449] Further, it has been held that disease includes neither heroin addiction[450] nor hypersensitivity[451] nor allergy to a drug prescribed by a doc-

442. p 181.
443. p 182.
444. *Excelsior Life Ins Co* v *Colby* (1979) 107 DLR (3d) 333, 339 (Alta—PA), applied in *Johnson* v *Mutual of Omaha Ins Co* (1982) 139 DLR (3d) 358, 369 (Ont—PA), affirmed (1984) 8 DLR (4th) 640 (Ont).
445. *Board of Governors of the University of Western Ontario* v *Yanush*, (1988) 56 DLR (4th) 552 (Ont—liability).
446. p 562.
447. *Manufacturers' Accident Indemnity Co* v *Dorgan*, 58 F 445, 456 (6 Cir, 1893—PA).
448. The Insurance Ombudsman, Annual Report 1991, para 2.7.
449. *Preferred Accident Ins Co* v *Combs*, 76 F 2d 775, 781 (8 Cir, 1935—PA).
450. *Miller* v *Continental Ins Co*, 389 NYS 2d 565 (1976—PA); *Botway* v *American Int Ins Co*, 543 NYS 2d 651 (1989—life).
451. See below, 17–5G2.

tor,[452] but that it does include a state of the body, genetically transmitted and thus present from birth, if, like haemophilia,[453] it is not a normal state of the body.

Disease is relative to the insured's calling in life. Tendonitis may be of no consequence to the solicitor but disastrous to the professional sportsman or to the barrister who must dash from court to court. There is much to be said for defining disease by asking whether the insured was able to carry on his normal life.[454] Subject to this, we may agree with Cardozo J[455]:

"In a strict and literal sense, any departure from an ideal or perfect norm of health is a disease or an infirmity. Something more, however, must be shown to exclude the effects of accident from the coverage of a policy. The disease or infirmity must be so considerable or significant that it would be characterized as disease or infirmity in the common speech of men."

The common speech of men changes and an example of change lies in the way we speak about mental illness. Early cases in the United States held that disease does not include mental illness: the insured who killed himself while insane was not diseased.[456] Later cases held[457] that disease does not include tension or anxiety. Today, it seems likely that courts in the United States would regard mental illness with physical manifestations as disease, although much will depend on the medical evidence, as courts are conscious that "no clear delimitation marks the boundary between demonstrated peculiarities of personality and similar manifestations of mental illness."[458] In England, insurance cases on this point have not been reported.

The meaning of disease is apparent in most situations. Disease is not regarded as a normal feature of the human condition and has been described as an *abnormality* in the human body which develops internally. However, it is fundamental to the law of insurance that it is distinguished from the injurious effect on the body of an accident (below 17–5G1) and, for the purpose of this distinction, it has been described as "the *natural* result of a *natural* cause": see above 17–5C. The need to draw this distinction has skewed the meaning of illness and disease.

For example, it has been held that, if the insured drinks poison by mistake, that is an accident,[459] but if he drinks contaminated water and contracts typhoid, that is not an accident but a case of disease. The court in one such case went on to say,[460] however, that if the typhoid bacillus had not entered the body "through normal channels

---

452. *Mutual Life Ins Co* v *Dodge*, 11 F 2d 486 (4 Cir, 1926—life).

453. *Cheney* v *Bell National Life Ins Co*, 556 A 2d 1135 (Md, 1989 – PA).

454. This was the question sent back to the trier of fact in *Sullivan* v *National Casualty Co*, 125 NYS 2d 851 (1953—professional disability), affirmed 128 NYS 2d 717 (1954). Specifically the question was whether the degree of vomiting and nausea suffered by a pregnant lady amounted to "sickness".

455. In *Silverstein* v *Metropolitan Life Ins Co*, 171 NE 914, 915 quoted in *Combs* (above). Health must be impaired in a "material" degree: *Zorn* v *Aetna Life Ins Co*, 260 F Supp 730, 733 (ED Tex, 1965—PA and PHI), affirmed 368 F 2d 1013 (5 Cir, 1966): impairment, it is submitted, is material only if the insured's normal life is impeded or prevented.

456. *Accident Ins Co of North America* v *Crandall*, 120 US 527 (1887—PA).

457. *Metropolitan Life Ins Co* v *Main*, 383 F 2d 952 (5 Cir, 1967—PA); in this case there were no significant physical manifestations of the tension and anxiety.

458. *Keller* v *Orion Ins Co Ltd*, 422 F 2d 1152, 1154 (8 Cir, 1970—occupational disability). On the meaning of "mental illness" in a health policy, see *Phillips* v *Lincoln National Life Ins Co*, 774 F Supp 495 (ND Ill, 1991).

459. Welford citing *Cole* v *Accident Ins Co* (1889) 61 LT 227, cited with approval by Mustill LJ in *De Souza* (below). USA idem: *Chase* v *Business Men's Assurance Co of America*, 51 F 2d 34 (10 Cir, 1931).

In *Sklar* v *Saskatchewan Govt Ins Office* (1965) 54 DLR (2d) 455 (Sask) it was held that, when a man sitting in his car stuck in a snowdrift died of carbon monoxide poisoning, that was an accident under his life policy.

460. *Chase* (above) p 36.

of entry", that would have been an accident. The line between illness and accident is considered next.

17–5G1 Disease as Cause of Injury is Not Accidental

In the law of insurance, the effect on the human body is not accidental if the chain of events consists of or is initiated by illness or disease. The cases, said the Court of Appeal, regarded simply as decisions, are difficult if not impossible to reconcile.[461]

In 1861, in Sinclair,[462] the insured was covered against personal injury or death "from, or by reason or in consequence of any accident" at sea. While master on board ship in India he suffered sunstroke and died. His death, it was held, was not an accident. Cockburn CJ[463] assumed that a line had to be drawn between death by accident and by "natural causes" and said that "some violence, casualty, or *vis major*, is necessarily involved. We cannot think that disease produced by the action of a known cause can be considered accidental . . . unless . . . the exposure is itself brought about by circumstances which may give it the character of accident". Cases on this question should be seen in their context[464] and Sinclair might be seen as a decision of its time. First, it shows a low level of sympathy for casualties of the work place on sea or on land. Second, it is not law now, as it seems to have been then, that the accident must be "some violence, casualty or *vis major*"; a mere slip on the floor is enough.[465] Third, *Sinclair* shows a high level of fatalism about the impact of nature, whereby disease and death were regarded as natural to a degree that modern man is less willing to accept. Nonetheless, in 1990, in De Souza,[466] the rule against disease as accident was affirmed. In De Souza, the insurance covered "accidental bodily injury caused solely and directly by outward violent and visible means". On the ordinary construction of these words and without regard to precedent, Mustill LJ, giving the judgment of the Court of Appeal, restated that heatstroke was not an "accidental bodily injury".[467] The insured, who intended to expose himself to the sun while on holiday but suffered sunstroke and died, did not die by accident. Once again, this is because "an injury is not caused by accident when it is the natural result of a natural cause".[468]

---

461. Mustill LJ in De Souza v Home & Overseas Ins Co Ltd, The Times, 19 September 1990.

462. *Sinclair v Maritime Passengers' Assurance Co* (1861) 3 El & El 478. This decision was followed in *Wyman v Dominion of Canada General Ins Co* [1936] 2 DLR 268 (Ont—PA) in respect of heatstroke suffered by a street cleaner. The decision might be distinguished, as the contract in *Wyman* required the accident to be solely by external means.

Cf USA: *semble* disease is not excluded by definition from accident. Certainly, sunstroke has been held to be accidental: Indiana—*Wiecking v Phoenix Mutual Life Ins Co*, 116 F 2d 90 (7 Cir, 1940); Ohio—*Hammer v Mutual Benefit Health & Accident Assn*, 109 NE 2d 649 (1952). A heart attack at work in hot weather was not accidental in *Thomas v Transamerica Occidental Life Ins Co*, 761 F Supp 709 (D Or, 1991—PA). However, in practice disease is not covered, either as a result of express exception of disease or by the requirement that the accident be external to the insured (below, 17–5H1).

463. p 485.

464. Mustill LJ in De Souza v Home & Overseas Ins Co Ltd, The Times, 19 September 1990.

465. For example *Hamlyn v Crown Accident Ins Co Ltd* [1893] 1 QB 750 (CA—PA); above, 17–5F1.

466. (above).

467. This view was reinforced by the words of the contract of insurance, in particular, by the requirement of "outward violent and visible means" and by the distinction drawn elsewhere in the policy between accident and injury on the one hand and illness on the other. Illness and disease were not expressly excluded, but that inference could be drawn from other clauses in which, for example, the recovery of expenses in respect of bodily injury and illness were distinguished and some of the latter excepted.

468. *Ibid*, quoting Welford p 269.

Compare and contrast *Ismay*,[469] decided in 1908. While working in the stokehole of a steamship the insured suffered heatstroke and died. It was argued for the insurers, *inter alia* by reference to *Sinclair* (above), that this was not a death by accident within the meaning of the Workmen's Compensation Act 1906. The House of Lords, without referring expressly to *Sinclair*, held that it was an accident. Lord Loreburn LC[470]: "What killed him was a heat-stroke coming suddenly and unexpectedly upon him while at work. Such a stroke is an unusual effect of a known cause . . . In common language, it was a case of accidental death."

Sinclair has been explained[471] on the basis that death was not accidental because the sunstroke was suffered in the ordinary course of the insured's work. But Mr Ismay was at work too, and this explanation of *Sinclair* appears to create as many problems as it solves. Injury from a radiation leak would be accidental or not, according to whether the victim was a patient or a radiographer.[472] Injury on the road would be accidental or not according to whether the victim was a taxi driver or his passenger. Nor is the suggestion[472a] convincing that, whereas lightning (although "natural") strikes accidentally,[473] it would cease to be accidental as regards persons whose duty it is to be out in the storm. It is very doubtful that a modern court would penalise members of the emergency services in such a way,[474] on the contrary, it is public policy that men should not be inhibited in their work by fear of the consequences of accidents.[475] If a man's employment is dangerous, that is a matter for disclosure, premium loading and exceptions (such as "wilful exposure", below, 19–2B), rather than a contrived construction of the word "accident".

Nonetheless, public policy favours the workplace rather than, for example, the beach and a more extensive and avowedly different meaning is given to accident when it occurs at work. This is the explanation of *Ismay* and the first part of the explanation of *De Souza*. Since 1897, accidents at work have been governed by the Workmen's Compensation Acts,[476] which, we are told by the Court of Appeal in *De Souza*,[476a] we must distinguish from the notion of accident at common law, because decisions under the Acts stretched the notion of accident to ensure that men were covered.

469. *Ismay, Imrie & Co* v *Williamson* [1908] AC 437. In the same sense: *Morgan* v *Owners of SS Zenaida* (1909) 25 TLR 446 (CA—workmen's compensation); *Davies* v *Gillespie* (1911) 105 LT 494 (CA—workmen's compensation). It might be different if the contract required external means (below, 17–5H1) for then it could be argued that the element of fortuity was not in the temperature of the stokehole, but internal to the body of the insured. *Cf Pyper* v *Manchester Liners* [1916] 2 KB 691 (CA).

470. p 439.

471. MacGillivray, No 1779. Also in this sense: *Thomas* v *Transamerica Occidental Life Ins Co*, 761 F Supp 709 (D Or, 1991—PA). *Cf Arthurs* v *Metropolitan Life Ins Co*, 760 F Supp 1095, 1100 (SD NY, 1991 – life).

472. *Cf King* v *Travelers' Ins Co*, 192 A 311 (Conn, 1937): dentist's over-exposure to radiation held accidental.

472a. MacGillivray, No 1779.

473. For example, *Andrew* v *Failsworth Industrial Sy Ltd* [1904] 2 KB 32 (CA—workmen's compensation).

474. For example, any suggestion that an occupier of land owed a lower duty of care to firemen than to other citizens, because it was their job to cope with fires, has been rejected: *Salmon* v *Seafarer Restaurants Ltd* [1983] 3 All ER 729, 735–736 *per* Woolf J, approved in *Ogwo* v *Taylor* [1988] AC 431, 436 *per* Dillon LJ (CA), 447–448 *per* Lord Bridge (HL).

475. *Fenton* v *Thorley & Co Ltd* [1903] AC 443, 447 *per* Lord Macnaghten (workmen's compensation).

476. Certainly, diseases or illness contracted at work have been held within the Acts: for example, rheumatism or pneumonia in a man required to stand in icy water or in draughts: Willis, *Workmen's Compensation Acts* (37th ed., 1945), pp 11–12.

476a. *De Souza* v *Home & Overseas Ins Co Ltd*, *The Times*, 19 September 1990. Other courts have taken a different view: see above, 17–5F2.

The second part of the explanation is that the rule, which excludes disease from accident, has less to do with the nature of insurance, with logic or with language than with what has "always been considered"[477] by insurers. For accident insurers, an accident does not include the effects of disease: the insurers have not calculated the risk on that basis. As with the inherent exclusion of explosion from fire cover (above, 17–2E), it is market custom that excludes disease. To those outside the market, it is not immediately obvious why a person who suffers heatstroke from the sun does not die by accident, while further down the same beach the person, who is overcome by cramp and drowns, suffers accidental death.[478] Does this really correspond to the reasonable expectations of the insured on holiday on the Costa Brava?[479] The Court of Appeal thought so in *De Souza*. True or not, it corresponds with the expectations of insurers and results in relatively cheap accident insurance. People must be advised that, in insurance law and practice, illness and disease are not accidents, unless they occur within the bounds of the workplace and are thus governed by the Acts.

17–5G2 Disease Predisposing to Accident

If disease leads inevitably to accident, as when a brain tumour causes a loss of consciousness and a fall, there is no accident in law. However, the courts are quick to find that the disease did not lead inevitably to the fall and that, therefore,it was the fall and not the disease that was the proximate cause of any injury.[480]

Nonetheless, it has been argued that an accident is not an accident if, although not inevitable the day before, on the day it was caused in part by the insured's predisposition to the events of the day. For example, it was argued in *Ismay*[481] that the death of the insured by heatstroke was not an accident, because of the insured's physical debility, i.e., because death was an inevitable result of his debility in the heat of the "kitchen". This was rejected.[482] Similarly, in the United States Justice Cardozo said[483]: "A policy of insurance is not accepted with the thought that its coverage is to be restricted to an Apollo or a Hercules." The frail condition of the insured at the time of the accident does not alter the character of the event as accident.[484] Moreover,

477. (1861) 3 El & El 478, 486 *per* Cockburn CJ.
478. *Trew* v *Railway Passengers Assurance Co* (1861) 6 H & N 839, 844–845 *per* Cockburn CJ.
479. In the USA it is sometimes said that "accident" should be understood in the sense understood by "the average insured when he purchased the policy": *Burr* v *Commercial Travelers' Mutual Accident Assn*, 67 NE 2d 248, 252 (NY, 1946—life); *Arthur A Johnson Corp* v *Indemnity Ins Co*, 175 NYS 2d 414, 417 (1958—liability); *American Casualty Co* v *Minnesota Farm Bureau Service Co*, 270 F 2d 686 (8 Cir, 1959—liability). On the relevance of "reasonable expectations" in English law see above, 15–5B2.
480. For example *Lawrence* v *Accidental Ins Co Ltd* (1881) 7 QBD 216. *Adkins* v *Reliance Ins Co*, 917 F 2d 794 (4 Cir, 1990—PA). See below, 17–5H2.
481. *Ismay Imrie & Co* v *Williamson* [1908] AC 437 (workmen's compensation). Note the debate concerning whether such cases are typical of PA insurance: above, 17–5F2 and 17–5G1.
482. p 439 *per* Lord Loreburn LC. See also *Jason* v *Batten (1930) Ltd* [1969] 1 Lloyd's Rep 281, 291 *per* Fisher J (PA). *Cf* Lord Macnaghten dissenting in *Ismay* (p 442): "The death was due to the physical state of the workmen and 'the nature' of the employment . . . It was, I think just what anybody would have expected who saw the man and knew what a trimmer has to do."
USA: hypersensitivity does not deprive death or injury of accidental character: *Mutual Life Ins Co* v *Dodge*, 11 F 2d 486 (4 Cir, 1926—life); *Preferred Accident Ins Co* v *Combs*, 76 F 2d 775 (8 Cir, 1935); *Berkowitz* v *New York Life Ins Co*, 10 NYS 2d 106 (1939—life); *Adlerblum* v *Metropolitan Life Ins Co*, 30 NE 2d 728 (NY 1940—life).
483. *Silverstein* v *Metropolitan Life Ins Co*, 171 NE 914, 915 (NY).
484. *Arthurs* v *Metropolitan Life Ins Co*, 760 F Supp 1095, 1100 (SD NY, 1991—life).

an accident which activates a latent physical infirmity is nonetheless an accident.[485] As always, the position may be changed by appropriate clauses. A predisposition to injury may exclude cover if there is an exception of "bodily infirmity".[486]

17–5G3 Disease as Link: The Injury may be Accidental

An injury does not cease to be an accident because one link in the chain is illness or disease in the insured.[487]

For example, the insured who is shipwrecked, catches pneumonia and dies, suffers accidental death.[488] Again, if something goes wrong in the course of medical treatment for the consequences of an accident, for example the patient contracts a virus or infection, the entire injury is attributable to the accident.[489] And, if the insured dies of blood poisoning caused by the slightest scratch, that is an accident: above, 17–5G. If, however, the effect of the accident is to accelerate the progress of an existing ailment, which leads to death, it has been held[490] that this is disease not accident. There is some attraction in the counter-argument[491] that, although the accident does not cause that death, it accelerates it and hence causes loss of (length of) life. In any case, decisions like this are subject to the terms of the policy, which often exclude cover of injury wholly or partly caused by illness and disease.[492]

485. *Bankers Life & Casualty Co* v *Crenshaw*, 483 So 2d 254 (Miss, 1985—PHI); also *Dickson* v *United States Fidelity & Guarantee Co*, 466 P 2d 515 (Wn, 1970—property AR).

486. For example, *Zorn* v *Aetna Life Ins Co*, 260 F Supp 730 (ED Tex, 1965), affirmed 368 F 2d 1013 (5 Cir, 1966).

487. *Mardorf* v *Accident Ins Co* [1903] 1 KB 584; *Brintons Ltd* v *Turvey* [1905] AC 230 (workmen's compensation); *Fidelity & Casualty Co* v *Mitchell* [1917] AC 592 (PC—PA). *Accident Ins Co of North America* v *Young* (1892) 20 SCR 280 (PA).

488. *Sinclair* v *Maritime Passengers Assurance Co* (1861) 3 El & El 479, 485 *per* Lord Cockburn CJ; *Isitt* v *Railway Passengers Assurance Co* (1889) 22 QBD 504; *Re Etherington and Lancashire & Yorkshire Accident Ins Co* [1909] 1 KB 591.
Cases under the Workmen's Compensation Acts in which, after an event in the course of employment initiated illness or disease, the death was held to be accidental include: *Drylie* v *Alloa Coal Co Ltd*, 1913 SC 549 (pneumonia); *Britons Ltd* v *Turvey* [1905] AC 230 (anthrax); *Coyle* v *John Watson Ltd* [1915] AC 1 (pneumonia); *Glasgow Coal Co* v *Welsh* [1916] 2 AC 1 (rheumatism); *Pyrah* v *Doncaster Corp* [1949] 1 All ER (CA) (tuberculosis). The "event" at work may pass unnoticed in the blinking of an eye, for example, the entry of noxious dust via an abrasion, causing death from blood poisoning: *Innes* v *Kynoch* [1919] AC 765. See also *Pyrah* (above). These have been called cases of assault by bacilli, but the use of the word "assault" is but a thin disguise for facts that would not pass the rule against disease in cases of private cover.

489. In *Cheney* v *Bell National Life Ins Co*, 556 A 2d 1135, 1137 (Md, 1989—PA) the court stated that, assuming 'that the transfusion of contaminated blood or blood products into the insured constituted an accidental injury within the meaning of the policy, the AIDS and pneumonia caused thereby are considered 'link(s) in the chain of causation,' and the accidental injury remains the cause of death." However, in that case the contract excluded injury caused by "medical or surgical treatment", the transfusion was part of treatment for haemophilia and, as the court decided that that was a disease (see above 17–5G) the claim failed. See further below, 17–5G4.

490. *McKechnie's Trustees* v *Scottish Accident Ins Co* (1889) 17 R 6: the insured was thrown from a cart. He then died from kidney disease, which had been accelerated by his fall. The Court of Session held that this was not an accident.
Quite apart from the meaning of accident, the common law does not see the fall as the cause of death: for example *Cutler* v *Vauxhall Motors Ltd* [1971] 1 QB 418 (CA).

491. Hart and Honoré, p 159.

492. *For example, Smith* v *Accident Ins Co* (1870) LR 5 Ex 302 where the decision against accident in such circumstances turned on the wording of the policy. This decision suggests that the position stated in the text might be changed by a policy requirement that the accident be "direct and sole cause" of injury or death (p 307 *per* Martin B). See also below, 17–5H2.

17–5G4 Accidents in Hospital

What if things go wrong in hospital? Welford, citing cases on workmen's compensation,[493] stated that, if it becomes advisable to perform an operation upon the insured and the insured dies, although it is the immediate cause of death in point of time, the operation is to be disregarded and the death is to be attributed to the circumstances giving rise to the operation. Indeed, as Welford's statement suggests, this may follow less from the meaning of disease or of accident than from the rules of causation.[494] So, if the operation arose out of a road accident, the death in hospital is by accident. But, if the operation was to remove a growth, it is death by disease. In *Allison*,[495] for example, the insured fell, broke her hip and was taken to hospital for an operation on the hip, during which she suffered cardiac arrest and died; this was held to be a "loss resulting from injury". But, in *Clark*,[496] the court said that "one who submits to a simple appendectomy, where the condition is not acute, knows that he may be one of the comparatively small number who will die as a result of the operation. He does not expect death but he knows it may occur. In such cases, we do not think an ordinary man would say that the death was accidental".

If, however, the death came about as a result of negligent hospital treatment, the law of tort would suggest a break in the chain of causation[497] between the circumstance that brought the person to hospital and the death, which is therefore a "new event". Welford[498] took the same view of insurance cover and drew the conclusion that, whatever the circumstance that brought the insured to hospital, the insured's death would be by accident.

17–5H Clauses[499]

The primary meaning of accident, discussed above, may be changed by the wording of the particular contract. This may be achieved, first, by exclusions or conditions, which are discussed elsewhere in this book.[500] For example, there may be cover against accidental death or injury, unless caused by wilful exposure to unnecessary danger[501] or by specific causes, such as hang-gliding or motor racing, or caused by negligence,[502] or intoxication.[503] Second, a similar effect may be achieved by adjectives or adverbs in the statement of accident cover itself. One example of this kind is cover against acci-

---

493. p 272, citing notably *Shirt* v *Calico Printers' Assn* [1909] 2 KB 51 (CA).
494. Below, 25–4A.
495. *Allison* v *Nationwide Mut. Ins Co* , 964 F 2d 291 (3 Cir, 1992—PA).
496. *Preferred Accident Ins Co* v *Clark*, 144 F 2d 165, 168 (10 Cir, 1944—PA). See also *Zinn* v *Equitable Life Ins Co*, 107 P 2d 921 (Wn, 1940—life); *Life & Casualty Co* v *Brown*, 98 SE 2d 68 (Ga, 1957—life). *Cf Senkier* v *Hartford Life & Accident Ins Co*, 948 F 2d 1050, 1052 (7 Cir, 1991—PA): "while injuries caused . . . by the treatment of the illness could be put in either bin, the normal understanding is that they belong with illness, not with accident". *Cf* further *Groves* v *AMP Fire & General Ins Co (NZ) Ltd* [1990] 1 NZLR 124 (PA): the insured died as a result of a reaction to anaesthetic prior to a hysterectomy, the chance of which was 1:125,000. Her death was held to be an accident, however, the present point was not addressed.
497. *Hogan* v *Bentinck Collieries* [1949] 1 All ER 588 (HL).
498. p 272 fn (s).
499. Generally, Appleman, Nos 758 ff.
500. Generally, see ch 19.
501. Below, 19–2B.
502. Below, 19–2A; courts are reluctant to apply this kind of exception.
503. Below, 19–2C.

dent causing incapacity for work.[504] Two other leading examples are examined in the following pages.

17–5H1 Cover against Bodily Injury by External, Violent and Accidental Means

(a) *Bodily Injury*. This includes any deleterious change in the body of the insured. In the United States a leading decision[505] defined bodily injury as "any localized abnormal condition of the living body". That case concerned liability insurance in respect of asbestosis; it has been questioned[506] whether, in general, "bodily injury" should have the same meaning in different types of insurance: there is some doubt and perhaps this should be kept in mind.

In Australia, it has been held[507] that "accidental bodily injury" includes nervous shock. In Canada, however, it has been decided[508] that bodily injury means physical harm to the body, as opposed to mental infirmity or illness. In England, Welford said[509]: "Mere mental pain or grief or shock does not constitute bodily injury, unless manifesting itself by operating upon the person of the insured and producing physical disease." In the United States, the same qualification is found: it is "well recognized" that "emotional distress can and often does have a direct effect on other bodily functions",[510] such as weight loss, headaches, muscle spasms and so on. That is bodily injury. However, while it has been held that "*personal* injury" includes mental anguish,[511] the argument, that the extension of liability in tort to cover the infliction of emotional distress has created a reasonable expectation in the liability insured that his insurance will cover that liability, has been rejected in New Jersey[512] although accepted in New York.[513] That argument is unlikely to succeed under PA insurance against bodily injury. In any event, the determined doctor can find a physical change that goes with psychological or emotional effects. It is probably enough that the event "operates"[514]

---

504. *Hooper* v *Accidental Death Ins Co* (1860) 5 H & N 546; *Fidelity & Casualty Co of New York* v *Mitchell* [1917] AC 592 (PC); *Pocock* v *Century Ins Co Ltd* [1960] 2 Lloyd's Rep 150.
505. *Insurance Co of North America* v *Forty-Eight Insulations Inc*, 633 F 2d 1212, 1222 (6 Cir, 1980—liability).
506. *Keene Corp* v *INA*, 667 F 2d 1034, 1043, 1045 (Colum, 1981—product liability).
507. *Boyle* v *Nominal Defendant* [1939] SR (NSW) 413 (liability); for the general position in Australia, see Derrington & Ashton, *The Law of Liability Insurance*, pp 316 ff. But *cf Jason* v *Batten (1930) Ltd* [1969] 1 Lloyd's Rep 281, 290 *per* Fisher J: "It seems to me to be a strained and unusual use of words to call the anxiety or the [consequent] change in the blood or the clot itself 'a bodily injury sustained in the accident'." *Idem Milashenko* v *Cooperative Fire & Casualty Co* (1968) 1 DLR (3d) 89, in which the Saskatchewan court declined to treat the effects of anxiety on the heart as bodily injury.
508. *Johnson* v *Mutual of Omaha Ins Co* (1982) 139 DLR (3d) 358, 365 (Ont—PA), affirmed (1984) 8 DLR (4th) 640 (Ont), holding death from an overdose of anaesthetic was an accidental bodily injury.
509. 2nd ed, p 268. USA *idem*: *SL Industries* v *American Motorists Ins Co*, 607 A 2d 1266 (NJ, 1992—liability).
510. *Vorheers* v *Preferred Mutual Ins Co* 607 A.2d 1255, 1261 (NJ, 1992—liability). See also *Allstate Ins Co* v *Biggerstaff*, 703 F Supp 23 (D SC, 1989—liability). However, physical manifestations of emotional distress will not be presumed: *Garvis* v *Employers Mutual Casualty Co*, 497 NW 2d 254, 258 (Minn, 1993—liability).
511. See, for example, *International Ins Co* v *Guaranty National Ins Co*, 780 F Supp 546 (ND Ill, 1991—liability)
512. *SL Industries* (above) p 1275.
513. *Lavanant* v *General Accident Ins Co*, 595 NE 2d 819, 823 (CA NY, 1992—liability).
514. *Pugh* v *London, Brighton & South Coast Ry Co* [1896] 2 QB 248 (CA—workmen's compensation).

on the insured by some discernible physical deterioration, although temporary.[515]

(b) *Violent*. Apart from obvious examples, such as being crushed by a train,[516] or falling to the ground,[517] violence connotes any physical accident, unless it occurs "without any violence at all".[518] So, it includes the action of pool water drowning an unconscious man and even, it has been held,[519] the case of a person who dies in bed from an overdose of sleeping pills and alcohol.[520]

(c) *External Means*. Means are often distinguished from results, *viz*, injury (see above, 17–5F1). The accidental means, containing an element of fortuity, must occur outside the body of the insured.[521] External is the antithesis of internal.[522] If outside the body, the means do not have to be far outside; thus the person who died because his pimple was pierced by an infected pin, died through external, violent and accidental means.[523] Indeed, it has been held in the USA that "if a foreign material causes death through mechanical action [such as choking] as it is being attempted to be taken into the body, this is an external cause of death".[524] However, a line has to be drawn somewhere and, "if food is taken into the body, digested, and regurgitated causing suffocation, this has been held not to be an external cause of death. The reason is that the body has internalized the substance that has, by then, lost its previous character".[525] The same was held of an artificial heart valve which failed seven years after implantation.[526]

Injury must be the result of something that operates *on* the insured and thus be external to his body. In a sense, a heart attack is an injury to the body but has been held outside accident cover on this ground: were it otherwise (relatively cheap) accident insurance would be converted, when death results, into life insurance, which is something quite different.[527]

17–5H2 *Independently of all Other Causes*

The function of this limit on cover is to increase the (limiting) effect of any causes that are excepted.

515. *Keating* v *National Union Fire Ins Co*, 754 F Supp 1431 (CD Cal, 1990—liability). However, when bodily injury was defined as any physical harm, sickness or disease, it does not cover a person's alleged humiliation, shame, emotional distress and mental anguish: *Mellow* v *Medical Malpractice Joint Underwriting Assn*, 567 A 2d 367 (RI, 1989—liability): these were the alleged effects on a patient, when the insured physician disclosed to a newspaper the blood-alcohol level of the patient.

516. *Lawrence* v *Accidental Ins Co* (1881) 7 QBD 216.

517. *Hamlyn* v *Crown Accidental Ins Co Ltd* [1893] 1 QB 750 (CA—PA).

518. *Ibid*, p 753 *per* Lord Esher MR. *Idem*: *Southard* v *Railway Passengers' Assurance Co*, 22 F Cas No 13, 182 (D Conn, 1868—PA); *Jensma* v *Sun Life Assurance Co*, 64 F 2d 457, 459 (9 Cir, 1933—PA), cert den 289 US 763 (1933); *Sanberg* v *Fidelity & Casualty Co*, 158 F 1, 5 (8 Cir, 1907—PA).

519. *Reynolds* v *Accidental Ins Co* (1870) 22 LT 820 (PA).

520. *Gay* v *Pacific Mutual Life Ins Co*, 237 F 2d 448 (5 Cir, 1956—PA).

521. *Hamlyn* v *Crown Accidental Ins Co Ltd* [1893] 1 QB 750, 753 *per* Lord Esher MR (CA). For example *Clidero* v *Scottish Accident Ins Co*, 1892 19 R (Ct Sess) 355; *Burridge* v *Haines & Son Ltd* (1918) 87 LJKB 641 (accident to a horse).

522. *Miss Jay Jay* [1987] 1 Lloyd's Rep 32, 39 *per* Slade LJ (CA—hull) approving statements in *Hamlyn*: above, 17–5F1.

523. *Iowa State Traveling Men's Assn* v *Lewis*, 257 F 552 (8 Cir, 1919).

524. *Century Cos* v *Krahling*, 484 NW 2d 197, 198 (Iowa 1992—life).

525. *Ibid*.

526. *Ibid*.

527. *Winchester* v *Prudential Life Ins Co*, 975 F 2d 1479, 1486 (10 Cir, 1992—PA).

In *Jason* v *Batten (1930) Ltd*,[528] six days after the insured was in a motor accident he suffered a coronary thrombosis which, it was found, he would have suffered in any event within three years. It was held that, assuming the thrombosis was a bodily injury, it was not an injury "independently of all other causes"; specifically, it was not independent of his pre-existing arterial disease. In *Travelers' Ins Co* v *Elder*,[529] the insured while drunk aimed a punch at a restaurateur, missed and injured his face on some glasses that fell in the fracas. It was held in Canada that this was not an accident occurring independently of other causes.

In other cases, however, the insured has evaded this clause by persuading the court to construe it strictly and to require that the other cause, of which the accident must be "independent", is not just any cause (such as a "but for" cause) but a cause relevant to the law of insurance, that is to say, an expressly excepted and proximate cause[530] leading inevitably to injury. For example, in *Lawrence* v *Accidental Ins Co Ltd.*,[531] the insured had a fit, while standing on a railway platform, fell under a train and was killed. The court held that this was an accident, even though the insurance required the accidental injury to be the "sole cause of death". The court reached this decision not by asking whether the impact of the train was the sole cause but by asking[532] whether the fit, the cause advanced by the insurer, was the proximate cause. Because, in the view of the court, the fit did not lead inevitably to injury, it was not the proximate cause and nor, the immediate point of interest, was it a cause of which the subsequent fall under the train had to be independent.[533]

---

528. [1969] 1 Lloyd's Rep 281 (PA). *Cf Fidelity & Casualty Co* v *Mitchell* [1917] AC 592 (PC—PA).

529. [1940] 2 DLR 444 (Quebec—PA); see also *Voison* v *Royal Ins Co* (1986) 26 DLR (4th) 637 (Ont—PA).

530. See below, 25–2. Alternatively, a literal application of the clause might be said to be contrary to the reasonable expectations of the insured: above, 15–5B1.

531. (1881) 7 QBD 216. See also *Winspear* v *Accident Ins Co Ltd* (1880) 6 QBD 42 (PA). These cases were approved by Lord Collins MR, in *Wicks* v *Dowell & Co Ltd* [1905] 2 KB 225, 229 (workmen's compensation). See also *Reynolds* v *Accidental Ins Co* (1870) 22 LT 820 (PA). See further below, 25–4(a).

532. (1881) 7 QBD 216, 221 *per* Watkin Williams J.USA: similar reasoning is found, for example, in *Life & Casualty Co* v *Brown*, 98 SE 2d 68 (Ga, 1957—life); and *Adkins* v *Reliance Ins Co*, 917 F 2d 794 (4 Cir, 1990—PA); but in other cases it has been overlooked that disease as a background or *causa sine qua non* is enough to defeat the claimant: for example, *Preferred Accident Ins Co* v *Combs*, 76 F 2d 775, 780 (8 Cir, 1935). For further references, see *Adkins* (above).

533. *Malley* v *Minnesota Mutual Life Ins Co*, 785 F Supp 605 (SD Miss, 1991—life).

CHAPTER 18

THE PERIOD OF COVER

18-1 THE IMPORTANCE OF THE INSURANCE PERIOD

Insurance cover is limited in time. It is limited to certain events occurring during a certain period of time[1] and whether the events, in a particular case, fall within the period raises a question of construction of the particular contract of insurance.[2]

18-1A Long Tail Insurance

Difficulty arises with long tail insurance, such as certain kinds of liability cover,[3] in respect of loss which may first appear years after the original cause. Is loss covered by insurance in force at the time of the cause or at some later time, such as the time when the consequences appear? The first step is to look at the event stated in the policy and to define it; and then to see if that event occurred during the insurance period.

If the event is relatively specific in point of time, such as a fire or an accident, it is usually obvious whether this is so. If, for example, the policy covers accidents, and if loss is suffered when an aircraft propellor fails after cover has ended, the accident occurred outside the insurance period and there is no cover, even though the cause of the failure was negligence occurring during the insurance period.[4]

If, however, the event is less specific in point of time, for example, the occurrence of injury or damage, and if the injury or damage develops slowly over many years, it may be difficult to establish which policy period (and which insurer) carries the loss.[5] Of the range of possibilities, the first is the time of the original cause, impact, for example, when the worker's lungs were exposed to asbestos dust.[6] The second is the period in which the loss was manifested:[7] for example, a fidelity policy may cover losses discovered during the policy period, although the theft occurred earlier. The

---

1. *Prudential Ins Co v IRC* [1904] 2 KB 658, 663 *per* Channell J (life).
2. *Kelly v Norwich Union Fire Ins Sy Ltd*, [1989] 2 All ER 888 (CA—property).
3. See further on liability cover, above, 17–4C.
4. *National Aviation Underwriters Inc v Idaho Aviation Center Inc*, 471 P 2d 55 (Idaho, 1970—liability). Keeton, s 5. 10(d). As regards the duration of insurance cover in general see Appleman, sections 101 ff, 6712 ff and 7171 ff.
   The same rule is found in England: *Hough v Head* (1885) 55 LJKB 43, 44 *per* Lord Esher MR (CA—freight); *Campbell & Phillips Ltd v Denman* (1915) 21 Com Cas 357 (war risks); *Fooks v Smith* [1924] 2 KB 508 (cargo). Everything turns on policy interpretation: *Kelly v Norwich Union Fire Ins Sy Ltd* [1989] 2 All ER 888 (CA—property).
5. See further, above, 17–4C2.
6. For example *Insurance Co of North America v Forty-Eight Insulations Inc* 451 F Supp 1230 (ED Mich, 1978); 633 F 2d 1212 (6 Cir, 1980), cert den 454 US 1109.
7. For example *Eagle-Picher Industries Inc v Liberty Mutual Ins Co*, 682 F 2d 12 (1 Cir, 1982—product liability).

third possibility is the triple trigger theory, which ensures the liability of insurers in long tail situations by fixing liability on any insurer whose policy was in effect (1) at the time of initial exposure, or (2) during continued exposure, or (3) at the time of manifestation.[8] The result is that, subject to "other insurance" clauses in the policies, the insurers on risk at any of those times are jointly and severally liable. A fourth possibility, in the case of liability insurance, has been to tie cover to the moment of a claim against the insured; this has not, as some hoped, avoided all ambiguity or doubt.[9]

18–1B Loss Before or After the Insurance Period

If loss insured occurs during the insurance period, the loss is covered to its full extent, although its extent is not ascertained or has not fully developed until after the period;[10] an instance is that of a house which began to move within the period as a result of an unstable land fill and heavy rain.[11]

"Once the contingent event has occurred during the policy period covered, the liability of the [insurer] becomes contractual rather than potential only, and the sole issue remaining is the extent of the obligation, and it is immaterial that it may not be fully ascertained at the end of the policy period."[12]

Argument, that in such cases loss occurs at the earlier time when it has become a latent inevitability, has been rejected: it occurs when the loss is manifested, as a manifestation rule promotes certainty.[13]

In contrast, continuing damage during one insurance period caused by an event, such as spillage of toxic material, in a previous period is not covered in the later period, unless there is a new, related but distinct development within that period.[14]

8. *Keene Corp* v *INA*, 667 F 2d 1034 (Colum, 1981—product liability): even though the policy provided that the "injury" and not the occurrence that causes injury must fall within the policy period.

9. See above, 17–4D. However, in many cases the insured will have sufficient knowledge of an impending claim to be in breach of his duty of disclosure when the policy is contracted or renewed: *Soole* v *Royal Ins Co Ltd* [1971] 2 Lloyd's Rep 332, 338 *per* Shaw J (liability).

10. *Knight* v *Faith* (1850) 15 QB 649, 666–667 *per* Lord Campbell CJ (hull); *Hough* v *Head* (1885) 55 LJKB 43, 45 *per* Bowen LJ (CA—freight); *Anderson* v *Marten* [1908] AC 334, 338 *per* Lord Loreburn LC (hull); *Daff* v *Midland Collier, Owners Mutual Indemnity Co* (1913) 109 LT 418, 427 *per* Lord Moulton (HL—employers' liability); *Mayer & Sherratt* v *Cooperative Ins Sy Ltd* [1939] 2 KB 627 (CA—employers' liability for lead poisoning).

11. *Snapp* v *State Farm Fire & Casualty Co*, 24 Cal Rptr 44 (Cal, 1962); see also as regards liability for pollution, *Aetna* v *Pintlar Corp*, 948 F 2d 1507, 1516 (9 Cir, 1991—liability); *Chemstar Inc* v *Liberty Mutual Ins Co*, 797 F Supp 1541 (CD Cal, 1992—liability).

12. *Snapp* (above), p 46.

13. *Prudential–LMI Commercial Insurance* v *Superior Court*, 274 Cal Rptr 387, 403 (Cal, 1990—fire), approving *Snapp* (above) and *Landmark* (below); Towner, 27 Tort & Ins L J 638 (1992).

14. For example, *Armotek Industries Inc* v *Employers Ins of Wausau*, 952 F 2d 756, 763 (3 Cir, 1991—liability). Old cases of this kind in England include: *Lockyer* v *Offley* (1786) 1 TR 252: the ship was seized after the voyage and cover had ended in respect of acts insured against occurring during the voyage. Holding the insurer not liable Willes J said (p 260): "Till the seizure of the ship, it was not certain that the officers of the Crown knew of the illicit trade carried on by the master, or whether they would take advantage of the forfeiture. It would be a dangerous doctrine to lay down that the insurer should in all cases be liable to remote consequential damages."

In *Fooks* v *Smith* [1924] 2 KB 508 (cargo) cargo was diverted within the period, a constructive total loss covered by the insurance, but requisitioned and sold outside the period; the latter was not covered, for in the words of Bailhache J (pp 515–516) "seizure and sale was a *nova causa superveniens*, and was not the necessary and direct result of the restraint of princes . . . by the time the seizure and sale took place the policy had long since run off, and . . . the seizure and sale were not so nearly connected with the restraint of princes that I can hold that the total loss was a completion of what was begun by the restraint of princes".

Distinguish, however, a new development from a loss that occurs in one period, which exposes the property insured to the possibility of (further) loss outside the period.

In *California Union Ins Co* v *Landmark Ins Co*[15] a swimming pool leaked over two consecutive periods covered by two different insurers and damaged adjacent property. The second insurer claimed that all loss was due to the occurrence of a leak during the first period. The first insurer argued that an attempted repair broke the chain of causation, and that later damage was a new occurrence falling in the second period. The court held that there was a single occurrence through the two periods, although not until the second period was the true cause discovered and the full extent of damage apparent; and that[16] the first insurer was liable because, if insurance is occurrence based, loss occurring in the insurance period must be compensated, even if the development of that loss continues after the period.

18–2 THE COMMENCEMENT OF COVER

The commencement of cover is governed by the contract of insurance: below, 18–2A. In the absence of any provision, cover begins not at the date of contracting but at the date of the policy[17]; but, if the policy date and the delivery date differ, it has been held[18] that the delivery date is the date on which cover begins. In the absence of a policy, cover will begin after a reasonable time.

18–2A Contract Terms

A contract term governing the commencement of cover is subject to normal rules of construction (above, chapter 15), in particular, construction *contra proferentem* in favour of the insured and against the insurer,[19] and in a way which advances the purpose of the insurance.

If the contract purports to cover loss occurring prior to the date of the contract, the courts will give effect to that intention, unless one of the parties was aware of the loss at the time of the contract: if the insured was aware even of facts suggesting that a loss might have occurred, failure to disclose these facts to the insurer could give rise to avoidance; if the insurer was in possession of the facts, he would be unlikely to underwrite the risk. The most common example of such cover is the marine example of property "lost or not lost",[20] but there is also the kind of liability insurance, which

15. 193 Cal Rptr 461 (Cal, 1983). Hook, 21 Tort & Ins L J 395 (1986).

16. However, the court also held the second insurer liable, jointly and severally with the first insurer, applying the triple trigger cases: see above, 17–4C and 18–1A. See also *Gruol Construction Co* v *Ins Co of North America*, 524 P 2d 427 (Wn, 1974—liability: dry rot).

17. *Silver Dolphin Products Ltd* v *Parcels & General Assurance Assn* [1984] 2 Lloyd's Rep 404 (cargo). *McMaster* v *New York Life Ins Co*, 183 US 25, 35–36 *per* Fuller CJ (1901—life); *Mutual Life Ins Co* v *Hurni Packing Co*, 263 US 167 (1923—life); *Williams* v *Employers' Liability Assurance Co Ltd*, 69 F 2d 285 (5 Cir, 1934—PA); *Hines* v *US*, 90 F 2d 957 (7 Cir, 1937—life).

Cf the view that normally "a lay person who pays his premium at the time an application for insurance is filed is justified in assuming that payment will bring immediate protection": *Crossley* v *State Farm Mutual Auto Ins Co*, 415 SE 2d 393, 395 (SC, 1992—PHI).

18. *Security Benefit Life Ins Co* v *Jackson*, 318 F 2d 846 (8 Cir, 1963—life).

19. For example *Klos* v *Mobil Oil Co*, 249 A 2d 889 (NJ, 1969—PA): in respect of insurance solicited by post by a credit card company the court held *inter alia* that, when the proposer was given a 10-day period during which to inspect the policy, he was held covered during that period.

20. MIA, section 6. *Sutherland* v *Pratt* (1843) 11 M & W 296 (cargo); *Bradford* v *Symondsen* (1881) 7 QBD 456 (CA—re). *US* v *Patryas*, 303 US 341 (1938—war risks); *Burch* v *Commonwealth County Mutual Ins Co*, 450 SW 2d 838 (Tex, 1970—motor). See also 18–2A4.

is triggered by claims made during the insurance period in respect of events causing material loss before that period.[21]

18–2A1　From 1 January

If cover is expressed to run "from 1 January 1994 to 1 January 1995," cover includes the last day but excludes the first: cover commences on 2 January 1994.[22] Much depends on the context in which words are used,[23] but there is attraction in the hetero-dox view of Rowlatt[24] that, according to the ordinary construction of the English language, when two days were mentioned as the days when a period began and ended both days are included in the period; that, for example, if it was said that the court sat from Monday to Friday each week, or that the calendar year ran from 1 January to 31 December, the days at each end of the period were included. But this is not the ortho-dox view of insurance periods: insurance from 1 January excludes 1 January. Reasons given are as follows:

(a) "Our law rejects fractions of a day . . . The effect is to render the day a sort of indivi-sible point; so that any act, done in the compass of it, is no more referrible [*sic*] to any one, than to any other portion of it; but the act and the day are co-extensive; and therefore the act cannot properly be said to be passed until the day is passed."[25]

This statement concerned a six-month period under a settlement. The force of the argument diminishes with the period of time in issue[26]; however, it has been applied[27] to contracts of insurance, although the insurance period may be measured in months.

(b) The "from date" construction might be supported as making a natural use of the word "from", which connotes an idea of separation:

"If space were in question, and a mile had to be measured 'from' a given place, it is obvious that no part of the place would be included in the mile. And, similarly, I can-not but think that, as regards time, 'from' is akin to 'after', and excludes the date fixed for the commencement of the computation."[28]

(c) The courts have been concerned to adopt a general rule for the construction of documents in the interests of certainty. This, of course, is an argument for a rule, but not necessarily for any particular rule.

---

21. Above, 17–4D.

22. In *Isaacs* v *Royal Ins Co* (1870) LR 5 Ex 296, 300 *per* Kelly CB (fire); *Cartwright* v *MacCormack* [1963] 1 All ER 11; [1962] 2 Lloyd's Rep 328 (CA—motor). The rule was affirmed in Scotland in *Sickness & Accident Assurance Assn Ltd* v *General Accident Assurance Corp Ltd*, 1892 19 R 977, 985 by Lord Robert-son (Ct Sess—liability). Levison no 13.08. *Contra: Scottish Metropolitan Assurance Co Ltd* v *Stewart* (1923) 39 TLR 407, 409 *per* Rowlatt J (hull), to whom the cases above were not cited.

23. *Pugh* v *Duke of Leeds* (1777) 2 Cowp 714, 717 *per* Lord Mansfield concerning a lease. See above, 15–3.

24. *Scottish Metropolitan Assurance Co Ltd* v *Stewart* (1923) 39 TLR 407, 409 (hull). *Polan* v *Travelers Ins Co*, 192 SE 2d 481 (Va, 1972).

25. *Lester* v *Garland* (1808) 15 Ves Jun 248, 257 *per* Sir William Grant. *Scottish Metropolitan* (above). Levison no 13.07.

26. Having booked a week's skiing from 1 January, the customer might not be very impressed, when told that in accordance with the courts of Chancery his holiday did not begin until January 2.

27. The words of Sir William Grant were applied by Harman LJ in *Cartwright* v *MacCormack* [1962] 2 Lloyd's Rep 328, 333–334 (CA—motor); also by Willmer LJ, *ibid*, p 334.

28. *South Staffordshire Tramways Co Ltd* v *Sickness & Accident Assurance Assn Ltd* [1891] 1 QB 402, 405 *per* Day J (liability); the decision was affirmed by the CA (*ibid*). *Cf* USA: this argument was rejected in *Polan* v *Travelers Ins Co*, 192 SE 2d 481 (Va, 1972).

Nonetheless, the "from date" construction is not a rigid rule but an inference about the intention of the parties[29]; any clear contrary intention to include the day first stated is given effect.[30] Further, the court is likely to construe the date in favour of the insured, as "the person primarily interested",[31]; and courts are readily persuaded that the parties intended to avoid an absurdity, for example, that of a gap in cover between one period of cover and its renewal.[32]

18–2A2 From 11 am

Any expression of time which occurs in a document for construction by the English courts is subject to the effect of section 3 of the Summer Time Act 1972, taken to refer to Greenwich mean time.[33]

As regards the terms of documents such as wills[34] it has been said that the law rejects fractions of a day. However, if the search for party intention is genuine, it is difficult to avoid the inference that insurance cover expressed to run from 11.00 am was intended to begin at 11.00 am; why else would the parties state the hour? Moreover, most insured, unversed in rules of construction conceived in Chancery in centuries past, would assume, for example in the case of motor insurance, that they were immediately covered and could lawfully drive the car that morning.

Yet, the "from date" construction (above, 18–2A1) was applied to the hour in *Cartwright* v *MacCormack*.[35] In that case, if 15 days motor insurance "from the commencement date of risk" in a cover note was measured so as to exclude the day of that date, it covered liability for injury to a third party, arising in the latter hours of the 15th day. If, as argued by the insurer, 15 days began from what the note called the commencement time, 11.45 am on the commencement date, there was no cover. The Court of Appeal decided there was cover both during the remainder of the commencement date and throughout the 15th complete day thereafter, when the accident occurred.

But for the mention of "11.45 am" in the cover note the case would have been a simple case of "from date" construction. As it could not be ignored, Nield J concluded "regretfully" for the insurer, for otherwise he could not explain "11.45 am".[36] On appeal there were two converging views. First, the leading judgment of Harman LJ found the note "tolerably clear"[37]: the 15 day cover note gave 15 days cover, as the risk was covered from 11.45 am on the commencement date, but the 15 day period

29. *Lester* v *Garland* (1808) 15 Ves Jun 248, 258 *per* Sir William Grant; *In re North* [1895] 2 QB 264, 274 *per* Rigby LJ (CA).

30. "1 January inclusive"—*Sickness & Accident Assurance Assn Ltd* v *General Accident Assurance Corp Ltd*, 1892 19 R 977 (Ct Sess—liability).

31. *In re North* [1895] 2 QB 264, 274 *per* Rigby LJ (CA), left open by Lord Collins MR in *Goldsmiths' Co* v *West Metropolitan Ry Co* [1904] 1 KB 1, 5 (CA) and discussed by Megarry J in *Re Figgis* [1969] 1 Ch 123, 133–134 in connection with the construction of a will. On construction *contra proferentem* in general see above, 15–5C.

32. *Cornfoot* v *Royal Exchange Assurance Corp* [1904] 1 KB 40, 44 *per* Mathew LJ (CA—hull); *Talbot* v *Metropolitan Life Ins Co*, 142 F 694, 699 (5 Cir, 1906—life). On construction by reference to the parties' objectives, and to avoid absurdity, see above, 15–3B and 15–4.

33. Interpretation Act 1978, sections 9 and 23(3). Levison no 13.06. In the USA, a time reference is usually taken to refer to standard time: Appleman, section 7174.

34. *Lester* v *Garland* (1808) 15 Ves Jun 248, 257 *per* Sir William Grant, cited above, 18–2A1(a).

35. [1963] 1 All ER 11. For a fuller report see [1962] 2 Lloyd's Rep 328.

36. [1962] 2 Lloyd's Rep 328, 331. In this sense: *Union Trust Co* v *Continental Gas Co*, 194 F 2d 901 (D Colum, 1952—PA).

37. p 333.

began on the day after. Second, Willmer LJ did not find the note clear, but continued[38]: "The cover note is in a form supplied by the [insurer], and the words used are their words. If there is any doubt as to its meaning, the document must, on well-known principles, be construed against the [insurer]."

18–2A3 On Delivery of the Policy

If the contract stipulates that cover shall commence on delivery of the policy, that stipulation will be enforced. If that policy is "delivered" by post to the insured, it has been held[39] that cover commences on the date of posting.

18–2A4 On Payment of Premium

A common provision is that the insurance cover shall not attach until premium is paid.[40] In the case of life insurance, at least, which can be obtained for an interim period while the risk is fully assessed, the purpose, it has been said,[41] is the purpose of prepayment in contracts generally: to ensure that the insurer does not have to commence performance by coming on risk, until he has had something in return. If the provision is clear, it will be applied by the courts.[42] However, a provision "no insurance until premium is paid" can be read in three different ways.[43] First, there may be no contract (or cover) until premium is paid.[44] Second, there may be a contract from the time of agreement, but no cover until premium is paid and then only for the future.[45] Third, in the second situation, when premium is paid, there may be cover retrospectively to some earlier date,[46] such as the date of agreement or, in the case of renewal, to the date on which the previous cover expired.[47]

---

38. p 334. This was also accepted by Harman LJ (p 333), albeit as a "last-ditch argument".

39. *North American Life Assurance Co Ltd* v *Elson* (1903) 33 SCR 383 (life); *Sharkey* v *Yorkshire Ins Co* (1916) 54 SCR 92 (stallion).

40. The meaning of payment depends on the context: Goode, *Payment Obligations in Commercial and Financial Transactions*, p 11. As to payment of premium, see above, 13–2 ff. Appleman, section 107.

A variation is that the insurance shall not attach until payment of premium and delivery of receipt. It has been held that the receipt was delivered at the time that it was sent by the company to its agent for delivery to the insured: *North American Life Assurance Co* v *Elson* (1903) 33 SCR 383 (life).

41. *Rosenthal* v *New York Life Ins Co*, 94 F 2d 675, 680 (8 Cir, 1938—life).

42. *Tarleton* v *Staniforth* (1796) 1 Bos & Pul 471 (fire); *Equitable Fire & Accident Office Ltd* v *The Ching Wo Hong* [1907] AC 96 (PC—fire).

43. Generally, see above, 11–2E.

44. *Canning* v *Farquhar* (1886) 16 QBD 727, 731 *per* Lord Esher MR (CA—life). See also *Ocean Accident & Guarantee Corp Ltd* v *Cole* [1932] 2 KB 100, 104 *per* Lord Hewart CJ (motor).

45. *Sickness & Accident Asurance Assn* v *General Accident Assurance Co* (1892) 19 R 977, 981–982 *per* Lord Low (Ct Sess—liability).

46. For example marine insurance on subject-matter "lost or not lost" necessarily contemplates cover in respect of events prior to the conclusion of the contract and payment of premium: *Bradford* v *Symondsen* (1881) 7 QBD 456 (CA—re). However, the rule is that the insured "is entitled to recover . . . notwithstanding that the fact that he may have acquired his interest only after the loss has already occurred", not that he "can recover in respect of a loss which has already occurred before the period of risk specified in the policy has ever commenced": *Reinhart Co* v *Joshua Hoyle & Sons Ltd* [1961] 1 Lloyd's Rep 346, 358 *per* Willmer LJ (CA–AR). In *New South Wales Leather Co Pty Ltd* v *Vanguard Ins Co Ltd* (1991) 25 NSWLR 699 (cargo) the rule was applied to enable recovery in respect of goods which were not damaged but stolen before the claimant acquired an interest and hence in which the claimant never acquired an interest; *sed quaere*: Davies 5 Ins L J 159 (1992).

The inference suggested in the text might arise in the case of compulsory cover such as motor insurance: *Ocean Accident & Guarantee Corp Ltd* v *Cole* [1932] 2 KB 100, 105–106 *per* Avory J (motor), but other members of the court did not agree.

47. *Salvin* v *James* (1805) 6 East 571, 582 *per* Lord Ellenborough CJ (fire).

18–2A5 From an Event

In the case of cover from an event, the "from date" rule (above, 18–2A2) does not apply; each case is considered in the light of the event and of the purpose of the insurance. In a case of aviation insurance, cover for 12 hours from the date and time of the first flight of an experimental aircraft began when the first flight began[48]: application of the "from date" rule would have postponed cover until the first flight was over, and would have defeated the manifest intention of the parties. However, for the same reason, burglary cover from the time that specified alarms were installed would not include the period of installation.

18–2A6 Cover During Transit

Insurance cover expressed to operate during a period or an event or operation depends for its commencement on the construction or meaning of the period, event or operation. A leading example is transit cover on goods.

Insurance of goods is often expressed to begin and end with transit. The same basic idea underlies the warehouse to warehouse clause, now called the transit clause.[49] In the interpretation of transit clauses the court's main concern is to give effect to the intention of the parties. In particular, the insured is presumed[50] to want to avoid a time gap in cover; the insurer is presumed to want to avoid a risk of a kind that he did not intend to undertake. With this in mind, the courts generally infer that transit cover begins when the custody and control of the goods[51] passes from the sender or his agent to the carrier or his agent; it is at this point that the nature of the risk usually changes.[52] If this interpretation enables the court to avoid a gap in cover, so much the better[53] but this factor tends to be secondary to the transfer of custody and control. Thus, goods, which have been loaded on the vehicle but remain in the control of the sender, for example, locked in his warehouse,[54] have not commenced transit. An exception arises when, although custody and control have passed to a carrier, the

---

48. *Dunn* v *Campbell* (1920) 4 Ll L Rep 36, 39 *per* Bankes LJ (CA—PA). *Marathon Ins Co* v *Arnold*, 433 P 2d 927 (Okl, 1967—motor).

49. A notable example is clause 8 of the Institute Cargo Clauses 1982.

50. *Cf Hirdes GmbH* v *Edmond* [1991] 2 Lloyd's Rep 546, 549 (hull), in which Hirst J, while accepting that this was a "relevant consideration", questioned whether it gave rise to a presumption.

51. *Crow's Transport Ltd* v *Phoenix Assurance Co Ltd* [1965] 1 Lloyd's Rep 139, 143 *per* Lord Denning MR (CA—goods in transit); *SCA (Freight) Ltd* v *Gibson* [1974] 2 Lloyd's Rep 533, 534 *per* Ackner J (goods in transit). Clarke (1988) 23 ETL 645; Merkin & McGee, p B.1.2–01. *Plata American Trading Inc* v *Lancashire* [1957] 2 Lloyd's Rep 347, 349 (NY, 1957—cargo). For a case involving the sender's shipping agent see *City Stores Co* v *Sun Ins Co*, 1973 AMC 44 (SD NY, 1972—cargo).

Cf an earlier tradition reflected in Rule 4 of the Rules of Construction in the first Schedule to the MIA, whereby insurance of goods "from the loading thereof" did not attach until goods were actually on board ship: Arnould, No 523. Also cases turning on the physical movement of goods: *Sadler Bros Co* v *Meredith* [1963] 2 Lloyd's Rep 293, 307 (goods in transit). *Hillcrea Export & Import Co Inc* v *Universal Ins Co*, 110 F Supp 204 (SD NY 1953—cargo).

52. *Re Traders & General Ins Assn Ltd* (1924) 18 Ll L Rep 450, 451 *per* Eve J (cargo).

53. *Salvin* v *James* (1805) 6 East 571, 582 *per* Lord Ellenborough CJ (fire); *Cornfoot* v *Royal Exchange Assurance Corp* [1904] 1 KB 40, 44 *per* Mathew LJ (CA—hull); *Symington & Co* v *Union Ins Sy of Canton Ltd* (1928) 31 Ll L Rep 179, 181 *per* Scrutton LJ (CA—cargo). *Lindo* v *Ocean Marine Ins Co*, 27 F 2d 956, 958 (ND Cal, 1928—cargo).

54. *Kessler Export Corp* v *Reliance Ins Co*, 207 F Supp 355 (ED NY 1962—cargo). See also *Hillcrea* (above).

goods have embarked on the wrong journey[55] or the wrong ship[56]: the cover contracted for has not commenced.

Transit cover continues until transit ends (below, 18–3C) or is interrupted. Transit includes the ordinary incidents of transit: "temporary stops, incidental delays, or some deviation from the planned route of travel".[57] It includes, therefore, stops while the driver of the vehicle sleeps[58] or takes refreshment,[59] but not an evening out in Rome.[60] It also includes, therefore, "normal" delay,[61] including but not confined to delay beyond the control of the insured,[62] but not indefinite delay[63] or delay ordered by the sender while he reconsiders the destination of the goods,[64] or a delay of more than a few hours for the operational convenience of the carrier.[64a] Moreover, it is common to exclude loss while the goods are "left unattended".[65]

18–3 TERMINATION OF COVER

Cover may end on a date or event stated in the contract (18–3A ff) or it may end prematurely. It ends prematurely, if the insured has failed to pay premium (chapter 13) or has broken a warranty (chapter 20), or when the parties agree to end it (18–3D), or when one of them exercises an option to end it (18–3E).

18–3A Expiry

As with the commencement of cover, so also with termination of cover: the contract ends in accordance with its own terms. If the contract provides cover for a certain period from a commencement date, what determines the end is calculation from the commencement date (above, 18–2A). Cover ends at midnight on the last day of the period, whether that day is deduced from the commencement date or the period is expressed to be "until" that day.[66] In the absence of an effective stipulation for the

---

55. *Israel & Co* v *Sedgwick* [1893] 1 QB 303 (CA—cargo); cited with approval in *Kallis (Manufacturers) Ltd* v *Success Ins Ltd* [1985] 2 Lloyd's Rep 8 (PC—cargo).

56. *Kallis* (above).

57. *Boontong Handbag Co Inc* v *Home Ins Co*, 310 A 2d 510, 511 (NJ, 1973). To avoid doubt the policy, such as the Lloyd's Goods in Transit (CMR) Policy, may specify that cover continues "whilst in the normal course of transit the goods or merchandise are temporarily housed on or off the vehicles".

58. *Ries & Sons Inc* v *Automobile Ins Co*, 3 A 2d 610 (NJ 1939).

59. *Sadler Bros Co* v *Meredith* [1963] 2 Lloyd's Rep 293, 307 *per* Roskill J (goods in transit). *Ries & Sons Inc* v *Automobile Ins Co*, 3 A 2d 610, 612 (NJ 1939).

60. *SCA (Freight) Ltd* v *Gibson* [1974] 2 Lloyd's Rep 533 (goods in transit).

61. As regards "normal" delay, see *Symington & Co* v *Union Ins Sy of Canton Ltd* (1928) 30 Ll L Rep 280, 283 *per* Roche J; (1928) 31 Ll L Rep 179, 181 *per* Scrutton LJ (CA—cargo); *Crow's Transport Ltd* v *Phoenix Assurance Co Ltd* [1965] 1 Lloyd's Rep 139, 144 *per* Danckwerts LJ (CA—goods in transit).

62. This is commonly dealt with by the contract terms; see the Termination of Adventure Clause, clause 9 of the Institute Cargo Clauses 1982.

63. *Fireman's Fund Ins Co* v *Service Transportation Co*, 466 F Supp 934 (D My, 1979)—public health authorities ordered the goods to be held until further notice.

64. *Safadi* v *Western Assurance Co* (1933) 46 Ll L Rep 140. Templeman, *Marine Insurance* (5th ed), p 102.

64a. For example, between two and six days on a trailer while the tractor was otherwise engaged: *Hartford Casualty Ins Co* v *Banker's Note*, 817 F Supp 1567, 1573 (ND Ga, 1993—property).

65. *Starfire Diamond Rings Ltd* v *Angel* [1962] 2 Lloyd's Rep 217 (CA—jewellers' block); *Plaistow Transport Ltd* v *Graham* [1966] 1 Lloyd's Rep 639 (goods in transit); *Ingleton of Ilford Ltd* v *General Accident Fire & Life Assurance Corp* [1967] 2 Lloyd's Rep 179 (goods in transit); *Langford* v *Legal & General Assurance Sy* [1986] 2 Lloyd's Rep 103 (market traders).

66. *Isaacs* v *Royal Ins Co* (1870) LR 5 Exch 296, 300 *per* Kelly CB (fire); *Hirdes GmbH* v *Edmond* [1991] 2 Lloyd's Rep 546 (hull). As regards the termination of motor cover, see Parsons, (1993) 3 Ins L & P 43.

termination of cover, it has been suggested that cover will continue indefinitely[67] how-ever, that suggestion was made *obiter* in a case in which the insurer was in a position to bring about the event which determined the period of cover.[68] In other cases, it is likely that, as in other kinds of contract,[69] the court will imply a term that cover shall not last beyond a reasonable time.[70]

Cover may end before the contract date, if there is a monetary limit on the liability of the insurer and aggregate loss reaches that limit. If cover ends before the full period, the insured has no general right to recover premium proportionate to the time remaining.[71]

18–3B End of Risk

If the contract covers only one occurrence of the specified risk, for example death of the life insured, the risk ends and the cover ends when the life ends.[72] Similarly, if the life (or property) insured ceases to exist by reason of an event that is not insured, the risk ends and the insurance ends. In each case, there is no right to demand return of premium proportionate to the unexpired period of cover.[73]

18–3C Stated Event

The termination of insurance may be fixed with reference to the occurrence of an event, so that cover ends at the time of the event or after a stated period following the event. For example, a life contract under an employer's group scheme may end when the insured employee leaves the employment.[74]

In the case of transit insurance on goods, transit ends and cover ends when custody and control of the goods pass from the carrier or his agent to the consignee or his agent.[75] If goods in transit are delivered to a third party, such as a customs authority, a port authority or a warehouseman, the position depends on whether the third party

67. *General Accident Fire & Life Assurance Corp v Robertson* [1909] AC 404, 411 *per* Lord Loreburn LC (PA).

68. *Robertson* (above).

69. *Hick v Raymond* [1893] AC 22, 32 *per* Lord Watson; *Carlton SS Co Ltd v Castle Mail Packet Co Ltd* [1898] AC 486, 490 *per* Lord Herschell.

70. *Allagar Rubber Estates Ltd v National Benefit Assurance Co Ltd* (1922) 12 Ll L Rep 110 (CA—cargo: transit clause).

71. *Tyrie v Fletcher* (1777) 2 Cowp 666. See further, above, 13–12.

72. Equally hull cover ends when the ship sinks: *Gorsedd SS Co v Forbes* (1900) 5 Com Cas 413, 415 *per* Bigham J (hull). As regards the termination of motor cover, see Parsons, (1993) 3 Ins L & P 43.

73. *Tyrie v Fletcher* (1777) 2 Cowp 666 (hull). See above, 13–12A.

74. *Lineberger v Security Life & Trust Co*, 95 SE 2d 501 (SC, 1956—life). This situation has generated considerable case law in the United States; see Appleman, section 122. On the option to leave a group scheme and convert to an ordinary life policy, see Appleman, section 126.

75. *Bartlett & Partners Ltd v Meller* [1961] 1 Lloyd's Rep 487, 489 *per* Sachs J (AR). *Budco Associates Inc v Royal Exchange Assurance Co of America*, 384 NYS 2d 819 (1976); *First American Artificial Flowers Inc v AFIA Worldwide Ins*, 1977 AMC 376 (NY, 1976—cargo); *Lumber & Wood Products Inc v New Hampshire Ins Co*, 807 F 2d 916 (11 Cir, 1987—cargo).

holds for the consignee or for the carrier.[76] For example, in one case,[77] goods arrived and for a month were left with a stevedore entirely for the convenience of the consignee and unrelated to any requirement of transportation: transit and transit insurance had ended.

If goods in transit never reach the custody and control of the consignee, insurance cover does not continue for ever. It has been suggested[78] that it will lapse after a reasonable time. In *Verna*,[79] the Australian court stated that "unduly protracted steps in the cargo's transportation are not within, and may terminate 'ordinary course of transit' ". He adopted the words of Ackner J in an earlier English case: "Goods cease to be in transit when they are on a journey which is not in reasonable furtherance of their carriage to their ultimate destination."[80] Moreover, in the case of movements governed by the Institute Cargo Clauses, cover ends, whether the goods have reached the custody and control of the consignee or not, "60 days after completion of discharge overside . . . from the oversea vessel at the final port of discharge".[81] All this is subject, of course, to the terms of the cover in question, so that, for example, if cover runs to or from a "warehouse"[82] or to "final warehouse",[83] goods remain covered until such place is reached, even if the consignee has obtained custody and control earlier.

18–3D Termination by Agreement

Like any other contract, a contract of insurance may be discharged by the agreement of the parties. The insured abandons his right to insurance cover for the unexpired period of the contract term, in return for which the insurer usually returns a proportionate part of the premium. The agreement is not binding unless it satisfies the usual requirements of a binding contract,[84] such as consideration and consent.[85] It will be recalled, no doubt, that, in principle, the law does not investigate the adequacy of consideration.

In *Liberty National Bank* v *Life Ins Co of Cincinnati*,[86] the insurer informed the insured, who was wondering whether to change his life cover, that his existing policy had a certain surrender value and, in reliance on this information, the insured let it

---

76. *Marten* v *Nippon Sea & Land Ins Co Ltd* (1898) 3 Com Cas 164; *Gagnière & Co* v *Eastern Co of Warehouses Ins and Transport of Goods with Advances Ltd* (1921) 7 Ll L Rep 188 (goods in transit). *Lindo* v *Ocean Marine Ins Co*, 27 F 2d 956 (ND Cal, 1928), affirmed 30 F 2d 782 (9 Cir, 1929—cargo); *St Maurice Valley Paper Co* v *Continental Ins Co*, 13 F Supp 346 (ED NY, 1936—cargo), affirmed 85 F 2d 1018 (2 Cir, 1936).
Cf cover which extends expressly to "loss in customs": *Saffadi* v *Western Assurance Co* (1933) 46 Ll L Rep 140 (cargo). *Industrial Waxes Inc* v *Brown* [1958] 2 Lloyd's Rep 626; 160 F Supp 230 (SD NY, 1957—cargo).
77. *Verna Trading* v *New India Assurance* [1991] 1 VLR 129 (Vict—cargo).
78. *Allegar Rubber Estates Ltd* v *National Benefit Assn* (1922) 10 Ll L Rep 564, 565 *per* Bailhache J.
79. *Verna* (above) p 168 *per* Ormiston J.
80. *SCA (Freight) Ltd* v *Gibson* [1974] 2 Lloyd's Rep 533, 535 (goods in transit).
81. Clause 8.
82. *Rapp Ltd* v *McClure* [1955] 1 Lloyd's Rep 292 (burglary, fire and theft); *Reinhart Co* v *Hoyle & Sons Ltd* [1961] 1 Lloyd's Rep 346 (CA—cargo). Cf *Plata American Trading Inc* v *Lancashire* [1957] 2 Lloyd's Rep 347, 349 (NY, 1957) in which the court was prepared to assume that a storage tank was a warehouse.
83. Clarke (1988) 23 ETL 645, 650.
84. *Baines* v *Woodfall* (1859) 6 CB (NS) 657 (hull); *Ingram-Johnson* v *Century Ins Co Ltd* 1909 SC 1032 (PA).
85. *Reyner* v *Hall* (1813) 4 Taunt 516 (hull); *Baines* v *Woodfall* (1859) 6 CB (NS) 657, 676 *per* Lord Cockburn CJ (hull); *Lowlands SS Co Ltd* v *North of England P & I Assn* (1921) 6 Ll L Rep 230.
86. 901 F 2d 539 (6 Cir, 1990—life).

lapse. The quoted value was mistaken, the true figure being zero. The insured died and his personal representative sought either the amount of the value quoted or the reinstatement of the policy (and hence payment of the sum insured). The court saw the quotation as an offer to buy the policy which the insured had accepted,[87] and this contract was enforced subject, however, to determination of the factual question whether the insured should have been aware of the true surrender value and hence of the error in the quotation.

The parties are free to terminate the contract of insurance, even though the effect is to defeat the legitimate expectations of a third party. For example, it has been held that group life insurance contracted between an employer and insurer may be terminated without the consent of the employee-beneficiary.[88] Again, the insolvent insured may terminate his contract with his liability insurer, even though the practical effect is to defeat the claim of a third party against him.[89] The law draws a distinction between rights, such as rights in tort against the insured, and the enjoyment of those rights. The third party may be unable to enjoy his rights because the tortfeasor has neither money nor insurance, but the rights themselves, although of no practical value, are unaffected.[90] This being so, the law will not intervene to prevent the discharge of the contract of insurance. A statutory exception appears in respect of motor insurance, whereby the rights of a third party against the insurer may be enforced notwithstanding that the insurer may be entitled to avoid or cancel the policy, for this situation is thought to include the case of discharge by agreement.[91]

18–3E Option to Terminate

An option to terminate insurance cover which has commenced may be found in the contract itself or in statute.

18–3E1 Statute: Second Thoughts

In the case of ordinary long-term insurance,[92] the insured has a statutory right of cancellation. The insurer is obliged to provide the insured with a statutory notice, to which a form of notice of cancellation is annexed.[93] The insured may serve the notice[94] of cancellation on the insurer, which has the effect of cancelling the contract or, if no contract has been concluded, revoking any offer to contract made by the pro-

---

87. p 547.

88. *Metropolitan Life Ins Co* v *Korneghy*, 71 So 2d 292 (Ala, 1954—life). *Cf* the group policy contracted by the employer as agent for the employee: *ex hypothesi* the employee is a party to his own insurance contract and it cannot be terminated without his consent.

89. *Rowe* v *Kenway* (1921) 8 Ll L Rep 225 (liability).

90. "No one's right was infringed"—*Quinn* v *Leathem* [1901] AC 495, 539 *per* Lord Lindley; see also *Allen* v *Flood* [1898] AC 1. *Cf Hood's Trustees* v *Southern Union General Ins Co* [1928] Ch 793 (CA—motor).

91. Shawcross, *Motor Insurance* (2nd ed, 1949), p 289, commenting on section 10 of the Road Traffic Act 1934, now replaced by provisions of the Road Traffic Act 1988: see above, 5–9.

92. Ordinary long-term business means long term business that is not industrial assurance business: Insurance Companies Act 1982, section 96(1). By section 1 of the Act long term business is business of any class specified in Schedule 1 to the Act, which includes such categories as life assurance and permanent health insurance.

93. Insurance Companies Act 1982, section 75. The form of the notice is established by regulations, currently the Insurance Companies Regulations 1981 (SI 1981, No 1654). Failure to provide the required notice is an offence, but does not render the insurance contract unenforceable: section 75(4)

94. The service of notice is defined in section 77.

posed insured.[95] To have this effect, the notice of cancellation must be served before the end of the tenth day after receipt of the statutory notice or before the end of the earliest day, on which the insured knows both that the insurance contract has been concluded and that the first or only premium has been paid.[96] Any sums previously paid by way of premium or insurance money may be recovered.[97]

18–3E2 Contract Option

The contract of insurance may provide that a party to the contract shall be entitled to cancel the contract, for example, by notice. In England, the court will not investigate or question the motives of the party exercising the right of cancellation. In *Sun Fire Office* v *Hart*,[98] the Privy Council rejected the argument that the insurer could exercise a contractual right to terminate only on reasonable grounds, concluding that "the sufficiency of the reasons moving them to desire the termination of the risk which they had undertaken is a matter of which the insurers are constituted the sole judges". In the United States, however, the right of the insurer to terminate the insurance in accordance with its terms may be limited by statute,[99] by public policy as applied by the courts,[100] or by the doctrine of good faith.[101]

In England, options to terminate are limited only by the normal rules of construction.[102] To take an extreme case, in which the right of cancellation once exercised purported to have retroactive effect, a court would be disinclined[103] to apply it literally, because the possibility of cancellation would deprive the contract of all binding effect at the discretion of the insurer. Further, the requirements of notice will have to be closely observed and are likely to be construed strictly against the insurer.[104] In some parts of the United States, courts have required that notice be actually received by the insured, as a matter of public policy, "to give the insured an opportunity to procure

---

95. Section 76(4).
96. Section 76(1).
97. Section 76(5).
98. (1889) 14 App Cas 98, 104–105 *per* Lord Watson; in 1885 there were nine fires destroying over half the plantation insured. After the eighth fire the insured received an anonymous letter threatening further fires, which he showed to the insurer who, while accepting liability in respect of the previous fires, promptly purported to end the cover in accordance with its terms. The Board held that the insurer had validly terminated the insurance prior to the ninth fire.
99. For example, California Ins Code, section 661.
100. *L'Orange* v *Medical Protective Co*, 394 F 2d 57 (6 Cir, 1968—liability) in which each party was entitled to cancel the policy by giving notice, but the court held (p 62) that it "is contrary to public policy to permit an insurance company to use policy cancellation as punishment against a doctor or dentist who appears as a witness to protect the rights of a plaintiff who has been wronged by another member of the profession. If the insurance industry can use the cancellation procedure to keep members of the medical profession from testifying as witnesses, malpractice litigation can be stifled." The court found (p 63) that cancellation thus motivated would be a breach of the insurance contract. This decision has been followed or accepted in other jurisdictions: *Spindle* v *Travelers Ins Co*, 136 Cal Rptr 404 (Cal, 1977—liability); *Coira* v *Florida Medical Assn*, 429 So 2d 23 (Fla, 1983—liability).
101. *Spindle* v *Travelers Ins Co*, 136 Cal Rptr 404, 408 (Cal, 1977—liability): the doctrine will be used to prevent cancellation by the insurer, if the effect is to deprive the insured of his bargain, i.e., of the cover for the period for which he has paid.
102. *Commercial Union Assurance Co PLC* v *Sun Alliance Ins Group PLC* [1992] 1 Lloyd's Rep 475, 480 *per* Steyn J (re), which concerned insurance intended to continue indefinitely "with 120 days NCAD", i.e. subject to notice of cancellation within 120 days of the anniversary date.
103. *Sun Fire Office* v *Hart* (1889) 14 App Cas 98, 103 *per* Lord Watson.
104. *Koehn* v *Central National Ins Co*, 354 P 2d 352 (Kan, 1960—motor).

other insurance".[105] In England, commercial good sense requires that a policy be construed with the same end in mind[106] and this, together with public policy, suggests a requirement that notice of cancellation by the insurer in any case of compulsory insurance, such as motor insurance, be actually received.[107] Less likely, though no less attractive, is an implied term in a group policy that notice of termination shall be received by the individual insured.[108]

Contractual cancellation by the insured is subject to the same rules. However, the exercise of a right of surrender, that is, surrender of a life policy in return for payment of the surrender value of that policy, has been analysed as something like discharge by agreement, namely the acceptance by the insured of a standing offer by the insurer.[109] It has also been described as the exercise of an option[110]; in the general law options must be exercised strictly in accordance with their terms.[111] In any event, the insured may be able to bring about the cancellation of the policy by refusing to pay further premiums, when they fall due.[112]

In the case of a composite policy with two or more co-insureds, it has been held by the High Court of Australia[113] that all the co-insured must join in cancelling the contract, unless it is clear that the contract gives one or more of them a unilateral right of cancellation. The latter would have to be very clear, as this is unlikely to be the intention of the insurer in view of the possible change in the nature of the risk, if a contract for A and B becomes a contract for B alone,[114] and in view of the practical difficulties involved. For example, it may well be that the amount of premium to be refunded is

---

105. *Koehn* (above) p 359, citing *Donarski* v *Lardy*, 88 NW 2d 7 (Minn, 1958—motor); the latter case was applied in *Government Employees Ins Co* v *Swanson*, 246 F Supp 698 (D Minn, 1965 motor), but the rule was later changed by statute which provided that proof of mailing of notice of cancellation shall be sufficient proof that notice has been given: Minn St 1971, section 65B.18. The *Donarski* rule is found in Iowa: *Selken* v *Northland Ins Co*, 90 NW 2d 29, 34 (Iowa, 1958 motor) and cases cited, in spite of statute: *Farmers Ins Group* v *Merryweather*, 214 NW 2d 184 (Iowa, 1974—motor); and also Ohio: *Smith* v *Globe American Casualty Co*, 313 NE 2d 21 (1973—motor). The *Donarski* rule has been rejected in, for example, Alaska: *Hartsfield* v *Carolina Casualty Ins Co*, 411 P 2d 396 (Alk 1966—motor); California: *Jensen* v *Traders & General Ins Co*, 345 P 2d 1 (Cal, 1959—motor); South Dakota: *Rumsey* v *St Paul Mercury Ins Co*, 242 NW 2d 677 (SD, 1976—motor) applying the law of Oregon; and Pennsylvania: *Mackiw* v *Pennsylvania Threshermen & Farmers Mutual Casualty Ins Co*, 193 A 2d 745 (1963—motor).

106. *Webb & Hughes* v *Bracey* [1964] 1 Lloyd's Rep 465, 468 *per* Sachs J (liability).

107. The word "notice" is generally construed to require receipt of the communication in question: below, 26–2D.

Cf the view that notice of cancellation will be effective if sent to the address of the insured indicated on the policy *Matthews* v *Fidelity & Guarantee Ins Underwriters Inc* 734 F Supp 755 (SD Miss, 1990—motor) or any subsequent address notified to the insurer, even if the insured has moved and does not receive the notice.

108. USA: such a right to notice may be provided by statute. Its purpose is to reinforce the statutory right of the insured to convert group cover, for example, on loss of associated employment, to personal cover. It remains unsettled whether, if notice is not given, he remains covered: Best, 90 Dick L Rev 101 (1985). See also Levy, 26 Tort & Ins L J 621 (1991).

109. *Ingram-Johnson* v *Century Ins Co Ltd* 1909 SC 1032 (PA). Also in this sense: *Zimmerman* v *American States Ins Co*, 763 F Supp 228, 231 (SD Ohio, 1990—life), indicating that, generally and in line with rules of contract law, notice will be effective when it is sent.

110. *Ingram–Johnson* (above) p 1037 *per* Lord Guthrie.

111. *United Dominions Trust (Commercial) Ltd* v *Eagle Aircraft Services Ltd* [1968] 1 All ER 104 (CA).

112. An exception may arise in the case of life policies under which the insurer is entitled to deduct accumulated benefits in order to fund premiums and maintain the policy. Generally, see above, 13–11B.

113. *Federation Ins Ltd* v *Wasson* (1987) 163 CLR 303 (motor), citing (p 310) with approval of the "well-known exposition by Sir Wilfred Greene MR" in *General Accident* v *Midland Bank* (below 30–4).

114. p 316.

not readily susceptible of calculation, if one co-insured alone terminates his separate insurance.[115]

18–3F Wrongful Termination by the Insurer

If the insurer purports to terminate the cover wrongfully, whether in the purported exercise of a contractual option or on the ground of misrepresentation, non-disclosure or breach of warranty, the insured may elect to accept the insurer's repudiation of the contract of insurance or to affirm the contract. If he affirms the contract and, in due time, tenders payment of premiums, the contract remains in force and any loss occurring is covered by the contract.[116] If the insurer refuses to pay the claim, the usual remedies follow.[117]

---

115. p 315.
116. *Arkwright–Boston Manufacturers Mutual Ins Assn* v *Calvert Fire Ins Co* 887 F 2d 437 (2 Cir, 1989—re).
117. Below, 30–7

CHAPTER 19

EXCEPTIONS

19–1 EXCEPTIONS IN GENERAL

19–1A The Nature of Exceptions

The scope of a contractual promise can be stated either in simple positive terms[1] or in a mixture of positive terms and negative terms such as exceptions.[2] The use of exceptions as tools of definition has been recognised in the general law,[3] and has been found in the law of insurance for longer.[4] Insurance cover may be defined positively by specifying the risks or circumstances in respect of which cover is provided; alternatively, cover may be expressed in broad terms, such as "property damage", subject to exceptions that subtract from the broad terms,[5] so that the precise cut of the insurer's liability, voluntarily assumed in broad terms, is "contractually tailored".[6] If exceptions are used in this way, the counsel of caution must be that they are to be regarded in most if not all respects like any other exceptions. This seems to be the current view of exceptions in general contract law,[7] and insurance contract law does not evidently differ.

Distinguish, however, the policy drafted with belt and braces, using so-called exceptions to spell out the negative corollary of terms stating cover, these "should be regarded as merely ensuring that the insured risk does not cover a particular situation" and "may fall to be regarded not as true exceptions in that they exclude a risk".[8]

Distinguish also an exception within the scope of an exception; that is not construed as providing cover, unless and to the extent that it is supported by positive statements of cover elsewhere in the contract. One might be forgiven for thinking that 5 minus (2 minus 1) came to 4, but it is not necessarily so; the cover may come to either 3 or 4.

---

1. For example, I promise to let the two upper floors of my house.
2. For example, I promise to let my entire (three storied) house except the ground floor.
3. Coote, *Exception Clauses* (London, 1964); Yates and Hawkins, *Standard Business Contracts* (London, 1986), No 6(B)1.
4. Talking of a clause requiring reasonable care on the part of the insured, Branson J in *Concrete Ltd* v *Attenborough* (1940) 65 Ll L Rep 174, 179 (liability) said:"It is the very function of conditions to limit the extent of the general undertaking which is given in the first instance". See also, for example, *Gray* v *Blackmore* [1934] 1 KB 95 (motor); *Davidson* v *Guardian Royal Exchange Assurance* [1979] 1 Lloyd's Rep 406 (Ct Sess—motor).
5. Although the resultant cover may be the same, whichever method of drafting is used, there is less chance of gaps in cover in the case of an all risks policy. Further the onus of proof is different. Keeton, pp 269–273
6. *Gulf Ins Co* v *Tilley*, 280 F Supp 60, 63 (ND Ind, 1967—liability), affirmed 393 F 2d 119 (7 Cir, 1968).
7. *Smith* v *Eric S Bush* [1990] 1 AC 831, 857 *per* Lord Griffiths; criticised by Macdonald (1992) 12 LS 277.
8. *Bell* v *Lothiansure Ltd* (Court of Session, 1 February 1991).

For example, an exception to cover in respect of "liability assumed by the insured under any contract", and which goes on to say that the exception "does not apply to a warranty that work performed by the insured will be done in a workmanlike manner" does not without more mean that there is cover for the latter, in particular, without close regard to other terms of the contract.[9]

In this book, exceptions, sometimes referred to as terms delimiting risk,[10] conditions, exclusions,[11] temporal exclusions,[12] or limitations of risk,[13] are terms of the insurance contract that reduce the extent of cover which, but for the exception, would be provided . . . with the exception, however, of one issue (below, 19–5), the application of the spirit of the Unfair Contract Terms Act, for which the definition of exception is reconsidered.

As a matter of form, exceptions may be express or implied. Express exceptions are found as terms written in the contract of insurance. Implied exceptions are found as limits inherent in the usual meaning of the cover written by the contract of insurance.[14] For example, it is implicit that a fire risk does not cover explosion[15]; and that "all risks" do not include inevitable deterioration.[16] An exception may concern the circumstances of cover[17] or the amount of cover.[18] In the former instance, the exception may or may not be drafted in terms that make it operate only if it is a cause of loss: below, 19–1C2.

19–1B Warranties Compared

19–1B1 The Effect on Risk

When an insurer defends a claim by pleading the operation of an exception to the scope (or amount of cover), if he sustains that plea, the effect is to defeat (or reduce the amount of) the claim but it leaves the insurance in force in respect of any other or later loss within the scope of the cover. When an exception operates, the insurer is off risk, usually because the circumstance of the exception has increased the risk to a

---

9. *Commercial Union Ins Co* v *John Massman Contracting Co*, 713 F Supp 1403, 1406 and references cited (D Kan, 1989—liability). See also *Continental Casualty Co* v *Pittsburgh Corning Corp*, 917 F 2d 297, 299 *per* Judge Posner (7 Cir, 1990—liability), in which it was held that an exclusion of office expenses in an exception of legal defence expenses did not provide cover for the former. On the onus of proof in such cases, see above 16–3C5.

10. Hence it is acceptable to refer to an exception as a term descriptive of the risk; for example, *De Maurier (Jewels) Ltd* v *Bastion Ins Co Ltd* [1967] 2 Lloyd's Rep 550, 559 *per* Donaldson J (motor). *Contra*, MacGillivray, No 550. *Cf* Birds [1976] JBL 231, 232.

It is not of course the only kind of contract term that is descriptive of the risk. When a motor car was described in the policy as a five seater, Mackinnon J observed that nobody "could suppose that if during the course of the policy the man altered the body and turned it into a two-seater car, the validity of the policy would then cease": *Roberts* v *Anglo-Saxon Ins Assn Ltd* (1926) 26 Ll L Rep 154, 157 (motor). Although the principle holds, it is not clear that that illustration holds good today.

11. Keeton, p 175.

12. For example Australian Law Reform Commission, Report No 20, para 217.

13. For example 45 CJS, section 473(4). *Cf* the discussion of terminology, distinguishing exceptions and exclusions, by Keeton, pp 306 ff.

14. Keeton, p 278.

15. Above, 17–2E.

16. Above, 17–3A1.

17. For example, whether my health insurance covers me while working in West Africa.

18. For example, other insurance provisions: below, 28–9.

degree which he has not contracted to assume. When the exception ceases to operate, the risk returns to the contract level and the cover continues.[19]

When an insurer defends a claim by pleading a breach of warranty, if he sustains that plea, the effect of the breach is not only the defeat of the particular claim but also that the insurance contract is discharged altogether;[20] the insurer does not come back on risk later, unless he is estopped from pleading the breach.[21] In the case of a "true" warranty,[22] breach of warranty has these effects because the breach has increased the risk insured, not just for the time being but for the rest of the contract period, to a level which the insurer has not contracted to assume,[23] or at least raised that possibility so that the insurer wishes to reconsider his position.

For example, if it is a term of the contract that property insured shall be kept in a certain place, cover ceases when it is removed from that place, but the term is generally an exception rather than a warranty, so that, if loss occurs to the property when it has been returned to the specified place, the loss is covered.[24] Again, if my van is insured for business use, it is off risk when I use it to travel to my golf club (unless for business); after I return to work the insurance resumes.[25] The argument that excepted use of that kind amounted to a breach of warranty that entitled the insurer to end the contract was firmly rejected in Australia[26] by reference to "the utter unreasonableness of a provision forfeiting the entire policy for an act which may not in any degree increase the risk of loss or accident and which may have no relation to the loss in fact claimed for". If, however, a vehicle is put to an excepted use so regularly that the exception becomes the rule,[27] or the excepted use, of which a notable example would

19. It is immaterial that the effect is that the vehicle is on and off risk in quick succession: *Samuelson* v *National Ins & Guarantee Corp Ltd* [1986] 3 All ER 417, 419 *per* O'Connor LJ (CA—motor).

20. Below, 20–6C.

21. Below, 20–7.

22. See below, 20–2B1.

23. *De Maurier (Jewels) Ltd* v *Bastion Ins Co Ltd* [1967] 2 Lloyd's Rep 550, 559 *per* Donaldson J (motor). In this sense Bennett [1991] JBL 592, 594; MacGillivray, No 779. *Britsky Building Movers Ltd* v *Dominion Ins Corp* (1981) 7 Man R (2d) 402, 411–412; *McKay* v *Ins Corp of British Columbia* (1984) 56 BCLR 391, 395 (BC—motor).

24. *Gorman* v *Hand in Hand Ins Co* (1877) IR 11 CL 224, 236 *per* Pallas CB (fire). *Cf Dawsons Ltd* v *Bonnin* [1922] 2 AC 413 (motor), which concerned a similar term, but one expressed to be a warranty.

Cf Patterson, 34 Colum L Rev 595, 599 ff (1934) for whom all exceptions must be excepted causes of loss, and it was this that distinguished exceptions from warranties. This distinction may not be useful in England today (a) because the requirement of cause is at the mercy of the draftsman (below, 25–9) and (b) the decision of the Court of Appeal in *Roberts* (below) was that there need be no causal connection between exception (if that was what it was in the case) and loss.

25. *Roberts* v *Anglo-Saxon Ins Assn Ltd* (1927) 27 Ll L Rep 313 (CA – motor). *Dawson* v *Mercantile Mutual Ins Co Ltd* [1932] VLR 380 (Vict—motor). *Hudson* v *Ins Corp of British Columbia* (1991) 83 DLR (4th) 377 (BC—motor). See also *Piddington* v *Cooperative Ins Sy Ltd* (1934) 48 Ll L Rep 235, 237 *per* Lawrence J (motor); *Provincial Ins Co* v *Morgan* [1933] AC 240 (motor); there is more than one possible *ratio* of *Morgan*, see Birds, pp 110–111. For "warranties" as to limits of navigation in marine policies, see Arnould, No 692, which sees these limits as exceptions delimiting the scope of the risk. Also in this sense: *Cory & Sons* v *Burr* (1883) 8 App Cas 393, 400 *per* Lord Blackburn (hull). *Conner* v *Manchester Assurance Co*, 130 F 743, 745 (9 Cir, 1904—fire).

In the United States restrictions on the use of motor vehicles are usually interpreted as suspensive of cover; see for example *American Lumberman's Mutual Casualty Co* v *Wilcox*, 16 F Supp 799 (ED NY 1936,—motor); *Fort Worth Lloyds Ins Co* v *Lane*, 189 SW 2d 78 (Tex, 1945—motor).

26. *Dawson* (above) p 388; the court did not deny that it was a question of interpretation.

27. *Murray* v *Scottish Automobile & General Ins Co Ltd*, 1929 SC 48, 53 *per* Lord Sands (motor): a vehicle insured for private use was mostly used for hire and thus, when used for hire, off risk. It was destroyed by fire when it was garaged for the night and thus, in a sense, not being used at all. The Court of Session held that the loss was not covered. Lord President Clyde (p 53): "It seems to me impossible to suggest that a car which is being regularly used for purposes of hire not only ceases to be so used while it is at

be motor rallying, is one that might permanently increase the level of risk and the substance of the situation is a breach of warranty, the effect is to end the cover altogether.

In the United States, the effect of exceptions is different in one or two respects. The first difference favours the insured. In England, the effect of an exception is that the insurer is liable, even though the operation of the exception did not cause the loss.[28] In the USA this is not necessarily so. Most states have "antitechnical" statutes, whereby "policy provisions; misrepresentations; warranties; conditions" do not defeat the policy unless their breach contributed to loss. However, exceptions have always been distinguished in that, as in England, they defined cover and, if loss fell within the scope of an exception, the insurer was not liable even though the excepted cause did not contribute to loss. Recently, however, the distinction has been blurred in a minority of states, which have construed their statute as applicable to exclusions.[29]

The second difference favours the insurer. If something unconnected with the exception occurs while the exception is operating and the insurer is off risk, so that, when the exception ceases to operate, the level of risk has increased, there is no cover. For example, in *Powell*[29a] a helicopter was insured while being used for work X and while piloted by A; pilot instruction was excepted. The insured argued that, although in the course of work X the helicopter was piloted by B under instruction and was therefore off risk, the controls were resumed by A just before the crash, and the helicopter came back on risk notwithstanding "that the aircraft was maneuvered (*sic*) into a dangerous and precarious condition while being piloted" by B. This contention was rejected because, when cover is validly suspended,[30] "the coverage is not reinstated if anything has taken place while the insurance was suspended that would increase the insurer's risk of loss". The claimant argued that that rule did not apply if, as he contended, the cause of loss was not pilot B but some unrelated cause, such as aircraft malfunction. But the court concluded[31] that it "matters not what caused the crash if the cause developed while the coverage was suspended". If, however, no danger had befallen the helicopter before A resumed control, the cover would have recommenced.[32]

In both countries the legal position may be altered by the terms of the contract[33]:

---

rest in its garage, but—so long as it remains there—is being used for the private personal purposes of its owner." Lord Sands (p 54) thought that the position at night was ancillary to the use in the day.

28. *Roberts* v *Anglo-Saxon Ins Assn Ltd* (1927) 27 Ll L Rep 313 (CA—motor).

29. For criticism see Bates, 52 J Air Law & Commerce 451 (1986).

29a. *Powell Valley Electrical Cooperative Inc* v *United States Aviation Underwriters Inc*, 179 F Supp 616 (WD Va, 1959). See also *Travelers Protective Assn* v *Prinsent*, 291 US 576 (1934—PA).

30. p 618. See also *Henjes* v *Aetna Ins Co*, 132 F 2d 715, 720 (2 Cir, 1943—hull); *Fidelity-Phenix Fire Ins Co* v *Pilot Freight Carriers Inc*, 193 F 2d 812, 817 (4 Cir, 1952—goods in transit).

Cf a case of motor insurance in which the danger arose while the vehicle was controlled by an unlicensed driver (cover excepted), but the instructor took control shortly before injuring a pedestrian: *Lumbermen's Mutual Casualty Co* v *McIver*, 27 F Supp 702 (Cal, 1939—motor), affirmed 110 F 2d 323 (9 Cir, 1940), cert den 311 US 653.

31. p 618.

32. *Fidelity-Phenix* (above) p 816 .

33. *Provincial Ins Co* v *Morgan* [1933] AC 240, 247 *per* Lord Buckmaster (motor).

the use of terminology such as "warranty" or "condition precedent" suggests that the term is not an exception but a warranty,[34] although terminology is not decisive.[35] Further, what is inherently an exception may be a warranty in the particular contract, because it is clear that "breach" gives the insurer the right to terminate the contract[36] or, it has been said,[37] because the insured has promised that a circumstance shall or shall not obtain throughout the period of cover. Close attention must be given to interpretation of the contract, a matter of some difficulty. For example, it has been said[38] that, while there may be a warranty in a fire contract that the building insured shall not be unoccupied for more than 30 days, a provision that the insurance shall not cover loss which occurs when the building has been unoccupied for more than 30 days is an exception.

19–1B2 The Effect of Waiver

Whereas the doctrine of waiver (or estoppel) can be invoked to prevent reliance by the insurer on a breach of warranty,[39] with the result that there is cover in circumstances in which the insurer was not obliged to provide it, it has been held in the United States that the doctrine cannot be used to prevent the insurer from relying on an exception. "While a forfeiture of benefits contracted for in an insurance policy may be waived, the doctrine of waiver or estoppel cannot create a liability for benefits not contracted for".[40] Waiver (or estoppel) may operate to nullify exceptions and thus to extend cover at the time of contracting[41] but not after that.

One reason, it is said, is that to hold the insurer to payment because he has "waived" an exception would be to increase the extent of cover without reciprocal

---

34. *Ellinger & Co* v *Mutual Life Ins Co* [1905] 1 KB 31, 38 *per* Stirling LJ (CA—life); *Palatine Ins Co Ltd* v *Gregory* [1926] AC 90, 93 *per* Viscount Cave LC (PC—fire).

35. *Barnard* v *Faber* [1893] 1 QB 340, 342 *per* Lindley LJ, 345 *per* A L Smith LJ (CA—fire); *Roberts* v *Anglo-Saxon Ins Assn Ltd* (1926) 26 Ll L Rep 154, 157 *per* Mackinnon J (motor); *Re Morgan and Provincial Ins Co* [1932] 2 KB 70 79–80 *per* Scrutton LJ (CA—motor), giving the illustration of the marine warranty free of particular average and "warranted no St Lawrence between October 1 and April 1". Also *Pictorial Machinery Ltd* v *Nicholls* (1940) 45 Com Cas 334, 342 *per* Humphreys J (liability); *CTN Cash & Carry Ltd* v *GAFLAC plc* [1989] 1 Lloyd's Rep 299 (burglary). This is consistent with the more general rule that, when interpreting contract terms, labels such as "condition" or "warranty" are not decisive: *Wickman Tools Sales Ltd* v *Schuler AG* [1974] AC 235.

A similar approach is found in the Supreme Court of Canada: *The Bamcell II, Century Ins Co of Canada* v *Case Existological Laboratories Ltd* (1983) 150 DLR (3d) 9, 15 (hull): see below, 20–2B.

36. *Provincial Ins Co* v *Morgan* [1933] AC 240, 255 *per* Lord Wright (motor).

37. *Palatine Ins Co Ltd* v *Gregory* [1926] AC 90, 93 *per* Viscount Cave LC (PC—fire); *Morgan* (above).

38. Australian Law Reform Commission, Report No 20, para 218. *Sed quaere*.

39. Below 20–7.

40. *Nieves* v *Intercontinental Life Ins Co*, 964 F 2d 60, 66 (1 Cir, 1992—life). See also *Kaminer* v *Franklin Life Ins Co*, 472 F 2d 1073 (5 Cir, 1973—life), cert den 414 US 840; *Aetna Casualty & Surety Co* v *Richmond*, 143 Cal Rptr 75, 79–80 (1977—liability); *Matia* v *Carpet Transport Inc*, 888 F 2d 118, 121 (11 Cir, 1989—motor); *Rhinebeck Bicycle Shop Inc* v *Sterling Ins Co*, 546 NYS 2d 499, 501 (1989—liability); *Shannon* v *Shannon*, 442 NW 2d 25, 33 ff (Wis, 1989—liability); *Underwriters at Lloyd's* v *Denali Seafoods Inc*, 729 F Supp 721 (WD Was, 1989—liability), affirmed 927 F 2d 459 (9 Cir, 1991); *Kane* v *Aetna Life Ins*, 893 F 2d 1283 (11 Cir, 1990—group health); *Nancarrow* v *Aetna*, 932 F 2d 742 (8 Cir, 1991—homeowner's); *Braun* v *Annesley*, 936 F 2d 1105 (10 Cir, 1991—motor); and cases cited by Appleman section 9090.

In *Shepard* v *Keystone Ins Co*, 743 F Supp 429, 433 (D Md, 1990—homeowner's) the rule was applied to what English law would see as breach of warranty, the warranty of occupancy (below, 20–5A3): "waiver and estoppel cannot be used to create liability where none previously existed, or to extend coverage beyond what was originally intended".

41. Above, 8–3C. The Couch rule is not applied to such cases, for example, *Standard Fire Ins Co* v *Marine Contracting & Towing Co*, 392 SE 2d 460 (SC, 1990—liability).

consideration (premium) from the insured.[42] But, to English eyes, this argument proves too much, for that is the effect of waiver (or estoppel) in many if not most of the cases, in which it is regularly and incontroversially applied; and, in any case, the law does not investigate the adequacy of consideration.

The main reason against waiver of exceptions, attributed to Couch, is that a cause of action cannot be based on waiver (or estoppel).[43] However, the same objection might be might be raised when the insured breaches a warranty, or fails to satisfy a condition precedent to cover,[44] although in these cases waiver (and hence cover) is often allowed. At first sight, however, the Couch proposition is more persuasive with regard to exceptions than warranties. Both are concerned with the scope of cover, however, whereas the true warranty says "yes if", the true exception says "not if". In other words, the warranty says that, as long as the warranty is fulfilled, there is cover. The exception says that, if X occurs or does not occur, there is no cover. Behind the warranty is cover, so, it seems, when the warranty is waived an obstacle is removed revealing the sculpted promise of cover behind. Behind the exception, however, is nothing: to waive the exception and cover the loss is to give life and force to something that was never there before.[45]

But, in English law, the Couch distinction and the explanation behind it will not do. First, on the one hand, although the role of exceptions is indeed best seen as definitional,[46] this view of exceptions is far from universal. Second, on the other hand, the role of warranties can also be seen as definitional[47] and thus similar to that of exceptions, albeit without ruling out the possibility of waiver.[48] The House of Lords has now insisted that the effect of breach of warranty is not that the insurer is entitled to elect to terminate the cover but that his promise of cover is discharged immediately and automatically.[49] If then there is waiver (or estoppel), the effect is that the insurer is prevented from pleading the absence of cover. This being so, the Couch explanation of the difference between the two cases does not hold for English law. Further, in the general law of contract in England, a person has a "right" to defend an action or resist a claim on the basis that he has no contract at all and, if he does not do so he may be estopped from asserting that "right" later, with the result that he is bound in contract

---

42. *Zappone* v *Home Ins Co*, 447 NYS 2d 911, 914 (1982—motor). So, a term that ended cover when the insured reached a certain age could be waived by the insurer's continued acceptance of premium: *Minnesota Mutual Life Ins Co* v *Larr*, 567 So 2d 239 (Miss, 1990—life).

43. *Kane* v *Aetna Life Ins*, 893 F 2d 1283, 1285 (11 Cir, 1990—group health), citing Couch, section 71:40 (ed 1983).

44. For example, a medical examination: *Rosenburg* v *Lincoln American Life Ins Co*, 883 F 2d 1328 (7 Cir, 1989—life).

45. *State Farm Mutual Automobile Ins Co* v *Elgot*, 369 NYS 2d 719, 722 (1975—motor). In these circumstances, the insurer is bound only if the claimant can establish that the contract of insurance has been varied (above, 11–4A) by deletion of the exception in question. Otherwise, there is no contractual right for the insurer to give up, waive or abandon: if under the initial contract there is no motor cover in Michigan, there is simply no cover there, not a right to refuse to provide cover, if the insured drives in Michigan.

46. Above 19–1A at note 3.

47. For example, Lord Goff: "the rationale of warranties in insurance law is that the insurer only accepts the risk provided that the warranty is fulfilled": *The Good Luck* [1992] 1 AC 233, 263 (hull). Moreover, it is clear from the same passage in the same judgment that, if the warranty is not fulfilled at the time of contracting, the non-fulfilment prevents the contract from coming into existence.

48. This was accepted by Lord Goff (above). As regards the scope of cover in point of time, see, for example, *Handler* v *Mutual Reserve Fund Assn* (1904) 90 LT 192, 193, 194 (CA—life): it was clearly the opinion of members of the Court of Appeal that the insurer could be estopped from setting up a requirement of payment of premium as a condition of cover.

49. *The Good Luck* (above). Generally, see below, 20–6C.

where he was not before.[50] Last but not least, waiver has actually been enforced by the House of Lords in respect of what can only be characterised as an exception.[51]

So, it seems that the Couch rule is not to be found in English law, and nor is it ubiquitous to the USA. In New York, for instance, if the insurer does not dispute the existence or extent of cover, he may find that he is estopped and his cover extended accordingly, whether the definition and scope of the cover in question is expressed in positive terms[52] or negative terms (exceptions):[53] "once the foundational facts for an estoppel have been established, liability of an insurer may be imposed, even for a loss falling outside the risks insured under the policy or beyond the policy limits."[54] However, in the case of exceptions, the New York rule has a base in statute, section 167(8) of the New York Insurance Law, whereby the insurer is required to give timely notice to the insured of any "disclaimer". Moreover, even in some other states, in which the Couch rule has taken root, it does not apply if, with knowledge that a liability policy does not cover the occurrence, the insurer assumes the defence of the insured without disclaiming liability and giving notice of reservation of rights: it appears that the insurer will not be allowed to rely on absence of cover.[55]

19–1C Interpretation

In the general law, exceptions are construed strictly against the profferor. In case of ambiguity, insurance exceptions are interpreted against the insurer,[56] not, however, because there is anything more objectionable about exceptions than other terms of the contract but because the entire contract is usually drafted by the insurer.

19–1C1 Mixed Use of Property

When an insured cause operates concurrently with an excepted cause, the proximate and effective cause in law is the exception.[57] If motor cover is confined *exclusively* to

---

50. *The Henrik Sif* [1982] 1 Lloyd's Rep 456; *The Uhenbels* [1986] 2 Lloyd's Rep 294; *A–G for Hong Kong* v *Humphrey's Estate* [1987] 1 AC 114, 127–128 *per* Lord Templeman (PC).

51. *The Kanchenjunga* [1990] 1 Lloyd's Rep 391 (HL): the carrier had waived his right not to take his ship into an unsafe port.

52. In *Boston Old Ins Co* v *Lumbermens Mutual Casualty Co*, 889 F 2d 1245 (2 Cir, 1989—motor) the insurer was estopped by delay from pleading that the loss fell outside the time period of cover. In *Mazzola* v *CNA Ins Co*, 548 NYS 610, 614 (1989—motor) the insurer was estopped from recovering a payment in excess of that required by the policy.

53. *Kamyr Inc* v *St Paul Surplus Lines Ins Co*, 547 NYS 2d 964 (1989—liability), in which the excess underwriter of product liability cover would, it was held, be estopped by delay from "asserting its coverage defences" (p 967), in particular, an exception of design error, if the claimant could show prejudice. *County of Chautauqua* v *International Ins Co*, 724 F Supp 112 (WD NY, 1989—liability) in which the insurer was estopped by delay from pleading an exception (in respect of claims arising out of personal injury).

54. *Bucon Inc* v *Pennsylvania Manufacturing Assn*, 547 NYS 2d 925, 927 (1989—liability): it was held that the insurer was estopped from denying that a particular contractor was covered by another contractor's insurance.

55. *INA* v *Atlantic National Ins Co*, 329 F 2d 769, 775–776 (4 Cir, 1964—motor); *Pennsylvania Nat. Mutual Cas Ins Co* v *Kitty Hawk Airways Inc*, 964 F 2d 478, 481 (5 Cir, 1992—liability).

56. See above, 15–5C. For example, *Gulf Ins Co* v *Tilley*, 280 F Supp 60, 63 (ND Ind, 1967—liability), affirmed 393 F 2d 119 (7 Cir, 1968): babysitting for reward is not within a "business pursuit" exception in a householder's liability policy!

57. *Wayne Tank & Pump Ltd* v *Employers' Liability Assurance Corp Ltd* [1974] QB 57 (CA). See below, 25–6.

one kind of use, and the use at the time of loss is mixed, there can be no cover.[58] If the insured use is not required to be exclusive, courts in both England and the United States look for the "essential or predominant character"[59] of the use, when loss occurred.

If a driver, who was insured for social, domestic and pleasure purposes, gave a lift out of kindness to one who happened to be on business, the use would remain social, even though the beneficiary of the kindness was on business.[60] On the same principle, when motor cover was excluded while the vehicle was operated by a person under age but the instructor (who was of age) attempted to take over to avoid a hazard, the Missouri court decided[61] against cover because the instructor, being "in such a position that it was impossible for him to assume control of substantially all the means of control, he relegated himself to the position of a helper or director of the physical operation".

If there is no essential or predominant use but dual use, there is no cover.[62] Thus when a driver, who was covered when driving for social, domestic and pleasure purposes, was driving home for lunch, but also taking a passenger for excluded business reasons, the English court held that there was no cover.[63]

The argument that an isolated or occasional excepted use (predominant or exclusive at the time) does not suspend cover, which has been successful in the United States, has been rejected in England.[64] However, the argument has succeeded in the United States, not because the prohibited use was occasional but because the exception was construed as applying only to regular, as opposed to occasional, use: "If insured's truck had been held out to the public, by advertisement or otherwise, for use as a vehicle for carrying passengers for hire . . . such use would have been an excluded use even if the accident happened on the first instance of such use. But words defining a particular excluded use . . . may be inapplicable to a particular single isolated transaction though applicable to a course of such transactions."[65]

---

58. *Passmore* v *Vulcan Boiler & General Ins Co Ltd* (1936) 54 Ll L Rep 92 (motor).

59. *Seddon* v *Binions* [1978] 1 Lloyd's Rep. 381, 385 *per* Roskill LJ (CA—motor). See also *Murray* v *Scottish Automobile & General Ins Co Ltd*, 1929 SC 48 (motor). In *Jones* v *Welsh Ins Corp Ltd* (1937) 59 Ll L Rep 13, 15 (motor), a case of dual purpose, Goddard J looked to the "real" purpose of the activity.

60. *Passmore* (above) p 94 *per* Du Parcq J (motor), approved in *Seddon* v *Binions* [1978] 1 Lloyd's Rep 381, 385 *per* Roskill LJ (CA—motor).

61. *State Farm Mutual Automobile Ins Co* v *Smith*, 48 F Supp 570 (WD Mo, 1942—motor).

62. *Seddon* (above). Also in this sense *Browning* v *Phoenix Assurance Co Ltd* [1960] 2 Lloyd's Rep 360, 367 *per* Pilcher J (motor) and *McGoona* v *MIB* [1969] 2 Lloyd's Rep. 34, 44 *per* Lawton J (motor), relying on *Passmore* (above) p 94 *per* Du Parcq J (motor). However, it is not altogether clear that Du Parcq J took the view attributed to him. (a) His illustrations suggest that he thought the normal rule looked only to the predominant purpose. (b) He observed (*loc cit*) that in the case of dual purpose "If the policy only said that [the insured] was to benefit by it so long as the car was being used for the purposes of her business, I think her position would be unassailable". He then appears to have decided the case against cover on the terms of the policy by treating the exception of use "otherwise than for the business of the insured" as limiting cover to use *solely* for the business of the insured.

USA: some courts have approached the construction of phrases like this by drawing an analogy with the more general notion of "course of employment": for example, *McMillan* v *State Mutual*, 922 F 2d 1073, 1079 (3 Cir, 1990—life).

63. *Seddon* (above).

64. *Wyatt* v *Guildhall Ins Co Ltd* [1937] 1 KB 653 (motor). *Cf Port-Rose* discussed below, 19–2A2.

65. *Stanley* v *American Motorists Ins Co*, 73 A 2d 1, 3 (Md, 1950—motor); applied in *St Paul Mercury Indemnity Co* v *Knoph*, 87 NW 2d 636, 638–639 (Minn, 1958 motor); *National Grange Mutual Ins Co* v *Cervantes*, 266 NYS 2d 163, 165 (1966—motor). The same interpretation has been put on warranties restricting use, even though breach was a cause of loss: see Appleman, section 4435.

19–1C2 Causation

In principle, an exception is not operative unless it is the proximate cause of loss. As a matter of strict interpretation of the contract of insurance, an exception is not proximate unless it is the inevitable cause of loss.[66] Insurers may increase the scope of exceptions by appropriate drafting,[67] not least by drafting an exception that is coincidental rather than causative: for example, the insurer may come off risk while the property insured is or is not in a certain location or certain condition, whether or not that location or condition causes loss.

This drafting is generally effective, unless the courts can be persuaded that loss, which occurs or appears while the property was off risk, was caused by an event insured against which had occurred before the property came off risk. For example, if a fishing boat loses its rudder in a collision and drifts helplessly out of the navigational limits imposed by the policy, the fact may be that further damage incurred outside the limits was caused by the collision within limits and thus covered.[68]

This possibility was taken a stage further in *United States Fire Ins Co* v *Cavanaugh*.[69] The skipper employed by the insured wrongfully took the vessel outside the navigational limits; this was an act of barratry, a peril covered. Outside the limit the vessel stranded and caught fire. The decision of the Court of Appeals was that[70] "Since barratry, grounding and fire were all covered perils and the act of barratry cannot operate to breach the warranty and void coverage, the decison of the district court that [the insurer] is liable under the policy for the loss must be affirmed". The basis of this conclusion appears to be the doctrine of concurrent causation,[71] found in some parts of the United States[72] but not in England. An English court is unlikely to reach the same decison, unless the barratry is seen as the proximate cause of stranding, perhaps because barratry was continuous from the time of the decison to breach the navigational limit until the time of stranding.[73] An English court is more likely to agree with the dissenting judge in *Cavanaugh*,[74] that the majority decision in that case could

"be predicated only upon a conclusion that the captain's barratry extended the insurance coverage. As I see it, the result of the barratry was the owner's loss of coverage. It was a grievous loss to the owner, but not one of the losses against which the policy provided coverage. The insurance policy did not provide coverage against the loss of its own coverage; it insured against loss of the vessel. In maritime matters, the insured may recover only if a peril covered under the policy proximately causes the loss of the vessel. In this case, the vessel was not lost as a proximate result of . . . barratry."

66. See below, 25–4.
67. See below, 25–9C.
68. By analogy with the rule that, if a peril occurs within the period of cover, the full loss is payable even though the full extent of the loss does not develop and manifest itself until outside the period; see above, 18–1B. In the present context the force of the analogy may depend on the wording. If the exception refers to loss sustained outside the limit the analogy is weaker than if it refers to perils occurring outside the limit.
69. 732 F 2d 832 (11 Cir, 1984—hull).
70. p 835.
71. This appears from the court's citation of an earlier case to the effect that when barratry is one of the causes, if the ultimate cause is not excluded, recovery may be based on barratry, whether or not the ultimate cause is a peril insured against.
Alternatively, the decision is a manifestation of a special rule for barratry, which was doubted by Blackburn LJ in *Cory & Sons* v *Burr* [1883] AC 393, 398 in a passage to which the dissenting judge referred in *Cavanaugh. Cf* Arnould, No 765.
72. See below, 25–3.
73. This kind of analysis can be found in *Yorkshire Dale SS Co Ltd* v *Minister of War Transport* [1942] AC 691 (hull); Clarke [1981] CLJ 284, 294.
74. 732 F 2d 832, 835–836.

The stranding was not, as English law requires,[75] caused by (the inevitable consequence) of the barratry. The English view of such cases has subsequently been taken in one decision in the United States.[76]

19–2 EXCEPTIONS CONCERNING THE CONDUCT OF THE INSURED

19–2A Negligence

"An overwhelming percentage of all insurable losses sustained because of fire can be directly traced to some act or acts of negligence. Were it not for the errant human element, the hazards insured against would be greatly diminished. It is in full appreciation of these conditions that the property owner seeks insurance, and it is after painstaking analysis of them that the insurer fixes his premiums and issues the policies. It is in recognition of this practice that the law requires the insurer to assume the risk of negligence of the insured."[77]

In England, in contrast with the United States from which this statement comes, the law does not "require" cover against negligence but, unless negligence is expressly excepted, the cover, whether against fire or any other hazard, is presumed and construed to cover loss caused by the negligence of the insured[78] or his employees.[79] Loss negligently caused may be excluded directly and expressly, or indirectly by a positive requirement of diligence,[79a] but courts are inclined to interpret insurance contracts against that result.

At this point, the distinction between exceptions and warranties (above, 19–1B) is particularly unclear. If the motor contract requires the insured to exercise care in the maintenance of the vehicle, that may be adjudged a warranty, even though it means that the negligent home mechanic loses cover. If, however, the motor contract requires reasonable precautions to prevent theft, negligence in that regard is, arguably at least, an exception. Terms of this kind are more likely to have the effect of exceptions than of warranties, and for that reason they are considered here.

---

75. Below, 25–7.
76. In *Tillery v Hull & Co Inc* 876 F 2d 1517 (11 Cir, 1989—hull), the vessel was covered for loss caused by acts of barratry, but the contract (in its FCS clause) excluded losses caused by seizure. In breach of instructions (barratry) the master took the vessel to Jamaica to pick up marihuana and was seized by the Jamaican authorities. Having quoted the judgment of Lord Blackburn in *Cory v Burr* [1883] AC 393, 400–401, but without citation of its own earlier decision in *Cavanaugh* (above), the court concluded that the loss was caused not by the barratry but by the seizure.
77. *Federal Ins Co v Tamiami Trail Tours Inc*, 117 F 2d 794, 796 (5 Cir, 1941—fire). In the same sense *Columbia Ins Co v Lawrence*, 10 Pet 507, 517 *per* Story J (Sup Ct 1836—fire); *State Farm Fire & Casualty Co v Von Der Lieth*, 802 P 2d 285 (Cal, 1991—AR).
78. *Shaw v Robberds* (1837) 6 Ad & E 75, 84 *per* Lord Denman CJ (fire); *Cornish v Accident Ins Co* (1889) 23 QBD 453, 457 *per* Lindley LJ (CA—PA); *Re Etherington and Lancashire & Yorkshire Accident Ins Co* [1909] 1 KB 591, 601 *per* Kennedy LJ (CA—PA); *Tinline v White Cross Ins Assn Ltd* [1921] 3 KB 327 (motor); *The Diane* [1977] 1 Lloyd's Rep 61 (guarantee).
Central Manufacturers Mutual Ins Co v Elliott 177 F 2d 1011 (10 Cir, 1949—fire); *Maryland Casualty Co v Nieman-Marcus Co*, 186 F 2d 140, 142 (5 Cir, 1951—boiler); *Chapin Lumber Co v Lumber Bargains Inc*, 11 Cal Rptr 634 (Cal, 1961—fire). Keeton, pp 285–286.
79. *Dixon v Sadler* (1839) 5 M & W 405, 414 *per* Parke B (hull and cargo); *Trinder Anderson & Co v Thames & Mersey Marine Ins Co* [1898] 2 QB 114 (CA—freight); *Re Etherington and Lancashire & Yorkshire Accident Ins Co* [1909] 1 KB 591, 601 *per* Kennedy LJ (CA—PA). MIA section 55(2)(a). *Phoenix Ins Co v Erie & Western Transportation Co*, 117 US 312, 224–325 *per* Gray J (1886—cargo); *Leavell & Co v Fireman's Fund Ins Co*, 372 F 2d 784 (9 Cir, 1967—contractors AR).
79a. On such clauses see Appleman, sections 531 ff.

19–2A1 Interpretation

In accordance with general rules of construction applicable to all insurance terms, an exception of negligence will be construed restrictively. Even if clearly worded to cover negligence, the exception will not be construed literally to exclude cover of common law negligence by the insured unless (a) there is still some insured loss without negligence and (b) insurance against loss without negligence is sufficient to achieve the purpose of the insurance contract.

In *Fraser* v *Furman (Productions) Ltd*[80] the employers' liability cover of a manufacturing company turned on the meaning of a "condition" in the insurance contract, that "the insured shall take reasonable precautions to prevent accidents and disease". The leading judgment was delivered by Diplock LJ who said this[81]: the condition

"must be construed, of course, in the context of a policy of insurance against specified risks. The risks so specified, which are 'liability at law for damages', are liability for breach of statutory duty, for which the owner or occupier of the factory would always be personally liable, negligence at common law of the employer, for which he would be personally liable, and also the negligence of his servants, for which he would be vicariously liable. Therefore, when one approaches the construction of the condition, one does so in this context, and applies the rule that one does not construe a condition as repugnant to the commercial purpose of the contract."

His Lordship then construed the condition restrictively and in the context of an insurance policy on liability for death or injury.

"(1) It is the insured personally who must take reasonable precautions. Failure by an employee to do so, although the employer might be liable vicariously for the employee's negligence or breach of statutory duty, would not be a breach of the condition. That was established in, and was the *ratio decidendi* of *Woolfall & Rimmer Ltd* v *Moyle*.[82] (2) The obligation of the employer is to take precautions to prevent accidents. This means in my view to take measures to avert dangers which are likely to cause bodily injury to employees."

His Lordship then construed the condition yet more restrictively in the light of the purpose of the contract to provide liability cover.[83] Interpreted in isolation, a duty to take reasonable precautions might be seen as one breached by ordinary negligence, but this interpretation would defeat the purpose of a liability insurance contract.

"'Reasonable' does not mean reasonable as between the employer and the employee. It means reasonable as between the insured and the insurer having regard to the commercial purpose of the contract, which is *inter alia* to indemnify the insured against liability for his (the insured's) personal negligence. That too is established by the case which I have cited.[84] Obviously, the condition cannot mean that the insured must take measures to avert dangers which he does not himself foresee, although the hypothetical reasonably careful employer would foresee them. That would be repugnant to the commercial purpose of the contract, for failure to foresee

80. [1967] 1 WLR 898 (CA); applied on this point in *Aluminium Wire & Cable Co Ltd* v *Allstate Ins Co Ltd* [1985] 2 Lloyd's Rep 280 (liability); it was influential in *Cee Bee Marine Ltd* v *Lombard Ins Co Ltd* [1990] 2 NZLR 1 (CA—fire). See also *Bedford* v *James* [1986] 2 Qd R 300 (liability).
81. [1967] 1 WLR 898, 905 (CA).
82. [1942] 1 KB 66 (CA); referred to with approval in *Gold Coast Bakeries (Qld) Pty Ltd* v *Heat & Control Pty Ltd* [1992] 1 Qd R 162, 172 (liability).
83. [1967] 1 WLR 898, 905–906 (CA).
84. *Woolfall & Rimmer Ltd* v *Moyle* [1942] 1 KB 66 (CA—employers' liability) where Goddard LJ observed (p 76) that, if the condition were seen in isolation "it would follow that the underwriters were saying: 'We will insure you against your liability for negligence on condition that you are not negligent,' because, if the [insured] had taken all reasonable precautions to prevent accidents in the widest sense, they could not be liable in negligence". The Diplock view has also been applied in Australia: *Vosten* v *The Commonwealth* [1989] 1 Qd R 693, 705 (liability), in a case of employer's liability for injury to a workman. See also *London Crystal Window Cleaning Ltd* v *National Mutual Indemnity Ins Co Ltd* [1952] 2 Lloyd's Rep 360 (employers' liability); and above 15–6A.

dangers is one of the commonest grounds for liability in negligence. What, in my view, is 'reasonable' . . . is that the insured should not deliberately court a danger, the existence of which he recognises . . . In other words, it is not enough that the employer's omission to take any particular precautions to avoid accidents should be negligent; it must at least be reckless, that is to say, made with actual recognition by the insured himself that a danger exists, and not caring whether or not it is averted. The purpose of the condition is to ensure that the insured will not, because he is covered against loss by the policy, refrain from taking precautions which he knows ought to be taken."[85]

Fraser v *Furman* concerned liability for injury to persons, but the Diplock approach has been taken to the insured's liability in negligence for damage to property in England[86] and also in Canada,[87] where the Supreme Court said of a comprehensive business liability policy that[88] "negligence is by far the most frequent source of exceptional liability which a businessman has to contend with. Therefore, a policy which would not cover liability due to negligence could not properly be called 'comprehensive' ".

More recently the Diplock approach was taken in *Sofi* v *Prudential Assurance Co Ltd*[89] This case concerned a composite "hearth and home" contract with a general condition requiring "reasonable steps to safeguard any property". The court concluded that the insured's conduct would be unreasonable only if it were "reckless". Lloyd LJ, giving the judgment of the Court of Appeal, thought that the condition did not apply to the liability section of the contract at all, because legal "liability in the great majority of cases depends on want of reasonable care. So a wide construction of [the condition] would be altogether repugnant to the cover apparently afforded by [the liability section] of the policy".[89a]

This reasoning has led to the suggestion that the Diplock standard should apply only to liability cover and not, for example, to theft cover.[89b] However, in *Sofi*, Lloyd LJ went on to say: "Similarly, the insurers would escape all liability . . . in the very ordinary case of damage to a house or its contents by fire (one of the insured perils) if the fire were caused by the negligence of the insured. That could not be right".[90] The court then applied the Diplock approach to the way the insured looked after the property in issue, jewellery.

In spite of this decision, the Diplock reference to the object of the insurance does invite a distinction between different kinds of insurance or even between different sections of the same policy. Within the bounds of a comprehensive motor policy, there may well be more than one level of care required of the insured. Whereas it is axiomatic that the negligence of the insured is covered as regards injury he causes to third parties, and any clause to the contrary may be repugnant to public policy,[91] it is possible to require reasonable care to safeguard the vehicle from theft or damage, as an exception to the liability of the insurer.[92] A similar view of a different kind of cover

85. Even "courting danger" may be part of the activity intended to be covered: *Golden Eagle Liberia Ltd* v *St Paul Fire & Marine Ins Co*, 685 F Supp 393 (SD NY, 1988—liability).
86. *Lane* v *Spratt* [1970] 2 QB 480 (goods in transit). This interpretation is broadly in line with the normal meaning of accident in PA insurance: above, 17–5C.
87. *Canadian Indemnity Co* v *Walkem Machinery & Equipment Ltd* [1976] 1 SCR 309.
88. p 316, *per* Pigeon J.
89. [1993] 2 Lloyd's Rep 559 (CA—AR).
89a. p 564.
89b. Tompkinson, BILA Journal No 76, p 8 (1991).
90. [1993] 2 Lloyd's Rep 559 at p 564.
91. Shawcross, *Motor Insurance* (2nd ed, 1948), p 611. *Cf* Ivamy, *Fire*, p 333.
92. It is also perhaps a duty the breach of which by the insured is actionable by the insurer: *National Farmers' Union Mutual Ins Sy Ltd* [1941] 2 KB 424, 430 *per* Viscount Caldecote CJ (motor).

was taken in *HTV Ltd v Lintner*.[93] It was argued of an entertainment risk policy, that a clause requiring due diligence of the insured applied equally to the section of the policy insuring persons (the cast) as it did to property (the props). Rejecting this argument, Neill J said[94] that "both in this policy and in insurance law generally a clear distinction can be drawn between the insurance of persons and the insurance of property". However, in general, this may be as far as the distinction will be drawn. In Canada, argument for different levels of care within a single policy for (a) liability insurance covering injuries to others and (b) accident insurance covering injury to the insured himself has been rejected by the Supreme Court.[95] Even so, if the condition requiring care or diligence were repeated in each section of the policy, its meaning might still be coloured by the immediate context and by the purpose of the particular section: see above, 15–3A. With the very high levels of car theft current in England, courts may be open to persuasion that the policy that covers the carelessness of the insured on the road does not cover his carelessness in the garage.

19–2A2 Application

Although unreported for some time, the *Sofi* case[96] has been said to have had "a devastating effect on the insurance industry".[97] It should not, however, have come as a devastating surprise to the industry's lawyers. Courts bring to the construction of words of this kind a certain frame of reference and this can be seen in decisions such as *Sofi*.

First, confronted with phrases such as "reasonable steps" or "reasonable care", the courts are likely to assess the conduct of the insured, as they might that of a person owing a duty of reasonable care in tort[98], in relation to the circumstances: the likelihood of loss, the gravity of loss,[99] the viability and expense of precautions against loss,[100] and the importance of any activity being pursued when the alleged negligence occurred.[101] The duty does not mean an obligation to take every practicable precaution.[102] Similarly, the Ombudsman, in his Reports for 1985 and 1986, set out "basic criteria", by which he assessed the care taken by the insured: "(a) the value of the goods at risk; (b) the reason for their being in the place from which they were stolen; (c) the actual precautions taken to safeguard them; and (d) the alternatives open to the policyholder."

93. [1984] 2 Lloyd's Rep 125.
94. p 127.
95. *Mutual of Omaha Ins Co v Stats* (1978) 87 DLR (3d) 169 (motor), discussed above, 17–5F3.
96. *Sofi v Prudential Assurance Co*, CA, [1993] 2 Lloyd's Rep 559 (CA—AR).
97. Cowan (1993) 3 Ins L & P 4.
98. For example, by reference to what would 'be expected of an ordinary competent person of that kind of profession: *The Talisman* [1989] 1 Lloyd's Rep 535 (HL—hull P & I).
99. See *Sofi v Prudential Ins Co* (below).
100. *Melik & Co Ltd v Norwich Union Fire Ins Sy Ltd* [1980] 1 Lloyd's Rep 523, 531 *per* Woolf J (burglary).
101. See above as regards the meaning of accident: 17–5E1.
102. *Melik* (above). See also the Report of the Ombudsman (quoted below). *Cf* "All reasonable endeavours", discussed in *Stephen v Scottish Boatowners Ins Mutual Assn*, 1989 SLT 52 (Ct Sess—hull). The words cannot "be read in a literal sense. The taking of one precaution might indeed preclude the taking of another" (p 66). Nor are the words "synonymous with taking all reasonable precautions and using all due diligence, and thus the converse of negligence . . . What is required . . . is that he must do everything to save the vessel which it was reasonable for him to do in the circumstances" (p 55); or "do everything which he reasonably could do in the circumstances to save the vessel from loss" (p 66).

Thus, in *Sofi*,[103] the small chance of theft (short absence from empty park) and the difficulty of taking adequate precautions counted in favour of the claimant, but the gravity of the risk (expensive jewellery) and the triviality of the occasion (a casual visit to Dover Castle) counted against.

Further as in actions in tort, the reasonable care required is relative to the person concerned.[103a] On the one hand, more is expected of the self-confessed expert. On the other hand, if the particular insured has become largely incapable of foresight on account of mental incapacity, the duty and thus the exception do not apply at all.[104] Negligence "implies at least a cognitive capacity to recognize alternative courses of conduct and the relative risks of choice between them, and the volitional capacity then to make conscious choice between them".[105]

Secondly, a distinction has been drawn between the kind of negligence, which since *Sofi* we must call gross negligence or recklessness and which is excepted, and "inadvertence", merely momentary carelessness, which is not.[106] In his 1986 Report,[107] the Ombudsman underlined that "I have always acknowledged a fundamental difference

---

103. *Sofi* v *Prudential Assurance Co Ltd*, [1993] 2 Lloyd's Rep 559 (CA—AR): a clause in the all risks section of a "Private Combined (Hearth and Home) Policy" required the insured to "take all reasonable steps to safeguard any property insured and to avoid accidents which may lead to damage or injury". One January, the insured and family set out by car for the south of France. In the locked glove compartment, he took valuable jewellery in a case measuring 12 inches by 6 inches—having told the insurer's agent that he would do so: he had had a burglary at home and felt safer taking the jewellery with him on holiday. En route, they stopped to look briefly at Dover Castle, leaving the car in a small unattended car park. Having discussed the safest thing to do, they took their money and travellers cheques but left everything else in the car which, on their return 15 minutes later, they found to have been broken into and ransacked.

The visit to the Castle was entirely casual and superfluous, a means of killing time before taking the ferry. In the circumstances, was it justifiable to leave the car with such valuable contents at all? This question was not directly addressed. The insurer argued that the insured had not taken all reasonable steps to safeguard the jewellery; that he should either have taken the jewellery with him, when he climbed the Castle mound, or left one of his party behind in the car. Lloyd LJ, giving the judgment of the Court of Appeal, accepted (p 566) that, as a matter of "common sense, the greater the value of the goods insured, the greater the risk that they will be stolen, and the easier it will be for the insurer to establish" recklessness. He also observed that the submission of recklessness might have succeeded, if the insured had given no thought at all to the jewellery or had left it exposed to view. However, he agreed with the judge below who, having found that "the car can only have been out of sight or sound for five to seven minutes" and that this was "not a case of a car being left unattended for a lengthy period of time in an obviously vulnerable place", concluded that the insured had not been reckless.

103a. See *The Talisman* (above).

104. *Erie Ins Exchange* v *Stark*, 962 F 2d 349 (4 Cir, 1992—fire).

105. p 355. In this case the insured was suffering severe reactive depression after his son's death and attempted to destroy himself by setting fire to the family home, but this alone was not evidence enough to take the case outside an exclusion of "loss resulting . . . from neglect . . . to use all reasonable means to protect covered property".

106. The distinction can be traced to *Port-Rose* v *Phoenix Assurance plc* (1986) 136 NLJ 333 , in which the claimant's handbag was stolen at Gatwick airport. Dismissing the insurer's defence that she had failed "to take reasonable steps to prevent loss", Hodgson J said that the defence came down "to a suggestion that, because this lady was inadvertent momentarily, for two or three seconds and took her eye off the handbag during two or three seconds, she was in breach of the condition of the policy. It seems to me inconceivable that such a let out could be open to an insurance company, and if any member of the public were told that if they insured with the Phoenix Insurance Company and had a handbag containing jewellery which, through fortuitous circumstances became such that it was difficult to carry, and they put it on a trolley being pushed by one of her teenage sons, and that during two or three seconds she took her eye off that trolley, she was thus taking herself outside the cover which she had, or thought she had had, for many years, and for which over many years she had paid substantial premiums, they would have been quite astonished."

The distinction between recklessness and mere inadvertence was also accepted in *Devco Holder Ltd* v *Legal & General Assurance Sy Ltd* [1993] 2 Lloyd's Rep 567 (CA—motor).

107. p 7. The Ombudsman has continued to distinguish inadvertence, which is covered, from conduct which is not: The Insurance Ombudsman, Annual Report 1991, para. 2.16.

between failing to take the care appropriate to the value of the property at risk, and taking such care and yet losing the property due to momentary inadvertence when one's attention is distracted". This is a distinction that turns not on the degree of risk but on whether the insured was aware of it. It is a distinction of a kind that has a long history in relation to the law of carriage of goods, which distinguishes negligence from wilful misconduct: see below, 19–2B. It is a distinction, which, as a commercial judge of great experience, Lloyd LJ in *Sofi* could not have forgotten. In the context of insurance, the insured is not covered if he deliberately "courts danger".[108] Thus, from the baseline that the insured with valuables knows that there is a risk of theft, if he does nothing at all to protect them or must have been aware that what he did was inadequate, that is reckless and, if theft occurs, he is not covered. If, however, he takes some steps which he, mistakenly and carelessly, believes to be sufficient to protect them, he is covered.[109] Further, even a high level of carelessness may be covered, if it can be called (momentary)[110] inadvertence, as in the case of the lady who took no care at all for her handbag for a moment or two while her attention had been distracted.[111]

Thirdly, whether expressed as a condition of due diligence or an exception of negligence, the term is more likely to be construed as an exception than as a warranty.[112] As an exception, it will be construed *contra proferentem*[113] and, moreover, it will not generally apply unless it causes loss.[114] In one case, for example, the judge considered a general liability policy and a term that the insured would exercise reasonable care to see that his plant machinery and appliances were in proper order, and observed that, if the term were a "condition precedent",[115] "if, for instance, the plaintiffs had neglected to keep their cellar flap in proper condition so that it might be that someone walking along the street might trip over it—and although no one complained about it at all . . . the insured could not recover on this policy in respect of a fire . . . a quarter of a mile away and which had no possible connexion with the cellar. To my mind that is an absurdity".

19–2B Wilful Exposure to Unnecessary Danger

Many ordinary activities of life, such as motoring, involve exposure to danger, many

---

108. *Fraser* v *Furman Ltd* [1967] 2 Lloyd's Rep 1, 12 *per* Diplock L J (CA—liability), applied in *Devco* (above), pp 569–570 *per* Slade LJ.
109. See *Sofi* (above). Also Cowan (1993) 3 Ins L & P 4, who refers to a number of decisions of the Ombudman's Bureau, as well as the case of *Devco* (above), in which the insured deliberately left the keys in the ignition of his (expensive) car, while he crossed the road to his office on the first floor: the theft was not covered.
110. But *cf* Cowan (1993) 3 Ins L & P 4, 5: "Decisions have been made at the Bureau that . . . inattention can continue for some hours without becoming gross negligence. As we understand the reasoning [of *Sofi* and *Port-Rose*], provided the property, for example a handbag in a car, was initially left due to mere inattention because the insured was distracted at the time, it does not become grossly negligent simply because its absence was not noticed for many hours". The writer of this book, who, it should be said, lacks personal experience of carrying handbags, wonders whether the insured should not have noticed the absence of the bag before many hours had passed and, if he or she does not, could it not be said that this shows a "couldn't care" attitude which has been characterised in the past as recklessness?
111. *Port-Rose*, (above).
112. *Pictorial Machinery Ltd* v *Nicholls* (1940) 45 Com Cas 334, 342 ff *per* Humphreys J (liability); *Lane* v *Spratt* [1970] 2 QB 480 (goods in transit); *HTV Ltd* v *Lintner* [1984] 2 Lloyd's Rep 125, 128 *per* Neill J (entertainment risks).
113. See above, 15–5C.
114. See above, 19–1C2.
115. *Pictorial Machinery* (above) p 343.

more, such as travel for pleasure,[116] are not strictly necessary and some, such as playing football, may be said to be both dangerous and unnecessary.[117] Hence, a literal reading of clauses excepting (wilful) exposure to unnecessary danger would remove most of the cover normally expected of accident insurance. The courts, however, have refused to take a literal view of such exceptions, which are construed *contra proferentem* and in the light of the main purpose of the insurance contract.[118] So, for example, "Cramp is a danger which attends all bathing in deep water, but it would be absurd to say, on that account, that all bathing in deep water is grossly imprudent"[119] and thus caught by the exception. If insurers wish to exclude particular activities, such as bungee jumping, they can (and do).

The effect of a clause excepting wilful exposure to unnecessary danger is to exclude death or injury brought about intentionally or recklessly[120] by the insured. In the case of accident insurance, that would take away nothing that is not already excluded by the inherent nature or meaning of accident,[121] unless there is something extra in the notion of wilfulness. If "wilful" meant no more than that the sequence of events was initiated or propelled by a voluntary act on the part of the insured, without more, the word would add little or nothing to the notion of accident; this interpretation has been rejected.[122] In the USA, "wilful" exposure connotes consciousness of the danger.[123] This is also the view in England of the Insurance Ombudsman[124] and of the courts concerning the analagous notion of "wilful misconduct" in other legal contexts.[125] It is now the view taken in England by the Court of Appeal.

In *Morley*,[126] the court accepted an analogy with the cases of wilful misconduct, although the *ratio* is not free from ambiguity. The case concerned a young man who, after drinking four to six pints of beer, jumped onto the rear bumper of a car being

116. *Sangster's Trustees* v *General Accident Assurance Corp Ltd* (1896) 24 R 56, 57 *per* Lord Stormonth-Darling. *Travelers' Ins Co* v *Randolph*, 78 F 754, 762 (6 Cir, 1897—PA).

117. *Morley* v *United Friendly Ins plc* [1993] 3 All ER 47, 52 *per* Neill LJ (CA—PA).

118. *Sangster's* (above) p 57 *per* Lord Stormonth-Darling; *Cornish* v *Accident Ins Co Ltd* (1889) 23 QBD 453, 456 *per* Lindley LJ (CA—PA). *Randolph* (above), p 762; *Morley* (above).

119. *Sangster's* (above) p 57 *per* Lord Stormonth-Darling.

120. *Glenlight Shipping Co Ltd* v *Excess Ins Co Ltd* 1983 SLT 241, 244 *per* Lord Robertson (Ct Sess—PA). The exception refers to conduct "so grossly imprudent as to infer utter recklessness" (*Sangster's, loc cit*); "a piece of gross carelessness"—*Manufacturers' Accident Indemnity Co* v *Dorgan*, 58 F 945, 952 (6 Cir, 1893).

In New York the phrase "willfully negligent" in a statute regulating accidental death benefit has been interpreted as meaning with "conscious disregard of the consequences of his actions"—*Ramsden* v *Regan*, 458 NYS 2d 1, 2 (1982), which approximates to gross negligence or recklessness. In the United States a variety of clauses are found in accident policies excluding loss intentionally incurred. See Wilcox, 32 Wayne L Rev 1523 (1986). This survey found that a minority of states apply these exclusions objectively, i.e., on the basis that the insured is presumed to intend the natural and probable consequences of his act; this is similar to the position in England. However, the survey concluded that a majority of states interpret the exclusion more narrowly, confining it to subjective intent to injure, with the qualification that, if harm was substantially certain, subjective intent will be inferred. Appleman, sections 531 ff.

Cf "conscious, reckless, wanton and wicked disregard for personal safety"—*Canadian Ry Accident Ins Co* (1902) 32 SCR 194, 202 *per* Sedgewick J.

121. See above, 17–5C.

122. *Morley* v *United Friendly Ins plc* [1993] 3 All ER 47, 52 *per* Neill LJ and 54 *per* Beldam LJ (CA—PA).

123. *Ashenfelter* v *Employers' Liability Assurance Corp Ltd*, 87 F 682 (9 Cir, 1898—PA). *Glenlight Shipping Co Ltd* v *Excess Ins Co Ltd*, 1983 SLT 241, 242 *per* Lord Hunter (Ct Sess—PA). *Cf* Lord Robertson (p 244): "Knowledge of the danger was not necessary for 'wilful exposure'; recklessness was enough".

124. The Insurance Ombudsman, Annual Report 1991, para. 2.8.

125. Carriage by air: *Horobin* v *BOAC* [1952] 2 All ER 1016, 1022. *Idem* as regards the carriage of goods: Clarke, *International Carriage of Goods by Road: CMR*, (2nd ed, 1991), pp 501 ff.

126. Above.

driven slowly by his fiancee and who did not expect what happened next—that the speed of the car would increase and that he would be thrown off and killed. Neill LJ concluded that the "exclusion clause should be reserved to deal with cases where either the occurrence of an insured injury is more likely *or* where the appreciation of the peril can be more clearly appreciated".[127] However, seen in the context of his judgment as a whole, these words do not indicate that objective likelihood, i.e. recklessness, alone makes it a case of wilful exposure but that the likelihood must be such that actual appreciation of the danger can be inferred. He also said, for example, that the court "must have regard to *all* the circumstances including (a) the likelihood of the insured injury being incurred if the risk is taken *and* (b) the opportunity for reflection before the risk is taken"[128] and his reference to cases on "wilful misconduct" makes little sense, unless actual "appreciation" of exposure is an essential element of the exclusion. The same is true of the judgment of Beldam LJ, who concluded that it "must be shown that . . . the insured was *mindful* of a real risk of the kind of injury . . . *and* that" he was, in effect, reckless. On the facts of the case, it was not "a reasonable inference from such a *thoughtless* act on the spur of the moment that he *appreciated* that he was exposing himself to the risk" in question.[129]

Examples of conduct caught by the clause include crossing a railway line without paying attention to the approach of a train,[130] and driving a vehicle without lights on the public highway at dusk.[131] Conduct not caught by the clause includes not only that found in *Morley* (above) but also swimming alone in deep water on the part of an expert swimmer[132] and driving a car over the ramp of a ferry in the mistaken belief, induced by alcohol, that the ferry had reached the pier.[133]

19–2C Intoxication

The exception of loss occurring while the insured is under the influence of alcohol or drugs is found, for example, in accident or travel insurance. In the absence of this exception loss while the insured is intoxicated is accidental loss.[134] If the contract contains the exception, much turns on the words of the exception.

In England, "under the influence of intoxicating liquor" means under the influence of alcohol to the extent that the "quiet and equable exercise of the intellectual faculties" of the insured is disturbed.[135] In Australia, the meaning is similar: it means that

127. p 52 (emphasis added).
128. *Ibid* (emphasis added). He also differed from the judge below "if in the context he equated recklessness with wilful exposure to peril": *ibid*.
129. p 55 (emphasis added).
130. *Cornish* v *Accident Ins Co Ltd* (1889) 23 QBD 453 (CA—PA). *Glass* v *Mason's Fraternal Accident Assn*, 112 F 495 (ND Iowa, 1901—PA).
131. *Re United Ins Co Ltd and Absalom* [1932] VLR 494 (Victoria—PA).
132. *Sangster's Trustees* v *General Accident Ins Corp Ltd* (1896) 24 R 56 (Ct Sess—PA).
133. *Glenlight Shipping Co Ltd* v *Excess Ins Co Ltd*, 1983 SLT 241 (Ct Sess—PA).
134. *Beller Ltd* v *Hayden* [1978] QB 694 (PA). *Miller* v *American Casualty Co*, 377 F 2d 479 (6 Cir, 1967—PA). *Contra: Hobbs* v *Provident Life & Accident Co*, 535 SW 2d 864 (Tenn, 1975—PA). See above, 17–5E3.
135. *Mair* v *Railway Passengers Assurance Co* (1877) 37 LT 356, 358 *per* Lord Coleridge CJ (PA); "disturbing the quiet, calm, intelligent exercise of the faculties"—*per* Denman J (p 359). These tests were applied in *Louden* v *British Merchants Ins Co Ltd* [1961] 1 WLR 798 (motor), where Lawton J observed (p 799) that he adopted those words "albeit they have been expressed in mid-nineteenth century idiom. I add no gloss, as to do so might add confusion where none may have existed among insurers and policy holders during the past 84 years".

the insured "has taken such a quantity of intoxicating liquor as disturbs the balance of his mind, or the quiet, calm, intelligent exercise of his faculties".[136] In the United States, however, some courts have taken a purposive view of the clause and found that the insured is "under the influence" whenever the drug or alcohol increases the relevant risk.[137] In one case[138] of accident insurance, the court tested the point by asking whether the insured had consumed enough alcohol to "impair in any degree his ability of protecting himself against accidents" at the time he was run down. By contrast, if the contract excludes cover while the insured is "intoxicated", that is "stronger than the term "under the influence" and describes a person who is under the influence of intoxicating beverages to such an extent that he has *lost the normal control* of his bodily and mental faculties",[139] without necessarily being drunk.[140]

As the exception is commonly drafted with reference to loss occurring *while* the insured is under the influence in question, the exception may apply although the loss was not caused by intoxication,[141] with potentially absurd consequences. In *Kennedy* v *Smith* ,[142] counsel for the insurer was forced to concede that the literal construction, for which he was contending, meant that the exception would apply to a claim arising in Scotland, when the car was being driven by the insured's wife in a state of complete sobriety, if it were proved that at that time the insured was under the influence of alcohol on a beach in Spain.

If, however, intoxication does contribute to loss, that is evidence of influence.[143] In *Mair*,[144] accident insurance excepted liability for "death or injury happening while the insured is under the influence of intoxicating liquor". The insured, who had been drinking liquor, rudely accosted a lady accompanied in the street by a large man. The large man pushed the insured to the ground, who broke his skull and died three weeks later. It was held that the exception applied.[145]

The modern court will take evidence of blood alcohol content, if available, and

136. *Forbes* v *Australian Associated Motor Insurers Ltd* (1990) 6 ANZ Ins Cases, no 61–015 (Tas—motor); and *Condon* v *Mercantile Mutual Ins (Australia) Ltd.*, (1991) 12 Qd Lawyer Rep 126 (motor), with reference to English decisions such as *Mair* (above).

137. For example, *Mackay* v *General Accident Ins Co* (1991) 6 ANZ Ins Cases, no 61–046 (NZ—motor); and *Flannagan* v *Provident Life & Accident Ins Co*, 22 F 2d 136, 138 (4 Cir, 1927—PA).

In the United States the argument of literal interpretation, that an insured is under the influence if affected to the slightest degree, has been rejected; the court held that it meant that the insured be injuriously affected: *Murdie* v *Maryland Casualty Co*, 52 F 2d 888, 892 (D Nev, 1931—motor), affirmed 57 F 2d 1081 (9 Cir, 1932).

138. *Murdie* (above) *loc cit.*

139. *Rivers* v *Conger Life Ins Co*, 229 So 2d 625, 628 (Fla, 1969—disability) (emphasis supplied).

140. *Young* v *All American Assurance Co*, 243 So 2d 894 (La, 1971—PA); *Richard* v *American Home Assurance Co*, 318 So 2d 613, 616 (La, 1975—PA).

141. *Louden* v *British Merchants Ins Co Ltd* [1961] 1 WLR 798 (motor): the exception applied to the insured who was a passenger in a vehicle driven by his drinking companion. *Givens* v *Baloise Marine Ins Co Ltd* (1959) 17 DLR (2d) 7 (Ont—PA). *Flannagan* v *Provident Life & Accident Ins Co*, 22 F 2d 136 (4 Cir, 1927—PA); *Order of United Commercial Travelers of America* v *Greer*, 43 F 2d 499 (10 Cir, 1930—PA); *Ludlow* v *Life & Casualty Co*, 217 SW 2d 361 (Tenn, 1948—PA), affirmed 218 SW 2d 65 (1949); *Harris* v *Carolina Life Ins Co*, 226 So 2d 710 (Fla, 1969—PA).

142. 1976 SLT 110, 115 (motor).

143. *Mair* v *Railway Passengers Assurance Co* (1877) 37 LT 356, 358 *per* Lord Coleridge CJ.

144. Above.

145. The suggestion that the court should adopt a literal interpretation, whereby death must "happen while" under the influence, so that, if the insured broke his skull while drunk but did not die until sober, there would be no cover, was rejected as "preposterous" by Lord Coleridge CJ (p 357); Denman J agreed (p 358). This view accords with the usual rule governing the time of cover: above, 18–1B.

draw conclusions from that.[146] However, there may still be some sympathy for the view that

"alcoholic beverages have a varying effect on different individuals. An amount of alcoholic liquor which would have a noticeably intoxicating effect on one individual would have no appreciable effect on another. The court is not aware of any rule which may be relied upon other than the appearance of and conduct of the party at the time in question and for a limited period prior to or subsequent thereto."[147]

Thus, in *Kennedy v Smith*[148] the Court of Session criticised the court below for inferring that a given quantity of alcohol would have a greater effect on a man because he had eaten little or had never taken alcohol before, without evidence that the effect had indeed been greater than usual in the particular case. Again, the court is not interested in evidence of the insured's general drinking prowess[149] but in his behaviour in the particular circumstances. A Louisiana court observed[150] that "the decedent's actions in driving at such a highly excessive rate of speed after consuming substantial quantities of alcohol constituted sufficient proof of the fact that he had lost control of at least some of his normal mental faculties". By contrast, the Court of Session[151] in Scotland, in a case in which it showed very little sympathy for the motor insurer's defence, declined to draw similar conclusions from the erratic course of the vehicle because, it decided, the cause was unknown and might have been other than the intoxication of the insured driver. Generally, if a person has been drinking and his behaviour is aggressive or abnormal, the court is likely to infer the influence of alcohol.

19–2D Unroadworthiness

A motor insurance contract commonly provides that the vehicle shall be efficient or roadworthy. Such terms may be either exceptions or warranties. For example, a term that the insurer shall not be liable while the vehicle is "being driven in an unsafe or unroadworthy condition" has been treated as an exception.[152] But a term, that the "insured shall take all reasonable steps to safeguard from loss or damage and maintain in efficient condition the vehicle" has been treated as a warranty. While the same level of care (to take all reasonable steps) applies to both "safeguard" and "maintain",[153] to "maintain" is a continuous process required throughout the period of cover, so that

---

146. *Louden v British Merchants Ins Co Ltd* [1961] 1 WLR 798, 802 per Lawton J (motor). See also *Givens v Baloise Marine Ins Co Ltd* (1959) 17 DLR (2d) 7, 12 (Ont—PA); *Kulbara v Ins Corp of British Columbia* (1981) 129 DLR (3d) 750 (BC—motor).

147. *Murdie v Maryland Casualty Co*, 52 F 2d 888, 893 (D Nev, 1931—motor), affirmed 57 F 2d 1081 (9 Cir, 1932).

148. 1976 SLT 110 (motor). In this case, a motor accident occurred shortly after the insured aged 39 had taken alcohol for the first time in his life—one or one and a half pints of lager to celebrate victory in a bowls match.

Cf Kulbara (above) in which the court accepted evidence that the driver's blood alcohol level (0.189%) was such as always impaired driving ability, and held that he was "under the influence", even though he showed no overt symptoms of intoxication.

149. *Richard v American Home Assurance Co*, 318 So 2d 613, 617 (La, 1975—PA).

150. *Ibid.*

151. *Kennedy v Smith*, 1976 SLT 110, 116 per Lord President Emslie (motor).

152. *Clarke v National Ins & Guarantee Corp Ltd* [1964] 1 QB 199 (CA—motor). On this exception see Ivamy, *Fire*, pp 248 ff. But in earlier times this kind of term was seen as a warranty, for example, Shawcross, *Motor Insurance* (2nd ed, 1948), p 607.

153. *Brown v Zurich General Accident & Liability Ins Co Ltd* [1954] 2 Lloyd's Rep 243 (motor).

the term appears to be a warranty rather than an exception.[154] In any event, the correct analysis is not always obvious, policies are often unclear on the matter and, although courts are non-committal, strict construction *contra proferentem*[155] suggests that, if there is ambiguity, the term should be treated as an exception.

19–2D1   The Meaning of Roadworthiness

As regards "efficient condition", it means "roadworthy—that is, in an efficient condition for the purpose for which it was going to be used, namely to run upon the roads".[156] It "does not mean a perfect condition".[157]

The exception concerns the efficiency of the vehicle against loss or damage of the kind insured against.[158] The level of mechanical and electrical efficiency required by the motorist to be achieved by his garage is higher than the level which is required of the motorist by his insurer[159]: "if the engine was not properly tuned or timed or was flooding and was consuming too much petrol or too much oil, it would be inefficient in one sense. But I do not think that is the type of inefficiency . . . which arises under this contract" of insurance.[160] However, efficiency is more than merely mechanical efficiency. A vehicle that is overloaded and hence unstable is in an unroadworthy condition.[161]

Efficiency is related to the use to which the vehicle is to be put. Thus a lower level of efficiency, for example as regards the condition of tyres, has been required of a taxi undertaking short trips at low speed, than of a powerful saloon used for long journeys on motorways.[162] In each case, the vehicle must be fit for the normal use[163] of such a vehicle.

---

154. This appears to have been the view taken, for example, in *Jones v Provincial Ins Co Ltd* (1929) 35 Ll L Rep 135 (motor). See also above, 19–1B.

155. Above, 15–5C.

156. *Brown* (above) p 246 *per* Sellers J (motor): a vehicle with treadless tyres is not roadworthy. The judge substantially repeated this view in *Conn v Westminster Ins Assn Ltd* [1966] 1 Lloyd's Rep 123, 127 (motor) holding (p 130) that, if one front tyre is treadless, a vehicle to be used at slow speeds is not unroadworthy; *sed quaere*.

A vehicle driven at night without lights is unsafe: *Trickett v Queensland Ins Co Ltd* [1936] AC 159, (PC—motor). A vehicle driven down a steep hill without a foot brake is not efficient: *Jones v Provincial Ins Co Ltd* (1929) 35 Ll L Rep 135 (motor). But a vehicle towing another with a defective tow rope is not unsafe, as the rope is not part of the vehicle: *Jenkins v Deane* (1933) 47 Ll L Rep 342 (motor). On this reasoning the same is true of the vehicle being towed; *sed quaere*.

157. *Conn v Westminster Ins Assn Ltd* [1966] 1 Lloyd's Rep 123, 126–127 *per* Sellers LJ (motor).

158. *Ibid*.

159. *Conn* (above), p 127 *per* Sellers LJ.

160. *Ibid*.

161. *Clarke v National Ins & Guarantee Corp Ltd* [1964] 1 QB 199, 210–211 *per* Sellers LJ (CA—motor). The court held that, while decisions on seaworthiness do not govern the meaning roadworthiness, they were of some assistance; see Harman LJ (p 205) and Sellers LJ (p 209). But in *Trickett v Queensland Ins Co Ltd* [1936] AC 159, 165 (PC—motor) Lord Alness said that "their Lordships think the analogue imperfect and indeed misleading". Contrast faulty loading which does not affect the handling of the vehicle but is unsafe to other road users because, for example, the load protrudes or falls off: the vehicle is not "in an unsafe condition"—*Salmon Contractors Ltd v Monksfield* [1970] 1 Lloyd's Rep 387 (motor). If the analogue is followed, a vehicle will be unroadworthy when driven by an incompetent or unqualified driver: *Hong Kong Fir Shipping Co Ltd v Kawasaki Kisen Kaisha* [1962] 2 QB 26 (CA).

162. *Conn* (above), pp 128–131 *per* Sellers LJ. However, if the tyres are bald, the vehicle is not "in a proper state of repair", regardless of the use made of the vehicle: *Lefevre v White* [1990] 1 Lloyd's Rep 569 (motor).

163. *Clarke* (above), p 212 *per* Havers J (CA—motor): thus an overloaded vehicle that is safe only when driven more slowly than normal is not roadworthy.

19–2D2 The Degree of Care Required

As regards the level of the duty of maintenance, the duty is to take reasonable care.[164] Argument based on *Woolfall* (above, 19–2A1), that it is no more than a duty not to be reckless, has been rejected.[165] Reasonable care requires regular servicing and that, if any signs of inefficiency should have been seen by the insured, they should be investigated and, if necessary, put right.[166]

19–2D3 The Timing of the Duty

Reasonable steps "to safeguard ... and maintain" must be taken at the time that reason dictates. By contrast, the exception relating to a vehicle "being driven in an unsafe condition" is tested by reference to the state of the vehicle when it is being driven and, usually therefore, when the accident occurs. Thus, it has been held that a vehicle driven on dry roads with tyres that would render it unsafe in the wet is not being driven in an unsafe condition.[167] However, it has also been held of this exception that it operates even though the insured is unaware that the vehicle is unsafe.[168]

19–3 EXCEPTIONS: PERILS OF SOCIETY[169]

19–3A War

Insurance contracts commonly except war risks. War is not defined, however, the word is not usually used in the sense of international law; the question, whether or not there is a state of war, is a question of fact in each case.[170]

---

164. *Brown* v *Zurich General Accident & Liability Ins Co Ltd* [1954] 2 Lloyd's Rep 243, 247 *per* Sellers J (motor).
Cf the exception "while being driven in a damaged or unsafe condition": in *Trickett* v *Queensland Ins Co Ltd* [1936] AC 159 (PC—motor) the Board rejected the argument that the exception only applied if the insured was aware of the defect.

165. *Brown* (above), *loc cit.*

166. *Conn* (above), pp 128–129 *per* Sellers LJ. See also *Lefevre* v *White* [1990] 1 Lloyd's Rep 569 (Motor).

167. *Bashtannyk* v *New India Assurance Co Ltd* [1968] VR 573 (motor), relying on *Trickett* (above) and *Clarke* (above). The court also suggested (p 575) that a vehicle with defective lights would not breach the condition, when driven in daylight. *Cf Lefevre* v *White* (above).

168. *Trickett* (above). *Cf Crossley* v *Road Transport & General Ins Co* (1925) 21 Ll L Rep 219 (motor); *Bonney* v *Cornhill Ins Co* (1931) 40 Ll L Rep 39, 45 *per* Charles J (motor). In *Barrett* v *London General Ins Co Ltd* (1934) 50 Ll L Rep 99, 101, Goddard J sought to improve the position of the insured by holding that the exception does not operate, unless the vehicle was unsafe not only at the time of the event but also at the time when it set out on its journey, on the basis of an analogy, specious on this particular point, with the duty of the shipowner to maintain his ship in a seaworthy condition; this reasoning was doubted in *Trickett* (above), p 165 *per* Lord Alness.

169. The property insurer generally classifies special perils as (a) social perils, such as riot and war; (b) perils of nature, such as earthquake, storm, flood, hail, subsidence, subterranean fire; (c) chemical perils, including explosion and spontaneous combustion; and (d) miscellaneous, such as the effect of aircraft and breaking mirrors.

170. *Kawasaki Kisen Kabushiki Kaisha of Kobe* v *Bantham SS Co Ltd* [1939] 2 KB 544, 558 *per* Greene MR (CA). Consequently insurance contracts are often detailed on this issue; see for example in connection with aviation risks in the Middle East *American Airlines Inc* v *Hope* [1974] 2 Lloyd's Rep 301 (HL). On war risks generally see Arnould, Nos 880 ff.
In the USA international law definitions do not necessarily govern the insurance meaning of a term such as "war" but provide a starting place for inquiry: *Pan American World Airways Inc* v *Aetna Casualty & Surety Co*, 505 F 2d 989, 1012 (2 Cir, 1974); [1975] 1 Lloyd's Rep 77, 93. See further *New York Life Ins Co* v *Bennion*, 158 F 2d 260 (1946—life), that there was war with Japan after the Pearl Harbour attack regardless of formal declaration; also *New York Life Ins Co* v *Durham*, 166 F 2d 874 (10 Cir, 1948).

War includes civil war,[171] unless the context clearly indicates otherwise,[172] as where civil war is separately mentioned: below, 19–3B. In *Curtis & Sons* v *Mathews*[173] Roche J considered fire insurance in respect of loss caused "by war, bombardment, military or usurped power", and said[174]:

"the Dublin rising was not merely felonious, but was treasonable. Further it had a distinct connection with the war in which this country was engaged against the Central Powers. The Provisional Government in their proclamation claimed 'to be supported by gallant allies in Europe'—that is to say, by Germans . . . It is true that the rising was in fact as hopeless as the proclamations of its leaders were vainglorious, but I am satisfied that Easter week in Dublin was a week not of mere riot but of civil strife amounting to warfare waged between military and usurped powers and involving bombardment."

One feature of war consistently required has been the involvement of a political entity, although not necessarily one formally recognised by the forum state. In *Pan Am* v *Aetna*,[175] the question was whether the hijacking (and subsequent destruction) of a passenger aircraft by two members of the PFLP[176] was excluded *inter alia* as a war risk. The United States Court of Appeals, accepting the view of the court below,[177] held[178] that war implied "hostility engaged in by entities that have at least significant attributes of sovereignty" and "that constitute governments at least *de facto* in character". The court concluded that the activities of guerrilla groups did not amount to a war risk.

19–3B Civil War

When the words civil war, revolution, rebellion, civil commotion and riot appear in conjunction in the same insurance contract, one view is that each connotes a disturbance less extensive than the one before,[179] but with a degree of overlap so that, for example, the same events may amount to both riot and civil commotion.[180] Mention

---

171. *Pesquerias y Secaderos de Bacalao de Espana SA* v *Beer* (1949) 82 Ll L Rep 501 (HL—hull).
172. p 514 *per* Lord Morton.
173. [1918] 2 KB 825, affirmed [1919] 1 KB 425 (CA); approved in *Pesquerias* (above).
174. p 829.
175. *Pan American* v *Aetna* (above).
176. Popular Front for the Liberation of Palestine.
177. 368 F Supp 1098, 1130 (SD NY, 1973); [1974] 1 Lloyd's Rep 207, 229
178. 585 F 2d 989, 1012 (2 Cir, 1974); [1975] 1 Lloyd's Rep 77, 93. The court cited with approval *Vanderbilt* v *Travelers' Ins Co*, 184 NYS 54 (1920—life), affirmed 139 NE 715 (1923), that the sinking of the liner *Lusitania* and consequent death of the insured passenger was an act of war, excluded by the policy. In the same sense: *Holiday Inns Inc* v *Aetna Ins Co*, 571 F Supp 1460, 1465 (SD NY 1983—AR).
179. *Republic of Bolivia* v *Indemnity Mutual Marine Assurance Co Ltd* [1909] 1 KB 785, 801 *per* Farwell LJ (CA—cargo). Also in this sense Arnould, No 905, but adopting the doubts of Mustill J in *Spinney's* (below) p 428: "I am not convinced that all the listed perils lie in a straight line with riot at the bottom and civil war at the top. Some appear to stand rather to one side."
Cf also *Pan American World Airways Inc* v *Aetna Casualty & Surety Co*, 505 F 2d 989, 1005 (2 Cir, 1974—aviation): the court rejected the argument that the terms define uninterrupted overlapping areas of exclusion on a continuum of violence. It preferred the view that each term has dimensions besides the level of violence, and that interpretation *contra preferentem*—shrinks the alleged overlapping areas to "mere points on a line of violence. The lacunae between these points include the vast number of nameless causes that are not precisely described by the terms actually employed."
180. *Motor Union Ins Co* v *Boggan* (1923) 130 LT 588, 591 *per* Lord Birkenhead LC (HL—motor). Events may also be both a riot and a mutiny: *Pitchers* v *Surrey CC* [1923] 2 KB 57, 71 *per* Lord Sterndale MR (CA).

of war, at least when civil war is not mentioned separately, includes civil war,[181] which is a war which is internal[182] to a state rather than external between two states or more.

Recognition by the government of the United Kingdom, that certain events amount to a civil war in the sense of international law, is not decisive.[183] And the courts have declined to offer a definition. In *Spinney's* case,[184] however, Mustill J suggested that a civil war should have certain characteristics.

(a) There must be opposing sides,[185] although the sides need not amount to quasi-states, so that it is possible "to say of each fighting man that he owes allegiance to one side or another, and it must also be possible to identify each side by reference to a community of objective, leadership and administration".[186]

(b) The objectives of the warring sides must be of a certain scale; (i) to seize or retain the whole or part of the state[187] or, if not, there may yet be civil war if, for example, (ii) one side sought "to force changes in the way in which power is exercised, without fundamentally changing the existing political structure",[188] or (iii) "if the participants were activated by tribal, racial or ethnic animosities".[189]

(c) As regards the character and scale of the conflict, there is a list of matters to be considered[190]: the number of combatants, the number of casualties, military and civilian, the amount and nature of the armaments involved, the relative size of the territory occupied by the opposing sides, the extent to which it is possible to delineate the territories occupied, the degree to which the populace as a whole is involved in the conflict and, in particular, whether there have been movements of population, the duration and degree of continuity in the conflict, the extent to which public order and the administration of justice have been impaired, the degree of interruption to public services and private life, the extent to which each side purports to exercise exclusive legislative, administrative and judicial powers.

19–3C Insurrection and Rebellion

"Sometimes the word 'insurrection' has been used to characterize an outbreak more limited in its objective than the forcible overthrow of government—for instance, where the civil authority in a community has been defied and temporarily rendered

---

181. *Pesquerias y Secaderos de Bacalao de Espana SA* v *Beer* (1949) 82 Ll L Rep 501, 514 *per* Lord Morton (HL—hull).

182. *Spinney's* (below), p 429 *per* Mustill J.

183. *Spinney's* (below), p 426 *per* Mustill J; cited with approval in *Holiday Inns Inc* v *Aetna Ins Co*, 571 F Supp 1460, 1464 (SD NY 1983—AR).

184. *Spinney's (1948) Ltd* v *Royal Ins Co Ltd* [1980] 1 Lloyd's Rep 406, 429–430 (fire). *The Amy Warwick*, 2 Black, 635, 666 ff (Sup Ct USA, 1862).

185. p 430. There may be more than two sides.

186. p 430: the community of objective may be merely substantial rather than identical.

187. This is the traditional concept of civil law in public international law expounded by Vattel, accepted in England, and applied, for example, in *Brown* v *Hiatt*, 4 F Cas No 2,011 p 384, 387 (D Kan, 1870). In the United States, civil war implies a "specific intent to overthrow established government": *Holiday Inns Inc* v *Aetna Ins Co*, 571 F Supp 1460, 1466 (SD NY 1983—AR).

188. *Spinney's*, p 430.

189. p 430.

190. p 430. Mustill J rejected the argument that each faction must hold a substantial portion of territory, citing *Curtis* (above, 19–3A).

impotent in consequence of a labor struggle"[191] or a politically motivated organisation has kidnapped someone.[192] But when used in conjunction with other events such as riot and civil commotion in an insurance contract, insurrection implies the overthrow of government.[193] It

"is no less an insurrection because the chances of success are forlorn . . . At the time of its breaking out, an insurrection may not necessarily look impressive either in numbers, equipment or organization. As the insurrection develops into an affair of greater magnitude, so the insurgents come into *de facto* control of a definite region of the country, the insurrection may be spoken of as a 'rebellion'.[194] If the insurrection or rebellion proceeds to the attainment of its objective, *viz*, the overthrow of the old constituted government and the establishment of a new one in its place, then the movement, retroactively, will be dignified by the characterization of a 'revolution'."[195]

Further, an insurrection is no less an insurrection because it was originally organised by an outside government (*in casu* Rhodesia) and was subsequently supported or even controlled by an outside government (South Africa), provided that the insurrection is not of outside mercenaries but has a sufficient number of disaffected locals (*in casu* between 5,000 and 8,000) and one of its objects was to overthrow the local government: *National Oil Co of Zimbabwe (Pte)* v *Sturge*.[196] Supporters of the Mozambique National Resistance (Renamo) blew up the pipeline between Beira and Feruka causing losses of gas oil, which were the subject of a subsequent insurance claim. The losses came within the Institute Strike Clauses (loss caused by "any terrorist or any person acting from a political motive"), but the insurers pleaded an exception of loss caused by "war, civil war, revolution, rebellion, insurrection, or civil strife". Saville J held[197] that "rebellion" and "insurrection" each meant an organised and violent internal uprising in a country with the main object of trying to overthrow or supplant the government of that country—though "insurrection" denoted a lesser degree of organisation and size than "rebellion". Such was the case before the court: the insurers were not liable.[198]

19–3D Civil Commotion

A civil commotion or civil disturbance is something less than a civil war,[199] but "something considerably more serious than a leaderless mob".[200] The "phrase is used to

---

191. *Home Ins Co* v *Davila*, 121 F 2d 731, 736 (1 Cir, 1954—fire); the case concerned events in Puerto Rico in October 1950.

192. *Beckman Instruments* v *OPIC*, 83 AJIL 112 (1989): the decision of an arbitral tribunal, applying *Pan-Am* v *Aetna*, 505 F 2d 989 (2 Cir, 1974—aviation).

193. *Davila* (above), *loc cit*. See also *The Amy Warwick*, 2 Black, 635, 666 (USA, 1862). *Pan American World Airways Inc* v *Aetna Casualty & Surety Co*, 368 F Supp 1098, 1124 (SD NY, 1973—aviation), affirmed 505 F 2d 989, 1005 (2 Cir, 1974); *Holiday Inns Inc* v *Aetna Ins Co*, 571 F Supp 1460, 1466 (SD NY 1983—AR).

For a similar view in England see *Spinney's (1948) Ltd* v *Royal Ins Co Ltd* [1980] 1 Lloyd's Rep 406, 437 *per* Mustill J (fire).

194. In the sense of this sentence: *Spinney's* (above) pp 436–437 *per* Mustill J.

195. *Davila* (above), *loc cit*.

196. [1991] 2 Lloyd's Rep 281.

197. p 282, with reference to *Davila*, (above).

198. Accordingly, the court did not find it necessary to decide whether the situation amounted to a "rebellion" or a "civil war".

199. *Brown* v *Hiatt*, 4 F Cas no 2,011 p 384, 388 (D Kan, 1870).

200. *Spinney's (1948) Ltd* v *Royal Ins Co Ltd* [1980] 1 Lloyd's Rep 406, 437 *per* Mustill J (fire). *Levy* v *Assicurazioni Generali* [1940] AC 791, 800 *per* Luxmoore LJ (PC—fire): "The element of turbulence or tumult is essential; an organised conspiracy to commit criminal acts, where there is no tumult or disturbance

indicate a stage between riot and civil war".[201] There is no exhaustive definition, but it does not imply the objective of supplanting governmental authority, but, in the view of Lord Mansfield,[202] "a rising of the people . . . for purposes of general mischief". Some degree of commotion and tumult is essential.[203]

19–3E Riot

The meaning of "riot" in English law is clear but curious; the word is used in the technical sense of the criminal law rather than a popular sense.[204] It is well illustrated by one of the leading cases: *Motor Union Ins Co Ltd* v *Boggan*.[205] A motor car was insured against a number of perils, including fire and theft; riot was excepted. One night in Ireland, the car was commandeered quietly and efficiently by four men with revolvers. The House of Lords held [206] that the loss fell within the exception of riot:

(a) At the time of *Boggan* there could be a riot with no more than three or more persons[207]; in *Boggan* there were four. The number has since been increased to twelve.[208]

(b) There must be a common purpose[209]; in *Boggan* there was the common purpose of commandeering the motor car.

(c) The purpose must be carried out or incepted; in *Boggan* the car was taken.

(d) There had to be an intent to help one another by force, if necessary, against any person who might oppose them in the execution of their common purpose. In *Boggan* this was inferred from the possession of revolvers. The law now requires the use or threat of unlawful violence[210]; this too was present in *Boggan*.

until after the acts, does not amount to civil commotion". In the latter sense *London & Manchester Plate Glass Co Ltd* v *Heath* [1913] 3 KB 411 (CA—plate glass); *Cooper* v *General Accident, Fire & Life Assurance Corp* (1922) 13 Ll L Rep 219, 220 (HL—theft). *Holiday Inns Inc* v *Aetna Ins Co*, 571 F Supp 1460, 1466 (SD NY 1983—AR).

201. Referred to by Luxmoore LJ (above), *loc cit*.

202. *Spinney's* (above), p 438 *per* Mustill J (fire), quoting the summary in *Lindsay & Pirie* v *General Accident Fire & Life Assurance Corp Ltd* (1914) SAR (App D) 574, 594 *per* Soloman JA (fire) of the opinion of Lord Mansfield in *Langdale* v *Mason* (1780) 2 Park on Ins 965, 968. Also in this sense Luxmoore LJ (above), *loc cit*. Lord Mansfield's view was adopted in *London & Manchester Plate Glass Co Ltd* v *Heath* [1913] 3 KB 411, 416 *per* Vaughan Williams LJ (CA—plate glass).

203. *Heath* (above). Merkin & McGee, pp B.11.2–21 ff.

204. *London & Lancashire Fire Ins Co Ltd* v *Bolands Ltd* [1924] AC 836, 847 (burglary); *cf* Lord Atkinson (p 845), who thought that the House was giving the word its ordinary sense.

Cf Canada and the USA where a popular sense is preferred: *Ford Motor Co of Canada Ltd* v *Prudential Assurance Co Ltd* (1958) 14 DLR (2d) 7, 13 (Ont—property, business interruption). *Pan American World Airways Inc* v *Aetna Casualty & Surety Co*, 368 F Supp 1098, 1134 (SD NY 1973—aviation), affirmed 505 F 2d 989 (2 Cir, 1974).

205. (1923) 130 LT 588 (HL).

206. See in particular p 592 *per* Lord Wrenbury who took the five requirements from *Field* v *Receiver of Metropolitan Police* [1907] 2 KB 853, 860 *per* Phillimore J.

207. USA in this sense: *Pan American World Airways Inc* v *Aetna Casualty & Surety Co*, 505 F 2d 989, 1005, 1020 (2 Cir, 1974—aviation).

It is irrelevant that the rioters are soldiers (in a demobilisation camp): *Pitchers* v *Surrey CC* [1923] 2 KB 57 (CA).

208. This is the effect of section 1(1) of the Public Order Act 1986, which replaces common law riot with a statutory offence of riot, on the assumption that courts in insurance cases will continue to follow the criminal law: see *Bolands* above; also 15–2B.

209. It has been held that the objective or purpose must be a private rather than a public purpose: *Pan American World Airways Inc* v *Aetna Casualty & Surety Co*, 368 F Supp 1098, 1135 (SD NY 1973—aviation), affirmed 505 F 2d 989 (2 Cir, 1974).

210. Public Order Act 1986, section 1(1).

(e) There must be a display of force or violence in such manner as to alarm at least one person of reasonable firmness and courage; or, in the language of the law today, "such as would cause a person of reasonable firmness present at the scene to fear for his personal safety".[211] In *Boggan*, Lord Wrenbury observed[212] that he had "no doubt that it was done in such a manner as to cause some alarm to the [chauffeur] who was blindfolded and kept for two hours in a cottage while they were getting away".

In the United States, the "ancient common law criminal definition of the term" found in *Boggan* has been rejected as too broad.[213] In the popular, common sense and usual meaning of the word, it has been held,[214] a riot requires an element of tumult. Hence the hijacking of an aircraft by two or three terrorists was not a riot, even with the help of more terrorists on the ground. The

"notion of a flying riot in geographic installments cannot be squeezed into the ancient formula. Among its other attributes . . . a riot is a local disturbance, normally by a mob, not a complex traveling (*sic*) conspiracy of the kind in this case . . . Riot is not like conspiracy. It may not be conducted by mail, by telephone, or as in the present case, by radio."[215]

That approach "attracts considerable sympathy"[216] in England, but bound, as they are, by decisions of the House of Lords on facts occurring in Ireland in the early part of this century, the English courts have applied a rule of riot without tumult. Since the Public Order Act 1986 there is still no requirement of tumult; however, the chance of a quiet riot with 12 persons is evidently less than the chance of a quiet riot with three.

19–4 WAIVER

The circumstances in which the insurer will be taken to have waived an exception as a defence or be estopped from raising an exception as a defence are broadly the same as those in relation to breach of warranty: below 20–7.

211. *Ibid*.
212. (1923) 130 LT 588, 592. *Quaere* whether at common law someone must have actually seen the display of force or whether it is enough that there was a display of force which, if someone had seen it, would have alarmed him. The former can be inferred from the decision in *The Andreas Lemos* [1982] 2 Lloyd's Rep 483, 492 *per* Staughton J (hull). The matter is settled by the Public Order Act 1986, section 1(4): "No person of reasonable firmness need actually be, or be likely to be, present at the scene."
213. In *Pan American World Airways Inc* v *Aetna Casualty & Surety Co*, 368 F Supp 1098, 1134 (SD NY 1973—aviation); affirmed 505 F 2d 989 (2 Cir, 1974) the District Court observed of the *Bolands* case: "With all the deference we accord the ancestral authorities on the old mysteries, the opinions of the House of Lords are not impressive . . . it is quite evident that the court was affected by its awareness of the disturbances in Dublin and elsewhere in Ireland at the time."
214. *Pan American World Airways Inc* v *Aetna Casualty & Surety Co*, 505 F 2d 989, 1005, 1020–1021 (2 Cir, 1974—aviation). An element of tumult was also required, for example, in *Hartford Fire Ins Co* v *War Eagle Coal Co*, 295 F 663, 665 (4 Cir, 1924—fire): when five men stealthily set fire to a mine, that was not a riot. Also see *Holiday Inns Inc* v *Aetna Ins Co*, 571 F Supp 1460, 1467 (SD NY 1983—AR).
215. *Pan Am* v *Aetna*, *loc cit*.
216. *The Andreas Lemos* [1982] 2 Lloyd's Rep 483, 492 *per* Staughton J (hull). In that case thieves boarded a ship stealthily, armed with knives, and made off with equipment, using force to escape. The court was able to find that the exception of riot did not apply because (*loc cit*) "A riot did occur. But it was not complete until after the loss." This was because the theft was complete before the thieves were discovered and force was used (pp 491–492).

19–5 EXCEPTIONS AND THE UNFAIR CONTRACT TERMS ACT 1977

So far in this chapter, exceptions have been identified by the "but for" test. This, how-ever, is admitted (above 19–1) to be a literal, mechanical approach to identifying an exception. It may be a matter of chance whether the scope of cover is defined purely positively or both positively with some subtraction by exceptions and, it has been sug-gested[217] that it would be anomalous, at least for some purposes, to treat these two approaches to drafting differently. One such purpose may be the application of the principles behind the Unfair Contract Terms Act 1977.[218]

The Act does not apply as such[219]: insurance contracts were excluded from the Act on the understanding that the industry would bring in codes of practice that reflected the spirit of the Act. Codes were published by the ABI but, more recently, the Insur-ance Ombudsman has indicated that the spirit of the Act will be applied to cases that come to his Bureau,[220] in particular, for example, a provision of the insurance con-tract, whether drafted in positive or negative terms, which produces an unexpected loss of cover.[221]

So, in these cases, insurance exceptions will not apply "except in so far as the con-tract satisfies the requirement of reasonableness".[222] The onus is on the person seek-ing to rely on the term,[223] hence the insurer, to show that the term "was fair and reasonable . . . having regard to the circumstances which were, or ought to have been, known to or in the contemplation of the parties when the contract was made."[224] Moreover, the insurer must show that the whole of the exception and not just the part of the exception that he relies on is reasonable.[225] Reasonableness is a matter of impression,[226] built up by reference to certain factors[227] as they affect the particular contract. The factors listed below are not in any order of precedence.

    (a) The relative bargaining strength of the parties[228]: the more of a match they are for each other, the less the inclination of the court to interfere. When assessing their relative strength, the courts have been invited[229] to have regard to whether the profferee (insured):

---

217. McGee (1992) 2 Ins L & P 86.

218. In assessing the nature of the term the court looks at the effect or substance of the term rather than its form: *Phillips Products* v. *Hyland* [1987] 2 All ER 620, 626, *per* Slade LJ (CA).

219. Schedule 1, para 1.(a).

220. The Insurance Ombudsman, Annual Report 1990, para 2.4.

221. *Ibid.* Macdonald (1992) 12 LS 277. On the doctrine of reasonable expectations, as it might apply to the interpretation of insurance contracts, see above, 15–5B.

222. By analogy with s 3(2) of the Act.

223. By analogy with s 11(5) of the Act.

224. By analogy with s 11(1) of the Act.

225. *Stewart Gill Ltd* v *Horatio Myer & Co Ltd* [1992] 2 All ER 257, 262–263 *per* Stuart–Smith LJ (CA).

226. Adams & Brownsword (1988) 104 LQR 94, 103.

227. *Smith* v *Bush* [1990] 1 AC 831, 858–859 *per* Lord Griffiths, 873–874 *per* Lord Jauncey (HL). Gener-ally see the Law Commission Report (No. 69), Second Report on Exemption Clauses, 1975, paras 169 *et seq*. Sched. 3 to the Act offers guidelines on reasonableness in the case of sales of goods, which the courts have applied freely to other kinds of contract: for example, *The Flamar Pride [1990] 1 Lloyd's Rep. 434, 439, per* Potter J. Generally, see Adams and Brownsword (1988) 104 LQR 94, 113; Treitel, pp 236–239; Yates, Exclusion Clauses in Contracts (2nd ed, 1982), pp 95 *et seq*.

228. Unfair Contract Terms Act 1977, Sched. 2(a). *Photo Production* v *Securicor Transport* [1980] AC 827, 843 *per* Lord Wilberforce; *Smith* v *Bush, loc cit*.

229. Law Commission Report (No. 69) Second Report on Exemption Clauses, 1975, para 189.

    (i) knew or should have known that he could enter into a similar contract with another insurer without having to agree to the exception;[230]

    (ii) was experienced in transactions of that kind; and

    (iii) had relied on the advice of the other party (the insurer).

(b) The party best able to insure against the loss or damage in question.[231] This factor, which is of the utmost importance for contracts in general, appears to have no direct relevance to contracts that are insurance contracts—except that it implies consideration for the wider matter of the best or most appropriate risk bearer and thus, it is submitted, for the (reasonable) expectations of the insured.

(c) Any inducement offered by the profferor: in the context of insurance, this factor invites attention to the level of premium paid for the level of risk which, it is contended, the insurer has assumed.[232]

(d) Whether and to what extent the insured had actual notice of the term.[233] Actual notice of an exception is not required for it to be part of the contract,[234] however, both at common law and also in the spirit of the Act, active steps to bring the exception to the mind of the insured, especially if the exception was in small print or difficult to understand,[235] or its content was unusual or unexpected,[236] are desirable if it is to be held to be reasonable.

(e) Whether the term is in established and widespread use in the trade context,[237] i.e., by other insurers.

(f) Any evidence of past practice or evidence in the instant case of settlement of or offers to settle claims without relying on the exception or at a level significantly above the amount of the monetary limit will suggest that the term is not fair and reasonable: this is the so-called "estoppel factor".[238]

(j) In the case of a limit on the time within which claims must be notified or suit may be brought, whether the limit is necessary to enable the carrier to safeguard his position.[239]

---

230. *Smith* v. *Bush* (above).

231. Unfair Contract Terms Act 1977, s 11(4). *George Mitchell (Chesterhall)* v *Finney Lock Seeds* [1983] 2 A.C. 803; *Smith* v *Bush*, *loc cit.*

232. Sched. 2(b). Also, general contract law recognises "proportionality": if the loss claimed against the defendant profferor is large in relation to the remuneration (premium) received by the defendant under the contract, the exception will receive favourable consideration: *George Mitchell (Chesterhall)* v *Finney Lock Seeds* [1983] 2 AC 803; see discussion of the case by Adams and Brownsword (above) p 101.

233. Sched. 2(c). *Phillips Products* v *Hyland* [1987] 2 All ER 620 (CA): if the contract is made at short notice and the profferee is unaware of the terms, he may have insufficient opportunity to take the appropriate action in response.

234. Above, 11–1A3.

235. *The Zinnia* [1984] 2 Lloyd's Rep 211, 222, *per* Staughton J. Further, the court will be influenced by whether the term was agreed on legal advice: *Walker* v *Boyle* [1982] 1 All ER 634, 644, *per* Dillon LJ (CA).

236. *Interfoto Picture Library* v *Stiletto Visual Programmes* [1989] QB 433 (CA).

237. Unfair Contract Terms Act 1977, Sched. 2(c). *George Mitchell (Chesterhall)* v *Finney Lock Seeds* [1983] 2 AC 803.

238. *George Mitchell (Chesterhall)* v. *Finney Lock Seeds* [1983] 2 AC 803, 817, *per* Lord Bridge. Adams and Brownsword (above) pp 100, 106 *et seq.* Of course, evidence of recent practice does not necessarily demonstrate that a term contracted prior to that practice was reasonable, as required by the Act, at the time of contract. Nor does non-reliance in the past preclude reliance in the present or the future: *The Scaptrade* [1983] 1 All ER 301 (CA), affirmed [1983] 2 All E.R. 763 (HL).

239. Law Commission Report (No. 69) Second Report on Exemption Clauses, 1975, para 188. See below, 26–2E4.

19–5A The EC Directive

The EC Directive on unfair terms in consumer contracts[240] is to be implemented by 31 December 1994. All contracts, which come within the scope of the Directive and are concluded after that date, will be subject to the regime.

19–5A1 The Scope of the Directive

The Directive is intended, according to Article 1.1, to approximate laws "relating to unfair terms in contracts concluded between a seller or supplier[241] and a consumer". Article 2 defines the former as "any natural or legal person who . . . is acting for purposes relating to his trade, business or profession" and the consumer as "any natural person . . . acting for purposes which are outside his trade, business or profession", "in transactions covered by this Directive".

The Directive applies to most consumer contracts.[242] Moreover, according to the preamble to the Directive, Member States have the option "to afford consumers a higher level of protection through national provisions that are more stringent" than those of the Directive. The context indicates that the provisions must be in "laws and regulations" and that statements of practice will not suffice.[243] The insurance industry failed to persuade the Commission that insurance contracts should be fully exempted, however, not all terms of the insurance contract are subject to scrutiny under the Directive.

First, the preamble (para 19) states that "assessment of unfair character shall not be made of terms which describe the main subject matter of the contract nor the quality/price ratio of the goods or services supplied; [but] the main subject matter of the contract and the price/quality ratio may nevertheless be taken into account in assessing the fairness of other terms; [and] it follows, *inter alia*, that in insurance contracts, the terms which clearly define or circumscribe the insured risk and the insurer's liability shall not be subject to such assessment since these restrictions are taken into account in calculating the premium paid by the consumer".

Secondly, the Directive applies only to non-negotiated terms of the contract.

Thirdly, however, Article 6.2 requires Member States to "take the necessary measures to ensure that the consumer does not lose the protection granted by this Directive by virtue of the choice of the law of a non-Member country as the law applicable to the contract if the latter has a close connection with the territory of Member States".

19–5A2 Unfairness

As to the central concept of unfairness, Article 3 provides:

"1. A contractual term which has not been individually negotiated shall be regarded as unfair

---

240. Council Directive 93/13/EEC of 5 April 1993 (OJ 21 April 1993 L95/29). See Dean (1993) 56 MLR 581; Duffy [1993] JBL 67; Maitland-Walker [1993] 3 ICCLR 91.
241. It can be inferred from clauses in the Annex that the Directive is to apply to suppliers of financial services.
242. The Directive does not apply to contracts of employment, contracts concerning succession and family matters, or the internal organisation of companies and partnerships. It does, however, apply to contracts relating to immovable property, except to the extent that timeshare contracts are intended to be the subject of a separate Directive.
243. Unusually, the draftsman has used the preamble to clarify (or qualify) the text of the Directive on the matter. This technique poses it own problems of interpretation: see Duffy p 71.

if, contrary to the requirement of good faith, it causes a significant imbalance in the parties' rights and obligations arising under the contract, to the detriment of the consumer.

2. A term shall always be regarded as not individually negotiated where it has been drafted in advance and the consumer has therefore not been able to influence the substance of the term, particularly in the context of a pre-formulated standard contract.

The fact that certain aspects of a term or one specific term have been individually negotiated shall not exclude the application of this Article to the rest of the contract if an overall assessment of the contract[244] indicates that it is nevertheless a pre-formulated standard contract.

Where any [insurer] claims that a standard term has been individually negotiated, the burden of proof in this respect shall be incumbent on him."

The first striking feature of Article 3 is the reference to good faith. The Directive does not define it, perhaps because it means rather different things in different legal systems. Although the existence of a general doctrine of good faith in English law has been denied, insurance contract law is one branch of English law to which a doctrine of this name is no stranger[245] and, in other branches of English law, other rules achieve results which, in other legal systems, are achieved in the name of a doctrine of good faith.[246]

Although the Directive does not define good faith, the preamble (para 16) indicates, in language already familiar to English lawyers (above 19–5), that

"in making an assessment of good faith, particular regard shall be had to the strength of the bargaining position of the parties, whether the consumer had an inducement to agree to the term and whether the [insurance cover was] to the special order of the consumer; [moreover] the requirement of good faith may be satisfied by the [insurer] where he deals fairly and equitably with the other party whose legitimate interests he has to take into account".

Through notions of what is fair and equitable, good faith is clearly related to the other striking feature of Article 3, that a term "shall be regarded as unfair if . . . it causes a significant imbalance in the parties' rights and obligations . . . to the detriment of the consumer". This has provoked the criticism that it is "vague and lacking in the sort of precision an English lawyer might expect", and the prediction that the notion of imbalance in combination with the reference to good faith is likely to lead to interpretation based on "the more familiar test of reasonableness".[247]

Article 3 is elaborated to a degree by Article 4, which indicates that unfairness is to be assessed (a) by taking into account the nature of the services contracted for; (b) by reference to all the circumstances attending the conclusion of the contract; and (c) by reference to all other terms of the contract or of any other contract on which it is dependent. Moreover, insurers should take particular note of the first two sentences of Article 5:

"In the case of contracts where all or certain terms offered to the consumer are in writing, these terms must always be drafted in plain, intelligible language. Where there is doubt about the meaning of a term, the interpretation most favourable to the consumer shall prevail."

Finally, the Annex to the Directive contains, in the language of Article 3.3, "an indicative and non-exhaustive list of the terms which may be regarded as unfair". This has been described as less a black list of unfair terms than a grey list.[248] *Prima facie*,

---

244. Compare the Unfair Contract Terms Act, 1977 (above 19–5), whereby the court is instructed to look at certain terms only (exclusion and limitation clauses) and, apparently, to consider them in isolation: Dean p 583.
245. See below, chapter 27.
246. See, for example, Clarke [1993] HKLJ 318.
247. Dean p 585.
248. Dean p 587.

few of the kinds of term listed will affect insurance contracts, however, attention might be given to the following categories. Category (i): terms with which the consumer "had no real opportunity of becoming acquainted before the conclusion of the contract"; category (m): terms giving the insurer "the exclusive right to interpret any term of the contract"; category (n): terms making the insurer's commitments "subject to compliance with a particular formality"; and category (q): terms "excluding or hindering the consumer's right to take legal action or exercise any other legal remedy, particularly by requiring the consumer to take disputes exclusively to arbitration not covered by legal provisions, unduly restricting the evidence available to him or imposing on him a burden of proof which, according to the applicable law, should lie with another party to the contract".

19–5A3 The Effect of Unfairness

Article 6.1 provides that unfair terms shall "not be binding on the consumer and that the contract shall continue to bind the parties upon those terms if it is capable of continuing in existence without the unfair terms". Evidently, it is open to the consumer to plead before a court that a term of his insurance contract is unfair, but the Directive takes the matter further, in at least two respects.

First, Article 7.1 provides that Member States shall ensure that "adequate and effective means exist to prevent the continued use of unfair terms" in contracts, to which the Directive applies. What is envisaged is measures to prevent sellers and suppliers ignoring particular decisions against particular terms, even perhaps by means of the criminal law.[249]

Second, Article 7.2 provides that the means of prevention, referred to in Article 7.1, "shall include provisions whereby persons or organizations, having a legitimate interest under national law in protecting consumers"—the Insurance Ombudsman, the Director General of Fair Trading, and the Consumers' Association come to mind—"may take action according to the national law concerned before the courts or before competent administrative bodies for a decision as to whether contractual terms drawn up for general use are unfair, so that they can apply appropriate and effective means to prevent the continued use of such terms".

---

249. Such as the Consumer Transactions (Restrictions of Statements) Order 1976.

CHAPTER 20

WARRANTIES[1]

20-1 TERMINOLOGY: THE NATURE OF WARRANTIES

A warranty[2] is a term of the contract of insurance. Breach of warranty automatically terminates the contract of insurance, subject, however, to the intervention of the insurer to keep it on foot by what is called, inaccurately perhaps, waiver of termination.[3]

Distinguish, first, the warranty of the Sale of Goods Act 1979,[4] a promise collateral to the main purpose of the contract which, if broken, gives the innocent party a right to damages but does not result in termination of the contract. Breach of the insurance warranty does not usually give the insurer a right to damages,[5] but does terminate[6] the contract of insurance.

Distinguish, second, a condition precedent, which must be satisfied before a contract comes into existence.[7] A warranty is part of an insurance contract, and its breach assumes the existence of a contract which obliges the insured to undertake the warranty. However, note that breach of warranty has now been characterised as the failure of a condition precedent,[8] with the result that, if breach occurs after cover has commenced, there is cover until the point of breach but the contract is then terminated automatically from that time. Further, note that in some contracts express words convert a promise, which is in essence a warranty, into a "condition precedent" in the different sense of something to be proved before a claim can be made; the intention is to reverse the normal onus of proof, so that it is the insured who must prove

---

1. Appleman, sections 7341 ff; Brown & Menezes, 5:2:4 and 7:5:20; Patterson, "Warranties in Insurance Law", 34 Colum L Rev 595 (1934); Law Reform Committee Fifth Report (Conditions and Exceptions in Insurance Policies), Cmnd 62 (1957); Hasson, "The 'Basis of the Contract Clause' in Insurance Law", (1971) 34 MLR 29; Birds, "Warranties in Insurance Proposal Forms" [1977] JBL 231.
2. The word warranty may also be used to mean an exception, although warranty and exception are distinct concepts: above, 19-1B. For example, "A warranty that a marine policy is free from particular average certainly does not mean that if there is a partial loss to the insured ship the whole policy is avoided. It merely describes the risk, . . . Again, if a time policy contains the clause 'warranted no St Lawrence . . . ' That is an example of a so-called warranty which merely defines the risk insured against"—*Re Morgan and Provincial Ins Co Ltd* [1932] 2 KB 70, 80 *per* Scrutton LJ (CA—motor).
3. On the precise effect of breach and the meaning of termination see 20-6C.
4. *Dawsons Ltd v Bonnin* [1922] 2 AC 413, 422 *per* Viscount Haldane (motor). For the purposes of the Act a warranty is defined in section 61(1) in language criticised by Benjamin, No 10-022.
5. Patterson, 34 Colum L Rev 595, 604 (1934), suggests that a promissory term, with no more than the attendant remedy in damages, would not have been sufficient to compensate the insurer; hence the insurance warranty was seen as something more than a promissory term.
6. On the precise effect of breach and the meaning of termination see below, 20-6C.
7. *Hurt v New York Life Ins Co*, 53 F 2d 453 (10 Cir, 1931—life).
8. *The Good Luck* [1992] 1 AC 233, 263 (hull)

that the warranty has been fulfilled, rather than the insurer who must prove that it has been broken.[9]

Distinguish, third, the condition of the Sale of Goods Act 1979[10] which, if broken, gives the innocent party not only a right to damages but also an option to terminate the contract of sale, which continues unless that option is exercised. The broken insurance warranty, although sometimes called a condition,[11] terminates the cover automatically[12] but does not usually give the insurer a right to damages.[13] The insurance warranty is said[14] to be conditional, but not promissory. In other contracts, a condition is generally a term which is part of the consideration and which, if broken, substantially deprives the promisee of what he contracted for.[15] An insurance warranty is not part of the consideration and, if it is broken, the insurer is not substantially deprived of what he contracted for—which is premium. The insurer wants the warranty in his contract not for its own sake but in order to limit the risk and so limit the burden or extent of his own promise of cover.[16] His promise of cover is conditional, first, on payment of premium: that is consideration, the price of his promise. It is conditional, second, on the risk covered being no greater than expected when he calculated the premium and being as defined in the contract. The risk is defined and proscribed by three kinds of contract term: terms descriptive of the risk, exceptions and warranties. For example, a voyage may be insured from Liverpool to a port on the east coast of Canada in January (description of risk), St Lawrence excepted (exception) in a seaworthy ship (warranty).

Distinguish, fourth, terms descriptive of risk (or subject-matter), which may or may not be relevant to the risk of loss. If relevant, the term will usually be treated as a war-

---

9. *Logan* v *John Hancock Mutual Life Ins Co*, 116 Cal Rptr 528, 531 (Cal, 1974—PA), citing Harnett & Thornton, 17 Fordham L Rev 220, 237 ff. Use of the words "condition precedent" may not succeed in reversing the onus; see below, 20–6A.

10. In this sense Lord Wright in *Provincial Ins Co Ltd* v *Morgan* [1933] AC 240, 253–254 (motor). For discussion of "condition" under the Act see Benjamin, Nos 10–024 ff. *Cf* Hasson, *op cit*, p 30: "warranty" is used "in the sense of being a term of the contract which has the force of a condition".

11. Lord Wright (above) regarded these words as "equivalent" in insurance law. In *Woolfall & Rimmer Ltd* v *Moyle* [1942] 1 KB 66, 71 (CA—employers' liability) Lord Greene MR left open the question whether "condition" or "condition precedent" was an accurate phrase to describe a warranty.

Cf Roskill J in *Lane* v *Spratt* [1969] 2 Lloyd's Rep 229, 236 (goods in transit) who invented his own distinction for the purposes of the case: a "warranty", he said, is a warranty that does not operate unless it causes loss, a "condition" is one that does. It appears from examples given (*ibid*) that his "warranty" is a term which in this book is referred to as an exception.

12. The "entitlement", a right of election, to accept or not a repudiation of contract condition, is relevant to breach of contracts in general lest the contract breaker be in a position to take advantage of his own wrong by unilaterally terminating the contract. This is not, however, a danger in the case of breach of warranty of insurance, as a breach of warranty is not a wrong in the general sense: if the insured chooses to take himself outside the scope of the cover, no rule of public policy is offended. See Bennett [1991] JBL 592, 596. On the precise effect of breach and the meaning of termination, see below, 20–6C.

13. In *West* v *National Motor & Accident Ins Union Ltd* [1955] 1 All ER 800 (CA—motor) the court held that in the case of a breach of contractual warranty the insurer could not reject the claim while keeping the contract alive; if he wished to reject the claim he must repudiate the policy altogether. See further Patterson, 34 Colum L Rev 595, 604 (1934). *Cf Mint Security Ltd* v *Blair* [1982] 1 Lloyd's Rep 188, 198–199 *per* Staughton J (cash in transit).

14. Patterson, loc. cit.

15. *Hongkong Fir Shipping Co Ltd* v *Kawasaki Kisen Kaisha Ltd* [1962] 2 QB 26 (CA).

16. *Woolfall & Rimmer Ltd* v *Moyle* [1942] 1 KB 66, 76-77 *per* Goddard LJ (CA—employers' liability), as regards a promise to take reasonable precautions; *The Vasso* [1993] 2 Lloyd's Rep 309, 313 *per* Hobhouse J (hull). See also *Ellinger & Co* v *Mutual Life Ins Co of New York* [1904] 1 KB 832, 837 *per* Bigham J (life); these words were cited with approval on appeal [1905] 1 KB 31, 37 *per* Collins MR (CA). Bennett [1991] JBL 592.

ranty.[17] An example discussed below (20–5B1) is that of property insured against fire and described as a two storied house; to raise a third storey is to break a continuing warranty of description. However, to describe a house by its correct name "Chez Moi" is unlikely to be relevant to risk, if the identity of the house is unambiguous, and to change it to "Chez Nous" is unlikely to be seen as a breach of warranty.

Distinguish, fifth, exceptions,[18] which have a functional similarity to warranties: each limits the cover promised by the insurer. It is sometimes difficult to know whether a term is the one or the other, but there is an important difference in their effect. If an exception operates cover is suspended; if a warranty is broken cover is immediately terminated. This difference in effect is the consequence of a difference in concept. While each is to provide against the possibility that the risk is or will be different from the risk expected, the exception concerns a temporary difference, but the true warranty[19] concerns a change or difference that is permanent or regular,[20] or gives rise to the possibility of such a change.[21]

Finally, distinguish the sort of undertaking contained in a warranty from (other) obligations assumed by the insured. In a broad sense, his obligations under the contract of insurance are of three kinds.[22] First, there is money consideration: the payment or promise of premium or calls. Second, there are warranties, whether true warranties or contractual warranties, the subject of this chapter. Third, there are claim conditions to be performed by the insured, such as notice of claims and the duty of co-operation, which are neither consideration nor warranties but terms inserted in the contract to make the main parts of the contract work properly,[23] when claims arise—not to limit the scope of the insurer's main promises (cover and payment) but to make those promises less difficult and less expensive for the insurer to perform.[24] Breach of a claim condition, such as notice,[25] may entitle the insurer to refuse pay-

17. *Yorkshire Ins Co Ltd* v *Campbell* [1917] AC 218, 224 *per* Lord Sumner (PC—cargo). See also *Sillem* v *Thornton* (1854) 3 El & Bl 868, 881 *per* Lord Campbell CJ (fire).

18. *Cf* note 2 (above).

19. *Cf* the contractual warranty which may or may not be a true warranty in this sense: once again the warranty limits the scope of the insurer's promise; however, it limits the promise to pay rather than risk (likelihood) of the event which triggers the duty to pay. See further below, 20–2B.

20. *De Maurier (Jewels) Ltd* v *Bastion Ins Co Ltd* [1967] 2 Lloyd's Rep 550, 558–559 *per* Donaldson J (jewellers' AR); approved in *The Good Luck* [1990] 1 QB 818 (CA—hull). See further above, 19–1B.

21. In many cases the risk has been increased. In other cases the risk may or may not have been increased, but there has been a change of risk which did not enter into the insurer's calculations, when making the contract, so he wishes to reserve the question whether he should continue to provide cover in the new situation. For example this appears to be the case when a restricted use clause has been held to be a warranty: *Provincial Ins Co Ltd* v *Morgan* [1933] AC 240 (motor).

22. Patterson, 34 Colum L Rev 595, 600 (1934), having referred to exceptions, continues: "The other conditions prescribed in insurance contracts may be grouped into three classes: 1. Payment (or non-payment) of premiums. 2. Conditions related to the risk as potential causes of the insured event. 3. Conditions in aid of loss-adjustment, that is, designed to aid the insurer in ascertaining whether the insured event has occurred, the observance of policy provisions, and the amount of loss."

23. Procedural conditions are found in other contracts: "cogwheels in the machinery"—*The Julia* (1949) 82 Ll L Rep 270, 284 *per* Lord Simonds (HL). Clarke [1981] LMCLQ 234, 237 ff.

24. Such conditions are "incidental to the subject-matter of the insurance . . . made with a view to fence round and protect the rights of the assurer, so as to enable him to require satisfactory evidence of, or to make due inquiry concerning, the facts upon which his liability depends. They do not alter the character of the risk upon which the assurance depends. Such conditions grow out of, and are subsidiary to, the subject-matter of the insurance"—*Lancashire Ins Co* v *IRC* [1898] 1 QB 353, 359 *per* Bruce J (employers' liability).

An example is a term, which required the insured to keep a wages book, designed to facilitate the adjustment of premium: *Re Bradley and Essex & Suffolk Accident Indemnity Sy* [1912] 1 KB 415 (CA—employers' liability).

25. *Hood's Trustees* v *Southern Union General Ins Co Ltd* [1928] Ch 793, 806–807 *per* Tomlin J (motor).

ment of loss, but does not normally justify termination of the insurance so as to defeat claims for subsequent loss. Claim conditions are discussed in chapter 26 and co-operation in chapter 27.

20–2 IDENTIFYING A WARRANTY

A warranty is a term of the contract, that is usually express, not implied. A "true" warranty (below, 20–2B1) is material to risk, but parties may create a "contractual" warranty (below, 20–2B2) which, if broken, has the same effect in law, although material to neither risk nor loss.

20–2A Part of the Contract

The warranty must be a term of the contract.[26] Oral warranties are unusual, writing is usual. The effect of the parol evidence rule (above, 14–1) is that, if there is a policy, the warranty must be found in the policy,[27] except in the cases of a proposal and attached documents such as a medical report,[28] with a basis clause (below, 20–2A1), and except in the case of implied terms (below, 20–2A2).

A warranty is part of the policy and thus part of the contract, wherever it is found in the document,[29] unless the presentation of the document is misleading. In particular, a document is held to end where it seems to end and, if the warranty is beyond that and out of sight, the courts will be reluctant to hold that the insured has sufficient notice of it for it to be a term of the contract.[30]

20–2A1 Warranties in the Proposal

The policy may incorporate terms by reference, including a reference to the proposal.[31] But, if statements by the insured in the proposal are stated in the proposal to be the "basis" of the contract of insurance, they have been held to be terms[32] of the

26. *Rice* v *Fidelity & Deposit Co of Maryland*, 103 F 427 (8 Cir, 1900—indemnity bond).
27. *Pawson* v *Watson* (1778) 2 Cowp 785, 786, 787 *per* Lord Mansfield (hull); *Pawson* v *Barnevelt* (1779) 1 Doug 12 n.4 (hull); *Lothian* v *Henderson* (1803) 3 Bos & Pul 499, 509–510 *per* Chambre J (HL—cargo).
28. *Home Life Ins Co* v *Fisher*, 188 US 726 (1903—life); *National Life & Accident Ins Co* v *Gorey*, 249 F 2d 388 (9 Cir, 1957—life).
29. *Thomson* v *Weems* (1884) 9 App Cas 671, 684 *per* Lord Blackburn (life); *Bensaude* v *Thames & Mersey Marine Ins Co Ltd* [1897] AC 609, 612 *per* Lord Halsbury LC (freight). This includes (a) a warranty written on a paper pasted to the policy (*ibid*); and (b) a warranty written on the margin of the policy, but not one in a separate document delivered with the policy: *Bean* v *Stupart* (1778) 1 Doug 11, 14 *per* Lord Mansfield (hull) and cases cited.
30. MacGillivray, No 730 as regards warranties on the back of the policy. Generally, see Clarke [1976] CLJ 51, 77 and citations, especially *Henderson* v *Stevenson* (1875) LR 2 Sc & Div 470 (HL). See also *Silvestri* v *Italia SpA di Navigazione* [1968] 1 Lloyd's Rep 263 (2 Cir, 1968).
31. *Worsley* v *Wood* (1796) 6 TR 710 (fire); *Yorkshire Ins Co Ltd* v *Campbell* [1917] AC 218, 221-222 *per* Lord Sumner (PC—cargo); *Provincial Ins Co Ltd* v *Morgan* [1933] AC 240, 252 *per* Lord Wright (motor).
An example, taken from *Dawsons* v *Bonnins Ltd* [1922] 2 AC 413 (fire), is a policy clause that refers to a proposal of a given date, "which proposal shall be the basis of the contract and be held as incorporated herein".
32. *Joel* v *Law Union & Crown Ins Co* [1908] 2 KB 431, 437 *per* Lord Alverstone CJ (CA—life), citing *Wood* v *Dwarris* (1856) 11 Ex 493 (life). See also *Condogianis* v *Guardian Assurance Co Ltd* [1921] 2 AC 125, 129 *per* Lord Shaw (PC—fire); *Rozanes* v *Bowen* (1928) 32 Ll L Rep 98, 103 *per* Scrutton LJ (CA—jewellery). *Phoenix Mutual Life Ins Co* v *Raddin*, 120 US 183, 189 *per* Gray J (1887—life), but it was held there (p 190) that the words in the proposal that the answers should "form the basis of the contract for insurance" were insufficient to make the answers warranties; see also *Home Life Ins Co* v *Fisher*, 188 US 726, 728 *per* Holmes J (1903—life).

contract of (non-marine[33]) insurance, although not referred to in the policy at all. While this rule is well established by insurance cases as being what the parties intend,[34] it is difficult to square the rule with the notion underlying the parol evidence rule, that a document such as a policy which looks like the whole of the contract should be treated as the whole of the contract and thus as being exclusive.[35] There are established exceptions to the parol evidence rule, but these do not explain why basic terms of a contract between the very same parties should be found not only in the formal policy but also in the proposal,[36] except by well worn resort to market practice. If the answer is indeed market practice, there must be doubt about its application to consumers. Basis clauses have been described as "objectionable",[37] "traps"[38] and "a major mischief in the present law".[39] Reform of the law has been recommended by the Law Commission,[40] and basis clauses are abjured by the Statement of General Insurance Practice[41]; however, they remain enforceable in law.

20–2A2 Implied Warranties: Aggravation of Risk

Terms may be implied in the contract of insurance, as in other contracts, if their implication is necessary to give the contract business efficacy.[42] In practice, this possibility is of little importance to insurance contracts. Undoubtedly, the insured has a duty of good faith which, it has been contended,[43] depends on an implied term, however the view of the majority is that, at the time of contracting at least, the basis of the duty is not an implied term but a rule of law.[44] Courts have been slow to interfere in this way with the contract of insurance, with the exception of marine contracts, in which terms were once implied by the courts but are now sanctioned by statute[45]

---

33. As regards marine contracts, the MIA, section 35(2) provides: "An express warranty must be included in, or written upon, the policy, or must be contained in some document incorporated by reference."

34. See below, 20–2B2.

35. See above, 14–1.

36. *Cf* Wedderburn, "Collateral Contracts" [1959] CLJ 57.

37. MacGillivray, No 728. See also Hasson, (1971) 34 MLR 29.

38. *Zurich General Accident & Liability Ins Co Ltd* v *Morrison* [1942] 2 KB 53, 58 *per* Lord Greene MR (CA—motor). For further judicial criticism: *Anderson* v *Fitzgerald* (1853) 4 HLC 484, 514 *per* Lord St Leonards (life); *Joel* v *Law Union & Crown Ins Co* [1908] 2 KB 863, 885 *per* Fletcher Moulton LJ (CA—life); *Provincial Ins Co Ltd* v *Morgan* [1933] AC 240, 252 *per* Lord Wright (motor).

39. Law Commission Report No 104 (Cmnd 8064), No 7.5.

40. *Ibid*, Nos 7.8 ff.

41. 1986, para. 1(b).

42. *Liverpool CC* v *Irwin* [1977] AC 239; *Euro-Diam Ltd* v *Bathurst* [1990] 1 QB 1, 41 *per* Kerr LJ (CA—goods). In contracts generally there are (a) terms which the parties really did intend; in the contract of insurance these are usually expressed. (b) Terms which would have been expressed, if the parties had thought about them; these have usually been thought of by insurers and expressed in their contracts. (c) Terms which have been implied by the courts as a matter of law in the guise of party intention; these are not generally found in insurance contracts. The classification is that of Glanville Williams in (1945) 61 LQR 385, 401, which is reflected in the judgment of Lord Wilberforce in *Irwin* (p 254). Cf Phang [1993] JBL 242.

43. Below, 27–1. *The Litsion Pride* [1985] 1 Lloyd's Rep 437 (hull). In this sense Ivamy, p 294. Professor Ivamy also contends (*ibid*) that the non-marine contract has these implied terms: (a) that the subject-matter of insurance exists when the policy is effective; and (b) that the subject-matter is so described as to clearly identify it and define the risk; and (c) that the insured has an insurable interest. These "terms" can be seen differently: (c) as a rule of law, and (a) and (b) as applications of rules of law.

44. Below, 23–1A.

45. MIA, section 39. Arnould, Nos 670 ff, 705 ff. MIA, section 41. Arnould, Nos 743 ff. See also MIA, sections 36–38 and 40. Corresponding warranties are not implied in non-marine contracts: for example *Euro-Diam Ltd* v *Bathurst* [1990] 1 QB 1 (CA—goods).

If the insured increases the risk fraudulently, the contract is avoided, however, fraud in this sense seems to refer to an increase to the point at which loss is so likely that it can be inferred that the object is to destroy the property insured in order to claim[46]; in these circumstances, one might speak of an implied warranty but there evidently is more than one reason in law why the insurance will not be enforced.[47]

If the insured increases the risk but without fraud in this sense, one might have expected a duty or rule of the kind found in some other legal systems[48] to discourage or prevent the aggravation of risk during the insurance period, a duty based perhaps on implied warranty—but there is none.[49] "If a person who insures his life goes up in a balloon, that does not vitiate his policy . . . A person who insures may light as many candles as he please in his house, though each additional candle increases the danger of setting the house on fire."[50] In practice, however, a similar effect is achieved by the combined effect of different and more specific contract terms: (a) continuing warranties,[51] (b) a restriction on the freedom of the insured to alter the identity of the property insured or the description of the risk,[52] (c) a term[53] that any increase in risk shall end the insurance or shall give the insurer the option of ending it, and (d) exceptions to cover in circumstances, seen by the insurer as likely to aggravate risk, notably a term, which might be seen as a warranty but which is better seen as an exception, requiring reasonable care on the part of the insured.[54]

20–2B The Language of Warranty

Not all terms that form part of the insurance contract are warranties. A term of the contract should not be construed as a warranty "except on very clear indications that it

---

46. *Pim* v *Reid* (1843) 6 Man & G 1, 22 *per* Maule J (fire); *Thompson* v *Hopper* (1858) El Bl & El 1038, 1049 *per* Willes J (Exch Ch—hull), cited with approval by Collins LJ in *Trinder Anderson & Co* v *Thames & Mersey Marine Ins Co* [1898] 2 QB 114, 127–128 (CA—freight). Also in this general sense *Denison* v *Modigliani* (1794) 5 TR 580 (hull) in which a ship on a trading voyage took a letter of marque against the express wishes of the insurer, although there was no clear evidence that the insured intended to bring about loss.

47. See, for example, above 17–3A.

48. For example, in France, if the aggravation of risk is such that, if it had been made known to the insurer at the time of the contract, he would not have concluded the contract or would have done so only at a higher premium, the insurer has the option forthwith to terminate the contract or to raise the premium: Insurance Code, Art L.113–4, as amended by the law of 31 December 1989. In Quebec, under the influence of French law and the general doctrine of good faith, the insured is obliged to inform the insurer of any aggravation of the risk *during* the insurance period: Dubreuil (1992) 37, McGill L J 1087, 1101; an exception is made in the case of life insurance !

49. *Pim* v *Reid* (1843) 6 Man & G 1, 22 *per* Coltman J and Maule J (fire); *Stokes* v *Cox* (1856) 26 LJ Ex 113 (Exch Ch—fire); *Trinder Anderson & Co* v *Thames & Mersey Marine Ins Co* [1898] 2 QB 114, 128 *per* Collins LJ (CA—freight); *Mitchell Conveyor & Transporter Co Ltd* v *Pulbrook* (1933) 45 Ll L Rep 239, 245 *per* Roche J (construction AR); *Exchange Theatre Ltd* v *Iron Trades Mutual Ins Co Ltd* [1984] 1 Lloyd's Rep 149, 151–152 *per* Eveleigh LJ (CA—fire).

Cf Toulmin v *Ingis* (1808) 1 Camp 421, 422–423 *per* Lord Ellenborough (cargo) that an increase in the risk did not "vacate" the insurance, unless it amounted to "culpable inattention". As to the impact of wilful default by the insured, see ch 24.

50. *Baxendale* v *Harvey* (1859) 4 H & N 445, 449, 452 *per* Pollock CB (fire), applied in *Dawson* v *Monarch Ins Co* [1977] 1 NZLR 372 (fire). *Albion Lead Works* v *Williamsburg City Fire Ins Co*, 2 F 479, 485 (D Mass, 1880—fire).

51. See below, 20–5.

52. See below 20–5B1.

53. Merkin & McGee, pp B.3.1–01 ff. Appleman, sections 2941 ff. Nicholson, *Mid-term Alterations In the Risk: What Can Be Done ?*, (1991) 4 ILJ 27.

54. See above, 19–2A, and below, 20–5A1.

was the intention of the contracting parties that it should have that effect . . . The effect of each contract must be determined by the instrument itself".[55] Before a term "is held to have the effect of a warranty it is necessary to see that the language is such as to shew that the assured as well as the insurer meant it, and . . . the language in the policy being that of the insurers, if there is any ambiguity, it must be construed most strongly against them".[56]

In *The Bamcell II*,[57] a claim for loss by perils of the sea was defended on the ground of breach of a term "warranted that a watchman is on board" between stated hours. The Court of Appeal for British Columbia adopted the view in an earlier case,[58] that policies should not be construed so as to substantially deprive the insured of the cover for which he had contracted, and accepted[59] the argument of counsel that the parties in the instant case "cannot have intended that if the watchman was late one night, or even missed a night, then the insurers should be discharged from liability for the remainder of the term of the policy". The decision, that the term was not a warranty but a suspensive condition[60] was affirmed by the Supreme Court of Canada.[61]

Use of the word "warranty" is indicative[62] but not decisive,[63] no particular form of words being required[64]; the same is true of the words "condition precedent".[65] Insurance warranties can best be identified by their function (below, 20–2B1) or by the drastic consequences ascribed by the contract to their breach: automatic and instant termination of cover (below, 20–2B2 and 20–6C).

20–2B1 The True Warranty

A true warranty, like an exception, concerns the level of risk. In the United States, Professor Patterson[66] defined a warranty as a term of an insurance contract which pre-

55. *Wheelton* v *Hardisty* (1857) 8 El & Bl 232, 300 *per* Bramwell B (life). Intention is decisive: *Union Ins Sy of Canton Ltd* v *Wills & Co* [1916 1 AC 281, 287 *per* Lord Parmoor (PC—cargo). *Sutton* v *Hawkeye Casualty Co*, 138 F 2d 781 (6 Cir, 1943—motor). However, the intention must be very clear: *Joel* v *Law Union & Crown Ins Co* [1908] 2 KB 863, 886 *per* Fletcher Moulton LJ (CA—life); *Re Bradley and Essex & Suffolk Accident Indemnity Sy* [1911] 1 KB 415, 430–433 *per* Farwell LJ (CA—employers' liability).

56. *Thomson* v *Weems* (1884) 9 App Cas 671, 682 *per* Lord Blackburn (life), adopting *Anderson* v *Fitzgerald* (1853) 4 HLC 484, 507 *per* Lord St Leonards. A more recent example is *CTN Cash & Carry Ltd* v *GAFLAC plc* [1989] 1 Lloyd's Rep 299 (burglary).

USA: warranties to be construed so that the policy is "of some value to the insured"—*Sutton* v *Hawkeye Casualty Co*, 138 F 2d 781, 783 (6 Cir, 1943—motor). Appleman, section 7342.

57. *Case Existological Laboratories Ltd* v *Century Ins Co* (1982) 133 DLR (3d) 727.

58. *Consolidated-Bathurst Export Ltd* v *Mutual Boiler & Machinery Ins Co* [1980] 1 SCR 888.

59. pp 740–741.

60. Also called an exception: above, 19–1A and 19–1B.

61. (1983) 150 DLR (3d) 9.

62. *Hambrough* v *Mutual Life Ins Co of New York* (1895) 72 LT 140, 141 *per* Lord Esher MR (CA—life); *Palatine Ins Co Ltd* v *Gregory* [1926] AC 90, 93 *per* Viscount Cave LC (PC—fire).

63. *Barnard* v *Faber* [1893] 1 QB 340, 342 *per* Lindley LJ, 345 *per* AL Smith LJ (CA—fire); *Dawsons Ltd* v *Bonnin* [1922] 2 AC 413, 428 *per* Viscount Finlay (motor); *Roberts* v *Anglo-Saxon Ins Assn Ltd* (1926) 26 Ll L Rep 154, 157 *per* Mackinnon J (motor); *Re Morgan & Provincial Ins Co Ltd* [1930] 2 KB 70, 79 *per* Scrutton LJ (CA—motor); *CTN Cash & Carry Ltd* v *GAFLAC plc* [1989] 1 Lloyd's Rep 299 (burglary).

Case Existological Laboratories Ltd v *Century Ins Co* (1982) 133 DLR (3d) 727, 740–741 (BC—hull), affirmed (1983) 150 DLR (3d) 9 (Sup. Ct.). *Moulor* v *American Life Ins Co*, 111 US 335, 342 *per* Harlan J (1884—life); *Sutton* v *Hawkeye Casualty Co*, 138 F 2d 781, 784 (6 Cir, 1943—motor); *Hall's Aero Spraying Inc* v *Underwriters at Lloyd's*, 274 F 2d 527, 529 (5 Cir, 1960—liability).

64. *Thomson* v *Weems* (1884) 9 App Cas 671, 684 *per* Lord Blackburn (life); *Union Ins Sy of Canton Ltd* v *Wills & Co* [1916] 1 AC 281, 287 *per* Lord Parmoor (PC—cargo).

65. *Re Bradley and Essex & Suffolk Accident Indemnity Sy* [1911] 1 KB 415 (CA—employers' liability). See above, 20–1.

66. 34 Colum L Rev 595, 602 (1934). *Cf* Arnould, No 681, that the distinction between material and non-material warranties is too troublesome to merit retention.

scribes, as a condition of the insurer's promise, a fact antecedent to or contemporaneous with an insured event, the existence of which, regarded as of the time of contracting, will or may render less probable than its absence the occurrence of an insured event. In England, Lord Blackburn observed[67] that in "marine insurance I think it is well settled by authority that any statement of a fact bearing upon the risk introduced into the written policy is, by whatever words and in whatever place, to be construed as a warranty." Lord Blackburn's use of the word "any" goes too far for the modern law, as it ignores the role of exceptions,[68] but we can still say that, in such a case, the possibility that the statement is a warranty must always be considered.[69]

20–2B2 The Contractual Warranty

A contractual warranty is a term of the contract in the form of an undertaking by the insured which, if broken, entitles the insurer to end the insurance or ends it automatically, whether or not breach is material to risk (below, 20–3A) or to loss (below, 20–3B). It is not necessary that the word "warranty" be used, as any form of words expressing the existence of a particular state of facts as a condition of the enforceability of the contract may be enough to constitute a warranty.[70]

An established example is the basis clause,[71] devised to relieve the insurer of the burden of proving the materiality (to either risk or loss) of statements made by the proposer in the proposal.[72] When "answers are declared to be the basis of the contract this can only mean that their truth is made a condition exact fulfilment of which is rendered by stipulation foundational to its enforceability."[73] "The basis of a thing is that upon which it stands, and on the failure of which it falls."[74]

The effect of the basis clause may be softened by other terms of the contract, but courts, although hostile to basis clauses,[75] have been slow to accept argument to that

---

67. *Thomson v Weems* (1884) 9 App Cas 671, 684 (life), cited with approval in *Ellinger & Co v Mutual Life Ins Co of New York* [1905] 1 KB 31, 36 *per* Lord Collins MR (life) and *Union Ins Sy of Canton Ltd v Wills & Co* [1916] 1 AC 281, 289 *per* Lord Parmoor (PC—cargo). See also *Barnard v Faber* [1893] 1 QB 340, 344 *per* Bowen LJ (CA—fire); *Lancashire Ins Co v IRC* [1898] 1 QB 353, 359 *per* Bruce J (employers' liability); *Bancroft v Heath* (1901) 6 Com Cas 137, 140 *per* Fletcher Moulton LJ (CA—fire); *Yorkshire Ins Co Ltd v Campbell* [1917] AC 218, 225 *per* Lord Sumner (PC—cargo); *Hadenfayre Ltd v British National Ins Sy Ltd* [1984] 2 Lloyd's Rep 393 400 *per* Lloyd J (contingency). *Allstate Ins Co v Boggs*, 271 NE 2d 855, 858 (Ohio, 1971—motor).
68. On the role of exceptions and the interplay with warranties, see above, 19–1B and 20–1.
69. *Prima facie* any "words qualifying the subject-matter of the insurance will be words of warranty"—*Yorkshire Ins Co Ltd v Campbell* [1917] AC 218, 224 *per* Lord Sumner (PC—cargo). See also *Sillem v Thornton* (1854) 3 El & Bl 868, 881 *per* Lord Campbell CJ (fire), discussed below, 20–5B1.
70. *Anderson v Fitzgerald* (1853) 4 HLC 484, 503 *per* Lord Cranworth LC (life); *Farr v Motor Traders Ins Sy Ltd* [1920] 3 KB 669, 673 *per* Bankes LJ (CA—motor); *Dawsons Ltd v Bonnin* [1922] 2 AC 413, 428–429 *per* Viscount Finlay (fire).
71. *Dawsons Ltd v Bonnin* [1922] 2 AC 413, 423–424 *per* Viscount Haldane (fire); see also pp 432–433 *per* Viscount Cave, citing *Thomson v Weems* (1884) 9 App Cas 671, 684 *per* Lord Blackburn (life). *Cf* p 430 *per* Viscount Finlay (dissenting).
72. *Dawsons* (above), pp 422–423 *per* Viscount Haldane.
73. *Dawsons* (above), p 425 *per* Viscount Haldane.
74. *Dawsons* (above), p 432 *per* Viscount Cave.
75. Above 20–2A1.

effect.[76] The clause will be modified only by a clause with which it is inconsistent,[77] or which, without modification, becomes meaningless.[78]

20–3 THE ABSOLUTE NATURE OF WARRANTIES

Breach of warranty entitles the insurer to terminate the contract of insurance, even though the breach is material neither to the risk nor to any loss that has occurred.

20–3A Risk

"It is competent to the contracting parties, if both agree to it and sufficiently express their intention so to agree, to make the existence of anything a condition precedent to the inception of any contract; and if they do so, non-fulfilment is a good defence. And it is not of any importance whether the existence of that thing was or was not material; the parties would not have made it a part of the contract if they had not thought it material, and they have a right to determine for themselves what they shall deem material."[79]

This statement by Lord Blackburn was cited with approval by Viscount Haldane,[80] who then put it in his own words[81]:

"if the [insurers] can show that they contracted to get an accurate answer to this question, and to make the validity of the policy conditional on that answer being accurate, whether the answer was of material importance or not, the fulfilment of this contract is a condition of the appellants being able to recover."

Reverence for the sanctity of contract was bolstered by the thought that, as the parties had stipulated the matter, they must have considered the matter material.[82] In

---

76. For example, *Condogianis* v *Guardian Assurance Co Ltd* [1921] 2 AC 125 (PC—fire); *Dawsons Ltd* v *Bonnin* [1922] 2 AC 413 (motor); *Holmes* v *Scottish Legal Life Assurance Sy* (1932) 48 TLR 306 (life).

77. *Holmes* (above). The court will seek to reconcile clauses when necessary: *Fowkes* v *Manchester & London Assurance Assn* (1863) 3 B & S 917, 926 *per* Lord Cockburn CJ, 927 *per* Compton J (life).

78. In *Fowkes* (above) the basis clause was followed in the same sentence by "if . . . any fraudulent concealment or designedly untrue statement shall be contained therein, then . . . the policy . . . shall be absolutely null and void". Lord Cockburn CJ (p 925) pointed out that these words would be superfluous unless they explained and qualified the basis clause by limiting its effect to fraud. See further below, 20–6B1.

79. *Thomson* v *Weems* (1884) 9 App Cas 671, 683 *per* Lord Blackburn (life). See also *ibid*, p 689 *per* Lord Watson; *Newcastle Fire Ins Co* v *Macmorran & Co* (1815) 3 Dow 255, 261–263 *per* Lord Eldon LC (HL—fire); *Anderson* v *Fitzgerald* (1853) 4 HLC 484, 503 *per* Lord Cranworth LC (life); *Union Ins Sy of Canton Ltd* v *Wills & Co* [1916] 1 AC 281, 286 *per* Lord Parmoor (PC—cargo); *Yorkshire Ins Co Ltd* v *Campbell* [1917] AC 218, 224 *per* Lord Sumner (PC—cargo); *Glicksman* v *Lancashire & General Assurance Co Ltd* [1927] AC 139, 143 *per* Viscount Dunedin (burglary); *Allen* v *Universal Automobile Ins Co Ltd* (1933) 45 Ll L Rep 55, 58 *per* Lord Wright (motor); *Hales* v *Reliance Fire & Accident Ins Corp Ltd* [1960] 2 Lloyd's Rep 391 395 *per* McNair J (fire); *New India Assurance Co Ltd* v *Chow* [1972] 1 Lloyd's Rep 479 (PC—motor); *Macphee* v *Royal Ins Co Ltd*, 1979 SLT 54 (yacht). The early cases do not support such a strict rule: Hasson, (1971) 34 MLR 29; Merkin & McGee, p B.2.3–03.

USA: early cases had the English rule; for example, *Knickerbocker Life Ins Co* v *Trefz*, 104 US 197, 202 *per* Matthews J (1881—life); also *Carrollton Furniture Mfg Co* v *American Credit Indemnity Co*, 124 F 25, 28 (2 Cir, 1903), cert den 192 US 605, citing *inter alia* from *Anderson* (above). However, now the trend is not to allow a breach of warranty to defeat cover unless it is material to the risk: Appleman, sections 4146 and 7354. In some states materiality is required by statute.

80. *Dawsons Ltd* v *Bonnin* [1922] 2 AC 413, 423 *per* Viscount Haldane (motor). In this case, a lorry was insured against fire on a proposal (stated to be the basis of the contract) containing an innocent misstatement about where the lorry was garaged. Although the lorry was probably no more at risk where it was than where stated in the proposal, the House of Lords held that the misstatement was a defence to a claim under the policy.

81. p 421.

82. For example *Yorkshire Ins Co Ltd* v *Campbell* [1917] AC 218, 225 *per* Lord Sumner (PC—cargo).

recent times, courts have shown rather less respect for the sanctity of contract and the opinion of particular insurers about what is material. As regards the opinion of insurers, see below.[83] As regards the sanctity of contract, early cases rest on the supposition that the warranty reflects the will of both parties, a matter of doubt as regards the insured.[84] Later judges were more cautious: there "is no objection whatever to the insertion of such conditions, so long as the intending [insured] has full and fair notice of them and consents to them."[85] Rules of construction are available to bring effect into line with the actual intention and consent of the insured. Without going as far as the rule of reasonable expectations,[86] courts have refused to apply a "condition" as a condition in law, if the effect is "so capricious and unreasonable that a Court of Law ought not to enforce it, or to be *sua natura* incapable of being made a condition precedent".[87]

20–3B Loss

Although the Statement of General Insurance Practice exhorts insurers not to take the point,[88] it is clear law that breach of warranty terminates the contract and vitiates cover, even though the breach is not material to the loss claimed.[89]

Thus, if a warranty of temperance has been broken, the insurer may refuse to pay, if the insured dies completely sober in a road accident.[90] If a warranty that a motor vehicle shall be maintained in an efficient condition has been broken, the insurer may refuse to pay for damage to the vehicle, even if the defect is not a cause of the

---

83. The current test is that of the prudent underwriter, evidence of which is open to critical scrutiny by the court: see below, 23–6.

84. Patterson, 34 Colum L Rev 595 (1934): "A rule of tight construction, devised for astute bargains between equals, and adapted to the protection of an infant industry, was slavishly followed by a timid judiciary which lacked the courage and resourcefulness to devise a technique for overhauling one-sided agreements".

85. *Re Bradley and Essex & Suffolk Accident Indemnity Sy* [1912] 1 KB 415, 431 *per* Farwell LJ (CA—employers' liability).

86. See above, 15–5B.

87. *London Guarantie Co v Fearnley* (1880) 5 App Cas 911, 919 *per* Lord Watson (fidelity) as regards a procedural condition. See also *Daff v Midland Colliery Owners Mutual Indemnity Co* (1913) 82 LJ KB 1340, 1352 *per* Lord Moulton (HL—employers' liability); *Wickman v Schuler AG* [1974] AC 235. Treitel, p 693.

On the other hand, the courts have declined to construe a term as less than a warranty, if that construction would be unreasonable: *Ellinger v Mutual Life Ins Co of New York* [1905] 1 KB 31, 38 *per* Stirling LJ (CA—life).

Cf statements that, however unreasonable the effect, a clear indication that the term is a warranty must be observed: *Farr v Motor Traders Mutual Ins Sy Ltd* [1920] 3 KB 669, 673 *per* Bankes LJ (CA—motor).

88. Clause 2(b)(iii) (1986).

89. *Thomson v Weems* (1884) 9 App Cas 671, 685 *per* Lord Blackburn (life). See also *Beacon Life & Fire Ins Co v Gibb* (1862) 1 Moore NS 73, 96 *per* Lord Chelmsford (PC—fire policy on hull); *Foley v Tabor* (1861) 2 F & F 663, 672 *per* Erle CJ (hull); *cf Weir v Aberdeen* (1819) 2 B & Ald 320, 323 *per* Lord Abbott CJ (hull).

Cf the contrary suggestion by Hodgson J in *Port-Rose v Phoenix Assurance plc* (1986) 136 NLJ 333 (AR) is difficult to square with precedent. The decision can be supported, however, as one of construction of the term, which was not a warranty but an exception; see above, 19–2A2. A contrary decision in Canada is *Long v Commercial Union Assurance Co* (1981) 121 DLR (3d) 623, 632 (Ont—motor).

Cf USA where the trend is not to grant forfeiture unless there was causal connection between breach of warranty and loss: *Home Ins Co v Ciconett*, 179 F 2d 892 (6 Cir, 1950—hull); *Coffey v Indiana Lumberman's Mutual Ins Co*, 372 F 2d 646 (6 Cir, 1967—fire). Appleman, section 4146. Most states have "antitechnical" statutes, whereby "policy provisions; misrepresentations; warranties; conditions" do not defeat the policy unless breach contributed to loss. A minority of states have construed their statute as applicable to exclusions: for criticism see Bates, 52 J Air Law & Commerce 451 (1986).

90. *Thomson v Weems* (1884) 9 App Cas 671, 685 *per* Lord Blackburn (life).

damage.[91] If a warranty to notify a change of use of premises insured has not been observed, the insurer may refuse to pay for fire damage, even though the change of use was not a cause of the fire.[92] If it is a condition of burglary insurance that the "alarm shall be in efficient working order", an insurer may refuse to pay in respect of loss while the alarm was in perfect working order because investigation revealed that for a day or two earlier in the year, when there was no burglary, the alarm was out of order.[93]

Decisions like these would not be reached, if the term were seen not as a warranty, breach of which terminates the contract altogether, but as an exception, which suspends cover only while the circumstance, for example inefficiency, lasts or when it has a causal connection with loss.[94]

20–4 SCOPE OF THE WARRANTY: CONSTRUCTION

The scope of the warranty, like that of any other term of the contract of insurance, is determined by construction, which allows the court to consider *inter alia* the purpose of the warranty.[95] "Policy defences are perhaps the most workable tool for enforcing compliance with the insurer's risk management standards."[96] At the same time, if policies are construed too strictly against the insured the function of insurance in seeking to prevent loss supersedes the primary function of loss distribution.[97] In the first place, however, the English court is likely to concentrate mainly on applying to a particular warranty in a particular case the general rules of construction that apply to all commercial documents.[98]

In a particular case, the English court seeks the intention of the parties to the contract, and presumes that words are used in their ordinary sense[99] and in accord with legal precedent.[100] The ordinary meaning of words read in isolation is displaced by any special meaning they acquire from the immediate context of the policy[101] or from the wider context of the trade or industry[102] and, closely related to the latter, words are construed in the light of the object or purpose of the contract of insurance as a whole (below, 20–4A). Whether or not there is ambiguity, the court seeks to avoid a

---

91. *Conn v Westminster Motor Ins Assn Ltd* [1966] 1 Lloyd's Rep 407 (CA—motor).
92. *Glen v Lewis* (1853) 8 Exch 607, 617 *per* Parke B (fire).
93. *Cf Melik & Co Ltd v Norwich Union Fire Ins Sy* [1980] 1 Lloyd's Rep 523 (burglary).
94. An example of the latter approach is *Lane v Spratt* [1969] 2 Lloyd's Rep 229, 236 *per* Roskill J (goods in transit).
95. Above, 15–3B.
96. Abraham, p 60.
97. *Ibid.*
98. *Hart v Standard Marine Ins Co Ltd* (1889) 22 QBD 499, 501 *per* Bowen LJ (CA—hull).
99. See above, 15–2.
100. See above, 15–2A.
101. For example, *Benham v United Guarantee & Life Assurance Co* (1852) 7 Ex 744 (guarantee); *Hales v Reliance Fire & Accident Ins Corp Ltd* [1960] 2 Lloyd's Rep 391, 396 *per* McNair J (fire); *De Maurier (Jewels) Ltd v Bastion Ins Co Ltd* [1967] 2 Lloyd's Rep 550, 560 *per* Donaldson J (jewellers' AR).

In particular, words will be construed *eiusdem generis*: *Re Bradley and Essex & Suffolk Accident Indemnity Sy* [1911] 1 KB 415 (CA—employers' liability); *Sweeney v Kennedy* (1949) 82 Ll L Rep 294 (motor). Generally, see above, 15–3A1.

102. For example, *Hart v Standard Marine Ins Co Ltd* (1889) 22 QBD 499, 500 *per* Lord Esher MR (CA—hull): "a warranty like every other part of the contract is to be construed according to the understanding of merchants, and does not bind the insured beyond the commercial import of the words." Generally, see above, 15–3B.

literal construction which gives absurd results (below, 20–4B).[103] If there is ambiguity, the words will be construed *contra proferentem* (below, 20–4C).[104]

20–4A Purpose

The court will consider the main purpose of the insurance contract and a warranty will be construed so as not to defeat it.[105] With this in mind, the Court of Appeal declined[106] to construe a provision in a liability policy, that the "assured shall take reasonable precautions to prevent accidents", as an undertaking to be performed not only by the insured but also by his employees. Were it so the insurer would be saying: " 'We will insure you against your liability for negligence on condition that you are not negligent' . . . That would be granting an indemnity with one hand and taking it away with the other . . . ".[107]

The court will also consider and respect the purpose of the warranty; purpose is central, for example, to continuing warranties: below, 20–5B. However, the court will construe the warranty in a way that goes no further than necessary to achieve that purpose. Thus, in theft insurance, "always occupied" does not mean "never unattended" but means "used as a residence", as this satisfies the purpose of the warranty to provide a deterrent to theft: to leave potential thieves unsure whether they would be disturbed, if they entered the premises insured.[108] Again, a warranty that no policy had been previously cancelled will be limited to adverse termination, which casts doubts upon the risk, and does not include voluntary surrender of a policy.[109]

20–4B Absurdity

Whether or not there is ambiguity, the court seeks to avoid a literal construction of warranties which would give absurd results.[110] To that extent, at least, the courts put upon words a "reasonable" construction.

In *Connecticut Mutual Life Ins Co* v *Moore*,[111] for example, the insured's answer to the question, "Have you had any other illness, local disease, or personal injury?" became a warranty. The judgment of the Privy Council was delivered by Sir Robert Collier, who said[112]:

103. Generally, see above, 15–4.
104. Generally, see above, 15–5C.
105. *Barnard* v *Faber* [1893] 1 QB 340 (CA—fire); *Re Bradley* (above) p 422 *per* Lord Cozens-Hardy MR.
106. *Woolfall & Rimmer Ltd* v *Moyle* [1942] 1 KB 66 (CA—employers' liability), in which the undertaking was a contractual warranty. Such provisions are sometimes seen as exceptions rather than as warranties: see above, 19–2A1.
107. pp 76–77 *per* Goddard LJ.
108. *Simmonds* v *Cockell* [1920] 1 KB 843, 845 *per* Roche J (burglary). See also *Australian Agricultural Co* v *Saunders* (1875) LR 10 CP 668, 678 *per* Pollock B (Exch Ch—fire); *Hart* (above) p 501 *per* Lord Esher MR.
109. *Smith* v *Dominion of Canada Accident Ins Co* (1902) 36 NBR 300, 312 (NB—PA). See also *National Protector Fire Ins Co Ltd* v *Nivert* [1913] AC 505, 511–512 *per* Lord Atkinson (PC—fire), in which a duty to give notice of other insurance on the same property was construed in the light of the insurer's concern about moral hazard and contribution.
110. Generally, see above, 15–4.
111. (1881) 6 App Cas 644 (life).
112. p 648. In a similar vein as regards the difficulty of remembering past insurance policies: *Broad & Montague Ltd* v *South East Lancashire Ins Co Ltd* (1931) 40 Ll L Rep 328, 331 *per* Rowlatt J (motor); and in *Hulton & Co* v *Mountain* (1921) 8 Ll L Rep 249, 250 (CA), Bankes LJ said that a condition of liability insurance that costs should not be incurred without the consent of the insurers "must be construed reasonably".

"Their Lordships agree . . . that this is a question of a somewhat embarrassing character, and one which the company could hardly have expected to be answered with strict and literal truth. They could not reasonably expect a man of mature age to recollect and disclose every illness, however slight, or every personal injury, consisting of a contusion, or a cut, or a blow, which he might have suffered in the course of his life. It is manifest that this question must be read with some limitation and qualification to render it reasonable; and that personal injury must be interpreted as one of a somewhat serious or severe character."

In *Australian Agricultural Co v Saunders*,[113] goods were insured under separate contracts for the land and sea phases of transit. The land contract required notice of any overlapping insurance as a condition precedent to recovery. Where land met sea there was indeed a possibility of overlap, of which the insured did not give notice and thus, argued the insurer, was not entitled to indemnity for fire loss in a store pending shipment. Having held that the loss came within the land contract but not the marine contract, the Court of Exchequer Chamber held that the action on the land contract succeeded. As to the condition precedent,

"there was a subsequent insurance of the goods, but the words must be read with some limitation, or the result would be absurd. The insurance elsewhere must, to be within the clause, be an insurance as to a portion of the risks covered by the policy sued on. If that is so, it seems to me this is not a case of double insurance such as was intended . . . I doubt whether a mere possibility that some portion of the risk covered by both policies might accidentally coincide constitutes such a double insurance as was meant."[114]

20-4C Contra Proferentem

In case of ambiguity,[115] warranties will be construed *contra proferentem*[116]—against the insurer. Further, as regards answers to questions in the proposal form, answers which may become warranties, the truth of an answer may depend on the meaning and scope of a question. If there is ambiguity in the question, it will be construed strictly against the insurer,[117] and it will be interpreted in the sense in which it was fairly and reasonably understood by the proposer.[118]

20-5 CONTINUING WARRANTIES

A warranty may apply not only to circumstances prevailing when the contract is made but also to circumstances arising during the period of cover and, if so, it is referred to

---

113. (1875) LR 10 CP 668.

114. p 674. See also in this sense Blackburn J, pp 674–675 and Pollock B, p 678. Further, *North British & Mercantile Ins Co v London, Liverpool & Globe Ins Co* (1877) 5 Ch D 569, 576–577 *per* Jessell MR (fire); *Re Bradley and Essex & Suffolk Accident Indemnity Sy* [1912] 1 KB 415, 422 *per* Cozens Hardy MR, 433 *per* Farwell LJ (CA—employers' liability); *Re Birkbeck Permanent Benefit Building Sy* [1913] 2 Ch 34, 38 *per* Neville J (credit); *Hair v Prudential Assurance Co Ltd* [1983] 2 Lloyd's Rep 667, 673 *per* Woolf J (houseowners').

115. On the meaning of ambiguity see above, 15–5.

116. *Anderson v Fitzgerald* (1853) 4 HLC 484, 507 *per* Lord St Leonards (life); *Fowkes v Manchester & London Assurance Assn* (1863) 3 B & S 917, 925 *per* Lord Cockburn CJ (life); *Thomson v Weems* (1884) 9 App Cas 671, 687 *per* Lord Watson (life); *Re Bradley and Essex & Suffolk Accident Indemnity Sy* [1911] 1 KB 415, 422 *per* Lord Cozens-Hardy MR, 430 *per* Farwell LJ (CA—employers' liability); *Simmonds v Cockell* [1920] 1 KB 843, 845 *per* Roche J (burglary); *De Maurier (Jewels) Ltd v Bastion Ins Co Ltd* [1967] 2 Lloyd's Rep 550 (jewellers' AR). See above, 15–5C.

117. *Zurich General Accident & Liability Ins Co Ltd* [1942] 2 KB 53, 57–58 *per* Lord Greene MR (CA—motor).

118. *Condogianis v Guardian Assurance Co Ltd* [1921] 2 AC 125, 130 *per* Lord Shaw (PC—fire). For example, a question about "sober and temperate habits" was reasonably understood to refer to alcohol and not to drugs: *Yorke v Yorkshire Ins Co Ltd* [1918] 1 KB 662, 666 *per* McCardie J (life). See below, 22–2D2.

as a continuing or promissory warranty.[119] The courts, however, construe warranties against this possibility, seeking to limit them to the time of contracting, for example the state of the premises at that time.[120] A warranty is construed as a continuing warranty only if, first, the words admit of no other construction (below, 20-5A); or, second, the warranty would have no purpose or function unless it continued during the period of cover (below, 20–5B).

20–5A Wording

The continuing nature of the warranty may be express, for example: this warranty "shall continue to be in force during the whole currency of the Policy".[121] Courts are influenced by whether the clause uses the future tense, indeed, it is so easy for the draftsman who wants a continuing warranty to use that tense, that courts are slow to find a continuing warranty, unless the future tense is used.[122] It is not, however, absolutely essential. Futurity may also be obvious from the nature of the undertaking.

20–5A1 Reasonable Precautions

If an employer insures his liability and undertakes to take reasonable precautions to prevent accidents, for which he might incur liability, it has been held that this undertaking must be performed throughout the period of cover.[123] The same is true of undertakings by the insured to safeguard the property insured or to maintain it (for example, a vehicle) in a safe or efficient condition. Insofar as the corollary of breach is that the insurer is not liable for the negligence of the insured, these clauses, although they can be classified as warranties, can also be classified as exceptions and are discussed in that context: above 19–2A.

20–5A2 Change of Use

The insured may warrant that the use of property insured shall be unchanged or, at least, undertake to notify the insurer of any change in the use of the subject-matter insured; these duties continue throughout the insurance period. Construction has

---

119. The latter phrase is more common in the USA, where the clause is also referred to as a condition subsequent: 45 CJS 536. A different meaning may be ascribed to "promissory warranty" in England; for example, Merkin & McGee, p B.2.3–01.

120. *Woodruff* v *Southeastern Fire Ins Co*, 426 F 2d 555, 562 (5 Cir, 1970—fire); or the insured's intention at that time: *Sutton* v *Hawkeye Casualty Co*, 138 F 2d 781, 784 (6 Cir, 1943—motor). Thus, a negative answer to "Will the car be driven by any person under 25 . . . ?" has been held to be a statement of current intention, rather than a continuing warranty: *Kirkbride* v *Donner* [1974] 1 Lloyd's Rep 549 (motor); *Huddleston* v *RACV Ins Pty Ltd* [1975] VR 683, 686–687 (Vict—motor): if a matter is declared and warranted to the best of the proposer's knowledge and belief, it can only refer to the proposer's state of mind at the time of the proposal.

121. *Hales* v *Reliance Fire & Accident Ins Corp Ltd* [1960] 2 Lloyd's Rep 391 (fire).
Cf "This declaration shall be held to be promissory." *Ceteris paribus* this does not refer to the future. "The most usual meaning of the word 'to promise' is 'to undertake to do or abstain from doing something in the future'. But there is a well-recognized second usage in which 'to promise' means 'to assert confidently, to declare'. Such an assertion usually refers to the present."—*Sweeney* v *Kennedy* (1949) 82 Ll L Rep 294, 299 (Eire—motor); the warranty was construed *contra proferentem* in the second sense.

122. *Weber & Berger* v *Employers' Liability Assurance* (1926) 24 Ll L Rep 321, 322 *per* Mackinnon J (burglary); *Woolfall & Rimmer Ltd* v *Moyle* [1942] 1 KB 66, 71 *per* Lord Greene MR (CA—employers' liability); *Kennedy* v *Smith*, 1976 SLT 110, 116 *per* Lord President Emslie (Ct Sess—motor); *Albion Lead Works* v *Williamsburg City Fire Ins Co*, 2 F 479, 485–486 (D Mass, 1880—fire); *Hosford* v *Germania Ins Co*, 127 US 399, 403–404 *per* Gray J (1888—fire).

123. This interpretation was not contested in *Woolfall & Rimmer Ltd* v *Moyle* [1942] 1 KB 66 (CA—employers' liability). USA: see Appleman, sections 3001 ff.

limited their scope to permanent or habitual change of use,[124] unless the wording is clearly broader, for example, that the insured use was warranted to be the only use[125] or that no change of use of any kind shall occur without the agreement of the insurer.[126] Construction has also limited their scope to changes not contemplated at the time of contract: in one case, "though apparently an alteration, there is no real alteration at all because the fact that such an alteration might take place was an element of the contract itself".[127]

20–5A3 Occupancy

A fire or burglary contract may provide that the insurance shall cease to attach (unless the insurer agrees to extend cover) if the building becomes unoccupied and remains so for a period of more than, say, 30 days.[128] The word "unoccupied"

"should be construed with reference to the nature and character of the building, the purpose for which it was designed, and the uses contemplated by the parties. It cannot be contended that a church is unoccupied because services are held therein only on Sunday, or that a school is unoccupied because school sessions are not held therein during school vacation."[129]

Much turns on what was contemplated at the time of the contract. In the case of an hotel, there must be a daily (though not continuous) physical presence in the building.[130] But, in the case of a dwelling house, it is not essential that it be occupied every day; the occupants may be absent from it, for reasons of health, pleasure, business or convenience for reasonable periods.[131] A person's dwelling is not the boundary of his life but its focal point; it is not continuous physical presence but the habitual recurrence of physical presence that makes a dwelling occupied.[132] Moreover, although occupation usually means actual not constructive occupation,[133] the occupation of the main building in a complex may amount to occupation of the whole.[134]

124. *Shaw v Robberds* (1837) 6 Ad & E 75 (fire). In *Exchange Theatre Ltd v Iron Trades Mutual Ins Co Ltd* [1984] 1 Lloyd's Rep 149 (CA—fire) it was held that an additional activity, which increased the risk of fire, did not alter the nature of the building itself. See also *Dobson v Sotheby* (1827) M & M 90 (fire); and for more examples, see Nicholson (1991) 4 ILJ 27, 30–31.
125. *Shaw* (above), p 83 *per* Denman CJ (fire). There is also a suggestion that the decision might have been different, if the different use had been for profit rather than an act of kindness. This view of *Shaw* was suggested in *Glen v Lewis* (1853) 8 Exch 607, 619 *per* Parke B (fire), however, it is doubtful in the light of the approval of *Shaw* by Lord Wright in *Provincial Ins Co Ltd v Morgan* [1933] AC 240, 255 (motor). USA: see Appleman, sections 2579 and 2876.
126. *Glen v Lewis* (1853) 8 Exch 607, 618–619 *per* Parke B (fire).
127. *Law Guarantee & Accident Sy v Munich Reinsurance Co* [1912] 1 Ch D 138, 153 *per* Warrington J (guarantee), cited with approval in *Exchange Theatre Ltd v Iron Trades Mutual Ins Co Ltd* [1984] 1 Lloyd's Rep 149, 152 *per* Eveleigh LJ (CA—fire); and in *Southern Cross Ins Co Ltd v Australian Provincial Assurance Assn Ltd* (1939) 39 SR (NSW) 174, 199–200 (life). See also reference to changes that might have been contemplated by the parties in *Linden Alimak Ltd v British Engine Ins Ltd* [1984] 1 Lloyd's Rep 416, 423 *per* Webster J (extraneous damage insurance).
128. See, for example, PM, 10 December 1992, p 17.
129. *Westchester Fire Ins Co v John Conlon Coal Co*, 92 F2d 160, 161 (3 Cir, 1937—fire), cert den 302 US 751; *Stivers v National American Ins Co*, 247 F 2d 921, 925 (9 Cir, 1957—fire). Appleman, sections 2581 and 2876.
130. *Marzouca v Atlantic & British Commercial Ins Co Ltd* [1971] 1 Lloyd's Rep 449 (PC—fire): it was not enough to have a policeman as night watchman who never entered the building nor had the means of doing so. See also *Simmonds v Cockell* [1920] 1 KB 843, 844–845 *per* Roche J (burglary).
131. *Foley v Sonoma County Farmers' Mutual Fire Ins Co*, 115 P 2d 1, 3 (Cal, 1941—fire). In *Winicofsky v Army & Navy General Assurance Co* (1919) 88 LJKB 1111 (fire) occupation does not cease if the occupiers leave the building empty for two hours during an air raid.
132. *Foley*, loc cit.
133. *Marzouca* (above); *Stivers* (above), p 926.
134. *Stivers* (above), p 925.

Occupation is assessed by reference to deeds rather than to words, and to people rather than to things. If a building has become unoccupied, intention to resume occupation cannot prevent a building being unoccupied, for "intention to resume occupation cannot affect the risk of fire during absence"[135]; but intention to abandon premises does not make them unoccupied, even after departure, if the 30-day period has not expired.[136] If people are there, a dwelling house may be unfurnished, yet "occupied"[137]; if there are none, the house may be furnished, yet "unoccupied".[138] "The terms 'vacant' and 'unoccupied' are not generally considered synonymous, since 'vacant' means without inanimate objects, while 'unoccupied' refers to the absence of animate objects."[139]

20–5A4 Alteration of Risk

The clauses that have just been considered are more or less concerned with alteration of the risk.[140] In addition, the draftsman may take the bull by the horns and confront, for example, "any alteration after the commencement of this insurance . . . whereby the risk of destruction or damage is increased", perhaps by stipulating for termination of the contract.[141] Courts construe these strictly[142] and thus the clause quoted was construed to refer to an alteration not in the risk,[143] which had occurred, but in the building, which had not. However, the draftsman's purpose might be achieved for fire or theft cover, for example, by a clause that cover shall cease to attach if, without the insurer's permission, "the nature of the occupation or other circumstances affecting the [subject-matter] be changed in such a way as to increase the risk of loss or damage".[144] Even so, as with clauses concerned with change of use (above, 20–5A2), courts are likely to confine a clause like this to changes which are more than temporary.[144a]

20–5B Purpose

The scope of a warranty and, in particular, whether it is a continuing warranty, will be determined in part by reference to the purpose of the warranty and the purpose of the insurance.[145]

---

135. *Marzouca* (above) p 453 *per* Lord Hodson.
136. *Laurentian Ins Co* v *Davidson* [1932] SCR 491.
137. *Page* v *Nationwide Mutual Fire Ins Co*, 223 NYS 2d 573, 575 (1962—fire).
138. *Foley* (above).
139. *Feinstein* v *Reliance Ins Co*, 380 NYS 2d 990, 992 (1976); Foley (above) p 2.
140. Above, 20–5A1 to 20–5A3; see also below, 20–5B1.
141. *Exchange Theatre Ltd* v *Iron Trades Mutual Ins Co Ltd* [1984] 1 Lloyd's Rep 149 (CA—fire).
142. Nicholson (1991) 4 ILJ 27, 33.
143. To provide power in a bingo hall, the insured brought in a petrol generator and a container of petrol; the hall was destroyed by a fire and explosion "attributable to petrol". The introduction of something such as the generator might change the use of the building (above, 20–5A2) but it does not necessarily change the building: p 151 *per* Eveleigh LJ; *cf Farnham* v *Royal Ins Co Ltd* [1976] 2 Lloyd's Rep 437 (fire).
144. Nicholson p 34.
144a. *Shaw* v *Robberds* (1837) 6 Ad & E 75 (fire); applied in *Barrett* v *Jermy* (1849) 3 Exch 535, 545 *per* Parke B (fire); applied in *Dawson* v *Monarch Ins Co* [1977] 1 NZLR 372 (fire), in which the court held (pp 376–377) that an increase in the likelihood of loss or damage is not an "increase in risk", because the "statements in the description are the definition of the risk undertaken by the insurer and the basis upon which alterations to it after the date of the policy are to be measured". See also 20–6B(a).
145. Generally, see above, 20–4A.

In a fidelity case, Goddard J said[146] that it was impossible to construe undertakings about the way the employee did his work as "a promise that during the currency of the policy [the employee] would faithfully carry out his duties, which is what the argument comes to, because that is the very thing against which insurance is being taken out".

In a liability contract, however, a warranty about *modus operandi*, such as the use of explosive during demolition, an activity which was to be covered by the insurance proposed and which the proposer had never pursued before, referred to the future.[147] But, in *Woolfall*[148] there was an undertaking that the insured's machinery, plant and ways were properly fenced and guarded, and otherwise in good order and condition. It was argued that, if the undertaking were limited to the time of the contract, it would be valueless to the insurer. This argument was rejected by Lord Greene MR[149]: "The value of the question to the underwriters, as I construe it, is that it enables them to find out with what sort of person they are dealing, that is, whether or not he keeps his machinery, plant and ways properly fenced and guarded and otherwise in good condition." The undertaking did not limit the risk to a safe workplace, but did provide some guarantee of a safe employer, thus affecting the moral hazard.

For fire and burglary insurance contracts, however, McNair J in *Hales*[150] accepted the proposition[151] that warranties as to the nature of the premises and precautions taken against loss will *prima facie* be read as applicable to the whole duration of the policy, as it would be of little value to take such a warranty unless it was effective to ensure those conditions throughout.

20–5B1 Change in the Risk: Change of Description

In fire insurance, matters of description are readily seen as the basis of a continuing warranty that the description of the property will remain unchanged. In *Sillem* v *Thornton*,[152] for example, within two months of taking fire insurance on a house cor-

---

146. *Hearts of Oak Building Sy* v *Law Union & Rock Ins Co Ltd* [1936] 2 All ER 619, 624. See also *Benham* v *United Guarantee & Life Assurance Co* (1852) 7 Ex 744 (guarantee).

But this does not mean that a court cannot be persuaded that some precautions were required (as warranties) during the insurance period: cf *Hawarth & Co* v *Sickness & Accident Assurance Assn Ltd*, 1891 18 R 563 (Ct Sess—fidelity); *Harbour Commissioners of Montreal* v *Guarantee Co of North America* (1893) 22 SCR 542 (fidelity); for example, counter-signature: *Rice* v *Fidelity & Deposit Co of Maryland*, 103 F 427 (8 Cir, 1900—indemnity bond).

147. *Beauchamp* v *National Mutual Indemnity Ins Co Ltd* [1937] 3 All ER 19, 22 *per* Finlay J (liability); accepted but distinguished in Eire in *Sweeney* v *Kennedy* (1949) 82 Ll L Rep 294 (motor) as a case in which words, literally applicable only to present circumstances, had to be construed in context.

148. *Woolfall & Rimmer Ltd* v *Moyle* [1942] 1 KB 66 (CA—employers' liability).

149. p 71. See also *Pim* v *Reid* (1843) 6 Man & G 1, 20 *per* Tindal CJ (fire) as regards a warranty of disclosure; *Kennedy* v *Smith*, 1976 SLT 110, 117 *per* Lord President Emslie (Ct Sess—motor) as regards a declaration that the proposer was a total abstainer from alcoholic drink. See also *Huddleston* v *RACV Ins Pty Ltd* [1975] VR 683, 687 (Victoria—motor); Sutton, Nos 2.57 and 10.87; *Sweeney* v *Kennedy* (1949) 82 Ll L Rep 294 (Eire—motor).

150. *Hales* v *Reliance Fire & Accident Ins Corp Ltd* [1960] 2 Lloyd's Rep 391, 395 (fire): the insured under a Retail Shopkeepers' Policy warranted in the proposal that no inflammable goods (except lighter fuel) were kept on the premises. That was true at the time of the contract in March, but in October a fire started in a tin of fireworks brought to the premises a few days before. The insurance claim failed for breach of a continuing warranty.

151. Taken from MacGillivray (4th ed, No 903); the proposition is repeated in the current edition (No 778). *Contra* Birds, p 125 and [1977] JBL 231, 237–238: there were better alternative grounds for the decision: (a) an express provision that warranties should continue in force during the currency of the policy and (b) breach of a duty to notify the insurer of an increase in risk. No reference was made in *Hales* to *Woolfall* (above).

152. (1854) 3 El & Bl 868 (fire). USA: see Appleman, sections 2571; 45 CJS, section 510.

rectly described as a two storey house in San Francisco, the insured added a third storey. Having found that the description was a warranty, Lord Campbell CJ continued[153]:

"In this case, the description is evidently the basis of the contract, and is furnished to the underwriter to enable him to determine whether he will agree to take the risk at all, and, if he does take it, what premium he shall demand. The assured no doubt wished him to understand that, not only such was the condition of the premises when the policy was to be effected, but, as far as depended upon them it should not be altered so as to increase the risk during the year for which he was to be liable, if a loss should accrue. Without such an assurance and belief, the statement introduced into the policy of the existing condition of the premises would be a mere delusion. Identity might continue, and yet the quality, condition and incidents of the subject matter insured might be so changed as to increase tenfold the chances of loss."

It would be strange, he said,[154] if a building, described as used by a butcher and thus attracting a low premium, could be converted for the manufacture of fireworks. He concluded[155] that "principles of justice" required an "implied engagement", derived from the warranty of description,[156] that the insured would not alter the premises from the policy description in a way that increased the risk.

In other kinds of insurance, a similar but unclear distinction has been drawn between a mere increase in the chance that the insured event will occur,[157] which does not affect the efficacy of cover, and an alteration in the nature of the risk, which takes it outside the cover promised by the insurer.[158]

20–6 BREACH OF WARRANTY

20–6A Onus of Proof

Although warranties are sometimes described by the policy as "conditions precedent to the insured's right to recover",[159] the onus of proving breach of warranty is usually on the insurer.[160] If the insurer seeks from the court a declaration that a breach of

---

153. pp 882–883.
154. p 884.
155. pp 887–888.
156. This apart, no warranty will be implied that the risk will not be increased: above, 20–2A2.

In *Pearson* v *Commercial Union Assurance Co* (1876) 1 App Cas 498 a fire policy covered a ship described as then "lying in the Victoria Docks", so that with one qualification, when she was moved, the insurance did not apply. Lord Chelmsford (p 505): "An insurance against fire necessarily has regard to the locality of the subject-matter of the policy, the risk being probably different according to the place where the subject of the insurance happens to be." In this case, however, *semble* (p 506) the term about location operated as an exception rather than as a warranty: the cover resumed when the ship returned to the named docks. *Cf* Lord O'Hagan (p 511) who spoke of deviation by the ship.

157. See above 20–2A2

158. For example, *Newcastle Fire Ins Co* v *Macmorran & Co* (1815) 3 Dow 255 (HL—fire); *Sillem* v *Thornton* (1854) 3 El & Bl 868 (fire), as distinguished by Willes J in *Thompson* v *Hopper* (1858) El Bl & El 1038, 1049 (Exch Ch—hull); *Mitchell Conveyor & Transporter Co Ltd* v *Pulbrook* (1933) 45 Ll L Rep 239, 245 *per* Roche J (construction AR).

Southern Cross Ins Co Ltd v *Australian Provincial Assurance Assn Ltd* (1939) 39 SR (NSW) 174, 199–200 (life), with reference to *Pearson* (above). Nicholson, *Mid-term Alterations In the Risk: What Can Be Done?*, (1991) 4 ILJ 27, 29.

159. *Bond Air Services Ltd* v *Hill* [1955] 2 QB 417 (aviation).

160. *Barrett* v *Jermy* (1849) 3 Ex 535, 542 *per* Parke B (fire); *Stebbing* v *Liverpool & London & Globe Ins Co Ltd* [1917] 433, 438 *per* Viscount Reading CJ (burglary); *Bennett* v *Yorkshire Ins Co Ltd* [1962] 2 Lloyd's Rep 270 (burglary); *Farnham* v *Royal Ins Co Ltd* [1976] 2 Lloyd's Rep 437, 441 *per* Ackner J (fire). *Anglo-American Fire Ins Co* v *Morton* (1912) 46 SCR 653 (fire); *Hanes* v *Wawanesa Mutual Ins Co* [1963] SCR 154 (motor).

warranty has terminated the insurance, there is little doubt that the insurer must prove breach. If, however, breach of warranty is raised as a defence to a claim under the policy, the position is a little less clear. In so far as warranties concern the circumstances in which the insurer has agreed to pay, there is some attraction in the argument that the insured must prove that those circumstances prevailed when the loss occurred, and thus offer some evidence that there was no breach of warranty. What the law requires, however, is that the insured prove loss caused by the peril insured against. The extent of the proof depends on the meaning of the peril. He must prove, for example, not damage to his roadworthy motor car but simply damage to his motor car. If the car was unroadworthy and that was a breach of warranty, this must be proved by the insurer. So, it appears that the onus of proof relating to warranties is broadly the same as the onus of proof relating to exceptions.[161] At all events, if in doubt, the inclination of the court is to put the onus on the insurer.[162] However, as with exceptions, the issue is one of construction of the contract and in theory the onus may be changed by clear words in the contract.[163]

20–6B The Meaning of Breach

Whereas, for a misrepresentation to make the contract voidable, the error must be substantial,[164] it takes only the slightest breach of warranty to terminate the contract—even though, as we have seen (above, 20–3), that breach may be quite immaterial to either risk or loss. The corollary is that a warranty must be strictly[165] and literally[166] observed.

For examples, a pipe between stove and chimney three feet long did not comply

161. *Bond Air* (above), p 427 *per* Lord Goddard CJ (aviation). Derrington, 59 ALJ 554, 557 (1985). On the onus of proof relating to exceptions see above, 16–3B2.

162. *Fraser* v *Furman (Productions) Ltd* [1967] 1 WLR 898, 905 *per* Diplock LJ (CA—liability). *Contra*: *Toikan International Ins Broking Pty Ltd* v *Plasteel Windows Australia Pty Ltd* (1989) 94 FLR 362 (fire). However, in subsequent litigation arising out of the same dispute the court observed that "the statements made in answer to questions in the proposal would, at common law, have constituted warranties and proof of their breach would have rested upon the insurer": *Plasteel Windows Australia Pty Ltd* v *C E Heath Underwriting Agencies Pty Ltd* (1990) 19 NSWLR 400, 408 (liability). Also in this sense: *Strang Pty Ltd* v *NZI Ins Australia Ltd* [1990] VR 1016 (liability).

163. *Bond Air* (above); and *Toikan* (above). To describe warranties as conditions precedent is insufficient to shift the onus from insurer to insured: *ibid*. *Contra*: *Logan* v *John Hancock Mutual Life Ins Co*, 116 Cal Rptr 528, 531 (Cal, 1974—PA).

164. See below, 22–2E.

165. *Pawson* v *Watson* (1778) 2 Cowp 785, 787–788 *per* Lord Mansfield (hull); *Newcastle Fire Ins Co* v *Macmorran & Co* (1815) 3 Dow 255, 262 *per* Lord Eldon (HL); *Re Universal Non-Tariff Fire Insurance Co* (1875) LR 19 Eq 485, 494 *per* Malins V-C (fire).

Canada: *Dunningham* v *St Paul Fire & Marine Ins Co*, 42 DLR (2d) 524 (BC—fire). However, a distinction is drawn between warranties, which must be strictly observed, and conditions which are only to be substantially complied with, and the courts tend to find that a term is a condition rather than a warranty: Brown and Menezes, 7:5:20. Moreover, state legislation may outlaw conditions that are "unjust or unreasonable". There is, however, no general doctrine of relief against forfeiture caused by breach of warranty: Baer, 17 Ottawa L Rev 631, 658 (1985).

USA: warranties must be strictly observed: *Moulor* v *American Life Ins Co*, 111 US 335, 342 *per* Harlan J (1884—life); *Phoenix Mutual Life Ins Co* v *Raddin*, 120 US 183, 189 *per* Gray J (1887—life). However, in the case of continuing or promissory warranties some courts have held that substantial compliance is enough: *Ortiz* v *National Liberty Ins Co*, 75 F Supp 550, 551 (D Puerto Rico, 1948—fire) and cases cited.

166. *De Hahn* v *Hartley* (1786) 1 TR 343, 346 *per* Lord Mansfield (hull). *Sovereign Fire Ins Co* v *Moir* (1887) 14 SCR 612 (fire). *Norwich Union Indemnity Co* v *Kobacher & Sons Ltd*, 31 F 2d 411 (6 Cir, 1929—burglary), cert den 280 US 558 (1929). As regards marine insurance in England, the rule is stated by MIA, section 33.

with a warranty in a fire policy that it was two feet long.[167] A warranty in another fire policy, that no inflammable goods were kept on the premises, was broken by the presence of fireworks for 17 days prior to 5 November.[168] In a case of motor insurance a warranty, that the price paid for a vehicle was £285, was broken because the price paid was £271.[169]

Substantial performance is not enough, as it is one of the purposes of a warranty "to preclude all questions whether it has been substantially complied with".[170] However, this assumes that the warranty has been broken. The strictness of the rule is softened by construction, leading to the conclusion that the warranty has not been broken:

(a) By strict construction against the insurer, occasional "non-compliance" is not breach. In *Dobson* v *Sotheby*,[171] a barn insured against fire was described as "where no fire is kept, and no hazardous goods are deposited". Deciding for the insured, Lord Tenterden CJ said[172]: "the condition must be understood as forbidding only the habitual use of fire, or the ordinary deposit of hazardous goods, not their occasional introduction, as in this case, for a temporary purpose connected with the occupation of the premises. The common repairs of a building necessarily require the introduction of fire upon the premises." In *Provincial Ins Co Ltd* v *Morgan*,[173] a warranty, that the purpose for which the vehicle insured was to be used was the carriage of coal, did not mean exclusively for coal and was not broken by the occasional carriage of timber. Occasional "non-compliance" may amount to a breach of warranty, but only if this is clear from the words of the contract.[174]

(b) By purposive construction, a literal construction which might indicate breach, can be ignored. In *Nivert*,[175] a literal reading of the warranty required the insured to declare to the insurer any (and every) subsequent policy on the property. The Privy Council held that the purpose of the warranty was satisfied as regards both a second and a third policy, if insurer knew of the second policy, which the undeclared third was intended to replace. Lord Atkinson said[176] that terms such as this "should always be interpreted in a reasonable sense, having regard to the business nature of insurance transactions". Again, in *Mammone*,[177] the person, who insured his vehicle with a warranty that it "has not been and will not be specially modified from the maker's original specification", fitted wider wheels and better

---

167. *Newcastle Fire Ins Co* v *Macmorran & Co* (1815) 3 Dow 255 (HL).
168. *Hales* v *Reliance Fire & Accident Ins Corp* [1960] 2 Lloyd's Rep 391.
169. *Allen* v *Universal Automobile Ins Co Ltd* (1933) 45 Ll L Rep 55.
170. *De Hahn* v *Hartley* (1786) 1 TR 343, 346 *per* Ashurst J (hull): not even performance which is better than that literally required, better in the sense that it better achieves the purpose of the warranty, for example security in a fidelity policy: *Benham* v *United Guarantie & Life Assurance Co* (1852) 7 Ex 744, 752 *per* Pollock CB (fidelity).
171. (1827) M & M 90. A similar decision on an exception of loss "while gasoline is stored or kept in the building" is *Thompson* v *Equity Fire Ins Co* [1910] AC 592 (PC—fire). See also *Mint Security Ltd* v *Blair* [1982] 1 Lloyd's Rep 188, 197 *per* Staughton J (cash in transit) that a warranty that security procedure will not be varied is not broken "merely because there is a casual non-observance of it by one of the [insured's] minions".
172. (1827) M & M 90, 92–93. See also *Shaw* v *Robberds* (1837) 6 Ad & E 75 (fire).
173. [1933] AC 240 (motor).
174. p 255 *per* Lord Wright (motor). For example *Glen* v *Lewis* (1853) 8 Ex 607 (fire).
175. *National Protector Fire Ins Co Ltd* v *Nivert* [1913] AC 507 (PC—fire).
176. p 513.
177. *Mammone* v *RACV Ins Pty Ltd* [1976] VR 617 (motor).

tyres. The Supreme Court of Victoria found the warranty slightly ambiguous and concluded that its purpose "was to ensure that the risk would not be materially altered to the detriment of the insurer. It could never have been intended that the . . . warranty was to prevent an alteration to the vehicle which would improve its performance from a safety angle and so lessen the risk covered by the underwriter".[178]

(c) Conversely, by literal construction, a purposive construction which might indicate breach, can be ignored. In a case of cargo insurance,[179] it was enough that the ship had the 20 guns warranted, even though it did not have the crew to man the guns, and therefore the purpose of the warranty could not be achieved. In a case of fire insurance, a warranty that the mill was worked only by day was not broken by work in part of the mill at night.[180] Again, when a warranty is based on a statement in the proposal, its scope is limited to the scope of the insurer's question, and the insured does not warrant the truth or fulfilment of extra statements, not required by the questions, but included in his answer.[181] And again, a basis warranty in the proposal,[182] that the insured intended to do X, is not broken, even if he did not do X at all, provided that the statement was *bona fide*, i.e., it was true of his intention at the time of the contract.[183] In contrast, a marine warranty "not to proceed east of Singapore" was construed narrowly as a warranty about the future, and the judge observed that, even if there was "an intention to commit a breach" of the warranty, that "does not itself constitute a breach" of the warranty itself.[184]

20–6B1 Knowledge

If the insured has warranted the truth of a statement, it is "not the less untrue because [he] is not apprized of its untruth",[185] or because he makes it in good faith.[186] How-

178. p 622.

179. *Hide* v *Bruce* (1783) 3 Doug 213.

180. *Mayall* v *Mitford* (1837) 6 Ad & E 670, 673 *per* Littledale J; see also *Equitable Fire & Accident Office Ltd* v *The Ching Wo Hong* [1907] AC 96 (PC—fire).

181. *Norwich Union Indemnity Co* v *Kobacker & Sons*, 31 F 2d 411 (6 Cir, 1929—burglary): when asked whether a watchman would be on duty, the proposer answered "Yes—two". It was held that the warranty was limited to one watchman, for (p 413) "the insurer was apparently indifferent as to the number so employed".

182. On basis warranties, see above, 20–2B2.

183. *Benham* v *United Guarantee & Life Assurance Co* (1852) 7 Exch 744, 752–753 *per* Pollock CB (fidelity); *Grant* v *Aetna Ins Co* (1862) 15 Moore 516 (PC—hull).

184. *Simpson SS Co Ltd* v *Premier Underwriting Assn Ltd* (1905) 10 Com Cas 198, 201 *per* Bigham J (hull).

185. *Duckett* v *Williams* (1834) 2 C & M 348, 351 *per* Lord Lyndhurst CB (life); see also *Newcastle Fire Ins Co* v *Macmorran & Co* (1815) 3 Dow 255, 261–262 *per* Lord Eldon LC (HL—fire); *Anderson* v *Fitzgerald* (1853) 4 HLC 484, 498–499 *per* Lord Cranworth LC (life); *Cazenove* v *Equitable Assurance Co* (1859) 6 CB (NS) 437 (life), affirmed (1860) 29 LJ CP 160 (Exch Ch); *Fowkes* v *Manchester & London Assurance Assn* (1863) 3 B & S 917, 929 *per* Blackburn J (life); *Macdonald* v *Law Union Ins Co* (1874) LR 9 QB 328 (Exch Ch—life); *Thomson* v *Weems* (1884) 9 App Cas 671, 682 *per* Lord Blackburn, 688 *per* Lord Watson (life); *Hambrough* v *Mutual Life Ins Co of New York* (1895) 72 LT 140 (CA—life); *Condogianis* v *Guardian Assurance Co Ltd* [1921] 2 AC 125, 129 *per* Lord Shaw (PC—fire).

Northern Life Ins Co v *King*, 53 F 2d 613, 617 (9 Cir, 1931—life), cert den 285 US 544; *Ettman* v *Federal Life Ins Co*, 48 F Supp 578 (ED Mo, 1942—life), affirmed 137 F 2d 121 (8 Cir, 1943), cert den 320 US 785.

186. *Thomson* v *Weems* (1884) 9 App Cas 671, 682 *per* Lord Blackburn (life). *Cf* ignorance not of the facts warranted but of the very existence of the warranty: below, 20–6B2.

ever, the courts are ready to construe against this conclusion, as an inference either from other clauses in the contract,[187] or as an inference from the nature of the warranty itself.

An instance of the latter is found in the judgment of Lord President Inglis in the Court of Session[188]:

"a person making a statement regarding his own health must be assumed generally to be speaking according to his own personal knowledge, and there are many facts regarding his health of which he cannot be ignorant, a misstatement of which would of course be fraudulent. But there may be many other facts, materially affecting his state of health and prospect of longevity, of which a person without medical skill or medical advice can know nothing. No doubt a contract of insurance may be so expressed as to make freedom from certain specified diseases, however latent, matter of warranty, but the contract will not so readily bear that construction in the case of a person insuring his own life, as in the case of one who makes such statements respecting the health of another for the purpose of obtaining a policy of insurance upon the life of that other person . . . It would never enter into the mind of a person of mere ordinary intelligence, being neither a medical man nor a lawyer, nor a director of an insurance company, that he was asked to warrant . . . that his mother, as in this case, died of old age at ninety-nine, and not of a fracture of the skull at ninety-eight."

Similarly, Mr Justice Harlan in the Supreme Court of the United States stated[189]:

"In the absence of explicit, unequivocal stipulations requiring such an interpretation, it should not be inferred that a person took a life policy with the distinct understanding that it should be void and all premiums paid thereon forfeited, if at any time in the past, however remote, he was, whether conscious of the fact or not, afflicted with some one of the diseases mentioned in the question to which he was required to make a categorical answer."

The current trend is to construe statements as warranties of opinion rather than as warranties of fact. Thus, if the insured states that he "believes"[190] something to be true, or is "not aware"[191] of some matter, the truth of these warranties is judged by the insured's state of mind. Further, as to his state of his mind, if the warranty or question on which the warranty is based is drafted by the insurer, the insured's answer will be construed in the light of construction of the warranty or question *contra proferen-*

---

187. For example, *Fowkes* v *Manchester & London Assurance Assn* (1863) 3 B & S 917 (life): if one part of the contract suggests an absolute warranty but another part does not, there is sufficient ambiguity to justify preference for the latter construction throughout. Also in this sense: *Moulor* v *American Life Ins Co*, 111 US 335, 342 *per* Harlan J (1884—life).

188. *Life Assn of Scotland* v *Foster* (1873) 11 Ct Sess (3rd) 351, 358—359 (life), a judgment approved by Lord Blackburn in *Thomson* v *Weems* (1884) 9 App Cas 671, 683 (life); see also p 693 *per* Lord Watson. Likewise *Wheelton* v *Hardisty* (1857) 8 El & Bl 232, 300 *per* Bramwell B (Exch Ch—life): "we ought not to adopt that construction except upon very clear indications that it was the intention of the parties." See also *Connecticut Mutual Life Ins Co* v *Moore* ((1881) 6 App Cas 644 (PC—life), discussed above, 20–4B.

189. *Moulor* v *American Life Ins Co*, 111 US 335, 341 (1884—life). However, literal effect has been given to the 'good health' clause, whereby the insured warrants that he is in the actual state of health represented in the application: *Ruwitch* v *Wm Penn Life Assurance Co*, 966 F 2d 1234 (8 Cir, 1992—life).

190. *Wheelton* v *Hardisty* (1857) 8 El & Bl 232 (Exch Ch—life). *Confederation Life Assn* v *Miller* (1887) 14 SCR 330 (life). *Aetna Life Ins Co* v *France*, 94 US 561 (1877—life); *Northwestern Mutual Life Ins Co* v *Gridley*, 100 US 614 (1880—life).

191. *Jones* v *Provincial Ins Co* (1857) 3 CB (NS) 65 (life): the insured warranted that he was "not aware of any disorder or circumstances tending to shorten his life". Counsel for the insurer argued that there was a breach of warranty, if the insured was aware of a disorder, whether or not he was aware of its effect. The judge held that, if the insured honestly believed that the disorder did not tend to shorten life, the policy could not be defeated, and this decision was upheld on appeal.

tem, i.e., in the sense in which the insured "should reasonably have understood it".[192] There is breach only if his answer is wilfully false.[193]

This is true not only in matters medical, such as the health of the proposer,[194] but also in matters more material, and even where the proposer has some knowledge. In a case in which the proposer was required to estimate and warrant the value of the subject-matter (a stamp collection), the Australian court held[195] that, as the value of such things was a matter of opinion, the *bona fide* estimate of an experienced person did not breach the warranty, although a subsequent valuation by an expert suggested that the original estimate was too low. The Statement of General Insurance Practice in England asserts[196] that, so far as is practicable, insurers will avoid asking questions which would require expert knowledge beyond that which the proposer could reasonably be expected to possess or obtain or which would require a value judgment on the part of the proposer.

20–6B2 Impossibility

Lord Kenyon CJ said[197] that, if it is impossible for the insured to perform a condition, that does not excuse the insured, unless it was always impossible from the time that it was contracted. This suggestion about the assumption of risk was made about a procedural condition concerning evidence of loss, but it applies also to warranties, particularly continuing warranties.[198] As the effect of impossibility at common law is termination of contract, the plea of impossibility is not often found. The insured seeks in vain[199] for a defence of impossibility, that excuses the breach of warranty but leaves his insurance cover in force, except as follows.

192. *Confederation Life Assn* v *Miller* (1887) 14 SCR 330, 344 *per* Gwynne J (life: "serious" injury), with whom the majority of the court concurred. See also below, 22–2D2.

193. *Ibid*—even though the insured warranted "to the *best* of my knowledge or belief" (emphasis added) that he had suffered no serious injury; this would be untrue only if "to his knowledge and belief he had received some other serious personal injury than stated" (*per* Gwynne J, p 344).

In *Akerhielm* v *De Mare* [1959] AC 789 (PC), which concerned an action for damages for fraudulent misrepresentation, Lord Jenkins said (p 805): "The question is not whether the defendant in any given case honestly believed the representation to be true in the sense assigned to it by the court on an objective consideration of its truth or falsity, but whether he honestly believed the representation to be true in the sense in which he understood it albeit erroneously when it was made".

194. *Joel* v *Law Union & Crown Ins Co* [1908] 2 KB 863, 885 *per* Fletcher Moulton LJ (CA—life). Hasson, (1971) 34 MLR 29, 34. *Keating* v *New Ireland Assurance Co plc* [1990] IR 383 (life). *Service Life Ins Co* v *McCullough*, 13 NW 2d 440, 444–445 (Iowa, 1944—life).

One might wonder whether the insured is justified in making such a statement without consulting a doctor, however, it is clear in the context of non-disclosure that the proposer is not required to improve his knowledge of material facts by investigation; see below, 23–8C. Further, if the statement is based on the opinion of a doctor it is enough that the doctor did give that opinion or an opinion from which the proposer's statement could reasonably be inferred, thus disregarding any latent conditions which the doctor could not be expected to discover: *Mitchell* v *Fidelity & Casualty Co* (1916) 37 Ont LR 335 (Ont—disability), affirmed [1917] AC 592 (PC).

195. *Timms* v *Fai Insurances Ltd* (1976) 12 ALR 506 (N Territory—AR).

196. Clause 1(e) (1986). See also the Statement of Long-Term Insurance Practice, clause 1(d).

197. *Worsley* v *Wood* (1796) 6 TR 710, 718–719 (fire). Arnould, No 687.

198. Ivamy, p 311. See further Arnould, No 687, n 44, citing *inter alia Continental Sea Foods Inc* v *New Hampshire Fire Ins Co*, 1964 AMC 196 (SDNY, 1963—cargo); this held that impossibility was not an excuse for the insured, on the basis (p 201) of the requirement of literal compliance with express warranties.

199. Generally, see *Fibrosa Spolka Akcyjna* v *Fairburn Lawson Combe Barbour Ltd* [1942] 1 KB 12 (CA). Cf *Minnevitch* v *Café de Paris (Londres) Ltd* [1936] 1 All ER 884; Treitel, p 734. Markesinis [1978] CLJ 53, 65.

First, section 34(1) of the MIA excuses breach of warranty, when "by reason of a change of circumstances, the warranty ceases to be applicable to the circumstances of the contract". Although the underlying principle, *cessante ratione, cessat lex*,[200] is a general principle of law, it is not clear that this provision will be applied to non-marine insurance contracts. Section 34(1) also provides that breach of warranty is excused when "compliance with the warranty is rendered unlawful by any subsequent law". This too is considered[201] to be an expression of a general principle of law, and the essence of this provision does affect all insurance contracts: see chapter 24.

Second, the insured may be excused by ignorance. If he failed from the start to comply with a warranty, not because it was inherently impossible to perform but because he neither knew of the warranty nor had the opportunity of knowing it, the insurance may be enforced without the warranty; this is not because the warranty is impossible to perform, but because the warranty was not a term of the contract or was not intended to apply, until the terms including the warranty had been communicated to the insured.[202] Further, it has been held[203] of a continuing warranty, that the insured will take reasonable care or reasonable precautions, that he is not in breach of the warranty, unless he has actual or constructive knowledge of circumstances giving rise to a need for care and precautions.

20–6C Breach of Warranty: Effect

The first edition of this book expressed the view, commonly held in the past, that breach of warranty entitled the insurer to exercise an option to repudiate his part of the contract of insurance (from then on).[204] This view has now been modified in the light of the judgment of Lord Goff, with whom the other members of the House of Lords agreed, in *The Good Luck*.[205]

In *The Good Luck*, the ship of that name was insured with the defendant club and mortgaged to the plaintiff bank. As required by the mortgage, the benefit of the insurance was assigned to the bank and the club gave a Letter of Undertaking to the bank, whereby the club promised to advise the bank promptly if the club should "cease to insure" the ship. The ship became a constructive total loss, having been sent to the Arabian Gulf in breach of warranty. Both club and bank knew of the loss but, whereas

In Canada there is legislation confirming the court's general equitable power to relieve against forfeiture. However, the courts have not used this power in cases of breach of insurance warranty or procedural condition. See *Johnston* v *Dominion of Canada Guarantee & Accident Ins Co* (1908) 17 OLR 462. Baer, 17 Ottawa L Rev 631, 661 ff. (1985).
    200. Arnould, No 688. In Canada this provision is found in state legislation, for example, in Ontario: RSO 1980, c 255, section 34.
    201. Arnould, No 688.
    202. *Re Coleman's Depositories Ltd and Life & Health Ins Assn* [1907] 2 KB 798, 805 *per* Vaughan Williams LJ, 812 *per* Buckley LJ (CA—employers' liability).
    203. In *Melik & Co Ltd* v *Norwich Union Fire Ins Sy* [1980] 1 Lloyd's Rep 523 (burglary) it was held that a term, that a burglar alarm should be kept in efficient order, was not broken until the insured was aware that it was out of order.
    204. Thus Lord Dunedin, interpreting the word "void" in a statute, said that it was not meant in a technical sense but that on the non-performance of the condition (payment of premium) the insurer would be "relieved from his liabilities under the policy"—*Equitable Life Assurance Sy* v *Reed* [1914] AC 587, 596 (life). In *Hadenfayre* v *British National Ins Co Ltd* [1984] 2 Lloyd's Rep 393, 401 Lloyd J spoke of "a warranty, for breach of which the [insurers] are discharged". See also *Sulphite Paper Co Ltd* v *Faber* (1895) 1 Com Cas 146, 152 *per* Lord Russell CJ (fire); *The Good Luck* (below).
    205. [1992] 1 AC 233 (hull). See also *Euro-Diam Ltd* v *Bathurst* [1990] 1 QB 1, 40 *per* Kerr LJ (CA—goods).

the club knew of the breach of warranty, the bank, which may well have been as well placed as the club to discover the truth, did not—and the club did not tell it. In the belief that the club had not ceased to insure the ship, the bank made further advances to the shipowners.

The bank sued the club for having broken its promise to give prompt notice that the club had ceased to insure the ship. The main issue in the House of Lords was whether the club had ceased to insure the ship at the time that the warranty had been broken, as argued by the bank, or at the later time, when the club took a formal decision not to indemnify the shipowners because of that breach, as argued by the club. Whether and when the club had "ceased" to insure the shipowner depended on the effect of the owner's breach of warranty.

Lord Goff, with whom other members of the House of Lords concurred, started with section 33(1) of the Marine Insurance Act 1906, which speaks of "a promissory warranty . . . by which the assured undertakes that some particular thing shall or shall not be done, or that some condition shall be fulfilled, or whereby he affirms or negatives the existence of a particular state of facts". Although section 34(3) provides that a "breach of warranty may be waived by the insurer", suggesting an election on his part, section 33(3) provides that, if a warranty is not "exactly complied with", "then, subject to any express provision in the policy, the insurer is discharged from liability as from the date of the breach of warranty, but without prejudice to any liability incurred by him before that date". "Those words", said Lord Goff,[206] "are clear. They show that discharge of the insurer from liability is automatic and is not dependent upon any decision by the insurer to treat the contract of insurance as at an end. . . . Section 33(3) of the Act reflects what has been described, in successive editions of Chalmers' *Marine Insurance Act 1906*, as the inveterate practice in marine insurance of using the term 'warranty' as signifying a condition precedent."

Clear indeed, but on the assumption, first, that the nature of a warranty depends solely on construction of the Act, without regard to other branches of the law of insurance. It does not. Nor, indeed, was it the view of Lord Goff,[207] and he continued in general terms: "the insurer is discharged from liability as from the date of the breach of warranty, for the simple reason that fulfilment of the warranty is a condition precedent to the liability or the further liability of the insurer. This moreover reflects the fact that the rationale of warranties in insurance law is that the insurer only accepts the risk provided that the warranty is fulfilled."[208] If this is true of marine warranties, then it is true also of non-marine warranties. The second assumption is that the question is uncluttered by previous authority. It is not. Indeed, the Court of Appeal in *The Good Luck* was, in the opinion of Lord Goff, "led astray by passages in certain books and other texts which refer to the insurer being entitled to avoid the policy of insurance, or to repudiate". This view, which was widely held in the past,[209] must now be revised.

---

206. p 262.
207. He referred to words of Lord Blackburn which, read in their own context, make it clear that Lord Blackburn thought that, as regards the effect of breach of warranty, the same principles applied, whether the insurance be marine or not: *Thomson v Weems* (1884) 9 App Cas 671, 684 (life).
208. pp 262–263. See Carter, *Conditions and Conditions Precedent*, (1991) 4 JCL 90.
209. If the Court of Appeal was led astray, it is hardly surprising, as the texts included (a) books written by Sir Mackenzie Chalmers between 1907 and 1933, with the view "that a breach of warranty in insurance law appears to stand on the same footing as the breach of a condition in any other contract"; (b) a report of the Law Reform Committee in 1957 based on the combined opinion of Lords Jenkins, Parker, Devlin and

If, then, breach of warranty is the failure of a condition precedent to cover, and this occurs when the contract is concluded, the contract ends as soon as it begins—if, indeed, it begins at all,[210] and, certainly, it is without (further) effect. If, however, a breach occurs during the insurance period, duties, especially duties of payment,[211] which had fallen due before breach remain due; and procedural conditions for the settlement of earlier claims must still be performed.[212]

If breach of warranty automatically terminates the contract of insurance, this affects not only the insured but also an assignee even though he is in no way responsible for the breach.[213] However, the effect of a breach is a matter based on the intention of the parties and their contract. So, when the insurance makes loss payable to a mortgagee, a mortgage clause, that the insurance shall not be invalidated by an act or neglect of the mortgagor of the property insured, is effective as regards acts or neglect after the insurance commences although not for earlier acts or neglects.[214] A similar clause may apply to the beneficial assignment of life insurance,[215] in each case, the clause is one that renders cover unconditional, i.e. independent of breach of warranty. Further, the contract may simply provide that a breach of warranty does not operate to terminate cover but that cover continues, perhaps on different terms. For example, in marine

Diplock, with the view "that any breach entitles the insurer to repudiate the contract": Fifth Report, Conditions and Exceptions in Insurance Policies 1957, Cmnd 62, para 8; and (c) a report of the Law Commission in 1980, with the view that "the insurer is entitled to repudiate the policy": Insurance Law, Non-Disclosure and Breach of Warranty, Cmnd 8064, para 104. Other academic authority ranged against Lord Goff includes Arnould, *The Law of Marine Insurance and Average* (16th ed., 1981) para 708 and *MacGillivray* para 790. Also in this sense: Lord Wright in *Provincial Ins Co* v *Morgan* [1933] AC 240, 255.

210. Fulfilment of the warranty is "a condition precedent to the inception" of the contract of insurance: *Thomson* v *Weems* (1884) 9 App Cas 671, 683 *per* Lord Blackburn (life). If the warranty is unfulfilled, "there is in reality no contract": *Newcastle Fire Ins Co* v *Macmorran & Co* (1815) 3 Dow 255, 259 *per* Lord Eldon (HL—fire).

The insurer may wait for a claim and repudiate liability on the ground of breach of warranty, or in advance of such a claim seek a declaration from the court: *Guarantee Trust Co of New York* v *Hannay & Co* [1915] 2 KB 536 (CA), approved by Lord Sumner in *Russian Commercial & Industrial Bank* v *British Bank for Foreign Trade Ltd* [1921] 2 AC 438, 452.

211. *Hare* v *Travis* (1827) 7 B & C 14 (cargo); *Baines* v *Holland* (1855) 10 Exch 802, 807–808 *per* Parke B (hull). See also *Daff* v *Midland Colliery Owners Mutual Indemnity Co* (1913) 82 LJKB 1342, 1344–1345 *per* Lord Shaw as regards the effect of non-payment of calls on employers' liability insurance. These citations indicate that the rule suggested in the text rests on the intention of the parties, so presumably the parties could stipulate that a breach should have retroactive effect to discharge liability for earlier claims. However, the courts will be reluctant to construe a warranty in this way: *Pim* v *Reid* (1843) 6 Man & G 1, 13 *per* Maule J (fire).

212. The ending of his promise would not end a contractual promise either to pay or to arbitrate an earlier claim under the policy: *Heyman* v *Darwins Ltd* [1942] AC 356; this is a consequence of the principle of separability of arbitration agreements, ancillary to the main contract of insurance: *Harbour Assurance Co (UK) Ltd* v *Kansa General International Ins Co Ltd* [1992] 1 Lloyd's Rep 81, 92 *per* Steyn J (re). Law Commission Report No 104 (Cmnd 8064), section 6.6. Cf *Jureidini* v *National British & Irish Millers Ins Co Ltd* [1915] AC 499 (fire), as distinguished in *Heyman* v *Darwins Ltd* [1942] AC 356, 364–365 by Viscount Simon LC.

Cf the effect in the case of rescission: 23–17C.

213. *Scottish Amicable Life Assurance Sy* v *Fuller* (1867) Ir 2 Eq 53 (life); *Scottish Equitable Life Assurance Sy* v *Buist*, 1877 4 R 1076 (Ct Sess—life); *Graham Joint Stock Shipping Co Ltd* v *Merchants Marine Ins Co Ltd* [1924] AC 294 (hull). As regards marine contracts, this is the effect of the MIA, section 50(2).

214. Whether the mortgagee has a distinct contract with the insurer or not: *Liverpool & London & Globe Ins Co* v *Agricultural Savings & Loan Co* (1903) 33 SCR 94, 110 *per* Davies J (fire). See also *Samuel & Co Ltd* v *Dumas* [1924] AC 431 (hull). In the USA a similar result is achieved by the union mortgage clause; see further, 45 CJS 545.

215. *Jackson* v *Forster* (1860) 1 El & El 470 (Exch Ch—life). See above, 6–6(d).

insurance, a breach of warranty or a change in risk may trigger a clause whereby the insured is held covered at a premium to be arranged (TBA).[216]

20–6C1 Composite Insurance

In the general law, it can be argued that, if A's promise 1 is dependent on fulfilment of B's promise 1, failure of the latter discharges A from promise 1, but not from A's promise 2, if A's promise 2 is independent of A's promise 1 and B's promise 1.[217] This argument provides an English explanation of decisions in the United States that,

"where a policy of insurance covers two classes of property which are clearly and definitely separated, each being made a distinct subject of insurance, and each being insured for a specified sum, the contract is divisible, and the insurance on one class is not invalidated by the breach of condition which applies to the other class alone; and . . . this rule will be applied in the case of a policy of insurance covering a building and its contents, where each is made a distinct subject of insurance."[218]

However, courts are not in agreement on what constitutes a distinct class and thus an independent promise; some have required that the property be subject to different risks,[219] others only that the classes be separately itemised and valued.[220]

20–7 WAIVER OF BREACH OF WARRANTY

20–7A The Nature of Waiver

Courts have spoken in the past of waiver[221] of a breach of warranty as if the rules are broadly the same as those governing waiver of rescission (affirmation) in respect of misrepresentation or non-disclosure,[222] waiver of claim conditions,[223] and waiver of forfeiture for non-payment of premiums.[224] The similarity must now be reconsidered, as it now appears that the nature of waiver of breach of warranty is that it is not waiver at all but estoppel.[225]

216. These clauses are discussed above, 11–1A4.
217. For example, Dawson, 91 LQR 380, 392 ff (1975).
218. *Northern Assurance Co Ltd* v *Case*, 12 F 2d 551, 552-553 (4 Cir, 1926—fire); *Payne* v *Eureka-Security Fire & Marine Ins Co*, 122 SW 2d 431 (Tenn, 1938—fire); ; *Roof* v *New York Federated Underwriters*, 201 NYS 2d 515 (1960—fire); even though everything is insured for a single entire premium: *Bennett* v *Cosmopolitian Fire Ins Co*, 50 F 2d 1017 (5 Cir, 1931—fire); *Bethune* v *New York Underwriters Ins Co*, 98 F Supp 366 (ED S Carolina, 1951—fire); *First Savings & Loan Assn* v *American Home Assurance Co*, 316 NYS 2d 233 (1970—fire).
219. *Payne*, above.
220. *Bethune*, above.
221. In cases of waiver of breach of insurance warranty, the courts have applied the rules of waiver or estoppel found in relation to other kinds of contract: *Ayrey* v *British Legal & United Provident Assurance Co Ltd* [1918] 1 KB 136, 142 *per* Atkin J (life); *Evans* v *Employers Mutual Ins Assn Ltd* [1936] 1 KB 505, 518 *per* Slesser LJ (CA—motor); *Barratt Bros (Taxis) Ltd* v *Davies* [1966] 2 Lloyd's Rep 1, 5 *per* Lord Denning MR (CA—motor).
222. In this sense Arnould, No 683, n 36. See also Lloyd J in *Hadenfayre* v *British National Ins Co Ltd* [1984] 2 Lloyd's Rep 393, 401 (contingency) who speaks in terms of "affirming" a breach of warranty. The analogy with waiver of rescission for misrepresentation is particularly close, as representations in the proposal form are often stated to be the basis of the contract of insurance and thus become warranties. For discussion of these rules see below, 23–18B.
223. See below, 26–4.
224. See above, 13–11A.
225. Courts have sometime spoken of "estoppel" in this context in the past, for example, in *Jones* v *Bangor Mutual Shipping Ins Sy Ltd* (1889) 61 LT 727, 729 *per* Mathew J (hull).

This is the conclusion tentatively taken from the decision of the House of Lords in *The Good Luck*,[226] that breach of warranty by the insured automatically terminates the contract of insurance. Both section 34(3) of the MIA and the leading judgment of Lord Goff in that case suggest that there can still be "waiver" of breach of warranty. But, as Arnould points out,[227] if the insurer "had once become 'discharged as from the date of breach' it would be logically impossible for the insurer to make himself liable by subsequent waiver". Cover has died, subject only to the insurer's power to revive the corpse before it is cold. But is this really the wand of waiver? Waiver concerns an election but, if the contract has been terminated automatically, the insurer has no election to make. One suggestion is that it is resurrection by reinstatement.[228] However, in terms of the law of today[229] and, indeed, of Lord Goff's own judgment in *The Kanchenjunga*,[230] it is submitted that (what was once) waiver of breach of warranty should now be regarded as a case of estoppel, whereby the insurer is estopped from pleading that the insurance has terminated by reason of the breach of warranty.[231] Accordingly, in the following pages, what has commonly been referred to in the past as waiver will be referred to as estoppel.

20–7B Proof

While breach of warranty must be proved by the insurer, estoppel must be pleaded[232] and proved[233] by the insured. However, when the policy governs waiver, the first point to note is that it is indeed likely to be a case of waiver rather than estoppel: the policy term modifies the default rule, that breach of warranty automatically discharges the contract. The second point is that it has been held that the insurer must not only prove breach of warranty but also that the breach has not been waived.

In *Marcovitch*[234] a life policy provided that, if the insured took an additional policy on her life without the permission of the (first) insurer indorsed on the policy, it should be void. Defending a claim on the policy the insurer proved the existence of other policies, *prima facie* a breach of the warranty. However, the Court of Appeal also required the insurer to prove that permission had not been given. The insurer pointed to the absence of indorsement on the policy, but the court held that this did not meet the burden of proof, for permission might have taken another form. The insurer's defence failed.

20–7C Knowledge

In a case of waiver, the election "does not arise (1) unless you know all the facts—being put on inquiry is not sufficient; you must know the facts—and (2) unless you

---

226. See above, 20–6C. Also Clarke [1991] LMCLQ 437.
227. no 708.
228. Birds (1991) 107 LQR 540, 542.
229. See below, 26–4A2.
230. [1990] 1 Lloyd's Rep 391, 399 (HL).
231. This was also the suggestion of Arnould no. 708. For cases in which a person might be estopped from pleading that he was bound to the other by contract, see *The Henrik Sif* [1982] 1 Lloyd's Rep 456; *The Uhenbels* [1986] 2 Lloyd's Rep 294; *A–G for Hong Kong* v *Humphrey's Estate* [1987] 1 AC 114, 127–128 *per* Lord Templeman.
232. *Brook* v *Trafalgar Ins Co Ltd* (1947) 79 Ll L Rep 365, 367 *per* Scott LJ (CA—motor).
233. *Bentsen* v *Taylor, Sons & Co (No 2)* [1893] 2 QB 274, 283 *per* Bowen LJ (CA), relied on in *Evans* v *Employers Mutual Ins Assn Ltd* [1936] 1 KB 505, 518 by Slesser LJ (CA—motor).
234. *Marcovitch* v *Liverpool Victoria Friendly Sy* (1912) 28 TLR 188.

have a reasonable time to make up your mind".[235] One of the key differences between waiver and estoppel, however, is that the law of estoppel is much less concerned with the knowledge of the insurer about the breach of warranty than with the effect of the insurer's words or conduct on the insured.[236] There must still be some concern with the insurer's knowledge, however, for, if the insured believes that the insurer is unaware of his breach of warranty, he will find it not entirely impossible but certainly rather difficult to convince a court, that he justifiably relied on the insurer's not pleading a breach, of which the insurer was unaware, and that the insurer is therefore estopped: below, 20–7C1. An exception will arise when the insurer's words or conduct suggest that he is indifferent to the possibility of breach. Nonetheless, the decisions and dicta[237] that underline requirements of knowledge on the part of the insurer must now be read with caution.

20–7C1 Apparent Knowledge

As indicated below (20–7D), any conduct relied by the insured as estoppel against the insurer must be unequivocal. As indicated above (20–7C), this may depend in part on what the insured is entitled to assume about what the insurer knows: clearly, there will be cases in which the insurer's words or conduct must be assessed in that light. This leads to a particular but very important question, the point at which any communication of information from insured to insurer is effective—the point at which the insurer can be assumed to know what has been communicated.

As to the mode of communication, the rule is that knowledge will be attributed to the insurer, if it has been given to an agent of the insurer, whose duty is *to communicate* such knowledge to the insurer—whether or not he carries out that duty, and whether or not the agent is fraudulent,[238] unless the insured is aware of it. From the insured's perspective, if information is put in the proper channel, that is enough, even if it does not actually reach the person within the insurer's organisation who is authorised to deal with the matter.[239] What happens to the information within the organisation is the insurer's concern alone and he cannot plead a breakdown of internal

---

235. *McCormick* v *National Motor & Accident Ins Union Ltd* (1934) 49 Ll L Rep 361, 365 *per* Scrutton LJ (CA—motor), a case of non-disclosure; see also pp 368–369 *per* Greer LJ; *Jones* v *Bangor Mutual Shipping Ins Sy Ltd* (1889) 61 LT 727, 729 *per* Mathew J (hull); *Hemmings* v *Sceptre Life Assn Ltd* [1905] 1 Ch 365, 369–370 *per* Kekewich J (life); *Peters (Jewellers) Ltd* v *Brocks Alarms Ltd* [1968] 1 Lloyd's Rep 387, 394–395 *per* Megaw J (burglary); *Melik & Co Ltd* v *Norwich Union Fire Ins Sy Ltd* [1980] 1 Lloyd's Rep 523, 533–534 *per* Woolf J (burglary); *Hadenfayre* v *British National Ins Co Ltd* [1984] 2 Lloyd's Rep 393, 401 *per* Lloyd J (contingency). *Phillips* v *Grand River Farmers' Mutual Fire Ins Co* (1881) 46 UCR 334, 362 (fire).

As regards the corresponding rule for waiver of disclosure, below, 23–9AZ; for waiver of rescission, below, 23–18B1; and for waiver of claim conditions, below, 26–4B.

236. See below, 26–4A1(b).

237. See the first edition of this book, 20–7C, notably, *Evans*, below 20–7C1.

238. See above, 8–3D.

239. Restatement 2d of the Law of Agency, section 278: a principal can be affected by the knowledge of an agent who "having the knowledge has committed a fault . . . in failing to communicate it to others who are to act upon it". Applied, for example, in *Kelley* v *British Commercial Ins Co Ltd*, 34 Cal Rptr 564, 567 (Cal, 1963—liability). See also *Nissho Iwai Petroleum Co. Inc.* v *Cargill International SA* [1993] 1 Lloyd's Rep 80, 84: where Hobhouse J noted that "it is an implied term of a contract that one party shall not obstruct or prevent the other from performing the contract". For this, he cited *The Aello* [1961] AC 135 and held in respect of a sale of goods fob that to "delay in answering the telephone so as to prevent a seller from giving a valid nomination under the contract is a breach of an implied term in the contract".

communication to deny knowledge.[240] As to the time of communication, the insurer is presumed to have knowledge of the information within a reasonable time after its receipt by the agent.[241]

In *Evans* v *Employers Mutual Ins Assn Ltd*,[242] untrue statements in a proposal of motor insurance became warranties. In the course of a claim the true facts were stated to a claims inspector, who passed the information back to other employees of the insurer, in particular, a clerk whose task was to check such information against the relevant proposal. The clerk noticed the discrepancy, but considered it unimportant, did not advise his superiors, and no steps were then taken to terminate cover. One month later, after the insurer had paid first party claims, another employee noticed the discrepancy and the breach of warranty was raised to repudiate liability. The claimant argued, as seemed best at that stage in the development of the law, that the point had been waived and succeeded on that ground. The insurer argued lack of knowledge of the truth but the Court of Appeal rejected the contention: the knowledge being possessed by the employees deputed to receive it, that knowledge must be imputed to the insurer. Of greater interest today is the alternative ground of decision,[243] that "if such information is invited by a company and is given and communicated to that company in the manner invited, that fact alone would be sufficient".

In principle, any notice or similar communication must be directed to the insurer at head office. This principle is modified by the policy or by practice, and the acceptability of a communication directed to the local office, as the appropriate channel of communication to head office, will be readily inferred.[244]

In *Wing* v *Harvey*,[245] a branch office with authority to receive premiums was the appropriate channel for information about a breach of warranty: the court apparently accepted the argument[246] that the claimant was entitled to assume that the insurer would be informed of all that was communicated to that office. In *Ayrey*,[247] the insured misdescribed his occupation in the proposal, which was the basis of the con-

---

240. *Evans* (below), 516 *per* Greer LJ, 518 *per* Slesser LJ (CA—motor). *Standard Plan* v *Tucker*, 582 So 2d 1024 (Ala, 1991—motor).
241. *Kelley* v *British Commercial Ins Co Ltd*, 34 Cal Rptr 564, 567 (Cal, 1963—liability).
242. *Evans* v *Employers Mutual Ins Assn Ltd* [1936] 1 KB 505, 515 *per* Greer LJ (CA—motor). See also *Holdsworth* v *Lancashire & Yorkshire Ins Co* (1907) 23 TLR 521 (employers' liability) in which the knowledge of the chief clerk at a branch office was treated as the knowledge of the company. In relation to companies generally see *Houghton & Co* v *Nothard, Lowe & Willis Ltd* [1928] AC 1, 14 *per* Viscount Dunedin.
   New York Life Ins Co v *Chapman*, 132 F 2d 688 (8 Cir, 1943—life), cert den 319 US 749; *Major Oil Corp* v *Equitable Life Assurance Sy*, 457 F 2d 596 (10 Cir, 1972—life). When the policy provides that an agent has no power to waive or modify the terms of the policy, the knowledge of that agent cannot be imputed to the insurer: *Cleaver* v *Traders Ins Co*, 40 F 711, 715 (ED Mich, 1889—fire). Knowledge of post contract breach by a soliciting agent is not attributed to the insurer: *Gawecki* v *Dubuque Fire & Marine Ins Co*, 72 F Supp 430 (SD Cal, 1947—fire), affirmed 167 F 2d 894 (9 Cir, 1948), not least because his mandate (solicitation) in respect of that policy has ended. However, knowledge of breach acquired by a loss adjuster has been attributed to the insurer: *Briney* v *Tri-State Mutual Grain Dealers Fire Ins Co*, 117 NW 2d 889, 894 (Iowa, 1962—fire).
243. p 521 *per* Roche LJ, in agreement with Greer LJ (p 516) who said that, if there were proper communication, the insurers "could not say they had no knowledge of its contents because no authorised official read it". A similar rule is found in relation to notice in other contexts; see, for example, *The Brimnes* [1975] QB 929 (CA); *Brinkibon Ltd* v *Stahag Stahl* [1983] 2 AC 34. See further below, 23–3B and 23–9A2.
244. Below, 26–2D. See also, below, 23–3C.
245. (1854) 5 De G, M & G 265 (life).
246. p 268: see p 271 *per* Turner LJ.
247. *Ayrey* v *British Legal & United Provident Assurance Co Ltd* [1918] 1 KB 136 (life). In Canada a similar decision is *Beasant* v *Northern Life Ins Co* [1923] 1 WWR 362 (Man—life).

tract and thus a warranty, but later gave the correct description to the insurer's district manager. The Divisional Court held that the insurer "knew" of the correction and would not be allowed to plead the original misdescription: "the district manager had no authority to make a new contract on behalf of the company, but it is not necessary, in order to hold the company liable to the plaintiff, to regard the district manager as having made a new contract". It was "a reasonable thing . . . to assume that the making of that communication to the district manager was equivalent to informing the company's head office".[248]

20-7D Unequivocal and Positive Conduct[249]

The representation by the insurer to found an estoppel, that he will not rely on a breach of warranty against the insured, must be clear and unequivocal,[250] as in the following cases.

(a) Instead of treating the insurance as having been terminated for breach of warranty, the insurer gave the insured 30 days notice of cancellation under a cancellation clause.[251]

(b) The insurer resisted a claim by the insured not, as he might have done, on the ground of breach of warranty but on a different ground altogether.[252]

(c) The insurer issued[253] or renewed[254] the policy.

(d) The insurer advised the insured about loss prevention in future.[255]

(e) The insurer responded to the insured's claim by paying money into court.[256]

(f) The insurer accepted further premiums under the contract of insurance.[257]

If, however, the insurer has disregarded a breach of warranty in the past, he is not barred from pleading a subsequent and similar breach as a ground for treating the

248. p 140 *per* Lawrence J. *Cf Melik & Co Ltd* v *Norwich Union Fire Ins Sy Ltd* [1980] 1 Lloyd's Rep 523, 533 *per* Woolf J (burglary), that it was not enough to tell a risk inspector that the burglar alarm, the efficiency of which had been warranted, was not working properly.

249. As regards corresponding rules for waiver of rescission, see 23–18B2, and for waiver of claim conditions, see 26–4C.

250. *Woodhouse AC Israel Cocoa Ltd* v *Nigerian Produce Marketing Co Ltd* [1972] AC 741; *The Scaptrade* [1983] 2 AC 694. For this kind of statement in respect of breaches of warranty, see *McCormick* v *National Motor & Accident Ins Union Ltd* (1934) 49 Ll L Rep 361, 371 *per* Slesser LJ (CA—motor). Also in this sense *Jones* v *Bangor Mutual Shipping Ins Sy Ltd* (1889) 61 LT 727, 729 *per* Mathew J (hull); *Mint Security Ltd* v *Blair* [1982] 1 Lloyd's Rep 188, 198 *per* Staughton J (cash in transit).

251. *Mint Security Ltd* v *Blair* [1982] 1 Lloyd's Rep 188 (cash in transit).

252. *Cleaver* v *Traders Ins Co*, 40 F 711, 715 (ED Mich, 1889—fire)this assumes that the waivor has the requisite knowledge: *Wyckoff* v *Standard Fire Ins Co*, 936 F 2d 1474, 1489 (6 Cir, 1991—fire). *Cf*, however, above, 20–7C4. In the general law of England the *Cleaver* point was confirmed in *The Wise, Vitol SA* v *Esso Australia Ltd* [1989] 2 Lloyd's Rep 451. *Idem* in New York as regards any grounds for refusing a claim or terminating the contract, if the insurer knew of one ground while (only) pleading another: *Guberman* v *William Penn Life Ins Co*, 538 NYS 2d 571, 573 (1989—life); *Firemans Fund Ins Co* v *Freda*, 548 NYS 2d 319 (1989—motor). Also in this sense *Brown* v *State Farm Mutual Automobile Ins Co*, 776 SW 2d 384, 386 (Mo, 1989—motor). *Idem*, if the insurer did not know of another ground but should have known: *Zumbrun* v *United Services Automobile Assn*, 719 F Supp 890, 895–896 (ED Cal, 1989—flood).

253. *Jones* v *Bangor Mutual Shipping Ins Sy Ltd* (1889) 61 LT 727 (hull); *Keeling* v *Pearl Assurance Co Ltd* (1923) 129 LT 573 (life).

254. *Sulphite Paper Co Ltd* v *Faber* (1895) 1 Com Cas 146, 153–154 *per* Lord Russell CJ (fire).

255. *De Maurier (Jewels) Ltd* v *Bastion Ins Co Ltd* [1967] 2 Lloyd's Rep 550, 559 *per* Donaldson J (jewellers' AR).

256. *Harrison* v *Douglas* (1835) 3 Ad & E 396, 402 *per* Lord Denman CJ (hull).

257. *Jones* v *Bangor Mutual Shipping Ins Sy Ltd* (1889) 61 LT 727, 729 *per* Mathew J (hull); *Hemmings* v *Sceptre Life Assn Ltd* [1905] 1 Ch 365, 369–370 *per* Kekewich J (life).

insurance as having been thereby terminated[258]: times, circumstances and attitudes may change.

A representation, although stated at the time to be "without prejudice", may still give rise to estoppel. "A man is bound by what he does, and he cannot alter what he does by saying he is doing it 'without prejudice'",[259] although, if it is very clear that it negates a representation on which reliance and thus estoppel might otherwise have been based, it will have this effect.[260] Unless it is clear, however, the courts look to the effect of his conduct as a whole. It has been suggested that, if the insurer's conduct makes it look as if he does not intend to take the point about the breach of warranty, the insured is entitled to infer this,[261] whatever the insurer's real intention. It is at this point that the line between waiver in the traditional sense of election, which focuses on the conduct and intention of the waivor, and promissory estoppel, which focuses on the effect of his conduct on the other party[262] and on reliance,[263] has been crossed.

20–7D1 Exceptions

The requirement of a positive representation, words or conduct indicating that in spite of the breach of warranty the insurance is to continue, may be relaxed in one instance: estoppel by convention.[264] Estoppel by convention differs from ordinary (promissory) estoppel, as well as waiver, in that it does not require an unequivocal representation, merely that the parties have proceeded on an assumed state of fact.[265] A court might decide, for example, that, if the insurer has not insisted on regular data, such as monthly value reports required by a fire contract, he has "waived" (the existence of) the promise, or is estopped from insisting on it, and the contract can be enforced on the basis of the last data supplied.[266]

A second exception applies to waiver and thus applied to breach of warranty—before the decision in *The Good Luck*. This was that, although mere inactivity on the part of the insurer is generally equivocal and hence could not constitute waiver,[267]

---

258. As regards past failure to plead an exception: *London & Manchester Plate Glass Co Ltd* v *Heath* [1913] 3 KB 411 (CA—plate glass). Generally, see *The Scaptrade, Scandinavian Trading Co A/B* v *Flota Petrolera Ecuatoriana* [1983] 1 Lloyd's Rep 146 (CA), affirmed on other points [1983] 2 AC 694. *Christian & Brough Co* v *St Paul Fire & Marine Ins Co*, 5 F 2d 489 (5 Cir, 1925—motor). Especially if the alleged waiver occurred under a previous policy: *Coleman Furniture Corp* v *Home Ins Co*, 4 F Supp 794 (WD Va, 1933—sprinkler leakage), affirmed 67 F 2d 347 (4 Cir, 1933), cert den 291 US 669.

259. *Craine* v *Colonial Mutual Fire Ins Co Ltd* (1920) 28 CLR 305, 324—325 *per* Isaacs J (HCA—fire) in relation to a procedural condition, citing *Matthews* v *Smallwood* [1910] 1 Ch 777, 786 *per* Parker J.

260. *Sun Fire Office* v *Hart* (1889) 14 App Cas 98, 102 *per* Lord Watson (PC—fire).

261. There must be "conduct showing an intention not to repudiate" the policy: *Murray* v *Scottish Boat-owners' Mutual Ins Assn*, 1986 SLT 329, 330 *per* Lord Murray (Ct Sess—hull).

262. The relation between waiver and estoppel is discussed below, 26–4A.

263. Below, 20–7E.

264. Treitel, pp 111 ff. The leading modern decisions are *Amalgamated Investment & Property Co Ltd* v *Texas Commerce International Bank Ltd* [1982] QB 84 (CA); and *The Vistafjord* [1988] 2 Lloyd's Rep 343 (CA).

265. "Fact" includes not only the existence of a promise but also its legal effect. *The Vistafjord* (above), p 352 *per* Bingham LJ.

266. In effect the decision in *Aetna Ins Co* v *Rhodes*, 170 F 2d 111 (10 Cir, 1948—fire). See also *Columbia Fire Ins Co* v *Boykin & Tayloe Inc*, 185 F 2d 771, 776 (4 Cir, 1950—fire); *American Eagle Fire Ins Co* v *Burdine*, 200 F 2d 26 (10 Cir, 1952—fire) in which such reports had been prepared not by the insured but by the insurer's agent.

267. *Melik & Co Ltd* v *Norwich Union Fire Ins Sy* [1980] 1 Lloyd's Rep 523, 534 *per* Woolf J (burglary). See also *CTN Cash & Carry Ltd* v *GAFLAC plc* [1989] 1 Lloyd's Rep 299, 303 *per* Macpherson J (burglary), suggesting that delay alone may amount to waiver.

delay would amount to waiver, if it was such as to "prejudice" the insured.[268] For example, if the insured read his policy, found a continuing warranty that he was unable to perform and told the insurer, who did nothing, the insurer, it was said, had "waived" the (potential breach of) warranty.[269] Silence in this context spoke with sufficient unambiguity for the inference to be drawn that the insurer had affirmed the contract. This seems to be good sense, but it may no longer be good law after the decision in *The Good Luck*.[270]

The most that can be inferred from silence is the maintenance of the *status quo*. As long as the *status quo* after a breach of warranty was an avoidable contract, the effect of the insurer's silence was that the insurance continued. If, however, as we now learn from *The Good Luck*, the position is that the contract has been automatically discharged from the time of breach, how can it be inferred from silence on the part of the insurer that the insurance survives? The cases allowing for "waiver" by silence must be reconsidered. In so far as they concern non-disclosure,[271] or breach of procedural condition,[272] and the *status quo* is that the contract goes on until rescinded or repudiated, the cases are not affected by *The Good Luck*, but in so far as they concerned breach of warranty, that contention is surely now untenable after *The Good Luck*. Estoppel in respect of breach of warranty can only be by conduct that is unequivocal and positive.

20–7E Reliance[273]

As long as the situation was seen as one of waiver the response of the waivee insured was secondary, if not irrelevant.[274] However, the insurance cases did not distinguish clearly between waiver and estoppel, for which reliance is required. So, it has been held that "waiver" is not irrevocable until it has been relied on by the insured[275]; and that the question for the court is whether the insurer did by acts or conduct lead the insured reasonably to suppose that the insurer did not intend to treat the contract for

---

Cf USA: in general a waiver does not result from mere silence or inaction; for example, *Robinson* v *Home Ins Co*, 73 F 2d 3, 4 (5 Cir, 1934—hull), cert den 294 US 712. However, it has been held, for example, that upon "notice informing them that the automobile was being used in violation of the terms of the policy, . . . the Company was under the duty of promptly notifying the assured that the accident in question was not covered", failing which they will be liable: *Commercial Standard Ins Co* v *Blankenship*, 40 F Supp 618, 620 (MD Tenn, 1941—motor), affirmed 134 F 2d 784 (6 Cir, 1943). In New York this rule has statutory force: Insurance Law, section 167; the onus is on the insurer to explain his delay, and he cannot extend the period by a letter reserving his rights: *Zappone* v *Home Ins Co*, 447 NYS 2d 911 (1982—motor).

268. *Murray* v *Scottish Boatowners' Mutual Ins Assn*, 1986 SLT 329, 330 *per* Lord Murray (Ct Sess—hull). As regards the effect of silence and delay, in relation to waiver of rescission see 23–18B4 and 23–18C, and in relation to waiver of claim conditions see 26–4C.

269. *Forsik Vesta* v *Butcher (No 1)* [1989] 1 All ER 402, 413 *per* Lord Lowry (re).

270. [1992] 1 AC 233 (hull). See above 20–6C.

271. *Morrison* v *Universal Marine* (1873) LR 8 Ex 197, 205–206; *Simon, Haynes, Barlas & Ireland* v *Beer* (1945) 78 Ll L Rep 337.

272. *Allen* v *Robles Cie Parisienne de Garantie* [1969] 2 Lloyd's Rep 61 (CA).

273. As regards the corresponding rule for waiver of rescission see 23–18B4, and for waiver of claim conditions see 26–4D.

274. See 26–4A. The traditional view, whereby waiver is "not dependent upon reliance on it by the other party", was confirmed by Lord Goff in a case of a charterparty, *The Kanchenjunga, Motor Oil Hellas (Corinth) Refineries SA* v *Shipping Corp of India* [1990] 1 Lloyd's Rep 391, 399 (HL).

275. *Phillips* v *Grand River Farmers' Mutual Fire Ins Co* (1881) 46 UCR 334, 362 (fire).

the future as at an end.[276] Now that it seems that the situation must be seen as one of estoppel (above 20–7A), some degree of reliance on the part of the insured is essential.[277]

Reliance must be reasonable. If, as is likely, reliance is placed on a representation by an agent, that agent must have actual or apparent authority to make it.[278] If the insured has notice, for example from the terms of the policy, that the agent lacks such authority, there is neither actual nor apparent authority in that agent, and any reliance by the insured is not reasonable.[279] Further, reliance is not reasonable, if the insured knows or suspects that the insurer is unaware of the breach of warranty; this is another aspect of the rule (above, 20–7C1) that waiver must be unequivocal.

Reliance means some action or inaction by the insured to his disadvantage.[280] Examples include the payment of further premiums,[281] not seeking alternative cover,[282] and failure to defend an action by a third party.[283]

20–7F Clauses

The automatic termination of the contract on the ground of breach of warranty is an inference about party intention, and thus the consequence may be affected by a term of the contract itself. This is the effect, if not the correct analysis, of a held covered clause[284] and of an "indisputable" clause—a clause that the insurer will not dispute the validity of a life contract, usually except on the ground of fraud.[285]

---

276. *Bentsen* v *Taylor, Sons & Co (No 2)* [1893] 2 QB 274, 283 *per* Bowen LJ (CA), relied on in *Evans* v *Employers Mutual Ins Assn Ltd* [1936] 1 KB 505, 518 by Slesser LJ (CA—motor).
   Concerning an alleged waiver of a 50-mile-radius warranty in a policy on a truck in *Chase* v *National Indemnity Co*, 278 P 2d 68, 72 (Cal, 1954) the court referred to the general law of contract and said: "In no case will a waiver be presumed or implied . . . unless by his conduct the [insured] has been misled to his prejudice, into the honest belief that such waiver was intended or consented to." See also *Cochran* v *Order of United Commercial Travelers* 143 F 2d 82, 86 (10 Cir, 1944—life); *Insurance Co of North America* v *National Steel Service Centre Inc*, 391 F Supp 512, 521 (ND W Va, 1975—liability), affirmed 529 F 2d 515 (4 Cir, 1976).
   277. See below, 26–4A.
   278. *Davies* v *National Fire & Marine Ins Co of New Zealand* [1891] AC 485, 496 *per* Lord Hobhouse (PC—cargo); *Levy* v *Scottish Employers' Ins Co* (1901) 17 TLR 229 (PA). Generally see above 8–2 and 8–3.
   279. *M'Millan* v *Accident Ins Co*, 1907 SC 484 (PA).
   280. *Western Canada Accident & Guarantee Ins Co* v *Parrott* (1921) 61 SCR 595, 600 *per* Idington J (liability); but *cf* p 606 *per* Mignault J; *Beasant* v *Northern Life Ins Co* [1923] 1 WWR 362, 365 (Man—life).
   281. *Wing* v *Harvey* (1854) 5 De G, M & G 265 (life); *Holdsworth* v *Lancashire & Yorkshire Ins Co* (1907) 23 TLR 521 (employers' liability); *Ayrey* v *British Legal & United Provident Assurance Co Ltd* [1918] 1 KB 136 (life).
   Receipt of premiums due before breach occurs is not inconsistent with a decision to terminate the insurance, so does not amount to waiver: *Wing* v *Harvey* (1854) 5 De G, M & G 265, 268 *per* Knight Bruce LJ (life).
   282. *Hargett* v *Gulf Ins Co*, 55 P 2d 1258, 1261 (Cal, 1936—fire).
   283. *Western Canada Accident & Guarantee Ins Co* v *Parrott* (1921) 61 SCR 595 (liability).
   284. See above, 11–1A4.
   285. *Anstey* v *British Natural Premium Life Assn Ltd* (1908) 24 TLR 871 (CA—life).
   In the case of a breach of warranty indorsement on a fire policy the insurer may agree not to raise a breach of warranty by the insured in respect of a claim by the mortgagee. As regards the effect of such indorsements on insurance of aircraft, see Case, 47 J Air Law & Commerce 729 (1982).
   Waiver is also the effect, though not the orthodox analysis, of section 20(3) of the Industrial Assurance Act 1923 as regards certain misstatements in a proposal of industrial assurance which are made conditions of the policy.

CHAPTER 21

MISTAKE

21–1 INTRODUCTION

A mistake by one or both parties to the contract of insurance will vitiate the contract, if the mistake is sufficiently serious. In this respect, the contract of insurance is like other contracts in that such mistakes do not arise very often. Further, circumstances giving rise to mistake will often give rise to other remedies, notably remedies for breach of warranty, misrepresentation or non-disclosure by the insured, remedies which are adequate and easier to obtain than relief based on mistake. The most important instance of mistake occurs when the policy does not accurately reflect the agreement of the parties, and the policy is rectified; *ex hypothesi* the contract is not vitiated.[1]

Traditionally, the law categorises mistakes[2] as common mistakes, where both parties made the same mistake, mutual mistakes, where the parties were at cross purposes, but were unaware of it, or unilateral mistakes, where one party alone was mistaken and the other was aware of it. In the case of unilateral mistake, there is a further distinction between cases in which a party signed a document under a mistake about its contents (*non est factum*) and cases in which there was no such signature.

21–2 COMMON MISTAKE

A common mistake[3] is one shared by both parties. It vitiates the contract of insurance, if the mistake is sufficiently serious. The person seeking relief will find that the rules of common mistake at common law are different from and more demanding than those of equity; each set of rules must be applied separately to a case, to see if the contract is vitiated.

21–2A Common Law

The contract of insurance will be void at common law, if there is common mistake as follows:

(a) The mistake must be fundamental: some aspect of the contract, usually the subject-matter, must be essentially different from what it is believed to be.[4]

---

1. Rectification is discussed in chapter 14.
2. The labels given to the different kinds of mistake are not terms of art; different courts and different writers use different labels. Generally see Treitel, ch 8; Williston, sections 1568–1570.
3. Sometimes called mutual mistake, especially in the United States: Williston, section 1570A.
4. *Bell* v *Lever Bros* [1932] AC 161.

In modern cases this requirement, the precise meaning of which is obscure, has rarely been met. The rarity of such cases in England has led to the suggestion that they are confined to cases in which, unknown to the insurer and proposer, the subject-matter of the insurance does not exist.[5]

In *Pritchard*,[6] the plaintiff renewed reinsurance of his risk on the life of J; both the plaintiff and the reinsurer were unaware that, between the expiry of the previous period of reinsurance and the renewal, J had died. Crowder J said[7] that "it is manifest that it was the essence of the contract that [J] should be alive and in good health at the time". The contract was held void.[8]

(b) Assumption of risk: if the mistake is fundamental, the contract is void, unless one party expressly or implicitly assumes the risk that the (mistaken) belief is false. Thus, in *Pritchard* (above), before holding the contract void, Byles J noted[9] that " 'Dead or alive' which would be equivalent to 'lost or not lost' in a marine policy, seems to be excluded by the terms of the policy". Otherwise, the effect would have been that the risk of mistake (about the survival of the life insured) would have been borne by the insurer, as it is in the case of hull or cargo insured "lost or not lost".[10] The insurer would have been bound by his contract of insurance, in spite of the mistake.

(c) The party mistaken must have reasonable grounds for holding his mistaken belief.[11]

21–2B Equity

A doctrine of common mistake is found also in equity. It differs from that at common law (above, 21–2A) in that it applies to mistakes that are less fundamental (below, (a)) and that the effect on the contract is less drastic: whereas the contract under the common law rules is void, in equity it is voidable (below, (d)). Consequently the remedy (rescission) may be barred.[12] The equitable doctrine of common mistake applies and the contract may be set aside, if the following requirements are satisfied.[13]

(a) The parties must make the contract under a misapprehension, which is fundamental, although less serious than the fundamental mistake operative at common law.[14]

---

5. *Contra* as regards other kinds of contract: *Associated Japanese Bk (International) Ltd* v *Crédit du Nord SA* [1988] 3 All ER 902 (guarantee).

6. *Pritchard* v *Merchants' & Tradesmen's Mutual Life Assurance Sy* (1858) 3 CB (NS) 622. See also *Scott* v *Coulson* [1903] 2 Ch 249 (CA—life), approved in *Bell* v *Lever Bros Ltd* [1932] AC 161, 236 by Lord Thankerton.

A similar decision in the USA is *Paine* v *Pacific Mutual Life Ins Co*, 51 F 689, 692 (8 Cir, 1892—life). See also *Independent Life & Accident Ins Co* v *Wiggins*, 139 So 2d 619, 626 (Ala, 1961—PA): a person who had already lost an eye could not insure against its future loss.

7. p 642.

8. p 640 *per* Williams J.

9. p 645. See also *Associated Japanese Bk* (above) p 912 *per* Steyn J.

10. MIA, section 6, and Rule 1 of the Rules for Construction of Policy. *Reinhart Co* v *Joshua Hoyle & Sons Ltd* [1961] 1 Lloyd's Rep 346 (CA—cargo). Arnould, No 31.

11. *Associated Japanese Bk* (above) p 913 *per* Steyn J.

12. See below, 23–18.

13. Cases in the Court of Appeal are *Solle* v *Butcher* [1950] 1 KB 671; *Peters* v *Batchelor* (1950) 100 LJ News 718; *Magee* v *Pennine Ins Co Ltd* [1969] 2 QB 507 (CA—motor).

14. Above, 21–2A(a). Compare *Bell* v *Lever Bros* [1932] AC and *Magee* v *Pennine Ins Co Ltd* [1969] 2 QB 507 (CA—motor). On the latter case see below, 30–6C.

In Illinois[15] a contract of fire insurance was rescinded, because the parties contracted in the mistaken belief that there was a sprinkler system in the building concerned. The result in the case, that the claimant had no building and no insurance, has been attacked.[16]

(b) Assumption of risk: if the misapprehension is fundamental, the contract is vitiated, unless, as at common law,[17] one party expressly or implicitly assumes the risk that the (mistaken) belief is false.

(c) No fault: being an equitable doctrine, he who seeks equity must do equity. One suggestion is that no remedy will be available to a party who was mistaken as a result of his own negligence.[18]

(d) Rescission is not barred.[19]

21–3 MUTUAL MISTAKE

There is mutual mistake, if one party is mistaken or both parties are mistaken but in different respects, and neither is aware of the other's belief on the matter. If, in these circumstances, there is genuine ambiguity in their dealings, so that a third party cannot determine the true sense of the "agreement" in some essential respect, there is no matching offer and acceptance and there is no contract, even if the parties thought otherwise.[20]

For example, if a fire contract is "concluded", the insured intending to insure number 16, Highfield Avenue but the insurer believing that the subject-matter is number 16, Highfield Close, there is no contract, provided that the reasonable observer would be left in genuine doubt about the true subject-matter.[21] If, however, the reasonable observer would have understood Highfield Avenue, there is a contract on 16, Highfield Avenue, i.e., in the sense (reasonably) understood by the insured.[22] If the reasonable observer would have understood Highfield Close, there is a contract on 16 Highfield Close, as understood by the insurer,[23] albeit a contract which is unenforceable for lack of insurable interest unless, of course, the insured has an interest in both properties.[24]

15. *Allstate Ins Co* v *National Tea Co*, 323 NE 2d 521 (Ill, 1975—fire). Having found that the insurer would not have accepted the risk, if it had known the truth, it "follows" (p 529) that there was a "material mistake of fact which operated to prevent the existence of a valid contract". In spite of this language, the remedy was rescission, which, the court indicated, would not have been available if the party seeking relief had been negligent.

16. Appleman, section 7122, n 4.

17. Above, 21–2A(b).

18. *Associated Japanese Bk (International) Ltd* v *Crédit du Nord SA* [1988] 3 All ER 902, 913 *per* Steyn J (guarantee). *Allstate* v *National* (above) p 529. Treitel, p 284.

19. On the bars to rescission, see below, 23–18.

20. *Mutual Life Ins Co* v *Young*, 90 US 85 (1875—life).

21. Treitel, p 267. For a mutual mistake about the identity of the subject-matter see *Hayford* v *Century Ins Co*, 209 A 2d 716 (NH, 1965—fire); for a mutual mistake about the identity of the insured see *Storer* v *Anderson*, 347 NE 2d 698 (Mass, 1976—life), in which the court declined to avoid the policy, as the mistake had not been made reasonably by the mistaken party seeking relief.

22. *Hayford* (above) p 718.

23. *Hayford*, p 718. In the USA, ambiguities are likely to be resolved against the insurer in favour of the insured: Williston, No 1568A, discussing *Ramco Inc* v *Pacific Ins Co*, 439 P 2d 1002 (Or, 1968—products liability).

24. *Zurich General Accident & Liability Ins Co Ltd.* v. *Rowberry* [1954] 2 Lloyd's Rep 55 (CA): the insured intended cover for air travel to Nice, the insurer reasonably inferred that he proposed cover for air travel to Paris. It was held that there was a contract for Paris and that the insurer was entitled to premium.

Mistakes which motivate the making of the contract are no different from other kinds of mistake. In practice, mistakes in motivation are unlikely to give rise to the kind of ambiguity which can vitiate contracts. Examples are the mistaken belief of the insured that his previous cover had come to an end,[25] or an error by the insurer in calculating the premium[26]: generally, such mistakes do not vitiate the contract.[27]

21–4 UNILATERAL MISTAKE

A unilateral mistake occurs when one party is mistaken and the other is aware of his mistake. In such cases, the insurance contract can often be avoided for misrepresentation or non-disclosure. For contracts generally, the main feature of unilateral mistake is that the contract is void and not merely voidable. Whereas a voidable contract cannot be rescinded, if third parties have acquired rights in property which must be restored as part of rescission, when the contract is void, no such bar can be raised. As it will be rare for third parties to acquire rights barring rescission of a contract of insurance, unilateral mistake has little impact on the law of insurance in England. It has more impact in the United States in respect of incontestable clauses, which can be pleaded if the contract is voidable but not if it is void.[28] The gravity of the mistake, that vitiates the contract on this ground, varies according to what the mistake is about.

21–4A Mistake of Identity or of Subject-Matter

If the contract is to be void for unilateral mistake, the party seeking to escape from the contract must show that he was mistaken and that the mistake was of vital importance.

Courts require evidence that the importance of the matter, about which he was mistaken, was reflected in his conduct at the time: that he took all reasonable steps to avoid the mistake or its consequences.[29] Hence, it will be very difficult for an insurer to plead successfully a mistake about the insured and the risk proposed, if the mistake was about something reasonably verifiable[30] but which had not been checked or had been overlooked. As to the insured, he might well be mistaken about the identity of the insurer, thinking, for example, that an agent represented insurer A rather than

25. *Vrabel* v *Scholler*, 85 A 2d 858 (Pa, 1952—motor).

26. *International Union of Operating Engineers, Local 953* v *Central National Life Ins Co*, 501 F 2d 902 (10 Cir, 1974—life), cert den 420 US 926.

27. In some parts of the United States, for example Illinois, this has been moderated: the mistaken party may obtain rescission of the contract, if the mistake was not negligently made, the enforcement of the contract would be unconscionable and the other party can be put back in *status quo ante: Local 953* (above), p 906. See also *People* v *South East National Bk* 266 NE 2d 778 (Ill, 1971).

28. *Obartuch* v *Security Mutual Life Ins Co*, 114 F 2d 873 (7 Cir, 1940—life): Mrs O's claim on a policy on the life of her husband was resisted on the ground that the policy had not been applied for by her husband, and that it had been obtained by the submission of a person other than Mr O to the necessary medical examination. The claimant relied on the incontestable clause in the policy, but, as the court observed (p 878) the clause "presupposes a valid contract and not one void *ab initio*. The court (p 877) cited *Maslin* v *Columbian National Life Ins Co*, 3 F Supp 368, 370 (SDNY, 1932—life) that "there cannot be the slightest doubt that the person whom an insurance company intends to make a contract with and intends to insure is the person who presents himself for physical examination." Vance, p. 590.

29. *Highland Ins Co* v *Allstate Ins Co*, 688 F 2d 398 (5 Cir, 1982—fire).

30. *Midland Bank plc* v *Brown Shipley & Co Ltd* [1991] 2 All ER 690. *Cf Obartuch* (above).

insurer B, but then doubt may arise not only about whether he has shown sufficient concern about the agency; but also about whether the mistake is material anyway.[31]

21–4B Mistake as to Terms of the Contract

If one party is mistaken about the terms of the contract of insurance and the other party is aware that he is mistaken, there is no contract.[32] However, distinguish two other situations. First, if there has been agreement on the terms of the insurance contract, but a mistake occurs in the policy or other document recording the agreement, the document may be rectified[33] and the contract may be enforced as rectified. Second, if the insured has agreed terms with an agent of the insurer acting with apparent authority, but terms not those intended by the insurer, there is a contract in the terms agreed with the agent.[34]

21-5 DOCUMENTS MISTAKENLY SIGNED

The importance attached to the more or less formal documents which people are called upon to sign is such that, if the signatory is mistaken, the circumstances in which the law will allow him to repudiate his signature are the subject of special rules and of distinct discussion in any commentary. So it is here, however, as the issue arises most pointedly in connection with the signature of the proposal form, the matter is considered in that context: see above, 10–3.

---

31. *Mackie* v *The European Assurance Sy* (1869) 21 LT 102 (fire): unknown to the insured, the agent, who had formerly dealt with insurer C, had become instead agent for the defendant. The latter's plea of contract vitiated by mistake failed. Malins VC (p 105): the insured's "intention was not to remain uninsured for an hour, in what office it was was a secondary consideration, provided it would meet its engagements". The decision might have been different, if the plaintiff had had insurance at the time of the proposal.

32. *Hartog* v. *Colin & Shields* [1939] 3 All ER 566. *Currier* v. *North British & Mercantile Ins Co*, 101 A 2d 266 (NH, 1953—fire), discussed in Williston, section 1570A.

33. Above 14–3C.

34. Above 8–3C.

CHAPTER 22

MISREPRESENTATION[1]

22-1 INTRODUCTION

A contract is voidable by a party to that contract, if he was induced to make the contract by misrepresentation; he may also have the remedy of damages. It is customary to separate discussion of misrepresentation and non-disclosure and this custom is observed in this book, except as regards remedies.[2] However, it should be remembered that the line between misrepresentation and non-disclosure cannot be clearly drawn; that some rules of law operate in both contexts; and that by the use of basis clauses[3] insurers have sought to remove questions of misstatement in the proposal from the legal area of misrepresentation (and non-disclosure) altogether to that of warranty: above, 20–2B2.

The onus of proving an operative misrepresentation is on the party alleging it,[4] in this context usually the insurer. The contract of insurance is most vulnerable to misrepresentations, which may be quite innocent, made by the insured, when seeking cover for the risk. However, there may also be misrepresentation by the insurer, for example, in literature promoting his product.[5] In that case, apart from civil liability now being considered, there may be criminal liability for misleading statements under section 133 of the Financial Services Act 1986.[6]

22-2 MISREPRESENTATION

A misrepresentation is a positive statement (22–2A) of fact (22–2B), which is made or adopted by a party to the contract (22–2C) and which is untrue (22–2D).

---

1. Generally, see Treitel, ch 9; Bower, *The Law relating to Estoppel by Representation*, (3rd ed, 1977); Appleman, Nos 7291 ff; also 12121 ff and 12428 ff. Farnham, 20 Forum 299 (1984–5).
2. Below, 23–14 ff.
3. Above, 20–2A1.
4. *Davies* v *National Fire & Marine Ins Co* [1891] AC 485, 489 *per* Lord Hobhouse (fire); *Craig* v *Imperial Union Accident Ins Co* (1894) 1 SLT 646 (Ct Sess—PA); *Stebbing* v *Liverpool & London & Globe Ins Co Ltd* [1917] 2 KB 433, 438 *per* Viscount Reading CJ (CA—burglary); *Arlet* v *Lancashire & General Assurance Co Ltd* (1927) 27 Ll L Rep 454 (motor); *Adams* v *London General Ins Co* (1932) 42 Ll L Rep 56 (motor). See also below, 23–2.
5. Below, 22–2C1.
6. If, as is the case of most insurance contracts, the contract is not an investment agreement, it is an offence to make fraudulently any misleading, false or deceptive statement, promise or forecast for the purpose of inducing a person to enter into or refrain from entering into an insurance contract, or to exercise or refrain from exercising any rights under an insurance contract. A statement, etc, is made fraudulently, if its character is known to the person making it or he makes it recklessly. An investment agreement is defined in section 44(9), and an insurance contract in section 207(7).

22–2A A Positive Statement

Misrepresentation may be in the spoken word, in writing, or by conduct. In any case, it must be positive: silence alone cannot be a misrepresentation—except in the law of insurance, where it is called non-disclosure or concealment: below, chapter 23.

Failure to answer a question in a proposal form is not regarded as a negative answer to the question,[7] unless a negative answer can be inferred when the blank is seen in the context of other words in the document.[8] Of course, if the matter is material, silence on the matter amounts to non-disclosure and the contract may be rescinded on that ground, unless the insurer's acceptance of an incomplete proposal form can be interpreted as waiver by the insurer of the missing information: below, 23–12B1.

22–2A1 Implication

A statement of fact, which is true in one case, may be untrue in another case, unless qualified with further or additional information; failure to supply the latter (silence) may mislead the person receiving the statement, usually the insurer. This is a case of half truth; see below, 22–2F.

22–2A2 Change of Circumstances

If a statement, although true when made, becomes false as a result of a change in the facts on which the statement was based, and this occurs before the contract is made, failure by the party who made the statement to correct it may be treated as misrepresentation. If, for example, the proposer of life insurance declares himself to be well but before contract becomes ill, he must tell the insurer. In the general law this will be seen as misrepresentation: the initial statement is regarded as continuing until contract and thus becomes false, when the illness develops.[9] In the context of insurance, however, it may be treated in the same way, as a misrepresentation of the old fact (fitness), but it may also be approached as non-disclosure of the new fact (illness).

Examples include not only a change in the proposer's health,[10] but also a change in his loss record[11] and a change in his previously stated intention (his current state of mind) to retain part of the risk himself[12] or not to insure the risk with another insurer.[13]

---

7. *Perrins* v *Marine & General Travellers' Ins Sy* (1859) 2 El & El 317, 323 *per* Wightman J (PA); *Marcovitch* v *Liverpool Victoria Friendly Sy* (1912) 28 TLR 188, 189 *per* Lord Alverstone CJ (CA—life).

8. *Roberts* v *Avon Ins Co Ltd* [1956] 2 Lloyd's Rep 240, 249–250 *per* Barry J (burglary), where the blank followed a declaration that the proposer had never sustained a relevant loss except as therein specified.

9. *Smith* v *Kay* (1859) 7 HLC 750, 769 *per* Lord Cranworth; *With* v *O'Flanagan* [1936] Ch 575 (CA). Hudson, 85 LQR 524 (1969).

10. *Mutual Benefit Life Ins Co* v *Higginbotham*, 95 US 380 (1877—life).

11. *Pan Atlantic Ins Co Ltd* v *Pine Top Insurance Co Ltd* [1992] 1 Lloyd's Rep 101, 109 per Waller J (re), affirmed [1993] 1 Lloyd's Rep 496 (CA).

12. *Trail* v *Baring* (1864) 4 De GJ & S 318 (re). However, in *Wales* v *Wadham* [1977] 2 All ER 125 the judge, to whom *Trail* was not cited, held that a person was not obliged to communicate a change of intention (whether to remarry), as the contract in that case (a maintenance agreement) was not a contract of utmost good faith; the decision on the point was approved briefly in *Livesey* v *Jenkins* [1985] AC 424, 439 *per* Lord Brandon, which also concerned a maintenance agreement.

13. *Re Marshall & Scottish Employers' Liability & General Ins Co Ltd* (1901) 85 LT 757 (PA).

22–2B A Statement of Fact

A statement of fact is defined negatively: it is any statement relating to the present or the past, which is not therefore a promise, and which is not a statement of opinion or a statement of law.

22–2B1 Promise

A promise is a statement about the future, which is therefore not a statement of (present or past) fact, and which cannot be true or false at the time it is made[14]: it cannot be a *mis*representation.

For example, an estimate of how much use of his car would be made by the proposer's son "can only be an estimate of future activity and not a representation of existing fact".[15] The same is true of an undertaking that certain security precautions would be taken.[16]

In exceptional cases, however, the present and the future meet, and statements which point to the future have nonetheless enough of the present in them for the law to treat them as statements of fact.

(a) A statement about the future conduct of the speaker can be seen as a statement of his current intention, his present state of mind. If he does not have that intention, that is a misrepresentation of his present state of mind, which will be actionable as such.[17] In other words, the statement is not made in good faith.[18]. Examples include the proposer's intention to retain part of the risk himself,[19] and not to insure the risk with any other insurer[20]; the insurer's current plans for future bonuses[21]; and a statement by a party to negotiations that, unless a particular term is assented to, negotiations will be broken off.[22] The practical impact of this kind of misrepresentation should not be exaggerated:

> "formidable difficulty . . . generally stands in the way of one who seeks, whether for purposes of misrepresentation or estoppel, to extract a representation from expressions of intention, the difficulty, that is, of proving that he regarded the supposed fact (that is, the existence of a then present intention on the part of the representor) as of the slightest importance. What the representee is generally found in the last resort to complain of, or to protest against, is that the representor is refusing to carry out his intention, not that he is setting up that he never had any such intention in the first instance."[23]

---

14. *Beattie* v *Ebury* (1872) 7 Ch App 777, 804 *per* Mellish LJ. Further, it is thought that promises should be not actionable, unless contracted for, which, *ex hypothesi*, is not the case of a representation.

15. *Milbank Mutual Ins Co* v *Wentz*, 352 F 2d 592, 596 (8 Cir, 1965—motor).

16. *Benham* v *United Guarantie & Life Assurance Co* (1852) 7 Exch 744 (fidelity); *Towle* v *National Guardian Assurance Sy* (1861) 30 LJ Ch 900, 908 *per* Stuart V-C (guarantee).

17. *Smith* v *Price* (1862) 2 F & F 748, 752 *per* Erle CJ; *Edgington* v *Fitzmaurice* (1885) 29 Ch D 459, 482 *per* Bowen LJ (CA): "the state of a man's mind is as much a fact as the state of his digestion". *New England Mutual Life Ins Co* v *Gillette*, 171 F 2d 500 (2 Cir, 1948—life).

18. *The Dora* [1989] 1 Lloyd's Rep 69, 90 *per* Phillips J (yacht).

19. *Trail* v *Baring* (1864) 4 De GJ & S 318 (re).

20. *Re Marshall & Scottish Employers' Liability & General Ins Co Ltd* (1901) 85 LT 757 (PA).

21. *Kettlewell* v *Refuge Assurance Co Ltd* [1908] 1 KB 545 (CA—life).

22. *Goff* v *Gauthier* (1991) 62 P & CR 388. *Idem* concerning a misstatement that, unless less onerous terms were accorded, one party would go into liquidation: *The Siboen* [1976] 1 Lloyd's Rep 293.

23. Bower, *Estoppel*, p 33, quoted with approval in *The Anemone* [1987] 1 Lloyd's Rep 546, 558 by Staughton J.

In the context of contracting insurance, if the insurer is really concerned about what the proposer will do during the insurance period, he can and will make it the subject of a warranty.[24]

(b) It has been suggested that there is an implied representation that the speaker has reasonable grounds for believing that he will be able to perform his promise. If no such grounds exist, there is a (negligent) misrepresentation. In the general law it is doubtful whether an implied representation of this kind is actionable.[25] As regards insurance, however, it may be material and hence important that a belief is held: see below, 22-2B2.

(c) A statement in terms about the present may be given primarily for its implications about the future, but be nonetheless a statement of present fact.[26] An assertion, that the house to be insured is in good repair, implies that it will withstand normal weather conditions in the future. Again, an account of the past performance of a company's endowment policies carries implications of future performance; nonetheless, as regards the past it is a representation of fact.[27] Moreover, a statement about the future effect of an insurance policy may be actionable as a statement of fact about the present terms of the policy.[28]

22–2B2 Opinion

Fact is distinguished from opinion. An opinion is a statement which, as it appears or should appear to the person to whom the statement is made, the speaker does not have sufficient information to guarantee.[29] Even where the statement is within the scope of the speaker's apparent expertise, if the statement is one on which there is not such unanimity of view that a contrary view could be described as unreasonable,[30] that statement may be opinion. Opinions are not usually actionable as such,[31] for reliance on them by the recipient plaintiff is not reasonable or, in other words, it is not a statement for which the speaker can usually be expected to take the legal responsibility associated with representations of fact.

For example, courts are reluctant to find that a proposer's statements about his medical history are statements of fact rather than of opinion.[32] Lord Mansfield spoke of the proposer, who says that he is in good health "knowing nothing about it, nor

---

24. See above, 20–5.

25. Treitel, p 297: while the suggestion is logical, the effect would undermine the law of bankruptcy.

26. For example, goods said to be in good order and condition on shipment: *Silver* v *Ocean SS Co* [1930] 1 KB 416 (CA).

27. *Grieb* v *Equitable Life Assurance Sy*, 189 F 498 (ED Pa, 1911—life).

28. For example, in the case of mutual insurance, as regards calls: *Cross* v *Mutual Reserve Life Ins Co* (1904) 21 TLR 15 (life); *Merino* v *Mutual Reserve Life Ins Co* (1904) 21 TLR 167 (life).

29. *Hubbard* v *Glover* (1812) 3 Camp 313, 314–315 *per* Lord Ellenborough (hull); *Brine* v *Featherstone* (1813) 4 Taunt 869, 873 *per* Lord Mansfield CJ (hull); *Anderson* v *Pacific Fire & Marine* (1872) LR 7 CP 65, 69 *per* Willes J (freight); *Bisset* v *Wilkinson* [1927] AC 177 (PC); *Zurich General Accident & Liability Ins Co Ltd* v *Leven*, 1940 SC 406, 415 *per* Lord Normand (motor).

30. *Irish National Ins Co Ltd* v *Oman Ins Co Ltd* [1983] 2 Lloyd's Rep 453, 462 *per* Leggatt J: that a description of insurance by a broker as excess of loss insurance was an opinion.

31. Greig, (1971) 87 LQR 179, 208–210. Opinions may be actionable in tort as negligent misstatements under the rule in *Hedley Byrne & Co* v *Heller & Partners* [1964] AC 465; however, for such an action to succeed, there must have been (reasonable) reliance by the plaintiff on the (expert) opinion of the defendant. See above, 9–2A.

32. The same is true when such statements have been converted into warranties by a basis clause: 20–6B1.

having any reason to believe the contrary; there, though the person is not in good health, it will not avoid the policy, because the underwriter takes the risk upon himself."[33] But a statement by one, who can be expected to have sufficient information to support the statement, is no less a statement of fact because he uses words such as "I think" or "in my opinion".[34]

Although the law does indeed draw a distinction between fact and opinion, in the context of contracting insurance it is of secondary importance.[35] Here, in particular, the opinions of others do have influence, because an opinion may be valued as an opinion, and such reliance may be reasonable.

"A statement as to a future state of affairs can in itself be neither true nor false at the time it is made, since the future cannot be foretold. However, such a statement can and often does carry with it a representation that the person making the statement has an honest belief or expectation, based on reasonable grounds, that events will turn out to be as stated or forecast."[36]

Behind every opinion is the implication of fact that the opinion is genuine, i.e., that it is actually held; if not, there is a fraudulent misstatement.[37] Further, if "the facts are not equally well known to both sides, then a statement of opinion by one who knows the facts best involves very often a statement of material fact, for he impliedly states that he knows facts which justify his opinion",[38] as an opinion.

If a statement is *prima facie* a statement of fact, it is nonetheless fact because, to the knowledge of the representee, the information contained in the statement is derivative.[39] In the case of facultative reinsurance, for example, the reinsurer knows that the description of the risk presented by the proposer (of reinsurance) is based partly on what he has been told by the primary insured. The description is fact nonetheless. The proposer is in a better position than the reinsurer to collect information about the risk, and the reinsurer is, at the very least, influenced by the fact that the proposer presents the information he does.[40]

22–2B3 Statements of Law

Misstatements of law are not actionable as misrepresentations,[41] if they concern the general law of the land. Distinguish misstatements of private rights[42] and incorrect

---

33. *Pawson v Watson* (1778) 2 Cowp 787, 788 (hull). Examples of opinion include "serious illness": *Delahaye v British Empire Mutual Life Assurance Co* (1897) 13 TLR 247 (CA—life); and "In good health": *United Benefit Life Ins Co v Knapp*, 51 P 2d 963 (Okl, 1935—life); *Franklin Life Ins Co v Champion & Co*, 350 F 2d 115 (6 Cir, 1965—life) and cases cited.

Cf "temperate in [my] habits", regarded as fact in *Thomson v Weems* (1884) 9 App Cas 671, 684–685 *per* Lord Blackburn (life), who drew a distinction between a statement that habits were temperate, and one that disease had not resulted from intemperate habits; see also p 690 *per* Lord Watson. "No illness of consequence" is fact: *Yorke v Yorkshire Ins Co Ltd* [1918] 1 KB 662 (life).

34. *Ionides and Chapeaurouge v Pacific Fire & Marine Ins Co* (1871) LR 6 QB 674, 683–684 *per* Blackburn J (cargo).

35. See below, 23–5.

36. *Bank Leumi Le Israel BM v British National Ins Co Ltd* [1988] 1 Lloyd's Rep 71, 75 *per* Saville J (contingency).

37. Treitel, p 296.

38. *Smith v Land and House Property Corp* (1884) 28 Ch D 7, 15 *per* Bowen LJ (CA); *Highlands Ins Co v Continental Ins Co* [1987] 1 Lloyd's Rep 109, 112 *per* Steyn J (re).

39. *Howard Marine & Dredging Co Ltd v Ogden & Sons (Excavations) Ltd* [1978] QB 574 (CA).

40. See the discussion of this issue by Steyn J in *Highlands* (above), pp 111 ff.

41. *Bilbie v Lumley* (1802) 2 East 469; *Brisbane v Dacres* (1813) 5 Taunt 143.

42. *Cooper v Phibbs* (1867) LR 2 HL 149, 170 *per* Lord Westbury.

conclusions about the effect of the general law in a particular situation, which are actionable. Misstatements of foreign law are treated as misstatements of fact.[43]

A mistake about what a document, such as a policy, says, its contents, is a mistake of fact[44] but a mistake about what it means, its interpretation, is a mistake of law [45]—if that mistake arises out of a mistake about the rules of law for the construction of documents, including previous cases deciding what particular words mean.[46] Otherwise, a mistake about the meaning of a document can be said to be concerned solely with private rights,[47] and not therefore a mistake of law.

The reason for the rule, that misstatements of law are not actionable as misrepresentations, is commonly said to lie in the general maxim, *ignorantia juris haud excusat*.[48] If so, a viable test[49] to identify a misstatement of law is to identify not the nature of the statement but the nature of the mistake: was it the rule of law itself which he understood wrongly,[50] or did his error lie in the operation of the rule, which he understood correctly, because of a mistake about the facts?

This reason for the rule, may, however, be historically unsound.[51] Moreover, it is patently unrealistic in a society with so much law. Perhaps a remedy for misstatements of law should be refused only when necessary to defend the social policy of the criminal law. This is now the view of the Supreme Court of Canada. In *Air Canada* v *British Columbia*,[52] adopting the dissenting judgment of Dickson J in an earlier decision of the same court,[53] who considered[54] that the rule was contrary to authority,[55] if it was based

"upon the maxim *ignorantia non excusat*. The maxim is a statement of general applicability of rules of law and operates to preclude individuals from seeking to excuse themselves from criminal or other liability. Lord Ellenborough imported into the law of contract a maxim of criminal

---

43. *André & Cie SA* v *Ets Michel Blanc* [1979] 2 Lloyd's Rep 427, 430–431 *per* Lord Denning MR (CA). Cf *The Amazonia* [1989] 1 Lloyd's Rep 403, 408 *per* Gatehouse J, affirmed [1990] 1 Lloyd's Rep 236 (CA).
44. For example, *Wilding* v *Sanderson* [1897] 2 Ch 534 (CA); *Curtis* v *Chemical Cleaning & Dyeing Co Ltd* [1951] 1 KB 805 (CA), misapplied in *Horry* v *Tate & Lyle Refineries Ltd* [1982] 2 Lloyd's Rep 416, 422 by Peter Pain J. Kelly (1989) 2 Ins L J 45, 68 ff.
45. *Cross* v *Mutual Reserve Life Ins Co* (1904) 21 TLR 15, 16 *per* Buckley J (life).
46. For example, *Ord* v *Ord* [1923] 2 KB 432 (previous cases construing "free of any deduction whatever").
47. *Cooper* v *Phibbs* (1867) LR 2 HL 149; *Beauchamp (Earl)* v *Winn* (1873) LR 2 HL 223; *Daniell* v *Sinclair* (1881) 6 App Cas 181 (PC); *Faraday* v *Tamworth Union* (1917) 86 LJ Ch 436. Winfield, (1943) 59 LQR 327.
48. *Bilbie* v *Lumley* (1802) 2 East 469, 472 *per* Lord Ellenborough; *Cooper* v *Phibbs* (1867) LR 2 HL 149, 170 *per* Lord Westbury.
49. *The Oro Chief* [1983] 2 Lloyd's Rep 509, 520 *per* Staughton J. *Solle* v *Butcher* [1950] 1 KB 671 (CA) can be reconciled with this view, albeit with difficulty. The test that separates statements of fact and law is a matter of controversy; it is not possible to reconcile all the cases. For a different test, see *Eaglesfield* v *Marquis of Londonderry* (1875) 4 Ch D 693, 703 *per* Lord Jessell MR.
50. *British Workman's & General Ins Co* v *Cunliffe* (1902) 18 TLR 425, 426 *per* Vaughan Williams LJ (CA—life).
51. This basis for the rule was doubted by Lord Atkin in *Evans* v *Bartlam* [1937] AC 473, 479. Goff & Jones (ch 4) argue that this was not the true basis of the rule and it has resulted in an unwarranted extension of the rule, which was originally intended to prevent recovery of sums paid under mistake of law to discharge an honest claim: the debtor had had his chance to dispute the claim at law.
52. (1989) 59 DLR (4th) 161, 187 ff
53. *Hydro Electric Commission of Township Nepean* v *Ontario Hydro* (1982) 132 DLR (3d) 193.
54. p 204
55. This basis for the rule rests on a dictum of Lord Ellenborough in *Bilbie* v *Lumley* (1802) 2 East 469, 472, but which is contradicted by a later statement of the same judge in *Perrott* v *Perrott* (1811) 14 East 423, 440, as well as the opinion of Lord Wright: *Legal Essays and Addresses* (1939) Preface, p xix; and of Williston: *Contracts* (3rd ed, 1957), para 1581, p 536. See also below, 30–5A.

or public law. As Lord Wright has written,[55a] one cannot escape the application of a rule of law by pleading ignorance of it, adding: 'Lord Ellenborough, however, stated as dogma that every man must be taken to be cognizant of the law. Whatever force may be given to this in criminal law, it is clearly not true as a general proposition. It is not only against principle and early authority but against common sense, and has been consistently disavowed by great judges, though often repeated by some who should have known better'. . . . In the case of contracts entered into under a mistake of law: 'Rather than trying to escape the consequences of a rule of law, the plaintiff is seeking to escape consequences that would not have occurred had the law been known and observed. In a general sense it can be said that he seeks to bring the situation into conformity with the rule of law, by asserting rights based upon it.'[56] Thus the maxim *ignorantia juris non excusat* cannot serve as the foundation for the rule barring recovery."

A similar view has prevailed for some time past in the United States:[57]

"It is urged that the tenant is presumed to know the law applicable to the facts, and that therefore it cannot rely on the guaranty as to the law applicable to the use of the building. No presumption exists that all men know the law. The maxim 'a man is presumed to know the law', is a trite, sententious saying, 'by no means universally true.' Ignorance of the law does not excuse persons so as to exempt them from the consequences of their acts, such as punishment for criminal offenses."

Indeed, it does little service to the law to hold, for example, that a misrepresentation by an insurer, that a person has an insurable interest, is a misstatement of law and thus not actionable as a misrepresentation by the person concerned.[58] There is much to be said for the alternative view of Bowen LJ,[59] who explained earlier cases on the matter as concerning a misstatement of law made by one who did not know the law very well, so that, if the recipient relied on it, he did so at his own peril. If this is right, when misstatements of law are not actionable, it is because they are statements of opinion (above, 22–2B2) and reliance is not reasonable. The corollary would be consistent with the opinion of the Privy Council,[60] that a mistake of law will give ground for relief, if the parties are not *in pari delicto*. In other words, a remedy may be available to the one who is less well informed and who, perhaps, acted reasonably in relying on the better knowledge of the other. People rarely have either equal access to or equal knowledge of the law,[61] not least, in most cases, insurer and insured.

Thinking of this kind may have led Professor Winfield to suggest[62] that the mistake of law rule does not apply, when the mistake has been induced by misrepresentation. So, if an insurer's agent misrepresents the legal effect of a policy, the court is likely to

55a. *Op cit* (above) p 43.
56. Palmer, *The Law of Restitution* (1978), vol III, para 14.27 at p 340.
57. *Municipal Metallic Bed Mfg Corp v Dobbs*, 171 NE 75, 76 *per* Pound J (NY, 1930), who continued: "If ignorance of the law did not in fact exist, we would not have lawyers to advise and courts to decide what the law is. Every one would know the law and it would be applied uniformly when the facts were known to the parties; yet the law of a particular case is often known only as the courts decide it." The view in *Dobbs* was accepted, for example, in *National Convention Corp v Cedar Building Corp*, 246 NE 2d 351 (NY, 1969). Moreover, Rest Contracts 2d, section 198 provides a claim for restitution, if the contract is unenforceable and (a) the claimant "was excusably ignorant of the facts or of legislation of a minor character, in the absence of which the promise would be enforceable, or (b) he was not equally wrong with the promisor".
58. *Tofts v Pearl Life Assurance Co Ltd* [1915] 1 KB 189 (CA—life).
59. *West London Commercial Bank v Kitson* (1884) 13 QBD 360, 362–363 *per* Bowen LJ. Also in this sense *Rashdall v Ford* (1866) LR 2 Eq 750, 754 *per* Sir W Page Wood V-C. MacGillivray, No 584. Bower, No 40.
60. *Kiriri Cotton Co Ltd v Dewani* [1960] AC 192.
61. *André & Cie SA v Ets Michel Blanc* [1979] 2 Lloyd's Rep 427, 431 *per* Lord Denning MR (CA).
62. (1943) 59 LQR 326.

find that the proposer is not *in pari delicto* and hence entitled to relief.[63] When an "innocent" misstatement of the legal validity of proposed insurance has been made by an agent of the insurer, one skilled in the matter, to an unskilled proposer, it has been held[64] that the premiums might be recovered as money paid under a mistake of fact. Similarly, the unskilled proposer, who is misled like this, should have a remedy in respect of misrepresentation.

22–2C The Maker of the Misrepresentation

Commonly, the misrepresentation concerned is made by the proposer seeking cover, but misrepresentations may also be made by the insurer and by third parties.

22–2C1 Misrepresentation by the Insurer

As regards the law of misrepresentation, the insurer is in the same position as the insured. Reported cases include misstatements about bonus quotations,[65] the conduct of the company itself,[66] the level of rates compared with those of other insurers,[67] the terms of the cover on offer,[68] and the amount of cover the insured would need.[69]

22–2C2 Misrepresentation by Third Parties

If A makes a misrepresentation to B which, as A should have anticipated, also reaches C, C may rescind a contract with A, which was induced by that misrepresentation, even though it was not made to him directly by A.[70]

If A enters a contract with B on the inducement of a misrepresentation made by C, of which B is unaware, A cannot rescind the contract with B (unless, of course, C is B's agent acting within the scope of his actual or apparent authority). Thus, if insurer A contracts life assurance with life B on the inducement of a misrepresentation made by C, B's family doctor, of which B is unaware, the contract stands.[71] The same should

---

63. *Defender Industries Inc* v *Northwestern Mutual Life Ins Co*, 727 F Supp 252, 256 ff (D SC, 1989—life). A more limited view of parties not *in pari delicto* was stated by Lord Collins MR in *Harse* v *Pearl Life Assurance Co* [1904] 1 KB 558, 563 (CA—life): there must be an "element of fraud, duress or oppression, or difference in the position of the parties which created a fiduciary relationship to the plaintiff [insured] so as to make it inequitable for the defendants to insist on the bargain". In *West London Commercial Bank* v *Kitson* (1884) 13 QBD 360, 362–363, Bowen LJ said *obiter* that a contract induced by wilful misrepresentation of law could be rescinded. See also in this sense *Hirschfield* v *London, Brighton & South Coast Ry Co* (1876) 2 QBD 1.
64. *British Workman's & General Ins Co* v *Cunliffe* (1902) 18 TLR 425 (CA—life). In such cases an equity may arise by reason of the conduct of the insurer's agent: *Rogers* v *Ingham* (1876) 3 Ch D 351, 356 *per* James LJ (CA). *Cf* Merkin & McGee, p A.5.1–04.
65. *Walker* v *Continental Life Ins Co*, 445 F 2d 1072 (9 Cir, 1971—re). Appleman, section 7312. *Cf Hale* v *Continental Life Ins Co*, 12 F 359 (D Vt, 1882—life).
66. *Pontifex* v *Bignold* (1841) 3 Man & G 63 (life).
67. *Mutual Reserve Life Ins Co* v *Foster* (1904) 20 TLR 715 (HL—life); *Molloy* v *Mutual Reserve Life Ins Co* (1906) 22 TLR 525 (CA).
68. *Cross* v *Mutual Reserve Life Ins Co* (1904) 21 TLR 15 (life); *Refuge Assurance Co Ltd* v *Kettlewell* [1909] AC 243 (life). A representation about the monies payable under endowment life assurance has been held to be part of the contract, so that the insured obtained rectification of the policy to conform to the representation: *Sun Life Assurance Co of Canada* v *Jervis* [1943] 2 All ER 425 (CA).
69. *Duffell* v *Wilson* (1808) 1 Camp 401 (insurance against call up for military service).
70. *Pilmore* v *Hood* (1838) 5 Bing NC 97; *Gross* v *Lewis Hillman Ltd* [1970] 1 Ch 445, 461 *per* Cross LJ (CA). Treitel, p 305. As regards misrepresentation by a co-insured see O'Donnell, 22 Tort & Ins L J 662 (1987).
71. *Jones* v *Pearl Assurance Co Ltd* [1927] IAC Rep 42 (life). *Wasbash Life Ins Co* v *Maguire*, 461 SW 2d 916 (Ky, 1970—life).

be true, if a firm takes out keyman life insurance on one of its executives: generally, the contract cannot be avoided on account of misrepresentation made by the executive, of which the firm is unaware.[72]

In contrast, if insured B is not only aware but also assumes responsibility for C's misrepresentation,[73] the misrepresentation is treated as B's misrepresentation and insurer A may avoid the contract. Similarly, if A contracts life insurance with life B on the inducement of misrepresentations in the proposal form which derived from beneficiary C, who helped B to complete the proposal, misrepresentation is a successful defence to an action on the policy.[74] A more difficult situation is that in which B insures the life of C as security in the knowledge or expectation that questions will be put to C by insurer A. Early cases[75] suggest that C will answer as the agent of B, but this suggestion was squashed by Lord Campbell CJ in *Wheelton v Hardisty*[76]:

"A policy may, no doubt, be framed which shall make the insured liable for any material misrepresentation or concealment by the 'life' or the referees; but what we have to consider is whether when the policy contains no express condition for this purpose, and is made on a declaration by the insured that they believe the statements of the 'life' and the referees to be true, the 'life' and referees are still the agents of the insured in the manner contended for . . . [Such a] doctrine would entirely prevent a life policy from being a security upon which a man could safely rely as a provision for his family, however honestly and however prudently he may have acted when the policy was effected. But the assurer and insured being equally ignorant of material facts to influence their contract, if the assurer asks for information and the insured does his best to put the assurer in a situation to obtain the information and form his own opinion as to whether the information is sincere, can it be permitted where the assurer, without any blame being imputable to the insured, has allowed himself to be deceived, that he shall be able to say to the insured: 'You warranted all the information I received to be true; and having received your premiums for many years . . . the policy I gave you is a nullity'?"

By contrast, in *Armstrong v North West Life Ins Co*,[77] a creditor seeking life insurance on the life of his debtor sent his own agent with a form, signed in blank by the creditor, to be completed by the agent on the basis of information elicited from the debtor. The information entered was false and the contract held voidable.

22–2D Untruth

The representation must be a misrepresentation: it must be false. Whether a statement is true or false depends on how it is interpreted. It will be interpreted in a fair and common sense way, objectively and in context.

---

72. Appleman, section 7306.5. This appears to follow from general rules of contract law: Williston, section 1518.

73. For example, when C is B's agent; or when he signs the proposal in blank and sends it to C to complete: *Armstrong v North West Life Ins Co* (1987) 34 DLR (4th) 757 (BC—life). In the general law of contract, see *Royscott Trust Ltd v Rogerson* [1991] 3 All ER 294 (CA). For arguments against this decision, see Brown and Chandler [1992] LMCLQ 40.

74. *Lamark v Lincoln Income Life Ins Co*, 169 So 2d 203 (La, 1964—life); *All American Life & Casualty Co v Krenzelok*, 409 P 2d 766 (Wy, 1966—life); *Elfstrom v New York Life Ins Co*, 63 Cal Rptr 35 (Cal, 1967—life).

75. Discussed and distinguished by MacGillivray, No 840.

76. (1858) 8 El & Bl 232, 269–270 (life). *Cf Keeling v Pearl* (1923) 129 LT 573, 574 *per* Bailhache J (life). *Parker Precision Products Inc v Metropolitan Life Ins Co*, 407 F 2d 1070 (3 Cir, 1969—life).

77. (1990) 72 DLR (4th) 410 (CA BC).

22–2D1 Common Sense Interpretation

Interpretation in a fair and common sense way, it is said,[78] avoids a literal construction of the insurer's question which might make the answer represented inaccurate by generality. No more detail is required of the answer than is required on a strict construction of the question.[79]

For example, the proposer, when asked whether he has consulted any doctors, does not have to state all those consulted in the course of his life. A true answer for practical purposes mentions those that were consulted recently and those who were consulted on major matters.[80] In contrast, a negative reply to a question about declinature was held false by the Court of Appeal, because the insured had previously been refused a renewal: "in the insurance world a transaction like that, though expressed in polite terms, would be treated by everybody as a declining to insure."[81]

A similar problem arises, if a proposer is asked about past illness. "Good health" has been described[82] as "the perfect, conscious enjoyment of all one's faculties and functions, and the conscious freedom from any ailment affecting them, or any symptom of ailment". But perfect health is not what is expected of the proposer. "Even a pessimist may be a fit subject of life assurance."[83] Illness and health are relative matters. It is a question of degree and the proposer's response must be construed in a fair business manner.[84]

22–2D2 Objective Interpretation

If, objectively interpreted, a statement is true, it is true in law, although it may have been understood in a different sense by the recipient.[85] If the representation is ambiguous, "it should be given the meaning intended by the maker, or which he knew or ought to have known the recipient would put upon it"[86] and will be true or false according to that meaning. However, representations are often made in response to questions asked by the insurer, from which the replies take their colour. If true in the sense in which it is reasonably intended as an answer to a question in the proposal

78. *Connecticut Mutual Life Ins Co* v *Moore* (1881) 6 App Cas 644, 650, 654 *per* Sir Robert Collier (PC—life); *Craig* v *Imperial Union Accident Assurance Co* (1894) 1 SLT 646 (Ct Sess—PA); *Condogianis* v *Guardian Assurance Co Ltd* [1921] 2 AC 125, 130 *per* Lord Shaw (PC—fire), applied in Australia in *Bradbury* v *London Guarantee & Accident Co Ltd* (1927) 40 CLR 127, 131 (HCA—fire).
79. *National Protector Fire Ins Co Ltd* v *Nivert* [1913] AC 507 (PC—fire).
80. *Joel* v *Law Union & Crown Ins Co* [1908] 2 KB 863 (CA—life). *Thompson* v *Occidental Life Ins Co*, 513 P 2d 353, 360 (Cal, 1973—life).
81. *Holt's Motors Ltd* v *SE Lancashire Ins Co Ltd* (1930) 35 Com Cas 281, 286 *per* Scrutton LJ (CA—motor). See also *Arthrude Press Ltd* v *Eagle Star & British Dominions Ins Co Ltd* (1924) 19 Ll L Rep 373 (CA—fire).
82. *Hutchison* v *National Loan Fund Life Assurance Sy* (1845) 7 D 467, 478 (Ct Sess—life).
83. *Yorke* v *Yorkshire Ins Co Ltd* [1918] 1 KB 662, 669 *per* McCardie J who, sadly, later committed suicide.
84. *Ibid* p 668. See also *Railway Passenger Assurance Co* v *Standard Life Assurance Co* (1921) 65 DLR 470, 478 (Sup Ct—fidelity): the meaning which a business man of ordinary intelligence would ascribe. See further, below, 22–2D3.
85. *McInerny* v *Lloyds Bank Ltd* [1974] 1 Lloyd's Rep 246, 254 *per* Lord Denning MR (CA).
86. *Ibid*. See also *Anderson* v *Fitgerald* (1853) 4 HLC 484, 507 *per* Lord St Leonards (life); *Anderson* v *Pacific Fire & Marine Ins Co* (1869) 21 LT 408, 410 *per* Sir Joseph Napier (re); *Thomson* v *Weems* (1884) 9 App Cas 671, 682 *per* Lord Blackburn (life); *Mutual Reserve Life Ins Co* v *Foster* (1904) 20 TLR 715 (HL—life); *Price Bros & Co Ltd* v *Heath* (1928) 32 Ll L Rep 166 (CA—fire).

form, the proposer's statement is true in law, for any ambiguity in the question results in construction of the question against the insurer.[87]

For example, in *Byers*,[88] the proposer who, when asked if he had consulted a doctor, did not mention a doctor who examined him but found nothing wrong, did not thereby answer inaccurately. In *Campbell*,[89] an accident proposal asked whether any life, health or accident insurer had ever rejected his application and, although the proposer's application for life cover had been refused by a life company, he answered "No". The court held that this was not a false answer, for he acted not unreasonably in interpreting the question as confined to (rejections of) accident cover. In *Bradbury*,[90] the proposer of fire insurance, when asked whether she or her husband had had a fire, answered it truthfully as regards her current husband but did not include the experience of her previous deceased husband. The High Court of Australia held that the question referred to her husband then alive. Isaacs ACJ[91] rejected the idea that "by association with a man who had had a fire . . . the wife might have become in some way affected so as to increase the risk of future fires". He continued: "Whether that assumes a moral deterioration or a sort of introduction to pyrotechnics, I am unable to conjecture. But it is too remote, in my opinion, to enter into the calculation of any reasonable insurer."

If, thus interpreted, the statement is untrue, it is false in law, but with one exception. If it is alleged that the misrepresentation was fraudulent, in view of the serious nature of the allegation, the statement will be interpreted in accordance with the honest but erroneous intention of the maker, rather than with the objective or reasonable meaning, which makes it false.[92]

22–2D3 Interpretation in Context

Statements are interpreted in context. The context may be the document in which the statement appears.[93] For example, a statement in a proposal form, that the property has not been insured before, refers only to the property subject of the proposal, and not to other property of the proposer.[94] The context may be a section of society. For example, the meaning of "temperate" must be seen in the context of the drinking or

87. *Corcos* v *De Rougement* (1925) 23 Ll L Rep 164 (motor); *Brewtnall* v *Cornhill Ins Co Ltd* (1931) 40 Ll L Rep 166, 168 *per* Charles J (motor); *Revell* v *London General Ins Co Ltd* (1934) 50 Ll L Rep 114, 116–117 *per* Mackinnon J (motor); *Hair* v *Prudential Assurance Co Ltd* [1983] 2 Lloyd's Rep 667 (fire).
On strict construction of this kind in the USA, see *Clark* v *Manufacturers'*, 8 How. 235 (1850—fire); *Wharton* v *Aetna Life*, 48 F 2d 37 (8 Cir, 1931—life), cert den 284 US 621; *Metts* v *Central Standard Life Ins Co*, 293 P 2d 621 (Cal, 1956—polio insurance); *Ashley* v *American Mutual Liability*, 167 F Supp 125 (ND Cal, 1958); *American Mutual Liability* v *Goff*, 281 F 2d 689 (9 Cir, 1960—liability), cert den 364 US 920; *Middlesex Mutual Assurance Co* v *Walsh*, 590 A 2d 957, 965 (Conn, 1991—motor).
88. *Byers* v *Pacific Mutual Life Ins Co*, 24 P 2d 829 (Cal, 1933—life).
89. *Business Men's Assurance* v *Campbell*, 32 F 2d 995 (8 Cir, 1929); in any event, the court found the life refusal non-material to accident cover. See also *Metropolitan Life Ins Co* v *Montreal Coal & Towing Co* (1904) 35 SCR 266 (life).
90. *Bradbury* v *London Guarantee & Accident Co Ltd* (1927) 40 CLR 127. See also *Revell* v *London General Ins Co Ltd* (1935) 50 Ll L Rep 114 (motor) and *Taylor* v *Eagle Star Ins Co Ltd* (1940) 67 Ll L Rep 136 (motor).
91. p 131.
92. *Akerhielm* v *De Mare* [1959] AC 789, 805 *per* Lord Jenkins (PC). In such a case the recipient's understanding will prevail, if the maker seeks specific performance of the contract: *New Brunswick & Canada Ry* v *Muggeridge* (1860) 1 D & S 363.
93. *Anderson* v *Pacific Fire & Marine Ins Co* (1869) 21 LT 408, 410 *per* Sir Joseph Napier (re).
94. *Golding* v *Royal London Auxiliary Ins Co Ltd* (1914) 30 TLR 350 (fire). See also *Business Men's Assurance* v *Campbell*, 32 F 2d 995 (8 Cir, 1929), discussed above, 22–2D2.

drug taking habits of the time and place.[95] The context may be that of the activity insured. For example, a representation, that the proposer of motor insurance does not have "defective vision", is true, even though he must wear spectacles to drive if, when he does wear them, his vision has been sufficiently enhanced or corrected for driving.[96]

22–2D4 True at the Time

A statement is true, if it is true when it is made[97] or if it will become true "so imminently that it did not really affect the accuracy of the answer that was given".[98] Conversely, it may be that a statement true when made is untrue (as a half truth), if the representor knows that it will become untrue in the near future. Certainly, it is treated as a false representation, if it becomes untrue before the contract is concluded: above, 22–2A2. If, however, it is true when the contract is made, unless it is also the subject of a continuing warranty,[99] its force is spent and, if it becomes untrue during the period of cover, the contract stands and the insured is not even obliged to notify the insurer.[100]

22–2E Three-quarter Truths: Substantial Truth

In marine insurance,[101] a "representation as to a matter of fact is true, if substantially true, if it be substantially correct, i.e., if the difference between what is represented and what is actually correct would not be considered material by a prudent insurer." The error must be material[102]; no account is taken of trivial errors. It has been suggested[103] that a similar rule applies to non-marine insurance.

For example, a material misstatement is made by the proposer of motor cover, who

---

95. *Thomson* v *Weems* (1884) 9 App Cas 671, 685 *per* Lord Blackburn (life)."Sober and temperate habits" in 1918 referred "only to the use or abuse of alcohol . . . not to the use of veronal or other soporific or narcotic drugs"—*Yorke* v *Yorkshire Ins Co Ltd* [1918] 1 KB 662, 666 *per* McCardie J (life).
96. *Austin* v *Zurich General Accident & Liability Ins Co Ltd* (1944) 77 Ll L Rep 409, 418 *per* Tucker J. The decision was affirmed [1945] KB 250 (CA), but this point was not appealed. Similarly, "convicted in connection with the driving of a motor vehicle" has been truthfully answered by reference to convictions involving careless driving, without reference to other convictions, which the court of the time did not consider relevant to care and skill as a driver, such as using a vehicle without an external mirror: *Revell* v *London General Ins Co Ltd* (1935) 50 Ll L Rep 114 (motor); or driving without a licence: *Taylor* v *Eagle Star Ins Co Ltd* (1940) 67 Ll L Rep 136 (motor); or driving without insurance cover: (*Revell* above).
97. *Laurentian Ins Co* v *Davidson* [1932] SCR 491 (fire). *De Camp* v *New Jersey Mutual Life Ins Co* (1873) F Cas No 3,719; *Mutual Benefit Life Ins Co* v *Higginbotham*, 95 US 380 (1877—life); *Zurich General Accident & Liability Ins Co* v *Flickinger*, 33 F 2d 853 (4 Cir, 1929—PA); *National Automobile Ins Co* v *Industrial Accident Commission*, 65 P 2d 128 (Cal, 1937—workmen's compensation); *Milbank Mutual Ins Co* v *Wentz*, 352 F 2d 592 (8 Cir, 1965—motor). Appleman, section 7309.
98. *Hair* v *Prudential Assurance Co Ltd* [1983] 2 Lloyd's Rep 667, 672 *per* Woolf J (fire).
99. Above, 20–5.
100. Unless, of course, the matter is material and must be disclosed on renewal; below, 23–4C.
101. MIA, section 20(4).
102. *Carter* v *Boehm* (1766) 3 Burr 1905, 1911 *per* Lord Mansfield (marine); *De Hahn* v *Hartley* (1786) 1 TR 343, 345 *per* Lord Mansfield (hull); *Newcastle Fire Ins Co* v *Macmorrow & Co* (1815) 3 Dow 255, 262 *per* Lord Eldon (HL—fire); *Re Universal Non-Tariff Fire Ins Co* (1875) LR 19 Eq 485, 493 *per* Malins V-C (fire).
  Buelli v *Connecticut Mutual Life Ins Co*, 4 F Cas No 2,104 (ND Ohio, 1877—life); *Carrolton Furniture Co* v *American Credit Indemnity Co*, 124 F 25 (2 Cir, 1903), *cert* den 192 US 605; *Zogg* v *Bankers' Life Co*, 62 F 2d 575 (4 Cir, 1933—life).
103. *Yorke* v *Yorkshire Ins Co Ltd* [1918] 1 KB 662, 669 *per* McCardie J (life). See also *Morrison* v *Muspratt* (1827) 4 Bing 60, 62 *per* Burrough J (life): "Advantage ought not to be taken of the omission of trifling circumstances". MacGillivray, No 592.

has been convicted of a motoring offence, but states that he has not. If, however, he states his conviction for speeding, but understates his speed or the amount of his fine by 5 per cent, it might be said that the representation (conviction) was material, but the untruth (by 5 per cent) was not and, hence, that the statement as a whole is not false.[104] The same has been held of a statement, that the vehicle will be used for business, when the proposer also intends to use it occasionally for recreation.[105] Again, it has been held that a statement, that the proposer has consulted a doctor on a stated number of occasions, is true, although it does not include visits in respect of "slight and temporary ailments which leave no trace of injury to health such as ordinary cold, inability to sleep because of occasional excesses".[106]

Substantial misstatements include a representation that a car, which in fact cost £271, cost £285.[107] However, courts are usually reluctant[108] to conclude that a statement of value is false, unless there is evidence of fraud or the true value is reasonably ascertainable with precision. One way out of that conclusion is to hold that, being incapable of precision, the statement of value was opinion,[109] not fact, and hence incapable of being a misrepresentation. In contrast, although an error in a Christian name might be thought trivial,[110] any error in a name, which makes it harder for the insurer to check records, is substantial.[111]

22–2F Half Truths

A statement which is literally true may be untrue because of what is left unsaid. It is untrue "when a person is asked how old he is, and he states, in answer, a number of years less than his true age. It is trifling to say that that is a true answer which requires something to be added to it to make it true".[112]

Examples include the response to a question about other insurance on the life, which mentions one policy but not another[113]; the answer to a question about previous

---

104. *Fowkes v Manchester & London Life Assurance & Loan Assn* (1863) 3 B & S 917, 924 *per* Blackburn J (life). However, in the case of insurance, the contract may still be avoided, if it can be said that the truth of the matter is relevant to the moral hazard.

105. *Dawson v Mercantile Mutual Ins Co Ltd* [1932] VLR 380, 386 (motor): "purpose" was held to mean "principal purpose".

106. *New York Life Ins Co v Levin*, 102 F 2d 403, 405-406 (8 Cir, 1939—life). See also *Zogg v Bankers' Life Co*, 62 F 2d 575 (4 Cir, 1933—life); *Metropolitan Life Ins Co v Goldberger*, 155 NYS 2d 305 (1956—life); *Cohen v Penn Mutual Life Ins Co*, 312 P 2d 241 (Cal, 1957—life); *Boulez v Continental Casualty Co*, 454 F 2d 85 (1 Cir, 1972—PHI).

107. *Allen v Universal Automobile Ins Co Ltd* (1933) 45 Ll L Rep 55, 58 *per* Lord Wright (motor).

108. For example, *Laidlaw v Liverpool & London Ins Co* (1867) 13 Gr 377 (fire). *St Paul Fire & Marine Insurance Co v St Clair*, 193 So 2d 821 (La, 1966—fire).

109. For example, *Hinson v British American Assurance Co*, 43 F Supp 951 (WD La, 1942—fire).

110. *Dawsons v Bonnin Ltd* [1922] 2 AC 413, 425 *per* Viscount Haldane (fire).

111. *Galle Gowns Ltd v Licenses & General Ins Co Ltd* (1933) 47 Ll L Rep 186 (fire).

112. *Cazenove v British Equitable Assurance Co* (1860) 29 LJ CP 160, 160 *per* Pollock CB (life). See also *Railway Passengers Assurance Co v Standard Life Assurance Co* (1921) 65 DLR 470 (Sup Ct—fidelity).

113. *Wainwright v Bland* (1836) 1 M & W 32 (life); *London Assurance v Mansel* (1879) 11 Ch D 363 (life).

accidents[114] or fires[115] or medical treatment,[116] which mentions one occasion but not others; the answer to a question about previous policies[117] or declinatures,[118] which mentions one but not others; and the answer to a question about past business, which gives one name under which the proposer has traded but not another.[119] Each case may be seen as one of non-disclosure or as one of disclosure by an answer which is false, as it carries an untrue implication that it is a complete answer to the question concerned.[120]

22–3 INDUCEMENT

22–3A Materiality

The representation must have been such as would affect the judgment of a reasonable man[121] which, in the typical insurance case, means the prudent insurer. The insurer may have a remedy for misrepresentation, whether or not it was material to loss which is the subject of dispute between insured and insurer.[122] For example, in 1874 Blackburn J stated that excessive valuation of the property to be insured "not only may lead to suspicion of foul play, but . . . has a direct tendency to make the assured less careful".[123] In 1988 a Californian court agreed: "it increases the risk, provides an inducement to fraud" and, the court added, it "changes the object of the insurance from indemnity to an outright gamble at stakes greatly favoring the insured".[124] So, a mis-

---

114. *Reid & Co Ltd* v *Employers' Accident & Livestock Ins Co Ltd*, 1899 1 F 1031 (Ct Sess—employers' liability); *Dent* v *Blackmore* (1927) 29 Ll L Rep 9 (motor).

115. *Condogianis* v *Guardian Assurance Co* [1921] 2 AC 125 (PC—fire); applied as regards fire history by the Supreme Court of South Australia in *Sheldon* v *Sun Alliance Australia Ltd* (1990) 53 SASR 97, 115 (fire). See also *Western Assurance Co* v *Harrison* (1903) 33 SCR 473 (fire). In contrast, a statement about the past losses of a partnership is not rendered false by omission of the past losses of the partners as individuals: *Davies* v *National Fire & Marine Ins Co of New Zealand* [1891] AC 485, 490 *per* Lord Hobhouse (PC—fire); as a matter of strict construction of the proposal against the insurer, this would seem to be correct, as the questions were limited to the history of the "proposer". Cf *Locker & Woolf Ltd* v *Western Australian Ins Co Ltd* [1936] 1 KB 408 (CA—fire).

116. *Cazenove* (above).

117. *Dent* (above).

118. *Broad & Montague Ltd* v *SE Lancashire Ins Co Ltd* (1931) 40 Ll L Rep 328 (motor). See also *Holt's Motors Ltd* v *SE Lancashire Ins Co Ltd* (1930) 35 Com Cas 281 (CA—motor), in which a negative reply to a question about declinature was false, in view of a previous refusal to renew.

119. *Galle Gowns Ltd* v *Licenses & General Ins Co Ltd* (1933) 47 Ll L Rep 186 (fire).

120. An illustration of the interchange of half-truth and non-disclosure is *Rozanes* v *Bowen* (1928) 32 Ll L Rep 98: the proposer of burglary insurance declared a small loss, but not two larger losses. The CA decided for the insurer on the ground of non-disclosure of the latter, but Sankey LJ observed that the declaration (of the smaller loss) was "not a correct one" (p 104).

121. *McDowell* v *Fraser* (1779) 1 Doug 260, 261 *per* Lord Mansfield; *Smith* v *Chadwick* (1882) 20 Ch D 27, 44–45 *per* Jessel MR (CA); *Mathias* v *Yetts* (1882) 46 LT 497, 502 *per* Jessell MR (CA). Treitel, p 301; Appleman, section 7294. *Dodge* v *Western Fire Ins Co (No 2)* (1912) 6 DLR 355 (Alta—fire); *Clarke* v *British Empire Ins Co (No 2)* (1912) 6 DLR 355 (Alta—stallion); *Taylor* v *London Assurance Corp* [1935] SCR 422 (fire), applying Lord Blackburn in *Smith* v *Chadwick* (1884) 9 App Cas 187, 195–197.

122. *New York Life Ins Co* v *Wittman*, 813 F Supp 1287 (ND Ohio, 1993—disability); but it has been argued that in practice courts only rescind for misrepresentation when there is a causal relationship between the misrepresentation and loss claimed: McDowell, 16 Conn L Rev 513, 527 (1984).

123. *Ionides* v *Pender* (1874) LR 9 QB 531, 538–539 (re).

124. *Hartford Ins Co* v *Garvey* 1989 AMC 652, 660 (yacht) with reference *inter alia* to Arnould. Cf *Evora* v *Henry*, 559 A 2d 1038, 1040 (1989—fire): although a house bought for 33,000 dollars was represented to have been bought for 50,000 dollars, the Supreme Court of Rhode Island held that the misrepresentation was not material, as the insurer would have accepted the application anyway.

representation of this kind grounds rescission, whether or not any insured loss has occurred or whether there was any connection between the misrepresentation and the loss.

The requirement of materiality has been doubted[125] and, indeed, in some cases the issue may became lost[126] in that of inducement in fact[127] (below, 22–3B). On the one hand, "if a man has a material misstatement made to him which may, from its nature, induce him to enter into the contract, it is an inference that he is induced to enter the contract by it".[128] On the other hand, a court which thinks that no reasonable man would have been affected by the representation in question (materiality), may proceed from the supposition that the particular recipient was a reasonable man, and infer that his judgment was not actually affected and that, therefore, it did not induce him to contract. Further, it is inherent in the meaning of representation of "fact", that it is reasonable for the recipient to rely on the statement (above, 22–2B2) so, in the modern law materiality, as a distinct requirement of inducement, appears to be superfluous. Even proponents of the rule of materiality concede two exceptions to it.

First, materiality is not required in a case of fraudulent misrepresentation.[129] Second, any statement is material, if the contract says so. Insurance provides a notable example of this rule. A provision, the "basis clause", that the statements of the proposer in the proposal form shall be the basis of the contract of insurance, a provision inserted by insurers to obviate the need to prove materiality of misrepresentation,[130] has precisely that effect. It converts the proposer's representation into a term (warranty) of the contract itself for which materiality is irrelevant: see 20–2A1.

22–3B Inducement in Fact

If the materiality of the representation is established (above, 22–3A), the effect is a presumption that the recipient (as a reasonable man) was indeed influenced by it, i.e., that there was inducement in fact.[131] It is then open to the representor to rebut that presumption, but the onus of proof is on him. This he may do in various ways, as follows.

22–3B1 Recipient Unaware

If the maker of the representation can prove that the representation did not reach the mind of the "recipient", i.e., that of the person responsible for contracting the insurance, it does not induce the contract.

---

125. For example, Goff & Jones, p 168.
126. For example, *Smith* v *Chadwick* (1884) 9 App Cas 187.
127. For example, Anson, p 214.
128. *Mathias* v *Yetts* (1882) 46 LT 497, 502 *per* Lord Jessel MR (CA). Carter, *Unequal Bargaining* (1991), p 82.
129. *Smith* v *Kay* (1859) 7 HLC 750.
130. *Anderson* v *Fitzgerald* (1853) 4 HLC 484, 503 *per* Lord Cranworth LC (life); *Stebbing* v *Liverpool & London & Globe Ins Co Ltd* [1917] 2 KB 433, 437 *per* Viscount Reading CJ (burglary).
131. *Redgrave* v *Hurd* (1881) 20 Ch D 1, 21 *per* Lord Jessell MR (CA), applied by Waller J in *Pan Atlantic Ins Co Ltd* v *Pine Top Insurance Co Ltd* [1992] 1 Lloyd's Rep 101, 112–113 (re), affirmed [1993] 1 Lloyd's Rep 496 (CA). See also *The Moonacre* [1992] 2 Lloyd's Rep. 501, 521 *per* Deputy Judge Colman (yacht). Appleman, section 7296.

22–3B2 Independent Judgement

If the maker can prove that the recipient, although aware of the representation, did not allow it to influence his judgement, there is no inducement in fact.

If, for example, a statement is made by the proposer on a matter of common knowledge, on which the insurer has no reason to think himself less informed than the proposer, there is *prima facie* no inducement,[132] as the insurer does not rely on the statement. If the proposer represents to the insurer that he is in good health, but the insurer relies solely on a medical report,[133] there is no inducement by the proposer. If the insurer's agent relies solely on his personal knowledge of the risk, there is no inducement.[134] If the proposer's representation is patently false, again there is no inducement.[135]

However, the degree of inducement required by the law is very slight (below, 22–3C), so, the argument, that the insurer was unaffected by what was said by the proposer, is hard to sustain. Moreover, an investigation of the risk by the insurer does not necessarily rule out all collateral reliance by the insurer on representations made by the proposer.

"The mere fact that in order to test the truth of the representations some independent inquiry is made, which necessarily is really in the nature of a fishing expedition rather than a systematic search that will necessarily reveal the truth if carried out with reasonable thoroughness, does not indicate lack of reliance; to hold so would enable a liar who falsifies facts peculiarly within his own knowledge to subject an insurance company to an unconscionable squeeze play: if the company makes any independent checks he would claim that it isn't 'relying' and thus the policy is not voidable . . . the only alternative for the company would be to indicate 100 per cent faith and reliance by making no investigation whatsoever, at the risk of having a court later determine that inconsistencies in the application or information otherwise brought to their attention should have caused them to make at least such an inquiry as a prudent man would have made."[136]

22–3C The Degree of Inducement[137]

The degree of inducement required by the law appears to be slight. The general law of contract suggests that it is enough that the representation was "actively present" to the mind of the representee,[138] when he decided to make the contract of insurance. On this basis, little or no causal connection is required between the misrepresentation and the making of the contract; however, that was said in a case of fraud, in which the

---

132. *Smith* v *Land & House Property Corp* (1884) 28 Ch D 7, 15 *per* Bowen LJ (CA).
133. *Franklin Life Ins Co* v *Champion & Co*, 350 F 2d 115 (6 Cir, 1965—life).
134. *Kinman* v *Ocean Accident & Guarantee Assn* (1913) 12 DLR 364 (BC—PA).
135. For example, the proposer who makes a misrepresentation, say, that he suffers from no physical infirmity, when the untruth of that statement is manifest to the insurer's agent. If the knowledge of the latter can be attributed to the insurer, the contract cannot be avoided for misrepresentation or non-disclosure: see *Bawden*, discussed above, 10–3A. *New York Life Ins Co* v *Strudel*, 243 F 2d 90 (5 Cir, 1957—life); *Apperson* v *United States Fidelity & Guarantee Co*, 318 F 2d 438 (5 Cir, 1963—motor); *Greene* v *United Mutual Life Ins Co*, 238 NYS 2d 809 (1963—life), affirmed 258 NYS 2d 323; *Parker Precision Products Co* v *Metropolitan Life Ins Co*, 407 F 2d 1070 (3 Cir, 1969—life).
136. *New York Life Ins Co* v *Strudel*, 243 F 2d 90, 93–94 (5 Cir, 1957—life). See also *Apperson* v *United States Fidelity & Guarantee Co*, 318 F 2d 438 (5 Cir, 1963—motor); *Parker Precision Products Co* v *Metropolitan Life Ins Co*, 407 F 2d 1070 (3 Cir, 1969—life).
137. See also the discussion of the related problem in connection with non-disclosure of material information: below, 23–7. Appleman, section 7294.
138. *Edgington* v *Fitzmaurice* (1885) 29 Ch D 459, 483 *per* Bowen LJ (CA).

court was little inclined to favour the defendant. As regards the degree of inducement, there are broadly four possibilities.

Type A is a misrepresentation such that, if the recipient had known the truth, he would not have made the contract at all. Some cases require type A.[139] For example, in *Evora v Henry*,[140] the Supreme Court of Rhode Island rejected a defence based on misrepresentation, because, it found, the insurer would have accepted the application even if the correct purchase price of the property to be insured had appeared on the insurance application. This is unlikely to be the decision in England. Even in early cases, in which a stricter test of materiality can be found, Blackburn J said that excessive valuation was material, for it "not only may lead to suspicion of foul play, but . . . has a direct tendency to make the assured less careful".[141]

Type B is a misrepresentation such that, if the recipient had known the truth, he would still have been willing to make the contract, but only on different terms,[142] notably but not only as to premium.

Type C is a misrepresentation such that, although it was relevant to the decision to contract, if the recipient had known the truth, he would still have made the contract and on the same terms.

Type D is a misrepresentation which, as regards the degree of inducement, might be placed between Type B and Type C. For example, in Missouri,[143] the "test of materiality is whether if stated truthfully the answer might reasonably influence an insurer to reject a risk or charge a higher premium"—a test which can be distinguished from one which asks whether it "would reasonably influence" an insurer.[144]

It is Type C that is the rule of English law, although not that of other countries, if the contract is to be avoided for non-disclosure: below, 23–7. It would be odd if an insurance contract could be avoided for a lesser degree of (passive) non-disclosure

139. Perhaps *Horry v Tate & Lyle Refineries Ltd* [1982] 2 Lloyd's Rep 416, 422 *per* Peter Pain J: "it has to be a factor without which the plaintiff would not have entered into" the contract. See also to this effect as regards misstatements about title or in a prospectus: Lord Romilly in *Jennings v Broughton* (1853) 17 Beav 234, 239 and *Pulsford v Richards* (1853) 17 Beav 87, 96; also Lord Chelmsford LC in *Re Royal British Bank* (1859) 3 De G & J 387, 422. *Vebeliunas v American National Fire Ins Co*, 549 NYS 2d 60 (1989—fire).

140. 559 A 2d 1038, 1040 (1989—fire): a house purchased for 33,000 dollars was stated to have been purchased for 50,000 dollars. *Idem: Knight v US Fire Insurance Co*, 651 F Supp 471 (SDNY, 1986—cargo): *Kentucky Central Life Ins Co v Jones*, 797 F Supp 53 (MD Tenn, 1992—life); *Utah Power & Light Co v Federal Ins Co*, 983 F 2d 1549, 1555 (10 Cir, 1993—liability).

141. *Ionides v Pender* (1874) LR 9 QB 531, 538–539 (re). See above, 22–3A.

142. There is some support for this position in *Re Universal Non-Tariff Fire Ins Co* (1875) LR 19 Eq 485, 493–493 *per* Malins VC (fire); and *Industrial Properties (Barton Hill) Ltd v AEI Ltd* [1977] QB 580, 597 *per* Lord Denning MR (CA).

Carrollton Furniture Co v American Credit & Indemnity Co, 124 F 25 (2 Cir, 1903), cert den 192 US 605; *Mutual Benefit Life Ins Co v JMR Electronics Corp*, 848 F 2d 30 (2 Cir, 1988—life); *William Penn Life Ins Co v Sands*, 912 F 2d 1359, 1361 (11 Cir, 1990—life); *Parker v Prudential Ins Co*, 900 F 2d 772, 778 (4 Cir, 1990—life); *New York Life Ins Co v Johnson*, 923 F 2d 279, 282 (3 Cir, 1991—life); *Massachusetts Mutual Life Ins Co v Manzo*, 584 A 2d 190, 195 (NJ, 1991—life); *Borden v Paul Revere Life Ins Co*, 935 F 2d 370, 377 (1 Cir, 1991—disability); *Bageanis v American Bankers Life Assurance Co*, 783 F Supp 1141, 1145 (ND Ill, 1992—life); *Goodwin v Investors Life Ins Co*, 419 SE 2d 766, 769 (NC, 1992—life); *Genovia v Jackson National Life Ins Co*, 795 F Supp 1036, 1041 (D Hawaii, 1992—life); *Wohlman v Paul Revere Life Ins Co*, 980 F 2d 283 (5 Cir, 1992—disability); *Berger v Manhattan Life Ins Co*, 805 F Supp 1097 (SD NY, 1992—life); *National Union Fire Ins Co v Sahlen*, 807 F Supp 743 (SD Fla, 1992—liability); *Saint Calle v Prudential Ins Co*, 815 F Supp 679 (SD NY, 1993—life); *Fidelity Federal Savings & Loan Assn v Felicetti*, 813 F Supp 332 (ED Pa, 1993—fidelity).

143. *Galvan v Cameron Mutual Ins*, 733 SW 2d 771, 773 (Mo, 1987—fire) (emphasis added). In that case, however, the misrepresentation was of type A.

144. *Meeker v Shelter Mutual Ins Co*, 766 SW 2d 733, 743 (Mo, 1989—fire), which concerned misrepresentation or non-disclosure of previous fire losses.

than of (active) misrepresentation, and this suggests that the minimum degree of inducement required by English law should be the same[145] in each case: Type C. If so, the possibility of avoidance on trivial grounds overshadows the contract, and like the similar rule for non-disclosure, is a subject of controversy. In actions for damages for deceit[146] or negligent misstatement,[147] the general law requires that loss should have been caused by the misstatement and, in effect, requires either inducement Type A or inducement Type B. Moreover, the general law on misrepresentation suggests that, when the courts state that the misrepresentation must be an inducement, it must be causal,[148] that is to say, that it must be of Type A or Type B: but for the misrepresentation the person misled would not have made the contract at all or, at least, not on the same terms.[149] If "he would have entered the contract even had he known the true facts", the person's mind was not "affected" and the misrepresentation is not an inducement.[150] This, it is submitted, is the better view but not, it must be conceded, the view that can be said with any confidence to reflect the current state of English law as regards insurance contracts.

22–3D The Negligent Recipient

In the general law of contract in England, it is irrelevant that the representee was careless in not discovering the untruth of the representation.[151] However, in the case of the careless insurer, the court may find that the insurer was not induced in fact or has waived the matter: below, 23–13A.

In the United States, if the insurer has facts, which should put him on inquiry about the truth of the misrepresentation, and if diligent inquiry would have revealed that the representation was untrue, courts have held the insurer to be estopped in equity from asserting the misrepresentation as a ground of rescission,[152] unless the misrepresentation was fraudulent.[153] Estoppel presupposes reliance by the proposer, which lies in his not obtaining alternative insurance.[154] Commonly, the insurer is put on inquiry by inconsistencies in the statements emanating from the proposer; but the insurer will also be put on inquiry, if a statement in the proposal form is inconsistent with other

---

145. In this sense: *Pan Atlantic Ins Co Ltd* v *Pine Top Ins Co Ltd* [1992] 1 Lloyd's Rep 101, 112 *per* Waller J (re), affirmed [1993] 1 Lloyd's Rep 496 (CA). An appeal to the House of Lords is to be heard in February 1994.

146. *Smith* v *Chadwick* (1884) 9 App Cas 187, 195–196 *per* Lord Blackburn.

147. *JEB Fasteners Ltd* v *Marks Bloom & Co* [1981] 3 All ER 289 (CA).

148. *Edgington* v *Fitzmaurice* (1885) 29 Ch D 459, 467 *per* Denman J; and 483 *per* Bowen LJ (CA). The misrepresentation must be of a nature to induce the representee "to alter his position": Bower, Representation, nos 137 ff. *Idem*: Halsbury, vol 31 no 1079.

149. *Pulsford* v *Richards* (1853) 17 Beav 87, 96 *per* Sir John Romilly; *Edgington* v *Fitzmaurice* (1885) 29 Ch D 459, 481 *per* Cotton LJ (CA); *The Siboen* [1976] 1 Lloyd's Rep 293, 324 *per* Kerr J; *Horry* v *Tate & Lyle Refineries Ltd* [1982] 2 Lloyd's Rep 416, 422 *per* Peter Pain J.

150. *Chitty on Contracts* (26th ed. by A.G. Guest and others, 1989) no 425.

151. *Redgrave* v *Hurd* (1881) 20 Ch D 1 (CA). *Cf McInerny* v *Lloyds Bank Ltd* [1974] 1 Lloyd's Rep 246, 254 *per* Lord Denning MR (CA): an action based on a negligent misstatement will fail, if the plaintiff recipient has himself been negligent, by analogy with the cases requiring intermediate examination of goods, such as *Lambert* v *Lewis* [1982] AC 225.

152. *Columbian National Life Ins Co* v *Rodgers*, 116 F 2d 705 (10 Cir, 1940—life), cert den 313 US 561; *Variety Homes Inc* v *Postal Life Ins Co*, 287 F 2d 320 (2 Cir, 1961—life); *Apperson* v *United States Fidelity & Guarantee Co*, 318 F 2d 438 (5 Cir, 1963—motor); *Greene* v *United Mutual Life Ins Co*, 238 NYS 2d 809 (1963—life), affirmed 258 NYS 2d 323.

153. *Koral Industries* v *Security–Connecticut Life Ins Co*, 802 SW 2d 650 (Tex, 1990—life).

154. *World Ins Co* v *Pipes*, 255 F 2d 464 (5 Cir, 1958—PHI).

information in the insurer's possession.[155] In the absence of circumstances putting the insurer on inquiry, he is not bound to check or investigate the proposer's statements.[156] For example, if it appears that past illness has been successfully treated,[157] the insurer is not obliged to investigate. "An insurance company has the right to rely on the truthfulness of the answers given by an insurance applicant" concerning his health record, and is not obliged to check the relevant hospital records.[158]

In England, the courts are unlikely to go this far, less likely, in particular, to find that the insurer is put on inquiry to this degree by inconsistencies in the proposer's statements.[159] However, many of the situations, in which the insurer might be estopped in the United States, could be seen as cases of waiver in England: below 23–13.

22–4 REMEDIES

The remedies for misrepresentation are damages, rescission or both. The remedy usually sought is rescission: avoidance of the contract of insurance. These remedies are common to both misrepresentation and non-disclosure and are discussed below, 23–14 ff.

---

155. For example, information that the proposer has been declined or loaded by another insurer: *Rodgers* (above). However, knowledge that the proposer has lied on one matter does not necessarily put the insurer on inquiry as regards all other statements by the proposer: *Provident Life & Accident Ins Co* v *Hawley*, 123 F 2d 479 (4 Cir, 1941—life).
156. *Apperson* v *US Fidelity & Guarantee Co* 318 F 2d 438 (5 Cir, 1963—motor); *Apolskis* v *Concord Life Ins Co*, 445 F 2d 31 (7 Cir, 1971—life).
157. *Michael* v *World Ins Co*, 254 F 2d 663 (6 Cir, 1958—life); *Variety Homes Inc* v *Postal Life Ins Co*, 287 F 2d 320 (2 Cir, 1961—life). See also *Arcese* v *Equitable Life Assurance Sy*, 223 NYS 2d 95 (1961—life). *Cf Cherkes* v *Postal Life Ins Co*, 138 NYS 2d 788 (1955—life), affirmed 132 NE 2d 328.
158. *Commercial Life Ins Co* v *Lone Star Life Ins Co*, 727 F Supp 467, 471 (ND Ill, 1989—health).
159. *Cf Panchaud Frères SA* v *Etablissements General Grain Co* [1971] 1 Lloyd's Rep 53 (CA).

PART I: NON-DISCLOSURE

23–1 INTRODUCTION

It is customary to discuss misrepresentation and non-disclosure separately, however, the line between the two may be barely discernible, for example, in the case of misrepresentation by half truth. The custom of separate discussion is followed in this book, except that the remedies, notably rescission, are so similar that they are considered together: below, 23–14 ff.

23–1A The Nature and Justification of the Rule

The basic rule, which is broadly the same in all branches of insurance,[1] is that the proposer is obliged to disclose to the insurer at the time of making (or remaking) the contract of insurance all material information affecting the risk.

Breach of the duty is sometimes called concealment—in early English insurance literature[2] and, especially, in current decisions in the United States. In English law, unlike that in parts of the United States,[3] the duty may be broken, even though the proposer is innocent; so, breach is referred to in this book as non-disclosure.

The duty is part, the most important part, of the general duty of good faith.[4] The

---

1. *London Assurance* v *Mansel* (1879) 11 Ch D 363, 367 *per* Jessell MR (life). The law is the same for reinsurance: *Sun Mutual* v *Ocean*, 107 US 485 (1883); *General Reinsurance* v *Southern Surety*, 27 F 2d 265 (8 Cir, 1928). The rule has also been applied to contracts of suretyship: *London General Omnibus* v *Holloway* [1912] 2 KB 72 (CA); but *cf Seaton* v *Burnand* [1899] 1 QB 782, 793 *per* Romer LJ (CA); *Re Denton's Estate* [1904] 2 Ch 178, 188 *per* Vaughan Williams LJ (CA).
   For a short essay on this topic in comparative law, see Rudden (1991) 1 Ins L & P 45. On the history of the duty of disclosure, see Holmes, 39 U Pittsburgh L R 381, 409 ff (1978). For requirements of disclosure in the general law of England, see Spencer Bower, Turner and Sutton, *The Law relating to Actionable Non-Disclosure* (2nd ed, 1990), ch 1–6 and 14. On concealment (non-disclosure) in the United States, see Appleman, sections 7271 ff; Williston, Vol 7, sections 502 ff. On this question in Canada, see Brown & Menezes, 5:2:1 ff. Although the matter has a common law base, the practical duty of disclosure in Canada has been modified by statutes governing particular classes of insurance. Examples are the Fire Insurance Policy Act 1876, Statutory Condition 1. As regards motor, PA insurance and PHI, states have similar statutes regulating this matter. "The courts have done little to modify this piecemeal pattern": Baer, 22 Ottawa L Rev 389, 405 (1990). It is marine insurance, also governed by statute, which is nearest to English law: Brown & Menezes, 5:3:41 ff.
2. For example, Park, *Marine Ins* (5th ed, 1802), ch 10.
3. See below, 23–8E and 23–17A. This is one factor that helps to account for the relative infrequence of litigation in the United States on non-disclosure.
4. *Seaton* v *Burnand* [1899] 1 QB 782, 792 *per* Romer LJ (CA—guarantee); *Greenhill* v *Federal Ins* [1927] 1 KB 65, 76 *per* Scrutton LJ. (CA—cargo). Achampong, (1987) 36 Int & Comp L Q 327. *Cf* Matthews, *Foundations*, pp 39 ff. *Mutual Life* v *Hilton-Green*, 241 US 613 (1916—life). If the insured is an insurance agent contracting with his own company, it has been said that his duty of good faith is higher than for other people: *Schrader* v *Prudential*, 280 F 2d 355 (1960—life). On the general duty of good faith, see chapter 27 (below).

duty of disclosure is justified on the basis of the assumption that the insured has the advantage of information. "Insurance is a contract of speculation. The special facts upon which the contingent chance is to be computed lie most commonly in the knowledge of the insured only; the underwriter trusts to his representation, and proceeds upon confidence that he does not keep back any circumstance . . . "[5] The duty is said to be necessary for the protection of insurers.[6]

The legal basis of the duty has been said to be an implied term in the contract of insurance. While this analysis has been rejected in recent cases,[7] it has impressive support in precedent[8] and no alternative has received universal recognition. Alternatives include some kind of fiduciary basis[9] or simply *lex specialis*.[10] Whatever the true basis of the duty, it is "an incident of the contract of insurance",[11] as well as reinsurance,[12] and a duty that does not apply between insurer and assignee of the benefit of the insur-

5. *Carter* v *Boehm* (1766) 3 Burr 1905, 1909 *per* Lord Mansfield. See also *London General Omnibus* v *Holloway* [1912] 2 KB 72, 86 *per* Kennedy LJ (CA—surety); *Rozanes* v *Bowen* (1928) 32 Ll L Rep 98, 102 *per* Scrutton LJ (CA—jewellers' block); *Greenhill* v *Federal* [1927] 1 KB 65, 77 *per* Scrutton LJ (CA—cargo). *Hare & Chase* v *National Surety*, 60 F 2d 909 (2 Cir, 1932—guarantee).

6. *Re Yager* (1912) 108 LT 38, 45 *per* Channell J (fire).

7. *Merchants' & Manufacturers' Ins Co* v *Charles & John Hunt* [1941] 1 KB 295, 313 *per* Scott LJ (CA—motor); *March Cabaret Club & Casino* v *London Assurance* [1975] 1 Lloyd's Rep 169, 175 *per* May J (fire); *Good Luck* [1990] 1 QB 818 (CA); *Banque Financière de la Cité SA* v *Westgate Ins Co Ltd* [1990] 1 QB 665, 777 *per* Slade LJ (CA), affirmed on other grounds [1991] 2 AC 249; *Pryke* v *Gibbs Hartley Cooper Ltd* [1991] 1 Lloyd's Rep 602, 615 *per* Waller J (re). *Saunders* v *Queensland Ins Co Ltd* (1931) 45 CLR 557 (HCA—fire); *Ogden & Co Pty Ltd* v *Reliance Fire Sprinkler Co Pty Ltd* [1975] 1 Lloyd's Rep 52 (HCA—liability); *Khoury* v *Govt Ins Office* (1984) 58 ALJR 502 (HCA).

Objections to basing the duty on an implied term are (i) that it is strained analysis. It could hardly be a genuine implied term, such as the nature of the contract implicitly requires (*Liverpool CC* v *Irwin* [1977] AC 239), for it should also be something so obvious that it goes without saying (*Shirlaw* v *Southern Foundries (1926) Ltd* [1939] 2 KB 206, 227 *per* Mackinnon LJ): most insureds would be most surprised at what the law tells them that they had meant but left unsaid. If it is to be an implied term, it will be a term implied by the courts to effect policy, judicial legislation (see G L Williams (1945) 61 LQR 401); (ii) *Ex hypothesi* the (contractual) term requiring disclosure comes into existence at a time after it has or has not been performed by the proposer: Bower, *Disclosure*, 2.01. It is possible to explain this as a warranty that you are in the position now of having done something in the past. Alternatively, the disclosure promise might be part of a contract collateral to the insurance contract. Again, this is said to be strained analysis.

8. For example *Blackburn Low & Co* v *Vigors* (1886) 17 QBD 553, 578 *per* Lindley LJ, 583 *per* Lopes LJ; (CA—1887) 12 App Cas 531, 539 *per* Lord Watson (re); *Jester-Barnes* v *Licenses & General* (1934) 49 LLR 231, 234–5 *per* Mackinnon J (motor); *The Litsion Pride* [1985] 1 Lloyd's Rep 437, 518–519 *per* Hirst J, whose opinion may be limited to the operation of the duty of good faith during the currency of the contract of insurance. See also *The Good Luck* [1988] 1 Lloyd's Rep 514, 547 *per* Hobhouse J (hull).

Arnould based the duty of disclosure on an implied term from the 2nd ed (1850) to the 12th ed (1939), para 780. It was also the view of other distinguished writers: Devlin, *The Enforcement of Morals* (Oxford, 1965), 45; Shawcross, *The Law of Motor Insurance* (2nd ed, 1948) p 645; Welford and Otter–Barry, *The Law Relating to Fire Insurance* (4th ed, 1948) p 5.

9. Matthews, *Foundations*, pp 39 ff. There are obvious attractions in bringing rogue doctrines back into established categories. However, this suggestion should be greeted cautiously. First, case support is confined to decisions in the United States concerned with punitive damages against insurers, or the conflict of interest that might arise when the insurer has a duty to defend. The invitation to follow courts that speak in this regard (for example *Gruenberg* v *Aetna Ins Co*, 510 P 2d 452 (Cal, 1979)) of "a cause of action in tort for breach of an implied covenant of good faith" is likely to meet with little enthusiasm in England: below, 30–10. Second, insurance contracts have in the past been cited as contracts *uberrima fidei* and distinguished from contracts between persons in fiduciary relationship: for example, Anson, pp 231 ff. Whereas both categories give rise to a duty of disclosure, the reason is said to be different. In the case of fiduciaries, it is said to stem from the equity of the special relationship of confidence. In the case of contracts of insurance, where no such relationship normally exists, it is said to stem from an imbalance of information.

10. Rudden, *Disclosure in Insurance: the Changing Scene* in Lectures on the Common Law, vol. 3 (Deventer 1991), p 1, 2.

11. *The Good Luck* [1988] 1 Lloyd's Rep 514, 546 *per* Hobhouse J (hull), affirmed [1989] 2 Lloyd's Rep 238 (CA), reversed on another ground [1992] 1 AC 233.

12. Butler & Merkin A.6.1.

ance[13] or between primary and excess insurer.[14] It has been suggested that the rule should apply differently between sophisticated parties[15] such as insurer and reinsurer and, in particular, that they should be able to bargain for the appropriate level of disclosure. To a degree, this is what happens: the application of the duty of disclosure depends on sub-rules about constructive knowledge (23–8 and 23–9) and waiver (23–12 and 23–13) and these matters are under the control of the parties:

The rule requiring disclosure was undoubtedly necessary to protect insurers when the context was marine and the year 1800. Communications were slow and unreliable. It was usually impossible to inspect the subject-matter or the scene of the risk. The insured usually knew much more about both. "In Lord Mansfield's time marine underwriting was a precarious infant industry, an important factor in the development of British overseas trade."[16] Today this is less true.[16a] It is not obvious to the consumer why, if he sells a car, he is not obliged to promise the buyer anything at all about the car but, if he insures the same car, he effectively guarantees all manner of things to the insurer.

"The basic policy premise in favor of maintaining the doctrine of [non-disclosure] is that insurance premiums are made commensurate with the risks undertaken, and that the selection and control of risks is therefore essential to the successful operation of the insurance enterprise. In as much as the nature of contractual subject matter is significant in adjusting the price term of most contracts, this is actually a statement that this type of contract is a special one, probably on the grounds that the insurance business is vital in modern social and economic equations, and therefore should be given extraordinary protection. This position becomes doubtful under careful scrutiny . . . [T]here is no provable basis for saying that insurance contracts are more important than brokerage contracts, or sales contracts . . . In recognizing the well-founded principle that premiums must be commensurate with the risk, it must not be forgotten that there are several principles operating in competition. Generally speaking, a promisor is under a duty to perform his contractual obligations even though he has made a bad bargain . . . [D]iscouragement of investigation by the insurer removes a factor which could materially improve the insurer's evaluation of the risk."[17]

Investigation, however, costs money. Some matters are best ascertained by the insured[18] but others by the insurer. In any event, perhaps the consumer should be better informed about his position in law.[19]

23–1B Mutuality of the Duty of Disclosure

Lord Mansfield said[20] that the insurance "would equally be void, against the underwriter, if he concealed; as, if he insured a ship on her voyage, which he privately knew

---

13. *The Good Luck* (above). If the insurer breaches his duty of good faith to the insured, the assignee may benefit from the rights and remedies arising from the breach, but the duty remains a duty to the assignor/insured: pp 546 ff.

14. Below 27–1.

15. Thomas, 41 Duke LJ 1548, 1574 ff (1992).

16. Patterson, 34 Colum L Rev, 595, 621–622 (1934). See, for example *Barclay v Cousins* (1802) 2 East 544, 547 *per* Lawrence J (profits insurance). On the history of the duty of non-disclosure, see Davis (1991) 4 ILJ 71.

16a. In this sense: *PJ & J Mchale Ltd v SIGM* (1991) 6 ANZ Ins Cases, no 61–022 (NZ—fire).

17. Harnett, 15 *Law & Contemporary Problems*, 391, 408 (1950). The writer demonstrates how the contract of insurance might be governed by ordinary rules of the law of contract.

18. The insurer lacks the time and the opportunity to learn by inquiry: *London General Omnibus v Holloway* [1912] 2 KB 72, 86 *per* Kennedy LJ (CA—surety).

19. For general criticism of English law see Hasson, 32 MLR 615 (1969); Law Commission Report No 104.

20. *Carter v Boehm* (1766) Burr 1905, 1909.

to be arrived: an action would lie to cover the premium." From this it has been concluded that the duty of good faith,[21] which gives rise to the duty of disclosure, is a
reciprocal duty owed not only by the insured to the insurer but also by the insurer to
the insured[22]; for ease of reference, however, it is non-disclosure by the insured to
which this chapter refers, unless otherwise indicated.

It has been suggested[23] that, when he made the statement quoted, Lord Mansfield
was thinking only of facts decreasing the risk and not of facts increasing the risk, of
which the insurer but not the insured was aware. Although breach of duty by the
insurer has rarely been argued in the courts, it arose over 200 years after Lord Mansfield in *Banque Keyser Ullmann SA* v *Skandia (UK) Ins Co Ltd*.[24] Steyn J held that the
insurer owed a duty of disclosure to the insured. On appeal this part of his decision
was affirmed.[25] Just as the insured must disclose to the insurer any facts known to him
but not to the insurer which increase the risk, so also the insurer must disclose to the
insured any facts known to the insurer but not to the insured which reduce the risk.

Although the duty of disclosure is indeed reciprocal and is limited in each case to
information that is material, materiality may mean something different according to
whether the duty in issue is that of the insured or that of the insurer. As regards the
insurer, the duty was tested by Steyn J by asking whether "good faith and fair dealing
require disclosure?" But on appeal, Slade LJ said[26] that this test

"is not entirely satisfactory," for "in the case of commercial contracts, broad concepts of
honesty and fair dealing, however, laudable, are a somewhat uncertain guide when determining
the existence or otherwise of an obligation which might arise even in the absence of any dishonest or unfair intent . . . More importantly, in our judgment, it would be too broad a proposition to state [in the language of the Marine Insurance Act] that any fact is material if it is
'calculated to influence the decision of the insured to conclude the contract of insurance'. To
give one example, it might well be that in a particular case proposed insurers would be aware of
another reputable insurer who would be prepared to underwrite the same risk at a substantially
lower premium. In our judgment the mere existence of the relationship of insurers and insured
would not place on them the duty to inform the insured of this fact.[27] . . . [The duty, however,]
must at least extend to disclosing all facts known to him which are material either to the nature
of the risk sought to be covered or the recoverability of a claim under the policy which a prudent
insured would take into account in deciding whether to place the risk for which he seeks cover
with that insurer."

If the cover proposed does not adequately meet the needs of the proposer, the
insurer may well have reason to point this out to the proposer. However, failure to do
so does not breach the duty of disclosure or, indeed, any other duty owed by the
insurer, unless the proposer places his insurance needs in the hands of the insurer, the
insurer accepts that trust and the insurer's response falls short of what can reasonably

21. See below, chapter 27.
22. *Carter* v *Boehm* (1766) 3 Burr 1905, 1909 *per* Lord Mansfield. MIA, section 17. *Goldshlager* v *Royal Ins Co Ltd* (1978) 84 DLR (3d) 355, 365 (Ont, 1977—fire).
23. Butler [1987] Insurance & Reinsurance International, p 14.
24. [1987] 1 Lloyd's Rep 69.
25. [1990] 1 QB 665 (CA); [1991] 2 AC 249; Hudson [1991] LMCLQ 18. The decision of Steyn J, that the insurer could be liable to the insured in damages, was reversed: see below 23–15C.
26. p 772.
27. Cf *United Fire Ins Co* v *McClelland*, 780 P 2d 193 (1989—PHI) in which the Supreme Court of Nevada held that the insurer was in breach of the duty in failing to disclose its own financial difficulties to the insured. The breach gave rise to substantial damages, a remedy not open to the insured under English law, which would allow no more than recovery of premium paid: below 23–15C.

be expected. In South Carolina[28], for example, no such duty is owed by the insurer through his agent, unless the insured can prove that "(1) the agent received consideration beyond a mere payment of the premium; (2) the insured made a clear request for advice[29]; or (3) there is a course of dealing over an extended period of time which would put an objectively reasonable insurance agent on notice that his advice is being sought and relied on".[30] In general, however, and in the absence of such special circumstances, the insurer has no duty to advise the proposer about the suitability or scope of cover.[31]

23–1C Summary of the Rules Governing Non-Disclosure

To rescind the contract of insurance or raise the defence of non-disclosure the onus is on the insurer (below, 23–2) to prove non-disclosure (23–3) of material fact (23–5) which is known to the proposer (23–8) and which would influence the judgement of a prudent insurer (23–7).

Nonetheless, the plea of non-disclosure will fail in the the following cases:
- (a) The information was not disclosed because its disclosure was waived by the insurer; below, 23–12.
- (b) The information was not disclosed because it was a matter which the insurer could be presumed to know already; below, 23–9.
- (c) The information was not disclosed because it was a matter in which the insurer was insufficiently interested, because it diminished the risk; below, 23–10.
- (d) The information was disclosed, but the insurer made an error of judgement, perhaps not appreciating the significance of the information, and ignored it: he was not a prudent insurer; below, 23–6.
- (e) The information was disclosed and was of a type that would put the prudent insurer on inquiry to make further investigations; but the particular insurer made no inquiry; below, 23–13.

23–2 THE ONUS OF PROOF

The onus of proving on the balance of probabilities, that there has been non-disclosure of a material fact, is upon the insurer who alleges it.[32] This he does in a typical

---

28. *Trotter* v *State Farm Mutual Automobile Ins Co*, 377 SE 2d 343 (SC, 1988—motor); Frederick, 41 S Carolina L Rev 119 (1989).

29. Thus, if the insured applies for a specific kind of cover and the insurer responds with a particular policy, it has been held that the insurer is estopped from denying that the policy offers the cover applied for: *Standard Fire Ins Co* v *Marine Contracting & Towing Co*, 392 SE 2d 460 (SC, 1990—liability).

30. p 347, with case references omitted. Where a state insurer provides motor cover, an area of acute public interest, directly to the insured motorist, it may bear a heavier duty to advise or, at least, to provide information, than would a private insurer: *Fletcher* v *Manitoba Public Ins Co* (1990) 74 DLR (4th) 636, 655–656 *per* Wilson J (Sup Ct—motor).

31. *Nelson* v *Davidson*, 456 NW 2d 343 (Wis, 1990—motor). If, however, advice is sought and given, liability arises: above, 9–5C.

32. *Butcher* v *Dowlen* [1981] 1 Lloyd's Rep 310 (CA—motor). *Murphy* v *Sun Life Assurance Co of Canada* (1964) 44 DLR (2d) 369 (Alta—life). *Mercantile Mutual Ins Co* v *Folsom*, 18 Wall 237 (Sup Ct, 1873—hull).

case by proving that material information existed at the time of contract, that it was known to the insured, and that this information was not disclosed. As the onus is on the insurer, it is the insured who receives the benefit of any doubt.

In *Joel* v *Law Union*,[33] action was brought to enforce insurance on the life of Robina Morrison. The contract had been made after she had answered a list of questions put to her, together with explanation of the questions, by a doctor appointed by the insurer. In answer to a question "What medical men have you consulted?" she named two but did not name a third, who had treated her for a nervous breakdown. Fraud was negatived by the jury. *Prima facie* this was non-disclosure or misrepresentation by half-truth.[34] However, in the circumstances of the case, the Court of Appeal considered it necessary to ask whether the nature of the question or the scope of the duty of disclosure had been changed by any explanation of the question given by the insurer's doctor.[35] The evidence provided no answer. This being so, the court held that the insurer had not discharged the onus of proving non-disclosure or misrepresentation.

It is generally difficult to prove a negative, to prove that the insured did not disclose a material fact. If the only communication between insured and insurer is a standard proposal form, however, the insurer simply produces the form for the court to read and invites it to infer non-disclosure. When there have been multiple communications, proof is less easy. But the insurer is often helped by the judge who, having listened to the evidence, may be persuaded that the particular insurer is indeed a prudent and reasonable insurer who, if the matter had been disclosed to him, would have responded differently to the risk proposed.

In *Greenhill* v *Federal Ins Co*,[36] a pre-contract voyage was material to cargo insurance. Neither party had a clear recollection of what was said when the contract was negotiated. The agent of the insured argued that the fact was so material that he (as an honest broker) must have disclosed it. The insurer argued that the fact was so material that, if it had been disclosed, he (as a competent underwriter) would never have written the risk. Both Branson J and the Court of Appeal decided for the insurer. In the Court of Appeal, Scrutton LJ found[37] that "it is inconceivable to me that the ordinary rate of premium should be charged for a cargo as to which an underwriter knew" the relevant facts.

33. [1908] 2 KB 863. See also *Dawsons* v *Bonnin* [1922] 2 AC 313, 429 *per* Viscount Finlay (motor); *Cornhill Ins Co Ltd* v *Assenheim* (1937) 58 Ll L Rep 27, 30 *per* Mackinnon J (motor); *Kreglinger and Fernau* v *Irish National* [1956] IR 116, 150 *per* Davitt P. *Murphy* v *Sun Life* (1964) 44 DLR (2d) 369 (Alta—life). *American Mutual Liability* v *Goff*, 281 F 2d 689 (9 Cir, 1960—liability), cert den 364 US 920.
34. Above, 22–2F.
35. p. 892 (Fletcher Moulton LJ); pp 895–896 (Buckley LJ). Vaughan Williams LJ (p 874) referred to the question about consultations and said: "Some limit to this question must have been intended. It could not have been expected that Miss Morrison's answer should extend to early childhood. I do not know what limit was set by [the doctor] in his explanation." He continued later (pp 881–882): "I do not think that by reason of her having so signed her name the onus shifted from the defendant company, on whom the onus lay to prove non-disclosure, to the plaintiff. I say this, amongst other reasons, because one does not know what the explanations were to the questions put . . . it is doubtful whether she may not have given [the doctor], if not full information, full means of information at this interview."
36. [1927] 1 KB 65.
37. p. 79. He was also impressed that the broker was unable to find any reference to the fact in his documents relating to transaction. However, it is not the broker, agent of the insured, but the insurer who must establish what did (or did not) occur.

23–3 COMMUNICATION OF MATERIAL INFORMATION

23–3A Comprehension

Communication implies comprehension. If the insurer receives information from a proposer, he will be taken to have understood what would be understood by a reasonable insurer of his kind, and to have drawn the inferences and conclusions that would be drawn by such an insurer.[38] In *Ionides* v *Pender*[39] Blackburn J stated that "in the absence of some active deception, the assured had a right to suppose that an underwriter read and understood the documents laid before him, and that if he did not understand the language in which they were written, he would ask for a translation". At the same time, however, the disclosure by the proposer must be clear and must be complete. The "artist's claim—'piece out our imperfections with your thoughts', – has no place".[40]

23–3B The Mode of Communication

The mode of communication is unrestricted. Completion of a proposal form does not preclude oral communication of facts omitted from the form.[41] However, the person to whom communication is made must be the right person, as it reasonably appears to the proposer. For example, in *Ayrey*[42] Lawrence J said that

"It was the duty of the district manager to supervise the company's subordinate agents, and he was the means of communication between them and the head office . . . it was a reasonable thing for [the proposer] to assume that the making of that communication to the district manager was equivalent to informing the company's head office."

23–3C The Meaning of Communication

In the nineteenth century communication was ineffective until brought to the mind of the human person to whom it was sent,[43] unless the parties had agreed otherwise.[44] But this rule was a product of judges mindful of *consensus ad idem* and, as we now see things, of small firms conducting business slowly. The current model includes larger firms and instantaneous international transactions in a compressed society, with the result that the law puts more emphasis on effects than on intentions. The court of today proceeds "by reference to the intentions of the parties, by sound business practice, and in some cases by a judgment where the risks should lie."[45]

A person in business, who has a telephone, telex or telefax and who lets the

---

38. For example *The Bedouin* [1894] P 1, 12–13 *per* Lord Esher MR (CA—freight); *Cohen* v *Standard Marine* (1925) 21 Ll L R 30, 38 *per* Roche J (hull).
39. (1874) LR 9 QB 531, 537 *per* Blackburn J (cargo).
40. Bower, *Disclosure*, 2.07.
41. See *Ayrey* v *British Legal* [1918] 1 KB 137 (life).
42. Above, p 140; he was speaking of post-contract communication, but the rule seems to be the same when making the contract. See further, above, 20-7C and below, 23–9A2 and 26–2D.
43. *Henthorne* v *Fraser* [1892] 2 Ch 27, 32 *per* Herschell LJ (CA).
44. *Holwell Securities* v *Hughes* [1974] 1 All ER 161 (CA).
45. *Brinkibon Ltd* v *Stahag Stahl und Stahlwarenhandelgesellschaft mbH* [1982] 1 All ER 293, 296 *per* Lord Wilberforce (HL).

numbers be known, is said to represent that any message sent there by that mode during business hours will be dealt with promptly.[46] The same can be said of a letter[47] or telemessage. Hence it is contended that communication occurs when the message reaches the recipient's number or address. First, by having the machine the user implies that "this is how you may (effectively) reach me". Second, the recipient, whose "house" it is, is the better risk avoider, so he naturally takes the risk of events, notably failures of communication, within those walls or, in the case of networks, within his firm. Third, such a rule meets the need for certainty.[48]

In *Hadenfayre*,[49] Lloyd J held that, when a message about a material change in the risk was sent to the insurer's office, "the person who answered the telephone had ostensible authority to accept the message and pass it on". The argument, that there had been no communication because the message had not been passed on and there was nobody in that office authorised to receive it, was rejected. Once the person, who answered the phone, indicated that he had noted the message, the insurer had "sufficient actual notice"[50] of the contents of the message. More recently, in *Nissho Iwai Petroleum Co. Inc.* v *Cargill International SA* Hobhouse J noted that "it is an implied term of a contract that one party shall not obstruct or prevent the other from performing the contract",[51] and held that to delay in answering the telephone so as to prevent the other party from doing what the contract required of him was a breach of an implied term in the contract.

23–3D The Target of Communication

Evidently, communication must be to the insurer or to his agent but the question remains, who is the insurer or agent for this purpose? It is not necessary that the communication be sent directly to a person who has discretion to assess and act on the information sent. It is enough to send it to an agent whose role is communication, one who has authority to pass it on to the right person, the proper channel of communication, hence to a local agent, if there is one. In that case, disclosure occurs not at once but within a reasonable time of receipt by the local agent, i.e. the time expected for communication to the right person within the insurance organisation.[52]

In some cases, however, the identity of the agent may be less than evident to persons unacquainted with the industry. "Full and frank disclosure to the Lloyd's broker concerned in presenting on behalf of the proposed assured the proposal to the insurers as against an insurer who complains of non-disclosure and repudiates on that ground avails the proposed insured in no sense at all. To the person unacquainted with the insurance industry it may seem a remarkable state of the law that someone who des-

---

46. *The Brimnes* [1975] QB 929 (CA); *Hadenfayre* v *British National Ins Sy* [1984] 2 Lloyd's Rep 393 (contingency). If a telex is sent overnight, it is not "received" until the office next opens in the normal course of business: *The Brimnes* (above).

47. The recipient "had impliedly invited communication by use of an orifice in his front door designed to receive communications"—*Holwell Securities Ltd* v *Hughes* [1974] 1 All ER 161, 164 *per* Russell LJ (CA).

48. Thus it is the kind of rule chosen by statutes such as the Law of Property Act 1925, s 196(4). A rule, that communication is not effective until it reaches the mind or the desk or the department of the recipient executive handling the matter, puts an impossible onus of proof on the sender.

49. (Above) p 401.

50. *Ibid*.

51. [1993] 1 Lloyd's Rep 80, 84, citing *The Aello* [1961] AC 135.

52. See above, 20–7C, and below, 26–2D.

cribes himself as a Lloyd's broker who is remunerated by the insurance industry and who presents proposals forms and suggested policies on their behalf should not be the safe recipient of full disclosure; but that is undoubtedly the position in law as it stands at the moment."[53] The reaction of the Insurance Ombudsman has been to hold that any person who solicits or negotiates a contract of insurance should be deemed to be the agent of the insurer.[54]

23–4 THE TIME OF DISCLOSURE

As the purpose of disclosure of material facts is to enable the insurer to decide whether to make the contract of insurance and, if so, on what terms, the duty of disclosure has to be performed whenever the insurer has that kind of decision to make: on new insurance (below, 23–4A), on renewal of insurance (23–4C) and in respect of any change in current insurance (23–4B). The corollary is that there is no duty of disclosure at any other time[55] and, in particular, unless the contract stipulates otherwise,[56] no duty to notify changes of risk during the insurance period.[57]

23–4A New Insurance

In the case of a new insurance contract, the duty matures when the contract is concluded and, unless the parties agree otherwise,[58] performance of that duty is assessed at that time.[59]

In particular, if temporary cover is granted while the main cover is negotiated, and during that time a material fact arises, and the insured fails to disclose it before the main cover is contracted, the latter can be avoided for non-disclosure.[60] Again, if, as is common with life insurance, there is no cover until payment of premium, there is no

---

53. *Roberts* v *Plaisted* [1989] 2 Lloyd's Rep 341, 345 *per* Purchas LJ (CA—fire).

54. The Insurance Ombudsman, Annual Report 1989, para 2.14.

55. *Cf* the duty of good faith, from which the duty of disclosure stems: the duty of good faith is a continuing duty in other respects: below, 27–1.

56. See above, 20–5A2.

57. *Cf* certain civil law systems which require, as a matter of law, that the insurer be notified of any aggravation of risk promptly during the insurance period; for example, Quebec: Dubreuil, (1992) 37 McGill L J 1087.

58. For example, the duty may be tied to the time of the proposal: *Mutual Benefit* v *Higginbotham*, 95 US 380 (1877—life).

59. *Re Yager* (1912) 108 LT 38. See also *Uzielli* v *Commercial Union* (1865) 12 LT 399 (hull); *Re Marshall* (1901) 85 LT 757 PA); *Whitwell* v *Autocar* (1927) 27 Ll L Rep 418 (motor); *CTI* v *Oceanus* [1984] 1 Lloyd's Rep 476, 486 *per* Kerr LJ (CA—marine: containers). *Khoury* v *Govt Ins Office* (1984) 58 ALJR 502 (HCA). *M'Lanahan* v *The Universal*, 1 Pet 170 (Sup Ct, 1828—hull); *Equitable Life Assurance Sy* v *McElroy*, 83 F 631 (8 Cir, 1897—life); *Stipcich* v *Metropolitan Life*, 277 US 311 (1928—life); *Mutual Life Ins Co of New York* v *Bohlman*, 328 F 2d 289 (10 Cir, 1964—life); *Disposable Services Inc* v *ITT Life Ins Co*, 453 F 2d 218 (5 Cir, 1971—life) cert den 409 US 1023 (1972). Generally, see Bookhout, 25 Cornell LQ 612 (1940).

It has been argued that in the case of treaty reinsurance the duty continues during the currency of the treaty; see Carter, *Reinsurance*, p 127.

60. *Re Yager* (above). By contrast, in the case of a Lloyd's slip, binding only in honour until a policy is issued, the duty of disclosure matures on issue of the slip, and there is no duty to disclose facts arising between then and the issue of the policy: *Lishman* v *Northern Maritime Ins Co* (1875) LR 10 CP 179, 180–181 *per* Bramwell B (Exch Ch—freight). Also in this sense: *Cory* v *Patton* (1872) LR 7 QB 304 (cargo); *Niger Co Ltd* v *Guardian Assurance Co Ltd* (1922) 13 Ll L Rep 75 (HL—cargo).

contract until payment and the duty of disclosure continues until then; the consequence is that any intervening change in the health of the life must be disclosed to the insurer.[61] The same may be true, even though the issue of the policy on payment of premium purports to provide cover retroactive to a time, such as the time of proposal, before the undisclosed fact arose.[62]

23–4B Modification or Extension of Existing Insurance

If a change in an existing insurance contract is agreed of such a kind "as to substantially alter the nature of the bargain as affecting both sides",[63] it appears that the old contract has been (or soon will be) terminated, a new contract is being made and the proposer is under a duty to disclose[64] all matters material to the new insurance: above, 23–4A.

If a change in an existing insurance contract is agreed of such a kind as does not "substantially alter the nature of the bargain", this is called modification or extension (or variation) of that contract. The contract continues, as modified, and, if the modification affects the risk,[65] there is a limited duty of disclosure as regards the change in the risk, a duty maturing when the change is agreed. Only facts material to the change have to be disclosed. If

"the alteration were such as to make the contract more burdensome to the underwriters, and a fact known at that time to the insured were concealed which was material to the alteration, I should say the policy would be vitiated. But if the fact were quite immaterial to the alteration, and only material to the underwriter as being a fact which shewed that he had made a bad bargain originally, and such as might tempt him, if it were possible, to get out of it, I should say there would be no obligation to disclose it."[66]

In particular, when the contract provides that the insured will be held covered at a premium to be agreed for a risk not part of the original cover, the insured who wishes to take advantage of that provision must, it has been held,[67] "act with the utmost good faith towards the underwriters". Accordingly the insured must disclose the relevant facts to the insurer.[68]

---

61. *British Equitable Ins Co* v *G W Ry Co* (1869) 20 LT 422 (CA—life); *Canning* v *Farquhar* (1886) 16 QBD 727 (CA—life), followed in *Harrington* v *Pearl Life Co* (1914) 30 TLR 613 (CA—life) and *Looker* v *Law Union & Rock Ins Co Ltd* [1928] 1 KB 554. *Dalgety* v *Australian Mutual* [1908] VLR 481. *Stipcich* v *Metropolitan Life*, 277 US 311 (1927—life).

62. *Strangio* v *Consolidated Indemnity*, 66 F 2d 330 (9 Cir, 1933—motor). *Contra: Grier* v *New York Mutual Life Ins Co*, 44 SE 28 (NC, 1903—life): the company was "estopped, in the absence always of fraud" by the issue of the policy.

63. *Lishman* v *Northern Maritime* (1875) LR 10 CP 179, 181 *per* Bramwell B (Exch Ch—freight).

64. *Sawtell* v *Loudon* (1814) 5 Taunt 359: subject-matter changed from hull to cargo.

65. *Lishman* (above), *loc cit*. Although most of the cases deciding this point have concerned marine insurance, there seems to be no reason in principle why the rule should not apply to other kinds if insurance; MacGillivray no 651 (also in this sense) points out that the rule has been applied to PA insurance.

66. *Lishman* (above), p 182, *per* Blackburn J.

67. *Overseas Commodities Ltd* v *Style* [1958] 1 Lloyd's Rep 546, 559 *per* McNair J (cargo). See also *The Litsion Pride* [1985] 1 Lloyd's Rep 437, 511 *per* Hirst J (hull); *The Good Luck* [1988] 1 Lloyd's Rep 514, 545 *per* Hobhouse J (hull).

68. *Liberian Ins Agency Inc* v *Mosse* [1977] 2 Lloyd's Rep 560, 568 *per* Donaldson J (cargo); *The Litsion Pride* (above), *loc cit*.

23–4C Renewal

"A renewal is a new contract for the renewal of an old bargain."[69] If the contract is new, the insurer must be given the information to decide[70] whether to make the new contract and, if so, on what terms. The duty of disclosure applies in full, when the new contract is made.

The obverse is that, if a fact, the non-disclosure of which could have vitiated the original contract, has ceased to be material,[71] the new contract is unaffected by the non-disclosure.[72] It remains to be seen whether the original non-disclosure, although inapplicable as such, survives in the ghost of moral hazard which, being undisclosed, continues to haunt and vitiate the new contract.[73]

23–4D Modification or Renewal?

Evidently, it is important to distinguish the modification of a contract of insurance, to which at most a limited duty of disclosure applies, and renewal, a new contract based on the old bargain, to which the duty applies in full. The distinction depends on the intention of the parties. If the original contract has run its course,[74] or has been cancelled,[75] and is silent on what follows, it is presumed that the insurer may refuse further cover and that, therefore, any further cover must be a matter of renewal.[76]

23–4D1 Extension of the Insurance Period

One kind of extension occurs when the insured has a right to continue the contract beyond a stated term[77]: a common example of extension is the "renewal" of a life contract. This kind of extension should be distinguished from renewal in the strict sense and from modification. Extension is as of right; modification, like any other variation of an existing contract, and renewal, like any other new contract, is a matter for agree-

69. Halsbury, Vol 25, para 491.
70. *Pim* v *Reid* (1843) 6 Man & G 1, 25 *per* Cresswell J. *Cf* USA: in the case of *pro forma* renewal, with no specific inquiries by the insurer, the insured has no duty of disclosure: *Zurich General Accident & Liability Ins Co* v *Flickinger*, 33 F 2d 853 (4 Cir, 1929—PA); *Patrons Mutual Ins Co* v *Rideout*, 411 A 2d 673 (Me, 1980—motor). This explained by the significance attached to the insurer's questions: below, 23–12B1
71. For example, when making the contract in the first place the insured is required to disclose all convictions within the last 10 years, but fails to disclose a conviction over nine years previously: on renewal one year later, that conviction will no longer be within the time range for which disclosure is required and, assuming that the general law is not more rigorous than the proposal form, its disclosure will not be necessary.
72. *Whytes Estate* v *Dominion*, 1945 TPD 382 (South Africa). *Cf Liverpool & London & Globe Ins Co* v *Agricultural Savings* (1902) 33 SCR 94 (fire).
73. This argument is likely to meet judicial scepticism: *Pengelly* v *British Empire* (1974) 38 DLR (3d) 624 (Sup Ct—motor).
74. *Royal Exchange Assurance* v *Hope* [1928] 1 Ch 179, 195 *per* Sargant LJ (CA—life). *Contra: Continental Casualty* v *Casey* [1934] 1 DLR 577 (Sup Ct—PA).
75. *Pengelly* (above).
76. *C E Heath Underwriting & Ins (Aust) Pty Ltd* v *Edwards Dunlop & Co Ltd* (1993) 67 Aust L J 395, 399, 402 (HCA—fidelity).
77. *Stokell* v *Heywood* [1897] 1 Ch 459: the insured assigned his property, including the benefit of his accident insurance, to his creditors. Subsequently he continued the cover by annual payments of premium. He was then struck dead by lightning, an event within the cover. If the money were payable under the original contract, extended from year to year, the money went to the creditors. If the money were payable under a subsequent contract, by way of renewal, it went to his estate. Kekewich J held the latter, stressing (p 464) that neither party to the contract of insurance was obliged to continue it at the end of each year period.

ment between the parties concerned. Both involve new terms: even extension will be new as to, notably, the insurance period but it may also be that the right of extension is conditional, for example, on payment of a new but predetermined (and usually higher) premium.[78] Nonetheless, extension is a matter for the unilateral decision of one party, usually the insured. As regards consequences in law, the key difference is that modification and renewal, being conditional on the insurer's consent, require disclosure; extension, not being conditional on the insurers' consent, does not require disclosure.

A second kind of extension occurs when a change is settled, not by one party (the insured) as a matter of right but by agreement of both parties. Strictly speaking, this is a modification, but it may be referred to as an extension because the modification concerns the insurance period: there is an extension of cover in point of time. In this situation, the change may be such as to require disclosure. This depends on the circumstances, especially, on whether there is a change in the risk. If so, the insured must disclose all information material to the change. Indeed, the change may be such that the case is not an extension (modification) at all but really a renewal. This depends on the degree of change in the risk: 23–4D2.

23–4D2 Change in the Quantum of Risk

"Strictly, a 'renewal' is descriptive of a repetition of the whole arrangement by substituting the like agreement in place of that previously subsisting, to be operative over a new period, whereas an 'extension' betokens a prolongation of the subsisting contract by the exercise of a power reserved thereby to vary one of its provisions, that is, by enlarging the period."[79]

In *Kensington* v *Inglis*,[80] however, Lord Ellenborough stated[81] that, if the amount of property at risk had been increased, "a new subject of insurance would be introduced". This statement is consistent with general law, that any increase in the amount of performance suggests a new contract rather than an extension or variation of the old one,[82] but it cannot be read literally: if it were, an extension (of the second kind described above, 23–4D1) would rarely exist and decisions, including the decision in the case itself, would be hard to explain.

In *Kensington* v *Inglis*,[83] insurance was taken on goods on ships sailing between 1 October 1799 and 1 June 1800, up to an overall amount of £45,000. Later the parties agreed to extend the time to 1 August 1800 but did not extend the amount. This, it was held, was not a new contract but an extension of the old one. In *Royal Exchange Assurance* v *Hope*[84] a man took insurance on his life for one year while he was abroad, without any right of renewal or extension. The benefit of the contract was assigned to Mrs Hope. As the year ended, he was still abroad and arranged further cover for three months, during which he died. If the original contract had been renewed, there was a

---

78. *Semble* this includes renewable increasable convertible term assurance, such as found in business life or "keyman" insurance. For a case of fire insurance see *Liverpool & London & Globe Ins Co* v *Agricultural Savings* (1902) 33 SCR 94.

79. *Re Kerr* [1943] SASR 8, 16 *per* Mayo J (South Australia—life).

80. (1807) 8 East 273. Cf *Cornhill Ins Co Ltd* v *Assenheim* (1937) 58 LLR 27, 29: Mackinnon J held that, when a lorry was taken off a motor policy, but that policy indorsed in respect of cover for two other lorries owned by the policyholder, this was a new contract (on the terms of the old policy).

81. (1807) 8 East 273, 293.

82. *Morris* v *Baron & Co* [1918] AC 1: change in the quantity of goods sold and delivered. Treitel, p 173.

83. (1807) 8 East 273.

84. [1928] Ch 179.

new contract, the benefit of which had not been assigned. If the original contract had been extended, the benefit of the extension, like the original, went to Mrs Hope—and this was the decision of the Court of Appeal.[85] In each case, the courts did not regard the extended risk as a different risk,[86] although the duration of the risk and hence the chance of loss had increased. In each case, significantly, the extension was for a period shorter than the original, and on the same subject–matter.

Party intention is decisive.[87] Intention is sometimes apparent from the contract itself. This is true, for example, of an extension of cargo cover to war risks, at a premium to be arranged.[88] This is also true of the guaranteed insurability option in a business or keyman life policy, although there may be a change in both the amount insured and in the premium.

23–5 MATERIAL FACT

The insured must disclose material fact; and fact, it is said, must be distinguished from opinion.[89] Materiality is discussed below, 23–6. The distinction between fact and opinion is similar to that made by the law of misrepresentation: above, 22–2B2. However, in the context of non-disclosure the distinction is perhaps superfluous for, although information may be no more than opinion, the insurer may be influenced by the fact that the opinion is held; if so, the existence of the opinion and its content should be disclosed.

In *British Equitable Ins Co* v *Great Western Ry*,[90] for example, the proposer consulted a specialist, who told him that he had a dangerous kidney condition. He did not disclose this when later taking life insurance because, he said, his general practitioner had insisted that the specialist was mistaken and that the condition was temporary. Nonetheless, the Court of Appeal in Chancery held that he should have disclosed the prognosis of the specialist (which later turned out to be correct).[91]

Again, if a man has been arrested, charged and committed for trial in respect of an offence, that is not a reasonable ground for concluding that he is guilty: that remains to be determined at the trial. However, these facts are still enough to give the insurer pause before rating the risk that the man presents (the moral hazard).[92] Hence, the

85. All the judges were influenced by the form: no new policy, but indorsement on the original. In modern practice this is not conclusive: see *Cornhill* v *Assenheim* (above).

86. p 191.

87. See in particular *Royal Exchange Assurance* v *Hope* [1928] Ch 179, 184 *per* Tomlin J, 191 *per* Lord Hanworth MR, 193 *per* Sargant LJ.

88. See above, 11–1A4.

89. For example, *CTI* v *Oceanus* [1984] 1 Lloyd's Rep 476, 506 *per* Kerr LJ (container insurance). See also *Cantiere Meccanico Brindisino* v *Janson* [1912] 3 KB 452, 471 *per* Buckley LJ (CA).

90. (1869) 20 LT 422 (life).

91. See also *Cantiere Meccanico Brindisino* v *Janson* [1912] 3 KB 452, 471 *per* Buckley LJ (hull), requiring disclosure of surveyors' reports; and *Shirley* v *Wilkinson* (1781) 3 Doug 41 (hull): the proposer did not disclose a letter from the ship's master indicating when the ship would be ready to depart, for the proposer thought that the master was mistaken. A court including Lord Mansfield held that the letter should have been disclosed.

92. In this sense *March Cabaret & Casino Club Ltd* v *London Assurance* [1975] 1 Lloyd's Rep 169, 177 *per* May J (traders combined); *The Dora* [1989] 1 Lloyd's Rep 69, 73 *per* Phillips LJ (yacht). *Contra: Reynolds* v *Phoenix Assurance Co Ltd* [1978] 2 Lloyd's Rep 440, 459–460 *per* Forbes J (fire). The latter is perhaps distinguishable because the judge concluded that the undisclosed allegation never had any sound basis (p 455). But *cf* also Newell (1993) 5 Ins L J 212.

fact of prosecution, based on the opinion of the prosecutor that the proposer is probably guilty, must be disclosed.

Opinion has been distinguished in this respect from rumour. "Loose rumours, indeed, which have gathered together, no one knows how, need not be communicated."[93] But, if they have any credence at all, the proposer would be well advised to disclose them—or any other "fact", which, although not in itself a sound basis for drawing conclusions, is enough to give the insurer pause for thought and suggests that he should inquire further before assuming the risk.

For example, in *Morrison* v *Universal Marine Ins Co*,[94] the proposer read newspaper reports to the effect that either his ship, for which he was seeking cover, or another ship were aground and in peril. His broker made inquiries at Lloyd's, concluded that it was not the proposer's ship that had grounded, and did not mention the newspaper report to the insurer. Without apparent regard for whether the broker was justified in drawing that conclusion, the Court of Exchequer held that it should have been disclosed.

The effect of the cases is that the duty of disclosure does not depend on any *a priori* classification of information as fact, opinion, rumour or moonshine. The only real question is whether the prudent insurer would consider the information to be material.[95]

23–6 THE PRUDENT INSURER

The materiality of information is a question of fact,[96] determined by reference to the judgement of the prudent insurer at the time that the proposer is obliged to disclose.[97]

"[W]hat is the Court to do? It cannot, as it seems to me, choose one prudent underwriter rather than another. The very choice of a prudent underwriter as the yardstick in my view indicates that the test intended was one which could be sensibly answered in relation to prudent underwriters in general."[98]

93. *Durrell* v *Bederley* (1816) Holt NP 283, 285 *per* Gibbs CJ.
94. (1872) LR 8 Ex 40; the decision was reversed on a different ground, *ibid*, p 197. See also *Leigh* v *Adams* (1871) 25 LT 566 (cargo); and *Lynch* v *Hamilton* (1810) 3 Taunt 37 (cargo), in which an eye-witness account that the ship, on which the goods insured were being carried, was leaking and labouring was posted in Lloyd's coffee house. The court held that the fact that the goods were on this ship should have been disclosed to the insurer.
95. See for example the approach taken by Cockburn CJ in *Leigh* v *Adams* (1871) 25 LT 566 (cargo); by Forbes J in *Reynolds* v *Phoenix Assurance Co Ltd* [1978] 2 Lloyd's Rep 440 (fire), and by Kerr LJ in *CTI* v *Oceanus* [1984] 1 Lloyd's Rep 476, 506 (CA—container insurance).
96. *M'Lanahan* v *Universal Ins Co*, 1 Pet 170 (Sup Ct, 1828—hull).
97. *Thompson* v *Liverpool & London & Globe Ins Co*, 23 F Cas No 13, 966 (D Me, 1879—fire).
98. *CTI* v *Oceanus* [1984] 1 Lloyd's Rep 476, 511 *per* Parker LJ, see also p 527 *per* Stephenson LJ (container insurance); *Rivaz* v *Gerussi* (1880) 6 QBD 222, 228 *per* Brett LJ (CA); *Samuel Hooper* v *Royal London General Ins Co Ltd* 1993 SLT 679 (fire), discussed by Forte: [1993] LMCLQ 557. For the common law in Ireland, see Ellis (1990) 8 ILT 45.
An objective test of similar kind is found in New Zealand: *State Insurance General Manager* v *McHale* [1992] 2 NZLR 399 (CA—fire), although the court was critical of the test; and in some decisions in the USA: *Penn Mutual Life* v *Mechanics' Savings Bk*, 72 F 413, 431 (6 Cir, 1896—life); *Sovereign Camp* v *McDaniel*, 64 SW 2d 581 (Ky, 1933—life); *New York Life Ins Co* v *Kuhlenschmidt*, 33 NE 2d 340 (Ind, 1941—life); *John Hancock Mutual Life Ins Co* v *Conway*, 240 SW 2d 644 (Ky, 1951—life); Couch, *Cyclopedia of Insurance Law* (2nd ed) para 69.121.
Cf the Cal Ins Code, in which the wording of section 334 concentrates attention on the judgement of the particular insurer: *Merchants Fire* v *Lattimore*, 263 F 2d 232 (9 Cir, 1959). See also in this sense Wilson, 73 Dick L Rev 250 (1968) discussing the law of Pennsylvania; and McDowell, 16 Conn L Rev 513, 523 (1984), citing *Employers Liability Assurance Corp* v *Vella*, 321 NE 2d 910 (Mass, 1975—motor); *Hollinger* v *Mutual Benefit Life Ins Co*, 560 P 2d 824 (Colo, 1977—life).

The term "prudent insurer" is used interchangeably with "reasonable insurer".[99] He has also been called the "reasonably prudent insurer".[100] The test purports to be an objective test.

Among other tests currently in eclipse in the courts is reference to the opinion of the reasonable insured.[101] However, "in order to mitigate the rigour of the law in favour of policy-holders", this test has been applied to consumer cases by the Insurance Ombudsman.[102] Moreover, this test has two secondary functions. First, if the insurer asks questions in a proposal form, they are construed not according to the intention of the (prudent) insurer, who framed them, but according to how they would be read by the reasonable proposer: above, 22–2D2. Second, as regards private insurance, the test of the reasonable insured has been adopted in the Statement of General Insurance Practice and of Long-Term Insurance Practice 1986. Under this voluntary code, it is provided that (a) matters which insurers have generally found to be material will be the subject of clear questions in proposal forms[103]; and (b) insurers will not repudiate liability on grounds of non-disclosure of a material fact, which the insured could not reasonably be expected to disclose.[104]

23–6A The Judgement of the Particular Insurer

In principle, the judgement of the particular insurer is irrelevant[105]: what counts is the opinion of prudent insurers in general: above, 23–6. In practice, however, the view of the particular insurer matters in various respects. First, brokers at Lloyd's admit to "broking the personality" of the particular underwriter. Second, some courts, while

---

99. *Mutual Life Ins Co* v *Ontario Metal Products* [1925] AC 344, 351 *per* Lord Salveson (life), adopted by Lord Greene MR, in *Zurich General Accident & Liability Ins Co Ltd* v *Morrison* [1942] 2 KB 53, 58 (CA—motor). See also *Rozanes* v *Bowen* (1928) 32 Ll L Rep 98, 110 *per* Scrutton LJ (CA—jewellers' block); *Lambert* v *Cooperative Ins Sy Ltd* [1975] 2 Lloyd's Rep 485, 492 *per* Cairns LJ (CA—AR).
100. Getz and Davis, *The South African Law of Insurance*, (3rd ed, Cape Town, 1983) p. 110.
101. The test was adopted, for example, in *Life* v *Foster* (1873) 11 M 351 (Ct of Sess—life); *Joel* v *Law Union & Crown Ins Co* [1908] 2 KB 863, 884 *per* Fletcher Moulton LJ (CA—life), but rejected by later cases, for example, *Lambert* v *Cooperative Ins Sy Ltd* [1975] 2 Lloyd's Rep 485 (CA—AR). In the USA, this test was rejected in *Apolskis* v *Concord Life*, 445 F 2d 31, 35 (7 Cir, 1971—life).
Even so, there has been some judicial sympathy for a test of this kind in England, e.g., McNair J in *Rose-lodge Ltd* v *Castle* [1966] 2 Lloyd's Rep 113, 129 (jewellers' AR); MacKenna J in *Lambert* p 491; and some authority for it in South Africa: Getz and Davis, *The South African Law of Insurance*, (3rd ed, Cape Town, 1983), p 109. Such a rule was recommended by the Law Reform Committee in its Fifth Report, *Conditions and Exceptions in Insurance Policies,* 1957 (Cmnd 62) 14. The Law Commission (Report No 104, para 4.51, Cmnd 8064) has recommended reference to "a reasonable man in the position of the proposer"; the position would relate, not only to the expertise of the proposer, but also to the circumstances in which the contract was made (e.g., by telephone, from an airport machine etc). A similar recommendation was made by the Law Reform Commission of Hong Kong in its report of 16 January 1986, para 7.03; and by the court in *State Insurance General Manager* v *McHale* [1992] 2 NZLR 399 (CA—fire).
Other tests rejected by the courts include: (i) The actual opinion of the insured: rejected in *Brownlie* v *Campbell* (1880) 5 App Cas 925, 954 *per* Lord Blackburn; and *Lindenau* v *Desborough* (1828) 8 B & C 586, 592 *per* Bayley J (life): such a rule "would lead to frequent suppression of information, and it would often be extremely difficult to show that the party neglecting to give the information thought it material". *Idem* Roskill J in *Godfrey* v *Britannic* [1963] 2 Lloyds Rep 515, 529 (life); McNair J. in *Roselodge Ltd* v *Castle* [1966] 2 Lloyd's Rep 113, 129 (jewellers' AR). (ii) The actual opinion of the insurer: rejected in *Glasgow Assurance Corp Ltd* v *Symondson & Co* (1911) 16 Com Cas 109 (re); *Zurich General Accident & Liability Ins Co Ltd* v *Morrison* [1942] 2 KB 53 (CA—motor). Cf *Berger* v *Pollock* [1973] 2 Lloyd's Rep 442, 463 *per* Kerr J (cargo): below, 23-6A2.
102. The Insurance Ombudsman, Annual Report 1989, para 2.16.
103. Clause 1(d). Forte, (1986) 49 MLR 754, 761. A study suggests that there is no adequate means of enforcing compliance with the Statement: Cadogan and Lewis (1992) 21 Angl-Am L Rev 123.
104. Clause 2(b)(i). Forte, *loc cit*, pp 764 ff.
105. *CTI* v *Oceanus* [1984] 2 Lloyd's Rep 476 (CA—containers).

paying lip service to the criterion of the prudent insurer, accept evidence of that standard from the practices of the particular insurer and little else.[106] Third, if information is objectively material but the particular insurer ignores it, that is waiver—by the particular insurer and the non-disclosure has no effect.[107] In addition, the opinion of the particular insurer may be relevant in two further ways that require some explanation.

23–6A1 Subjective Materiality

If a particular insurer has a particular bee in his bonnet about some matter, which most insurers would regard as immaterial, that bee is irrelevant, whether the insured knows that the bee is there or not. If the matter is the subject of a question in the proposal form, the proposer must answer it truthfully. In relation to misrepresentation it has been argued[108] that "the special susceptibility of the representee" (the bee in the insurer's bonnet) "and the representor's knowledge of it, may be of importance, because these facts will make a representation material which would not be material in other circumstances". But, if there is no inquiry by the insurer, and no representation on the matter by the proposer, it is very doubtful that the proposer must volunteer information of that kind.[109]

23–6A2 Subjective Immateriality

If the information is objectively material, it will be presumed that disclosure would have influenced the particular insurer or, as it is sometimes put, that the opinion of the particular insurer is irrelevant. In the law of misrepresentation, however, it is open to the insured to prove that material statements did not in fact induce the contract with the particular insurer: above, 22–3B2. By analogy, should it not be possible to offer the same kind of proof in a case of non-disclosure?

In *Berger* v *Pollock*[110] a claim was made on open cover in respect of steel injection moulds damaged in transit from Melbourne to London. One of the defences was non-disclosure that the bill of lading issued in respect of the moulds was claused. Although there was evidence from an independent (and prudent) insurer that the fact was material, there was also evidence that the particular insurer would not have been influenced by the fact. Kerr J rejected the defence: the court must determine not only the standard of the judgement of a prudent insurer but whether "the insurer in question would have been influenced by the fact undisclosed". If he would not have been

---

106. In *Henwood* v *Prudential Ins Co of America* (1967) 64 DLR (2d) 715, 720 (life) the Supreme Court of Canada adopted the standard of the reasonable insurer, but accepted the uncontradicted evidence of the insurer's own medical adviser on that question. This has been criticised as putting the onus on the insured to prove that the practices of the insurer were unreasonable: Trakman, 34 U Toronto LJ 421, 431 (1984). The court relied in part on statements in *Zurich General Accident & Liability Ins Co Ltd* v *Leven* [1940] SC 407 (Ct Sess—motor).

107. See below, 23–12 and 23–13.

108. Bower, *Misrepresentation*, No 127; see also No 129. The cases cited by the learned authors were ones in which either (a) the fact was objectively material: *Whurr* v *Devenish* (1904) 20 TLR 385, or (b) the representor was fraudulent: *Phillips* v *Duke of Buckingham* (1683) 1 Vern 227; *Higgins* v *Samels* (1862) 2 J & H 460; *Archer* v *Stone* (1898) 78 LT 34; *Gordon* v *Street* [1899] 2 QB 641 (CA); *Said* v *Butt* [1920] 3 KB 497; *Lake* v *Simmons* [1927] AC 487; *Sowler* v *Potter* [1940] 1 KB 271. Apart from *Higgins* v *Samels* these cases concerned fraudulent misrepresentations of the identity of a party to the contract, a matter of known importance to the representee.

109. *Beachey* v *Brown* (1860) El Bl & El 796, 803–804 *per* Crompton J.

110. [1973] 2 Lloyd's Rep 442.

influenced, it "would then be a very odd result if [he] could nevertheless avoid the policy".[111] As non-disclosure vitiates contracts because it affects consent, it would indeed be odd if, in a particular case, a contract was avoided for a non-disclosure which, *ex hypothesi*, had had no effect on consent. Later, as Kerr LJ in *CTI* v *Oceanus*, the judge appeared to resile from his view in *Berger* v *Pollock*.[112] Perhaps this illustrates what Lord Mansfield had in mind, when he said[113] that "It is certainly true, in many instances, that first thoughts are best . . . Sometimes you miss the mark by taking too long an aim". Be that as it may, in the present state of the law, the safer view is that set out at the beginning of this discussion: If the information is objectively material, the opinion of the particular insurer is irrelevant.

23–6A3 Particular Questions

If the insurer puts a question to the proposer, it does not follow without more that the subject–matter of the question is material,[114] but "it must take the asker part of the way". Although in the end materiality "must depend on a general assessment of all the circumstances of the case",[115] notably market opinion (below, 23–6B), the view of the particular insurers, as reflected in the question, is not irrelevant.

23–6B The Search for the Prudent Insurer

What is material, what would have influenced a prudent insurer, depends on the following factors.

23–6B1 The Branch of Insurance

Underwriters of one kind of risk may be influenced by information that would not influence those writing other kinds of risk. The main division is between marine insurance and non-marine insurance. In *Glasgow Assurance Corp Ltd* v *Symondsen*[116] Scrutton J said:

"The ordinary man in the street would, I am sure, think it material to know that the risk he was offered had been previously refused by six other underwriters; and many life insurance offices expressly ask the question: 'Has your life been refused by any other office?' But it is elementary marine insurance law that such refusals need not be disclosed to another underwriter. The ordinary business man would, I am sure, think it material to know that the underwriter wanting to reinsure thought so badly of the risk that he was ready to pay a higher premium than he received to get rid of [it]; but no one has ever suggested that this need be disclosed."

This factor, the branch of insurance, can be seen as a case of the second and more important factor: general practice.

---

111. p 463. In this sense *Western Australian Ins Co Ltd* v *Dayton* (1924) 35 CLR 355, 379–380 *per* Isaacs A-CJ (motor), Arnould, No 641; Sutton, No 3.56; and, especially, Kelly, 1 Ins L J 30 (1988). *Contra: Zurich General Accident & Liability Ins Co Ltd* v *Morrison* [1942] 2 KB 33, 60 *per* Mackinnon LJ (CA—motor). Also *contra*: Ivamy, p 128. MacGillivray, No 663, is doubtful.
112. [1984] 1 Lloyd's Rep 476, 495 (CA—container insurance).
113. *Lowery* v *Bourdieu* (1780) 2 Dougl 468, 470.
114. *Dawsons Ltd* v *Bonnin* [1922] AC 413 (motor).
115. Bower, *Disclosure*, 3.13.
116. (1911) 16 Com Cas 109, 119 (CA—re). See also *London Assurance Co* v *Mansel* (1879) 11 Ch D 363, 367 Lord Jessel MR (CA life); *New York Life Ins Co* v *Kuhlenschmidt*, 33 NE 2d 340 (Ind, 1941—life). In a large jurisdiction the answer may vary according to the locality: *ibid*, p 347.

23–6B2 General Practice

The prudent insurer is no less a myth than the reasonable man of tort. In the view of a leading broker, the prudent underwriting of fire risks may be little more reasonable than the conduct of the man in the street in the face of the fire.[117] To determine the view of the prudent underwriter, the court hears evidence from insurers[118] of the relevant branch of insurance—evidence less, it sometimes appears, about what insurers do than about what they think that they should do.

In England, although the questions put to the proposer by the particular insurer have no more than a very limited bearing on the issue,[119] the court does look to the questions put by insurers in general.[120]

In the United States, the significance of the questions put to the proposer is greater than in England. The Supreme Court has said[121] that the "practice of requiring the applicant for life insurance to answer questions prepared by the insurer has relaxed [the rule of disclosure] to some extent, since information not asked for is presumably deemed immaterial". But this presumption is not universal. It applies when the proposer "may honestly consider himself discharged from any duty of affirmative disclosure about matters concerning which he has not been interrogated".[122] While the presumption applies to fire, life and accident[123] insurance, it does not apply to marine.[124] The presumption might have been confined to ordinary consumer insurance; however, it has been applied to professional liability insurance,[125] fidelity insurance,[126] and to a floating policy taken by a warehouseman for goods in his charge.[127] In any case, the presumption does not apply to unusual facts increasing the risk which "could not, with reasonable diligence, be discovered by the insurer, or anticipated as a foundation for specific inquiry".[128]

---

117. A broker's view: Madge, BILA Journal 1992 No 80 p 37.

118. *Glasgow Assurance Corp Ltd* v *Symondson* (1911) 16 Com Cas 109, 120 *per* Scrutton J (re); *Associated Oil Carriers Ltd* v *Union Ins Sy of Canton Ltd* [1917] 2 KB 184, 192 *per* Atkin J (freight); *Yorke* v *Yorkshire Ins Co* [1918] 1 KB 662, 670 *per* McCardie J (life).

119. See above, 23–6A3. Cf *Golding* v *Royal London Auxiliary Ins Co Ltd* (1914) 30 TLR 350, 351 *per* Bailhache J (fire).

120. *Symondson* (above) p 119 *per* Scrutton J (re); *Re Yager* (1912) 108 LT 38, 43 *per* Lord Alverstone CJ (CA—fire); *Associated Oil Carriers Ltd* (above) *loc cit*; *Mann Macneal & Steeves* v *Capital & Counties Ins Co* [1921] 2 KB 300, 307 *per* Bankes LJ (CA—hull); *Becker* v *Marshall* (1922) 11 LLR 114, 117 *per* Salter J (burglary); *Glicksman* v *Lancashire & General Assurance Co* [1925] 2 KB 593, 605 *per* Bankes LJ, 609 *per* Scrutton LJ (CA—burglary).

121. *Stipcich* v *Metropolitan Life Ins Co*, 277 US 311, 316 *per* Stone J (1928—life).

122. *Hare & Chase* v *National Surety*, 60 F 2d 909, 911 (2 Cir, 1932), cert den 287 US 662.

123. *Columbian National Life Ins Co* v *Harrison*, 12 F 2d 986 (6 Cir, 1926); *Ellis* v *Standard Accident Ins Co*, 27 F 2d 544 (SD Tex, 1928); *Prentiss* v *Mutual Benefit Health & Accident Assn*, 109 F 2d 1 (7 Cir, 1940—PHI).

124. *Hare & Chase* (above).

125. *Roess* v *St Paul Fire & Marine Ins Co*, 383 F Supp 1231 (D Fla, 1974—liability). *Idem: Ashley* v *American Mutual Liability*, 167 F Supp 125 (ND Cal, 1958—liability) in which it was suggested that this presumption would apply even to failure to ask about and to disclose even the most obvious matters such as previous insurance history.

126. *United States* v *Howard*, 67 F 2d 382 (5 Cir, 1933); *First State Bank of Gustine* v *New Amsterdam Casualty*, 83 F 2d 992 (5 Cir, 1936).

127. *American Eagle Fire Ins Co* v *Peoples Compress Co*, 156 F 2d 663 (10 Cir, 1948).

128. *Transcontinental Ins Co* v *Minning*, 135 F 2d 479, 481 (6 Cir, 1943—fire).

It has also been suggested that there is an exception in case of fraud: *Roberto* v *Hartford Fire Ins Co*, 177 F 2d 811 (7 Cir, 1949—fire).

23–6B3 Context

The general practice and opinion of underwriters is gauged at the time that the duty of disclosure has to be performed.

In *Associated Oil Carriers* v *Union of Canton*,[129] on 31 July 1914, the claimant insured freight to be earned on a ship charter. On 4 August 1914, war broke out with Germany and the freight could not be earned. The insurer pleaded non-disclosure by the claimant that the charterer was German. The plea was rejected. The fact was material when the claim was brought; but, when the insurance was contracted, the German nationality of the charterer would not have been considered material by prudent insurers.

Further, it is submitted, that when assessing the materiality of facts undisclosed, they should be "located in the web of surrounding circumstances which explain their true significance".[130] Evidently, a fact viewed in isolation may assume an importance, which it lacks, when seen in its entire context.

23–6B4 Judicial Control

The evidence of general practice provided by insurers in court may be a defensive "post mortem" response[131] to the risk in the particular case. This being so, the court asks whether the evidence presented is the evidence of a reasonably prudent insurer? "The word 'reasonably' is necessary to maintain control over the evidence of possibly absurdly stringent insurance practice . . . It achieves the purpose of the 'reasonable insured' test, but fixes the area of judgement where it properly belongs—that is, with the insurer"[132] or, we might say, with the court. Even so, the court may also ask whether some scope should be reserved for instinctive underwriting based on "hunch".[133]

In *Roselodge Ltd* v *Castle*,[134] the judge heard evidence from an "expert" that "a man who stole apples at the age of 17 and had led a blameless life for 50 years is so much more likely to steal diamonds at the age of 67 that . . . he would not have insured him". Having observed[135] "that even under the present practice of admitting expert evidence from underwriters as to materiality, the issue as to disclosability is one

129. [1917] 2 KB 184. See also *Lynch* v *Hamilton* (1810) 3 Taunt 37 (cargo), affirmed *sub nom Lynch* v *Durnsford* (1811) 14 East 494 (cargo); *Roberts* v *Plaisted* [1989] 2 Lloyd's Rep 341 (CA—fire).
130. *Barclay Holdings (Australia) Pty Ltd* v *British National Ins Co Ltd* (1987) 8 NSWLR 514, 519 *per* Kirby P (fire); see also *Western Australian Ins Co Ltd* v *Dayton* (1924) 35 CLR 355, 359 *per* Isaacs ACJ (motor).
131. *Long* v *Commercial Union Assurance Co* (1981) 121 DLR (3d) 623, 634 (Ont—motor). *Thompson* v *Occidental Life Ins Co*, 513 P 2d 353, 360 (Cal, 1973—life).
132. *Mayne Nickless* v *Pegler* [1974] 1 NSWLR 228, 239 (motor). A similar insistence that the court will not accept the insurers' evidence uncritically is found in *Yorke* v *Yorkshire Ins Co* [1918] 1 KB 662, 670 *per* McCardie J (life), as well as in *Roselodge* v *Castle* (below). See further Evans, [1984] Austl Bus L Rev 4.
133. Abraham, 71 Va L Rev 403, 414 (1985).
134. [1966] 2 Lloyd's Rep 113, 132: A claim in respect of theft of diamonds was resisted for non-disclosure of two matters. One was that a director of the insured company had been convicted of an attempt to bribe a policeman 18 years before the insurance was made, namely that (p 127) "Mr Rosenberg who at the time was a young man of 26 years of age and had only been in this country for a few years, had parked his car for too long in a proper parking place in Glasshouse Street. When he came down to his car and was about to drive away, he was stopped by a police officer, and, after offering the police officer a cigarette, he passed him 5s, which the police officer took". The defence was successful with regard to the other matter undisclosed.
135. p 131. See also *The Dora* [1989] 1 Lloyd's Rep 69, 93 *per* Phillips J (yacht).

which has to be determined as it was in Lord Mansfield's day by the view of the jury of reasonable men" and thus, today, the view of the court, the judge rejected the expert evidence on this point and found the conviction not material.

In *Reynolds* v *Phoenix Assurance Co Ltd*,[136] Forbes J said that

"the evidence of insurers called in this way is expert evidence in the sense that such witnesses are assisting the court in deciding what a reasonable and prudent underwriter would or would not do. They are not to give evidence of what they themselves would do, because their evidence is expert, that is opinion evidence and not factual . . . Further, in giving expert evidence such witnesses are only assisting the court not deciding it."

On the issue of moral hazard, he observed[137] that he had "no doubt that every insurer would like to have the most complete information about the moral make-up of each proposer, but that is not the test. The test is whether the circumstances in question would influence his judgement in determining whether he will take the risk". He then noted that, as regards the materiality of past convictions, the underwriters expressed in evidence a wide range of differing views, and chose the view that he preferred.[138]

The duty of disclosure "is analogous to a duty to do an act which you undertake with reasonable care and skill, a failure to do which amounts to negligence".[139] Indeed, the courts look to the reasonable insurer of the relevant kind (aviation, marine etc), as in a negligence case they might to medical men (anaesthetist or surgeon) to establish the appropriate standard. The courts look to the state of the art[140] at the relevant time; and the courts show considerable respect for the general practices of the insurance industry.[141] In the guise of the reasonable man, the judge retains control of the standard required.

In practice, the opinion of the judge is likely to be most significant in the following cases: (a) when it is argued that a fact is immaterial as a matter of law[142]; (b) when the evidence of the experts is patently absurd[143]; (c) when evidence from experts is lacking; (d) when evidence from experts is in conflict[144]; and perhaps, (e) when the answer to the question of materiality seems obvious to the court.[145] Further, the court must ultimately ensure that underwriting is not contrary to public policy: below, 23–6B5. In other cases, considerable deference is paid to evidence from the insurance industry of what is material to the prudent insurer.

---

136. [1978] 2 Lloyd's Rep 440, 457–458 (fire). The judge adopted (p 458) the view of Lord President Cooper in *Davie* v *Edinburgh Magistrates*, 1953 SC 34, 40, that the duty of expert witnesses is "to furnish the judge or jury with the necessary scientific criteria for testing the accuracy of their conclusions so as to enable a judge or jury to form their own independent judgment".
137. p 458.
138. p 459. The insurer pleaded non-disclosure of a conviction eight years earlier for receiving stolen property. The court held that this was not material.
139. *Joel* v *Law Union & Crown Ins Co Ltd* [1908] 2 KB 863, 883 *per* Fletcher Moulton LJ (CA—life).
140. See above, 23–6B3. In tort see, for example, *Roe* v *Minister of Health* [1954] 2 QB 66 (CA).
141. Above, 23–6B2. In tort see, for example, *Brown* v *Rolls Royce Ltd* [1960] 1 WLR 210 (HL); *Sidaway* v *Board of Governors of the Bethlem Royal Hospital* [1985] AC 871. *Cf Luxmore–May* v *Messenger May Baverstock* [1990] 1 All ER 1067 (CA).
142. *Scottish Shire Line* v *London & Provincial Marine and General Ins Co* [1912] 3 KB 51, 70 *per* Hamilton J.
143. For example, *Roselodge Ltd* v *Castle*, discussed above.
144. For example, *Reynolds* v *Phoenix Assurance Co Ltd*, discussed above.
145. *Glicksman* v *Lancashire & General Assurance Co Ltd* [1925] 2 KB 593, 609 *per* Scrutton LJ (CA—burglary).

23–6B5 Public Policy

In England, pricing insurance by reference to sex does not infringe legal rights.[146] However, under the Rehabilitation of Offenders Act 1974, criminal convictions are spent and need not be disclosed after a stated period of time, which varies according to the sentence. A conviction resulting in a sentence of two-and-a-half years' imprisonment or more is never spent. Further, there is a general exception,[147] whereby the court has discretion to admit evidence of a conviction if "justice cannot be done in the case except by admitting it".

23–7 MATERIALITY—DEGREE

The insured must disclose information which is material, material to the prudent insurer (above, 23–6). Further, it is sometimes said that the presentation of the proposal must be fair.[148] This may be another way of saying the same thing. If it is not, it will be difficult to advise proposers. If, in a counsel of caution, they are advised to say everything and thus to make a presentation, in which facts material are buried in facts immaterial, is the presentation fair?

Information is material if, in the words of section 18(2) of the MIA, it "would influence the judgment of a prudent insurer in fixing the premium, or determining whether he will take the risk".[149] This statement is ambiguous as regards influence.

23–7A The Degrees of Influence

As regards the degree of influence that an undisclosed fact might have had on the prudent insurer, there are broadly speaking four possibilities and four types of information:

Type A is information such that, if the insurer had known it, after due consideration[150] he would have refused to make the contract at all. This is the rule in certain jurisdictions[151] of the United States.

146. See below, 24–4C. *Cf* USA: pension arrangements that discriminate on the basis of sex have been declared invalid: *City of Los Angeles, Dept of Water & Power* v *Manhart*, 435 US 702 (1978); *Arizona Governing Commission* v *Norris*, 463 US 1073 (1983).

147. Section 7(3).

148. For example, *CTI* v *Oceanus* [1984] 1 Lloyds Rep 476 (CA—container insurance), below, 23–7B.

149. This rule applies also to non-marine insurance: *Equitable Life Assurance Sy* v *General Accident Assurance Corp*, 1904 12 SLT 348, 349 *per* Lord Pearson (life); *Joel* v *Law Union & Crown Ins Co Ltd* [1908] 2 KB 863 (CA—life); *Cantiere Meccanico Brindisino* v *Janson* [1912] 3 KB 452, 467 *per* Fletcher Moulton LJ (CA—hull); *Locker & Woolf Ltd* v *Western Australian Ins Co Ltd* [1936] 1 KB 408, 415 *per* Scott LJ (CA—motor); *Godfrey* v *Britannic Assurance Co Ltd* [1963] 2 Lloyd's Rep 515, 528, 530 *per* Roskill J (life); *March Cabaret Club & Casino Ltd* v *London Assurance* [1975] 1 Lloyd's Rep 169 (fire); *Lambert* v *Cooperative Ins Sy Ltd* [1975] 2 Lloyd's Rep 485 (CA—householder's AR); *Marene Knitting Mills Pty Ltd* v *Greater Pacific General Ins Ltd* [1976] 2 Lloyd's Rep 631 (PC—fire); *Highlands Ins Co* v *Continental Ins Co* [1987] 1 Lloyd's Rep 109, 114 *per* Steyn J (re).

150. For example, *Anglo-African Merchants* v *Bayley* [1970] 1 QB 311, 319 *per* Megaw J (cargo).

151. *Roberto* v *Hartford Fire Ins Co*, 177 F 2d 811, 814 (7 Cir, 1949—fire), cert den 339 US 920; *Mavros* v *St Paul Fire & Marine Ins Co*, 296 F 2d 271, 272 (7 Cir, 1961—fire); *Knight* v *United States Fire Ins Co*, 651 F Supp 477, 481 (SD NY 1986—cargo). "To be material, the fact must be 'something which would have controlled the underwriter's decision' to accept the risk": *Hartford Ins Co* v *Garvey* 1989 AMC 652, 659 (ND Cal—yacht) and cases cited; *idem*: *American Home Assurance Co* v *Fremont Indemnity Co*, 745 F Supp 974, 977 (SDNY, 1990—re).

See also in this sense, for example, Argentina, Insurance Act, article 5; For a more general survey see the UNCTAD Working Paper TD/B/C.4/ISL/46, paras 88 f. In Australia, however, this test was rejected in *Elston* v *Phoenix Prudential Australia Ltd* [1987] 2 Qd 354 (fire).

Type B is information such that, if the insurer had known of it, he would have made a contract of insurance but only on terms, especially (but not only) as to premium, different from that which he did make.[152] This seems to be the rule in Australia,[153] Canada,[154] New Zealand,[155] and most jurisdictions of the United States.

In *Penn Mutual Life* v *Mechanics' Savings Bank*,[156] Taft J considered many of the English cases of the time and said that the test of the materiality of a fact was "whether reasonably careful and intelligent men would have regarded the fact . . . as substantially increasing the chances of the loss insured against". Evidence should be taken of insurance practice, and the question for an expert witness, he said,[157] was, "Are you able to say, from your knowledge of the practice and usage among life insurance companies generally, that information of this fact would have enhanced the premium to be charged, or would have led to a rejection of the risk?"

Type C is information such that, if the insurer had known it, he would have considered it relevant but, unlike Type A, not so relevant that he would have refused to contract or, unlike Type B, so relevant that he would have insisted on different terms. It would have "affected" his judgement perhaps by reinforcing it or in that, together with other facts, it might have been sufficient to lead to different contract terms, but, considered alone in the particular case, it would have made no difference to the contract or its terms. This has been referred to as the "awareness" test of materiality.

Type D might be placed between Type B and Type C. In Missouri, for example, the "test of materiality is whether if stated truthfully the answer *might* reasonably influence an insurer to reject a risk or charge a higher premium".[158] The words "might

---

152. Some support for this rule can be found in England (and Scotland), mostly in older cases: *Quin* v *National Assurance* (1839) Carey & Jones Rep 316 (Exch Ch (Ireland)—fire); *Stribley* v *Imperial Marine Ins Co* (1875) 1 QBD 507, 512 *per* Blackburn J (hull); *Blackburn, Low & Co* v *Vigors* (1886) 17 QBD 553, 562 *per* Lord Esher MR, whose dissenting judgment was upheld by the House of Lords without comment on this *dictum:* (1887) 12 App Cas 531 (re); *Laing* v *Union Marine Ins Co* (1895) 1 Com Cas 11, 17–18 *per* Mathew J (hull); *London General Omnibus Co Ltd* v *Holloway* [1912] 2 KB 72, 77 *per* Vaughan Williams LJ (CA—surety); *Cantiere Meccanico Brindisino* v *Janson* [1912] 3 KB 452, 467 *per* Fletcher Moulton LJ (CA—hull). As regards "material" increase in risk, see *Shanly* v *Allied Traders Ins Co Ltd* (1925) 21 Ll L Rep 195, (fire). On the early cases see Brooke [1985] LMCLQ 437. A more recent statement of this kind was made by Kerr J, who later took a very different view in *CTI* v *Oceanus* (below, 23–7B), in *Berger* v *Pollock* [1973] 2 Lloyd's Rep 442, 463 (cargo). See also cases cited in relation to materiality of misrepresentation above, 22–3C. This also appears to be the rule in Scotland: *M'Cartney* v *Laverty*, 1968 SC 207, 213 *per* Lord Fraser (motor).
153. *Southern Cross Assurance Co Ltd* v *Australian Provincial Assurance Assn Ltd* (1939) 39 SR (NSW) 174, 187–188; *Barclay Holdings (Australia) Pty Ltd* v *British National Ins Co Ltd* (1987) 8 NSWLR 514, 523, with reference to *Mayne Nickless Ltd* v *Pegler* [1974] 1 NSWLR 228, 239 (motor).
154. *Gauvremont* v *Prudential Ins Co of America* [1941] SCR 139, 156—157 *per* Rinfret J (life);
155. *FAME Ins Co Ltd* v *McFadyen* [1961] NZLR 1070, 1074 (Sup Ct—motor); also in Belgium and Switzerland: Sent Anvers [1987] ETL 752, 756.
156. 72 F 413, 429 (6 Cir, 1896); rehearing denied 73 F 653. The action on the policy depended on the construction of a statute in force in Pennsylvania, which avoided a policy if it had been obtained by a misrepresentation "material to the risk". For discussion of the law in Pennsylvania see Wilson, 73 Dick L Rev. 250 (1968). More generally see Appleman, section 7294 and, as regards what is regarded as material information for personal lines, Appleman, section 1917.
157. p. 430. *Idem: New York Life Ins Co* v *Kuhlenstadt*, 33 NE 2d 340, 347–348 (Ind, 1941); *Firemen's Ins Co of Newark* v *Smith*, 180 F 2d 371 (8 Cir, 1950—fire), cert den 339 US 980; *Garvey* v *Old Colonial Ins Co*, 153 F Supp 755 (ED NC, 1957—fire), affirmed 253 F 2d 299 (4 Cir, 1958); *Franklin Life Ins Co* v *Champion & Co*, 350 F 2d 115, 129 (6 Cir, 1965—life); *Parks* v *Federal Crop*, 416 F 2d 833, 840 (7 Cir, 1969—crop insurance); *Parker* v *Prudential Ins Co*, 900 F 2d 772 (4 Cir, 1990—life); *Petersen* v *Mutual Life Ins Co*, 803 P 2d 406, 409 (Alaska, 1990—life); *Stephens* v *American Home Assurance Co*, 811 F Supp 937, 955–956 (SD NY, 1993—re); *Saint Calle* v *Prudential Ins Co*, 815 F Supp 679 (SD NY, 1993—life).
158. *Galvan* v *Cameron Mutual Ins*, 733 SW 2d 771, 773 (Mo, 1987—fire) (emphasis added). In that case, however, the dispute concerned a misrepresentation of type A.

reasonably influence" do not mean "*would* reasonably influence".[159] In England, the Law Reform Committee stated the law in similar terms.[160] So, Type D may be information such that, it might be classed as information Type B or as Type C, because the evidence from the market is that some prudent insurers would have insisted on different terms but some would not: market practice is not universal or uniform but, even so, there is a sufficiently established practice among a respectable body of prudent underwriters for the information to be held material.[161]

The key to the difference between a rule with reference to Type B and a rule with reference to Type C, lies with the purpose of disclosure to enable the insurer to make a decision and the information on which he is to make it. If it is to enable the insurer to decide more or less at once whether to take the risk and on what terms, the rule should require Type B. If, however, the purpose is wider, if it is not only that but also to enable the insurer to decide whether to undertake further investigation of the risk as regards the information in question, then a case can be made for Type C.[162] That said, in England, as a result of the decision of the Court of Appeal in *CTI* v *Oceanus*,[163] the current rule would appear to require disclosure of information Type C – subject, however, to recent reconsideration of *CTI* in *Pan Atlantic Insurance Co Ltd* v *Pine Top Ins Co Ltd*.[164] In this case, Steyn LJ, who gave the judgment of the Court of Appeal, reviewed and, as he saw it, reinterpreted *CTI*.

Reinterpretation was possible, in his view, because the judges in *CTI* v *Oceanus* had been so concerned with whether the law required information of Type B, which had been the decision of the court below, that they did not decide between two further alternatives. The first, the "awareness" test (above), would require disclosure of all information of Type C; in other words, those of Steyn LJ,[165] the rule required that "a prudent insurer would wish to be aware of it in reaching his decision". However, he was not prepared to agree that the "immensely experienced judges, who decided *CTI* v *Oceanus*, consciously decided to make a ruling in favour of the [this] solution". He saw a second and different interpretation of *CTI*,[166] the "increased risk" test, which

159. *Meeker* v *Shelter Mutual Ins Co*, 766 SW 2d 733, 743 (Mo, 1989—fire), which concerned misrepresentation or non-disclosure of previous fire losses.

160. 5th Report 1957 (Cmnd 62), para 4. *Cf Reynolds* v *Phoenix Assurance Co Ltd*, discussed above, 23–6B4.

161. There is an approximate analogy here with the generality of practice which, in the law of negligence, has an important bearing on whether a doctor (*Brown* v *Rolls Royce Ltd* [1960] 1 WLR 210 (HL) or an art expert (*Luxmore–May* v *Messenger May Baverstock* [1990] 1 All ER 1067 (C.A.)) has followed prudent and careful practice.

162. In *Barclay Holdings (Australia) Pty Ltd* v *British National Ins Co Ltd* (1987) 8 NSWLR 514, 523 (fire) Glass JA first quoted from the judgment of Kerr LJ in *CTI* v *Oceanus* (below, 23–7B, p 492), including these words: "The word 'influenced' means that the the disclosure is one which would have had an impact on the formation of [the insurer's] opinion and *on his decision-making process*" (emphasis added). Glass JA continued: "The difference is whether the relevance of the hypothetical facts, assuming that they had been disclosed, is judged at the moment the underwriter is deciding whether or not to accept the risk or at the moment when he undertakes an investigation of the risk. The former is the [Australian] view and is binding upon us. The latter advanced in *Container Transport International* is not binding on us and should in my view be disregarded."

163. [1984] 1 Lloyd's Rep 476. Such a rule has been rejected in Scotland: *M'Cartney* v *Laverty*, 1968 SC 207, 213 *per* Lord Fraser (motor).

164. [1993] 1 Lloyd's Rep 496 (CA—re). An appeal to the House of Lords is to be heard in February 1994.

165. p 505.

166. *Ibid.* Based on words of Lord Mansfield, in *Carter* v *Boehm* (1766) 3 Burr 1905, 1909, which were also cited by Kerr LJ in *CTI* v *Oceanus* [1984] 1 Lloyd's Rep 476, 493, 496.

"is whether a prudent underwriter, if he had known the undisclosed facts, would have regarded the risk as increased beyond what was disclosed on the actual presentation".

The second interpretation, it is submitted, is not significantly different from the first.[167] If the risk is a "different and increased risk" to the degree that, if the information had been disclosed, the terms offered by the prudent underwriter, if any, would have been different, this does not differ from a test with Type B, explicitly rejected in *CTI*. But evidently this was not what Steyn LJ had in mind, as he ended his deliberation thus: "the question is whether the prudent insurer would view the undisclosed material as probably tending to increase the risk. That does not mean that it is necessary to prove that the underwriter would have taken a different decision about the acceptance of the risk. After all, there may be many commercial reasons for still writing the risk on the same terms".[168] But this being so, is the law really much of an improvement on the "awareness" test? Steyn LJ noted that "*CTI* v *Oceanus* has proved to be a remarkably unpopular decision",[169] but he dealt with none of the criticisms directly or, it is submitted, indirectly by the interpretation that he adopted. At the time of going to press an appeal to the House of Lords is in prospect. The crucial case for review remains *CTI* v *Oceanus*.

23–7B CTI v Oceanus[170]

CTI leased out containers and insured them with insurer A who, unhappy with the subsequent claims experience, sought to change the terms of the cover in a way unacceptable to CTI. CTI insured with insurer B and the same occurred. CTI then insured with Oceanus on the basis of an account of their past claims record which, in the view of all the judges, was not complete or entirely fair. Oceanus sought to avoid the policy for misrepresentation and non-disclosure. Lloyd J held[171] that, if all the relevant information had been disclosed, the insurer would have made the same contract on the same terms, that such information (Type C) was not material and that therefore the contract could not be avoided.

This decision was reversed by the Court of Appeal. First, on the facts, the undisclosed information was not of Type C but of Type B. Secondly, in any event, there "is no requirement that the particular insurer should have been induced to take the risk or charge a lower premium than he would otherwise have done as a result of the non-disclosure".[172] So, information of Type C (or perhaps Type D) is material in English law and the non-disclosure of such information entitles the insurer to avoid the con-

---

167. See, for example, the subsequent application of the test by Potter J in *St Paul Fire & Marine Ins Co (UK) Ltd* v *McConnel Dowell Contractors Ltd* [1993] 2 Lloyd's Rep 503 (contractors AR).
168. p 506.
169. p 504. See Brooke [1985] LMCLQ 437; Diamond [1986] LMCLQ 25, 29; Kelly, (1988) 1 Ins L J 30, 35 ff; Borrowdale, *Essays in Commercial Law* (ed Borrowdale and Rower, Auckland 1991) p 72. *Cf* Khan [1986] JBL 37. For discussion of public policy considerations, see Clarke [1988] JBL 298, 305.
170. [1984] 1 Lloyd's Rep 476. The decision was followed in *Highlands Ins Co* v *Continental Ins Co* [1987] 1 Lloyd's Rep 109 (re).
The decision was accepted in *Amo Containers Ltd* v *Drake Ins Co Ltd* (1985) 51 Nfld & PEIR 55 (container insurance).
171. [1982] 2 Lloyd's Rep 178. The judge held the same in *Commonwealth Ins Co* v *Groupe Sprinks SA* [1983] 1 Lloyd's Rep 67.
172. [1984] 1 Lloyd's Rep 476, 510 *per* Parker LJ.

tract of insurance, certainly in commercial insurance and perhaps also on personal business.[173] The decision is open to question on a number of grounds.

23–7B1 Precedent

Although described[174] as the "only discordant note" in "a stream of decisions reaching back to *Carter* v *Boehm*",[175] the decision of the Court of Appeal purported to rest largely on previous cases, and the belief that precedent must be respected. But precedent for the court's decision is far from clear. There are cases supporting a test based on information Type B (above, 23–7A), not least the statement of Lord Mansfield[176] that a contract of insurance could not be set aside for non-disclosure unless the "risk run is really different from the risk understood and intended to be run, at the time of the agreement". Moreover, it is submitted that the cases said to support the view taken in *CTI* v *Oceanus* might be distinguished on one or more of the following grounds.

A first ground of distinction is that the decisions did not concern information Type C and therefore did not concern the materiality of such information; most concerned information of type B.[177] Second, in some cases the materiality of the information was admitted and thus not the subject of searching debate by the court.[178] Third, some cases concerned fraud, to which courts have usually responded with a rule more favourable to the insurer.[179] In cases of misrepresentation, in which the information misrepresented must likewise be material, the impact of fraud is more evident. "Once make out that there has been anything like deception, and no contract resting in any

173. Kerr LJ (p 491) suggested that the rule might differ in cases of consumer insurance. *Cf* Law Commission Report No 104, paras 4.34 ff.

174. *Barclay Holdings (Australia) Pty Ltd* v *British National Ins Co Ltd* (1987) 8 NSWLR 514, 522–523 *per* Glass JA (fire).

175. *Carter* v *Boehm* (1766) 3 Burr 1905.

176. pp 1909–1910.

177. *Carter* v *Boehm* (1766) 3 Burr 1905 (that "Fort Marlborough" was effectively without defence against a European enemy); *Traill* v *Baring* (1864) 4 De G J & S 318 (whether the person taking out reinsurance would bear part of the risk himself); *Harrower* v *Hutchinson* (1870) LR 5 QB 584 (that the ship was calling at port L, in respect of which the prudent insurer would have required a higher premium); *Ionides* v *Pender* (1874) LR 9 QB 531 (whether goods insured were greatly over valued in the policy thus making it a speculative risk); *Rivaz* v *Gerussi* (1880) 6 QBD 222 (whether, when taking out open cover, previous open cover was nearly exhausted, thus affecting how soon the new cover would become operative); *Tate* v *Hyslop* (1885) 15 QBD 368 (whether there would be recourse against lightermen who damaged the goods insured); *Glicksman* v *Lancashire & General Ins Co Ltd* [1927] AC 139 (whether the insured had previously been refused such (burglary) cover); *Greenhill* v *Federal Ins Co Ltd* [1927] 1 KB 65 (that the goods to be insured had just travelled on deck and been exposed to sea water); *McCormick* v. *National Motor & Accident Ins Union Ltd* (1934) 49 Ll L Rep 34 (that the proposer of motor insurance had been convicted of dangerous driving); *Anglo-African Merchants* v *Bayley* [1970] 1 QB 311 (that the "new" leather jerkins being insured were government surplus 20 years old, such goods being regarded as "hot" i.e., that there was an abnormally high risk of theft); *Marene Knitting Mills Pty Ltd* v *Greater Pacific General Ins Ltd* [1976] 2 Lloyd's Rep 631 (fire insurance: the same company had previously suffered four serious fires); *Mayne Nickless* v *Pegler* [1974] 1 NSWLR 228 (motor insurance: previous accident causing extensive damage to three vehicles).

178. *Bates* v *Hewitt* (1867) LR 2 QB 595 (hull); *Greenhill* v *Federal Ins Co Ltd* [1927] 1 KB 65 (CA—cargo); *Marene Knitting Mills Pty Ltd* v *Greater Pacific General Ins Ltd* [1976] 2 Lloyd's Rep 631 (PC—fire); *Reynolds* v *Phoenix Assurance Co Ltd* [1978] 2 Lloyd's Rep 440 (fire).

179. Such a case was *Rivaz* v *Gerussi* (1880) 6 QBD 222 (CA—cargo). See also *The Bedouin* [1894] P 1, 12 *per* Lord Esher MR (CA—freight).

degree on that foundation can stand."[180] It is submitted that, whether the allegation be one of misrepresentation or of non-disclosure, cases of fraud provide little guidance on materiality in cases where there is no fraud.

In *CTI* v *Oceanus* Lloyd J had been influenced by two decisions, each of which was distinguished and disregarded by the Court of Appeal. The first was *Mutual Life Ins Co* v *Ontario Metal Products Co Ltd*,[181] in which Lord Salveson accepted[182] the contention of counsel for the insurer that "the test was whether, if the fact concealed had been disclosed, the insurers would have acted differently, . . . by declining the risk at the proposed premium . . . " Deciding that failure by the insured to disclose certain visits to his doctor did not avoid life insurance, the Privy Council in *Mutual Life* did not regard non-disclosure type C as sufficient for avoidance. This decision was distinguished by the Court of Appeal in *CTI* v *Oceanus*[183] as a case about the meaning of material misrepresentation in a Canadian statute. But, as Kerr LJ observed, on the question of materiality "there is no difference between allegations of non-disclosure and misrepresentation."[184] Further, the Ontario statute was drafted in the language and image of English law, and clearly both the Board and later courts thought that there was no (material) difference between the law in Ontario and in England. Indeed, in 1957 the definition of materiality in the *Mutual Life* case was adopted as a statement of English law by a Law Reform Committee[185] with some of the finest legal minds of the time.[186]

The second case was *Zurich General Accident & Liability Ins Co Ltd* v *Morrison*,[187] in which the issue was whether a judgment obtained against the insured by the victim of a motor accident could be enforced against the insurer under the Road Traffic Act 1934, section 10. The insurer pleaded non-disclosure that the insured had failed the driving test. The Court of Appeal rejected this defence. Lord Greene MR said[188]: "The evidence entirely fails to convince me that the insurers, had they known of the failure to pass the test, would have declined to issue a policy on precisely the same terms as those on which they did issue the policy in question." In *CTI* v *Oceanus*[189] Kerr LJ distinguished the *Morrison* case as turning on the particular statute: for a plea of non-disclosure the statute required not one thing but two: not only objective materiality (potential influence) but also subjective materiality (actual influence).[190]

---

180. *Reynelle* v *Sprye* (1852) 1 De GM & G 600, 708 *per* Lord Cranworth; see also *Attwood* v *Small* (1838) 6 Cl & Fin 232, 444, 466 *per* Lord Brougham (HL); *Kennedy* v *Panama Royal Mail* (1867) LR 2 QB 580, 587 *per* Blackburn J. In early days fraud was a prerequisite of rescission in such cases: *Higgins* v *Samels* (1862) 2 J & H 460, 467 *per* Wood V-C. A similar severity in response to fraud is seen, for example, in *Smith* v *Kay* (1859) 7 HLC 750, 759 *per* Lord Chelmsford LC, applied in *Gordon* v *Street* [1899] 2 QB 641, 646 by A L Smith LJ (CA); *Dimmock* v *Hallett* (1866) 2 Ch App 21, 29 *per* Sir G J Turner LJ; *Herring* v *Janson* (1895) 1 Com Cas 177.

181. [1925] AC 344.

182. p 351.

183. [1984] 1 Lloyd's Rep 476, 495.

184. p 490.

185. Fifth Report (Conditions and Exceptions in Insurance Policies) Cmnd 62. It was also adopted by the Australian Law Commission Report No 20 on Insurance Contracts, 1982, para 175.

186. Including Jenkins LJ, Parker LJ, Devlin J, Diplock J, RE Megarry QC (as they then were). It was also adopted more recently by Bower, *Disclosure*, 3.07, however the learned editors appear to have ignored *CTI* v *Oceanus* (above).

187. [1942] 2 KB 53.

188. p 58. See also Goddard LJ at p 65.

189. [1984] 1 Lloyd's Rep 476, 495.

190. [1942] 2 KB 53, 60 *per* Mackinnon LJ. In any event, there is authority that subjective materiality is also required by common law: see above, 23–6A2.

In *Oceanus* there was one question to be answered, and in *Morrison* there were two, but the sole question in *Oceanus* and the first question in *Morrison*, the question of objective materiality, were the same.[191] On that question *Morrison* was and is good precedent in England.

23–7B2 Practicality

"It is possible to say that prudent underwriters in general would consider a particular circumstance as bearing on the risk and exercising an influence on their judgment towards declining the risk or loading the premium. It is not possible to say, save in extreme cases, that prudent underwriters in general would have acted differently, because there is no absolute standard by which they would have acted in the first place or as to the precise weight they would give to the undisclosed circumstance."[192]

To this statement, the first objection is that, although there is no "absolute standard" (a loaded phrase), the test of materiality is that of the prudent insurer,[193] an objective test controlled and applied by the court[194] in the light of expert evidence, like that of the reasonable man in tort.[195]

Second, given the objective nature of the materiality test, it is not very much easier (and thus more practical and more certain) to say that a fact has some influence (Type C) than to say that it has a decisive influence (Type A or Type B), unless information Type C means any information having the slightest connection with the risk, in which case, there is a third objection.

Third, if the proposer must disclose information Type C, potential insureds will be advised to play safe by total disclosure. Over 100 years ago, Blackburn J said[196] that "it would be too much to put on the insured the duty of disclosing everything which might influence the mind of an underwriter. Business could hardly be carried on if this was required". No less today, the London tradition of the rapid placement of risks would be blocked by an avalanche of information. The placing file in *CTI* v *Oceanus* itself was over 100 pages in length; yet the Court of Appeal held that the insurer had not been told enough! The relentless march of the megabyte, of the machine that copies, stores and faxes to foreign parts, may be such that it is now too late.[197]

23–7C Principle

In recent years, the trend of the law has been to make it not easier but harder to end contracts. A contract can be terminated for breach of contract, but only if the breach is serious[198] or if the contract itself provides for termination in very clear terms.[199] Since 1967, the right to rescind a contract for misrepresentation is only absolute, i.e., free of court discretion to refuse rescission, in cases of fraud.[200]

191. Also in this sense, Brooke, *op cit.*
192. *CTI* v *Oceanus* [1984] 1 Lloyd's Rep 476, 510 *per* Parker LJ (CA).
193. Above, 23–6.
194. Above, 23–6B4.
195. *Ibid.*
196. *Ionides* v *Pender* (1874) LR 9 QB 531, 539 (re). In this sense *CTI* v *Oceanus* [1982] 2 Lloyd's Rep 178, 187 *per* Lloyd J. *Barclay Holdings (Australia) Pty Ltd* v *British National Ins Co Ltd* (1987) 8 NSWLR 514, 518 *per* Kirby P (fire). *Contra: CTI* v *Oceanus* [1984] 1 Lloyd's Rep 476, 496 *per* Kerr LJ (CA).
197. See further, Arnould, No 646; Baer, 12 Ottawa L Rev 610, 644.
198. *Hongkong Fir Shipping Co Ltd* v *Kawasaki Kisen Kaisha Ltd* [1962] 2 QB 26 (CA); *Cehave NV* v *Bremer Handelsgesellschaft mbH* [1976] QB 44 (CA).
199. *Wickman Machine Tools Sales Ltd* v *Schuler AG* [1974] AC 235.
200. Misrepresentation Act 1967, section 2(2).

In the law of tort, no action for damages will lie in respect of negligent misstatement, unless that statement contained material information of Type A or Type B. In *Jeb Fasteners Ltd* v *Marks Bloom & Co*,[201] Donaldson LJ thought immaterial all information which "will not affect the essential validity of [the] decision in the sense that if the truth had been known or suspected before the decision was taken, the same decision would still have been made." In other words, the act impugned must be in some sense a cause of the loss or damage.

The decision in *CTI* v *Oceanus* ignores the underlying reason for granting a remedy in cases of misrepresentation and non-disclosure, that they vitiate consent, in the present case, the consent of the insurer. As Steyn LJ recently underlined, account should be taken in this context of "the fact that avoidance for non-disclosure is the remedy provided by law because the risk presented is different from the true risk".[202] How can it be said that the consent of the insurer has been vitiated, if he would have made the same contract on the same terms, even if the information had been disclosed?

23–8 FACTS KNOWN TO THE PROPOSER

The proposer is required to disclose only material information known to him.[203] However, he may be deemed to know things, which he does not actually know, if they are known to his agents (below, 23–8A) or if he should have known them (below, 23–8B, 23–8C):[204] either because he failed to make himself aware of certain information available to him or because, having become aware of it, he had forgotten it at the time of contracting the insurance.[205] Moreover, he is deemed to know things that he should have inferred them from things he actually did know (below, 23–8D).

23–8A The Knowledge of Agents

Whether or not the proposer actually knows it, he is deemed to know what is known or should be known to any servant or agent who is his "agent to know".[206] This is because the agent is presumed to have performed his duty to pass the information back to his principal—a presumption that is said to be irrebuttable except when the agent is acting fraudulently to his principal.[207] As to the identity of the "agent to know", in marine insurance,

---

201. [1983] 1 All ER 583, 588 (CA).

202. *Pan Atlantic Insurance Co Ltd* v *Pine Top Ins Co Ltd* [1993] 1 Lloyd's Rep 496 (CA—re).

203. *Lindenau* v *Desborough* (1828) 8 B & C 586 (life); *Swete* v *Fairlie* (1833) 6 Car & P 1; *Joel* v *Law Union & Crown Ins Co* [1908] 2 KB 863, 884 *per* Fletcher Moulton LJ (CA—life); *Lee* v *British Law Ins Co Ltd* [1972] 2 Lloyd's Rep 49, 56 *per* Davies LJ (CA—PA). *Cleveland* v *Sunderland Marine Mutual Ins Co* (1987) 45 DLR (4th) 340 (NS—hull); *Dyck* v *Poirier* (1988) 47 DLR (4th) 193 (Sask—motor). *American Employers' Ins Co* v *Cable*, 108 F 2d 225 (5 Cir, 1939—fidelity); *Brayer* v *John Hancock Mutual Life Ins Co*, 179 F 2d 925 (2 Cir, 1950—life). *Keating* v *New Ireland Assurance Co plc* [1990] IR 383 (life).

204. Canada in this sense: *Turgeon* v *Fortin* (1968) 13 DLR (3d) 308 (Sup Ct—motor). But in certain cases, such as fire insurance, statute has changed the common law rule: the insurance can be avoided only if the proposer was fraudulent: for example, Ontario Insurance Act, RSO c 218, section 125. USA *idem*: below, 23–8E.

205. Bower, *Disclosure*, 4.08.

206. *Blackburn* v *Vigors* (1887) 12 App Cas 531, 537 *per* Lord Halsbury LC (re). As regards the duties of the insured's agent, including duties affecting disclosure, see above, 9–5D.

USA in this sense: *Merchants Fire Assurance Corp* v *Lattimore*, 263 F 2d 232 (9 Cir, 1959—personal property floater).

207. See Bower, *Disclosure*, no 4.26; Bowstead pp 412 ff.

"it is not the knowledge of all agents and servants that is imputed to the proposer of any marine insurance, but only the knowledge of quite a limited class, namely, the broker who actually places the insurance, the master or the shipowner, or, to use Lord Halsbury's phrase 'his general agent for the management of his shipping business'."[208]

In non-marine insurance, Pearson J said[209] that

"one should consider, mainly at any rate, (1) the position of the agent in relation to the principal and whether the agent had a wide or narrow sphere of operations, and (2) the position of the agent in relation to the relevant transaction and whether he represented the principal in respect of that transaction."

This statement suggests that two kinds of person may be the proposer's "agents to know", the agent mandated specifically to contract the insurance and the more general agent, who is the *alter ego* of the insured, especially inside companies, and whose function is to receive and, in appropriate circumstances, to communicate relevant knowledge to the insured.

23-8A1 Contracting Agents

The relevant agents include a person who is commissioned to make the insurance contract[210] and does so. If that agent himself employs a further agent to make the contract, he is an agent of the proposer too, and so is any other agent in the chain of commission leading to the making of the contract,[211] as well as persons "specially employed for the purpose of communicating to him the very facts which the law requires him to divulge to his insurer"[212] in relation to that contract.

In contrast, the knowledge of agents operating independently does not come together. If two insurances are contracted "in parallel" on the same risk, one through agent A and the other through agent B, the insured may enforce B's contract, regardless of any knowledge possessed by agent A.[213] A further distinction is made between "parallel" insurance and joint insurance because, in the case of joint insurance, non-disclosure by one co-insured affects the other: the insurer is entitled to avoid the contract as regards both of them.[214] Where the insurance is not joint but composite,[215] the position is less clear, however, as composite insurance concerns a single contract of insurance albeit on multiple interests, perhaps the governing principle is that, if a con-

---

208. *Australia & New Zealand Bank Ltd* v *Colonial & Eagle Wharves Ltd* [1960] 2 Lloyd's Rep 241, 254 *per* McNair J (goods AR).

209. *Regina Fur Co Ltd* v *Bossom* [1957] 2 Lloyds Rep 466, 484 (AR).

210. USA: for cases concerning brokers, see *Hamblet* v *City Ins Co*, 36 F 118 (WD Pa, 1888—hull); *Merchants Fire Assurance Corp* v *Lattimore*, 263 F 2d 232 (9 Cir, 1959—personal property floater); *Breiling* v *Maciuszek*, 780 F Supp 535 (ND Ill, 1991—yacht).

211. In *Blackburn* v *Haslam* (1888) 21 QBD 144, the proposer employed broker A, who employed his London agent, who in turn had the contract of reinsurance concluded by a London broker. The proposer was fixed with knowledge possessed by A.

212. *Blackburn* v *Vigors* (1887) 12 App Cas 531, 541 *per* Lord Watson (re).

213. *Blackburn* v *Vigors* (above).

214. *Woolcott* v *Sun Alliance & London Ins Co Ltd.* [1978] 1 Lloyd's Rep 629, 632 per Caulfield J (fire), with reference to the judgment of Sir Wilfred Greene MR quoted below 30-4.

A similar decision was reached as regards the duty of the "insured" to disclose in section 21 of the Insurance Contracts Act 1984 (Cth): a wife, jointly insured with her husband, was affected by non-disclosure by her husband of facts known only to him: *Advance (NSW) Insurance Agencies Pty Ltd* v *Matthews* (1989) 63 ALJR 365 (HCA—house contents).

215. See Sir Wilfred Greene MR, *loc cit.*

tract cannot be rescinded *in toto* it cannot be rescinded at all. The result would be the rescission of composite insurance for non-disclosure by one alone of the co-insured.[216]

In any case, if the agent of the proposer has material knowledge, the insurer does not need to prove that he acquired the knowledge while actively engaged in concluding the contract.[217]

23–8A2 The Knowledge of Companies: the Alter Ego

The agents include any person, servant or agent, who is the proposer's *alter ego*[218]—a reference suggesting an analogy with the *alter ego* doctrine in the general law of companies.[219] The functions of that doctrine are various,[220] but include one germane to contracting insurance: to ensure that "the device of incorporation is not a bolt-hole for people who commit offences".[221] So too here, the notion of constructive knowledge is to ensure that delegation is not a bolt-hole for people who make contracts of insurance without sufficient disclosure. Generally, "one hand of the company must be charged with what the other knows and does."[222]

In *Regina Fur Co Ltd* v *Bossom*,[223] the insured was a company with two directors, A and B. Financially the company belonged to A, who was also chairman. It was operated by B, and it was he who insured some furs. The insurance claim was defeated on the ground of non-disclosure of moral hazard known only to A. Pearson J[224]:

"The difficulty arises here because the person who actually negotiated the insurance with the underwriters was [B], and [A] did not participate in those negotiations; but there are other factors, namely (i) [A]'s predominant position in the plaintiff company, as previously set out; (ii) the fact (if relevant) that in similar policies in previous years [A] had been joined with the company as co-insured; (iii) his knowledge that the company's property was being insured year after year; (iv) the fact that he regularly, year after year, joined with [B] in signing the company's cheques for the insurance premiums."

Again, in Australia, having considered the English cases, a judge has decided[225] that the "managing agent of a block of shops and offices is . . . such an agent. His knowledge of matters relating to the property which impact on the insurance risk ought to be imputed to the owners. In other words, by delegating the management of the property to an agent, the owners cannot avoid having knowledge of matters which might result in a proposal being refused or a higher premium being imposed". This

---

216. Nicholson (1990) 3 Ins L J 218, 227 ff.

217. Arnould, No 637. However, it may be open to the insured to prove that the agent did not acquire the information while acting for him: Bowstead, p 415.

218. The phrase "*alter ego*" was used by Lord Watson in *Blackburn* v *Vigors* (1887) 12 App Cas 531, 540 (re).

219. This is suggested by the language used in, for example, *Australia & New Zealand Bank Ltd* v *Colonial & Eagle Wharves Ltd* (below) and by Lord Halsbury in *Blackburn* v *Vigors* (above).
In relation to companies, the rule looks to any person who has the power to make managerial decisions without further reference. See *R* v *Stanley Haulage* (1964) ICL case No 421; *The Lady Gwendolen* [1965] P 294 (CA); *Tesco* v *Nattrass* [1972] AC 153; *The Marion* [1984] 2 All ER 343 (HL).

220. Including to ensure that a company may be liable under rules of law requiring intent or *mens rea* by attributing the mental state of certain people to the company, for "corporate responsibility in crime has social utility in promoting obedience to the law"—Glanville Williams, *Textbook of Criminal Law*, p 975.

221. Williams, *op cit*, p 970.

222. *State Farm Mutual Ins Co* v *Bockhurst*, 453 F 2d 533, 536 (10 Cir, 1972—motor). See also *London General* v *General Marine* (below, 23–8C).

223. [1957] 2 Lloyd's Rep 466; an appeal on other points was not allowed: [1958] 2 Lloyd's Rep 425.

224. p 484. See Bowstead pp 395–396; but *cf* Bower, *Disclosure*, 4.24.

225. *Lindsay* v *CIC Ins Ltd* (1989) 16 NSWLR 673, 684 (fire). On this point he considered that the common law rule had been adopted by s 21(1) of the Insurance Contracts Act (Cth) 1984.

opinion is entirely consistent with the *alter ego* doctrine of company law, which has been applied to insurance cases in Australia.

Moreover, knowledge, like the corporate entity, survives the demise or departure of the human beings who acquired it. In the USA, in the case of the acquisition of the insured company by another company, it has been held that it was not inequitable to impute the insured company's preacquisition knowledge to its postacquisition existence. "Where a corporation is acquired by the purchase of all its outstanding stock, the corporate entity remains intact and retains its liabilities . . . The process of acquisition simply does not sanitize the acquired corporation, notwithstanding . . . the fact that it has gained new owners and a fresh management", who were justifiably ignorant of the relevant information.[226]

In contrast, clearly the insured is not obliged to disclose material facts known only to junior staff, such as clerical workers. Speaking of a chief entry clerk at a warehouse, the only person aware of the actual system of control, McNair J said[227]: "Though, in a sense, the key man in the sense that a mistake by him would mean the failure of the system, his duties were almost entirely clerical; it was not established that he had any discretion or executive authority."

In conclusion and in principle, one can only say that knowledge is attributable to the insured company, if "it is within the scope of the employee's employment to receive such knowledge and he is therefore under a duty to communicate it to his employer".[228] He may be a channel for information in general or only as regards matters relating to a specific department, such as the consignment of goods.[229]

23–8B The Knowledge of Experience

The law makes assumptions about what the proposer knew or should have known himself, simply as a human being in his position. Cockburn CJ talked of his being taken to know that of which he "ought to have knowledge"[230]; Lord Halsbury emphasised the appearances, looking to what the insurer was entitled to assume about the knowledge of the proposer.[231] It is likely that what the law expects of the commercial proposer (below, 23–8C) is greater than what it expects of a consumer; otherwise, the duty of knowledge is objectively assessed.

For example, the proposer who insures a cohabitee may be deemed to know material facts about that person. In the United States, it has been held that a husband, who insures his wife, should know about her "female troubles"[232]: "Mrs Straub testified that she did not communicate to her husband the fact that she was suffering from

---

226. *Fireman's Fund Ins Cos* v *Meenan Oil Co*, 755 F Supp 547, 553 (ED NY, 1991—liability).

227. *Australia & New Zealand Bank Ltd* v *Colonial & Eagle Wharves Ltd* [1960] 2 Lloyd's Rep 241, 254: a claim was made under all risks insurance on goods in the insured's warehouse. The insurer pleaded non-disclosure of a practice at the warehouse, unknown to the directors of the insured company but known to persons at the warehouse, of releasing goods without the authority of the bank for which they were being held. The most senior person in the know was the chief entry clerk. McNair J held that his knowledge could not be attributed to the insured.

228. *South Australian Housing Trust* v *State Government Ins Commission* (1989) 51 SASR 1, 23 (liability), with reference *inter alia* to *Tesco* v *Nattrass* [1972] AC 153. See also on this point below 26–2D.

229. *Proudfoot* v *Montefiore* (1867) LR 2 QB 511.

230. *Proudfoot*, p 521.

231. *Blackburn* v *Vigors* (1887) 12 App Cas 531 (re).

232. *Straub* v *Mutual of Omaha*, 335 F Supp 892, 896 (D Canal Zone, 1971): a claim under a health policy in respect of the cost of treating the claimant's wife for cancer of the breast was defeated for non-disclosure. Generally, the proposer in the United States is only required to disclose what he knows: below, 23–8E.

fibroid tumours, but it was his responsibility to know whether or not she had such condition and convey the information to the insurer before the insurer was bound."

The proposer knows only what his doctor tells him. At common law, he is not deemed to know what his doctor does not tell him, because his doctor is not his "agent to know"[233] and because, in England, the doctor-patient relationship is not such as to require the doctor to tell the patient the whole truth about his investigation.[234] This is no less true, when the proposal is on the life or health of a third party. In *Wheelton* v *Hardisty*[235] the plaintiff, who lent money to X on the security of the reversionary interest of X in his father's estate, insured the life of X. The jury found fraud by X and by his doctor but the court held that the plaintiff was not affected.[236] For Lord Campbell CJ,[237] the test was whether

"the assurer and the insured being equally ignorant of material facts to influence their contract, . . . the assurer asks for information, and the insured does his best to put the assurer in a situation to obtain the information, and to form his own opinion as to whether the information is sincere".

This position may have been changed, however, by the proposer's right of access to information about himself under the Data Protection Act 1984, the Access to Medical Reports Act 1988 and the Access to Health Records Act 1990. For example, under the 1988 Act he has only to "request" the information of the person who made the report (s 6(2)), and under the 1990 Act to apply to the person who holds the records,[238] to obtain the relevant information. Even so, it is not clear that he will be deemed to have the information. First, these persons are neither the agent nor the *alter ego* of the proposer. Second, although the proposer can be expected to check in his own records the accuracy of what he says, it has been held that he is not obliged to initiate an (outside) investigation of matters relevant to the risk proposed.[239] One reason is cost: a premise of the duty of disclosure is that it is cheaper and more efficient that the proposer should tell the insurer all he knows about the risk than that the insurer should have to "discover the wheel" for himself, however, if the proposer must blunder around collecting information, the balance of cost and convenience has swung against him. The law is slow to put upon a contracting party the duty and expense of seeking information.[240] Yet, it might be thought that the statutes provide a relatively cheap and easy means of checking one's records. There is doubt.

If the proposer has conducted an investigation leading to knowledge (or means of

---

233. *Keating* v *New Ireland Assurance Co plc* [1990] IR 383 (life).See also above, 23–8A.

234. For example *Godfrey* v *Britannic Assurance Co Ltd* [1963] 2 Lloyd's Rep 515 (life). Generally, see *Sidaway* v *Bethlem Royal Hospital Governors* [1985] AC 871.

235. (1857) 8 E & B 232. See also *Joel* v *Law Union & Crown Ins Co* [1908] 2 KB 863 (CA—life).

236. The doctor was employed and paid by the insurer but this was, in the view of Lord Campbell CJ (p 274) irrelevant. The fraud lay in non-disclosure when questioned by the insurer, notably concerning the intemperate habits of X. It was argued by the defendant insurer that X and the doctor were agents of the plaintiff insured in giving answers to all material questions, so that their knowledge (and fraud) was his knowledge (and fraud). This contention was rejected by the Court of Queen's Bench and by the Exchequer Chamber.

237. p 269. The answer expected was, of course, negative. This is consistent with the rule that if an insurer conducts an investigation or examination he assumes responsibility for what is or is not revealed.

238. In certain circumstances the information can be withheld. Moreover, under the 1988 Act the reporter is not obliged to retain the information for more than six months from the date on which it was "supplied".

239. *Australia & New Zealand Bank Ltd* v *Colonial & Eagle Wharves Ltd* [1960] 2 Lloyd's Rep 241.

240. For example, *Reid* v *Rush & Tompkins Group* [1989] 3 All ER 240 *per* Ralph Gibson LJ (CA); Collins (1992) 55 MLR 556.

knowledge) of the risk greater than would normally be expected of him, and the insurer is unaware of this investigation and its findings, is the proposer obliged to disclose them to the insurer? The law is normally reluctant to reward diligence with the crown of heavier duties than those generally imposed on the reasonable man in his position,[241] lest it discourage the voluntary investigation of risks which might better prevent loss.[242] However, in insurance law it appears that, if the proposer has arranged an investigation, the results of that investigation must be made known to the insurer, whether the insurer could have expected the proposer to make the investigation or not.[243]

23–8C Knowledge of Businesss

The proposer is not expected to conduct a special investigation of, for example, security in his business,[244] unless and to the extent specifically demanded by the insurer—any more than a consumer is expected to initiate himself a medical examination before applying for life or accident insurance. However, if he has conducted such an investigation, it seems that he must disclose the results: above, 23–8B. In any event, the businessman, who proposes insurance, is taken to know what is going on, both in his line of business generally and within the walls of his own firm.

In *London General* v *General Marine*,[245] the plaintiff insured was himself an insurer with separate departments for underwriting and for reinsurance. When the Lloyd's casualty list came, as usual, to the underwriting department, which was busy, it was put in a drawer. The list contained information material to a risk which was reinsured by the reinsurance department, unaware of the information, that afternoon. The Court of Appeal held that the plaintiff should be deemed to know the information. Lord Sterndale MR[246]:

"If it were a question of their having done their best, so far as the pressure of business would allow, to make themselves acquainted with the casualty slips, and of their not being able to do so in time to stop the broker's instructions, I think it might have been difficult to deal with such a case, but there is no such case before us. They never did anything at all."

This decision suggests an objective test of what the proposer in business should know, but Arnould takes a different view[247]:

"The test of what 'ought to be known' by the insured is not, therefore, an objective test of what ought to be known by a reasonable, prudent insured carrying on a business of the kind in question, but a test of what ought to be known by the insured in carrying out his business in the manner in which he carries on that business; the underwriter takes the risk that the business may be run inefficiently unless the circumstances are such that the insured knows or suspects facts material to be disclosed. To hold otherwise would be tantamount to saying that underwriters only insure those who conduct their business prudently, whereas it is commonplace that one of

---

241. The duty of care in tort, for example, is assessed with reference to objective categories such as layman, nurse, doctor, surgeon, and a higher standard is not expected of a layman who happens to have gone on a first aid course.

242. *The Hoyanger* [1979] 2 Lloyd's Rep 79, 89 (Canada—Fed Ct).

243. For example, the report of a specialist doctor; see cases discussed above, 23–5.

244. *Australia & New Zealand Bank Ltd* v *Colonial & Eagle Wharves Ltd* [1960] 2 Lloyd's Rep 241 (above, 23–8A2).

245. [1921] 1 KB 104.

246. P 110. See also Warrington LJ (p 111) who decided against the proposer because "they were either too busy or too careless"; and Younger LJ (p 113) who said that the proposer's business practice was "neglect to their own undoing".

247. No 640.

the purposes of insurance is to obtain cover against the consequences of negligence in the management of the insured's affairs."

While it is true that in principle cover extends to negligence by the insured, once the cover has been contracted, it does not follow from that that the insurer assumes the risk of negligence in the presentation of information, on the basis of which the insurer will decide whether to take or how to rate the risk. It would be odd, if the law applied an objective standard to inferences that the proposer draws from what he knows,[248] as well as an objective standard of materiality by reference to the prudent insurer or, sometimes, the reasonable insured,[249] and yet allowed the proposer to conduct his business in such a negligent way that facts never come to his attention in the first place, so that the objective rules are never allowed to bite. It is submitted that he is taken to know what he should know in the ordinary course of his kind of business.

23–8D Inference

For the purposes of disclosure, there are first the facts that the proposer actually knows or ought to know, his primary knowledge, and then, in addition, the law takes him to know what the reasonable man would infer from his primary knowledge.

In *Fowkes*,[250] Cockburn CJ addressed the jury in these terms:

"As to the first answer, to the question whether he had ever been afflicted with gout? no doubt it must be considered with some reasonable latitude, and the answer would not be false, merely because he had some symptoms which an experienced medical man might see indicated the presence of gout in the system. You will probably consider whether there was gout in a sensible appreciable form . . . "

But in *Godfrey*,[251] the insured was told by his doctors that he had a kidney complaint and that he could return to work, if he took care.[252] Roskill J said[253]: "I cannot think that a reasonable man, with no specialist knowledge of any kind, could have failed to appreciate that he was possessed of knowledge and information relating to his health . . . " However, it is doubtful whether a proposer must mention routine visits for a check-up. He must disclose only if there was "something that should have stuck in his mind and was quite different from the ordinary routine visits that one makes to an eye surgeon when he examines a patient and perhaps prescribes altered lenses."[254]

248. Below, 23–8D.

249. Above, 23–6.

250. *Fowkes* v *Manchester & London Life Assurance & Loan Assn* (1862) 3 F & F 440, 443–4 (life); the contract was avoided on other grounds.

251. *Godfrey* v *Britannic Assurance Co Ltd* [1963] 2 Lloyd's Rep 515. See also *Life Assn of Scotland* v *Foster*, 1873 11 Macph 351 (Ct Sess—life); *Joel* v *Law Union & Crown Ins Co Ltd* [1908] 2 KB 863, 884 *per* Fletcher Moulton LJ (CA—life); *Lee* v *British Law Ins Co Ltd* [1972] 2 Lloyd's Rep 49 (CA—PA). *Murphy* v *Sun Life Assurance Co* (1964) 44 DLR (2d) 369 (Alta—life). *Life Ins Co of North America* v *Capps*, 660 F 2d 392 (9 Cir, 1981—life). *Cf Hudson* v *Mutual of Omaha Ins Co* (1974) 55 DLR (3d) 115 (BC—life): held that cover on a person, who had been treated for depression and anxiety, was not vitiated by a negative answer to a question in the proposal form asking about "mental or nervous disorder". *Cf* also *Rivera* v *Benefit Trust Life Ins Co*, 921 F 2d 692 (7 Cir, 1991—PHI).

252. To the knowledge of the doctors, the complaint was more serious (a mild degree of chronic nephritis) and led to his death six months after he took insurance on his life. Nothing of this was disclosed to the insurer and, on this point, Roskill J decided that the insurer could avoid the contract: the patient must have known that all was not well with him. *Aliter*, when the proposer with an eye defect was given no warning at all about his condition: *Dyck* v *Poirier* (1988) 47 DLR (4th) 193 (Sask—motor).

253. [1963] 2 Lloyd's Rep 515, 532.

254. *Lee* v *British Law Ins Co Ltd* [1972] 2 Lloyd's Rep 49, 55 *per* Davies LJ (CA—PA).

The standard is the objective standard of the reasonable man, who is neither the stoic who shrugs off pain nor the hypochondriac who lives a life of apprehension. As Bower suggests,[255] "as the scale is traversed, a state of mind will be reached in which such an apprehension is seen to be sufficiently acute to impose a duty of disclosure".

23-8E United States: Fraud

The corresponding rule in the United States is quite different. In California, for example, a court would decide against the insurer if "the applicant for insurance had no present knowledge of the facts sought, or failed to appreciate the significance of the information related to him."[256] Again, "an applicant for life insurance is not faulted for failing to disclose a material fact when, because he or she fails to appreciate the significance of certain information, the existence of a condition queried on the application is not known."[257] In the USA, the English rule is found only in marine insurance.[258] In other cases, the rule, sometimes modified by state legislation, is that, if the insurer wishes to avoid the contract for non-disclosure (concealment), he must prove "fraud".[259] Fraud has been defined in the USA[260] in terms familiar to the English lawyer: "(1) Where insured, having actual knowledge of material facts, has intentionally failed to disclose them truthfully. (2) Where insured, though not having actual knowledge of material facts, yet has intentionally, and in bad faith, refused to become acquainted with the facts."

23-9 FACTS KNOWN TO THE INSURER

The insured is not obliged to disclose information already known to the insurer.[261] For this purpose, information is information actually known by the insurer (below,

255. Bower, *Disclosure*, 3.05; see also *ibid* 4.09.

256. *Thompson* v *Occidental Life Ins Co*, 513 P 2d 353, 360 (Cal, 1973—life).

257. *Life Ins Co of North America* v *Capps*, 660 F 2d 392, 394 (9 Cir, 1981—life).

258. *M'Lanahan* v *Universal Ins Co*, 1 Pet 170 (Sup. Ct., 1828—hull); *Alexander, Ramsay & Kerr* v *National Union Fire Ins*, 104 F 2d 1006 (2 Cir, 1939—hull); *Fireman's Fund Ins Co* v *Wilburn Boat Co*, 300 F 2d 631 (5 Cir, 1962—hull); *Gulfstream Cargo Ltd* v *Reliance Ins Co*, 409 F 2d 974 (5 Cir, 1969—hull). For the view that there is insufficient justification for the marine rule, see Harnett, 15 *Law & Contemporary Problems* 391 (1950).

259. *General Reinsurance* v *Southern Surety*, 27 F 2d 265, 273 (8 Cir, 1928—re); *Blair* v *National Security Ins Co*, 126 F 2d 955 (3 Cir, 1942—jewellery-fur floater); *Transcontinental Ins Co* v *Minning*, 135 F 2d 479 (6 Cir, 1943—fire); *Harris* v *State Farm Mutual*, 232 F 2d 532 (6 Cir, 1956—motor); *National Aviation Underwriters Inc* v *Fischer*, 386 F 2d 582 (8 Cir, 1967—aviation); in life insurance cases conflict: 45 CJS, section 594. *Cf Straub* above, 23-8B.

The onus is on the insurer: *Wharton* v *Aetna Life*, 48 F 2d 37 (8 Cir, 1931—life), cert den 284 US 621; *North American Accident Ins Co* v *Tebbs*, 107 F 2d 853 (10 Cir, 1939—PA).

260. *General Reinsurance* v *Southern Surety*, 27 F 2d 265, 273 (8 Cir, 1928). In England see *Derry* v *Peek* (1889) 14 App Cas 337; and in Canada: *Taylor* v *London Assurance Corp* [1935] SCR 422 (fire).

However, it is clear from *New York Life Ins Co* v *Cohen*, 57 F 2d 494, 495, (6 Cir, 1932—disability) and from other cases there cited that "falsely" means, not simply untrue, but in circumstances amounting to presumed or constructive fraud: the cases concerned a "no" answer to a question (in a proposal of life insurance) about previous visits to doctors. The proposer being of apparently sound memory, the appeal courts refused to accept a finding of the trial court that the proposer lacked intention to deceive. Moreover, it has been held that constructive knowledge of materiality may arise through the knowledge of the insured's agent: *Merchants Fire Assurance Corp* v *Lattimore*, 263 F 2d 232 (9 Cir, 1959—personal property floater). On this basis, the law begins to look more like English law.

261. *Carter* v *Boehm* (1766) 3 Burr 1905, 1911 *per* Lord Mansfield (marine); *St Margaret's Trust Ltd* v *Navigators & General Ins Co Ltd* (1949) 82 Ll L Rep 752 (hull). MIA, section 18(3)(b).

23–9A), information that he is deemed to know, first, because he is an insurer of that kind (23–9B) and, second, because he is a member of society—matters of common knowledge (23–9C). He is taken to know such things to prevent his closing his eyes,[262] and thereby providing himself with a means of escape from the contract. In all three cases, it is necessary to identify the person whose knowledge, actual or constructive, is taken to be the knowledge of the insurer.[263]

While the onus of proof of non-disclosure is on the insurer,[264] the onus of proof, that the insurer already knew or should have known the information, is on the insured.

23–9A The Actual Knowledge of the Insurer

If the insurer has the information because he has been given the information by the proposer, the proposer has performed the duty of disclosure and the present question, whether the proposer is dispensed from performing the duty, does not arise. We are here concerned with the different argument, that the proposer did not need to tell the insurer at all, because the insurer already knew. The difference may be less obvious, however, when it is argued that the insurer knew because he was told by the proposer sometime previously, for example, when a previous insurance contract was concluded. In any event, the source of the information must have been reliable.

23–9A1 Reliable Sources

Does it matter where the insurer gets the knowledge from? Apparently not, as long as the source is reliable. Usually, the source is his own agent.

In *Pimm* v *Lewis*,[265] Martin B addressed the jury about fire insurance on a mill[266]: "The mill had been used for years for the grinding of rice-chaff, and used publicly and openly, and the company's officer resident in the neighbourhood well knew the mill . . . Did the plaintiff, then, omit to communicate the matter which he might well presume they knew?" The jury returned a verdict for the plaintiff. Again, in *Woolcott* v *Excess Ins Co Ltd*,[267] once satisfied that the insurer's agent knew about the proposer's criminal record, the Court of Appeal was ready to reject the defence of non-disclosure: although the information had not come from the proposer himself, it had come from a reliable alternative source.

23–9A2 The Mind of the Insurer

If the insurer can be said to have the information already, who exactly represents the insurer for this purpose? If the insurer is a company, it is the *alter ego* : the highest person authorised to take the (managerial) decision, whether to accept or reject the proposal, or any (lower) person to whom that decision has been delegated. Such persons may be difficult for the proposer to identify and reach and so, if the insured's con-

---

262. *Bates* v *Hewitt* (1867) LR 2 QB 595, 605 *per* Cockburn CJ (hull).
263. *Mutual Life* v *Hilton-Green*, 241 US 613, 620 (1916—life).
264. Above, 23–2.
265. (1862) 2 F & F 778. USA in this sense: *Casey Enterprises Inc* v *American Hardware Mutual Ins Co*, 655 F 2d 598 (5 Cir, 1981—fire).
266. (1862) 2 F & F 778, 780.
267. [1979] 1 Lloyd's Rep 231, 241 *per* Megaw LJ (CA—fire).

tention is that the information has already reached the insurer, whether from the insured himself or from elsewhere, the contention becomes that the information reached the right channel of communication to such persons; in other words, the information has been received by the right agent in or for the insurance company.

The agent must be the right person to receive on behalf of the insurers that kind of information,[268] whether to deal with it himself or to pass it on: the insurer's antenna. The insurer's doorman is not the right channel nor, in general, is his lawyer.[269] The agent may or may not be an employee of the insurer.[270] If not, perhaps a broker, he must have undertaken an obligation [271] to channel information of the relevant kind to the particular insurer. In either case, the agent must have acquired the information while acting in his capacity as agent. Most information relating to the risk proposed is acquired when an agent is procuring the proposal for transmission to the insurer; he is then acting in his capacity as authorised agent of the insurer.[272] From this, two conclusions are said to follow.

The first conclusion is that information acquired at other times,[273] for example, off duty on Sunday, is not attributed to the insurer. This logic is sometimes lost on the insured, not least on the businessman who sees the 19th hole of his golf club as an extension of the office. It means, for example, that if the information is in an envelope handed to the agent at the club on Sunday, it is attributable or not according to whether the agent reads it then or waits until he arrives at the office on Monday; the position, if he reads it on the way to the office on Monday, is unclear. Also unclear is the impact of information acquired while on duty, the significance of which does not become apparent to the agent until he is off duty, or *vice versa*. The agent, it appears, is a robot operated by a time switch.

The second conclusion is that information acquired before he became the insurer's

---

268. *Bancroft* v *Heath* (1901) 6 Com Cas 137 (CA—fire); *Equitable Life Assurance Sy* v *General Accident Assurance Corp*, 1904 12 SLT 348, 351–352 *per* Lord Pearson (life). *Stipcich* v *Metroplitan Life*, 277 US 311 (1927—life); *Strangio* v *Consolidated Indemnity*, 66 F 2d 330 (9 Cir, 1933—motor); *Schrader* v *Prudential*, 280 F 2d 355 (5 Cir, 1960—life); *Contractors Realty Co* v *Ins Co of North America*, 469 F Supp 1287 (SDNY, 1979—hull). See also, above 20–7C and below 23–18B1 and 26–4B.
Notice to a soliciting or procuring agent, which would have been attributable to the insurer had it been given during the negotiations, is not attributable after the contract has been concluded: *Hare & Chase* v *National Surety*, 49 F 2d 447 (SDNY, 1931—guarantee). This rule may not apply to a general agent, whose authority is normally greater than that of a procuring or soliciting agent. The knowledge of an agent, who buys insurance from his own company, is not attributable to the company, if the agent is "fraudulent" (above, 23–8E) in the sense required, if a plea of concealment is to succeed: *Hartford Accident & Indemnity Co* v *Hartley*, 275 F Supp 610, 618 (MD Ga, 1967—fidelity), affirmed 389 F 2d 91 (5 Cir, 1968).
269. *Tate* v *Hyslop* (1885) 15 QBD 368, 378 *per* Lord Brett MR (CA—cargo).
270. *McGehee* v *Farmers Ins Co Inc*, 734 F 2d 1422 (10 Cir, 1984—fire). See further above, 23–3B. A leading case in Scotland is *Cruikshank* v *Northern Accident* (1895) 23 R 147: the insurer's agent, who was employed by the insurer as an inspector of agents but who was encouraged to procure business directly, if chance arose, obtained a proposal of accident cover. The proposal mentioned "slight lameness from birth", and was accepted by the insurer. The insurer resisted a claim on the ground of non-disclosure of the full extent of lameness. The claimant countered that this had been apparent to the agent when obtaining the proposal. The Court of Session decided for the claimant. See further, on the role of agents at the time of proposal, above, chapter 10.
271. Obliged, for example, by contract; thus, a doctor commissioned by an insurer to examine the proposer is the agent of the insurer: *Joel* v *Law Union & Crown Ins Co* [1908] 2 KB 863 (CA—life). *Idem*: *Life Ins Co of New York* v *Bohlman*, 328 F 2d 289 (10 Cir, 1964—life). *Cf California Reclamation Co* v *New Zealand Ins Co*, 138 P 960 (Cal, 1914—hull).
272. Generally, see chapter 8.
273. *Wilkinson* v *General Accident Fire & Life Assurance Corp Ltd* [1967] 2 Lloyd's Rep 182 (motor).

agent is not attributable to the insurer. In *Taylor* v *Yorkshire Ins Co*,[274] however, Palles CB said[275] that "recollection or forgetfulness by the agent of matters known previous to the relation ought not to affect the principal, save in cases . . . in which the principal purchases the previously obtained knowledge of the agent in relation to a particular subject-matter", perhaps only on the same risk, "or where the agent is—to use the emphatic words of Lord Halsbury—'an agent to know'[276]."

23–9B The Constructive Knowledge of the Insurer: Business

The "means of information may be equally open to both parties, and where concerning such matters, each professes to act from his own skill and sagacity, there is no need for either to communicate to the other party matters of general knowledge known to the enlightened or mercantile community at large, including well-established customs and usages, geography and natural perils, and political and international conditions. Silence in such matters does not affect the validity of the contract".[277] This has been the rule as regards the insurer's knowledge of the trade he insures since at least the time of Lord Mansfield: "Every underwriter is presumed to be acquainted with the practice of the trade he insures, and that whether it is established [practice] or not."[278] More recently, however, it has been held that the practice must be consistent,[279] but the real question seems to be whether the insurer should have realised that the practice would be followed as regards the risk under consideration.

  Most of the cases for this rule concern marine insurance,[280] but it probably extends to other branches of insurance. For example, the "reinsured ordinarily has no obligation to disclose the terms upon which insurance has been granted where those terms are generally to be found in policies of that nature, for the reinsurer ought to be aware of such standard terms. Where the reinsured has offered extended coverage or an unusual term, however, that is a material fact which, if not disclosed, would render

---

274. [1913] 2 IR 1, 20–21; see also p 30 *per* Gibson J. In this case, when acting as agent (in the view of the court—there was doubt) for insurer A, the agent learned that A had refused to insure a stallion. Ten months later he had become agent for insurer B, with whom he arranged to insure the same stallion. The claimant, who had insured the stallion through that agent on four occasions before he had started acting for insurer B, understandably left the agent to fill up the form. There was no mention of the refusal by insurer A. The Divisional Court of the Queen's Bench in Ireland held that the agent was acting for the proposer in filling the form; and (p 16) that knowledge acquired before he became agent for insurer B was not attributable to B, who could therefore avoid the contract on the ground of non-disclosure of the refusal.

275. See also *Banque Keyser Ullmann SA* v *Skandia (UK) Ins Co Ltd* [1985] 1 Lloyd's Rep. 69, 95 *per* Steyn LJ: "If [D] acted wrongfully or in breach of duty failed to act, during the course of his employment with [the insurer], it does not matter whether he acquired the relevant knowledge before or after the commencement of the employment."

276. *Blackburn* v *Vigors* (1887) 12 App Cas 531, 537.

277. *Anne Quinn* v *American Manufacturers*, 369 F Supp 1312, 1315 (SDNY, 1973—hull).

278. *Noble* v *Kennaway* (1780) 2 Doug 511, 513 (hull and cargo); the practice concerned was that of the fishing trade off Newfoundland and Labrador.

279. *Tate* v *Hyslop* (1885) 15 QBD 368, 378 *per* Lord Brett MR (CA—cargo).

280. For example, *Salvador* v *Hopkins* (1765) 3 Burr 1707 (hull insurer taken to know the practice of the East India Company); *Planche* v *Fletcher* (1779) 1 Doug 251 (cargo insurer taken to know "the constant course of trade, and notoriously so to everybody" (*per* Lord Mansfield, p 253) of clearing goods through customs for destination A, when in fact they were going to destination B). More recently, in *The Moonacre* [1992] 2 Lloyd's Rep 501, 517 (yacht) the insured (on renewal) was not required to disclose a minor theft as it was one "of the ordinary incidents to be anticipated during lay-up" of a yacht for the winter in Spain.

USA *idem*: *Buck & Hadnick* v *Chesapeke Ins Co*, 1 Pet 151, 160 *per* Justice Johnson (Sup Ct, 1828—hull); *Hazard* v *New England Marine Ins Co*, 8 Pet 557, 582 *per* Justice M'Lean (Sup Ct, 1834—hull); *Clark* v *Manufacturers'*, 49 US 235, 248 (1850), applied in *Anne Quinn* v *American Manufacturers*, 369 F Supp 1312 (SDNY, 1973—hull).

the reinsurance agreement voidable".[281] In any case, a similar idea is found in all branches of insurance in the proposition that the proposer need not disclose the ordinary attributes of the risk.[282]

23-9B1 Events Affecting the Business

If the insurer is taken to know the practices of the trade or context that he insures, it is but a small step to say that he should also be aware of particular events, notably catastrophes, affecting that trade or context. This small step is one that the courts have been reluctant to take.

Much depends on the way the idea is put to the court. In *Lean v Hall*[283] the court asked, what should be known to an insurer who had covered that kind of risk in that area in the recent past, and had little hesitation in attributing knowledge of events two months before. Avory J said[284] that

"Underwriters had been effecting these insurances in this part of Ireland since about November 1920, and it was for the jury to judge whether *the underwriters doing this business* up to May 1921 must not have known that premises of this character might probably have been occupied for a short time by the Crown forces or used for the internment of Sinn Fein prisoners".

But in the better known case of *Bates v Hewitt*[285] the court put the question in more general terms and the hull insurer there was not expected to remember events, even matters of great notoriety affecting shipping, occurring merely four months earlier. In *Bates v Hewitt*, a notorious Confederate cruiser put into Liverpool on 2 May 1864 and was converted for commercial use, an event of general notoriety at that time. She was insured under the same name on 6 August 1864 on the basis of a slip with an accurate description of her size and machinery, but no mention of her Confederate past. At the trial this was admitted to be material. On her first voyage she was seized by an American warship. The insurer defended the claim by a plea of non-disclosure. The judge entered a verdict for the insurer, which the Court of Queen's Bench would not disturb.[286]

---

281. *Sumitomo Marine* v *Cologne Reinsurance*, 552 NE 2d 139 (NY, 1990—re), with reference to Butler & Merkin, p A6.4–04 and Carter, *Reinsurance*, pp 125–126.
282. *Hales* v *Reliance Fire & Accident Ins Corp Ltd* [1960] 2 Lloyd's Rep 391 (fire).
283. (1923) 16 Ll L Rep 100: shortly after an Elizabethan house in County Kerry was insured against fire it was burned down by Sinn Fein rebels. The insurer pleaded non-disclosure that two months previously British troops had interned Sinn Fein prisoners in the house.
284. p 103 (emphasis added).
285. (1867) LR 2 QB 595.
286. The questions left to the jury were as follows:
"1. Whether the defendant had a present knowledge of the identity of the vessel.
2. If not, whether taking the previous knowledge of defendant as to the Confederate *Georgia* being at Liverpool, and the particulars disclosed by the slip and memorandum accompanying it, defendant, by the exercise of ordinary intelligence and knowledge of his business, might have known that this was the Confederate."
"Verdict: The jury are not satisfied that defendant was aware of the fact that the *Georgia* proposed for insurance was the former Confederate cruiser; but their verdict is, that he had abundant means [in the particulars] of identifying the ship at the time of underwriting the ship." This finding could mean one of two things. First, literally, the defendant had "means", and thus "might have known", but does not tell us whether the defendant did know or should have known. Second, the finding could mean that the insurer had sufficient means of identifying the ship and, by implication, should have known. As the slip did not mention her Confederate past, the jury must have made some assumptions about what the insurer should have remembered about recent events: constructive knowledge. Mellor J (p 609) appears to have rejected this as mischievous.

Cockburn CJ reasoned as follows[287]: the plaintiff could only succeed, if the insurer knew the recent history of the ship. Knowledge meant (a) "matters common to the knowledge of both parties", (b) a fact of "public notoriety" or (c) a fact "where it is one which is a matter of inference, and the materials for informing the judgment of the underwriter are common to both"; (b) suggests the possibility of constructive knowledge, but the case for the plaintiff, said the judge,[288] could be put in only two ways:

"either, that, if the previous knowledge which the defendant had with reference to the vessel *had been present* to his mind, that with the particulars before him, *would* have brought to his mind the fact that he was then asked to insure the Confederate steamship *Georgia*; or that, if he had carefully studied the particulars . . . those particulars *would* have brought back to his mind the knowledge which had been previously present to it, which, for the moment had been forgotten, and the combination of the knowledge thus resuscitated and revived with the particulars . . . *would* have led him to the conclusion that the vessel offered for insurance was the Confederate steamer."

The second way of putting the plaintiff's case indicates that a degree of constructive knowledge was contended for but rejected: "the facts are to the contrary; the previous knowledge that the defendant may have had *was not* present to his mind; and . . . the particulars *did not* bring back that knowledge to his mind." On this basis the decision below was upheld.

Cockburn CJ was clearly opposed to the idea that the insured should be entitled to make suppositions about what the insurer knew, saying[289]:

"We should be sanctioning an encroachment on a most important principle, and one that is vital in keeping up the full and perfect faith which there ought to be in contracts of marine insurance, if we were to hold that a party . . . may speculate as to what may or may not be in the mind of the underwriter, or as to what may or may not be brought to his mind by the particulars disclosed to him by the insured, if those particulars fall short of the fact which the insured is bound to communicate. If we were to sanction such a course, especially in these days, when parties frequently forget the rules of mercantile faith and honour which used to distinguish this country from any other, we should be lending ourselves to innovations of a dangerous and monstrous character, which I think we ought not to do."

This statement shows that the decision is one of its time. Further, the argument on speculation proves too much, for it also rules out *any* kind of constructive knowledge, including knowledge of trade practice, which has been assumed of the insurer in many cases before and since. It is surely odd that the insurer is taken to know the practices of the trade context, in which he operates (above, 23–9B1), including matters reported in *Lloyd's List*,[290] yet events, however well publicised, affecting that trade context can be conveniently forgotten. Moreover, it is doubtful whether the distinction between practices and events can be practicably made.

In modern Canada, in contrast, the insurer is expected to keep abreast of developments, not least in the area of industrial disease. Prior to 1970, many articles had been published in Canada and the United States on the health hazards of asbestos, scientific papers on the subject were in the public domain and the risk of asbestosis from inhalation of asbestos fibres was mentioned in the 1963 edition of *Encyclopedia Britannica*.

287. p 605.
288. p 606 (emphasis supplied); see also p 608. A similar statement of the law was given by Mellor J (p 610) on a selective view of Lord Mansfield's judgment in *Carter* v *Boehm* (1766) 3 Burr 1905 (marine). A view closer to that of the law today is found in the judgment of Shee J (p 610).
289. pp 606–607; similar reasons are given by Mellor J, pp 608–609.
290. *Mackintosh* v *Marshall* (1843) 11 M & W 116 (cargo).

Nonetheless, in *Canadian Indemnity Co* v *Canadian Johns-Manville Co*,[291] the under-writers argued that it was for the proposer to disclose these matters to them as late as 1973. The claimant's reply was that, in terms of the Quebec Civil Code,[292] these were facts "known to the insurer or which from their public character and notoriety he is presumed to know" and thus matters, which the proposer did not have to disclose. As to the latter, the underwriters argued that the standard of knowledge to be expected of them was that of the general public. The claimant argued that it was a standard by reference to common knowledge in the industry, in which the risk of asbestosis occurred. Delivering the judgment of the Supreme Court, Gonthier J rejected both positions, the standard being that of "a reasonably competent underwriter insuring similar risks".[293] Looking at the authorities drawn on, when the law of Quebec was codified, in particular *Carter* v *Boehm*, he concluded[294] that "an insurer was expected to know facts which went beyond political and natural perils and generally matters known to all and included a certain amount of information regarding the activity which was being insured". The press reports were in prominent publications and that the scientific papers "were easy to obtain by anyone interested and just as easy to read and understand",[295] the seriousness of the risk was a matter of "public character" and "notoriety". All of the material "was at hand and available to anyone who was inter-ested in the details" and that "an insurance underwriter ought to have known of their existence and their seriousness".

23–9B2 The Means of Knowledge

If the law sometimes expects the insurer to remember what he read in the news-paper[296] on the way to the office, why not also expect him to know what was in his desk, when he arrives? If the insurer cannot plead non-disclosure of information, if he has been put on inquiry,[297] that is, if he has been provided with the means of acquiring it by the proposer, why should the rule be different, when he has failed to use means of acquiring knowledge with which he has provided himself? The law of England, unlike that in the United States, answers both questions against the proposer.

Early statements are in the proposer's favour. In 1861, Erle CJ said this[298]: "actual knowledge is not essential if the insurer knew he had the means of knowing the fact, and it was within his knowledge. If, for example, he knew that he could learn the exact

---

291. (1988) 54 DLR (4th) 468 (CA Quebec); (1990) 72 DLR (4th) 478 (Sup Ct).

292. Civil Code of Lower Canada (1886) art 2486. The CA left open the question, raised by the insurer, whether this provision differed from the English rule, that allows a court to "presume than an insurer had knowledge of the risks in a particular industry that it insured" (p 479). Nor was this nettle firmly grasped in the Supreme Court, however, citations suggest that the court considered the law to be the same at least at the time of codification (1886) and, by implication from its conclusions, also at the period (1970s) on which the dispute centred.

293. pp 495–496; also p 506 and p 508.

294. p 500.

295. (1988) 54 DLR (4th) 468, 478–480. Although the risk was written in Canada, the sources included *The New York Times*, the *Wall Street Journal*, *The New Yorker Magazine* and *The Washington Post*, as well as *Encyclopedia Britannica*.

296. Above, 23–9B1.

297. Below, 23–13.

298. *Foley* v *Tabor* (1861) 2 F & F 663, 672 (hull). See also *Mackintosh* v *Marshall* (1843) 11 M & W 116 (cargo).

Aliter, if the proposer were fraudulent, for it has been held with regard to the issue of shares, that it is no answer to the party seeking rescission that the fraud might have been discovered by a proper inquiry: *Central Ry of Venezuela* v *Kisch* (1867) LR 2 HL 99.

cargo at Lloyd's, and chose not to ascertain it . . . it was *within* his knowledge." Indeed, a careful reading of the leading case of *Carter* v *Boehm*[299] suggests that Lord Mansfield was of the same view, and that the proposer in that case was not required to disclose his fears that the French might attack his "fort", because the insurers in London were better placed to discover the political facts than the insured. Be that as it may, the law was restated in favour of insurers in two much more recent decisions of the Court of Appeal: *Greenhill* v *Federal Ins Co*[300] and *London General* v *General Marine*.[301]

In *London General* v *General Marine*,[302] the court first held that the proposer of reinsurance should have known the contents of casualty slips received from Lloyd's: above, 23–8C. The proposer then argued that by the same token there was no need to disclose the contents to the reinsurer, for the latter should also have known the contents. The argument was rejected, for "the defendants, supposing they had these slips could not be expected to have always present to their mind information which at the time they got it would have no interest for them at all".[303] "The defendants cannot be presumed to have had knowledge of this casualty merely because they had the opportunity of ascertaining it."[304]

So, there is little or no duty on the insurer to look in his desk; in his memory, perhaps, but not his files. This reflects a fear that originates in marine insurance of the eighteenth and nineteenth centuries,[305] when the world was larger and the stories were taller. Surely, the insurer no longer needs quite as much protection. Just as man's legs have been extended by modern means of transport, his memory been extended by the computer. Now that vast amounts of information can be summoned at the touch of a keypad on a desk, perhaps it is time to reconsider in England the rule settled many years ago in the United States, that "an insurance company is charged with knowledge of what appears in his own records".[306]

In the leading American case of *Columbia National Life* v *Rodgers*,[307] action was brought on a life policy by the beneficiary. The defence was non-disclosure of an unsuccessful application for cover to another company. The insurer had cards, derived from a reporting system set up by life companies which pooled information, that indicated a criticism of the insured which, if it had been seen, would have put the insurer on inquiry and which, if pursued, would have revealed the unsuccessful application. The court held that the insurer was deemed to know this information; by failing to

---

299. (1766) 3 Burr 1905. See discussion of the case by Holmes, 39 U Pittsburgh L R 381, 426 ff.
300. [1927] 1 KB 65 (cargo).
301. *London General Ins Co* v *General Marine Underwriters' Assn* [1921] 1 KB 104.
302. Above.
303. p 110, *per* Lord Sterndale MR.
304. p 112, *per* Warrington LJ. *Cf Stone* v *Reliance Mutual Ins Sy Ltd* [1972] 1 Lloyd's Rep 469, 474 *per* Lord Denning MR (CA—fire & theft).
305. Park, *Marine Ins* (5th ed, 1802), p 178.
306. *Washington National Ins Co* v *Reginato*, 272 F Supp 1016, 1021 (ND Cal, 1966—life). See also *Boyd Co* v *United States*, 94 P 2d 1046 (Cal, 1939—surety); *Newman* v *Firemen's Ins Co*, 154 P 2d 451 (Cal, 1944—fire); *Metropolitan Life Ins Co* v *Goldberger*, 155 NYS 2d 305 (1956—life); *Haas* v *Integrity Mutual Ins Co*, 90 NW 2d 146, 150 (Wis, 1958—motor); *Trawick* v *Manhattan Life Ins Co*, 447 F 2d 1293, 1295–1296 (5 Cir, 1971—life); *Highlands Ins Co* v *Allstate Ins Co*, 688 F 2d 398, 404 (5 Cir, 1982—fire); *Haley* v *Continental Casualty Co*, 749 F Supp 560 (D Vt, 1990—liability).
Cf Michigan: "even its own earlier records do not put the insurer upon notice of the falseness in an application unless there is some circumstance which directs attention to them"—*Great Northern Life Ins Co* v *Vince*, 118 F 2d 232, 236 (6 Cir, 1941—life), cert den 314 US 637.
307. 116 F 2d 705 (10 Cir, 1940), cert den 313 US 561.

investigate his own files, he waived matters which investigation would have revealed. "Knowledge which is sufficient to lead a prudent person to inquire about the matter, when it could have been ascertained conveniently, constitutes notice of whatever the inquiry would have disclosed, and will be regarded as knowledge of the facts."[308]

The fear expressed in England,[309] that to impose any duty of investigation on the insurer would destroy the duty of disclosure, is unfounded. First, there will usually be material facts not on the insurer's files and, in many cases, it would be a foolish proposer who omitted facts on the assumption that the insurer already had the information. Second, in case of fraud, the fraudulent insured would not be able to plead the insurer's failure to look at the files and consequent failure to uncover false statements in the proposal.[310] Third, the insurer would be required to make only such searches as are reasonable in the circumstances, considering the cost of searching, the equipment available[311] and current business practice. Thus, in a case in Tennessee, when two insurance companies had recently merged, the one was not charged with knowledge of the records held by the other.[312]

In the *Taku Air Case*,[312a] the Canadian Supreme Court, by what was described as "no more than a reasonable incremental change in the existing law",[313] has taken a clear step in the direction of the American rule. Canadian legislation designed to protect passengers required that, as a licence condition, every commercial air carrier should obtain liability insurance cover in respect of passengers killed or injured. Against this background, the Court took the view that the scheme demanded "the active participation of the insurance companies".[314] Whereas the common law enunciated by Lord Mansfield might "hold true today where the policy is for the exclusive benefit of the insured", it was different as regards insurance "primarily for the benefit of the flying public" rather than the insured carrer.[315] In a case like this, "the insurer must take some basic steps to investigate the flying record of the air carrier applying for insurance. At a minimum, it should review its own files on the applicant. Further, the insurer should make a search of the public record of accidents of the air carrier".[316]

---

308. p 707.   309. *Greenhill* v *Federal Ins Co Ltd* [1927] 1 KB 65 (CA—cargo).

310. *US* v *Willoughby*, 250 F 2d 524 (9 Cir, 1957—life).

311. In *Schrader* v *Prudential*, 280 F 2d 355 (5 Cir, 1960) an insurance agent, already insured under his employer's group hospitalisation policy, obtained insurance from his employer on his life. He fraudulently concealed information about the removal, the cost of which had been covered by the group policy, of a malignant tumour from his back. When the insurer pleaded non-disclosure, the claimant beneficiary argued *inter alia* that the insurer's left (underwriting) hand should have known what was known to its right hand dealing with claims, in particular, that the life had been hospitalised for removal of the tumour. The court rejected the argument and the claim. The court noted that the insurer did maintain files recording significant information, which had been checked in respect of the life proposal, but that these files did not contain information about impairments stated in claims under the group policy. The court concluded (p 361) that "it seems unreasonable to hold this insurer to a knowledge of the information in its group hospitalization records when, as appears here, it was so impracticable and costly to transcribe the records of physical impairments from the group policy claims to the underwriting department". *Semble*, in view of the information technology available today, the decision might now be different.

312. *Lane* v *Travelers Indemnity Co*, 499 SW 2d 643 (Tenn, 1973—motor). *Cf Fireman's* v *Meenan Oil* (above, 23–8A2).

312a. *Coronation Ins Co* v *Taku Air Transport Ltd* (1991) 85 DLR (4th) 609 (Sup Ct — liability).

313. 85 DLR (4th) 609, 625 *per* Cory J, with whose judgment three other members of the Court agreed (Sup Ct, 1991—liability).

314. p 621, *per* Cory J.

315. pp 622–623 *per* Cory J.

316. p 623 *per* Cory J. He stressed that the records were easily available on a public database. In the end, the cover was vitiated by another misrepresentation altogether.

23–9C Common Knowledge

It has been often said,[317] that the insured need not disclose to the insurer matters known to both of them, in particular matters of common or general notoriety. In practice, the courts are more likely to hold that such information, although it may have been known to the man in the street, should have been known to the man in Lime Street[318] as a matter of professional knowledge of an event affecting his business: above, 23–9B1. Although there are undoubtedly matters of common knowledge, if they affect the business that the insurer writes, he will be expected to have a better knowledge of them than the layman—as appears to be the case, for example, of health risks.

23–10 MATERIAL FACTS: EXCEPTIONS

The meaning of material information[319] is wide enough to include three types of information to which, however, the duty of disclosure does not extend.

23–10A Inferences from Facts

The proposer must disclose material facts but he is not obliged to state or speculate on inferences, that might be drawn from those facts,[320] even though, perhaps, the materiality of the facts depended on those very inferences: above, 23–8D. Nor is the proposer obliged to state or speculate on the legal consequences of those facts.[321]

In *Bell* v *Bell*,[322] for example, Lord Ellenborough said that the "assured are only bound to communicate facts. The broker did communicate the fact of the ship's papers being sent to Petersburgh for examination. He was not bound to communicate the sensations and apprehensions which that fact produced at Riga", where the ship was situated.

This rule is based on the assumption that each professes to act from his own skill and sagacity.[323] The same assumption is found in the idea that each is taken to know the "natural consequences" of a material fact[324] but not, by inference, any other consequences. The line between fact and inference becomes unclear, however, when the proposer is much better placed to appreciate the significance of the facts (notably facts

---

317. *Carter* v *Boehm* (1766) 3 Burr 1905 (marine); *Planche* v *Fletcher* (1779) 1 Doug 251, 253 *per* Lord Mansfield (cargo); *Bates* v *Hewitt* (1867) LR 2 QB 595, 605 *per* Cockburn CJ (hull); *Buck & Hedrick* v *Chesapeke Ins Co*, 1 Pet 151, 160 (Sup. Ct., 1828—cargo); *Anne Quinn Corp* v *American Manufacturers Mutual Ins Co*, 1974 AMC 655, 659–660 (SD NY, 1973—hull).

318. For example, in *Hales* v *Reliance Fire & Accident Ins Corp Ltd* [1960] 2 Lloyd's Rep 391 (fire) knowledge that a small shop selling groceries, newspapers and tobacco might also stock fireworks in October/November was presumed of the fire insurer as "an ordinary attribute of the risk".

319. Above, 23–6.

320. *Carter* v *Boehm* (1766) 3 Burr 1905, 1911 *per* Lord Mansfield; *Bates* v *Hewitt* (1867) LR 2 QB 595, 604 *per* Lord Cockburn CJ (hull), followed in *Gandy* v *Adelaide Ins Co* (1871) LR 6 QB 746 (hull).

321. *The Bedouin* [1893] P 1, 12 *per* Lord Esher MR (CA—freight).

322. (1810) 2 Camp 475, 479 (marine).

323. *Carter* v *Boehm* (1766) 3 Burr 1906, 1911 *per* Lord Mansfield (marine), quoted above, 23–9B.

324. *Greenhill* v *Federal Ins Co* [1927] 1 KB 65, 84 *per* Scrutton LJ (CA—cargo).

of a technical kind): his opinion, although in a sense a matter of inference, is regarded as a fact[325] and must be disclosed.[326]

23–10B Warranties

Matters, however material, which are the subject of an express or implied warranty in the contract of insurance, need not be disclosed.[327] This, it is said, is because, first, the requirement of disclosure is made to protect the insurer; if he has a warranty, he does not need such protection. Second, if there is a warranty on the matter, his judgement would not be influenced by its disclosure.[328] The rule does not apply in the face of clear evidence of contrary intention, as where, notwithstanding the warranty, the insurer specifically asks about the matter.[329]

23–10C Facts that Diminish the Risk

Facts diminishing risk are material in the sense that they would influence in some degree the mind of the prudent insurer. However, the insurer does not need protection from the proposer, who fails to disclose such facts. The law is clear: there is no duty to disclose "any circumstances which diminish the risk".[330]

23–11 WAIVER AND NON-DISCLOSURE: INTRODUCTION

In respect of non-disclosure, waiver arises principally at three points:
- (a) *Waiver of the Duty*. Before the contract of insurance has been concluded, there may be a total or partial waiver by the insurer of the duty of disclosure: below, 23–12.
- (b) *Waiver of Further Information*. Before the contract of insurance has been concluded, material information may be disclosed by the proposer but not in sufficient detail to allow the prudent insurer to assess its significance. At this point, the insurer may indicate that he does not wish to hear more on the subject from the proposer. If so, the result is that, although the undisclosed detail may be material, the insured has waived performance of the rest of the duty, as regards that information. This type of waiver, which sometimes shades into type (a), waiver of duty, is discussed below, 23–13.
- (c) *Waiver of Rescission*. After the contract of insurance has been concluded,

---

325. Above, 23–5.

326. In *Cantiere Meccanico Brindisino* v *Janson* [1912] 3 KB 452, 461–462, Vaughan Williams LJ approved this statement by Scrutton J in the court below: "if the insured knows or believes that the dock [subject-matter of the insurance] is not fit to go to sea owing to the absence of some strengthening usually added, or has a report or opinion to that effect, though he thinks it erroneous, he must . . . disclose his knowledge or his unfavourable report".

327. MIA, section 18(3)(d). *Ross* v *Bradshaw* (1761) 96 ER 175 (life). *Gulfstream Cargo Ltd* v *Reliance Ins Co* [1970] 1 Lloyd's Rep 178 (5 Cir, 1969).

328. *De Maurier (Jewels) Ltd* v *Bastion Ins Co Ltd* [1967] 2 Lloyd's Rep 550, 557 *per* Donaldson J (jewellers' AR).

329. *Haywood* v *Rodgers* (1804) 4 East 590, 597–598 *per* Lord Ellenborough CJ (marine). The MIA, section 18(3) applies only "in the absence of inquiry" by the insurer.

330. MIA, section 18(3)(a). *Carter* v *Boehm* (1766) 3 Burr 1905, 1911 *per* Lord Mansfield (marine); *The Dora* [1989] Lloyd's Rep 69, 89 *per* Phillips J (yacht). *Cf Transcontinental Ins Co* v *Minning*, 135 F 2d 479 (6 Cir, 1943—fire).

the insurer may discover non-disclosure by the insured but, nonetheless, wish to affirm the contract and keep it in force. In these circumstances, the insurer has waived his remedy, his right to rescission: below, 23–18B.

For example, if the insurer offers cargo insurance "seaworthiness admitted", there is waiver type (a) of the duty of disclosure as regards any material information known to the proposer about the condition of the ship to be used. If the proposer identifies the ship and the insurer makes no further inquiry about it, there is waiver type (b) of any matters, whether affecting the condition of the ship or any other material information, which further inquiry of the proposer would have revealed. If, in the absence of waiver of disclosure, the insurer discovers that the proposer knew but failed to disclose material facts about the ship, and the insurer nonetheless indicates that he wishes to go on with the contract, there is waiver type (c) of rescission.

23–12 WAIVER OF THE PROPOSER'S DUTY OF DISCLOSURE

23–12A No Questions

If there is evidence that insurers in general do not inquire about a particular matter, that indicates that the matter is not material.[331] If, on the contrary, the evidence is that most insurers (and thus the prudent insurer) would regard the matter as material, is there waiver, if the particular insurer does not ask about it? In England, the usual answer has been negative[332]; thus, in a motor case in 1934, Scrutton LJ said[333] of the proposer that "it does not matter whether he is asked questions about it, he must tell every material fact". This orthodoxy seems, however, to have overlooked some observations of Lord Mansfield, who said[334] in 1782 that the underwriter "waived the inquiry by putting no questions to him, though they naturally arose from the subject-matter". Today in England, there is some movement back to Lord Mansfield. The position of the Insurance Ombudsman, as regards the insurance contracts of consumers that are within the Bureau's remit, is that the scope of the proposer's duty of disclosure is determined by the questions put by the insurer.

In 1934 in the USA, life insurers, "by their practice, of making medical examinations and asking detailed questions in applications, practically have extinguished the place of concealment at the time of application . . . Thus, it has been held that concealment of a material fact about which the company does not inquire does not avoid

---

331. *Mann Macneal & Steeves Ltd* v *Capital & Counties Ins Co Ltd* [1921] 2 KB 300, 307 *per* Bankes LJ (CA—hull).

332. *Becker* v *Marshall* (1922) 11 Ll L Rep 114 (fire and burglary), affirmed 12 Ll L Rep 413 (CA); *Bond* v *Commercial Union Assurance Co Ltd* (1930) 35 Com Cas 171; *Taylor* v *Eagle Star Ins Co Ltd* (1940) 67 Ll L Rep 134 (motor); *Roselodge Ltd* v *Castle* [1966] 2 Lloyd's Rep 113, 133 *per* McNair J (jewellers' block policy). Ivamy, *Fire*, p 58. For example, in *Godfrey* v *Britannic Assurance Co Ltd* [1963] 2 Lloyd's Rep 515 there was no suggestion that a life company, which did not require a medical examination of a proposed life over 40, thereby waived information about his health. Generally, see Lluelles, 67 Can Bar Rev 258 (1988).

333. *McCormick* v *National Motor & Accident Ins Union Ltd* (1934) 49 Ll L Rep 361, 363 (CA—motor). Scrutton LJ (*ibid*) also hinted that the rule might be different in other kinds of insurance. However, the same rule was stated for fire insurance in *State Insurance General Manager* v *McHale* [1992] 2 NZLR 399, 409 (CA NZ—fire).

334. *Court* v *Martineau* (1782) 3 Dougl 161, 163 (hull). Also in this sense *Dyck* v *Poirier* (1988) 47 DLR (4th) 193, 206 (Sask—motor), citing *Carter* v *Boehm* (1766) 97 ER 1162, 1169 *per* Lord Mansfield (marine), a *dictum* that is perhaps better seen as concerning waiver of further disclosure: below, 23–13C.

the policy".[335] There, the position has not changed. For example, it was reaffirmed in 1989 that "Virginia law is clear that an insured 'is bound only to disclose such matters as may be inquired about' . . . To hold, as INA urges, that an insured is under a general duty of affirmative disclosure would, in effect, be to place the burden on underwriting decisions upon the insured and not the insurer. This would turn the relationship on its head and nullify the duty of an insurer to act reasonably to protect its own interests".[336]

This proposition appears to apply to all branches of insurance, except reinsurance. In the USA, as in England, normal practice is that the reinsurer does not duplicate the investigation of the basic risk undertaken by the reinsured as insurer. Reinsurance is an international market and it would make little sense for a reinsurer based in London or Munich to investigate a risk reinsured from, for example, Singapore.[337] It does not follow, however, that the reinsurer should disregard the reinsured and, in particular, the methods of investigation used by the reinsured or the results of his investigation in a particular case.

23–12B Limited Questions

If the insurer asks a question of limited scope, by implication his restraint excludes and thus waives related matters outside the scope of the question: the implication rests on the rule of construction *expressio unius*. In *Schoolman* v *Hall*[338] this application of the principle was accepted by the Court of Appeal. Asquith LJ said[339]:

"questions in a proposal form may be so framed as necessarily to imply that the underwriter only wants information on certain subject-matters, or that within a particular subject-matter their desire for information is restricted within the narrow limits indicated by the terms of the question, and, in such a case, they may *pro tanto* dispense the proposer from what otherwise at common law would have been a duty to disclose everything material."

Thus, if a motor insurer asks about convictions in the last five years, he waives disclosure of any convictions before that time.[340] Again, in *Roberts* v *Plaisted*,[341] the insurer asked about one kind only of ancillary activity that might be conducted on part of the motel premises to be insured against (running a casino) and thus waived disclosure about another kind of ancillary activity (running a discotheque for non-residents).[342] In *Kelleher*,[342a] a form of offer "for any member who is under 60 years old and who satisfactorily completed the declaration of health below" waived related matters not covered by the declaration. The implication, however, must be clear. For

335. Wilcox, 9 Tul L Rev 449, 454–455 (1934–5).
336. *INA* v *US Gypsum Co*, 870 F 2d 148, 153 (4 Cir, 1989—AR). In that case the insurer was keen to increase revenue for reinvestment and, perhaps, to save costs.
337. Thomas, 41 Duke LJ 1548, 1556 ff (1992).
338. [1951] 1 Lloyd's Rep 139 (CA—jewellery).
339. p 143. See also *Joel* v *Law Union & Crown Ins Co Ltd* [1908] 2 KB 863, 878 *per* Vaughan Williams LJ (CA—life).
340. *Jester-Barnes* v *Licenses & General Ins Co Ltd* (1934) 49 Ll L Rep 231, 237 *per* Mackinnon J (motor). See also *Hair* v *Prudential Assurance Co Ltd* [1983] 2 Lloyd's Rep 667, 673 *per* Woolf J (fire); for criticism of the application of the proposition to the facts, see Birds [1984] JBL 163.
341. [1989] 2 Lloyd's Rep 341 (CA—fire).
342. p 347 *per* Purchas LJ. In view of the terms of the particular form, this construction was generous to the claimant: see (1991) 1 Ins Law & Practice 28. A better ground for the decision is that discussed below 23–13C, namely that the very fact that the risk proposed was stated to be on a motel was a sufficient disclosure of all activities currently incidental to the operation of a motel of that kind, including a discotheque for non–residents.
342a. *Kelleher* v *Irish Life Assurance Co Ltd* [1993] ILRM 643 (Sup Ct, Ireland—life).

example, questions seeking trade references do not waive information about convictions relating to moral hazard.[343]

23–12B1 Questions Unanswered

When the insurer asks questions, which the proposer does not answer, the situation is ambiguous. If the question is posed, then it cannot be said that the information was never material to the insurer. But equally, if the question goes unanswered, it cannot be readily assumed that the insurer is satisfied with the (failure to) answer and has waived the matter. Nor does a failure to answer amount to a negative answer[344]; it is equivocal. What might be said[345] is that, when the proposal is received with the question unanswered or incompletely answered, the insurer's acceptance of the proposal without objection is a waiver of further information: below, 23–13. This is the view taken in the United States. "By issuing the policy without requiring an answer to the question, the company waived answer to the inquiry and elected to treat it as immaterial."[346]

In *Phoenix Mutual Life* v *Raddin*,[347] the 28th question in a life proposal form was not one question but four questions in three sentences: "Has any application been made to this or any other company for assurance on the life of the party? What amounts are now insured on the life of the party, and in what companies? If already insured in this Company, state the No of policy?" The proposer's answer, "$10,000 Equitable Life Assurance Society", might have been construed as the only positive information relevant to all three questions, and thus as a negative (and untrue) answer to, for example, the first question.[348] But the Supreme Court saw it as a (true) answer to the third question, and no answer at all to the first and fourth, Justice Gray saying[349]: "wherever on the face of the application a question appears to be not answered at all, or to be imperfectly answered, and the insurers issue a policy without further inquiry, they waive the want or imperfections in the answer, and render the omission to answer more fully immaterial."

23–12C Waiver by the Nature of the Insurance

In cargo insurance, the clause "seaworthiness admitted" is commonly found[350]: the seaworthiness of the ship is clearly material, but it is equally clear that the insured may have no knowledge of the ship to be used or of its condition. In these circumstances, a clause like this spells out what is obvious. It is an express waiver[351] but it is also a

343. *Schoolman* v *Hall* [1951] 1 Lloyd's Rep 139 (CA—jewellery).
344. *Perrins* v *Marine & General Travellers' Ins Sy* (1859) 2 El & El 317, 323 *per* Wightman J (PA); *Marcovitch* v *Liverpool Victoria Friendly Sy* (1912) 28 TLR 188, 189 *per* Lord Alverstone CJ (CA—life).
345. A case cited against this view is *Arterial Caravans Ltd* v *Yorkshire Ins Co Ltd* [1973] 1 Lloyd's Rep 169, but this is a case in which the relevant question was never put to the proposer, so the proposer had no reason to think that the insurer's mind was brought to bear on a blank answer, and Chapman J (p 180) did not tackle the present issue.
346. *Bowles* v *Mutual Benefit Health & Accident*, 99 F 2d 44 (4 Cir, 1938—PHI). See also *Phoenix Mutual* v *Raddin* (1886) 120 US 183 (life); *Mutual Reserve Fund Life* v *Farmer*, 47 SW 850 (Ark, 1898—life). Cf *Rutherford* v *Prudential Ins Co*, 44 Cal Rptr 697 (Cal, 1965—life).
347. (1886) 120 US 183.
348. As in *Roberts* v *Avon Ins Co Ltd* [1956] 2 Lloyds Rep 240 (burglary).
349. p 189.
350. *Cantiere Meccanico Brindisino* v *Janson* [1912] 3 KB 452 (CA).
351. pp 472–473.

reflection of a broader proposition, that waiver may arise by the very nature of the insurance. For example, under a floating policy on goods the insurer undertakes to cover all goods of a stated kind and within stated limits, for example of value, regardless of factors affecting any particular consignment, such as the ship.[352]

Under certain kinds of life insurance, the insured may have options,[353] which entitle the insured to increase the amount of insurance without, for example, further medical examination of the life. Similar issues arise in respect of floating fidelity policies on, for example, all (unnamed) employees of the insured employer, or on all persons occupying defined positions in the firm. Again, under a treaty of reinsurance, whatever the primary risk, the reinsurer may be obliged to accept a risk undertaken by the prime insurer, provided that it falls within the terms of the treaty, regardless of facts material to the particular risk.[354]

In such cases, it is not suggested that the insurer waives his right to avoid the contract in case of fraud, whether occurring before or after the contract is made. Nor is it suggested that the insurer waives information, for example, concerning moral hazard: this is material information which is available when the contract is first made. The suggestion is that he waives information, which is not or not readily available when the contract is made, for example, the name of the ship on which the goods insured will be consigned. In the case of a treaty or of a floating policy, binding contracts between insurer and insured, it is said that the insurer has agreed to cover all subject-matter properly declared; that he has therefore given up any discretion to decline a particular risk falling within the scope of the policy; that the duty of disclosure implies that the insurer, to whom a duty of disclosure is owed, has a decision to make, to accept or decline the proposal or to accept it on terms, but that in these situations the insurer has to a degree given up his discretion, has no decision to make, and has thus waived disclosure. This view of the law is entirely consistent with the rules governing the timing of the duty of disclosure: above, 23–4.

A further case of waiver by the nature of the insurance arises, when the insurer has authorised an agent to contract insurance business rapidly, precluding normal inquiries. This case differs from those above in that, although material information is available, in the interests of expedition, the insurer takes a risk, both commercially and legally. This was the case[355] of an insurance taken at short notice by the hirer of a car through the agency of the car company, in which the court said that it "is part of the scenario that no question of any sort is asked of the prospective renter by the person in charge of the rental office". The inference is that the insurer classifies and assumes the risk mainly by reference to the car company rather than the individual hirer as such.

---

352. See further, Arnould, No 274 and the MIA, section 29(1). Nonetheless, the insurer may reasonably wonder just how exposed he had really been during the last period of cover. Hence the insured under a floating policy will be required to declare specified details about the consignments he has sent under the cover. This, however, is a duty put upon him by the contract and is quite distinct from the extra-contractual duty of good faith that requires disclosure. See *Robinson* v *Tourey* (1811) 3 Camp 158 (cargo); *Ionides* v *Pender* (1871) LR 6 QB 674, 682, 685 *per* Blackburn J; (1872) 7 QB 517, 525 *per* Kelly CB (Exch Ch—cargo); *Davies* v *National Fire & Marine Ins Co* [1891] AC 485 (PC—cargo).

As regards the application of the rule for floating policies to open cover on cargo, see *Berger* v *Pollock* [1973] 2 Lloyd's Rep 442 (cargo). *La Pointe* [1986] 2 Lloyd's Rep 513 (BC—hull).

353. For example the GIO (guaranteed insurability option) or the RPI option with inflation in mind, which links the amount of insurance to the retail price index.

354. Carter, pp 126–127.

355. *Dyck* v *Poirier* (1988) 47 DLR (4th) 193, 207 (Sask—motor).

23-13 WAIVER OF FURTHER INFORMATION

It has sometimes been held that, if the proposer discloses information, the insurer is on inquiry about related information and, if the insurer makes no inquiry about the latter, he has waived its disclosure. Moreover, Lord Esher MR said[356] that it

"is not necessary to disclose minutely every material fact; assuming that there is a material fact which he is bound to disclose, the rule is satisfied if he discloses sufficient to call the attention of the underwriters, in such a manner that they can see that if they require further information they ought to ask for it."

On this basis, if the proposer discloses information, for example about a past fire, it is for the insurer to seek the details. However, the courts' response has not been consistent. One court may take a narrow view and hold that there has been non-disclosure of the detail or of the related fact.[357] Another court either in a similar case takes a general view and finds that disclosure has been "fair", or finds that the insurer has waived further or related information about the matters disclosed. The second approach, more evident in the United States than in England, favours the insured.[358]

23-13A Documents Tendered

If the proposer effects disclosure by tendering one or more documents, it can be inferred that there has been disclosure of the contents of that document.[359] For example, if a broker comes to a meeting with his client's full record but the agent of the insurer looks only at a document summarising the short record, that is enough: the insurer has waived matters stated in the full record.[360] If information is made readily available to the insurer, but the insurer does not trouble to look at it, the insurer cannot complain. Again, it has been held[361] that when the proposer signed a form permitting the insurer to consult his medical records but the insurer did not do so, the insurer waived matters which consultation would have revealed.

If, however, the proposer misrepresents the nature or contents of the document, the document may be taken to state (and disclose) only what it was represented to state,[362] provided that the representation was plausible, i.e., consistent with what is usual or to be expected in such a case and subject to any verification that can be reasonably expected of the profferee insurer.[363]

356. *Asfar* v *Blundell* [1896] 1 QB 123, 129 (CA—freight). This statement was applied in *Roumeli Food Stores* v *New India* [1972] 1 NSWLR 227, 234 (fire).

357. Both approaches are in evidence, but the first more prominent in *CTI* v *Oceanus* [1984] 2 Lloyd's Rep 476 (CA—containers).

358. See in particular, below, 23-13D.

359. See *Kreglinger* and *Asfar* v *Blundell*, below, 23-13B.

360. *Pan Atlantic Ins Co Ltd* v *Pine Top Insurance Co Ltd* [1992] 1 Lloyd's Rep 101 (re), affirmed on this point [1993] 1 Lloyd's Rep 496 (CA). An appeal to the House of Lords is to be heard in February 1994. *Aliter*, if the information is present but not reasonably accessible: *CTI* v *Oceanus* [1984] 2 Lloyd's Rep 476, 497 per Kerr LJ (CA—re).

361. *Ellingwood* v *NN Investors Life Ins Co*, 805 P 2d 70, 77 (NM, 1991—life). But *cf Massachusetts Mutual Life Ins Co* v *Nicholson*, 775 F Supp 954 (ND Mass, 1991—life), that the insurer does not waive the contents unless he has been put on sufficient inquiry to have reason to investigate.

362. *Curtis* v *Chemical Cleaning & Dyeing Co Ltd* [1951] 1 KB 805 (CA).

363. What is usual is discussed below. In the general law a misrepresentee is entitled to rely on a misrepresentation, even though it was negligent on his part not to check it and even though the misrepresentee was not a consumer. But it is doubtful whether the courts will be quick to allow an insurer to benefit from this rule: above, 22-3D.

23–13B Documents Mentioned

In *Kreglinger*[364] Davitt P said[365] that

"the insured does not have to conduct the insurer's business for him. Where the contract, the performance of which the insurer is asked to cover, contains a clear intimation that a matter which is specially referred to but not fully set out, is of importance and full information is to be had for the asking, it would seem quite unreasonable and unjust to allow the insurer to repudiate liability on the grounds that he did not know and was not told the details of something he was in fact told about. What [the underwriter] was told by the terms of the contract was, in my opinion, clearly sufficient to put him upon inquiry."

In *Asfar & Co* v *Blundell*[366]

"the plaintiffs disclosed that there was a charterparty in existence . . . and that the subject-matter which the underwriters were asked to insure was the difference between the chartered freight payable by the insured to the shipowner, and the bill of lading freights which they were to obtain from the consignees of the goods. But having given this information, they did not tell the underwriters whether the chartered freight was a lump sum, or whether it was a tonnage freight depending upon the delivery of the goods to the consignees. But that the freight must be a lump sum was almost certain; and if the underwriters wanted to be sure on the point, they could have immediately acquired the knowledge by asking the question."

In *Asfar*[367] it was "almost certain" that the freight would be a lump sum freight, and this influenced the court.[368] The implication is that the insurer was taken to know this kind of thing.[369] When there are no usual terms, the decision will be the same but, when the actual terms are unusual, the decision will be different. In a reinsurance case,[370] Scrutton J said that

"obviously twelve months' time policies on ships differ so very much in their terms that I am inclined to think with regard to a great many of those terms, the man writing the risk is put on inquiry, and, if he wants to know the terms and conditions on which he is purporting to write, he should ask. But I think it is quite clear that the policy may be for such an extraordinary risk, as where the ship may have liberty to do unusual and dangerous things, that there may be clauses in the original policy which an underwriter offering ought to disclose because they are so out of the usual that a reinsuring underwriter would not expect them."

That was so in the case, because the primary hull insurance covered navigation in the Canadian lakes.[371] However, the judge decided that there had been sufficient

---

364. *Kreglinger and Fernau Ltd* v *Irish National Ins Co Ltd* [1956] IR 116; note Hudson, 38 MLR 212. The case concerned a performance bond, which was treated as an insurance contract in that it gave rise to a duty of disclosure. See also *Freeland* v *Glover* (1806) 7 East 457, 463 *per* Lord Ellenborough CJ (marine) in which disclosure of a letter, which referred to an earlier letter, was held sufficient disclosure of the latter.

365. p 151.

366. [1896] 1 QB 123, 129–130 *per* Lord Esher MR (CA—freight). Some of the goods arrived damaged and, while he still had to pay the full charter freight, he could not earn all the bill of lading freight and so made a loss, in respect of which he made the disputed claim. The insurers defended the claim *inter alia* on the ground that the claimant had not specifically informed them of the terms in the charter about freight. The Court of Appeal rejected this defence. *Asfar* was applied in *Mann, Macneal & Steeves* v *Capital & Counties Ins Co* [1921] 2 KB 300, 309 *per* Bankes LJ (CA—hull). See also *Atlantic Mutual Ins Co* v *Cooney*, 303 F 2d 253 (9 Cir, 1962—cargo).

367. [1896] 1 QB 123.

368. p 131 *per* Lopes LJ.

369. See above 23–9B.

370. *Property Ins Co Ltd* v *National Protector Ins Co Ltd* (1913) 108 LT 104, 106.

371. As to unusual terms, see also *Charlesworth* v *Faber* (1900) 5 Com Cas 408 (re); *CTI* v *Oceanus* [1984] 1 Lloyds Rep 476, 498 *per* Kerr LJ (CA—container insurance). This is consistent with general rules of notice: *Interfoto Picture Library Ltd* v *Stiletto Visual Programmes Ltd* [1989] QB 433 (CA).

notice, for the normal rule, to which the passage from his judgment refers, was over-ridden by a clause[372] of the reinsurance contract in issue.

23–13C The Nature of the Risk Proposed

The insurer is taken to draw the usual inferences from what he is told about the risk proposed. If accident cover is sought by a professional stuntman, the insurer must draw his own conclusions.

In the leading case of *Carter* v *Boehm*,[373] Lord Mansfield stated the law like this[374]:

"If an underwriter insures private ships of war, by sea and on shore, from ports to ports, and places to places, anywhere—he need not be told the secret enterprises they are destined upon; because he knows some expedition must be in view; and *from the nature of his contract*, without being told, he waives the information."

Turning to the facts he said[375]:

"The underwriter knew the insurance was for the governor. He knew the governor must be acquainted with the state of the [fort]. He knew the governor could not disclose it, consistently with his duty. He knew the governor, by insuring, apprehended, at least, the possibility of an attack. With this knowledge, without asking a question, he underwrote. By so doing, he took the knowledge of the state of the place upon himself. It was a matter, as to which he might be informed in various ways: it was not a matter, within the private knowledge of the governor."

According to one report[376] of the case, Lord Mansfield concluded that the proposer is obliged to disclose only facts which he "privately knows, and the [insurer] is ignorant of, and *has no reason to suspect*".

23–13D Inference from Facts Disclosed: Insurer on Inquiry

Whatever is disclosed to the insurer, the question arises of the knowledge and experience that the insurer should bring to its appreciation, so that the proposer might say, "I told you enough; as to what I did not say, you should have realised, you were put on inquiry". This argument is closely related to the argument that information does not have to be disclosed, because it was information that the insurer knew or should have known.[377] In a simple case, for example, the proposer responds to a question from the insurer about past loss with "Known to insurer": the insurer is on inquiry to look at his records.[378]

The insurer is only expected to assume or infer what can readily and confidently be assumed or inferred. The corollary is that the insurer is not expected to fear the worst

---

372. "subject without notice to the same clauses and conditions as the original policy". However unusual the clauses of the latter, this, it was held, amounted to waiver of disclosure. Scrutton J observed (p 106) that the clause "is probably put in by the person who tenders the risk as a measure of precaution to avoid points like this: 'Oh, on now carefully considering the policy I think that clause 22 is an unusual one, and you ought to have told me of it . . . ' . . . it gives the certainty of being paid without a lawsuit."

373. (1766) 3 Burr 1905.

374. p 1911. See also *Greenhill* v *Federal Ins Co* [1927] 1 KB 65, 73 *per* Lord Hanworth MR (CA—cargo), quoted below, 23–13D.

375. p 1915.

376. Park, *The Law of Marine Ins* (1787) p 220, reported by Hasson (1969) 32 MLR 615, 617. Emphasis added.

377. Above, 23–9. Information that the insurer should have known may be derived not only from things disclosed by the proposer but also other sources.

378. *Framar Money Management Pty Ltd* v *Territory Ins Office* (1986) 87 FLR 251 (N Terr—fire). It has been suggested (above, 23–9B2), that the insurer should consult his records anyway.

and seek confirmation of his fears. In the absence of grounds for suspicion, the insurer is entitled to assume without investigation that the proposer has told the truth.[379] According to Scrutton LJ, it is only the "natural consequences"[380] of facts stated by the proposer that the insurer should deduce and which might put the insurer on inquiry. Any other rule, he said, "would entirely destroy the obligation to disclose . . . because if you insure a ship, of course it is a *possibility* that anything may have happened to her."[381] The English courts have been slow to conclude that the insurer was put on inquiry.

In the leading case of *Greenhill* v *Federal Ins Co*,[382] the insured argued that, knowing that the goods were to be sent from Halifax, the insurer should have inferred a preliminary journey by rail or by sea—the goods did not start life in Halifax and must have got there one way or the other—and should have asked about it, if he wanted to know. This argument was rejected by the Court of Appeal. Lord Hanworth, MR, said[383] that it "may well be . . . that if an underwriter is told of the cargo, a cargo (we will say) of some chemical substance of which he has had no previous experience, and makes no inquiry about it, then from the nature of his contract,[384] without being told, he waives the information. But . . . we are dealing with a cargo which has had a history, which has had pre-carriage with many incidents . . . " He then concluded that these incidents were not "in the nature of the contract", that is not something the insurer should have "supposed to have taken place".[385]

Other cases suggest that the more commonplace the risk proposed, the more that the insurer can be supposed to know and to infer. An associated suggestion is that more will be expected of the insurer, when dealing with a consumer.

In the case of motor insurance, if the proposer describes the make, model and year of the vehicle, he can assume that the insurer knows enough about the characteristics of a vehicle of that type. Moreover, as regards his previous road accidents, the proposer is only "bound to disclose enough to enable the company to inquire".[386]

In the case of life or PHI insurance, the insurer, once alerted that the proposer has undergone medical treatment, is on notice, "for the hospital records or the attending

---

379. *Duren* v *Northwestern National Life Ins Co*, 581 So 2d 810 (Ala, 1991—life).

380. [1927] 1 KB 65, 84; see also p 89 *per* Sargant LJ. *Charlesworth* v *Faber* (1900) 5 Com Cas 408 (re). *Apperson* v *US Fidelity & Guarantee Co*, 318 F 2d 438 (5 Cir, 1963—motor); *Union Ins Exchange Inc* v *Gaul*, 393 F 2d 151 (7 Cir, 1968—motor); *Apolskis* v *Concord*, 445 F 2d 31 (7 Cir, 1971—life); *Adamson* v *Home Life Ins Co*, 508 F 2d 766 (5 Cir, 1975—life).

For example, in *Major Oil Corp* v *Equitable Life Assurance Sy*, 457 F 2d 596 (10 Cir, 1972—life) the insurer was told that the life had been treated for excessive drinking, and was taken to know what he would have discovered (a liver disorder), if he had made further inquiries; but in *Pacific Queen Fisheries* v *Symes* [1963] 2 Lloyd's Rep 201, 208–209; 307 F 2d 700, 709 (9 Cir, 1962) to disclose that the ship subject of insurance is the mother ship to small fishing vessels does not disclose that she carries petrol fuel for them, for they could have got such a fuel from various places.

381. *Loc cit* (emphasis added).

382. [1927] 1 KB 65. See also *Laing* v *Union Marine* (1895) 1 Com Cas 11 (hull).

383. p 73; *idem* pp 84–85 *per* Scrutton LJ. See also in this sense *Harrower* v *Hutchinson* (1870) LR 5 QB 584, 590 *per* Kelly CB (cargo).

384. This phrase comes from Lord Mansfield in *Carter* v *Boehm* (1766) 3 Burr 1905, 191: above, 23–13C.

385. *Cf*: "a creditor must reveal to the surety every fact which under the circumstances the surety would expect not to exist"—*London General Omnibus Co Ltd* v *Holloway* [1912] 2 KB 72, 79 *per* Vaughan Williams LJ (CA—suretyship).

386. *Mayne Nickless Ltd* v *Pegler* [1974] 1 NSWLR 228, 240. In the same sense *Brayer* v *John Hancock Mutual Life Ins Co*, 179 F 2d 925 (2 Cir, 1950—life).

physicians would disclose the true cause of the insured's stay" in hospital.[387] However, to name the doctor with whom the proposer is registered, and to authorise the doctor to supply the insurer with necessary information, may not be sufficient unless the insurer has reason to contact the doctor.[388]

In the case of property insurance, if the insurer makes a physical inspection of relevant property, there is disclosure only of those things which such an inspection should have revealed.[389] However, he is not obliged to conduct an inspection, unless put on inquiry.[390]

387. *Prudential Ins Co of America* v *Saxe*, 134 F 2d 16, 29 (D Colum, 1943—life). *Cf Duren* v *Northwestern National Life Ins Co*, 581 So 2d 810 (Ala, 1991—life).
In *Joel* v *Law Union & Crown Ins Co Ltd* [1908] 2 KB 863 the Court of Appeal had to consider the insurer's defence, that the proposer had mentioned two doctors, whom she had consulted, but failed to disclose a third, who had treated her for influenza. The case was sent back for a new trial. Vaughan Williams LJ said (p 882) that "she gave information that Dr T B Scott had attended her as her medical attendant. It is true she says for colds, but this put the insurance office in a position in which, if they had chosen to make inquiries of Dr T B Scott, they could have got full information" about the influenza. See also p 897 *per* Buckley LJ.
388. See above, 23–13A.
389. *Pacific Queen Fisheries* v *Symes* [1963] 2 Lloyd's Rep 201; 307 F 2d 700 (9 Cir, 1962): a claim in respect of total loss of a ship, resulting from explosion and fire, was resisted *inter alia* on the ground of non-disclosure of structural changes in the ship to enable her to carry more petrol. The insured argued that the insurer had waived disclosure of these matters by making a survey of the ship, which had not revealed the changes. The court rejected this argument, because the changes were unusual and not observable by a reasonable inspection.
390. Above, 22–3D. A similar rule governs the duty of the seller in respect of the merchantability of goods which the buyer has inspected: the seller can disclaim responsibility for defects only if (a) the buyer chose to inspect and (b) in respect of defects which an inspection of that kind should have revealed. Benjamin, No 11–055.

PART II: THE EFFECT OF MISREPRESENTATION AND NON-DISCLOSURE

23–14 REMEDIES

The remedy for misrepresentation and for non-disclosure of material information is generally the same: although theoretically damages might be awarded, the remedy is usually rescission and it is usually sought by the insurer in respect of misrepresentation or non-disclosure by the insured. This part of the chapter describes the law in those terms, however, the same rules apply, if the roles are reversed and remedies are sought by the insured.

If cover is obtained by fraud, the proposer will have committed an offence, if he, in the language of section 16(1) of the Theft Act 1968, "by any deception dishonestly obtains for himself or another any pecuniary advantage". Under section 16(2), a pecuniary advantage is obtained when he is "allowed to take out any policy of insurance or annuity contract, or obtains an improvement of the terms on which he is allowed to do so".[391]

23–15 DAMAGES

23–15A Fraud

If either party has suffered loss as a result of fraudulent misrepresentation or non-disclosure by the other, he may recover damages to compensate him for that loss.[392] No insurance case has been reported in England,[393] but it has been suggested[394] that an action by the insurer could be based on the tort of deceit.

In the United States, it appears that this possibility may have been rediscovered in the guise of a "reverse bad faith suit". "Reverse bad faith suits are not so much new doctrinally, as newly recognized for their practical potential. For various reasons, they have been 'sleepers' in the law until recently: but now, they are an idea whose time has come."[395] In many instances, these suits are no more than what is known in Eng-

---

391. For example, *R* v *Alexander* [1981] Crim L R 183.
392. Generally see Treitel, pp 307 ff. In the USA, where the duty to disclose is based on contract, there appears to be no tortious action for negligent misstatement; for example, under New York law: *Nordstein Allgemeine Versicherungs AG* v *m/v Lauriergracht*, 1984 AMC 2826 (SD NY).
393. In *De Campos* v *State Compensation Fund*, 265 P 2d 617 (Cal, 1954) the underwriter who had paid workmen's compensation to an employee of the insured was able to recover the amount as damages from the insured.
394. *London Assurance Co* v *Clare* (1937) 57 Ll L Rep 254, 270 *per* Goddard J (fire).
395. Tierney, *Tort and Insurance Pleadings & Briefs*, January 1987, iii, iv-v.

land as a breach of the duty of co-operation by the insured.[396] In *Federal Ins Co* v *Wagner*,[397] for example, the California District Court awarded damages to the insurer against the insured in respect of fraud and bad faith. The sums awarded included not only the amount of insurance monies paid but also exemplary damages, which included a sum representing attorneys' fees. Whether the basis of the successful action was an implied term in the contract or in tort is unclear, but the obvious analogy with bad faith actions by insured against insurers suggests that the basis is tortious or possibly hybrid.[398]

23–15B The Misrepresentation Act

Damages may be awarded for a negligent misrepresentation inducing a contract of insurance. No such case has been reported. If the insurer has suffered loss as a result of negligent non-disclosure by the insured, then it is conceivable that he might recover damages to compensate him for that loss under section 2(1) of the Misrepresentation Act 1967. No reported case has been found. It has been suggested that the language of the Act limits the right to cases of positive conduct, misrepresentation, and excludes by implication a remedy for negative conduct such as non-disclosure.[399] Moreover, no damages can be recovered for non-disclosure as a breach of the duty of good faith: below 23–15C. That leaves the case of the half-truth,[400] the positive statement which is true when taken in isolation but which becomes untrue in context because of what has been left unsaid. For this damages should, in principle, be recoverable.[401]

23–15C Good Faith

In the *Westgate case*[402] Steyn J held that the insurer had broken a duty of disclosure to the insured. In spite of a *dictum* of Scrutton J,[403] Steyn J held that damages could be awarded against the insurer. His decision was reversed on appeal.[404] While acknowledging the existence of a duty of good faith, the higher courts considered that breach of that duty was not actionable in damages.

In that case, banks lent large sums to B on the security of some gemstones, which proved less valuable than the banks were led to believe, and of credit insurance guaranteeing repayment, which turned out to be worthless, because the policies excluded cover in the event of fraud. B, who committed the relevant fraud, did not repay the loan, and the banks sought to recover what they had lost from the insurers not as insurance money but as damages for breach of duty. The breach alleged was failure to

---

396. For example, *Liberty Mutual Ins Co* v *Altfillisch Construction Co*, 139 Cal Rptr 91 (1977); Karanian, 18 Pacific L J 307, 320 ff (1986). See further, below, chapter 27.

397. No 82 4339 LTL (BX) (Central District, California), reported by Tierney, *loc cit*.

398. Chutorian, 86 Colum L Rev 377 (1986).

399. *Westgate* (below, note 340); Hudson (1969) 85 LQR 524; Treitel, pp 360–361.

400. Above 22–2F.

401. Treitel, *loc cit*.

402. *Sub nom Banque Keyser Ullmann SA* v *Skandia (UK) Ins Co Ltd* [1990] QB 665.

403. *Glasgow Assurance Corp Ltd* v *Symondsen* (1911) 16 Com Cas 109, 121: that there was no breach of contract giving rise to a claim for damages; in this case, however, there was no finding of non-disclosure and no claim for damages for non-disclosure. For grounds on which this statement might be distinguished, see Matthews, *Foundations*, p 53. Also against an award of damages, however: *Khoury* v *GIO (N.S.W.)* (1984) 165 CLR 622, 636 (HCA).

404. *Sub nom Banque Financière de la Cité* v *Westgate Ins. Co* [1990] QB 665 (CA), affirmed on different grounds: [1991] 2 AC 249.

disclose to the banks, as insured, what the insurers' agent had discovered about the dishonesty of L, an agent of the banks' brokers,—dishonesty having no direct connection with that of B but dishonesty concerning the extent of the credit insurance in place.[405]

If the banks had known the truth, argued the banks, they would have lost some money to B but would not have advanced (and lost) a further sum of money to B, the amount of which they sought to recover as damages from the insurers. This premise was accepted by the lower courts,[406] but not by the House of Lords. In the view of the House,[407] the agent's failure to tell the banks about L's dishonesty was not a significant cause of the banks' loss.[408] The banks' argument to the contrary confused a cause of the advance (L's dishonesty) with the cause of the loss of the advance (B's dishonesty, which caused both that loss and the rejection of the insurance claim).

In any event, the insurers' duty of good faith to the insured banks had not been broken: L's dishonesty was not fraud within the meaning of the exclusion clause,[409] and it was not a matter which the agent was obliged to disclose to the banks.[410] However, Lord Templeman, with whom other members[411] of the House agreed, thought that, although not necessary to a decision now based on (lack of) causation, it would be helpful to observe[412] that he agreed that a breach of the obligation does not sound in damages, for "the cogent reasons advanced by Slade LJ", who delivered the only reasoned judgment of the Court of Appeal.

Slade LJ began from the position that any right to damages had to rest on an established category of duty.[413] "If the banks' right to full disclosure of material facts is founded neither on tort nor on contract nor on the existence of a fiduciary duty nor on statute, we find it difficult to see how as a matter of legal analysis it can be said to found a claim for damages."[414] The court first rejected a duty of disclosure based on implied contract. Later, the court rejected a duty of care in tort.[415] As regards breach of the duty of disclosure, which existed independently of contract and tort, the reasons against damages were as follows.

First, the power of the court to grant relief in a case of non-disclosure, together with duress and undue influence, stemmed from the jurisdiction originally exercised by courts of equity to prevent imposition. As no damages could be awarded in the cases of duress and undue influence, the court could "see no reason in principle" for doing so in the case of non—disclosure.[416] Does this argument by the court assume perhaps what it seeks to prove? In any event, it must be said that the origin of relief for non-

---

405. L was not involved with B's fraud but with a dishonesty of his own, aimed at obtaining commission.
406. p 686 and p 716 per Steyn LJ, p 806 per Slade LJ.
407. The clearest account of the view of the House can be found in the short judgment of Lord Ackner.
408. pp 957–958 *per* Lord Templeman: the argument, accepted in the courts below, "confuses the cause of the advance and the cause of the loss of the advance. The cause of the advance was the fraud of [L] . . . . The fraud of [B] caused the loss of the advance".
409. As had apparently been assumed by the lower courts.
410. It was not material to the risk: p 960 *per* Lord Jauncey.
411. Lord Brandon, Lord Ackner and Lord Jauncey. Lord Bridge (p 951) reserved his opinion on this question.
412. p 959.
413. p 776.
414. p 776. This has been described (Birds [1988] JBL 421, 422) as "a very conservative approach to the development of the common law", which overlooks the possibility of other bases, notably something akin to a fiduciary relationship with the possibility of damages, if a fiduciary duty is broken.
415. Below, 27–1A..
416. p 780.

disclosure in the courts of equity, at a time well before the Judicature Acts when and where no damages were possible, is not an overwhelming argument for refusing that remedy 100 years after fusion.[417]

The same can be said of the second of the court's arguments, that, as the Marine Insurance Act 1906 mentions avoidance but not damages, "we think the clear inference from the Act of 1906 is that Parliament did not contemplate that a breach of the obligation would give rise to a claim for damages in the case of such contracts".[418] True, no doubt, but it does not follow from this that there is or should be no right of action today.

The third reason lies in "the conceptual difficulties involved in a decision that a remedy by way of damages lies in this class of case".[419] In particular, Slade LJ noted the rule of materiality[420] and that, where an insured is seeking avoidance of the contract, the "court will be concerned not so much with the effect of the non-disclosure on his mind as that of the mind of the prudent notional insured". This being so, "it could legitimately be asked how damages could be awarded if the non-disclosure had no effect on the insured. In my judgment the only conceivable answer is that the requirements for avoidance are less than for an action for damages".[421]

An alternative, conceivable and simpler answer, it is submitted, lies in the basic rule that a claimant cannot recover damages unless and to the extent that he has suffered loss, which has been caused by the breach in question.[422] The grounds on which the law allows a contract to be rescinded or terminated and those on which damages are awarded are quite different—a premise, indeed, of the fourth reason (below), and difficulties in the one area should not be allowed to obstruct relief in the other.

Fourth, an action in damages might "give rise to great potential hardship to insurers and even more perhaps, to insured persons. An insured who had in complete innocence failed to disclose a material fact when making an insurance proposal might find himself subsequently faced with a claim by the insurer for a substantially increased premium by way of damages before any event had occurred which gave rise to a claim."[423] Indeed, it is one thing to say to a man that, if he does not disclose the whole truth as he knows it, the other will be able to withdraw from the contract because he did not know enough to give informed consent, but another thing to say to the first man that he assumes responsibility for consequential loss suffered by the other and will be liable to pay damages for it.[424] Contract apart, a person who makes a (positive) misrepresentation is only liable in damages to the full extent of the law, if he has been fraudulent or negligent. It might be thought odd that there should be such liability for (negative) non-disclosure, and in a wider range of cases—because non-disclosure

417. "How can anyone sensibly justify an English insurance policy to a foreign would-be user by explaining that the obligation to make full disclosure is still solely based upon the special powers of some separate system of courts which has not existed for over a century?"—Davenport [1989] LMCLQ 251, 258.

418. p 781.

419. p 780.

420. Above, 23–7B.

421. Words of Steyn J (p 706), who was undeterred by the difficulty which, indeed, is little greater than that confronting any court that must first apply the rule of remoteness of damage to the hypothetical defendant and then the rule of measure to the loss suffered by the actual plaintiff.

422. *Woodar Investment Development Ltd* v *Wimpey Construction UK Ltd* [1980] 1 All ER 571 (HL). As to the requirement of causation, this, of couse, was reaffirmed by the House in *Westgate* itself.

423. p 781.

424. See also Rudden, *Disclosure in Insurance: the Changing Scene* in Lectures on the Common Law, vol 3 (Deventer 1991), p 1, 8, who points out that most systems of law shrink from requiring compensation in such circumstances.

might be innocent; and that, whereas the liability for misrepresentation was the special work of Parliament in the Misrepresentation Act of 1967, the liability for damages for non-disclosure would have to be dredged up from the residue of common law.

23–15D Tort

In the *Westgate case* [425] it was held also that the insurer did not owe the insured a duty of care such that, in the event of non-disclosure, the insurer would be liable to the insured in tort. Further, the insurer is not obliged to investigate a risk and, if he does so, it is doubtful that he owes the insured any duty of care as to the way in which it is done.

In *Boerner*,[426] assuming that the insurer was negligent when inspecting the insured's elevator, the property insured, the Ohio court held that an employee of the insured, who was injured in the elevator, had no right of action against the insurer. The insurer had a contractual right of inspection but no duty (either in contract or in tort) to inspect the elevator. The inspections were part of the insurer's loss control programme and, but for the regularity of the inspections over seven years, this might have been the end of any argument that a duty was owed to anyone other than the insurer's own shareholders. In Ohio as in England,[427] however, a case might be made that, once a duty has been undertaken voluntarily, it must be performed with reasonable care. Moreover, there was some evidence in that case that the insurer saw them also as a service to the insured, to whom the inspector made a report and, in the opinion of the court, this service was more than merely incidental.[428]

"The policy considerations regarding a private party's voluntarily undertaking inspections differ from policy considerations regarding the state's establishment of standardized inspections, at least in part because of the nature of the relationship of the parties. The relationship between an insurer such as Defendant and the insured is of a voluntary, commercial nature which arises through arms (*sic*) length negotiation, and within which the parties may bargain for the assignment of risks and costs. The relationship is defined and may be freely modified by contract or a course of dealing, to suit the needs of the parties according to the nature of their business."[429]

Nonetheless, it was possible that the insurer had voluntarily assumed a duty of the kind alleged, and the case was sent for trial on the relevant issues of fact.

23–16 MISREPRESENTATION OR NON-DISCLOSURE AS A DEFENCE

The victim of misrepresentation or of non-disclosure may await action by the person responsible and plead the matter as a defence.[430] This is seen as a sort of passive rescission, and is subject to the same rules (below, 23–17) with one exception: the insurer may defend an action on an extension of cover under a held covered clause by reference to misrepresentation or non-disclosure in relation to the extension, without

425. Above 23–15C and below 27–1A.
426. *Boerner* v *Liberty Mutual Ins Co*, 748 F Supp 535 (WD Ohio, 1989).
427. On the contention that English law recognises a duty to warn others of danger, see Logie [1989] CLJ 114.
428. pp 539–540.
429. p 540.
430. *Redgrave* v *Hurd* (1881) 20 Ch D 1 (CA).

having to avoid the policy altogether; the misrepresentation or non-disclosure is treated as post-contract breach.[431]

23–17 THE RIGHT OF RESCISSION

The usual remedy for misrepresentation or non-disclosure is rescission of the contract.[432]

23–17A The Relevance of Fraud

Until the Misrepresentation Act 1967, the law distinguished fraudulent misrepresentations from innocent misrepresentation. Misrepresentations were fraudulent, as defined at common law,[433] if made with knowledge that the statement was untrue, without belief that it was true, or with recklessness as to whether it was true or false. A misrepresentation was innocent, if it was not fraudulent. Since the 1967 Act, however, innocent misrepresentations have been divided into those made with carelessness and those made without carelessness. The same divisions might be made in cases of non-disclosure, but as it appears that the Act does not apply to non-disclosure,[434] the division post 1967 does not matter.

In common law of the nineteenth century, a contract could be rescinded for misrepresentation only if the misrepresentation was made fraudulently or if it became a condition of the contract. After the fusion of law and equity, however, the remedy of rescission[435] was extended to the case of truly innocent misrepresentation,[436] although the court has now a discretion to refuse rescission and award damages in lieu: Misrepresentation Act 1967, section 2(2). Equally, non-disclosure gives rise to rescission as regards facts which the insured knew or should have known (above, 23–8), although he was "innocent" in that he totally failed to appreciate the materiality of those facts (above, 23–6).

Under the Statements of General Insurance Practice and Long-Term Insurance Practice, 1986, the declaration in the proposal form should be restricted to completion according to the proposer's knowledge and belief.[437] Moreover, insurers should not repudiate liability on grounds of non-disclosure of a material fact, which the insured could not reasonably be expected to have disclosed; and on grounds of misrepresentation, unless it is a deliberate or negligent misrepresentation of a material fact.[438]

---

431. *The Litsion Pride* [1985] 1 Lloyd's Rep 437, 515–516 *per* Hirst J (hull).
432. Generally, see Treitel, pp 329 ff. Appleman, sections 1831 ff.
433. *Pawson* v *Watson* (1778) 2 Cowp 785, 788 *per* Lord Mansfield (hull); *Derry* v *Peek* (1889) 14 App Cas 337.
434. Above, 23–15B.
435. *Redgrave* v *Hurd* (1881) 20 Ch D 1 (CA).
436. *Graham* v *Western Australian Ins Co Ltd* (1931) 40 Ll L Rep 64, 66 *per* Roche J (re); *Versicherungs und Transport AG Daugava* v *Henderson* (1934) 48 Ll L Rep 54, 58 *per* Roche J (re). Affirmed on other grounds (1934) 49 Ll L Rep 252 (CA). *Jordan* v *Provincial Provident Institution* (1898) 28 SCR 554 (life); *Murphy* v *Sun Life Assurance Co* (1964) 44 DLR (2d) 369 (Alta—life).
   USA: in many states, in the absence of statutory modification, there is rescission in cases of innocent misrepresentation: Keeton, p 323. See further, Appleman, sections 7297 ff. However, some states have passed "anti-technical" statutes, such as that in Alabama: a contract may be avoided for misrepresentation or concealment only if there is fraud: 1975 Ala Acts, ha 27–14–7. See further Brennan & Hanson, 21 Tort & Ins LJ 451 (1986).
437. Statement cl 1(a). Forte, 49 MLR 754, 757 (1986).
438. Cl 2(b). Forte, *loc cit* pp 764 ff.

23–17A1 Basis Clauses

If a misrepresentation is converted into a term of the contract by a basis clause,[439] the insurer may terminate the contract of insurance, whether the misrepresentation was innocent, negligent or fraudulent.[440] Most of the cases concerned misrepresentations that were apparently careless,[441] but nothing turned on this, for on a proper construction of the basis clause and the resulting contract term the representations had to be true. There are exceptions:

(a) If the terms of the basis clause limit its effect to, say fraudulent misstatements, so be it.

(b) If the proposer's statement is expressed to be accurate only to the best of the proposer's knowledge or belief, the contract can be avoided only if the statement was made fraudulently or negligently.[442]

(c) If the contract provides that its validity shall be indisputable after (x) years, except in case of fraud,[443] this provision will be applied. In case of doubt or ambiguity the contract would be construed against the insurer.[444]

23–17B The Mode of Rescission: Election

"[I]f there was non-disclosure, nevertheless non-disclosure does not automatically avoid the contract. It gives the insurers a right to elect. They can either avoid the contract or affirm it."[445] There can be no election without knowledge of the truth; this is discussed in connection with affirmation: below 23–18B1.

Rescission may be effected by notice to the insured, confirmed, if desired, by a court order. The rescission dates from the time of notice.[446]

23–17C The Effect of Rescission: Total Retroactivity

Rescission, sometimes referred to as avoidance, "if justified by the facts, terminates the contract, puts the parties in *statu quo ante* and restores things, as between them, to the position in which they stood before the contract was entered into".[447] Rescission, therefore, is retroactive. In particular, the insurer is not liable for claims arising

---

439. Generally, see 20–2A1.
440. Above, 20–6B1.
441. *Macdonald v Law Union Fire & Life Ins Co* (1874) LR 9 QB 328 (life); *Thomson v Weems* (1884) 9 App Cas 671 (life); *Reid & Co v Employers' Accident & Live Stock Ins Co*, 1899 1 F (Ct of Sess) 1031 (liability). There was no carelessness apparent in *Duckett v Williams* (1834) 2 C & M 348 (life) and carelessness was not discussed. See also *Holmes v Scottish Legal Life Assurance Sy* (1932) 48 TLR 306 (life).
442. *Wood v Dwarris* (1856) 11 Exch 493 (life); *Scottish Provident Institution v Boddam* (1893) 9 TLR 385 (life); *Hemmings v Sceptre Life Assn Ltd* [1905] 1 Ch 365 (life). For other decisions to this effect, see above, 20–6B1.
443. *Anstey v British Natural Premium Life Assn Ltd* (1908) 99 LT 765 (CA—life). Hasson (1987) 13 Can Bus L J 93, 102 ff.
444. *Joel v Law Union & Crown Ins Co* [1908] 2 KB 863, 886 *per* Fletcher Moulton LJ (CA—life). *Maye v Colonial Mutual Life* (1924) 35 CLR 14, 26–27 *per* Isaacs ACJ (HCA).
445. *Mackender, Hill & White v Feldia AG* [1966] 2 Lloyd's Rep 449, 455 *per* Lord Denning MR (CA—jewellers' block). *Stipcich v Metropolitan Life*, 277 US 311 (1927—life); *New York Life Ins Co v Cohen*, 57 F 2d 494 (6 Cir, 1932—death & disability).
446. *Reese Silver Mining Co v Smith* (1869) LR 4 HL 64.
447. *Abram v Westville* [1923] AC 773, 781 *per* Lord Atkinson; see also *Johnson v Agnew* [1980] AC 367, in which the House of Lords drew a clear distinction between "rescission" for breach, which operates prospectively, and rescission for misrepresentation, which operates retrospectively.

between the making of the contract and the moment of avoidance,[448] and the insurer must return premium.[449]

Further, rescission of the contract must be total, not partial.[450] Unless the contract provides otherwise,[451] the insurer cannot refuse to pay a claim on the ground of misrepresentation or non-disclosure, yet keep the contract alive for the future.[452]

An exception may exist, first, for extensions of cover, such as are achieved by the activation of held covered clauses, the extension being treated as a severable part of the contract so that what happens to the extension does not necessarily affect the rest of the contract.[453]

An exception may also exist, second, if under one policy there are two distinct classes of property, which are clearly and definitely separated, each being made a distinct subject of insurance, and each being insured for a specified sum. In such a situation it has been held in the United States[454] that the contract is divisible, and a ground of rescission for one part may be pleaded without affecting the other part of the contract.

Third, there may be an exception as regards arbitration. If an insurance contract is void from the beginning, a procedural clause such as an arbitration clause falls with the contract. However, when the contention is that the contract is voidable for misrepresentation or non-disclosure, "a widely drawn arbitration clause will survive avoidance of the contract. When the arbitrator declares that the contract is avoided it operates retroactively, i.e. it operates *ab initio*. [Nonetheless, having] declared the contract avoided, the arbitrator may proceed in the same or a subsequent award to unscramble the monetary consequences in the light of claims and cross claims".[455] For this purpose, it makes no difference whether the misrepresentation is fraudulent, negligent or innocent.[456]

23–18 LIMITS ON RESCISSION

The insurer's right to rescind may be barred, notably, by affirmation of the contract, or, possibly, lapse of time, or performance of the contract. These bars derive from the general law. The right may also be barred by the court acting under statutory power.

---

448. *Standard Accident* v *Pratt*, 278 P 2d, 489 (Cal, 1955—motor).
449. *Cf* above, 13–12.
450. *Urquhart* v *Macpherson* (1878) 3 App Cas 831. *Liverpool & London & Globe Ins Co* v *Stuart*, 14 SE 2d 98 (Ga, 1941—fire).
451. The contract may contain a "discretion" clause, whereby, if the insurer becomes entitled to avoid the contract, the insurer has the discretion, exercised by notice to the insured, to treat the contract as in force, excluding any claim relating to facts which should have been disclosed; for example, see *Tilley & Noad* v *Dominion Ins Co Ltd* (1987) 284 EG 1056 (liability).
452. *West* v *National Motor & Accident Union* [1955] 1 Lloyd's Rep 207 (CA—burglary).
453. This was the decision as regards an extension of cover to war risks in the Arabian Gulf in *The Litsion Pride* [1985] 1 Lloyd's Rep 437 (hull).
454. *Northern Assurance Co Ltd* v *Case*, 12 F 2d 551 (4 Cir, 1926—fire); *Bethune* v *New York Underwriters Ins Co*, 98 F Supp 366 (ED SC, 1951—fire): The cases concerned breach of warranty (see further, above 20–6C), but the rule is regarded as applicable equally to misrepresentation. *Aliter* if the misrepresentation affects all parts of the contract, any rescission must be total: *Hesselberg* v *Aetna Life Ins Co*, 102 F 2d 23 (8 Cir, 1939—life). See further above, 13–12A.
455. *Harbour Assurance Co (UK)* v *Kansa General Int Ins Ltd* [1992] 1 Lloyd's Rep 81, 91 *per* Steyn J (re). See also *Metal Products Ltd* v *Phoenix Assurance Co Ltd* (1925) 23 Ll L Rep 87 (CA—fire).
456. *Harbour* (above), with reference to *Mackender* v *Feldia AG* [1967] 2 QB 590 (CA).

23–18A Statute

Under the Misrepresentation Act 1967, section 2(2), in the case of misrepresentations made "otherwise than fraudulently", i.e., those made negligently or innocently, the court has a discretion to refuse rescission and to award damages instead. The sub-section operates in respect of a person who "has entered into a contract after a misrepresentation has been made to him" and hence, it has been argued,[457] whereas it will apply to the half truth—the statement that is literally true but rendered false by related omission—,[458] it does not apply to "pure" non-disclosure.

When exercising its discretion the court is directed by the sub-section to have regard, *inter alia*, to the nature of the misrepresentation and to the loss that rescission would cause to the party against whom rescission is sought. It seems possible that a court would refuse rescission of a contract of insurance against an insured, who had made an innocent misrepresentation on a matter which, if correctly stated, would have affected the terms of the cover but not led to declinature.[459]

23–18B Affirmation

The remedy of rescission may be barred by affirmation of the contract, sometimes called waiver of the right to rescind,[460] or election[461] not to rescind. There are two, perhaps three, requirements for such affirmation.

23–18B1 *Knowledge*

As regards his right to rescind "whether you treat it as an election or whether you treat it as a ratification" a person seeking relief must "know all the facts—being put on inquiry is not sufficient".[462] Election must, in general, "be an informed choice, made with knowledge of the facts giving rise to the right".[463] However, if he knows all the facts from which a reasonable man would deduce the truth, he may be presumed to know the truth.[464]

In Australia, it has been held that the person must know not only the facts giving

---

457. Above, 23–15B.
458. Above, 22–2F.
459. *The Lucy* [1983] 1 Lloyd's Rep 188, 202 *per* Mustill J. But *cf* Steyn J in *Highlands Ins Co* v *Continental Ins Co* [1987] 1 Lloyd's Rep 109, 118 (re): "Where a contract of reinsurance has been validly avoided on the grounds of a material misrepresentation, it is difficult to conceive of circumstances in which it would be equitable within the meaning of s 2(2) to grant relief from such avoidance".
460. *West* v *National Motor & Accident* [1955] 1 Lloyd's Rep 207 (CA). Bower, pp 304 ff.
461. To be distinguished from equitable election: Bower, *Estoppel*, No 309. See below, 26–4A.
462. *McCormick* v *National Motor & Accident Ins Union Ltd* (1934) 49 Ll L Rep 361, 365 *per* Scrutton LJ (CA—motor); see also *Russell* v *Thornton* (1860) 6 H & N 140 (Exch Ch—marine); *General Accident Fire & Life Assurance Corp* v *Campbell* (1925) 21 Ll L Rep 151 (re); *CTI* v *Oceanus* [1984] 1 Lloyd's Rep 476, 498 *per* Kerr LJ, 529 *per* Stephenson LJ (CA—containers); *Hadenfayre* v *British National Ins Sy Ltd* [1984] 2 Lloyd's Rep 393 (contingency); *The Litsion Pride* [1985] 1 Lloyd's Rep 437, 516 *per* Hirst J (hull). In English law generally see *Kendall* v *Hamilton* (1879) 4 App Cas 504, 542 *per* Lord Blackburn; *Kammins* v *Zenith* [1971] AC 850, 884 *per* Lord Diplock.
    Ogden & Co Pty Ltd v *Reliance Fire Sprinkler Co Pty Ltd* [1975] 1 Lloyd's Rep 52, 65 *per* Macfarlan J (HCA—liability). *Knights of Pythias of the World* v *Kalinski*, 163 US 289, 298 *per* Brown J (1898—life); *Moore* v *Prudential Ins Co*, 166 F Supp 215 (NC, 1958—life).
463. *Motor Oil Hellas (Corinth) Refineries SA* v *Shipping Corp of India, The Kanchenjunga* [1990] 1 Lloyd's Rep 391, 399 (HL). *American Franklin Life Ins Co* v *Galati*, 776 F Supp 1054, 1062 (ED Pa, 1991—disability).
464. *Long* v *Lloyd* [1958] 1 WLR 753 *per* Pearce LJ (CA).

rise to the right to rescind but also that those facts give him that right,[465] although the point has not been settled.[466] In England too, it has been decided that the knowledge required is knowledge of rights,[467] however, it is submitted that that decision must be seen in the context of its special facts. Other cases hold that it is enough that he knows or has obvious means of knowing his legal rights, whether or not he realises, to take the present case, that he is entitled to rescind the contract. It is enough that he has "knowledge of the facts giving rise to the right".[468] This is the better view, as the alternative by reference to knowledge of rights, makes it very difficult for the other party to decide whether he can safely rely on what appears to be affirmation.[469] As to the person whose knowledge counts as the knowledge of the insurer, see above, 23–9A2.

In the USA, consistently with decisions there that the proposer need not disclose information already on the insurer's files, it has been held that, if the insurer has already been given information contradicting the misrepresentations of the proposer, failure to rescind within a reasonable time amounts to waiver of rescission, i.e. to affirmation, even though the insurer had no actual knowledge of the information in his possession.[470] In England, a decision of this kind seems unlikely at the moment.[471]

23–18B2 Affirmation must be Unequivocal

Affirmation must be clear and unequivocal[472]: the relevant conduct must be consistent only with the exercise of the right to affirm rather than the right to rescind.[473] For example, affirmation by an insurer with knowledge of one ground for rescission does

---

465. *Elder's Trustee* v *Commonwealth Homes* (1941) 65 CLR 603 (HCA).

466. *Cf Sargant* v *ASL* (1974) 131 CLR 634. *Contra: Coastal Estates Pty Ltd* v *Melevende* [1965] VR 433 (Vict). Carter ((1992) 5 J Cont L 199, 216.

467. *Peyman* v *Lanjani* [1985] Ch 457 (CA).

468. *Eagle Star Ins Co Ltd* v *National Westminster Finance Australia Ltd* (1985) 58 ALR 165, 174 *per* Lord Roskill (PC). See also *Bremer Handelsgesellschaft mbH* v *Mackprang Jr* [1979] 1 Lloyd's Rep 221 (CA), applied in *The Eurometal* [1981] 1 Lloyd's Rep 337. *Idem* in *California: Prudential–LMI Commercial Insurance* v *Superior Court*, 274 Cal Rptr 387, 394 (Cal, 1990—fire). Generally, Rest Contracts 2d, section 84b.

Cf Kelly v *Solari* (1841) 11 LJ Ex 10, 12 *per* Lord Abinger CB (life) and more recently *Peyman* v *Lanjani* [1985] Ch 457 (CA) in which Stephenson LJ said (p 483) that "knowledge of the right to choose is essential to the loss of the right". Although the case concerned termination for breach the court considered that on this issue there was no difference between that and rescission for fraudulent misrepresentation (p 489 *per* Stephenson LJ).

Cf Goldsworthy v *Brickell* [1987] Ch 378, 411–412 (CA): Nourse LJ doubted whether there is a "hard and fast rule that ignorance of the right is a bar to the defence of acquiescence . . . the whole of the circumstances must be looked at to see whether it is just" that rescission be ordered.

469. Carter (1992) 5 J Cont L 199, 216.

470. *Foremost Guarantee Corp* v *Meritor Savings Bank* 910 F 2d 118 (4 Cir, 1990—mtge)—a case of an offering memorandum given to the insurer which contradicted oral representations. The court placed some emphasis on the fact that the memorandum was written, whereas the misrepresentations were oral: p 126.

471. See above, 23–9B2.

472. *Bremer Handelsgesellschaft mbH* v *Vanden Avenne-Izegem* [1978] 2 Lloyd's Rep 109 (HL); *Motor Oil Hellas (Corinth) Refineries SA* v *Shipping Corp of India, The Kanchenjunga* [1990] 1 Lloyd's Rep 391, 399 (HL). See also in relation to waiver of procedural conditions below, 26–4D.

Sargant v *ASL* (1974) 131 CLR 634 (HCA); *Ogden & Co Pty Ltd* v *Reliance Fire Sprinkler Co Pty Ltd* [1975] 1 Lloyd's Rep 52, 65 *per* Macfarlan J (HCA—liability). *Continental Casualty Co* v *Casey* [1934] SCR 54 (PA).

473. Bower, *Estoppel*, No 310. The test of a person's intention is objective rather than subjective: *Peyman* v *Lanjani* [1985] Ch 457, 488 *per* Stephenson LJ (CA).

not amount to affirmation of the same contract in respect of another ground of rescission, of which the insurer was unaware.[474]

23–18B3 Reliance

It has been argued that affirmation by one party does not bar rescission, unless the other has altered his position in reliance on the affirmation. If there is reliance, however, affirmation is permanent and irrevocable; the insurer cannot resume his right to rescind by giving the insured notice.[475] Certainly, in the United States some insurance decisions have required reliance.[476] But, in England the view is that reliance is a feature, not of affirmation, waiver or election, but of estoppel; that, if a clear election has been made, it cannot be withdrawn, whether there has been reliance or not.[477] Still, reliance does have the lesser function that, if present, it will clinch the matter, for example, in cases of affirmation by silence; but in such cases the courts are as likely to talk of estoppel as of waiver or affirmation.

However, reliance will be decisive in certain cases, in which rescission would not otherwise have been barred by affirmation. There is authority that, if the insurer delays his decision to rescind or to affirm—negative conduct not normally amounting to affirmation—but the delay prejudices the insured, it may bar the right to rescind. In *Clough* v *LNWR*, Mellor J said this[478]:

"The party defrauded may keep the question open so long as he does nothing to affirm the con-

---

474. *American Franklin Life Ins Co* v *Galati*, 776 F Supp 1054, 1062 (ED Pa, 1991—disability).

475. *Hartley* v *Hymans* [1920] 3 KB 475, 495 *per* McCardie J; *Bentsen* v *Taylor* [1893] 2 QB 274, 279 *per* Lord Esher MR, 283 *per* Bowen LJ (CA); in the latter case, the representee could not in any event have resumed his former position.

476. In the USA promissory estoppel differs from that in England, for it provides a cause of action independent of any contractual principles, more akin to a tort of inducing detrimental reliance: Morgan, 15 Melb U L Rev 134 (1985). As to the circumstances giving rise to an estoppel, there are similarities in England and the USA, not least on the diverse views of the relationship with waiver.

One view, like the orthodox view in England (below, 26–4A), is that, while estoppel requires reliance, waiver does not; estoppel emphasises the effect of conduct, hence the requirement of reliance, but waiver emphasises the intention of the actor: *John Alt Furniture Co* v *Maryland Casualty Co*, 88 F 2d 36 (8 Cir, 1937—liability); *American Home Assurance Co* v *Harvey's Wagon Wheel Inc*, 398 F Supp 379 (D Nev, 1975—fire), affirmed 554 F 2d 1067 (9 Cir, 1977); *Providence Washington Ins Co* v *Stanley*, 403 F 2d 844 (5 Cir, 1968—fire); *Hully* v *Aluminium Co of America*, 143 F Supp 508 (SD Iowa, 1956—liability), affirmed 245 F 2d 1 (8 Cir, 1957); *Souter* v *State Mutual Life Ins Co*, 273 F 2d 921 (4 Cir, 1960—life). See generally, 45 CJS, section 673.

A second view is that estoppel is the result of waiver and that for present purposes, whether the phenomenon is called waiver or estoppel, there must be reliance by the insured before the insurer is unable to rescind: *Globe Mutual Ins Co* v *Wolff*, 95 US 326, 333 *per* Justice Field (1877—life); *Equitable Life Assurance Sy* v *McElroy*, 83 F 631 (8 Cir, 1897—life); *Greyhound Corp* v *Excess Ins Co of America*, 233 F 2d 630 (5 Cir, 1956—liability); *US* v *Willoughby*, 250 F 2d 524 (9 Cir, 1957—life); *Blanton* v *John Hancock Mutual Life Ins Co*, 345 F Supp 168 (ND Tex, 1971—life), affirmed 463 F 2d (5 Cir, 1972).

Similarly when a suit for reformation (rectification) has been defended on the ground of affirmation, courts have said that the defence will fail unless there has been prejudice to the defendant: *Columbian National Life Ins Co* v *Black*, 35 F 2d 571 (10 Cir, 1929—life); *Kansas City Life Ins Co* v *Cox*, 104 F 2d 321 (6 Cir, 1939—life); *Preferred Accident Ins Co* v *Onali*, 43 F Supp 227, 231 (D Minn, 1942—motor), affirmed 125 F 2d 580 (8 Cir, 1942); *Mutual Life Ins Co of New York* v *Simon*, 151 F Supp 408 (SDNY, 1957—life). Generally, see Rest Contracts 2d, section 84b; Spry, *Equitable Remedies* (2nd ed), pp 217 ff.

477. See 26–4A. Brown & Menezes, No 14:4:2.

478. (1871) LR 7 Ex 26, 34–5; see also *Lindsay Petroleum* v *Hurd* (1874) LR 5 PC 221, 239–240 *per* Sir Barnes Peacock; *Simon, Haynes, Barlas & Ireland* v *Beer* (1945) 78 Ll L Rep 337, 369 *per* Atkinson J (liability). In *Clough*, Mellor J said (p 35) that to issue a writ against the person alleged to have waived his rights did not amount to sufficient reliance.

tract . . . We think that as long as he has made no election, he retains the right to determine it either way, subject to this, that if, in the interval whilst he is deliberating, . . . in consequence of his delay, the position even of the wrongdoer is affected, it will preclude him from exercising his right to rescind."

This statement was applied more recently by the Court of Appeal in *Peyman* v *Lanjani*.[479] Stephenson LJ stated[480] that "acts which on the face of them are referable only to an intention to affirm the contract" do not affirm the contract, in the absence of the required knowledge, unless, however, "those acts are 'adverse to' the opposite party, as e.g., if the defrauded party goes into possession of property sold to him by the contract or accepts some other benefit thereunder. This is a form of estoppel, for the other party has in such a case acted to his prejudice upon a representation".

Neither *Clough* nor *Peyman* concerned insurance contracts. In *Morrison* v *Universal Marine*,[481] however, the judgment of Mellor J (above) was accepted in relation to marine insurance. The insured's broker failed (without fraud) to disclose information indicating that the relevant ship had stranded. Although the insurer saw the entry of the stranding in the loss book at Lloyd's, he waited until the loss was confirmed before seeking to rescind the contract of insurance. The insured's argument, that by remaining quiescent for eight days the insurer had allowed him to think himself insured and had thus lost the right of rescission, was rejected by the Court of Exchequer Chamber. Honyman J, however, cited the passage from the judgment of Mellor J in *Clough* (above) and concluded[482] that, if the plaintiff had indeed abstained from taking insurance elsewhere as a result of the insurer's quiescence, there would have been a loss of the right of rescission. While that seems just, however, if the courts are too quick to find affirmation or waiver, it would "have a tendency to require insurance companies to be unduly cautious in the settlement of claims, and put insureds to unnecessary trouble, delay and expense in obtaining funds rightfully due to them."[483]

23–18C Lapse of Time

In the absence of fraud,[484] lapse of time alone is sometimes stated to be a bar to rescission, a bar distinct from affirmation. There is uncertainty, but the better view of the insurance cases may be that it is a kind of affirmation: if an insurer has knowledge[485] of the facts giving rise to the right to rescind, he is entitled to take time to consider whether to avoid the contract or not.[486] After that, further delay may amount to affirmation, but only if it can be "said to evidence acceptance of liability".[487]

---

479. [1985] Ch 457. The Court was persuaded by *Coastal Estates Pty Ltd* v *Melevende* [1965] VR 433 (Vict), in which the court applied *Clough*.
480. [1985] Ch 457, 487, with whom other members of the court agreed.
481. (1873) LR 8 Ex 197 (freight).
482. pp 205–206; see also p 206 *per* Honeyman J.
483. *Moore* v *Prudential Ins Co of America*, 166 F Supp 215, 219 (MD NC, 1958—life).
484. *Clough* v *LNWR* (1871) 7 Ex 26, 35 *per* Mellor J. The courts are generally less willing to allow any of the bars to rescission to operate in favour of a fraudulent party.
485. Above, 23–18B3.
486. *Pan Atlantic Ins Co Ltd* v *Pine Top Insurance Co Ltd* [1992] 1 Lloyd's Rep 101, 107 *per* Waller J (re), affirmed [1993] 1 Lloyd's Rep 496 (CA); an appeal to the House of Lords is to be heard in February 1994.
487. *Ibid.*

In *Clough* v *LNWR*[488] Mellor J first said that a person "may keep the question open so long as he does nothing to affirm the contract" but later continued: "And lapse of time without rescinding will furnish evidence that he has determined to affirm the contract, and, when the lapse of time is great, it would probably in practice be treated as conclusive evidence to shew that he has so determined." In *Allen* v *Robles Cie Parisienne de Garantie*[489] Fenton Atkinson LJ said that rescission would be barred if "delay was so long that the court felt able to say that the delay in itself was of such a length as to be evidence that they had in truth decided to accept liability".

In the general law of contract, there is little authority for a distinct bar by lapse of time alone, without the knowledge which might give rise to affirmation. Authority is limited to one decision of the Court of Appeal[490] and the rationale appears to be that "it behoves the [representee] either to verify or, as the case may be, to disprove the representation within a reasonable time, or else stand or fall by it."[491] This reasoning is plausible when related, as it was in that case, to a man who pays the market price for a work of art. It is less convincing, when the misrepresentation is just one part of a proposal of insurance, and still less so when the case for rescission is based on non-disclosure: insurers cannot be presumed to check the truth of what proposers do not say. So, it is submitted, this very isolated decision on contracts to sell goods is of little relevance to contracts of insurance. Moreover, the cases on waiver of rights and remedies, other than rescission, show that the courts are very slow to construe waiver from negative conduct.[492] Given a sensible statute of limitation, there is little to justify such a decision in the general law, still less with respect to contracts of insurance. "If Achilles wakes up in time to beat the tortoise at the winning-post, the law has no business to inquire how long it was before he woke up."[493] In practice, the point will not often arise, for usually the insurer will have the requisite knowledge for affirmation, and the longer the delay or inactivity by the insurer, the more likely that there will be reliance by the insured, which will bar rescission on the ground suggested above, 23–18B3.

488. (1871) 7 Ex 26, 34–35: applied in *The Scaptrade* [1981] 2 Lloyd's Rep 425, 430 by Lloyd J. *Cf March Cabaret Club & Casino* v *London Assurance* [1975] 1 Lloyd's Rep 169, 178 *per* May J (fire).

In the USA many jurisdictions allow lapse of time as a bar: for example, *Fountain & Herrington Inc* v *Mutual Life Ins Co*, 55 F 2d 120, 125 (4 Cir, 1932—life); *Prentiss* v *Mutual Benefit Health & Accident Assn*, 109 F 2d 1 (7 Cir, 1940—accident & sickness benefit); *Milbank Mutual Ins Co* v *Schmidt*, 304 F 2d 640 (8 Cir, 1962—motor); *American Home Assurance Co* v *Harvey's Wagon Wheel Inc*, 398 F Supp 379 (D Nev, 1975—fire), affirmed 554 F 2d 1067 (9 Cir, 1977). In general, however, the insurer is entitled to a reasonable time to investigate and reach a decision: *Shaner* v *West Coast Life Ins Co*, 73 F 2d 681, 685 (10 Cir, 1934—life).

489. [1969] 2 Lloyd's Rep 61, 64 (CA—motor). In that case, the Court of Appeal applied the judgment of Mellor J (above) in *Clough* but held that two to three months was not enough to bar rescission.

Cf Simon, Haynes, Barlas & Ireland v *Beer* (1945) 78 Ll L Rep 337 (liability): it was held as an alternative ground for the decision that lapse of time, either of six months or of 18 months, would suffice to bar rescission.

490. *Leaf* v *International Galleries* [1950] 2 KB 86 (CA). *Idem*, Rest Contracts 2d, section 381; Williston, section 683 n 8.

491. *Leaf* p 92 *per* Jenkins LJ.

492. *Woodhouse A C Israel Cocoa Ltd* v *Nigerian Produce Marketing Co* [1972] AC 741 (PC), applied in cases in which by accepting part delivery the buyer does not waive rights in respect of the undelivered balance: for example, *Bremer Handelsgesellschaft mbH* v *Westzucker GmbH* [1981] 1 Lloyd's Rep 207. See also *Burrow* v *Subsurface Surveys* (1968) 68 DLR (2d) 354 (SC). See further, below, 26–4D.

493 Bower, *Misrepresentation*, No 311.

23–18D Performance

Performance of the contract does not bar rescission of insurance contracts obtained by fraudulent misrepresentation or non-disclosure[494] and, whether such a bar operates in other cases, is doubtful.

Before 1967, it was believed that there was a bar to rescission of contracts generally, if the contract had been executed;[495] and there were signs of such a bar in cases on insurance.[496]

After 1967, any such bar to rescission of contracts in general was apparently abolished by section 1 of the Misrepresentation Act 1967, when "a person has entered into a contract after a misrepresentation has been *made* to him".[497] However, it has been argued[498] that, although this wording extends to misrepresentation, it does not extend to non-disclosure, because the latter is not "made", except in the case of a half-truth[499]: a representation which has become untrue because of what has been left unsaid. Hence the possibility of such a bar to rescission for non-disclosure cannot be ruled out.

23–18E Restitution

Normally a person seeking to rescind a contract must give back as well as take back what has been transferred under the contract to be rescinded, failing which rescission may be barred. Thus, the insurer who seeks rescission for misrepresentation or non-disclosure must hand back the premiums. This requirement gives little difficulty in the law of insurance.

23–18F Third Party Rights

A person seeking recission finds the remedy barred, if a third party has acquired rights in property transferred under the contract to be rescinded. This bar does not affect insurance. The insurer, who rescinds and must therefore return premium, is not required to return notes or coins in specie. If the insured has assigned the policy of insurance, the assignee is not a third party in the sense of the bar; he takes subject to equities, including the right of the insurer to rescind.[500]

---

494. *Kettlewell* v *Refuge Assurance Co Ltd* [1908] 1 KB 545 (CA—life).

495. The leading case is a first instance decision: *Seddon* v *North Eastern Salt Co Ltd* [1905] 1 Ch 326; see also *Angel* v *Jay* [1911] 1 KB 666; *Edler* v *Auerbach* [1950] 1 KB 359, 373 *per* Devlin J. *Contra*: *Mackenzie* v *Royal Bank of Canada* [1934] AC 468 (PC).

496. The bar was argued unsuccessfully in *Kettlewell* v *Refuge Assurance Co Ltd* [1908] 1 KB 545 (CA—life). Lord Alverston CJ (p 549) indicated that, in any event, the insurer's coming on risk would not amount to performance. Also cited in this connection is *Lowry* v *Bourdieu* (1780) 2 Dougl 468 (marine), however, that decision can be explained and distinguished as concerning illegality and repentance.

497. Emphasis added.

498. For example, Treitel, p 310. See further, above, 23–15.

499. Above, 22–2F.

500. See above, 6–6.

CHAPTER 24

ILLEGAL INSURANCE

24-1 ILLEGAL CONTRACTS

Illegality usually arises as a defence raised by the insurer to an insurance claim. The onus of proof lies on the party who alleges illegality.[1] Conviction in a criminal court is no more than *prima facie* evidence of events in civil proceedings.[2] If evidence of illegality emerges in the course of a hearing, the court must take it into account, whether that is the wish of the parties or not.[3]

Cases of illegal contract are usually classified, originally by Sir Frederick Pollock, according to the source of the rule infringed, common law, statute, or judicial intervention.[4] The case law is so unsettled that any classification is arbitrary and of limited conceptual significance. The classification adopted in this chapter is purely for exposition, chiefly to make the text intelligible to the reader who has come from general books on the law of contract. Yet, what is said in this chapter is good, if at all, only for insurance contracts.

The key to the confusion is public policy. The courts start from the policy position that contracts should be enforced.[5] They then retreat from this position according to the force of other factors, including justice to the individual insured,[6] but the most prominent factor is the contention that enforcement of the contract will encourage unlawful conduct. Hence, courts are least disposed to enforce the contracts of those whose unlawfulness is intentional or reckless than of those whose conduct is negligent or innocent. Courts are also influenced by the effect that non-enforcement would have on third parties and the more so, if those third parties are innocent. The effect of these competing factors is uncertainty in the law. Although "general principles of insurance

---

1. *Stormont* v *Waterloo Life & Casualty Assurance Co* (1858) 1 F & F 607 (life).
USA: there are cases to similar effect: *US* v *Kwasniewski*, 91 F Supp 847 (ED Mich, 1950—life); but the case law is not entirely consistent; see, *Minasian* v *Aetna Life Ins Co*, 3 NE 2d 17 (Mass, 1936—life).
2. Civil Evidence Act 1968, section 11. *Cf Prince of Wales Ins Assn* v *Palmer* (1858) 25 Beav 605 (life): Sir John Romilly MR was appreciably, but not exclusively, influenced by the finding of a coroner's jury that the insured had been murdered by the claimant. In the modern law it is clear that such evidence is insufficient: *Bird* v *Keep* [1918] 2 KB 692 (CA—workmen's compensation). See also *In Re Crippen* [1911] P 108. *Cf Gray* v *Barr* [1971] 2 QB 554 (liability) in which members of the Court of Appeal were reluctant to accept a jury verdict acquitting the insured of manslaughter.
3. *Gedge* v *Royal Exchange Assurance Co* [1900] 2 QB 214 (hull), applying Lindley LJ in *Scott* v *Brown, Doering, McNab & Co* [1892] 2 QB 724, 728 (CA).
4. Treitel, p 377. *Cf* Williston, section 1628: "There seems to be no importance to these distinctions." Concerning insurance contracts, see McNair, *Legal Effects of War* (4th ed, 1966), ch 11; Webber, *The Effect of War on Contracts* (1940), ch 9 and ch 11.
5. See below, 24-5A3(c)
6. A court may be reluctant to allow an insurer the defence of lack of interest, if the insurer knew or should have known of the matter, but yet took premiums: *Holmes* v *Nationwide Ins Co* (1963) 244 NYS 2d 148, 152 (life).

law should be the same wherever they are applied, the overlay of public policy entails that the actual decisions may well differ from time to time and place to place".[7] This suggests caution not only with decisions of other countries but also with those of other periods of social history in England.

24–2 ILLEGALITY WHEN MAKING THE CONTRACT OF INSURANCE

24–2A Contracts with Persons Lacking Insurable Interest

A contract of insurance made by an insurer with a person, who lacks the insurable interest required by law[8] is void; it can also be said that it is contrary to public policy and thus illegal.[9]

24–2B Contracts with Enemy Aliens

Common law forbids contracts with enemy aliens; any such contract is said to be void.[10] An enemy alien is a person with a significant connection with an enemy state (below, 24–2B1) in time of war (24–2B2).

24–2B1 Enemy Connection

At common law, an enemy alien is not solely or necessarily a national of the enemy state but also any person, of whatever nationality, voluntarily resident or carrying on business in the enemy state or in enemy occupied territory.[11] An enemy national, who is not an enemy in the sense just described, may bring action in the English courts, if he is an "enemy in protection"[12]; usually, this means that he must be registered.[13]

The common law definition was supplemented by statute,[14] whereby enemy means:

" . . . (b) any individual resident in enemy territory,

---

7. Mustill [1988] LMCLQ 310, 320.
8. See chapter 3 and chapter 4.
9. For example, *Spare* v *Home Mutual Ins Co*, 15 F 707 (D Or, 1883—fire).
10. *Janson* v *Driefontein Consolidated Mines Ltd* [1902] AC 484, 499 *per* Lord Davey, 506 *per* Lord Lindley (cargo).
11. *Sovfracht (V/O)* v *Van Udens Scheepvaart en Agentuur Maatschappij (N V Gebr)* [1943] AC 203; see also *Porter* v *Freudenberg* [1915] 1 KB 857 (CA); *The Anglo-Mexican* [1918] AC 422 (PC). Generally, see Halsbury, Vol 49, Nos 146 ff.
Cf Eastern Carrying Ins Co v *The National Benefit Life & Property Assurance Co Ltd* (1919) 35 TLR 292 (re): an insurer in Bolshevik Petrograd was not treated as an enemy alien, apparently because he was not a supporter of the Bolsheviks; this alone would not now be decisive, so that, if he nonetheless carried on his business there voluntarily, he would be seen as an enemy alien in this context, as his business activity helped the enemy economy. In *Bromley* v *Haseltine* (1807) 1 Camp 75, 77, Lord Ellenborough indicated that a contract with a person in enemy occupied Livorno would be enforced only if that person were "entrapped and confined" there.
12. *Porter* v *Freudenberg* [1915] 1 KB 857, 874 *per* Lord Reading CJ (CA). See further *Schaffenius* v *Goldberg* [1916] 1 KB 284 (CA). *Ex P Kawato*, 317 US 69 (1942). McNair, *op cit*, pp 120–1;
13. Registration is governed by regulations made under the Aliens Restriction Acts 1914 and 1919.
14. Section 2(1) of the Trading with the Enemy Act 1939, as amended by the Emergency Laws (Miscellaneous Provisions) Act 1953, section 2.
Parliament also may modify the consequences at common law of the prohibition on dealing with the enemy. The basis for this power is now the Insurance Contracts (War Settlement) Act 1952, "an Act to provide for carrying into effect Agreements with certain foreign governments with respect to contracts of insurance and reinsurance made by persons who subsequently became enemies". Such agreements have been made, for example, with Finland, Italy and Germany and published as statutory instruments.

(c) any body of persons (whether corporate or unincorporate) carrying on business in any place, if and so long as the body is controlled by a person who, under this section, is an enemy . . .

(d) any body of persons constituted or incorporated in, or under the laws of, a State at war with Her Majesty; and

(e) as respects any business carried on in enemy territory, any individual or body of persons (whether corporate or unincorporate) carrying on that business."

This provision exists solely for the purposes of the Act, namely, to indicate the extent of the prohibition contained in the Act on dealings with enemies.[15] The common law definition is unaffected[16]; in any event, it is thought to be substantially the same as the definition in the Act.[17]

(a) *Enemies.* Enemies, therefore, include persons voluntarily resident *or* carrying on business in enemy or enemy occupied territory. A person resident there is an enemy even as regards business, including insurance transacted in neutral territory, and even if that business is his entire business.[18] Conversely, a person is also an enemy if, although not resident in enemy territory, he does business there.[19] Arnould objects[20] that "residence is no more a satisfactory test than nationality, and business activity seems to provide the best criterion". However, the double rule makes sense as public policy for, in the case of business in neutral territory, profit generated may well be remitted to the place of residence and thus to territory of the enemy and thus to the benefit of the enemy. Moreover, business in neutral territory by a person resident there may support another arm of the business conducted in enemy territory.

(b) *Agents.* If an enemy insurer has a branch in England or in neutral territory, it is now established law[21] that the branch will have enemy character, if the *de facto* control of the branch still lies with the enemy parent.[22] If the insurer has no more than an agent in these places, the first question is whether the agency survives the outbreak of war. Generally, the agency is abrogated by the outbreak of war: "when the principal becomes an enemy the authority of the agent ceases on the ground that it is not permissible to have intercourse with an enemy alien, and the existence of the relationship of principal and agent necessitates such intercourse."[23] Even in the rare case in which the agency can function without intercourse,[24] there remains the objection that an arrangement, that would benefit the enemy principal after the war as a source of credit, is of benefit to the principal (and the enemy economy) during the war.[25]

In the case of life insurance, it is not "manifestly" in the interest of the enemy

15. *Sovfracht* [1942] 1 KB 222 (CA).

16. *Sovfracht* [1943] AC 203, 235 *per* Lord Wright.

17. *Ibid*, p 219 *per* Lord Wright. See also McNair, *op cit*, pp 106–108. *Cf* Parry (1941) 4 MLR 161 suggesting some differences between the Act and common law.

18. *Porter* v *Freudenberg* [1915] 1 KB 857, 869 *per* Lord Reading CJ (CA); *The Anglo-Mexican* [1918] AC 422, 427 *per* Lord Parker; *Sovfracht* [1943] AC 203, 209 *per* Viscount Simon LC.

19. *Sovfracht* [1943] AC 203, 229 *per* Lord Wright.

20. No 147, note 31.

21. *Cf Ingle Ltd* v *Mannheim Ins Co* [1915] 1 KB 227, in which Bailhache J held that a branch in England of an insurance company, the head office of which was in enemy territory, was not itself an enemy as regards business transacted in England. He applied a notion of commercial domicil, and ignored the enemy connection, which current law sees as important.

22. *Daimler Co Ltd.* v *Continental Tyre & Rubber Co (Great Britain) Ltd* [1916] 2 AC 307; *The Hamborn* [1919] AC 993 (PC). See also the the Trading with the Enemy Act 1939, section 2.

23. *Sovfracht* [1943] AC 203, 254 *per* Lord Porter. See also *The Panareiellos* (1916) 85 LJ (P) 112, 116 *per* Lord Sumner (PC); *Hugh Stenson & Co* v *AG fur Cartonnagen-Industrie* [1917] 1 KB 842 (CA).

24. *Tingley* v *Miller* [1917] 2 Ch 144 (CA). See discussion of this case in *Sovfracht* [1943] AC 203, 254 *per* Lord Porter.

25. This objection is discussed below, 24–4B1.

insurer,[26] that he should continue to cover lives, the ending of which is being actively sought by his compatriots and has been made more likely by the war. On the other hand, it may be manifestly in the interest of an insured here, who has paid premium for many years before the war, that the insurance should be maintained.[27] The Supreme Court of the United States envisaged that life insurance might be maintained during wartime by payment to an agent in the forum state, but thought[28] it a condition of any valid agency that funds were not remitted to the enemy principal during the war.

(c) *Disconnection*. Although a company may acquire enemy character by enemy connection, such as doing business in enemy territory, it has been held in the United States that the company does not cease to be an enemy simply by ceasing such business, at least as regards the consequences of enemy character prior to cessation.

In *Swiss National Ins Co Ltd* v *Crowley*[29] the plaintiff corporation was organised under the laws of Switzerland, with shares largely owned by German nationals, and had branches doing insurance business in the United States and in (enemy) Germany. The plaintiff sought to recover assets, which had been seized in the United States, because since the seizure the corporation had ceased to do business in Germany. The action failed in the Supreme Court of the United States because, in the words of Chief Justice Taft,[30] the cessation of business "could not take away the status of the seized property as enemy property. The withdrawal from business in Germany might well involve the transfer of something of value from the plaintiff to enemy citizens or subjects, and strengthen the enemy resources."

It will be observed that the Chief Justice framed the decision in terms of the status of the property, rather than the status of the corporation. The reasons of policy for not enforcing contracts with enemy aliens and the reasons given by the Chief Justice for the decision of the court suggest the possibility that the enemy status of the corporation might end, not at the end of the war, but at the earlier date, when the corporation was no longer in a position to "strengthen the enemy resources", unless it is still resident there. This is probably the rule in England. Enemy alien is usually defined in the present tense: for example, Viscount Simon LC in *Sovfracht*: someone who "*is* carrying on business in, or *is* voluntarily resident in, the enemy's country".[31] He went on to suggest[32] that, if the company concerned had lost its commercial domicil in (enemy occupied) Rotterdam, the decision that it had enemy status would have been different. So also, Lord Wright thought,[33] that in the case of occupied territory the company trading there loses enemy character, if the occupation ceases.

(d) *Enemy Territory*. Enemy territory comprises all territory which is recognised by international law, at the outbreak of war, as belonging to the enemy state. For the present rule, it extends also to territory occupied by the enemy, although perhaps illegally. To be occupied, the territory

---

26. *New York Life Ins Co* v *Davis*, 95 US 453, 454 and 455 *per* Bradley J (1877—life). See also *Tait* v *New York Life Ins Co*, 23 F Cas No 13,726 (WD Tenn, 1873—life).

27. Webber, *op cit*, p 151.

28. *Davis* (above) p 454.

29. 267 US 42 (1924).

30. p 44.

31. [1943] AC 203, 209 (emphasis added).

32. p 210. See also p 237 *per* Lord Porter; and *Tingley* v *Miller* [1917] 2 Ch 144, 174–175 *per* Scrutton LJ (CA).

33. p 229.

"must be subjugated, not merely occupied. It must be held under the dominion and control of the enemy for a period sufficient to give the occupation a settled and relatively permanent character and to show the intention to keep it. I do not think that the cases require that there should be formal acts, such as cession by treaty or a public declaration of annexation. The matter must be decided as a question of fact with due regard to the character, purpose and intention of the occupation and the degree of dominion exercised . . . there is a sharp distinction between an occupation of territory by armed forces for strategical and temporary purposes and an occupation of territory as being a settled acquisition."[34]

This statement reflects the stringent requirements of international law[35] for the acquisition of territory by states, stringent particularly when, as in the present hypothesis, the territory is already settled. To set up title against another state, with the concomitant rights and duties of statehood, it is evident that the requirements should be strict. But it is doubtful whether the requirements should be as strict in the present context: it is easy to imagine "occupation", which would not satisfy these rules, but during which civilian commercial activity is both possible and beneficial to the "occupying" power.[36] Hence, it should be enough, in words approved by Lord Wright,[37] that the enemy can use the place for the purposes of his war.

24–2B2 Time of War

At one time war was strictly defined. Thus, in spite of considerable military commitment by the British Government to the White Russians, there was no war against the Bolsheviks, as the British Government had not recognised their government.[38] Since the First World War, a more flexible definition has been accepted in commercial cases.[39] War is not limited to a formal declaration of war, nor does it extend to a state of "strained relations"; war must have been heralded by some belligerent "act of the nation".[40] There is much to be said for the certainty, which was the product of the more cautious approach at the turn of the century.[41]

A person, whether a neutral or a national of the forum state at war, has a reasonable time in which to leave and dissociate himself from the enemy state. In *Nigel Gold Mining Co Ltd v Hoade*,[42] insurance was taken on the contents of a gold mine in Transvaal, which were seized shortly after the beginning of the Boer war. This loss was held to be covered, even though it occurred in enemy territory. In a short judg-

---

34. *Sovfracht* [1943] AC 203, 220; see also p 225 and p 226.
35. Acknowledged by Lord Wright, p 227.
36. Thus Webber, *op cit*, p 15: "The occupation of territory increases the capacity of the enemy for prolonging the war, and therefore, during the war . . . territory—while temporarily occupied—must be considered as belonging to the enemy".
37. Hall, *International Law*, 6th ed, p 505, cited by Lord Wright in *Sovfracht* [1943] AC 203, 227.
38. *Eastern Carrying Ins Co v The National Benefit Life & Property Assurance Co Ltd* (1919) 35 TLR 292 (re).
39. *Kawasaki Kisen Kabushiki Kaisha v Bantham SS Co* [1938] 2 KB 790 (CA).
40. *Janson v Driefontein Consolidated Mines Ltd* [1902] AC 484, 492–493 *per* Lord Halsbury LC, 498 *per* Lord Macnaghten (cargo); the House held that even an act of seizure by a state in anticipation of a declaration of war nine days later did not amount to war for the purposes of this rule; the House was anxious to avoid uncertainty: see p 491 *per* Lord Halsbury LC, p 500 *per* Lord Davey, p 507 *per* Lord Lindley.
41. *Janson* (above).
42. [1901] 2 KB 849. This case is cited by MacGillivray, No 522 for the broader proposition that insurance on non-commercial property against non-war risks is valid; *sed quaere*. In *Hoad* the illegality, if any, would have intervened after the lawful conclusion of the contract; such cases of intervening illegality are considered below, 24–4B.

ment, Mathew J said[43]: "The subject of one country, surprised by a declaration of war in the country where he has a commercial domicil, ought to have time allowed to free himself from his commercial engagements and effect a removal of his property." Such a rule is supported not only by the duty to do justice to the individual but also, it has been argued, by reference to the longer term interests of the state.

"The nation which takes an interest in the prosperity of its commerce can feel no inclination to restrain its citizens from residence abroad for the purposes of commerce; nor will it hastily construe such residence into a change of national character, to the injury of the individual. It is not the policy of such a nation, nor can it be its wish, to restrain its citizens from pursuing abroad a business which tends to enrich it."[44]

24–3 ILLEGAL MODE OF CONTRACTING

The insurance industry has been the subject of regulation, which has been consolidated in the Insurance Companies Act 1982 and supplemented by the Financial Services Act 1986. Some regulations concern the making of contracts of insurance.

Section 75 of the 1982 Act requires the insurer under a long term contract to give the other party a statutory notice. If the insurer contravenes the section, it is provided in section 75(4) that the contract of insurance shall not be invalidated by reason of the contravention.

Section 74 of the 1982 Act requires an intermediary to give prescribed information about his connection with the insurer. If an agent of the insurer contravenes section 74, a subsequent contract of insurance might be avoided for misrepresentation or non-disclosure.

An uncertain case is that of section 72, which regulates the form and content of advertisements. If the breach amounts to a misrepresentation, the effect will be like that of section 74. If not, then the breach is unlikely to be grave and, it is submitted, the validity of any contract of insurance made on the faith of the offending advertisement is unlikely to be impugned: this question will be regulated by the rules of law on implied statutory prohibition.[45] Further, section 130 of the 1986 Act provides that investment insurance[46] may be advertised only by authorised persons. Section 133 of that Act applies to non-investment insurance, creating an offence of making misleading statements as to insurance contracts; no civil law consequences for the contract are specified, but the effect appears to be like that of section 72.

---

43. pp 853–854. See also in this sense *The Gerasimo* (1857) 11 Moo PC 88, 96 *per* Lord Kingsdown; *The Anglo-Mexican* [1918] AC 422, 425–427 *per* Lord Parker (PC); *Sovfracht* [1943] AC 203, 237 *per* Lord Porter.

USA *idem* as regards temporary residents: *The John Gilpin*, 13 F Cas No 7,344. A similar notion was accepted by the Supreme Court in respect of blockade running in *The Grey Jacket*, 5 Wall 342 (1867). *Cf* the contrary view in *The Venus* (1814) 8 Cranch 253; and *The Frances* (1814) 8 Cranch 363. *Cf* also *Swiss National Ins Co Ltd* v *Crowley*, discussed above, 24–2B1.

44. *The Venus* (above), p 293 *per* Marshall CJ (dissenting).

45. Below, 24–3A.

46. Long term insurance contracts, except contracts whereby payment is to be made only on death or disability: Financial Services Act 1986, Schedule 1, para 10. See McGee (1988) 1 Ins L J, 61, 64.

24–3A Unlicensed Insurers

In *Phoenix General Ins Co* v *Adas*[47] the view was taken that, as section 2 of the Insurance Companies Act 1982 prohibited the making of contracts of insurance by an unlicensed insurer, any contract concluded in contravention of that section was "void". In New York, this controversial decision has provided the court with a reason for steering clear of the application of English law, "given New York's strong and long-standing policy of enforcing such insurance contracts".[48] As regards unlicensed insurance in England, however, the decision[49] was overturned by section 132 of the Financial Services Act 1986.[50]

At common law, an action on the contract of insurance by the insured, although ignorant that the insurer lacked a licence, failed because the contract was "void".[51] Section 132(6) of the 1986 Act[52] provides that contravention of section 2 of the 1982 Act "shall not make a contract of insurance illegal or invalid to any greater extent than" provided in section 132. Section 132 limits enforceability by the insurer, but not by the insured, who may enforce the contract, subject to the usual common law defences, such as non-disclosure.[53] Alternatively, the insured may elect not to maintain or enforce the contract and, if so, it is provided by section 132(1) that the insured "shall be entitled to recover any money or other property paid or transferred by him under the contract, together with compensation for any loss sustained by him as a result of having parted with it".[54] In that case, he must return to the insurer any money or other property received from the insurer under the contract: section 132(4).

At common law, reinsurance contracts could not be enforced, if either party lacked a licence. It is provided by section 132(6) that a contravention of section 2 "in respect of a contract of insurance shall not affect the validity of any reinsurance contract entered in respect of that contract".

At common law, no action was available to the unlicensed insurer against the

---

47. [1988] QB 216 (CA—re). The considered *obiter* view of the court was followed without enthusiasm in *Re Cavalier Ins Co Ltd* [1989] 2 Lloyd's Rep 430 as regards unlicensed extended warranty insurance.

48. *Curiale* v *D R Ins Co*, 1992 NY Misc LEXIS 588 (re).

49. See Clarke [1987] LMCLQ 201. The main argument against the decision concerns the interpretation of section 2: see Clarke, pp 205–206. As regards such prohibitions generally:

(a) It does not follow from a prohibition of unlicensed activity (insurance) that contracts concluded in breach of the prohibition are "void" or "avoided" or unenforceable: Clarke pp 203–204 and cases cited. Also in this sense: *Ashton Jenkins Ins Co* v *Layton Sugar Co*, 39 P 2d 701 (Utah, 1935—fire); *Pyramid Life Ins Co* v *Patten*, 110 SW 2d 526 (Ark, 1937—life); *Virginia Surety Co* v *Knoxville Transit Lines*, 135 F Supp 606 (ED Tenn, 1955—motor); *General Casualty Co* v *Arkansas*, 316 SW 2d 704 (Ark, 1958—bailbonds); *Holmes* v *Nationwide Ins Co*, 244 NYS 2d 148, 151–152 (1963—life).

(b) If (a) is accepted, the contract should be enforced, unless its enforcement would undermine the purpose of the prohibition. For example, since the main purpose of requiring insurers to be licensed, is to protect the insured, his protection is better served by enforcing his insurance contracts than by refusing to enforce them. Thus in *Jackson National Life Ins Co* v *Receconi*, 827 P 2d 118, 130–131 (NM, 1992—life) it was said with reference *inter alia* to *Holmes* (above) that "an insurance policy which violates a statute designed for the protection of the insured is nevertheless enforceable against the insurer . . . [A] holding that such contracts were unenforceable by the insured would thwart the purpose of the statutes". Similar reasoning can be found in England: Treitel p 437.

50. The section does not have retroactive effect: *D R Ins Co* v *Seguros America Bananex* [1993] 1 Lloyd's Rep 120 (re).

51. *Phoenix* (above).

52. Section 132 does not apply to investment insurance, which is governed in this respect by section 5 of the Act.

53. *Quaere* the effect, if the insured was aware that the insurer was unlicensed.

54 McGee, (1988) 1 Ins L J 61, 62, contends that the right may be exercised after the contract period has expired.

insured, for example, for instalments of premium. That is confirmed by section 132(1), however, section 132(3) provides that a contract affected by section 132(1) may be permitted by the court "to be enforced or property paid or transferred under it to be retained", if the court is satisfied (a) that it is just and equitable, and (b) that the insurer reasonably believed that in entering the contract he was not in breach of section 2.

24–4 ILLEGAL PROMISES

If a contract contains an illegal promise, the illegal promise will not be given effect. If such an insurance promise is illegal by the public policy of the forum, it is still without effect, even if valid by the law of the place where the contract was made or where the insurance policy was issued.[55]

24–4A Indemnity Clauses

Whether or not it is described as insurance, a promise, made by A to indemnify B in respect of liability incurred by B in the commission of a deliberate tort or crime, will not be enforced.

For example, if A promises B indemnity in respect of any liability incurred by B in issuing a document, known to be false and intended to be acted upon by third parties, the promise is unenforceable: this is a contract to commit the tort of deceit.[56] The result is the same, if A promises B to indemnify B in respect of liability as underwriter of a share issue under a prospectus known to be false[57]; or to indemnify a publisher against libel damages.[58] Further, the law has the same attitude to an action by B for damages from A, being the amount of compensation[59] or of a criminal penalty paid by B in respect of a wilful wrong to a third party: the court must have regard "to the necessity of deterring him and others from doing the same thing again, to reform him and, in cases such as this, to make him and others more careful in their dealings."[60]

---

55. *Watson* v *Employers Liability Corp*, 348 US 66 (1954—products liability); *Seligman* v *Tucker*, 362 NYS 2d 881 (1975), affirmed 335 NE 2d 844 (1975).

56. Such as a bill of lading: *Brown Jenkinson & Co* v *Dalton (Percy) (London)* [1957] 2 QB 621 (CA).

57. *Globus* v *Law Research Service Inc*, 418 F 2d 1276 (2 Cir, 1979), cert den 397 US 913.

58. *Shackell* v *Rosier* (1836) 2 Bing (NC) 634. In *Smith (W H) & Sons* v *Clinton* (1909) 99 LT 840 it was agreed that the plaintiff B would publish "Vanity Fair" for defendant A in return, *inter alia*, for a promise of indemnity against the consequences of any libel that might appear in the paper. When B sought to enforce this promise, the action was defended mainly on other grounds, but Coleridge J (p 841) also said this: "To indemnify against publishing a libel is to indemnify against doing a wrongful and illegal act . . . This, then, being an action brought by one party who has committed a wrongful and illegal act against another party who has committed the same wrongful and illegal act, to indemnify the one party in respect of the wrongful or illegal act committed by both, . . . such a contract cannot be enforced by law."

59. *Weld-Blundell* v *Stephens* [1919] 1 KB 520 (CA): B, who published a libel about C to A, failed to recover damages from A for A's admitted negligence in allowing the libel to come to the attention of C, who consequently obtained a libel award from B; the case went to the House of Lords on a different point: [1920] AC 956.

60. *Askey* v *Golden Wine Co Ltd* (1948) 64 TLR 379, 380 *per* Denning J. In that case the plaintiff, who sold a cocktail containing methylated spirit, failed to recover the amount of the fine as damages from his supplier: he had closed his eyes to the contents and been grossly negligent.

Cf Osman v *J Ralph Moss Ltd* [1970] 1 Lloyd's Rep 313: the plaintiff, who had been fined for driving while uninsured, recovered the amount of the fine from his insurance broker, who had negligently led him to believe that he was insured. The Court of Appeal distinguished *Askey* on the ground that Mr Osman had been "entirely free of culpable negligence" (*per* Edmund Davies LJ, p 318). See further, *R Leslie Ltd* v *Reliable Advertising & Addressing Agency Ltd* [1915] 1 KB 652, 659 *per* Rowlatt J; *Simon* v *Pawsons & Leafs Ltd* (1932) 38 Com Cas 151, 158 *per* Scrutton LJ (CA).

Such cases differ from enforceable liability insurance in that the wrong was likely or intended to occur,[61] and the "insurer", A, was a "participator" in the wrongful act.[62] Indeed, the consideration received by A may be not money but the performance of the very acts, which amount to tort or crime.

The main reason given for such decisions, for example concerning indemnity for criminal libel, is that it "would be productive of great evil if the courts were to encourage such an engagement as this and thereby hold out inducement to the propagation of illegal and unfounded charges".[63] This same reason is given for refusing to enforce ordinary liability insurance in respect of wrongs deliberately committed: below, 24–5A1.

Distinguish cases, in which the insurer is in no such sense a "participator" in the wrongful act, but public policy argues that to allow insurance indemnity takes the sting out of a penalty and deprives the punishment of its power for deterrence.

In the case of persons who, having been convicted in respect of driving a motor vehicle while having a blood alcohol level above that permitted by law, are disqualified from driving, insurance providing compensatory benefits, such as the provision of a chauffeur, has been enforced.[64] In more recent times hostility to such behaviour has increased and a proposal to outlaw such insurance by statute has been given serious consideration.[65]

In the case of punitive damages, courts in the United States are divided on whether to enforce insurance against these awards of damages.[66] Some courts have taken the view that to allow the defendant to shift the burden to an insurance company would defeat the purpose of such damages and so refuse effect to the policy to that extent.[67] However, Appleman[68] suggests that the current trend is to enforce liability insurance of this kind. In certain cases and in spite of the view of the lower court, that the decision would defeat "the dual purpose of punitive damages to punish the wrongdoer and to deter similar conduct in future"[69] it has been held, for example, in North Carolina that such insurance could be inforced even as regards intentional conduct by the

---

61. *Westinghouse, Church, Kerr & Co* v *Long Island Ry Co*, 145 NYS 201 (1914), affirmed 110 NE 1051 (1915).

62. *Clinton* (above, note 56), p 841 *per* Coleridge J.

63. *Shackell* v *Rosier* (1836) 2 Bing (NC) 634, 648 *per* Park J. *Cf South Carolina State Budget & Control Board* v *Prince*, 403 SE 2d 643 (SC, 1991—liability), in which the liability cover expressly included liability for defamation: there was no evidence that anyone intended acts of defamation when the insurance was contracted and the insurance covered subsequent defamation, even though it was intentional and malicious at the time.

64. *Dept of Trade & Industry* v *St Christopher Motorist Assn Ltd* [1974] 1 All ER 395. In early 1987 the Minister of State was reported (PM, 12 Jan 1987, p 3) as saying that such insurance was not contrary to public policy.

65. PM, 16 March 1989, p 13.

66. Kenney, 48 J Air Law & Commerce 754 (1983). For example, in Minnesota, insurance of liability for punitive damages will not be enforced: *US Fire Ins Co* v *Goodyear Tyre & Rubber Co*, 726 F Supp 740 (D Minn, 1989—liability). The position in Massachusetts, for example, is less clear: Boyle and O'Malley, 25 New England L Rev 827 (1991). Generally, see [1994] IJIL 5 and 44.

67. For example, *American Surety Co* v *Gold*, 375 F 2d 523 (10 Cir, 1966).

68. Section 7031. For example *Ohio Casualty Ins Co* v *Welfare Finance Co*, 75 F 2d 58 (8 Cir, 1934—motor), cert den 295 US 734; *Price* v *Hartford Accident & Indemnity Co*, 502 P 2d 522, 524 (Ariz, 1972—motor).

69. *St Paul Mercury Ins Co* v *Duke University*, 670 F Supp 630, 637 (MD NC, 1987—liability). The deterrence argument is not taken seriously by many courts, but the punitive function survives: Burrows 67 NCLRev 1410, 1414 (1989).

insured. The countervailing factors were the desire to avoid the unjust enrichment of insurers and commercial uncertainty.[69a]

24–4B Payment to Enemy Aliens

To contract with an enemy alien is illegal and void: above, 24–2B. A contract with a non-enemy, who later becomes an enemy on the outbreak of war, is usually abrogated by the outbreak of war.[70] In any case, public policy prohibits the payment of money, whether premium to the insurer or insurance money to the insured, while the war lasts.

24–4B1 Commercial Insurance

In the middle of the eighteenth century, a contract made with a person who later became an alien enemy was valid and enforceable, if it was profitable to England.[71] "If we don't trade with them, neutrals will. Why should not our merchants get the benefit?"[72] In France, commentators found this hard to understand: "One part of that nation restored to us by the effects of insurance, what the other took from us by the rights of war."[73] The more recent view in England, however, is that "the presumed object of war being as much to cripple the enemy's commerce as to capture his property",[74] the balance of benefit was taken to be against the continuation of commercial relations, including insurance.

For these reasons, it is better that the contract be discharged than suspended.[75] In *Ertel Bieber*[76] Lord Dunedin said that suspension

"hampers the trade of the British subject, and through him the resources of the kingdom. For he cannot, in view of the certainly impending liability to deliver (for the war cannot last forever), have a free hand as he otherwise would . . . It increases the stocks of the enemy, for if the enemy knows that he is contractually sure of getting the supply as soon as the war is over, that not only allows him to denude himself of present stocks, but it represents a present value which may be realized by means of assignation to neutral countries."

69a. 849 F 2d 133, 136–137 (4 Cir, 1988);

70. See below, 24–4B1 and 24–4B2. *Cf* MacGillivray, No 530: "a contract of insurance is never dissolved by war."

71. For example, *Henkel* v *Royal Exchange Assurance Co* (1749) 1 Ves Sen 317, 320 *per* Lord Hardwicke LC (hull).

72. Lord Mansfield, quoted by McNair, p 259.

73. Valin, *Des Assurances*, art 3, p 215, writing in 1756. This observation formed part of the reasoning of Lord Alvaney CJ in a decisive case: *Furtado* v *Rogers* (1802) 3 Bos & Pul 191 (hull), 198; see also *Kellner* v *Le Mesurier* (1803) 4 East 396. The decision was followed in *Gamba* v *Le Mesurier* (1803) 4 East 396, 401 *per* Lord Ellenborough (cargo); and *Brandon* v *Curling* (1803) 4 East 410 (cargo). See also *Janson* v *Driefontein Consolidated Mines* [1902] AC 484, 499 *per* Lord Davey, 507 *per* Lord Lindley (cargo).

74. *Esposito* v *Bowden* (1857) 7 E & B 763, 779 *per* Willes J; see also the *Sovfracht* case [1943] AC 203, 213 *per* Lord Atkin; *Schering* v *Stockholms Enskilda Bank A/B* [1946] 1 AC 219, 253 *per* Lord Macmillan.

75. It has been held that, if an insured loss occurs before the outbreak of war, rights in respect of that loss are suspended and may be enforced after the war: *Flindt* v *Waters* (1812) 15 East 260.

76. *Ertel Bieber & Co* v *Rio Tinto Co Ltd* [1918] AC 260, 275. See also *Furtado* v *Rogers* (1802) 3 Bos & Pul 191 (hull); *Brandon* v *Curling* (1803) 4 East 410 (cargo); *Sovfracht* [1943] AC 203, 212 *per* Viscount Simon LC, 236 *per* Lord Wright. *Tait* v *New York Life Ins Co*, 23 F Cas No 13, 726 (WD Tenn, 1873) p 624.

One exception is the contract of a shareholder with the company in which he holds shares: *Robson* v *Premier Oil & Pipeline Co* [1915] 2 Ch 124 (CA). *Quaere* whether the same rule might apply to reinsurance; see *Eastern Carrying Ins Co* v *The National Benefit Life & Property Assurance Co Ltd* (1919) 35 TLR 292 (re).

Benefit to the enemy is the dominant consideration, qualified, however, by Lord Porter[77] as follows: "The prohibition against doing anything for the benefit of an enemy contemplates his benefit during the war and not the possible advantage he may gain when peace returns", except insofar as that possible advantage works to benefit him, for example his credit, during the war.

In any case, at common law, the prime consideration is national interest. In *Robinson* v *Continental Ins Co of Mannheim*[78] there was a claim by a British national under a contract of marine insurance, when the First World War began, and the defendant insurer, who had become an alien enemy, applied for the proceedings to be stayed during the war. It was argued[79] by the insurer that "by the common law of England all actions between British subjects and alien enemies are suspended during the war, and further that an alien enemy cannot appear and cannot be heard in [British] courts during hostilities". Some support for this view could be found in a statement of Lord Davey in *Janson*[80] but this statement was not essential to that case. The application was dismissed: "to hold that a subject's right of suit is suspended against an alien enemy is to injure a British subject and to favour an alien enemy and to defeat the object and reason of the suspensory rule. It is to turn a disability into a relief".[81]

For a particular contract to be illegal on this basis, it is enough that the contract is of a class that is likely to assist the enemy; it does not have to be proved that the particular contract did or would have this effect.[82] In modern times, however, the question turns mainly on the construction of legislation dealing with trade and trade sanctions.[83]

24–4B2 Life Insurance

Non-enforcement, it has been argued, should be confined to commercial contracts. In the United States, this argument has succeeded in the corollary, that "subsistence" contracts made in enemy territory were enforceable.[84] Corbin states[85] this as a rule with the qualification, that the subsistence contract must not aid the enemy or injure the United States. In England, however, a rule of this kind has been rejected[86] on the grounds that no workable or significant distinction could be drawn between subsistence contracts and commercial contracts, and that public policy required that, generally, no contracts with an alien enemy should be enforced.

Fire insurance is another exception suggested by the Supreme Court of the United

---

77. *Daimler Co Ltd* v *Continental Tyre & Rubber Co (Great Britain) Ltd* [1916] 2 AC 307, 347.

78. [1915] 1 KB 153. See also *R A Kohnstamm Ltd* v *Ludwick Krumm (London) Ltd* [1940] 2 KB 359 in which it was held that to receive payments from an alien enemy, payments made under a contract of guarantee in respect of goods supplied by the payee before the war, was not trading with the enemy contrary to the Trading with the Enemy Act 1939, s 1(2)(*a*)(iii).

79. [1915] 1 KB 153, 158.

80. *Janson* v *Driefontein Consolidated Mines* [1902] AC 484, 499 (cargo).

81. p 159 *per* Bailhache J, who relied on a decision of the United States Supreme Court relating to an action in respect of real property: *McVeigh* v *United States*, 11 Wall 259 (1871).

82. *Central India Mining Co* v *Sté Coloniale Anversoise* [1920] 1 KB 753, 763 *per* Bankes LJ (CA); *Sovfracht* [1943] AC 203, 252 *per* Lord Porter.

83. Firth (1991) 1 Ins L & P 2.

84. *Kershaw* v *Kelsey*, 100 Mass 561 (1868), approved in *Williams* v *Paine*, 169 US 55 (1897); see also *Tait* v *New York Life Ins Co*, 23 F Cas No 13,726 (WD Tenn, 1873—life).

85. Section 1517.

86. *Robson* v *Premier Oil & Pipe Line Co Ltd* [1915] 2 Ch 124, 135–136 *per* Pickford LJ (CA).

States, provided that no profit was remitted to the enemy until after the war. In England, however, the view taken in *Ertel Bieber* (above, 24–4B1), that the prospect of more funds after the war helps to mobilise funds during the war, suggests that the House of Lords would not agree, although the same objection could be made[87] to the one exception, for which there is some authority in England: life insurance.[88]

Life insurance, it is said, survives the outbreak of war, if the essential nature of the contract is unchanged[89] and if, in addition, (a) there is no benefit to the enemy economy and (b) it does not give rise to intercourse with the enemy during the war. With these qualifications life insurance as an exception to abrogation is perhaps more apparent than real.[90]

As to condition (a), in *Seligman* v *Eagle Ins Co*,[91] L took out two policies on his own life and assigned them to a company to secure a loan. He and two sureties covenanted jointly and severally to repay the loan with interest and to pay the premiums necessary to maintain the policies. On the subsequent outbreak of war, L became an alien enemy and left the United Kingdom. The premiums were thereafter paid by one of the sureties, who also paid off the loan and then sought assignment of the policies to him, which the company refused. Neville J declared the policies valid, saying[92] that "there is nothing in the nature of the contract to put an end to it upon the outbreak of war", unless performance of the contract involved "unlawful intercourse with the enemy . . . [T]he receipt of money from an enemy involves no unlawful intercourse . . . I can see nothing illegal in the acceptance of the premiums by the company because no benefit can accrue to the enemy alien at all as the result of the payment of his premium." *Seligman* is an isolated case. It is significant that there was neither intercourse with the enemy nor apparent benefit to the enemy economy. It was a decision to do justice between Englishmen.

As to condition (b), intercourse with the enemy must be avoided although, in general, the insurance cannot be maintained without payment of premium. It has been held that the English branch of an enemy insurer may continue to conduct business, but the decision is doubtful.[93] If the insured is unable to pay premium, because there is no agent of the insurer that he can lawfully pay, in principle, the contract is discharged. Only rarely is a party excused by impossibility of performance, without discharge of the contract. Moreover, failure to pay a renewal premium for life insurance is failure to exercise an option, and the terms of options must be strictly observed.[94] Again, the option granted by the life insurer can be seen as an offer sub-

---

87. The objection is found in, for example, *Tait* v *New York Life Ins Co*, 23 F Cas 620, 624–625 (WD Tenn, 1873) in which the court held that life policies were abrogated by outbreak of war between the state of the insured and that of the insurer. *Contra: Hamilton* v *Mutual Life Ins Co*, 11 F Cas No 5, 986 (SDNY, 1871).

88. McNair (p 284) suggests that the key to life insurance is that it is sufficiently analogous to contracts of lease, which also survive the outbreak of war between the states of the parties; and (p 285) that the same rule would prevail if the life were to drop in the course of British military action.

89. The possibility of no change has been doubted: *Tait* v *New York Life Ins Co*, 23 F Cas 620, 623 (WD Tenn, 1873—life).

90. McElroy & G L Williams, *Impossibility of Performance* (1941), pp 42–43. *Cf* MacGillivray, Nos 518 and 520.

91. [1917] 1 Ch 519.

92. p 525–526.

93. See above, 24–2B1.

94. *United Dominions Trust (Commercial) Ltd* v *Eagle Aircraft Ltd* [1968] 1 WLR 74 (CA). Treitel, pp 707–708. *New York Life Ins Co* v *Statham*, 93 US 24 (1876); 23 L Ed 789, 793 *per* Strong J (life); also *Tait* v *New York Life Ins Co*, 23 F Cas No 13,726 pp 631–632 (life).

ject to an implied condition, that circumstances have not radically changed since the offer was made.[95]

The argument, that the contract was not discharged by war and that non-payment of premium was excused until after the war, when the contract would continue or revive, has been rejected by the Supreme Court of the United States. The cases[96] concerned persons in the Confederacy, who did not pay premiums to Northern insurers because of the Civil War. The court rejected the argument because it was based on consider-ations of justice and equity, which should not be invoked, it was said, to revive a con-tract, which it would be unjust or inequitable to revive.

"The business of insurance is founded on the law of averages . . . By spreading their risks over a large number of cases, the companies calculate on this average with reasonable certainty and safety. Anything that interferes with it deranges the security of the business. If every policy lapsed by reason of the war should be revived, and all the back premiums should be paid, the companies would have the benefit of this average amount of risk."[97]

Not, however, the benefit of the interest on premium invested, so important in some modern markets.[98] The judgment continued:

"But the good risks are never heard from; only the bad are sought to be revived, where the per-son insured is either dead or dying. Those in health can get new policies cheaper than to pay arrearages on the old."[99]

24–4C Discrimination

Premium rating may infringe legislation against discrimination, such as the Sex Dis-crimination Act 1975, if a person is treated less favourably than persons of the opposite sex.[100] As regards the provision of insurance, however, less favourable treat-ment is not unlawful, if "effected by reference to actuarial or other data from a source on which it was reasonable to rely, and was having regard to the data and any other relevant factors.[101]

Insurers might wish to discriminate not only in the terms offered but also in the investigation of the risk. In New York, for example, the practice of considering HIV tests to determine insurability for health insurance was condemned by the Superinten-dant of Insurance as discriminatory, but his decision was challenged and the practice upheld by the court.[102] The court observed that "valid underwriting practices promote fairness to the policyholder in not requiring him or her to bear in premiums the costs of insuring others in higher risk categories, and solvency of the insurer, another goal

---

95. *Financings Ltd* v *Stimson* [1962] 3 All ER 386 (CA).

96. Notably *New York Life Ins Co* v *Statham*, 93 US 24 (1876); 23 L Ed 789; approved in *New York Life Ins Co* v *Davis*, 95 US 425 (1877).

97. p 792 *per* Bradley J.

98. The importance of having the use of premium income was stressed, for example, in *Tait* v *New York Life Ins Co*, F Cas No 13,726 (WD Tenn, 1873) p 636.

99. This argument is overstated, for it may not be cheaper in the case of a short war (and thus low arrears) or of a person of an age to have paid premiums for many years, or for any person at all, if market conditions had changed to a degree that raised premiums appreciably.

100. Sections 1(1)(*a*) and 2. As regards Canada, see Wiegers, 39 U Toronto L J 149 (1989).

101. Section 45. In *Pinder* v *The Friends Provident Life Office* (1985) 5 EOR 31 a self-employed lady den-tist was required to pay PHI premiums 50 per cent higher than those that would have been asked of a man in similar circumstances. Her claim in the Westminster County Court, that the requirement was unlawful dis-crimination, was rejected on the basis that the case fell within section 45. For critical comment on the evi-dence in this case, see Thornton (1990) 3 Ins L J 12. See also Wiegers, (above) (1989).

102. *Health Ins Assn* v *Corcoran*, 551 NYS 2d 615 (1990—PHI), affirmed 565 NE 2d 1264 (1990).

of insurance regulation".[103] The practice was upheld as having a sound actuarial basis, except perhaps, a question not before the court, "where large group insurance policies and the like are involved since, in those instances, the insurer is assessing the risk characteristics of the group as a whole, rather than that of the individual applicant".[104]

24–5 ILLEGAL PURPOSE

If a contract of insurance, although lawfully concluded and lawful in its terms, is designed to serve an illegal purpose, the party with that design[105] is unable to enforce the contract. For example, "if the motorist intended from the beginning to make a criminal use of the vehicle . . . and the insurers knew that that was his intention, the policy would be bad in its inception. No one can stipulate for iniquity."[106]

More commonly, the insured has no unlawful purpose when the insurance is contracted but that same insurance, if enforced, sustains a later purpose that is unlawful. In the example of motor insurance, a comprehensive policy will cover events that are regrettable but lawful, such as fire or collision. The present issue is whether it may also cover, for example, loss caused when the driver is in breach of the criminal law—driving without due care or robbing a bank.

24–5A Rationale

In a rational system, the line might be drawn between enforceable and non-enforceable insurance by reference to the reasons for non-enforcement; however, in this context reasons and hence results differ.

24–5A1 Deterrence

Non-enforcement of insurance is said to help to deter crime. In *Gray* v *Barr*,[107] the Court of Appeal was asked to enforce insurance in respect of the liability of the insured for having killed his wife's former lover. Although he had been acquitted of manslaughter, the court refused to enforce the insurance. "Crimes of violence . . . are among the worst curses of this age. It is very much in the public interest that they should be deterred."[108]

The main objection to a rule based on deterrence is that there is scant evidence that the deterrent works, that the thought of losing cover will attenuate the desire to do wrong. Can it really be supposed that a cheated spouse, inflamed by jealousy and a glass or two of wine, will be deterred by thoughts of insurance from assaulting the

103. pp 618–619. See also in this sense: *Life Ins Assn* v *Commissioner of Insurance*, 530 NE 2d 168, 171 (Mass, 1988).
104. p 619, with reference to Clifford and Iucculano, "Aids and Insurance", 100 Harv L Rev 180 (1987).
105. The same is true of the other party, if the latter is aware of the design.
106. *Hardy* v *Motor Insurers' Bureau* [1964] 2 QB 745, 760 *per* Lord Denning MR (CA—motor), in a passage cited with approval by Lord Hailsham LC in *Gardner* v *Moore* [1984] AC 548 (motor). *Idem: Burrows* v *Rhodes* [1899] 1 QB 816, 828 *per* Kennedy J.
107. [1971] 2 QB 554; see further on this case below, 24–7B.
108. p 581 *per* Salmon LJ. See also *Amicable Society* v *Bolland* (1830) 4 Bligh NS 194, 211 *per* Lord Lyndhurst LC (life).

other man or woman? Or a heroin addict deterred from heroin by the effect of an overdose on his accident insurance?[109] As Diplock LJ observed in a motor case,[110] it is

"slightly unrealistic to suggest that a person who is not deterred by the risk of a possible sentence of life imprisonment from using a vehicle with intent to commit grievous bodily harm would be deterred by the fear that his civil liability to his victim would not be discharged by his insurers".

In the early days of motorists' liability insurance, the matching argument, that cover would encourage careless driving, was rejected by the Supreme Court of the United States.[111] Earlier still, the courts there had rejected the argument, that insurance against the consequences of negligence would make railroads more careless.[112] With one possible exception, neither the availability of insurance nor the non-enforcement of existing insurance, it seems, has significant impact on unlawful or irresponsible behaviour. The exception may be the case of fire insurance and arson,[113] if the likelihood of detection is perceived as being high. Otherwise, deterrence alone neither justifies the rule of non-enforcement nor indicates its bounds. If deterrence is to be achieved at all, it is a function of the criminal law and detection, rather than that of the law of contract or the law of insurance.[114]

24–5A2 No Man Shall Profit from His Own Wrong[115]

This maxim has been described[116] as "a heart-warming phrase but too imprecise for analysis". We shall nonetheless try to analyse it to see what it means and whether it provides a workable basis for the law.

(a) *"No Man"*. One thing, at least, is clear: the maxim applies equally to men and to women. A wife who poisons her husband to death cannot claim under his life insur-

109. *Miller* v *Continental Ins Co*, 389 NYS 2d 565, 568 (1976—PA).

110. *Hardy* v *MIB* [1964] 2 QB 745, 770 (CA—motor). See Fleming, who describes the deterrence theory articulated by Salmon LJ as bizarre and unrealistic: (1971) 34 MLR 176, 178. See also Shand [1972A] CLJ 144, 152 ff; Clarke [1981] CLJ 284, 301; Mustill [1988] LMCLQ 310, 319.

In the same sense: *Prudential Ins Co* v *Goldstein*, 43 F Supp 765, 767 (ED NY, 1942), quoted below, 24–6A; *Miller* v *Continental Ins Co*, 389 NYS 2d 565, 568 (1976—PA); *Harrington* v *New England Mutual Life Ins Co*, 873 F 2d 166, 168 (7 Cir, 1989—life). See also Schwarz, 75 Cornell L Rev 313, 336 ff (1990).

111. *Merchants' Mutual Auto Ins Co* v *Smart*, 267 US 126 (1925). See McNeely, 41 Colum L Rev 26, 33 (1941).

112. *Trenton Passenger Railroad Co* v *Guarantors' Liability Indemnity Co*, 37 Atl 609 (NJ, 1897). Appleman, section 7031.

What is believed to improve standards of behaviour of the rational insured is the prospect, not of non-enforcement, but of higher premiums: "Accurate insurance pricing and risk classification can encourage the insured to invest in a more efficient combination of loss prevention and insurance"—Abraham, p 44. *Aliter*, perhaps, if the insured is a large concern and competition between insurers is fierce: R Derham, *Subrogation in Insurance Law* (Sydney, 1985) p 155; or the insured is in a position to pass on increases in the cost of insurance: *ibid*; or, if premium increases depend or are believed to depend not on the record of the individual insured but on that of the rating group (the "risk community"): *ibid* p 156. *Cf* also Hasson, 14 Osgoode Hall L J 769, 773 (1976); Sugarman, 73 Cal L Rev 555, 579 (1985). In any event, this prospect is unlikely to influence persons about to commit serious crimes.

113. *Brown* v *American Int Life Co.*, 778 F Supp 912 (SD Miss, 1991—PA), discussed above 17–5E3(d).

114. Devlin, *The Enforcement of Morals* (Oxford, 1965), ch 3. *Cf* Shand [1972A] CLJ 152.

115. Applied, for example, in *Cleaver* v *Mutual Life Fund Association* [1892] 1 QB 147, 152 *per* Lord Esher MR (CA—life); *Beresford* v *Royal Ins Co Ltd* [1938] AC 586, 596–597 *per* Lord Atkin (life). See also *Euro-Diam Ltd* v *Bathurst* [1990] 1 QB 1, 35 *per* Kerr LJ (CA—goods AR).

The maxim has been recognised in Canada in, for example, *Shaw* v *Gillan* (1982) 143 DLR (3d) 232, 234 (Ont—life) and cases cited; and in the USA, see Reager, 39 U Fla L Rev 971, 973 (1987) and cases cited.

116. Mustill [1988] LMCLQ 310, 318.

ance.[117] A wife, however, who poisons her husband short of death but is forgiven, is likely to benefit by the enforcement of the husband's health or accident insurance, albeit indirectly via the family budget; but this does not matter. What matters in the maxim is that she does not herself enforce any right in law under the insurance. "No man shall profit" means that the courts will not enforce the profit at the suit of the wrongdoer. So, the man in the maxim is the wrongdoer who seeks to enforce a right under the contract of insurance, as well as any person claiming through him, such as his personal representative,[118] his agent,[119] or a neutral insurer who has paid an enemy alien and is subrogated to his rights.[120]

The maxim is "applied so as to exclude from benefit the criminal and all claiming under her, but not so as to exclude alternative or independent rights". This was stated in *Cleaver*,[121] in which the claimant was executor of a man who had been murdered by his wife, as well as assignee from the wife under an assignment made after she had been convicted and sentenced to death.[122] His claim was enforceable as executor but not as assignee.

If the policy is assigned *bona fide* and for valuable consideration or if a lien is acquired upon it *bona fide* and for valuable consideration, the insurance is enforceable by the assignee or the lienor, notwithstanding any later illegality by the insured.[123] In *Moore* v *Woolsey*,[124] a life policy provided that

"Policies effected by persons on their own lives, who shall die by duelling or by their own hands, or by the hands of justice, will become void, so far as regards the executors or administrators of the person so dying, but will remain in force only to the extent of any *bona fide* interest which may have been acquired by any other person under an actual assignment . . . or by virtue of any legal or equitable lien as security . . . "

The Court of King's Bench held that, in spite of the suicide of the insured, an equitable lien on his policy to secure an obligation under a marriage settlement could be enforced. Lord Campbell CJ referred to the clause and noted[125] that "No authority has been cited in support of the position that such a condition is illegal".

(b) *"Profit"*. The wise man profits from his mistakes and wrongs by changing his ways but, in the maxim, the profit is profit measurable in terms of money. The profit may be momentary, as the money passes on to his debtors or friends,[126] but it must have existed, however briefly. Whether it has to be a net profit is unclear. If a wife

---

117. *Cleaver* v *Mutual Reserve Fund Life Assn* [1892] 1 QB 147 (CA—life).
118. *Beresford* v *Royal Ins Co Ltd* [1938] AC 586 (life).
119. *The Palm Branch* [1916] P 230 (cargo).
120. *The Gothland* [1916] P 239n (cargo).
121. *Cleaver* (above), p 159 *per* Fry LJ (CA—life). Also in this sense *Hardy* v *MIB* [1964] 2 QB 745, 760 *per* Lord Denning MR, 768–769 *per* Diplock LJ (CA—motor). *MacDonald* v *Prudential Assurance Co Ltd* (1972) 24 DLR (3d) 185, 192 (NB).
122. Her sentence was later commuted to one of life imprisonment.
123. *Moore* v *Woolsey* (1854) 4 El & Bl 243, 255 *per* Lord Campbell CJ (life).
124. Above.
125. p 255. Cf *Burt* v *Union Central Life Ins Co*, 187 US 362 (1902—life), where a claim by assignees failed because (p 365) "the rights of the plaintiffs depend mainly, if not wholly, upon the fact of the assignment made by the insured after the killing of his wife and prior to his execution, and the further fact that they are his sole heirs. The plaintiffs, therefore . . . claim directly under the insured, and sought to recover on a policy obtained by him, the maturity of which was accelerated by his execution for crime". In *Burt*, the Supreme Court had followed the similar English case, *Amicable Society* v *Bolland* (1830) 4 Bligh NS 194, in which, having committed the felony of forgery, the insured assigned the benefit of his life policy to trustees on behalf of a lady beneficiary. When he was later executed for his crime, the House of Lords held that her claim on the policy failed, being a claim by persons representing the deceased felon and claiming under him.
126. *Beresford* v *Royal Ins Co Ltd* [1938] AC 586 (life).

poisons her husband, it seems that she will be unable to enforce his life policy, even if it can be shown that its enforcement would leave her less well off financially than if he had been alive and earning.[127] The reference to profit, sometimes referred to as an "advantage",[128] means no more than that the relief sought from the court has money value.

(c) *"From His Wrong"*. It is doubtful that the courts would decline to enforce insurance in respect of a tort,[129] if it did not also amount to a crime. Wrong means an infringement of the criminal law,[130] with the reservation that "there are many statutory offences which are the subject of the criminal law, and in that sense crimes, but which would, it seems, afford no moral justification for a court to apply the maxim".[131] Whether moral justification can be found or not is a question of balancing factors of public policy (24–5A3).

The main difficulty about the maxim is that the profit impugned must be *from* the wrong. One can conceive a status of wrongdoer, like that of enemy alien, which would carry disabilities including one that all his insurance contracts were unenforceable; thus a burglar would lose his life cover and so on. This is not the law. The law requires some connection between the wrong and the insurance, if enforcement is to be refused. The difficulty is in defining the connection.

In *Geismar* v *Sun Alliance & London Ins Ltd*,[132] the plaintiff imported items of jewellery, on which he did not pay the required customs duty and which were later stolen from his house. His insurance claim failed *inter alia* because, said the judge,[133] "Where there is a deliberate breach of the law I do not think that the court ought to assist the plaintiff to derive a profit from it, even though it is sought indirectly through an indemnity under an insurance policy". The profit was the amount of the unpaid duty. The assistance was, not assistance to acquire the profit, for the claimant had already had the profit, but assistance to retain the profit or to obtain indemnity for its loss. It appears essential to the decision that, whereas the customs authority could have seized the jewellery, they could not have seized the insurance money[134]; and that, even if he were still liable to prosecution, the amount of the fine would have been

127. *Cf Geismar*, below, (c).
128. For example *Gardner* v *Moore* [1984] AC 548 (motor).
129. For example *Shaw* v *Gillan* (1982) 143 DLR (3d) 232, 237 (Ont—life).
130. *Cleaver* v *Mutual Reserve Life Fund Association* [1892] 1 QB 147, 152 *per* Lord Esher MR (CA—life); see also *In Re Crippen* [1911] P 108, 112 *per* Sir Samuel Evans P; *Hall* v *Knight & Baxter* [1914] P 1, 8 *per* Swinfen Eady LJ (CA).
131. *Beresford* v *Royal Ins Co* [1937] 2 KB 197, 219 *per* Lord Wright MR (CA—life), affirmed [1938] AC 586. Lord Wright was cited with approval in *Fire & All Risks Ins Co* v *Powell* [1966] VR 513, 522 (Vict—liability).
132. [1978] QB 383. In *Parkin* v *Dick* (1809) 11 East 501, goods were exported in breach of statute, which provided for forfeiture of the goods and payment of a penalty three times the value of the goods. It was accepted that the statute "impliedly avoids all contracts made for protecting the stores so exported", including insurance.
133. p 395 *per* Talbot J, quoted with approval in *Euro-Diam Ltd* v *Bathurst* [1990] 1 QB 1, 39 *per* Kerr LJ (CA—goods AR).
134. See the Customs and Excise Act 1952, section 44. As to powers of confiscation that might affect insurance on the property concerned, see the Misuse of Drugs Act 1971, section 27, the Powers of the Criminal Courts Act 1973, section 43, and the Criminal Justice Act 1988, section 69.
Cf Ardekany v *Dominion of Canada General Ins Co* (1986) 32 DLR (4th) 23 (BC—personal property floater), in which the claimant declared two rugs orally but not in writing, as required by law, and was allowed to proceed without payment of duty. His insurance was enforced, as the chance of confiscation was slight.

less than the profit.[135] In one respect, he would have been better off with the insurance money than with the jewellery; in short, he would have profited from his wrong.

If Mr Geismar had sold the jewellery (profitably) for cash but the cash had been stolen, would his insurance claim have failed in respect of the cash? Probably not. In *Bird* v *Appleton*,[136] the plaintiff shipped an illegal cargo to Canton and sold it there. The proceeds were used to buy part of a lawful cargo, which was lost on the return voyage. His insurance claim was defended on the ground that the insurance was illegal and unenforceable, because the cargo was bought with the proceeds of illegality on the previous voyage. Rejecting this defence, Lord Kenyon CJ said[137]:

"If this objection were well founded, it would go to an alarming extent. In deciding on a claim made on the policy of insurance, it would be necessary to examine and scrutinize the past conduct of the insured, in order to see whether or not, by their former transactions in life, they had illegally acquired the funds with which the particular goods were purchased; but we cannot enter into considerations of that kind; we must confine ourselves to the immediate transaction before us; . . . "

Indeed, the commercial courts will not view with enthusiasm a process like that of tracing in equity.

By contrast, in *Thackwell* v *Barclays Bank plc*,[138] an action against the bank for conversion of a cheque failed, because it represented the proceeds of a fraud in which the claimant was involved. Again, it is hard to believe that a court would enforce AR insurance on the immediate proceeds of traffic in heroin or, perhaps, fire insurance on property bought with the proceeds.[139] In *Gardner* v *Moore*,[140] the defending insurer, facing a liability claim by a motorist who had deliberately driven at a third party, argued that no claimant should be allowed to gain an advantage from the consequences of his own wrong. This argument was rejected, for the maxim "ought not to be stretched beyond what is necessary for the protection of the public".[141] How far? As a predictor of a court's willingness to enforce an insurance contract, the maxim sounds better than it works; we must look further.

---

135. He was subject to a maximum fine of £100, but he could have been sent to prison for up to two years: Customs and Excise Act 1952, section 44.

136. (1800) 8 TR 562.

137. p 566; cited with approval in *Geismar* (above) p 392. See also Grose J (p 568) who thought the plea "inconvenient and absurd".

138. [1986] 1 All ER 676, a decision approved in *Euro-Diam Ltd* v *Bathurst* [1990] 1 QB 1, 35 *per* Kerr LJ (CA—goods AR). See further, Clarke [1988] LMCLQ 124.

139. Clarke [1987] LMCLQ 201, 213 ff. But *cf Tinsley* v *Milligan* [1993] 3 All ER 65, in which a majority of the House of Lords reaffirmed the principle that, when property interests are acquired as a result of an illegal transaction, a party to the illegality can recover by virtue of the interest acquired.

140. [1984] AC 548, 558 (motor).

141. *Ibid per* Lord Hailsham LC, with whom other members of the House agreed. Thus the wife, whose husband is killed by her careless driving, will be allowed to enforce his life insurance in her favour, even though she "profits" thereby: *Minasian* v *Aetna Life Ins Co*, 3 NE 2d 17, 19 (Mass, 1936—life). *Shaw* v *Gillan* (1982) 143 DLR (3d) 232 (Ont—life).

It has been suggested by MacGillivray, No 485, that in such cases, even if the policy money is paid to an assignee creditor, that does not discharge the debt, for that would enable the debtor to profit from his wrong. It is true that discharge leaves the debtor better off, and the courts accept this: *City Bank* v *Sovereign Life Assurance Co* (1884) 50 LT 564, 566 *per* Pearson J; but this is just the debit side of the balance of policy in favour of enforcement: below, 24–5A3. See *White* v *British Empire Mutual Life Assurance Co* (1868) LR 7 Eq 394, 396, 398 *per* Sir R Malins V-C; also *Solicitors & General Life Assurance Society* v *Lamb* (1864) 1 H & M 716, 725 *per* Sir W Page Wood V-C, followed in *City Bank* v *Sovereign Life Assurance Co* (1884) 50 LT 564.

24–5A3 Balance of Policy Factors

The most convincing approach to a theory of non-enforcement and hence to some kind of rule is this: "The court has to weigh the gravity of the anti-social act and the extent to which it will be encouraged by enforcing the right sought to be asserted against the social harm which will be caused if the right is not enforced."[142]

The judges are not entitled to decide cases according to their own views of what is good for society,[143] but may apply public policy, if it is reduced to the form of rules or if it is supported by precedent.[144] However, within these constraints there is still room for change as the times change.[145] "The principles of public policy, which I suppose are only a branch of the principles of ethics, are themselves unchanging, but their applications may be infinitely various from time to time and from place to place."[146]

In many cases the abhorrence of the court is spontaneous and no evidence is needed to establish, for example, that murder is bad for people. However, to say that death by gunshot is more damaging to society than death by motor vehicle is less obvious, but the courts have said it, as something apparently too obvious to require supporting evidence, statistical or otherwise.[147] When deciding what is good for people, the legal system expects judges to rely as much on instinct as on information.[148] Inevitably, there is a degree of uncertainty in the law. Nonetheless, it is possible to identify a number of factors that influence the courts.

(a) *The Gravity of the Crime.* The courts are influenced by the gravity of the crime in issue. Public policy is strong against violence or human injury. Further, the courts are more hostile to deliberate conduct than to conduct which is merely negligent: below, 24–5B.

By contrast, infringement of foreign law will be disregarded, if the law is chiefly a trade law and, particularly, if it is aimed against English traders. Speaking of a device to reduce the amount of duty payable not in England but in France, Lord Mansfield said[149] that this was not fraud in England and that "One nation does not take notice of

---

142. *Hardy* v *MIB* [1964] 2 QB 745, 760 *per* Diplock LJ (CA—motor); this kind of approach was approved in *Gardner* v *Moore* [1984] AC 548 (motor). See also *Fire & All Risks Ins Co* v *Powell* [1966] VR 513, 521–522 (Vict—liability). In the general law see *Weld-Blundell* v *Stephens* [1919] 1 KB 520, 547–548 *per* Scrutton LJ (CA); *Shaw* v *Groom* [1970] 2 WLR 299, 304 *per* Harman LJ (CA). In the USA, *idem*: for example, *Vorheers* v *Preferred Mutual Ins Co*, 607 A.2d 1255, 1263–1264 (NJ, 1992—liability). As to the impact on this test of the decision in *Tinsley* v *Milligan* [1993] 3 All ER 65 (HL), see below, 24–9D5.

143. *Egerton* v *Brownlow* (1853) 4 HLC 1.

144. *Janson* v *Driefontein Consolidated Mines Ltd* [1902] AC 484 (cargo); *Fender* v *St John-Mildmay* [1938] AC 1. Lord Wright, *Legal Essays and Addresses*, ch 3.

145. Lord Wright, *loc cit*, p 77.

146. *James* v *British General Ins Co Ltd* [1927] 2 KB 311, 322 *per* Roche J (motor). *Trenton Passenger Railroad Co* v *Guarantors' Liability Indemnity Co*, 37 Atl 609 (NJ, 1897—liability).

147. See *Gray* v *Barr*: below, 24–7B. Contrast the citation of data to the Supreme Court of the United States: *Merchants' Mutual Auto Ins Co* v *Smart*, 267 US 126 (1925).

148. The commercial courts in England face a dilemma between expertise and expedition. Lord Mansfield, described as "the founder of commercial law in England" believed in taking advice from experts. But a great modern commercial judge, Lord Justice Scrutton, has said that "the system does not work very well if your judge is too conscientious"—[1921] CLJ 6, 14.

149. *Planché* v *Fletcher* (1779) 1 Doug 251, 253. See also *Rossano* v *Manufacturers' Life Ins Co* [1963] 2 QB 352, 376–377 *per* McNair J (life). *Btesh* v *Royal Ins Co Ltd*, 40 F 2d 659 (SDNY, 1930—cargo), affirmed 49 F 2d 720 (2 Cir, 1931).

the revenue laws of another." This statement has been controversial[150]: read literally, it goes too far.

English courts will not enforce the revenue law of another state, that is, will not require a non-contractual payment of money in favour of its central or local government.[151] However, in other ways foreign revenue laws will be applied or respected,[152] if relevant to the issue before the court and if not contrary to English public policy.[153] Thus, whether the law is a revenue law or a trading law,[154] the court will not enforce a contract to import goods into another country contrary to a local law designed to protect people there from those goods,[155] although it may be different, if the law is to protect local society from English traders or if the law is viewed here as an "instrument of oppression and discrimination"[156]; on this Lord Mansfield's view[157] may still represent English law, if the English courts are able to identify the public policy in point.[158]

(b) *Encouragement of Crime.* Much importance is attached to the possibility that, if the contract of insurance is enforced, illegality will be encouraged.

The greater the gravity of the wrong the smaller the degree of encouragement that will influence the court against enforcement. Generally, however, it is not enough that the insurance *may* encourage illegality; the very existence of insurance on goods in transit may encourage the buyer who has made a bad bargain to throw the goods away. This factor becomes important only if,

"taking that class of contract as a whole the contracting parties will generally, in a majority of cases, or at any rate in a considerable number of cases, be exposed to a real temptation by reason of [the contract] to do something harmful, i.e., contrary to public policy; and that it is likely that they will yield to it. All kinds of contracts provide motives for improper actions, e.g., benefits deferred until the death of a third party, and contracts of insurance. To avoid a contract it is not enough that it affords a motive to do wrong; it must surely be shown that such a contract generally affords a motive and that it is likely to be effective."[159]

These are the words of Lord Atkin in England in 1938. Whether in England or abroad, courts today are still not easily convinced that insurance tends to motivate people to irresponsible action: "the existence of insurance coverage does not necessarily promote the abdication of personal responsibility . . . Damage awards may result in increased insurance premiums, inability to obtain insurance coverage, and injury to a defendant's reputation. Furthermore, damage awards may exceed the limit of insurance coverage".[160]

(c) *Sanctity of Contract.* Promises must be kept. It is a premise of policy, that, in

---

150. *Ralli Bros* v *CN Sota y Aznar* [1920] 2 KB 287, 300 *per* Scrutton LJ (CA); *Foster* v *Driscoll* [1929] 1 KB 470, 516–519 *per* Sankey LJ (CA). *Re Emery's Investment Trusts* [1959] Ch 410. The view of Lord Mansfield reflects a view, originally attributed to Emerigon, that smuggling is a vice common to all nations, if not a sport for small coastal communities and, today, for holidaymakers.

151. *Govt of India* v *Taylor* [1955] AC 491 (capital gains tax).

152. *Regazzoni* v *Sethia (K C) (1944) Ltd* [1956] 2 QB 490, 520 *per* Birkett LJ. (CA).

153. *Regazzoni* v *Sethia (K C) (1944) Ltd* [1958] AC 301, 325 *per* Lord Reid, 330 *per* Lord Somervell; F A Mann (1956) 21 MLR 130.

154. See Mann, *loc cit.*

155. For example, liquor: *Foster* v *Driscoll* [1929] 1 KB 470 (CA).

156. *The Playa Larga* [1983] 2 Lloyd's Rep 171, 190 *per* Ackner LJ (CA).

157. *Planché* v *Fletcher* (above).

158. *Cf Foster* v *Driscoll* [1929] 1 KB 470, 517–518 *per* Sankey LJ (CA).

159. *Fender* v *St John-Mildmay* [1938] AC 1, 13 *per* Lord Atkin.

160. *Loveridge* v *Chartier*, 468 NW 2d 146, 157 (Wis, 1991—liability).

general, contracts should be enforced[161]; and "you have this paramount public policy to consider—that you are not lightly to interfere with this freedom of contract".[162]

(d) *Third Parties*. The court will consider the effect of non-enforcement on third parties, which may mean the effect on the public at large. In particular, the court will consider the overriding need to compensate victims, which will not be met unless the insurance is enforced.[163] Also, courts have considered the effect of insurance on the availability of information about the spread of disease.[164]

(e) *Deliberate Damage*. It has been suggested in Australia[165] that the insured cannot recover in respect of damage to property inflicted intentionally. In the United States, a claim was rejected[166] because to "allow the plaintiff, with the knowledge that it had of contamination . . . to take a chance that the contamination would not be discovered and then impose the loss upon the insurer when the gamble failed would be to countenance insurance against one's deliberate misconduct". That statement concerned reckless disregard of the integrity of the property of someone else. If no infringement of the criminal law is involved, however, there is much to be said for the view expressed in Canada,[167] that "the right to destroy one's [own] property is a basic incident of ownership and without it we would be overwhelmed by garbage". It appears that, unless the act is a crime, the question whether the deliberate destruction of insured property is covered by insurance, is not an issue of public policy but is solely a matter of the construction of the insurance contract.[168] By inference, for example, cover of all risks (above, 17–3A2) or of death or injury (above, 17–5B) excludes loss caused intentionally. Whenever, however, the act is a crime, if the loss or damage was wilfully or deliberately incurred or inflicted, this is a factor against enforcement of the insurance. In the United States, there is said in such a case to be an implied excep-

---

161. *Cowie* v *Barber* (1814) 4 Camp 100, 102–103 *per* Lord Ellenborough CJ (cargo); *James* v *British General Ins Co Ltd* [1927] 2 KB 311, 321 *per* Roche J; *Bell* v *Lever Bros* [1932] AC 161, 224 per Lord Atkin; *Beresford* v *Royal Ins Co* [1938] AC 586, 604 *per* Lord MacMillan; *Vita Food Products Inc* v *Unus Shipping Co Ltd* [1939] AC 277, 293 *per* Lord Wright; *Shiloh Spinners Ltd* v *Harding* [1973] AC 691, 727 *per* Lord Simon; *SCF Finance Co Ltd* v *Masri (No 2)* [1987] QB 1002, 1025–1026 *per* Slade LJ (CA).
Lord Wright's dictum has been applied in Canada, for example, *Ardekany* v *Dominion of Canada General Ins Co* (1986) 32 DLR (4th) 23, 37 (BC—personal property floater). USA: see, for example, *Miller* v *Continental Ins Co*, 389 NYS 2d 565, 568 (1976—life).
162. *Printing & Numerical Registering Co* v *Sampson* (1875) LR 19 Eq 462, 465 *per* Sir George Jessel.
163. See *Gardner* v *Moore* [1984] AC 548 (motor); and discussion of *Gray* v *Barr* below, 24–7B. *Ranger Ins Co* v *Bal Harbour Club Inc*, 509 So 2d 945 (Fla, 1987—liability); Reager, 39 U Fla L Rev 971 (1987).
164. In *Loveridge* v *Chartier*, 468 NW 2d 146, 157 (Wis, 1991—liability), the court said that it would enforce liability insurance in respect of the negligent transmission of a disease (herpes), provided that this would not inhibit identification and treatment of persons suffering from serious contagious diseases, or encourage people to act irresponsibly.
165. *Fire & All Risks Ins Co* v *Powell* [1966] VR 513, 517 (Vict—marine cargo).
166. *Industrial Sugars Inc* v *Standard Accident Ins Co*, 338 F 2d 673, 675–676 (7 Cir, 1966): the maker of liquid sugar allowed a batch to be contaminated by chlorine, and failed to warn customer Pepsi Cola. When sued by the customer, the maker sought a declaration that his product liability insurer should defend him. It was held that the proximate cause of loss was deliberate failure to notify the customer, and the declaration was refused.
167. Brown & Menezes, No 6:4:6.
168. In this sense *Beresford* v *Royal Ins Co Ltd* [1938] AC 586 (life), for example, p 595 *per* Lord Atkin, *Liverpool & London & Globe Ins Ltd* v *Canadian General Electric Co Ltd* (1981) 123 DLR (3d) 513, 529 *per* Estey J (Sup Ct, Canada—fire).

tion[169] to cover but in England, when the act is a crime, the matter is as much one of public policy as of contract interpretation; in any event, some attention must be given to what it means: 24–5B.

24–5B Wilful or Deliberate Loss or Damage

Loss or damage may be wilful and deliberate not only when it is inflicted by the insured himself, but also when it is done intentionally by someone else for whom he is responsible (24–5B1).

24–5B1 The Acts of Others

When the insured is responsible for the illegal acts of others, the degree of control that the insured is able to exercise over such acts is directly reflected in the degree to which their acts might affect the enforceability of his insurance.[170]

Courts in early times readily enforced insurance taken by a shipowner against the consequences of the misconduct of his master and crew[171] and, more recently, of employees on land whose work is (justifiably) unsupervised.[172] In the United States, it has been held that an employer may enforce indemnity for punitive damages awarded against him in respect of the tort of his servant[173]; and that a corporation may insure liability for assault even by its president.[174] However, the more prevalent view is that the acts of elevated managerial persons must be regarded as the acts of the corporation,[175] so that insurance in such cases is enforceable, only if it expressly covers the deliberate act of the insured.

An insurance claim is not affected by the unlawful conduct of those close to the

---

169. Keeton, p 292; the exception is often express in standard policies: Fleming (1971) 34 MLR 176, 177. See, for example, above 17–5H3.

In some countries cover of wilful loss may be prohibited by legislation. The French Insurance Code contained in the *Décret* 16.7.1976, article L113–1(2) provides that, notwithstanding any agreement to the contrary, the insurer shall not be liable for loss or damage caused by a "*faute intentionelle ou dolosive de l'assuré*". See also in Switzerland *la loi fédérale sur le contrat d'assurance*, 2.4.1908, article 14; Brehm, *Le Contrat d'Assurance RC*, Nos 517 ff.

170. McNeely, 41 Colum LR 26, 30–31 (1941).

171. MIA, section 3.

172. For example a theatre manager: *Floralbell Amusement Corp* v *Standard Surety & Casualty Co*, 9 NYS 2d 524 (1939—liability); a taxi driver: *Huntingdon Cab Co* v *American Fidelity & Casualty Co*, 155 F 2d 117 (4 Cir, 1946—motor). However, the cases in the United States are not consistent, see 72 ALR 3d, pp 1142 ff.

173. *Ohio Casualty Ins Co* v *Welfare Finance Co*, 75 F 2d 58 (8 Cir, 1934—motor), cert den 295 US 734.

174. *Western Casualty & Surety Co* v *Aponaug Mfg Co*, 197 F 2d 673 (5 Cir, 1952—liability). See also *Morgan* v *Greater New York Taxpayers Mutual Ins Assn*, 112 NE 2d 273 (NY, 1953): one partner covered in respect of partnership liability for assault by another partner: the policy was construed as creating separate and distinct obligations on the insurer to each partner.

175. In this sense *S & Y Investments (No 2) Pty Ltd* v *Commercial Union Assurance Co Ltd* (1986) 82 FLR 130 (NT—liability). *Glen Falls Indemnity Co* v *Atlantic Building Corp*, 199 F 2d 60 (4 Cir, 1952—liability); *Greater New York Mutual Ins Co* v *Perry*, 178 NYS 2d 760 (1958—liability). See further, Witten, 22 Tort & Ins L J 511 (1987).

claimant, such as a spouse,[176] son,[177] aunt,[178] or co-trustee,[179] unless, of course, the claimant commissions their conduct.

24–5B2 Wilful or Deliberate

In principle, conduct is deliberate, if it is so reprehensible in its conception (as opposed to its effects alone) that the courts must weigh it against the enforcement of insurance. However, in practice, loss is deliberate or wilful if it is not accidental, so it is best defined as the obverse of accident: for the case of PA insurance, see above, 17–5B and 17–5C. The precise meaning is affected by public policy considerations and, therefore, varies according to the context. Attempts by the draftsman to clarify the matter, by defining accidental loss or damage as that which is "neither expected nor intended" by the insured, have failed to keep the question out of the courts.[180]

While that is generally true, deliberate loss or damage may still have an element of fortuity. It is still deliberate, if (a) the kind of loss was intended but not the extent; or (b) the loss was intended in full but the chance of achieving it was small. For example, the golfer in Japan, who sinks a ball in one, is expected to celebrate the event in style with a dinner and gifts to all and sundry. Japanese insurers offer insurance against the expense of this intended "loss". However, whereas loss (a) is also deliberate in the sense that its character will weigh against the enforcement of insurance, that is not true of (b). It is submitted that there is no reason of public policy why an English court would not enforce the Japanese golf insurance. The same is true of insurance offered to sponsors who incite and induce the loss insured against: the firm that offers a prize to those who "hole in one" can insure against having to pay the prize.[181]

For this purpose, the object or focus of deliberation or wilfulness is the injury, damage or loss in question. It is irrelevant whether the insured intended to break the law. What counts is whether he knew or should have known enough about the circumstances to have intended the illegal act and loss.[182] Ignorance of the relevant law is no

176. See also above, 17–2G, and below, 27–2D.

177. *Podmore* v *Tunstall & District Assurance Collecting Sy* [1930] IAC Rep 38: when a man was executed for murder, his mother could enforce an industrial policy on his life, taken out to cover funeral expenses.

178. *Jernigan* v *Allstate Ins Co*, 269 F 2d 353 (5 Cir, 1959), reh den 272 F 2d 857 (1959): the insured permitted his aunt to drive his car when, unknown to him, she was legally insane. She drove at her victim and then to and fro over his prostrate body. The insurer pleaded that the death was brought about intentionally. The court held the insurer liable, upholding a clause in the policy whereby cover extended to assault and battery, hence intentional conduct, unless committed by or at the direction of the insured. For a similar result under employers' liability insurance see *Georgia Casualty Co* v *Golden Mills*, 127 So 555 (Miss, 1930).

Cf Farm Bureau Mutual Auto Ins Co v *Hammer*, 177 F 2d 793 (4 Cir, 1949), cert den 339 US 914 (1950); *Culp* v *Northwestern Pacific Indemnity Co*, 365 F 2d 474 (10 Cir, 1966).

179. *Giacobetti* v *Insurance Placement Facility*, 457 A 2d 853 (Pa, 1983—fire).

180. USA: As regards liability for injuries to other people, see McKenzie and Johnson, 51 La L Rev 251, 252 (1990); and Boyle & O'Malley, 25 New England L Rev 827, 831 ff (1991). As regards liability for the cost of cleaning up pollution, see Marrs 26 Tort & Ins L J 662 (1991); Silverman, 90 Mich L Rev 2113 (1992); and Kolesar, 68 Notre Dame L Rev 549 (1993).

181. For example, the motor dealer who advertises by offering the prize of a vehicle: *Crawford Chevrolet* v *National Hole–In–One Association*, 828 P 2d 952 (NM, 1992).

182. *Burrows* v *Rhodes* [1899] 1 QB 816, 828 ff *per* Kennedy J; the question for the court was whether there could be an "action for indemnity, grounded on deceit or warranty" for the plaintiff, who had been induced to break the law (Foreign Enlistment Act 1870) "in honest ignorance of the particular circumstances which constituted its unlawfulness". The court held that there could, provided the mistake was "justified" (p 831).

Cf R Leslie Ltd v *Reliable Advertising & Addressing Agency Ltd* [1915] 1 KB 652: plaintiff moneylenders were convicted of the offence of sending a circular advertising their services to a minor, which occurred

excuse.[183] By contrast, when the actor is aware of the law, but makes an error of judgement concerning the relevant facts such that he does not realise that he is breaking the law, his conduct may be covered by liability insurance.[184]

24–6 ILLEGALITY AND LIFE INSURANCE

24–6A Murder

A person who murders the life insured cannot benefit under the insurance. In *Cleaver*,[185] it was held that, while the wife who murdered her husband could not claim the amount of a life policy in her favour, that did not prevent enforcement of the policy by the executors of the deceased.[186] Nor would it have prevented enforcement by a mortgagee, in possession of the policy as security for a loan.

In *Davitt* v *Titcumb*,[187] the defendant bought a house, by means of a mortgage secured by endowment insurance on the life of himself and of a lady, and later murdered the lady. The mortgagee used the insurance money to pay off the mortgage. The mortgagee, said the court,[188] "was innocent of any wrongdoing, and no rule of public policy required that it should be deprived of its security by reason of the defendant's criminal act. Moreover, the repudiation of the policy . . . would have been unfairly prejudicial to the estate of [the deceased], which would have remained liable jointly with the defendant to repay" the mortgagee. The murderer, however, is not to benefit at all, not even indirectly. The house in that case was sold and the question for the court was whether the defendant could share in the net proceeds. That surplus would not have existed but for the reduction of indebtedness achieved by the application of the insurance money, which would not have become available for that purpose but for the defendant's criminal act. If he were entitled to claim the surplus, he would benefit from his criminal act and that, it was held, would be contrary to public policy.[189]

In the past, courts have refused to enforce insurance on the life of one who is

---

through the negligence of the defendants, to whom the task of checking the addressees had been entrusted. Rowlatt J found that the plaintiffs had not acted reasonably (p 661) and that their action for an indemnity failed.

183. *Haseldine* v *Hosken* [1933] 1 KB 822 (CA—liability).

184. For example *Sommer* v *New Amsterdam Casualty Co*, 171 F Supp 84 (ED Mo, 1959): when a psychiatrist faced suit for assault in committing a person to mental hospital, it was held that his malpractice insurer should have been prepared to defend the suit.

185. *Cleaver* v *Mutual Reserve Fund Life Assn* [1892] 1 QB 147. Recently, in *Brissette* v *Westbury Life Ins Co* (1989) 60 DLR (4th) 78 (life), *Cleaver* was applied by the High Court of Ontario to enable enforcement of a policy on the life of M at the suit of her executor because, although M had been murdered by her husband, the court was satisfied that her husband would not be permitted to receive any part of the insurance money. On appeal, enforcement was refused on other grounds, although the public policy behind *Cleaver* was approved: (1993) 96 DLR (4th) 609, 613 (Sup Ct, 1992).

USA in this sense: *Mutual Life Ins Co of New York* v *Armstrong*, 117 US 591 (1886); *Austin* v *US*, 125 F 2d 816 (7 Cir, 1942). In cases of murder the insurer is not bound by an incontestability clause: *Austin* (above).

186. *Quaere*, if the motive of the wife had been to enrich her children by the marriage.

187. [1990] Ch 110.

188. p 112 *per* Scott J, sitting as Vice-Chancellor of the County Palatine of Lancaster.

189. p 114, in application of public policy as expressed by Lord Esher MR in *Cleaver* v *Mutual Reserve Fund Life Assn* [1892] 1 QB 147, 152 (CA—life).

executed for the crime that he has committed.[190] One reason was said[191] to be that enforcement of the insurance would "take away one of those restraints operating on the minds of men against the commission of crimes, namely, the interest we have in the welfare and prosperity of our connections." However, deterrence is a weak basis for a rule of non-enforcement[192] and in New York, for example, insurance on the lives of executed murderers has been enforced:

"the granting of recovery in a case like the present one in no way benefits the criminal who is now dead and at least benefits his named beneficiaries who in most instances will be the persons deprived of support and maintenance by his death. On the other side of the ledger is the purely speculative possibility that a man who knows his kin are cared for by his insurance is more apt to commit a crime punishable by death. In reply to such an assumption, it may well be asked what sort of crime deterrent the voiding of a man's life insurance may be, when the penalty of death does not halt his criminal act."[193]

24–6B Manslaughter

In *Gray* v *Barr*,[194] Salmon LJ suggested that the effect of manslaughter on liability insurance would depend on the case and on the (variable) gravity of the killing. In the United States, the general rule is that enforcement of the insurance will not be refused, if the killing by the beneficiary was unintentional[195]; however, like "accident",[196] "intent" is a flexible notion that bends with the feelings of the court about the particular case.

In *Hall* v *Knight & Baxter*[197] the Court of Appeal held that a legatee, convicted of manslaughter of the testator, could not take the legacy. No doubt the same would be held in respect of the benefit of a life policy. In *Gray* v *Barr*,[198] Salmon LJ suggested that *Hall* should be seen as a case in which the killing, although labelled manslaughter, was akin to murder; and that it did not follow that all persons guilty of manslaughter would be deprived of a bequest from the victim or could not enforce life insurance.[199]

24–6C Suicide

If the insured committed suicide when it was a crime, his life insurance was not enforceable.[200] Suicide ceased to be crime with the passing of the Suicide Act, 1961,

190. *Amicable Society* v *Bolland* (1830) 4 Bligh (NS) 194 (HL). *Bolland* was followed in *Burt* v *Union Central Life Ins Co*, 187 US 362 (1902); see also *Northwestern Mutual Life Ins Co* v *McCue*, 223 US 234 (1911).
Cf Podmore v *Tunstall & District Assurance Collecting Sy* [1930] IAC Rep 38.
191. *Bolland*, p 211 *per* Lord Lyndhurst LC.
192. Above, 24–5A1.
193. *Prudential Ins Co* v *Goldstein*, 43 F Supp 765, 767 (ED NY, 1942); approved in *John Hancock Mutual Life Ins Co* v *Tarrence*, 244 F 2d 86 (6 Cir, 1957).
194. [1971] 2 QB 554, 581 (CA—liability).
195. For example, self defence: *Mahar* v *Metropolitan Life Ins Co*, 23 NYS 2d 299 (1940), app den 25 NYS 2d 1015; *Burns* v *US*, 200 F 2d 106 (4 Cir, 1952); *Taylor* v *US*, 113 F Supp 143 (WD Ark, 1953) affirmed 211 F 2d 794 (8 Cir, 1954); criminal negligence: *Lake* v *New York Life Ins Co*, 194 NYS 2d 1006 (1959); manslaughter: *Minasian* v *Aetna Life Ins Co*, 3 NE 2d 17 (Mass, 1936); *Tippens* v *Metropolitan Life Ins Co*, 99 F 2d 671 (5 Cir, 1938); *McClure* v *McClure*, 403 SE 2d 197, 200 (W Va, 1991 – life); somnambulism: *Re Eckardt*, 54 NYS 2d 484 (1945).
196. See 17–5E.
197. [1914] P 1.
198. [1971] 2 QB 554, 581 (CA—liability).
199. *Cf Re Giles* [1971] 3 WLR 640, 646 *per* Pennycuick J, who doubted the parallel between inheritance and insurance cases.
200. *Beresford* v *Royal Ins Co Ltd* [1938] AC 586.

and the decision today would be different.[201] The Act was "a mark of changing public attitudes to suicide. In times gone by an act of suicide may well have met with universal condemnation and serious consequences, but nowadays society has a different view. With the development of medical science a much greater understanding has been achieved of those who are driven to act in this way. In cases where grave mental instability on the part of the victim has been proved it could hardly be said that any action brought in respect of the suicide, or for that matter the attempt, is grounded in immorality. The position may well be different where the victim is wholly sane".[202]

To deal with the insured who makes a life contract with a view to committing suicide, the policy may contain a clause whereby the insurance is invalid, if the insured commits suicide within a stated period (often a year) of the making of the contract.[203] Alternatively, cover may be defined in a way that excludes suicide,[204] expressly or by implication; for example, in the case of accident cover, a deliberate act of suicide is not accidental.

24–6D Immorality

Common law refused to enforce contracts which, although unconnected with any infringement of the criminal law, were thought to promote sexual immorality, including property contracts that facilitated immoral activity.[205] However, insurance contracts are unlikely to be impugned on this basis. First, it has been strongly argued that the common law rule has died in its sleep.[206] Second, even if the common law rule survives, the rule makes a curious distinction, whereby gratuities to lovers are enforceable,[207] even if contracts with lovers are not. It is likely that insurance made by the insured in favour of a lover as beneficiary would be enforceable, even if, in the case of life insurance, the insured were also survived by a lawful spouse and children.[208]

24–7 ILLEGALITY AND LIABILITY INSURANCE

When liability insurance is compulsory, "the need to assure compensation for the injured is recognised as so peremptory that it should be universal rather than left to the chance initiative of" the person responsible for the injury.[209] The force of this fac-

---

201. *Gray* v *Barr* [1971] 2 QB 554, 582 *per* Salmon LJ (CA—liability). A woman who was injured or who died during an illegal abortion would be covered: *Carlson* v *Travelers Ins Co*, 316 NYS 2d 398 (1970). But if cover is limited to accidental death, the decision might be different. For example, *Stokley* v *Hartford Accident & Indemnity Co*, 321 F Supp 18 (WD Miss, 1978—life). See further, 17–5E.

202. *Kirkham* v *Chief Constable of the Greater Manchester Police* [1990] 2 QB 283, 296 *per* Farquharson LJ (CA); see also in this sense Lloyd LJ (p 292).

203. Clause held valid in *Ellinger & Co* v *Mutual Life Ins Co* [1905] 1 KB 31 (CA); the clause was framed as a warranty, but this does not seem to have been decisive. See also *White* v *British Empire Mutual Life Assurance Co* (1868) LR 7 Eq 394.

204. *Beresford* (above).

205. *Upfill* v *Wright* [1911] 1 KB 506.

206. See *Tanner* v *Tanner* [1975] 1 WLR 1346 in which the Court of Appeal went to some lengths to enforce an arrangement by a man with his mistress. Generally see Dwyer (1977) 93 LQR 386; Poulter (1974) 124 NLJ 999.

207. *Ayerst* v *Jenkins* (1873) LR 16 Eq 275.

208. So held in *Prudential Ins Co* v *Taylor*, 46 F Supp 115 (WD La, 1942—life), the court being influenced by the fact that the proceeds of the policy went directly to the beneficiary and formed no part of the insured's estate.

209. Fleming (1971) 34 MLR 176, 179.

tor generally overcomes any scruples in the court about the advantage to the wrong-doer of enforcing his insurance, which is seen as incidental.

24–7A Compulsory Liability Insurance

"At the beginning of the nineteenth century, liability insurance would have been unthinkable. It would have been considered as immoral to take out an insurance against the consequences of civil liability as to take out one against the consequences of criminal liability."[210] At the beginning of the twentieth century, this was true no longer, yet the courts were at pains to distinguish motoring offences as not really criminal.[211] Later courts, faced with the defence that there could be no insurance for loss deliberately inflicted, were at pains to find that, although the insured may have deliberately got drunk and then deliberately driven his car at speed, the final error of judgement was not deliberate and that therefore his liability could be validly insured.[212] However, it is now clear that the public policy in favour of the third party victim is so strong that the insurance is valid, whether the damage was done deliber-ately or not; and, in any event, studies suggest that the existence of liability cover has had little effect on the behaviour of the individual insured.[213]

"The primary purpose of compulsory motor vehicle liability insurance is to compensate inno-cent victims who have been injured by the negligence of financially irresponsible motorists. Its purpose is not, like that of ordinary insurance, to save harmless the tortfeasor himself. There-fore, there is no reason why the victim's right to recover from the [insurer] should depend on whether the conduct of the insured was intentional or negligent. In order to accomplish the objective of the law, the perspective here must be that of the victim and not that of the aggressor for whom the law provides criminal penalties calculated to minimise any profit he might derive from the insurance."[214]

In *Gardner* v *Moore*,[215] M had an "altercation" with G. He then got into his van and drove at G on the pavement, dragging him along the road. G went to hospital. M went to prison. M was unable to pay damages to G and was uninsured. The House of Lords rejected a defence by the Motor Insurers' Bureau based on the wilful and crimi-nal nature of M's conduct, accepting both the decision and the reasoning of the Court of Appeal in *Hardy* v *Motor Insurers' Bureau*.[216] In *Hardy*, a similar defence had been

210. Tunc, *Encyclopedia of Comparative Law*, vol IX part 1 no 90.
211. *Robertson* v *London Guarantee & Accident Co Ltd*, 1915 1 SLT 195: the insured injured two lady cyclists, while he "was driving with criminal negligence, being in an extreme state of drunkenness and quite unfit to drive". He was prosecuted but committed suicide on the eve of his trial. The action against his liab-ility insurer succeeded in the Outer House of the Court of Session, in spite of a defence based on the insured's crime. Lord Ormidale (p 196): "I assume that the insured could not have insured against the con-sequences of his own unlawful (in the sense of criminal) act . . . but . . . I have some difficulty in holding that a man who drives a car recklessly because he is drunk is a criminal in the sense of the law . . . although he may be guilty of a statutory offence".
212. *Tinline* v *White Cross Ins Assn Ltd* [1921] 3 KB 327; *James* v *British General Ins Co Ltd* [1927] 2 KB 311.
213. Tunc, *op cit*, no 93.
214. *Nationwide Mutual Ins Co* v *Roberts*, 134 SE 2d 654, 659 (NC, 1964).
215. [1984] AC 548. See also *MacDonald* v *Prudential Assurance Co Ltd* (1972) 24 DLR (3d) 185 (NB).
Cf *McCarthy* v *United Services Auto*, 204 NYS 2d 420 (1960) as viewed in *McCarthy* v *Moto-Vehicle Acci-dent Indemnification Corp*, 224 NYS 2d 909 (1962) affirmed 238 NYS 2d 101 (1963); see also *Moto-Vehicle Accident Indemnification Corp* v *Kilgallon*, 244 NYS 2d 123 (1963—motor).
216. [1964] 2 QB 745; applied in *Suncorp Ins* v *Ploner* (1989) 12 Qd Lawyer Reps 57, 66 (motor), affirmed [1991] 1 Qd R 69 (FC). A similar decision is *Wheeler* v *O'Connell* 9 NE 2d 544 (Mass, 1937).

rejected as the "court has to weigh the gravity of the anti-social act and the extent to which it will be encouraged by enforcing the right sought to be enforced against the social harm which will be caused if the right is not enforced."[217]

The result of these decisions is, first, that insurance is enforceable by the victim, even though the harm was deliberately inflicted and even though the insured benefits by the discharge of a civil liability, which he otherwise would have had to bear. It may, however, have been significant that in motor cases the claim against the insurer is seen not as a claim by the insured, who is guilty of the wrong, but as a claim by a third party, who is not, a third party who is given a right of action by statute.[218] This may distinguish motor insurance from cases, in which the victim has no direct action against the insurer but must bring an action against the insured, who must then seek indemnity from the insurer.

Second, there is nothing in these decisions to suggest that the insured wrongdoer may recover for damage to his own vehicle[219] but, as motor cover against liability for damage to the property of third parties is now compulsory, indemnity for damage to somebody else's vehicle is likely to be enforced.

24–7B Other Liability Insurance

Liability for acts which are torts or lesser crimes is a proper subject of insurance.[220] Were it otherwise, professional negligence cover would be as restricted as the enthusiasm of the professional to take on all but the safest work. On a graph the cases form a curve, one toe of which is staked down by legislation so that, however great the revulsion of the courts, cover is compulsory and enforceable. The other toe of the curve represents liability so inoffensive that the enforcement of insurance is not questioned. The peak of the curve, however, is the point at which the wrong goes above the treeline of judicial tolerance and is a clear target for non-enforcement.

Before motorists' liability insurance became compulsory, the courts drew a distinction between liability based on negligent and even grossly negligent conduct, which was insurable,[221] and liability based on acts done "knowingly" or which were "wilful and advertent",[222] which was not. Since motor cover became compulsory,[223] a similar distinction has been drawn for other kinds of liability insurance that is not compulsory, a distinction that corresponds roughly with the line between accidental and non-accidental loss.[224] The precise line wavers with the winds of policy and with the context. For example, it appears that the courts have always responded as if mayhem by

217. pp 767–768 *per* Diplock LJ. As to the impact on this test of the decision in *Tinsley* v *Milligan* [1993] 3 All ER 65 (HL), see below, 24–9D5.
218. Above, 5–9.
219. In this sense *Hardy* (above) pp 760–761 *per* Lord Denning MR (CA—motor). *Acme Finance Co* v *National Ins Co*, 195 P 2d 728 (Colo, 1948—motor). But the joint (not guilty) insured may recover: *Gill* v *Ins Corp of British Columbia* (1988) 50 DLR (4th) 148 (BC—motor).
220. For example, *Big Town Nursing Homes Inc* v *Reserve Ins Co*, 492 F 2d 523 (5 Cir, 1974): liability insurance in respect of false imprisonment by a doctor was enforceable in Texas.
221. *Tinline* v *White Cross Ins Assn Ltd* [1921] 3 KB 327; *James* v *British General Ins Co Ltd* [1927] 2 KB 311. In New York, similar reasoning is found in cases of drunken driving, for example, *Cooperative Fire Ins Co* v *Vondrak*, 346 NYS 2d 965 (1973).
222. *Tinline*, p 331 *per* Bailhache J.
223. Above, 24–7A.
224. See above, 17–5B, 17–5C and 24–5B2.

motor vehicle were quite different from other kinds of violence[225] and that, therefore, cases on the roads should be considered apart.[226]

In *Haseldine* v *Hosken*,[227] the plaintiff solicitor settled an action against him for champerty and sought to recover the amount under his solicitors' indemnity policy. The Court of Appeal held that his claim failed: "It is clearly contrary to public policy to insure against the commission of an act, knowing what act is being committed, which is a crime . . . "[228] There was no third party who, as a result of the decision, went without compensation; and public policy required that such agreements should be discouraged.[229] The absence of a third party distinguishes the situation, though not in the event the decision, from the next.

In *Gray* v *Barr*,[230] B thought mistakenly that his wife was with G, with whom she had had an affair. He took a shotgun to G's house and, when entry was refused, tried to push past G; the gun went off and G was killed. B was acquitted of manslaughter. B had liability insurance, but the action against his insurer for damages payable to B's wife failed in the Court of Appeal, which thought that killing with cars was one thing, killing with guns another.

"Crimes of violence, particularly when committed with loaded guns are amongst the worst curses of the age. It is very much in the public interest that they be deterred . . . no one who threatens unlawful violence with a loaded gun should be allowed to enforce a claim for indemnity against any liability that he may incur as a result of having so acted. I do not intend to lay down any wider proposition . . . Manslaughter is a crime which varies infinitely in its seriousness."[231]

It has been shown[232] that the deterrence argument is weak. The House of Lords has decided[233] that the compensation of third parties is important. This being so, if crimes of violence were indeed a curse of the age, the argument in *Gray* v *Barr* can be turned on its head to favour insurance protection for the victims of (unmotorised) crimes of violence: there are more victims in need of protection.[234] The decision has been

---

225. See *Gray* v *Barr* (below) and *Robertson* v *London Guarantee*, footnoted under 24–7A, above.

226. Hasson, 14 Osgoode Hall L J 769, 777 (1976). In this sense as regards the development of liability insurance in the United States, McNeely, 41 Colum L Rev 26, 41 (1941).

Indemnity for liability for rape would be refused: *Haser* v *Maryland Casualty Co*, 53 NW 2d 508, 512 (ND, 1952—motor). As regards liability for intentional acts of (religious) discrimination, see *Ranger Ins Co* v *Bal Harbour Club Inc*, 509 So 2d 945 (Fla, 1987—liability); Reager, 39 U Fla L Rev 971 (1987). As regards liability to the victims of arson, see Appleman, section 7031 at n 14.

227. [1933] 1 KB 822. *Cf* Cal Ins Code, section 533: the liability insurer is not bound to pay in respect of loss caused by the wilful act of the insured, but loss is distinguished from legal expenses, and the insurer is bound to defend the insured against a third party; see *Gray* v *Zurich Ins Co*, 419 P 2d 168 (Cal, 1966—liability). See also *Conner* v *Transamerica Ins Co*, 496 P 2d 770, 775 (Okl, 1972—liability).

228. p 833 *per* Scrutton LJ.

229. p 836 *per* Greer LJ.

230. [1971] 2 QB 554. A similar reluctance to enforce such insurance is found in *Farm Bureau Ins Co* v *Hammer*, 177 F 2d 793, 795 (4 Cir, 1949), cited with approval in *Kraus* v *Allstate Ins Co*, 379 F 2d 443 (3 Cir, 1967—motor). But *cf Zurich General Accident & Liability Co* v *Flickinger*, 32 F 2d 853, 856 (4 Cir, 1929—PA).

231. p 581 *per* Salmon LJ.

232. Above, 24–5A1.

233. Above, 24–7A.

234. In England in 1970, when the case was decided, there were 30 known cases of homicide by firearms, but 685 cases of causing death by reckless or dangerous driving. Such statistics, published annually by the Home Office, do not appear to have been put before the court.

severely criticised.[235] In cases like this, it is perhaps less a belief in deterrence than downright distaste that explains judicial recoil and refusal to enforce insurance.[236]

Compare *New Amsterdam Casualty Co v Jones*,[237] in which J, the owner of a petrol station, had cover against liability for bodily injury as the result of an accident on the premises. A man came to the station, who J thought was a racketeer employed to ruin his business during a price-cutting war in Detroit, and J shot him. The insurance was enforced.

"By no stretch of the imagination can it be said that the shooting, or unlawful conduct, could have been previously within the contemplation of Jones at the time he procured the policy insuring himself . . . The execution of the policy did not place a premium on the wrongful assault. It did not tend to encourage unlawful conduct. It did not arouse an illegal temptation. Viewed from a common sense standpoint, neither the contract, nor a recovery thereunder by [the victim], can be held to be against public policy . . . The vague possibility of benefit to Jones—that some time in the distant future, when he may have accumulated a sum of money equal to the amount of the damages assessed against him he will be saved from payment of [the victim's] judgment against him—is too remote, and uncertain to require that a court hold that such nebulous consequences (not induced by the stipulated protection from financial liability) are sufficient to void the insurance contract on grounds of public policy."[238]

In the past, it should be noted, the possibility has been canvassed[239] that D & O liability insurance contracted by a company for its officers might be invalidated by section 310 of the Companies Act 1985, which nullifies provisions which purport prospectively to indemnify an officer against liability. This possibility has been removed by section 137 of the Companies Act 1989, which enacts a new section 310(3) of the Act of 1985, to the effect that nothing in section 310 prevents a company from "purchasing or maintaining for any such officer or auditor insurance against such liability".

24-8 INSURANCE OF PROPERTY ILLEGALLY USED OR ACQUIRED

Under section 41 of the MIA, there is "an implied warranty that the adventure is a lawful one".[240] No such warranty is implied in non-marine insurance contracts.[241] Nonetheless, enforcement of property insurance may be refused by reference to the unlawfulness surrounding its use or acquisition.

235. For example Fleming (1971) 34 MLR 176; Shand [1972A] CLJ 144, 152 ff; Hasson, 14 Osgoode Hall L J 769, 776 ff (1976). Yet the decision has been accepted in Canada: Hasson, *loc cit* and cases cited; and in Australia: *S & Y Investments (No 2) Pty Ltd v Commercial Union Assurance Co Ltd* (1986) 82 FLR 130 (NT—liability).
Criticism would be less, if the insurance were purchased as part of planned wrongdoing, in case the wrongdoer is apprehended and punished: *Jernigan v Allstate Ins Co*, 272 F 2d 857, 859 (5 Cir, 1959—motor). Appleman, section 7031 at n 14. MacGillivray, No 447. This is also the fear underlying English cases against indemnity for fines: above, 24–4A.
236. This may explain *Gray v Barr*, as well as cases in which the courts have refused to enforce insurance against liabilty to the victim in respect of sexual offences: *JC Penney Cas Ins Co v MK*, 52 Cal 3d 1009 (1993—liability).
237. 135 F 2d 191 (6 Cir, 1943). See also *Barry v Romanosky* 538 NYS 2d 14 (1989—liability).
238. p 195. Cf *S & Y Investments (No 2) Pty Ltd v Commercial Union Assurance Co Ltd* (1986) 82 FLR 130 (NT—liability): the person insured, who shot an intruder, in the circumstances a dangerous and unlawful act, and was guilty of manslaughter, could not enforce the insurance.
239. See Stanbury, BILA Journal, No 73, p 17 (1990).
240. Arnould, No 744.
241. *Euro-Diam Ltd v Bathurst* [1990] 1 QB 1 (CA—goods AR).

24–8A Past Illegality

Although property was illegally used or acquired in the past, current insurance may be enforced. If enforcement is to be refused, the insurance cover and the illegality must in some sense be concurrent or connected in point of time.

The Supreme Court of the United States has said[242] that "a new contract, founded on a new consideration, although in relation to property respecting which there had been unlawful transactions between the parties, is not itself unlawful". Likewise, the English courts have held that the illegal employment of a ship on one voyage does not invalidate hull insurance on the next.[243]

In England, however, the connection in time between the illegality and the insurance may be made, although tenuous. A voyage is illegal from the beginning, if it is made with the purpose of illegal importation later in the voyage.[244] Again, in *Geismar*,[245] although illegal importation had taken place in the past, it had created a continuing and connected state of affairs, the liability of the jewellery imported to confiscation, which vitiated cover on the jewellery contracted some time later.

24–8B Future Illegality

In the case of future illegality, the decisive question is whether the property insured has been marked for or appropriated to the illegal activity.[246] If so, the court is unlikely to enforce the insurance. If not, although illegal use is possible, the insurance is likely to be enforced. When something can be done legally or illegally, something used lawfully or unlawfully, the courts presume, in the absence of clear evidence to the contrary, that the lawful course or use will be pursued: people are given the benefit of any doubt.[247]

In *Erb*,[248] the insurer defended a fire claim on the contents of a retail outlet on the ground that the claimant pharmacist sold alcoholic liquor without the required licence. None of the property destroyed in the fire had (yet) been used for illegal activity or marked out for illegal use, and the court enforced the claim. "The issuing of

---

242. *Armstrong* v *Toler*, 11 Wheat 258, 269 (1826). See also *Clark* v *Scott*, 5 F Cas No 2,832 (D Mass, 1840—hull). In *Transcontinental Ins Co of New York* v *Minning*, 135 F 2d 479 (6 Cir, 1943): a fictitious conveyance of property to defraud a potential creditor did not invalidate fire insurance on the property for (p 481) "the entire transaction was completed a considerable period of time prior to the fire and it had no relation to the insurance contract".

243. *Lubbock* v *Potts* (1806) 7 East 449, 456 *per* Lord Ellenborough CJ (hull and cargo); *Gibson* v *Service* (1814) 5 Taunt 433 (hull); *Bird* v *Appleton* (1800) 8 TR 562 (cargo).

244. *Lubbock* v *Potts* (above). This is one of a number of cases in which trading which infringed current statutes to promote war against France invalidated marine insurance.

245. *Geismar* v *Sun Alliance & London Ins Ltd* [1978] 1 QB 383, discussed more fully above, 24–5A2(c). Cf *Howard* v *Refuge Friendly Society* (1886) 54 LT 644, 646 *per* Mathew J (life).
In *Clark* v *Scott*, 5 F Cas No 2,832 (D Mass, 1840) Justice Story rejected the argument that, when a ship with an anchor on which American duty had not been paid, was lost (a) the entire cover was void or (b) there could be no recovery for the smuggled anchor, because (p 916) "Suppose goods, smuggled on a former voyage, were afterwards embarked on a new, and lawful voyage, never having been seized, it seems clear, that they would be insurable. The contract is one degree removed from the illegality . . . the illegality did not attach to the voyage on which it was used."

246. This is one view of *Lubbock* v *Potts* (above).

247. *Foster* v *Driscoll* [1929] 1 KB 470, 498 *per* Scrutton LJ (CA); *Clark* v *Scott*, 5 F Cas No 2,832 (D Mass, 1840) p 913 *per* Justice Story; *Fidelity & Deposit Co* v *Moore*, 3 F 2d 652 (D Or, 1925—fidelity); 272 US 317 (1926); *Craig* v *United States Ins Co*, 6 F Cas No 3,340 (D Pa, 1817—freight).

248. *Erb* v *German-American Ins Co*, 67 NW 583 (Iowa, 1896).

the policy did not necessarily have the effect to encourage and promote an unlawful purpose."[249]

In decisions[250] of this kind and time, the court relied on a test of contract law, asking whether the claimant required the aid of the illegal transaction to establish his right,[251] for example, whether he needed to rely on the (unlawful) sale to enforce the insurance? Evidently not, and so Williston asserted in general terms that "a contract of insurance is not invalidated by the fact that the property insured is used for an illegal purpose."[252] In England, the same test has been applied and called the *Bowmaker* principle.[253] The relevance of the test to the recovery of property has recently been confirmed.[254] So, insurance on goods or ships to be employed in smuggling into another country will not be enforced, even if in the event the smuggling is not carried out.[255]

24–8C Concurrent Illegality

24–8C1 Illegal Use

The use of property for an illegal purpose does not invalidate current insurance on the property, unless the illegal purpose is serious, such as murder: if the car used deliberately to injure or kill is damaged in the process, the damage will not be covered.[256] But fire insurance on premises used for unlawful activity may well be enforced.[257]

24–8C2 Illegal Mode of Managing Property

In the nineteenth century the English courts decided that, if a voyage was carried out in a manner forbidden by statute and this was known to the insured, his insurance on the adventure was invalid.[258] The less draconian approach found in the balancing

---

249. *Erb* v *Fidelity Ins Co*, 69 NW 261, 263 (Iowa, 1896), a similar decision arising out of the same facts as the previous case. See also *Brown* v *New Jersey Ins Co*, 14 P 2d 272, 273 (Or, 1932): a claim under fire insurance on the insured's stock of goods was resisted as to part of the claim on the ground that the part concerned false labels to be used in the unlawful sale of "moonshine whisky". The court noted that no unlawful use had (yet) been made of the goods in question and that there was no law making the possession, sale or insurance of such goods unlawful, and enforced the claim.

250. For example, *Brown* (above).

251. Page, *Contracts*, para 1103; Williston, *Contracts* (2nd ed), section 1752; the third edition, para 1752, contains the same proposition.

252. *Ibid*.

253. *Euro-Diam Ltd* v *Bathurst* [1990] 1 QB 1, 35 *per* Kerr LJ (CA—goods AR), by reference to *Bowmakers Ltd* v *Barnet Instruments Ltd* [1945] KB 65 (CA).

254. See below, 24–9D5.

255. *Foster* v *Driscoll* [1929] 1 KB 470 (CA); *Mackender* v *Feldia AG* [1967] 2 QB 590 (CA—jewellers' block).

256. See above, 24–7A. A similar but more questionable severity has been shown to ships trading in breach of trade laws: *Gray* v *Sims*, F Cas No 5,729 (D Pa, 1814—hull). However, in *Northwest Amusement Co Inc* v *Aetna Casualty & Surety Co*, 107 P 2d 110, 114 (Or, 1940) a claim under burglary insurance failed because the goods lost were gambling machines, the possession of which was illegal. See also *Trinity Universal Ins Co* v *Cunningham*, 107 F 2d 857 (8 Cir, 1939—motor) cert den 310 US 654.

257. See *Brown* (above).

258. For example, cargo loaded on deck without required certificate: *Cunard* v *Hyde* (1859) 2 El & El 1 (cargo); *Wilson* v *Rankin* (1865) LR 1 QB 162 (cargo); carriage of passengers without the required certificate: *Dudgeon* v *Pembroke* (1874) LR 9 QB 581, 585 (hull).

Cf Ocean Ins Co v *Polleys*, 13 Pet 157 (Sup Ct, 1839): Story J held that insurance on a ship, which was subject to forfeiture for breach of regulations in its American port of registry, was valid. See also *Trinity Universal Ins Co* v *Cunningham*, 107 F 2d 857 (8 Cir, 1939—motor), cert den 310 US 654.

rule,[259] which is adopted today, asks whether non-enforcement of the insurance is necessary to promote the policy of the prohibition.[260] If so, only then will the claim not be enforced.

In *Fire & All Risks Ins Co v Powell*,[261] the claimant deliberately overloaded his lorry in breach of statute. He then (negligently) drove the lorry under a bridge, which was too low for the load. He sought to recover the amount of his liability to the owner of the damaged load under a (marine) cargo policy. The insurer argued that it would be contrary to public policy to allow him to recover for damage inflicted while deliberately engaged in an operation contrary to law, but the action succeeded. The court relied on English cases,[262] which might have been distinguished as cases of compulsory insurance; but Smith J thought[263] that

"as the legislature has adopted in the field of death and bodily injury the view that the interests of the victim and the general public interest in having contracts performed outweigh any danger there may be that the enforcement of liability insurance extending to the criminal use of a motor car would tend to promote crime, there is no justification for taking a different view of the matter in the field of damage to property."

24–8C3 Guilt by Association

If goods are lawfully used, acquired or designated, it is irrelevant that other goods in the immediate vicinity, even perhaps in the same ownership, are illegally used, acquired or designated: there is no guilt by association.

In *Pleschell v Allnutt*,[264] the claimant had insured lawful merchandise for transport from Hamburg to London. Also on board the ship was unlawful merchandise, which was neither his property nor insured under his policy. The insurer claimed that the presence of unlawful merchandise rendered the entire venture illegal and insurance thereon void. It was argued for the claimant that it

"would fall extremely hard upon the commercial interests of the country, if the innocent goods of one merchant should be confiscated on account of the misconduct of another. Such a position would carry the doctrine of infection beyond what is done even in cases of contraband, where the penalty attaches only to the property of the same owner."

The court decided for the claimant. Moreover, as regards goods in the same ownership, in *Geismar*,[265] while the burglary claim on the uncustomed jewellery failed, it appears that the claim in respect of other goods burgled at the same time was not contested.

24–9 THE EFFECT OF ILLEGALITY ON THE CONTRACT OF INSURANCE

The effect of illegality on the contract of insurance varies from total nullity of the con-

---

259. Above, 24–5A3. *Leggate v Brown* (1950) 66 (2) TLR 281 (motor) might be explained on this basis.
260. *Redmond v Smith* (1844) 7 Man & G 457, 474 *per* Tindal CJ (hull). See also *St John Shipping Corp v Joseph Rank Ltd* [1957] 1 QB 267.
261. [1966] VR 513 (Vict).
262. *Tinline v White Cross Ins Assn Ltd* [1921] 3 KB 327 (motor) and *James v British General Ins Co Ltd* [1927] 2 KB 311 (motor).
263. p 527.
264. (1813) 4 Taunt 792.
265. See above, 24–5A2(c).

tract to non-enforceability of a particular claim, without prejudice to the validity of the contract as regards other claims.

24–9A Illegality When Making the Contract of Insurance[266]

Illegality at this stage, if it gives rise to non-enforcement at all, means that the contract is totally without effect, as follows.

The insured has no insurance. However, there is venerable authority[267] that, if the insurer nonetheless pays the broker involved, the insured may recover the money from the broker as money had and received.

The insured is unable to recover any premiums paid to the insurer under the illegal contract of insurance. Thus in *Harse v Pearl Life Assurance Co*[268] the plaintiff contracted life insurance, in which he had no interest, and was unable to recover premium paid. This decision was based on rules applicable to all contracts,[269] as was *Vandyck v Hewitt*,[270] in which premium could not be recovered in respect of cargo part owned by enemies and, for that reason, not lawfully insurable in England. This is a simple application of the general rule against the recovery of money paid or property transferred in performance of an illegal contract.[271]

24–9B Illegal Promises[272]

An illegal promise may be but a small part of the promised consideration. If the main purpose of the contract can be carried out without the illegal part, the latter is ignored and the contract is performed as far as possible without contravening the law.[273] As regards the illegal part unperformed, liability is exempted by operation of law.[274] If, on the other hand, the illegal part, although one illegal promise among many lawful promises, is one without which a substantial part of the rest cannot be performed, the whole contract is discharged or dissolved.[275] Insurance promises, to pay loss or to pay premium, are likely to be put in the latter category [276] but, in relation to claims conditions, the position may be different.

---

266. Above, 24–2.

267. *Tenant v Elliott* (1797) 1 Bos & Pul 3 (cargo).

268. [1904] 1 KB 559 (CA—life); applied in *Evanson v Crooks* (1911) 106 LT 264 (life); *Goldstein v Salvation Army Assurance Sy* [1917] 2 KB 291 (life). See also *Howard v Refuge Friendly Society* (1886) 54 LT 644 (life).

In the USA, premium is irrecoverable in principle unless, as is readily found by the courts in such cases, the parties are not *in pari delicto*: *Holland v Pyramid Life Ins Co*, 199 F 2d 926 (5 Cir, 1952—life); *Magers v Western & Southern Life Ins Co*, 344 SW 2d 312 (Mo, 1961—life).

269. p 563 *per* Lord Collins MR. Romer LJ stressed (p 564) that in this case the parties to the contract were *in pari delicto*: cf below, 24–9D.

270. (1800) 1 East 96, Lord Kenyon CJ saying that "the rule has been settled at all times, that where both parties are *in pari delicto*, which is the case here, *potior est conditio possidentis*". See also *Morck v Abel* (1802) 3 Bos & P 35 (cargo).

271. Treitel, p 436. *Cf Tinsley v Milligan* [1993] 3 All ER 65 (HL).

272. Above, 24–4.

273. Treitel, pp 446 ff and cases cited.

274. Treitel, pp 446–447 and cases cited.

275. The *Fibrosa* case [1942] 1 KB 12 (CA); reversed on a different point [1943] AC 32

276. It is different in the United States, where state law dictates the terms of insurance contracts. Contract terms in breach of such rules have been disregarded and the contract enforced as if they had not been included: *Equitable Life Assurance Society v Pettus*, 140 US 226 (1891—life); *Bersano v General Accident Fire & Life Corp*, 330 NE 2d 68 (NY, 1975—fire).

For example, in *Watson* v *Employers Liability Ins Co*,[277] liability insurance contained a clause, that no action could be brought against the insurer until the liability of the insured had been determined, which was valid in Massachusetts, where the policy was issued, but not in Louisiana, where the action was brought. The Supreme Court of the United States held that the court in Louisiana could apply the insurance contract without applying the clause.

24–9C Illegal Purpose[278]: Partial Enforcement

If a contract of insurance is concluded with an illegal purpose as the main objective, the contract is entirely unenforceable. If, as is more likely to occur, the contract is concluded with lawful purposes in mind, but appears to cover an activity conceived later to serve an unlawful purpose, the question arises, whether it is the entire contract, which is unenforceable from then on, or just the claim or part of the claim arising out of the unlawful activity.

In *Parkin* v *Dick*,[279] insurance was taken on goods to be subsequently specified. Goods were shipped to a total value of £10,000, of which goods to the value of £600 were naval stores shipped in breach of statute. The entire consignment was seized by an enemy and lost. The insured argued that, although the insurance was inoperative to cover the naval stores, it was valid for the rest; that the policy was like a deed containing a number of covenants, in which illegal covenants might be severed, but the rest enforced. The court rejected the argument and held that the entire claim failed. The contract was construed as an entire contract, so that illegality in part infected the whole.[280]

In the process of construction, the court is influenced by the gravity of the illegality and, perhaps, also by the other factors[281] affecting the preliminary question, whether (and in the present context to what extent) the contract should be enforced. *Parkin* is typical of English marine insurance cases at the time[282] and its severity may reflect the particular context, legislation to further the wars against Napoleon. It is not clear that such cases are a reliable guide to decisions today.

277. 348 US 66 (1954). See also, in New York, *London Guarantee & Accident Co Ltd* v *Marine Repair Corp*, 199 NYS 237 (1923—liability); *Seligman* v *Tucker*, 362 NYS 2d 881 (1975—motor), affirmed 335 NE 2d 844 (1975).
278. Above, 24–5.
279. (1809) 11 East 502. See also *Bird* v *Appleton* (1800) 8 TR 562, 566 *per* Lord Kenyon CJ (hull).
280. p 503 *per* Lord Ellenborough CJ. Generally, see Treitel, pp 449 ff.
Cf Keir v *Andrade* (1816) 6 Taunt 498: the insured exported 300 barrels of gunpowder, but was licensed to export only 150. His insurance on the entire consignment was valid as regards 150 barrels. The decision proceeds, it is submitted correctly, by regard to the inferences of the statute in question: as the insured was only liable to forfeit the excess, but could keep the rest, the court inferred (p 504) that insurance on the latter was not meant to be invalid. See also *Glaser* v *Cowie* (1813) 1 M & S 52; *Butler* v *Allnutt* (1816) 1 Stark 222. *Clark* v *Scott*, 5 F Cas No 2,832 (D Mass, 1840).
281. Above, 24–5A3.
282. See also *Wilson* v *Marryat* (1798) 8 TR 31, 46 *per* Lord Kenyon CJ (hull and cargo); *Chalmers* v *Bell* (1804) 3 Bos & Pul 604 (cargo); *Gibson* v *Service* (1814) 5 Taunt 433 (hull): *Cunard* v *Hyde* (1859) 2 El & El 1, 8 *per* Lord Campbell CJ (cargo).
The rule was different, if the voyage was in two or more distinct stages, separately insured: *Sewell* v *Royal Exchange Assurance Co* (1813) 4 Taunt 855, 858 *per* Sir John Mansfield CJ (hull & cargo). *Cf Geismar*, 24–5A2 (c) and 24–8C3.

24–9D Plaintiff Not in Pari Delicto

In *Harse*,[283] Lord Collins MR stated that relief would have been granted, if there had been "fraud, duress, oppression, or a difference in the position of the parties which created a fiduciary relationship to the plaintiff so as to make it inequitable for the defendants to insist on the bargain". He was referring, although incompletely, to the general law of contract and to the exceptions to the rule, that money transferred in performance of an illegal contract is irrecoverable. The exceptions can be explained as cases, in which the parties to the contract are not *in pari delicto*, and, where appropriate, this principle will be applied to illegal insurance contracts, as follows.

24–9D1 Innocence

Obviously, the parties are not *in pari delicto*, if one party, not being implicated in the illegality at all, is innocent. He may be able to enforce the contract or obtain restitution, with two qualifications. First, no remedy will be granted, however innocent the supplicant, if that is required by the public policy in issue. Second, his innocence must be justifiable. It is justifiable, if he is unaware of facts,[284] for example, that the vehicle lacked the required certificate,[285] but not, perhaps, if he knew or should have known the facts but was ignorant of the existence, content or true meaning of the relevant rule of law being infringed: *ignorantia juris haud excusat*.[286]

24–9D2 Relative Turpitude

The parties are not *in pari delicto*, if, although both are implicated in the illegality, the behaviour of one, the defendant, is significantly worse than that of the party seeking relief,[287] notably, where the defendant has been guilty of fraud,[288] duress or oppression against the plaintiff. An example would be the fraud of an agent of the insurer who, seeking greater commission, misrepresented facts about the company.

24–9D3 Class Protection

The parties are not *in pari delicto*, if one belongs to a class which the law seeks to protect from the other.[289] If an insurance contract should be vitiated by infringement of

---

283. *Harse* v *Pearl Life Assurance Co* [1904] 1 KB 559, 563 (CA—life). Treitel, p 437.

284. *Pearce* v *Brooks* (1866) LR 1 Exch 213; *Fielding & Platt Ltd* v *Najjar* [1969] 1 WLR 357 (CA). *Wolk* v *Benefit Association of Railway Employees*, 172 F Supp 62 (WD Pa, 1959—life); *Motel Manager Training School Inc* v *Merryfield*, 347 F 2d 27 (9 Cir, 1965).

285. *Wilson* v *Rankin* (1865) LR 1 QB 162, 164 *per* Erle CJ in the Exchequer Chamber (freight); see also *Dudgeon* v *Pembroke* (1874) LR 9 QB 581 (hull).

Further, premium has been recovered, when the insured paid premium in ignorance of the outbreak of war, which rendered performance illegal: *Oom* v *Bruce* (1810) 12 East 225 (cargo); *Hentig* v *Stanforth* (1816) 5 M & S 122 (cargo); or, if the war breaks out between the time of payment and the time that cover begins, as the consideration has totally failed: *Fibrosa* case [1943] AC 32.

286. For further discussion of this rule see above, 22-2B3 concerning misstatements of law. It will be seen that mistakes of law, as distinguished from misstatements of law, can be identified only by reference to the traditional approach found in *British Workman's & General Ins Co* v *Cunliffe* (1902) 18 TLR 425, 426 *per* Vaughan Williams LJ (CA—life).

287. *Saunders* v *Edwards* [1987] 2 All ER 651 (CA), approved in *Euro-Diam Ltd* v *Bathurst* [1990] 1 QB 1 (CA—goods AR), but doubted as regards actions to recover property in *Tinsley* v *Milligan* [1993] 3 All ER 65 (HL).

288. *Hughes* v *Liverpool Victoria Legal Friendly Sy* [1916] 2 KB 482 (life).

289. *Browning* v *Morris* (1778) 2 Cowp 790, 792 *per* Lord Mansfield; *Kiriri Cotton Co Ltd* v *Dewani* [1960] AC 192 (PC).

statute,[290] it is submitted that in many cases a remedy should be available to the "insured" under this exception.[291] More generally, equity may afford remedy in the case of "an advantage taken by a clever man over an ignorant one".[292]

In *Cunliffe*,[293] the plaintiff, a collier, took insurance on the life of his brother-in-law, induced by the fraudulent misstatement by the insurer's agent that such insurance was valid. The court allowed his action, because the statement had been made by a person skilled in insurance to one who was not. This decision was affirmed by the Court of Appeal.[294] The case might also have been decided under 24–9D1 or, in view of the agent's fraud, under 24–9D2.

24–9D4 Repudiation

A person implicated in the illegality may recover, if he repudiates the venture in time.[295] Repudiation is in time if it occurs before the illegal conduct has begun.[296] Although repudiation is sometimes called repentance, with the implication that the parties are not *in pari delicto*, a safer basis for the right of recovery in such cases is pragmatism: the existence of the right may encourage parties to pull back from an illegal design,[297] whether the motive be moral regeneration or fear of apprehension.

24–9D5 Independent and Untainted Cause of Action

If a policy was deposited as security for a debt, the debt repaid but the return of the policy refused, the policy can be recovered, even though the security was given in furtherance of some illegal purpose of transaction. This is "sometimes called the *Bowmaker* rule, under which a claimant's claim is enforceable when he has either to found his claim on an illegal transaction or plead its illegality in order to support his claim",[298] but not otherwise. The depositor rests his claim to recover the policy on his ownership of the document because he can establish his title "without pleading or leading evidence of his illegality".[299]

290. Above, 24–3.
291. So held as regard unlicensed extended warranty in *Re Cavalier Ins Co Ltd* [1989] 2 Lloyd's Rep 430.
292. *Harse v Pearl Life Assurance Co* [1904] 1 KB 559, 564 *per* Romer LJ (CA—life); this had been the view of the case taken by the court below—[1903] 2 KB 92—but the Court of Appeal took a different view of the facts. *Washington v Atlantic Life Ins Co*, 136 SW 2d 493 (Tenn, 1940—life); *Ross v Producers Mutual Ins Co*, 295 P 2d 339 (Utah, 1956—life).
293. *British Workman's & General Assurance Co Ltd v Cunliffe* (1902) 18 TLR 425, cited with approval in *Harse v Pearl Life Assurance co* [1904] 1 KB 559 (CA—life).
294. (1902) 18 TLR 502. The court was at pains to find that the misstatement was one of fact rather than law. *Cf* above, 22–2B3.
295. *Morck v Abel* (1802) 3 Bos & P 35, 39 *per* Chambre J (cargo); *Palyart v Leckie* (1817) 6 M & S 290, 293 *per* Lord Ellenborough CJ (cargo): the main reason given was that the insured had given no notice of renunciation to the insurer, until he started the action; a modern court might prefer the reason that he had lost the opportunity to carry out the illegal venture, and therefore that the reason for allowing recovery (to encourage second thoughts) did not arise: *Bigos v Bousted* [1951] 1 All ER 92.
296. The cases are inconsistent on this point: Merkin, 97 LQR 920 (1981).
297. Treitel, p 379. Rest Contracts 2d, section 199, provides for a *locus poenitentiac* if the person "did not engage in serious misconduct and . . . he withdraws from the transaction before the purpose has been achieved". His motive is irrelevant.
298. *Tinsley v Milligan* [1993] 4 All ER 65, 74 *per* Lord Goff (HL), with reference to *Bowmakers Ltd v Barnet Instruments Ltd* [1945] KB 65 (CA).
299. *Ibid* p 85 *per* Lord Browne-Wilkinson, with whom Lords Jauncey and Lowry agreed. *Cf* the view of the minority (Lords Keith and Goff) that in equity the rule against recovery is wider, because the court is sensitive to the fact that the hands of the claimant are not clean. The view of the majority (p 90) was that the fusion of law and equity resulted in the narrower *Bowmaker* rule.

A literal reading of these statements from *Tinsley* v *Milligan*[300] suggests that, when the issue is not recovery of the policy but its enforcement as insurance, fire insurance on buildings used for an illegal purpose will usually be enforced[301] but that insurance of liability amounting to a crime will not.[302] However, the question before the House of Lords in that case was a narrow one[303] of the recovery of an interest in land. With one exception, the insurance cases were not examined. In particular, there was no mention of the decision of the House in *Gardner* v *Moore*.[304] The exception was *Euro-Diam Ltd* v *Bathurst*[305] which was doubted by Lord Goff[306] in so far as it applied a so-called public conscience test. The reference is to the test applied in *Tinsley* by Nicholls LJ[307] and which was based in part on the balancing test of Diplock LJ for insurance in *Hardy*.[308] It should be noted that the Diplock test was also applied by the House in *Gardner* v *Moore*. In these circumstances, it is submitted that the decision in *Tinsley* does not bar the Diplock balancing approach to insurance claims which might be thought to serve an illegal purpose.

---

300. Above.
301. *Cf* above, 24–8.
302. *Cf* above, 24–7.
303. For example, p 83 *per* Lord Jauncey, who also underlined (p 82) that it was "important to distinguish between the enforcement of executory provisions under an illegal contract or other transaction and the enforcement of rights already acquired under the completed provisions of such a contract or transaction". See also Berg [1993] JBL 513, 516.
304. Above, 24–7A.
305. [1990] 1 QB 1 (CA).
306. p 77.
307. [1992] 2 All ER 391, 396 ff. (CA).
308. See above, 24–5A3.

CHAPTER 25

CAUSATION[1]

25-1 INTRODUCTION

The insured is allowed to recover from the insurer only that loss, which is caused by an event covered by the insurance contract. Subject to contrary terms in the contract, the cause, whether an event covered (peril) or an event excluded (exception), is the so-called proximate cause, "the dominant or effective or operative cause". What does this mean? The pragmatic Englishman prefers to avoid the philosophical maze,[2] to cut through to a practical solution. The proximate cause is found, said Lord Denning,[3] by the application of common sense.

Resort to "common sense", however, is sometimes a cloak for intuition, when data is lacking.[4] Law based on common sense has been viewed with suspicion: a remit for judicial discretion without external control[5] or for the application of personal values without the requirement of justification.[6] Or, as it was put by Sir John Vinelott,[7] "to abandon the search for guiding principles and to say that the decision in every case must rest on its own particular facts is the last refuge of the intellectually idle". Worse, perhaps, in the context of commerce, psychologists tell us that there is little or no consistency in what the ordinary man means by common sense[8] and Hart and Honoré tell us[8a] "that it is impossible to characterise any principles on which common sense pro-

---

1. Generally, see Hart and Honoré, *Causation in the Law* (2nd ed, 1985); this important book has attracted much comment, for example, Culp, 49 Law & Contemporary Problems 23 (1986). For less sympathetic comment see Dray, *ibid*, p 13; Howarth, 96 Yale LJ 1389 (1987).
    On causation in insurance law, see Muchlinski, *New Foundations*, p 102; Brown & Menezes, ch 10; Appleman, section 362 (PA); section 3083 (fire).
2. *Inman SS Ltd* v *Bischoff* (1882) 7 App Cas 670 *per* Lord Blackburn (freight); see also more recently in the United States, Parks, "Marine Insurance: Proximate Cause", 10 JMLC 519, 521 (1979): "no attempt has been made to work out any philosophical theory of cause and effect and . . . it is probably just as well for commerce that the attempt has not been made".
3. *Wayne Tank & Pump Co Ltd* v *Employers' Liability Assurance Corp Ltd* [1973] 2 Lloyd's Rep 237, 240 (CA—liability); in the same sense p 241 *per* Cairns LJ. Also, *Leyland Shipping Co Ltd* v *Norwich Union Fire Ins Sy Ltd* [1918] AC 350, 362 *per* Lord Dunedin (hull); *Athel Line Ltd* v *Liverpool & London War Risks Ins Assn Ltd* [1946] 1 KB 117, 122 *per* Lord Greene MR (CA—hull); *Miss Jay Jay* [1987] 1 Lloyd's Rep 32, 37 *per* Lawton LJ, 39 *per* Slade LJ (CA—yacht). Tarr p 216.
4. Fraser and Howarth, 4 *Legal Studies* 131, 138 (1984).
5. Howarth, 96 Yale LJ 1389, 1391 (1987) and references cited. See also Muchlinski, *New Foundations*, p 91.
6. Mullany (1992) 12 OJLS 431, 436.
7. 6 Co Law 31 (1985), speaking of section 75 of the Companies Act 1980.
8. Mullany p 436 and references cited.
8a Causation in the Law (2nd ed, 1985), p 26. See also *ibid*, pp. 91–92; and Lawson and Markesinis, *Tortious Liability for Unintentional Harm in the Common Law and the Civil Law*, Preface, xvi, condemning English law for "ignoring logic, symmetry and elegance for the sake of practical solutions."

ceeds". Impossible to characterise but not, it seems, to state in general terms. They continue:

"We must not think of a common sense notion as necessarily a matter of mere impression, or so intuitive that it cannot further be elucidated, at least in its application to standard cases, however vague a penumbra may surround it. Common sense is not a matter of inexplicable or arbitrary assertions, and the causal notions which it employs . . . can be shown to rest, at least in part, on stateable principles."

25–2 CAUSES AND CONDITIONS: RELEVANT EVENTS

In the scene of loss or damage, circumstances or conditions form the stage set into which new active forces, the causes, are interjected.[9] The difficulty is to separate causes from conditions, to draw up the short list of candidates for the title of proximate cause.

A "common sense" view of causation says[10] that "a cause is something which intrudes into a settled state of affairs or which interferes with ongoing processes"—a conclusion from common sense that is not disputed here: cf 25–1, above. This conclusion suggests[11] that causes are either abnormal events or voluntary human actions. For example,[12] if a severe storm occurs where such storms are rare, the storm is likely to be considered a cause and perhaps the cause of personal injury to a hillwalker. If, however, such storms are common in that place, a cause and perhaps the cause might be seen as the walker's decision to walk there at that time.

Nonetheless, this approach may not be appropriate for the search for the proximate cause of insurance loss. Generally, the relevance of one cause rather than another depends on the purpose of the inquiry.[13] If we seek a cause of loss because we do not understand what has happened, we may arrive at a cause of one kind; whereas, if we seek the cause of loss in order to attribute responsibility, as in the law of tort, we may arrive at a cause of quite a different kind. A distinguishing feature of the search for the proximate cause of insurance loss is that it is a search for the meaning of a contract, the contract of insurance.[14] Hence, rules of causation in other branches of the law, such as tort, are of limited assistance; and it is a key feature of the present search that the court rarely looks further for causes than the causes highlighted by the contract

9. Beale, 33 Harv L R 633, 643 (1920).
10. Dray, 49 Law and Contemporary Problems 13, 14 (1986).
11. Hart and Honoré, *Causation in the Law* (2nd ed, 1985), pp 32 ff.
12. Adapted from Dray, *loc cit*.
13. Culp, 49 Law and Contemporary Problems 23, 24 ff (1986).
14. In this sense Muchlinksi, *New Foundations*, p 83, citing *Leyland Shipping Co Ltd* v *Norwich Union Fire Ins Sy Ltd* [1918] AC 350, 369 *per* Lord Shaw (hull). See also *Becker, Gray & Co* v *London Assurance Corp* [1918] AC 101, 113–114 *per* Lord Sumner (cargo). *Consolidated-Bathurst Export Ltd* v *Mutual Boiler & Machinery Ins Co* [1980] 1 SCR 888 (accident, property damage).
Contrast the court that sees insurance as an instrument of economic efficiency: Abraham, pp 10 ff. This perspective will incline the judge to apply different rules of causation from those suggested here in the text: Culp, *loc cit*, pp 33 ff, especially p 35, with reference to the views of Calabresi on tort: "the causal decision maker would choose the factor (or factors) that, if altered, would have imposed the lowest social cost on society." This results in "causal minimalism", i.e., once there is a "but for" link between the various possible "causes" and loss, no further selection of the dominant or proximate cause need be made, for the role of the court is deterrence and the efficient distribution of cost; it may be doubted whether the courts have the training, inclination or information to undertake this role.

itself, the perils and the exceptions stated in the contract of insurance. That is the short list, ready drawn for the court.'

If, for example, cover is expressed to be in respect of loss caused by the careless operation of machinery and this occurs, *prima facie* there is cover, the machinery being no more than part of the stage set in which the cause (carelessness) occurs. If, however, the carelessness and loss would not have happened but for the (defective) state of the machinery, such defects become causes, when *expressly excepted*, and are, potentially, the proximate cause of loss.[15]

Again, if a yacht breaks up in moderate seas and the yacht was negligently designed or constructed, a tort inquiry is likely to point to the designer or constructor. But, when the question arose in the *Miss Jay Jay*[16] in connection with insurance against perils of the sea, the search for a proximate cause went no further back than the peril, the incursion of seawater. How far back the search goes depends on the events highlighted in the contract of insurance. If there are a number of possible causes, and if "one of these causes is insured against under the policy, and none of the others is expressly excluded from the policy, the insured will be entitled to recover".[17] If, as in *Miss Jay Jay*, "there were no relevant exclusions or warranties in the policy the fact that there may have been another proximate cause did not call for specific mention since proof of *a* peril which was within the policy was enough to entitle the plaintiffs [insured] to judgment".[18] If, on the other hand, "the policy had contained a relevant exception which related to loss caused by the unseaworthiness of the vessel, the plaintiffs' claim might well have been unsustainable".[19]

The characteristic emphasis on the contract of insurance and on party intention[20] affects not only the selection of potential causes but also proximity, that is, the degree of connection required between cause and loss. Insurers wish to know as accurately as possible the extent of the risk written.[21] Too loose a connection between peril and recoverable loss, it is said, would make underwriting difficult, except on terms that would drive away business; insurers want to write risks that are actuarial rather than entrepreneurial.[22] Consequently, the proximity required between cause and loss is

---

15. *Wayne Tank & Pump Co Ltd* v *Employers Liability Assurance Corp Ltd* [1974] QB 57 (CA—liability), discussed below, 25–6.

16. *Miss Jay Jay* [1987] 1 Lloyd's Rep 32 (CA—yacht).

17. Halsbury, Vol 25, para 181, cited with approval in *Miss Jay Jay* [1987] 1 Lloyd's Rep 32, 36 by Lawton LJ, p 40 by Slade LJ (CA—yacht). See also in this sense *Bell* v *Lothiansure Ltd* 1993 SLT 421 (Ct Sess —liability).

A similar approach is found in Australia: *Gold Coast Bakeries (Qld) Pty Ltd* v *Heat & Control Pty Ltd* [1992] 1 Qd R 162, 171 (liability); and in Canada: *Saskatchewan Wheat Pool* v *Royal Ins Co*; (1989) 64 DLR (4th) 135. Brown & Menezes, 10:2:9. Similarly, in the United States, if a collision leads necessarily to fire on a ship, the fire damage is recoverable under fire policy, unless collision damage is expressly excluded: *Howard Fire Ins Co* v *Norwich & New York Transportation Co*, 79 US 194; 20 L Ed 378, 379–380 *per* Strong J (1877—fire). In the same sense: *Northwest Agricultural Coop Assn* v *Continental Ins Co*, 769 P 2d 218, 220 (Or, 1989—fire). Bragg, 20 Forum 385, 387 (1984–5)

18. p 37 *per* Lawton LJ. In that case there was a design defect, but the policy exception was limited to defects which were the *sole* cause of loss, an exception which therefore was not relevant to what occurred.

19. p 40 *per* Slade LJ, referring to Arnould, No 776. One qualification is that in marine insurance, at least, wilful misconduct is treated as a relevant exception, whether expressly mentioned in the contract of insurance or not: *Samuel & Co Ltd* v *Dumas* [1924] AC 431 (hull). *Waters* v *Merchants' Louisville Ins Co*, 11 Pet 213 (1837—hull).

20. For example, *Becker, Gray & Co* v *London Assurance Corp* [1918] AC 101, 112 *per* Lord Sumner (cargo).

21. In this sense: Muchlinski, *New Foundations*, pp 81–82.

22. For discussion and criticism of this viewpoint, see Morris, "Enterprise Liability and the Actuarial Process—The Insignificance of Foresight", 70 Yale LJ 554 (1961).

close. The main rule, Rule (a),[23] limits the range of loss that is recoverable. Courts have responded with the *contra proferentem* rule of construction and produced Rule (e),[24] a rule for exceptions that is similarly narrow.

25–3 THE PROXIMATE CAUSE

In England the proximate cause is said to be the efficient or dominant cause.[25] A change of words does not necessarily achieve a change of rule. The words "'caused by' and 'arising from' do not give rise to difficulty. They are words which have always been construed as relating to the proximate cause".[26] Similarly, the "direct"[27] cause, the "dominant" cause,[28] the "effective" cause,[29] the "immediate" cause,[30] each is the proximate cause; and "the consequences of" and "the consequences on" an event are those proximately caused by the event.[31]

In the United States, at least three rules of causation are to be found. First, the general rule, superficially similar to that in England, is that the cause is the proximate cause[32] and cover depends on whether that cause is (a) covered, (b) excluded, or (c) neither expressly covered nor excluded. However, a distinction is sometimes made[33] according to whether the contract covers loss "directly caused" by a given peril or loss merely "caused" by a peril, the former requiring a closer connection and one more akin to that in English law.

Second, "New York courts give especially limited scope to the causation inquiry . . . cases establish a mechanical test of proximate causation for insurance

23. Below, 25–4.
24. Below, 25–5.
25. *Leyland Shipping Co Ltd* v *Norwich Union Fire Ins Sy Ltd* [1918] AC 350 (hull), applied in Canada in *Cooperative Fire & Casualty Co* v *Saindon* [1976] 1 SCR 735 (liability).
26. *Coxe* v *Employers' Liability Assurance Corp* [1916] 2 KB 629, 634 *per* Scrutton J. See also *Motor Union Ins Co Ltd* v *Boggan* (1924) 130 LT 588, 590 *per* Lord Birkenhead LC (motor: "arising during"); *Bell* v *Lothiansure Ltd* (Inner House of the Court of Session, 1 February 1991, unreported). *Canadian Bank of Commerce* v *London & Lancashire Guarantee & Accident Co* (1958) 14 DLR (2d) 623 (Ont—liability). *Cf Toll Bridge Authority* v *Aetna Ins Co*, 773 P 2d 906, 909–910 (Wash, 1989—liability): "'Arising out of' and 'proximate cause' describe two different concepts."
27. *Coxe* (above); *Oei* v *Foster* [1982] 2 Lloyd's Rep 170, 174 *per* Glidewell J (liability); *Miss Jay Jay*, [1987] 1 Lloyd's Rep 32, 37 *per* Lawton LJ, 39 *per* Slade LJ (CA—yacht). *Ford Motor Co of Canada Ltd* v *Prudential Assurance Co Ltd* (1958) 14 DLR (2d) 7 (Ont), affirmed [1959] SCR 539 (business interruption and property damage). *Lipshultz* v *General Ins Co*, 96 NW 2d 880, 883–884 (Minn, 1959—fire).
Cf "immediate cause": this has been interpreted as the last cause in time: *Sabella* v *Wisler*, 377 P 2d 889, 897 (Cal, 1962—homeowners' AR).
28. *Miss Jay Jay* [1987] 1 Lloyd's Rep 32, 37 *per* Lawton LJ (CA—yacht). Arnould, No 762, suggests that this is the most useful synonym.
29. *Miss Jay Jay*, p 37 *per* Lawton LJ.
30. *Shera* v *Ocean Accident & Guarantee Corp Ltd* (1900) 32 Ont R 411 (PA): the Divisional Court held that "immediate" was the language not of time but of causation.
31. Arnould, No 778.
32. United States cases applying such a rule are mentioned below in connection with English law; in particular, see 25–3.
33. For example, *Graff* v *Farmer's Mutual Home Ins Co*, 317 NW 2d 741 (Neb, 1982—windstorm). Direct cause is sometimes equated with the last cause in time, and distinguished from a tort rule of causation, which looks further back. See the New York cases in the next note; also *Bruener* v *Twin City Fire Ins Co*, 222 P 2d 833 (Wn, 1950—motor): collision was excluded; when a car skidded and collided, the court held that the damage was caused by the collision not the skidding. This rule is discussed, e.g., by Squires, 59 Washington L Rev 565 (1984), in the light of later cases more akin to the English cases: *Graham* v *PEMCO*, 656 P 2d 1077 (Wash 1983—homeowner's AR).

cases, a test that looks only to the causes nearest to the loss."[34] In so far as this test rules out excepted causes further back, it is said to be justified by interpretation *contra proferentem*.[35] Further, it is contended[36] that such a rule favours the insured, for the last direct physical cause can be easily determined, facilitating prompt disposition and payment of claims.

Third, California applies the concurrent causation rule, which looks to all potential proximate causes; if any one of them is not excepted, the loss is covered.[37] The rule is also found in some decisions in other states. For example, in *Braxton* v *United States Fire Ins Co*,[38] a man was shot by a drunken petrol station attendant. The station's insurer was liable, even though the policy excluded injury "arising out of the use of any firearm", because one cause of the loss was held to be negligent supervision of the attendant, which had not been excluded.

25-4 PROXIMITY: INEVITABLE LOSS

Rule (a): In England, the proximate cause is the event, whether peril or exception, which, in all the circumstances prevailing at the time of the event, led inevitably[39] to the kind of loss in question. Nothing in life, it may be said, is inevitable in an absolute sense; God may reach down and stop the train or the chain. However, the word "inevitable" is used here at the level of current human capacity. A cause is proximate if it "operated with reasonable certainty to occasion the loss".[40]

The judgments of the House of Lords in *Leyland Shipping Co Ltd* v *Norwich Union*

---

34. *Pan American World Airways Inc* v *Aetna Casualty & Surety Co*, 505 F 2d 989, 1006–1007 (2 Cir, 1974—aviation). See also *Bird* v *St Paul Fire & Marine Ins Co*, 224 NY 47 (1918—fire), in which fire led inevitably to explosion and the concussion damaged property insured; held that the loss was not caused by fire.

35. *Pan American* v *Aetna* (above), p 1007.

36. Squires, 59 Washington L Rev 565, 576 (1984).

37. *Sabella* v *Wisler*, 377 P 2d 889 (Cal, 1962—homeowners' AR); *State Farm Mutual Automobile Ins Co* v *Partridge*, 514 P 2d 123 (Cal, 1973—liability); *Safeco Ins Co* v *Guyton*, 692 F 2d 551 (9 Cir, 1981—homeowners' AR). Brewer, 59 Mich L Rev 1141 (1961); Bragg, "Concurrent Causation and the Art of Policy Drafting", 20 Forum 385 (1984–5); Cozens & Hardy, *ibid*, 222, 245; Katofsky, 20 Pacific LJ 783 (1989). The application of doctrine has been described as "trying to pick up a jellyfish by the corners": Knoll and Arthur, 26 Tort & Ins LJ 97 (1990); indeed, there is probably no single view of causation in California: Risley, 40 UCLA L Rev 1145, 1155 ff (1993).

38. 651 SW 2d 616 (Mo, 1983—liability); see further cases cited pp 619–620.

39. Generally in this sense MacGillivray (6th ed), No 1552, speaking of an "inevitable sequence"; *cf* the version in the 8th ed, No 1552: "a chain of events leading naturally and in the ordinary course to loss".

In the United States, the most common rule is that the proximate cause is "the one that necessarily sets the other causes in operation"—*Aetna Ins Co* v *Boon*, 95 US 117 (1877—fire), 24 L Ed 395, 398 *per* Strong J; loss must be the "natural and necessary consequence of the peril insured against"—*Peters* v *Warren Insurance Co*, 14 Pet 99, 109 *per* Strong J (1840—hull); if fire is the "inevitable consequence of the hostile seizure" the proximate cause is not the fire but the seizure: *Dole* v *New England Mutual Marine Ins Co*, 7 F Cas No 3,966 (D Mass, 1864—hull). See also *Lanasa Fruit SS & Importing Co* v *Universal Ins Co*, 302 US 556, 562 ff (1938—cargo), citing with approval *Reischer* v *Borwick* (below, 25–4A) and *Leyland* (below, 25–4(c)); and *Safeco Ins Co* v *Hirschmann*, 773 P 2d 413 (Wash, 1989—homeowner's): storm (peril) led to landslide (excluded) and to house destruction, which was held to be covered. Again, if peril x (fire) makes it "impossible to control or prevent" the effect of exception y (flood) the proximate cause is x: *Princess Garment Co* v *Fireman's Fund Ins Co*, 115 F 2d 380, 383 (6 Cir, 1940). Similar decisions in Canada are *Drumbolus* v *Home Ins Co* (1916) 37 OLR 465 (Ont—fire); *Filkow* v *Gore Mutual Ins Co*, 55 DLR (2d) 258 (Man, 1965—fire). *Cf Canada Rice Mills Ltd* v *Union Marine & General Ins Co Ltd* (below, 25–4C1).

40. *Ore* v *Aetna Life Ins Co*, 435 F 2d 957, 959 (6 Cir, 1970—life).

Fire Ins Sy Ltd[41] mark the end in England of an earlier rule that looked to the last cause in point of time; cases decided before *Leyland* should be treated with caution, unless cited with approval in that or later cases. Leading cases include the following:

(a) *Personal Accident*. In *Lawrence v Accidental Ins Co Ltd*,[42] the deceased had insurance against death in case of personal injury caused by accidental means, but excluding death from injury caused by fits. When standing on a platform at Waterloo station, the deceased had a fit, fell under a passing train and was killed. In a decision that some think kind to the claimant, the court held that the proximate cause was the impact with the train (peril) and not the fit (exception).[43] If a man has a fit on a station platform, it is not inevitable that he will fall under a train. If a man does fall under a train, injury is inevitable and death not unlikely.

(b) *Fire*. In *Louisiana Mutual Ins Co v Tweed*,[44] explosion caused fire on property in the neighbourhood of the property insured. The direction and intensity of the wind at the time was such that the fire spread to the property insured. The United States Supreme Court held that the loss was caused not by fire (peril) but by explosion (exception).

(c) *Hull*. In *Leyland*,[45] a ship was torpedoed during the First World War. She was towed to a quay in the outer harbour at Le Havre but, being low in the head, she could not be brought to safety in the inner harbour. It was the end of January and the weather, already rough, deteriorated and caused the ship to bump the quay. The port authorities, fearful that she would sink there and obstruct a quay needed for Red Cross embarkation, ordered the ship out. She was taken out to a breakwater, where the master hoped to continue to take off cargo but, buffeted by the heavy seas, she soon sank. The shipowners contended that this was a loss by perils of the sea (peril). The insurers argued that this loss was a consequence of hostilities (exception). The House of Lords, like the courts below, held that the proximate cause was the torpedo and, therefore, that the claim failed. Some loss by explosion and incoming seawater was the inevitable consequence of the torpedo.[46]

41. [1918] AC 350, (hull). A rule that looks to the last cause in time survives in parts of the United States; see above, 25–3.

42. (1881) 7 QBD 216. In *Commercial Casualty Ins Co v Stinson*, 111 F 2d 63 (6 Cir, 1940—PA), cert den 311 US 667, the decision was the same, when the insured fell while intoxicated.

43. See also *Winspear v Accident Ins Co Ltd* (1880) 6 QBD 42: the deceased was insured against "personal injury caused by accidental, external and visible means" having as its direct effect death within three months, but excluding such an accident if caused by disease. While fording a small river, the insured had an epileptic fit and was drowned. The court held that the loss was caused by the peril insured against. It is not clear how deep the water was (one judge says "shallow") or whether he was near the edge or whether other people were at hand. See also *Montoya v London Assurance Co* (1851) 20 L J Exch 254 (cargo); *Fooks v Smith* (1924) 132 LT 486 (cargo). Cf *Wadsworth v Canadian Railway Accident & Ins Co* (1914) 49 SCR 115 (PA) discussed below, 24–5.

44. 7 Wall 44 (1869—fire). Cf *Russell v German Fire Ins Co*, 111 NW 400 (Minn, 1907—fire): a fire on an adjoining building left a high wall unsupported, which collapsed seven days later in a wind which was strong but not unusual at that time of year, damaging the property of the insured. The court held that the loss was proximately caused by the fire. This decision is regarded as orthodox. An English court might well agree but on a different ground: it was not inevitable at the time of the fire that such loss would occur, however, the very definition of fire includes (as cause) associated collapse of masonry, whether or not collapse was inevitable: above, 17–2C2.

45. *Leyland Shipping Co Ltd v Norwich Union Fire Ins Sy Ltd* [1918] AC 350.

46. What was not inevitable was that the ship would sink: but given the time of year and the wartime conditions this was a "natural consequence" (p 362 *per* Lord Haldane) in the circumstances. Once there is (some) inevitable loss, the natural consequences, including an increase in the extent of the loss, are covered under Rule (b): below, 25–4A. See also *ibid*, p 355 *per* Lord Finlay; and discussion of the case by Clarke [1981] CLJ 284, 286.

(d) *Liability*. In *Bell* v *Lothiansure Ltd* the Inner House of the Court of Session[47] considered the liability of a professional indemnity insurer (the second defenders) in respect of the negligence of insurance brokers (the first defenders), who had induced and advised the claimant (and many others) to invest in a company which was practically insolvent. The issue was perceived to be whether the claimants' claim against the brokers for negligence, which was covered, was caused by the negligence of the brokers, as argued by the claimants, or by the insolvency of the company, which was expressly excluded, as argued by the insurers. The court concluded that it would not disturb the decison of the Lord Ordinary that the cause of the claim was the negligence of the brokers and not the insolvency of the company. But, given the pitfalls of litigation and the difficulty of proving negligence, the claim was not (as it is submitted the law requires) the inevitable consequence of the negligence of the insured. However, it is submitted that the court reached the right result albeit by asking, in part at least, the wrong question. The event insured, the peril, was not the negligence of the brokers but a claim in respect of negligence by the brokers: the insurer promised to "indemnify the Assured in respect of [for loss caused by]:—1A. Claims . . . for any negligent act, error, omission" and so on. The real question was whether the insured's loss was the inevitable consequence of the peril and the answer was clear. If there was a claim for negligence, in the particular circumstances of the case against the brokers, it was practically inevitable that the brokers would suffer some loss, if liability were established (and perhaps anyway).[47a] Hence the insurers were liable unless the peril (the claim for negligence) was itself proximately caused by an exception (the insolvency of the company) and thus subject to Rule (c).[48] In other words, of a kind used by Lord Cullen, was the claim (and consequent loss) proximately caused by i.e. the inevitable result of the insolvency of the company or, as the policy put it, was it a "claim or loss arising from [proximately caused by] . . . The insolvency of any company"? The court held not and, with respect and for the reasons mentioned above, this is right.

(e) *Perils of Nature*. In *Mork*,[49] a fire contract covered an explosion, which occurred in the oil-burning furnace of a private house when the occupants were absent. The court held that it also covered[50] "what inevitably must follow such an explosion if it occurs in sub-zero weather", namely loss caused by frozen water in pipes. Again, in *Lipshultz* v *General Ins Co*,[51] fire insurance also covered windstorms. A storm cut off

47. 1993 SLT 421 (Ct Sess—liability). See also *Gray* v *Barr* [1971] 2 QB 554. One issue was whether, when G shot B in a scuffle, this was "bodily injury caused by accident" (peril), that is to say, an accidental event leading inevitably to loss. Lord Denning MR first identified the act which caused the loss. In his view this was the threatening and deliberate approach of G holding a gun. He then turned to the question of proximate cause, and found that G's (non-accidental) conduct, the "dominant cause", was what led "inexorably" to the loss: pp 566–567. It is respectfully submitted that this approach to the issue of causation in general is right, although in PA cases causation is often dealt with differently (see above, 17–5A(b) and below, 25–9B), as exemplified by the other judges in the case. Salmon LJ (p 579) took such a broad view of the "accident" that he did not need to isolate any particular act as the cause of death. Phillimore LJ (p 586) on the other hand, refused to isolate particular acts in the sequence, preferring to assess the character, accidental or not, of the incident as a whole. *Gray* v *Barr* was followed in *Cooperative Fire & Casualty Co* v *Saindon* [1976] 1 SCR 735 (liability).
47a. See above, 17–4A.
48. Below 25–5.
49. *Mork* v *Eureka-Security Fire & Marine Ins Co*, 42 NW 2d 33 (Minn, 1950—fire).
50. p 36; see also cases cited p 37.
51. 96 NW 2d 880, 883–884 (Minn, 1959—fire).

electric power, with the result that the insured lost refrigerated stock. This loss was proximately caused by the windstorm.

25–4A The Extent of Loss

Rule (b): If under Rule (a) loss was the inevitable result of a peril, the full extent of that kind of loss will be recoverable, if the extent, although not inevitable at the time of the peril, was not unlikely to result[52] or, in other words, was a natural consequence in the circumstances.[53]

In *Reischer* v *Borwick*,[54] a ship was covered against collision with any object but there was no mention, whether as peril or as exception, of perils of the sea or water. On the Danube, she struck a "floating snag", was holed and began to sink. The master managed to plug the gaps and it seems possible that, with the use of the pumps and in calm water, she would not have sunk. However, perhaps on account of the extra pressure of water while the ship was being towed to be repaired, one of the plugs was forced out, it proved impossible to staunch the flow of water and the vessel was lost. It was held that the loss was covered. The initial damage to the hull and the engines through the immediate instrumentality of the snag was an inevitable result of the collision. The sinking and the full extent of actual loss was not then inevitable but, at the time, it was not unlikely that it would occur and, although parasitic on the earlier and inevitable damage, the full extent of loss was recoverable.

> "The rule must be applied with good sense, so as to give effect to (the parties') intentions . . . She was injured by a peril insured against, and liability to make good that injury has arisen and is not denied. The extent of that liability is the matter in dispute . . . If the ship had sunk and been lost under such circumstances as to render the inference unavoidable that the collision caused the loss, it is plain that the cost of repairing the (initial) damage would not be the (only) liability of the underwriters . . . it is difficult to see on what principle liability for loss occasioned by that injury can be excluded, *except upon the ordinary principles applicable to remoteness of damage*. The fact that some fresh cause arises, without which the injury would not have led to further loss, is, I think, in such a case far from conclusive. Assume that this ship would have floated in calm water notwithstanding the injury she had sustained by the collision, and suppose that, before such injury could be made good, the water became so rough as to get into her and sink her, by reason only of her injured condition, such loss would, in my opinion, be proximately, though not exclusively, caused by the collision."[55]

If a peril covered leads inevitably to a peril expressly excepted and on inevitably to loss, the loss is fully covered: below, 25–7. If, however, a peril excepted is no more than the probable result of the peril covered, the excepted peril is the proximate cause of all or part of the subsequent loss which, therefore, is not covered. So, the decision in *Reischer* would have been different, if the incursion of water (when the plug was forced out) had been expressly excepted.

This explains *Ford Motor Co of Canada Ltd* v *Prudential Assurance Ltd*.[56] Ford had property damage and business interruption cover against *inter alia* riot, but excepting loss "caused by cessation of work or . . . by change in temperature". Dismissal of

---

52. *Reischer* v *Borwick* [1894] 2 QB 548 (CA—hull). See also *Re Etherington and Lancashire & Yorkshire Accident Ins Co* [1909] 1 KB 591, 598–599 *per* Vaughan Williams LJ (CA—PA). *Accident Ins Co* v *Young* (1892) 20 SCR 280, 294 *per* Patterson J (PA).

53. *Leyland* (above), p 362 *per* Lord Haldane (emphasis added).

54. Above. The decision has survived the review of the law in *Leyland* (above, (c)): *Heskell* v *Continental Express Ltd* [1950] 1 All ER 1033, 1048 *per* Devlin J.

55. pp 550–551 *per* Lindley LJ (emphasis added).

56. (1958) 14 DLR (2d) 7 (CA Ont), affirmed [1959] SCR 539.

workers led to industrial action, including a riot, during which rioters cut off the electrical power in Ford's plant. As soon as the riot broke out or soon afterwards, there was a cessation of work and lack of maintenance, with damage immediately caused by a fall in temperature a day or two later. But for the exception in respect of cessation of work, it appears that the entire loss might have been recovered under Rule (a) and Rule (b): some loss was inevitable and, in all the circumstances, the rest of the loss was not unlikely to occur.[57] However, the courts inferred from the contract,[58] that the parties had had precisely this possibility in mind when they agreed the exception, and held that the temperature damage was not recoverable.[59]

25–4B Negligence of the Insured

Rule (c): The application of Rule (a) and Rule (b),[60] is not affected by the negligence of the insured or his servants, either in the face of the peril[61] or in the events leading up to the operation of the peril,[62] unless the negligence is itself the subject of a peril or exception.

For many years, it has been true to say with Lord Denman "that one of the objects of insurance against fire is to guard against the negligence of servants and others: and therefore the simple fact of negligence has never been held to constitute a defence."[63] Moreover, neither negligence nor anything else is a relevant cause of insurance loss, unless specified as a peril or as an exception by the contract.[64] So, unless the contract provides otherwise,[65] negligence in the face of the peril is treated as part of the peril insured.[66] As part of the peril,[67] the negligence is not in competition with the peril for the role of proximate cause. Thus, in *The Warilda*,[68] the House of Lords held that a collision was caused by the warlike operation, on which the ship was engaged, and not

---

57. It did not follow inevitably from the riot and loss of power, for the mild weather might have continued and other workers might have remained to carry out maintenance and prevention.

58. p 18; and, less explicitly, p 543.

59. At least some of the cessation of work loss was not consequent on the riot but concurrent with the riot and thus had an independent causal effect (p 16).

60. Above, 25–4 and 25–4A.

61. *Yorkshire Dale SS Co Ltd v Minister of War Transport* [1942] AC 691. *General Mutual Ins Co v Sherwood*, 14 How 351, 365 (1852—hull); *New York, New Haven & Hartford Railroad Co v Gray*, 240 F 2d 460 (2 Cir, 1957—cargo), cert den 353 US 966; *Lipshultz v General Ins Co*, 96 NW 2d 880, 886 (Minn, 1959—fire), above, 25–4(e).

62. *Shaw v Robberds* (1837) 6 Ad & El 75 (fire); *Dixon v Sadler* (1839) 5 M & W 405 (hull); *Harris v Poland* [1941] 1 KB 462 (fire); *Trinder Anderson & Co v Thames and Mersey Marine Ins Co* [1898] 2 QB 114 (CA—freight), applied in *Global Tankers Inc v Amercoat Europa NV* [1977] 1 Lloyd's Rep 61, 66 *per* Kerr J (guarantee). MIA, section 55(2)(*a*). See also above, 19–2A.

63. *Shaw v Robberds*, p. 84.

64. Above 25–2. *Yorkshire Dale Steamship Co v Minister of War Transport* [1942] AC 691, 711 *per* Lord Wright: "Negligence is not a cause for this purpose."

65. The definition of the peril insured is of prime importance, as this may exclude negligence by the insured.

66. The peril, however, must be a reality. The rule "does not touch losses incurred in a mistaken attempt to avoid a peril in fact non–existent": *Watson & Son Ltd v Firemen's Fund Ins Co* [1922] 2 KB 355, 359 *per* Rowlatt J (fire), applied in *Liverpool & London & Globe Ins Ltd v Canadian General Electric Co Ltd*, (1981) 123 DLR (3d) 513 (Sup Ct—fire); above 17–2C2. Unless specifically covered, negligence is parasitic: it is covered only if associated with some (other) peril.

67. Appleman, section 763A.

68. *A-G v Adelaide Steamship Co* [1923] AC 292; also *Canada Rice Mills Ltd v Union Marine and General Ins Co Ltd* [1941] AC 55, 69 *per* Lord Wright.

by the negligence in navigation immediately before the impact. "Negligence is a quality of the navigation as carried out . . . but is not a distinct operation in itself."[69]

Distinguish loss that is intended. In cases such as *The Warilda*, the act of navigation was an intentional act, which was negligent in view of its consequences. If, however, an act is not only intentional as an act but also as to its consequences, either because the consequences are the natural consequences of the act or because they are sufficiently probable that to disregard them can be characterised as reckless, the act is treated as a cause either as a matter of public policy or as a matter of construction of the contract. "For the purposes of the law of insurance, in the absence of an express agreement to the contrary, a policy should not be construed as covering the ordinary consequences of voluntary conduct of the assured."[70]

25–4C Reasonable Efforts to Avoid or Minimise Loss

Rule (d): The application of Rule (a)[71] and, possibly, Rule (b)[72] is not affected by the reasonable efforts of the insured or his servants to avoid the peril or to minimise its effects, unless those efforts are themselves the subject of a peril or an exception. As regards causation, such action is generally seen as part of the peril insured.[73] Rule (d) is believed to encourage the insured to take such action. If the insured, no longer in the face of the insured peril, fails to take steps (such as repair) to minimise loss and, for example, vulnerable insured property suffers further damage, the insured's failure may break the chain of causation between the initial insured peril and the further damage.[73a]

25–4C1 Damage Limitation

In *Canada Rice Mills Ltd* v *Union Marine and General Ins Co*,[74] the master of a ship, which was carrying rice in heavy seas, ordered the ventilators to the holds to be closed to prevent the incursion of sea-water. The lack of ventilation in the holds led to damage to the rice. The Privy Council held that this was a loss through perils of the sea and that it was covered by the respondents' insurance. Lord Wright said[75]:

"Where the weather conditions so require, the closing of the ventilators is not to be regarded as a separate or independent cause, interposed between the peril of the sea and the damage, but as

69. p 301 *per* Lord Sumner. This part of his judgment was approved by Lord Wright in *Yorkshire Dale* (above) p 711. See also *The St Oswald* [1917] 2 KB 769. *Cf* cases like *Becker, Gray & Co* v *London Assurance Corp* [1918] AC 101 (cargo); Clarke [1981] CLJ 284, 291.

70. *Ikerigi CN SA* v *Palmer* [1991] 1 Lloyd's Rep 400, 416 *per* Hobhouse J (freight), affirmed on other grounds: [1992] 2 Lloyd's Rep 566 (CA). See also above, 24–5B, and below, 25–8.

71. Above, 25–4.

72. Above, 25–4A.

73. Note, however, that the cost of prevention may not be insured loss: below, 28–8G. Note also that efforts of a third party may not be part of the peril insured: *Cleland Simpson Co* v *Firemen's Ins Co Newark*, 140 A 2d 41 (Pa, 1958—business interruption). *Cf Liverpool & London & Globe Ins Co Ltd* v *Canadian General Electric Co Ltd* (1981) 123 DLR (3d) 513 (Sup Ct—fire).

73a. See, for example, *EK Nominees Pty Ltd* v *Indemnity Corp Pty Ltd* (1990) 6 ANZ Ins Cases, no 61–008 (NSW—Flood). As to the insurer's liability to pay for the cost of mitigation, see below, 28–8G.

74. [1941] AC 55. *Glen Falls Ins Co* v *Spencer* (1956) 3 DLR (2d) 745 (NB—fire); *Liverpool & London & Globe Ins Co Ltd* v *Canadian General Electric Co Ltd* (1981) 123 DLR (3d) 513, 528 *per* Estey J (Sup Ct—fire). *Fruit Distributing Co* v *Boag*, 93 F Supp 431 (SD Ala, 1950—cargo). *Cf Princess Garment Co* v *Fireman's Fund Ins Co*, 115 F 2d 380, 383 (6 Cir, 1940).

75. p 70.

being such a mere matter of routine seamanship necessitated by the peril that the damage can be regarded as the direct result of the peril."

In another case, Lord Finlay LC,[76] talking of *Reischer*,[77] said that "the fact that ineffectual attempts had been made to stop the hole, and that the plug came out, did not introduce any new element of causation"; and, in *Stanley*,[78] describing the scope of standard fire cover, Kelly CB said:

"Any loss resulting from an apparently necessary and *bona fide* effort to put out a fire, whether it be by spoiling the goods by water, or throwing articles of furniture out of a window, or even the destroying of a neighbouring house by an explosion for the purposes of checking the progress of the flames, in a word, every loss that clearly and proximately results, whether directly or indirectly from the fire, is within the policy."

Compare *NOW* v *Dol*,[78a] in which the judge referred to section 78(4) of the MIA as containing "the fairly obvious proposition that if after the advent of an insured peril . . . the assured or his agent failed to act to avert or minimize loss in circumstances where any prudent uninsured would have done so, the chain of causation between the insured peril and the loss will be broken".

25-4C2 Avoiding the Peril

If, for example, a fire (peril) has begun to damage the property insured, the water damage incurred by soaking the property to prevent further fire is recoverable loss.[79] The decision is the same, if the entire damage to the property insured was water damage incurred to prevent loss from a fire nearby.[80] However, the fire must exist and be imminent.

Compare *Becker*, in which the master of a ship changed his route to avoid capture. The House of Lords held that consequent loss was not covered by insurance against restraint of princes.[81] That might be explained on the ground that capture was not inevitable.[82] It has also been explained as a case in which the peril did not yet exist (sufficiently) or operate (imminently).[83] Another explanation, however, is that the issue before the court in such cases is not one of causation but one of construction:

76. *Leyland* [1918] AC 350, 358.
77. Above, 25–4A.
78. *Stanley* v *The Western Ins Co* (1868) LR 3 Exch 71, 74. This statement was approved in *Symington & Co* v *Union Ins Sy of Canton Ltd* (1928) 139 LT 386 (CA—fire). On firefighting see above, 17–2F.
Also in this sense: *Northwest Transportation Co* v *Boston Marine Ins Co*, 41 F 793 (ED Mich, 1890—hull); *Goodyear Rubber & Supply Inc* v *Great American Ins Co*, 545 F 2d 95 (9 Cir, 1976—fire).
Cf Liverpool & London & Globe Ins Co Ltd v *Canadian General Electric Co Ltd* (1981) 123 DLR (3d) 513 (Sup Ct—fire).
78a. *National Oilwell (UK) Ltd* v *Davy Offshore Ltd* [1993] 2 Lloyd's Rep 582, 604, 618 *per* Colman J (builders' AR). The judge also thought the "proposition" applicable to negligent failure to avert the peril; however, this is doubtful (i) in view of section 55(2)(a) to which he refers and (ii) in view of the presumption that negligence is covered: above, 25–4B. "Theoretically, the cover for negligence and the duty [in s 78(4)] appear incompatible", unless the negligence itself is seen as (part of) a peril, to which *ex hypothesi*, and the duty restricted to the aftermath of the peril: O'May, *Marine Insurance* (London, 1993) p 142; see also pp 327 ff: the duty can only arise after an insured loss has occurred. The entire "proposition" is doubtful and, in any event, does not apply to cases not governed by the MIA and s 78(4).
79. Above, 25–4C1.
80. *Symington & Co* v *Union Ins Sy of Canton Ltd* (1928) 31 Ll L Rep 179 (CA—cargo). *Dube* v *Norwich Union Fire Ins Co* (1964) 42 DLR (2d) 489 (Ont—motor).
81. *Becker, Gray & Co* v *London Assurance Corp* [1918] AC 101, 113–114 *per* Lord Sumner (cargo).
82. For example, p 110 *per* Lord Sumner.
83. *Watson & Son Ltd* v *Fireman's Fund Ins Co* [1922] 2 KB 355, 359 *per* Rowlatt J (cargo). *Liverpool & London & Globe Ins Co Ltd* v *Canadian General Electric Co Ltd* (1981) 123 DLR (3d) 513 (Sup Ct—fire).

whether these parties, in particular, and the insurance market, in general, consider that that kind of loss is intended to be covered.[84]

25–5 SUCCESSIVE CONNECTED CAUSES:
EXCEPTION—PERIL—LOSS

Rule (e): A peril which is proximate under Rule (a)[85] is not the proximate cause, if it is preceded by an excepted cause which is also proximate under Rule (a).[86] If an excepted cause leads inevitably and in the same chain of causation to both peril and loss, the proximate cause is the excepted cause.

For example, in *Samuel* v *Dumas*,[87] scuttling (excepted) was immediately followed by the incursion of seawater (peril).[88] Viscount Finlay was in no doubt[89]: "It is obvious that the proximate cause . . . was . . . the act of scuttling. It was for the purpose of letting in the sea-water that the holes were made, and all that followed was the inevitable consequence of what had been done."

For an exception to operate in this way, the causal connection with the peril and hence with the loss must be close. In *Lawrence*,[90]: when the insured had a fit (exception) on a busy railway platform, it was not inevitable that he would fall on to the line, rather than away from it, when a train was passing and unable to avoid him. By contrast, in *Wadsworth*,[91] the insured went to an outside water-closet made of wood; he had a fit (exception), dropped his lantern and died of the burns sustained in the ensuing fire. The Supreme Court of Canada held that the proximate cause of the burns was the fit.[92]

---

84. For example, *Becker* (above) p 108 *per* Lord Dunedin; pp 114–115 *per* Lord Sumner. See further, on this case and on the apparent conflict with *British & Foreign Marine Ins Co Ltd* v *Sanday* [1916] 1 AC 650 (cargo), Muchlinski, *op cit*, pp 86 ff; and Arnould, Nos 766 ff.

85. Above, 25–4.

86. Obviously, the co-existence in time of an exception leading to a different peril is irrelevant—even an exception leading to the same peril at a later date. Thus, when the insured died as a result of a fall (covered), it was irrelevant that he was also suffering from a disease (excepted) which might or would have killed him some time later: *Hope's Trustees* v *Scottish Accident Ins*, 1896 3 SLT 252 (PA). See also *Marks* v *Commercial Travelers Mutual Accident Assn* (1956) 4 DLR (2d) 113 (Sup Ct—life).

87. [1924] AC 431. See also the exception to liability for damage to property caused by natural decay: Sassoon (1965) 28 MLR 180.

88. [1924] AC 431, 446 *per* Viscount Cave.

89. pp. 452–453. It was sufficient that some loss by perils of the sea was inevitable, and that the full loss (sinking) was not unlikely.

Cf cases, in which the exception was insufficiently proximate, e.g., *Winicofsky* v *Army & Navy Ltd* (1919) 88 LJKB 1111; *Marsden* v *City & County Assurance Co* (1865) LR 1 CP 232 (plate glass); *The Salem, Shell International Petroleum Co Ltd* v *Gibb* [1983] 1 Lloyd's Rep 342, 350 *per* Lord Roskill (HL—cargo); Clarke [1983] LMCLQ 576.

In *Soya GmbH* v *White* [1980] 1 Lloyd's Rep 491, 505 Lloyd J said that inherent vice (excepted) was the proximate cause, only if the soya beans were such that they *could* not withstand any normal voyage of that duration. In other words, in those circumstances, the state of the beans (exception) led inevitably to loss: the state of cargo has to be such that such loss "must occur" or is the "necessary result": *British & Foreign Marine Ins Co Ltd* v *Gaunt* [1920] 1 KB 903, 910, 911 *per* Lord Sterndale MR (CA—cargo); but *cf* Donaldson LJ in *Soya* v *White* [1982] 1 Lloyd's Rep 136, 150 (CA), a statement that was not essential to his judgment. This issue was left open in the House of Lords: [1983] 1 Lloyd's Rep 122, 124 *per* Lord Diplock. See further, above 17–3A1.

90. Above, 25–4(a).

91. *Wadsworth* v *Canadian Railway Accident & Ins Co* (1914) 49 SCR 115.

92. In which case, the amount payable under the policy was reduced to one-tenth.

25–6 CONCURRENT CAUSES

If there are two or more causes, operating concurrently, their effect depends on whether they cause loss independently of each other. In any case, they do not have to be exactly co-extensive in time: a later cause may join with a previous and continuing cause and hence be concurrent.[93]

25–6A Concurrent and Interdependent Causes

Rule (f): If the application of Rule (a)[94] gives two concurrent and proximate causes, one a peril and the other an exception, and if these causes are interdependent, in that neither would have caused loss without the other, the exception prevails.[95]

In *Wayne Tank*,[96] a fire started in equipment installed by the insured. The equipment was switched on to warm up overnight prior to a trial run and was left unattended, so that nobody noticed that piping, part of the equipment and wholly unsuitable for the use to which it was put, melted and ignited. But for that kind of piping (exception, cause A), there would have been no fire. But for the absence of proper supervision overnight (peril, cause B), the fire would not have occurred, as the melting would have been observed in time to prevent the fire.

According to Rule (a), there were two proximate causes. First, there was the unsuitable piping, cause A, a continuing state of affairs in circumstances, which included, it might be said,[97] an unsupervised trial at night (cause B) and which thus led inevitably to fire.[98] Second, there was the lack of supervision, cause B, a continuing state of affairs, in circumstances, which included unsuitable piping being warmed up at night (cause A) and thus led inevitably to a fire. So, there were two concurrent causes, one covered and the other excepted. They were independent, in that one did not lead to the other, but also interdependent, in that neither would have led to the fire but for the other.

Faced with two proximate causes, one a peril and the other an exception, the Court of Appeal held that the exception must prevail. This is because exceptions in contracts, including insurance contracts, define the extent of the obligations assumed.[99] As Lord Denning put it,[100] "Seeing that they have stipulated for freedom, the only

---

93. *Jason* v *British Traders' Ins Co Ltd* [1969] 1 Lloyd's Rep 281 (PA).

94. Above, 25–4.

95. *Samuel & Co Ltd* v *Dumas* [1924] AC 431, 467 *per* Lord Sumner (hull); *Wayne Tank & Pump Co Ltd* v *Employers' Liability Assurance Corp Ltd* [1974] QB 57 (CA—liability); *Miss Jay Jay* [1987] 1 Lloyd's Rep 32, 36 *per* Lawton LJ, 40 *per* Slade LJ (CA—yacht).

96. *Wayne Tank & Pump Co Ltd* v *Employers' Liability Assurance Corp Ltd* [1974] QB 57. See also *Taylor* v *Dunbar* (1869) LR 4 CP 206 (cargo); *Saqui & Lawrence* v *Stearns* [1911] 1 KB 426 (CA—burglary).

97. Strictly speaking, B was not a circumstance but a cause: see above, 25–2.

98. As a first ground of decision, the court preferred cause A as the single proximate cause of the fire. This view premises that cause A continued to operate until the fire had begun; however, the court did not satisfactorily explain why cause B, the lack of supervision, which also continued until the fire broke out, was not a cause competing with cause A at all. The better view (see above, 25–2), that there were two concurrent causes, was an alternative ground of the decision.

99. Above, 19–1A.

100. [1973] 2 Lloyd's Rep 237, 240, citing *inter alia Board of Trade* v *Hain SS Co Ltd* [1929] AC 534, 541 *per* Lord Sumner.

Cf tort cases with concurrent but dependent causes: *Hale* v *Hants & Dorset Motor Services Ltd* [1947] 2 All ER 628 (CA). The contractual basis of the insurance action justifies a different result: above, 25–2.

way of giving effect to it is by exempting them altogether." If the exception does not operate when it is proximate, it is deprived of contractual effect.

25–6B Concurrent and Independent Causes

Rule (ff): If the application of Rule (a)[101] gives two concurrent and proximate causes, one a peril and the other an exception, and if these causes are independent, in that each would have caused loss without the other, the insured may recover only that part of the entire loss attributable to the peril covered.

In *Ford Motor Co of Canada Ltd* v *Prudential Assurance Co Ltd*,[102] some loss to the plant was caused both by riot (peril) and cessation of work or change in temperature (exception), operating concurrently and independently; each would have produced part of the loss (property damage and business interruption) without the operation of the other. It was held by the Supreme Court of Canada that the insured could recover only in respect of the (small) part of the total loss which would have been caused by the riot alone.

Contrast *Guaranty National Ins Co* v *North Rivers Ins Co*,[103] in which the insured hospital was liable for the death of a psychiatric patient, who jumped from the window of her room on the fourth floor of the hospital. The relevant causes were (a) failure to maintain the window in a secure state (peril covered) and (b) failure to keep the patient under proper observation (exception). Each cause operating alone would have been a sufficient cause of the liability. The US federal court held that, under the law of Texas, the insurer was liable in full.

In English law, it is submitted, the decision would have been different. If a person fails to perform a contract as a result of (a) a cause for which he is liable and (b) a cause for which he is not liable, each cause being sufficient to cause non-performance, that person is not liable.[104] One reason for that is that it cannot be said, as English law requires,[105] that but for cause (a), the contract would have been performed. Similarly, it cannot be said of the *Guaranty* case that, but for the failure to maintain the window, the death and the resulting liability would not have occurred. In the eyes of English law, the hospital in that case failed to prove that the loss, the liability, was caused by the negligence covered by the insurance.

25–7 SUCCESSIVE CONNECTED CAUSES:

PERIL—EXCEPTION—LOSS

Rule (g): If an insured peril leads inevitably to an exception and then to loss, the proximate cause is the peril.

---

101. Above, 25–4.
102. 14 DLR (2d) 7 (Ont, 1958), affirmed [1959] SCR 539. More facts are found above, 25–4A. See also *Crutchfield, Coyle, Niagara Fire Ins Co* v *Muhle*, 208 F 2d 191 (8 Cir, 1953): while still under water from a flood six days earlier, a farm was struck by a cyclone. Loss was covered by insurance against windstorm, excepting water damage, and was recoverable only to the extent that it would have occurred without the presence of water.
103. 909 F 2d 132, 137 (5 Cir, 1990—liability).
104. *Avery* v *Bowden* (1855) E & B 714; (1856) 6 E & B 953; *The Simona* [1989] AC 788.
105. *Wilsher* v *Essex Area Health Authority* [1988] AC 1074.

In *Mardorf* v *Accident Ins Co*,[106] the insured came home from work and, while removing his socks, scratched his leg with his thumb nail. Six days later, a doctor pronounced that the wound was septic. On the tenth day septicaemia set in and, on the twentieth day, in spite of the efforts of his doctors, he died of septic pneumonia. His insurance covered death by accident but not death by disease.[107] Wright J held the insurers liable: once the germs had been introduced at the time of the scratch (accident), death was in the circumstances, including the current state of the art of medicine, inevitable.

25–8 WILFUL MISCONDUCT

Rule (h): Loss which is recoverable under Rules (a) to (g) will not be recoverable, if it was the result of unlawful misconduct by the insured or by those for whom he is responsible.

Difficulty turns on the connection required between misconduct and loss. The man convicted of assault in May will still recover under his motor insurance in June, as there is *prima facie* no causal connection between the assault and the motor loss. All agree that such a connection must exist, if recovery is to be refused. Agreement is absent, however, on (a) what that connection must be and (b) how bad the conduct must be before it affects the insurance. The answer to question (a) depends on the answer to question (b). It is not a question that can be answered by the rules suggested in this chapter. Indeed, no clear rule of causation can be found for such cases: the greater the strength of public policy against the conduct in question, the weaker the connection required between the wilful misconduct of the insured and loss, if recovery is to be refused by the court. However, there is no clear agreement about the wilful

---

106. [1903] 1 KB 584. See also *Re Etherington and Lancashire & Yorkshire Accident Ins Co* [1909] 1 KB 591 (CA—PA); *Fitton* v *Accidental Death Ins Co* (1864) 17 CB (NS) 122 (PA); *Abasand Oils Ltd* v *Boiler Inspection & Ins Co* (1949) 65 TLR 713, 716 *per* Lord Porter (PC—business interruption); *Boiler Inspection & Ins Co* v *Sherman-Williams Co Ltd* [1951] AC 319 (PC—accident). *Marks* v *Commercial Travelers Mutual Accident Assn* (1956) 4 DLR (2d) 113 (Sup Ct—life).

In the United States, if peril x (fire) makes it "impossible to control or prevent" the effect of exception y (flood) the proximate cause is x: *Princess Garment Co* v *Fireman's Fund Ins Co*, 115 F 2d 380, 383 (6 Cir, 1940). See also *Colonial Fire* v *Utica Mutual Ins Co*, 69 NYS 2d 623 (motor, 1947); *Tonkin* v *California Ins Co*, 62 NE 2d 215 (NY, 1945, fire); *Franklin Packaging Co* v *Californian Union Ins Co*, 408 A 2d 448 (NJ, 1979—fire); *Graham* v *PEMCO*, 656 P 2d 1077 (Wn, 1983—homeowners' AR).

Cf Smith v *Accident Ins Co* (1870) LR 5 Ex 302 (PA)—although the disease (exception) was the probable result of the wound (accident, peril), it was not the inevitable result, so the insurer was not liable. Also *Accident Ins Co* v *Young* (1892) 20 SCR 280, 294–295 (PA).

Cf also *Cory & Son* v *Burr* (1883) 8 App Cas 393: the barratry of the captain (peril) was smuggling, which gave rise to capture (exception) and so to loss, the expense of obtaining the ship's release. The capture would not have occurred at all but for the smuggling, so it was not a case for Rule (f) (above, 25–6A). The House of Lords held that the proximate cause of loss was the capture. *Prima facie*, this is a case like *Smith*, in which the peril (barratry) did not lead inevitably to capture (exception), so the exception prevails; but cf the view of Lord Blackburn (p 399), that the capture was "a direct and immediate consequence of the barratrous act of the captain". Another explanation of the case, which does not run against Rule (g), is that the question of causation was subsumed by the need to interpret and define the terms of cover: to give the exception any practical effect, it was necessary to define the peril as "barratry not giving rise to capture": in this sense Earl of Selborne LC (p 397), with whom Lord Fitzgerald concurred (p 404). On this basis the loss was not within the terms of cover.

107. The exception read "death caused by or arising wholly or in part from disease or other intervening cause, even although the disease or other intervening cause may either directly or otherwise be brought on or result from accident". In view of the last part of the exception, it is not clear that a court today would take the same view of the clause.

misconduct that will have this effect.[108] Consequently, although other branches of the law also have a rule, superficially similar, whereby, in the event of wilful misconduct, the guilty party loses some legal right or advantage,[109] analogy with those rules is probably unsafe.

25–9 THE FLEXIBLE CHAIN: BENDING THE RULES

The rules set out above (25–4 to 25–8) can be adapted or in some cases avoided by the draftsman or by the court.

25–9A Causes, Consecutive or Concurrent

As has been seen, the rules differ according to whether competing causes are consecutive or concurrent. So, the result of a case may turn on whether the court sees one of the causes as an event that occurred and finished before another competing cause came into operation,[110] or as continuing, concurrently with the later cause.[111] In many cases, both views of the facts are possible and the court has room to manoeuvre and outflank the peril or the exception, as desired. This is well illustrated by the next case.

In *Miss Jay Jay*,[112] after crossing the English Channel in moderate seas, a yacht was found to be damaged. A design defect made the yacht unseaworthy and this had produced loss of watertight integrity (peril) with consequent damage. *Prima facie* the loss was covered, unless, as argued by the insurers, the real cause was unseaworthiness. The Court of Appeal, affirming the decision of Mustill J, decided that the proximate cause of damage was the peril. It was essential to the decision, that unseaworthiness had not been expressly excepted.[113] If it had been excepted, there would have been two possibilities, and the decision might have been different, as follows.

One view of the facts was the Mustill chain[114]: "it is clearly established that a chain of causation running—(i) initial unseaworthiness; (ii) adverse weather; (iii) loss of watertight integrity of the vessel; (iv) damage to the subject-matter insured—is treated as a loss by perils of the sea". On this view of events, stage (i) was a single event, the creation of a defect in design and construction, which had occurred and finished before stage (ii).[115] On this view, the defect in design was not the proximate cause of loss, for it was not possible to say that it led inevitably to damage: the defect

---

108. See chapter 24, in particular, 24–5A2 and 24–5A3. Arnould, No 764.
109, For example, under certain carriage conventions, the carrier guilty of wilful misconduct or equivalent default loses the right to rely on certain defences or liability limits: the Warsaw Convention art 25 and the CMR Convention art 29. On these provisions, see Clarke, *International Carrige of Goods by Road: CMR* (2nd ed, 1991), ch 8.
110. And thus subject to Rule (e) (25–5) or Rule (g) (25–7).
111. And thus subject to Rule (f) (25–6).
112. *Lloyd Instruments Ltd* v *Northern Star Ins Co Ltd* [1985] 1 Lloyd's Rep 264, affirmed [1987] 1 Lloyd's Rep 32.
113. See above, 25–2.
114. [1985] 1 Lloyd's Rep 264, 271 *per* Mustill J, citing *Dudgeon* v *Pembroke* (1874) 9 QB 581, 595 *per* Blackburn J; (1877) 2 App Cas 284, 296 *per* Lord Penzance (hull); and *Frangos* v *Sun Ins Office Ltd* (1934) 49 Ll L Rep 354, 359 *per* Roche J (hull).
115. *Cf* cases such as *Jason* (below, 25–9C2) where one of the competing causes is latent illness, such as atheroma or cancer: it is harder to say that that has already "occurred" and harder to deny that its effects are continuing. But *cf* also epilepsy, in respect of which the relevant cause has been seen as a finite fit, an event which occurs and is finished soon after it begins: *Lawrence* (above, 24–4(a)).

might have been discovered and rectified before loss occurred. The only proximate cause was the action of the sea (peril).

A second view of the facts was the Lawton tandem. Stage (i) unseaworthiness was a continuing state of affairs, the operation of which had not finished, when the vessel was damaged by the sea. On this view, there were "two concurrent and effective causes of the loss. One was the unseaworthiness due to the design defects, the other the action of the adverse sea."[116] On this view, there were two proximate causes and, applying Rule (f) and *Wayne Tank*,[117] "if the policy had contained a relevant express exception [design defect or unseaworthiness] the plaintiffs' claim might well have been unsustainable".[118]

25–9B Stretching the Cause to Cover Weakness in the Chain

Any gap between cause and loss may be closed by expanding the definition and scope of the cause itself. Events prior to loss, which in isolation are too remote to be causes, may yet be part of a larger composite event which does cause loss.[119] This may be achieved by the draftsman [120] or, in a few instances, by the way that the courts have defined the insured event.[121]

25–9B1 Accident

An expanded notion of cause is sometimes found in personal accident cover. The event (accident) is looked at broadly and the effect is to overlay and shorten the chain of causation between the initial or initiating event and loss.[122] For example, the chain is initiated (at point 1) when insured driver A begins to overtake B, then finds that driver C has emerged from a side road to the right (point 2), but neither A nor C are able to control their vehicles (point 3) sufficiently to avoid collision (loss). At point 1, the loss is not inevitable but that does not matter. In PA cases, the main question is not whether loss is inevitable at point 1 or point 2 or even point 3, but whether at point 1 it is probable; only if it is not, is the entire sequence an accident and, in PA cases, the question of proximate cause is often forgotten. If it is addressed at all, it is enough that loss is inevitable when the cause (accident) is complete, at point 3.

In contrast, the courts have applied a restricted definition of the exception of inherent vice of goods: only if loss is the inevitable and thus proximate consequence of natural deterioration of the goods, is there an inherent vice at all. Inherent vice might have been defined as any natural deterioration and the question of causation then addressed, as usual, as a distinct question. However, inherent vice is defined as such deterioration of goods as will inevitably lead to loss (during the transit insured); thus,

116. [1987] 1 Lloyd's Rep 32, 35 *per* Lawton LJ.

117. p 40 *per* Slade LJ. See also Lawton LJ (p 37): "As there were no relevant exclusions or warranties in the policy the fact that there may have been another proximate cause did not call for specific mention since proof of a peril which was within the policy was enough to entitle the plaintiffs to judgment."

118. Above, 25–6A, a case cited with approval by Lawton LJ (p 36) and Slade LJ (p 40).

119. Arnould, No 763.

120. For example, fire cover might be extended to include all consequential or incidental loss, such as looting; see below, 25–9C1 and note 122.

121. See also "warlike operations": *Yorkshire Dale Steamship Co Ltd v Minister of War Transport* [1942] AC 691, discussed by Clarke [1981] CLJ 284, 294 ff; and "civil commotion", discussed in the footnotes to *Spinney's* case, below, 25–9C1.

122. See, for example, *Smith v Accident Ins Co* (1870) LR 5 Ex 302, 308 *per* Martin B (PA), discussing *Fitton v Accidental Death Ins Co* (1865) 17 CB (NS) 122 (PA).

the causal requirement is built in to the definition of inherent vice.[123] In the result, the general rules of causation[124] are observed but the approach is different and it does make the matter more confusing.

25–9C Particular Wording

As the "rules" of causation rest on the supposed intention of the parties to the contract, they can change them by appropriate wording.

25–9C1 The Proximate Cause Bypassed: Areas of Risk

(a) *"Occasioned by . . . "*. These words stretch the connection between cause and loss, thus increasing the power of the cause. For example, loss occasioned by civil commotion "means that there must be a civil commotion somewhere, and that the act [causing the loss] must be an act which is attributable to that commotion, but nothing more."[125] Loss is occasioned by a peril, if there is a sufficient connection, not in the sense of causation, but of coincidence—coincidence in time and space.

In *Spinney's (1948) Ltd* v *Royal Ins Co Ltd*[126] Mustill J observed, with reference to an exception of loss occasioned by civil commotion in Beirut, that the

"turbulence and collapse of public order attendant upon the civil commotion permitted and even encouraged the acts of looting and vandalism of which the incidents at Spinney's were examples. Unless rebutted, this would in my view be sufficient to establish that the loss was occasioned indirectly . . . [127] by, through or in consequence of the civil commotion."

Again, in *Cooper* v *General Accident Fire & Life Assurance Co*,[128] the insurer pleaded an exception of "loss or damage occasioned through Riot or Civil Commotion occurring within the land limits of Ireland". The subject of the claim was a car, which was taken one evening from the insured's garage in Cork by two (possibly more) persons, who threatened the insured, when he tried to intervene. The House of Lords held that the exception applied. The act of theft itself was neither riot nor civil com-

---

123. For example, *The Barcore* [1896] P 294, 297 *per* Gorell Barnes J; *Albacora SRL* v *Westcott & Laurance Line Ltd* [1966] 2 Lloyd's Rep 53, 59 *per* Lord Reid, 62 *per* Lord Pearce. *Cf Soya* v *White* [1980] 1 Lloyd's Rep 491, 505 *per* Lloyd J (cargo); [1983] 1 Lloyd's Rep 122, 124 *per* Lord Diplock (HL). See further, above 17–3A1.

124. Above, 25–4.

125. *Cooper* v *General Accident Fire & Life Assurance Co* (1923) 128 LT 481. *Cf Coxe* v *Employers' Liability Assurance Corp* [1916] 2 KB 629, 634 *per* Scrutton J, that the word "arising" did not change the basic rule (24–5A). However, later cases suggest that it may allow a more tenuous connection: "arising during": *Motor Union Ins Co Ltd* v *Boggan* (1924) 130 LT 588, 590 *per* Lord Birkenhead LC (HL—motor); or "arising out of the use of": *Dickinson* v *Motor Vehicle Ins Trust* (1987) 61 ALJR 553 (HCA—motor). *Cf* also *Storrie* v *Newman* (1982) 139 DLR (3d) 482 (BC—motor).

126. [1980] 1 Lloyd's Rep 406, 442 (fire).

127. The words omitted are "(or directly by)", not easy to reconcile with Rule (a) (above, 25–4), except in the light of the judge's view (p 442) that he "would if necessary have been prepared to hold that the events at [the property insured] were themselves part of a continuous state of civil commotion". This view may be seen as an illustration of 25–9B. The main ground in *Spinney's* was that the causal link between cause (exception of civil commotion) and loss was stretched by the wording "occasioned by". But the judge's view (at p 442) is that it is not the link but the meaning of the cause that is given an expanded definition, so that civil commotion includes incidental events, such as looting, that experience shows to be more likely to occur at the time and area of commotion.

128. (1923) 128 LT 481.

motion,[129] but this did not matter, if there were some connection with such events. There was civil commotion in Cork at that time, and it was probable that the men took the car for some purpose connected with the civil commotion.[130] The loss of the car was not proximately caused by the civil commotion, for it was not inevitable that that car would be taken as a result of the commotion.[131] The House might have construed "occasioned by" as "directly or proximately caused by". The House did not, partly on construction of the words and partly in awareness of the difficulties that face insurers assessing risk. Lord Atkinson said[132]: "it would be really absurd to hold that you must have some civil commotion at the very place where the theft is committed, no matter whether the civil commotion is for the purpose for which theft was committed or to serve the civil commotion." Insurers know that most claims of this kind are associated with civil commotion and that a proximate causal link is hard to prove.

(b) *"Directly or indirectly caused by . . . "*. The direct cause has been held to mean the proximate cause.[133] By implication, "indirectly caused" refers to something less proximate but, it seems, something more than a mere "but for" cause.[134]

In *Oei* v *Foster*,[135] public liability cover excepted "damage arising directly or indirectly from . . . ownership or occupation of any land or building". The insured's wife left some fat heating on an electric cooker in a borrowed house, while she went out; the fat ignited and caused fire damage in the house. Glidewell J held that the fire was not the proximate result of occupation. "The proximate cause was [her] action in turning on the heat on the cooker and then failing to turn it off when she went out to take the daily help home." Indeed, fire is not the inevitable result of occupation of a building; it is not even a reasonably foreseeable result within anything but a fairly long period of time. Nonetheless, the judge held that the damage arose "indirectly" from occupation.

In *Spinney's*,[136] shops in Beirut were covered against damage by riot unless "in consequence directly or indirectly of . . . civil commotion". As to causation, Mustill J said[137] that the commotion "permitted and even encouraged" looting and that this was enough for the exception to apply.

In such cases, the exception applies, if it is a normal or usual incident of the immediate or direct cause of loss. For example, looting[138] and theft[139] are normal incidents of civil commotion; (careless) cooking is a normal incident of house occupation[140]; and guard duty in difficult or dangerous circumstances is a normal incident of war.[141]

The insurer wants his contract to reflect his categories of risk. The direct cause is an

---

129. See above, 19–3C and 19–3D.
130. (1923) 128 LT 481, 483 *per* Lord Cave, LC; p 484 *per* Lord Finlay; p 485 *per* Lord Atkinson.
131. *Cf* note 122 above.
132. p 485.
133. Above, 25–3.
134. *Spinney's (1948) Ltd* v *Royal Ins Co Ltd* [1980] 1 Lloyd's Rep 406, 441 *per* Mustill J (fire); *Coxe* v *Employers' Liability Assurance Corp* [1916] 2 KB 629, 633 *per* Scrutton J (life).
135. [1982] 2 Lloyd's Rep 170. See also *Marcel Beller Ltd* v *Hayden* [1978] 1 Lloyd's Rep 472.
136. *Spinney's (1948) Ltd* v *Royal Ins Co Ltd* [1980] 1 Lloyd's Rep 406 (fire).
137. p 442 quoted above, 25–9C1(a).
138. *Spinney's* (above).
139. *Cooper* v *General Accident Fire & Life Assurance Co* (1923) 128 LT 481.
140. *Oei* v *Foster*, p 176; "cooking meals is a necessary, indeed, inevitable incident of the . . . occupation of the house".
141. *Coxe* v *Employers' Liability Assurance Corp* [1916] 2 KB 629, 634 *per* Scrutton J (life): "he was placed in a position of special danger—namely, he had to be about the railway line performing his military duties at night with the lights turned down, in consequence of war".

"incident" of the indirect (excepted) cause, if it brings the loss within the zone of risk which, according to the insurer's classification of risks, was not one intended to be covered. The real task may be to find that intention and then, in the case of an exception to cover, to answer the further question, whether that intention has been made sufficiently clear to the insured.

For example, once street violence has reached the level of civil commotion, the insurer's statistics show that property damage rises to such a degree, that he should not accept the risk at all or not without a higher premium. From his point of view a causal link in a particular case between civil commotion and loss is irrelevant; what matters is the statistical connection and that, as regards the particular loss, the insurance risk has moved from one category to another. For him, it is enough that loss is related in time and space to civil commotion; that it is within the area of risk categorised as civil commotion. As regards the contract, the insurer's intention can be achieved either by stretching the causal link between exception and loss, or, better perhaps, expanding the definition of the exception.[142]

25–9C2   The Proximate Cause Restricted: Sole Cause

To avoid doubt or difficulty arising from concurrent causes, a technique used by some draftsmen is to require that the peril or exception be the sole or independent cause of loss.

In *Jason* v *British Traders' Ins Co Ltd*,[143] the policy covered accidents and excepted "death, injury or disablement directly or indirectly caused by or arising or resulting from or traceable to . . . any physical defect or infirmity which existed prior to the accident". As the result of a car accident, the insured suffered a coronary thrombosis, which would not have occurred if he had not been suffering at the time of the accident and unknown to him from an arterial disease, atheroma. Fisher J concluded that there were two interdependent and concurrent causes. Given the state of the arteries it was inevitable that the accident would cause this man a thrombosis; and given the shock of the accident it was inevitable that the state of the arteries would cause a thrombosis. As one cause (atheroma) was excepted, the loss was not covered (Rule (f)).[144] But, in view of the wording of the contract as interpreted by the court, there could be no possible doubt. As another cause of the thrombosis was the atheroma, the accident was not "independently of all other causes the *exclusive* . . . cause of the disablement".[145]

These clauses can severely restrict cover. No cause operates in total isolation and there will always be the temptation to argue that it was not therefore exclusive. At the very least, that argument should be tempered by the distinction between causes and conditions (above, 25–2). "Other causes", surely, as a normal matter of construction *contra proferentem*, means not *any* other possible cause (conditions) but only the

---

142. See, for example, footnote discussion of civil commotion, above, 25–9C1(a).

143. [1969] 1 Lloyd's Rep 281. *Cf Preston* v *Aetna Life Ins Co*, 174 F 2d 10 (7 Cir, 1949—PA), cert den 338 US 829; *Continental Casualty Co* v *Jackson*, 400 F 2d 285 (8 Cir, 1968—PA).

144. Above, 25–6A.

145. Italics supplied. See also *Re Scarr and The General Accident Assurance Corp Ltd* [1905] 1 KB 387 (PA), which might be explained on this ground but, in that case, the court defined accident in such broad terms that the issue of causation was diminished. *Cf* Arnould, No 362; MacGillivray, No 1800 and No 1803.

In Canada see *Marks* v *Commercial Travelers' Mutual Accident Assn* (1956) 4 DLR (2d) 113 (Sup Ct—life). Brown & Menezes, 10:2:9.

causes specified in the contract as (excepted) causes.[146] Thus, a latent condition of ill-ness which is activated by an external accident may not be viewed as a cause at all, unless expressly excepted.[147] Likewise, in property insurance, the court may take the view, that "the latent defect was not an efficient cause, but merely an inert condition contributing to the final result".[148]

146. *Fidelity & Casualty Co* v *Mitchell* [1917] AC 592, 596 *per* Lord Dunedin (PC—PA). The other cause must itself be potential proximate cause: *Voisin* v *Royal Ins Co* (1988) 53 DLR (4th) 299, 305 (Ont-PA).
147. *Mitchell* (above). *Bankers Life & Casualty Co* v *Crenshaw*, 483 So 2d 254 (Miss, 1985—PIII).
148. *Dickson* v *United States Fidelity & Guarantee Co*, 466 P 2d 515, 520 (Wash, 1970—AR).

CHAPTER 26

CLAIMS PROCEDURE

26-1 INTRODUCTION

Conditions of the insurance contract govern claims procedure. Procedural conditions are "machinery"[1] to make the contract work as intended. The principal conditions, discussed in this chapter, are terms governing notice of loss, particulars and proof of loss, and arbitration clauses.

26-2 NOTICE OF LOSS

26-2A The Basis of the Duty

Most contracts require and regulate notice of loss to the insurer.[2] There is disagreement about whether, in the absence of such a requirement, the claimant must take any special steps to notify the insurer of loss. In practice, of course, he must do so, if he wants payment but, if there is a legal duty to do so, the law may also govern the speed and particularity of notice.

On one view,[3] there is no legal obligation to give notice and a term about notice cannot be implied, because a term is not necessary to give the contract of insurance business efficacy[4] and because it is easy for the insurer to stipulate for notice, if he wants it.[5] However, courts do imply terms, even though many of them might easily have been stipulated.[6] Business efficacy is an elusive concept. Whereas business efficacy must surely require that, if there is to be payment, the claim must be notified and particularised,[7] what is less obvious is that it must be done in a time that is reasonable from the insurer's point of view. A further argument against the implication of a duty

---

1. *Re Bradley* [1912] 1 KB 415, 432 *per* Farwell LJ (CA—employers' liability). Other contracts too have "cogwheels in the machinery"—*The Julia* (1949) 82 Ll L Rep 270, 284 *per* Lord Simonds, 290 *per* Lord Mac-Dermott (HL)
2. In Canada, there is a statutory requirement of notice for fire, accident, health, motor and liability insurance: Brown & Menezes, ch 11. For law in the USA, see Appleman, sections 1391 ff, 3481 ff, 4731 ff.
3. MacGillivray, No 1585.
4. Or to fill a gap, as is necessary to the operation of "held covered" clauses: *The Litsion Pride* [1985] 1 Lloyd's Rep 437, 469 *per* Hirst J (hull). Cf *Nilsen* v *Mutual Marine Office Inc*, 428 F Supp 1375 (D Mass, 1977—hull): the primary policy contained a notice clause but the excess of loss policy did not; the court declined to imply a notice term in the latter, given that the primary insurer would investigate loss and its report become available to the excess insurer.
5. *Nilsen* v *Mutual Marine Office Inc*, 428 F Supp 1375, 1379 (D Mass, 1977—hull).
6. This is implicit in the "officious bystander test", used by courts to test whether a term should be implied: *Shirlaw* v *Southern Foundries (1926) Ltd* [1939] 2 KB 206, 227–228 *per* Mackinnon LJ (CA), affirmed [1940] AC 701
7. In this sense: *Olin Corp* v *INA* 743 F Supp 1044, 1051 (SDNY, 1990—liability).

677

arises from the premise that the insurer is obliged to pay the instant that the loss occurs and, therefore, before he has notice of it. From this premise, it must be conceded, that notice is hardly necessary in law, however, the premise is controversial: below, 30–2.

An alternative view is that a duty of notice exists as an aspect of the duty of good faith.[8] Against this view, it has been argued[9] that the duty of good faith arises only when the contract is made or renewed. However, in *The Litsion Pride*[10] it was held that the duty of good faith continued during the insurance period; and that the duty, together with "commercial good sense", obliged the insured to give the insurer "relevant information". Much of the relevant information in that case concerned a war risk extension, a situation analogous to that when the insurer makes or renews an insurance contract. Nonetheless, there are clear statements,[11] that the duty of good faith runs throughout the insurance period. The effect is that the insured must disclose relevant information not only when the contract is made or renewed but also whenever the insurer has to take a decision, which cannot be taken properly without information from the insured. This occurs not only when the insured invokes a held-covered clause,[12] or when the contract entitles the insurer to charge an additional premium[13]; but also when the insured gives notice of loss. When the contract is made, the duty of disclosure is strict.[14] It is not clear that the same strictness will be shown at later moments of truth.[15]

26–2B The Form of Notice

Notice must be in the form required by the contract, for example, in writing.[16] If no form is stipulated, it may be oral;[17] all that matters is that the claimant's notice has the content required.

The content required depends on the context. A request for arbitration, for example, might amount to a "notice" but not to a "notice of claim arising through any accident or disease covered under the . . . policy".[18] Generally, it is sufficient that the contents serve the purpose of notice, without having to be couched in technical terms[19] or, perhaps, even being complete.

8. Ivamy, p 421. For discussion of cases in the USA in this sense, see Thomas, 41 Duke LJ 1548, 1589 ff. (1992).
9. MacGillivray, No 1585.
10. *Black King Shipping Corp* v *Massie* [1985] 1 Lloyd's Rep 437, 512 *per* Hirst J (hull).
11. Below, 27–1.
12. *Overseas Commodities Ltd* v *Style* [1958] 1 Lloyd's Rep 546 (cargo); *Liberian Ins Agency Inc* v *Mosse* [1977] 2 Lloyd's Rep 560 (cargo).
13. *The Litsion Pride* [1985] 1 Lloyd's Rep 437 (hull).
14. Above, 23–5.
15. In this sense, *The Litsion Pride* (above) p 512; Hirst J spoke of a "remarkable dearth of authority, which no doubt stems from the fact that in the vast majority of cases this matter is dealt with in the express conditions of the policy": ibid.
16. *Cawley* v *National Employers' Accident & General Assurance Assn Ltd* (1885) 1 TLR 255 (PA); *Brook* v *Trafalgar Ins Co* (1946) 79 Ll L Rep 365 (CA—motor).
17. *Re Solvency Mutual Guarantee Sy* (1862) 31 LJCh 625 (credit). *Gill* v *Yorkshire* (1913) 24 WLR 389, 396 (Man—livestock).
18. *Wilkinson* v *Car & General Ins Corp Ltd* (1914) 110 LT 468 (CA—workmen's compensation).
19. In *Boyle* v *Yorkshire Ins Co Ltd* [1925] 2 DLR 596, 598, a car was covered against theft but the Supreme Court of Ontario rejected the contention, that the claimant's declaration should have sworn that the taking of the car constituted theft, because the "ordinary man is not sufficiently versed in the technicalities of the law properly to swear to the nature of the offence". See also *Duggan* v *Travelers Indemnity Co*, 383 F 2d 871 (1 Cir, 1967—liability).

In *Duggan* v *Travelers Indemnity Co*,[20] the claimant contracted liability policy A and, later, increased the cover with the same insurer under policy B. The subsequent claim mentioned policy A but not policy B. The United States Federal Court reversed the decision of the lower court, that the notice of claim was effective under policy A but not policy B, saying that[21]

"once a notice of claim is filed, is it too much to ask that an insurer have a reasonable filing system, that its employees check the files for more than one policy covering the same insured for the same risk, and that, if questions arise over coverage, it surface them . . . ? We think not. And we are confident that contemporary office systems and management are up to the task."

26–2C The Giver

Notice must be given by the claimant or by a person acting on his behalf,[22] for these reasons.[23] First, the insured may prefer to retain a "no claim bonus" and carry a particular loss himself.[24] Second, it would put an unreasonable burden and expense on the insurer, if he had to react to every information suggesting a loss, whatever the source. Nonetheless, notice is valid if it comes from a third party, if the source is reliable[25] and if it is clear from the nature of the case that a claim by the insured is likely.[26]

26–2D The Recipient

It is in the nature of notice that it should be actually brought to the attention of the proper recipient,[27] although there is a case for saying that it is enough to put it into the post.[28] As to the destination, if the contract requires that notice be sent to the insurer

---

20. 383 F 2d 871 (1 Cir, 1967).

21. p 874. Policy B had been contracted shortly before the occurrence, and was not in the hands of the claimant; it was possible that the claimant expected not a new policy but an extension of policy A.

22. *Shiells* v *Scottish Assurance Corp Ltd* (1889) 16 R 1014, 1020 (Ct Sess—livestock); *Davies* v *National Fire & Marine Ins Co* [1891] AC 485, 490 *per* Lord Hobhouse (PC—fire); *The Vainqueur José* [1979] 1 Lloyd's Rep 557, 564–565 *per* Mocatta J (P & I). *Yale* v *National Indemnity Co*, 664 F 2d 406 (4 Cir, 1981—liability).

23. *The Vainqueur José* (above) p 565.

24. This reason does not, of course, apply to information required of the insured after he has initiated a claim: *Barratt* v *Davies* [1966] 2 Lloyd's Rep 1 (CA—motor), below, 26–2E.

25. For example, the police: *Barratt* v *Davies* (above); or "any person involved"—*Republic Mutual Ins Co* v *State Farm Mutual Automobile Ins Co*, 413 F Supp 649, 653 (SD W Va, 1976—motor), such as the third party victim: *Carter* v *Aetna Casualty & Surety Co*, 473 F 2d 1071, 1076 (8 Cir, 1973—motor).

26. For example, the loss of a ship reported at Lloyd's: *Abel* v *Potts* (1800) 3 Esp 242; notice from a victim: *Elmuccio* v *Allstate Ins Co*, 540 NYS 2d 465, 467 (1989—liability). See also *Hassett* v *Legal & General Assurance Sy Ltd* (1939) 63 Ll L Rep 278, 283 *per* Atkinson J (liability).

Cf Reeves v *State Farm Fire & Casualty Co*, 539 So 2d 252 (Ala, 1989—liability): the insurer's agent cut out the newspaper report that the insured had a shot and killed someone but, it was held, although the agent was aware that the killer was a client, the report did not amount to notice of a liability claim.

27. *Holwell Securities Ltd* v *Hughes* [1974] 1 All ER 161 (CA).

28. In *Milinkowich* v *Canadian Mercantile Ins Co* (1960) 25 DLR (2d) 481 (fire) the Supreme Court of Canada held that it was enough that the claimant prove that the notice was posted in good time, without having to prove actual receipt. The decision was based on the English rule (in *Household Fire Ins Co* v *Grant* (1879) 4 Ex D 216) about postal acceptance of offers to contract. While the main reason for *Grant*—implicit assumption of risk by the recipient offeror—does not apply to notices, the subsidiary reason is relevant: it is unreasonable to require the claimant to prove actual receipt at a distant office. The *Milinkowich* rule is also found in the USA: *General Motors Acceptance Corp* v *American Ins Co*, 50 F 2d 803 (5 Cir, 1931—fire); *Universal Underwriters Ins Co* v *Patriot Ambulette Inc*, 539 NYS 2d 981 (1989—motor); and, in respect of a requirement to "furnish" proofs of loss: *Ball* v *Allstate Ins Co*, 611 NE 2d 750 (NY, 1993—theft). Appleman, section 4736.

at a particular place, such as the head office of the insurance company, that requirement must be observed.[29]

The argument, that a local agent has authority to waive such a requirement, has been described[30] as "ridiculous". Sometimes, however, a local agent[31] of the insurer has actual or apparent[32] authority to receive such notice. Moreover, even if receipt at head office is required, if the local agent is authorised to transmit (but not formally receive) notice, it is enough to give notice to that agent for transmission to head office,[33] provided that it is given to the agent in time for it to reach head office in the normal course of business within the contract notice period.[34] The "*prima facie* inference in such a case is that the responsible agent does what duty to his principal may seem to require".[35] If A holds B out as a proper channel of communication, it is A who bears the risk that the channel does not work as it should. If, however, the local agent is not held out as a channel of communication, then to give notice to him for transmission is not enough[36]; but, if in fact he transmits it to head office in time, it is effective, the local agent having acted as the agent of the sender.[37] In practice, there is a strong presumption that, at the very least, the agent is an agent for transmission of notice.

---

29. *Cawley* v *National Employers' Accident & General Assurance Assn Ltd* (1885) 1 TLR 255 (PA); *Roche* v *Roberts* (1921) 9 Ll L Rep 59 (greyhound); *Brook* v *Trafalgar Ins Co Ltd* (1946) 79 Ll L Rep 365 (CA—motor).

30. *Brook* (above) p 368 *per* Scott LJ (CA—motor). On the authority of agents to waive procedural conditions in the USA, see Appleman, sections 3486–3487.

31. For example, the agent who effected the insurance: *Herbert* v *Railway Passengers Assurance Co* [1938] 1 All ER 650, 653 *per* Porter J (motor); *Re Solvency Mutual Guarantee Sy* (1862) 31 LJ Ch 625 (notice of termination of credit insurance). *McQueen* v *Phoenix Mutual Fire Ins Co* (1880) 4 SCR 660, 678 *per* Ritchie CJ (notice of assignment of fire insurance). In the case of group disability insurance arranged by an employer for his employees, notice to the employer may suffice: *Workman* v *Continental Ins Co*, 538 F 2d 619 (4 Cir, 1976).

32. Apparent authority may exist because the insurer has dealt with previous claims sent via the agent: *Dunphy* v *Scottish Metropolitan Assurance Co Ltd* [1928] 1 DLR 420 (NS—motor). There may be apparent authority, even though the agent has ceased to represent the insurer, unless the claimant has notice of the change: *Marsden* v *City & County Assurance Co* (1866) LR 1 CP 232, 239 *per* Erle CJ (plate glass).

In *Tannenbaum* v *Cosmopolitan Mutual Ins Co*, 318 NYS 2d 205 (1971—motor) it was held that for a person who hired a vehicle it was enough to give notice of an accident to the local office of the hire company, even though the hire contract stipulated for notice to head office.

33. *A/S Rendal* v *Arcos Ltd* (1937) 58 Ll L Rep 287 (HL). *Gill* v *Yorkshire* (1913) 24 WLR 389, 396 (Man—livestock). *General Accident Fire & Life Assurance Corp* v *Johnson*, 177 NYS 2d 90, 93 (1958—motor). *Idem, Tannenbaum* (above) p 207. *Sumitomo Canada Ltd* v *Canadian Indemnity Co* (1981) 125 DLR (3d) 356 (BC—liability). Treitel, p 22. See also above, 20–7C1.

Cf Sheills v *Scottish Assurance Corp Ltd* (1889) 16 R 1014, 1020 (Ct Sess—livestock) where it was suggested that, in sending notice to an agent for transmission to head office, the claimant took the risk that it would not be passed on and, therefore, could not presume that it would be; this may be explained as an inference from the particular notice clause.

34. *Gill* (above).

35. *A/S Rendal* v *Arcos Ltd* (1937) 58 Ll L Rep 287, 296 *per* Lord Wright (HL), concerning notice under a charterparty; see also p 300, *per* Lord Maugham. Current law puts the risk of the mode on the person who authorised its use: Treitel, p 24. In *Rendal* (ibid) Lord Wright went on: "I do not put this as a rule of law, but as a presumption of fact. The presumption can no doubt be rebutted by evidence of failure so to act on the part of the agent." The last sentence is hard to reconcile with more recent statements on the allocation of risk between sender and recipient: *The Brimnes* [1975] QB 929 (CA); *Hadenfayre Ltd* v *British National Ins Sy Ltd* [1984] 2 Lloyd's Rep 393, 401 *per* Lloyd J (contingency). Bowstead, pp 419–420. See also *Aetna Life Ins Co* v *Moyer*, 113 F 2d 974, 981 (3 Cir, 1940—life).

36. This appears to have been the position in *Re Williams and Lancashire & Yorkshire Ins Co* (1902) 19 TLR 82 (employers' liabilty); also *Accident Ins Co* v *Young* (1891) 20 SCR 280 (PA).

37. *Sheills* (above).

26–2E The Time of Notice

Notice must be given within the time prescribed by the contract or, in the absence of prescription, within a reasonable time.[38] Time usually runs from an event, such as the loss, accident, or occurrence. If a time is prescribed, the term is strictly construed against the insurer but must be strictly observed by the claimant.

For example, if the insurer of cash in transit excludes liability for loss not notified "within 14 days of its occurrence", he is not liable for systematic embezzlement in the months prior to the 14 days before notice, although notified as soon as it was discovered.[39] In Canada, it has been held that a time period will be applied strictly against the beneficiary under a policy, even though the beneficiary was unaware of the term[40]; and that notice under a liability contract had to be given "as soon as practicable" after "the occurrence of an accident", even though the insured had no reason to think it would give rise to liability, and the liability claim, successfully defended, was not made until 10 months after the accident.[41]

Much depends on the definition of the event which triggers the duty to give notice. If notice is required "within 14 days of the accident", notice months later, when the claimant is first aware of his injury, is too late.[42] If, however, the duty is to give notice of an "accident causing disability", it has been held[43] that it is not every accident that is envisaged but only one causing disability and that, until there is disability, there is no such accident and no duty to give notice.

26–2E1 Impossibility

As regards notice, it has been held that impossibility and ignorance are no excuse.[44] It is no excuse that the claimant unconscious in hospital could not give notice of the accident that put him there.[45] He who insures himself against accidental injury or death is expected to arrange that, if he is unable to give notice, it will be given by somebody else.[46] To temper the strictness of this rule, some courts have insisted that the insurer can defend on lack of notice, only if the insurer has been prejudiced thereby: below, 26–2E2. In addition, the strict rule has been softened in two further ways.

First, as regards the impossibility of providing a certificate of loss, required by fire

---

38. *Hadenfayre Ltd* v *British National Ins Sy Ltd* [1984] 2 Lloyd's Rep 393, 402 *per* Lloyd J (contingency). *Idem* as regards proof of loss: *Kaplan* v *Guardian Life Ins Co*, 231 F Supp 874, 878 (WD Mo, 1964—life).

39. *Adamson & Sons* v *Liverpool & London & Globe Ins Co Ltd* [1953] 2 Lloyd's Rep 355.

40. *Youlden* v *London Guarantee* (1913) 12 DLR 433 (Ont—PA).

41. *Glenburn Dairy Ltd* v *Canadian General Ins Co* [1953] 4 DLR 33 (BC—liability), following *Marcoux* v *Halifax Fire Ins Co* [1948] SCR 278 (motor).

42. *Cassel* v *Lancashire & Yorkshire Accident Ins Co Ltd* (1885) 1 TLR 495 (PA).

43. *Rorick* v *Railway Officials'*, 119 F 63, 66 (9 Cir, 1902—PA); see also in this sense *Western Commercial Travelers' Ins Co* v *Smith*, 85 F 401, 403 (8 Cir, 1898—PA); and in Canada *Gill* v *Yorkshire Ins Co* (1913) 24 WLR 389, 396 (Man—livestock); *Treeland Motor Inn Ltd* v *Western Assurance Co* (1985) 17 DLR (4th) 572 (Sask—business interruption).

44. *Cassel* (above); *Re Carr and Sun Fire Ins Co* (1897) 13 TLR 186 (CA—fire); *Adamson* v *Liverpool & London & Globe Ins Co* [1953] 2 Lloyd's Rep 355 (cash in transit). *Accident Co* v *Young* (1891) 20 SCR 280, 284 *per* Ritchie CJ (PA).
Cf USA: in certain states notice "as required by the policy may be excused by circumstances that render strict compliance therewith impossible or unreasonable"—*Barco* v *Pennsylvania Mutual Life Ins Co*, 126 F 2d 56 (5 Cir, 1942—life). Appleman, section 1416.

45. *Evans* v *Railway Passengers* (1912) 3 DLR 61 (Ont—PA), following *Gamble* (below).

46. *Gamble Assurance Co* v *Accident* (1870) IR 4 CL 204, 214 *per* Pigot CB (PA).

insurance in *Worsley* v *Wood*,[47] Lord Kenyon CJ said that "If there be a condition precedent to do an impossible thing, the obligation becomes single: but however improbable the thing may be it must be complied with". It is clear from context that Lord Kenyon would delete a condition that was incapable of being performed by its very nature[48] or, perhaps, was impossible for the particular parties from the time of the contract but would apply a condition, which had become impossible to perform as things turned out later for the person required to perform it.[49]

Second, it has been held that notice need not be given if notice has become pointless. In one case,[50] Lord Denning MR observed[51]: "Seeing that [the insurers] had received the information from the police, it would be a futile thing to require the motor cyclist himself to give them the selfsame information. The law never compels a person to do that which is useless and unnecessary." In the same case, however, Salmon LJ[52] did not agree. Indeed, Lord Denning's view is not easily reconciled with decisions (below, 26–2E2) that require notice, whether the insurer has been prejudiced or not, and thus appear to reject the argument that notice should not be required when it would not have served its purpose. However, in one case, it is clear that notice or, indeed, the performance of any other procedural condition is pointless and the claimant has complete dispensation—when it is clear that the insurer will refuse to pay, anyway: below, 26–4D(c).

26–2E2 Prejudice to the Insurer

If the notice condition has been broken, indemnity may be refused, even though the insurer has not been prejudiced by the breach. In England, the point was left open by Mocatta J in *The Vainqueur José*,[53] who observed that, if prejudice were necessary, "relatively little prejudice has to be shown". In *Pioneer Concrete*,[54] Bingham J reviewed English precedent and concluded that prejudice was not required. In the United States, however, the trend is away from the strict application of notice clauses,[55] according to what is sometimes called the traditional contract analysis.

47. (1796) 6 TR 710, 718–719 (fire).
48. In this sense Halsbury (4th ed), Vol 25, para 437.
49. Such distinctions were ignored by the Court of Appeal in *The Fanti*; see above, 5–8E3.
50. *Barratt Bros (Taxis) Ltd* v *Davies* [1966] 2 Lloyd's Rep 1 (CA—motor).
51. [1966] 2 Lloyd's Rep 1, 5. Danckwerts LJ (*ibid*) agreed with Lord Denning on this point; it was an alternative ground of decision.
52. p 6. See also *The Vainqueur José* [1979] 1 Lloyd's Rep 557, 565 *per* Mocatta J (P & I), however, much may depend on the wording of the notice clause. The Denning view on futility was applied to a charterparty by Mustill J in *The Mozart* [1985] 1 Lloyd's Rep 239, 245.
53. [1979] 1 Lloyd's Rep 557, 566 *per* Mocatta J (P & I).
54. *Pioneer Concrete (UK) Ltd* v *National Employers' Mutual General Ins Assn Ltd* [1985] 2 All ER 395, 400 ff *per* Bingham J (accident). See also *Barratt Bros (Taxis) Ltd* v *Davies* [1966] 2 Lloyd's Rep 1 (CA—motor); *Farrell* v *Federated Employers Ins Assn Ltd* [1970] 1 All ER 360, 364 *per* Mackenna J (employers' liability), affirmed [1970] 2 Lloyd's Rep 170 (CA). Australia: see Tarr p 221.
55. Some states require prejudice, for example California: *Sinton* v *Hartford Accident & Indemnity Co*, 261 Cal Rptr 163 (1989—liability); Iowa: *Estate of Wade* v *Continental Ins Co*, 514 F 2d 304 (8 Cir, 1975—PA); Michigan: *West Bay Exploration Co* v *AIG*, 915 F 2d 1030 (6 Cir, 1990—liability); and New Mexico: *Yarbrough* v *State Farm Ins Co*, 730 F Supp 1061 (D NM, 1990—motor). In California, it has been argued, albeit unsuccessfully, that the rule does not apply to reinsurance, however, it appears that actual prejudice may be harder to show in such cases: *Ins Co of Pennsylvania* v *Associated International Ins Co*, 922 F 2d 516 (9 Cir, 1991—re).
Other states do not require prejudice, for example, Connecticut: *National Semiconductor Corp* v *Allendale Mutual Ins Co*, 549 F Supp 1195, 1198 (D Conn, 1982—business interruption); Louisiana: *Jackson* v *Transportation Leasing Co* 893 F 2d 794 (5 Cir, 1990—liability); and New York: *Kason* v *City of New York*, 373 NYS 2d 456 (1975—liability); *Heydt Contracting Corp* v *American Home Assurance Co*, 536 NYS 2d

One court spoke of "the modern view that this provision, although denominated by the policy as a condition precedent, should be construed in accord with its purpose and with the reasonable expectations of the parties".[56] As to its purpose, on the one hand, another court said that the "reasonable notice clause is designed to protect the insurance company from being placed in a substantially less favorable [sic] position than it would have been in had timely notice been provided, e.g., being forced to pay a claim against which it has not had an opportunity to defend effectively. In short, the function of a notice requirement is to protect the insurance company's interests from being prejudiced. Where the insurance company's interest have not been harmed by a late notice, even in the absence of extenuating circumstances to excuse the tardiness, the reason behind the notice condition in the policy is lacking, and it follows neither logic nor fairness to relieve the insurance company of its obligations under the policy in such a situation".[57] On the other hand, "limitation periods on suits are designed to promote justice by preventing surprises through revival of stale claims, to protect defendants and courts from handling matters in which the search for truth may be impaired by loss of evidence, to encourage plaintiffs to use reasonable and proper diligence in enforcing their rights, and to prevent fraud. The presence or absence of prejudice is not, nor should it be, a factor in deciding whether an insurer may effectively assert this defence."[58]

Even in states, in which the insurer has been required to prove prejudice, a different rule has been applied to liability insurance. If the insurance is based on claims made *and* reported in the insurance period, the report (notice) has been seen as a description of the risk. Consequently, the claimant must establish loss within the scope of the cover thus described and, if he cannot establish notice within the period, he has not established insured loss and the insurer is entitled to refuse payment, without proof of prejudice.[59]

When prejudice is required, it must be proved by the insurer. In the case of liability insurance, for example, the principal factors concerning prejudice are, first,[61] whether "substantial rights pertaining to a defense of a claim have been irretrievably lost"—as in the case of a cold trail,[62] or of notice after judgment has been given against the liab-

770, 772 (1989—AR); *Ins Co of Pennsylvania* v *Associated International Ins Co*, 922 F 2d 516 (9 Cir, 1991—re). In New York, however, decisions conflict on whether the same rule applies to reinsurance: *Travelers Ins Co* v *Buffalo Reins Co* 739 F Supp 209, 213(1990—re); *cf Christiana General Ins Corp* v *Great American Ins Co* 745 F Supp 150, 159 (1990—re) requiring prejudice because reinsurers "have no duty to defend claims, nor is the potential staleness of a claim as significant a concern to a reinsurer as to a primary insurer"; affirmed: 979 F 2d 268, 274 (2 Cir, 1992); see also *Unigard Security Ins Co* v *North River Ins Co*, 584 NYS 2d 290 (1992—re). See also Works 70 Neb L Rev 229 (1991); but *cf* Appleman, section 4732: to require proof of prejudice by the insurer is unworkable, for *ex hypothesi* in many cases the evidence of prejudice will be unobtainable.

56. *Great American Ins Co* v *Tate Construction Co*, 279 SE 2d 769, 771 (1981—liability); 61 NCL Rev 167 (1982–3); the policy required notice "as soon as practicable". More recently, in *Estes* v *Alaska Ins Guaranty Assn* (SC, Alaska, 26 May 1989—fire) the court premised that the purpose of such notice clauses was to prevent prejudice to the insurer, and concluded that, absent such prejudice in fact, the clause would not be enforced against a claimant who did not knowingly agree to the clause and whose reasonable expectations were that late notice in such circumstances would not defeat a claim.

57. *Brakeman* v *Potomac Ins Co*, 371 A 2d 193, 197 (1977—motor). See also in North Carolina: *Great American Ins Co* v *Tate Construction Co*, 279 SE 2d 769, 771, 776 (1981—liability). Pierce, 19 Western Univ L R 165, 169 ff. (1992).

58. *Zieba* v *Middlesex Mutual Ass Co*, 549 F Supp 1318, 1321 (D Conn, 1982—fire).

59. *Pacific Employers Ins Co* v *Superior Court* 270 Cal Rptr 779, 784 (Cal App, 1990—liability).

61. *Morales* v *National Grange Mutual Ins Co*, 423 A 2d 325, 329 (NJ, 1980—motor).

62. *Steinbach* v *Aetna Casualty & Surety Co*, 440 NYS 2d 637 (1981—liability), applying the law of New Hampshire.

ility insured; and, second,[63] the "likelihood of success of the insurer in defending against the accident victim's claim"—if the victim's claim is clear the courts are less likely to hold that the insurer has been prejudiced by late notice of the claim. It is unclear whether extra expense amounts to prejudice.[64]

26–2E3 "Immediate" Notice; Notice "As Soon as Possible"

A policy requirement of "immediate notice" is not read literally: even if he had a mobile telephone, it would be absurd to expect the victim of an accident to contact his insurer before calling an ambulance.[65] Such notice is said to be a question of fact depending on the circumstances of the case[66] and to mean with due diligence,[67] with "all reasonable speed" in the circumstances,[68] at the first reasonable opportunity.[69]

A requirement of notice "as soon as possible" is not read literally either; it requires what is reasonably possible for a person in the position of the claimant. Thus, notice of accidental death a year after it occurred was sufficient, when the claimant was unaware until then of the existence of the policy.[70] The same has been held of notice "as soon as reasonably practicable"[71]; "regardless of the language used, whether 'immediate', 'prompt', 'forthwith',[72] 'as soon as practicable' or words of similar import, the courts are generally in agreement that reasonable notice is sufficient."[73] In England, it is a requirement of notice "as soon as reasonably possible" that is indicated by the Statement of General Insurance Practice.[74]

---

63. *Morales* (above), p 330.

64. NCL Rev 167, 175 (1982–3).

65. *Accident Ins Co* v *Young* (1891) SCR 280, 291 *per* Patterson J (PA).

66. *Re Williams* (1902) 19 TLR 82 (employers' liability), in which the clause also said that time was of the essence; notice seven weeks after knowledge of the accident was held too late. A similar delay was held too long in *Farrell* v *Federated Employers Ins Assn Ltd* [1970] 1 All ER 360 (employers' liability); and 39 days was too long in *Accident Ins Co* v *Young* (1891) 20 SCR 280 (PA).

67. *Shera* v *Ocean Accident* (1900) 32 OR 411 (Ont—PA).

68. *Re Coleman's Depositories and Life & Health Assurance Assn* [1907] 2 KB 798, 807 *per* Fletcher Moulton LJ (CA—employers' liability), and Lord Denning MR appeared to accept argument to this effect in *Farrell* (above), p 173.

Idem, Johnston v *Dominion of Canada Guarantee & Accident Ins Co* (1908) 17 OLR 462 (Ont—PA); *Shera* v *Ocean Accident* (1900) 32 OR 411 (Ont—PA); *Merchants'* v *Parent* (1918) 48 DLR 96 (Que—PA); *Sumitomo Canada Ltd* v *Canadian Indemnity Co* (1981) 125 DLR (3d) 356 (BC—liability). *Stargatt* v *Avenell*, 434 F Supp 234, 247 (D Del, 1977—liability); *National Semiconductor Corp* v *Allendale Mutual Ins Co*, 549 F Supp 1195, 1199 (D Conn, 1982—business interruption). It is a question of fact on which there are many decisions: Appleman, sections 1391, 4734. The matter may be governed by statute: Appleman, sections 1394, 4735.

A similar view is found of the term in other kinds of contract: *Garcia* v *Page* (1936) 55 Ll L Rep 391, 392 *per* Porter J in relation to the duty to open a bankers' credit. See also *Pybus* v *Mitford* (1793) 2 Lev 74, 77; *Alexiadi* v *Robinson* (1861) 2 F & F 679, 684 *per* Cockburn CJ.

69. *Newnham* v *Baker* [1989] 1 Qd R 393 (fire).

70. *Verelst's Administratrix* v *Motor Union Ins Co* [1925] 2 KB 137, 142–143 *per* Roche J (PA). See also *Price* v *Dominion* [1940] 3 DLR 244, 259 (NB—PA).; and *Glenburn Dairy Ltd* v *Canadian General Ins Co* [1953] 4 DLR 33 (BC—liability).

71. *Heydt Contracting Corp* v *American Home Assurance Co*, 536 NYS 2d 770 (1989—AR); *Reeves* v *State Farm Fire & Casualty Co*, 539 So 2d 252 (Ala, 1989—liability); *St Clare's Hospital* v *INA*, 934 F 2d 15 (2 Cir, 1991—liability). See also *Glenburn* (above).

72. *Roberts* v *Brett* (1865) 11 HLC 337. In statutes, however, the word is given a more demanding construction; for example *R* v *Berkshire Justices* (1878) 4 QBD 469, 471 where Cockburn CJ said in relation to a rule of criminal procedure that "The words 'forthwith' and 'immediately' have the same meaning. They are stronger than the expression 'within a reasonable time', and imply prompt, vigorous action, without any delay".

73. *State Auto Mutual Ins Co* v *Youler* 396 SE 2d 737, 742 (W Va, 1990—motor).

74. Clause 2(a).

26–2E4 Reasonable Time

"There is of course no such thing as a reasonable time in the abstract . . . the only sound principle is that the 'reasonable time' should depend on the circumstances which actually exist,"[75] no allowance being made to the claimant for delay which he has (unreasonably) caused.[76] Although a reasonable time must be calculated with a view to the particular circumstances, there are certain general factors to be considered.

   (a) The insurer wants notice as soon as possible: to enable him to test the genuineness of the claim before the trail becomes cold[77] and to avoid the extra expense in following a trail obscured by time.[78] "The purpose of a provision for notice and proofs of loss is to allow the insurer to form an intelligent estimate of its rights and liabilities; to afford it an opportunity for investigation; and to prevent fraud and imposition upon it."[79]

     If the insurer is liable on the insurance, there is the further purpose to minimise loss[80] or, in the case of liability insurance, to enable the insurer to perform his role as *dominus litis*[81] or to participate in negotiations to settle the claim.[82] If the potential claim is a large one, the insurer may require time to provide a sufficient reserve fund[83] or, if no claim is made, to know when he can disregard the possibiity with a view to fixing an appropriate level of reserves and of premiums for future liabilities.[84]

   (b) The court will consider the knowledge available to the claimant. If the claimant was totally unaware of the possibility of a claim, unaware perhaps of the facts giving rise to a claim,[85] the court will be reluctant to find that a reason-

75. *Hick* v *Raymond* [1893] AC 22, 29 *per* Lord Herschell LC; *Verelst* (above) *loc cit; Ets Chainbaux SARL* v *Harbormaster Ltd* [1955] 1 Lloyd's Rep 303, 311 *per* Devlin J. Appleman sections 1411 ff.
76. Lord Herschell LC, *loc cit*.
77. *Mason* v *Harvey* (1853) 8 Ex 819, 821 *per* Pollock CB (fire); *Gamble* v *Accident Assurance Co* (1870) IR 4 CL 204, 214 *per* Pigot CB (PA); *Hassett* v *Legal & General Assurance Sy Ltd* (1939) 63 Ll L Rep 278, 281 *per* Atkinson J (liability); *Re Coleman's Depositories and Life & Health Assurance Assn* [1907] 2 KB 798, 807 *per* Fletcher Moulton LJ (CA—employers' liability); *The Vainqueur José* [1979] 1 Lloyd's Rep 557, 565 *per* Mocatta J (P & I); *Pioneer Concrete (UK) Ltd* v *National Employers' Mutual General Ins Assn Ltd* [1985] 2 All ER 395, 400 *per* Bingham J (accident).
   Johnston v *Dominion* (1908) 17 OLR 462, 465 (Ont—PA); *Sproul* v *National Fire* [1925] 1 DLR 1152, 1155 (Nova Scotia—fire); *Marcoux* v *Halifax Fire Ins Co* [1948] SCR 278, 282 *per* Taschereau J (motor); *National Semiconductor Corp* v *Allendale Mutual Ins Co*, 549 F Supp 1195, 1199 (D Conn, 1982—business interruption); *Federal Deposit Ins Co* v *Aetna*, 744 F Supp 729, 734 (ED La, 1990—fidelity).
78. *Stoneham* v *Ocean Ry & General Accident Ins Co* (1887) 19 QBD 237, 240 *per* Mathew J (PA).
79. *Kaplan* v *Guardian Life Ins Co*, 231 F Supp 874, 878 (WD Mo, 1964—life).
80. Thus under a guarantee policy a reasonable time for notice that an employee has committed a criminal offence is likely to be short: *Harbour Commissioners* v *Guarantee Co* (1893) 22 SCR 542. See also *The Vainqueur José* [1979] 1 Lloyd's Rep 557 (P & I).
81. *Pioneer Concrete* (abovc), *loc cit. Stargatt* v *Avenell*, 434 F Supp 234, 247 (D Del, 1977—liability); *State Farm Fire & Casualty Co*, 539 So 2d 252, 256 (Ala, 1989—liability).
82. *Hefner* v *Republic Indemnity Co*, 773 F Supp 11 (SD Tex, 1991—liability).
83. *Heydt Contracting Corp* v *American Home Assurance Co*, 536 NYS 2d 770, 772 (1989—AR); *Christiana General Ins Corp* v *Great American Ins Co*, 979 F 2d 268, 275 (2 Cir, 1992—re).
84. *Federal Savings & Loan Ins Corp* v *Heidrick*, 774 F Supp 352, 358 (D Md, 1991—liability); *Olin Corp* v *INA*, 966 F 2d 718, 723 (2 Cir, 1992—liability).
85. *Travelers Ins Co* v *Buffalo Reinsurance Co*, 735 F Supp 492, 500 (SD NY, 1990—re); *Allstate Ins Co* v *Fitzgerald*, 743 F Supp 539, 542 (WD Tenn, 1990—liability).
   For example, a claimant may be excused, if his doctor fails to diagnose an injury, provided that "the claimant, in the exercise of ordinary care, believes and relies upon that advice"—*Texas Employers Ins Assn* v *Daniels*, 257 SW 2d 150, 153 (Tex, 1953—workmen's compensation); see also *Brown* v *Einbinder*, 172 NYS 2d 928 (1958—liability).

able time has passed.[86] Ignorance by a personal representative of the existence of a policy taken out by the deceased is an excuse for delay,[87] but not ignorance by the insured of the existence of the policy[88] or of the terms of his policy,[89] unless there is reasonable doubt about its scope.[90] If, however, he is ignorant because the insurer has retained the policy[91] or because he has not been given notice of the condition in issue, he cannot be held to it[92] but, if it is because he has mislaid the policy,[93] the court will be less sympathetic. In Texas,[94] the youth and inexperience of the claimant are relevant factors, although they do not provide an automatic excuse for breach of condition. Moreover, it is no excuse, it has been held,[95] that the claimant did not give notice under policy A because he believed in good faith that he was fully covered under policy B.

If knowledge comes gradually, reasonable time may begin to run with a speed that increases with knowledge. In the case of liability insurance, it has been held that the insured knew enough to give notice, if he "ought to have contemplated that it was an occurrence which might result in a claim for compensation"[96]; "the mere possibility of a claim should have alerted plaintiff to the necessity of promptly informing his insurance carrier".[97] Commonly, the policy deal with the matter by requiring notice when a liability claim against the insured is "likely".[98] But other cases have held that there

86. *Verelst's Administratrix* v *Motor Union Ins Co Ltd* [1925] 2 KB 137 (PA); *Baltic Ins Assn Ltd* v *Cambrian Coaching & Goods Transport Ltd* (1926) 25 Ll L Rep 195 (motor). *Subia* v *Cosmopolitan Mutual Ins Co*, 364 NYS 2d 118, 120 (1975—motor): it may be ignorance of the injury, the accident, the identity of the insurer (*ibid*); or incapacity: *Estate of Wade* v *Continental Ins Co*, 514 F 2d 304 (8 Cir, 1975—PA).

87. *Verelst* (above). In the case of an insured firm, the knowledge that counts is generally that of persons in a managerial or executive position: Appleman, section 4742 pp 151 ff. As to third party beneficiaries, see Appleman, section 1419.

88. *Olin Corp* v *INA*, 966 F 2d 718, 724–725 (2 Cir, 1992—liability).

89. *USLIFE Savings & Loan Assn* v *National Surety Corp*, 171 Cal Rptr 393, 398 (1981—fidelity); *Reeves* v *State Farm Fire & Casualty Co*, 539 So 2d 252, 255 (Ala, 1989—liability). The insured has a duty to make himself familar with the contents of his insurance contract: *Shindler* v *Mid-Continent Life Ins Co*, 768 SW 2d 331, 334 (Tex, 1989—life); *Greene* v *Lilburn Agency Inc*, 383 SE 2d 194 (Ga, 1989—theft). Allowance will be made for the ignorance of an employee of his rights under a group policy: *Jarka Corp* v *American Fidelity & Casualty Co*, 241 NYS 2d 546 (1963—liability).

90. *Olin* (above).

91. *Caldwell* v *Stadcona Fire & Life Ins Co* (1883) 11 SCR 212, 225 *per* Ritchie CJ (fire). *Aliter* if the policy is in the hands of the insured's agent: *Northern Assurance Co* v *Standard Leather Co*, 165 F 602 (3 Cir, 1908—fire).

92. *Re Coleman's Depositories and Life & Health Assurance Assn* [1907] 2 KB 798 (CA—employers' liability); in this case, of course, the notice condition may not be a term of the contract at all: p 812 *per* Buckley LJ.

93. *Accident Ins Co* v *Young* (1891) 20 SCR 280, 284 *per* Ritchie CJ (PA).

94. *Dairyland County Mutual Ins Co* v *Roman*, 498 SW 2d 154, 158 (Tex, 1973—motor). In Illinois, it was held in *Grasso* v *Mid-Century Ins Co*, 536 NE 2d 977 (Ill, 1989—liability) that a claimant, aged 19 at the time of a road accident, was able to plead ignorance of excess liability insurance, contracted by her father but covering her own liability arising out of the accident, and claim notwithstanding a two year delay in giving notice to the insurer. "Her ignorance of potential coverage under a policy held by another for a car she neither owned nor operated when the accident occurred is not, under Illinois law, unreasonable." (p 980).

95. *Gardner-Denver Co* v *Dic-Underhill Construction Co*, 416 F Supp 934 (SD NY, 1976—contractors' equipment).

96. *General Motors Ltd* v *Crowder* (1931) 40 Ll L Rep 87, 89 *per* Hawke J (workmen's compensation).

97. *Heydt Contracting Corp* v *American Home Assurance Co*: 536 NYS 2d 770, 773 (1989—AR); *Avondale Industries Inc* v *Travelers Indemnity Co* 774 F Supp 1416, 1433 (SD NY, 1991—liability).

98. *Moore* v *Canadian Lawyers Ins Assn* (1992) 95 DLR (4th) 365 (NS—liability).

was no duty to notify the insurer, until it was "plain" that there would be a claim under the policy.[99] To the extent that the notice clause requires specific details of the event or the claim, the claimant must be allowed the time necessary to gather the information.[100]

(c) *Industry practice.* Although in one decision,[101] the New York court accepted that in this matter reinsurance was governed by the same considerations as other kinds of insurance, in a more recent decision,[102] the court accepted that it could hear evidence of industry custom and practice which, it was alleged, would show that longer lapses of time were acceptable in the reinsurance industry. Reinsurance contracts require "a more relaxed approach to interpretation than direct insurance contracts. The traditional reasons for this difference in approach have been the small numbers of the reinsurance fraternity, a desire to avoid burdensome transaction costs, and the perception that, by their nature, reinsurance contracts cannot provide for every eventuality at the outset".[103]

In particular, it has been held in New York that, whereas prompt notice is a condition precedent to a successful claim, whether the insurer has been prejudiced or not, in the case of reinsurance a claim is not barred by late notice unless the reinsurer has suffered prejudice.[104] And in *Unigard Security Ins Co* v *N River Ins Co*,[105] the court noted the reasons for notice in primary insurance but observed that the purpose of notice to a reinsurer is different, that is, "to allow the reinsurer to post reserves, to allot it to associate in the resolution of the underlying claims, and to enable it to determine under what conditions it wishes to renew the reinsurance coverage. A comparison of the needs of direct insurers and reinsurers indicates that only an insurer faces irreparable harm from untimely notice of a claim". Whereas an insurer may have difficulty in proving the existence and extent of prejudice as a result of late notice, that is less likely to be true of the reinsurer. The court continued[106] that, "while a reinsurer may have difficulty establishing damages arising from an inability to associate in the resolution of an underlying claim, it is important to note that the right to associate is not a right of control, and under the 'follow the fortunes' doctrine,[107] the mere fact that a reinsurer might have disagreed with its cedent's handling of the claim does not permit it to avoid liability on the reinsurance agreement".

99. *Ward* v *Law Property* (1856) 4 WR 605, 606 *per* Crompton J (guarantee); *Smellie* v *British General Ins Co*, 1918 2 SLT 58, 60 *per* Lord Anderson (Ct Sess—employers' liability). *Lemar Towing Co Inc* v *Fireman's Fund Ins Co*, 352 F Supp 652 (ED La, 1972—hull), affirmed 471 F 2d 609, cert den 414 US 976. On the meaning of liability, see above, 17–4C and 17–4D.

100. *V/O Exportkhleb* v *m/v Anpa*, 773 F Supp 832 (ED La, 1991—liability).

101. *Travelers Ins Co* v *Buffalo Reinsurance Co*, 735 F Supp 492, 498 (SD NY, 1990—re).

102. *Travelers Ins Co* v *Buffalo Reinsurance Co*, 739 F Supp 209, 212 (SD NY, 1990—re); *Christiana General Ins Corp* v *Great American Ins Co*, 745 F Supp 150, 159 (SD NY, 1990—re).

103. Sehr, Blume and Elenius 27 Tort & Ins L J 226, 237 (1992). See also Thomas, 'Utmost Good Faith in Reinsurance: A Tradition in Need of Adjustment' 41 Duke LJ 1548, 1576 ff (1992).

104. *Christiana* (above).

105. 762 F Supp 566, 592 (SD NY, 1991—re). See also in this sense: *Unigard Security Ins Co* v *N River Ins Co*, 594 NE 2d 571, 574 (CA NY, 1992—re); Ritter (1992) 4 Ins L & P 114.

106. pp 592–593.

107. As to this doctrine, see below 27–4.

26–2F Particulars

The insured must give all information necessary to the purpose of the notice,[108] such as time, place, circumstances, and other information, on which the insurer can base an investigation.[109] These are the particulars and the requirement of particulars, although ancillary to the requirement of notice, is distinct. In general, a notice of claim "does not mean a precisely formulated claim with full details, but it must be such a notice as will enable the party to whom it is given to take steps to meet the claim by preparing and obtaining appropriate evidence for that purpose".[110] It is enough for notice, if the claimant indicates clearly,[111] that there will be a claim under a particular clause of the contract.[112] It is then for the insurer to indicate, if the policy does not do so, what further particulars he requires, for example, by sending a claim form.

Distinguish proof. On the one hand, it is not necessary that the loss claimed should have been quantified[113] or proved[114] at the time of initial notice or particulars. On the other hand, when later submitting proof, the claimant is not estopped by particulars previously submitted and has a reasonable opportunity to submit amended or additional information.[115] Moreover, when a claimant submitted a revised estimate of the amount of loss, it was held[116] that that was not a new claim falling outside the policy limit for claims.

Provisions of the policy and, sometimes, of statute[117] are important on this question. The words, "full particulars of loss", mean "the best particulars the assured can reasonably give . . . that the assured will, within a convenient time after the loss, produce to the company something which will enable them to form a judgment as to whether or not he has sustained a loss".[118] When the contract requires particulars to be "true" particulars, this probably means "true" to the best of the claimant's belief;

---

108. *The Litsion Pride* [1985] 1 Lloyd's Rep 437, 511–512 *per* Hirst J (hull).

109. *General Accident Fire & Life Assurance Corp Ltd* v *Dickinson*, 61 F Supp 153, 155 (ND Cal, 1945—motor). Appleman, section 4739.

110. *A/S Rendal* v *Arcos Ltd* (1937) 58 Ll L Rep 287, 292 *per* Lord Wright (HL).

111. Not casually: *Herbert* v *Railway Passengers Assurance Co Ltd* [1938] 1 All ER 650 (motor), in which the notice was required under statute. There is a suggestion that notices required by statute must be "strictly", perhaps more strictly, complied with: *Weldrick* v *Essex & Suffolk Equitable Ins Sy Ltd* (1949) 83 Ll L Rep 91, 102 *per* Birkett J (motor).

112. *A/S Rendal* v *Arcos Ltd* (1937) 58 Ll L Rep 287, 299 *per* Lord Maugham.

113. *A/S Rendal* (above) p 293 *per* Lord Wright.

114. *Johnston* v *Dominion of Canada Guarantee & Accident Ins Co* (1908) 17 OLR 462 (Ont—PA).

115. In the United States, the claimant may correct earlier misstatements inadvertently made: *Hirsch* v *New York Life Ins Co*, 45 NYS 2d 892 (1944—disability); *Chase Rand Corp* v *Central Ins Co*, 63 F Supp 626 (SD NY, 1945—jeweller's block), affirmed 152 F 2d 963 (2 Cir, 1945). But in Canada, the claimant may be bound by premature particulars of loss: *Kent* v *Ocean Accident & Guarantee Corp* (1909) 20 OLR 226 (Ont—PA).

116. *Northern Suburban Property* v *British Law Fire Ins Co* (1919) 1 Ll L Rep 403 (fire). *Cf Elliott* v *Royal Exchange Assurance Co* (1867) LR 2 Ex 237 (fire), in which the insurer's promise was to pay the adjusted loss: once paid it would be too late to claim further items arising from that loss (p 247 *per* Pigott B).

117. For example, "notice of the action": *Ceylon Motor Ins Assn Ltd* v *Thambugala* [1953] AC 584 (PC—motor) and "notice of proceedings": *McGoona* v *MIB* [1969] 2 Lloyd's Rep 34 (motor).

118. *Mason* v *Harvey* (1853) 8 Exch 819, 820–821 *per* Pollock CB (fire). See also "such an account as the nature and circumstances of the case would admit of, or (in other words) the best account they could", discussed by Lord Davey in *Hiddle* v *National Fire & Marine Ins Co* [1896] AC 372, 375 (PC—fire). *Cinqu-Mars* v *Equitable Ins Co*, 15 UCQB 143, 148 (fire); *Mulvey* v *Gore* (1866) 25 UCQB 424, 430 (fire); *Fowlie* v *Ocean Accident & Guarantee Corp Ltd* (1902) 4 OLR 146 (PA), affirmed (1902) 33 SCR 253.

and if his particulars contain a deliberate untruth, these are not particulars within the meaning of the condition.[119]

26–2F1 Proof of Loss

The requirement of particulars, which specify loss, is distinct from the requirement of proof, which must establish loss on the balance of probabilities. Whereas proof of loss includes particulars,[120] particulars of loss do not necessarily amount to proof.[121] As to the time of proof, see the rules above (26–2E) governing notice.

Proof must be furnished in the way stipulated by the contract, such as a certificate from some reputable source that the loss has occurred in the amount claimed.[122] The words, "all such proofs and information with respect to the claim as may reasonably be required",[123] have been applied literally. The words, "proof satisfactory to" the insurer, have been held to mean the same: such particulars as the insurer "might reasonably require",[124] thus ensuring an element of good faith. In Australia, the same decision has been reached, when the relevant degree of disablement was to be determined "in the opinion of" the insurer.[125]

If it is necessary to establish the cause of death, the insurer may require a post mortem examination of the deceased[126] within a reasonable time[127] and the insurer may demand particulars of an insured doctor, even though disclosure by the doctor might be a breach of professional etiquette, if necessary to enable the insurer to test the claim.[128] Again, it has been held in the USA that a fire insurer was entitled to refuse to pay a claim because the insured claimant refused to comply with a contract duty to submit to an examination under oath directed at the claimant's financial circumstances.[129] However, the court also cautioned that it was "not suggesting, nor do the

119. *Cox* v *Orion Ins Co Ltd* [1982] RTR 1 (CA—motor).

120. *Conlon* v *Northern Life Ins Co*, 92 P 2d 284 (Mo, 1939—life).

121. *Schoenholtz* v *Travelers Ins Co*, 30 NYS 2d 642 (1940—life). In the USA, substantial (not literal) compliance with contract stipulations is sufficient: *Globe & Rutgers Ins Co* v *Prairie Oil & Gas Co*, 248 F 452, 455 (2 Cir, 1917—fire). Generally, see Appleman, sections 1443 ff, 3505 ff, 3531 ff.

122. *Worsley* v *Wood* (1796) 6 TR 710 (fire); approved in *London Guarantie Co* v *Fearnley* (1880) 5 App Cas 911, 916 *per* Lord Blackburn (fidelity); *Burridge & Sons* v *Haines & Sons* (1918) 118 LT 681, 684 *per* Avory J (livestock); *Welch* v *Royal Exchange Assurance* [1939] 1 KB 294, 315 *per* Finlay LJ (CA—fire). Canada: see *Anderson* v *Stevenson* [1943] 3 DLR 301 (Ont—fire) and cases discussed. Brown & Menezes, 11:3:9.

123. For example, *Welch* v *Royal Exchange Assurance* [1939] 1 KB 294 (CA—fire).

124. *Braunstein* v *Accidental Death Ins Co* (1861) 1 B & S 782, 794–795 *per* Wightman J (PA). See also in this sense *Moore* v *Wolsey* (1854) 4 El & Bl 243, 256 *per* Lord Campbell CJ (life); *London Guarantie Co* v *Fearnley* (1880) 5 App Cas 911, 916 *per* Lord Blackburn (fidelity); *MacDonald* v *Refuge Assurance Co* (1890) 17 R 955 (Ct Sess—life).

125. *Edwards* v *Hunter Valley Co–op Dairy Co* (Supreme Court, NSW, 22 April 1992), reported by Sckar, 5 Ins L J 171 (1992).

In the general law, see *Niarchos (London) Ltd* v *Shell Tankers* [1961] 2 Lloyd's Rep 496. *Renard Constructions (ME) Pty Ltd* v *Minister for Public Works* (1992) 26 NSWLR 234.

126. *Ballantine* v *Employers Ins Co Ltd* (1893) 21 R 305, 316-317 *per* Lord Young (Ct Sess—PA).

127. *Maryland Casualty Co* v *Harris*, 60 F 2d 810 (3 Cir, 1932—PA).

128. *A B* v *Northern Accident Ins Co Ltd* (1896) R 258, 266, *per* Lord Trayner (PA): the claimant alleged that he contracted syphilis while treating a patient. For the requirement of an independent medical examination to establish bodily injury, see *Vanhaaren* v *State Farm Mutual Automobile Ins Co*, 989 F 2d 1 (1 Cir, 1993—motor).

129. *Allison* v *State Farm Casualty Co*, 543 So 2d 661 (Miss, 1989—fire). *Idem* when the insured refused access to books and papers in breach of the contract: *Ganz* v *Public Service Mutual Ins Co*, 551 NYS 2d 437 (1989—property).

authorities support, a rule that the insurer may ask anything of the insured as part of the examination and refuse coverage because of any refusal to answer. We reject the notion that the insurer is the sole judge of materiality" in these matters.[130]

26–2G The Effect of Breach of Procedural Condition

Notice is not something to be proved by the claimant as part of his insurance claim, but its absence may be a defence for the insurer,[131] on whom therefore falls the onus of proving breach.[132] This is generally true of all procedural conditions, unless it is clear from the contract that performance, for example, specified proof of death, is a condition precedent to any claim.[133] The inclination of the courts is to place the onus on the insurer, as he is seeking to escape an obligation, which he has been paid to undertake.[134]

If breach of condition is established, it is a matter of construction[135] of the condition whether it is (a) a condition precedent to payment by the insurer, (b) a suspensive condition or (c) a minor contract duty, breach of which does not prevent recovery, but may render the insured liable in damages to the insurer for loss (if any) caused to the latter by the breach.[136] If it is a condition precedent, the insurer in England may refuse payment, even though he has suffered no prejudice from the breach.[137] If it is a suspensive condition, the claimant may recover when the condition is performed, even though performance was late.[138] Case (c) seems to be rare in insurance cases and this feature inclines the courts to construction (a).

The condition is construed in accordance with general rules of construction.[139] If the contract states that the condition is a condition precedent (or that breach shall bar

---

130. p 664.
131. *Baker* v *Provident* [1939] 2 All ER 690, 697 *per* Cassels J (motor).
132. *Baltic Ins Assn Ltd* v *Cambrian Coaching & Goods Transport Ltd* (1926) 25 Ll L Rep 195, 197 *per* Mackinnon J (motor); *Pioneer Concrete (UK) Ltd* v *National Employers' Mutual General Ins Assn Ltd* [1985] 2 All ER 395 (accident). But *cf Mount Vernon Fire Ins Co* v *Creative Housing Ltd*, 797 F Supp 176, 184 (ED NY, 1992—liability), that it is the duty of the insured to show that the required notice was given in a reasonable time.
133. *Home Life Ins Co* v *Randall* (1899) 30 SCR 97, 103–104 *per* Ritchie CJ (life). *Maynard* v *National Fire Ins Co*, 129 SE 2d 443 (Va, 1963—fire). *Cf American Guarantee Ins Co* v *Chandler Mfg. Co*, 467 NW 2d 226, 228 (Iowa 1991—liability).
134. *Great American Ins Co* v *Tate Construction Co*, 279 SE 2d 769, 775 (1981—liability), especially if the breach does not defeat the claim, unless the insurer has been prejudiced (above, 26–2E1): the insurer is in a better position to establish prejudice.
135. *Stoneham* v *Ocean, Railway & General Accident Ins Co* (1887) 19 QBD 237, 239 *per* Mathew J (PA); *Scott Lithgow Ltd* v *Secretary of State for Defence* (1989) 45 BLR 1, 10 *per* Lord Keith (HL). *Patterson* v *National Life & Accident Ins Co*, 183 F 2d 745 (6 Cir, 1950—life).
136. *Re Coleman's Depositories Ltd and Life & Health Assurance Assn* [1907] 2 KB 798, 807 *per* Fletcher Moulton LJ (CA—employers' liability): it was suggested that the very difficulty in specifying the damages that flowed from the breach supported the contention that the term (notice of loss) was intended to be a condition precedent. See also *London Guarantie Co* v *Fearnley* (1880) 5 App Cas 911, 916 *per* Lord Blackburn (fidelity).
137. See above, 26–2E.
138. For example, *Western Australian Bk* v *Royal Ins Co* (1908) 5 CLR 533 (HCA—fire), in which the contract required notice of loss within 15 days, and continued that "unless and until" the information was given no claim should be payable. See also *Maynard* v *National Fire Ins Co*, 129 SE 2d 443, 448 (Va, 1963—fire).
139. Chapter 15.

recovery),[140] that is influential[141]; but it is not decisive, especially when the label "condition precedent" is attached generally to a number of terms of different nature and importance.[142] However, when some terms are labelled "condition precedent" and others are not, the label is likely to be respected.[143] In one case, when it was admitted that the receipt of particulars of loss was essential, the court inferred that the time for submission was also important and, therefore, a condition precedent.[144] When there is doubt about the meaning of the term in its immediate context, the court will consider the purpose of the condition.[145]

For example, in *Welch* v *Royal Exchange Assurance*,[146] the English Court of Appeal held it to be in the very nature of the obligation, which was to provide such proofs and information as the insurer might reasonably require, that it was a condition precedent to payment. Generally, it makes little sense that the insurer should intend to pay before receipt of the stipulated proofs from the claimant: it "is a necessary preliminary to his right to recover on the agreement".[147]

In *Commercial Union* v *Margeson*,[148] a claimant was required to give certain particulars of fire loss within 14 days and King J, in the Supreme Court of Canada, observed[149]:

"Where, from a consideration of the whole instrument, it appears that the one party relied upon his remedy and not upon performance of the condition by the other, the performance is not a condition precedent; but where it appears that the intention most probably was to rely substantially upon the performance of the condition rather than upon a remedy in damages for its breach, then the reasonable view is that performance is a condition precedent. Looking at the nature of the requirement here, and the close connection between performance and the principal obligation of the company, it does not seem at all likely that the company was stipulating for an independent advantage, or intending to rely on what in any event must prove a barren remedy. The more reasonable construction is that performance was meant to be a condition precedent."

In *Newnham* v *Baker*,[150] having referred to English authorities, Derrington J, in the Supreme Court of Queensland, said:

"Although it is true that there is a general tendency to regard a term requiring notice to the

140. Or that in the case of notice "time is of the essence"—*Re Williams* (1902) 19 TLR 82 (workmen's compensation); *Re Coleman's Depositories Ltd and Life & Health Assurance Assn* [1907] 2 KB 798 (CA—employers' liability).
141. *Stoneham* v *Ocean, Railway & General Accident Ins Co* (1887) 19 QBD 237, 240 *per* Mathew J (PA).
142. *Re Bradley and Essex & Suffolk Accident Indemnity Sy* [1912] 1 KB 415 (CA—employers' liability).
143. *Stoneham* (above); *In Re Coleman's* (above), p 813 *per* Buckley LJ. *Employers' Liability Assurance Corp* v *Taylor* (1898) 29 SCR 104, 109 *per* Gwynne J dissenting (PA).
144. *Roper* v *Lendon* (1859) 1 El & El 825, 829, 830 *per* Lord Campbell CJ (fire).
145. *Stoneham*, (above) *loc cit; Re Bradley* (above) p 422 *per* Cozens-Hardy MR. In New York it has been held that the importance of a clause requiring prompt notice of loss is such that observance is a condition precedent: *State of New York* v *Amro Realty Corp*, 745 F Supp 832, 835 (ND NY, 1990—liability).
146. [1939] 1 KB 294, 313 *per* Mackinnon LJ, p 315 *per* Finlay LJ (CA—fire); *cf* p 307 *per* Slesser LJ. Also in this sense *Employers' Liability Assurance Corp* v *Taylor* (1898) 29 SCR 104, 107 *per* Taschereau J (PA). *Cf Scott Lithgow Ltd* v *Secretary of State for Defence* (1989) 45 BLR 1, in which the House of Lords held that the wording of the clause was such that it did not amount to a condition precedent, however, Lord Keith (pp 10–11) was apparently unaware of the case law, above 26–2E3.
147. *Roberts* v *Brett* (1865) 11 HLC 337, 351 *per* Lord Westbury LC.
148. (1899) 29 SCR 601 (fire).
149. p 607, citing *Roberts* v *Brett* (1856) 18 CB 561, affirmed (1859) 6 CB (NS) 611, (1865) 11 HLC 337.
150. [1989] 1 Qd R 393, 402 (PA), citations omitted. Although notice had not been given to the insurer until some five months after the initial injury, it was held that the requirement was not a condition precedent and did not bar the claim.

insurer to be a condition precedent, it is also true that the resolution of the point depends upon the construction of the particular policy. While the usual considerations favouring the desirability of the insurer's being promptly informed apply in the present case, there are certain features attenuating the force of this. First, the loss relates to personal injury to the insured. Factors which might be relevant to investigation in such types of insurance as fire cover, where the cause of the fire and the extent of the damage may need investigation, or liability insurance, where questions of defence of the third party's claim may be urgent, do not have application in this case, the risk is injury to the insured which is usually not deliberately self-inflicted. Moreover, in cases of injury to the person as contrasted with property damage, the extent of the injury is usually ascertainable objectively at a later stage . . . [In] respect of this particular contract, it was part of a scheme where the insured persons were expected to be at sea for an extended period of time so that it might well occur, as in the present case, that an injury might not be capable of investigation until the insured's return to port. Although the term requires 'immediate notice', however, in the circumstances of a policy such as this that must be construed as meaning notice at the first reasonable opportunity. Even so, the point is that the insurer must be deemed to have known the general nature of the plaintiff's work with its prospect that an injury might not be capable of early investigation. This factual situation reduces the efficacy of notice in this case . . . In these circumstances, there is added force in the proposition that, if the insurer wished to endow the term with the force of a condition precedent, it could easily have said so, whilst the imposition upon the insured of such a drastic result in the event of his failure to comply should be avoided if the position is not made clear.''

26–3 ARBITRATION

If a difference arises between insurer and insured, a contract condition may require the difference to be litigated[151] or arbitrated[152] within a stated period of time. A clause requiring an award, as "a condition precedent to the commencement of any action upon the policy", has been enforced.[154]

In the case of arbitration, a poor claimant is prejudiced by the lack of legal aid.[155] In *Clough*,[156] a clause, which required differences to be referred to arbitration, also required the insured to pay one half of the costs. The Court of King's Bench, while upholding the decision of the County Court judge not to apply the clause, rejected one of his grounds—that the clause was unfair and oppressive: the insured is bound by clear contract terms. Arbitration and "other referral procedures" are countenanced by the Statement of General Insurance Practice.[157] However, it is possible that a court

---

151. Clause upheld in *Walker* v *Pennine* [1980] 2 Lloyd's Rep 156 (CA—motor).
152. Clause upheld in *Scott* v *Avery* (1856) 5 HLC 810 (hull). *Aliter* if (a) the clause purports to oust the jurisdiction of the courts (in subsequent proceedings): *Scott* v *Avery* (1856) 5 HLC 811; or (b) it is contended that the contract of insurance, in which the clause is found, is void or voidable: *Heyman* v *Darwins Ltd* [1942] AC 356; *cf* breach of warranty which terminates the primary duties under the contract but not, it is submitted, secondary duties such as the duty to arbitrate: see above, 20–6C; in this sense Birds, p 239. USA: concerning arbitration provisions in insurance contracts, see Sehr, Blume and Elenius 27 Tort & Ins L J 226, 237 ff (1992).
154. *Caledonian Ins Co* v *Gilmour* [1893] AC 85 (fire).
155. In *Smith* v *Pearl* [1939] 1 All ER 95 (CA—motor) the contention, that an application by the insurer to have court proceedings stayed so that the dispute might be arbitrated, because financial assistance, available to the claimant in court proceedings, was not available to him in the arbitration, was rejected. The court (e.g., Slesser LJ, p 97) felt obliged to give literal effect to the clear words of the arbitration clause. Such clauses have been criticised as a possible means of abuse by insurers by the Law Reform Committee (5th Report), Cmnd 62, para 13; and by The Australian Law Commission (Report No 2), para 332.
156. *Clough* v *County Live Stock Ins Assn Ltd* (1916) 32 TLR 526 (livestock).
157. Clause 6. Appraisal, an informal procedure has been upheld, being "favored (*sic*) by the law because it serves as an inexpensive and speedy means of settling disputes over matters such as the amount or value of the property" insured: *Central Life Ins Co* v *Aetna*, 466 NW 2d 257, 260 (Iowa, 1991—fire). It has been regarded in the same light as arbitration: *Northeast Financial Corp* v *INA*, 757 F Supp 381, 384 (D Del, 1991—fire).

will not allow the insurer to exercise an option of arbitration in a way prejudicial to the insured, for example, to delay exercise of the option for tactical reasons until a point when the insured has incurred expense preparatory to litigation.[158]

In many contracts, the promise to refer differences to arbitration is distinct from the promise to pay insurance money, so that the latter may be enforced regardless of the former. In other cases, the arbitration clause has been construed as more than mere machinery, as being an inherent part of the insurer's promise of payment, without which the promise cannot be ascertained or enforced. In a fire case,[159] Lord Herschell LC stated:

"The question is . . . whether where the only obligation created is to pay a sum ascertained in a particular manner, where, in other words, such ascertainment is made a condition precedent to the obligation to pay, the courts can enforce an obligation without reference to such ascertainment? If they could do so, they would not be enforcing the contract made by the parties."

26-3A The New York Convention

Commercial contracts, including insurance contracts, may be enforced under the Convention on the Recognition and Enforcement of Foreign Arbitral Awards,[160] known as the New York Convention, to which effect is given in England by the Arbitration Act 1975. The Convention applies, first, to "foreign" awards, that is, "awards made in the territory of a State other than the State where the recognition and enforcement of such awards are sought".[161] Second, for the application of the Convention, the arbitration agreement must be valid "under the law to which the parties subjected it or, failing any indication thereon, under the laws of the country where the award was made".[162]

An award is made, according to one view, at the "seat" of arbitration, i.e. the place of arbitration stipulated by the parties in their arbitration agreement or determined for them by third parties.[163] In *Hiscox* v *Outhwaite*,[164] however, the House of Lords rejected the seat of the arbitration, as well as the place where the award was published, and held that an award is made where it is signed, even though the place of signature in that case (Paris) was entirely fortuitous. The decision was based on "the ordinary, common and natural construction of the word 'made'. A document is made

158. This was the basis of a decision against the insurer in *Chandler v Blue Cross Blue Shield*, 833 P 2d 356 (Utah, 1992—PHI).

159. *Caledonian Ins Co v Gilmour* [1893] AC 85, 90 (fire); Lord Watson (p 95) said that the arbitration clause had been "made an integral part of the obligation of indemnity". The House distinguished policies with two independent promises, first, a promise of indemnity and second, a promise to refer differences to arbitration. See also *Elliott v Royal Exchange Assurance Co* (1867) LR 2 Exch 237 (fire).

160. For example, *Meadows Indemnity Co Ltd v Baccala & Shoop Ins Services Inc*, 760 F Supp 1036 (ED NY, 1991—re). Evidently, international arbitration is attractive as a means of settling reinsurance disputes. Generally, see Ward Atterbury 32 Va J Int L 471 (1992); Diaconis 28 Tort & Ins L J 109 (1992). For a list of signatories to the Convention, see (1993) J Int'l Arb 105.

161. Article I(1) of the Convention,

162. Article V(1)(a).

163. Chukwumerije, 20 Can Bus L J 305 (1992). This is also the view of various commentators referred to by Hirst J ([1991] 2 Lloyd's Rep 1, 7) in his decision on this issue, which was reversed by the Court of Appeal.

164. [1991] 2 Lloyd's Rep 435 (re). In this case, the agreement provided for arbitration in London and the contract of reinsurance in dispute was governed by English law. The award was faxed from Paris to 4, Essex Court, London, where the arbitrator was a door tenant and from which it was made available to the parties.

when and where it is perfected. An award is perfected when it is signed, at any rate in the absence of something in the arbitration agreement or the rules under which the arbitration is conducted requiring some further formality before the award becomes effective".[165] Further, a distinction is drawn by article V of the Convention between the place where the arbitration took place and the place where the award was made: "it is with the making, not the evolution, of the award that the Act is concerned, and that has nothing to do with where the arbitration takes place".[166] This was an "anomalous"[167] decision, which the court reached with "regret".[168]

Against the decision, the obvious objection is that the place of signature is arbitrary and, worse, creates uncertainty, as that place may be unknown when the dispute is submitted to arbitrators and when the arbitrators proceed to business. FA Mann[169] gave an example which tells against the decision: "If there are three arbitratators who hold an arbitration in London, but meet in Paris to consider their award, and sign it at their respective residences, *viz*, New York, Geneva and Tokio, the award should be treated as 'made' in London, even if each arbitrator has indicated the place where he has signed it." Hirst J thought this problem insoluble, however, Lord Donaldson MR, found the solution that the award would not be made until the last arbitrator signed it and that, therefore, his place of signature would be the place of the award.[170]

In favour of the decision, Legatt J thought that "the disadvantages of an occasional capricious solution are outweighed by the advantages of simplicity and consistency", adopted by the Convention "as being precise, and not susceptible to any real difference of approach between the Courts of different countries".[171]

26–4 WAIVER OF PROCEDURAL CONDITIONS[172]

26–4A Waiver and Estoppel

In cases of waiver of breach of procedural conditions in insurance contracts, the courts have applied the general rules of waiver or estoppel[173]; and the rules applied have been treated as broadly the same as the rules of waiver (or estoppel) for rescission for misrepresentation or non-disclosure.[174] However, as regards contracts in general,

---

165. p 439 *per* Lord Oliver. Hirst J, at first instance ([1991] 2 Lloyd's Rep 1, 8) thought this interpretation, being "highly unreasonable" and "absurd", was one he could avoid by a purposive view of the Act and of the Convention, as taken by FA Mann, which sought to avoid uncertainty.
166. [1991] 2 Lloyd's Rep 1, 20 *per* Leggatt J (CA), reversing Hirst J (*ibid*) on this issue.
167. p 439 *per* Lord Oliver.
168. *Ibid*; also [1991] 2 Lloyd's Rep 1, 12 *per* Lord Donaldson MR.
169. quoted by Hirst J (p 7).
170. *Ibid* p 12.
171. p 20. See also p 12 *per* Lord Donaldson MR.
172. USA: see Appleman, sections 1420, 1449, 4747.
173. For example *Ayrey* v *British Legal & United Provident Assurance Co Ltd* [1918] 1 KB 136, 142 *per* Atkin J (life); *Evans* v *Employers Mutual Ins Assn Ltd* [1936] 1 KB 505, 518 *per* Slesser LJ (CA—motor); *Barratt Bros (Taxis) Ltd* v *Davies* [1966] 2 Lloyd's Rep 1, 5 *per* Lord Denning MR (CA—motor).
174. In this sense Arnould, No 683, n 36. The analogy was accepted in *Allen* v *Robles* [1969] 2 Lloyd's Rep 61 (CA—motor). See also Lloyd J in *Hadenfayre* v *British National Ins Co Ltd* [1984] 2 Lloyd's Rep 393, 401 (contingency), speaking of "affirming" a breach of warranty.

most English courts,[175] many writers in countries of common law,[176] as well as courts Australia[177] and in the United States,[178] indicate that the doctrines of waiver (used here in the sense of election)[179] and estoppel (in the sense of promissory estoppel[180]) are not the same.

26–4A1 Waiver and Estoppel: The Distinction

Waiver and estoppel were distinguished by the High Court of Australia in *Craine* v *Colonial Mutual Fire Ins Co Ltd*,[181] in which a "waiver clause" provided that any waiver by the insurer had to be in writing. As the alleged waiver was not in writing, the claimant pleaded it as estoppel and the court was asked to distinguish estoppel from waiver. While accepting[182] that many cases could be decided on either basis, Isaacs J distinguished waiver and estoppel along lines that have support in England, as follows:

(a) For waiver, the court pays particular attention to the conduct of the waivor[183] (insurer), to see "whether he has elected to get some advantage to

---

175. See *The Athos* [1981] 2 Lloyd's Rep 74, 87–88 *per* Neil J, citing *Kammins Ballrooms Co Ltd* v *Zenith Investments (Torquay) Ltd* [1971] AC 850, 882–883 *per* Lord Diplock; *Motor Oil Hellas (Corinth) Refineries SA* v *Shipping Corp of India, The Kanchenjunga* [1990] 1 Lloyd's Rep 391, 399 *per* Lord Goff (HL); Clarke [1990] CLJ 206.

176. Anson says (p 436): "Waiver was developed by the common law mainly as a device for evading the Statute of Frauds; little attempt was made to explain why a gratuitous promise should thus be binding. If it is to be justified analytically, it may be more satisfactory to regard waiver as a species of estoppel." Waiver and estoppel are "closely akin" to promissory estoppel: Waddams, *The Law of Contracts* (2nd ed), p 147; see also pp 152–153. See also, in this camp rather than the other, Lucke 21 W Austral L R 149 (1991).

Writers who distinguish waiver and estoppel include Stoljar (1957) 35 Can Bar Rev 485, 490–491; Adams, 36 Conv 244 (1972); Lindgren, (1989) 12 Univ NSW L J 153; Carter (1992) 5 JCL 198, 210; Arjunan (1993) 21 ABLR 86; Bower & Turner, *Estoppel by Representation* (3rd ed, 1977) distinguish estoppel by representation from estoppel by convention, election and promissory estoppel. Treitel (pp 709 ff), distinguishes waiver of the right to rescind (waiver in the sense of election) from other kinds of waiver. Treitel, however, concedes (p 110) that promissory estoppel has "close affinities" with waiver in the sense of forbearance. Brown & Menezes, 14:1:2, speak of a "lack of consensus in the courts and among writers" on the issue, and argue (14:7:5) for a distinction between waiver and estoppel in order to give sense to Canadian uniform legislation on insurance.

177. *Commonwealth of Australia* v *Verwayen* (1990) 170 CLR 394.

178. In *Globe Mutual Life Ins Co* v *Wolff* (1877) 95 US 326, 333 (life) Field J stated that waiver is only another name for estoppel; see also *Cochran* v *Order of United Commercial Travelers*, 143 F 2d 82, 85 (10 Cir, 1944—life). But the more general view is that "Although waiver and estoppel are terms used interchangeably, they represent distinct concepts of law. A waiver is a voluntary act of election between two or more courses of action. An estoppel . . . is an abatement of rights through the intervention of law because of equitable considerations; it contemplates an act to the prejudice of one party in reliance on the conduct of another"—*Prudential Ins Co* v *Brown*, 215 NYS 2d 652 (1961—life). See also in this sense *Providence Washington Ins Co* v *Stanley*, 403 F 2d 844, 850 (5 Cir, 1968—fire); 31 CJS, section 61. On the distinction in the USA, see further above, 23–18B3.

179. Common law election is distinguished from the equitable doctrine of election which, in Scotland, is referred to in the phrase "approbate and reprobate"—*Lissendon* v *Bosch Ltd* [1940] AC 412, 417 ff *per* Viscount Maugham. Bower, No 311.

180. *The Kanchenjunga* [1990] 1 Lloyd's Rep 391, 399 *per* Lord Goff (HL).

181. (1920) 28 CLR 305, affirmed [1922] 2 AC 541 (PC—fire). Sutton 11.9. The question in *Craine* was whether the insurer could reject a claim because notice (required within 15 days of loss) was three hours late. The High Court held that the insurer was estopped from raising the defence. The *Craine* distinction was accepted in *Deaves* v *CML Fire & General Ins Co Ltd* (1979) 59 ALJR 382, 388 *per* Gibbs ACJ (HCA—fire). See also Sutton, 11.10. In the context of insurance the distinction in *Craine* appears to have lost importance in Australia since the enactment of the Insurance Act 1984, in particular, sections 14 and 54.

182. (1920) 28 CLR 305, 326–327, 328.

183. (1920) 28 CLR 305, 326.

which he would not otherwise have been entitled, so as to deny to him a later election to the contrary".[184] For estoppel, while looking for a representation on the part of the person estopped (insurer), the court pays particular attention to the effect of the representation, usually reliance, on the insured. Whereas waiver "is not dependent upon reliance upon it by the other party",[185] equitable estoppel requires "such reliance by the representee as will render it inequitable for the representor to go back upon his representation".[186]

(b) For waiver, the court is concerned with the intention and knowledge[187] of the waivor, whereas the knowledge and intention of the person estopped are irrelevant.[188] Waiver must generally "be an informed choice, made with knowledge of the facts giving rise to the right" and, in the view of some courts[189] but not others,[190] made with knowledge of the legal right, to which the facts give rise. In contrast, in the case of estoppel, no "question arises of any particular knowledge on the part of the representor",[191] although, of course, for reliance, there must be knowledge of the representation on the part of the representee.[192]

---

184. (1920) 28 CLR 305, 326.

185. *The Kanchenjunga* [1990] 1 Lloyd's Rep 391, 399 *per* Lord Goff (HL); waiver "involves both knowledge and intent. Estoppel may arise when there is no intent to mislead. A waiver does not necessarily imply that one has been misled to his prejudice or altered his position. An estoppel always involves this element": *Brown* v *State Farm Mutual Automobile Ins Co*, 776 SW 2d 384, 387 (Mo, 1989—motor). See also in this sense: *Saunders* v *Lloyd's of London*, 779 P 2d 249, 254–255 (Wash, 1989—property); *Pitts* (below). See also *Peyman* v *Lanjani* [1985] Ch 457 (CA); and *Craine* (1920) 28 CLR 305, 327, citing *Sarat Chunder Dey* v *Gopal Chunder Laha* (1892) LR 19 Ind App 203 (PC) in which it was premised (p 215 *per* Lord Shand) that the law of India and the law of England on this point were the same. The distinction is accepted by Birds, pp 240 ff. See also Carter (1992) 5 JCL 199, 215. Estoppel is concerned to avoid inequity to the person induced by the conduct of the person estopped (pp 215–216 *per* Lord Shand).

Contra Bower, *Estoppel*, no 310. Also—"It is only when the waiver causes the other party to the contract to change his position to his detriment, which he would not have done save for his reliance upon the conduct of the other party, that an estoppel results"—*Alexander* v *Standard Accident Ins Co*, 122 F 2d 995, 997 (10 Cir, 1941—liability); see further in this sense *Providence Washington Ins Co* v *Stanley*, 403 F 2d 844, 850 (5 Cir, 1968—fire); *Pitts* v *American Security Life Ins Co*, 931 F 2d 351, 357 (5 Cir, 1991—group health). 31 CJS, section 61.

186. *The Kanchenjunga* [1990] 1 Lloyd's Rep 391, 399 *per* Lord Goff (HL); see also *Ajayi* v *Briscoe (Nigeria) Ltd* [1964] 3 All ER 556, 559 *per* Lord Hodson (PC); *The Post Chaser* [1982] 1 All ER 19 (CA). Reliance must give rise to inequity (sometimes called detriment) which is assessed at the time the representor seeks to resile from his representation.

187. *Craine* v *Colonial Mutual Fire Ins Co Ltd* (1920) 28 CLR 305, 326, citing *Earl of Darnley* v *Proprietors of the London, Chatham & Dover Ry* (1867) LR 2 HL 43, 57 *per* Lord Chelmsford LC. See also *The Mihalios Xilas* [1979] 1 WLR 1018, 1023 *per* Lord Diplock (HL); and, in Australia, *Deaves* v *CML Fire & General Ins Co Ltd* (1979) 59 ALJR 382, 388 *per* Gibbs ACJ (HCA—fire).

Contra as regards intention: *Donnison* v *Employers' Accident & Life Stock Ins Co Ltd*, 1897 24 R 681, 685 (Ct Sess—PA); *Toronto Ry Co* v *National British & Irish Millers Ins Co Ltd*, (1914) 111 LT 555, 563 *per* Scrutton J (CA—fire), an opinion which might be seen as concerned with estoppel rather than waiver (in the sense of election).

188. *Sarat Chunder Dey* v *Gopal Chunder Laha* (1892) LR 19 Ind App 203, 215 *per* Lord Shand (PC); *Blow* v *Guardian Assurance Co Ltd* (1922) 22 SR (NSW) 154, 170 (fire); *Reece* v *Pearl Assurance Co Ltd* (1934) 34 SR (NSW) 124, 129 (PA).

189. *The Uhenbels* [1986] 2 Lloyd's Rep 294, 298 *per* Hirst J, relying mainly on *Peyman* v *Lanjani* [1985] Ch 457 (CA).

190. See above, 23–18B1.

191. *The Kanchenjunga* [1990] 1 Lloyd's Rep 391, 399 *per* Lord Goff (HL); *Youell* v *Bland, Welch & Co Ltd, The Superhulls Cover Case*, [1990] 2 Lloyd's Rep 431, 449–450 *per* Phillips J (re).

192. *Lark* v *Outhwaite* [1991] 2 Lloyd's Rep 132, 142 *per* Hirst J (re).

(c) A further point of distinction, which was not raised in *Craine*,[193] is that waiver, at least waiver of past breaches of duty, cannot be revoked,[194] whereas it has been said[195] that promissory estoppel can always be revoked by reasonable notice, unless it is impossible to resume the previous position. Whereas "election once made is final", in general, "estoppel may be suspensory only".[196]

26–4A2 Waiver and Estoppel: When do they Apply?

In the general law, one answer to this question was given by Lord Diplock, as follows. Waiver arises when a person is entitled to alternative rights inconsistent with one another, as on forfeiture of a lease or rescission of a contract for wrongful repudiation,[197] and that person chooses one and waives the other. By contrast, estoppel debars a person from raising a defence to a claim against him.[198] The Diplock answer indicates that the procedural conditions in insurance contracts, which provide the insurer with defences, must be within the area of estoppel; and that forfeiture for non-payment of premium, rescission for misrepresentation or non-disclosure give rise to alternative and inconsistent rights (rescission or affirmation) and are thus within the area of waiver. However, misrepresentation and non-disclosure also commonly arise as defences to claims; and breach of procedural conditions presents the defending insurer with the alternative of raising the defence to a claim or not. For insurance contracts, the Diplock answer does not seem to work. Another answer has been given by Lord Goff:

193. In *Craine* v *Colonial Mutual Fire Ins Co Ltd* (1920) 28 CLR 305, 326 (HCA), the court did add a further point of distinction, that waiver required positive acts, whereas estoppel did not, citing decisions on leases: *Doe* v *Birch* (1836) 1 M & W 402, 406 *per* Parke B; *Perry* v *Davis* (1858) 3 CB (NS) 769, 777 *per* Williams J. *Sed quaere*.

194. *Central Estates (Belgravia) Ltd* v *Woolgar* (No 2) [1972] 1 WLR 1048, 1054 *per* Buckley LJ (CA), with reference to *Scarf* v *Jardine* (1882) 7 App Cas 345, 360 *per* Lord Blackburn; see also *The Kanchenjunga* [1990] 1 Lloyd's Rep 391, 399 *per* Lord Goff (HL); *Cia Tirrena di Assicurazioni SpA* v *Grand Union Ins Co Ltd* [1991] 2 Lloyd's Rep 143, 153 *per* Waller J (re). Thompson [1983] CLJ 257, 261; Carter (1992) 5 JCL 199, 217. *Aliter*, of course, if it is expressed as a temporary concession. See Anson, p 436.

Cf USA where it has been held that "waiver" of non-coverage is irrevocable: *Consolidated Electric Cooperative* v *Employers Mutual Liability Ins Co*, 106 F Supp 322 (ED Mo, 1952—liability); *Salerno* v *Western Casualty & Surety Co*, 336 F 2d 14 (8 Cir, 1964—liability); *Employers' Liability Assurance Corp* v *Royals Farm Supply Inc*, 186 So 2d 317 (Fla, 1966—fire)—waiver of formal proof of loss is irrevocable.

195. *Ajayi* v *Briscoe (Nigeria) Ltd* [1964] 1 WLR 1326, 1330 *per* Lord Hodson (PC). Treitel pp 106–107. It is far from clear that this distinction holds good when the promise is clearly intended to be permanent: Clarke [1974] CLJ 260, 287 ff. Much depends on the scope of the decision in *Foakes* v *Beer* (1884) 9 App Cas 605, which can be cited against estoppel of permanent effect; the better view may be that that decision does not touch the present question: Anson, p 102. The possibility of permanent promissory estoppel has some support: *D & C Builders Ltd* v *Rees* [1966] 2 QB 617, 624 *per* Lord Denning MR; *Alan & Co Ltd* v *El Nasr Export & Import Co* [1972] 2 QB 189, 218 *per* Megaw LJ (CA). Anson, p 105.

196. *Finagrain SA* v *Kruse* [1976] 2 Lloyd's Rep 508, 545 *per* Browne LJ (CA); *The Kanchenjunga* [1990] 1 Lloyd's Rep 391, 399 *per* Lord Goff (HL). See also Carter (1991–2) 4 JCL 59. For Australian decisions supporting this point of distinction between waiver and estoppel, see Carter (1992) 5 JCL 198, 217.

197. See *The Athos* [1981] 2 Lloyd's Rep 74, 87–88 *per* Neil J, citing *Kammins Ballrooms Co Ltd* v *Zenith Investments (Torquay) Ltd* [1971] AC 850, 882–883 *per* Lord Diplock. These statements were adopted in *Cia. Tirrena di Assicurazioni SpA* v *Grand Union Ins Co Ltd* [1991] 2 Lloyd's Rep 143, 153 *per* Waller J (re). Brown & Menezes, 14:4:2.

198. See *The Athos*, *loc cit*. The distinction made by Neil J was adopted by Lloyd J in *The Scaptrade* [1981] 2 Lloyd's Rep 425, 430; but, on appeal, the contention that the owners had lost the right to forfeit the charter for late payment of hire was treated as one of estoppel: [1983] QB 529, 536 *per* Robert Goff LJ; *cf The Athos* [1981] 2 Lloyd's Rep 74, 88 *per* Neil J. Loss of a right to avoid a contract under Italian law: estoppel: *Janred Properties Ltd* v *ENIT* [1989] 2 All ER 444 (CA).

"In the context of a contract, the principle of election applies when a state of affairs comes into existence in which one party becomes entitled to exercise a right, and has to choose whether to exercise that right or not . . . On the other hand, equitable estoppel requires an unequivocal representation by one party that he will not insist upon his legal rights against the other party".[199]

Unlike the Diplock answer, the Goff answer is easily applied to insurance cases. When the insurer knows something which entitles him to rescind the contract (misrepresentation, non-disclosure) or to repudiate a claim (breach of procedural condition), he "has to choose whether to exercise that right or not" and his choice of one course is waiver of the other. When, however, at a time *before* disclosure is due or a condition has to be performed, the insurer indicates that he *will* not insist on disclosure or performance of the condition, that is a case of estoppel. This is, it is submitted, the better answer. In practice, it must be said, the insurance cases in England show little trace of the distinction at all. Cases of one often involve the other,[200] and what starts as estoppel ("I shall not insist . . . ") may progress to waiver ("I shall not enforce my remedy for your past failure. . . "). The two doctrines may be applied in quick succession to the same facts by judges disinclined to draw lines between them. Although the judgment in *Craine* was largely on the basis of English precedent and the decision was affirmed by the Privy Council,[201] the judgment and the distinction have been largely ignored in insurance cases in England.[202] Why so? Perhaps because the distinction

---

199. *The Kanchenjunga* [1990] 1 Lloyd's Rep 391, 399 (HL).This answer was anticipated by Bower, *Estoppel*, no 310. A similar distinction was drawn by Thompson ([1983] CLJ 257) between pre-breach representations, which can be withdrawn, and post-breach representations, which cannot be withdrawn: the former, made in circumstances which do not call for an election, go to variation of contractual rights and are generally temporary, while the latter go to waiver of contractual remedies and are permanent (p 262).

200. *Peyman* v *Lanjani* [1985] Ch 457, 493 *per* May LJ (CA). Even when the distinction is drawn, the one tends to roll into the other, for example: *Dalzell* v *Northwestern Mutual Ins Co*, 32 Cal Rptr 125 (1963—motor). Having referred to waiver by a seller of payment as a condition precedent, 3 Corbin, section 752, continues that if "it causes the purchaser to change his position materially in reliance upon it, this too deprives the vendor of his power of retraction for, at the least, a reasonable time. The vendor is then said to be estopped; his own action can still be described as a 'waiver', while the resulting action of the purchaser justifies the added description of estoppel. By the usage thus explained, it appears that 'waiver' consists of the voluntary action of the obligor alone . . . To create an 'estoppel' . . . action by both parties is required."

201. *Sub nom Yorkshire Ins Co Ltd* v *Craine* [1922] 2 AC 541 (PC), on the basis of estoppel by conduct: pp 546–547 *per* Lord Atkinson, who did not discuss the distinction between waiver and estoppel.

202. For example, in *Jones* v *Bangor Mutual Shipping Ins Sy Ltd* (1889) 61 LT 727, 729 (hull) it was said that, as the insurer had taken premium in knowledge of the breach of warranty, he was estopped. In *Toronto Ry Co* v *National British & Irish Millers Ins Co Ltd* (1914) 111 LT 555, 653 (CA—fire), Scrutton J said that a condition could be waived for the future, especially if the conduct of the insurer led the other to spend time or incur expense—a passage relied on in *Burridge* v *Haines* (1918) 87 LJKB 641, 644 by Avory J. In *Barratt Bros (Taxis) Ltd* v *Davies* [1966] 2 Lloyd's Rep 1, 5 (CA—motor), Lord Denning MR said that waiver of past breach became effective when acted on.

Outside the field of insurance in *Rickards Ltd* v *Oppenhaim* [1950] 1 KB 616, 623 (CA), Denning LJ referred to waiver as kind of estoppel. In *Bremer Handelsgesellschaft mbH* v *Westzucker GmbH* [1981] 1 Lloyd's Rep 207, 212–213, Robert Goff J spoke of waiver of a right to object to a notice, as requiring reliance, basing his view *inter alia* on *Bremer Handelsgesellschaft mbH* v *Vanden Avenne-Izegem PVBA* [1978] 2 Lloyd's Rep 109, 126–127 *per* Lord Salmon (HL); the review of the issue by Robert Goff J was approved in *Cook Industries Inc* v *Tradax Export SA* [1985] 2 Lloyd's Rep 454, 462 by Kerr LJ (CA). In *Bunge SA* v *Cie Européene de Céréales* [1982] 1 Lloyd's Rep 306, 308 Mustill J considered an alleged waiver by a buyer of the seller's duty to ship on time and required the seller to show that it would be "unjust to allow the buyer to resume" his rights.

In Canada it has been suggested that waiver is a branch of estoppel: *Teasdall* v *Sun Life Assurance Co* [1927] 2 DLR 502, 509 (Ont—life); *Tarr* v *Westchester Fire Ins Co* [1953] 2 DLR 655, 665 (Ont—fire); *Ashe Trucking Ltd* v *Dominion Ins Corp* (1966) 56 DLR (2d) 730, 745 (BC—motor); *Chiasson* v *Century Ins Co*

owes more to legal history than to functional necessity. In each situation, the question is usually whether the insurer is to be prevented (for the time being or for ever) from raising a defence to a claim. It is a matter of little importance to the courts and still less to the parties, whether a sensible answer is found on the basis of waiver or of estoppel.

For example,[203] if the claimant fails to produce the evidence of fire loss required by the contract and the insurer does not insist on it until it is too late for the claimant to obtain it, the insurer will not be allowed to refuse the claim on that ground. According to the Goff distinction, that is waiver and, as such (above, 26–4A1(c)), is irrevocable. However, even if it is called estoppel, the result is the same; estoppel, although generally only suspensory, is also irrevocable, if the representee claimant cannot resume his former position, i.e., in this example, cannot obtain the evidence of the fire loss. So, in the discussion that follows, "waiver", the term most commonly used by the judges, is used to cover both concepts.

26–4B Proof of Waiver

While breach of condition must be proved by the insurer, waiver of that breach must be proved by the claimant.[204]

26–4C Knowledge

For waiver, the insurer must have sufficient knowledge of the breach, past or prospective.[205] It is probably enough that he has knowledge of the facts giving rise to the right of election,[206] whether or not he appreciates their legal significance.[207]

26–4D Unequivocal Conduct

Waiver by the insurer must take the form of unequivocal words[208] or conduct suggesting that he will not enforce the strict rights arising out of the breach of procedural condition, which usually means that he will not plead breach of condition as a defence to a claim. The waiver must be by the insurer or an authorised agent of the insurer.[209]

(1978) 86 DLR (3d) 342, 350 (NB—household) "waiver by estoppel"; see also *Phillips v Grand River Farmers' Mutual Fire Ins Co* (1881) 46 UCR 334, 362 (fire).

203. See *Toronto Ry Co v National British & Irish Millers Ins Co Ltd* (1914) 111 LT 555 (CA—fire), below, 26–4D and 26–4E.

204. *Home Indemnity Co v Allen*, 190 F 2d 490, 491 (7 Cir, 1951—liability); *Dalzell v Northwestern Mutual Ins Co*, 32 Cal Rptr 125, 131 (1963—motor). Cf above, 20–7B.

205. *Donnison v Employers' Accident & Life Stock Ins Co Ltd* (1897) 24 R 681 (Ct Sess—PA). *Craine* (above, 26–4A). See also *Deaves v CML* (1979) 59 ALJR 382, 388 *per* Gibbs ACJ (HCA—fire). *Canadian Ry Accident Ins Co v Haines* (1911) 44 SCR 386, 392 *per* Duff J (PA). *Keehn v Express Ins Co*, 129 F 2d 503 (7 Cir, 1942—re). Cf *Dalzell v Northwestern Mutual Ins Co*, 32 Cal Rptr 125, 128 (1963—motor): it is "sufficient if the insurer has information which if pursued would lead to the discovery of the breach".

206. *The Kanchenjunga* [1990] 1 Lloyd's Rep 391, 399 *per* Lord Goff (HL).

207. By analogy with cases of affirmation: above 23–18B1.

208. *The Kanchenjunga, loc. cit, Youell v Bland, Welch & Co Ltd, The Superhulls Cover Case*, [1990] 2 Lloyd's Rep 431, 450–451 *per* Phillips J (re). *Travellers Indemnity Co v Maracle*, (1991) 80 DLR (4th) 652, 657 (Sup Ct, Canada—fire). See also Carter (1991–2) 4 JCL 59.

209. It has been held that a loss adjuster may have actual or apparent authority to waive conditions of proof: *Hartford Fire Ins Co v Kiser*, 64 F 2d 288, 290 (4 Cir, 1933—fire); *Connecticut Fire Ins Co v Fox*, 361 F 2d 1 (10 Cir, 1966—fire); *Jackson v National Flood Insurers Assn*, 398 F Supp 1383 (SD Tex, 1974—flood).

In *Toronto Ry*,[210] the policy conditions concerning proof of fire loss were ignored by the claimant, who offered an alternative procedure. The insurer raised no objection, but replied that they would await receipt of the proof offered. The Court of Appeal held that the insurer had waived the conditions: "Conditions precedent may be waived by a course of conduct inconsistent with their continued validity, even though the contracting party does not intend his conduct to have that result."[211] So, if, for example, the insurer exercises contract rights such as a right of salvage,[212] that is an unequivocal act capable of amounting to waiver.

(a) *Investigation*. An appraisal or investigation of his own, while it may amount to waiver of formal notice of loss or of particulars of loss,[213] is not waiver by the insurer of conditions requiring proof of loss by the claimant[214] or of a time limit for claims,[215] unless the investigation is directed not to whether the insurer is liable but to matters which assume his liability[216]; or unless, as a result of the investigation, the insurer offers to settle the claim.[217]

(b) *Silence*. Generally, silence cannot constitute waiver; "it is difficult to imagine how silence and inaction can be anything but equivocal."[218] "A renunciation of a right is never to be presumed."[219] Total silence and inactivity, even with knowledge that a claim is pending cannot be waiver.[220] However, silence in context, such as failure to reply to the claimant's letter asking what information he should supply,[221] or failure to respond to requests for claim forms,[222] may be construed as waiver of the relevant information. Again, delay by the insurer will give rise to waiver "if thereby there was prejudice to [the claimant] or if in some other way rights of third parties intervened or if their delay was so long that the court felt able to say that the delay in itself was of such a length as to be evidence that they had in truth decided to accept liability".[223]

Failure to object to non-performance of a procedural condition, while handling the

---

210. *Toronto Ry Co v National British & Irish Millers Ins Co Ltd* (1914) 111 LT 555 (CA—fire). Similar conduct constituted waiver in *Webster v GAFLAC* [1953] 1 QB 520 (motor).

211. p 563 *per* Scrutton J; see also *Donnison v Employers' Accident & Life Stock Ins Co Ltd* (1897) 24 R 681, 685 (Ct Sess—PA); *Burridge v Haines* (1918) 87 LJKB 641; *Webster v GAFLAC* [1953] 1 QB 520, 532 *per* Parker J (motor).

212. *Yorkshire Ins Co Ltd v Craine* [1922] 2 AC 541 (PC—fire).

213. *King v Commercial Union Ins Co*, 306 F Supp 9 (ND Tex, 1969—liability).

214. *Maple Leaf Milling Co v Colonial Assurance Co* (1917) 36 DLR 202 (Man—fire). *Alexander v Standard Accident Ins Co*, 122 F 2d 995 (10 Cir, 1941—liability).

215. *Washington v Allstate Ins Co*, 901 F 2d 1281 (5 Cir, 1990—homeowner's).

216. *Security Ins Co v White*, 236 F 2d 215 (10 Cir, 1956—motor); *Allstate Ins Co v Flaumenbaum*, 308 NYS 2d 447 (1970—motor).

217. *Concordia Ins Co v School District No 98*, 282 US 545 (1931—fire); *Karp v Fidelity-Phenix Fire Ins Co*, 4 A 2d 529 (Tenn, 1939—motor).

218. *The Leonidas D* [1985] 2 All ER 796, 805 *per* Robert Goff LJ (CA). *Jackson v National Flood Insurers Assn*, 398 F Supp 1383 (SD Tex, 1974—flood).

219. *Accident Ins Co v Young* (1891) 20 SCR 280, 290 *per* Taschereau J (PA).

220. *Ibid*, p 284 *per* Ritchie CJ (PA); *Hyde v Lefaivre* (1902) 32 SCR 474 (fire). *State Farm Mutual Automobile Ins Co v Elgot*, 369 NYS 2d 719, 722 (1975—motor). *Cf Scali, McCabe, Sloves Inc v North River Ins Co*, 532 F Supp 203 (SD NY, 1981—liability), affirmed 681 F 2d 802, *cert den* 456 US 976, in which the insurer's lack of response to a letter from the insured's lawyer, announcing what the insurer later argued was a breach of condition, amounted to waiver.

221. *Jackson v National Flood Insurers Assn*, 398 F Supp 1383 (SD Tex, 1974—flood).

222. *Staff Jennings Inc v Fireman's Fund Ins Co*, 218 F Supp 112 (D Or, 1962).

223. *Allen v Robles* [1969] 2 Lloyd's Rep 61, 64 *per* Fenton Atkinson LJ (CA—motor), cited in *Reid v Campbell Wallis Moule & Co Pty Ltd*, [1990] VR 859, 874 (liability). Prejudice: *Brown v State Farm Mutual Automobile Casualty Ins Co*, 506 F 2d 976 (5 Cir, 1975—motor). See above, 23–18B3.

claim as if it were in all other respects correctly presented, may amount to waiver.[224] In *Barratt Bros (Taxis) Ltd* v *Davies*,[225] the insurers wrote to the claimant asking why he had not sent them documents, as required by the policy, but the tenor of the letter was that they were not rejecting the claim on that ground. Lord Denning MR observed[226]: "By not asking for the documents, they as good as said they did not want them . . . I think they waived the condition." In such a case, the insurer must expressly reserve his position on the breach of condition, if he is not to lose the option of pleading the breach.[227] By contrast, it has been accepted that insurers may deal with all aspects of a claim concurrently; so, to ask for an appraisal of the property damaged[228] or to investigate the facts supporting a claim[229] does not necessarily waive a limitation period or notice condition: see (a), above.

(c) *Inferences from Rejection.* If the insurer rejects the claim altogether on another ground, such as lack of cover, the insurer does not thereby waive the possibility of pleading a breach of condition at a later stage,[230] if that breach occurred prior to the rejection of the claim; the rejection did not prompt the breach. By contrast, if the insurer repudiates liability under the policy before performance of a procedural condition is due, it is generally held[231] that the claimant is dispensed from the duty to perform the condition.[232] In a liability case[233] the court said that

"a claimant should not be required to approach his insurer, hat in hand, and request consent to settle . . . when he has already been told, in essence, that the insurer is not concerned, and he is

---

224. *Donnison* v *Employers' Accident & Life Stock Ins Co Ltd* (1897) 24 R 681 (Ct Sess—PA). *Ocean Accident & Guaranty Corp* v *Fowlie* (1902) 33 SCR 253 (PA); *Canadian Ry Accident Ins Co* v *Haines* (1911) 44 SCR 386 (PA); *Sproul* v *National Fire Ins Co* [1925] 1 DLR 1152 (NS—fire).
    The retention of proofs of loss without objection may amount to waiver: *General Motors Acceptance Corp* v *American Ins Co*, 50 F 2d 803 (5 Cir, 1931—fire), *cert den* 284 US 676; *Muntwyler* v *Ranger Ins Co*, 393 F Supp 795 (ND Ill, 1975—aviation).
    225. [1966] 2 Lloyd's Rep 1 (CA—motor). See also *Glagovsky* v *National Fire Ins Co* [1931] 1 WWR 573 (Man—fire).
    226. p 5. See also *Fowlie* v *Ocean Accident & Guarantee Corp Ltd* (1902) 4 OLR 146, 158 (PA), affirmed (1902) 33 SCR 253.
    227. *Donnison* (above). For example, judicious use of the hallowed phrase "without prejudice" which was held effective for this purpose in *National Trust* v *Sterling Accident* (1916) QR 51 SC 481 (PA); *Marcoux* v *Halifax Fire Ins Co* [1948] SCR 278, 283–284 *per* Taschereau J (motor).
    228. *Gillis* v *Bourgard* (1983) 145 DLR (3d) 570 (Ont—fire).
    229. *Boyer* v *American Casualty Co*, 332 F 2d 708, 711 (2 Cir, 1964—motor).
    230. *Welch* v *Royal Exchange Assurance* [1939] 1 KB 294 (CA—fire). *Accident Ins Co* v *Young* (1891) SCR 280 (PA). *Allied Steel Construction Co* v *Employers Casualty Co*, 422 F 2d 1369 (10 Cir, 1970—liability); *Stargatt* v *Avenell*, 434 F Supp 234, 246 (D Del, 1977). *Idem* in New York as regards any grounds for refusing a claim or terminating the contract, unless the insurer knew of one ground while pleading (only) the other: *Guberman* v *William Penn Life Ins Co*, 538 NYS 2d 571, 573 (1989—life). Appleman, sections 3631 ff. This appears to be consistent with general principle in England: *The Mihalis Angelos* [1971] 1 QB 164, 183 (CA); *cf The Wise, Vitol SA* v *Esso Australia Ltd* [1989] 2 Lloyd's Rep 451 (CA).
    231. For example *Re Coleman's Depositories* [1907] 2 KB 798, 805–806 *per* Vaughan Williams LJ (CA—employers' liability); *Jureidini* v *National British & Irish Millers Ins Co Ltd* [1915] AC 499 (fire).
    Ross v *Scottish Union & National Ins Co* (1918) 58 SCR 169, 182 *per* Anglin J (fire); *Magrath* v *Sydenham Mutual Fire Ins Co* [1923] 3 DLR 44 (Ont—fire); *Pickford & Black Ltd* v *Canadian General Ins Co* (1973) 42 DLR (3d) 360, 397 (NS—liability).
    D'Aquilla Bros Contracting Co Inc v *Hartford Accident & Indemnity Co*, 193 NYS 2d 502 (1959—liability); *Stout* v *Grain Dealers Mutual Ins Co*, 201 F Supp 647 (MD NC, 1962—liability), affirmed 307 F 2d 521 (4 Cir, 1962); *Bluff Ventures Ltd* v *Chicago Title Ins Co*, 950 F 2d 139 (4 Cir, 1991—title). Appleman, sections 3631 ff, 4747.
    232. As to whether the claimant must have been ready and willing to perform the condition, see *The Simona* [1989] AC 788.
    233. *Stephens* v *State Farm Mutual Automobile Ins Co*, 508 F 2d 1363, 1366 (5 Cir, 1975—motor). Williston, section 699.

to go his way. It is difficult to see why an insurer should be allowed to, on the one hand, deny liability and thus, in the eyes of the insured breach his contract and, at the same time, on the other hand, be allowed to insist that the insured honor all his contractual commitments".

The insurer may reserve his position by making an offer of settlement without prejudice to any right to reject the claim altogether. If the insurer reserves his position as regards specified defences, his failure to include other potential defences may be seen as waiver of those defences.[234]

26–4E Reliance[235]

Regardless of the conceptual difference between waiver and estoppel,[236] courts usually require reliance by the claimant.[237] Courts look to whether the claimant has been "lulled to sleep . . . or was induced to act in a particular way in reliance"[238] on what the insurers had done. If the alleged waiver occurred after the time for notice had passed, it cannot be said to have induced the lateness.[239] It is implicit that the insurer's conduct must have been aimed at the claimant. Thus a concession of extra time made to the insured cannot be pleaded by an assignee.[240]

Finding waiver in *Toronto Ry*,[241] Kennedy LJ said that observance of the condition, requiring a magistrate's certificate of loss,

"had become impracticable owing to the rebuilding or reconstruction of the premises and the replacement of the destroyed or damaged rolling stock, and this consideration appears to me materially to confirm the opinion [that the insurer] had so indicated to the plaintiffs their intention not to insist upon the stipulations of the policy as to the ascertainment of the amount of loss, and so led them to act and to abstain from acting . . . as to debar them from afterwards insisting upon adherence to those stipulations".

In the same case, Scrutton J[242] adopted this statement by the Supreme Court of Maine[243]:

"if the conduct and declaration of the insurer are of such a character as to justify the belief that waiver was intended, and, acting upon this belief, the insured is induced to incur trouble and expense and is subjected to delay to his injury and prejudice, the insurer may be prohibited from claiming a forfeiture for such a breach upon the principle of equitable estoppel."

---

234 *Vitol SA* v *Esso Australia Ltd, The Wise* [1989] 2 Lloyd's Rep 451 (CA). *Johnston Equipment Corp* v *Industrial Indemnity*, 489 NW 2d 13, 17 (Iowa, 1992—liability). As to "non-waiver" agreements, see above, 17–4F.

235. See also 20–7E and 23–18B3.

236. See above, 26–4A1.

237. For example, finding waiver in *Barratt Bros (Taxis) Ltd* v *Davies* [1966] 2 Lloyd's Rep 1, 6 (CA—motor), Salmon LJ looked at the response of the reasonable person receiving the letter said to contain the waiver; *idem*, p 5 *per* Lord Denning MR, with whom Danckwerts LJ concurred.

Atlas Assurance Co v *Brownell* (1899) 29 SCR 537, 544 *per* Sedgewick J (fire); *Gillis* v *Bourgard* (1983) 145 DLR (3d) 570, 572 (Ont—fire). *Globe Mutual Life Ins Co* v *Wolff* (1877) 95 US 326, 333 (life); applied in *Home Indemnity Co* v *Allen*, 190 F 2d 490, 491 (7 Cir, 1951—liability).

238. *Webster* v *GAFLAC* [1953] 1 QB 520, 532 *per* Parker J (motor). *Merchants Mutual Casualty Co* v *Wildman*, 197 NYS 2d 925, 928 (1960—liability); and *Alliance Ins Co* v *Enders*, 293 F 485, 488 (9 Cir, 1923—fire).

239. *Sheet Metal & Roofing Contractors' Assn* v *Liskany*, 369 F Supp 662 (SD Ohio, 1974—fidelity).

240. *Re Carr and Sun Fire Ins Co* (1897) 13 TLR 186 (CA—fire).

241. *Toronto Ry Co* v *National British & Irish Millers Ins Co Ltd* (1914) 111 LT 555, 561 (CA—fire).

242. p 593; applied in *Burridge* v *Haines* (1918) 87 LJKB 641.

243. *Hanscom* v *Ins Co*, 90 Me 333, 339 (1890).

26–4F The Effect of Waiver

As regards past breaches of condition by the insured, waiver is permanent; it cannot be revoked.[244] As regards conditions, performance of which is not yet due, much turns on the terms of the waiver. If the waiver is a temporary concession, such as an extension of time, the waiver expires with the time granted and, thereafter, the condition must be observed.[245] If the performance of the condition is no longer possible and, therefore, the former position cannot be resumed, the effect of the waiver is permanent[246]; if not, the concession may be withdrawn by reasonable notice to the insured.[247]

26–5 TIME OF SUIT

By section 5 of the Limitation Act 1980, all actions founded on a contract not under seal shall not be brought after the expiration of six years from the date on which the cause of action accrued. If the contract is under seal, by section 8 of the Act the period is 12 years. The effect on contracts is not to prescribe or extinguish the right but to bar the remedy. In the case of all insurance contracts, *prima facie* the cause accrues on the happening of the event covered. The period may be shortened by clear terms of the contract.

When the insurance claim is characterised as a debt,[248] the effect of section 29(5) is that, if the insurer "acknowledges the claim or makes any payment in respect of it the right shall be treated as having accrued on and not before the date of the acknowledgement or payment".

26–5A Ignorance

In England, the statutory period runs even though the claimant may be unaware of his cause of action. This was the intention behind the legislation[249] and is the implication of those provisions of the Limitation Act 1980, whereby a longer time limit is provided for certain cases—negligence actions (s 14A), fraud and concealment (s 32)—in which the facts relevant to the cause of action are not known at the date of accrual, but not in other cases such as that of an insurance claim, in which there has been no fraud or concealment.[250] The same rule prevails in parts of the USA.[251] In other parts of the USA a more lenient rule prevails. In California, in *Prudential–LMI Commercial Insurance* v *Superior Court*,[252] the Supreme Court considered a limitation period in the light of the purpose of limitation: "to promote justice by preventing surprises through the revival of claims that have been allowed to slumber until evidence has been lost, memories have faded, and witnesses have disappeared. The theory is that even if one has a just

---

244. Thompson [1983] CLJ 257, 261.
245. *Re Carr* (1897) 13 TLR 186 (CA—fire).
246. *Burridge* v *Haines* (1918) 87 LJKB 641 (livestock).
247. See above at note 155.
248. Below, 30–7.
249. Law Revision Committee, Fifth Interim Report, 1936 (Cmd 5334).
250. See *Chandris* v *Argo Ins Co* [1963] 2 Lloyd's Rep 65, 73 *per* Megaw J, and cases cited; the judgment of Megaw J was approved in *Castle Ins* v *Hong Kong Shipping* [1984] AC 226 (PC).
251. For example, Illinois.
252. 274 Cal Rptr 387, 393 (1990—fire); Towner, 27 Tort & Ins L J 638 (1992).

claim it is unjust not to put the adversary on notice to defend within the period of limitation and that the right to be free of stale claims comes to prevail over the right to prosecute them." From this perspective, the court concluded that the "inception of loss", the moment from which time ran under the statutory policy form, "should be determined by reference to reasonable discovery of the loss and not necessarily turn on the occurrence of the physical event causing the loss".[253] The purpose of the English Act is similar, however, the express provision for cases of justifiable ignorance on the part of the claimant must make it difficult to argue a "Californian" extension by inference.[254] Moreover, the statutory period in England (six years) is longer than the one year period in California for insurance contracts.

26–5B Quantification

In Canada, it has been held that as "the very nature of a contract of indemnity is that it is a reimbursement obligation for an amount of damages that has actually been suffered . . . no cause of action can even arise until the extent of the loss has been quantified"[255] and, consequently, a limitation period does not begin to run, at the very earliest, until the loss has been discovered. Alternatively, it might be held in such a case that liability has been admitted and that, in the event of a dispute about quantum, the insurer is estopped from pleading the limitation period.[256]

Apart from estoppel, the rule in England is different. A cause of action arises upon the existence of every fact which the plaintiff must allege in his statement of claim[257]; and that proof is a condition precedent not to the cause of action but to enforcement. The period runs regardless of difficulties of proof or of whether the claim has been quantified[258] and, therefore, runs under an insurance contract from the time of the event which triggers the insurer's obligation to pay insurance money. English decisions to this effect, however, have been in relation to the relatively long statutory period.[259] In the case of a short contractual period, especially in an insurance contract with clauses about proof and claims procedure, the latter may be used as the basis of a construction argument to soften the effect of the former, if not by postponing the starting date, then by suspension or waiver.

26–5C Investigation and Suspension

For waiver or estoppel in this context,[260] the usual rules apply. Whereas an admission of liability with investigation of the claim on the issue of quantum may amount, for example, to waiver of notice of loss,[261] it does not amount to waiver of the limitation

---

253. p 395.
254. See also the strict view taken by English courts of notice clauses: 26–2E.
255. *Callaghan Contracting Ltd* v *Royal Ins Co of Canada* (1989) 59 DLR (4th) 753, 757 (New Brunswick—liability).
256. *Maracle* v *Travellers Indemnity Co* (1989) 62 DLR (4th) 570 (Ont—fire).
257. *Coburn* v *Colledge* [1897] 1 QB 702, 706–707 *per* Lord Esher MR, with whom other members of the court agreed. See Mullaney [1993] LMCLQ 34.
258. *Coburn* v *Colledge* [1897] 1 QB 702 (CA); *RB Policies at Lloyd's* v *Butler* [1950] 1 KB 76.
259. When the statutory period (for a particular kind of contract) is short, it may be linked with a provision for suspension, for example, the Carriage of Goods by Road Act 1965, Schedule, article 32.2.
260. Generally, see above 26–4.
261. Above 26–4D.

period: for that, it has been held,[262] there must be a distinct representation.[263] Were it otherwise, the possibility of waiver would jeopardise dealings to resolve claims and would not be in the interests of claimants.[264] The English view appears to be the strict view, also found in some parts of the United States,[265] that the time runs while the claim is being investigated and regardless of the insurer's response. In contrast, in California the contractual limitation period is construed in the light of other clauses of the contract contemplating claims procedure and investigation, and time is suspended from the time of notice to the time of the insurer's formal denial of the claim.[266] The Supreme Court found it "anomalous . . . that an insured must file a lawsuit before the insurer has completed its investigation and denied the claim",[267] and that the purpose of the limitation period, to "permit complete and adequate defense" had been achieved by the notice of claim.[268] Nonetheless, states such as New York have found it expedient to provide for suspension of time in insurance claims by statute.

---

262. *Travellers Indemnity Co* v *Maracle*, (1991) 80 DLR (4th) 652 (SC Canada—fire).
263. For example, from decisions in California: leading the insured to believe that an amicable settlement will be reached, accepting informal proof of loss and negotiating the settlement of a claim after the time for suit had passed: *Prudential–LMI* (above) p 397.
264. *Maracle* (above) p 657.
265. For example, decisions in Pennsylvania.
266. *Prudential–LMI* (above).
267. p 395.
268. p 397.

CHAPTER 27

CLAIMS CO-OPERATION AND GOOD FAITH

27–1 THE CONTINUING DUTY OF GOOD FAITH

27–1A The Nature of the Duty

In England, it "is an essential condition of the policy of insurance that the underwriters shall be treated with good faith, not merely in reference to the inception of the risk, but in the steps taken to carry out the contract."[1] In California,[2] there is "an implied covenant of good faith and fair dealing *in every contract* that neither party will do anything which will injure the right of the other to receive the benefits of the agreement". This implied covenant requires, for example, "that the insurer conduct a reasonable investigation into the insured's claim".[3]

The language of the Californian court points up the connection with more general rules of contract law in the USA,[4] as well as in England where there is a "positive rule of the law of contract that conduct of either [party] which can be said to amount to . . . bringing about the impossibility of performance is itself a breach".[5] This proposition has also been turned around and stated in positive terms, as a duty of co-operation, that, when "it appears that both parties have agreed that something shall be done, which cannot be effectually done unless both parties concur in doing it, the construction of the contract is that each agrees to do all that is necessary to be done on

---

1. *Boulton v Houlder Bros & Co* [1904] 1 KB 784, 791–792 *per* Mathew LJ (CA—hull); see also *Leon v Casey* (1932) 43 Ll L Rep 69, 70 *per* Scrutton LJ (CA—cargo).
   The *Boulton* dictum has been applied in Australia: *Maraitis v Harvey Trinder (Queensland) Pty Ltd* [1969] Qd R 226, 236 (fire); and in *Trans-Pacific Ins Co (Australia) Ltd v Grand Union Ins Co Ltd* (1989) 18 NSWLR 675, 702–703 (re). Also in this sense: *Distillers-Bio-Chemicals (Australia) Pty Ltd v Ajax Ins Co Ltd* (1973) 130 CLR 1, 31 *per* Stephen J (HCA—liability); *Deaves v CML Fire & General Ins Co Ltd* (1979) 23 ALR 539, 580 *per* Murphy J (HCA—fire). *Dawson v Monarch Ins Co Ltd* [1977] 1 NZLR 372, 378 (fire); *Sampson v Gold Star Ins Co Ltd* [1980] 2 NZLR 742, 746 (motor); *cf FAME Ins Co Ltd v McFayden* [1961] NZLR 1070, 1074 (motor); and *Guardian Royal Exchange Ins Ltd v Ormsby* (1982) 29 SASR 498 (theft), criticised by Tarr, (1988) 1 Ins LJ 42, 57 (1988).
2. *Comunale v Traders & General Ins Co*, 328 P 2d 198, 200 (Cal, 1958—motor), emphasis added. See Shipstead and Thomas, 23 Tort & Ins LJ 215, 218 (1987). As regards the continuing duty of good faith between insurer and reinsurer, see Marick, 26 Tort & Ins LJ 231, 233 ff (1991).
3. *Hydro Systems Inc v Continental Ins Co*, 929 F 2d 472, 477 (9 Cir, 1991—liability).
4. *Kirke La Shelle Co v Paul Armstrong Co*, 263 NY 79, 87 (1933); *Beck v Farmers Ins Exchange*, 701 P 2d 795 (Utah, 1985). In Australia, see *Secured Income Real Estate (Australia) Ltd v St Martin's Investments Pty Ltd* (1979) 144 CLR 596 (HCA). See also below, 30–10, concerning the "tort" of bad faith.
5. *Southern Foundries Ltd v Shirlaw* [1940] AC 701, 717 *per* Lord Atkin, with reference to a statement by Cockburn CJ in *Stirling v Maitland* (1864) 5 B & S 840, 852. See also *Nissho Iwai Petroleum Co. Inc. v Cargill International SA* [1993] 1 Lloyd's Rep 80, 84, *per* Hobhouse J, citing *The Aello* [1961] AC 135.

his part for the carrying out of that thing, though there may be no express words to that effect".[6]

As regards insurance contracts, the duty of good faith continues throughout the contractual relationship at a level appropriate to the moment. In particular, the duty of disclosure, most prominent prior to contract formation,[7] revives whenever the insured has an express or implied duty to supply information to enable the insurer to make a decision.[8] Hence, it applies if cover is extended[9] or renewed.[10] It also applies when the insured claims insurance money: he must make "full disclosure of the circumstances of the case".[11] It is less clear but arguable that, if good faith requires a degree of disclosure by claimant to insurer, in view of the generally mutual character of the duty (below 27–1B), the insurer owes a corresponding duty to the claimant, for example, a duty to disclose adjusters' reports.[12] The degree of disclosure, however, varies according to the phase in the relationship. It seems that the level of disclosure appropriate to a claim is different from that at the time of contract: an innocent misrepresentation or non-disclosure in the claim does not defeat a claim; there must be fraud in the sense discussed below: 27–2A.

If a claim by the insured against his insurer is settled, any compromise must be *bona fide* and honest[13] and, if the insurer exercises rights in subrogation, he must exercise them in good faith.[14] If, however, the relationship has fallen to the point that the insured institutes action against the insurer to sustain a claim, the nature of the relationship has changed, at least as regards that claim. It has been held in Connecticut that, although the claimant must not commit perjury, that is a matter for the criminal law; and that when "settlement fails and suit is filed, the parties no longer deal on the non-adversary level required by [good faith]. If the insurer denies liability and compels the insured to bring suit, the rights of the parties are fixed as of that time for it is assumed the insurer, in good faith, then has sound reasons based upon the terms of the policy for denying the claim of the insured. To permit the insurer to await the testimony at trial to create a further ground for escape from its contractual obligation is inconsistent with the function a trial normally serves".[15]

---

6. *Mackay* v *Dick* (1881) 6 App Cas 251, 263 *per* Lord Blackburn. See also *Mona Oil Equipment & Supply Co Ltd* v *Rhodesia Railways Ltd* [1949] 2 All ER 1014, 1018 *per* Devlin J; *The World Navigator* [1991] 1 Lloyd's Rep 277, 282; and *Nissho* (above). In the past, the duty of co-operation has been limited; it has been mostly a duty to desist. It becomes a duty to act only in cases of necessity: Burrows, 31 MLR 392, 393, 404 (1968); or, as it was put more recently and more positively, where it is necessary to make the agreement work: Treitel 186.

7. Above, ch 23.

8. *The Litsion Pride* [1985] 1 Lloyd's Rep 437, 511 *per* Hirst J (hull). *New Medial Defence Union Ltd* v *Transport Industries Ins Co Ltd* (1985) 4 NSWLR 107: the insured has no duty to *volunteer* information which the insurer would consider relevant to an option to terminate the cover. See also *Cory* v *Patton* (1872) LR 7 QB 304, cargo.

9. See above, 23–4B.

10. See above, 23–4C.

11. *Shepherd* v *Chewter* (1808) 1 Camp 274, 275 *per* Lord Ellenborough (hull); and somewhat more recently, for example: *Action Scaffolding Ltd* v *AMP Fire Ins & Gen Ins Co* (1990) 6 ANZ Ins Cases, No 60–970 (motor). See below, 27–2. As to the doctrine of reverse or comparative bad faith affecting the claimant in the USA, see below, 30–10.

12. Pincott (1988) 1 Ins LJ 27, 34. Further, it is clear that the liability insurer who defends the insured has a duty of good faith: above, 17–4E1.

13. See below, 30–6A and 30–10.

14. See Mullins (1991) 4 Ins LJ 83. However, it has been held that the insurer, when performing its duties under the contract, is not liable for failing to protect the "commercial image" of the insured: *Vacuum Industrial Pollution Inc* v *Union Oil Co*, 764 F Supp 507 (ND Ill, 1991—liability).

15. *Rego* v *Connecticut Insurance Placement Facility*, 593 A 2d 491, 497 (Conn, 1991—fire).

27–1B To Whom the Duty is Owed

In England, the duty exists mutually between insurer and insured, however, it has been held that the duty of good faith owed by the insurer to the insured is owed to the insured only and not, for example, to a bank which, having lent money to the insured, takes an assignment of the benefit of the contract of insurance[16]; any rights that the bank might have against the insurer derive from the insured.

Similarly, it has been held in Oklahoma that there is no duty of good faith without "either a contractual or statutory relationship between the insurer and the party" in question.[17] The corollary is, first, that a duty of good faith does exist between a primary insurer and his reinsurer.[18] Second, however, it has been held, in Arizona[19] and Louisiana[20] in cases of liability insurance, that a primary insurer owes no such duty of good faith to an excess insurer on the same risk. The courts wished to avoid "the injustice and efficiency that may be produced by encouraging insurers with independent rights to intervene in litigious matters in competition with their insureds, and the effect upon insurance administration and rates of requiring a primary insurers' attorneys to serve three masters".[21] Courts reason[22] that the excess insurer can protect its position by contract terms and has a right of subrogation through the insured against the primary insurer, in the event of bad faith.[23]

27–1C A Duty of Care in Tort

In *Banque Financière de la Cité* v *Westgate Ins Co*,[24] it was held that the insurer does not owe the insured a duty of care actionable in tort. According to the general guidelines for the existence of a duty,[25] first, loss of the type alleged must be a foreseeable consequence of the failure alleged.[26] Second, there must be proximity: "such close and direct relations that the act complained of directly affects a person whom the person alleged to be bound to take care would know would be directly affected by his

16. *The Good Luck* [1988] 1 Lloyd's Rep 514, 546–547 *per* Hobhouse J (hull). This view was approved on appeal: [1989] 2 Lloyd's Rep 238, 264 *per* May LJ. That decision was affirmed on other grounds: [1992] 1 AC 233. Hobhouse J continued: "A different situation may arise where the assignee steps into the shoes of the assignor and takes over the conduct of the contract. Under those circumstances, where the assignor ceases to be the person dealing with the insurer, the duty of utmost good faith has to be discharged by reference to the assignee. However, that was not the case here".

17. *Roach* v *Atlas Life Ins Co*, 769 P 2d 158, 161 (Okl, 1989—life). In that case, however, the latter was the statutory beneficiary of life insurance and thus (*ibid*) "meets both criteria for assertion of the right". See also *Burley* v *Homeowners Warranty Corp*, 773 F Supp 844, 859 (SD Miss, 1990—liability).

18. In England this is accepted but it is also recognised that reinsurance, especially treaty reinsurance, may give rise to special problems: Butler & Merkin A.6.1. USA: see, for example, Thomas, 41 Duke LJ 1548, 1553 (1992).

19. *Twin City Fire Ins Co* v *Superior Court*, 792 P 2d 758 (Ariz, 1990—liability). But *cf* New York where such a duty is owed: *General Star Nat. Ins Co* v *Liberty Mutual Ins Co*, 960 F 2d 377 (3 Cir, 1992—motor).

20. *Great Southwest Fire Ins Co* v *CNA Ins Cos*, 557 So 2d 966 (La, 1989—liability).

21. p 971.

22. For example, *Twin City* (above) pp 759–760.

23. For example, *Hartford Accident & Indemnity Co* v *Aetna Casualty & Surety Co*, 792 P 2d 749 (Ariz, 1990—motor). Courts in the USA divide on whether the primary insurer owes to the excess insurer a duty of care actionable in tort: Sehr, Blume and Elenius 27 Tort & Ins L J 226, 227 (1992).

24. [1990] QB 665 (CA), affirmed mainly on other grounds: [1991] 2 AC 249; however, it is clear (e.g. p 273) that the House agreed with the Court of Appeal that the insurer did not owe the insured a duty of care.

25. See for example *Caparo Industries plc* v *Dickman* [1989] 1 All ER 798, 802 *per* Bingham LJ (CA); [1990] 2 AC 605, 633 *per* Lord Oliver. On the duty of care in general, see also as regards the duty of insurance agents above 9–2,

26. This requirement is usually easy to satisfy: *Banque Financière* p 768 *per* Slade LJ.

careless act.";[27] Third, the imposition of a duty of care must be fair and reasonable. However, Lord Goff has referred[28] to proximity, the second requirement, as "an expression which refers to such a relation between the parties as renders it just and reasonable that liability in negligence may be imposed". The second and third requirements, distinguished in theory, are often applied together in practice and, so it was in *Westgate*, in which Slade LJ dealt with proximity in connection with what was fair and reasonable.[29]

In a case of purely economic loss, as is likely to occur between insurer and insured, the imposition of a duty is regarded as neither fair nor reasonable, unless brought within very limited categories, notably the category of negligent misstatement.[30] In *Westgate*, it was held that the insurance relationship did not come into these categories.

First, there could be no duty in respect of misstatements and consequent economic loss, without a voluntary assumption of responsibility by the obligor,[31] a feature which, as Slade LJ observed,[32] will be more difficult to infer in a case of silence than in a case of misrepresentation, in which there is reliance by the plaintiff. "For better or worse, our law of tort draws a fundamental distinction between the legal effects of acts on the one hand and omissions on the other."[33]

Second, the Court of Appeal was reluctant to impose a duty to speak between parties who were in the course of negotiating a (further) contract.[34] It quoted[35] the opinion of Lord Scarman[36] that their "Lordships do not believe that there is anything to the advantage of the law's development in searching for a liability in tort where the parties are in a contractual relationship . . . it is a relationship in which the parties have, subject to a few exceptions, the right to determine their obligations to each other". As Slade LJ observed,[37] it "should be no part of the general function of the law of tort to fill in contractual gaps".

Third, at a practical level, Lord Templeman in the House of Lords thought that a duty to speak "would give rise to great difficulties. The information may be unreliable or doubtful or inconclusive. Disclosure may expose the informer to criticism or litigation".[38]

---

27. *Donoghue* v *Stevenson* [1932] AC 562, 581 *per* Lord Atkin; *Caparo* (above), *loc cit.*

28. *Davis* v *Radcliffe* [1990] 2 All ER 536, 540 (PC). *Idem* in Caparo (above) p 633 *per* Lord Oliver.

29. The writer has some sympathy with Buckley, (1991) 6 Professional Negligence, p 98, who refers to "the current tendency to conceal judicial reasoning behind such sublimely meaningless ritual incantations as 'proximity' and 'just and reasonable' ". See also Howarth [1991] CLJ 58, 72 ff, who argues persuasively that the courts are confusing the duty of care with breach of duty. *Idem* Tettenborn [1991] LMCLQ 445.

30. See above, 9–2.

31. pp 794 ff. Other judges prefer to see the key to the situation as reasonable reliance by the party to whom the duty is owed: for example, *Smith* v *Bush* [1990] 1 AC 831, 846 *per* Lord Templeman, 864 *per* Lord Griffiths. This difference is unlikely to affect the result between insurer and insured.

32. p 794.

33. p 797. The court found no such assumption of responsibility in the case, in particular, no assumption of responsibility by the insurers for the honesty of the (dishonest) agent or reliance on that by the banks. *Idem* in the House of Lords: [1991] 2 AC 249, 275 *per* Lord Templeman (HL), with whom Lord Brandon, Lord Ackner and Lord Jauncey concurred.

34. p 798.

35. p 800.

36. *Tai Hing Cotton Mill Ltd* v *Liu Chong Hing Bank Ltd* [1986] AC 80, 107 (PC).

37. p 800.

38. [1991] 2 AC 249, 274. As regards justice in the particular case, the banks were not left without remedy as their brokers were vicariously liable for the relevant dishonesty and a claim against the brokers had been brought and settled.

The decision against the existence of a duty of care was reached in spite of a "most forceful submission"[39]: given the admitted duty of disclosure between insurers and banks, why should the court not treat the insurers "as having in law voluntarily assumed responsibility to make full disclosure of material facts to the banks, not only for the purpose of the principles of *Carter* v *Boehm*, but also for the purpose of the law of negligence in tort? The very nature of the contract which was being negotiated . . . gives rise to a special relationship between the negotiating parties which justifies the imposition of a duty of care". The Court of Appeal answered this submission in substantially the same way that it answered the submission, that damages should not be awarded for breach of the duty of disclosure as such,[40] concluding that it did "not think that the nature of the contract as one of the utmost good faith can be used as a platform to establish a common law duty of care".

27–2 FRAUDULENT CLAIMS

The duty of good faith between insurer and insured is sometimes specified as the foundation,[41] although not the only foundation, of the rule that fraud in a claim by the insured defeats the claim[42] and terminates the contract of insurance. The rule is often spoken of as a contract term but a term that is "in accordance with legal principle and sound policy".[43]

Although, at the time of the claim as at other times, the duty of good faith is most apparent as it affects the insured claimant, the duty must also be observed by the insurer.[44] In the United States, for example, "good faith requires the insurer to notify the insured of its objections within a reasonable time".[45] In England, however, although the duty is indeed mutual, the court is more likely to see that particular situation as raising an issue not of good faith as such but an issue of waiver or estoppel.[46]

27–2A The Fraud

The onus of proving fraud is on the insurer. In cases of fraudulent misstatement about the extent of loss, there may be little doubt that the statement was made, but the insurer must also prove that it was false and that the claimant knew it was false: below, 27–2B. In other cases, the insurer's allegation of fraud may be more serious: that the loss occurred as claimed but was deliberately caused by the claimant. In all cases of

---

39. p 800.
40. See above above 23–15C. Courts in the USA divide on whether the primary insurer owes to the excess insurer a duty of care actionable in tort: Sehr, Blume and Elenius 27 Tort & Ins L J 226, 227 (1992).
41. *Britton* v *Royal Ins Co* (1866) 4 F & F 905, 909 *per* Willes J (fire); *The Litsion Pride* [1985] 1 Lloyd's Rep 437, 512 ff *per* Hirst J (hull); *The Captain Panagos DP* [1986] 2 Lloyd's Rep 470, 512 *per* Evans J (hull). *Harris* v *Waterloo Mutual Fire Ins Co* (1886) 10 OR 718, 723 (fire). Brown & Menezes, 11.5.2. Appleman, sections 3587 ff.
42. *Britton, loc cit.*
43. *Britton, loc cit. Maraitis* v *Harvey Trinder (Queensland) Pty Ltd* [1969] Qd R 226, 236 (fire); *Dawson* v *Monarch Ins Co Ltd* [1977] 1 NZLR 372, 378 (fire); *Guardian Royal Exchange Ins Ltd* v *Ormsby* (1982) 29 SASR 498, 505 (theft).
44. See *Dercoli* v *Pennsylvania National Mutual Ins Co*, 554 A 2d 906, 909 (Pa, 1989—motor).
45. *Federal Savings & Loan Ins Corp* v *Burdette*, 718 F Supp 649 (ED Tenn, 1989—liability).
46. Above 20–7D and 23–18C.

alleged fraud, the onus, while not that of the criminal law,[47] is greater than the usual balance of probabilities, because the "more serious the allegation the higher the degree of probability"[48] to be established. Indeed, if the allegation of fraud is that the insured fired his own property, the onus is close to that facing the prosecution in a criminal case on the same facts,[49] involving a "high degree of probability".[50]

Although it has been suggested that the insurer owes a duty to the public to expose a fraud such as arson,[51] it is also a recognised[52] reality that the insurer may prefer to defend a claim by assuming the lesser burden of showing fraud in some other aspect of the claim, such as the amount of loss[53] or to establish an easier "technical" defence such as non-disclosure. In any event, "recession induced claims" is a phrase on so many lips, that it has acquired an acronym (RIC) and there is some evidence that the attitudes of insurers are hardening, not least because there is evidence that fraudsters have identified and targeted insurers believed to be "soft" or sloppy about fraud.[54]

27–2B Wilful Falsehood

A statement known to be false is fraudulent; it is also clear that a misstatement made inadvertently or carelessly is not.[55] Early cases, stating that to be fraudulent a claim must be "wilfully false in any substantial respect"[56] or "a claim he knew to be false and unjust",[57] were made before the definition of fraud in *Derry* v *Peek*[58] and do not now limit fraudulent claims to those that are known to be false. Between knowledge and negligence, there is the authority of Lord Sumner[59] that a claim is knowingly "false and fraudulent", if it is made recklessly, not caring whether it is true or false. Thus, insurance fraud appears to be common law fraud.[60]

A contract term may ground the avoidance of cover, if a statement in a claim is

---

47. *The Litsion Pride* [1985] 1 Lloyd's Rep 437, 479 *per* Hirst J (hull). *Maple Leaf Milling Co* v *Colonial Assurance Co* [1917] 2 WWR 1091, 1097 (Man—fire).

48. *Hornal* v *Neuberger Products Ltd* [1957] 1 QB 247, 258 *per* Lord Denning MR (CA). See further above, 17–2G4.

49. *Thurtell* v *Beaumont* (1823) 1 Bing 339 (fire); *Herbert* v *Poland* (1932) 44 Ll L Rep 139, 142 *per* Swift J (fire); *S & M Carpets (London) Ltd* v *Cornhill Ins Co Ltd* [1981] 1 Lloyd's Rep 667 (fire), affirmed [1982] 1 Lloyd's Rep 423 (CA).

50. *Slattery* v *Mance* [1962] 1 Lloyd's Rep 60, 63 *per* Salmon J (yacht); *Watkins & Davies Ltd* v *Legal & General Assurance Co Ltd* [1981] 1 Lloyd's Rep 674, 677 *per* Neill J (fire).

On the difficulty of proving fraud and concomitant disincentives in England, see Michael Clarke, *Insurance Fraud*, (1989) 29 Brit. J Criminology 1; Sayer, BILA Journal No 81, January 1993, p 47; in France, *La Lutte contre la Fraude à l'Assurance, Actes du Colloque Organisé à Niort les 28 et 29 juin 1990* (Paris, 1991); and in the USA: Emerson, *Insurance Claims Fraud Problems and Remedies*, 46 U Miami L Rev 907 (1992).

51. *Worsley* v *Wood* (1796) 6 TR 710, 722 *per* Lawrence J (fire). *Taschuk* v *Sun Alliance Ins Co* (1979) 27 NBR (2d) 596, 604 (fire). The Insurance Ombudsman, Annual Report 1992, para 6.1.

52. *Britton* v *Royal Ins Co* (1866) 4 F & F 905, 909 *per* Willes J (fire); criticised by the Insurance Ombudsman, Annual Report 1985, p 15.

53. *Michael Clarke* (above). *Idem*: Cadogan and Lewis (1992) 21 Angl–Am L. Rev. 123, 131.

54. Mann, PM Supplement, *Claims in the '90s*, Winter 1993 p 3.

55. *Cann* v *Imperial Fire Ins Co* (1875) 10 NSR 240 (fire).

56. *Goulstone* v *Royal Ins Co* (1858) 1 F & F 276, 279 *per* Pollock CB (fire); *Britton* v *Royal Ins Co* (1866) 4 F & F 905, 908 *per* Willes J (fire).

57. *Chapman* v *Pole* (1870) 22 LT 306, 307 *per* Cockburn CJ (fire).

58. (1889) 14 App Cas 337.

59. *Lek* v *Mathews* (1927) 29 Ll L Rep 141, 145 (HL—theft); also *Dome Mining Corp Ltd* v *Drysdale* (1931) 41 Ll L Rep 109, 121–122 *per* Branson J (hull); *Haase* v *Evans* (1934) 48 Ll L Rep 131, 148 *per* Avory J (AR). *Truglia* v *Travelers Indemnity Co* (1966) 53 DLR (2d) 309, 320 (Ont—fire); *Direct Investments Ltd* v *Dominion Ins Corp* (1968) 68 DLR (2d) 278, 286 (Ont—fire); *Taschuk* v *Sun Alliance Ins Co* (1979) 27 NBR (2d) 596, 604 (fire).

60. *Derry* v *Peek* (1889) 14 App Cas 337.

simply "false", but this has been restrictively interpreted as "fraudulently false".[61] A trend, typified by terms of that kind, has been discerned, whereby the insurer seeks to draft the claim form in such a way that the claimant guarantees the truth of information solicited by the insurer. Just as that trend has been resisted in respect of proposals and basis clauses,[62] we can expect a similar antipathy in the judges towards these clauses at the point of claim.[63]

Restrictive interpretation is found in two further respects. To defeat a claim, first, the falsehood must be substantial (below, 27–2C); incidental inaccuracy is ignored. Second, the fraud must have been intended to obtain an advantage, generally monetary, or to put someone else at a disadvantage.[64] The corollary is that some licence is allowed in negotiating claims with the insurer.

For example, it has been held[65] that the claimant who valued used goods on the basis of the price of new goods, although advancing a total that was "preposterously extravagant", was not acting fraudulently but merely taking a bargaining position. This distinction may be hard to draw. If fraud requires no more than "a specific intent to recover more than he is entitled to",[66] surely a person who takes a bargaining position may be fraudulent,[67] for example, if he does so in the knowledge that he may well be entitled to less but hopes that, in the interests of good will or administrative economy, the insurer will not dispute his claim.

The court will decide case by case in the light of the demeanour of witnesses, on which its view is unlikely to be disturbed on appeal,[68] and of the degree of exaggeration, which may speak for itself. A claim of £200 for furniture worth £50 suggests fraud[69]; even though gross overvaluation is not considered to furnish conclusive evidence of fraud,[70] it raises a strong presumption of fraud.[71] However, a finding of fraud is a serious matter, it is the claimant's idea of truth which counts[72] and the courts are

---

61. *Kostuk v National Ben Franklin Fire Ins Co* [1927] 1 DLR 1145, 1146 (Ont—fire).

62. See above no 20–2A1.

63. Courts in New Zealand have read in these words a requirement of "moral obliquity", although it is not entirely clear what this means: Borrowdale [1987] NZLJ 76. See also Borrowdale, *Essays in Commercial Law* (ed Borrowdale and Rowe, Christchurch 1991) pp 80 ff. Cf Tarr, pp 225 ff.

64. *Wisenthal v World Auxiliary Ins Corp Ltd* (1930) 38 Ll L Rep 54, 61–62 *per* Roche J (burglary).

65. *Ewer v National Employers' Mutual General Ins Assn Ltd* [1937] 2 All ER 193, 203 *per* MacKinnon J (fire). Similarly, it seems that in the USA a mild degree of claim inflation is accepted as a tactic in negotiating a claim: Emerson, 46 U Miami L Rev 907, 952 (1992).

66. Birds, p 244. Conduct is fraudulent, if there is an intention to get out of the insurer money to which the insured knew he had no right: *Norton v Royal Fire & Accident Life Assurance Co* (1885) 1 TLR 460, 461 *per* Lord Coleridge CJ (fire), applied in *Guardian Royal Exchange Assurance Co v Ormsby* (1982) 29 SASR 498, 503 (theft).

67. *Norton v Royal Fire & Accident Life Assurance Co, The Times*, 12 August 1885 (CA—fire). *Taschuk v Sun Alliance Ins Co* (1979) 27 NBR (2d) 596, 604 (fire). *Dawson v Monarch Ins Co Ltd* [1977] 1 NZLR 372, 379 (fire). *Dunn v State Farm Ins Co*, 927 F 2d 869, 874 (5 Cir, 1991—fire).

68. *Herman v Phoenix Assurance Co Ltd* (1928) 18 Ll L Rep 371 (CA—fire). *Kostuk v National Ben Franklin Fire Ins Co* [1927] 1 DLR 1145, 1146 (Ont—fire). *Meagher v London & Lancashire Fire Ins Co* (1881) 7 VLR 390, 397 (fire). *Soler & Co v United Firemen's Ins Co*, 299 US 45 (1936—fire).

69. *Goulstone v Royal Ins Co* (1858) 1 F & F 276, 279 *per* Pollock CB (fire). See also *Etterman v London & Scottish Ins Corp* [1936] 4 DLR 43, 50 (Man—fire); and *Pogo Holding Co v New York Property Ins Underwriting Assn*, 467 NYS 2d 872 (1983, fire), concerning a claim five times the appraised value of the property damaged.

70. *London Assurance v Clare* (1937) 57 Ll L Rep 254, 268 *per* Goddard J (fire). Cf *Dunn v State Farm Ins Co*, 927 F 2d 869, 874 (5 Cir, 1991—fire).

71. *Mamco Inc v American Employers Ins Co*, 736 F 2d 187, 191 (5 Cir, 1984—fire).

72. *Akerhielm v De Mare* [1959] AC 789 (PC). *Reddick v Saugeen Mutual Fire Ins Co* (1888) 15 OAR 363, 369 (fire).

inclined to give him the benefit of doubt[73]; good faith is presumed.[74] In a leading case, the Supreme Court of the United States said: "Policy holders may present inaccurate proofs of loss without conscious dishonesty or intent to defraud; different views of values are common; memory is faulty; insurance company and assured often entertain widely different views concerning the policy."[75] Evidently, the claimant is not fraudulent, if he relies *bona fide* on the erroneous valuation of an apparently competent third party.[76]

27–2C Substantial Falsehood

The falsehood must be more than trivial[77]; it must be material.[78] A falsehood is material, if it would influence a prudent insurer's decision to accept, reject or compromise the claim,[79] *prima facie* the kind of materiality required when a contract is vitiated by misrepresentation or non-disclosure at the time of formation.[80] In the latter context, however, English law[81] is unduly strict. When it comes to a false claim, it is submitted, the "substantial" falsehood required by Baron Pollock[82] should be preferred to the "full disclosure of the circumstances of the case" required by Lord Ellenborough[83]; a falsehood is material, if the statement or omission in question affects the readiness of the insurer to pay the amount to be paid or the person to whom it is to be paid.[84]

One corollary of this submission is that it is not material, for example, if a claimant presents false evidence to bolster a valid claim or to conceal facts, which have nothing to do with the claim but which he finds embarrassing.[85] Although perhaps dishonest, this behaviour should not defeat the claim[86]: it is not fraudulent in the sense of an intention to obtain money, to which he knows that he is not entitled.[87]

This issue divides courts in the United States, where, on the one hand, it has been

73. *Newcastle Fire Ins Co* v *Macmorran* (1815) 3 Dow 255, 262, 266 *per* Lord Eldon (HL—fire).
74. *Street* v *Royal Exchange Assurance* (1914) 111 LT 235, 239 *per* Phillimore LJ (CA—re), applied in *Guardian Royal Exchange Assurance Co* v *Ormsby* (1982) 29 SASR 498, 503 (theft).
75. *Soler & Co* v *United Firemen's Ins Co*, 299 US 45, 50 *per* McReynolds J (1936—fire). See also *Cann* v *Imperial Fire Ins Co* (1875) 10 NSR 240 (fire).
76. *American Central Ins Co* v *Harmon Knitting Mills,* 39 F 2d 21, 23 (7 Cir, 1930—fire). However, if the third party is his agent, the knowledge of the agent is attributed to the claimant: *Hyland* v *Millers National Ins Co*, 58 F 2d 1003, 1006 (ND Cal, 1932—fire), affirmed 91 F 2d 737, cert den 303 US 645.
77. So that the maxim *de minimis* is inapplicable: *Lek* v *Mathews* (1927) 29 Ll L Rep 141, 145 *per* Lord Sumner (HL—theft).
78. *Globe & Rutgers Fire Ins Co* v *Stallard*, 68 F 2d 237, 241 (4 Cir, 1934—fire). Cf *The Litsion Pride* [1985] 1 Lloyd's Rep 437, 513 *per* Hirst J (hull): the falsehood does not have to relate specifically to the claim.
79. *Royal Ins Co* v *Byers* (1885) 9 Ont 120, 135 (fire).
80. *The Litsion Pride, loc cit.* See further 22–3A and 23–5 *et seq.*
81. See above 23–7.
82. *Goulstone* v *Royal Ins Co* (1858) 1 F & F 276, 279 (fire). Merkin & McGhee, p C.1.3–03; Pincott, (1988) 1 Ins LJ 27, 32. On the role of the loss assessor, who acts for the claimant, see Wilson, PM, 21 January 1993, p 10.
83. *Shepherd* v *Chewter* (1808) 1 Camp 274, 275 (hull).
84. *People* v *Hardy*, 825 P 2d 781, 810 (Cal, 1992—life).
85. *Longobardi* v *Chubb Ins Co*, 560 A 2d 68, 77 (NJ Super AD, 1989—burglary); but *cf Pacific Indemnity Co* v *Golden*, 791 F Supp 935 (D Conn, 1991—fire), in which the fire claimant lied about his reasons for having gasolene on the premises, the real reason being to pour it on a colleague's lawn as an act of revenge.
86. *Guardian Royal Exchange Ins Ltd* v *Ormsby* (1982) 29 SASR 498 (theft). *Maple Leaf Milling Co* v *Colonial Assurance Co* [1917] 2 WWR 1091 (Man—fire). *American Paint Service Inc* v *Home Ins Co*, 246 F 2d 91 (3 Cir, 1957—fire).
87. *Ormsby* (above) p 503, citing *Norton* v *Royal Fire & Accident Life Assurance Co* (1885) 1 TLR 460, 461 *per* Lord Coleridge LCJ (fire).

stated[88] that a misstatement is material, only if it would "cause the insurer to do other than that which would have been done had the truth been told". If "to do other" refers only payment, the rule is narrow like that in England. On the other hand, some decisions in the United States take a broader view of materiality. For example, the "right rule of law . . . is one that provides insureds with an incentive to tell the truth"[89] and which helps "to keep an insured from making false statements . . . and misleading an insurance investigation", as that wastes the insurer's time and resources.[90] Moreover, materiality is to be assessed not with the benefit of hindsight but on the basis of things as they appeared (not to the insured but) to the insurer at the time.[91] "An insured's misstatement is material if *when made* a reasonable insurer would have considered the misrepresented fact relevant to its concerns and important in determining its course of action."[92] Thus, the broad view is that a statement is material if it affects not only whether the insurer will pay but also if it affects the course of the investigation, even if later the statement turns out to be irrelevant or even if later the claimant has corrected it.[93] One can see that a court might be ill disposed to a careless claimant who wasted the insurer's time and money but, surely, a more important consideration is that to hold such misstatements material and fatal to the claim "would encourage an insurer, after the loss, to continually attempt to question its insured in the hope of obtaining misstatements."[94] The narrow view found in England is, it is submitted, to be preferred.

27–2D The Effect of Fraud

27–2D1 *Termination of Contract or Rejection of Claim.*

The conceptual basis of the duty of good faith is uncertain. At the time of contracting it is based, in the view of a minority, on an implied term. Although there are difficulties about that view[95] as regards the time of contracting, it is submitted that that is the better view as regards the duty during contract performance.[96] If that is right, one alternative, as in the case of any other serious breach of contract, is termination of the contract at the option of the insurer.[97] As to the future, the effect is to terminate the

---

88. *Berkshire Mutual Ins Co* v *Moffett* 378 F 2d 1007, 1012 (5 Cir, 1967—fire). *Cf Mamco Inc* v *American Employers Ins Co*, 736 F 2d 187 (5 Cir, 1984—fire): whether or not the falsehood had any actual effect on the insurer's response; *Longobardi* v *Chubb Ins Co*, 560 A 2d 68, 77 (NJ Super AD, 1989—burglary): "Except for fraud in the origin or existence of a claim, a misstatement would seem to have greater significance to the insurer when made before the policy is written" than at the time of a claim.

89. *Longobardi* v *Chubb Ins Co*, 582 A 2d 1257, 1263 (NJ, 1990—burglary). "It would dilute that incentive to allow an insured to gamble that a lie will turn out to be unimportant": *ibid*.

90. *Pacific Indemnity Co* v *Golden*, 791 F Supp 935, 940 (D Conn, 1991—fire).

91. *Longobardi* (above) p 1263.

92. *Ibid* (emphasis added). There is some dispute over whether this must amount to "prejudice".

93. *Golden* (above); the claim failed, even though the court acknowledged (p 939) that its decision provided little incentive for claimants to correct false statements.

94. *Longobardi* v *Chubb Ins Co*, 560 A 2d 68, 83 (NJ Super AD, 1989—burglary). According to the decision in that case, the claimant's concealment of his past association with persons subsequently convicted of insurance fraud did not defeat his claim, but this judgment was reversed on appeal: 582 A 2d 1257 (NJ, 1990).

95. See above, 23–1A.

96. This view finds tentative support in the *Banque Financière case* [1990] 1 QB 665, 777 per Slade LJ (CA); the point was not taken up in the House of Lords.

97. *Reid & Co* v *Employers' Accident & Live Stock Ins Co* (1899) 1 F (Ct Sess) 1031, 1036 *per* Lord Trayner (liability). *Gore Mutual Ins Co* v *Bifford* (1987) 45 DLR (4th) 763, 765 (BC—fire). Nicholson (1990) 3 Ins L J 218, 250 ff. *Contra: Stebbing* v *Liverpool & London & Globe Ins Co Ltd* [1917] 2 KB 433, 438 *per* Ridley J (burglary). Also *The Litsion Pride* [1985] 1 Lloyd's Rep 437, 515 *per* Hirst J (hull), that

primary duties but secondary duties, such as a duty to arbitrate an earlier honest claim,[98] remain. As to the past, if honest claim A is followed by fraudulent claim B, the contract may end but claim A remains enforceable[99]; and the insurer cannot recover insurance money paid in respect of earlier loss, or even payments on account of present loss made prior to the fraud.[100] The other alternative is that post-contract breach of the duty of good faith in relation to a claim defeats only the claim, perhaps at the option of the insurer, and that the contract remains in force.[101] As no damages are recoverable for this breach of duty (below), observance of the duty seems to be a condition precedent, on the first alternative, a condition precedent to the continuance of the contract and, on the second alternative, a condition precedent to recovery of the amount of the claim.

27–2D2 Single, Joint and Composite Insurance

If a single claim is honest in part and fraudulent in part, the entire claim fails, the honest with the dishonest.[102] This is because the contract is a single contract[103] and because, if the fraud justifies termination, all primary duties, including the insurer's duty to pay claims, are ended.[104] There is also a reason of public policy, the traditional distaste of the courts for fraud. "Fraud in any part of his formal statement of losses taints the whole. Thus corrupted, it should be wholly rejected and the suitor left to repent that he destroyed his actual claim by the poison of his false claim."[105]

avoidance means "avoidance *ab initio*", by analogy with avoidance for breach of the duty at the time of contract. The obvious objection to this analogy is that the breach of duty (fraudulent claim), unlike misrepresentation or non-disclosure, does not vitiate consent. In general, post contract breach does not rescind the contract *ab initio*: *Johnson* v *Agnew* [1980] AC 367. See above, 20–6C.

98. *Heyman* v *Darwins Ltd* [1942] AC 356; *The Captain Panagos DP* [1986] 2 Lloyd's Rep 470, 512 *per* Evans J (hull), affirmed [1989] 1 Lloyd's Rep 33. The contrary decision in *Jureidini* v *National British & Irish Millers Ins Co Ltd* [1915] AC 499 (PC—fire) can be explained by a term of the contract that, in the event of a fraudulent claim, "all benefit" under the contract should be "forfeited": p 505 *per* Viscount Haldane LC. In so far as statements (*ibid*) base that decision on general principle, they must be regarded as doubtful in the light of observations in *Heyman* v *Darwins Ltd* [1942] AC 356, 364, *per* Viscount Simon LC, and 372 *per* Lord Macmillan.

The survival of the duty to arbitrate may be explained on the basis that the agreement to arbitrate is a self-contained and separate agreement: *Harbour Assurance Co (UK) Ltd* v *Kansa General Int Ins Co Ltd* [1992] 1 Lloyd's Rep 81, 88–89 *per* Steyn J (re).

99. *Lehmbecker's Earthmoving & Excavators (Pty) Ltd* v *Incorporated General Ins Ltd* [1983] 3 SA 513 AD (machinery), in spite of a clause that in the event of a fraudulent claim "all benefit under this policy shall be forfeited". *Cf* Merkin & McGhee, p C.1.3–03.

100. *Gore Mutual Ins Co* v *Bifford* (1987) 45 DLR (4th) 763 (BC—fire).

101. *The Litsion Pride* [1985] 1 Lloyd's Rep 437, 515 *per* Hirst J (hull), citing *Reid & Co* v *Employers' Accident & Livestock Ins Co Ltd*, 1899 1 F (Ct Sess) 1031, 1036 *per* Lord Trayner (liability).

102. *Lek* v *Mathews* (1927) 29 Ll L Rep 141 (HL—theft); *The Captain Panagos DP* [1986] 2 Lloyd's Rep 470, 512 *per* Evans J (hull), affirmed [1989] 1 Lloyd's Rep 33.

USA *idem*: see Appleman, section 3595. *Cf Johnson* v *South State Ins Co*, 341 SE 2d 793 (SC, 1986—household contents), that when the contract covers separately valued items, the policy is divisible. See Dickman, 39 S Carolina L Rev 1 (1987).

Cf Australia: section 56 of the Insurance Contracts Act 1984 provides: "(1) Where a claim under a contract of insurance . . . is made fraudulently, the insurer may not avoid the contract but may refuse payment of the claim. (2) In any proceedings in relation to such a claim, the court may, if only a minimal or insignificant part of the claim is made fraudulently and non-payment of the remainder of the claim would be harsh and unfair, order the insurer to pay, in relation to the claim, such amount (if any) as is just and equitable in the circumstances." See further Tarr, (1988) 1 Ins LJ 42; Scotford, (1988) 1 Ins LJ 1, 19 ff.

103. *Cashman* v *London & Liverpool Fire Ins Co* (1862) 10 NBR 246, 249 (fire), applied in *Harris* v *Waterloo Mutual Fire Ins Co* (1886) 10 OR 718, 723 (fire).

104. *Cf Gore*, above, note 53.

105. *Maple Leaf Milling Co* v *Colonial Assurance Co* [1917] 2 WWR 1091, 1104 (Man—fire).

These reasons are not compelling in the case of a composite policy: a fraudulent claim by insured A does not affect an honest claim by insured B.[106] When, however, "two persons are jointly insured and their interests are inseparably connected so that loss or gain necessarily affects them both",[107] it may well be that "the misconduct of one is sufficient to contaminate the whole insurance".[108] In *Scott v Wawanesa*[109], however, this statement by Viscount Cave in *Samuel v Dumas* was regarded by the Supreme Court of Canada as a statement of the "old" approach:

"As noted, a minority of state courts still follow that approach. This line of authority is premised on several considerations of public policy. Chief among them is the principle that a wrongdoer must not be allowed to profit, be it directly or indirectly, from his act [as well as] the desire to deter crime and to avoid fraud against insurers. I agree . . . that the latter considerations are 'not very persuasive' . . . The modern approach, followed in *Hedtcke*,[110] focuses, first and foremost, on the contract of insurance. The result is made to depend upon whether 'the insureds have promised the same performance, or a separate performance as to each, that is, whether each insured has promised that all insured parties will use reasonable means to preserve the property, or whether each has promised that he or she will protect the property'.[111] This depends on the language of the policy. This approach, however, takes as its starting point the 'fundamental principle of individual responsibility for wrongdoing'.[112] Consequently in the interpretation of the insurance contract the courts have held that, absent unambiguous provisions to the contrary, the reasonable person, . . . would view the obligations of the insurer as several to each of the persons involved . . . [In] construing an insurance policy, the courts must be guided by the reasonable expectation and purpose of an ordinary person in entering such a contract . . . [R]easonable persons would expect that they would lose the right to recover for their own wilful destruction. But the same persons would find it an anomalous result if informed that they stood to lose all if their spouse burned down the house."

So, the "modern approach" is that the claim is defeated only if, as a matter of construction, that result is clear from the contract.[113]

Indeed, not only is the example quoted by the court anomalous but in some cases an injustice bordering on the absurd, particularly, if the effect is a bar to recovery by an innocent insured, when the arson appears to have been an act of retribution against the innocent insured. "Having lost the property, the innocent insured is victimized once again by the denial of the proceeds forthcoming under the fire insurance policy."[114]

---

106. *General Accident Fire & Life Assurance Corp Ltd v Midland Bk Ltd* [1940] 2 KB 388, 417 *per* Sir Wilfred Greene MR (CA—fire). See also *Samuel & Co Ltd v Dumas* [1924] AC 431, 445 *per* Viscount Cave (hull); *AGC Ltd v Western Underwriters Ins Ltd* [1988] 2 Qd R 119 (motor). The view of Sir Wilfred Greene, MR, was applied in *VL Credits Pty Ltd v Switzerland General Ins Co*, [1990] VR 938 (fire). See also Brown & Menezes, 11:5:9. Nicholson (1990) 3 Ins L J 218, 242 ff.

107. On the distinction between joint and composite insurance, see Sir Wilfred Greene MR, *loc cit*, set out below 30–4.

108. *Samuel & Co Ltd v Dumas* [1924] AC 431, 445 *per* Viscount Cave. See further Nicholson, *op cit*.

109. (1989) 59 DLR (4th) 660, 667 *per* La Forest J, dissenting, but with whom two judges concurred. The majority (of four judges) did not disagree with the "modern" construction approach here quoted, but considered that the policy contained an exclusion clause which was too clear (p 674) to allow that approach in the particular case. But nor did their decision turn on the "old" approach (p 675). Subsequently in *Walsh v Canadian General Ins Co* (1989) 60 DLR (4th) 358, the Newfoundland Court of Appeal reached a similar decision on the wording of the contract, while expressing (p 368), however, a preference for the "old" approach.

110. *Hedtcke v Sentry Ins Co*, 326 NW 2d 727 (Wis, 1982).

111. *Hedtcke* p 739. Generally, on a duty to preserve property, see 28–8G.

112. *Hedtcke*, p 740.

113. *Atlas Assurance Co v Mistic*, 822 P 2d 897 (Alaska, 1991—fire).

114. *Hedtcke* at p 740.

The "modern" approach can also claim antecedents in a statement by Lord Sumner in *Samuel* v *Dumas*,[115] and appears to have been anticipated in *Peters* v *Fireman's Fund Ins Co of Canada*,[116] a Canadian case decided shortly before the decision of the Supreme Court in *Scott*. A fire policy issued jointly to husband and wife was held enforceable by the wife, even though the jointly-owned house was deliberately fired by the husband, because as a matter of construction she was individually insured.[117] The court was careful to note that there was no suggestion that the husband would benefit from the wife's recovery of indemnity.[118] In Victoria, however, although a trace of the "modern" approach can be discerned, it is the older approach of Viscount Cave based on separate interests that was more evident in *V L Credits Pty Ltd* v *Switzerland General Ins Co*.[119] The "modern" approach concentrates less on concepts of property law and more on the language and scope of the contract of insurance[120] and, for this reason, is attractive. If the "old" approach is followed, it is the innocent co-insured that may suffer; if the "modern" approach is taken, it is the insurer that may suffer but only to the extent of an action in subrogation against the guilty co-insured.

27–2D3 The Liability of the Claimant

If the insurer has paid a fraudulent claim, he has an action to recover the money as money paid by mistake.[121] However, Goddard J held[122] that the insurer has no action for breach of contract to recover damages for the cost of investigating a fraudulent claim. The objections were, first, that the insurers were not "in any worse position than they would have been if it had been an honest claim".[123] As an argument from causation, this is sound only on the premise that, in the absence of fraud, there would still have been a claim to investigate. As an inference about the allocation of risk, it is one thing to infer that the insurer is to bear the cost of handling honest claims, it is another to infer that he is to bear the cost of investigating fraud. Second, the loss was said[124] to be too remote. This is hard to follow because, if loss has been caused by the fraud and the first objection does not apply, it must surely be within the contemplation of the insured that, if he makes a fraudulent claim for loss that has not occurred, the insurer will incur expense handling the claim, whether it is investigated or not.[125] In

---

115. [1924] AC 431, 469.
116. (1989) 58 DLR (4th) 727, 736 (NW Territories—fire).
117. This possibility has been described as an insoluble conundrum by Nicholson (1990) 3 Ins L J 218, 249, who also points out that, when the parties, whether spouses or business partners, remain together after the event, many insurers will be justifiably suspicious of the innocent parties' innocence. Still, the indications in England are that the insurer will pay rather than seek to prove connivance: Michael Clarke, (1989) 29 Brit J Criminology 1.
118. *Cf* the case of communal or community property, in which the guilty spouse benefits from insurance payment to the innocent spouse: payment was refused in *Webster* v *State Farm Fire & Casualty Co*, 953 F 2d 222 (5 Cir, 1992—fire).
119. [1990] VR 938 (fire).
120. Nicholson (above) p 247.
121. See below, 30–5.
122. *London Assurance* v *Clare* (1937) 57 Ll L Rep 254 (fire); however, Goddard J suggested (p 270) that an action might lie in the tort of deceit.
123. p 270 *per* Goddard J.
124. *Ibid.*
125. It is submitted that a court is likely to see the cost of investigation as an aggravated kind of handling cost and, therefore, as not too remote, rather than as a distinct head of loss, to which the remoteness rule must be separately applied.

any event, the insurer faces the further difficulty that, in general, damages are not recoverable for breach of the duty of good faith.[126]

27-3 NOTICE OF LOSS

Almost invariably the contract requires the insured to give notice of loss or of events likely to give rise to loss covered by the insurance; see above, 26–2.

27-4 CO-OPERATION

27-4A The Co-operation Clause

As regards any kind of insurance claim by the insured against the insured, the insured may be required to co-operate by providing particulars of loss: above, 26–2F. He may also be required, expressly or perhaps even implicitly, to protect both his own position and that of the insurer by taking steps to limit the extent of the loss: below 28–8G. In the USA, property insurance contracts commonly require the insured to participate in an examination under oath, if required by the insurer. Examination under oath has been seen as an efficient device for expediting the assessment and adjustment of claims, as well as for detecting and discouraging exaggerated or fraudulent claims.[127]

In the case of liability insurance, the contract commonly contains a co-operation clause, whereby the insured promises not to admit liability[128] or to settle a claim, without the consent of the insurer,[129] and promises to secure information or evidence required by the insurer to defend a claim against the insured[130] and to render the insurer all reasonable assistance.

"The insurer is entitled to know from the assured the true facts (of which he may have knowledge) underlying an accident and upon which the injured person bases his claim in order that it may determine for itself, in the light of such information, whether it should contest or attempt to settle the claim".[131]

Co-operation "does not mean that the insured is to aid and assist the insurer in the maintenance of a sham defense. It does, however, imply good faith".[132]

---

126. Above 23–15C. *Quaere* whether damages would be recoverable, if the insurer framed his claim as one in respect of breach of the duty of co-operation: below 27–4.

127. Hamilton, 97 Dick L Rev 329, 332 (1993). For the requirement of an independent medical examination to establish bodily injury, see *Vanhaaren* v *State Farm Mutual Automobile Ins Co*, 989 F 2d 1 (1 Cir, 1993—motor).

128. The court will be slow to find that an employee has authority to bind his employer by an admission, lest the policy be avoided by an unguarded remark: *Tustin* v *Arnold & Son* (1915) 84 LJKB 2214, 2216 *per* Bailhache J (motor).

129. For example: "No liability shall be admitted or legal expenses be incurred nor any offer promise or payment made to Third Parties without the Company's written consent . . . " This clause was applied in *Terry* v *Trafalgar Ins Co Ltd* [1970] 1 Lloyd's Rep 524 (motor).

130. The insurer's duty, if any, to defend an action against the insured is discussed above: 17–4E.

131. *Valladao* v *Fireman's Fund Indemnity Co*, 89 P 2d 643, 646 (Cal, 1939—motor). To require the insurer to direct all inquiries to the insured's solicitor is not a failure of co-operation: *Van de Ven* v *SIGM* (1990) 6 ANZ Ins Cases, No 61–016 (NZ—motor).

132. *Valladao*, p 647. In *Terry* (above), it was argued that such a clause was prejudicial to the administration of justice, tending to cause the insured to lie or to conceal the truth, and hence contrary to public policy. The argument was rejected (p 526) as "fanciful".

As regards the obligation of the insured not to admit liability to a third party or to settle, breach of this term may defeat cover, whether the insurer intended to dispute the third party's claim or not.[133] If the insurer has wrongfully repudiated cover, the insured is released from the obligation.[134] A dilemma confronts the insured when the insurer has neither repudiated cover nor undertaken to defend or settle an action against the insured by a third party. This was explained by Stephen J in an Australian case in which, as is also common in England,[135] the insurer had a right to defend the insured but no obligation to do so[136]:

"The insured will be anxious to settle the claim at a figure within [the policy] limit; the insurer, however, will gain little from a settlement close to the limit and may prefer to have the case fought out rather than have it settled on such terms. An immediate conflict of interests then arises. Where settlement for less than the upper limit appears unattainable and the third party's case is a strong one the insurer's immediate financial interests would be better served if he could successfully resist the insured's claim to indemnity instead of accepting liability to indemnify and conducting an inauspicious defence. [The condition against settlement] may afford to an insurer a means of attaining this result; if the insured is anxious to settle and the insurer, while refusing to take over the conduct of the defence, witholds its consent to a settlement, a breach of the condition against settlement without consent may be procured and subsequent liability to indemnify may be avoided. An insured's anxiety to settle will, of course, be acute if his entitlement to indemnity is in doubt and will in any event be substantial if the likely amount of any judgment against him far exceeds the limit of his entitlement to indemnity under the policy."

However, the judge concluded,[137] that the dilemma facing the insured was less stark than at first appeared:

"Its power of restraining settlement by the insured must be exercised *in good faith* having regard to the interests of the insured as well as to its own interests and in the exercise of its power to withhold consent the insurer must not have regard to considerations extraneous to the policy of indemnity".

27–4B Breach of the Duty of Co-operation

Breach of the duty of co-operation defeats the claim,[138] except that in some parts of the USA, such as California, the claim is defeated only if the insurer proves that he

---

133. *Distillers-Bio-Chemicals (Australia) Pty Ltd* v *Ajax Ins Co Ltd* (1973) 130 CLR 1 (HCA—liability).
134. *Stevenson* v *Reliance Petroleum Ltd* [1956] SCR 936, 948 *per* Locke J (motor), applied in *Shore Boat Builders Ltd* v *Canadian Indemnity Co* (1974) 51 DLR (3d) 628 (BC—liability). *General Omnibus Co Ltd* v *London General Ins Co Ltd* [1936] IR 596 (motor).
135. Above, 17–4E.
136. *Distillers* (above), pp 23–24.
137. pp 26–27 (emphasis added), citing *Groom* v *Crocker* [1939] 1 KB 194, 203 *per* Sir Wilfred Greene MR (CA—motor), discussed above 17–4E1; *Beacon Ins Co Ltd* v *Langdale* [1939] 4 All ER 204, 206 *per* Slesser LJ (CA—motor). These passages appear to refer to the decision whether to defend the third party action as well as conduct of the defence. Stephen J also relied on decisions in New York, such as *Gordon* v *Nationwide Mutual Ins Co*, 334 NYS 2d 601, 608 (1972—motor), where the court awarded damages against the insurer for "a breach of implied conditions of the contract to act in its performance in good faith in refusing to settle within policy limits". The other members of the HCA did not express a view on this issue.
138. *Valladao* v *Fireman's Fund Indemnity Co*, 89 P 2d 643 (Cal, 1939—motor).

has been prejudiced.[139] In other parts, courts consider that proof of prejudice, which can be difficult,[140] should not be required and prejudice is presumed.[141]

In Australia, in *Trans-Pacific* v *Grand Union*,[142] the Supreme Court of New South Wales has taken an intermediate position. It held that breach of the co-operation clause, a failure to provide information requested by the reinsurer, does not necessarily entitle the reinsurer to terminate the contract of reinsurance. The question is one of construction of the relevant documents, however, the court observed of the breach by the reinsured in that case that "it must have been obvious that there could be major or minor failures to co-operate, disagreement on what did or did not amount to co-operation, or breach which was readily rectified without any prejudice to reinsurer".[143] The court concluded[144] that, in the language of the general law of contract, the obligation to co-operate was "innominate". There is more than a hint in this case, however, that, as in California, the reinsurer could only have terminated the contract, if he had been prejudiced.[145]

27–4C The Reinsurer's Duty to Follow Settlements

Whereas an insurer seeks to control or monitor the steps taken by the primary insured by means of a co-operation clause (above 27–4A), especially as regards the settlement of claims, a reinsurer may promise very largely to surrender discretion[146] and to follow the settlements of the primary insurer, his insured. The background to this kind of promise is that the

"original insurer of today might be the reinsurer of tomorrow; and trusting each other to act in the utmost good faith and saving the expense to reinsurers of disputing claims which the original insurers did not dispute, they agree to insert in policies of reinsurance a clause applying their

---

139. *Campbell* v *Allstate Ins Co*, 32 Cal Rptr 827 (Cal, 1963—motor): an action by the injured third party, and this influenced the decision (p 829). The insurer had not been prejudiced by lack of information from the insured, for the insurer "had access" to the information and a "sufficient opportunity to verify" it (p 829). *Campbell* was followed in *Billington* v *Interinsurance Exchange*, 79 Cal Rptr 326 (Cal, 1969—motor), in which the insured failed to appear to give evidence. It was held that the insurer had failed to prove prejudice, unless he could show a "substantial likelihood" that, if the evidence had been available, the trier of fact would have reached a different decision. Generally see Haydel & Shaver, 13 Pac L J 943 (1982).
In England, in *Terry* v *Trafalgar Ins Co Ltd* [1970] 1 Lloyd's Rep 524 (motor), the court left open whether prejudice was required. Generally see above, 26–2E2.
140. *Purze* v *American Alliance Ins Co*, 781 F Supp 1289, 1292 (ND Ill, 1991—fire).
141. *Valladao* (above), p 648. *Contra: Campbell* (above), p 829.
142. *Trans-Pacific Ins Co (Australia) Ltd* v *Grand Union Ins Co Ltd* (1989) 18 NSWLR 675, 701 ff (re). In this case, the court also found (p 693) that in "the course of arriving at settlements, the reinsured must co-operate with the reinsurer, so that the reinsurer is aware of what is occurring and has at least the opportunity to be heard on the course being followed by the reinsured towards a settlement". *Cf* below, 27–4C.
143. p 702.
144. p 702, with reference to *Phoenix General Ins Co* v *Halvanon Ins Co Ltd* [1988] QB 216, 241 *per* Hobhouse J; and *Hongkong Fir Shipping Co Ltd* v *Kawasaki Kisen Kaisha Ltd* [1962] 2 QB 26 (CA).
145. For example, p 703.
146. The reinsurance contract may well give the reinsurer a right to inspect the books and other documents of the reinsured and, if not, it has been held that such a right will be implied: *Phoenix General Ins Co* v *Halvanon Ins Co Ltd* [1988] QB 216 (CA—re); and that the reinsurer may exercise the right, whether or not it has paid all outstanding claims by the reinsured: *In Re a Company No 008725/91 and 008727/91* [1992] BCLC 633. It has also been held, however, that, if the reinsurer invokes this right, this may be interpreted as affirmation of the contract, which thus bars him from avoiding the contract on the ground of misrepresentation of non–disclosure: *Iron Trades Mutual Ins Co Ltd* v *Cia de Seguros Imperio* (31 July 1990, unreported).

reinsurance to the original insurer's policies subject to the same terms and conditions 'and to pay as might be paid thereon'".[147]

In *Scor*,[148] the Court of Appeal concluded that the effect of the clause is

"that the reinsurers agree to indemnify insurers in the event that they settle a claim by their assured, i.e., when they dispose, or bind themselves to dispose, of a claim, whether by reason of admission or compromise, provided that the claim so recognized by them falls within the risks covered by the policy of reinsurance as a matter of law, and provided also that in settling the claim the insurers have acted honestly and have taken all proper and businesslike steps in making the settlement".

The essential element of the clause being that the reinsurer puts his trust in the reinsured, it would be inconsistent to require the reinsured to prove each time that the trust had been justified. Moreover, in many if not most cases, the reinsured would be constrained to prove it by establishing that liability existed in fact, which may be difficult, if a settlement had been agreed with the original insured. Hence, there is a presumption, that the reinsured is entitled to call upon the reinsurer to follow the settlement, not only as regards the quantum of liability but also as regards the very existence of liability.[149] It is for the reinsurer to prove, if so minded, that the settlement does not satisfy one of the three conditions (quoted above) in the *Scor* proviso.[150] Like any claimant, the reinsured must prove his loss, however, that is not the loss of the original insured but his own: the claim upon him and his reasonable settlement of it, although, in order to reach a reasonable settlement, he will also have required some proof of loss, at least, from the original insured.[151]

As to the first condition of the proviso, that the claim falls within the risks covered, if "there is genuine ambiguity over what a settlement covers, a 'follow the fortunes' clause may oblige a reinsurer to contribute to a settlement even though it might encompass excluded items".[152] The "insurer may not second guess the cedent's good faith decision to pay any claim that is arguably subject to coverage".[153] Cover is a matter for careful construction of the reinsurance contract. An important distinction has been drawn between cover of loss in the form of legal liability to the primary insured and the rather wider cover of loss in the form of payments made in good faith in connection with claims made by the primary insured.[154] However, the argument,

---

147. *Insurance Co of Africa* v *Scor (UK) Reinsurance Co Ltd* [1985] 1 Lloyd's Rep 312, 319 *per* Stevenson LJ (CA—re). On the meaning of the phrases "pay as may be paid" or "pay as might be paid", see also *ibid* pp 327 ff *per* Robert Goff LJ; *Hong Kong Borneo Services Co Ltd* v *Pilcher* [1992] 2 Lloyd's Rep 593 (marine); and above, 5–8E3. See further, Butler & Merkin, C.1.3. For a comparative study, see Hoffman, 28 Tort & Ins LJ 659 (1993).

148. Above, p 330, *per* Robert Goff LJ, with whom Fox LJ (p 334) agreed. The decison was cited in *American Marine Ins Group* v *Neptunia Ins Co*, 775 F Supp 703, 708 (SD NY, 1991—re), together with *Ins Co of the State of Pennsylvania* v *Grand Union Ins Co* [1990] 1 Lloyd's Rep 208 (CA Hong Kong—re), in which *Scor* was also applied.

149. *Scor* (above) p 330 *per* Robert Goff LJ; cf *Toomey* v *Eagle Star Ins Co Ltd*, [1993] 1 Lloyd's Rep 429 (re).

150. *Charman* v *GRE Assurance plc* [1992] 2 Lloyd's Rep 607, 613 *per* Webster J (re).

151. *Ibid* pp 613–614. However, the reinsurer may be entitled to required the reinsured to provide him with information and documents showing, but not necessarily in detail, how the claim was dealt with: *ibid*.

152. *American Ins Co* v *North American Casualty Co*, 697 F 2d 79, 81 (2 Cir, 1982—re). However, this does not make the reinsurer liable in an amount exceeding any limit on amount to be found in the reinsurance contract: *Bellefonte Reinsurance Co* v *Aetna Casualty & Surety Co*, 903 F 2d 910, 913 (2 Cir, 1990—re).

153. *Unigard Sec Ins Co* v *North River Ins Co*, 762 F Supp 566, 587 (SD NY, 1991—re), affirmed 949 F.2d 630 (2 Cir, 1991—re).

154. In *Toomey* v *Eagle Star Ins Co Ltd* [1993] 1 Lloyd's Rep 429 (re), the latter construction was taken of a stop loss policy. It has been doubted whether this is a viable distinction in practice.

that, as the clause stopped a defence based on the underlying contract, it also stopped the reinsurer from raising the same kind of defence in the context of an identical reinsurance contract, has been rejected: "the reinsurer is always entitled to raise issues as to the scope of the reinsurance contract".[155]

As to the second condition of honesty, the reinsurer must follow the settlement even though there has been fraud by the primary insured.[156] However, good faith in the reinsured implies a belief that the claim had sufficient substance for compromise to be prudent.

As to the third condition of proper and businesslike steps, to add the words "liable or not liable" to the clause may clarify it but does not qualify or limit the obligations of the reinsured; in particular, the words do not remove the requirement of a business-like settlement or allow the reassured to settle a claim, for which he knew that he was not liable.[157] Even so, payment might be thought prudent and made in good faith, although not a payment that the insurer was legally obliged to make.

For example, large claims, in respect of liability for bodily injury through contact with asbestos, gave rise to generic sharing arrangements between primary insurers under the 1985 Wellington Agreement, to reduce legal and other service costs and to avoid cross-claims between the insured, in cases of uncertainty about which insured was liable to which victim. However, this has meant that sometimes an insurer has made a payment which, on a strict application of his policy, he was not obliged to make. In these circumstances, most reinsurers have not disputed the settlement made by the reinsured, however, a small number have done so and their refusal to pay was upheld in *Hiscox* v *Outhwaite (No 3)*.[158]

Each clause must be considered in context. In *Scor*,[159] the Court of Appeal had to consider a cocktail of clauses, containing not only a follow settlements clause but also a condition against settlement without the consent of the reinsurer. The solution[160] of this apparent conflict was that the reinsurer was obliged to follow only those settle-ments which had received their approval: "the follow settlements clause must be con-strued in its context in the policy, containing as it does a claims co-operation clause in this form, as only requiring reinsurers to follow settlements which are authorized."[161]

---

155. *Hiscox* v *Outhwaite (No 3)* [1991] 2 Lloyd's Rep 524, 530 *per* Evans J (re).

156. *Scor* (above), pp 321–322 *per* Stevenson LJ, and p 330 *per* Robert Goff LJ, who continued: the rein-surers "must have recourse to their rights of subrogation, arising upon payment of the claim under the policy of reinsurance, in order to seek to rescind the settlement with the assured and to recover the money paid by the insurers under that settlement".

157. *Charman* v *GRE Assurance plc* [1992] 2 Lloyd's Rep. 607, 612 *per* Webster J (re). In this case, it was held that it was not sufficient without more to appoint a competent loss adjuster: "the reassured are to be identified with the conduct of their loss adjusters and any other agents they employ for the purpose of making the settlement", who must also act in a businesslike way (p 612).

158. *Hiscox* (above). See also: *INA* v *US Fire Ins Co*, 322 NYS 2d 520, 523 (1971—re), affirmed 348 NYS 2d 122 (1973). *Cf Unigard* (above) in which the court observed *(loc cit)* that the cedent's participation in the Wellington Agreement was in good faith, however, that it might have required disclosure to the reinsurer, if participation had altered the risk (p 588). See further "*Unigard II*": *Unigard Security Ins Co* v *North River Ins Co*, 4 F 3d 1049 (2 Cir, 1993—liability) and *North River Ins Co* v *Philadelphia Re Corp*, 831 F Supp 1132 (D NJ, 1993—liability).

159. Above.

160. Robert Goff and Fox LJJ, Stevenson LJ dissenting.

161. p 331 *per* Robert Goff LJ. See also p 334 *per* Fox LJ. Much depends on the wording of the clause. *Cf Trans-Pacific Ins Co (Aust) Ltd* v *Grand Union Ins Co Ltd* (1990) 6 ANZ Ins Cases, No 60–949 (NSW—re), in which it was held that the insurer must keep the reinsurer informed and listen to his views about the settlement in prospect.

Moreover, the court would not imply a term that, in the absence of approval, the reinsurers would indemnify the reinsured against any loss or expense incurred.[162]

27–5 ENTRY ON PREMISES

After a fire claim, the insurer has a right to enter the premises, inspect the damage and, if necessary, take possession of the premises. This right is usually given and governed by the contract, however, a right of entry will also be implied by law, to be exercised within and for a reasonable time.[163] Damages have been awarded against an insurer who was too slow.[164] An insurer will not be allowed to prolong an investigation in the hope of turning up evidence for its unsupported suspicion that a claim is fraudulent.[165] Moreover, if a fire insurer enters premises to minimise loss, the loss recoverable as indemnity is measured at the time the insurer returns possession to the insured; thus, the insurer will have to pay for progressive damage, for example, damage initiated by water used to extinguish the fire and spreading or augmenting while he is in possession.[166]

27–6 SUBROGATION

The insured is obliged by law and by contract terms to assist the insurer to exercise any rights of subrogation available to the insurer against a third party responsible for the loss insured. This duty is discussed below, 31–5.

162. p 332 *per* Robert Goff LJ, p 334 *per* Fox LJ. For criticism see Shadler [1986] LMCLQ 145, pointing *inter alia* to market practice whereby reinsurers share expenses, such as claims investigation, in proportion to their share of the risk and above the limit of indemnity under the reinsurance contract. See also above, note 142.
163. *Oldfield* v *Price* (1860) 2 F & F 80 (fire). On the law of contract see Burrows, (1968) 31 MLR 392, 401 ff and cases cited.
164. *Norton* v *Royal Fire & Accident Life Assurance Co* (1885) 1 TLR 460 (fire), affirmed (1885) *The Times*, 12 August 1885 (CA).
165. *Livingston* v *Auto Owners Ins Co*, 582 So 2d 1038, 1042 (Ala, 1991– fire).
166. *Ahmedbhoy Habbibhoy* v *Bombay Fire & Marine Ins Co Ltd* (1912) 29 TLR 96 (PC—fire): Lord Moulton (p 97) made it clear that the decision awarding indemnity to the insured was based not on any breach of duty by the insurer to the insured but on the loss caused by the fire.

CHAPTER 28

INDEMNITY

28–1 ACTUAL LOSS

In the case of non-indemnity insurance, the claimant recovers the amount stated in the policy.[1] In the case of indemnity insurance, the claimant recovers the amount of his actual loss and this chapter is concerned with the assessment of actual loss. He may not recover more than his actual loss,[2] even if the sum insured is greater (below, 28–1A). Moreover, the amount recoverable from the insurer is reduced by any indemnity for the same loss already obtained from a third party.[3]

The claimant may recover a sum greater than his own actual loss, if he is a person with a limited interest in the subject-matter of the insurance, such as a bailee of goods; the courts have accepted that full recovery is justifiable on grounds of commercial convenience. This is exceptional, however, and when full recovery is permitted, the claimant holds the insurance money in excess of his actual loss for others interested, such as the bailor.[4]

The claimant may recover a sum less than his actual loss (a) to the extent that he is his own insurer (below, 28–8), (b) if he is unable to prove his actual loss,[5] (c) when his actual loss is greater than the sum insured (below, 28–1A), or (d) when his actual loss is consequential loss (below, 28–8E) and not covered by the insurance.

The claimant may recover more or less than his actual loss, in the case of valued policies (below, 28–7), according to the case.

28–1A The Sum Insured: Independent Loss

The sum insured is a ceiling on the amount of actual loss recoverable,[6] it is not necessarily the amount payable in case of total loss.

---

1. *Ex hypothesi*, it is not a measure of actual loss. The amount recoverable may vary according to the circumstances of loss. For example, (i) a PA contract may pay on a scale of sums according to the nature of the injury; (ii) a life contract may reduce the amount payable, if the life drops in specified (usually hazardous) circumstances.

A PA contract may be a non-indemnity contract, as regards cover payable for death and injury, but pay an indemnity as regards medical and other consequential expenses covered: *Glynn* v *Scottish Union & National Ins Co Ltd* (1963) 40 DLR (2d) 929 (Ont—motor).

2. *Castellain* v *Preston* (1883) 11 QBD 380, 386 *per* Brett LJ (CA—fire). USA: generally, see Appleman, sections 3821 ff.

3. *British Traders' Ins Co Ltd* v *Monson* (1964) 111 CLR 86, 95 (HCA—fire). See below, 28–9 and 31–4.

4. See above, 5–6; below, 28–1B and 28–2A.

5. *Williams* v *Atlantic Assurance Co* [1933] 1 KB 81, 90 *per* Scrutton LJ (CA—cargo).

6. *Hercules Ins Co* v *Hunter*, 1836 14 Sh (Ct Sess) 1137 (fire); *Curtis & Sons* v *Mathew* (1918) 24 Com Cas 57, 67 *per* Roche J (fire); *Reynolds* v *Phoenix Assurance Co Ltd* [1978] 2 Lloyd's Rep 440, 450 *per* Forbes J (fire); *Leppard* v *Excess Insurance Co Ltd* [1979] 2 Lloyd's Rep 91, 95 *per* Megaw LJ (CA—fire).

"You must not run away with the notion that a policy of insurance entitles a man to recover according to the amount represented as insured by the premiums paid . . . he can only recover the real and actual value of the goods. The law will not allow gambling in the form of insurance. Insurance companies are subject to fraud enough as it is, and if a person were allowed to insure goods to a greater amount than the real value, it is obvious that a door would be open to fraud and wickedness of the most abominable description."[7]

The contract may contain more than one ceiling, one lower than the other; the lower ceiling is usually for loss in circumstances in which the risk is greater.[8]

Unless the contract provides otherwise,[9] the insurer is liable for any number of successive losses caused by insured perils during the period of cover,[10] even though the aggregate of amounts payable exceeds the ceiling; there is a presumption in favour of full indemnity. The ceiling is applied to each separate loss; hence, it is important to ask whether an item of loss is a separate loss for this purpose or whether it is one of a number of items of loss, amounting to a combined single loss at a total figure, which exceeds the sum insured and is thus affected by the ceiling. The answer depends on the interpretation of the contract[11] and, in appropriate cases, on the intentions of reasonable businessmen[12] and on evidence of commercial custom.[13]

In a leading case, when the insured's tram overturned and the tramway met the claims of 40 people affected, a liability policy limit of "£250 in respect of any one accident" applied, it was held, not to the aggregate of sums claimed but to the sum claimed by each person.[14] The context was a policy against "claims for personal injury and damage to property made against the assured in respect of accident caused by vehicles". The word "accident" might have refered to the tram or to the claimant; the court preferred the second construction.[15]

28–1B Limited Interests

Persons with a limited interest in property may insure the full value of the property, however, unless they have insured not only for themselves but also for other persons

---

British Traders' Ins Co Ltd v Monson (1964) 111 CLR 86, 92 (HCA—fire); *Lucas v New Zealand Ins Co Ltd* [1983] VR 698 (fire). *Citizens Ins Co v Foxbilt Inc*, 226 F 2d 641, 645 (8 Cir, 1955—fire); *Apparel City Sewing Machine Co Inc v Transamerica Ins Group*, 181 Cal Rptr 64 (1982—fire).
7. Cockburn CJ addressing the jury in *Chapman v Pole* (1870) 22 LT 306, 307 (fire).
8. For example, *Mint Security Ltd v Blair* [1982] 1 Lloyd's Rep 188, 193 *per* Staughton J: in a cash in transit policy a lower sum was insured in respect of loss "between vehicles and premises and vice versa".
9. For example, the insurer may be liable for successive losses with a ceiling on each and a global limit on accumulated losses; once the latter figure has been reached, the policy is exhausted. *Cf Crowley v Cohen* (1832) 3 B & Ad 478, 487-488 *per* Parke B: the ceiling applied to successive cargoes.
10. *Re Law Car and General Ins Corp Ltd* [1913] 2 Ch 103, 118 *per* Cozens-Hardy MR (CA—employers' liability). MIA, section 77. Anderson, 16 JMLC 553 (1985).
11. *South Staffs Tramways Co Ltd v Sickness & Accident Assurance Assn Ltd* [1891] 1 QB 402, 407 *per* Bowen LJ (CA—liability); *Pennsylvania Co for Ins on Lives v Mumford* [1920] 2 KB 537, 543 *per* Lord Sterndale MR, 547 *per* Warrington LJ, 552 *per* Scrutton LJ (CA—theft).
12. *Stewart & Co v Merchants Marine Ins Co Ltd* (1885) 16 QBD 619, 623, 627 *per* Lord Esher MR (CA—hull).
13. *Blackett v Royal Exchange Assurance Co* (1832) 2 C & J 244, 251 *per* Lord Lyndhurst CB (hull).
14. *South Staffs Tramways* (above).
15. *Ibid* p 405 *per* Bowen LJ: the words meant accidents caused by vehicles to persons; see also p 408 *per* Fry LJ.

interested in the property,[16] the amount recoverable is limited to the value of their interest.[17] Instances are creditors with a security interest and tenants, however, they recover the actual value of their interest, even though, in the case of a creditor, the aggregate amount recovered by several creditors may exceed the value of the property: a particular insurance contract is concerned only with the actual recoverable loss of the particular claimant.[18] As regards the measure in particular cases of limited interest, see below, 28–2A.

28–2 THE BASIS OF ASSESSMENT

Property, real or personal, may be totally lost or it may be partially lost, which means either that a part is missing or that there is damage. In each case, insurance loss is economic without regard to sentimental value.[19] The court seeks the actual monetary value of the property to the insured at the time of the loss.[20] The purpose is indemnity: to put the claimant in the position he would have been in, if the insured loss had not occurred.[21]

As regards the measure or assessment of loss, as distinguished from questions of remoteness of loss and causation,[22] the rule of indemnity in insurance contract law is analogous[23] to that found in the law of tort. In the case of a tort causing damage to real or personal property, the purpose of indemnity

"is achieved by the application of one or other of two quite different measures of damage, or, occasionally a combination of the two. The first is to take the capital value of the property in an undamaged state and to compare it with its value in a damaged state. The second is to take the cost of repair or reinstatement. Which is appropriate will depend on a number of factors, such

---

16. See above, 4–5F, 4–5G, and 5–6.

17. *British Traders Ins Co Ltd v Monson* (1964) 111 CLR 86, 100–101 *per* Menzies J (HCA—fire). *Peerless Ins Co v Bailey Mortgage Co*, 345 F 2d 14, 17 (5 Cir, 1965—fire); *Cherokee Ins Co v Koenenn*, 536 F 2d 585 (5 Cir, 1976—fire).

18. *Westminster Fire Office v Glasgow Provident Investment Sy* (1888) 13 App Cas 699, 713 *per* Earl of Selborne (fire).

19. *Richard Aubrey Film Productions Ltd v Graham* [1960] 2 Lloyd's Rep 101, 103 *per* Winn J, concerning the loss of a film. See also *Crisp v National Security Co*, 369 SW 2d 326, 328 (Tex, 1963—fire). In practice, there may be some leeway in the valuation of collections, for example, of ephemera: PM 11 March 1993, p 27.

20. For example, *Canadian National Fire Ins Co v Colonsay Hotel Co* [1923] SCR 688, 694 *per* Angin J (fire).

21. *Dominion Mosaics & Tile Co Ltd v Tralgar Trucking Co Ltd* [1990] 2 All ER 246 (CA). *Matergio v Canada Accident & Fire Assurance Co* [1926] 1 DLR 1002, 1004 (NS—fire). *Citizens Ins Co v Foxbilt Inc*, 226 F 2d 641, 645 (8 Cir, 1955—fire); *Crisp v National Security Co*, 369 SW 2d 326, 328 (Tex, 1963—fire); *Incardona v Home Indemnity Co*, 400 NYS 2d 944, 945 (1977—fire).

22. Chapter 25.

23. Analogy accepted in *Reynolds v Phoenix Assurance Co Ltd* [1978] 2 Lloyd's Rep 440, 450 ff by Forbes J (fire); and in *Montreal Trust Co v Hercules Sales Ltd* (1968) 3 DLR (3d) 504, 506 (Ont). The analogy is confined to direct loss; consequential loss, which may be recoverable in tort, is not normally recoverable under an insurance contract: below, 28–8E.

as the plaintiff's future intentions as to the use of the property and the reasonableness of those intentions."[24]

28–2A Real Property

In the case of real property, the appropriate basis of indemnity depends mainly on the intention of the insured at the time of the loss.[25]

If the insured intended the property for sale, the basis of assessment is the market value of the property[26] and, if a sale price had been agreed before the loss, that is likely to be taken as the value of the property, unless the sale was a forced sale.[27] Even if the insurer stipulates that the property be insured for the amount of the estimated cost of reinstatement,[28] that is influential but not decisive of the basis of assessment,[29] which may nonetheless be done on the basis of the likely sale price on the open market.

If the insured did not intend the property for sale immediately prior to loss but that becomes his intention as an immediate consequence of the loss, perhaps because he needs alternative accommodation quickly, the basis of indemnity is the cost of finding alternative property.

In *Dominion Mosaics*,[30] the plaintiff's premises were business premises, needed to earn income, and the Court of Appeal held that the appropriate measure of loss was the cost of acquiring new premises, thus mitigating the loss of income that would otherwise ensue while the original premises were rebuilt. "Where business premises are concerned, the need to carry on the business and to mitigate the loss of earnings is

24. *Dodd Properties (Kent) Ltd* v *Canterbury CC* [1980] 1 All ER 928, 938 *per* Donaldson LJ (CA). See also *Radford* v *De Froberville* [1978] 1 All ER 33; *Ward* v *Cannock Chase DC* [1986] Ch 546; *Minscombe Properties Ltd* v *Sir Alfred McAlpine & Son Ltd* [1986] 2 EGLR 15 (CA). However, there is no discount for betterment: *Harbutt's "Plasticine" Ltd* v *Wayne Tank & Pump Co Ltd* [1970] 1 QB 447 (CA). McGregor, Nos 946 ff, 1392 ff; Harris, Ogus and Phillips, 95 LQR 581 (1979).
USA *idem*: as appropriate, on the basis of (a) market value, known as the California rule, or (b) replacement cost less depreciation, known as the Pennsylvania rule, or (c) "the broad evidence rule", known as the New York rule, in which (a) and (b) are just factors among others that a court will consider: Fischer, 56 Ind L J 445, 463 (1982); Reader, 22 Tort & Ins L J 282 (1987). However, the New York rule is criticised as being no more than the court's view of the market value, a method of evaluation that lacks certainty: Reader pp 286–287. Generally, see Appleman, sections 3823 ff.
25. *Leppard* v *Excess Insurance Co Ltd* [1979] 2 Lloyd's Rep 91, 96 *per* Megaw LJ (CA—fire), with whom the other members of the court agreed. See also *Canadian National Fire Ins Co* v *Colonsay Hotel Co* [1923] SCR 688, 692 *per* Duff J (fire); *McLachlin* v *Dunwich Fire Ins Co* [1935] 3 DLR 194 (Ont—fire); *idem* even though the claimant's intention may have changed later, as a result of delay in payment of the insurance money: *Jauvin* v *L'Ami Michel Automobile Canada Ltée* (1986) 33 DLR (4th) 576 (Ont—fire).
26. *Leppard* (above); on the basis of the market in this case, the loss of a cottage was an amount less than half the cost of reinstatement.
A third basis has been suggested for old buildings, namely the value of equivalent modern replacement by a building serving the same purpose. This basis was adopted by Lawson J in *Exchange Theatre Ltd* v *Iron Trades Mutual Ins Co Ltd* [1983] 1 Lloyd's Rep 674, 688–689 (fire), as there was not "anything that could be called a market in old converted Victorian public halls". In *Reynolds* v *Phoenix Assurance Co Ltd* [1978] 2 Lloyd's Rep 440, 448, 451 (fire), Forbes J considered that equivalent modern replacement was not a separate basis of assessment but a valuer's device, an alternative way of arriving at the market value of an old building or of one subject to a compulsory purchase order.
27. *Garcia* v *Société Nationale d'Assurance* (1992) 94 DLR (4th) 245 (Que, 1991—fire).
28. For example, *Leppard* v *Excess Insurance Co Ltd* [1979] 2 Lloyd's Rep 91 (CA—fire). See also *Reynolds* v *Phoenix Assurance Co Ltd* [1978] 2 Lloyd's Rep 440, 453 *per* Forbes J (fire); *Pleasurama Ltd* v *Sun Alliance & London Ins Ltd* [1979] 1 Lloyd's Rep 389, 393 *per* Parker J (fire).
29. *Reynolds* (above), p 450 *per* Forbes J.
30. *Dominion Mosaics & Tile Co Ltd* v *Tralgar Trucking Co Ltd* [1990] 2 All ER 246 (CA).

an important factor."[31] Moreover, in this case the cost of acquiring new premises was less than the cost of rebuilding the old premises.

Subject to this, if at the time of the loss the insured intended to retain and use the insured property, the measure of indemnity is the cost of reinstatement. Further, if he intends to spend insurance money, although not his own money, on reinstatement of buildings, that is nonetheless a genuine intention to reinstate and the cost of reinstatement is the measure, provided that that intention is not merely eccentric.[32]

The degree and thus the cost of reinstatement depend on the objectives of reinstatement. If at the time of the loss the insured intended property for use or occupation, the basis is the cost of reinstatement to a condition in which it can be used or occupied.[33] So also with a farm barn in full and normal use at the time of the fire[34]; but it would usually be different, if the barn were not in use[35] or not in normal use.[36] In Oklahoma, for example, the appraiser takes account of "functional obsolescence"[37] but this does not include the likelihood of demolition.[38] Functional obsolescence "refers to a condition existing at the time of loss and not to the probable diminution of value at a date subsequent to loss".[39] On the time of assessment, see below, 28–4. As to the mode and materials of reinstatement, see below, 28–3A; and, as to the quality of reinstatement, see below 29–2D.

Among claimants with limited interests, a tenant, who has covenanted to insure or to repair the property leased, suffers loss based not on the market value of the property but on the cost of the covenanted reinstatement.[40] The same may be true of a lessor who, although he has sold the reversion, remains obliged under the lease to use

31. p 249 *per* Taylor LJ. Also in this sense: *INA* v *US Gypsum Co*, 870 F 2d 148 (4 Cir, 1989—AR), in which the cost of relocating and rebuilding a mill were recoverable, as the cost was less than that of reinstating the original, which had been affected by subsidence.

32. *Reynolds* (above), p 453 *per* Forbes J. *Cf Murphy* v *Wexford CC* [1921] 2 IR 230, 240 *per* O'Connor LJ (CA).

USA: courts are more ready to apply the measure of reinstatement, if there is some guarantee that the insurance money will be spent on reinstatement, thus reducing the moral hazard of arson: for example, *Higgins* v *INA*, 469 P 2d 766, 773–774 (Or, 1970—fire). Other courts go further and require actual reinstatement before insurance money has to be paid: *Lerer Realty Corp* v *MFB Mutual Ins Co*, 474 F 2d 410 (5 Cir, 1973—windstorm).

33. *Lucas* v *New Zealand Ins Co Ltd* [1983] VR 698 (fire).

34. *McLachlin* v *Dunwich Fire Ins Co* [1935] 3 DLR 194 (Ont—fire).

35. *Vanderburgh* v *Oneida Farmers' Mutual Fire Ins Co* [1935] 1 DLR 257 (Ont—fire). Likewise in the case of a redundant hotel: *Canadian National Fire Ins Co* v *Colonsay Hotel Co* [1923] SCR 688 (fire); a barn in use but intended for demolition: *Montreal Trust Co* v *Hercules Sales Ltd* (1968) 3 DLR (3d) 504, 506 (Ont); and buildings not being "economically utilized at the time of their damage", being "for all practical purposes non-existent": *Chicago Title & Trust Co* v *US Fidelity & Guarantee Co*, 376 F Supp 767, 770 (ND Ill, 1973—fire).

36. In *Ziola* v *Cooperative Fire & Casualty Co* [1976] 6 WWR 159 (Sask—fire), the insured occupied a new farmhouse and used the old one as a store; in determining the "actual cash value" of the latter, the court rejected reference to the cost of replacement as a farmhouse, as no reasonable person in those circumstances would reinstate it as such.

37. *First National Ins Co* v *Norton*, 238 F 2d 949 (10 Cir, 1956—fire).

38. *Bailey* v *Gulf Ins Co*, 406 F 2d 47 (10 Cir, 1969—fire). In this sense in Canada: *Leger* v *Royal Ins Co Ltd* (1968) 70 DLR (2d) 344, 351 (NB—fire). *Cf Lucas* v *New Zealand Ins Co Ltd* [1983] VR 698, 701 (fire).

39. *American Ins Co* v *Treasurer School Dist No 37*, 273 F 2d 759, 757 (10 Cir, 1959—windstorm). See also *Knuppel* v *American Ins Co*, 269 F 2d 163 (7 Cir, 1959—fire). Fischer, 56 Ind L J 445, 459 ff (1982). "Courts disregard the economic fact that a building about to be demolished is a liability rather than an asset because of the cost of demolition and removing debris and that the expectancy of any recovery for fire loss encourages arson"—*ibid*, pp 470–471. But some cases have held that, if demolition is certain or in course, the building has no economic value and therefore the insured has no insurable interest: *Lieberman* v *Hartford Ins Co*, 287 NE 2d 38 (Ill, 1972—fire).

40. *Castellain* v *Preston* (1883) 11 QBD 380, 400 *per* Bowen LJ (CA—fire).

insurance money for reinstatement.[40a] His recoverable loss may be the whole of the insurance money but, if so, usually "the reason would have been that the fire had cast upon him a liability of at least that amount".[41] However, even if he has not covenanted to insure or to repair, his recoverable loss may still be the full amount, if there is nowhere else he can reasonably be expected to go. This is the position of the tenant for life.[42]

As regards claimants with a security interest in property, their loss is the amount of their debt outstanding, whether or not the value of what remains of the property insured is such that the property could still be sufficient security for the debt.[43]

28–2B Other Property

What is true of real property (above, 28–2A) is broadly true also of other kinds of corporeal property.

"[T]he market value of the particular article destroyed or the price for which it could have been sold at the time of loss, is not necessarily the true measure of indemnity. To be restored to his original position, the insured must replace what he has lost, and he is not fully indemnified unless the amount recoverable under his policy is sufficient for the purpose. It may therefore be concluded that the rule in this case is the same as in the case of buildings, and that the true measure of indemnity is based on the cost of reinstatement and not the market value of the property destroyed."[44]

If the insured has something to sell and it is totally lost, its value, for the purpose of indemnity, is the price he could have got for it in the market. If he has it to use and it can be repaired at a reasonable cost, i.e. it is not a "write–off", indemnity is the cost of repair. If he has it to use and it is totally lost or cannot be repaired at a reasonable cost, indemnity is the price in the market to get another similar one to use—provided that a market exists.[45] If the thing is one for which there is a second hand market, the basis is indeed the market[46]; but, if there is no such market,[47] the only way to indemnify the claimant may be to repair it (at unreasonable cost) or to replace it with a new one.

In *Dominion Mosaics*,[48] the plaintiffs lost some machines in a fire, machines which they had bought only a few months earlier at a bargain price. That price was one-fifth of the cost of replacement after the fire, which the plaintiffs claimed and recovered.

40a. *Lonsdale & Thompson Ltd* v *Black Arrow Group* [1993] 2 Lloyd's Rep 428 (fire).

41. *British Traders' Ins Co Ltd* v *Monson* (1964) 111 CLR 86, 93 (HCA—fire). As regards the measure of recovery by a tenant for loss which the landlord has repaired, see Fischer, 56 Ind L J 445, 451 (1981).

42. *Castellain* v *Preston* (1883) 11 QBD 380, 400–401 *per* Bowen LJ (CA—fire). *Cf British Traders' Ins Co Ltd* v *Monson* (1964) 111 CLR 86 (HCA—fire).

USA: the measure for the life tenant is usually the cost of reinstatement and not the actuarial value of the life interest: *Convis* v *Citizens' Mutual Fire Ins Co*, 86 NW 994 (1901—fire). See further, Fischer, 56 Ind L J 445, 449 (1981).

43. *Westminster Fire Office* v *Glasgow Provident Investment Sy* (1888) 13 App Cas 699, 713 *per* Earl of Selborne (fire). USA: see Fischer, 56 Ind L J 445, 455–456 (1981).

44. Ivamy, *Fire*, p 174. Ivamy's view was quoted with approval in *Fire & All Risks Ins Co Ltd* v *Rousianos* (1989) 19 NSWLR 57, 67 (fire).

45. Logically, this should apply to partial as well as total loss, so that if my car is damaged I am left with the damaged car and the difference between the market price before and after damage; for example *Patriotic Ins Co* v *Franciscus*, 55 F 2d 844, 850 (8 Cir, 1932—fire). In practice in England the insurer pays the cost of repair. USA *idem*: Appleman, section 3861.

46. *Lucas* v *New Zealand Ins Co Ltd* [1983] VR 698, 700 (fire).

47. *Calder* v *Batavia Sea & Fire Ins Co Ltd* [1932] SASR 46. *Wisconsin Screw Co* v *Fireman's Fund Ins Co*, 193 F Supp 96 (ED Wis, 1960—fire), affirmed 297 F 2d 687 (7 Cir, 1962).

48. *Dominion Mosaics & Tile Co Ltd* v *Trafalgar Trucking Co Ltd* [1990] 2 All ER 246 (CA).

Taylor LJ observed[49] that, where there is no supply of second hand goods "and the only way the owner of destroyed chattels can replace them is by buying new ones, the measure of damages is the cost of doing that, unless the result would be absurd", for example, the case of a machine on its last legs. On the question of a discount for betterment in cases like this, see below, 28–3C.

Generally, the insured cannot expect indemnity sufficient to buy, for example, a brand new household arm-chair; but, as Mackinnon J observed,[50] he can expect "the reasonable value of the second-hand armchair that has been destroyed". As the only market may be the junk shop or the car-boot sale, the market value may not be the reasonable value and, in England, the law is perhaps not far from that stated by the Supreme Court of Texas[51]:

"household goods, clothing and personal effects have no market value in the ordinary meaning of that term. They may be sold but only at a considerable sacrifice which by no means represents the value of the articles to the owner. We find no recognized authority which would hold the insured to a recovery based solely on the proceeds obtainable on a secondhand market. Likewise, replacement costs do not afford a fair test. In some instances on account of obsolescence, change in style and fashion, this measure might represent an economic gain to the insured quite aside from the difficulty of application and proof. The measure . . . is the actual worth or value of the articles to the owner for use in the condition in which they were at the time of the fire excluding any fanciful or sentimental considerations."

Similarly, in the case of commercial property, for which there is no real market of any kind, the court must consider all the evidence available and find the reasonable value of the item as a thing in use. In particular, the value of commercial property is said[52] to be the value of the thing as part of a going concern and not the price that might have been obtained upon a "break-up sale" of the insured's business.[53] Similarly, the true value of components may be their value as part of a greater manufactured product.[54]

28–3 THE MODE OF ASSESSMENT

28–3A Reinstatement

When damages are awarded for tort or for breach of contract on the basis of reinstatement, the plaintiff's stated desire to reinstate must be reasonable, having regard to the relation between the cost of reinstatement and the market value of the property.[55] As to the legitimate objectives of reinstatement, see above, 28–2A. Reasonableness of

---

49. p 255.
50. *Ewer* v *National Employers' Mutual General Ins Assn Ltd* (1937) 157 LT 16, 21 (fire).
51. *Crisp* v *Security National Ins Co*, 369 SW 2d 326, 328 (Tex, 1963—fire). See also *Fisher* v *Indiana Lumbermen's Mutual Ins Co*, 456 F 2d 1396, 1400 (5 Cir, 1972—fire). Appleman, section 3825.
52. *Roumeli Food Stores (NSW) Pty Ltd* v *New India Assurance Co Ltd* [1972] 1 NSWLR 227 (fire). Tarr, p 258. *Ziola* v *Cooperative Fire & Casualty Co* [1976] 6 WWR 159, 165 (Sask—fire). In this sense in the absence of a market: *The Harmonides* [1903] P 1, 6 *per* Gorell Barnes J.
53. *Fire & All Risks Ins Co Ltd* v *Rousianos* (1989) 19 NSWLR 57, 67 (fire), with reference to the principle of indemnity in *Castellain* v *Preston* (1883) 11 QBD 380 (CA—fire). The case concerned a used automatic carwash.
54. Generally, see Tarr, 2 Canterbury L Rev 107, 118 (1983).
55. *Lodge Holes Colliery Co Ltd* v *Wednesbury Corp* [1908] AC 323. McGregor, No 1396.

reinstatement is also required in respect of *how* it is done and, therefore, how much it costs. In a tort case,[56] the judge said that the claimants were

"not bound to accept a shoddy job or put up with an inferior building for the sake of saving the defendants' expense. But I do not consider that they are entitled to insist on complete and meticulous restoration when a reasonable building owner would be content with less extensive work . . . and when there is also a vast difference in the cost of such work and the cost of meticulous restoration."

The same is true of insurance: the mode of reinstatement must be reasonable; it may not be reasonable to replace marble with marble. In the case of the reinstatement of old buildings, there must be appropriate economies in the use of materials,[57] however, reinstatement must meet current standards set by fire or other relevant regulations.[58] Machine parts may be replaced by cheaper parts made by a different manufacturer, if the replacements are of the same general kind and quality as the original.[59] In Louisiana, for example, the benchmark is what a reasonably prudent uninsured owner would do in the circumstances.[60] Indeed, in principle, reinstatement is a matter for the initiative of the insured but it is obviously wise to agree it first with the insurer; contract terms may regulate this process, for example, by requiring the claimant to submit estimates to the insurer.

28–3B Market Value

In principle, market value is measured at the time[61] and the place of loss. It is sometimes said[62] that the market value is the cost of replacement. The market place is the one nearest the place of loss or discovery of loss; in the case of goods in transit, it is usually the place of intended destination.[63]

When there is no market in which substitute goods can be bought, as when the property is unique and must be remade, some other criterion of value, such as the price at which the property could have been sold immediately before loss, must be sought. The court will use whatever evidence of value it can get.

For example, a work of art may be worth less than the cost of production. In *Richard Aubrey Film Productions Ltd v Graham*[64] the insured claimed £18,000, the cost of making[65] a film, described as the "child of his artistic creation", which had been lost, but Winn J observed[66]: "One could hardly say that an alchemist who had

---

56. *Dodd Properties (Kent) Ltd v Canterbury CC* [1979] 2 All ER 118, 124 *per* Cantley J, reversed on other grounds [1980] 1 All ER 928 (CA). As to the quality of reinstatement work, see below, 29–2D.

57. *Reynolds v Phoenix Assurance Co Ltd* [1978] 2 Lloyd's Rep 440, 453 *per* Forbes J (fire).

58. *Jacobsen Co v Commercial Union Assurance Co Ltd*, 83 F Supp 674 (D Minn, 1949—fire); *Reliance Ins Co v Orleans Parish School Bd*, 201 F Supp 78, 80 (ED La, 1962—fire), affirmed in part 322 F 2d 803 (5 Cir, 1963), cert den 377 US 916. This has been held, although the relevant regulations—*in casu* an earthquake code—did not come into effect until after the insured earthquake: *Vintix Pty Ltd v Lumley General Ins Ltd* (1991) 6 ANZ Ins Cas 61–050 (NSW—fire); Sutton (1992) 20 Austl Bus L Rev 262.

59. *Sachs v American Central Ins Co*, 227 NYS 2d 873 (1962—fire).

60. *Reliance* (above), *loc cit*.

61. Below, 28–4.

62. For example *Rice v Baxendale* (1861) 7 H & N 96, 100 *per* Bramwell B (goods in transit).

63. *Rice* (above). *Prussian National Ins Co v Lawrence*, 221 F 931 (4 Cir, 1915—fire). *Cf* Bramwell B in *Rice* (above), p 102, who preferred to award the price at the place of consignment plus the cost of getting them to destination.

64. [1960] 2 Lloyd's Rep 101 ("All risks of loss or damage . . . to . . . exposed film").

65. *Semble* the insured did not intend to use the money to reshoot the film; if he had intended to do so, and this intention was not unreasonable, it appears that he would have been entitled to the cost of doing so.

66. p 105.

spent large sums of money on base metal, trying to turn it into gold, had thereby increased correspondingly the value of the base metal on which he had unsuccessfully worked." The judge awarded a lesser sum, the estimated market value of the film at the time of loss.

When reference is made to market value, the law starts from the position that this means the value of the property as it was at the time of loss, in many cases property that has been used. An exception arises, of course, if the policy expressly provides for payment of the cost of replacement with unused goods of the same kind; the insured gets "new for old". More difficult is the suggestion that a similar provision can be implied. The main obstacle to that suggestion is the doctrine of betterment.

28-3C Betterment

When property is replaced or reinstated, the amount recoverable, it has been said,[67] should be subject to a discount for depreciation—an allowance or deduction for the betterment of the thing reinstated. In relation to buildings, however, Widgery LJ once objected that deduction "would be the equivalent of forcing the plaintiffs to invest money in the modernising of their plant which might be highly inconvenient for them".[68] On this ground, no deduction was made, in one case, in respect of the replacement for an essential machine part, for which there was no used market and without which the claimant's business could not be carried on[69]; and, in another case, in respect of the reinstatement of a factory after a fire.[70] In these cases, however, the action was based not on an insurance contract but in tort.

Whether the doctrine of betterment still applies to insurance cases is not entirely clear, but a recent dictum in the Court of Appeal suggests that it does.[71] Indeed, in Australia, the English tort cases have been distinguished convincingly and a line drawn at this point between tort and insurance. First, the modernisation forced upon the claimant is caused, in the case of tort, by the fault of the tortfeasor but, in the case

---

67. In this sense as regards partial loss of buildings: *Reynolds v Phoenix Assurance Co Ltd* [1978] 2 Lloyd's Rep 440, 450 ff *per* Forbes J (fire): "the principle of betterment is too well established in the law of insurance". No cases were mentioned; no reference was made to *Harbutt* (below). *Cf Hercules Ins Co v Hunter*, 1836 14 Sh (Ct Sess) 1137 (fire); *The Harmonides* [1903] P 1, 6 *per* Gorell Barnes J.

The *Reynolds* assumption is found in Canada: *McLachlin v Dunwich Fire Ins Co* [1935] 3 DLR 194 (Ont—fire); *Walker & Sons Ltd v Cooperative Fire & Casualty Co* (1966) 58 DLR (2d) 10, 13 (fire); and in Australia, if the insured is obliged to reinstate: *British Traders' Ins Co Ltd v Monson* (1964) 111 CLR 86, 92 (HCA—fire).

68. *Harbutt's "Plasticine" Ltd v Wayne Tank & Pump Co Ltd* [1970] 1 QB 447, 473 (CA). McGregor, No 1395. MacGillivray, No 1568 *dubitante*.

USA *idem*: *Glen Falls Ins Co v Gulf Breeze Cottages Inc*, 38 So 2d 828, 830 (Fla, 1949—hailstorm). However, many decisions in the USA have required an allowance for depreciation: Fischer, 56 Ind LJ 445, 463 (1982); Reader, 22 Tort & Ins L J 282 (1987).

Cf Ontario: recent cases on damages map a *via media*, whereby the onus is on the defendant to prove betterment and *semble* to quantify it, which may be difficult. If he does, the onus shifts to the plaintiff to prove loss associated with the extra expenditure incurred to bear his share of the reinstatement or replacement: Berryman (1993) 72 Can B Rev 54. For example, if it can be shown that a part was replaced 10 years before replacement would have been due, a deduction will be made for betterment but, as the plaintiff has to outlay that amount 10 years earlier, it is offset by the cost of borrowing that amount for a period of 10 years.

69. *Bacon v Cooper (Metals) Ltd* [1982] 1 All ER 397, 401 *per* Cantley J; the judge accepted (p 402) that each case depended on its facts and that his decision would have been different if, for example, the damaged part had been at the end of its useful life.

70. *Harbutt's* (above), p 473 *per* Widgery LJ.

71. *Dominion Mosaics & Tile Co Ltd v Trafalgar Trucking Co Ltd* [1990] 2 All ER 246, 255 (CA).

of insurance, not in any sense by the insurer but by the insured event.[72] Second, the victim of tort has no reason to anticipate the tort and the need for reinstatement. The insured, who thinks about insurance indemnity, might also be expected to think about betterment[73] and, indeed, can deal with the matter by covering replacement cost (below). Third, the wrongdoer is liable in tort to indemnify the victim against all foreseeable consequences of the tort. The insurer is liable in contract to indemnify the insured against no more than the immediate and proximate consequences of the insured event,[74] which include neither consequential loss nor attendant obstacles to obtaining substitute property which is no better than that lost. Lest the insured receive more than a simple indemnity and lest the insurer be burdened with a risk greater than he has contracted to bear, an allowance for betterment should be made.

If any uncertainty remains, it is tolerable, perhaps, because of the common use of clauses ("replacement cost basis" cover), whereby the actual replacement cost is the stipulated measure of indemnity, with the result that the insured does not have to find the funds to cover the betterment that the fire (or other insured event) has forced upon him. Another consequence, however, is increased moral hazard: the temptation to cast off the old and bring in the new.[75]

28–4 THE TIME OF ASSESSMENT

In principle, loss is assessed on the basis of values at the time loss occurred.[76] It is irrelevant that the values have changed since the time the insurance was contracted,[77] or since the time of loss,[78] or that they are likely to change in the foreseeable future.

"Whether the insured may have only a few days in which to make use of the structure because it has been condemned, or because it has been sold, is of little consequence. The liability of the insurer is for indemnity against loss to the property and attaches upon the occurrence of the loss. Because the amount of the loss is determined at that time, to open the question of [the future] would be but to open a field of speculation and conjecture that would cloud the issue of actual loss in a maze of collateral issues."[79]

Hence, in *Rayner* v *Preston*,[80] the insured, who had agreed before the fire to sell the

---

72. *Vintix Pty Ltd* v *Lumley General Ins Ltd* (1991) 6 ANZ Ins Cas 61–050 (NSW—fire); Sutton (1992) 20 Austral Bus L Rev 262. The idea of a "new-for-old" allowance was also accepted in *Fire & All Risks Ins Co Ltd* v *Rousianos* (1989) 19 NSWLR 57, 66 (fire), in which the appeal court (pp 67–68) declined to disturb the "broad factual judgment" value made by the court below.

73. See *The Gazelle* (1844) 2 W Robb 279, 281 *per* Dr Lushington.

74. Above 25–4 and below 28–8E.

75. On clauses designed to reduce moral hazard, see Bauer, 22 Ottawa L Rev 389, 420 ff (1990).

76. *Canadian National Fire Ins Co* v *Colonsay Hotel Co* [1923] SCR 688 (fire). *Citizens Ins Co* v *Foxbilt Inc*, 226 F 2d 641, 645 (8 Cir, 1955—fire): the claimant lessee recovered the insurance money, even though the premises were later repaired by the lessor at no cost to the lessee; the judgment reviews conflicting cases on this question.

77. *Re Wilson and Scottish Corp Ltd* [1920] 2 Ch 28 (motor); for cogent criticism of the reasoning in this case see Birds, p 253. See also *Leppard* v *Excess Insurance Co Ltd* [1979] 2 Lloyd's Rep 91 (CA—fire).

78. As regards consequential loss, see below, 28–8E.

79. *Bailey* v *Gulf Ins Co*, 406 F 2d 47, 49 (10 Cir, 1969—fire), quoting *American Ins Co* v *Treasurer School Dist No 37*, 273 F 2d 759, 757 (10 Cir, 1959—windstorm). See also above, 28–2A.

80. (1881) 18 Ch D 1 (CA). However, when the insured-vendor later received the purchase price, it was held that the insurer was entitled to recover a sum equal to the insurance money from the insured: *Castellain* v *Preston* (1883) 11 QBD 380 (CA—fire).

Cf USA: Fischer, 56 Ind L J 445, 456 ff (1982): in most states, the vendor must credit insurance money to the purchase price, holding the money as trustee for the vendee; for example, *Dubin Paper Co* v *INA*, 63 A 2d 85, 94 (Pa, 1949—fire).

property insured, recovered the insurance money in full. And, in *Adler*,[81] the insured tenant for life died in the fire in question 19 minutes after the fire began, however, her estate recovered the full value of the insured loss, for "the insurer's liability attached . . . the moment the fire started" and "that loss necessarily accrued in [her] favor prior to her demise, without regard to the length of time she lived after the fire began".[82]

If the insurer fails to pay promptly after loss, the claimant may be out of pocket as a result. As to the possibility of an action for damages against the insurer, see below, 30–9.

28–5 SALVAGE

The doctrine of constructive total loss and associated doctrine of salvage do not apply as such to non-marine insurance.[83] However, salvage "is an incident of every kind of insurance which is held by law to be a contract of indemnity".[84] If an insurer pays as on a total loss, "on general principles of equity not at all peculiar to marine insurance, he who recovers on a contract of indemnity must . . . cede all his right (*sic*) in respect of that for which he obtains indemnity",[85] including anything by way of salvage, for "otherwise the assured would be more than indemnified".[86]

In non-marine insurance, therefore, the insurer who pays as on a total loss is then entitled to what is left or recovered of the property insured.[87] In the case of fire insurance, the right may be reinforced by a contractual right to enter, inspect or possess the premises.[88] In the case of theft insurance, if the stolen object is recovered, it belongs to the insurer but, as it may still be of interest to the insured, in practice the insurer may choose to sell it back to the insured. Indeed, in the case of fine art insurance, the contract may contain a clause giving the insured a right of "first refusal". Being an option, the terms of the clause must be strictly observed.[89]

The effect is that there is no profit from the loss for the insured or, indeed, for the insurer. In *Mueller*,[90] on the total loss of a vehicle, the insurer paid 800 dollars, being the value of the vehicle (900 dollars) minus an excess (100 dollars), and also retained the salvage. In an action by the insured to recover the value of the excess or of the salvage, the Alberta court deduced from English cases[91] that the insurer was entitled to salvage, only if he had paid the full value of the property insured. It was held[92] that, in view of the excess, the insured was in the position of co-insurer entitled to a share in the salvage; and that, as the insurer had elected to keep the whole of the salvage, he

---

81. *Home Ins Co* v *Adler*, 309 A 2d 751 (My, 1973—fire).
82. p 754.
83. In marine insurance, in the case of constructive total loss, the insured has a unilateral right to abandon the property to the insurer and claim as if on a total loss: MIA, sections 61 ff. This is beyond the scope of this book; see Arnould, Nos 1160 ff; 1283.
84. *Dane* v *Mortgage Ins Corp* [1894] 1 QB 54, 61 *per* Lord Esher MR (CA—insurance of securities).
85. *Rankin* v *Potter* (1873) LR 6 HL 83, 118 *per* Blackburn J (freight), with which Brett LJ in *Kaltenbach* v *Mackenzie* (1878) 3 CPD 467, 470–471 (CA—hull) concurred.
86. *Dane* (above), *loc cit*.
87. *Skipper* v *Grant* (1861) 10 CB 237, 245 *per* Williams J (fire).
88. Above, 27–5. See also the Metropolitan Fire Brigade Act 1865, section 29.
89. See Treitel p 708.
90. *Mueller* v *Western Union Ins Co* [1974] 5 WWR 530 (Alta).
91. p 533 by reference to MacGillivray (5th ed), No 1790.
92. p 537.

must pay to the insured the full value of the vehicle, hence a further 100 dollars. This is consistent with principle and in the same spirit as the rule, that the insurer is entitled to rights in subrogation, only if he has paid a full indemnity.[93]

28–6 PARTIAL LOSS

In a case of partial loss, which refers not only to total loss of part but also to damage, the amount recoverable by the claimant is usually assessed on the basis of the cost of reinstatement[94]: above, 28–3A. The amount recoverable may be subject to a deduction for betterment, a discount to the extent that the property reinstated is better than it was prior to loss: above, 28–3C.

28–7 THE VALUED POLICY

The principle of indemnity, by reference to actual loss, is a matter of contract[95] and it may be altered by contract. If, therefore, the contract stipulates that the property insured shall be assumed to have a stated value,[96] that value is taken[97]: it is conclusive for both parties without further investigation.[98] The sum payable is based on the stated value, whether or not that sum equals the actual loss suffered by the claimant.

Being a matter of contract, whether a policy is a valued policy or not is a matter of construction. Merely to state a value may not be enough.[99] A policy is more likely to

93. Brown & Menezes, 13:3:4. *Cf* below, 31–3B1.

94. *Glasgow Provident Investment Sy* v *Westminster Fire Office* (1887) 14 R 947, 989 *per* Lord Young (Ct Sess—fire); *Reynolds* v *Phoenix Assurance Co Ltd* [1978] 2 Lloyd's Rep 440 (fire); *Pleasurama Ltd* v *Sun Alliance & London Ins Ltd* [1979] 1 Lloyd's Rep 389 (fire).

Walker & Sons Ltd v *Cooperative Fire & Casualty Co* (1966) 58 DLR (2d) 10, 14 (fire). *Jacobsen Co* v *Commercial Union Assurance Co Ltd*, 83 F Supp 674 (D Minn, 1949—fire). *Cf* Wisconsin: the cost of repair not exceeding the actual cash value of the entire building—*Wisconsin Screw Co* v *Fireman's Fund Ins Co*, 193 F Supp 96, 121 (ED Wis, 1960—fire), affirmed 297 F 2d 697 (7 Cir, 1962). *Cf* Iowa: it has been held that the measure is normally the difference between the fair market value of the property before the loss and its fair market value immediately thereafter, not exceeding the cost of repair: *Citizens Ins Co* v *Foxbilt Inc*, 226 F 2d 641, 644 (8 Cir, 1955—fire).

95. *Irving* v *Manning* (1847) 1 HLC 287, 308 *per* Lord Campbell (hull); *North of England Iron SS Ins Assn* v *Armstrong* (1870) LR 5 QB 244, 250 *per* Lush J (hull). *British Traders' Ins Co Ltd* v *Monson* (1964) 111 CLR 86, 93 (HCA—fire).

96. Whether a value has been stated with sufficient certainty is an issue analogous to whether parties to a sale have agreed a price. The parties may agree a figure or (*id certum est* . . .) refer to the market price: *Loders & Nucoline Ltd* v *Bk of New Zealand* (1929) 33 Ll L Rep 70, 73 *per* Wright J (cargo).

Cf the sum insured, a ceiling on recovery, which does not make the policy a valued policy: above, 28–1A.

97. *Feise* v *Aguilar* (1811) 3 Taunt 506, 507 *per* Mansfield CJ (cargo); *Burnand* v *Rodocanachi Sons & Co* (1882) 7 App Cas 333, 335 *per* Lord Selborne LC (cargo). *Holden* v *Hanover Ins Co*, 128 F Supp 527 (WD SC, 1955—fire); *Nichols* v *Hartford Fire Ins Co*, 403 NYS 2d 335 (1978—personal property). Cal Ins Code, section 412. Appleman, section 3827.

The stated or agreed value governs all questions of value arising under the policy, including for example subrogation: *North of England Iron SS Ins Assn* v *Armstrong* (1870) LR 5 QB 244 (hull); see also *Burnand* v *Rodocanachi Sons & Co* (1882) 7 App Cas 333, 342 *per* Lord Blackburn; but not the ascertainment of a constructive total loss in marine insurance: *Irving* v *Manning* (1847) 1 HLC 305; MIA, section 27(4). A valued policy does not cease to be a contract of indemnity in other respects: *British Traders' Ins Co Ltd* (1964) 111 CLR 86, 93 (HCA—fire).

98. *Re Freesman and Royal Ins Co* (1986) 29 DLR (4th) 621, 624 (Ont—homeowners').

99. For example *Blasheck* v *Bussell* (1916) 33 TLR 74 (CA—PA). In *Re Freesman and Royal Ins Co* (1986) 29 DLR (4th) 621, 625–626 (Ont—homeowner's) the High Court adopted the view expressed in the USA, that a mere statement of amount is not enough for there to be a valued policy, but that the words "valued at" or equivalent must have been used. However, that view may be confined to insurance of real property: *Garcia* v *Société Nationale d'Assurance* (1992) 94 DLR (4th) 245, 248 (Que, 1991—fire).

be construed as a valued policy in cases in which a valued policy is most useful, such as the insurance of property, the value of which fluctuates considerably or is a matter or debate,[100] or in cases in which it may be difficult to assess the actual amount of loss. In the latter cases, the role of the statement of value has been likened to that of a liquidated damages clause[101]: it is to save some of the expense[102] of settling the amount of actual loss, and the result will sometimes favour the insurer and sometimes the insured.[103]

In a case of total loss, therefore, the sum payable is the stated value. In a case of partial loss, however, the sum payable is a proportion of the stated value, but a proportion which is determined by the ratio of the actual value of the property after loss to the actual value of the property before loss.[104] In a case of property with a stated value of 6x, for example, and an actual value before loss of 4x and after loss of 2x, the claimant recovers 3x, being one half (2:4) of the stated value of 6x. Hence, in the case of partial loss, although the policy is valued, the actual loss in the sense of damage or depreciation must be proved and the role of the agreed value is limited in that respect.

28–7A Exceptions

In four cases, the stated value is not applied. As the value stated in a valued policy is a matter of contract, three of the exceptions concern cases when consent is flawed: in these three cases, the contract is usually vitiated altogether. The four exceptions are as follows:

(a) *Mistake*[105]: the value is stated on the basis of a mistake.

(b) *Fraud*[106]: "Where there is *heavy* over-valuation fraud is, *a priori*, not very far to seek."[107]

(c) *Misrepresentation*: The value of property insured is material to risk. Misrepresentation or non-disclosure of value may make the policy voidable.[108]

(d) *Wagering*: If the effect of over-valuation is that the claimant recovers signifi-

---

100. *Garcia* (above) p 247.

101. *Irving* v *Manning* (1847) 1 HLC 287, 307 *per* Patteson J (hull); *Elcock* v *Thomson* [1949] 2 KB 755, 761 *per* Morris J (fire); *Gambrell* v *Campbellsport Mutual Ins Co*, 177 NW 2d 313, 318 (Wis, 1970—fire).

102. *Irving* v *Manning* (1847) 1 HLC 287, 305 *per* Patteson J (hull); *North of England Iron SS Ins Assn* v *Armstrong* (1870) LR 5 QB 244, 250 *per* Lush J (hull); *Thames & Mersey Marine Ins Co Ltd* v *"Gunford" Ship Co Ltd* [1911] AC 529, 549 *per* Lord Robson (hull); *Elcock* v *Thomson* [1949] 2 KB 755, 761 *per* Morris J (fire).

103. *Maurice* v *Goldsbrough, Mort & Co* [1939] AC 452, 466–467 *per* Lord Wright (PC); *Elcock* v *Thomson* [1949] 2 KB 755, 760 *per* Morris J (fire).

104. *Irving* v *Manning* (1847) 1 HLC 287, 306 *per* Patteson J (hull); *Elcock* v *Thomson* [1949] 2 KB 755, 765 *per* Morris J (fire). *Re Art Gallery of Toronto and Eaton* (1961) 27 DLR (2d) 321 (Ont—AR paintings). A similar rule governs marine cargo insurance: MIA, sections 27 and 71. Arnould, Nos 423 ff.

105. *Elcock* v *Thomson* [1949] 2 KB 755, 760 *per* Morris J (fire). The contract will be vitiated only if the mistake is fundamental: see chapter 21. *Nichols* v *Hartford Fire Ins Co*, 403 NYS 2d 335, 337 (1978—personal property).

106. *Thames & Mersey Marine Ins Co Ltd* v *"Gunford" Ship Co Ltd* [1911] AC 529, 542 *per* Lord Shaw (hull); *Elcock* v *Thomson* [1949] 2 KB 755, 760 *per* Morris J (fire). *Nichols* v *Hartford Fire Ins Co*, 403 NYS 2d 335, 337 (1978—personal property).

107. Lord Shaw, *loc cit*, with emphasis added, as it seems that there may be legitimate business reasons for over-valuation: Arnould, No 428. For example, the sender of goods writes in his expected profit at destination: Arnould, Nos 428 and 442. For the suggestion that valued policies promote fraud by the insured, see Tarr, p 244.

108. For example, *Ionides* v *Pender* (1874) LR 9 QB 531 (cargo).

cantly more than his actual loss, this may infringe the rules of insurable interest against wagering.[109]

28–8 OWN INSURER

In a number of situations, the claimant recovers less than his actual loss. This is because the effect of the contract is that, to that extent, he remains his own insurer (below, 28–8A to 28–8D) or because the loss, while caused by the insured event, was not insured loss: an important case is consequential loss (below, 28-8E).

28–8A Under Insurance: Average

Subject-matter is often insured on the basis of an estimate of value, which has been provided by the insured or has been based on data provided by the insured. If the estimate understates the true value, the possibilities are as follows. (a) The insurer may be entitled to avoid the contract on the ground of misrepresentation or non-disclosure.[110] (b) The insured's information may be warranted at the time of contract and, if the information is incorrect or if it becomes incorrect during the period of cover without, for example, notice to the insurer, the effect may be to terminate cover. (c) Undervaluation is often accidental, so the insurer may prefer not to avail himself of possibility (a), to waive (b) and to pursue possibility (c), to pay subject to average.

Payment subject to average means payment limited to the proportion of actual loss, which the sum insured bears to the actual value of the property insured at the time of the loss.[111] If, for example, property insured for 10x is actually worth 12x, actual loss of 6x is subject to average (10:12) and the amount payable is limited to 5x (10 x 6/12). In such circumstances, the insured "is deemed to be his own insurer for the residue".[112] As it is a feature of average that the insurer pays less than the sum insured, which in any event is a ceiling on the payment of indemnity, and, as under insurance only arises when the sum insured is less than the actual value, average applies to partial loss but not to total loss.[113]

Average is not required by law, except in the case of marine insurance.[114] It has been suggested,[115] that average will be implied in commercial insurance of goods; but,

---

109. *Lewis* v *Rucker* (1761) 2 Burr, 1167 1171 *per* Lord Mansfield (cargo); *Lidgett* v *Secretan* (1871) LR 6 CP 616, 629 *per* Willes J (hull).

Quaere whether, in the case of buildings insured subject to section 3 of the Life Assurance Act 1774, the claimant can never recover more than the actual value of his loss: Birds, p 260.

110. *Re Wilson and Scottish Ins Corp Ltd* [1920] 2 Ch 28 (motor).

Cf the New York Standard Coinsurance Clause, part of which reads: "This Company shall not be liable for a greater proportion of any loss or damage to the property described herein than the sum hereby insured bears to the percentage specified on the first page of this policy of the actual cash value of said property at the time such loss shall happen, nor for more than the proportion which this policy bears to the total insurance thereon." Keeton, pp 137 ff. The result is that the insured contracts to insure to a minimum amount, failing which he becomes in part his own insurer.

111. *Crowley* v *Cohen* (1832) 3 B & Ad 478, 486 *per* Lord Tenterden CJ.

112. *British & Foreign Ins Co Ltd* v *Wilson Shipping Co Ltd* [1921] 1 AC 188, 214 *per* Lord Sumner (hull).

113. In the case of total loss of property worth 12x, but insured for 8x, the application of average gives 8/12 of 12x, i.e., 8x, the sum insured.

114. MIA, section 81.

115. *Carreras* v *Cunard SS Co Ltd* [1918] 1 KB 122–123 *per* Bailhache J (fire).

in the case of fire insurance[116] and, probably, other cases, there is average only if there is a clause to that effect, a clause commonly known as the "first" or "*pro rata*" condition of average and sometimes known as a coinsurance clause.[117] In the case of a Lloyd's policy said to be "subject to average", that form of words is sufficient to incorporate a condition of average.[118]

28–8B The Excess Clause

An excess clause or deductible is a clause, whereby the insured is to bear the first part of any loss, expressed as an amount of money or as a percentage of loss. In the case of separate successive losses,[119] the clause applies to each loss. These clauses are enforced in accordance with their terms.[120] Although the effect is that the insured is his own "insurer" to the extent of the excess, this does not make the insured an insurer within the meaning of an "other insurance clause" in another contract on the same risk.[121]

28–8C The Franchise Clause

A franchise clause[122] is a clause, whereby the insured is to bear the first layer of loss but, once the amount of loss exceeds that layer, the insurer becomes liable for that layer, together with any further layers covered by the insurance.

Whether the amount of loss exceeds the franchise (the first layer) depends *inter alia* on whether the items of loss are seen as a single loss or as a number of independent losses, some or all of which taken in isolation do not exceed the franchise: see above, 28–1A. This is a question of interpretation of the contract[123] but, as the franchise clause is seen as an exclusion of liability drafted by the insurer, it will be construed strictly against him.[124]

28–8D Warranted Part Uninsured

The main purpose of excess or franchise clauses is to eliminate the relatively high cost of handling small claims. These clauses may also succeed in promoting risk avoidance

---

116. *Sillem* v *Thornton* (1854) 3 El & Bl 868, 888 *per* Lord Campbell CJ (fire). Moreover, some insurers have issued houseowners' policies with "no-sum insured". These are the result of the difficulty (a) of persuading the insured to raise the sum insured to a realistic level in times of inflation, and (b) of predicting in a particular case the cost of reinstatement. One company surmised that given a broad statistical base on which to assess historical experience, an accurate monitor of inflation, and a rough description of the house, such as the number of rooms, premiums could be calculated without reference to an estimate of value by the insured: Ford, PM 8 Oct 1987. However, more recently, some insurers, who offered this kind of cover, have made such an underwriting loss on the cover that they have withdrawn it.

117. For example, *Carley Capital Group* v *Fireman's Fund Ins Co*, 877 F 2d 78 (D Colum, 1989—builders' risks). *Cf* Nicholson (1990) 3 Ins L J 218.

118. *Acme Wood Flooring Co Ltd* v *Marten* (1904) 9 Com Cas 157 (fire).

119. This is a question of interpretation of the contract; for example *Equitable Trust Co of New York* v *Whittaker* (1923) 17 Ll L Rep 153 (forged documents policy); see further, above, 28–1A.

120. *Beacon Ins Co Ltd* v *Langdale* (1939) 65 Ll L Rep 57 (CA—motor).

121. *State Farm Mutual Automobile Ins Co* v *Universal Atlas Cement Co*, 406 So 2d 1184 (Fla, 1981—motor). See further, Kahn, 19 Forum 591, 612 ff (1983–4). Such clauses are discussed below, 28–9.

122. In the past, these clauses have been most common in marine insurance, for example, in *Paterson* v *Harris* (1861) 1 B & S 336, 354 *per* Cockburn CJ (marine). Such a clause is found in the original Lloyd's form of policy set out in Schedule 1 to the MIA.

123. For example, *Philadelphia National Bk* v *Price* (1938) 60 Ll L Rep 257 (CA—forged documents policy).

124. *Blackett* v *Royal Exchange Assurance Co* (1832) 2 C & J 244, 251 *per* Lord Lyndhurst CB (hull).

on the part of the insured. There is another clause, for example,[125] that "it shall be a condition of this insurance that the assured shall keep one-fifth uninsured", the main purpose of which is risk avoidance by encouraging due care and attention on the part of the insured[126]; or, in the case of reinsurance, by encouraging a satisfactory investigation of the risk by the reinsured.[127] In the light of this purpose, the clause is construed as a continuing warranty[128] about the extent of cover, both with the obligee insurer and other insurers.[129] Breach[130] of this warranty terminates the insurance.[131]

28–8E Consequential Loss

Unless the contract provides otherwise, the actual loss recoverable by the claimant is limited to loss, which is "immediately connected with"[132] the insured event and, in the case of property insurance, "an incident of the property" insured.[133] In other words, the insurer of property is not liable for consequential loss: loss which, although resulting from loss or damage to the property insured, is not itself loss in the value of that property.

For example, fire damage to an inn may lead inevitably to loss of business but, although loss of business is insurable loss, it is not fire loss and it is not recoverable under fire insurance on the inn.[134] In *Leger*,[135] therefore, the claimant, whose block of flats was damaged by fire, could not recover "future profit or other consequential loss" such as lost rents.

Yet, in *Leger*, the New Brunswick court stressed[136] that the actual value of the loss to the claimant depended on the circumstances of the case; and that the court might refer to market value or to replacement cost or even to "investment value based on the capitalized value of the income". In England, lost profit on the property destroyed

---

125. Taken from *Muirhead* v *Forth & North Sea Steamboat Mutual Ins Assn* [1894] AC 72 (hull).
126. p 77 *per* Lord Herschell LC; *General Ins Co of Trieste* v *Cory* [1897] 1 QB 335, 338 *per* Mathew J (hull).
127. *Traill* v *Baring* (1864) 4 De GJ & S 318 (re).
128. As regards continuing warranties, see above, 20–5.
129. *Muirhead* (above), p 77 *per* Lord Herschell LC.
130. If the insured takes second insurance to cover that permitted by the clause, in case the first insurer is unable to pay in full, that is not breach of the clause: *General Ins Co of Trieste* v *Cory* [1897] 1 QB 335, 341 *per* Mathew J (hull); the judge assumed that it was not practicable to take a policy on the solvency of the first insurer. If, however, the insured insures the same risk in full with an honour policy, although the policy is not enforceable in law, it is honoured in practice and he may be in breach of the clause: *Roddick* v *Indemnity Mutual Marine Ins Co Ltd* [1895] 1 QB 335, 839 *per* Kennedy J (hull).
131. *Traill* (above); *Muirhead* (above). On termination of contract for breach of warranty, see above, 20–6.
132. *Theobald* v *Railway Passengers Assurance Co* (1854) 10 Ex 45, 58 *per* Pollock CB (PA). In that case the claimant was unable to recover the earnings that he had lost as a result of his injury. Counsel for the insurer successfully argued that the "*contract* limits the compensation to personal injury" (p 55, emphasis added). Although the argument relied on the rule of remoteness of damage and, one might say, that is a rule of law, the scope of what can be recovered within the framework of that rule depends on the will of the parties.
133. *Castellain* v *Preston* (1883) 11 QBD 380, 395 *per* Cotton LJ (CA—fire).
134. *Re Wright and Pole* (1834) 1 A & E 621 (fire).
135. *Leger* v *Royal Insurance Co Ltd* (1968) 70 DLR (2d) 344, 349 (NB—fire).
136. *Ibid*. See also *Matergio* v *Canada Accident & Fire Assurance Co* [1926] 1 DLR 1002, 1004 (Ont—fire). In *Leger*, the court accepted (p 350) evidence that value averaged five to seven times the gross annual rent received for the entire property, five to seven being approximately the minimum period of years that a prudent purchaser of the building would allow to recoup his investment. See further, *Falcon Investments Corp (NZ) Ltd* v *State Ins General Manager* [1975] 1 NZLR 520 (fire).

has been covered in the past by putting an agreed valuation on the property, which takes lost profit into account.[137]

It has been contended[138] and, it is submitted, correctly denied[139] that, if fire damage to property A is the sole cause of a fall in the value of property B, also owned by the insured owner of A, that fall is loss recoverable under insurance on property A. Equally, it has been denied that the amount of actual loss covered and payable is reduced by consequential benefit to the insured:

"If one of two unique china vases is insured and destroyed, it does not avail the underwriter that by the destruction the second vase has become more unique and more valuable. If profits of a business in Old-street are insured and lost, it does not matter that the assured makes profits from a business in New-street".[140]

In contrast, Lord Blackburn has said[141] that, where there is a contract of indemnity "and a loss happens, anything which reduces or diminishes that loss reduces or diminishes the amount which the indemnifier is bound to pay". But the word "loss" has no useful meaning without reference to its context in the contract of insurance and, generally, loss in this context means loss not to the insured but to the subject-matter of the insurance. As Scrutton LJ observed,[142] "What is insured is not the loss to the assured, but the loss of *the property*". Anything else is consequential.

28–8F Loss of Value

In the case of physical damage to insured property, clearly that is insurable loss and, moreover, the consequent reduction in the market value of that property may be the appropriate measure of indemnity.[143] If, however, property loses value without having suffered physical damage, is that insurable loss? And, is a contract to indemnify that kind of loss a contract of insurance? These questions have arisen in relation to "residual value insurance" (RVI),[144] whereby the lessor of an aircraft, whose charges depend in part on the (residual) market value of the aircraft at the end of the lease, is promised indemnity, if the value of the aircraft has fallen below a certain figure.

137. Above, 4–5N and 28–7.
138. *Westminster Fire Office* v *Glasgow Provident Investment Sy* (1888) 13 App Cas 699, 712 *per* Earl of Selborne (fire).
139. *Glasgow Provident Investment Sy* v *Westminster Fire Office* (1887) 14 R 947, 989 *per* Lord Young (Ct Sess—fire). *Firemen's Ins Co* v *Houle*, 69 A 2d 696 (NH, 1949—fire).
140. *City Tailors Ltd* v *Evans* (1921) 126 LT 439, 443 *per* Scrutton LJ (CA—fire); the policy was a valued policy but that does not appear to qualify his statement, in view of his citation of *Jebsen* v *East & West India Dock Co* (1875) LR 10 CP 300.
141. *Burnand* v *Rodocanachi Sons & Co* (1882) 7 App Cas 333, 339 (cargo).
142. *City Tailors* (above), p 443 (emphasis added). Moreover, consequential benefit is irrelevant unless, in the words of Lord Blackburn, it "reduces or diminishes *that loss*": *Burnand* (above), *loc cit* (emphasis added). The benefit must be an "incident of the property at the time when the loss takes place"—*Castellain* v *Preston* (1883) 11 QBD 380, 395 *per* Cotton LJ (CA—fire). *Tees* v *Great American Ins Co* (1972) 30 DLR (3d) 488 (Northwest Territories—fire).
143. See above 28–2A.
144. RVI is defined in section 1113(a)(22) of the New York Insurance Law as "insurance issued in connection with a lease or contract which sets forth a specific termination value at the end of the term of the lease or contract for the property covered by such lease or contract, and which insures against loss of economic value of tangible personal property or real property or improvements thereto except loss due to phsyical damage to property, excluding any lease or contract which falls within the definition of financial guaranty as set forth . . . " I am grateful to Rod Margo of Messrs Condon & Forsyth, for drawing my attention to this provision, as well as other related matters.

Underwriters agree to pay the difference or to buy the aircraft at the specified figure. It has been suggested that this arrangement is not insurance.

Reduction in value has been compensated in actions for damages, as a logical application of general principles such as *restitutio in integrum* or the rule in *Robinson* v *Harman*.[145] The reported cases have concerned motor vehicles[146] and ships[147] and, presumably, might also include aircraft. If loss of value is the proper subject of an award of compensation by way of damages, it is not obvious why it should not also be the subject of compensation by way of indemnity insurance, if that is what the contract covers and that is the risk assumed by the insurer.[148] It is not loss consequential on loss insured but the very loss insured against. Indeed, a mortgagee of realty is allowed to insure the property mortgaged and, if it is physically damaged, he is allowed to enforce the insurance (though not necessarily keep all the money), even though the property is still a sufficient security for the outstanding debt; this is because the property has become less valuable as a security.[149] Against this background, it would be strange if the law did not allow insurance of capital profits—or losses. It would be strange if English courts did not enforce RVI as valid insurance, as courts have done in the USA.[150]

A degree of doubt may have arisen from an ellipsis of ideas, whereby loss of value appears to be the loss insured as well as the peril or contingency, against which insurance is taken. Doubt might be removed, if that is thought necessary, by RVI which clearly separates those ideas and specifies the events that might give rise to the loss of value.

28–8G The Cost of Prevention

In *New Netherlands Ins Co* v *Karl Ljungberg & Co*,[151] a term of the contract obliged the insured to minimise loss but said nothing about who bore the expense of such action. The Privy Council implied an obligation on the part of the insurer to reimburse the cost. Is this decision part of a general rule? In an action for breach of contract, the cost of preventing loss, which would otherwise flow from the breach of contract, and

---

145. (1848) 1 Exch 850: the object of damages for breach of contract is to put the claimant, so far as money can do it, in the same situation as if the contract had been performed.

146. *Payton* v *Brooks* [1974] 1 Lloyd's Rep. 241, 244 *per* Edmund Davies LJ (CA). See also *Woods* v *Parkinson* 1985 (unreported except by The Insurance Ombudsman, Annual Report 1990, para 2.6). Moreover, for the purposes of carriage by road, damage means diminution in the market value of goods: Clarke, *International Carriage of Goods by Road: CMR* (2nd ed, 1991) para 59.

147. *The Helgoland*, 79 F 123 (SD NY, 1897).

148. *Cf* the distinction between insurance indemnity and tort compensation, drawn above, 28–3C.

149. *Royal Ins Co* v *Mylius* (1926) 38 CLR 477, 489 *per* Isaac J (HCA): "Where mortgagees insure tangible security against the risk of fire 'as mortgagees', they insure, not their debt, but their security". See also Rich J (pp 504–505). Isaacs J quoted *Excelsior Fire Ins Co* v *Royal Ins Co* (1873) 55 NY 343, 359 *per* Folger J: "The undertaking is that the property shall not suffer loss by fire; that is, in effect, that its capacity to pay the mortgage debt shall not be diminished". See also *Wilson* v *Jones*, in which Willes J, with whom the other members of the Court of Exchequer Chamber agreed, said that the "thing insured was the value of the plaintiff's shares, or rather his interest in the profits to be successfully derived from his shares": (1867) LR 2 Ex 139, 145–146 (discussed above 4–5N1).

150. *State* v *Hogan*, 8 ND 301 (1899); *Commonwealth* v *Fidelity Land Value Assurance* 312 Pa 425 (1933).

In *Glen Falls Ins Co* v *Covert* 526 SW 2d 222 (Tex, 1975), a claim in respect of the fall in value of stock-in-trade failed but this was because the contract covered (and by implication was limited to) "physical loss".

In *Seattle First National Bank* v *Washington Ins Guaranty Assn*, 804 P 2d 1263 (1991), RVI was upheld in respect of the lease of vehicles and characterised not as surety insurance but as casualty insurance.

151. [1986] 3 All ER 767 (cargo).

the cost of mitigating further loss, when some such loss has occurred, are recoverable from the party in breach.[152] In marine insurance, costs like these can be recovered under a "sue and labour" clause,[153] but it is less clear that they can be recovered as insured loss under other kinds of insurance contract.

In liability insurance, it is implied, if not expressed, that the cover extends to the reasonable cost incurred by the insured in defending a claim against him[154]; but this is just one kind of damage limitation. In fire insurance, measures to prevent fire damage are covered,[155] provided that the risk of fire damage (or of more fire damage) is actually imminent.[156] The measures, however, can be seen as part of the traditional definition of fire cover rather than as a distinct head of insured loss. Moreover, the fire rule may be limited to physical damage inflicted to prevent fire and it is unclear whether it extends to expense. The fire rule, therefore, is not necessarily the expression of a more general principle, of the kind which has been suggested,[157] unless it has some basis other than the traditional definition of the peril.

Another view of the fire rule is that the costs are recoverable, because the fire is the proximate cause of the measures taken to prevent it.[158] This is a view which could be extended to other cases: the cost is not merely consequential but "can be regarded as the direct result of the peril".[159] Insurance normally covers loss which has arisen by reason of the insured's negligence or which his negligence has failed to prevent,[160] so it would be curious and contrary to the interests of both parties to the contract, if it did not cover the cost of measures taken to mitigate loss. Whether the issue arises as one of the definitions of the peril insured or as an aspect of causation, it is ultimately a question of construction of the contract.[161]

Another view, which finds some support in the marine cases, is that the foundation for recovery of these costs lies in restitutionary principles[162]; this view too could be extended to other cases. The insurer has been enriched, to the extent that the insured's conduct avoided or mitigated loss,[163] and justice requires that the benefit should not be retained entirely by the insurer.

---

152. McGregor No 322.
153. Arnould, ch 25. A common law rule to this effect was rejected (7 October 1993) by the Court of Appeal for British Columbia in *McMillan Bloedel Ltd* v *Youell*, which concerned charterers' liability insurance.
154. See above, 17–4E3.
155. Above, 17–2C2 and 17–2F. See also above, 25–4C1.
156. *Liverpool & London & Globe Ins Co Ltd* v *Canadian General Electric Co Ltd* (1981) 123 DLR (3d) 513 (Sup Ct—fire).
157. Birds, p 216; MacGillivray para 1877.
158. *Symington* v *Union Ins Co of Canton* (1928) 34 Com Cas 23.
159. Lord Wright, quoted above, no 25–4C1. *Peters* v *Warren Ins Co*, 39 US 99, 112 (1840)
160. Below, 24–5B.
161. *Schlosser* v *INA*, 600 A 2d 836 (Md, 1992—liability), which concerned the meaning of "damage" to property; on this particular question, see above, 16–2C. In the USA, in *Leebov* v *US Fidelity & Guaranty Co*, 165 A 2d 82, 84 (Pa, 1960—liability) it was held that the cost of prevention was recoverable. At first, the decision was said to be exceptional: Anon, 71 Colum L Rev 1309, 1316 (1971); but that cases *contra* were often based on what is clearly a mistaken application to insurance of the general duty to mitigate loss: *ibid* 1320. In the insurance cases there was no breach of contract. More recently, the *Leebov* view began to find support in other states: *Slay Warehousing Co* v *Reliance Ins Co*, 471 F 2d 1364 (8 Cir, 1973); *Aetna Casualty & Surety Co* v *Eberheim*, 556 A 2d 1067 (Conn, 1988—liability); *INA* v *US Gypsum Co*, 870 F 2d 148 (4 Cir, 1989—AR).
162. *Aitchison* v *Lohre* (1879) 4 App Cas 755, 766 *per* Lord Cairns, LC. See also in this sense: Gilmore & Black, *Law of Admiralty* (2nd ed 1975), p 76 n 93.
163. Anon, 71 Colum L Rev 1309, 1318 (1971).

28–9 DOUBLE INSURANCE: CONTRIBUTION OR
CO-INSURANCE CLAUSES

If the loss is covered by more than one insurance contract, there is double insurance. The insured may recover his entire loss from any one or more of his insurers[164]; but, in the case of indemnity insurance, having recovered his entire loss from insurer A, he is unable to recover any more money from insurer B.[165] This is the basic rule as regards the insured.

From the point of view of the insured, the basic rule is simple and perhaps that is how it should be. Nonetheless, the underlying assumption seems to be that there neither is nor should be a strategy of co-ordination.[166] Take, for example, a camera covered against theft by two contracts, householder's AR and a policy for photographers. If the photographers' policy, being more specific and based on a more sophisticated risk classification, were exhausted first, this would lead to premium increase and encourage care by photographers, so promoting better loss prevention than if the householder's policy came first or loss was carried by both policies. As the law stands, however, English law is likely to see the stolen camera as a case of double insurance and to spread risk over the two contracts, promoting loss spreading rather than loss prevention, householder-photographers being subsidised by other householders.

The position between insurers is governed by the equitable doctrine of contribution, which is of little or no concern to the insured.[167] The position may also, however, be affected by any relevant clauses in the contract of insurance. These clauses, variously described as "contribution" clauses, "co-insurance" clauses, or "other insurance" clauses, also affect the insured. In particular, the insurance contract may provide that, in cases of double insurance, the insurer's liability shall be reduced to a rateable proportion of loss (below, 28–9A); or that the insurer's liability shall be limited to loss in excess of that covered by another contract of insurance (below, 28–9B); or that the contract shall be avoided, in the absence of notice to and consent of the insurer whose contract contains the clause (below, 28–9C). "Apart from the obvious advantage derived from extinguishing or limiting liability in respect of certain claims, [such clauses] protect insurers from fraudulent over-insurance, facilitate the investigation of claims, and enable the insurers to seek contributions where appropriate from one another."[168] As these clauses are inserted by and for the benefit of the insurer, they are construed *contra proferentem*[169] and, if unintelligible, may be disregarded.[170]

---

164. *Godin* v *London Assurance Co* (1758) 1 Burr 489 (cargo). MIA, section 32(2). *York-Buffalo Motor Express Inc* v *National Fire & Marine Ins Co*, 63 NE 2d 61 (NY, 1945—motor). Appleman, section 3902.
165. Life Assurance Act 1774, section 3. *Hebdon* v *West* (1863) 3 B & S 579 (life), applied in *Sims* v *Scottish Imperial Ins Co* (1902) 10 SLT 286 (Ct Sess—life).
166. Generally, see below, 28–9C, and Abraham, ch 6.
167. As regards contribution between insurers, when one insurer has paid the insured in full, see *Legal & General Assurance Sy* v *Drake Ins Co Ltd* [1992] 1 All ER 283 (CA—motor). Contribution is outside the scope of this book. See Goff & Jones, ch 13; Ivamy, ch 48; MacGillivray, Nos 1729 ff. *Eagle Star Ins Co Ltd* v *Provincial Ins plc* [1993] 3 All ER 1 (PC—motor).
168. Tarr, 2 Canterbury L Rev 107, 120 (1983). See also Kahn, 19 *Forum* 591 (1983–4). Tarr also points to traps for the insured, where the clauses are framed to operate not only where there is substantial double insurance but also marginal overlap of cover, overlap of which neither the insured nor his broker may be aware.
169. *Jauvin* v *L'Ami Michel Automobile Canada Ltée* (1986) 33 DLR (4th) 576 (Ont—fire).
170. *Jauvin* (above).

28–9A Rateable Proportion Clauses

The contract may provide that, if there are other contracts of insurance covering the loss, the insurer shall be obliged to pay only his proportion of the loss. Where

"there are several policies, and where there, in point of fact, is double insurance, then in order to do away with the old practice of the insured recovering the whole from one of the several insurance offices, and then the one from whom it is recovered being put to obtain contribution from the others, this clause was put in to say that the insured should, in the first instance, proceed against the several insurance companies for the aliquot parts for which they are liable in consequence."[171]

The clause operates[172] only when it is proved by the insurer[173] that the same property[174] is the subject-matter of "a subsisting insurance covering the loss;"[175] and that the interests are the same.[176] It applies "where there is the same person insuring the same interest with more than one office"[177] and the respective offices are legally liable to contribute to the same loss in respect of the same risk.[178] Were it otherwise, it would enable insurance companies to evade fulfilment of their obligations, and the rights of the insured could be diminished by the subsequent acts of persons not under his control:[179] persons concluding insurance contracts, to which the first insured was not a party and from which he could not benefit.[180]

171. *North British & Mercantile Ins Co* v *London, Liverpool & Globe Ins Co* (1877) 5 Ch D 569, 588 *per* Baggallay LJ (CA—fire). USA: on *pro rata* liability and coinsurance clauses, see Appleman, section 3905; 45 CJS, sections 917b, and 922; Kahn, 19 *Forum* 591 (1983-4).

172. For example, *Gale* v *Motor Union Ins Co Ltd* [1928] 1 KB 359 (motor). *Commercial Union Assurance Co* v *Aetna Casualty & Surety Co*, 455 F Supp 1190 (D NH 1978—motor).

173. *Jenkins* v *Deane* (1934) 47 Ll L Rep 342 (motor).

174. This refers to the property lost or damaged. It is not usually necessary that the range of items insured, whether lost or damaged or not, be exactly the same under each contract: 45 CJS, section 922(4). See also Appleman, sections 3056 and 3908. *Cf* "the Pennsylvania rule . . . that, where the insured has a policy covering several parcels of property and also specific insurance covering only one parcel, the latter must be entirely exhausted before the other policies can be called upon for contribution"—*Turk* v *Newark Fire Ins Co*, 4 F 2d 142, 145 (ED Pa, 1925—fire), affirmed 6 F 2d 533 (3 Cir, 1925). Appleman, section 3912.

175. *Jenkins* v *Deane* (1933) 47 Ll L Rep 342, 346 *per* Goddard J (motor). "Other contract of insurance" means a binding contract of insurance, hence one which is in force at the relevant time: *Equitable Fire & Accident Office Ltd* v *The Ching Wo Hong* [1907] AC 96 (PC—fire); *Cheshire & Co* v *Vaughan Bros & Co* [1920] 3 KB 240 (CA—cargo). *Western Assurance Co* v *Temple* (1901) 31 SCR 373 (fire); "two policies valid on their face and actually subsisting"—*Manitoba Ins Co* v *Whitla* (1903) 34 SCR 191, 198 *per* Taschereau CJ (fire).

The contract must be "subsisting and valid"—*Carpenter* v *Providence Washington Ins Co*, 16 Pet 495, 508–509 *per* Story J (1842—fire). Appleman, sections 3060, 3061 and 3096: subsisting insurance does not include insurance taken by the insured's agent, of which the insured is unaware, or the renewal of existing insurance which does not infringe the clause in question.

In *Carpenter* the United States Supreme Court held that the mere possibility of rescission for misrepresentation does not make the contract any the less a contract for this purpose, unless rescission actually occurs before loss. However, in England in *Jenkins* v *Deane* (1934) 47 Ll L Rep 342, 346 (motor), Goddard J said that the insurers "must prove not merely that there is another policy in existence, but that there is one under which the insurers can be called upon to pay" in respect of the loss.

176. *North British & Mercantile Ins Co* v *London, Liverpool & Globe Ins Co* (1877) 5 Ch D 569, 577 *per* Jessell MR (CA—fire); *Scottish Amicable Heritable Securities Assn Ltd* v *Northern Assurance Co*, 1883 11 R 287, 294 *per* Lord Craighill, 303 *per* Lord Moncrieff (Ct Sess—fire); *American Surety Co* v *Wrightson* (1910) 16 Com Cas 37, 56 *per* Hamilton J (fidelity). *Lititz Mutual Ins Co* v *Lengacher*, 248 F 2d 850 (7 Cir, 1957—builder's risk); *Modern Scaffold Co Inc* v *Karell Realty Corp*, 279 NYS 2d 436 (1967—fire). Appleman, sections 3507 and 3909.

177. *North British* (above), p 581 *per* James LJ.

178. *Wrightson* (above), *loc cit*; also *North British* (above) p 582 *per* James LJ; *Edwards* v *Commonwealth Mutual Fire Ins Co*, 197 F 2d 62 (3 Cir, 1952—fire). On identity of risk, see Appleman, sections 3055 and 3907.

179. *Scottish Amicable* (above), p 290 *per* Lord M'Laren.

180. *Scottish Amicable* (above), p 294 *per* Lord Craighill.

In the case of fire insurance on a particular building, for example, although the property and the risk are the same, the corollary is that no contribution is required when the interests insured are different: the interests of owner and bailee of goods,[181] successive mortgagees,[182] mortgagor and mortgagee,[183] landlord and tenant,[184] seller and purchaser,[185] tenant for life and remainderman,[186] homeowner and building contractor.[187] However, it has been held[188] that, if husband and wife insure property jointly, later insurance by one is double insurance, even though confined to his or her own interest in the property.

Again, no contribution is required between insurers of different layers of the same risk[189] or different phases of the same operation, such as transport. Moreover, in the case of transport, no contribution is required even between insurers, one a warehouse fire insurer and the other a transit insurer, of the same goods, as regards the risk of fire, when the contracts overlap slightly in point of space and time.[190]

28–9B Excess of Loss Insurance

The contract of insurance may exclude any loss "in respect of which the insured is entitled to indemnity under any other insurance except in respect of any excess beyond the amount which would have been payable under such insurance, if this policy had not been effected". The effect of this clause is to convert the contract into an excess of loss contract[191]: a contract on a different layer of risk from any other covering the same risk and, therefore, one designed to exclude contribution.[192]

"Liability under an excess policy attaches only after all primary coverage has been exhausted".[193] If the primary insurer is insolvent, the excess insurer has no duty to "drop down" to cover loss in the primary layer.[194] "Construing the [excess] policy to require indemnification would essentially make the policy a guarantee of the solvency of [the primary insurer]. Excess policies are intended to provide low cost coverage for

181. *North British & Mercantile Ins Co* v *London, Liverpool & Globe Ins Co* (1877) 5 Ch D 569, 577 *per* Jessell MR (CA—fire).
182. *North British* (above), *loc cit; Scottish Amicable Heritable Securities Assn Ltd* v *Northern Assurance Co*, 1883 11 R 287, 294 *per* Lord Craighill (Ct Sess—fire).
183. *Nichols & Co* v *Scottish Union & National Ins Co*, 1885 14 R 1094 (fire)
184. *Portavon Cinema Co Ltd* v *Price & Century Ins Co Ltd* [1939] 4 All ER 601 (fire).
185. *Economic Mutual Ins Co* v *Federation Ins Co* (1961) 27 DLR (2d) 539 (BC—fire). In *Portavon* (above), Branson J also rejected the contention that a person with a right to request reinstatement under the Fires Prevention (Metropolis) Act 1774 (discussed above, 5–7) is not thereby "insured" in the sense of double insurance.
186. *North British* (above), *loc cit*.
187. *Lititz Mutual Ins Co* v *Lengacher*, 248 F 2d 850 (7 Cir, 1957—builder's risk); *Modern Scaffold Co Inc* v *Karell Realty Corp*, 279 NYS 2d 436 (1967—fire); *Mission National Ins Co* v *Hartford Fire Ins Co*, 702 F Supp 543 (ED Pa, 1989—AR, builders' risk).
188. *Graham* v *American Eagle Fire Ins Co*, 182 F 2d 500 (4 Cir, 1950—fire).
189. *North River Ins Co* v *American Home Assurance Co*, 257 Cal Rptr 129 (1989—liability).
190. *Australian Agricultural Co* v *Saunders* (1875) LR 10 CP 668, 676 *per* Blackburn J (Exch Ch—fire). *Zeeb* v *National Farmers Union Co*, 946 F 2d 601 (8 Cir, 1991—fire).
191. On the meaning of excess of loss insurance and first loss insurance, see *Irish National Ins Co Ltd* v *Oman Ins Co Ltd* [1983] 2 Lloyd's Rep 453, 460–461 *per* Leggatt J (re).
192. *New Brunswick Fire Ins Co* v *Bauer-Gressman Co Inc*, 78 F Supp 343, 346 (WD Mo, 1948—fire).
193. *North River Ins Co* v *American Home Assurance Co* 257 Cal Rptr 129, 131 (1989—liability). See also *Allstate Ins Co* v *The 65 Security Plan*, 879 F 2d 90, 92 (3 Cir, 1989—motor).
194. *Central Waste Systems Inc* v *Granite State Ins Co*, 437 NW 2d 496 (Neb, 1989—liability); *Hudson Ins Co* v *Gelman Sciences Inc*, 706 F Supp 25 (ND Ill, 1989—liability).

catastrophic losses beyond the bounds of ordinary primary limits, and the insurer must be able to ascertain the point at which its liability will attach in order to evaluate the insurable risk and its cost of coverage. We should not construe a policy to subject the insurer to unforeseeable and variable risks."[195]

Being ultimately a matter of contract construction, exceptions have been identified, when the excess insurer does dropdown: for example, when the excess contract provides for liability in excess of sums "recoverable"[196] or "collectible"[197] from the primary insurer. In such cases, if the primary insurer is insolvent and primary loss cannot be recovered, the excess insurer may become liable for that loss. Whether the primary insurance is "collectible" has been determined at the time of the insured event.[198]

If both contracts contain the "other insurance" clause, *prima facie* the result is that neither insurance pays,[199] a result referred to in one case[200] as "the absurdity and injustice of holding that a person who has paid premiums for cover by two insurers [is] left without insurance cover because each insurer has excluded liability for the risk against which the other has indemnified him". Any such result is avoided by a rule of construction[201] that, in such a case, "you look at each policy independently and if each would be liable but for the existence of the other, then the exclusions would be treated as cancelling each other out, both insurers are then liable", and the one who pays can claim contribution from the other[202] as if no clause existed and the basic rule (above, 28–9) applied. In the United States also, the clauses have been condemned as mutually repugnant and have been disregarded.[203]

195. *Interco Inc* v *National Surety Corp*, 900 F 2d 1264, 1268 (8 Cir, 1990—liability). In view of their purpose, such policies are sometimes referred to as "umbrella" or "catastrophe" policies: *Le Mars Mutual Ins Co* v *Farm of City Ins Co*, 494 NW 2d 216 (Iowa, 1992—motor).

196. Hudson (above) p 27. *Cf* "coverage" which refers not to "recovery" but to the scope of the risks insured against; a loss may be covered, although indemnity is not paid, because the insurer is insolvent: *Central Waste* (above), pp 499–500.

197. *Alabama Ins Guarantee Assn* v *Magic City Trucking Service Inc*, 547 So 2d 849 (Ala, 1989—liability).

198. *Shapiro* v *Associated International Ins Co*, 899 F 2d 1116 (11 Cir, 1990—liability). For a review of conflicting cases in the USA see Sehr, Blume and Elenius 27 Tort & Ins L J 226, 230 ff (1992).

199. *National Employers' Mutual General Ins Assn Ltd* v *Haydon* [1979] 2 Lloyd's Rep 235, 238 *per* Lloyd J (liability).

200. *Haydon* (above) [1980] 2 Lloyd's Rep 149, 152 *per* Stephenson LJ (CA).

201. *Weddell* v *Road Transport & General Ins Co Ltd* [1932] 2 KB 563, 567–568 *per* Rowlatt J (motor): "the reasonable construction is to exclude from the category of co-existing cover any cover which is expressed to be itself cancelled by such co-existence . . . In other words [the insured] is not 'entitled to indemnity under any other policy' within the meaning of [the first policy] when the other policy negatives liability when there are two policies. At that point the process must cease. If one proceeds to apply the same argument to the other policy and lets that re-act upon the policy under construction, one would reach the absurd result that whichever policy one looks at it is always the other one which is effective". This decision was applied in *Austin* v *Zurich General Accident Ins Co Ltd* (1944) 77 Ll L Rep 409 (motor). The view of Rowlatt J in *Weddell* has been applied in Australia in *General Accident Ins Co* v *Sun Alliance Ins Ltd* (1989) 17 NSWLR 80, 84–85.

202. *Haydon* (above) p 152 *per* Stephenson LJ (CA—liability); the rule was applied by the court below but, on appeal, the court took a view of the clause that made application unnecessary. See also *Wawanesa Mutual Ins Co* v *Cooperative Fire & Casualty Co* (1981) 119 DLR (3d) 188 (Sask—liability).

203. *Lamb-Weston Inc* v *Oregon Auto Ins Co*, 341 P 2d 110, 119 (Or 1959—motor); *Sifers* v *General Marine Catering Co*, 892 F 2d 386 (5 Cir, 1990); *Argonaut Ins Co* v *US Fire Ins Co*, 728 F Supp 298 (SD NY, 1990—liability); *Cargill Inc* v *Commercial Union Ins Co*, 889 F 2d 174 (8 Cir, 1989—cargo), account being taken of the deductible in one of the policies. Kahn, 19 Forum 591, 596 ff (1983–4).

When contract A contains a *pro rata* clause and contract B an excess clause, the claim is paid under contract A, without contribution from contract B: *Jones* v *Medox Inc*, 430 A 2d 488 (App D Colum, 1981—liability).

28–9C Notice and Consent: Escape Clauses

The contract of insurance may provide that, in the absence of notice to and consent of the insurer,[204] the contract shall be avoided by subsequent insurance of the same risk; or that the insurer shall not be liable for loss previously insured. These provisions are sometimes called "escape clauses".[205] If, however, contract B follows contract A, each on the same risk and each with the same escape clause, the courts have held that B is not subsequent insurance within the terms of the escape clause in A: the effect of the clause in B is that the second insurer has not come on risk[206]: the loss is covered by A but not by B.

Concerning conflict between "other insurance" clauses generally, Abraham[207] has distinguished (a) decisions that allocate liability to the first contract concluded, (b) decisions that allocate liability to the insurance that most specifically covers the risk in question, (c) decisions that disregard conflicting provisions and prorate in proportion to the limits on cover in each insurance, and (d) decisions that disregard conflicting provisions but allocate liability primarily to the insurance most closely related to the risk. He points out that (b) incline to loss prevention, that (c) and (d) serve a distributive purpose, but that none of the rules adopted provides sufficient certainty to minimise resort to the courts.

204. Through the appropriate agent: *Western Assurance Co* v *Doull* (1886) 12 SCR 446 (fire).

205. These clauses have been enforced, for example, *Deaves* v *CML Fire & General Ins Co Ltd* (1979) 53 ALJR 382 (HCA—fire). *Allstate Ins Co* v *The 65 Security Plan*, 879 F 2d 90, 92 (3 Cir, 1989—motor).

206. *Equitable Fire & Accident Office Ltd* v *The Ching Wo Hong* [1907] AC 96 (PC—fire). *Steadfast Ins Co Ltd* v *F & B Trading Co Pty Ltd* (1971) 125 CLR 578 (HCA—fire). *Home Ins Co* v *Gavel* [1927] SCR 481, affirmed (1928) 30 Ll L Rep 139 (PC—fire); *cf Re Tinmouth and Groupe Desjardins* (1986) 32 DLR (4th) 621 (Ont—liability); *Crowley Milk Co Inc* v *American Mutual Liability Ins Co*, 426 F 2d 752 (2 Cir, 1970—motor). Appleman, sections 3051 ff, in particular section 3060.

207. pp 160–161. As to the interplay of an escape clause with an excess clause, see Kahn, 19 Forum 591, 604 ff (1983–4), and *Northeast Dept ILGWU Health & Welfare Fund* v *Teamsters Local Union No 229 Welfare Fund*, 764 F 2d 147, 159 ff (3 Cir, 1985); usually liability falls on the contract with the escape clause. As to the interplay of an escape clause with a *pro rata* clause, see *Farmers Mutual Ins Co* v *Summers*, 241 NE 2d 154 (Ind, 1968—fire).

CHAPTER 29

REINSTATEMENT

29-1 INTRODUCTION

There is reinstatement when, instead of paying the insured money,[1] the insurer pays[2] for the replacement or repair of the subject-matter of the insurance. Unless the context otherwise requires, in this chapter reinstatement refers to both replacement of property destroyed and repair of property damaged.[3] Reinstatement is generally an option given to the insurer, rather than the insured,[4] and, except when given by statute,[5] that option is available only if expressly given by the contract of insurance. The purpose is to protect the insurer from excessive claims,[6] to offer him a course that may be more economic than paying insurance money[7] and, especially in cases governed by the statute, to discourage arson and fraud.[8]

29-2 REINSTATEMENT: CONTRACT

If the contract allows the insurer to choose between payment of insurance money to the claimant and full reinstatement, these are mutually inconsistent duties in a contract of indemnity and hence subject to the doctrine of election.[9]

1. If the insurer pays insurance money to the insured, the insurer cannot require the insured to spend the money in the reinstatement of the property: *Rayner* v *Preston* (1881) 18 Ch D 1, 6 *per* Cotton LJ (CA—fire); *Re Law Guarantee Trust & Accident Sy Ltd* [1914] 2 Ch 617, 639 *per* Kennedy LJ (CA); *Reynolds* v *Phoenix Assurance Co Ltd* (1978) 2 Lloyd's Rep 440, 462 *per* Forbes J (fire). A contract to insure does not imply that the insured is obliged to apply the insurance money to reinstatement: *Lees* v *Whitely* (1866) LR 2 Eq 143. Nonetheless, the insured may not be free to dispose of the money as he pleases.
   (a) By the Law of Property Act 1925, section 108(3), the mortgagee of property has the right to compel the morgagor, who has insured the property and received the insurance money, to apply it to reinstatement.
   (b) The insured may be contractually obliged (for example in a lease or mortgage) to a person other than the insurer to reinstate the property insured: *Mumford Hotels Ltd* v *Wheler* [1964] Ch 117.
2. Usually, the insurer pays a third party to do the work but, in an attempt to control costs, some insurers operate, for example, vehicle or house repair businesses.
3. *Cf Anderson* v *Commercial Union Assurance Corp* (1885) 55 LJQB 146, 149 *per* Cotton LJ (CA—fire) as regards the terms of the particular contract.
4. *Leppard* v *Excess Ins Co Ltd* [1979] 2 Lloyd's Rep 91 (CA—fire). *Aliter* if the contract clearly gives the option to the insured; see for example *Carlyle* v *Elite Ins Co* (1984) 56 BCLR 331 (BC—fire).
   When making his election, the insurer may seek to serve his own interests; he may, for example, threaten reinstatement to put pressure on the insured to settle a claim: Watson PM 25 January 1990 p 59.
5. Fires Prevention (Metropolis) Act 1774: below 29–3.
6. Birds, p 264.
7. *Anderson* v *Commercial Union Assurance Corp* (1885) 55 LJQB 146, 149 *per* Bowen LJ (CA—fire). *Allwright* v *Queensland Ins Co Ltd* (1966) 84 WN (Pt 1) (NSW) 378, 390 *per* Isaacs J (motor).
8. *Simpson* v *Scottish Union Ins Co* (1863) 1 H & M 618, 628 *per* Sir W Page Wood V-C (fire); *Reynolds* v *Phoenix Assurance Co Ltd* [1978] 2 Lloyd's Rep 440, 462 *per* Forbes J (fire). *Kennedy* v *Boolarra Butter Factory Pty Ltd* [1953] VLR 548, 551 (fire).
9. *Kammins Ballrooms Co Ltd* v *Zenith Investments (Torquay) Ltd* [1971] AC 850, 883 *per* Lord Diplock. *Transit Casualty Co* v *Transamerica Ins Co*, 387 F 2d 1011, 1018 (8 Cir, 1967—fire).

29–2A The Act of Election

Election, to reinstate or not, must be made within a reasonable time.[10] Whether by word or by act, election must be unequivocal and it must be communicated to the person affected.[11] The election must be made with knowledge not only of the right to elect[12] but also of the facts affecting choice.[13] A court will be slow to see a move to investigate the nature and extent of the loss claimed as an act of election.[14] Election usually occurs when the insurer indicates to the claimant, that he intends to reinstate rather than to pay insurance money or vice versa.[15] However, an initial offer of money by the insurer may be seen as a first move in negotiations and does not rule out a later election to reinstate, if the initial offer is refused.[16]

It has been suggested in an Australian motor case[17] that the choice is not absolute, that the insurer may, if he chooses,

"do some repair and reinstatement so far as circumstances permit and compensate as to the balance—that course might, in some circumstances, be more economical to the insurer rather than treat it as a total loss. If a complete loss, it may replace with another vehicle of similar condition, vintage and value or if that be not possible and the replacement be worth less than the lost vehicle it may pay the insured the difference between the total loss and the value of the replaced vehicle."

When the insured has a clear preference for reinstatement rather than insurance money, the insurer may offer to elect reinstatement as part of a compromise, whereby the insured agrees to accept something less than full repair or restoration; this appears

10. This can be inferred from the duty to pay punctually: below 30–2. In the sense of the text: *Home Mutual Ins Co v Stewart*, 100 P 2d 159, 160–161 (Colo, 1940—motor); *Smith v Farm Bureau Ins Co*, 101 A 2d 778 (NH, 1953—motor); *Howard v Reserve Ins Co*, 254 NE 2d 631, 635 (Ill, 1969—fire).

11. *Lakshimijit v Sherani* [1974] AC 605, 616 *per* Lord Cross (PC). *Lake v Hartford Fire Ins Co* [1966] WAR 161, 163 (WA—motor): there must be "some unequivocal act on the part of the insurer which commits him to his choice under the policy". *Home Mutual* (above), *loc cit*; *Smith v Farm Bureau* (above); *Cameron v Virginia Surety Co*, 423 SW 2d 218 (Mo, 1967—motor); *Howard* (above), *loc cit*.

12. *Young v Bristol Aeroplane Ltd* [1946] AC 163, 176 *per* Lord Russell. *Cf* discussion of waiver in the sense of election between remedies, above, 26–4B ff.

13. *Matthews v Smallwood* [1910] 1 Ch 777, 786 *per* Parker J; *Sutherland v Sun Fire Office* (1852) 14 D (Ct Sess) 775, 777 *per* Lord Anderson (fire).

14. Tarr, p 273 citing *Sutherland* (above).

15. As in *Scottish Amicable Heritable Securities Assn Ltd v Northern Assurance Co*, 1883 11 R (Ct Sess) 287 (fire). An example is a statement to the insured that the insurer has been advised that it is not an economical proposition to repair the property: *Lake v Hartford Fire Ins Co* [1966] WAR 161, 167 (WA—motor).

16. *Sutherland* (above).

17. *Allwright v Queensland Ins Co Ltd* (1966) 84 WN (Pt 1) (NSW) 378, 391 (motor). *Cf Bowes v National Fire & Marine Ins Co of New Zealand* (1888) 7 NZLR 27 (fire) that, if a house and contents are insured for separate amounts but for a single premium in a single policy, the contract is indivisible and, absent a term to that effect, the insurer is not allowed to reinstate in part (house) and to pay in part (contents). *Cf* also *Globe & Rutgers Ins Co v Prairie Oil & Gas Co*, 248 F 452, 457 (2 Cir, 1917—fire) that it is "difficult to see how the oil could be replaced without at the same time replacing the tanks to receive it . . . It is not permissible to replace in part and pay in part." But all depends on the terms of the contract, which may allow the insurer to repair a building and pay for its contents, if insured in separate amounts: *DeSantis v Michigan Basic Property Ins Assn*, 265 NW 2d 634 (Mich 1978—fire).

acceptable in principle,[18] subject to the normal constraints on unfair contracts of compromise.[19]

29–2B The Effect of Election

The effect of election is that the insurer "is in the same position as if he had originally contracted to do the act which he has elected to do".[20] Election "does not constitute a fresh contract between the insured and the insurer, but the policy relates back and will be read as if it had originally been one simply for reinstatement".[21] An election once made is said to be irrevocable.[22]

29–2C Impossibility of Performance

As with any kind of contract, the question whether performance has become impossible turns on careful comparison of the terms of the promised performance[23] and the nature of the alleged obstacle. A contract is not discharged because it has become unexpectedly difficult or expensive to perform.[24] If in the course of reinstatement a fire breaks out destroying some of the work, the insurer must start again and is not excused from completing the work.[25]

If the insured event destroys both the machinery insured together with the building in which it was placed, reinstatement is possible in the new building[26] or at a convenient place nearby,[27] unless the locality or manner of reinstatement is so closely defined in the contract of insurance that the reinstatement required cannot be achieved.[28]

Replacement has been construed to mean "replacement according to law",[29] so reinstatement has to be effected in accordance with building regulations brought into force between the time of the contract and the time of reinstatement, even though

18. *Cf* USA: courts have stated that such an agreement is not consistent with an election to reinstate: *Home Mutual Ins Co* v *Stewart*, 100 P 2d 159, 161 (Colo, 1940—motor); *Smith* v *Farm Bureau Ins Co*, 101 A 2d 778 (NH, 1953—motor); *Cameron* v *Virginia Surety Co*, 423 SW 2d 218 (Mo, 1967—motor); *Howard* v *Reserve Ins Co*, 254 NE 2d 631, 636 (Ill, 1969—fire). The reasoning is not clear.

19. See below, 30–6.

20. *Brown* v *Royal Ins Co* (1859) 1 El & El 853, 858–859 *per* Lord Campbell CJ (fire). This statement was applied in *Maher* v *Lumbermen's Mutual Casualty Co* [1932] 2 DLR 593, 600–601 *per* Cannon J (Sup Ct—motor); and *Carlyle* v *Elite Ins Co* (1984) 56 BCLR 331, 335 (BC—fire), where it was said that the effect is that the contract of indemnity is "replaced" by a new contract of reinstatement; *sed quaere* as regards English law: below 29–2C. But *cf* also *Globe & Rutgers Ins Co* v *Prairie Oil & Gas Co*, 248 F 452, 456 (2 Cir, 1917—fire) that "the contract of insurance becomes converted into a new and independent undertaking . . . to replace"; *idem*: *Transit Casualty Co* v *Transamerica Ins Co*, 387 F 2d 1011, 1016 (8 Cir, 1967—fire).

21. *Robson* v *New Zealand Ins Co Ltd* [1913] NZLR 35, 37 *per* Ostler J (motor). See also *Langan* v *Aetna Ins Co*, 99 F 374, 379 (ND Iowa, 1900—fire), affirmed 108 F 985 (8 Cir, 1901), cert den 183 US 701, for discussion of the problems posed by multiple insurance, the court preferring the view that "election to rebuild . . . does not merge, convert, or affect the contract for indemnity contained in the policy".

22. *Scarf* v *Jardine* (1882) 7 App Cas 345, 360 *per* Lord Blackburn. See further below, 29–2C.

23. *Anderson* v *Commercial Union Assurance Corp* (1885) 55 LJQB 146 (CA—fire).

24. *Brown* v *Royal Ins Co* (1859) 1 El & El 853, 860 *per* Crompton J (fire); *Tsakiroglou & Co Ltd* v *Noblee Thorl GmbH* [1962] AC 93, 115 *per* Viscount Simonds. *Carlyle* v *Elite Ins Co* (1984) 56 BCLR 331 (fire).

25. *Smith* v *Colonial Mutual Fire Ins Co* (1880) 6 VLR (L) 200 (Sup Ct—fire).

26. *Anderson* v *Commercial Union Assurance Corp* (1885) 55 LJQB 146 (CA—fire).

27. *Anderson* (above). *Globe & Rutgers Ins Co* v *Prairie Oil & Gas Co*, 248 F 452, 457 (2 Cir, 1917—fire).

28. *Anderson* (above), p 148 *per* Lord Esher MR.

29. *Carlyle* (above), p 338. See also *D'Aloia* v *Colonial Mutual Gen Ins Co Ltd* (1990) 6 ANZ Ins Cases, No 61–009 (Vict—fire).

unexpectedly expensive for the insurer and putting the insured in a building that is better than before. For betterment the insurer gets no credit or allowance, it has been said,[30] unless provided for in the contract. As to the quality of reinstatement required by the contract, see below 29–2D.

If reinstatement really does becomes physically or legally impossible prior to election, the insurer no longer has a choice to make and must pursue the remaining option: to pay insurance money.[31] If impossibility occurs after an election to reinstate, the contract of reinstatement is subject to the general rules of discharge of contract.[32] As the contract of insurance has become for present purposes a contract of reinstatement, the situation is governed both by common law and also by the Law Reform (Frustrated Contracts) Act 1943.[33] *Prima facie*, therefore, if the impossibility has been caused by the insurer's breach of contract, such as delay, the insurer is liable to the insured in damages.[33a] If the impossibility has its cause in something for which neither party is responsible, the contract of reinstatement is discharged from the time it becomes impossible to perform. However, in spite of statements that an election once made is irrevocable, another and better view is that the contract of insurance remains in force and that the obligation to pay the loss in question as insurance money revives.[34] Although the insurance cases are unclear, this conclusion appears to be consistent with principle.

On the one hand, when the charterer of a ship refuses to load but the shipowner elects to affirm the contract, the contract is discharged by the subsequent outbreak of war, with liability on neither side.[35] If a seller of land elects to treat the purchaser's breach as repudiatory and disaffirms the contract, he cannot later seek specific performance; but that is because the contract has "gone",[36] whereas a contract of insurance, under which reinstatement has become impossible, has not "gone".[37] On the other hand, a party who obtains an order for specific performance, which later becomes impossible, may nonetheless recover damages instead.[38] Moreover, a distinction can be drawn between the kind of choice facing the shipowner and the seller of land,

---

30. MacGillivray, No 1681. See above, 28–3C.

31. Subject to the terms of the contract: *Anderson* (above), p 150 *per* Bowen LJ (CA—fire).

32. *Cf Brown* v *Royal Ins Co* (1859) 1 El & El 853, 859 *per* Lord Campbell CJ (fire), that the insurer would be liable in the case of physical (but not legal) impossibility. As Birds (p 266) and Tarr (p 275) point out, this was said prior to the development of the general doctrine of discharge by impossibility or frustration, and is now open to doubt.

33. The Act is inapplicable to contracts of insurance as such: section 2(5)(b).

33a. *Bland* v *South British Ins Co Ltd* (1990) 6 ANZ Ins Cases, No 60–998 (High Ct, NZ—fire).

34. In this sense Birds, p 267; Merkin & McGee, C.4.5–06; Sutton, No 15.74; Tarr, p 248. Some writers find support in *Anderson* v *Commercial Union Assurance Corp* (1885) 55 LJQB 146 (CA—fire), but the decision in that case was that reinstatement, as required by the terms of the particular policy, was possible; *dicta* beyond the decision (notably p 150 *per* Bowen LJ) do not make the necessary distinction between the effect of impossibility to reinstate arising before election and after election. *Cf* also *Brown* v *Royal Ins Co* (1859) 1 El & El 853, 859 (fire) in which, in such a case, Lord Campbell CJ did not consider either frustration or a revival of the duty to pay insurance money, which in his view (p 858) had been superseded by the duty to reinstate, but said that the insurer who failed to reinstate was liable in damages. However, *Brown* was cited with approval by Willmer LJ in *Reardon Smith Line Ltd* v *MAFF* [1962] 1 QB 42, 115 (CA), in support of his view, that once a port had been nominated under a charterparty, there was no duty to nominate another port, if the first became impossible.

35. *Avery* v *Bowden* (1855) E & B 714; (1856) 6 E & B 953, referred to with approval *inter alia* in *The Simona* [1989] AC 788, 800 *per* Lord Ackner (HL).

36. *Johnson* v *Agnew* [1980] AC 367, 392 and 398 *per* Lord Wilberforce.

37. Above, 29–2B.

38. *Johnson* (above).

which is an election between remedies, and that of an election between rights [39] or between modes of performance, as found in the case of reinstatement. A second distinction is that, in the case of reinstatement, it is not the elector who wishes to reverse the election.

As regards insurance, if not other situations, it is submitted that the statement that in all cases an election is irrevocable goes too far: the operation of election is based on considerations "of common sense and equity".[40] The case of the insurer, who elects to reinstate and then finds it impossible to do, is that of anyone whose contract allows him to choose to perform in one way or another[41]: if he chooses a mode of performance and that becomes impossible, he must perform by some other mode permitted by the contract,[42] even if he informs the other party of the chosen mode.[43] In these cases, it might be said, the contract did not require a (formal) election of mode. However, if a charterer nominates a port, which later becomes unsafe, the balance of authority[44] is that there is an (implied secondary) obligation to nominate another port, which is safe. To require the insurer neither to reinstate, which is impossible, nor to pay, which is still possible, is neither sensible nor equitable. The question is ultimately one of party intention.[45] There is a presumption that parties do not intend senseless or absurd results.[46] So, it is submitted that this part of insurance law accords with the view of Lord Wilberforce,[47] that election is irrevocable only where it "creates a new situation from which subsequent departure would be impossible".

29–2D The Quality of Reinstatement

The legal basis of the insured's rights with regard to reinstatement is found in the contract, subject in certain cases to the Supply of Goods and Services Act 1982.[48] Further, as the rights and duties are derived from a contract of reinstatement, albeit one derived from a contract of insurance, the better view[49] is that any exemption clauses are subject to the Unfair Contract Terms Act 1977.

To appoint a competent contractor to undertake the reinstatement is not enough: the insurer is responsible for the quality of the contractor's work.[50] The insurer has promised, not merely to arrange reinstatement of the property by someone else, but to reinstate it. The work must be done and done properly. The insurer must replace property destroyed "by other things which are equivalent to the property des-

---

39. p 396 *per* Lord Wilberforce.
40. p 398 *per* Lord Wilberforce.
41. *Robson* v *New Zealand Ins Co Ltd* [1931] NZLR 35, 37 *per* Ostler J (motor).
42. *Vantol Ltd* v *Fairclough Dodd & Jones Ltd* [1955] 1 Lloyd's Rep 546, 552 *per* McNair J.
43. As in the case of an FOB buyer who nominates a ship: that is only a matter of courtesy: *Agricultores Federados Argentinos* v *Ampro SA* [1965] 2 Lloyd's Rep 157, 167 *per* Widgery J.
44. Scrutton, *Charterparties* (19th ed), p 127. *The Evia* [1983] 1 AC 736.
45. *Anderson* v *Commercial Union Assurance Co* (1885) 55 LJQB 146, 150 (CA—fire).
46. Above,15–4.
47. *Johnson* v *Agnew* [1980] AC 367, 399.
48. See, for example, Miller & Harvey, *Consumer and Trading Law* (1985), ch 3.
49. In this sense Merkin & McGee, p C.4.5–04. The Act does not apply to contracts of insurance: Schedule 1, section 1(*a*).
50. *Thurston* v *Northwestern Fire & Marine Ins Co*, 9 F Supp 848, 852 (ND NY, 1934—hull): the insurer must see that the work of reinstatement is done in an ordinarily skilful and workmanlike manner; *Buerkle* v *Superior Court of Los Angeles County*, 379 P 2d 941 (Cal, 1963—motor); *Venable* v *Import Volkswagen Inc*, 519 P 2d 667, 674 (Kan, 1974—motor).

troyed",[51] even if the cost of reinstatement proves to be greater than the sum insured[52] or than the amount of the loss measured on the basis of depreciation.[53] But, a house must be put "substantially in the same state as before the fire",[54] and that state includes any faults in construction[55] or style,[56] which the insurer is not, therefore, obliged to have put right. Property must be "as serviceable and valuable" as before the loss.[57] Hence used parts may be replaced with used parts.[58] As to the general objective of reinstatement, see above, 28–2A; as to the mode and materials of reinstatement, see above, 28–3A; and, as to impossibility of reinstatement, see above 29–2C.

The insurer must reinstate within a reasonable time[59] and, if he fails to do so, will be liable to pay damages to the insured for loss of use.[60] If the insurer fails to reinstate at all, as reinstatement is generally an option for the insurer not the insured, the rights of the insured depend on whether the insurer is obliged to reinstate and, therefore, whether a clear election has been made.[61] If, however, the insurer attempts to reinstate but the work is defective, the insured has an action for damages in the amount necessary to put the defect right,[62] an amount that may exceed the sum insured; in this respect, the insurance contract has been superseded by the contract of reinstatement.

29–2E The Co-operation of the Insured

It is an inference from the insured's general duty of good faith and co-operation that he must assist the process of reinstatement, for example, by providing plans and relevant information,[63] and permitting entry on premises. In the case of fire insurance, the right of entry is usually governed by a term of the contract.[64] In the case of motor insurance, if the claimant refuses to hand over the insured vehicle for repair, thereby making it impossible for the insurer to perform his obligation, in principle, the insurer

---

51. *Anderson* v *Commercial Union Assurance Corp* (1885) 55 LJQB 146, 148 *per* Lord Esher MR (CA—fire).

52. *Brown* v *Royal Ins Co* (1859) 1 El & El 853 (fire); *Argy Trading Development Co Ltd* v *Lapid Developments Ltd* [1977] 1 Lloyd's Rep 67, 74 *per* Croom-Johnson J (fire). *Hartford Fire Ins Co* v *Peebles' Hotel Co*, 82 F 546, 548 (6 Cir, 1897—fire); *Samuels* v *Illinois Fire Ins Co*, 354 SW 2d 352, 358 (Mo, 1961—fire).

53. *Swift* v *New Zealand Ins Co Ltd* [1927] VLR 249 (fire).

54. *Times Fire Assurance Co* v *Hawke* (1858) 1 F & F 406, 407 *per* Channell B (fire).

55. *Ibid*: the insurer "was not bound to pull down the old walls and rebuild them entirely on account of any defect in their foundation. It was enough if, incorporating what remained of them, the new walls were as secure as the old ones were." See also *Braithwaite* v *Employers' Liability Assurance Corp Ltd* [1964] 1 Lloyd's Rep 94, 98 *per* MacKenna J (burglary). *Moriatis* v *Harvey Trinder (Qld) Pty Ltd* [1969] QdR 226, 233 (fire).

56. *Braithwaite* (above) *per* MacKenna J, concerning a replica brooch.

57. *Globe & Rutgers Ins Co* v *Prairie Oil & Gas Co*, 248 F 452, 457 (2 Cir, 1917—fire).

58. *Williams* v *Farm Bureau Mutual Ins Co*, 299 SW 2d 587, 589 (Mo, 1957—motor).

59. *Davidson* v *Guardian Royal Exchange Assurance* [1979] 1 Lloyd's Rep 406 (Ct Sess—motor). *Lake* v *Hartford Fire Ins Co* [1966] WAR 161, 166 (WA—motor). *Langan* v *Aetna Ins Co*, 99 F 374, 380 (ND Iowa, 1900—fire), affirmed, 108 F 985 (8 Cir, 1901), cert den 183 US 701; *Home Indemnity Co* v *Bush*, 513 P 2d 145, 149 (Ariz, 1973—motor); *Venable* v *Import Volkswagen Inc*, 519 P 2d 667 (Kan, 1974—motor).

60. *Davidson* (above). *Maher* v *Lumbermen's Mutual Casualty Co* [1932] 2 DLR 593, 601 *per* Cannon J (Sup Ct—motor). *Home Indemnity Co* v *Bush*, 513 P 2d 145, 150–151 (Ariz, 1973—motor), i.e., the reasonable rental value of the property; *Venable* v *Import Volkswagen Inc*, 519 P 2d 667 (Kan, 1974—motor). *Aliter* if the property proves unrepairable: *Owens* v *Pyeatt*, 57 Cal Rptr 100, 106 (Cal, 1967—motor).

61. Merkin & McGee, p C.4.5–02. Reinstatement is not the kind of duty of which the court will order specific performance. In the sense of the text: *Langan* v *Aetna Ins Co*, 99 F 374, 379 (ND Iowa, 1900—fire).

62. *Robson* v *New Zealand Ins Co Ltd* [1931] NZLR 35 (motor). *Samuels* v *Illinois Fire Ins Co*, 354 SW 2d 352, 359 (Mo, 1961—fire).

63. Above 27–1.

64. Above 27–5.

is discharged from his duty.[65] However, it has been held[66] in the United States that, in such a case, the claimant may recover the amount of the lowest firm repair estimate obtained in good faith.

29–3 REINSTATEMENT: STATUTE

Quite apart from any right of reinstatement in the contract, the insurer[67] (a) may elect to reinstate, if he suspects fraud or arson, and (b) must reinstate, if he is requested to reinstate by a person other than the insured and who is interested in or entitled to premises[68] damaged by fire.[69] This is the effect of the Fires Prevention (Metropolis)[70] Act 1774, section 83. The degree of reinstatement, unlike that of contractual reinstatement,[71] is limited by the amount of the "insurance money"[72]; and, if the insurance contract is unenforceable by the insured, there is no insurance money and the person interested has no right to request reinstatement from the insurer.[73] Section 83 may be a regular ghost at the feast of negotiations but rarely materialises in the courts. Moreover, as regards (a), the insurer usually has a right of election under the terms of the contract of insurance.[74]

29–3A The Request of Persons Interested

The request for reinstatement must come from a person interested. The scheme of this part of section 83 is to prevent insurance money being paid to and retained by the insured, when another person will be damnified if the money is not spent on reinstatement.[75] Hence, persons interested are all persons with an insurable interest in the

---

65. *Cf* impossibility, above, 29–2C.

66. *Williams* v *Farm Bureau Mutual Ins Co*, 299 SW 2d 587, 590 (Mo, 1957—motor) and cases cited.

67. The rules apply to the "governors and directors of the several insurance offices" and have been held inapplicable to individual underwriters at Lloyd's: *Portavon Cinema Co Ltd* v *Price & Century Ins Co Ltd* [1939] 4 All ER 601, 608 *per* Branson J (fire).

68. The Act does not apply to insurance of personal property: *Re Quicke's Trusts* [1908] 1 Ch 897 (fire).

69. The Act is confined to fire insurance: *Ex p Gorely* (1864) 4 De GJ & S 477 (insurance of personal property).

70. Notwithstanding the title of the Act, its scope is not limited to the Metropolis of London but, being concerned with "a general and universal evil", is "intended to be of general and universal application"—*Ex p Gorely* (above) p 481 *per* Westbury LC; however, not in Scotland: *Westminster Fire Office* v *Glasgow Provident Investment Sy* (1888) 13 App Cas 699, 714 *per* Earl Selborne, p 716 *per* Lord Watson (fire); or in Ireland: *Andrews* v *Patriotic Assurance Co* (1886) 18 LR Ir 355, 366 *per* Palles CB (fire). The same rules were enacted in parts of Australia: Sutton, No 6.11; Tarr, p 276.

71. Above, 29–2D.

72. *Semble* this is not the sum insured, the maximum amount which the insurer has undertaken to pay, but the amount which the contract obliges him to pay in the particular case: *Royal Ins Co Ltd* v *Mylius* (1926) 38 CLR 477, 504 *per* Rich J (HCA—fire); *Auckland City Corp* v *Mercantile & General Ins Co Ltd* [1930] NZLR 809 (fire); *Kennedy* v *Boolarra Butter Factory Pty Ltd* [1953] VLR 548 (fire).

73. *Matthey* v *Curling* [1922] 2 AC 180, 219 *per* Younger LJ (CA). *Auckland City Corp* v *Mercantile & General Ins Co Ltd* [1930] NZLR 809 (fire). See also *Kern Corp Ltd* v *Walter Reid Trading Pty Ltd* (1987) 61 ALJR 319 (HCA—fire).

74. Above, 29–2. As the statute is in the public interest, it has been suggested that it overrides the contract and that, on suspicion of fraud, the insurer is obliged to reinstate, whether he wishes to do so or not: Merkin & McGee, p C.4.5–19.

75. *Reynolds* v *Phoenix Assurance Co Ltd* [1978] 2 Lloyd's Rep 440, 462 *per* Forbes J (fire); it also discourages fraud: *Sinnott* v *Bowden* [1912] 2 Ch 414, 420 *per* Parker J (fire).

property,[76] whether a full interest or a limited interest, except the insured himself.[77] Persons held to be persons interested include owners,[78] landlords,[79] tenants,[80] lessees,[81] mortgagees,[82] the purchaser of land prior to completion,[83] and remainder-men.[84]

The request for reinstatement must be a distinct and clear request, which refers to the rights under the statute[85] and which is made before the insurance money has been paid.[86] In response to such a request, the insurer is obliged by section 83 to effect reinstatement, unless within 60 days after the adjustment of the claim the insured gives to the insurer sufficient security that the insurance money will be spent on reinstatement, or unless the insurance money is distributed among "all the contending parties",[87] to the satisfaction of the insurer.

If the insurer does not comply with such a request, the person interested is not entitled to reinstate himself and claim the cost from the insurer,[88] nor claim from the insurer the money to do it himself.[89] The remedy, it has been said,[90] is a mandatory injunction. But there is force in the objection[91] that there may be no adequate means to carry out or enforce the mandate, such as plans or a right of entry on the land. Moreover, the insurer would not be permitted to interplead,[92] because any competing claims are not adverse claims but merely inconsistent claims and interpleader, whereby payment of the insurance money into court would discharge the insurer, would be inappropriate in respect of a statutory duty on the insurer to see that money

76. See ch 4.
77. *Reynolds* (above).
78. *Ex p Gorely* (1864) 4 De G J & S 477. *Re Alliance Assurance Co Ltd* (1960) 25 DLR (2d) 316 (BC).
79. *Vernon* v *Smith* (1821) 5 B & Ald 1 (fire); *Simpson* v *Scottish Union Ins Co* (1863) 1 H & M 618; *Sun Fire Office* v *Galinsky* [1914] 2 KB 545 (CA); *Matthey* v *Curling* [1922] 2 AC 180, 198 *per* Lord Atkin.
80. *Wimbledon Golf Club* v *Imperial Ins Co* (1902) 18 TLR 815 (fire).
81. *Portavon Cinema Co Ltd* v *Price & Century Ins Co Ltd* [1939] 4 All ER 601; *Lonsdale & Thompson Ltd* v *Black Arrow Group* [1993] 2 Lloyd's Rep 428 (fire); Oakley, [1993] CLJ 387.
82. *Sinnott* v *Bowden* [1912] 2 Ch 414 (fire). The category probably includes the mortgagor. The contrary view, expressed by Lord Selborne LC in *Westminster Fire Office* v *Glasgow Provident Investment Sy* (1888) 13 App Cas 699, 714, by reference to the closing words of section 83, was convincingly refuted by Parker J in *Sinnott* v *Bowden* [1912] 2 Ch 414, 420 by reference to both the wording and the purpose of the section.
83. *Rayner* v *Preston* (1881) 18 Ch D 1, 15 *per* James LJ (CA—fire). *Royal Ins Co Ltd* v *Mylius* (1926) 38 CLR 477, 491 ff (HCA—fire); *Kennedy* v *Boolarra Butter Factory Pty Ltd* [1953] VLR 548 (fire); and *Kern Corp Ltd* v *Walter Reid Trading Pty Ltd* (1987) 61 ALJR 319 (HCA—fire), where the purchaser's action against the insurer failed, as, the insured vendor having been paid the full purchase price, he had suffered no loss recoverable against the insurer.
84. *Re Quicke's Trusts* [1908] 1 Ch 897 (fire).
85. *Simpson* v *Scottish Union Ins Co* (1863) 1 H & M 618 (fire). See above, 5–7D.
86. p 628 *per* Sir W Page Wood V-C.
87. These "include the persons who, though not interested in the policy moneys, are interested in the subject-matter of the insurance and are insisting on the insurance money being laid out in rebuilding"—*Sinnott* v *Bowden* [1912] 2 Ch 414, 420 *per* Parker J (fire).
88. *Simpson* v *Scottish Union Ins Co* (1863) 1 H & M 618 (fire).
89. *Matthey* v *Curling* [1922] 2 AC 180, 219 *per* Younger LJ (CA).
90. *Simpson* (above) p 629 *per* Sir W Page Wood V-C. See also *Mylius* (below) pp 493 ff on the basis of *ubi ius ibi remedium*, as expounded, for example, in *Bradford Corp* v *Myers* [1916] 1 AC 242, 263 *per* Lord Shaw.
91. *Wimbledon Golf Club* v *Imperial Ins Co* (1902) 18 TLR 815 (fire). For an explanation of this case which undermines this opinion, see Isaac J in *Royal Ins Co* v *Mylius* (1926) 38 CLR 477, 493–494 (HCA). In *Wimbledon*, Wright J refused *mandamus* against the insurer because (a) although all concerned agreed that the premises should not be reinstated exactly as before, they had not agreed on the (new) form that reinstatement should take; and (b) the insurer had no right to enter the building and execute the work of reinstatement.
92. *Sun Fire Office* v *Galinsky* [1914] 2 KB 545 (CA).

was spent as prescribed. A better remedy may be an injunction to restrain the insurer from paying the insured,[93] at least until the insured gives security, such as a performance bond. In any case, it has been held that no action lies under section 83 against the insurer to recover damages for loss of profits pending reinstatement of the property.[94]

93. *Wimbledon Golf, loc cit.*
94. *Mylius* v *Royal Ins Co Ltd* [1928] VLR 126, 130 (fire), as the purpose of the Act is not to compensate persons interested, but to remove any inducement to arson. *Cf Royal Ins Co Ltd* v *Mylius* (1926) 38 CLR 477, 493 (HCA—fire).

CHAPTER 30

PAYMENT AND NON–PAYMENT

30-1 PAYMENT

In the event of insured loss, the insurer discharges his duty under the contract of insurance by payment or, in the appropriate case, reinstatement.[1] The amount of payment has been discussed in chapter 28. This chapter is concerned, first, with the time and legal nature of payment (30–2), the mode of payment (30–3), and the identity of the payee (30–4). These matters are determined primarily[2] by the contract of insurance, subject to general rules of law governing payment.[3] This chapter is also concerned with payment by mistake (30–5), compromise payment (30–6), and, last but not least, the effect of non–payment (30–7 ff).

30-2 THE TIME OF PAYMENT

If there is no express term[4] in the contract of insurance governing the time of payment, the time is determined by the nature of insurance as "an agreement to pay a sum on the happening of an event".[5]

According to a literal view, this means that the indemnity insurer is in breach of contract as soon as the loss occurs: "where the claim is for unliquidated damages, it is not a condition precedent . . . that the plaintiff has quantified the amount of his claim . . . The claim, since it is not for a debt or liquidated sum due under the contract, is presumably a claim for breach of contract. If so, the insurer may technically be in breach of his contract before any demand is made on him".[6] This analysis "may be thought to produce curious results",[7] not least that the insurer is considered to have undertaken a duty that both parties know he cannot possibly perform, namely to indemnify the insured in respect of loss before the insurer (and sometimes even the

---

1. See chapter 29.
2. *General Accident Fire & Life Assurance Corp Ltd* v *Midland Bk Ltd* [1940] 2 KB 388 (CA—fire).
3. *Brainard* v *Brainard*, 62 P 2d 403. 404 (Cal, 1936—life).
4. Such as within x days of proof of loss. In Canada, state legislation on insurance sets time limits for the payment of insurance money, time from the completion of proof of loss: Brown & Menezes, 12:1:12. The same is true in the United States; for example, Cal Ins Code, section 2057.
5. *Pape* v *Home Ins Co*, 139 F 2d 231, 234 (2 Cir, 1943—fire).
6. *Chandris* v *Argo Ins Co Ltd* [1963] 2 Lloyd's Rep 65, 74 *per* Megaw J (hull), applied in *The Potoi Chau, Castle Ins Co Ltd* v *Hong Kong Islands Shipping Co Ltd* [1984] AC 22 (PC—cargo). *Cf Jabbour* v *The Custodian of Absentee Israeli Property* [1954] 1 WLR 139, 144 *per* Pearson J, that, in the case of the insurance claim for unliquidated damages, "the word 'damages' is used in a somewhat unusual sense".
7. *Chandris, loc cit.*

insured) knows that it has happened and, in many cases, before the extent of the loss can possibly be quantified.

A second and more sensible view can be based on the terms, as well as the nature, of the contract of insurance.[8] It is clear from commonplace terms of the contract that payment, on the happening of the insured event, does not mean immediate payment but payment after the procedural conditions,[9] such as notice and proof, have been satisfied.[10] Moreover, a reasonable time must be allowed for the adjustment of the amount due,[11] although, when precise adjustment gives rise to no diffiuclty, payment should be at the time when the insured has satisfied the conditions of notice and proof.[12] If there is real doubt about the amount, the claim may be "settled" and paid much later.

That does not alter the fact that the insured has contracted for a sum upon the happening of an earlier event. If a claim goes to court, this fact is recognised in that the court has power to order the insurer to pay interest from the time of the event: below 30–8. Indeed, it has been suggested that insurers should do so as a matter of course.[13] In any case, an award of interest from the time of the event is based not on the premise that the insurer is in breach of contract from that time but, it is submitted, on the insurer's promise of payment with effect from that time.

30–3 THE MODE OF PAYMENT

If the contract is silent on the point, payment must be in cash,[14] unless payment by cheque is implicitly authorised[15]; in practice, it will be readily inferred that the strict right to cash has been waived[16] and that payment may be by cheque. If the payee accepts a cheque, that is conditional payment,[17] which becomes actual payment when the cheque is honoured.[18] The currency of payment is ascertained by construction of the contract, in accordance with the proper law of the contract.[19]

It is open to the parties to make a further agreement, whereby the insurer discharges his duty of payment in a way other than lump sum cash[20]: not only discharge by cheque, which is usually implicit anyway (above), but also discharge in kind,[21] pay-

---

8. Cf *The Italia Express (No 2)* [1992] 2 Lloyd's Rep 281 (hull), below 30–9B.
9. See chapter 26.
10. *Chandris* (above), *loc cit.*
11. *Macbeth & Co Ltd* v *Maritime Ins Co Ltd* (1908) 24 TLR 599, 560 *per* Walton J (hull); *Burts & Harvey Ltd* v *Vulcan Boiler & General Ins Co Ltd* [1966] 1 Lloyd's Rep 354 (consequential loss).
12. *Macbeth* (above), *loc cit. State Farm Casualty Co* v *Thain*, 132 SE 2d 148, 150 (Ga, 1963): in the absence of an express term, "the loss is payable immediately after the proof of loss is made and filed". In June 1988, Lloyd's settled a 45m dollar hull claim (arising out of the crash in France of an A320 Airbus) in seven days. See further, Appleman, sections 4007 ff, 6452.
13. Editorial (1992) 142 NLJ 445.
14. *Sweeting* v *Pearce* (1861) 9 CB (NS) 534, 540 *per* Bramwell B (hull); *Hine Bros* v *Steamship Ins Syndicate Ltd* (1895) 72 LT 79, 81 *per* Lord Esher MR (CA—hull).
15. See Appleman, sections 1667 ff, 4006 ff, 6452.
16. Mann, pp 70 ff.
17. *D & C Builders Ltd* v *Rees* [1966] 2 QB 617 (CA).
18. *Hine* (above), p 82.*per* Lord Esher MR. See above, 13–4.
19. See above, 2–3C.
20. In the absence of special agreement the insurer's duty is to pay a single lump sum: *Prudential Ins Co* v *Faulkner*, 68 F 2d 676 (10 Cir, 1934—disability).
21. *Holmes* v *Payne* [1930] 2 KB 301: substitute jewellery.

ment against a loan receipt[22] or by periodic payments, in particular, periodic payments under a structured settlement.[23]

30-4 THE PAYEE

Unless the contract provides otherwise, payment must be to the insured[24] or his duly authorised agent or, in appropriate cases, to his personal representative,[25] assignee,[26] trustee in bankruptcy[27] or some other person designated by the insured,[28] such as a loss payee (below, 30–4A). Payment in good faith to the person designated discharges the insurer,[29] notwithstanding that the insured was insane at the time of designation[30] or that he later made a different designation, of which the insurer did not have sufficient notice.[31]

In the case of a joint policy, payment may be to any one of the joint insured.[32] Contrast *General Accident Fire & Life Assurance Corp Ltd* v *Midland Bk Ltd*,[32a] in which a single fire policy was taken by three persons for their respective rights and interest. The judgment of Sir Wilfred Greene MR, from which the following passage is taken, has been cited and applied[33] far and wide:

"If A and B are joint owners of property—and I use that phrase in the strict sense—an under-

22. A device whereby the insurer pays and obtains from the payee a loan receipt, whereby the money is treated as a loan without interest, repayable from any net recovery that the insured makes in respect of the loss insured against the third party responsible for the loss. It "permits the insurance company to speedily pay its insured and yet press in court to recoup its losses from the wrongdoer without the company appearing by name, trying in that way to avoid unmerited disadvantages" that might arise, if the jury is aware that an insurer is involved—*Merrimack Mfg Co* v *Lowell Trucking Group*, 46 NYS 2d 736, 738 (1944—fire). See further, *Luckenbach* v *McCahan Sugar Refining Co*, 248 US 139 (1918—cargo); *Watsontown Brick Co* v *Hercules Powder Co*, 201 F Supp 343 (MD Pa, 1962).

23. Compensation, usually to a third party to whom the insured is liable, through periodic payments free of tax to the payee, by means of an annuity; see further, Allen, (1988) 104 LQR 448; Lewis, (1988) 15 J Law & Soc 392.

24. *Swan & Cleland's Graving Dock & Slipway Co* v *Maritime Ins Co* [1907] 1 KB 116 (hull). Cf *Brissette* v *Westbury Life Ins Co* (1993) 96 DLR (4th) 609 (1992—life): a life policy joint between spouses made the money payable to the "survivor". The husband murdered the wife and could not, therefore, claim the money and, indeed, renounced any such claim. However, the Supreme Court held that the policy was unambiguous and declined to find a constructive trust of the money in favour of the wife's estate: the insurer had not been unjustly enriched, it was simply that the contingency, upon which payment was to be made, had not occurred!

25. *Durrant* v *Friend* (1852) 5 De G & Sm 343 (marine).

26. Law of Property Act 1925, section 136(1)(c). *Desborough* v *Harris* (1855) 5 De GM & G 439 (life).

27. *McEntire* v *Potter & Co* (1889) 22 QBD 438 (marine); *Hood's Trustees* v *Southern Union General Ins Co Ltd* [1928] Ch 793 (CA—motor).

28. *Bates* v *Equitable Fire & Marine Ins Co* (1870) 10 Wall 33 (USA); *Mercantile Credit Corp* v *Downey*, 238 NYS 2d 630 (1962—fire).

29. *Manhattan Life Ins Co* v *Hennessy*, 99 F 64 (5 Cir, 1900—life); *Weed* v *Equitable Life Assurance Sy*, 288 F 2d 463 (5 Cir, 1961—life), cert den 368 US 821; *Butternut Enterprises Inc* v *Travelers Indemnity Co*, 412 NYS 2d 185 (1979—fire), affirmed 431 NYS 2d 528.

If, however, less than the full sum is paid to the designee, who signs a release, the balance is still owed to the insured: *McCaffry* v *Metropolitan Life Ins Co*, 25 NYS 2d 926 (1941—life).

30. There is no duty on the insurer to inquire into the mental capacity of the insured and, if he pays in good faith and ignorance of the incapacity, he is discharged: *New York Life Ins Co* v *Federal National Bk*, 151 F 2d 537 (10 Cir, 1945—life), cert den 327 US 778.

31. As to whether a designation is sufficently clear to put the insurer on notice, see *Custer* v *Metropolitan Life Ins Co*, 286 NYS 2d 416 (1968—life).

32. *Penniall* v *Harborne* (1848) 11 QB 368, 376 *per* Lord Denman CJ (fire).

32a. [1940] 2 KB 388.

33. For example in Australia: Nicholson (1990) 3 Ins LJ 218, 221 and cases listed.

taking to indemnify them jointly is a true contract of indemnity in respect of a joint loss which they have suffered. Again, there can be no objection to combining in one insurance a number of persons having different interests in the subject matter of the insurance, but I find myself unable to see how an insurance of that character can be called a joint insurance. In such a case the interest of each of the insured is different. The amount of his loss, if the subject matter of the insurance is destroyed or damaged, depends on the nature of his interest . . . In such a case there is no joint element at all . . . Such a policy, in my judgment, may be more accurately described as a composite policy, because it comprises, for reasons of obvious convenience, in one piece of paper the interests of a number of persons whose connection with the subject matter of the insurance makes it natural and reasonable that the whole matter should be dealt with in one policy.[34] It follows that in such a case, when property the subject of insurance is damaged or destroyed, the claim of each of the insured will fall to be determined by reference to the obligation to indemnify 'the insured' against loss or damage to their respective interests in the property."[35]

The decision in the *General Accident* case, as a matter of construction, was that this was not a joint policy but a "composite" policy, for there "is no joint risk; there is no joint interest; the measure of loss suffered by those . . . parties will be different, calling for a different indemnity,"[36] different not only in amount but also in payee. If the loss is a loss which has been suffered by only one of the persons insured, the undertaking to pay must be construed as an obligation to pay that person only.[37] To the extent that money is paid to a party who has not suffered the loss in question, the party to whom it was owed can recover it from the party who has received it.[38]

The place of payment is usually determined by the identity of the payee. If the contract is silent, general principles suggest that payment must be made at the residence or place of business of the payee.[38a]

30–4A The Loss Payee

The contract of insurance may stipulate that the insurance money shall be paid to a third party, a person other than the original insured. In general, that stipulation may be enforced against the insurer by the insured but not by the third party[39]; if the insured obtains the money, the third party has no claim on the proceeds, unless he has a claim by statute or by contract against the insured.[40] In the case of insurance of property mortgaged, the insurance may stipulate that the insurance money shall be payable to a specified mortgagee or to the mortgagee "as his interest may appear". If so, the mortgagee is not a party to the contract of insurance[41] but the clause has been construed as effecting an assignment of (the right to) the insurance money to the mortgagee,[42] with the result that, in Canada at least, the mortgagee can sue to enforce the

34. pp 404 ff.
35. *Federation Ins Ltd* v *Wasson* (1987) 163 CLR 303, 310 (HCA – motor) with reference to the judgment of Sir Wilfred Greene MR.
36. p 405.
37. p 408 *per* Sir Wilfred Greene MR.
38. p 415 *per* Sir Wilfred Greene MR.
38a *Busto* v *Manufacturers Life Ins Co*, 556 P 2d 96, 99 (Or, 1978—life).
39. *Guerin* v *Manchester Fire Assurance Co* (1898) 29 SCR 139, 149 *per* Strong CJ (fire): the rule of privity of contract. On this rule and exceptions to it see ch 5 and ch 6.
40. *Sinnott* v *Bowden* [1912] 2 Ch 414, 419 *per* Parker J; *Halifax Building Sy* v *Keighley* [1931] 2 KB 248 (fire).
The Law of Property Act 1925, section 47, provides for a claim by the purchaser of land to insurance money received by the seller of the property in respect of damage to the property.
41. *Bank of Toronto* v *West Kildonan* [1937] 1 DLR 331 (Man—fire).
42. MacGillivray, No 1643. Above, ch 6.

liability of the insurer.[43] The Canadian courts have spoken of "the absolute rights of a mortgagee in such circumstances to control the destination of insurance proceeds untrammelled by any adjustment made [by the insurer] direct with the insured without the intervention of the mortgagee".[44]

30–5 PAYMENT BY MISTAKE

If the insurer pays insurance money by mistake, at least two questions arise. First, if he has paid the wrong person, is the insurer still obliged to pay the right person? Second, if the insurer has paid the right person but on the mistaken assumption that the money was due under the contract, can the insurer recover the money?

As to the first question, the rights of the proper payee are not affected either by the mistakes of the insurer or by the misstatements of third parties. Thus, the Insurance Ombudsman takes the view[44a] that, if the insurer pays the surrender value of a policy, on presentation of a forged authority by a person with neither actual nor ostensible authority from the insured or from the proper payee, the forgery is null and void and the policy must be reinstated. Equally, if the insurer pays insurance money to the wrong person in similar circumstances, he is entitled to recover the money from the miscreant[45] but he is not discharged from his duty to pay the right person: above 30–4.

As to the second question, if insurer A pays money to insured B by mistake as to B's entitlement under the contract of insurance, the chances that A be entitled to recover the money depend mainly on (a) whether B induced the mistake[46]; and (b) whether the money has passed from B to an innocent third party C—if so, whether or not A's mistake was induced by B, A's chances of recovering the money will be reduced by C's claim to retain it and the court must compare their respective merits.

A further question is whether B obtained the money from A with A's apparent consent, under a transacton that is or is like a contract—if so, this is best treated separately as case (c), in which A's chances of relief are seriously reduced by the fact that recovery will mean vitiating a contract (or something like it).[47] This is because, in case (c), whether the money has been actually paid or merely promised,[48] the mistake must in some sense be "fundamental" whereas, in case (b), the mistake that suffices for relief is less serious, for relief does not negative a contract (or something like it) and

43. *Re Liverpool & London & Globe Ins Co Ltd and Canadian Fire Ins Co* [1918] 2 WWR 429, 430–431; affirmed *ibid*, p 727 (Alta—fire); *London & Lancashire Guarantee & Accident Co v M & P Enterprises Ltd* (1969) 69 DLR (2d) 461, 465 (Man—fire), affirmed (1969) 1 DLR (3d) 731.
44. *M & P Enterprises Ltd* (above), *loc cit*.
44a. Annual Report 1991, para 2.2.
45. Goff and Jones pp 710–711.
46. See *Barclays* v *Simms* (below).
47. Goff & Jones, pp 87 ff. See also in this sense: Stoljar, *The Law of Quasi-Contract* (2nd ed, 1989, Sydney) p 20. Robert Goff J in *Barclays Bank Ltd* v *Simms Son & Cooke (Southern) Ltd* [1980] QB 677, 695: "1. If a person pays money to another under a mistake of fact which causes him to make the payment, he is *prima facie* entitled to recover it as money paid under a mistake of fact. 2. His claim may however fail if: . . . (b) the payment is made for good consideration, in particular if the money is paid to discharge, and does discharge, a debt to the payee. . . ." Moreover, the distinction is implicit in the approach of the House of Lords to the mistaken payments made in *Bell v Lever Bros* [1932] AC 161: Andrews [1989] LMCLQ 431, 441, 447.
48. Andrews p 439.

the expectations that go with it.[49] In case (b), relief merely seeks to prevent the unjust enrichment of the payee insured and any mistake which causes payment should suffice,[50] whether it is fundamental or not.

In the context of insurance claims, case (c) is that of the disputed claim, which is settled or compromised and thus the subject of a contract closely related to but quite distinct from the contract of insurance. The obvious point bears emphasis: if the insurer has paid money by mistake, he will find it less difficult to get it back, if he has simply paid it more or less without demur than if he has paid it in performance of a contract of settlement or compromise; see below, 30–6. From this perspective, closer examination of case (c) reveals that it is not one case but two.

In case (ca), A seeks to have the contract declared vitiated, in the sense of totally void, in order to recover the money from a third party C. The rules are rules of common law and they are strict. Case (ca) usually concerns mistakes about the personal identity of B, however, there is no reason in principle why other kinds of mistake should not count. In practice, the identity cases tend to stand out because, in practical terms, if the mistake has concerned human identity, it is generally hard to show that the mistake was not careless, as the law requires, if relief is to be granted to A.

In case (cb), A seeks to have the contract declared vitiated, but in the lesser sense of voidable, in order to recover the money from payee B. No third party is involved, so the mistake required is less fundamental than that in case (ca).[51] Typical of case (cb) is one in which a contract of settlement is set aside, because it was made by insurer A on the mistaken assumption of both parties that B's insurance claim was valid[52] or that the full extent of B's insured loss or injury had been taken into account.[53] "The general words in a release are limited to that thing or those things which were specially in the contemplation of the parties at the time when the release was given."[54] Case (cb) also includes mistakes of calculation.[55]

Case (c) is examined below, 30–6C. Turning first of all to case (b), in which relief does not entail the vitiation of any contract, the action by insurer A to recover money paid to B by mistake is restitutionary. A, must establish that his mistake was (i) a mistake not of law but of fact (below 30–5A); (ii) an essential mistake (below, 30–5B);

49. Moreover, it is public policy to uphold bargains and hence to require a narrow or strict doctrine of mistake if the effect is to upset or rescind a bargain: Andrews p 432. See also *Bell* v *Lever Bros* [1932] AC 161, 224 *per* Lord Atkin. Stoljar, *loc cit*. Above 24–5A3(c).

50. Goff & Jones, p 89; cf p 100.

51. *Magee* v *Pennine Ins Co Ltd* [1969] 2 QB 507 (CA—motor). See also *Solle* v *Butcher* [1950] 1 KB 671, 693 (CA). Cf *Bell* v *Lever Bros* [1932] AC 161.

52. *Magee* (above). The insurance contract could have been avoided for non-fraudulent misrepresentation in the proposal. *Cf* the view of Winn LJ (dissenting p 516) that operative mistakes are confined to subject-matter and do not embrace mistakes about rights.

53. *Roberts* v *Eastern Counties Ry Co* (1859) 1 F & F 460 (PA). Other cases of mistake about the extent or amount of recoverable loss, in which a settlement was not enforced for that reason include: *Kent* v *Ocean Accident & Guarantee Corp* (1909) 20 OLR 226 (PA). *Hind Ltd* v *Silva*, 75 F 2d 74 (9 Cir, 1935—motor); *United States* v *Drake & Beemont Mutual Aid Sy*, 218 F Supp 155 (ED Mo, 1963—fire), affirmed 330 F 2d 548 (8 Cir, 1964).

54. *London & SWR Co* v *Blackmore* (1870) LR 4 HL 610, 623 *per* Lord Westbury. See also *Kent* v *Ocean* (above), p 232.

55. For example, price. Thus, specific performance was refused in *Webster* v *Cecil* (1861) 30 Beav 62. An action (for damages) to enforce a contract concluded on the basis of an erroneous quotation by the defendant was refused in *Hartog* v *Colin & Shields* [1939] 3 All ER 566; the court decided that there was "no contract" (p 567), however, the better view of the case is that a contract existed at the "correct" price: Treitel p 273.

and (iii) an excusable mistake (30–5C). Recovery, it has been held,[56] does not extend to investment profit on the money earned by the payee.

30–5A Mistake of Fact

In England, money may be recovered on the basis of a mistake of fact but not a mistake of law.[57] The rule against relief for mistakes of law has been abandoned in other countries[58] and attacked in England,[59] where courts sometimes pass it by.[60] The rule was a ghost at the recent feast before the House of Lords in *Woolwich Building Society* v *Inland Revenue Commissioners (No 2)*[61] and, although it was not necessary to the decision[62] and was not laid to rest, it did not escape to the more murky shades of the law without comment.

Lord Keith thought that the rule "was too deeply embedded in English jurisprudence to be uprooted judicially"[63] but Lord Slynn thought it "open to review".[64] Moreover, Lord Goff referred with apparent approval to the "devastating analysis"[65] of the rule by Dickson J in Canada,[66] which led to the decision of the Supreme Court there that the distinction between mistake of fact and mistake of law should play no further part in the law of restitution in Canada.[67] Its role in the law of England must now be largely past.

---

56. *Glover* v *Metropolitan Life Ins Co*, 698 F 2d 947 (8 Cir, 1983—life).

57. *Kelly* v *Solari* (1841) 9 M & W 54, 58 *per* Lord Abinger CB (life); *Home & Colonial Ins Co Ltd* v *London Guarantee & Accident Co Ltd* (1928) 32 Ll L Rep 267 (re). The very difficulty of drawing the distinction between fact and law (above 22–2B3) is itself an argument against the rule: see *Nepean Hydro Electric Commission* v *Ontario Hydro* (1982) 132 DLR (3d) 193, 201 ff *per* Dickson J. Moreover, in *Harnischfeger Corp* v *Harbor Ins Co*, 927 F 2d 974, 977 (7 Cir, 1991—liability) the court adopted the doubts of the American Law Institute that a tenable line existed between fact and law.

58. *David Securities Pty Ltd* v *Commonwealth Bk of Australia* (1992) 66 ALJR 768; Watt [1993] LMCLQ 145. *Air Canada* v *British Columbia* (1989) 59 DLR (4th) 161, 187 ff by LaForest J, with whom Lamer and L'Heureux-Dubé JJ concurred and with whom Wilson J (p 168) agreed on this point. Zweigert & Kötz, *An Introduction to Comparative Law* (2nd ed, Oxford, 1987, transl Weir) p 261: "No comparable rule is to be found in Continental legal systems".

Cf USA: early cases bar recovery for mistake of law, for example, *Eifert* v *United States Fidelity & Guarantee Co Inc*, 31 NYS 2d 148 (1940—liability); but later courts, hostile to unjust enrichment, are less sympathetic to this defence: "the rule is harsh and should be abandoned when independent equitable considerations warrant"—*Glover* v *Metropolitan Life Ins Co*, 664 F 2d 1101, 1103 (8 Cir, 1981—life). See also *Handy* v *Lyons*, 475 SW 2d 451, 462–463 (Mo, 1971—life).

59. In Consultation Paper No 120, *Restitution of Payments Made Under a Mistake of Law*, 1991, the Law Commission considered (p 133) that the different treatment given to mistakes of law and mistakes of fact is inconsistent and arbitrary; and reached a provisional conclusion that the rule against recovery should be abolished. Arrowsmith (1990) 106 LQR 28. See also above, 22–2B3.

60. In *Rover International Ltd* v *Cannon Film Sales Ltd (No 3)* [1989] 3 All ER 423 (CA) the mistake of "fact" was that the contract in pursuance of which the sums had been paid was a valid contract, whereas in reality it was not. See also *Gibbon* v *Mitchell* [1990] 3 All ER 338. See further, Goff & Jones, pp 87 ff.

61. [1993] AC 70 (HL). An account of earlier litigation in this case is given by Birks [1991] LMCLQ 473, 497.

62. See, for example, p 176 *per* Lord Goff

63. p 154, however, his reluctance to intervene was evidently influenced by the particular context—overpayment of tax and, associated with that situation, the "nice considerations of policy which are properly the province of Parliament" (p 161).

64. p 199.

65. p 174.

66. *Nepean Hydro Electric Commission* v *Ontario Hydro* (1982) 132 DLR (3d) 193, 201 ff, in which the judge (p 206) adopted the position of Goff and Jones.

67. *Air Canada* (above).

30–5B: Essential Mistake

A mistake is an essential mistake, if the insurer would not have paid with knowledge of the truth[68]; the mistake must be "a mistake in respect of the underlying assumption of the contract or transaction or as being fundamental or basic".[69] Although, in the past, it has also been said that the mistake must have been essential to liability,[70] it does not have to be fundamental in the sense required to vitiate a contract.[71] Any mistake which causes the mistaken payment should suffice.[71a]

Cases include mistakes about entitlement, such as payment to the wrong person,[72] payment on a policy that has lapsed for non-payment of premium,[73] payment in the mistaken belief that the loss was covered by the insurance,[74] that the insured had an insurable interest,[75] and that the insured event has occurred,[76] as well as mistakes about the extent of loss[77] and mistakes in calculating the benefit payable.[78]

30–5C: Excusable Mistake

The mistake must be an excusable mistake. A mistake is excusable, said the court in *Kelly* v *Solari*,[79] though careless[80] or forgetful[81]: below, 30–5C1. Also, a mistake is not excusable, if the insurer intends to "waive all inquiry" into the matter,[82] in which case, the insurer deliberately assumes the risk of mistake: below, 30–5C2. In addition, a related but distinct bar to recovery by the insurer is reliance: that, on receipt of the insurance money, the payee has altered his position, in the belief that the money is his, to such a degree as to make recovery by the insurer inequitable: below, 30–5C3.

30–5C1 Carelessness

In *Kelly* v *Solari*,[83] a life policy lapsed because the insured, by mistake, failed to pay the quarterly premium. Although this was noted by the insurer, who marked "lapsed"

---

68. *Kelly* v *Solari* (1841) 9 M & W 54, 58 *per* Parke B (life); so, not if he would have paid anyway: *Home & Colonial Ins Co Ltd* v *London Guarantee & Accident Co Ltd* (1928) 32 Ll L Rep 267, 270 *per* Wright J (re). The principle in *Kelly* v *Solari* was applied in *Jones Ltd* v *Waring & Gillow Ltd* [1926] AC 670.

69. *Norwich Union Fire Ins Sy Ltd* v *Price Ltd* [1934] AC 455, 463 *per* Lord Wright (PC—cargo). See also *Piper* v *Royal Exchange Assurance* (1932) 44 Ll L Rep 103, 117 *per* Roche J (yacht).

70. *Aiken* v *Short* (1856) 1 H & N 210, 215 *per* Bramwell B.

71. Such as a contract of settlement: below 30–6C1.

71a. Goff & Jones p 89; cf p 100.

72. *Glover* v *Metropolitan Life Ins Co*, 698 F 2d 947 (8 Cir, 1983—life); *Faircloth* v *Northwestern National Life Ins Co*, 809 F Supp 46 (SD Ohio, 1992—life).

73. *Kelly* v *Solari* (1841) 9 M & W 54 (life).

74. *Norwich Union Fire Ins Sy Ltd* v *Price Ltd* [1934] AC 455 (PC—cargo); *London Assurance* v *Clare* (1937) 57 Ll L Rep 254 (fire).

75. *Piper* v *Royal Exchange Assurance* (1932) 44 Ll L Rep 103 (yacht).

76. For example, death: *Pilot Life Ins Co* v *Cudd*, 36 SE 2d 860 (SC, 1945—life).

77. *London Assurance* v *Clare* (1937) 57 Ll L Rep 254 (fire). *St Paul Fire & Marine Ins Co* v *Pure Oil Co*, 63 F 2d 771 (2 Cir, 1933—cargo).

78. *Mutual Life Ins Co* v *Kessler*, 202 NYS 2d 92 (1960—life).

79. (1841) 9 M & W 54, 59 *per* Parke B (life), cited with approval by Lord Wright in *Norwich Union Fire Ins Sy Ltd* v *Price Ltd* [1934] AC 455, 462 (PC—cargo).

Also in this sense: *Mutual Life Ins Co* v *Kessler*, 202 NYS 2d 92 (1960—life); *Graphic Arts Mutual Ins Co* v *Monello*, 246 NYS 2d 645, 649 (1963—workmen's compensation): this is seen as an aspect of the equitable principle underlying restitution.

80. p 59 *per* Parke B.

81. p 59 *per* Lord Abinger CB.

82. p 59. *New York Life Ins Co* v *Guttenplan*, 30 NYS 2d 430, 433 (1940—life).

83. (1841) 9 M & W 54 (life).

on the policy, when the insured died three months later and his widow—in good faith and unaware that the premium had not been paid—claimed the insurance money, the insurer paid it to her. Later, having discovered the mistake, the insurance company sought to get the money back. For the widow, it was argued that, although the company was not legally obliged to pay the money, having paid it with knowledge or the means of knowledge of the circumstances, it could not recover the money. However, ordering a new trial, the court held that the money could be recovered unless, on a new trial, it was found that the directors of the company had actual knowledge of the lapse. Baron Parke said that

"where money is paid to another under the influence of a mistake, that is, upon the supposition that a specific fact is true, which would entitle the other to the money, but which fact is untrue, and the money would not have been paid if it had been known to the payer that the fact was untrue, an action will lie to recover it back, and it is against conscience to retain it; . . . if it is paid under the impression of the truth of a fact which is untrue, it may, generally speaking, be recovered back, however careless the party paying may have been, in omitting to use diligence to inquire into the fact."[84]

Moreover, the law may be the same, if payment is made by insurer A not to B but to an innocent third party, C. In one case, that argument was accepted in principle but failed on the facts of the case, because the payment was one of insurance money on the life of B and C was B's child, for whose benefit payment was made on trust, as part of B's scheme to defraud the insurer.[85]

30–5C2 Assumption of Risk

The second point, made in *Kelly* v *Solari*,[86] was that money will not be recoverable, if the insurer has waived all inquiry into the matter. In general, if one party to a contract has taken the risk that an assumption is mistaken, the contract stands, if the assumption proves false.[87] So, if, in a spirit of compromise, perhaps to avoid uncomfortable litigation, the insurer does not dispute a claim, he cannot recover the money paid, in the absence of fraud.[88]

30–5C3 Reliance

Certain decisions of the courts, which have something of the flavour of estoppel, have barred recovery of money paid by an insurer who otherwise would have been entitled to recover that money on the ground that it had been paid by mistake.

---

84. pp 58–59, adopted in *Rover International Ltd* v *Cannon Film Sales Ltd* (*No 3*) [1989] 3 All ER 423, 441–442 by Dillon LJ (CA). See also *Prudential Ins Co* v *Harris*, 748 F Supp 445, 448 (MD La, 1990—life). *Idem*, even though the means of knowledge are such that "very slight inquiry" would have revealed the truth: *Home & Colonial Ins Co Ltd* v *London Guarantee & Accident Co Ltd* (1928) 45 TLR 134, 135 *per* Wright J (*re*).
85. *Prudential Ins Co* v *Harris*, 748 F Supp 445 (MD La, 1990—life).
86. Above, 30–5C.
87. This is true in both law and equity; see *McCrae* v *Commonwealth Disposals Commission* (1950) 84 CLR 377 (HCA); *Associated Japanese Bank* v *Credit du Nord SA* [1988] 3 All ER 902. See below, 30–6C2
88. *Da Costa* v *Firth* (1766) 4 Burr 1966 (marine); *Herbert* v *Champion* (1809) 1 Camp 134, 136 *per* Lord Ellenborough CJ (hull).
Cf Southern Farm Bureau Life Ins Co v *Burney*, 590 F Supp 1016 (ED Ark, 1984—life), affirmed 759 F 2d 658 (8 Cir, 1985) in which the insured faked his own death and disappeared. It was held that the insurer had a right to recover the amount of the insurance money from the insured, but could not rescind a settlement with beneficiaries, even though one of them was a company operated by the insured and in financial difficulty at the time of the faked death.

First, a mistake that was excusable may cease to be excusable if the insurer, after discovery of the mistake, "by neglect or unnecessary delay" allows the payee, who is "not responsible for the mistake to alter his position for the worse".[89] This may be seen as the defence of laches or delay whereby, once he knows or should have known of the mistake, time runs against the insurer.[90] Second, it has been held[91] that an employer, who overpaid his employee, could not recover the overpayment because the employee, in reliance on the representation of his employer that the money was the right wage, had spent it.[92] This was treated as a case of estoppel by representation.

These decisions may be manifestations of a wider rule, which is said[93] to go beyond estoppel, that money paid cannot be recovered, if the payee has altered his position in good faith and it would be inequitable to require repayment. A rule of this kind, which has been found for some time in Canada[94] and in the United States,[95] has now been accepted in England. Essentially, this is because the action to recover money paid by mistake is restitutionary and has its basis in the idea of unjust enrichment.[96] The decision is *Lipkin Gorman*,[97] in which Lord Goff, with whom other members of the House of Lords agreed, said this:

"[T]he defence is available to a person whose position has so changed that it would be inequitable in the circumstances to require him to make restitution in full. I wish to stress however that the mere fact that the defendant has spent the money, in whole or in part, does not of itself render it inequitable that he should be called upon to repay, because the expenditure might in any event have been incurred by him in the ordinary course of things."[98]

Further, if the person receiving money from the insured payee knows the facts which entitle the insurer to restitution before the money is dispersed, that knowledge will preclude the defence.[99] As constructive knowledge is sufficient to bar the defence of *bona fide* purchaser for value in equitable restitutionary claims, the same may be true of the defence of reliance.[100] It remains to be seen how this defence will be developed by the courts.[101]

---

89. *General Accident Fire & Life Assurance Corp Ltd* v *National Bk of New Zealand Ltd* [1932] NZLR 1289, 1292 *per* Ostler J (Sup Ct—fire).
90. Limitation Act 1980, section 32(1)(c). Goff & Jones, pp 723 ff.
91. *Avon CC* v *Howlett* [1983] 1 All ER 1073 (CA).
92. Even though the employee could not establish the full extent of his reliance, i.e. how he had spent the excess.
93. Cornish [1991] CLJ 407, 409.
94. *Storthoaks, Rural Municipality of* v *Mobil Oil Canada Ltd* [1976] 2 SCR 147: but merely to spend the money was insufficient to give rise to the defence.
95. *Mutual Life Ins Co* v *Kessler*, 202 NYS 2d 92 (1960—life); *Strubbe* v *Sonnenschein*, 299 F 2d 185 (2 Cir, 1962—life); *Glover* v *Metropolitan Life Ins Co*, 698 F 2d 947 (8 Cir, 1983—life); *Harnischfeger Corp* v *Harbor Ins Co*, 927 F 2d 974, 978 (7 Cir, 1991—liability). Rest Restitution, section 142.
Cf Allcity Ins Co v *Bankers Trust Co*, 364 NYS 2d 791 (1975—motor): the insurer, who had paid the loss payee in the mistaken belief that the insurance had not expired at the time of loss, was unable to recover from the payee, which had altered its position, but could recover from the insured, who had not.
96. *Lipkin Gorman* v *Karpnale Ltd* [1991] 2 AC 548, 559 *per* Lord Templeman, by reference to Lord Wright in the *Fibrosa case* [1943] AC 32, 61 but without awkward reference to the views of Lord Diplock in *Orakpo* v *Manson Investments Ltd* [1978] AC 95, 104.
97. Above. See Birks [1991] LMCLQ 473; McKendrick (1992) 55 MLR 377. See also *Rover International Ltd* v *Cannon Film Sales Ltd* (*No 3*) [1989] 3 All ER 423 (CA).
98. p 580 *per* Lord Goff.
99. Watts (1991) 107 LQR 521, 523.
100. *Ibid*. The answer is not apparent from the judgment of Lord Goff in *Lipkin Gorman* (above).
101. For conjecture on how such a defence might be developed, see Birks [1991] LMCLQ 473, 486 ff.

30–6 SETTLEMENT OR COMPROMISE OF CLAIMS

If an insurer declines to meet the claim in full, he may agree with the claimant a compromise or settlement of the claim and pay (less) on that basis. If the insurer pays the agreed lesser sum on the basis of a mistake and wants to recover that sum or part of it, the rules of recovery are stricter, because there is a contract of settlement[102] to be vitiated, than in a case in which there is no such contract: above, 30–5. So, it is first necessary to establish what is meant by a contract of compromise or settlement. In this context, the words compromise and settlement are often used interchangeably.[103]

The insurance claim, which is scrutinised by the insurer and then paid with the common formula "in settlement of your claim . . . ", has been said to be[104] the classic instance of implied settlement and, therefore, a contract. However, there is a difference between settling a claim and settling a dispute. In most cases, the settlement of a claim is no more than the customary language of the insurance world for the normal routine, whereby the insurer considers the claim presented in the light of the evidence and of the terms of the policy concerned, before "clearing the desk of the file" by payment.[105] Something more than this is implied by a contract of compromise or settlement. Compromise has been defined by Lord Asquith "as strictly confined to disputed rights".[106] He was concerned with the jurisdiction of the court in Chancery but there are at least three reasons for adopting a definition of this kind in the present context.

First, the very real reluctance of courts to set aside a compromise of claim is based on the desire to avoid litigation: below, 30–6C2(b). In some degree, therefore, litigation must be in prospect, when a claim is compromised, although it is not essential that litigation has been actually threatened[107] or that each party's position could have been sustained in a court of law.[108] Second, the concern of the law to ensure the reality of consideration,[109] when claims are compromised by contract, indicates a very real element of give and take and, therefore, a very real (although perhaps misguided or trivial) dispute. Third, if compromise is given a broader meaning than suggested by Lord Asquith, the obstacles in law to a subsequent plea of mistake might make the insurer unduly cautious about paying the sum claimed in the first place, in case his compliance be seen as a compromise of that kind,[110] with the associated difficulty of recovering sums paid by mistake. So, if there is no dispute in a real sense, the better

---

102. *Harnischfeger Corp* v *Harbor Ins Co*, 927 F 2d 974, 978 (7 Cir, 1991—liability).

103. *Goldbard* v *Empire State Mutual Life Ins Co*, 171 NYS 2d 194 (1958—PA). This usage is accepted also in England: Andrews [1989] LMCLQ 431, 435.

104. Andrews p 436.

105. For example, *Prudential Ins Co* v *Harris*, 748 F Supp 445 (MD La, 1990—life), in which the court rejected the argument that payment of a £250,000 under a life contract, when the life had apparently been drowned after being swept overboard from a ferry off the coast of New Zealand, was payment by way of settlement, as there was no "underlying dispute" (p 448). See also *Pilot Life Ins Co* v *Cudd*, 36 SE 2d 860, 865 (SC, 1945—life): the death of missing seaman was not denied but uncertain, as no body had been found; after two years the insurer paid, but then the life turned up in a Japanese PoW camp; the insurer recovered the payment.

106. *Chapman* v *Chapman* [1954] AC 429, 470.

107. Foskett, The Law and Practice of Compromises (London, 3rd ed, 1991) p 5.

108. Andrews [1989] LMCLQ 431, 435. *Cf Chapman* v *Chapman*, *loc cit*.

109. Below 30– 6D.

110. *Phoenix Indemnity Co* v *Steiden Stores Inc*, 267 SW 2d 733, 735 (Ky, 1954—theft); *Harnischfeger Corp* v *Harbor Ins Co*, 927 F 2d 974, 977 (7 Cir, 1991—liability).

view is that, by payment, the insurer is performing the contract of insurance itself and not a subsequent contract of settlement.[111]

In *Magee v Pennine Ins Co*,[112] for example, the claimant put in a "hopeful" claim of £600. The insurer did not expostulate, but simply responded with an "offer" of £385—which the claimant accepted. For a while there was a wide disagreement and the agreement that followed, although reached swiftly with scarcely a crossing of letters still less a crossing of swords, was treated as a contract of compromise. Sometimes, the line between a dispute and an undisputed settlement may be fine[113] but a line there is.

If a compromise there is, the compromise reached must appear to have been final. So, the claimant, who cashes a cheque from the insurer marked "in full settlement of all claims", does not thereby accept an offer of compromise for (no more than) the amount of the cheque, unless an intention to accept on those terms was clear in all the circumstances.[114] The degree of compromise must also be clear; any ambiguity will be construed against the insurer.[115] If an agreement is discernible, there is a strong presumption that, like any commercial contract, it is intended to be binding in law.[116]

As contract, a compromise or settlement must be based on mutual consent.[117] It will usually be in writing. He who signs a document setting out the terms of the settlement is bound by his signature,[118] unless the other induced consent by misrepresen-

111. A contract of settlement is one of the few instances in which the law questions the adequacy of consideration. What is true of potential claimants (for example *Poteliakoff v Teakle* [1938] 2 KB 816 (CA)) should also be true of those against whom the claim is brought: Treitel pp 82–83.
112. [1969] 2 QB 507, 513 (CA—motor)
113. Settlement is said to be "implied" when the parties sense an underlying problem, which might grow into an articulated dispute, but, notwithstanding the circumstances of doubt, one party pays and the other accepts the payment: Andrews pp 437–438; *sed quaere.*
114. *Bremer Handelsgesellschaft v Westzucker GmbH* [1981] 1 Lloyd's Rep 207, affirmed [1981] 2 Lloyd's Rep 130 (CA). *Decelle v Lloyd's of London* (1973) 33 DLR (3d) 743, 746 and cases cited (Sask—fire). *Cheek v Commonwealth Life Ins Co*, 126 SW 2d 1084 (Ky, 1939—life); *Baker v Hartford Ins Co*, 152 NYS 2d 1003 (1956—fire). However, in the case of a written contract, intention is governed by the terms of the document and the court will not consider evidence of what was said to the claimant, except on issues of misrepresentation and *non est factum*: *Arrale* (below). Also *ACF Produce Inc v Chubb/Pacific Indemnity Group*, 451 F Supp 1095 (ED Pa, 1978—goods in transit).
115. *Arrale v Costain Civil Engineering Ltd* [1976] 1 Lloyd's Rep 98 (CA). *Continental Ins Co v Dunne*, 226 F 2d 471 (9 Cir, 1955—fire).
116. However, courts have recognised that sometimes parties prefer to avoid lawyers and "the accompanying necessity of expressing themselves so precisely that outsiders may have no difficulty in understanding what they mean", and to rely on each other's good faith and honour: *Rose & Frank Co v Crompton & Bros Ltd* [1923] 2 KB 261, 288 *per* Scrutton LJ (CA), applied in *Orion Ins Co plc v Sphere Drake Ins plc* [1992] 1 Lloyd's Rep 239, 263 *per* Lloyd LJ (CA), concerning the outstanding liabilities of companies withdrawing from a pool in the London market.
117. *Rideal v GWR Co* (1859) 1 F & F 706, 707–708 *per* Erle CJ (PA); *Lee v Lancashire & Yorkshire Ry Co* (1871) LR 6 Ch 527, 533 *per* Sir William James LJ (PA). *Goldbard v Empire State Mutual Life Ins Co*, 171 NYS 2d 194 (1958—PA); *Ben-Morris Co v Hanover Ins Co*, 333 NE 2d 455 (Mass, 1975—fire). Appleman, sections 3921 ff.
118. *Arrale v Costain Civil Engineering Ltd* [1976] 1 Lloyd's Rep 98, 105 *per* Stephenson LJ (CA). *Wells v Progressive Ins Co* (1954) 35 MPR 234 (Nfdl—motor). *ACF Produce Inc v Chubb/Pacific Indemnity Group*, 451 F Supp 1095 (ED Pa, 1978—goods in transit). It is in the public interest to encourage settlements: *Allstate Ins Co v Riverside Ins Co*, 509 F Supp 43, 48 (ED Mich, 1981—motor).

tation,[119] including misleading him about the contents of the document,[120] failed to disclose material information (below, 30-6A), or exercised undue influence to obtain agreement (30-6B). In these cases the contract is voidable. Further, the contract may be void or voidable on the ground of mistake (below, 30–6C). However, the argument, that a settlement or compromise of claim can be impugned under section 10 of the Unfair Contract Terms Act 1977, as being an unreasonable exemption of liability, has been rejected: the Act is concerned solely with clauses that affect prospective liability and does not concern settlements of retrospective claims.[121]

30–6A Good Faith: Disclosure

When a claim of any kind is compromised, the claim must be *bona fide* or "honest"; and, as Cotton LJ observed,[122] "if both parties know all the facts, and with knowledge of those facts obtain a compromise, it cannot be said that that is dishonest". As regards contracts of insurance, the duty of good faith is mutual duty and a continuing one.[123] The duty continues during the currency of the contract, at a level appropriate to the moment, and it applies to claims and to the compromise of claims.

On the claimant's side, a compromise of claim will not be binding, if the claim was fraudulent[124] but, further, as Lord Ellenborough said,[125] an insurer is not bound by an adjustment "unless there was full disclosure of the circumstances of the case" by the claimant.

On the insurer's side, clearly there is a duty of disclosure in the sense of a duty to explain the terms of settlement proposed. In England, a claimant workman is not bound by a compromise or settlement, unless the insurer made it "clear to the workman that it was a once and for all payment and no more could be obtained".[126] In Illinois, when the claimant is a person "with little education and with little or no experience with insurance contracts, the insurance carrier owed him the utmost good faith in its dealings with him after the loss".[127] In Ontario,[128] even when the signatory

---

119. *Saunders* v *Ford Motor Co Ltd* [1970] 1 Lloyd's Rep 379 (employers' liability); *Arrale* v *Costain Civil Engineering Ltd* [1976] 1 Lloyd's Rep 98, 101 *per* Lord Denning MR, 105 *per* Stephenson LJ (CA), with reference to *Curtis* v *Chemical Cleaning & Dyeing Co* [1951] 1 KB 805 (CA).

United States v *Home Ins Co*, 142 F Supp 478 (SD Ill, 1956—fire); including an inadvertent misrepresentation of law by the insurer's agent: *Dixon* v *Pacific Mutual Life Ins Co*, 268 F 2d 812, 815 (2 Cir, 1959—disability). On whether the claimant is bound by misrepresentations made by his own agent, see O'Donnell, 22 Tort & Ins L J 662, 663 ff (1987).

120. *Lee* v *Lancashire & Yorkshire Ry Co* (1871) LR 6 Ch 527, 532–533 *per* Sir William James LJ, 534 *per* Sir G Mellish LJ (PA); *Curtis* v *Chemical Cleaning & Dyeing Co* [1951] 1 KB 805 (CA).

121. *Tudor Grange Holdings Ltd* v *Citibank NA* [1991] 4 All ER 1.

122. *Miles* v *New Zealand Alford Estate Co* (1886) 32 Ch D 266, 284 (CA).

123. *The Litsion Pride* [1985] 1 Lloyd's Rep 437, 511 *per* Hirst J (hull). See above, ch 27.

124. *Stanley Trucking Co Inc* v *National Indemnity Co*, 136 NW 2d 101 (Minn, 1965—theft).

125. *Shepherd* v *Chewter* (1808) 1 Camp 274, 275 (hull).

126. *Saunders* v *Ford Motor Co Ltd* [1970] 1 Lloyd's Rep 379, 386 *per* Paull J (employers' liability); also *Horry* v *Tate & Lyle Refineries Ltd* [1982] 2 Lloyd's Rep 416, 422 *per* Peter Pain J. In so far as the insurer is obliged to provide the claimant with information, the relationship has been described as a fiduciary relationship: *Horry, loc cit*. But note also the (questionable) view, that inequality of information gives rise to a presumption of (undue) influence, below 30–6B.

127. *United States* v *Home Ins Co*, 142 F Supp 478, 479 (SD Ill, 1956—fire).

128. *Stevens* v *Howitt* (1969) 4 DLR (3d) 50, 52 (Ont—motor). See also *Beach* v *Eames*, 82 DLR (3d) 736, 741 (Ont, 1976—motor).

had "ample time to read and study the document" and there was no misrepresentation or fraud on the part of the adjuster,

"his experience and knowledge makes it incumbent upon him to take care to explain the nature and contents of the document which he is requesting persons who are inexperienced and ignorant in the area of insurance and indemnity to sign. . . . [T]here is a very heavy responsibility in these circumstances upon the representative of the insurance company when dealing with unknowledgeable parties to see to it that the terms of the agreement itself and their ramifications are clearly understood".

In Puerto Rico, however, when the claimant was a person of limited formal education but a practical and successful businessman with the opportunity to take legal advice, he negotiated with the insurer's adjuster at arm's-length.[129] And, whatever the education of the claimant, if the document is fully explained to him, he is bound by it notwithstanding his misconceptions about the nature of the document, misconceptions of which the insurer's representative was unaware.[130]

It seems safe to conclude that, when there is inequality of bargaining power between insurer and insured, the insurer has a duty to explain the terms of the settlement proposed. What is less clear is whether the insurer's duty goes further than this and extends, for example, to the advisability of settlement.

In Pennsylvania in *Dercoli*,[131] a majority of the judges asserted that the "duty of an insurance company to deal with the insured fairly and in good faith includes the duty of full and complete disclosure as to all the benefits and every coverage that is provided . . . along with all requirements, including any time limitations for making a claim. This is especially true where the insurer undertakes to advise and counsel the insured in the insured's claim for benefits". This is perhaps the most expansive application yet of what has been called the "Tennessee Rule".[132] Other courts have been more cautious. Dissenting judges in *Dercoli*[133] argued persuasively that, if the Tennessee Rule applies, insurers will be reluctant even to talk to claimants, except perhaps to point them to a professional legal advisor, lest an "undertaking to advise and counsel" be inferred. Moreover, if insurers do talk to claimants, "what will their obligations be? Are they obliged to advise of innovative claims against themselves? Are they obligated to inform claimants of an improbable but perhaps conceivable claim that they themselves would not agree to pay? Are they, as in this case, obligated to be on the lookout for changes in the law which might be favourable to a claimant?"

In general, if the insured is unaware of the terms of his insurance contract, he cannot blame his agent or his insurer,[134] and it seems safer to take the side of the

---

129. *Home Ins Co* v *Davila*, 212 F 2d 731, 741 (1 Cir, 1954—fire).

130. *Bradley* v *Southern Farm Bureau Casualty Ins Co*, 392 F Supp 478 (ED Ark, 1975—motor); *Elson* v *Delaney*, 365 NYS 2d 572 (1975—motor).

131. *Dercoli* v *Pennsylvania National Mutual Ins Co*, 554 A 2d 906, 909 (Pa, 1989—motor); the claimant was severely injured in the relevant accident. She was referred to (p 911) as "a bereaved, defenseless, unsuspecting and trusting widow". To some members of the court, it was significant that the insurer offered advice and "talked the widow out of seeking independent legal counsel" (*ibid*).

132. *Darlow* v *Farmers Ins. Exchange*, 822 P 2d 820, 827 (Wyo, 1991—motor), with reference to *Gatlin* v *Tennessee Farmers Mutual Ins Co*, 741 SW 2d 324 (Tenn, 1987—motor).

133. p 912.

134. *Perkins* v *Shelter Ins Co*, 540 So 2d 488, 490 (La, 1989—group health and accident): "The insured is presumed to know the provisions of his policy and the insurer is not statutorily bound to send written notice of conversion rights." Generally on this point, see above, 11–2A2.

dissenters: the insurer has no duty to provide this kind of tactical advice unless he has clearly assumed the responsibility for providing it. If the insurer in England has assumed and broken a duty of this kind, he may be estopped from raising a defence, such as a time bar.[135] In England, unlike the USA, he will not be liable in damages.

30–6A1 Good Faith between Insurers

Between insurer and excess insurer in New York, "the primary carrier owes to the excess insurer the same fiduciary obligation which the primary insurer owes to the insured". The courts recognise "a direct and independent relationship between primary and excess insurance carriers" of this kind.[136] But, in Michigan, it has been held that, when negotiating a compromise with the insured, the primary insurer owes no duty to an excess insurer of the same risk to "bargain with the insured in good faith",[137] except to keep the excess insurer informed of the negotiations and provide him with an opportunity to participate in the negotiations[138]; in this situation, the principal duty of the primary insurer is to the insured.[139] Equally, when negotiating a settlement with his insurer, the liability insured owes no duty to the person to whom he is liable, unless such a duty has been assumed; that person will be refused an injunction to restrain a settlement that is too low.[140]

30–6B Undue Influence

If a contract is concluded between two persons, one of whom has undue influence over the other, the court has power to set the contract aside, unless it appears that, in spite of the influence, the person subject to the influence exercised independent judgement in the matter.

Undue influence does not mean improper influence but influence to a degree that is not usual; this is a question of fact.[141] Certain relationships give rise to a presumption

---

135. As in *Davis* v *State Farm Ins Co*, 262 Cal Rptr 595 (1989—AR).

136. *Hartford Accident & Indemnity Co* v *Commercial Union Ins Co*, 772 F Supp 741 (ED NY, 1991—liability).

137. *Allstate Ins Co* v *Riverside Ins Co*, 509 F Supp 43, 46 (ED Mich, 1981—motor); in that case the compromise did not have the effect of enlarging the liability of the excess insurer to the insured (pp 47–48). Indeed, the excess contract may stipulate that the excess insurer is not liable at all, unless the primary insurer is liable for the full sum insured, i.e., for an amount greater than the compromise sum agreed by the latter with the insured: for example, *United States Fire Ins Co* v *Lay*, 577 F 2d 421 (7 Cir, 1978—liability). As to the possibility of a duty of care owed by the primary insurer to the excess insurer and actionable in tort, see Sehr, Blume and Elenius, 27 Tort & Ins L J 226, 227 (1992).

138. *Allstate* (above), p 47.

139. *Ibid.*

140. *Normid Housing Assn Ltd* v *Ralphs* [1989] 1 Lloyd's Rep 265 (CA—liability); *aliter* perhaps if the settlement is fraudulent.

141. *National Westminster Bk* v *Morgan* [1985] AC 686, 708 *per* Lord Scarman. Such statements suggest that the mere existence of a certain kind of relationship cannot give rise to a presumption of undue influence, but may give rise to a presumption of influence, which together with unfair terms may be enough to make a case for avoidance of the contract.

of undue influence but the relationship between insurer and insured is not one of them; there is undue influence only if it can be shown that "by reason of the trust and confidence" of such a nature that one did or can fairly be presumed to have abused that relationship in procuring the impugned transaction.[142] However, actual abuse such as unfair settlement terms does not have to be shown.[143]

If there is undue influence whether or not the settlement was unduly favourable to the insurer,[144] or to the "manifest disadvantage" of the claimant insured,[145] equity will intervene. The contract will be set aside at the suit of the claimant, unless the insurer can prove that the compromise was agreed by the claimant by the "free exercise of an independent will"[146]; in practice this means that the claimant must have had independent advice from a competent person based on knowledge of all relevant facts.[147]

In particular, if the insurer does no more than explain the legal effect of the proposed compromise, that without more does not indicate undue influence.[148] If the insured takes advice from the insurer on general matters germane to the wisdom of the compromise, that indicates but does not necessarily prove undue influence,[149] but when a claimant *relies* on the insurer for guidance and advice and the insurer knows this,[150] he has crossed the line, it seems, and the insurer is in a position of undue influence. This was the position in *Horry*[151] between the employer's liability insurer and the employee claimant; and is generally the position of any insurer dealing with claimants, who are "poor and ignorant persons acting without independent advice",[152] and perhaps also with claimants in pressing need of speedy payment.[153]

---

142. *Barclays Bank plc* v *O'Brien* [1993] 4 All ER 417, 423 *per* Lord Browne-Wilkinson (HL).

In California, it has been held of settlements that in cases affording an opportunity for "overreaching", the law demands good faith on the part of the insurer and full understanding on the part of the claimant: *DuBois* v *Sparrow*, 154 Cal Rptr 717, 722 (Cal, 1979—motor).

143. *CIBC Mortgages plc* v *Pitt* [1993] 4 All ER 433 (HL).

144. In Arkansas, if the amount settled is grossly inadequate, that raises an inference of fraud: *Bradley* v *Southern Farm Bureau Casualty Ins Co*, 392 F Supp 478 (ED Ark, 1975—motor).

145. *Bank of Credit & Commerce International SA* v *Aboody* [1990] 1 QB 923 (CA) was overruled in this respect by *CIBC* (above).

146. *Inche Noriah* v *Shaik Allie bin Omar* [1929] AC 127, 135 *per* Lord Hailsham LC (PC).

147. *Horry* v *Tate & Lyle Refineries Ltd* [1982] 2 Lloyd's Rep 416, 421 *per* Peter Pain J (employers' liability).

148. *Cornish* v *Midland Bank plc* [1985] 3 All ER 513 (CA).

149. *Morgan* (below).

150. *Horry*, p 421 *per* Peter Pain J, relying on the judgment of Sachs LJ in *Lloyds Bk Ltd* v *Bundy* [1975] QB 326, 341 (CA). *Quaere* whether this part of the judgment of Sachs LJ was unscathed by Lord Scarman in *National Westminster Bk* v *Morgan* [1985] AC 686, 708. See also *Pridmore* v *Calvert* (1975) 54 DLR (3d) 133, 140–141 (BC—motor).

151. Above, note 98.

152. *Towers* v *Affleck* [1974] 1 WWR 714, 720 (BC—motor). In the same sense: *Arrale* v *Costain Civil Engineering Ltd* [1976] 1 Lloyd's Rep 98, 102 *per* Lord Denning MR (CA). See also the contention that, if one party consciously takes advantage of the other's ignorance and lack of advice, this is "unconscionable" to a degree "which might have justifed the intervention of equity": Beale, (1986) 6 OJLS 123, 126; this is a startling contention, inasmuch as it refers to any kind of contract, however, it is much less so as regards contracts compromising insurance claims.

153. *D & C Builders Ltd* v *Rees* [1966] 2 QB 617 (CA); *Multiservice Bookbinding Ltd* v *Marden* [1979] Ch 84, 111. *Cf Lobb (Garages) Ltd* v *Total Oil GB Ltd* [1983] 1 All ER 944. *Reliable Furniture Co* v *Fidelity & Guarantee Ins Underwriters Inc*, 398 P 2d 685, 687 (Utah, 1965—business interruption).

These claimants are not on equal footing with the insurer.[154] If so,[155] it may be set aside. This is the remedy of rescission, which is barred, if the contract has been affirmed[156] and, generally, if the person seeking rescission cannot hand back what he has received; in the case of undue influence, however, it has been held that the requirement of restitution does not apply.[157]

30–6C Settlement by Mistake

At common law, a contract of settlement or compromise is void, if made on the basis of a fundamental mistake[158] and if neither party has assumed the risk of the mistake.[159] With one exception,[160] it is some years since a court has found a mistake fundamental to the degree required by common law,[161] and one reason for this may be the development of a more flexible doctrine of mistake in equity.[162]

In equity,[163] there is an operative mistake, if there is a fundamental mistake (below, 30–6C1), if neither party has assumed the risk of the mistake (30–6C2), and if the person seeking relief is not at fault (30–6C3). The contract is then liable to be set aside by the court, subject, however, to the usual bars to rescission.[164] (30–6C4)

If the contract is embodied in a formal document, which has been signed by the person mistaken, a distinct but strict doctrine of common law declares the document void on the ground of *non est factum* (30–6C5).

30–6C1 *Fundamental Mistake*

For a contract to be declared void (common law) or voidable (equity), there must be, it has been said, a fundamental mistake (common law) or a fundamental misappre-

---

154. A general doctrine of inequality of bargaining power was advanced by Lord Denning in *Lloyds Bk Ltd* v *Bundy* [1975] QB 326, 339 (CA); it is found in Canada but was later rejected in England by Lord Scarman in *National Westminster Bk* v *Morgan* [1985] AC 686, 708. See Enman, "Doctrines of Unconscionability in Canadian, English and Commonwealth Contract Law", 16 Anglo-American L Rev 191 (1987), and Clark, *Inequality of Bargaining Power*, (Toronto, 1987) who show that, as regards contracts generally, the courts of Canada are more likely to set a contract aside than are the courts in England.

In the USA, settlements have been subject to the doctrine of inequality of bargaining power for some time: Schulz, 15 *Law & Contemporary Problems* 376, 387 (1950).

155. *Pridmore* v *Calvert* (1975) 54 DLR (3d) 133 (BC—motor).

156. Above, 23–18B.

157. *O'Sullivan* v *Management Agency & Music Ltd* [1985] QB 428 (CA).

158. *Bell* v *Lever Bros Ltd* [1932] AC 161. See further, Andrews [1989] LMCLQ 431.

159. For example, *McCrae* v *Commonwealth Disposals Commission* (1950) 84 CLR 377 (HCA).

160. *Associated Japanese BK (Int) Ltd* v *Crédit du Nord SA* [1988] 3 All ER 902.

161. The last reported case in which a contract was declared void on this ground without controversy was *Cundy* v *Lindsay* (1878) 3 App Cas 459.

162. Other reasons are that whereas courts in the last century sought the true intention of the parties, courts today are more concerned with the appearance of consent and its effect on third parties.

163. The legitimacy of a separate doctrine in equity is a matter of doubt: for example, Goodhart, (1950) 66 LQR 169; Cartwright, (1987) 103 LQR 594; but the doctrine cannot be ignored as it has been applied three times by the Court of Appeal: *Solle* v *Butcher* [1950] 1 KB 671; *Peters* v *Batchelor* (1950) 100 LJ 718; *Magee* v *Pennine Ins Co Ltd* [1969] 2 QB 507 (motor). See above, chapter 21.

164. Treitel, pp 338 ff.

hension (equity). A fundamental misapprehension in equity is less fundamental than a fundamental mistake at common law; beyond this, there is little to be said without resorting to cases.

In *Magee* v *Pennine Ins Co Ltd*[165] a compromise of claim was agreed on the mistaken assumption that the insurance contract was enforceable.[166] An action by the insured to enforce the compromise failed. While the compromise was not void at common law, it was voidable in equity by reason of a common and fundamental misapprehension as to the rights of the parties.[167] Again, cases not concerning insurance establish that a mistake about the value of the property contracted for may be fundamental.[168] This suggests the same for a serious mistake about the extent or amount of the insured's recoverable loss.[169]

30–6C2   Assumption of Risk

If one party has taken the risk that an assumption was mistaken, in general the contract stands in spite of the mistake.[170] However, as regards the compromise of claims, it should be recalled that the "general words in a release are limited to that thing or those things which were specially in the contemplation of the parties at the time when the release was given".[171]

(a) *Risks Assumed by the Claimant*. If, in the absence of fraud, misrepresentation, non-disclosure or undue influence, the claimant signs a document compromising a claim as regards "all unknown and unanticipated injuries and damages", the claimant assumes the risk of mistake and is bound by his agreement.[172]

For example, in *Kitchen Design & Advice Ltd* v *Lea Valley Water Co*[173] the action turned on a form of discharge, which was expressed to be "in full satisfaction, liquidation and discharge of all claims . . . in connection with a burst water main". QBE, with whom the plaintiffs were insured against both physical damage and business interruption, indemnified the plaintiffs in respect of physical damage caused by the burst water main, for which the defendants were responsible, and, as empowered by the terms of the insurance contract, settled the plaintiffs' claim against the defendants

---

165. [1969] 2 QB 507 (CA—motor).

166. It could have been avoided for non-fraudulent misrepresentation in the proposal.

167. p 514 *per* Lord Denning MR, applying his own statement in *Solle* v *Butcher* [1950] 1 KB 671, 693 (CA). *Cf* the view of Winn LJ (dissenting p 516) that operative mistakes are confined to subject-matter and do not embrace mistakes about rights.

168. For example *Re Garnett* (1885) 31 Ch D 1 (CA); *Grist* v *Bailey* [1967] Ch 532.

169. Cases, in which the settlement by a claimant unaware of the full extent of his injury was not binding, include: *Roberts* v *Eastern Counties Ry Co* (1859) 1 F & F 460 (PA). There is some authority that, while a mistake about the quality of the subject-matter of the contract does not make a contract void, a mistake about quantity does. See Treitel, p 257.

Also in the sense of the text: *Kent* v *Ocean Accident & Guarantee Corp* (1909) 20 OLR 226 (PA). *Hind Ltd* v *Silva*, 75 F 2d 74 (9 Cir, 1935—motor); *United States* v *Drake & Beemont Mutual Aid Sy*, 218 F Supp 155 (ED Mo, 1963—fire), affirmed 330 F 2d 548 (8 Cir, 1964). *Cf* below, 30–6C2.

170. This is true in both law and equity; see *McCrae* v *Commonwealth Disposals Commission* (1950) 84 CLR 377 (HCA).

171. *London & SWR Co* v *Blackmore* (1870) LR 4 HL 610, 623 *per* Lord Westbury. See also *Kent* v *Ocean* (above), p 232.

172. *Berry* v *Struble*, 66 P 2d 746 (Cal, 1937—motor).

173. [1989] 2 Lloyd's Rep 221.

on the terms of the form of discharge. Then, the plaintiffs submitted a further claim to QBE in respect of lost profits. QBE turned to the defendants, who pleaded the settlement. Deciding for the defendants, Phillips J held that "the natural meaning and effect of the form of discharge was that the defendants were to be discharged of all liability in respect of claims by QBE's assured to which QBE were, or might become, subrogated . . . The risk of further claims was, however, one of the very matters against which the discharge was intended to protect the defendants and their underwriters, and there is no doctrine of mistake that the plaintiffs can invoke which avoids the effect of the form of discharge".[174]

Some courts, however, have been reluctant to infer an assumption of risk, if the injury was unknown and unanticipated and, therefore, was "not within the contemplation of the parties when the settlement was agreed upon"[175]; that is a question of fact in the particular case.[176] Some decisions distinguish a mistake about the existence of injury, which avoids the contract, and mistake about the extent of a known injury, which does not.[177]

(b) *Risks Assumed by the Insurer.* If it is the insurer's business practice to compromise doubtful claims, this may be seen as an assumption of risk. In the absence of fraud,[178] he is bound by settlements agreed. When

"the insurer makes a mistake as to the existence of a material fact, although the insurer recognizes the possibility of its non-existence, and is fully conscious that there is an uncertainty as to whether or not the money is due, voluntarily makes the payment at the request of the beneficiary, it will be assumed that the payment is made to avoid difficulty which might arise from its non-payment".[179]

Again, when the insurer, who "could have drafted the release contract on the assumption by both parties that [the insured] was dead . . . made a 'business decision to settle the case' ", he could not repudiate the settlement with the beneficiary, when the insured was discovered alive.[180] There had been an assumption of risk by the insurer. Moreover, when there is dispute and compromise on some matters but not on others, it seems that the insurer may have assumed the risk of some matters germane to compromise but not of all matters affecting his liability to pay. Thus, if there is a dispute and compromise over the amount of loss, it does not follow that the insurer has assumed the risk that the contract of insurance was voidable from the beginning.[181]

---

174. p 224.

175. *Aronovitch* v *Levy*, 56 NW 2d 570, 576 (Minn, 1953—employers' liability).

176. *Ibid.*

177. For example, *Aronovitch* (above); *Kostick* v *Swain*, 253 P 2d 531 (Cal, 1953—motor); *Elson* v *Delaney*, 365 NYS 2d 572 (1975—motor). However, in some courts the reason is that a mistake about the likely development of an injury is a mistake of opinion, rather than a mistake of present or past fact: *Turner* v *Mutual Benefit Health & Accident Assn*, 160 NYS 2d 883, 890 (1957—PA). Yet, in one case, a compromise of a claim for landslide loss did not end the liability of the insurer, when the insured was quite unaware that the slide was continuing: *General Ins Co* v *Lapidus*, 325 F 2d 287 (9 Cir, 1963). *Cf* also cases such as *Roberts* v *Eastern Counties* above.

178. *Da Costa* v *Firth* (1766) 4 Burr 1966 (marine); *Re Norske Lloyd Ins Co Ltd* [1928] WN 99 (re); *Holmes* v *Payne* [1930] 2 KB 301 (jewellery), which concerned replacement, but Roche J said (p 309) that he saw "no distinction between payment and replacement". In *Prudential Ins Co* v *Harris*, 748 F Supp 445 (MD La, 1990—life), the insurer recovered from an innocent minor insurance money on the life of his father obtained by the fraud of the parents.

179. *Phoenix Indemnity Co* v *Steiden Stores Inc*, 267 SW 2d 733, 734–735 (Ky, 1954—theft). See also *New York Life Ins Co* v *Chittenden*, 112 NW 96 (Iowa, 1907—life).

180. *Southern Farm Bureau Life Ins Co* v *Burney*, 590 F Supp 1016, 1020 (ED Ark, 1984—life), affirmed 759 F 2d 658 (8 Cir, 1985).

181. The situation in *Magee* v *Pennine Ins Co Ltd*, above, 30–6C1.

In England, the assumption of risk by the insurer is confirmed by social policy. There is one factor of "peculiar importance",[182] that "money paid under the pressure of legal process cannot be recovered"[183] on the ground of mistake, provided that the payee has acted in good faith.[184] "The principle is based upon this, that when a person has had an opportunity of defending an action if he chose, but has thought proper to pay the money claimed by the action, the law will not allow him to try in a second action what he might have set up in the defence to the original action."[185] In other words, the principle is based on finality and the desire to avoid unnecessary litigation which is vexatious and wasteful.[186]

30–6C3   Fault

When the insurer brings an action to recover a payment by mistake, the action may succeed, even though he has been negligent: above, 30–5B. However, when a party seeks to have a contract set aside in equity for mistake, that party must not have been "at fault".[187] It is not clear what this means[188] but it is possible that relief will be refused to one who has been negligent.[189]

In Illinois, it has been held that a settlement, made on the basis of a negligent miscalculation by the insurer in favour of the claimant, will not be rescinded on the ground of mistake.[190] In New York also, a negligent overpayment by the insurer could not be recovered, although in that case it was a condition of the court's decision that the payee was unaware of the error.[191]

30–6C4   Bars to Rescission

If, as is likely, the insurer's right to recover the money depends on rescission of the contract of compromise on the ground of the equitable doctrine of mistake, rescission and thus recovery will be blocked by the usual bars to rescission.[192] To judge by decisions in New York, this may be a considerable obstacle. In one case, *Mazzola*,[193] the insurer's argument for rescission failed *inter alia* because the parties could not be put in *status quo ante*: rescission

"would mean that plaintiff could be put into a position of trying her case more than one year after it has originally been scheduled for trial. If plaintiff were placed in such a position, it is

---

182. Goff & Jones, p 107.

183. *Moore* v *Vestry of Fulham* [1894] 1 QB 392, 401 *per* Lord Halsbury (CA). It is not necessary that judgment has been delivered, only that proceedings have been commenced (p 402).

184. *Ward & Co* v *Lewis* [1900] 1 QB 675, 678 *per* Kennedy J.

185. *Moore* (above), *loc cit*.

186. Andrews [1989] LMCLQ 431, 432 ff and references given. USA *idem*: Fischer, 27 Tort & Ins L J 82, 85 (1991).

187. *Solle* v *Butcher* [1950] 1 KB 671 (CA).

188. Treitel, p 284.

189. *Cf Laurence* v *Lexcourt Holdings Ltd* [1978] 2 All ER 810 and *The Lloydiana* [1983] 2 Lloyd's Rep 313, 318 *per* Sheen J. *Associated Japanese Bk (Int) Ltd* v *Crédit du Nord SA* [1988] 3 All ER 902, 913 *per* Steyn J.

190. *Keller* v *State Farm Ins Co* 536 NE 2d 194 (Ill, 1989—tornado). *Semble* it was relevant in this case that the claimant had relied on the agreed settlement to the extent of contracting to buy a house to replace the house destroyed by the insured event (p 201).

191. *Mazzola* v *CNA Ins Co*, 548 NYS 2d 610, 613 (1989—motor): the mistaken payment (in excess of the policy limit) was to a third party injured by the insured motorist.

192. Treitel p 285. Generally, see above 23–18.

193. *Mazzola* (above).

clear that she would not be in status quo since at best the memories of her witnesses would be diminished by the passage of time and, at worst, her witnesses may be totally unavailable for trial. In addition, to allow defendant to void (sic) the settlement and put the plaintiff through the expense of renegotiation and possibly a trial would subject plaintiff to additional and costly legal fees. Finally, if the settlement were voided (sic), plaintiff would be at a tactical disadvantage having already disclosed to defendant the value of her claim".[194]

In a general way, this kind of bar to rescission shadows the defence to an action in restitution based on the payee's reliance: above, 30–5C3.

30–6C5 Documents Mistakenly Signed

If a signatory is fundamentally mistaken about the contents of the document signed, the document is void, unless he is negligent in signing.[195] This mistake is one about what the document says or means, rather than one about suppositions of fact that lie behind consent (above, 30–6C1). In an old case, in which relief was granted, the claimant had reason to believe that the document was no more than a receipt for part payment.[196] Today, the law is strict and even the uneducated and vulnerable find it hard to obtain relief, as the attitude is taken that they should understand that they are taking an important step in a matter which, perhaps, they do not understand and, therefore, take advice before signature.[197]

30–6D Consideration

The contract of compromise must be supported by consideration from each party.[198] Each party renounces his original (bargaining) position and accepts a compromise. Although generally the law does not question the adequacy of consideration, an exception applies to contracts of compromise: it is in the public interest[199] to ensure that the position abandoned was a *bona fide* position, lest improper pressure (threat of litigation, refusal to pay and fund starvation) be brought to bear on a weaker party. Accordingly, the general law requires of the claimant that he has reasonable (objective) grounds for the claim[200] and that he has an honest (subjective) belief in its chances of success.[201] The claim must have been put forward in good faith.[201a] Less

---

194. pp 613–614.
195. *Gallie* v *Lee* [1971] AC 1004.
196. *Rideal* v *GWR Co* (1859) 1 F & F 706 (PA); see also *Lee* v *Lancashire & Yorkshire Ry Co* (1871) LR 6 Ch 527, 533 *per* Sir William James LJ (PA).
197. *Norwich and Peterborough Building Sy* v *Steed (No 2)* [1993] 1 All ER 330 (CA). Generally, it will be negligent to trust the profferor of the document to explain the contents, unless the signatory is of low education and intelligence, as in *Beach* v *Eames*, 82 DLR 3d 736 (Ont, 1976—motor); see further, above, 10–3A.
198. *Arrale* v *Costain Civil Engineering Ltd* [1976] 1 Lloyd's Rep 98 (CA).
  Occidental Life Ins Co v *Eiler* 125 F 2d 229 (8 Cir, 1942—PA), cert den 316 US 688; *Continental Ins Co* v *Dunne* 226 F 2d 471 (9 Cir, 1955—fire).
199. *Poteliakoff* v *Teakle* [1938] 2 KB 816, 824 *per* Slesser LJ (CA).
200. He does not, however, have to prove his case on the balance of probabilities, otherwise there would be nothing to be gained by a compromise: *Miles* v *New Zealand Alford Estate Co* (1886) 32 Ch D 266, 284 *per* Cotton LJ (CA). There must be "some prospect of success"—*Horton* v *Horton* [1961] 1 QB 215, 221 *per* Upjohn LJ (CA).
201. Treitel, pp 82 ff. In other words there must be a "real" dispute: *Piper* v *Royal Exchange Assurance* (1932) 44 Ll L Rep 103, 117 *per* Roche J (yacht)
201a. *Keller* v *State Farm Ins Co*, 536 NE 2d 194, 198 (Ill, 1989– tornado).

clearly, the same is true of the other party, here the insurer, and his defence to the claim.[202]

For example, the courts in England today are likely to concur with courts in the United States in the 1950s, that settlement of a total loss under a valued policy for less than the policy value is an agreement for which the insurer provides no consideration.[203] Today, however, the courts in the United States are likely to approach this kind of case as raising an issue of the duty of good faith (below, 30–10).

30–6E Economic Duress

A contract is voidable,[204] if concluded by one party under "economic" duress.[205] Economic duress is just one kind of common law duress,[206] which was originally limited to the obvious cases of actual or threatened physical force, but then expanded to other cases. Economic duress "is now the principal control device which places limits upon the conduct of the parties during the negotiation of a contract"[207] and, we may add, the contract whereby an outstanding insurance claim is settled.

Duress is said to have two elements: "(1) pressure amounting to compulsion of the will of the victim; and (2) the illegitimacy of the pressure exerted."[208] Pressure alone is not enough to justify avoidance of the contract: life is full of pressures of one kind or another and commercial pressure is just one of them: below, 30–6E1.[209] For relief in law, the pressure on the person seeking relief, here the claimant, must have been illegitimate,[210] a "threat of unlawful damage to his economic interest"[211]: below, 30–6E2. Further, we may add, the pressure must have been applied by the person against whom relief is sought, the insurer: below, 30–6E3. Finally, the pressure must have induced the claimant to make the contract in question, the settlement or compromise: below, 30–6E4.

30–6E1 Compulsion

The compulsion in question has been referred to as "coercion of the will such that there was no true consent". In this connection, "it is material to enquire whether [the

202. *Yancey* v *Central Mutual Ins Assn*, 77 SW 2d 149, 154 (Mo, 1934—life); *Home Ins Co* v *Davila*, 212 F 2d 731, 742 (1 Cir, 1954—fire); *Stanley Trucking Co Inc* v *National Indemnity Co*, 136 NW 2d 101, 104 (Minn, 1965—theft).

Cf Ledingham v *Bermejo Estancia Co Ltd* [1947] 1 All ER 749, 751 *per* Atkinson LJ (CA). Kelly, (1964) 27 MLR 540.

203. *Holden* v *Hanover Fire Ins Co*, 128 F Supp 527 (WD SC, 1955—fire); *Baker* v *Hartford Ins Co*, 152 NYS 2d 1003 (1956—fire).

204. Not void: Treitel p 363 citing *Pao On* p 634; *The Universe Sentinel* [1983] 1 AC 366, 383, 400. *Cf Barton* v *Armstrong* [1976] AC 104 (PC).

205. *Pau On* v *Lau Yiu* [1980] AC 614, 635–6 *per* Lord Scarman (PC); *The Evia Luck (No 2)* [1992] 2 AC 152, 165, *per* Lord Goff (HL). Generally, see Birks, [1990] LMCLQ 342; Halson, (1991) 107 LQR 649; Macdonald, [1989] JBL 460; Nicholls, (1990–1) J Cont L 132 and 163, who lists (pp 170–1) Commonwealth cases and other articles.

206. Treitel p 363

207. McKendrick, *Force Majeure and Frustration of Contract* (ed McKendrick, London, 1991) p 48.

208. *Pau On* (above) p 400 *per* Lord Scarman. *Cf The Olib* [1991] 2 Lloyd's Rep 108, 114, in which Webster J stated three requirements: (1) commercial pressure, (2) illegitimacy, and (3) that the person seeking relief had no practicable alternative. This is out of line: (a) the higher courts have accepted that the doctrine is not limited to commercial pressure. (b) Most commentators see (1) and (3) as a single requirement of coercion.

209. *Atlas Express* v *Kafco* [1989] QB 833, 839 *per* Tucker J.

210. *Universe Tankships Inc* v *ITWF* [1983] AC 366, 384 *per* Lord Diplock.

211. *B & S Contracts* v *Victor Green Publications* [1984] ICR 419, 423 *per* Eveleigh LJ (CA).

claimant] did or did not protest; whether, at the time he was allegedly coerced into making the contract, he did or did not have an alternative course open to him such as an adequate legal remedy; whether he was independently advised; and whether after entering the contract he took steps to avoid it."[212] These are indicators of compulsion, of which the most significant is said[213] to be whether there was no alternative course: no reasonably practical alternative open to the claimant but to submit.[214]

Among the other indicators, importance was attached in the past to whether there was any legal remedy available to the victim, with which to resist the coercion.[215] For example, in the United States, if the threat was non-payment of a debt, it was presumed to be a sufficient alternative to sue for it, ignoring the reality that the creditor might be in desperate need of immediate cash and unable to wait upon the due process of law. Courts are now less sanguine. Similarly, the presence or absence of protest is far from decisive today: the pressure itself may produce not only payment but also numbed silence: "The victim's silence will not assist the bully, if the lack of any practicable choice but to submit is proved."[216] And, as to whether (or not) active steps were taken to avoid the impugned contract, if any were available, this can be seen as an aspect of the main question of reasonably practicable alternatives. However, it should not be forgotten that a failure to seek to rescind the contract may be seen as affirmation of the contract that bars relief.[217]

30–6E2 Illegitimacy

In general, it is not illegitimate simply to threaten to withhold *future* business[218]: the insurer who indicates that, unless settlement is agreed on his terms, he will not insure the claimant in future does not, for that reason alone, apply illegitimate pressure. Nor is it illegitimate simply to threaten to break an existing contract.[219] If

"economic duress could be successfully claimed after any illegitimate threat then it would undermine the security of any transaction caused by [a persons's] announcement of his intention to breach his contract and . . . the law has an interest in ensuring that many such transactions are regarded as binding. First, the functioning of the legal system depends upon such 'compromises' being made. Not all such disputes could be litigated without overloading the legal system. Secondly, if the parties can reach agreement themselves then they are more likely to be able to continue to do business with one another."[220]

---

212. *Pau On* (above), *per* Lord Scarman.
213. See Halson and Macdonald (above).
214. *Pau On*, p 400 (Lord Scarman). See also *B & S Contracts* (above), p 428 *per* Kerr LJ; and p 426 *per* Griffiths LJ. Cf *Hennessy* v *Craigmyle* [1986] ICR 461 (CA).
215. *Pau On* (above), pp 626 and 635. "It is incumbent . . . on one so coerced to resort to legal remedies; if he yielded he must be considered as doing so voluntarily": *Wou* v *Galbraith-Ruffin Realty Co*, 195 NYS 2d 886, 888 (1959); see also *Tri–State Roofing Co* v *Simon*, 142 A 2d 333, 336 (Pa, 1958). Goff and Jones (p 225): "The absence of an effective adequate remedy is most significant".
216. *The Universe Sentinel* [1983] 1 AC 366, 400 *per* Lord Scarman. Courts have also been influenced by whether it was the creditor or the debtor who initiated the settlement: *Williams* v *Roffey* [1990] 1 All ER 512, 526 *per* Purchas LJ (CA). Also in this category: *Alec Lobb (Garages) Ltd* v *Total Oil GB Ltd* [1985] 1 All ER 303 (CA).
217. For example, *The Atlantic Baron, North Ocean Shipping* v *Hyundai Construction* [1979] QB 705. Generally, see above, 23–18B.
218. *Eric Gnapp* v *Petroleum Bd* [1949] WN 180 (CA); *Smith* v *Charlwick* (1924) 34 CLR 38. For more cases, see Goff and Jones pp 236 ff; and Halson p 660.
219. *The Siboen* [1976] 1 Lloyd's Rep 293, 335 *per* Kerr J. Treitel pp 364–365. This is an implication of the secondary promise theory of contract. *Idem* in New York: *Wou* v *Galbraith–Ruffin Realty Co*, 195 NYS 2d 886 (1959).
220. MacDonald, p 466.

Moreover, the law must be sensitive to the possibility that the threat was a mistake.[221] If the courts are too responsive to complaints of economic duress, they reduce the role of the economically "efficient" breach, as well as the economically "efficient" compromise to avert that breach. Operative economic duress is a question of degree and, therefore, a source of uncertainty. The line, between what is legitimate and what is not, is fine but must be found.

What makes the pressure illegitimate, in one view at least, is that it is applied in bad faith: that it amounts to "the deliberate exploitation of the difficulties of the other party".[222] By contrast, the hallmark of a legitimate settlement "is that, in the absence of [the demanded] payment, the opportunist will prefer [the threatened] breach to performance".[223]

For example, no debtor should be too aggressive in reminding the creditor of the advantages of a bird in hand over the possibility of two birds much later after the creditor has been through the judicial bush. In *D & C Builders* v *Rees*,[224] debtors, knowing that their creditors were in desperate need of cash, told them that, unless they settled for less than the full debt, they would get nothing; the creditors settled for less. The Court of Appeal declined to enforce this compromise. The decision was later explained in terms of duress: "there was no 'true accord' because . . . 'no person can insist on a settlement procured by intimidation' ".[225]

30–6E3 The Source of Pressure

Relief is available only, it seems, if illegitimate pressure is applied by the person against whom relief is sought,[226] in this context, the insurer. This probably includes an agent acting for the insurer. If, however, the pressure on the claimant to settle the claim comes from his creditors, for example, *prima facie* he cannot impugn a settlement agreed with the insurer, on the ground of economic duress.[227]

30–6E4 Inducement

For relief, the duress must have been a "significant cause inducing" the claimant to make the agreement,[228] without having to be the sole cause.[229] This requirement is not satisfied automatically or easily; the situation may have been such that it made business sense for the claimant to agree anyway.[230] The onus of proof is on the insurer to show that pressure did not induce the settlement.[231] This issue is not easy to separate from the first element of duress, proof of coercion.[232]

221. For example, a mistake about rights: *ibid*. Goff and Jones pp 224–225.
222. Birks, p 346. *Cf* Goff and Jones (p 229) who are not persuaded that bad faith is at all decisive.
223. Halson, p 675.
224. [1966] 2 QB 617;
225. *The Siboen* [1976] 1 Lloyd's Rep 293, 335 *per* Kerr J.
226. Birks, p 343
227. See *Alec Lobb (Garages) Ltd* v *Total Oil GB Ltd* [1985] 1 All ER 303 (CA).
228. *The Evia Luck (No 2)* [1992] 1 Lloyd's Rep 115, 120 *per* Lord Goff (HL).
229. *Barton* v *Armstrong* [1976] AC 104, 120 *per* Lord Cross (PC). Nicholls, p 176; Birks, p 344; this is why the "coercion of the will" view is too strong: *The Evia Luck* (above). Consent can still be vitiated, as it is with misrepresentation, if the pressure (misrepresentation) is (just) one inducing cause. *Idem* Macdonald p 472.
230. Goff and Jones, p 223. For example, *Crescendo Management* v *Westpac Banking* (1989) 63 ALJ 504 (NSW).
231. Nicholls, p 176, citing *Barton*, p 120, and *Pao On*.
232. Goff and Jones, pp 224–225.

30–7 NON-PAYMENT

If the insurer fails to pay money due to the insured, the insured has a right of action to recover money from the insurer. This is scarcely surprising; what is surprising is that, in the case of indemnity insurance, the nature and thus the extent of that right are not clear.

30–7A Indemnity Insurance

In the case of indemnity insurance, it has been said,[233] actions against insurers "sound in unliquidated damages *rather* than debt". The emphasis in this statement, which might otherwise be misleading, should be on the contrast with debt and on the unliquidated nature of the claim. As Pearson J has observed, in this context "the word 'damages' is used in a somewhat unusual sense"[234] and should not be taken absolutely literally. The insurer promises, as a primary contractual promise, that the insured shall enjoy "the right to be indemnified by a payment of money"[235]; the promise is "a promise of indemnity giving a right of action for unliquidated damages *in case of non-payment*"[236]; and none the less so, if the claim has been adjusted and agreed,[237] the adjustment being no more than evidence of the amount to be paid.[238]

In *The Italia Express*,[239] however, Hirst J accepted a different view of the insurer's promise. He held that the insurer's obligation was to "prevent" the insured from suffering the loss in question; that "as soon as the loss has occurred . . . the primary obligation is broken, giving rise to the secondary obligation to pay damages"; and that the insured "had an immediate right of action the moment the loss occurred, no prior demand was necessary, and no separate subsequent breach was constituted by the underwriters' failure to respond immediately to the demand for payment".[240] This construction of the contract as containing a central and contingent promise which, if the contingency occurs, both parties know the promisor cannot possibly perform, invites reflection. The consequence, that any insurance payment is a payment of damages for breach of contract, follows from and is closely bound up with the premise that the insurer is obliged to indemnify the insured as soon as the loss occurs.

30–7A1 *When is the Insurer Obliged to Pay?*

The premise, it is submitted, is false. First, as regards liability insurance, it is clear law that the insurer is not obliged to pay until the insured's loss, i.e. his liability, has been

---

233. *Forney* v *Dominion Ins Co Ltd* [1969] 1 Lloyd's Rep 502,509 *per* Donaldson J (liability) (emphasis added), a view to which he made passing reference in *Edmunds* v *Lloyd Italico* [1986] 1 Lloyd's Rep 326, 327 (CA—re); see also *Irving* v *Manning* (1847) 1 HLC 287, 306 *per* Patteson J; *Chandris* v *Argo Ins Co Ltd* [1963] 2 Lloyd's Rep 65, 73–74 *per* Megaw J (hull), above 30–2; the judgment of Megaw J was approved in *Castle Ins* v *Hong Kong Shipping* [1984] AC 226 (PC). See also *The Fanti* [1991] 2 AC 1, 35 *per* Lord Goff (P & I). However, in few of these cases was the description of the money as damages examined, and in none of them did the present point arise. Moreover, *Chandris* (and approval of it in *Castle*)) have been distinguished and limited to marine insurance: *Penrith City Council* v *GIO of NSW* (1991) 24 NSWLR 564, 570 (liability).
234. *Jabbour* v *Custodian of Israeli Absentee Property* [1954] 1 WLR 139, 144 and cases cited.
235. *Ibid* p 145.
236. *Pickersgill & Sons Ltd* v *London & Provincial Marine & General Ins Co* [1912] 3 KB 614, 622 *per* Hamilton J (hull) (emphasis added), with reference to *Pellas & Co* v *Neptune Marine Ins Co* (1879) 5 CPD 34 (CA—cargo).
237. *Luckie* v *Bushby* (1853) 13 CB 864.
238. p 878 *per* Jervis CJ.
239. [1992] 2 Lloyd's Rep 281; [1992] LMCLQ 287.
240. p 286.

ascertained and determined, even though the insured may suffer measurable economic loss at an earlier time.[241] Second, in the case of *non*-indemnity insurance, the insurer is not regarded as in breach of his duty to pay until any genuine dispute about whether he is obliged to pay has been resolved: below, 30–8B. Third, as Hirst J had to concede, "it is commercially inconceivable that in a large total loss case like the present, or in a complex claim for partial loss or damage, the underwriter would pay up in full by return of post without any investigation".[242] If, as is commonly provided, the insured is required to give notice and particulars of loss, it is scarcely surprising that performance of these duties has been held to be a condition precedent to the insurer's obligation to pay.[243] The same view has been taken in other countries. In Colorado, for example, a "title insurance policy does not guarantee title or the enforceability of a mortgage lien, but is instead a contract of indemnity . . . The contract is breached only if the insurer does not pay for the loss or damage under the terms of the contract. Thus, the contract cannot be breached until after the insured makes a claim for loss *and* the insurer refuses to pay".[244] With this background of law and practice, surely, as a matter of common sense and construction, if not also of common law, this is the effect of any notice of loss clause: the insurer is not actually obliged to pay (and not in breach if he does not) until the conditions precedent to payment, such as notice, particulars and proof of loss, have been performed.

In a recent case, Lord Donaldson MR observed that the insurance money was due but not payable.[245] This, however, appears to be a contradiction—of terms, as the terms are commonly used interchangeably,[246] and of at least one old precedent (also about an insolvent insurance company), in which James V-C held that a debt is due when it is payable.[247] In the years between, an Irish judge observed[248] that "'Due' may mean immediately payable (its common signification), or a debt contracted but payable *in futuro*". Even on the latter view, the insurer is in breach of contract not at the time of the loss insured but when the debt becomes payable *in futuro*.

30–7A2 The Nature of the Insurer's Duty to Pay: Insurance Money or Damages?

It follows from what has been just said that, if the insurer pays on time, payment is performance of the insurance contract. In Scotland, at least, it was recently reaffirmed by the House of Lords that the "right of action is here a contractual one, not one in reparation".[249] This, however, was on the *obiter* supposition that, in English law, the position is different and that the law of Scotland "has not adopted the English view that the right of action is one for unliquidated damages". This supposition, however, has never been closely examined in the English courts and, it is submitted, the law of Scotland is to be preferred.

---

241. Above 17–4A. See also *Penrith City Council* v *GIO of NSW* (1991) 24 NSWLR 564 (liability).
242. p 291.
243. Above 26–2G. See also *Hunter* v *Stronghold Ins Ltd*, Sup Ct Victoria, 18 January 1991 (burglary); and *New Zealand Ins Co Ltd* v *Harris* [1990] 1 NZLR 10, 17 (CA—motor).
244. *First Federal Savings & Loan Assn* v *Transamerica Title Ins Co*, 793 F Supp 265, 270 (D Colo, 1992—title).
245. *Ackman* v *PPB* [1992] 2 Lloyd's Rep 321, 349 *per* Lord Donaldson MR (CA—liability).
246. For example, Benjamin no 16–021.
247. *Re European Life Assurance* (1869) LR 9 Eq 122. See also *Dibble* v *Bowater* (1853) 2 E & B 570; *Re Stockton Malleable Iron Co* (1875) 2 Ch D 101; *Potel* v *IRC* [1970] TR 325.
248. *Irish Land Commission* v *Massereene* [1904] 2 Ir 502, 513 *per* Gibson J, in a case about rent.
249. *Scott Lithgow Ltd* v *Secretary of State for Defence* (1989) 45 BLR 1, 8 *per* Lord Keith (HL).

If, however, this submission is rejected, it is further submitted that, in the case of indemnity insurance, the term "damages" should not be taken too literally. McGregor[250] defines damages as "Pecuniary compensation . . . for a wrong which is either a tort or a breach of contract" but goes on to say[251] that the "usual and strictly correct meaning of the term" excludes *inter alia* "actions for money payable by the terms of a contract" and thus, excludes "actions to recover money payable under insurance policies".[252] "These", he says, "are to be distinguished from actions for damages or breach of a contract". The

"explanation of the use of the expression 'unliquidated damages' to describe a claim for an indemnity under an insurance policy may be wholly or partly afforded by the old form of pleading in assumpsit. But as the only wrong admitted by the insurer is his failure to pay a sum due under a contract, the amount of which has to be ascertained, he seems to be in much the same position as the person who owes and has failed to pay a reasonable price for goods sold and delivered or a reasonable remuneration for work done or services rendered. The claim is for unliquidated damages but the word 'damages' is used in a somewhat unusual sense."[253]

30–7B Non-Indemnity Insurance

In the case of non-indemnity insurance, such as life insurance, the claim has been seen as one for a contract debt and an action as one to recover a liquidated sum[254] or, if payment has been delayed, as an action for damages for detention of the debt. When the action is for damages, the amount recoverable is not limited to the sum insured, for that restricts "the amount the insurer may have to pay in the performance of the contract, not the damages that are recoverable for its breach".[255] If the insurer does not pay when he should,[256] principles of compensation permit a further award to the claimant of general damages by way of interest on the sum due (below, 30–8) and special damages for special loss (30–9).

30–8 INTEREST

Under section 35A(1) of the Supreme Court Act 1981,[257] simple interest may be awarded on all or part of any debt or damages. Although the controlling principle is

---

250. Para 1, adopted (as stated in an earlier edition) in *Broome* v *Cassell* [1972] AC 1027, 1070 by Lord Hailsham LC.
251. Para. 2
252. Para 3.
253. *Jabbour* v *Custodian of Israeli Absentee Property* [1954] 1 WLR 139, 144 *per* Pearson J, approved in *Forney* v *Dominion Ins Co Ltd* [1969] 1 Lloyd's Rep 502. Cf *The Italia Express (No 2)*, discussed below, 30–9B1.
254. *Blackley* v *National Mutual Life Assn Ltd (No 2)* [1973] 1 NZLR 668, 672 *per* Mahon J (Sup Ct—life).
255. *Lawton* v *Great Southwest Fire Ins Co*, 392 A 2d 576, 579 (NH, 1978—fire), followed in *Salamey* v *Aetna Casualty & Surety Co*, 741 F 2d 874, 877 (6 Cir, 1984—fire).
256. As to when payment is due, see above, 30–2.
257. Superseding section 3(1) of the Law Reform (Miscellaneous Provisions) Act 1934, which had repealed section 29 of the Civil Procedure Act 1833, whereby "the Jury on the Trial of any Issue" had been empowered to "give Damages in the Nature of Interest . . . over and above the Money recoverable in all Actions on Policies of Assurance." As to the latter, James LJ in *Webster* v *British Empire Mutual Life Ins Co* (1880) 15 Ch D 169, 174 (CA—life) said that "anything in the nature of interest can only be given . . . as damages for the wrongful detention of money which ought to have been paid"—but in that case the insurer

"that a successful plaintiff should be compensated for the loss involved in being kept out of his money",[258] the power to award interest only arises "in proceedings . . . for the recovery of a debt or damages"; if the insurer pays late but before proceedings have been commenced, interest cannot be obtained against him under this section.[259] This rule "places the small creditor at grave disadvantage *vis-à-vis* his substantial and influential debtor. The former may fear to offend the latter by instituting legal proceedings either swiftly or at all and it is notorious that some substantial and influential debtors are not slow to take advantage of this tactical strength, especially in times of financial stringency".[260]

3–8A The Amount of Interest

Recovery of interest is subject to the discretion of the court whether to award interest at all and, if so, at what rate.[261] Generally, if, but for the non-payment, the creditor would have had the use of the money, interest should be awarded.[262] If awarded, interest may be at different rates for different periods.[263] In a commercial case, the rate of interest should reflect the commercial value of money,[264] "the average borrowing rate or lending rate for a sound lender and borrower . . . the full compensation for being out of your money".[265] Recently, courts have awarded the base rate plus one per cent.[266]

30–8B The Interest Period

Interest may be awarded for all or any part of the time between the date, when the cause of action arises, and the date of judgment.[267] The cause of action arises when

was not detaining the money wrongfully, i.e., was not in breach. He also said (*ibid*) that insurance policies did not bear interest as such. Generally see McGregor, ch 14.

At common law, there was a very limited right to interest, including (a) where the contract was for the payment of money on a certain day and (b) where the money had been used and interest earned: *De Havilland v Bowerbank* (1807) 1 Camp 50, 51 *per* Lord Ellenborough. These rights did not extend to insurance, being confined to mercantile securities and where interest was awarded by trade usage: *Higgins v Sargant* (1823) 2 B & C 348, 349–350 *per* Abbott CJ (life). In general and in the absence any agreement or statute for the payment of interest, a court had no common law power to award interest by way of damages for the detention of a debt: *London, Chatham & Dover Ry Co v SE Ry Co* [1893] AC 429; *President of India v La Pintada Cia Nav SA* [1985] AC 104, 115 *per* Lord Brandon.

In the USA there is no general right to interest before judgment on unpaid insurance money; however, a right may be found in the contract of insurance or in state legislation; see Appleman, section 8878.15; 46 CJS, sections 1391 ff.

258. *Blackley v National Mutual Life Assn Ltd (No 2)* [1973] 1 NZLR 668, 671 *per* Mahon J (Sup Ct—life).

259. *President of India v La Pintada Cia Nav SA* [1985] AC 104, 129 *per* Lord Brandon.

260. p 112 *per* Lord Roskill. For discussion of problems associated with this position, see the Law Commission Report No 88, sections 70 ff (Cmnd 7229); Law Commission WP No 66; Australian Law Reform Commission Report No 20, sections 319 ff.

261. Supreme Court Act 1981, section 35A(1).

262. McGregor, No 578, citing *Kemp v Tolland* [1956] 2 Lloyd's Rep 681, 691 *per* Devlin J.

263. Section 35A(6).

264. *Re Roberts* (1880) 14 Ch D 49, 52 *per* Jessel MR (CA); *Burts & Harvey Ltd v Vulcan Boiler & General Ins Co Ltd* [1966] 1 Lloyd's Rep 354, 355 *per* Lawton J (consequential loss).

265. *De Maurier (Jewels) Ltd v Bastion Ins Co Ltd* [1967] 2 Lloyd's Rep 550, 561 *per* Donaldson J (jewellers' AR).

266. See McGregor, No 607 and cases cited. *Cf* Lord Denning MR in *Jefford v Gee* [1970] 2 QB 130, 148 (CA) that the bank rate fluctuates too much and that, for longer periods of time (e.g. two years), the yardstick should be the rate of interest payable on money placed in a short term investment account; see also *The Dona Mari* [1973] 2 Lloyd's Rep 366, 376–377 *per* Kerr J.

267. Or the date of payment, if it occurs, prior to judgment: section 35A(1).

the creditor should have received the money,[268] so, generally, interest is payable from the time when the insurance money became due.[269] "Where a wrong-doer has failed to pay money which he should have paid, justice, in principle, requires that he should pay interest over the period for which he has withheld the money."[270] Moreover, if an interim payment which the insurer makes or is ordered to make turns out to be excessive or recoverable, the court has a discretion to award interest to the insurer on the amount recovered.[271]

If there is a *bona fide* dispute over proof of loss, interest will not be awarded against the insurer until the dispute has been resolved[272]; "until the claim has been presented, and he has investigated it, it is not fair to regard him as withholding payment".[273] Contrast a *bona fide* dispute not over the amount of loss but over the extent of cover: if the issue is decided against the insurer, interest may become payable from a time prior to judgment on the issue,[274] in many cases from the time when the insurer should have paid.[275] If the insurer disputes cover, the duty of the insurer is to pay into court or interplead. There will be less sympathy for an insurer, when the dispute turns on the meaning of contract terms that he has drafted, than for the insurer who disputes liability by reference to the conduct of the insured. In general, the question is whether the insurer was justified in refusing to pay before the matter had been investigated or litigated,[276] or whether "the payment of a just debt has been improperly withheld".[277]

30–9 SPECIAL DAMAGES

30–9A Contingency Insurance

In the case of contingency (non-indemnity) insurance, an action against the insurer for insurance money is an action for debt, and may involve a claim for damages for the wrongful detention, non-payment or late payment, of the debt.[278] The traditional rule was that, in the absence of any agreement or statute for the payment of interest, a court had no common law power to award interest by way of damages for the deten-

268. *Cf* the view that interest should not be awarded for the period prior to the issue of the writ, discussed critically by McGregor, No 601.
269. *Re Waterhouse's Policy* [1937] 1 Ch 415, 421 *per* Farwell J (life). See also *Forney v Dominion Ins Co Ltd* [1969] 1 Lloyd's Rep 502 (liability). As to when insurance money is due, see above, 30–2 and 30–7A1.
270. *General Tire & Rubber Co v Firestone Tyre & Rubber Co Ltd* [1975] 2 All ER 173, 188 *per* Lord Wilberforce (HL).
271. *City of London v New Hampshire Ins Co* [1992] 1 Lloyd's Rep 431.
272. *Knoller v Evans* (1936) 55 Ll L Rep 40 (burglary); *De Maurier (Jewels) Ltd v Bastion Ins Co Ltd* [1967] 2 Lloyd's Rep 550, 561 *per* Donaldson J (jewellers' AR).
273. Law Commission Report No 88, *Law of Contract: Report on Interest* (1978), section 72.
274. *Gliksten & Sons v State Assurance Co* (1922) 10 Ll L Rep 604 (fire).
275. *Mackie v European Assurance Sy* (1869) 21 LT 102 (fire). *Kazacos v Fire & All Risks Ins Co Ltd* (1970) 92 WN (NSW) 397, 404 (fire). *Chenier v Madill* (1973) 43 DLR (3d) 28 (Ont—fire). *Blackley v National Mutual Life Assn Ltd (No 2)* [1973] 1 NZLR 668 (Sup Ct—life). *American Eagle Fire Ins Co v Burdine*, 200 F 2d 26 (10 Cir, 1952—fire). Cal Ins Code, section 2057.
276. *Nishina Trading Co Ltd v Chiyoda Fire & Marine Ins Co Ltd* [1968] 2 Lloyd's Rep 47, 56 *per* Donaldson J (cargo). *Roumeli Food Stores (NSW) Pty Ltd v New India Assurance Co Ltd* [1972] 1 NSWLR 227, 251–252 (fire).
277. *Toronto Ry Co v City of Toronto* [1906] AC 117, 121 *per* Lord Macnaghten (PC); this is the governing principle in insurance cases in Canada, for example, *Chenier v Madill* (1973) 43 DLR (3d) 28, 50 (Ont—fire). The same view was expressed by Lord Herschell LC in *London, Chatham & Dover Ry Co v S E Ry Co* [1893] AC 429, 437, and, it is said, was given effect in the Law Reform (Miscellaneous Provisions) Act 1934.
278. McGregor, No 1058.

tion of a debt.[279] Statute modified the position by allowing the court a discretion to award interest (above, 30–8) but has left at least two kinds of unsatisfied claimant to scour the common law for a remedy. First, the court has no statutory power to award interest, if the debtor pays late but before proceedings for recovery have been begun and, second, an award of interest does not compensate special damage over and beyond loss of the normal use of the money.

The common law has always recognised exceptions to the traditional rule, when special damage was within the contemplation of the parties.[280] This has been confirmed.[281] For special damage, the "test in all cases is whether the loss was within the contemplation of the parties".[282] The distinction "between general and special damages is the difference between damages recoverable under the first part of the rule in *Hadley* v *Baxendale* . . . (general damages) and damages recoverable under the second part of the rule (special damages)",[283] i.e. a distinction between loss arising in the usual course of things, for which, in the case of non-payment of insurance money, interest is usually adequate compensation, and any additional loss suffered by the creditor, the likelihood of which was or should have been in the reasonable contemplation of the debtor.

In *Wadsworth* v *Lydall*,[284] for example, the defendant owed the plaintiff a sum of money which, to the knowledge of the defendant, the plaintiff needed in order to buy something, something which he had agreed to buy in the reasonable belief that he would have the money in time from the defendant. When the defendant did not pay on time, the plaintiff had to borrow to buy and, in this action, recovered the cost of borrowing as special damages from the defendant. In principle, this is the law applicable to non-indemnity insurance, such as life and PA insurance, but the principle has not been tested in this context in England.

30–9B Indemnity Insurance

30–9B1 Failure to Pay

If in *Wadsworth* (above, 30–9A), the plaintiff had not agreed to buy the thing but, to the knowledge of the defendant, urgently needed to do so to carry on normal life or business, it appears that the decision would have been the same. If, in such a case, the defendant were a motor insurer, who delayed payment of insurance money due, and the plaintiff his insured, who urgently needed the money to replace a stolen van essen-

279. *London, Chatham & Dover Ry Co* v *SE Ry Co* [1893] AC 429; *President of India* v *La Pintada Cia Nav SA* [1988] AC 395, 424 *per* Lord Brandon; applied in *Norwest Refrigeration Services Pty Ltd* v *Bain Dawes Pty Ltd* (1984) 157 CLR 149 (HCA—hull).
280. See McGregor, Nos 1061 ff.
281. *Wadsworth* v *Lydall* [1981] 2 All ER 401 (CA), approved in *La Pintada* (above), p 127 *per* Lord Brandon. See also *Trans Trust SPRL* v *Danubian Trading Co Ltd* [1952] 2 QB 297, 306 *per* Denning LJ (CA). *Reichert* v *General Ins Co*, 428 P 2d 860, 866 (Cal, 1967—fire). Holmes, 65 Cornell L Rev 330, 337 (1980).
There is, however, no power in England to award (further) damages for the late payment of damages, even of liquidated damages, from which therefore debt must be distinguished: *President of India* v *Lips Maritime Corp* [1988] AC 395; criticised by Mann, (1988) 104 LQR 3.
282. McGregor, No 1064. This, of course, is the general rule for remoteness of damage found in *Hadley* v *Baxendale* (1854) 9 Ex 341; *Victoria Laundry (Windsor) Ltd* v *Newman Industries Ltd* [1949] 2 KB 528 (CA); and *Koufos* v *Czarnikow Ltd* [1969] 1 AC 350.
283. *La Pintada* (above), p 127 *per* Lord Brandon.
284. [1981] 2 All ER 401 (CA).

tial to his business, the decision should be the same—but this cannot be predicted with confidence.

General rules of damages were applied to indemnity insurance in *Grant* v *Cooperative Ins Sy Ltd*.[285] For the period between (fire) loss and judgment, Hodgson J awarded the claimant damages for the cost of protecting the premises insured from vandals, while it was unoccupied pending repair, as well as the cost of alternative accommodation or the amount of rent obtainable from the premises during the same period, even though the period was extended by reason of the impecuniosity of the claimant and his inability to reinstate without the insurance money.[286]

In *The Italia Express (No 2)*,[287] however, Hirst J decided that no damages could be awarded for breach of contract by the insurer. Among the objections to this decision are, first, that it proceeded from a very literal view of the description of insurance indemnity as an obligation to pay damages.[288] Second, it rested on an unsupported dictum of Lord Brandon[289] made in a different context, that there is "no such thing as a cause of action in damages for late payment of damages". If, as we have been told,[290] the obligation to pay damages is a secondary contractual duty, it is not immediately obvious why (tertiary) damages should not be payable for breach of the secondary duty. The decision in *The Italia Express (No 2)* can be justified on a narrow ground of construction of the MIA,[291] however, the general reasoning employed is difficult to reconcile with the decision in *Grant* (above), which seems preferable.

Damages have been awarded in other countries, including the USA. The Supreme Court of California said in *Reichert*,[292] that where

"the owner of a heavily mortgaged motel or other business property suffers a substantial fire loss, the owner may be placed in financial distress, may be unable to meet his mortgage payments, and may be in jeopardy of losing his property and becoming a bankrupt. A major, if not the main, reason why a businessman purchases fire insurance is to guard against such eventualities if his property is damaged by fire. Certainly, the property owner who purchases fire insurance may reasonably expect that if a fire occurs, the insurance proceeds will be promptly available to protect him from those eventualities. The business of the fire insurer is to provide such protection. Insurers are, of course, chargeable with knowledge of the basic reasons why fire insurance is purchased, and of the likelihood that an improper delay in payment may result in the very injuries for which the insured sought protection by purchasing the policies".

In that and other cases in the United States, the insured has recovered damages in

---

285. (1983) 134 NLJ 81 (fire), with reference to the leading cases, *Hadley*, *Victoria Laundry* and *Koufos* (above). An alternative strategy in some cases might be an action based in the tort of negligence against the insurance adjuster. See below 30–12.

286. On the facts he refused an award for the effect of inflation on the cost of reinstatement, and for damage to the premises inflicted by vandals, as being not in the reasonable contemplation of the insurer, when the contract was concluded in 1962. However, it is submitted that the contemplation of the insurer should have been assessed as of the date of the current contract of insurance, i.e., of the last renewal in 1973; from that perspective the judge might have reached a different decision.

287. *Ventouris* v *Mountain* [1992] 2 Lloyd's Rep 281 (hull); Clarke [1992] LMCLQ 287.

288. It has been submitted that this is a mistaken view: above, 30–7A2.

289. *The Lips, President of India* v *Lips Maritime Corp* [1988] AC 395, 424. The context was a decision that there could be no action for damages for non-payment of a liquidated damages clause. Given the nature and purpose of such clauses, that is scarcely surprising and the decision has no necessary impact on the present question.

290. *Photo Production Ltd* v *Securicor Transport Ltd* [1980] AC 827, 848 *per* Lord Diplock.

291. According to sections 67 and 68 of the MIA, the measure of indemnity shall be "the sum fixed by the policy" and this, decided the court, is conclusively definitive of the extent of the liability of the insurer for loss under a valued policy.

292. *Reichert* v *General Ins Co*, 428 P 2d 860, 864 (Cal, 1967—fire).

respect of consequential damage to his business,[293] when this "resulted naturally and proximately from breach" and was "such as might reasonably have been expected to result".[294] In fire cases, on this basis and with reference to the rule in *Hadley* v *Baxendale*,[295] the insured has recovered as damages from the insurer profits lost when the insurer refused to indemnify him for destruction by fire of the insured business premises. And, in a case of health insurance, it has been held[296] that, when, in breach of contract, the insurer did not pay the insured's hospital bills, the insured could recover "damages for loss of credit or injury to credit reputation", if "that loss of credit was a natural, probable and foreseeable consequence of the defendant's breach".

30–9B2 Liability Insurance: Failure to Settle

In England, it has been held that the insured has no right to damages for breach of the duty of good faith—as regards the principal case of a breach of the duty of disclosure.[297] However, that may not rule out damages for other breaches of the duty of good faith, such as may arise when the liability insurer is in breach in respect of a settlement of a claim with a third party in respect of the latter's rights against the insured. The reasons against damages for breach, which are good in the case of the duty of disclosure, are less convincing in other cases of breach of the duty of good faith.

In *Diblasi*,[298] for example, in which the insurer failed to settle an action against the insured, the insured was awarded by the court in New York contractual damages in "the amount by which the judgment in the underlying tort action exceeded the insured's policy coverage". It is open to the English court, it is submitted, to reach a similar decision.

30–9C Inconvenience and Mental Distress

In *Grant*,[299] a fire case, Hodgson J held that damages for hardship, inconvenience and mental distress were not recoverable in law, applying the decision in *Addis* v *Gramo-*

---

293. *Alliance Ins Co* v *Alper-Salvage Co*, 19 F 2d 828 (6 Cir, 1927); *Venturi* v *Zurich General Accident & Liability Co*, 57 P 2d 1002 (Cal, 1936—motor); *Asher* v *Reliance Ins Co*, 308 F Supp 847 (ND Cal, 1970—fire); *Lawton* v *Great Southwest Fire Ins Co*, 392 A 2d 575 (NH, 1978—fire); *Royal College Shop Inc* v *Northern Ins Co*, 895 F 2d 670 (10 Cir, 1990—fire); *Pacific Employers Ins* v *PB Hoidale Co*, 789 F Supp 1117, 1124 (D Kan, 1992—liability). In *Hochman* v *American Family Ins Co*, 673 P 2d 1200 (Kan, 1984—fire) the insured recovered the cost of borrowing money to reinstate. In *Standard Fire Ins Co* v *Fraiman*, 588 SW 2d 681 (Tex, 1979—fire) the court denied that consequential damages could be recovered for the insurer's refusal to pay, but awarded such damages (telephone and travel expenses) for the insurer's breach of a procedural condition. In *Venturi* (above) the insured also recovered damages for injury to his credit rating. Generally, see Freemon, 21 Tort & Ins LJ 108 (1985).

294. *Alliance Ins Co* (above), p 831. Surprisingly, some courts have held that loss of use of a motor vehicle when the insurer wrongfully refused to pay for its repair was too remote: *Leonard* v *Fireman's Ins Co*, 111 SE 2d 773 (Ga, 1959—motor).

295. For example, *Salamey* v *Aetna Casualty & Surety Co*, 741 F 2d 874, 877 (6 Cir, 1984—fire).
For decisions of this kind in Canada see, for example, *Carlyle* v *Elite Ins Co* (1984) 56 BCLR 331, 340 (fire); and in New Zealand, see *New Zealand Ins Co Ltd* v *Harris* [1990] 1 NZLR 10 (CA—motor); also, Borrowdale, *Essays in Commercial Law* (Christchurch 1991), 88 ff and cases cited.

296. *Paramount National Life Ins Co* v *Williams* 772 SW 2d 255, 266 (Tex, 1989). Further, *Hadley* was expressly applied to loss resulting from a forced sale of assets to meet a judgment in *Pennsylvania Threshermen & Farmers Mutual Casualty Ins Co* v *Messenger*, 29 A 2d 653, 656 (Md, 1943—motor).

297. Above 23–15C.

298. *Diblasi* v *Aetna Life & Casualty Co*, 542 NYS 2d 187, 192 (1989—liability).

299. *Grant* v *Cooperative Ins Sy Ltd* (1983) 134 NLJ 81 (fire).

phone Co.[300] However, first, *Addis* concerned injured feelings and, clearly, does not apply to other kinds of non-pecuniary injury, such as physical inconvenience.[301] Second, even as regards injured feelings, *Addis*, which concerned a contract of employment, does not apply to every other kind of contract.

As regards mental distress, damages are now recoverable for breach of certain kinds of contract,[302] These are contracts, in which at least part of the object was to secure mental satisfaction,[303] peace of mind or freedom from distress.[304] Peace of mind and at least a degree of freedom from distress, surely, are the object of many insurance contracts: there is a widespread perception[305] that when a person, particularly a consumer, buys insurance, he buys not just a promise of indemnity in the future but also of peace of mind now. "A contract of insurance differs from most commercial contracts, in that the insured is offered and buys peace of mind against the designated risks".[306] If distress is not too remote,[307] damages for distress should be recoverable against an insurer who unreasonably delays payment and thus causes that distress.[308]

---

300. [1909] AC 488, in which the plaintiff was a servant wrongfully dismissed. See also *Groom v Crocker* [1939] 1 KB 194 (CA).

301. For example *Bailey v Bullock* [1950] 2 All ER 1167; for other decisions to this effect see McGregor, No 92.

302. For example *Jarvis v Swans Tours Ltd* [1973] QB 233 (CA); *Heywood v Wellers* [1976] QB 446 (CA). Bourne [1992] Bus L Rev 88; McGregor, No 97.

303. *Hayes v Dodd* [1990] 2 All ER 815 (CA). McGregor, No 99. USA: damages for mental suffering have been awarded against insurers, but as damages for the tort of bad faith: *Gruenberg v Aetna Ins Co*, 510 P 2d 1032, 1041 (1973—fire); see below, 30–10.

304. *Bliss v SE Thames Regional Health Authority* [1985] IRLR 308, p 316 *per* Dillon LJ CA).

305. *Crisci v Security Insurance Co*, 426 P 2d 173, 179 (Cal, 1967—liability): "Among the considerations in purchasing liability insurance, as insurers are well aware, is the peace of mind and security it will provide in the event of an accidental loss." See also *Fletcher v Western National Life Ins Co*, 89 Cal Rptr 78, 95 (Cal, 1970—disability); *Eckenrode v Life of America Ins Co*, 470 F 2d 1, 5 (7 Cir, 1972—PA); *Feathers v State Farm Fire & Casualty Co*, 667 SW 2d 693 (Ky, 1983—fire); *Andrew Jackson Life Ins Co v Williams*, 566 So 2d 1172, 1179 (Miss, 1990—life). The "fundamental role of insurance" is "in replacing uncertainty with certainty"—*anon*, 91 Yale LJ 1642, 1660 (1982). See also in this sense Abraham, p 178; McDowell, 16 Conn L Rev 513, 518 (1984); Paterson, 34 Colum L Rev 595, 599 (1934); Tartaglio, 56 S Cal L Rev 1345 (1983).

On the Social Readjustment Rating Scale for events inflicting stress, severe financial loss is comparable with the death of a close friend: Holmes & Rahe, 11 J Psychosomatic Research 213 (1967).

306. *Mortensen v Laing* [1992] 2 NZLR 282, 313 (CA—fire).

307. I.e., when it should have been in the contemplation of the defendant at the time of the insurance contract, as not unlikely to occur, if he were to break his contract in the way he eventually did, almost *ex hypothesi* the case of many kinds of breach of contract by an insurer.

308. So held in *Edwards v AA Mutual Ins Co* (1985) 3 ANZ Ins Cases 60–668, cited by Tarr, p 271.

Cf The Italia Express (No 2) [1992] 2 Lloyd's Rep 281, 293, where Hirst J held that such damages could not be recovered for breach of a hull insurance contract, because "in the vast majority of marine insurance contracts the assured is not an individual but a company, which could never invoke the 'peace of mind' test".

In the USA cases are divided. Some courts have followed Professor Corbin in the view that all insurance contracts are commercial contracts, to which such damages are inappropriate: *Dawkins v National Liberty Life Ins Co*, 252 F Supp 800, 802 (D SC, 1966—PHI); *Pendelton v Aetna Life Ins Co*, 320 F Supp 425, 432 (ED La, 1970—disability). *Cf Crisci v Security Insurance Co*, 426 P 2d 173, 179 (Cal, 1967—liability): "recovery of damages for mental suffering has been permitted for breach of contracts which directly concern the comfort, happiness or personal esteem of one of the parties". See also *Eckenrode v Life of America Ins Co*, 470 F 2d 1, 5 (7 Cir, 1972—PA); and *Universal Life Ins Co v Veasley*, 610 So 2d 290 (Miss, 1992—life), in which such damages were awarded against insurers. The line that separates the cases is that in the latter the suffering is foreseeable, while in the former it is not: Holinka, 48 Notre Dame L Rev 1303 (1973).

Contra text: *Kewin v Massachusetts Mutual Life Ins Co*, 295 NW 2d 50 (Mich, 1980—disability); however, the case is distinguishable as the court premised (pp 53–54) that the contract was commercial and that special damages were not within the reasonable contemplation of the parties. For early cases against recovery see Freemon, 21 Tort & Ins LJ 108, 117 (1985).

30–9D Time of Assessment

Whether the damages be general or special, the time of assessment is important. When the insurer performs his promise of indemnity, the amount of indemnity is normally calculated (above, 28–4) on values at the time of loss (point 1), even though the insurer may not be obliged to pay until later (point 2), when the claim has been investigated (above, 30–2). The traditional rule of contract law is to assess damages at the time of breach (point 2). Recently, however, courts mindful of inflation have stressed the basic aim of contract damages to put the plaintiff in as good a position as if the contract had been performed, and have based damages on values at the date of the hearing (point 3), "unless it can be said that the plaintiff ought reasonably to have mitigated by seeking an alternative performance at an earlier date, in which event the appropriate measure would . . . be the cost of the alternative performance at that date".[309] When the buyer, whose seller has defaulted, is required to mitigate by seeking alternative performance, i.e., to go into the market and buy substitute goods, this requirement assumes that he still has the money with which to do this.[310] When the insured takes cover against storm damage, for example, it is usually because he does not expect to have the money available to pay for the repair himself. Hence it appears that, if his wall is blown down in a storm but his insurer wrongfully refuses to pay, the amount of damages recoverable against the insurer should be assessed at point 3 rather than point 2, unless, it can be shown clearly that the insured ought reasonably to have found other money to have the wall rebuilt earlier than point 3.

30–10 THE TORT OF BAD FAITH

At one time in many parts of the United States, if payment was wrongly refused by the insurer, there could be no compensation at all in respect of pre-judgment interest, consequential economic loss or distress.[311] Insurers

"were insulated from liability for special damages resulting from their failure to settle or defend claims in accordance with policy obligations. That is, in a suit against the insurer for breach of a policy obligation, the insured was entitled only to have the obligation performed. This remedy gave the insured no compensation for any losses he suffered as a result of breach, and it provided the insurer with little additional incentive to perform."[312]

In *Eichenseer* v *Reserve Life Ins Co*,[313] the court said:

"If an insurance company could not be subjected to punitive damages it could intentionally and unreasonably refuse payment of a legitimate claim with veritable impunity. To permit an

---

309. *Radford* v *De Froberville* [1978] 1 All ER 33, 56–57 *per* Oliver J. See also *Dodd Properties (Kent) Ltd* v *Canterbury City Council* [1980] 1 All ER 928 (CA); *Ward* v *Cannock Chase DC* [1986] Ch 546. McGregor, Nos 619 and 949; Treitel, pp 849 ff.

310. See McGregor, No 301.

311. There were some exceptions, courts awarding damages for breach of contract: see above, 30–9B. Appleman, section 8878.15

312. Abraham, p 173. This produces what Professor Abraham calls (p 176) the reverse moral hazard: the insurer has an incentive to underallocate resources to reliability, while the insured may be encouraged to overallocate resources to loss prevention, which may amount to an inefficient use of resources (p 178). The cost to the insurer of increased reliability by, for example improving his methods of claims investigation, is likely to be less than the cost to the insured of finding or negotiating reliable insurance (p 184). See also Burton, 94 Harv L Rev 369, 393 (1980); Tartaglio, 56 S Cal L Rev 1345, 1350 (1983). This factor influenced the court in *Arnold* v *County Mutual Fire Ins Co*, 725 SW 2d 165 (Tex, 1987—motor).

313. 881 F 2d 1355, 1359–1360 (5 Cir, 1989—health), quoting *Standard Life Ins Co* v *Veal*, 354 So 2d 239 (Miss, 1977).

insurer to deny a legitimate claim, and thus force a claimant to litigate with no fear that claimant's maximum recovery could exceed the policy limits plus interest, would enable the insurer to pressure an insured to a point of desperation enabling the insurer to force an inadequate settlement or avoid payment entirely."

The courts responded to this situation, first in California and in relation to third party liability claims, with the "tort of bad faith".[314] In *Gruenberg*,[315] the Supreme Court of California analysed[316] earlier decisions[317] imposing liability on the insurer as being "not for a bad faith breach of contract but for failure to meet the duty to accept reasonable settlements, a duty included within the implied covenant of good faith and fair dealing", and continued: "in the case before us we consider the duty of an insurer to act in good faith and fairly in handling the claim of an insured, namely a duty not to withold unreasonably payments due under a policy. These are merely two different aspects of the same duty."

Although described as an implied covenant, it appears that the duty is not consensual but tortious in nature.[318] Although the duty arises out of a contractual relationship between insurer and insured,[319] the duty is independent of the contract and breach of that contract by one party does not release the other from the duty of good faith.[320] However, it has been held in California[321] that rules of "comparative" and "reverse" bad faith enable the insurer to plead the bad faith of the insured as a ground for reducing the damages for which the insurer is liable.

314. "Every contract imposes upon each party a duty of good faith and fair dealing in its performance and enforcement"—Rest 2d Contracts, section 205. Yet good faith bears little resemblance to the English notion of good faith in insurance contracts; for a comparative study see Hasson, 13 Can Bus L J 93 (1987–8). See further, Rest 2d Contracts, section 231. The extensive literature includes Burton, 94 Harv L Rev 369 (1980); Holmes, 65 Cornell L Rev 330 (1980); McMains, 53 J Air Law & Commerce 901 (1988); Herrin, 59 Miss LJ 537 (1989); "Good Faith: A Mini–Symposium", 26 Tort & Ins L J 560 (1991). On bad faith in Kentucky, see Harvey & Wiseman, 72 Kentucky L J 141 (1983–4); in Mississippi, Gibson, 55 Miss L J 485 (1985); in Montana, Graham & Luck, 45 Mont L Rev 43 (1984); in Nebraska, Fillman, 27 Neb L Rev 608 (1993); and in respect of workers' compensation see Kiser, 22 Tort & Ins L J 147 (1987); in respect of bond sureties: Balkin and Witten, 28 Tort & Ins L J 611 (1993). For the jurisdiction of courts in the USA over non-resident insurers, see Soiret, 28 Tort & Ins L J 533 (1993).
315. *Gruenberg* v *Aetna Ins Co*, 510 P 2d 1032 (Cal, 1973—fire).
316. p 1037.
317. Notably *Communale* v *Traders & General Ins Co*, 328 P 2d 198 (Cal, 1958 motor); and *Crisci* v *Security Ins Co*, 426 P 2d 173 (Cal, 1967—liability).
The original formulation of the doctrine is said to be that in *Kirke La Shelle Co* v *Paul Armstrong Co*, 263 NY 79, 87 (1933): "In every contract there is an implied covenant that neither party shall do anything which will have the effect of destroying or injuring the right of the other party to receive the fruits of the contract, which means that in every contract there exists an implied covenant of good faith and fair dealing." The contractual basis was retained in *Beck* v *Farmers Ins Exchange*, 701 P 2d 795 (Utah, 1985—motor). 5 Williston, section 670, p 159. In England *cf Southern Foundries (1926) Ltd* v *Shirlaw* [1940] AC 701, 707 *per* Lord Atkin; and in Australia *Secured Income Real Estate (Australia) Ltd* v *St Martin's Investments Pty Ltd* (1979) 144 CLR 596 (HCA). Lewison no 5.11. See also above, chapter 27, note 3.
318. *Gruenberg* (above), *loc cit*, citing *Richardson* v *Employers' Liability Assurance Corp Ltd* 102 Cal Rptr 547, 552 (Cal, 1972—liability). See further Cohen, 73 Cal L Rev 1291, 1302 ff. (1985). *Cf* Holmes, 65 Cornell L Rev 330, 367 ff (1980) who argues that the remedy is based in neither contract nor tort, but that when such damages are awarded "the wrong that occurred was equitable" (p 375).
319. *Gruenberg* (above), pp 1038–1039. It is confined to "special relationships" such as that between insurer and insured: *Seaman's Direct Buying Service Inc* v *Standard Oil Co*, 686 P 2d 1158 (Cal, 1984). Contra: Cohen, 73 Cal L Rev 1291 (1985).
320. *Gruenberg* (above), p 1040.
321. *California Casualty General Ins Co* v *Superior Court of San Bernadino County*, 218 Cal Rptr 817 (Cal, 1985—motor). Karanian, 18 Pacific L J 307 (1986); Shipstead & Thomas, 22 Tort & Ins L J 215 (1987). No case has yet been reported in which the insurer recovered damages against the insured on this ground: Shipstead & Thomas, p 225. The existence of a tort of reverse bad faith was denied in *Tokles & Son* v *Midwestern Indemnity Co*, 605 NE 2d 936 (Ohio, 1992—property).

As to the meaning of bad faith, the court in *Brown*[322] advanced a number of factors, none decisive, to be considered:

"(1) the strength of the injured claimant's case on the issues of liability and damages; (2) attempts by the insurer to induce the insured to contribute to a settlement; (3) failure of the insurer properly to investigate the circumstances so as to ascertain the evidence against the insured; (4) the insurer's rejection of advice of its own attorney or agent; (5) failure of the insurer to inform the insured of a compromise offer; (6) the amount of financial risk to which each party is exposed in the event of a refusal to settle; (7) the fault of the insured in inducing the insurer's rejection of the compromise offer by misleading it as to the facts; and (8) any other factors tending to establish or negate bad faith on the part of the insurer."

Having considered these matters, the court must still set a level of culpability for bad faith. While early courts required "substantial" culpability, later courts in California hinted at strict liability.[323] Between these positions there is the "negligence standard"; the court asks "whether the insurer's denial of the claim was reasonable, in light of the facts revealed by the insurer's investigation, the specificity of the policy terms, and the coverage expectations of reasonable insureds".[324]

In the USA, the significance of the tort of bad faith is not only that it provides the insured with compensation, in cases when the contract does not, but also that it has enabled courts to award punitive damages[325] against the insurer, when they consider that the insurer was guilty of malice, oppression, or intent to vex, harass or annoy the insured.[326] If something is too closely controlled or kept in check, even a benevolent control may kill it. There are now signs of something like a reaction in both the courts and the insurance industry. Some courts are overtly seeking to restore a balance in "the scales of justice between a claimant's right to recover on a policy when a claim is intentionally and wrongfully denied and the insurance company's right to question arguable claims".[327] In the industry, not only have certain kinds of cover been withdrawn but apprehension of large damages for bad faith has led to reluctance on the part of insurers to investigate or report fraudulent claims.[328] "Recognizing good faith as a matter of law is the long-term interest of premium-paying insureds and the financial predictability and stability of insurance companies . . . Insurance companies have a good faith right to be wrong!"[329] In England, the insurer, who unreasonably delays payment, is liable, if at all, only in contract; exemplary or punitive damages cannot generally be awarded against him, whether the action is based in contract or in tort.[330]

In Canada, the situation is more like that in the USA than that in England. No damages will be awarded for breach of contract by the insurer but punitive damages have been awarded, in respect of conduct which is "harsh, vindictive, reprehensible and malicious . . . extreme in its nature and such that by any reasonable standard it is

322. *Brown* v *Guarantee Ins Co*, 319 P 2d 69, 75 (Cal, 1958—motor).

323. For example *Crisci* v *Security Ins Co*, 426 P 2d 173, 177 (Cal, 1967—liability).

324. Abraham, p 187. See further *Seaman's Direct Buying Service Inc* v *Standard Oil Co*, 686 P 2d 1158 (Cal, 1984), *Arnold* (above), p 167). Burton, 94 Harv L Rev 369, 378 ff (1980); Holmes, 65 Cornell L Rev 330, 377 ff (1980). *Cf* Dobbyn, 62 N Dak L Rev 355, 363 (1986), who considers that the "negligence standard" is a minority view among the courts outside California.

325. Punitive damages are not awarded for breach of contract, unless the conduct constituting breach is also a tort: Rest 2d Contracts, section 355. "To speak of a tort of good faith . . . is to indulge in a legal fiction so that courts may award punitive damages"—Holmes, 65 Cornell L Rev 330, 385 (1980).

326. *Silberg* v *California Life Ins Co*, 521 P 2d 1103 (Cal, 1974—PHI).

327. Hauser, 27 Tort & Ins L J 665, 673 (1992).

328. Emerson, 46 U Miami L Rev 907, 942 ff (1992).

329. Hauser, *loc cit*.

330. *Rookes* v *Barnard* [1964] AC 1129. McGregor, nos 406 ff.

deserving of full condemnation and punishment".[331] Moreover, in Quebec damages may be awarded in such circumstances on the ground of *abus de droit*.[332] In this state of the law, given "the narrow circumstances in which punitive damages can be awarded, they may have little actual impact on the conduct of insurers. A more significant incentive for the insurer to negotiate and settle without delay may be found in the courts' discretion in awarding costs. This discretion is more often exercised against insurers than the award of punitive damages".[333]

30–11 THE POLICYHOLDERS PROTECTION ACT

If the insurer is insolvent, the claimant should consider resort to the Policyholders Protection Board under the Policyholders Protection Act 1975.[334] The Act offers protection in respect of United Kingdom policies, i.e., if the performance by the insurer "of any of his obligations under the contract evidenced by the policy" at any time "would constitute the carrying on by the insurer of insurance business of any class in the United Kingdom".[335] The latter phrase is also found in the Insurance Companies Act 1982,[336] where it means "the effecting and carrying out of contracts of insurance". Insurance business "is normally indivisible. The insurer who effects the contract carries it out".[337] Under the 1975 Act, eligibility for protection is determined at the "material time",[338] which is the beginning of the insurer's liquidation. For eligibility at that time, four conditions must be satisfied.[339]

The first condition is that the policy is a "United Kingdom policy", as defined by section 4(2) of the 1975 Act. A policy is a United Kingdom policy if, had any of the obligations under the contract evidenced by the policy (notably payment) been performed at the relevant time, such performance would have formed part of an insurance business which the insurer was authorised to carry on in the United Kingdom, whether or not such obligation(s) would have been performed in the United Kingdom.[340] Thus, in *Scher*,[341] although Parliament had had in mind mainly the protection of policyholders in the United Kingdom and had not appreciated the full financial burden of its enactment, the effect of the Act was also to protect policyholders in other countries and thus to "operate to underpin the London insurance market".[342]

---

331. *Vorvis* v *Ins Corp of BC* [1989] 1 SCR 1085, 1108 *per* McIntyre J.

332. Dubreuil (1992) McGill L J 1087, 1107.

333. Baer, (1990) 22 Ottawa L Rev 389, 417.

334. Generally, see Hodgin, *Protection of the Insured* (London, 1989), chapter 3.

335. Section 4(2). The umbrella of the Act was extended to members of friendly societies by the Friendly Societies Act 1992. Concerning the 1992 Act, see McGee, (1993) 3 Ins L & P 9.

336. Section 2. See above 24–3A.

337. *Ackman* v *Policyholders Protection Board* [1992] 2 Lloyd's Rep 321, 347 *per* Lord Donaldson MR (CA—liability), with whom Russell LJ (p 352) concurred; the case was a test case, in which, to assist the court, the intervention of the Secretary of State for Trade and Industry had been allowed. It was underlined (p 349) that the court was not concerned with long term insurance and capital redemption business.

338. section 4(1).

339. The conditions are those that emerged from *Ackman* (above), which went to the House of Lords *sub nom Scher* v *Policyholders Protection Board* [1993] 3 All ER 384 and *Scher* v *Policyholders Protection Board (No 2)* [1993] 4 All ER 840.

340. p 416 *per* Lord Goff.

341. Above.

342. p 413 *per* Lord Goff.

The second condition is that the claimant is a "policy-holder", as defined in section 96(1) of the Insurance Companies Act 1982, i.e., a person to whom a sum is due under the policy, or a person who is the "legal holder" of the policy. The "legal holder" of a policy is either

(i) a person who is not a party to the contract of insurance recorded in the policy but who nonetheless stands in a sufficiently close relationship to the policy to be (a) spoken of as the "holder" of the policy and (b) capable of having a sum due to him under the policy or

(ii) a person towards whom the insurer will in practice be able to fulfil the obligations, for example, the furnishing to policyholders of notices, accounts and reports, which are owed to policyholders under the 1982 Act.[343]

The third condition is that the claimant is a "private policyholder", as defined in section 6(7) of the 1975 Act. From this, the House in *Scher* concluded[344] that "a partnership loss is to be recoverable only if the partnership has no corporate member". This conclusion is in "broad conformity"[345] with part of the declaration on the point made by the Court of Appeal.[346] The points of agreement were as follows. First, no partnership, one or more of whose partners is a professional corporation, can be a private policyholder nor can any individual in his capacity as a partner in such a partnership. Second, being in partnership with a professional corporation does not disqualify an individual from being a private policyholder, if he contracts with the insurance company in a capacity other than as a partner.

The fourth condition is that the claim has reached the stage of creating a liability under the terms of an insurance policy, as required by section 8(2) of the 1975 Act. A corollary of this requirement is that a person whose claim is merely contingent at the material time (the beginning of the liquidation) is not eligible to claim.[347]

30–12 ACTION AGAINST AN ADJUSTER OR INVESTIGATOR

If an insurer rejects a claim as the result of a report by an adjuster or other investigator, does the claimant have any basis in law for action against the investigator? In the absence of a contract between claimant and investigator, the action must be based in tort. In the case of fire claims, the tort might be defamation, however, as a means of indemnity, the more salient question is whether the tort might be negligence.

The first question is whether the investigator owes the claimant a duty of care. Prima facie not, as the claimant's loss is economic, however, an exception is recognised in some cases when the negligence takes the form of misstatement.[348] The possi-

---

343. pp 853–854 *per* Lord Mustill.
344. p 851 *per* Lord Mustill.
345. p 852 *per* Lord Mustill.
346. p 350 *per* Lord Donaldson MR.
347. pp 857 ff *per* Lord Mustill.
348. See above, 9–2.

bility has been recognised in the USA and this was put to the New Zealand Court of Appeal in *Mortensen* v *Laing*.[349]

"In favour of a duty", said Cooke P, "is the close proximity between the investigators and the insured"; by "entering into the contract of insurance the insured has placed himself in a position where he must submit to investigation by the insurer's representatives in the event of a claim. Inevitably an honest insured has to rely to a considerable extent on the probity and carefulness of the insurer's investigators. The element of reliance is thus present. In turn those representatives must be well aware that a report by them adverse to the insured is likely to be seriously damaging to the interests of the insured".[350] In this connection, Hardie Boys J spoke of "the vulnerability of the insured", who is "highly dependent on the investigator carrying out his task carefully".[351] Cooke P also observed that the proximity between claimant and adjuster was at least as great as that in certain celebrated decisions of the House of Lords, *Smith* v *Eric S Bush*,[352] in which a valuer owed a duty to a prospective mortgagor, and *Arenson* v *Arenson*,[353] in which an auditor of a company owed a duty to the seller of shares in that company, as the auditor's valuation of the shares was to determine their price. Moreover, Sir Richard Bisson was impressed[354] by *Ministry of Housing and Local Govt* v *Sharp*,[355] in which the clerk, who prepared a certificate of entries in a register of land charges, was held to owe a duty of care to the person who had registered a charge. Also in favour of a duty, in the view of Sir Richard Bisson,[356] was the "social objective . . . of promoting professional competence" among investigators.

Against a duty were "formidable objections arising because the duty asserted would cut across established principles of law in fields other than negligence".[357] These include, firstly, defamation: the suggested cause of action in negligence would "impose a greater restriction on freedom of speech than exists under the law worked out over many years".[358] Secondly, a negligence action "could give rise to certain heads of damage not recoverable from the insurer",[359] as insurance money. This also appears to have been in the mind of Richardson J, who said: "where, as here, con-

---

349. [1992] 2 NZLR 282. As regards the USA, citations to the Court included *Continental Ins Co* v *Bayless*, 608 P 2d 281 (Ala, 1980); *Morvay* v *Hanover Insurance Cos*, 506 A 2d 333 (NH, 1986); and Hoey, 23 Tort & Ins L J 405 (1988), who concluded against the existence of a duty of care in most states. See also, against a duty: *Bui* v *St Paul Mercury Ins Co*, 981 F 2d 209 (5 Cir, 1993—yacht); Todd (1992) 108 LQR 360.

The court gave concurrent consideration to another action, *sub nom South Pacific Manufacturing Co Ltd* v *New Zealand Security Consultants & Investigations Ltd*, in which the action was brought not by the insured but by a creditor and shareholder of the insured and this was reason enough to dismiss the action: "even if the investigators owed a duty of care to the insured, such a duty would not extend to persons financially interested in the insured": *per* Cooke P, p 299.

350. p 302.
351. p 318.
352. [1990] 1 AC 831.
353. [1977] AC 405.
354. p 325.
355. [1970] 2 QB 223 (CA).
356. p 325.
357. p 301.
358. The report would attract qualified privilege, a defence to an action for defamation, which cannot be defeated by proving negligence—but by proving malice. *Idem*, p 309 *per* Richardson J and p 319 *per* Hardie Boys J. In this connection, see *Evans* v *London Hospital Medical College* [1981] 1 All ER 715. Cooke P also pointed out (p 303) that, for similar reasons, "to impose a duty of care would tend to cut across the law of malicious prosecution".

359. p 303. Cooke preferred to damages for delay and vexation, which, he assumed without deciding, were not available to the insured in a contractual action against the insurer. A similar assumption was made by Hardie Boys J (p 319). On these questions, see above, 30–9.

tracts cover the two relationships, those contracts should ordinarily control the allocation of risk unless special reasons are established to warrant a direct suit in tort. That accords, too with *Simaan General Contracting Co v Pilkington Glass Ltd (No 2)* [1988] QB 758", given that there were no "special factors such as those discussed in *Smith* v *Bush* . . . . In particular, it was not suggested [here] that through oligopolistic trade practices or other market failure the parties to such commercial insurance arrangements could not be expected to arrive at commercially acceptable bargains and that state intervention through the imposition of legal obligations in tort was required in the public interest to redress that kind of imbalance."[360] Thirdly, Richardson J took a "floodgates" point: "the imposition of the duty of care contended for could not reasonably be confined to insurance investigators and other related professionals and its ambit would be inherently expansive and unacceptably indeterminate . . . . Credit reports and media investigations and reports of events are obvious examples".[361] Fourthly, one judge at least,[362] considered that the duty owed by the investigators to the insurer "is necessarily inconsistent with the interest of the insured". The relationship between the investigator and the insured "takes on a 'mildly adversarial flavour'. It becomes a direct confrontation if arson is suspected. The imposition of a duty of care to the insured could well inhibit the investigators' ability to discharge their primary responsibility to the insurer".

A majority of the members of the Court considered that there was sufficient proximity between the claimant and adjuster, but the view was unanimous that, as regards public policy, the "balance of public interest . . . would be unjustifiably disturbed by superimposing the claimed duty of care".[363] There is more than a hint in the judgments that members of the court perceived relevant differences between England and New Zealand. Still, it is perhaps worth a moment's reflection on whether the four main reasons that persuaded the New Zealand court would also persuade a court in England.

First, certainly, an English court would not allow actions in negligence to disturb the balance of interests that must be maintained by the special rules of defamation and malicious prosecution. Certainly, an English court would not allow actions in negligence to inhibit or discourage the making of reports, the making of which is in the public interest.[364] However, it should not be forgotten that the action in *Mortensen* v *Laing* was preceded by the (unsuccessful) prosecution of Mrs Laing for arson. Many if not most reports by adjusters are more prosaic and less damaging than that on the Laings, concerning for example the extent of damage, and, if adverse, are unlikely to reflect in any way on the reputation of the claimant. Even an exaggerated insurance claim is not regarded by the courts as dishonest.[365]

Secondly, it was assumed in *Mortensen* v *Laing* that, if a negligent report led to declinature, a viable and sufficient action lay against the insurer. This may be true, but it

360. p 304.
361. pp 308–309. See also p 314, *per* Casey J. Whereas in *Smith* v *Bush*, the claimant was a private person seeking a mortgage loan to enable private house purchase, in *Mortensen v Laing*, Mr and Mrs Laing were the insured under a fire policy on a retail clothing business. On the last point made by Richardson J, it is submitted that much depends on the view taken of whether an insured could or should be able to get damages from an insurer who (unwarrantably) pays late: see above, 30–9.
362. p 314 *per* Casey J.
363. p 309 *per* Cooke P.
364. *Spring* v *Guardian Assurance plc* [1993] 2 All ER 273 (CA).
365. See above, 27–2B.

is not immediately or always self-evident. For most claimants, an action against an insurer is a daunting prospect, of the kind faced by David against Goliath. There is some evidence that Goliath does not like to be seen in public combat with David and prefers to back away from confrontation in the courts,[366] as it is bad for business; but there is also some evidence that Goliath is now inclined to take a harder line *pour décourager les autres*. If the insurer does take a firm line against payment, the claimant may not have to go to court for redress. If he has the patience to wait upon the final decision of the insurer, he may then (but only then) seek redress in another and more friendly field, that of the Ombudsman. But not every insurer has submitted to the scrutiny of the Ombudsman and it may well be precisely those who have not, who are most likely to prove obdurate, to play a dead bat and wear down the claimant. In any event, all this takes not only persistence but also time, during which the claimant may be both out of pocket[367] and eventually out of business. This brings us back to a related assumption underlying *Mortensen* v *Laing* that, at the end of the day in court, the insured may recover damages against the insurer for vexation and delay. Indeed, in New Zealand, there are decisions to this effect but in England, this is much less clear.[368]

Thirdly, the fear of floodgates must be seen in the context of a court which, unlike the House of Lords, has shown less deference to the idea that courts should proceed "incrementally" in developing and extending duties of care. The English courts may have less difficulty in distinguishing the reports of surveyors, auditors and adjusters from those of investigative journalists and the media at large and, therefore, less fear of floodgates that cannot stem the tide of litigation.

Fourthly, however, the adversarial relationship between adjuster and claimant is no less true in England[369] than in New Zealand. It is the very vulnerability of the claimant to the honesty and carefulness of the adjuster, which prompted the New Zealand court to point up the proximity between them, that has prompted the rise in England of investigators to act for the claimant, David can now pay his own warrior to meet Goliath and keep his distance.

In conclusion, although there are difference in the weight given to policy factors in New Zealand and in England, there is little reason to think that, when they are placed in the balance, the verdict of the court in England is likely to be different.

---

366. For example, *Post Magazine*, 1 April 1993, p 1; *Post Magazine*, 24 June 1993, p 2. See further, above, 27–2A.

367. *Cf Giles* v *Thompson*, [1993] 3 All ER 321, in which the House of Lords rejected argument of the insurer of the person responsible for the damage to the claimant's car, that the help and assistance provided by a car hire company in an action against the insurer was champertous and thus unlawful. Such assistance seems likely to be confined to motoring cases in which it is very likely that the action will establish the negligence of the person responsible, without contributory negligence on the part of the claimant.

368. See above, 30–9.

369. For example, *Post Magazine*, 15 April 1993, p 6, and 6 May 1993, p 3.

CHAPTER 31

SUBROGATION

31-1 INTRODUCTION

When A (the insurer) has conferred a benefit (insurance money or reinstatement) on B (the insured), B may be obliged by law to transfer to A some asset, including rights to salvage in the remains of insured property,[1] or to make available some right against a third party, including rights of action. This is to enable A to recoup, as far as possible, the loss or expense suffered or incurred by A in conferring the benefit on B.[2] This principle applies not only to insurers[3] but also, for example, to sureties and to indorsees of bills of exchange.

Underlying subrogation is the principle of indemnity (below, 31–3A) and the aim of preventing the insured from being over-compensated, by his getting both insurance money and compensation from a third party.[4] Over-compensation might have been avoided in a number of different ways but the means adopted by English law are as follows.

First, if, before he has been paid the insurance money, the insured has received compensation which diminishes his insured loss, the insurance money payable is reduced by that amount.[5]

Second, if the insurer has paid the insurance money due, the insurer may exercise any rights or remedies of the insured arising out of the event insured against.

Third, if the insurer has paid the insurance money due and then finds that the insured has already exercised rights or remedies arising out of the event, the insurer may reclaim from the insured a sum not greater than the amount the insured recovered by such exercise or the amount of the insurance money paid, whichever is the lesser sum. To that extent, a constructive trust may be impressed on money

---

1. As regards subrogation, fire and marine insurance do not differ: *Page v Scottish Ins Corp* (1929) 140 LT 571, 575 *per* Scrutton LJ (motor). *Mobile & Montgomery Ry Co v Jurey*, 111 US 584 (1884—cargo).
   MIA, section 79(1): "Where the insurer pays for a total loss, either of the whole, or in the case of goods of any apportionable part, of the subject-matter insured, he thereupon becomes entitled to take over the interest of the insured in whatever may remain of the subject-matter so paid for, and he is thereby subrogated to all the rights and remedies of the insured in and in respect of that subject-matter as from the time of the casualty."
2. Generally, see Goff & Jones, ch 27; Derham, *Subrogation in Insurance Law* (1985); Hasson, "Subrogation in Insurance Law, A Critical Evaluation", (1985) 5 OJLS 416. Appleman, sections 4051 ff.
3. *Rankin v Potter* (1873) LR 6 HL 83, 101–102 *per* Brett J (hull); *Simpson v Thompson* (1877) 3 App Cas 279, 284 *per* Lord Cairns LC (hull). MIA, section 79(2).
4. *Castellain v Preston* (1883) 11 QBD 380, 387 *per* Brett LJ (CA—fire).
5. *Hamilton v Mendes* (1761) 2 Burr 1198, 1210 ff *per* Lord Mansfield CJ (hull); *Burnand v Rodocanachi* (1882) 7 App Cas 333, 339 *per* Lord Blackburn (hull); *J Nelson & Sons Ltd v Nelson Line (Liverpool) Ltd* [1906] 2 KB 217, 223 *per* Lord Collins MR (CA—liability).

received by the insured from a third party[6]: this has the important consequence that, if the insured becomes insolvent, the insurer is entitled to that money in priority to other creditors of the insured.[7]

Fourth, in an appropriate case the insurer has the benefit of salvage.[8] Salvage is distinct from subrogation.[9] Indeed, strictly speaking only the second measure is one of subrogation, the first and third being loosely associated with subrogation and sometimes referred to as the "incidentals" of subrogation.[10]

31–2 THE LEGAL BASIS OF SUBROGATION

There are two main theories about the basis of subrogation in the law of insurance. One is that subrogation is based on a rule of equity; the other that it is based on an implied term in the contract of insurance. The former theory prevails but, in any case, the rules of subrogation may be confirmed or changed by express terms in the contract of insurance.

31–2A Equity

To avoid over-compensation of the insured is not to deny him good fortune but to avoid unjust enrichment of the insured,[11] unjust because he would be enriched at the insurer's expense. This is said to be a rule of equity.[12] It is the basis of subrogation most widely accepted in England,[13] as well as in the United States[14] where "the insurer's right of subrogation exists as a matter of equity, and is not dependent upon the reservation of the right in the contract of insurance."[15] The doctrine is equitable,[16] even when subrogation is the subject of express terms in the contract of insurance:

---

6. *Commercial Union Assurance Co* v *Lister* (1874) LR 9 Ch App 483, 484 *per* Sir G Jessel, MR (CA—fire); *King* v *Victoria Ins Co Ltd* [1896] AC 250, 255–6 *per* Lord Hobhouse (PC—cargo); *Morley* v *Moore* [1936] 2 QB 359, 366 *per* Merriman P (CA—motor); *Re Miller, Gibb & Co Ltd* [1957] 1 WLR 703 (export credit). *Cf Stearns* v *Village Main Reef Gold Mining Co Ltd* (1905) 10 Com Cas 89, 98 *per* Stirling LJ (CA—insurance of gold). *Cf* the view, that a proprietary right is inappropriate where the insured receives the money *before* he is paid by the insurer and that the appropriate action is a personal claim for money had and received: Mitchell [1993] LMCLQ 192, 195. However, this view, which was taken in the lower courts in the case, was rejected in favour of a proprietary claim in *Napier* v *Hunter* [1993] 1 All ER 385 (HL—re).
7. *Re Miller* (above).
8. Above, 28–5.
9. *Page* v *Scottish Ins Corp* (1929) 140 LT 571, 575 *per* Scrutton LJ (motor).
10. Mitchell [1993] LMCLQ 192, 194.
11. *Cf Randal* v *Cochran* (1748) 1 Ves Sen 99 (cargo) *per* Lord Hardwicke LC (p 99): the insurers "had the plainest equity that could be. The person originally sustaining the loss was the owner; but after satisfaction made to him, the insurer". See also *Burnand* v *Rodocanachi* (1882) 7 App Cas 333, 339 *per* Lord Blackburn, 344 *per* Lord Fitzgerald (hull); *Morris* v *Ford Motor Co Ltd* [1973] QB 792, 801 *per* Lord Denning MR, 805 *per* Stamp LJ. Also in favour of an equitable basis: Derham, *op cit* (note 1), p 22; Goff & Jones, p 524; Bowe, 53 J Air Law & Commerce 999, 1003 (1988) and citations.
12. Objections to a theory of subrogation based on a rule of equity are chiefly historical—the rule was applied by courts of common law before the fusion of law and equity: see further, MacGillivray, Nos 1164 ff.
13. *Napier* v *Hunter* [1993] 1 All ER 385 (HL—re).
14. *Hall* v *Nashville & Chattanooga Railroad Co*, 13 Wall 367 (1872—cargo); *Wager* v *Providence Ins Co*, 150 US 99, 108 *per* Shiras J (1893—cargo); *Employers Health Ins* v *General Cas Co*, 469 NW 2d 172, 180 (Wis, 1991—PHI); *Gibbs* v *Hawaiian Eugenia Corp*, 966 F 2d 101, 106 (2 Cir, 1992—freight).
15. *National Garment Co* v *New York C & St L R Co*, 173 F 2d 32, 37 (8 Cir, 1949—cargo).
Cf Farmers Elevator Mutual Ins Co v *Jorski Mill & Elevator Co*, 404 F 2d 143 (10 Cir, 1968), where it was said that the doctrine was based either on equity or on implied contract.
16. *Atlantic Mutual Ins Co* v *Cooney*, 303 F 2d 253 (9 Cir, 1962—cargo).

"Unless the contract indicates otherwise contractual subrogation is examined within the framework of the doctrine of equitable subrogation and is subject to conformity with its principles".[17] In the United States, there are

"at least three equitable reasons traditionally advanced for permitting subrogation: (1) that the person who in good faith pays the debt or obligation of another has equitably purchased (quasi-contractually), or at least is entitled to, the obligation owed by the debtor or tortfeasor; (2) that the third party (tortfeasor) is not entitled to a windfall release from his obligation simply because the injured party had the foresight to obtain insurance; and (3) that public policy is served by allowing insurers to recover and thus reduce insurance rates generally."[18]

31–2B Implied Term

In words of Lord Diplock,[19]

"there is no general doctrine of unjust enrichment recognised in English law . . . [Subrogation] embraces more than a single concept in English law. It is a convenient way of describing a transfer of rights from one person to another, without assignment or assent by the person from whom the rights are transferred and which takes place by operation of law in a whole variety of widely different circumstances. Some rights by subrogation are contractual in their origin, as in the case of contracts of insurance. Others . . . are in no way based on contract and appear to defeat classification except as an empirical remedy to prevent a particular kind of unjust enrichment."

This view of subrogation, which acquired some prominence when it was espoused by Lord Diplock, is of doubtful origin in the common law[20] and is not widely held today. Still less tenable today is the premise that English law does not recognise a doctrine of unjust enrichment.[21] The Diplock view of subrogation was largely consigned to the bin of legal history by the decision of the House of Lords in *Napier* v *Hunter*.[22]

In *Napier* v *Hunter*, Lloyd's members reinsured with "stop loss" insurers, claimed and were paid. Money was then recovered from third parties responsible for the loss and was held by solicitors. The main question was whether the reinsurers' right to part of that money was merely a personal common law right, enforceable by an action for money had and received, or a proprietary right in equity. The House of Lords held the latter and that, although the money was not impressed with a trust, the insurers had a lien or charge on the money, which gave them priority over other creditors of the insured.[23]

17. *Foremost County Mutual Ins Co* v *Home Indemnity Co*, 897 F 2d 754, 762 (5 Cir, 1990—motor). See also *Travelers Indemnity Co* v *US*, 543 F 2d 71 (9 Cir, 1976—casualty). *Cf Northwestern Mutual Ins Co* v *Jackson Vibrators Inc*, 402 F 2d 37 (6 Cir, 1968—fire).

18. *Stafford Metal Works Inc* v *Cook Paint & Varnish Co*, 418 F Supp 56, 58 (ND Tex, 1976—fire). The effect on premium rates appears to be small: see above, 31–1.

19. *Orakpo* v *Manson Investments Ltd* [1978] AC 95, 104. *Idem: Yorkshire Ins Co* v *Nisbet Shipping Co Ltd* [1962] 2 QB 330, 339–342 *per* Diplock J (hull), approved by Widgery LJ in *Cousins & Co Ltd* v *D & C Carriers Ltd* [1971] 2 QB 230, 242 (cargo). Lord Diplock reiterated the same view briefly in *Hobbs* v *Marlowe* [1978] AC 16, 39 in a speech with which Lord Elwyn-Jones LC (p 32) and Lord Salmon (p 42) agreed. *Cf Orakpo* (above) [1977] 1 WLR 347, 368 *per* Goff LJ.

The contractual basis derives some support from *Darrell* v *Tibbitts* (1880) 5 QBD 560, 562 *per* Brett LJ, p 565 *per* Cotton LJ, p 568 *per* Thesiger LJ (CA—fire); *John Edwards & Co* v *Motor Union Ins Co Ltd* [1922] 2 KB 249, 254–255 *per* McCardie J (hull); *Boag* v *Standard Marine Ins Co Ltd* [1937] 2 KB 113, 122, 125 *per* Lord Wright MR, 128 *per* Scott LJ (CA—cargo).

20. Derham, *op cit* (note 2), pp 9 ff. The view has been rejected in the USA, for example, in *Gibbs* v *Hawaiian Eugenia Corp*, 966 F 2d 101, 106 (2 Cir, 1992—freight).

21. *Lipkin Gorman* v *Karpnale Ltd* [1991] 2 AC 548; see above, 30–5C3.

22. [1993] 1 All ER 385.

23. It was not necessary to decide whether the insurers had an "equitable" right to sue third parties in the name of the insured.

31–2C Express Term

Whatever the basis of the law of subrogation, the rules may be modified by the express terms of the contract of insurance. Such terms are commonly found, many of them restating the rules of law.[24] By contrast but still on the basis of the contract, the insurer may seek to bypass subrogation, by stipulating that the insured shall assign to him the relevant rights. Assignment has potential advantages over subrogation: the insurer may exercise the rights without first indemnifying the insured and, if there is a windfall, it remains with the insurer. Even so, this device does not appear to be widely used.

31–3 WHEN? THE CONDITIONS OF SUBROGATION

31–3A Indemnity Insurance

The primary purpose of subrogation here is to vindicate the principle of indemnity[25] and it applies only to contracts of indemnity[26]: traditionally, all contracts of insurance except life and PA insurance.[27] If a contract is of a kind that is traditionally categorised as indemnity insurance, it remains an indemnity contract for the purpose of this rule, even though in a particular case the sum payable is less than the actual loss.[28]

In the leading case of *Bradburn* v *GWR*,[29] the insured was injured in a railway accident and was awarded damages against the railway company. The company's contention, that the damages should be reduced by the amount of his insurance cover for the injury, was rejected by the court.

In the face of new insurance products, courts may have to look behind the traditional categories, in order to draw a rational and predictable line between indemnity insurance, to which subrogation applies, and non-indemnity insurance,[30] to which it does not. Possible lines are as follows.

31–3A1 Benefit Purchased

In *Bradburn* (above),[31] the company's contention was rejected because "one who pays premiums for the purpose of insuring himself, pays on the footing that his right to

---

24. For discussion of such terms, see Birds [1979] JBL 124. USA: "conventional subrogation"; see Kimball & Davis, 60 Mich L Rev 841, 860 ff. (1962). As to whether the equitable character of subrogation limits the freedom of the insurer to alter the rules in his own favour, see Veal, 28 Tort & Ins L J 69, 74 (1992).

25. Fleming, 54 Calif L Rev 1478, 1499 (1966).

26. *Simpson & Co* v *Thomson* (1873) 3 App Cas 279, 284 *per* Lord Cairns LC (hull); *Burnand* v *Rodocanachi* (1882) 7 App Cas 333, 339 *per* Lord Blackburn (hull); *Finlay* v *Mexican Investment Corp* [1897] 1 QB 517, 522 *per* Charles J (credit); *Morris* v *Ford Motor Co Ltd* [1973] QB 792, 800 *per* Lord Denning MR, 804–806 *per* Stamp LJ, 812 *per* James LJ (CA); *Borserine* v *Maryland Casualty Co*, 112 F 2d 409, 414 (8 Cir, 1940); *Crab Orchard Improvement Co* v *Chesapeake & O Ry Co*, 115 F 2d 277, 281 (4 Cir, 1940—employers' liability), cert den 312 US 702.

27. *Theobald* v *Railway Passengers Assurance Co* (1854) 10 Exch 45, 53 *per* Alderson B (PA); *Meacock* v *Bryant & Co* [1942] 2 All ER 661. *Crab Orchard* (above); *South Central Bell Telephone Co* v *City of Columbia*, 641 F 2d 1192 (6 Cir, 1980—PA).

28. See above, 28–1.

29. (1874) LR 10 Exch 1. See also *Dufourcet & Co* v *Bishop* (1886) 18 QBD 373 (freight); *Parry* v *Cleaver* [1970] AC 1; *Cousins & Co Ltd* v *D & C Carriers Ltd* [1971] 2 QB 230, 240 *per* Widgery LJ (CA—cargo); *Hobbs* v *Marlowe* [1978] AC 16 (motor); *Mobile & Montgomery Ry Co* v *Jurey*, 111 US 584 (1884, cargo).

30. Non-indemnity insurance is sometimes called contingency insurance, for example, *Medical Defence Union Ltd* v *Dept of Trade* [1979] 1 Lloyd's Rep 499, 502 *per* Megarry V-C.

31. Above, note 27.

be compensated when the event insured against happens is an equivalent for the premiums he has paid."[32] The insured has bought something, a contingent benefit, of which he should not be deprived. Moreover, in many cases of life insurance, the purpose is investment: the insurer has had the use of the insured's money for a period of time and the insured reasonably expects an eventual return, for which he has paid. However, a principle based on the idea of purchase or investment presents difficulties.

First, while the element of investment may distinguish some life insurance[33] from traditional indemnity insurance, it does not distinguish personal accident insurance. That has been distinguished from indemnity insurance on the basis that to reduce the damages by the amount of the insurance money would be to deprive the victim insured of the full benefit of his premiums, of his providence, and hand it over to the third party wrongdoer in the form of reduced damages.[34] But this alone is unconvincing, for the same is true of traditional indemnity insurance, such as fire cover.

Second, the reference to the purchase of cover by the insured has led inevitably to the argument, that the rule against subrogation does not apply when the insurance cover has been paid for not by the insured himself but by somebody else. Thus, in *The Yasin*,[35] it was argued that the principle in *Bradburn* (above), that the proceeds of insurance should be disregarded when assessing damages, "only applies when it is the plaintiff himself who has paid the premium, thereby purchasing for himself the benefit of which he would be deprived if the proceeds of insurance were taken into account". It would be odd, if the application of the principle to life or accident insurance depended on whether the premiums were paid by the insured or, for example, his employer,[36] and in *The Yasin* a distinction of that kind was rejected.[37]

Third, the assumption that, if the damages are reduced by the amount of the insurance or vice versa, the insured would have paid something for nothing, is false. The insured buys accident cover, which includes not only cover against tortious injury but cover against accidental non-tortious injury, the latter being more common than the former. This he would have got, even if his accident is a tort and a reduction is made in the award.[38]

31–3A2 Objective: Compensation

A safer basis for the principle in *Bradburn* (above, 31–3A) is that insurance is indemnity insurance, when it is (reasonably and realistically) intended to compensate the

---

32. *Ibid*, p 2 *per* Bramwell B. For investment as a criterion in the USA, see Kircher, *op cit* (note 2), pp 34 ff.

33. Not all: for example, term insurance; also insurance taken by a creditor on the life of his debtor, which is like indemnity insurance, though the courts will probably not permit subrogation: the decision of Lord Ellenborough in *Godsall* v *Boldero* (1807) 9 East 72, that such insurance was a contract of indemnity, was overruled in *Dalby* v *India & London Life Assurance Co* (1854) 10 CB 365 (life).

34. This has been affirmed in cases of personal injuries: *Shearman* v *Folland* [1950] 2 KB 43, 46 *per* Asquith LJ (CA); *Parry* v *Cleaver* [1970] AC 1, 14 *per* Lord Reid; *ibid* p 37 *per* Lord Pearce; *Smoker* v *London Fire & Civil Defence Authority* [1991] 2 AC 502. *Mandas* v *Thomschke* (1983) 145 DLR (3d) 530, 536 (BC—disability).

35. [1979] 2 Lloyd's Rep 45, 48 (cargo).

36. In any event, the insured often pays for the cover indirectly, for example, through his work for the employer: *Parry* v *Cleaver* [1970] AC 1, 16 *per* Lord Reid; p 37 *per* Lord Pearce. *Cf Smith* v *Canadian Pacific Ry Co* (1964) 41 DLR 249 (Sask): *idem* only if pension contributory.

A similar view of the facts was taken in *The Yasin* (above): the insured "paid" for the insurance by agreeing to take a reduced benefit (older ship) from the shipowner, who paid the premiums.

37. p 48 *per* Lloyd J.

38. Fleming, 54 Calif L Rev 1478, 1500 (1966).

insured, and it is non-indemnity insurance, when it is not. This basis is brought back from the brink of tautology by the emphasis on intention.

"Life insurance, though based on the indemnity principle, is not itself a contract of indemnity. One of the chief reasons for this is the difficulty involved in placing any pecuniary value upon life. Indemnity insurance looks to a reimbursement of the actual loss sustained. It is this difficulty of appraising human suffering, similar to the difficulty of appraising the value of human lives, that has prompted most of the courts to deny the subrogation feature to accident, as well as life insurance."[39]

The amount of insurance money is determined not by actual loss but by the amount of cover purchased. The amount of damages awarded for injury is determined by reference to a tariff, the purpose of which is not to ensure compensation for the victim but consistency between awards. It is very hard to put a price on a life or a leg and very hard, therefore, to say whether a victim with insurance has been unjustly enriched or not.[40] So, as writers put it in the United States,[41] the "distinction is not between indemnity and investment but between a policy that merely makes the policyholder whole and one that pays a specified sum on the happening of the event insured against"; or, as Vice-Chancellor Megarry put it in England[42]: non-indemnity insurance provides "payment upon a contingent event".

The traditional categories will continue to speak for themselves: life and PA insurance will not normally be seen as indemnity insurance. Insurance of medical expenses[43] and disability insurance[44] have been held to be indemnity insurance. New lines and new policies will be looked at separately and each case treated on its merits.[45]

31–3B The Insurer must Pay

To have a right of subrogation a person must have conferred a benefit. This means that the insurer must have paid the insured[46] and, moreover, the rule is that he must have paid all sums due under the contract of insurance before he can exercise the right of subrogation.

In *Page* v *Scottish Ins Corp*,[47] the defendant drove the insured's Buick negligently

---

39. *Crab Orchard Improvement Co* v *Chesapeake & O Ry Co*, 115 F 2d 277, 281 (4 Cir, 1940—employers' liability). In France, an ordinance of 1681 forbade life assurance, because *liberum corpus aestimationem non habet*.

40. *Cf* property insurance at an agreed value, because value is hard to agree or assess; logically, this should be non-indemnity insurance, but usually it is not: Fleming 54 Calif L Rev 1478, 1499 (1966).

41. Kimball & Davis, *op cit*, p 851.

42. *Medical Defence Union Ltd* v *Dept of Trade* [1979] 1 Lloyd's Rep 499, 502 *per* Megarry V-C.

43. *Glynn* (below). *Employers' Liability Assurance Corp Ltd* v *Daley*, 51 NYS 2d 567 (1944); *Silinsky* v *State-Wide Ins Co*, 289 NYS 2d 541 (1968—motor); *Faust* v *Luke*, 364 NYS 2d 344 (1975). See further Kircher, *op cit*, pp 34 ff and cases cited. It has been argued that subrogation should not apply to medical expenses insurance, because thrift and foresight in taking the insurance should not be unrewarded: Baron 96 Dick L Rev 581, 588 (1992). This, of course, is an argument against subrogation altogether.

44. *Gibson* v *Sun Life Assurance Co* (1984) 6 DLR (4th) 746 (Ont).

45. *Glynn* v *Scottish Union & National Ins Co Ltd* (1963) 40 DLR (2d) 929 (Ont—motor). *Idem* pluvious insurance, *ibid*, p 938.

46. *Page* (below). See also *The Millwall* [1905] P 155 (CA); *Scottish Union & National Ins Co* v *Davis* [1970] 1 Lloyd's Rep 1 (CA—motor).

Globe & Rutgers Fire Ins Co Ltd v *Truedell* [1927] 2 DLR 659 (Ont—fire). *Bunge Corp* v *London & Overseas Ins Co*, 394 F 2d 496 (2 Cir, 1968), cert den 393 US 952; *Fifty States Management Corp* v *Public Service Mutual Ins Co*, 324 NYS 2d 345 (1971—fire); *Gibbs* v *Hawaiian Eugenia Corp*, 966 F 2d 101, 106 (2 Cir, 1992—freight).

47. (1929) 140 LT 571; 33 Ll L Rep 138.

and damaged not only the Buick but also a passing Rolls Royce.[48] With the consent of the insurer, the defendant himself repaired the Buick and then, as repairer, claimed the cost from the insurer, who counter-claimed in the name of the insured for the same sum from the defendant, as wrongdoer. However, pending settlement of a claim by the owner of the Rolls Royce, the insurer had yet to pay the insured. The defendant's plea, that the insurer was not subrogated to the rights of the insured until he had paid the insured, was upheld by the Court of Appeal.[49]

"if you get one car, one accident, one policy, one premium, I do not think the underwriter can claim to be subrogated until he has satisfied all the claims arising under that policy and paid for by that one premium in respect of that one accident and that one car."[50]

In the United States, a loan or advance by the insurer to the insured, on terms, for example, that it is to be repaid only from what may be recovered from a third party, is not a payment which entitles the insurer to subrogation.[51]

31–3B1 Full Indemnity

In *Page*[52] the court left open the question, whether the insurer "is not subrogated though he has paid the whole amount due on his policy if the insured has a further loss". This seems to envisage loss, which arises out of the same event but for which the insurer was not liable because, for example, the amount insured under the policy was less than the actual loss of the insured.

In English law, however, although there is some authority,[53] that the insured may apply any recovery from a third party first to his own uninsured loss, before accounting to the insurer, the answer to this question was not clear,[54] unless settled by the contract of insurance or unless it was a case of marine insurance,[55] until the decision of the House of Lords in *Napier* v *Hunter*.[56]

48. Scrutton LJ (p 574): "Unfortunately Mr Page belongs to that class of persons who drive very fast when the road is greasy—who go at a pace of about forty miles an hour round a curve on a greasy day. He skidded . . . He has been fined for furious driving."

49. On the authority of *Simpson* v *Thompson* (1877) 3 App Cas 279, 284 *per* Lord Cairns LC (hull); *Darrell* v *Tibbitts* (1880) 5 QBD 560, 563 *per* Brett LJ (CA—fire); *Castellain* v *Preston* (1883) 11 QBD 380, 389 *per* Brett LJ (CA—fire).

50. p 138; p 576 *per* Scrutton LJ; see also p 577 Sankey LJ. It made no difference that the insurer paid the third party claim between the time that the action was begun and the trial (*ibid*).

51. *Luckenbach* v *McCahan Sugar Refining Co*, 248 US 139, 149 *per* Brandeis J (1918—cargo); *Eber Bros Wine & Liquor Corp* v *Firemen's Ins Co*, 30 F Supp 412 (SDNY, 1939—liability); *Home Ins Co* v *Rosenfeld*, 56 NYS 2d 454 (1945); *Rosenfeld* v *Continental Building Operating Co*, 135 F Supp 465 (WD Mo, 1955—jeweler's block). *Contra: Neuss, Hesslein & Co* v *380 Canal St Realty Corp*, 168 NYS 2d 579 (1957). On the loan receipt agreement and its development, see Derham, *op cit* (note 2), ch 9.

52. *Page* v *Scottish Ins Corp* (1929) 33 Ll L Rep 134, 138; 140 LT 571, 576 *per* Scrutton LJ.

53. *Tunno* v *Edwards* (1810) 12 East 488 (cargo). *Re Driscoll* [1918] 1 IR 152, 159 *per* O'Connor MR (fire). *Globe & Rutgers Fire Ins Co Ltd* v *Truedell* [1927] 2 DLR 659 (Ont—fire). Tarr, 11 Adel L Rev 232, 233 ff (1987), and cases cited. USA: most courts allow the insured to cover the amount of a deductible: Veal, 28 Tort & Ins L J 69, 72 (1992). This is unlikely to be so, if the contract contains an average clause: in that case the recovery must be shared between insured and insurer in proportion to their share of the entire risk, to which the recovery relates.

54. Derham, *op cit* (note 2) p 53, reviews the cases. *Cf Commercial Union Assurance Co* v *Lister* (1874) LR 9 Ch App 483 (fire), deciding that the insured, whose insurance is only a partial indemnity and who sues a third party in respect of the loss, remains *dominus litis*. The court discussed the duty of the insured to the insurer in terms of the relationship found in a case of subrogation.

55. In marine insurance, the insurer is subrogated, whether the insured has been fully indemnified or not: *North of England Ins Assn* v *Armstrong* (1870) LR 5 QB 244 (hull); *Goole & Hull Steam Towing Co Ltd* v *Ocean Marine Ins Co Ltd* [1928] 1 KB 589 (hull). For criticism of these cases, see Goff & Jones, p 542, n 39. See further Arnould, No 1306.

56. [1993] 1 All ER 385 (HL—re).

According to the prevailing equitable theory of subrogation[57] and the underlying principle of unjust enrichment, which was approved in general terms in that case, the main concern should be against unjust enrichment of the insured and it has caused some surprise that an equitable doctrine of this kind should deprive the insured of indemnity.[58] Indeed, it is on equitable grounds like these, that the point has been decided against the insurer in Canada. In one case, the insured lost wages in a motor accident in an amount greater than that recovered from the insurer and the party at fault. The court picked out the basic idea of subrogation, on the basis of the English authorities, as being to prevent the insured being paid twice over for the same loss,[59] "a doctrine in favour of the underwriters or insurers in order to prevent the assured from recovering more than a full indemnity".[60] In a second case, the insured was injured in a motor accident and recovered less than the actual cost of hospital expenses. The court concluded that a "plaintiff is not to be unjustly enriched by an overpayment but he is entitled to full payment before the subrogation claimant is paid anything".[61] Although the insurer in each case had paid the full amount due under the contract of insurance, it was held that no right of subrogation arose in favour of the insurer.

The approach taken by the House of Lords in *Napier* v *Hunter* (above) is starkly different, as regards the case of an excess clause. The issue was seen not as one of unjust enrichment but as one of contract and the assumption of risk. As a matter of contract, the insurer has promised indemnity only in respect of loss greater than the excess. If the insured's actual loss is 10X, the excess is 2X, and the insurer pays 8X, but then the insured recovers 6X from a third party, the insured's actual loss (insurance money apart) has shrunk to 4X (10 minus 6); in these circumstances, the insurer's obligation, had he not paid already, would have been to pay only 2X (4 minus the excess of 2) and, having paid 8X, the insurer should recover 6X, leaving the insured with a final net loss of 2X (the excess) not, as held at first instance, a recovery of 4X, leaving the insured without loss. Is this really what both parties intended? Can one really say that this was a risk assumed by the insured, when one of the main reasons for taking insurance is to avoid risk and to avoid loss? The excess is stipulated not by the insured but by the insurer, to reduce transaction costs and to encourage the insured to be risk averse. Without an excess, the cover would cost more, so the insured does agree to bear that layer of risk but only because he cannot cover it without disproportionate expense. But does it follow that, if compensation is available from the wrongdoer, he intends it to go (top down) to the insurer first?

31–3B2 Doubtful Insurance Claims

If the insurer pays a claim, which is doubtful but which he does not consider worth contesting, can it be said that, not having been strictly obliged to pay under the con-

---

57. Above, 31–2A.
58. Birds [1993] JBL 294, 298.
59. *Confederation Life Ins Co* v *Causton* (1989) 60 DLR (4th) 372, 374 (CA BC).
60. p 375, quoting *Castellain* v *Preston* (1883) 11 QBD 380, 387 *per* Brett LJ (CA). Moreover, "the cost incurred in effecting recovery from a third party—be it legal fees or a *bona fide* compromise of a claim—are properly to be taken into account in determining the amount of the recovery or indemnification that the insured achieves" (p 382).
61. *Re Bigl* (1989) 60 DLR (4th) 438, 441 (CA Alta); Harris, (1993) 22 Can Bus L J 308. New Zealand: see Borrowdale, [1993] NZ Recent L Rev 297. USA: *Powell* v *Blue Cross*, 581 So 2d 772 (Ala, 1990—motor); *Sharpley* v *Sonoco Products Co*, 581 So 2d 792 (Ala, 1990—medical); *Peck* v *Dill*, 581 So 2d 800

tract of insurance, the insurer is not subrogated to the rights of the insured to recover an amount equivalent to that payment? According to the equitable theory of subrogation, if the insured has been fully indemnified, the possibility of unjust enrichment exists and the insurer should be entitled to subrogation.[62] In practice, this issue may be governed by contract terms, ensuring that the insurer has rights of subrogation as soon as he has paid.[63]

The question arose in *King* v *Victoria Ins Co Ltd*,[64] on a motion by a third party, responsible for damage to wool in lighters, to set aside a judgment against him. He argued that, although the insurers of the wool had paid, the insurance had not attached. The Board found[65] it a "startling proposition" that the judgment should be set aside by means of "a highly technical rule of law which has no bearing upon his own wrongful act". Lord Hobhouse pointed out[66] that, if the third party's contention were good law, "the consequence would be that insurers could never admit a claim on which dispute might be raised except at the risk of finding themselves involved in the very dispute they have tried to avoid, by persons who have no interest in that dispute." The Board concluded that, the claim having been honestly and reasonably made and honestly settled by the insurers, the insurers were subrogated to the rights of the insured against the third party.

The decision can be supported on the grounds, first, that it is in the public interest against unnecessary litigation and, second, that it is not open to a third party to raise a defence, which is based on a contract to which he is not a party, a defence which the parties to the contract have chosen not to raise[67] and which, certainly, they did not intend to enure for his benefit. The result would be different, whether based on equity, implied contract or public policy, if the settlement between insurer and insured was not an honest settlement[68] or if the insurance contract was illegal[69] or if the payment to the insured was evidently *ex gratia*.

(Ala, 1991—motor); *Sanders* v *Scheidler*, 816 F Supp 1338 (WD Wis, 1993—medical). But *cf Vesta Ins Co* v *Amoco Production Co*, 986 F 2d 981 (5 Cir, 1993—liability).

62. In this sense, Goff & Jones, p 529, citing *Boney* v *Central Mutual Ins Co*, 197 SE 122 (NC, 1938). See also *Ledingham* v *Ontario Hospital Services Commission* (1974) 46 DLR (3d) 699 (Sup Ct—medical expenses). *Nord-Deutscher Lloyd* v *INA,* 110 F 420 (4 Cir, 1904—cargo); *Gradmann & Holler* v *Continental Lines*, 504 F Supp 785 (D P Rico, 1980—cargo). *Cf Ambrosy* v *Oklahoma Union Ins Co*, 42 P 2d 849 (Okl, 1935).

63. Birds [1979] JBL 124.

64. [1896] AC 250; applied in *Austin* v *Zurich General Accident & Liability Ins Co* [1944] 2 All ER 243 (motor); the question did not arise on appeal: [1945] KB 250. The decision in *King* was accepted as correct in *John Edwards & Co* v *Motor Union Ins Co Ltd* [1922] 2 KB 249, 256 by McCardie J (hull).

A similar decision was reached in *Nord-Deutscher Lloyd* v *President Ins Co*, 110 F 420 (4 Cir, 1901—cargo); *Gradmann & Holler* v *Continental Lines*, 504 F Supp 785 (D P Rico, 1980—cargo)

65. [1896] AC 250, 254 *per* Lord Hobhouse.

66. p 255.

67. *King* (above), p 254 *per* Lord Hobhouse. *Sun Mutual Ins Co* v *Mississippi Valley Transport Co*, 17 F 919, 923 (ED Mo, 1883—cargo).

As to privity of contract, see *Scruttons Ltd* v *Midland Silicones Ltd* [1962] AC 446.

68. *King* (above). An example occurs if the lack of cover was clear: *Standard Marine Ins Co Ltd* v *Scottish Metropolitan Assurance Co Ltd*, 283 US 284, 289–900 *per* Stone J (1931—cargo). See also *Ambrosy* v *Oklahoma Union Ins Co*, 42 P 2d 849 (Okl, 1935).

69. *John Edwards & Co* v *Motor Union Ins Co Ltd* [1922] 2 KB 249 (hull—honour policy): the decision was based less on public policy than on the ground that the right to subrogation must derive from a contract of indemnity and that an honour policy was not a contract of indemnity (p 255).

Cf USA: an honour policy is valid and enforceable, and subrogation is permitted: *Frank B Hall & Co Inc* v *Jefferson Ins Co*, 279 F 892 (SDNY, 1921—hull).

31–3C Contractual Exclusion

Rights of subrogation may be limited or excluded by the contract of insurance.[70] Moreover, the exercise of the right may be excluded by agreement with a third party, such as the "knock-for-knock" agreements which, until recently, were commonplace between motor insurers.[71]

31–4 THE RIGHTS OF THE INSURER

The insurer may take "advantage" of any rights, which the insured has against a third party and which, if exercised, have the effect of diminishing the loss insured. The insurer does this by compelling the insured to enforce those rights, subject to indemnity provided by the insurer against costs,[72] or, if the insured has already done so, by requiring the insured to repay the insurer, to the extent that the loss covered by insurance money paid has been recouped from the third party.

In *Castellain* v *Preston*,[73] a house was insured against fire by its owner. After he had contracted to sell it but before completion of the sale, the house was damaged by fire. The seller received, first, the insurance money and then, after completion, the full purchase price of the house, to which the seller was entitled in spite of the fire. The Court of Appeal held that the insurer was entitled to recover from the insured seller a sum equal to the insurance money. In particular, the court rejected a narrow view of subrogation, that the right of the insurer was limited to proceeding in the name of the insured against a third party, who might be liable for the loss. The insurer's right extended to recovering from the insured money recovered from a third party, if that money diminished the insured loss. Brett LJ said[74] that the insurers "were not subrogated to a right to enforce the remedy, but what they were subrogated into was the right to receive *the advantage* of the remedy which had been applied".

In the case of double insurance, each insurer's enjoyment of the rights of subrogation will be affected by the right of the other to contribution. In the case of successive insurance on different layers of the same risk, the first insurer, having paid the insured, is served first by any advantages of subrogation:

In *Boag*,[75] wheat was insured on a voyage with insurer A. Later, its value increased and the extra value was insured with insurer B. The wheat was totally lost by jettison to save the ship. Having been paid in full by A and B, the insured received general average in respect of the jettison in an amount, however, less than that paid by A.

---

70. *Morris* v *Ford Motor Co Ltd* [1973] QB 792, 812 *per* James LJ (CA).

71. *Bell Assurance Assn* v *Licenses & General Ins Corp & Guarantee Fund* (1923) 17 Ll L Rep 100 (CA—motor); *Morley* v *Moore* [1936] 2 KB 359 (CA—motor). Another important example of such agreements is the agreement of insurers in respect of claims against employees of the insured employer concluded by members of the British Insurance Association. See further Lewis (1985) 48 MLR 275.

72. *Yorkshire Ins Co Ltd* v *Nisbet Shipping Co Ltd* [1962] 2 QB 330, 341 *per* Diplock J (hull).

73. (1883) 11 QBD 380; applied to a case of compulsory purchase in *Phoenix Assurance Co* v *Spooner* [1905] 2 KB 753. See also *Stearns* v *Village Main Reef Gold Mining Co Ltd* (1905) 10 Com Cas 89; and LPA, section 47. For criticism of the effect of subrogation on contracts to sell land, see Hasson, *op cit*, pp 428–429; Thompson (1984) Conv 43, 50. *Cf* in Australia the Insurance Contracts Act 1984, s 50(1)(*c*).

74. p. 391 (emphasis added).

75. *Boag* v *Standard Marine Ins Co Ltd* [1936] 2 KB 121, affirmed [1937] 2 KB 113 (CA). There is a suggestion (p 124 *per* Lord Wright MR) that the decision would have been different, if the general average had been adjusted on the basis of a value higher than that in the (valued) policy of insurer A.

Branson J held that the general average belonged entirely to A and rejected the claim of B to a proportionate part. His decision was affirmed by the Court of Appeal.

Both Branson J[76] and Lord Wright MR[77] adopted this passage from *Phillips on Insurance*[78]:

"The right of an underwriter cannot be affected by any contract made by the insured with another underwriter or any other person, except so far as the insured is supposed to reserve the right of making such other contract, and the underwriter to subscribe the policy under an implied condition that the insured may avail himself of such right."

31–4A The Nature of the Insurer's Rights

The judgments in *Castellain* (above) contain classic statements of the law of subrogation, as it relates to insurance. For instance, Brett LJ said[79] that subrogation "is a doctrine in favour of the underwriters or insurers in order to prevent the assured from recovering more than a full indemnity." He continued[80] that

"as between the underwriter and the assured the underwriter is entitled to every right of the assured, whether such right consists in contract, fulfilled or unfulfilled, or in remedy for tort capable of being insisted on, or in any other right, whether by condition or otherwise, legal or equitable, which can be, or has been exercised or has accrued, and whether such right could or could not be enforced by the insurer in the name of the assured by the exercise of or acquiring of which right or condition the loss against which the assured is insured, can be, or has been diminished".

In the same case Cotton LJ said[81] that the question turns on

"what a policy of insurance against fire is, and on that the right of the [insurer] depends. The policy is really a contract to indemnify the person insured for the loss which he has sustained in consequence of the peril insured against which has happened . . . it is only to pay that loss which the assured may have sustained by reason of the fire which has occurred. In order to ascertain what that loss is, everything must be taken into account which is received by and comes to the hand of the assured, and which diminishes that loss."

These statements can be interpreted in a way that is too literal and too wide. In the example of fire damage to a block of flats, if the insurer is subrogated to literally every right "by . . . which . . . the loss . . . can be, or has been diminished" (Brett LJ), or if "everything must be taken into account which is received by and comes to the hand of the assured which diminishes that loss" (Cotton LJ), the insurer would be subrogated to the right of the insured owner to any rent from his tenants, to which he was entitled notwithstanding the fire damage. In a sense the rent diminishes the loss to the insured; and, if handed over to the insurer, it diminishes the loss to the insurer—but at the expense of the insured, for it leaves the insured worse off than if the fire had not occurred. This is not the object of subrogation in the context of insurance. That is why it has been held that the insurer subrogated to the rights of his insured/shipowner, can-

---

76. p 127.
77. pp 124–125; see also Scott LJ, p 128.
78. (5th ed, 1867), Vol ii, para 1715.
79. *Castellain* v *Preston* (1883) 11 QBD 380, 387 (CA—fire).
80. p. 388. See also p 404 *per* Bowen LJ.
81. p 393. *Idem: Burnand* v *Rodocanachi* (1882) 7 App Cas 333, 339 *per* Lord Blackburn (cargo). See also Bowen LJ in *Castellain* (above) pp 397–399, who stresses the nature of fire insurance as a contract of indemnity and the necessity to prevent the insured recovering more than he has lost, so as not to promote wagering.

not enforce the owner's rights to freight[82]: it was not part of the salvage, it was something independent of the ship, capable of being separately insured.[83] Freight "is a payment for work and labour done".[84] Equally, rent is a payment for a facility or service provided by the landlord, which he has earned quite apart from the fire and which, *ceteris paribus*, he would have earned even if there had been no fire.

How is a line to be drawn between rights which are "independent" and rights which are not, rights to which the insurer is subrogated and rights to which he is not? One answer was firmly rejected by Bowen LJ in *Castellain* v *Preston*[85]: "It is said that the law only gives the underwriters the right to stand in the insured's shoes as to rights which arise out of . . . the loss. I venture to think there is absolutely no authority for that proposition."

A better answer lies in the underlying principle of indemnity. The insurer is entitled to an "advantage", if his taking it does not leave the insured worse off than he would have been, if the event insured against had not occurred, having taken account of any loss arising out of the event the risk of which was borne by the insured himself or by another insurer.

So, in the example of the fire in the flats, but for the fire, the owner would have had both flats and rent. Any rent, which the insured owner is able to recover notwithstanding the fire damage, is not an "advantage" which the insurer can take in subrogation. If the insured retains the rent, he is no better off on that account than if the fire had not occurred.[86] The same is true of the insured shipowner and freight.[87] The rights to rent or to freight are independent rights and the corollary is that, in the example of freight lost as a result of the event insured, if the insured shipowner has failed to take valid freight insurance, he cannot deduct the amount of lost freight before accounting to his hull insurer for the damages recovered from a third party responsible for the event insured,[88] unless the damages are or include an element for loss of freight.[89]

---

82. Even though the ship had been abandoned to the insurers: *Sea Ins Co* v *Hadden* (1884) 13 QBD 706 (CA—hull); except in the circumstances of MIA, section 63. See also *Glen Line Ltd* v *AG* (1930) 36 Com Cas 1 (HL—hull): the insurer could not recover compensation paid to insured shipowner in respect of lost operating profit.

83. pp 712–715 *per* Lord Brett MR.

84. p 716 *per* Lord Brett MR.

85. (1883) 11 QBD 380, 404 (CA—fire).

86. *Cf* the owner in *Castellain* (above, 31–4), who, if he had retained the purchase money calculated on the basis of an undamaged property, as well as the insurance money for the damage, would have been much better off than if no fire had occurred.

Cf also the mortgagee who, for the same reason, having been fully indemnified by the fire insurer, must pay the insurer any part of the mortgage debt later received from the mortgagor: *North British & Mercantile Ins Co* v *London, Liverpool & Globe Ins Co* (1877) 5 Ch D 569, 584 *per* Mellish LJ (fire); *Samuel & Co* v *Dumas* [1924] AC 431, 445–446 *per* Lord Cave (hull). *Carpenter* v *Providence Washington Ins Co*, 16 Pet 495, 501 *per* Story J (1842—fire).

Cf the owner of gold in *Stearns* v *Village Main Reef Gold Mining Co Ltd* (1905) 10 Com Cas 89 (CA), who, having been paid by the insurer as on a total loss, was paid a sum by the South African government, which had commandeered the gold. Having stressed that the owner had given no *quid pro quo* for the government payment, the court held that the insurer could recover from the insured.

87. By contrast, the insurer is subrogated to any rights of the insured landlord against the tenants to have the fire damage repaired; the benefit of enforcing those rights would not have come in, if the fire had not occurred: *Re King* [1963] Ch 459, 499–500 *per* Diplock LJ (fire).

88. *Cf* MIA, section 63(2) giving statutory effect to *Stewart* v *Greenock Marine Ins Co* (1848) 2 HLC 159 (hull), that, if the ship is abandoned, hull insurers may claim freight "in course of being earned, and which is earned by her subsequent to the casualty . . . " It is usual for insurers to contract out of this right: Arnould, No 1254.

89. *Sea Ins Co* v *Hadden* (1884) 13 QBD 706 (CA—hull).

31–4B Rights in Contract

If the insured has any contractual right to compensation in respect of the loss, its reinstatement[90] or diminution,[91] the insurer may enforce that right, if the insured has not already done so. If the insured has done so, he must account to the insurer.

An example of rights in compensation is found in *Darrell* v *Tibbitts*.[92] Having paid the insured lessor in respect of fire damage to his house, the insurer discovered that the insured had been compensated in respect of the same loss by his lessee in accordance with the terms of the lease. The Court of Appeal held that the insurer could recover the amount he had paid to the insured. Otherwise, the insured "would be not merely indemnified, he would be paid twice over".[93]

An example of rights in diminution may arise in the case of fidelity insurance: the insured may well benefit by being discharged from a duty to pay wages to the unfaithful employee. To the extent that this benefit is the consequence of the event insured, the act of infidelity, it is a benefit of which the insurer is entitled to the "advantage".[94]

31–4C Rights in Tort

The insurer may be subrogated to rights in tort against a third party, who wronged the insured, torts such as negligence[95] or deceit.[96] In the case of negligence, the rights of the insurer, being no greater than those of the insured, will be limited by any contributory negligence on the part of the insured.[97]

31–4D Statute

The insured may have rights by statute, the enforcement of which diminishes his loss. For example, under the Riot (Damages) Act 1886, section 2(1), the owner of any building damaged in a riot is entitled to compensation from the local authority.[98]

90. For example, *West of England Fire Ins Co* v *Isaacs* [1897] 1 QB 226 (CA—fire).
91. For example, *Castellain* v *Preston* (above, 31–4).
92. (1880) 5 QBD 560 (fire).
93. p 562 *per* Brett LJ. As regards rights against a tenant or lessee, see also *Andrews* v *Patriotic Assurance Co* (1886) LR Ir 355, 369 *per* Pallas CB (fire); *Re King* [1963] Ch 459, 499–500 *per* Diplock LJ (fire). Other rights to which the insurer might be subrogated include: (a) rights of a creditor against debtor and sureties—*Parr's Bk Ltd* v *Albert Mines Syndicate Ltd* (1900) 5 Com Cas 116 (credit); (b) rights of a shipper against a carrier—*Dufourcet* v *Bishop* (1886) 18 QBD 373 (cargo); (c) rights of a customer against his bank—*Bank of Montreal* v *Dominion Gresham Guarantee & Casualty Co Ltd* [1930] AC 659 (PC—fidelity): (d) rights of a creditor under a scheme of arrangement—*Dane* v *Mortgage Ins Corp* [1894] 1 QB 54 (CA—debt), applied in *Meacock* v *Bryant & Co* (1942) 74 Ll L Rep 53 (debt).
As regards specific performance, in *Castellain* v *Preston* (1883) 11 QBD 380, 390 and 405, Brett LJ and Bowen LJ, respectively, left open whether an insurer subrogated to the rights of the seller of land could enforce specific performance against the buyer. Cf *Gill* v *Yorkshire Ins Co* (1913) 24 WLR 389 (Man—livestock), in which it was held that the insurer was subrogated to the rights of a seller of the insured stallion to enforce promissory notes against the buyer.
94. *Fifth Liverpool Star-Bowkett Building Sy* v *Travellers' Accident Ins Co* (1893) 9 TLR 221.
95. For example, *Groom* v *GWR* (1892) 8 TLR 253 (fire); *King* v *Victoria Ins Co* [1896] AC 250 (PC—cargo); *The Charlotte* [1908] P 206 (CA—cargo); *Lister* v *Romford Ice & Cold Storage Co Ltd* [1957] AC 555 (employers' liability).
96. *Assicurazioni Generali di Trieste* v *Empress Assurance Co Ltd* [1907] 2 KB 814: the defendant insurer recovered damages in respect of a fraudulent insurance claim. Pickford J held that the reinsurer was subrogated to the defendant's right to the extent of the reinsurance cover.
97. *Insurance Co of N America* v *US*, 527 F Supp 962 (ED Ark, 1981—aviation).
98. For an early case under the Riot Act 1714, see *Mason* v *Sainsbury* (1782) 3 Dougl 61. USA: see *US* v *American Tobacco Co*, 166 US 468 (1897—fire).

31–4E Interest

If the insured recovers interest from the third party, such part of the interest as corresponds to the period since (and the extent of) the indemnification of the insured by the insurer can be claimed by the insurer. The amount of interest, awarded in the discretion of the court,[99] does not depend on the profit earning potential of any property insured and lost in the case; generally, the insurer will receive interest at the commercial rate.[100]

In *Cousins*,[101] goods in transit disappeared in December 1965. The owners were indemnified by their insurer in August 1966. In November 1969, the owners recovered the value of the goods from the carriers. On the question of interest, the Court of Appeal held that interest was recoverable; that in order to give business efficacy to the contract of insurance and to ensure that the plaintiffs were not over-compensated, it was necessary to imply a term into the contract of insurance, that the plaintiffs could retain any interest awarded for the period before August 1966 but that interest awarded for the period after that date should go to the insurer.

31–4F Costs

Cousins (above) rests on the principle of indemnity. On the same principle, any litigation costs recovered from the third party should be distributed between insured and insurer, according to their outlay[102] or their interest in the litigation, as appropriate. See further, below, 31–6B3.

31–4G Gifts to the Insured

If the insured receives a voluntary payment in respect of the loss from a third party, usually a person other than a wrongdoer, the question, whether the insurer has any subrogation rights in respect of that sum, turns on the intention of the donor. The answer is usually negative.

In *Randal* v *Cochran*,[103] decided in 1748, when the King of England proclaimed that one-half of certain prize money should go to those who had suffered from the depredations of the Spanish, the proclamation was construed by the court as operating "in favour of the insurers, who having paid the loss were entitled to be recouped".[104] But in 1881 in *Burnand* v *Rodocanachi Sons & Co*,[105] the decision was different. Cargo was destroyed by a Confederate cruiser and the cargo insurers paid the insured the amount fixed by the policy, an amount less than the actual loss. The difference was made up by a gratuitous payment to the insured from a fund, set up by the United

---

99. Above, 30–8.
100. *Metal Box Ltd* v *Currys Ltd* [1988] 1 All ER 341 (fire).
101. *H Cousins & Co Ltd* v *D & C Carriers Ltd* [1971] 2 QB 230.
102. *Cousins* (above), p 242 *per* Widgery LJ. The insured should be allowed to retain, from what he recovers from the tortfeasor, the cost of recovering it: *Fisher* v *Keller Industries*, 485 NW 2d 626 (Iowa, 1992—worker's compensation).
103. (1748) 1 Ves Sen 99.
104. *per* Lord Selborne LC in *Burnand* (below), p 338. See also Lord Blackburn, *ibid*, p 341.
105. (1882) 7 App Cas 333. *Cf Stearns* v *Village Main Reef Gold Mining Co Ltd* (1905) 10 Com Cas 89 (CA—insurance of confiscated gold).

States Congress, in terms that "underwriters are not to receive any benefit from the funds . . . and that the compensation given to any claimant must be given to compensate him for any [uninsured] loss".[106] In this case, the House of Lords held that the insurer was not entitled to recover from the insured the amount of the gratuity.

Burnand is easily explained, in the words of Lord Selborne LC, on the ground that "the fund awarded by the Act of Congress is only for that part of the actual loss which the [policy] valuation did not cover and which the insurers have not paid."[107] However, even if the fund had doubled with the insurance cover, the decision would have been the same, on account of the intention of Congress that the insured should have the benefit of the money anyway.

"[W]hen a gift is made afterwards in order to diminish the loss, it is bestowed in such terms as to shew an intention to benefit the insured, and to give the insurer the benefit of that would be to divert the gift from its intended object to a different person. That really was what was decided in *Burnand* v *Rodocanachi*. There the money bestowed, not as a matter of right but as a gift, was intended to benefit the insured beyond the amount which they got in consequence of the insurance."[108]

More recently, in *Merrett* v *Capitol Indemnity Corporation*,[109] the reinsured, liability insurers at Lloyd's, suffered a reinsured loss, which was partly "funded" by payment to them of a smaller sum by their brokers. The brokers were not obliged to pay the money but did so for their own commercial purposes, namely, to save themselves work and to keep the goodwill of the insurers. It was intended not as a loan[110] but as an outright gift. On a subsequent claim by the reinsured, arbitrators deducted from their award against the reinsurer an amount equivalent to the gift. On appeal from the arbitrators, Steyn J found that the award disclosed an error of law and remitted the award for reconsideration by the arbitrators. The error lay in the deduction. With passing reference to words of Lord Reid,[111] that "the common law ought never to produce an unreasonable result", Steyn J applied established principle: if "the payment was intended solely for the benefit of the assured, it has not been paid in diminution of the loss. In that event it must be disregarded in assessing the assured's recoverable loss".[112] In general, in the absence of clear intention by the donor, it will be presumed that he did not intend to benefit the insurer.[113]

---

106. p 343 *per* Lord Watson.
107. p 336 *per* Lord Selborne LC.
108. *Castellain* v *Preston* (1883) 11 QBD 380, 395 *per* Cotton LJ (CA—fire); see also pp 404–405 *per* Bowen LJ. *Cf* Cotton LJ, *loc cit*: "There is another ground which may possibly exclude gifts. It may be that the right of the insurer to have a sum brought into account in diminution of the loss . . . is confined to that which is a right or other incident belonging to the person insured, as an incident of the property at the time when the loss takes place." This ground would not explain *Randal* (above, note 94).
109. [1991] 1 Lloyd's Rep 169.
110. Thus ruling out, in this case, the practice of funding by brokers in the nature of a loan "subject to collection", i.e. subject to repayment by the insurers, if the broker failed to collect from the reinsurer concerned. However, it was the stated intention of the insurers that, if the reinsurance money were paid by the reinsurer in full, the gift would be repaid to the brokers, in which event, none of those involved would receive an uncovenanted windfall.
111. *Cartledge* v *Jopling & Sons Ltd* [1963] AC 758, 772.
112. p 171 by reference to *Burnand* v *Rodocanachi & Sons* (1882) 7 App Cas 333 (cargo).
113. *Stearns* v *Village Main Reef Gold Mining Co Ltd* (1905) 10 Com Cas 89, 95–96 *per* Romer LJ (CA—insurance on gold).

31–5 LIMITS ON THE INSURER'S RIGHTS

The insurer's rights against a third party are those of the insured himself[114] and, there-fore, they are limited in two respects.

First, the insurer is not subrogated to the rights of associated third parties, such as a loss payee. The same is probably true, if the insured insures his own interest and that of others and the latter, although beneficiaries of the insurance, are not parties to the contract.[115]

Second, the insurer's rights can be no better than those of the insured and the insurer's position to enforce them can be no better than that of the insured. "The insurer, seeking to step into the insured's shoes after payment . . . , may find that the laces already have been tied together."[116] So, in an "extreme" case, if the insured has perished and can exercise the rights no longer, the insurer cannot either.[117] For other instances of this rule, see below, 31–5A ff.

31–5A Contractual Exemption or Limitation

If the insured has agreed with a third party, that the liability of the latter shall be excluded or limited, the rights enforceable through subrogation by the insurer are restricted to the same extent.[118]

31–5A1 The Benefit of Insurance

A "waiver of subrogation" clause, as the title implies, bars the insurer's right of subro-gation. The purpose of such a clause has been said to be to ensure that the benefit of the insurance is extended to persons in the situation other than the insured.[119] So, if a contract provides expressly that a party shall have the benefit of insurance, this has been construed as exempting the beneficiary from any liability for loss to be covered by the insurance.[120] Further, if one party to a contract undertakes to insure against a

114. The insurer's rights may be less than those of the insured, for the right of subrogation may be limited by the contract of insurance: *Thomas & Co v Brown* (1899) 4 Com Cas 186 (insurance of cargo "without recourse to lightermen").

115. For example, the commercial trust: above, 5–6. See *Northern Assurance Co Ltd v Wolk*, 49 NYS 2d 754 (1944—goods in transit); *Ohio Casualty Ins Co v Ford Motor Co*, 502 F 2d 138 (6 Cir, 1971—motor); *Atlas Assurance Co Ltd v Harper, Robinson Shipping Co*, 508 F 2d 1381 (9 Cir, 1975—cargo).

In the case of goods insured by the carrier for the benefit of the owner, it has been argued that, on equit-able grounds, the insurer should be allowed to take advantage of the rights of the beneficiary: MacGillivray, No 1226. USA: see *Lititz Mutual Ins Co v Barnes*, 248 F 2d 241 (5 Cir, 1957—fire).

116. Veal, 28 Tort & Ins L J 69, 80 (1992).

117. *Smith (Plant Hire) Ltd v Mainwaring* [1986] 2 Lloyd's Rep 244 (CA): the insured company had been liquidated, so it was too late for subrogation. The insurer is advised to obtain an assignment of rights prior to the liquidation.

118. *Lister v Romford Ice & Cold Storage Ltd* [1957] AC 555, 600 *per* Lord Somervell. *Savannah Fire & Marine Ins Co v Pelzer Manufacturing Co*, 60 F 39 (SC, 1894—fire: exclusion of liability for negligence); *Tenneco Oil Co v Tug "Tony"* [1972] 1 Lloyd's Rep 514 (SD Tex, 1971—cargo: waiver of subrogation clause).

119. *Industrial Risk Ins v Garlock Equipment Co*, 576 So 2d 652, 656 (Ala, 1991—builder's risks).

120. *The Auditor* (1924) 18 Ll L Rep 464 (cargo). *Phoenix Ins Co v Erie & Western Transportation Co*, 117 US 312 (1886—cargo). Derham, *op cit* (note 2), pp 83 ff: the clause has its origin in contracts for the carriage of goods by sea, whereby the carrier stipulated for the benefit of the cargo insurance of the goods owner. See further, *Williams v Globe Indemnity Co*, 507 F 2d 837 (8 Cir, 1974—fidelity), cert den 421 US 948; *Great American Ins Co v US*, 575 F 2d 1031 (3 Cir, 1978—fire); *Silva v Home Indemnity Co*, 416 A 2d 664 (RI, 1980—motor).

particular risk, that undertaking may be seen as an assumption of that risk by that party with the corollary, that the other party is not liable in respect of the loss to be insured.[121]

In *Mark Rowlands Ltd* v *Berni Inns Ltd*,[122] the plaintiff was the landlord of a building, the basement of which was leased to the defendant restaurateur. The defendant covenanted to repair the basement and to pay to the landlord an insurance rent related to the premium to be paid by the landlord for insurance of the whole building. The lease contained a common provision that, in the event of fire, the tenant was to be relieved of his duty to repair and that the landlord was to use the insurance money to repair the building. The landlord insured the whole building, which was later destroyed by fire. The insurer paid the landlord and brought action in his name against the tenant who, for the purpose of this litigation only, admitted that his negligence had caused the fire.

Having found that the tenant was not a party to the insurance but that, under the lease, the insurance was taken for the joint benefit of landlord and tenant, the Court of Appeal held that the effect was to substitute the fire insurance for the tenant's liability for fire loss; it followed that the landlord had no right of action against the tenant, to which the insurer could be subrogated.

The main issue in *Mark Rowlands* was exemption: whether the lease precluded the landlord from recovering damages from the tenant. The court relied chiefly on reasoning of the Supreme Court of Canada,[123] which was in two parts. The first was an inference about the parties' allocation of risk and consequential reliance: as the tenant can reasonably "rely on the landlord's covenant to insure and can refrain from insuring against any liability to the landlord for its own negligence", the "landlord must then look to its own insurance if it suffers loss and cannot sue the tenant for loss that it had promised to insure".[124]

The second and main part of the reasoning was that[125] "where the covenant to insure is not at large, but is, as in this case, a covenant with the lessee that the landlord will keep the buildings on the premises insured against loss by fire, it must be given effect against liability for fires arising from the tenant's negligence because otherwise,

---

121. *Archdale Ltd* v *Comservices Ltd* [1954] 1 WLR 459 (CA—fire); *Coupar Transport (London) Ltd* v *Smiths (Acton) Ltd* [1959] 1 Lloyd's Rep 369 (goods in transit). Yates & Hawkins, *Standard Business Contracts* (London, 1986), pp 18, 292.

122. [1986] 1 QB 211 (CA); Clarke [1986] CLJ 22. The issue has also arisen in relation to carriage of goods by sea: *The Yasin* [1979] 2 Lloyd's Rep 45 (cargo). *New England Fish Co* v *Western Pioneer Inc*, 509 F Supp 865 (WD Wash, 1981—cargo); *Ferromontan Inc* v *Georgetown Steel Corp*, 535 F Supp 1198 (D SC, 1982—cargo).

123. *Agnew-Surpass Shoe Stores Ltd* v *Cummer-Yonge Investments Ltd* (1975) 55 DLR (3d) 676 (fire insurance contracted and paid for by landlord); *Ross Southward Tire Ltd* v *Pyrotech Products Ltd* (1975) 57 DLR (3d) 248 (fire insurance contracted by landlord, part of premiums paid by tenant); *Eaton & Co Ltd* v *Smith* (1977) 92 DLR (3d) 425 (fire insurance contracted and paid for by landlord).

Cf Greenwood Shopping Plaza v *Beattie* (1980) 111 DLR (3d) 257: by a strict application of the rule of privity of contract, the Supreme Court of Canada allowed a subrogated action, not against the tenant, but against the (negligent) tenant's employees. See Hasson, *op cit*, pp 431 ff.; Huband, 9 Man L J 147 (1979); Yates, 3 OJLS 431 (1983).

Cases of this kind in the USA, deciding against subrogation, include *General Mills Inc* v *Goldman*, 184 F 2d 359 (8 Cir, 1950—fire), cert den 340 US 947; and *Safeco Ins Cos* v *Weisgerber*, 762 P 2d 271 (Idaho, 1989—fire).

124. *Greenwood Shopping Plaza Ltd* v *Neil J Buchanan Ltd* (1979) 99 DLR (3d) 289, 291. Such reliance may have been lacking in the *Berni* case, for the tenant's liability insurer was standing behind him in the action. Moreover, risk was not solely on the landlord, for it was the tenant who paid the premium relating to the basement.

125. *Eaton & Co Ltd* v *Smith* (1977) 92 DLR (3d) 425, 428–430 *per* Lasking CJC.

as a covenant expressly running to the benefit of the tenant, it would have no subject matter."

The result is that, if one party to a lease is to have the benefit of insurance and the insurer is to be deprived of the benefit of subrogation against him, it is enough that the lease should contain a covenant to insure[126]; a warning to insure, as distinct from an obligation, is not enough.[127] Even if there is an obligation to insure, however, the result is not automatic: everything depends on the proper construction of the lease.[128] On the one hand, the Supreme Court of Canada[129] was apparently willing to hold that the covenant to insure did not amount to an exemption of the covenantee, if another explanation of the covenant could be found. On the other hand, it is not essential for exemption, that the premiums should be paid by the (tenant) beneficiary of the insurance.[130]

If the circumstances indicate exemption, the tenant in England "is entitled to say that the landlord has been fully indemnified in the manner envisaged by . . . the lease and that he cannot therefore recover damages from the tenant in addition".[131] Similar decisions can be found in the USA, where courts have emphasised that it would "be an undue hardship to require a tenant to insure against his own negligence, when he is paying, through his rent, for the fire insurance which covers the premises".[132] There, however, the inference is taken one step further and the tenant is considered to be co-insured with the landlord.[133]

31–5A2 Estoppel

If the insured is estopped from asserting his strict rights against the third party, the rights of the insurer in subrogation are limited in the same way.[134] If, however, the estoppel takes the form of a release after the right has arisen and after the insurance has been contracted, this is likely to be a breach of contract on the part of the insured: below, 31–6C1.

31–5A3 Time

If the insured's action is out of time, whether by contract term or by statute, the right of the insurer is limited in the same way.[135] In particular, time runs against the insurer

---

126. *Eaton & Co Ltd* v *Smith* (1977) 92 DLR (3d) 425, 428 *per* Laskin CJC; *Matthews* v *Andrew* (1986) 25 DLR (4th) 452 (BC—fire).

Cf Lister v *Romford Ice & Cold Storage Ltd* [1957] AC 555: an employer took (compulsory) insurance against employers' liability. A majority of the House of Lords declined to imply a term in the contract of employment that the employee in question, whose act gave rise to the employer's liability, should have the benefit of that insurance and hence be immune to suit by the employer (or his liability insurer). On public policy, see Viscount Simmonds, pp 576 ff. On why such a term is not necessary to give the contract of employment business efficacy, see Lord Morton, p 583.

127. Yates & Hawkins, *Standard Business Contracts* (London, 1986), pp 293–294.

128. In other contexts, however, English courts have shown little willingness to infer exemption of liability for negligence: Yates (above) p 293 and also 3 OJLS 431 (1983).

129. *Eaton* (above).

130. *Eaton* (above).

131. [1986] 1 QB 211, 233 *per* Kerr LJ.

132. *Community Credit Union* v *Homelvig*, 487 NW 2d 602, 605 (ND, 1992—fire); *Dix Mutual Ins Co* v *LaFramboise*, 597 NE 2d 622, 626 (Ill, 1992—fire).

133. *Ibid* and cases cited.

134. *Northern Assurance Co* v *Wolk*, 49 NYS 2d 754 (1944—goods in transit). See also *Greenwood Shopping Plaza Ltd* v *Neil J Buchanan Ltd* (1979) 99 DLR (3d) 289, 291 (Sup Ct—fire).

135. *Seven Sixty Travel Inc* v *American Motorists Ins Co*, 414 NYS 2d 254 (1979—liability).

not from the time that he indemnifies the insured but from when time begins to run against the insured.[136]

31–5A4 Earlier Proceedings

It is "a well settled rule of law that damages resulting from one and the same cause of action must be assessed and recovered once for all".[137] *Nemo pro eadem causa debet vexari.* There is public interest in avoiding any possibility of two courts reaching inconsistent decisions on the same facts and the same issue,[138] in there being finality in litigation and in protecting citizens from being "vexed" more than once by what is really the same claim.[139]

It follows that the insurer may be unable to take advantage of a cause of action against a wrongdoer, if that cause of action has already been "prosecuted to judgment"[140] by the insured. However, a single incident will give rise to more than one cause of action, if different evidence is needed to support the different causes of action[141] (and the evidence exists) or if distinct legal rights have been affected. A clear example is that, in a motor accident, damage to property and injury to the person give rise to different causes of action.[142]

Doubt has arisen about the case of different layers of insurance loss stemming from the same damage. In *Taylor* v *Wray Ltd*,[143] the insured commenced suit against the wrongdoer for his uninsured loss, which included the first £10 of damage to his vehicle; his action was settled before judgment. When, later, the insurer sought to sue the wrongdoer in the name of the insured for the insured damage to the vehicle, the defendant pleaded the earlier action as a defence. The defence was dismissed as "a mere technicality of no merit or substance".[144] It was conceded that a claim for personal injuries might be split as regards different items of injury[145] and Edmund Davies LJ[146] repeated the earlier opinion of Bowen LJ,[147] that demands could be split, if they are "essentially separable", subject to the inherent power of the court to prevent vexation and oppression. In so far as the decision in *Taylor* decides that the claim for the excess was separable from the claim for the insured loss, the decision is doubtful. This aspect of the decision has been described as "out of line with the general stream of authority",[148] the "joker in the pack".[149]

---

136. *Canadian Transport* v *Court Line Ltd* [1940] AC 934, 939 *per* Lord Atkin (P & I). As regards insurance of real property, see the Law of Property Act 1925, section 47. *Inman* v *S Carolina Ry Co*, 129 US 128 (1889); *Wager* v *Providence Ins Co*, 150 US 99 (1893, cargo); *Fidelity & Deposit Co* v *Smith*, 730 F 2d 1026 (5 Cir, 1984 —fidelity).
137. *Brunsden* v *Humphrey* (1884) 14 QBD 141, 147 *per* Bowen LJ. Also *Fetter* v *Beale* (1701) 1 Ld Raym 339.
138. [1984] 3 All ER 554, 558 *per* Sir John Donaldson MR (CA—motor).
139. pp 558–559.
140. *Taylor* v *Wray & Co Ltd* [1971] 1 Lloyd's Rep 497, 500 *per* Edmund Davies LJ (CA—motor).
141. p 499 *per* Harman LJ.
142. *Ibid.*
143. [1971] 1 Lloyd's Rep 497 (CA—motor).
144. p 500 *per* Harman LJ.
145. p 500 *per* Edmund Davies LJ.
146. p 501.
147. *Brunsden* v *Humphrey* (1884) 14 QBD 141, 151.
148. *Buckland* v *Palmer* [1984] 3 All ER 554, 560 *per* Griffiths LJ (CA—motor).
149. p 558 *per* Sir John Donaldson MR.

In *Taylor*,[150] the defendant's insurer had been aware of the plaintiff's insurer's claim well before settlement of the uninsured loss. Given that knowledge, together with the terms of the settlement agreed with the insured, the inference could be drawn that the claim for insured loss was distinct and "kept open".[151] Further, Widgery LJ admitted[152] that the obstacles to the suit by the insurer would have been greater, if the earlier action, instead of being determined by settlement, had ended in judgment, so that the cause of action had been merged in the judgment.

These factors distinguish the later cases of *Buckland v Palmer*[153] and *Hayler v Chapman*.[154] In *Hayler*, an insured motorist sued another motorist, with whom he had been in collision, for his uninsured loss (his excess, car hire charges and telephone calls) and obtained judgment. Unaware of this, his insurer brought an action in his name against the same defendant, whose insurer pleaded the earlier judgment as a bar to further proceedings in the name of the plaintiff. The County Court held that the later proceedings were an abuse of process and should be struck out. This, said the Court of Appeal, was plainly right, as two actions cannot be brought in respect of the same cause of action.[155]

Further, the County Court in *Hayler* had refused to set aside the award in the first action and it was this that was the subject of the appeal. On this issue,[156] the Court of Appeal noted that it was no more than possible that the defendant's insurer had been aware of the earlier action and that there was no suggestion that the insurer had misled anyone. The court cited *Buckland v Palmer*,[157] in which Sir John Donaldson MR said that he should

"be surprised and disappointed if this left the courts powerless to do justice if, for example, advantage had been taken of an ill-informed plaintiff by an experienced defendant who offered to submit to judgment in a small sum, well knowing that the plaintiff was under some misapprehension as to the effect on his right thereafter to proceed with his substantial claim".

The Court of Appeal in *Hayler* also cited its previous decision in *Burns v Cotton*,[158] in which it upheld the decision of a County Court judge setting aside a default judgment for the plaintiff's uninsured loss, which the defendant insurer had satisfied well knowing that a claim for the insured loss was outstanding and being actively pursued. The facts of *Hayler* were quite different. Taylor LJ said that, before a court takes the unusual step of setting aside an earlier judgment, given after a contested hearing, there must be evidence of the conduct of the parties showing that it was unjust and inequitable that the judgment should stand. Here there was no such evidence. In particular, there was no evidence that the defendant's insurer knew of the earlier action or believed that the later action would be brought, or that the insurer in any way exploited the situation.

---

150. [1971] 1 Lloyd's Rep 497, 500 *per* Harman LJ (CA—motor).
151. See p 501 *per* Edmund Davies LJ.
152. p 501.
153. Above.
154. [1989] 1 Lloyd's Rep 490 (CA).
155. Citing *Derrick v Williams* [1939] 2 All ER 559 (CA—motor); and *Buckland v Palmer* [1984] 3 All ER 554 (CA—motor).
156. See RSC, Ord 13 r 9. *Jonesco v Beard* [1930] AC 298.
157. (Above) p 559.
158. 3 February 1987 (unreported).

31–5B Windfalls

Windfalls belong to the insured. Rights of subrogation arise when and to the extent that there would otherwise be enrichment of the insured at the *insurer's expense*.[159] If the action against the third party produces more than the amount of the insurance money paid or payable, the balance is retained by the insured, except that, in the case of an action paid for by the insurer, the insurer can recover his costs.

In *Yorkshire Ins Co Ltd* v *Nisbet Shipping Co Ltd*,[160] the insurer paid the insured for a total loss of his ship in a collision. The insured recovered damages in Canadian dollars from the owner of the other ship responsible; by the time that the damages had been paid, the pound sterling had been devalued and the damages, when converted to sterling, exceeded the insurance money paid in sterling before devaluation. Diplock J held[161] that the "excess" could be retained by the insured owner:

"the only terms to be implied to give business efficacy to the contract between the parties are those necessary to secure that the insured shall not recover from the insurer an amount greater than the loss which he has actually sustained. The insurer has contracted to pay to the insured the amount of his actual loss. If, before the insurer has paid under the policy, the insured recovers from some third party a sum in excess of the actual amount of the loss, he can recover nothing from the insurer because he has sustained no loss, but it has never been suggested that the insurer can recover from the insured the amount of the excess. It is difficult to see why a term should be implied in a contract of insurance which would involve a fundamentally different result merely because the insurer had already paid for the loss under the policy before the insured had recovered any sum from the third party."

This rule, like other rules of subrogation, is subject to the terms of the contract of insurance, which may stipulate that any excess shall go to the insurer.[162]

31–5C No Rights Against the Insured

The insured has no right of action against himself and nor does his insurer.[163] In the leading case of *Simpson* v *Thomson*,[164] two ships in the ownership of the insured collided. The House of Lords held that, having indemnified the owner in respect of one ship, the insurer could not proceed against him as owner of the other ship, which was at fault.

The first reason given for the rule concerns the nature of subrogation: the right of action for damages must be asserted, "not in their own name but in the name of the person insured, and if the person insured be the person who has caused the damage",

---

159. Goff & Jones, p 528.

160. [1962] 2 QB 330. See also *Glen Line Ltd* v *AG* (1930) 36 Com Cas 1, 14 *per* Lord Atkin (hull). *The Livinstone*, 130 F 746 (2 Cir, 1904—hull), cert den 194 US 637; *Risdal* v *Universal Ins Co*, 232 F Supp 472 (D Mass, 1964—hull). For criticism of *Nisbet*, see Derham, *op cit* (note 2), pp 135 ff.

As regards valued policies, see *North of England Iron Steamship Ins Assn* v *Armstrong* (1870) LR 5 QB 244 (hull), discussed by Diplock J in *Nisbet* (above), pp 343 ff.; *Thames & Mersey Marine Ins Co* v *British & Chilian SS Co* [1916] 1 KB 30 (CA—hull). Arnould, Nos 1302 ff.

161. p 340.

162. *Lucas Ltd* v *ECGD* [1973] 1 Lloyd's Rep 549 (CA—guarantee).

163. Or against the co-insured: below, 31–5D

164. (1877) 3 App Cas 279. See also *Midland Ins Co* v *Smith* (1881) 6 QBD 561 (fire); *Ellerbeck Collieries Ltd* v *Cornhill Ins Co Ltd* [1932] 1 KB 401, 411 *per* Scrutton LJ (CA—employers' liability). *Wager* v *Providence Ins Co*, 150 US 99, 109 *per* Shiras J (1893, cargo); *Builders & Manufacturer's Mutual Casualty Co* v *Preferred Automobile Ins Co*, 118 F 2d 118 (6 Cir, 1941—motor); *Stafford Metal Works Inc* v *Cook Paint & Varnish Co*, 418 F Supp 56 (ND Tex, 1976—fire); *Farr Man & Co Inc* v *m/v Rozita*, 903 F 2d 871 (1 Cir, 1990—cargo).

it is impossible "to see how the right can be asserted at all."[165] The insurer's right is no more than "to make such claim for damages as the insured himself could have made."[166]

The second reason concerns the nature and scope of the cover. "Either the policy by which the underwriters are bound is an insurance against perils of the seas arising from the negligent navigation of any other vessel, even although that vessel belong to the person insured, or it is not."[167] In principle, insurance extends to loss caused by the negligence of the insured.[168] If he is intended to be covered in respect of loss caused by his own negligence by the insurance in question, he would lose that cover, if the insurer could take back with the hand of subrogation what he had given with the hand of insurance. If the insured keeps the insurance money, far from being unjustly enriched at the expense of the insurer, he has got the indemnity he contracted for[169] and has paid for.[170]

A third reason is to preserve the fiduciary relationship between insurer and insured from the deleterious effects of conflicting interests. Otherwise, for example, the insurer would be able to secure information, while representing the insured, for later use in a subrogation action against him.[171]

31–5D No Rights Against the Co-Insured[172]

If insurance is taken in the joint names of two persons for their respective interests as co-insured, such as mortgagor and mortgagee,[173] and, if insured loss is caused by one of them, the insurer usually has no rights in subrogation against the co-insured who caused the loss. Indeed, in the United States, the widespread adoption of mortgage clauses requiring joint insurance has virtually eliminated subrogation from that context.[174]

Also in the United States, the same rule against subrogation has been applied to a claim by a motor insurer against a tortfeasor, who was driving the vehicle with the consent of the insured and who was covered by the same insurance contract[175]; and to a claim by a cargo insurer, who sought to exercise subrogation rights against a carrier,

165. *Simpson* (above) p 284 *per* Lord Cairns LC. See also p 290 *per* Lord Penzance
166. Above, 31–5.
167. *Simpson* (above) p 286 *per* Lord Cairns LC. See also p 291 *per* Lord Penzance
168. See above, 19–2A.
169. Meagher, Gummow & Lehane, *Equity—Doctrine and Remedies* (2nd ed, 1984), No 948; *cf* James, "The Fallacies of *Simpson* v *Thomson*", (1971) 34 MLR 149.
170. *Stafford Metal Works Inc* v *Cook Paint & Varnish Co*, 418 F Supp 56, 58 (ND Tex, 1976—fire).
171. *Stafford Metal* (above), *loc cit*. *Home Ins Co* v *Pinski Bros Inc*, 500 P 2d 945, 949 (Mt, 1972—boiler), cited in *Royal Exchange Assurance Inc* v *s/s President Adams*, 510 F Supp 581, 584 (WD Wash, 1981—cargo). In some jurisdictions, however, it is precisely because of the potential for conflicts of interest, that the courts have concluded that the relationship between insured and insurer is not fiduciary at all: see above, 17–4E4.
172. Derham, *op cit* (note 2), ch 7. Co–insurance often refers to a single insured who takes two or more contracts of insurance on the same risk: see 28–9. Here, however, the co–insured is one of two or more persons insured under a single contract of insurance.
173. Other leading instances of joint insurance are between contractor and sub-contractor and between landlord and tenant.
174. Hasson, *op cit*, p 430. But *cf* decisions that a loss payee, for whose benefit insurance is taken, cannot claim immunity from subrogation: Bowe, 53 J Air L & Com 999 (1988).
175. *Carolina Casualty Ins Co* v *Underwriters Ins Co*, 569 F 2d 304 (5 Cir, 1978—motor); *cf Carolina Casualty Ins Co* v *Transport Indemnity Co*, 488 F 2d 790 (10 Cir, 1973—motor).

who was also insured by the same cargo insurer but under a different contract of insurance.[176]

If, however, one co-insured has ceased to be covered by the insurance, the rule against subrogation does not apply. In England in *Samuel* v *Dumas*,[177] there was co-insurance by the owner and the mortgagee of a ship, until wilful misconduct (scuttling) by the owner ended his cover. In these circumstances, the innocent mortgagee could enforce the insurance and, if he did so, the insurer would be subrogated to the rights of the mortgagee against the owner.[178]

31–5D1 Reasons for the Rule

The first reason for this rule against subrogation stems from the view that each co-insured is taking insurance for the benefit of the other, so that the one co-insured has no rights against the other, to which the insurer can be subrogated.[179]

"If a valid claim by the underwriters to be subrogated to the rights of the [cargo] owner will not arise where the carrier has contracted with the owner that he, the carrier, shall have the benefit of any insurance, it would seem to be clear that where the carrier actually and in terms is the party insured [as well as the cargo owner], the underwriter can have no right to recover against the carrier."[180]

The second reason is closely related to the first.

"The starting point . . . is the basic principle that subrogation cannot be obtained against the insured himself [above, 31–5C]. In the case of true joint insurance there is, of course, no problem; the interests of the joint insured are so inseparably connected that the several insureds are to be considered as one with the obvious result that subrogation was impossible. In the case of several insurance, if the different interests are pervasive and if each relates to the entire property, albeit from different angles, again there is no question that the several insureds must be regarded as one and that no subrogation is impossible."

It was this passage, from a Canadian case,[181] that persuaded Lloyd J in *Petrofina (UK)*

---

176. *Royal Exchange Assurance Inc* v *s/s President Adams*, 510 F Supp 581 (WD Wash, 1981—cargo). As regards the lender/loss payee, see *Rocky Mountain Helicopters Inc* v *Bell Helicopters Textron*, 805 F 2d 907 (10 Cir, 1986—aviation), discussed by Bowe, 53 J Air L & Com 999 (1988). As regards mortgagees, see Bowe, pp 1006 ff.

177. [1924] AC 431 (hull).

178. p 445 *per* Viscount Cave; *National Oilwell (UK) Ltd* v *Davy Offshore Ltd* [1993] 2 Lloyd's Rep 582, 616 *per* Colman J (builders' AR). *Idem* concerning fraud by the co-insured: *Transamerica Ins Co* v *Gage Plumbing & Heating Co*, 433 F 2d 1051 (10 Cir, 1970—fire); see also *Shelby County Trust & Banking Co* v *Security Ins Co*, 66 F 2d 120 (6 Cir, 1933—fire); *United States of America Inc* v *Fireman's Fund Ins Co*, 290 F Supp 61 (ED Mo, 1968—fire), affirmed 420 F 2d (8 Cir, 1970); *Larchmont Federal Savings & Loan Assn* v *Ebner*, 454 NYS 2d 450 (1982—fire).

179. On benefit of insurance clauses, see above, 31–5A1.

180. *Wager* v *Providence Ins Co*, 150 US 99, 108–109 *per* Shiras J (1893): charterers insured wheat owned by X, shipped by canal from Buffalo to New York on a ship hired by the charterers. The insurance required the insurer to pay the charterers or their order: the charterers transferred the insurance to the owner, to whom the insurers paid the insurance money. The Supreme Court held that the insurer could not sue the charterers (as the persons responsible for loss).
Also in this sense, MacGillivray, (7th ed), No 1213, a view from which the editors appear to have resiled in the 8th ed, No 1243.

181. *Commonwealth Construction Ltd* v *Imperial Oil Ltd* (1976) 69 DLR (3d) 558, (Canada—contractors AR); criticised by Brownlie (1990) 3 Ins L J 48, 56 ff, but *cf* Baer, 22 Ottawa L Rev 389, 394 ff (1990). See also *Mattera* v *Mack Trucks Inc*, 235 NYS 2d 89 (1962—motor); *Transamerica Ins Co* v *Gage Plumbing & Heating Co*, 433 F 2d 1051 (10 Cir, 1970—fire); *New Amsterdam Casualty Co* v *Homans-Kohler Inc*, 305 F Supp 1017 (D RI, 1969—fire); 310 F Supp 374 (D RI, 1970). *Cf Travelers Ins Co* v *Dickey*, 799 P 2d 625, 629 (Okl, 1990).

Ltd v *Magnaload Ltd*[182] to consider the rule against subrogation to be applicable to "every case of bailment, whether it is the goods which the bailee has insured, or his liability in respect of the goods" and, moreover, to apply the same rule "in the case of contractors and sub-contractors engaged on a common enterprise under a building or engineering contract".

A third reason, which, like the second, rests on contractual intention about the scope of the cover,[183] has been put forward in the United States.[184] The proposition is that, if the contract covers negligence, by insuring the co-insured, the insurer accepts the risk of the negligence of each of them not only towards third parties but also in their relations with each other. A similar view was expressed in England in *Stone Vickers Ltd* v *Appledore Ferguson Shipbuilders*.[185] Although the judge mentioned the fourth reason (below), he also said that to allow insurers to exercise rights of subrogation in respect of the same loss and damage against the co-assured sub-contractor would be "so inconsistent with the insurer's obligation to the co-assured . . . that there must be implied into the contract of insurance a term to give it business efficacy that an insurer will not in such circumstances use rights of subrogation in order to recoup from a co-assured the indemnity which he has paid to the assured. To exercise such rights would be in breach of such a term".[186] Moreover, in *Fireman's Ins Co* v *Wheeler*,[187] the court in New York observed that, if subrogation against a corporate insured is to be barred because "an insurer completely assumes the risk of a fire loss due to the negligence of the insured, at the very least the risk assumed must extend to the negligence of a corporate officer of the insured", thus barring the insurer's subrogated claim against the latter.

A fourth reason, said to be the English reason,[188] refers to circuity of action: "where a bailee is insured against liability to the bailor and the bailor is insured under the same insurance, it is obvious that the insurer could not exercise a right of subrogation against the bailee; circuity would be a complete answer".[189] The argument

---

182. [1983] 2 Lloyd's Rep 91, 98 (contractors AR). The decision was approved in *Mark Rowlands Ltd* v *Berni Inns Ltd* [1986] 1 QB 211, 229 *per* Kerr LJ (CA—fire).

183. See the judgment of Lord Cairns, quoted above 31–5C.

184. *New Amsterdam Casualty Co* v *Homans-Kohler Inc*, 305 F Supp 1017, 1020 (RI, 1969—fire contract taken by sub-contractors on construction site).

185. [1991] 2 Lloyd's Rep 288. The rule was applied to defeat an action against a sub-contractor on a shipbuilding, even though the sub-contractor's work (in supplying the propellor and tailshaft) was performed not at the yard of the insured but on the premises of the defendant co-insured. The decision was reversed ([1992] 2 Lloyd's Rep 578), however, the Court of Appeal did not comment on the present point.

186. p 302 *per* Deputy Judge Anthony Colman QC. *Idem*: *National Oilwell (UK) Ltd* v *Davy Offshore Ltd* [1993] 2 Lloyd's Rep 582, 604, 613–614 *per* Colman J (builders' AR), where the judge also discussed the effect of a waiver of the subrogation clause.

187. 566 NYS 2d 692 (1991—fire); in this case, the defendant officer was a co-insured under certain sections of the policy, which covered various risks apart from fire, but this does not appear to have determined the court's view; the company was, however, a closely held corporation, of which the officer was the president and principal shareholder.

188. MacGillivray, No 1244.

189. *Petrofina (UK) Ltd* v *Magnaload Ltd* [1983] 2 Lloyd's Rep 91, 98 *per* Lloyd J (contractors AR). See also *The Yasin* [1979] 2 Lloyd's Rep 45, 55 *per* Lloyd J (cargo), who relied on words of Viscount Cave in *Samuel & Co Ltd* v *Dumas* [1924] AC 431 (hull). *Sylvan Industries Ltd* v *Fairview Sheet Metal Ltd* (1993) 96 DLR (4th) 277, 283 (BC, 1992—builders' risks).

USA in this sense: *Employers' Fire Ins Co* v *Behunin*, 275 F Supp 399 (D Colum, 1967—builders' risks); *Public Service Co of Oklahoma* v *Black & Veatch Consulting Engineers*, 328 F Supp 14 (ND Okl, 1971—property floater); *Tishman & Co* v *Carney & Del Guidice Inc*, 320 NYS 2d 396 (1971—builders' risks), affirmed 359 NYS 2d 561 (1974). As regards builders' risks cover and the position of subcontractors, see Bowe, *op cit*, pp 1010 ff.

against circuity is an argument against waste: if the insurer must pay in the end, let him pay sooner (as property insurer) rather than later (as liability insurer).[190]

31–5D2 Different Contracts of Insurance

If the cover, albeit with the same insurer, is obtained not under one single contract of insurance but two, the second and third reasons (above) for the rule against subrogation indicate the same decision against subrogation. *In National Union Fire Ins* v *Engineering-Science Inc*,[191] the rule was raised to defeat an action in subrogation under a builders' risks contract against an alleged wrongdoer, who was insured not under that contract but under a separate (errors and omissions) contract with the same insurer. The court adopted the reasons of a lower court[192] in that case, including not only the second reason (above) but also that, if action in subrogation were permitted, it would "permit the insurer to secure information from its insured under the guise of policy provisions available for later use in the insurer's subrogation action against its own insured; [and] allow the insurer to take advantage of its own conduct and conflict of interest with its insured." The court did not accept the argument of the claimant insurer that policy was satisfied by the existence of Chinese walls between different departments of its business. Of course, the argument by reference to conflict of interest applies also to the single contract situation.[193]

31–5D3 Different Exposure

If the insurer's exposure as liability insurer is less than his exposure as property insurer, can he claim, in his role as property insurer, the difference from a co-insured, whose liability he did not insure to the extent of the difference? Certainly, the argument based on circuity falters,[194] unless perhaps the difference is small. Moreover, the answer may also depend on whether the wrongdoer has paid premium not to the subrogated insurer but to another excess insurer, for liability insurance cover on the difference.

The question arose in *Stafford Metal Works Inc* v *Cook Paint & Varnish Co*.[195] The common insurer argued for subrogation to avoid a large windfall to the liability insured, and to avoid the necessity of higher rates to compensate for its insurance loss; and that realism required its action to be allowed in view of the increasing incidence of the large insurance company, which insures both sides of an accident and "meets itself at the top". The court rejected, first, the windfall argument[196]:

"This . . . is not a positive windfall, but merely a question of who is to assume responsibility for

---

190. When there is not one insurer but two insurers, the courts have taken a different tack, in particular, when the prospect is that the property insurer will seek to bring an action in subrogations against the wrongdoer and hence the liability insurer: the court may leave the loss where it lies by limiting or eliminating any duty of care owed by the "wrongdoer" to the property insured, so that the property insurer has no action: for example *Norwich CC* v *Harvey* [1989] 1 All ER 1180 (CA); Markesinis, 25 Int'l Law 953, 961 (1991).

191. 884 F 2d 1208 (9 Cir, 1989—builders' risks).

192. F Supp 380, 382 (ND Cal, 1987).

193. *Sylvan* (above) pp 282–283.

194. Falter it does, as, traditionally, the defence based on circuity assumes not only identity of parties but also claims identical in amount: *Walmesley* v *Cooper* (1839) 11 Ad & E 216, 221–222.

195. 418 F Supp 56 (ND Tex, 1976). CP as supplier of defective foam insulation was liable for a fire in SM's plant. The fire insurer to SM was also liability insurer to CP under separate insurance contracts.

196. p 62.

a certain loss. Since this is a products liability case under the laws of the State of Texas, the principal basis of action is strict liability, not negligence. The concept of strict liability negates any notion of moral fault or equitable wrongdoing and robs the 'windfall' argument of its traditional validity."

Second, as regards premium rates, the court said:

"Since the loss, no matter which insurance company bears it, must be compensated for by increased premiums, it makes no difference as a matter of public policy whether [CP] or the excess liability carrier bears the loss. Public policy is influenced, however, by whether [U] is allowed to subrogate. Such subrogation creates administrative costs in shifting the loss between insurance carriers, which costs must be borne by the public in the form of increased insurance rates."

Although the court recognised the relevance of circuity and cost, the main ground in the judgment was the conflict of interest which subrogation would create.[197]

31–5E Public Policy

The right of subrogation may be refused on grounds of public policy. Arguments against subrogation altogether are considered below, 31–7. English law does all subrogation and here we are concerned only with specific grounds that might defeat the insurer in certain kinds of situation.

It is likely that particular policy grounds against subrogation will be expressed by the court in the language of the basis of the doctrine: that, in the situation before the court, subrogation would not be equitable.

31–5E1 Labour Relations

In England, in *Morris v Ford Motor Co Ltd*,[198] cleaners contracted to clean Ford's factory and to indemnify Ford against liability for any negligence by Ford's employees, which might arise out of the cleaning operations. The plaintiff, who worked for the cleaners, was injured by the negligence of a Ford employee and obtained damages from Ford, as employer, which then sought indemnity from the cleaners. The cleaners, in turn, claimed to be subrogated to the rights of Ford against Ford's employee but failed in the Court of Appeal.

Lord Denning MR[199]: "Fords would not themselves have dreamt of suing their [employee]. If they did so, all the men would have come out on strike . . . If the cleaners . . . can thus force [the employee] to pay the damages personally—it would imperil good industrial relations." He noted the gentleman's agreement between insurers, whereby the insurer of employer's liability agrees not to exercise surrogate

---

197. pp 62–63: one of the main reasons for not allowing subrogation against the sole insured: above, 31–5C. In *Commonwealth Construction* (above 31–5D1), the Supreme Court of Canada reached a similar decision but on the ground that, in view of the physical context (a large construction site), the co-insured should be regarded as one person.

198. [1973] QB 792, noted critically by Powles, (1974) 90 LQR 34.

See also *The Palm Beach* [1916] P 230: the insurer, who had paid the insured on a total loss of cargo, could not exercise the insured's rights to claim in the prize court because the insurer, unlike the insured, was an enemy alien.

199. p 798.

rights of action against an employee responsible for the loss. He concluded that the cleaners should not be permitted to sue the employee by reference to equity; but this was less the equity of the particular case than of the situation in general and, to this extent, it is overtly a decision of public policy. Lord Denning MR also said[200] that in the contract with the cleaners,

"Fords advised the cleaners to arrange with their insurance company to cover their liability under the indemnity. I expect they did so. Their insurance company has received the premiums, and should bear the loss. It should not seek to make [the employee] liable personally. Everyone knows that risks such as these are covered by insurance. So they should be; when a man is doing his employer's work, with his employer's plant and equipment, and happens to make a mistake, to make the servant personally liable would not only lead to a strike. It would be positively unjust."

For reasons of a similar kind, the English court might align itself with the law of other countries,[201] and refuse the exercise of rights in subrogation against members of the insured's family circle.

31–5E2 Conflict of Duty and Interest

In Connecticut, in *Pullman*,[202] a medical malpractice suit against insured, X, was defended by P, an attorney appointed by primary insurer A. The judgment against X was well above the primary layer and the excess was paid by an excess insurer, C. In respect of C's action against P, alleging negligence, the court held, first, that P owed no duty of care to C; and, second, that, although it was assumed that X had a right of action against P, C could not exercise X's rights in subrogation against P. The reason was that the interests of X and C might conflict. To hold otherwise, would "acknowledge a direct duty owed by the insured's attorney to the excess insurer and would be tantamount to saying that insurance defense attorneys do not owe their duty of loyalty and zealous representation to the insured client alone".[203] Moreover, a direct duty would "encourage excess insurers to sue defense attorneys [who] would come to fear such attacks, and the attorney–client relationship would be put in jeopardy".[204]

31–6 THE DUTIES OF THE INSURED

The insured is obliged to assist the insurer to exercise his rights of subrogation. Such a duty is implied in law[205] and often amplified or extended by the contract of insurance.

200. p 801. *Cf* James LJ (pp 814–815) who saw this as background information known to the parties to the indemnity, so as to justify an implied term excluding rights of subrogation.
   In Australia, as regards employees of the insured, the right of subrogation against such employees has been abolished: Insurance Contracts Act 1984 (Cth), section 66.
201. For example, Australia: Insurance Contracts Act (1984) (Cth), section 65, excepted as regards defendants with their own insurance; and Germany: VVG art 67(2), except as regards loss intentionally caused.
202. *Continental Casualty Co v Pullman, Comley, Bradley & Reeves*, 709 F Supp 44 (D Conn, 1989—liability).
203. p 50.
204. *Ibid*. See below 31–7B2.
205. This is an aspect of the duty of good faith and co-operation, discussed in chapter 27.

31–6A Commencement of Suit

In the absence of any initiative by the insurer, it is undecided[206] whether the insured must commence suit against a third party wrongdoer.[207] This matters in cases in which the limitation period barring action is short. It is submitted that the insured has no such duty. If subrogation were based on implied contract, it is doubtful whether a duty, that the insured must preserve the insurer's position by commencing action, would be implied.[208] The insurance contract usually contains a notice of loss clause with a period shorter than the limitation period operating in favour of the wrongdoer. As the insurer's position is sufficiently protected by the clause, a duty to commence suit does not have to be implied to give the contract of insurance business efficacy.[209] If, as now appears, subrogation is based on equity, the insured might reasonably respond with astonishment or even outright hostility to the suggestion that he is obliged to sue. The desire to avoid litigation is one of the reasons why people take insurance.[210]

31–6B Conduct of Suit

31–6B1 Suit Initiated by the Insurer

The insured must permit the insurer to use his name to bring an action against the third party. Such an action must be in the name of the insured with his consent or, if he does not consent, under compulsion by the court[211]; since the Judicature Act 1873, the insurer has been able to bring an action in his own name, joining the insured as co-defendant. Whether the insurer's rights in this respect can be described as equitable rights is unclear.[212] If the insured has been fully indemnified by the insurer and action against the third party is begun by the insurer in the name of the insured, it is the insurer who is *dominus litis* and who bears the costs of litigation. In any event, just as it is the duty of the insured not to prejudice the position of the insurer,[213] it is the duty of the insurer not to prejudice the position of the insured, for example, by an unfa-

---

206. In practice the question may be governed by the express terms of the contract of insurance. For example the Institute Cargo Clauses (A) 1982, cl 16: "It is the duty of the Assured . . . to ensure that all rights against carriers, bailees or other third parties are properly preserved and exercised and the Underwriters will, in addition to any loss recoverable hereunder, reimburse the Assured for any charges properly and reasonably incurred in pursuance of these duties."

207. Cf *Yorkshire Ins Co Ltd* v *Nisbet Shipping Co Ltd* [1962] 2 QB 330, 341 *per* Diplock J (hull). *Prima facie* against any such duty: *Andrews* v *Patriotic Assurance Co* (1886) 18 LR Ir 355, 369 ff *per* Pallas CB (fire); however, in this case, the bar was not time but the bankruptcy of the wrongdoer, and the court was influenced by the view that time had passed as a result of the insurer's wrongful refusal to pay under the policy.

208. *Contra*, MacGillivray, No 1201.

209. As the law requires for implied terms: see above, 11–1A3.

210. This point was recognised by Pallas CB in *Andrews* (above), *loc cit*.

211. *Wilson* v *Raffalovich* (1881) 7 QBD 553 (CA—cargo); *King* v *Victoria Ins Co Ltd* [1896] AC 250, 255–256 *per* Lord Hobhouse (PC—cargo); *Yorkshire Ins Co Ltd* v *Nisbet Shipping Co Ltd* [1962] 2 QB 330, 341 *per* Diplock J (hull); *Esso Petroleum Co Ltd* v *Hall Russell & Co Ltd* [1989] AC 643. *Aliter*, if the insured has assigned his rights to the insurer: the latter may sue in his own name: *King* (above), applied in *Cia Colombiana de Seguros* v *Pacific SN Co* [1965] 1 QB 101 (cargo).

As to whether discovery of documents may be ordered against the insurer, although not formally a party to the action, see *James Nelson & Sons Ltd* v *Nelson Line (Liverpool) Ltd* [1906] 2 KB 217 (CA—cargo).

212. There was some discussion of this issue in *Napier* v *Hunter* [1993] 1 All ER 385 (HL—re), however, it was not necessary to decide the question. On the difficulties of this view, see also Birds [1993] JBL 294.

213. Below, 31–6C.

vourable settlement. If that occurs, the insurer will be liable to the insured in damages.[214]

31–6B2 Suit Initiated by the Insured

If the insured has begun suit on his own initiative, he cannot be restrained by the insurer; the insured remains *dominus litis*.

In *Commercial Union Assurance Co* v *Lister*,[215] the insured's mill was destroyed by a gas explosion. The insured, whose loss was only partly covered by fire insurance, commenced an action against the person responsible for the explosion. His fire insurer sought to restrain him and to dictate the conduct of the action but the insured, having undertaken to sue for the full amount of the loss, was held by the Court of Appeal in Chancery to be "left free to go on and to conduct this action. If he does anything in the conduct of the action inconsistent with his duty [to the insurer] . . . he will have to make good any loss thereby incurred."[216]

31–6B3 Costs

Any reasonable costs, which cannot be recovered in an action against the wrongdoer, may be deducted by whoever sues from the damages recovered in that action, before accounting to the other.[217] If the contract of insurance obliges the insured to preserve rights against a third party, it will be implied that the cost of preservation will be reimbursed by the insurer,[218] lest the insurer be tempted to stand by for as long as possible and let the insured shoulder the burden and cost of preservation.[219]

If action is brought by an insured, whose loss is only partly covered by insurance, the costs of the action will be borne in accordance with agreement between them or, in the absence of agreement, in proportion to their respective interests in the litigation.[220] In any particular case, however, the rules of the court will determine whether the court has power to settle a dispute over costs, when one party to that dispute (the insurer) is not formally party to the litigation.[221]

31–6C Information and Assistance

The insured must give such information and assistance as will facilitate the recovery of the loss. The corollary is that the insured must not prejudice the insurer's position.

If the insured has agreed to the exclusion or limitation of the liability of a third party, against whom rights might otherwise have been exercisable in subrogation,

---

214. Generally, in this sense Arnould, No 1320. As regards liability insurance, and the duty of the insurer to defend the insured, see above, 17–4E.

215. (1874) LR 9 Ch App 483. See also *Morley* v *Moore* [1936] 2 KB 359 (CA—motor). *Cf Law Fire Ins Co* v *Oakley* (1888) 4 TLR 309 *per* Mathew J (fire).

216. p 486 *per* Sir W M James LJ.

217. For example, insured accounting to insurer: *Hatch Mansfield & Co Ltd* v *Weingot* (1906) 22 TLR 366 (fidelity guarantee); *Assicurazioni Generali di Trieste* v *Empress Assurance Corp Ltd* [1907] 2 KB 814 (cargo). *Baloise Fire Ins Co* v *Martin* [1937] 2 DLR 24 (Ont—fire).

218. *Netherlands Ins Co Ltd* v *Ljunberg & Co AB* [1986] 3 All ER 767 (PC—cargo). See also above, 28–8G.

219. p 771 *per* Lord Goff.

220. *Duus Brown & Co* v *Binning* (1906) 11 Com Cas 190, 195 *per* Walton J (cargo). As regards the circumstances in which such assistance might be champertous, see *Giles* v *Thompson* [1993] 3 All ER 321.

221. *Re Taxation of Costs* [1937] 2 KB 491 (CA—motor).

prior to making the contract of insurance, that is something that the insured may have to disclose at the time of the insurance contract; see above, chapter 26. The immediate issue is the abandonment or compromise of rights in respect of insured loss, after the loss has occurred.

31–6C1 Abandonment

If, after insured loss, the insured renounces or abandons unilaterally a right against a third party, the consequences are as follows.

First, as the insurer can have no better right than the insured, the insurer cannot be subrogated to the abandoned right,[222] unless, perhaps, the third party has notice of the insurer's rights and notice that the renunciation is prejudicial to the insurer.[223]

In *Morganite Ceramic Fibres Pty Ltd* v *Sola Basic Australia Ltd*,[224] the Supreme Court of New South Wales held that, if a third party liable in respect of loss settled with the insured and thus discharged his liability, the insurer's right of subrogation insurer would not be defeated, if, at the time of the settlement, the third party was aware of the payments made by the insurer to the insured and of the insurer's rights of subrogation. The same conclusion has been reached in Washington State,[225] after a survey suggesting that this is now the legal position in most parts of the USA. As to the equities of the situation, while "validating the release and destroying the insurer's subrogation rights might encourage settlement and avoid litigation between tort-feasors and insureds, such a speculative result is not equitably purchased at the price of either abandoning the subrogation rights of the insurer or limiting recovery to reim-bursement from the injured insured . . . We concur with the reasoning of the Illinois Supreme Court that allowing a general release between the tortfeasor and the insured 'may constitut[e] a trap for the unwary insured plaintiff' and 'encourag[e] . . . sharp practice on the part of the tortfeasor or his insurance carrier'."[226]

Second, abandonment by the insured is a breach of his contract with the insurer. The consequences of that breach are that the insurer is discharged from his duty to pay the relevant claim[227] or, if he has paid, that the insurer may recover from the insured damages to the extent of the prejudice consequential on the breach.

---

222. *West of England* v *Isaacs* (below). Also in this sense: *Harter* v *American Eagle Fire Ins Co*, 60 F 2d 245 (6 Cir, 1932—fire); *Bunge Corp* v *London & Overseas Ins Co*, 394 F 2d 496 (2 Cir, 1968); *Sears, Sucsy & Co* v *INA*, 392 F Supp 398 (ND Ill, 1975—fidelity).

223. This point is unsettled in England. The position suggested in the text is supported by the County Court decision in *Haigh* v *Lawford* (1964) 114 LJ 208 (motor); also, by inference, *Smidmore* v *Australian Gas Light Co* (1881) 2 NSWLR 219. Arnould, No 1320.
   This is also the position in the some parts of the United States, on the basis of the fairness and equity of the situation: *Ocean A & G Corp* v *Hooker Electrochemical Co*, 240 NY 37, 47 (1925). See also *Home Ins Co* v *Bernstein*, 16 NYS 2d 45 (1939—motor); *Potomac Ins Co* v *MacNaughton*, 77 NYS 2d 110 (1948—motor); *US* v *Guinn*, 259 F Supp 771 (D NJ, 1966—hospital); *Keystone Ins Co* v *US*, 332 F Supp 74 (ED Pa, 1971—motor); *Kozlowski* v *Briggs Leasing Corp*, 408 NYS 2d 1001 (1978—motor). Veal, 28 Tort & Ins L J 69, 81 (1992).

224. (1987) 11 NSWLR 189.

225. *Leader National Ins Co* v *Torres*, 779 P 2d 722 (Wash, 1989—motor). See also in this sense: *Martin* v *Commercial Union Ins Co*, 935 F 2d 235 (11 Cir, 1991—motor); *Gibbs* v *Hawaiian Eugenia Corp*, 966 F 2d 101, 107 (2 Cir, 1992—freight).

226. *Torres* (above) p 725, quoting from *Home Ins Co* v *Hertz Corp*, 375 NE 2d 115, 117 (Ill, 1978—motor).

227. *Andrews* v *Patriotic Assurance Co* (1886) LR Ir 355, 371 *per* Pallas CB (fire), assuming that in this respect the position of an insurer was the same as that of a surety: *cf* Goff & Jones, p 547, n 77.

In *West of England Fire Ins Co* v *Isaacs*,[228] a sub-lessor was obliged by the sub-lease to insure the premises for £100 and, in the event of loss, to lay out the insurance money in reinstatement. The defendant sub-lessee also insured the premises and his insurer, the plaintiff, paid him when the premises were damaged by fire. When the defendant renounced his rights under the sub-lease, the Court of Appeal held that the defendant sub-lessee was bound to make good to the plaintiff insurer the value of the rights against his lessor, which he had renounced and to which, but for renunciation, the insurers would have been subrogated.

31–6C2 Settlement

By contrast with abandonment or renunciation (above, 31–6C1), which is unilateral and for nothing, *bona fide* (bilateral) settlement by the insured of his claim against the third party is not a breach of the contract of insurance,[229] even though the settlement prevents subrogation against the third party. Settlement does not prejudice the insurer, provided that the settlement is indeed *bona fide*: the court will be alert to the possibility of collusion between victim and tortfeasor.

The same is true, if the insured releases the defendant subject to the continuance of the insurer's rights of subrogation[230] or if the insured releases the defendant only in respect of the uninsured part of his claim against the defendant.

In *Taylor* v *Wray & Co Ltd*,[231] the plaintiff was responsible under his motor cover for the first £10 of loss and was not insured at all against personal injury or consequential loss. Following a collision with a lorry, which was at fault, his claim against the owner of the lorry, which included items for the excess and for consequential loss, was settled. In a subsequent action in respect of the insured loss, the owner of the lorry defended, saying that the right of action in respect of that loss had been lost, when the previous claim had been settled. However, as "neither party to [the settlement] could have been in any doubt that the settlement then negotiated intended to exclude what I may call the insured claim and to be confined to the uninsured claim",[232] the Court of Appeal rejected the defence.

---

228. [1897] 1 QB 226; approved in *Boag* v *Standard Marine Ins Co Ltd* [1937] 2 KB 113, 128 *per* Scott LJ (cargo) and in *Canadian Transport Co Ltd* v *Court Line Ltd* [1940] AC 934, 945 *per* Lord Wright (P & I). See also *Phoenix Assurance Co* v *Spooner* [1905] 2 KB 753 (fire); *The Millwall* [1905] P 155 (CA—indemnity); *Horse, Carriage & General Ins Co Ltd* v *Petch* (1916) 33 TLR 131 (motor). As regards settlements and associated breach of the duty of co-operation, see above 27–4.
USA in this sense: *Freund Inc* v *INA*, 261 F Supp 131 (WD La, 1966); *Howarth* v *Druggists' Mutual Ins Co*, 485 F 2d 34 (8 Cir, 1973—fire).

229. *Globe & Rutgers Fire Ins Co* v *Truedell* [1927] 2 DLR 659 (Ont—fire); *Cansulex Ltd* v *Reed Stenhouse Ltd* (1986) 70 BCLR 273 (liability). There is some suggestion in the USA that *bona fide* settlement is possible only when the insurer has denied liability: *Amalgamet Inc* v *Underwriters at Lloyd's*, 724 F Supp 1132, 1141 (SD NY, 1989—cargo).
Cf Horse, Carriage & General Ins Co Ltd v *Petch* (1916) 33 TLR 131 (motor), in which the insured settled an action in respect of both personal injury and damage to his car; the insurer of the car was held entitled to recover from him the full amount previously paid by the insurer in respect of the damage to the car.
Cf The Southlands, 27 F 2d 1010 (SD Tex, 1928—cargo), affirmed 37 F 2d 474 (5 Cir, 1930), in which, the insurer having paid the insured, it was held that the latter had no authority to settle with the wrongdoer, and the settlement was not binding on the insurer.

230. *Taylor* v *Wray & Co Ltd* [1971] 1 Lloyd's Rep 497, 501 *per* Edmund Davies LJ (CA—motor).

231. [1971] 1 Lloyd's Rep 497.

232. p 500 *per* Harman LJ.

31-7 WHY SUBROGATION?

This chapter has been carried forward on the assumption that an insurer has rights of subrogation and, indeed, so he does—in the present state of the law. However, the chapter should not end without mention of the debate about whether subrogation, as a vehicle of recovery for the insurer, should be withdrawn from service and scrapped altogether.[233] At the very least, the court that has doubts may wish to consider the broader implications before driving the law in new directions or taking marginal points in favour of the insurer's rights in subrogation. Does the doctrine do what is claimed for it? Is it worth doing, anyway?

31-7A The Case for Subrogation

31-7A1 *Preserving the Principle of Indemnity*

The main object of subrogation (and of the incidents of subrogation) is to prevent over compensation of the insured[234] and thus to respect the underlying principle of indemnity.[235] This is a central principle of the law of insurance and, if there is no better way of respecting it, subrogation *to a degree* appears justified on that ground alone.

Alternative ways of maintaining the principle of indemnity have been considered and rejected. The money recoverable under the contract of insurance might have been reduced by the amount which the insured could be expected to recover in the future from a third party; this solution has been rejected in England.[236] A related possibility would have been to require the insured to claim from a third party liable for his loss before he claimed from his insurer; this too has been rejected.[237] In each case, the effect would have been to throw the burden of recovery, litigation perhaps, on the insured, who was probably less able to bear it and who, by taking insurance, might reasonably have hoped to avoid it.

A further possibility is to reduce the compensation, which is available to the insured from a person other than the insurer, to the extent of the insured's indemnity from the insurer. This possibility was firmly rejected in *Bradburn* v *GWR*.[238] Courts have recoiled from the idea that the providence of the victim, in buying insurance, should relieve the wrongdoer of the burden of damages which, in part, are felt to be a punishment he deserves.[239] This feeling is strongest, when the wrong is committed deliberately or recklessly and, moreover, in such cases, subrogation is said to be "justifiable in order to promote accident prevention or deter outright anti-social behaviour as an

---

233. Abolition in most cases is favoured, for example, by P Cane (ed), *Atiyah's Accidents, Compensation and the Law*, (4th ed, Oxford 1987), p 395. On public policy and subrogation, generally, see Abraham, pp 154–155; Derham, ch 14; Hasson, *op cit*.

234. Above, 31–3A2.

235. Above, 31–1.

236. *Collingridge* v *Royal Exchange Assurance Corp* (1877) 3 QBD 173 (fire). *Contra: British Traders Ins Co Ltd* v *Monson* (1964) 111 CLR 86, 95 (HCA—fire).

The contract may provide otherwise: *Construction Finance Co Ltd* v *English Ins Co Ltd* (1924) 19 Ll L Rep 144 (HL—contract guarantee policy).

237. *Cullen* v *Butler* (1816) 5 M & S 461, 466 *per* Lord Ellenborough (cargo); *Dickenson* v *Jardine* (1868) LR 3 CP 639 (cargo); *London Guarantie Co* v *Fearnley* (1880) 5 App Cas 911, 916 *per* Lord Blackburn (fidelity).

238. Above, 31–3A. See also *Mason* v *Sainsbury* (1782) 3 Dougl 61, 64 *per* Lord Mansfield CJ (fire).

239. Fleming, 54 Calif L Rev 1478, 1499 (1966).

adjunct to the criminal law".[240] Indeed, in the case of fidelity insurance in times of apparently high infidelity, there is some attraction in enabling the insurer to transfer the loss to a villain, if one can be found and is able to pay.[241] In these cases, more than in cases of mere negligence, there is some plausibility in arguments based on deterrence.[242] Accordingly, it might be thought bizarre, if not also invidious, that a tortfeasor's liability should vary according to whether his victim happens to be insured or not, so that he is let off the hook in the one case (more likely in prosperous communities) but not in the other.[243]

Insofar as it is an incident of subrogation that the insurer can recover any excess from an insured compensated both by the insurer and by a third party, the main purpose, preservation of the principle of indemnity, has been achieved. Insofar as subrogation allows the insurer to initiate proceedings against a third party, however, proceedings which the insured has not and would not have brought, some other justification for subrogation is required.

31–7A2 Deterrence

Subrogation has been defended as a tool of social engineering. Wrongdoers brought to justice are more likely to mend their ways. An associated argument is the economic argument, based on the theory of "general" deterrence, that the cost of accidents should be placed upon those who can avoid the accidents most cheaply[244] because that will encourage them to avoid accidents; and that this suggests placing the cost on a wrongdoer through subrogation.[245]

Against this argument is that, sometimes, the wrongdoer is a producer or supplier in a position to pass the cost on to another group, such as consumers of his product or his services, and thus back to the insured; in these situations, evidently, subrogation is wasteful.[246]

A more serious objection is that subrogation does not deter wrongdoing at all. In England, in only a tiny proportion of claims is there any prospect of recovery and, if rights in subrogation were abolished, there would be little effect on premiums.[247] The "conjectural and remote nature of subrogation militates against including it as a factor

---

240. Fleming, p 1537. For example, in Germany, whereas VVG art 67(2) does not allow actions in subrogation within the family, an exception is made as regards loss intentionally caused.

241. Veal, 28 Tort & Ins L J 69, 89 (1992).

242. Derham (above, note 2) p 154. *Cf* above, 24–5A1.

243. Fleming p 1538.

244. Calabresi, *The Cost of Accidents* (New Haven, 1970). The premise is that the person will respond to the burden by reducing the amount of activity which gives rise to accidents of that kind or pursue the activity with more care or better precautions. Loss distribution is achieved by insurance and deterrence theory is accommodated by premium differentials. The theory makes a number of questionable assumptions, for example, that people behave "rationally" and respond to greater cost (such as higher motoring charges) by reduced activity (less driving); that the person with the burden is (adequately) insured; and that the risk communities will be accurately and precisely defined and rated by insurers. For insurers, there is safety in large numbers; "any multiplication of component factors to be considered rapidly reduces the size of the class to numbers which are not statistically reliable": Cane p 534. For the literature, as well as discussion of this theory from an "English" perspective, see Cane pp 519 ff and, especially, pp 532 ff.

245. Derham (above, note 2) p 157.

246. Cane p 514.

247. Hitcham in *The Law of Tort (Policies and Trends in Liability for Damage to Property and Economic Loss)*, ed Furmston, London, 1986, p 198; see also Abraham, p 154; Derham p 153.

in premium setting".[248] In the USA, as well, suits in subrogation are few and far between,[249] which suggests that it is of no great importance to insurers.[250] Moreover, apart from the disputed case of the deliberate wrongdoer, the possibility of action in subrogation does not seem to have much effect on the conduct of the wrongdoer,[251] although it is still felt in some quarters that, if there were no possibility of action by his victim's insurer, that would engender an attitude of irresponsibility and, ultimately, more wrongdoing.

31–7B The Case Against Subrogation

31–7B1 Cost

In practice, subrogation is exercised by the insurer mostly when the wrongdong defendant is insured. Thus, it is said, subrogation allows a wasteful distribution of loss between insurers,[252] which the insurers themselves admitted by making "knock-for-knock" agreements between themselves.[253] Resort to legal process "must carry its own burden of self-justification", so transfer to the wrongdoers should not be allowed, unless that is a more efficient form of loss distribution.[254] To pass the cost to the wrongdoer assumes that his (liability) insurance is a more efficient way of distributing loss than leaving it where it lies with the victim and his insurer; and often it is not.[255]

If action in subrogation is brought against a wrongdoer, who is uninsured, it is he who bears the loss rather than the insurer. In this situation, the objection is that it is the insurer who has been paid to assume the risk and to distribute it among that part of the public which pays premiums. The benefits of loss spreading are lost.[256] An associated objection is that, if the insurer recovers all or part of the insurance money by means of subrogation, to the extent that he has received premium for a risk on which he has not "lost", he has an unmerited windfall.[257] Fleming responds[258] that the statement, that the insurer has assumed the risk, is a conclusion rather than a reason

---

248. Baron, 96 Dick L Rev 581, 582 (1992). However, in *The Icebird, Helicopter Resources Pty Ltd* v *Sun Alliance Australia Ltd* [1992] LMCLQ 21 (cargo), the Supreme Court of Victoria held that the fact, that the insurers' rights of subrogation were virtually valueless, was a material fact that should have been disclosed.

249. Meyers, 9 *Forum* 83 (1973).

250. *Cf* Abraham, pp 154–155.

251. Abraham, p 54; Derham, *op cit* (note 2) p 154.

252. Cane p 397; Fleming, 54 Calif L Rev 1478, 1537 (1966).

253. Found where there might be a myriad of small claims. The absence of such an agreement in other contexts does not indicate necessarily that insurers are enthusiastic about the possibility of subrogation; more likely, it is a reflection of competition and of a reluctance to shoulder the burden of bad underwriting by other insurers. Nor does the termination of such agreements between motor insurers mean that litigation has become more attractive. Agreements premised that each insurer carried a proportionate share of bad risks, a premise which, in current market conditions, is no longer believed to be true: *Sunday Times*, 1 August 1993, section 4 p 1.

254. Fleming, p 1535.

255. There is considerable opinion in common law countries too in favour of first-party (rather than third-party) cover: for example, *Iligan Integrated Steel Mills Inc* v *SS John Weyerhaeuser* 507 F. 2d 68, 73 (2 Cir., 1974), with reference to Diplock, 1 JMLC 525, 528–529 (1970). See also Alexander (1972) 12 JSPTL 112; Calabresi, 69 Iowa L Rev 833 (1984); Rea (1987) 12 Can Bus LJ 444; O'Connell and Guinivan, 49 Ohio State LJ 757 (1988); Fleming, 24 UBCL Rev. 1, 5 *et seq.* (1990). *Cf* also the view that discussion of (and preference) for first party insurance has been skewed by emphasis on motor cover, for which the classification of risk is relatively precise: Hanson and Logue, 75 Cornell L Rev 313 (1990). Something of a *via media* is mapped by Gilles, 78 Va L Rev 1291 (1992).

256. Abraham, p 155; Cane p 396.

257. *In re Future Manufacturing Cooperative*, 165 F Supp 111 (ND Cal, 1958—fire).

258. p 1500.

against subrogation. Evidently, the insurer did assume the risk but did he assume it *without recourse*? The answer, as subrogation is not often pursued by insurers and has little or no effect on premiums, may well be affirmative.

31-7B2 *Conflicts of Interest*

Occasionally, the possibility of rights in subrogation can give rise to a conflict of duty and interest on the part of the insurer. In *National Union Fire Ins Co v Aetna*,[259] an employer, A, had not only liability insurer, B, but also a promise of indemnity from a contractor, C, who had his own liability insurer, D. The court pointed out[260] that B would have no incentive to mount a vigorous defence of A, if the loss could be passed via C to D. Morever, B declined to settle the action against A until D contributed to the settlement. In this situation, the court was moved to find co-insurance, with the result that rights in subrogation did not exist.[261]

259. 790 F Supp 491 (SD NY, 1992—liability).
260. p 492.
261. See above, 31–5D3 and 31–5E2.

INDEX